ISBN 978-0-428-33434-5
PIBN 11306352

1 MONTH OF
FREE
READING

at

www.ForgottenBooks.com

By purchasing this book you are
eligible for one month membership to
ForgottenBooks.com, giving you
unlimited access to our entire
collection of over 1,000,000 titles via
our web site and mobile apps.

To claim your free month visit:

www.forgottenbooks.com/free1306352

English
Français
Deutsche
Italiano
Español
Português

www.forgottenbooks.com

Mythology Photography **Fiction**
Fishing Christianity **Art** Cooking
Essays Buddhism Freemasonry
Medicine **Biology** Music **Ancient
Egypt** Evolution Carpentry Physics
Dance Geology **Mathematics** Fitness
Shakespeare **Folklore** Yoga Marketing
Confidence Immortality Biographies
Poetry **Psychology** Witchcraft
Electronics Chemistry History **Law**
Accounting **Philosophy** Anthropology
Alchemy Drama Quantum Mechanics
Atheism Sexual Health **Ancient History**
Entrepreneurship Languages Sport
Paleontology Needlework Islam
Metaphysics Investment Archaeology
Parenting Statistics Criminology
Motivational

SESSIONAL PAPERS

VOL. XLIX.—PART IX.

THIRD SESSION

OF THE

FOURTEENTH LEGISLATURE

OF THE

PROVINCE OF ONTARIO

SESSION 1917

TORONTO:
Printed and Published by A. T. WILGRESS, Printer to the King's Most Excellent Majesty
1917

Printed by
WILLIAM BRIGGS,
Corner Queen & John Sts.,
Toronto.

LIST OF SESSIONAL PAPERS

TITLE.	No.	REMARKS.
Accounts, Public, 1916	1	*Printed.*
Agricultural College, Report	30	"
Agricultural and Experimental Union Report	32	"
Agricultural Societies, Report	42	"
Agriculture Department, Report	29	"
Archivist, Provincial, Report	51	"
Auditor, Provincial, Report	53	"
Bee-Keepers', Report	35	*Printed.*
Birth, Marriages and Death, Report	20	"
Blind, School for, Report of Commission	57	"
British Red Cross, Report	55	"
Burwash Prison Farm, buildings, etc., on	70	"
Canada Copper Company, Correspondence	65	*Printed.*
Canada Copper Company, Statements	69	*Not Printed.*
Canadian Northern Railway Co'y, application by, re lands	73	*Printed.*
Children, Dependent, Report	27	*Not Printed.*
Civil Service, Number of Members of Inside Service	86	"
Corn Growers' Association, Report	33	*Printed.*
Dairymen's Associations, Report	37	*Printed.*
Devonshire Race Track Company, Correspondence	81	*Not Printed.*
Division Courts, Report	5	*Printed.*
Education, Report	17	*Printed.*
Education, Orders-in-Council	61	*Not Printed.*
Education, re Public, Separate or High Schools	79	*Printed.*
Elections, Returns from Records	50	"
Entomological Society, Report	36	"
Estimates	2	"
Experiment Station, Vineland, Report	83	"
Experimental Union, Report.	32	"
Factories, Report	46	*Printed.*
Farmers' Institutes, Report	40	*Not Printed.*
Feeble-Minded, Report	24	*Printed.*
French, Fred W., Correspondence	78	*Not Printed.*
Friendly Societies, Report	11	*Printed.*
Fruit Growers, Report	44	"

TITLE.	No.	REMARKS.
Game and Fish, Report.............................	14	*Printed.*
Gore Bay Riding and Driving Association, Charter, etc....	82	*Not Printed.*
Guelph Prison Farm, Capital-Expenditure	75	*Printed.*
Gunn, Richards & Company, Amounts Paid to	74	*Not Printed.*
Health, Board of, Report	21	*Printed.*
Highway Improvement, Report	15	"
Hill, Fred., Correspondence *re* Dismissal of	88	*Not Printed.*
Horticultural Societies, Report	43	*Printed.*
Hospitals and Charities, Report	25	"
Hydro-Electric Power Commission, Report	48	"
Idiots and Epileptics, Report	23	*Printed.*
Industries, Report of Bureau	45	"
Insane Hospitals, Report	22	"
Insurance, Report	10	
International Nickel Co'y., Correspondence *re* Injured Lands, etc..................................	65	"
International Nickel Company, Statements Furnished ..	69	*Not Printed.*
Jackson, Willis K., Acres Occupied by *bona fide* Settlers on Lands Purchased by	68	*Not Printed.*
Labour, Report of Bureau	16	*Not Printed.*
Lands, Forests and Mines, Report..................	3	*Printed.*
Legal Offices, Report	6	"
Librarian, Report	52	*Not Printed.*
Liquor License Acts, Report	28	*Printed.*
Live Stock Branch, Report	38	"
Loan Corporations, Statements	12	"
McPherson, Alexander, Correspondence, etc.	78	*Not Printed.*
Machine Guns Purchased	63	*Not Printed.*
Mercer Reformatory, Cost of Knitting Plant	76	"
Mines, Report of Bureau	4	*Printed.*
Mond Nickel Company, Statements by, etc.	69	*Not Printed.*
Monteith Demonstration Farm, Report	56	*Printed.*
Nickel Commission, Report	62	*Printed.*
Nickel Commission. Cost of, etc.	80	*Not Printed.*
Nickel Companies. Damage to Lands	65	*Printed.*
Ontario Nickel Commission, Report	62	*Printed.*
Ontario Railway and Municipal Board, Report	49	"
Ontario Reformatory, Pay Rolls of Industrial Department	67	*Not Printed.*

Title.	No.	Remarks.
Paper Mills, Contracts with	72	*Printed.*
Prisoners in Gaols and Reformatories	85	*Not Printed.*
Prisons and Reformatories, Report	26	*Printed.*
Provincial Auditor, Report	53	"
Provincial Municipal Auditor, Report	8	"
Provincial War Tax, Amount Paid Under	89	*Not Printed.*
Public Accounts	1	*Printed.*
Public Highways, Report	15	"
Public Works, Report	13	"
Queen Victoria Niagara Falls Park, Report	9	*Printed.*
Racing Associations, Charters to	64	*Printed.*
Railway and Municipal Board, Report	49	"
Registrar General. Report	20	"
Registry Offices, Report	7	..
Secretary and Registrar, Report	19	*Printed.*
Soldiers' Aid Commission, Report	84	*Not Printed.*
Soldiers, Returned, Correspondence	77	"
Stallion Enrolment Board, Report	39	*Printed.*
Statute Distribution, Statement	59	*Not Printed.*
Surrogate Courts, Orders-in-Council	58	"
Temiskaming and N. O. R. Commission, Report	47	*Printed.*
Temiskaming and N. O. R., *re* Special Rate Quoted	60	*Not Printed.*
Temiskaming and N. O. R., Names of Townsites	71	"
Temiskaming and N. O. R., Tenders Received for Lots	87	"
Toronto University, Report	18	*Printed.*
Vegetable Growers' Association, Report	34	*Printed.*
Veterinary College. Report	31	"
Vineland Station, Report	83	"
War Tax, Provincial, Amount Paid Under	89	*Not Printed.*
Whitby Asylum, Patients Cared for in	66	*Printed.*
Women's Institutes, Report	41	"
Workmen's Compensation, Report	54	"

LIST OF SESSIONAL PAPERS

Arranged in Numerical Order with their Titles at full
length; the dates when presented to the Legislature;
the name of the Members who moved the same,
and whether ordered to be Printed or not.

CONTENTS OF PART I.

No. 1 Public Accounts of the Province for the year ending 31st October,
1916. Presented to the Legislature, February 22nd, 1917.
Printed.

No. 2 Estimates—Supplementary. for the service of the Province for the
year ending 31st October, 1917. Presented to the Legislature,
February 22nd, 1917. *Printed.* Estimates, Supplementary,
for the year ending October 31st, 1917. Presented to the
Legislature. March 26th, 1917. Estimates for the year ending
31st October. 1917. *Printed.* Presented to the Legislature.
April 2nd, 1917. *Printed.*

CONTENTS OF PART II

No. 3 Report of the Department of Lands, Forests and Mines for the
year 1916. Presented to the Legislature, March 16th. 1917.
Printed.

No. 4 Report of the Bureau of Mines for the year 1916. Presented to the
Legislature, April 6th, 1917. *Printed.*

No. 5 Report of the Inspector of Division Courts for the year 1916. Presented to the Legislature, March 2nd, 1917. *Printed.*

No. 6 Report of the Inspector of Legal Offices for the year 1916. Presented to the Legislature. March 23rd, 1916. *Printed.*

No. 7 Report of the Inspector of Registry Offices for the year 1916. Presented to the Legislature, March 23rd, 1917. *Printed.*

No. 8 Report of the Provincial Municipal Auditor for the year 1916.
Presented to the Legislature, April 6th, 1917. *Printed.*

No. 9 Report of the Queen Victoria Niagara Falls Park Commission for
the year 1916. Presented to the Legislature. April 6th, 1917.
Printed.

CONTENTS OF PART III.

No. 10   Report of the Superintendent of Insurance for the year 1916. Presented to the Legislature, April 6th, 1917. *Printed.*

No. 11   Report of the Registrar of Friendly Societies for the year 1916. Presented to the Legislature, April 6th, 1917. *Printed.*

No. 12   Loan Corporations' Statements, being Financial Statements made by Building Societies, Loan Companies, Loaning, Land and Trust Companies for the year 1916. Presented to the Legislature, April 6th, 1917. *Printed.*

CONTENTS OF PART IV.

No. 13   Report of the Department of Public Works for the year 1916. Presented to the Legislature, March 21st, 1917. *Printed.*

No. 14   Report of the Department of Game and Fisheries for the year 1916. Presented to the Legislature, April 6th, 1917. *Printed.*

No. 15   Report of the Department of Public Highways for the year 1916. Presented to the Legislature, April 6th, 1917. *Printed.*

No. 16   Report of the Bureau of Labour for the year 1916. Presented to the Legislature, April 6th, 1917. *Not Printed.*

No. 17   Report of the Department of Education for the year 1916. Presented to the Legislature, April 6th, 1917. *Printed.*

No. 18   Report of the Board of Governors of the University of Toronto for the year 1916. Presented to the Legislature, February 20th, 1917. *Printed.*

No. 19   Report of the Secretary and Registrar of the Province for the year 1916. Presented to the Legislature, April 6th, 1917. *Printed.*

CONTENTS OF PART V.

No. 20   Report of the Registrar-General upon Births. Marriages and Deaths for the year 1916. Presented to the Legislature, April 6th, 1917. *Printed.*

No. 21   Report of the Provincial Board of Health for the year 1916. Presented to the Legislature, April 6th, 1917. *Printed.*

No. 22   Report upon the Hospitals for the Insane for the year 1916. Presented to the Legislature, April 6th, 1917. *Printed.*

No. 23   Report upon the Hospitals for Feeble-minded and Epileptics for the year 1916. Presented to the Legislature, April 6th, 1917. *Printed.*

CONTENTS OF PART VI.

No. 24 | Report upon the Feeble-Minded of the Province for the year 1916. Presented to the Legislature, April 6th, 1917. *Printed for distribution.*

No. 25 | Report upon the Hospitals and Charities of the Province for the year 1916. Presented to the Legislature, April 6th, 1917. *Printed.*

No. 26 | Report upon the Prisons and Reformatories of the Province for the year 1916. Presented to the Legislature, April 6th, 1917. *Printed.*

No. 27 | Report upon the Neglected and Dependent Children of the Province for the year 1916. Presented to the Legislature, April 6th, 1917. *Not Printed.*

No. 28 | Report upon the operation of the Liquor License Acts in the Province for the year 1916. Presented to the Legislature, March 2nd, 1917. *Printed.*

No. 29 | Report of the Department of Agriculture for the year 1916. Presented to the Legislature, April 6th, 1917. *Printed.*

No. 30 | Report of the Ontario Agricultural College and Experimental Farm for the year 1916. Presented to the Legislature, April 6th, 1917. *Printed.*

No. 31 | Report of the Ontario Veterinary College for the year 1916. Presented to the Legislature, April 6th, 1917. *Printed.*

No. 32 | Report of the Ontario Agricultural and Experimental Union for the year 1916. Presented to the Legislature, April 6th, 1917. *Printed.*

No. 33 | Report of the Ontario Corn Growers' Association for the year 1916. Presented to the Legislature, April 6th, 1917. *Printed.*

No. 34 | Report of the Ontario Vegetable Growers' Association for the year 1916. Presented to the Legislature, April 6th, 1917. *Printed.*

No. 35 | Report of the Bee-Keepers' Association for the year 1916. Presented to the Legislature, April 6th, 1917. *Printed.*

No. 36 | Report of the Entomological Society of the Province for the year 1916. Presented to the Legislature, April 6th, 1917. *Printed.*

No. 37 | Report of the Dairymen's Association of the Province for the year 1916. Presented to the Legislature, April 6th, 1917. *Printed.*

CONTENTS OF PART VII.

No. 38   Report of the Live Stock Branch of the Department of Agriculture for the year 1916. Presented to the Legislature, April 6th, 1917. *Printed.*

No. 39   Report of the Stallion Enrolment Board for the year 1916. Presented to the Legislature, April 6th, 1917. *Printed.*

No. 40   Report of the Farmers' Institutes for the year 1916. Presented to the Legislature, April 6th, 1917. *Not Printed.*

No. 41   Report of the Women's Institutes of the Province for the year 1916. Presented to the Legislature, April 6th, 1917. *Printed.*

No. 42   Report of the Agricultural Societies of the Province for the year 1916. Presented to the Legislature, April 6th, 1917. *Printed.*

CONTENTS OF PART VIII.

No. 43   Report of the Horticultural Societies of the Province for the year 1916. Presented to the Legislature, April 6th, 1917. *Printed.*

No. 44   Report of the Fruit Growers' Association of the Province for the year 1916. Presented to the Legislature, April 6th, 1917. *Printed.*

No. 45   Report of the Bureau of Industries of the Province for the year 1916. Presented to the Legislature, April 6th, 1917. *Printed.*

No. 46   Report of the Inspectors of Factories in the Province for the year 1916. Presented to the Legislature, April 6th, 1917. *Printed.*

CONTENTS OF PART IX.

No. 47   Report of the Temiskaming and Northern Ontario Railway Commission for the year 1916. Presented to the Legislature, April 6th. 1917. *Printed.*

No. 48   Report of the Hydro-Electric Power Commission for the year 1916. Presented to the Legislature, April 3rd, 1917. *Printed.*

CONTENTS OF PART X.

No. 49   Report of the Ontario Railway and Municipal Board for the year 1916. Presented to the Legislature, April 6th. 1917. *Printed.*

No. 50   Return from the Records of the several By-Elections. Presented to the Legislature, February 15th, 1917. *Printed.*

No. 51 | Report of the Bureau of Archives for the year 1916. Presented to the Legislature, April 6th, 1917. *Printed.*

No. 52 | Report of the Librarian upon the state of the Library. Presented to the Legislature, February 15th, 1917. *Not printed.*

No. 53 | Report of the Provincial Auditor for the year 1916. Presented to the Legislature, February 22nd, 1917. *Printed.*

No. 54 | Report of the Workmen's Compensation Board for the year 1916. Presented to the Legislature, April 6th, 1917. *Printed.*

No. 55 | Report of the British Red Cross Fund for the year 1916. Presented to the Legislature, March 2nd, 1917. *Printed.*

No. 56 | Report upon the Monteith Demonstration Farm for the year 1916 Presented to the Legislature, April 6th, 1917. *Printed.*

No. 57 | Report of the Commission to investigate the administration, management, progress and welfare of the Ontario School for the Blind Presented to the Legislature, February 20th, 1917. *Printed.*

CONTENTS OF PART XI.

No. 58 | Copy of Order-in-Council under section 78 of the Surrogate Courts Act. Presented to the Legislature, February 20th, 1917. *Not Printed.*

No. 59 | Statement as to distribution of the Revised and Sessional Statutes for the year 1916. Presented to the Legislature, February 20th, 1917. *Not printed.*

No. 60 | Return to an Order of the House of April 19th, 1916, that there be laid before the House:—A Return shewing, 1. If the T. & N. O. Railway quoted any special rate not authorized by its tariff or has been a party to the quotation of a special rate from any point or points in Ontario or Western Canada. 2. If so, to what shipper or shippers has such rate been given. Presented to the Legislature, February 20th, 1917. Mr. *Munro.* *Not Printed.*

No. 61 | Copies of Orders-in-Council made under the authority of the Department of Education Act, or of the Acts relating to Public Schools, Separate Schools or High Schools. Presented to the Legislature, February 20th, 1917. *Not Printed.*

No. 62 | Report of the Nickel Commission. Presented to the Legislature, March 26th, 1917. *Printed.*

No. 63 | Return of an Address to His Honour the Lieutenant-Governor of the 16th February, 1917, praying that he will cause to be laid before this House, a Return:—1. Shewing all correspondence (including telegrams) since January 1st, 1916, passing between the Government of the Province of Ontario or any member, officer or official thereof, and the Government of the Dominion of Canada and any officer or official thereof in reference to the machine guns purchased out of the moneys of the Province of Ontario. 2. All correspondence since January 1st, 1916, passing between the Government of the Province of Ontario, or any member, officer or official thereof, and the Imperial Government, and any officer or official thereof, in reference to machine guns purchased out of the moneys of the Province of Ontario. Presented to the Legislature, March 1st, 1917. Mr. *Bowman.* *Not Printed.*

No. 64   Return to an Order of the House of the 26th February, 1917, for a Return shewing:—1. How many charters or licenses have been issued to racing associations operating in Ontario since the year 1912. 2. What are the names of the racing associations or companies and the dates of the issue of the licenses or charters respectively. Presented to the Legislature, March 1st, 1917. Mr. *Carter. Printed.*

No. 65   Return to an Address to His Honour the Lieutenant-Governor of the 11th April, 1916, praying that he will cause to be laid before this House a Return shewing:—1. Copies of all letters or telegrams, since the 1st January, 1915, which have passed between the Government or any official or agent thereof, and the International Nickel Company or the Canadian Copper Company or any officers or officials thereof, in reference to the damages done to the property of the farmers and others interested in the lands adjacent to the plant of the Canadian Copper Company. 2. Of all letters and telegrams which have passed between the Government, or any officer or official thereof—and particularly the Departments of Lands, Forests and Mines and of Agriculture—and Mr. Chas. McCrea, M.P.P., of Sudbury, in reference to the matters aforesaid or the operations of the International Nickel Company or the Canadian Copper Company, and the damage being done to the property in the vicinity of the operations of the said companies; and particularly the correspondence between either of the Departments and Mr. McCrea and Mr. Ponton and Mr. Jarvis, Valuators for the Canadian Copper Company. 3. Of all Orders in Council withdrawing lands from sale for agricultural purposes, at the instance or suggestion of the Canadian Copper Company. Presented to the Legislature, March 2nd, 1917. Mr. *Carter, Printed.*

No. 66   Return to an Order of the House of the 19th February, 1917 for a Return shewing how many patients were regularly cared for in the Whitby Asylum during the year 1916. Presented to the Legislature, March 2nd, 1917. Mr. *Wigle. Printed.*

No. 67 | Return to an Order of the House of the 23rd February, 1917, for a Return of copies, 1. Of the pay-rolls of the Industrial Department of the Reformatory for the Porvince of Ontario, commencing November 1st, 1915, and ending October 31st, 1916, specifying the nature of the services rendered by those whose names appear in the Return. 2. Of the monthly payments by the Industrial Department of the Reformatory for the Province of Ontario to persons whose names do not appear upon the monthly pay-roll of the Industrial Department, specifying the nature of the services rendered by those whose names appear in the Return. Presented to the Legislature, March 2nd, 1917. Mr. *Bowman. Not Printed.*

No. 68 | Return to an Order of the House of the 3rd April, 1916, for a Return shewing: 1. The number of acres occupied by *bona fide* settlers on the lands purchased from the Government by Willis K. Jackson *et al.* under agreement bearing date the 14th day of June, 1912, particularizing the number of acres occupied each year since the date of the said agreement. 2. The number of settlers occupying such lands since the date of such agreement and the number respectively occupying the same for each year since the date of said agreement and the number of acres occupied by each settler. 3. The number of settlers who have lived up to the requirements of The Free Grant and Homestead Act and the regulations thereunder, and the number in default. 4. The number of farms required to be cleared by the Minister under Clause 4 of said agreement, and the actual number of such farms cleared, the amount of work performed, and the number and kind of buildings erected in accordance with the request of said Minister. 5. The number and extent of roads, bridges and other improvements, designating the nature of such improvements, required by the Minister to be done under Clause 5 of said agreement and the number and extent of such roads, bridges and other improvements completed in accordance with such request. 6. The number of schools and school buildings erected under Clause 6 of said agreement, and whether same are established and erected to the satisfaction of the Minister, also the location of such schools, particularizing those which are not satisfactory to the Minister and the reason for such dissatisfaction. 7. The amount of work required to be performed under Clause 7 of said agreement that has actually been performed, particularizing the nature and cost of such work, and the date each work was commenced and completed. 8. The number of acres cut over by the purchaser under Clause 8 of said agreement, and whether same cleared in accordance with the terms of said clause and to the satisfaction of the Minister; and whether the terms of said clause as to leaving 20 acres of wood for each farm have been complied with, and the kind of wood so left. 9. Whether all the timber cut by the purchaser has been manufactured in the townships of Kendry and Haggart, and if not, the amount not so manufactured and the amount of timber disposed of outside of such townships, and to whom the same was sold. 10. The amount of timber that has been purchased from the settlers by the purchaser, and upon what terms were such purchases made; and how much and at what rate were the settlers paid for cutting and removing timber; and what was the rate charged to the settler for the use of the purchaser's teams. 11. The number and date of sales that have been made by the purchaser to settlers and the terms of such sales and copies of all agreements between such settlers and purchasers and as to whether the same have been approved of by the Minister. 12. The number of patents issued to settlers under Clause 13 of said agreement. 13. The extent of the lands upon which patents have been issued to the purchaser under Clause 14 of said agreement, and the nature and cost of the buildings built on same for which such patents granted. 14. All correspondence between the Government or any officer or official thereof and the purchaser or any of them, or any officer or official of such purchaser, and between the Government or any officer or official thereof and any settlers, relating to the whole or any part of the subject matter of the said agreement. Presetned to the Legislature, March 6th, 1917. Mr. *Lang*. *Not Printed.*

No. 69   Return to an Order of the House of the 16th February, 1917, for a Return shewing:—1. All statements furnished by the Canada Copper Company, International Nickel Company, Mond Nickel Company, and any other company producing nickel, under section 8 of The Mining Act, respecting taxation since the 1st of January, A.D. 1915. 2. All reports from any Government Mine Assessor, made under the provisions of The Mining Act. in respect to the mining operations of the Canada Copper Company. the International Nickel Company or the Mond Nickel Company. particularly with reference to the taxes to be paid by the said companies, or any of them, under The Mining Tax Act. 3. All correspondence since the 1st day of January, 1915, between the Minister of Lands, Forests and Mines, or the Provincial Treasurer, or any officer or official of the Government, and the Canada Copper Company. the International Nickel Company, the Mond Nickel Company, and any other companies producing nickel, or any officer or solicitor for or on behalf of the said companies, or any of them, with reference to the amount of taxes or royalties paid or to be paid by the said companies or any of them, to the Provincial Treasurer of the Province, in respect of the ore mined or the mining operations carried on by them in the Province of Ontario. Presented to the Legislature, March 16th, 1917. Mr. *Carter*. *Not Printed.*

No. 70   Return to an Order of the House of the 9th March, 1917, for a Return shewing:—1. The number, kind and cost of buildings comprised in the Burwash Prison Farm property. 2. What is the number of acres of land belonging to or included in the Burwash Prison Farm property, and of such land, how many acres are under cultivation, and how many acres are used for the purpose of pasture. 3. How many prisoners are there at Burwash Prison Farm. 4. What is the number of employees at the Burwash Prison Farm, and what is the amount of salary paid to each employee. 5. Were cattle or other animals shipped from the Burwash Prison Farm in the year 1916, and if so, what was the number so shipped, the total value of such shipments and the amount paid as freight charges thereon. 6. Were cattle or other animals brought to the Burwash Prison Farm from other places in the year 1916, and if so, what was the number so brought, and what were the names of the places from which said cattle or other animals were brought. Presented to the Legislature, March 16th, 1917. Mr. *Mageau*. *Printed.*

No. 71 | Return to an Order of the House of the 16th February, 1917, for a Return:—1. Shewing the names of all the Townsites established by the T. & N. O. Ry. Commission. 2. Shewing all the townsite lands sold by the T. & N. O. Ry. Commission on or after July 29, 1916, the towns in which they were situated, and the amounts received for each. Presented to the Legislature, March 20th, 1917. Mr. *Bowman*. *Not Printed.*

No. 72 | Copies of contracts with The Kinleith Paper Company, Limited, St. Catharines, Ontario; The Georgetown Coated Paper Mills, Limited, Georgetown; The Provincial Paper Mills Company, Limited, Toronto; authorized by Order in Council dated February 20th, 1917. Presented to the Legislature, March 21st, 1917. *Printed.*

No. 73 | Return to an Order of the House of the 19th February, 1917, for a Return shewing if the Canadian Northern Railway Company applied to the Minister of Lands, Forests and Mines to designate the lands or any part of the lands to be granted to the said railway as provided in section 3, 9 Edw. VII., chap. 71. 2. Has the Minister of Lands, Forests and Mines designated any such lands or any part of the same. 3. If such lands or any part of the same have been so designated, what is the total acreage so designated, and of what townships or part of townships does the same consist. 4. Have the said lands or any part of the same been surveyed. 5. If the said lands have not been so designated, why have they not been designated. Presented to the Legislature, March 21st, 1917. Mr. *Davidson*. *Printed.*

No. 74 | Return to an Order of the House of the 23rd February, 1917, for a Return shewing:—1. What amounts have been paid and upon what dates since January 1st, 1916, to the firm of Gunn, Richards and Company, Production Engineers and Public Accountants of 43 Wall Street, 43 Exchange Place, New York, or to any one acting for them, or on their behalf, on account of any

Department of the Government. 2. What amounts, if any, are still owing to the said firm or any one acting for them or on their behalf. 3. What were the services rendered in respect to which such payments were made or liability incurred. 4. By what authority was the employment of the said firm authorized. Presented to the Legislature, March 21st, 1917. Mr. *Richardson. Not Printed.*

No. 75 | Return to an Order of the House of the 19th February, 1917, for a Return shewing:—1. The total capital expenditure to the end of the fiscal year for all purposes in respect to the Guelph Prison Farm. 2. Any further capital expenditures contemplated, and if so, to what amount. 3. How many prisoners, on the average, have been accommodated at the Guelph Prison Farm during the year 1916. 4. How many prisoners are now at the Guelph Prison Farm for offences against the criminal law. 5. What was the average number of prisoners at the Guelph Prison Farm · during the year 1916 for offences against the criminal law. Presented to the Legislature, March 28th, 1917. Mr. *Ferguson (Kent.) Printed.*

No. 76 | Return to an Order of the House of the 28th March, 1917, for a Return shewing:—1. What was the total cost of the knitting plant installed at the Mercer Reformatory, Toronto. 2. From whom was such knitting plant purchased and what was the date of purchase. 3. When was the said knitting plant installed. 4. What amount was paid to operatives up to the 1st of March, 1917, for operating the said plant. 5. What is the value of the goods produced from the knitting plant. 6. Have the goods produced by the said plant been sold, and if so, to whom. Presented to the Legislature, March 29th, 1917. Mr. *Ferguson (Kent.) Not Printed.*

No. 77 | Return to an Address to His Honour the Lieutenant-Governor of the 19th February, 1917, praying that he would cause to be laid before this House a Return:—1. Of copies of all correspondence passing between the Government of this Province, or any member, officer or official thereof, and the Government of the Dominion of Canada, or any officer or official thereof, in reference to the care of Returned Soldiers. 2. Of all correspondence passing between the Government of this Province, or any member, officer or official thereof, and the Government of the Dominion of Canada, or any officer or official thereof, in reference to the establishment of Convalescent Homes for the care of Returned Soldiers. 3. Of all correspondence passing between the Government of this Province, or any member, officer or official thereof, and the Government of the Dominion of Canada, or any officer or official thereof, in reference to the relations between the Soldiers' Aid Commission and the Military Hospitals Commission of the Army Medical Service Corps. Presented to the Legislature, April 2nd, 1917. Mr. *Rowell. Not Printed.*

No. 78	Return to an Order of the House of the 21st March, 1917, for a Return of copies: 1. Of all correspondence and documents at any time passing between the Director of Industries, Ontario Reformatory, and the Assistant Provincial Secretary, referring to Alexander McPherson, foreman, Ontario Reformatory Industries, and Fred. W. French, Assistant Director of Ontario Reformatory Industries, or either of them, or relating to any matters arising between the said Alexander McPherson and Fred. W. French. Presented to the Legislature, April 2nd, 1917. Mr. *Richardson*. *Not Printed.*
No. 79	Copies of all Orders-in-Council made under the authority of the Department of Education Act or of the Acts relating to Public Schools, Separate Schools or High Schools, passed since the opening of the present Session of the Legislative Assembly. (*See No. 61.*) Presented to the Legislature, April 2nd, 1917. *Printed.*
No. 80	Return to an Order of the House of the 30th March, 1917, for a Return shewing: 1. What has been the cost of the Ontario Nickel Commission since the 1st day of February, 1917: (*a*) For salaries or payments by way of remuneration or honorarium to each member of the Commission respectively; (*b*) For travelling expenses of each member of the Commission respectively; (*c*) For allowance in lieu of travelling expenses to each member of the Commission respectively; (*d*) For other purposes, specifying such purposes and amounts. 2. What honorarium, remuneration or salary is payable or to be paid to the members of the Commission other than G. T. Holloway. 3. Is the Chairman, G. T. Holloway, still in the Government employ at $20,000 *per* year and $10.00 *per* day in lieu of travelling expenses, and if so when will the obligation of the Government cease. 4. Are the travelling expenses of the said G. T. Holloway from Toronto to Great Britain to be paid by the Government in addition to the allowance made to him. 5. What were the services rendered by each of the following parties in respect of which payments were made to them for salary as shown in the Return of the 16th February, 1916, respectively: Professor George A. Guess, salary, $1,250; F. Clithero, salary, $388.54; G. W. Dixon, salary, $359.03; A. L. Clark, salary, $600.00; R. N. Dickson, salary, $485.00; A. Stanfield, salary, $200.00; E. M. Tozer, salary, $306.60; E. A. Wilson, salary, $210.73. Presented to the Legislature, April 4th, 1917. Mr. *Dewart*. *Not Printed.*
No. 81	Return to an Order of the House of the 19th March, 1917, for a Return of copies of all correspondence between the Government of Ontario or any Member, officer or official thereof, and the Devonshire Race Track Company or any member, officer or official thereof, and in particular the correspondence between J. T. White, Esq., Solicitor to the Department of the Provincial Treasurer, and Hon. Dr. Reaume. Presented to the Legislature, April 4th, 1917. Mr. *Wigle*. *Not Printed.*

No. 82 | Return to an Order of the House of the 28th March, 1917, for a Return of:—1. Copies of: (1) Charter of the Gore Bay Riding and Driving Association. (2) Supplementary Letters Patent, dated 17th November, 1915, increasing capital stock to $25.000, and changing name to " Northern Riding and Driving Association." (3) Supplementary Letters Patent, dated 12th February, 1916, increasing capital stock to $200,000. 2. Copies of all annual returns made by the said company. 3. Copies of all correspondence, and documents filed with the Government on the application for the issue of said Supplementary Letters Patent. 4. Copies of application for license to the Provincial Treasurer, and all correspondence and communications in connection with the issue of said license to hold a race meeting at Windsor. Presented to the Legislature, April 6th, 1917. Mr. *Wigle. Not Printed.*

No. 83 | Report of the Horticultural Experiment Station, Vineland Station, Ontario, 1906-1915. Presented to the Legislature, April 6th, 1917. *Printed.*

No. 84 | Report of the Soldiers' Aid Commission of Ontario, 1916. Presented to the Legislature, April 6th, 1917. *Not Printed.*

No. 85 | Return to an Order of the House of the 12th March, 1917, for a Return shewing what was the number of prisoners in all gaols, reformatories and prisons in the Province of Ontario, on the thirtieth day of September, 1916. Presented to the Legislature, April 6th, 1917. Mr. *Parliament. Not Printed.*

No. 86 | Return to an Order of the House of the 26th March, 1917, for a Return shewing:—1. What was the total number of members of the Inside Civil Service of the Government of the Province of Ontario and the total number in each department thereof on the 31st day of July, 1914, the 31st day of July, 1916, and the 28th day of February, 1917, respectively. Presented to the Legislature, April 6th, 1917. Mr. *Elliott. Not Printed.*

No. 87 | Return to an Order of the House of the 16th March, 1917, for a Return shewing:—1. What tenders were received for each and every of the lots advertised for sale by George W. Lee, Commissioner of the Temiskaming and Northern Ontario Railway in the " North Bay Times " on Thursday, October 12th, 1916. 2. Which of the said lots have been sold by the said George W. Lee, the Temiskaming and Northern Ontario Railway Commission or any officer or official thereof. 3. What were the prices and terms at and upon which each and every of the said lots were sold by the said George W. Lee, the said Commission or any officer or official thereof. 4. Which of the said lots sold by the said George W. Lee, the said Commission, or any officer or official thereof, within the municipalities of Porquis Junction, Matheson, Cochrane, and Englehart, or what proportion of each and every lot so sold lies within the municipalities. Presented to the Legislature, April 6th. 1917. Mr. *Mageau. Not Printed.*

No. 88   Return to an Order of the House of the 21st March, 1917, for a Return of copies:—1. Of all reports for the year ending October 31st, 1916, of the superintendents of each and all the asylums, government prisons and reformatories in Ontario. 2. Of letters between Assistant Provincial Secretary and Fred Hill, relating to the dismissal of the said Fred Hill from the staff of the Ontario Reformatory at Guelph. Presented to the Legislature, April 6th, 1917. Mr. *Grieve. Not Printed.*

No. 89   Return to an Order of the House of the 16th February, 1917, for a Return shewing:—1. What amount has actually been paid since January 1st, 1916, for war purposes, by the Government, out of the proceeds of the Provincial War Tax. 2. For what particular purposes have such payments been made and what are the date of such payments. Presented to the Legislature, April 6th, 1917. Mr. *Bowman. Not Printed.*

Cutting First Crop of Oats on Farm of Mr. H. Hackford. East part, South half Lot 12, Con. 1, Township Marter.

FIFTEENTH ANNUAL REPORT

OF THE

Temiskaming and Northern Ontario Railway Commission

ONTARIO GOVERNMENT RAILWAY

SIR WILLIAM H. HEARST, PREMIER

For Year Ended October 31st

1916

PRINTED BY ORDER OF

THE LEGISLATIVE ASSEMBLY OF ONTARIO

TORONTO:

Printed and Published by A. T. WILGRESS, Printer to the King's Most Excellent Majesty

1917

Printed by
WILLIAM BRIGGS
Corner Queen and John Streets
TORONTO

To His Honour Sir John Strathearn Hendrie, C.V.O., a Lieutenant-Colonel in the Militia of Canada.

Lieutenant-Governor of the Province of Ontario.

May it Please Your Honour:

The undersigned has the honour to present to Your Honour the Fifteenth Annual Report of the Temiskaming and Northern Ontario Railway Commission for the fiscal year ended October 31st, 1916.

Respectfully submitted,

F. G. MACDIARMID,

Minister of Public Works and Highways.

Department of Public Works, Ontario,
March 7th, 1917.

HON. FINLAY MACDIARMID,

> *Minister of Public Works and Highways,*

> *Toronto.*

SIR,—I have the honour, by direction, to submit to the Legislature the Fifteenth Annual Report of the Temiskaming and Northern Ontario Railway Commission for the fiscal year ended October 31st, 1916.

I have the honour to be, Sir,

Your obedient servant,

W. H. MAUND,

Secretary-Treasurer.

Temiskaming and Northern Ontario Railway Commission.

J. L. ENGLEHART............Chairman..............................Petrolia.
DENIS MURPHY..............Commissioner.........................Ottawa.
GEO. W. LEE...............Commissioner and General Agent.........North Bay.

CHIEF OFFICERS.

W. H. MAUND...............Secretary-Treasurer....................Toronto.
S. B. CLEMENT ....Chief Engineer and Supt. of Maintenance. North Bay.
W. A. GRIFFIN.............Superintendent of Traffic...............North Bay.
T. J. GRACEY..............Auditor of Disbursements and Accountant.Toronto.
A. J. PARR................General Freight and Passenger Agent.....North Bay.
W. A. GRAHAM..............Purchasing Agent and Storekeeper........North Bay.
W. J. HARPER..............Auditor of Receipts and Car Accountant..North Bay.
C. L. FERGUSON............Paymaster...............................North Bay.
T. ROSS...................Master Mechanic.........................North Bay.
H. L. RODGERS.............Mechanical Engineer.....................North Bay.
C. BATTLEY................Air-brake Inspector.....................North Bay.
S. H. RYAN................Trainmaster.............................North Bay.
R. L. LAMB................Chief Train Despatcher..................North Bay.
WM. YOUNG.................Roadmaster—District No. 1...............North Bay.
S. J. FAUGHT, SR..........Assistant Roadmaster—District No. 1.....North Bay.
J. DRINKWATER.............Roadmaster—District No. 2...............Cochrane.
ADAM EDWARDS..............Assistant Roadmaster—District No. 2.....Cochrane.
W. J. OLDHAM..............Bridge and Building Master..............North Bay.
J. J. DOUGLASS............Road Foreman, Locomotives...............North Bay.
W. J. KELLY...............Supt. Telegraphs and Telephones.........North Bay.
ARTHUR A. COLE............Mining Engineer.........................Cobalt.
J. G. G. KERRY............Consulting Engineer.....................Toronto.

TEMISKAMING AND NORTHERN ONTARIO RAILWAY COMMISSION.

General Remarks.

Accounts and statistics for year ending October 31, 1916, herewith:

Mileage in operation on October 31st, 1916:—

Main Line.

	Miles.	Miles.
North Bay to Cochrane	252.29	252.29

Branch Lines.

Charlton Branch	7.60	
Porcupine Branch (includes Iroquois Falls Branch)..............	40.11	
Elk Lake Branch	28.50	
		76.21
Nipissing Junction Spur (leased to Grand Trunk Railway).......	......	2.10

Yards and Sidings.

Yards and sidings, main and branch lines........................	107.63	
Liskeard Spur	1 12	
		108.75
Double track, North Cobalt to Haileybury	......	1.70

Subsidiary Lines.

Nipissing Central Railway	13.26	13.26
Total mileage		454.31

Following condensed statement of Revenue Account for fiscal year ended October 31, 1916, compared with 1914 and 1915. The sub-divisions of the condensed statement for 1916 are shown in full detail in the financial part of this report:—

	1914.	1915.	1916.
Revenue from transportation	$1,580,668 28	$1,483,923 07	$2,044,808 99
Revenue other than transportation	90,230 59	66,480 26	93,312 96
Total operating revenue	$1,670,898 87	$1,550,403 33	$2,138,121 95
Operating expenses	1,468,574 23	1,356,049 87	1,594,177 46
Net operation revenue	$202,324 64	$194,353 46	$543,944 49
Ore royalties	$55,874 45	$26,268 74	$49,877 62
Rent from joint facilities	....	13,815 26	18,620 45
Rent from lease of road	....	16,601 37	13,347 04
Interest	....	....	1,736 36
Miscellaneous income	......	2,857 98	1,029 78
	$253,199 09	$253,896 81	$628,555 74
Deductions from income—hire of equipment, etc.	29,221 86	43,358 18	99,850 28
Total earnings	$228,977 23	$210,538 63	$528,705 46

Operating expenses amount to 75.1 per cent. of the gross earnings, the net earnings to 24.9 per cent., as compared with 85.6 per cent., and 14.4 per cent. respectively, for the twelve (12) months ended October 31st, 1915, and 87.8 per cent. and 12.2 per cent. for the twelve months ended October 31, 1914.

Earnings and expenses of Nipissing Central Railway are not included, but shown separately on page 423 of this report.

Total of pay rolls for the year amounted to............ $1,127,885 74

Comparison of Pay Rolls since Commencement of Operation.

1905	$216,119 37
1906	450,214 02
1907	574,959 09
1908	687,541 66
1909	681,072 47
1910	878,192 07
1911	783,218 89
1912	1,090,310 65
1913	1,218,473 04
1914	1,112,866 73
1915	953,209 41
1916	1,127,885 74

Total $9,774,063 14

The various statements contained in the financial part of report, fully itemized, will show:

| | November 1st to October 31st. | | |
	1916.	1915.	1914.
Revenue per mile of road	$6,508 74	$4,719 64	$5,061 18
Expenditure per mile of road	4,852 90	4,128 00	4,448 06
Net revenue per mile of road	$1,655 84	$591 64	$613 12
Miles of road operated	328.5	328.5	330.14

A betterment in net revenue in 1916 of $1,064.30 per mile operated over that of 1915 and an increase of $1,042.72 over 1914.

RECEIPTS.

	1916.	1915.	1914.
Revenue from transportation	$2,044,808 89	$1,483,923 07	$1,580,668 28
Revenue from other than transportation...	93,312 96	66,480 26	90,230 59
Total	$2,138,121 95	$1,550,403 33	$1,670,898 87

Increase over 1915 .... $587,718 62
Increase over 1914 .... 467,223 08

EXPENDITURES.

November 1 to October 31.

	%	1916.	%	1915.	%	1914.
Maintenance of way and structures	16.3	$349,024 48	21.5	$333,686 06	24.2	$408,046 15
Maintenance of equipment	11.6	248,702 04	17.5	271,335 10	17.	284,935 87
Traffic expenses	1.1	22,465 69	1.2	18,320 66	1.1	18,872 65
Transportation expenses.	39.4	842,058 75	40.9	634,160 64	39.	651,687 20
Miscellaneous operations.	2.0	42,562 89	1.9	28,701 40	....	....
General expenses	4.3	91,317 74	4.6	70,994 15	6.5	105,032 36
Transptn for Invstmt. Cr.	.1	1,954 13	.1	Cr. 1,148 44	....	....
Total operating exp..	74.6	$1,594,177 46	87.5	$1,356,049 57	87.8	$1,468,574 23
Balance	....	$543,944 49	....	$194,353 46	....	$202,324 64

MAINTENANCE OF WAY.

Renewal of rails, ties, ballast, etc., is fully detailed in report of Chief Engineer and Superintendent of Maintenance. The following statement shows distribution of the sums expended under the above heading, comparative 1914-15-16:

	1916.	1915.	1914.
Ballast	$5,935 63	$3,659 33	$15,470 56
Ties	32,643 42	28,845 05	34,700 65
Rails	4,732 84	8,725 46	21,429 22
Track material—frogs, switches, etc.	12,817 12	7,990 63	11,003 27
Roadway material and track repairs	176,661 89	166,392 62	196,797 43
Removal snow and ice	36,473 71	15,022 37	18,322 82
Bridges, trestles and culverts	9,099 40	30,421 75	30,142 15
Crossings, fences and signs	3,322 63	5,429 50	5,094 70
Telegraph and telephones, railway	5,681 91	3,283 81	7,894 22
Buildings, fixtures and grounds	29,670 93	28,238 13	44,939 89
Roadway tools and supplies	3,868 46	4,756 17	5,882 65
Miscellaneous expenses	*28,116 54	†30,921 24	16,368 59
Total	$349,024 48	$333,686 06	$408,046 15

MAINTENANCE OF EQUIPMENT.

The equipment has been maintained as heretofore to the highest standard of efficiency. In addition to maintenance statement below, there is shown a charge of $44,931.51, which has been added to reserve fund to cover depreciation on rolling stock, and to provide for the renewal of cars and locomotives retired, sold or destroyed.

EQUIPMENT REPAIRS.

	November 1st to October 31st.		
	1916.	1915.	1914.
Locomotives—repairs	$93,935 90	$86,269 58	$85,611 36
Passenger train cars—repairs	61,449 35	47,890 37	64,287 32
Freight train cars—repairs	34,778 69	16,208 51	32,106 29
Work equipment—repairs ....Cr.	8,876 79	53,658 55	15,472 12
Total	$181,287 15	$204,027 01	$197,477 09

DEPRECIATION.

	1916.	1915.	1914.
Locomotive—depreciation	$15,034 59	$14,845 56	$14,828 22
Passenger train cars—depreciation	13,373 40	14,040 84	9,012 36
Freight train cars—depreciation	12,462 60	12,327 36	12,727 08
Work equipment—depreciation	▶ 4,060 92	3,337 44	3,337 44
Total	$44,931 51	$44,551 20	$39,905 10

RETIREMENT.

	1916.	1915.	1914.
Locomotive—retirement	....	....	$8,391 12
Passenger train cars—retirement	....	....	3,859 40
Freight train cars—retirement	$418 72	....	21,548 25
Work equipment—retirement	....	....	....
Total	$418 72	....	$33,798 77

*Includes insurance of $7,820.20; † includes insurance of $29.484.84. Under old classification, year 1914, these items were chargeable to general expenses.

SUMMARY.

	1916.	1915.	1914.
Equipment repairs	$181,287 15	$204,027 01	$197,477 09
" depreciation	44,931 51	44,551 20	39,905 10
" retirement	418 72	....	33,798 77
	$226,637 38	$248,578 21	$271,180 96

Total for years 1914, 1915, 1916 .... $746,396 55

ADDITIONS AND BETTERMENTS.

During the fiscal year 1916 there have been expended the amounts as shown in following statements under above heading. Similar statements for 1914-1915 are appended for comparative purposes.

	1916.	1915.	1914.
Shops, engine houses, etc.	$15,294 65	$9,251 93	$5,759 55
Water and fuel stations	7,444 64	16,606 53	197 71
Shop machinery	2,413 44	3,403 95	....
Station and roadway buildings	47,270 96	23,327 08	53,298 63
Miscellaneous structures	6,801 49	....	651 64
Steam locomotives—additional	205,580 09	....	....
Steam locomotives—improvements	....	6,000 00	5,671 00
Passenger cars—additional	77,500 58	....	254,399 43
Passenger cars—improvements	4,952 46	1,393 27	1,021 10
Freight cars—additional	....	6,763 28	....
Work equipment—additional	40,923 03	1,407 06	....
Work equipment—improvements	....	....	1,410 35
Replacing wooden bridges with steel	2,674 43	752 73	71,560 06
Filling trestles—new culverts	24,839 02	15,331 10	21,268 62
Replacing wood trestles with concrete	....	1,749 16	....
Ties	4,170 53	4,764 52	11,063 42
Rails	14,205 76	8,570 98	37,310 46
Track materials, switches, etc.	9,533 07	13,599 96	25,098 78
	$463,604 15	$112,921 55	$488,710 75

GENERAL.

For year under review, as compared with 1914-1915, the percentages of operating expenses to operating revenue, are as follows:—

1916 . . .. 74.6%
1915 . . .. 87.5%
1914 . . .. 87.8%

Balance brought down from result of operation for year:—

1916 .... $543,944 49
1915 .... 194,353 46
1914 .... 202,324 64

Above comparative results show that 1916 betterment over 1915 is $349,-591.03, and over 1914, $341,619.85.

Ore Royalties.

1916 .... $49,877 62
1915 .... 26,268 74
1914 .... 55,874 45

An increase in 1916 of $23,608.88 over 1915.

Net earnings for fiscal year 1916	$528,705 46
Net earnings for fiscal year 1915	210,538 63
Net earnings for fiscal year 1914	228,977 23

Increase 1916 over 1915, $318,166.83—151 per cent.
Increase 1916 over 1914, $299,728.23—131 per cent.

We have transmitted to Provincial Treasurer for the year under review cheque for one million dollars—$1,000,000.

WAGES—INCREASE.

During the year practically all freight clerks, checkers, truckers and general station staffs, have been granted increases ranging from $5.00 to $10.00 per month. Laborers, North Bay, rate per hour increased from 18c. to 25c., with increase each employee in this class averaging approximately $20.00 per month.

Increase in wage to employees, Maintenance of Way Department, average $4,500.00 per month; Motive Power and Car Department employees $1,500.00 per month, and station agents' staffs about $500.00 per month.

Increased traffic necessitated employment of additional help at various stations, with wage increase allowed employees holding similar positions at other points.

Thus general increases were granted covering practically all branches of the service.

Full details with percentages are contained in report of Chief Engineer and Superintendent of Maintenance, page 21.

MINES AND MINERALS.

Mining Engineer's preliminary report only included herein. Regular complete report for year 1916 will be specially published in usual form.

HEAD OFFICE—TORONTO.

In September of present year Commission removed executive offices from 25 Toronto Street to 56 Church Street, City.

RELIEF FOR FIRE SUFFERERS.

During the period of distress immediately following the forest fires of July 29th-30th last, Commission put every facility of the Road at the disposition of those in charge of relief matters, et al. The following is a condensed statement of cost to Commission therein:—

Fire Sufferers, July 29-30, 1916.

Relief trains, men and materials	$1,491 53
Telegraph messages, transmitted free	105 33
Shipments in transit, diverted to use	540 56
Transportation tickets, issued free	7,656 75
Long distance telephone messages	27 90
Cost to Commission	$9,822 07

Farm of Mr. Oscar Prevost, Marter Township.

PATRIOTIC ASSOCIATION.

The employees of Commission formed themselves into a body known as " T. & N. O. Railwaymen's Patriotic Association," and through this source the following sums have been subscribed and paid to " Canadian Red Cross Society " and " Canadian Patriotic Fund " :—

Total subscription to Red Cross Society	$10,245 36
Total subscription to Canadian Patriotic Fund	12,064 52
Commission's subscription	10,000 00
Total	$32,309 88

The above is exclusive of many personal subscriptions made direct by members of Commission and employees, and is exclusive of monthly subscriptions to the "50,000 Club" by entire office staff, Toronto.

ROLL OF HONOUR.

Since the commencement of the war in August, 1914, up to date of October, 1916, a total of 91 employees joined the Canadian Expeditionary Forces, equivalent to over eleven per cent. (11%) of the entire number in Commission's service. In addition to this, very many men in the employ belonging to foreign nations as reservists, joined the colours of the respective countries—particularly Russians and Italians. To those joining the ranks of the Canadian Expeditionary Forces the Commission have instituted an honorary recognition therein in the form of a donation to each member, and to this end the sum of Eleven thousand five hundred and ninety-eight dollars and sixty-six cents ($11,598.66) has been disbursed.

WORKMEN'S COMPENSATION ACT.

Since the inception of the Act in January, 1915, the Commission voluntarily placed themselves under the jurisdiction of the Board, and during period under consideration—January, 1915, to October, 1916, inclusive, twenty-two months—the results are as follows:

Ninety-two (92) claims registered on Commission's book and submitted to Workmen's Compensation Board for adjustment:

48 Claims passed and paid.
40 Claims disallowed.
4 Claims in abeyance.

The forty-eight claims passed and paid amount to $3,807.15, an average of $70.17.

Liability insurance based on Commission's pay rolls for period would have cost $29,311.05, to protect above loss, or an average premium cost of $732.37 to protect an average award of $70.17.

Insurance premium during period would be	$29,311 05
W. C. Board's awards amount to	2,807 15
Cost reduction available	$26,503 90

FIRE RANGING.

From 1909 to 1916 inclusive, for the service of fire ranging, Commission have received from the Department of Lands, Forests and Mines the following accounts, same having been paid in due course:—

Year.
1909 .... $16,963 86
1910 .... 10,000 00
1911 .... 20,000 00
1912 .... 5,000 00
1914 .... 5,000 00
1915 .... 10,000 00
1916 .... 29,374 00

    Total $96,337 86

FOREST FIRES—NORTHERN ONTARIO, JULY 29-30TH, 1916.

Following is a statement of Commission's loss under above heading showing value of property destroyed and insurance recovered thereon. All claims presented and paid up to date of October 30th, 1916, are included herein:—

Buildings and structures $33,874 10
Damage to bridges and culverts 1,091 85
Fencing destroyed, right of way 3,001 00
Ties destroyed in track 2,334 35
Ties destroyed, right of way 976 61
Rails destroyed 2,038 40
Track material 520 04
Telegraph and telephone 2,688 06
Claims presented and paid 12,485 70
Claims under adjustment 28,531 84
Relief to fire sufferers 9,822 07
Miscellaneous, fighting fires, clearing burned area, etc.. 14,897 23
    Total $112,261 25
    Insurance recoverable 61,336 97

    Uncontrollable loss $50,924 28

In addition to above there are ninety-four freight cars of foreign roads destroyed for which claims will be presented in due course; also adjustment of values of contents of buildings destroyed, damage to work equipment and many other claims yet to be dealt with.

We have pleasure in directing attention to report of Edwards, Morgan & Co., Chartered Accountants, with reference to the accounts.

J. L. ENGLEHART, ESQ., Chairman,

    Temiskaming and Northern Ontario Railway Commission,

Toronto, Ont.

DEAR SIR,—Under instructions from the Commissioners we have maintained a running audit of the accounts of the Commission for the year ending October 31st, 1916. Our examination has included the Cash Receipts and Disbursements, Accounts Collectible, Accounts Payable, Agents' and Conductors' Accounts, Foreign Tickets, Foreign Freights, Car Mileage Accounts and Bank Balances.

We certify that all transactions relating thereto have been properly vouched, and that the Cash and Bank Balances have been duly accounted for. We have verified the balances of accounts outstanding and have ascertained that they correspond with the General Ledger Accounts.

We find the books in good order and all information asked for has been promptly given.

We are,

Yours faithfully,

(Sgd.) EDWARDS, MORGAN & CO.

NEW SCHEDULE—ORDER OF RAILROAD TELEGRAPHERS.

Commission have now arrived at a satisfactory conclusion with Operators, Station Agents, etc., and this is embodied in an agreement between Commission and Order of Railroad Telegraphers, effective December 1st, 1916.

This agreement provides for a general increase in all salaries under above heading, amounting approximately to $7,000.00 per annum—equal to 11.7 per cent.

Fine yield on Farm of Mr. Wm. Schell.   North half Lot 1, Con. 4, Dack Township.

Annual Report 1916.

Insurance—Fire.

During the year, fire insurance has been maintained on Commission's property to the extent of $1,948,895, valuation under the following headings:—

BUILDINGS AND CONTENTS.

Division No. 1—buildings	$259,230 00	
" 1—contents	157,300 00	
" 2—buildings	96.775 00	
" 2—contents	27,400 00	
Kerr Lake Br. —buildings	600 00	
" —contents	100 00	
Charlton Br. —buildings	7,100 00	
" —contents	1,300 00	
Porcupine Br.—buildings	45,300 00	
" —contents	17,000 00	
Elk Lake Br. —buildings	16,100 00	
" —contents	3,250 00	
Electric Ry. —buildings	10,425 00	
" —contents	23,040 00	$664,920 00

BRIDGES AND TRESTLES.

Division No. 1	$4,600 00	
Division No. 2	16,950 00	
Kerr Lake Branch	5,000 00	
Charlton Branch	10,150 00	
Porcupine Branch	11,750 00	
Elk Lake Branch	12,400 00	$60,850 00

FREIGHT.

Merchandise in transit	$200,000 00	$200,000 00

ROLLING STOCK.

Locomotives and tenders	$210,000 00	
Passenger equipment	317.700 00	
Freight equipment	319,300 00	
Work equipment	81,075 00	
Electric railway equipment	45,050 00	
Foreign equipment	50,000 00	$1,023,125 00

Total	$1,948,895 00

The rate on above insurance is $1.50 per $100.00 for a period of three years, or 50c. per $100.00 per annum for period 1915-1917, inclusive.

Therefore, present rate of insurance expires at end of November, 1917.

Insurance under joint schedule is divided as follows:—

Western Assurance Co., 50 per cent.; Home Insurance Co., 35 per cent.; Norwich Union Fire Insurance Society, 15 per cent.

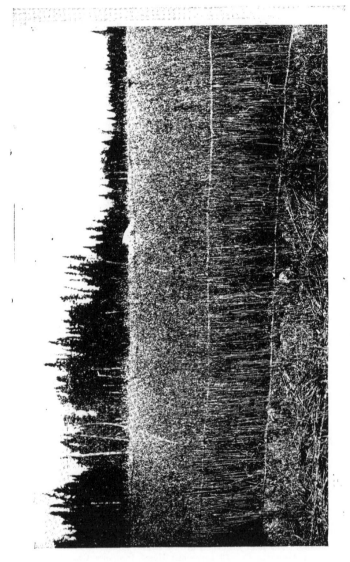

Oats six feet high, yielding 75 bushels per acre, on Farm of Mr. H. Hackford.   South half Lot 12, Con. 1, Township Marter.

COUNSEL'S REPORT—D. E. THOMSON, K.C.

Litigation.

At the end of the financial year there were no actions pending in which the Commission was defendant. During the year the threatened litigation with one Balaban, administrator of the estate of Evan Koptonchuk and Messrs. Morrow & Beatty, arising out of an accident on the siding of the Abitibi Pulp and Paper Company, was compromised.

There is only one action pending in which the Commission is plaintiff, namely:

T. & N. O. vs. Abitibi Pulp and Paper Company. Action for indemnity under siding agreement in respect of the amounts paid in settlement of the Balaban and Morrow & Beatty claims above mentioned.

T. & N. O. vs. Abitibi Pulp and Paper Company No. 1. Action for compensation for lands in the Townsite of Matheson flooded by the defendant. Satisfactory settlement arrived at.

Damage Claims.

A large number of claims have arisen during the year in respect of freight, baggage, etc., lost, destroyed, delayed, mislaid or damaged, also claims for cattle killed on the Commission's right-of-way. Most of these claims have been adjusted or abandoned while others are still pending. None have been placed in suit.

Fire Claims.

A considerable number of claims have arisen in respect of baggage, etc., damaged or destroyed by the forest fires in July last. Some of these claims have been adjusted or abandoned while others are still pending. None have been placed in suit.

Cobalt Intercepting Sewer

Application pending before Mining Commissioner to compel Town of Cobalt to enter into an agreement indemnifying the Commission against liability by reason of the construction or operation of the intercepting sewer laid under the right-of-way and station grounds of the Commission at Cobalt.

Agreements, Contracts, etc.

A considerable number of agreements, leases and contracts covering various matters between the Commission and others have been prepared and executed.

Nipissing Central Railway

A number of claims, including those for personal injuries, were made during the year. Some have been settled and others abandoned, but in no case has a writ been issued.

Grand Trunk Railway Company—Grand Trunk Pacific and National Transcontinental Railway.

This matter is still standing for adjustment. Meantime the Commissioners of the National Transcontinental Railway are operating a temporary through train service over the Commission's line on terms suitable for such limited service.

Miscellaneous.

Numerous other questions on various subjects have arisen during the year calling for consideration by the Legal Department.

Wheat in the Shook on Mr. D. Stewart's Farm at Earlton.

ʹANNUAL REPORT OF CHIEF ENGINEER AND SUPERINTENDENT OF MAINTENANCE T. N. & O. RAILWAY.

Year ended October 31st, 1916.

W. H. Maund. Esq.,

Secretary-Treasurer;
Toronto, Ontario.

Dear Sir,—I beg to submit the following report of the Engineering, Maintenance of Way and Mechanical Departments of the Temiskaming and Northern Ontario Railway, for the fiscal year ended October 31st, 1916.

Mileage and Equipment.

There has been no change in the main track mileage, but a slight net decrease in the mileage of yard tracks, railway sidings and private sidings.

OPERATED BY THE COMMISSION:	Oct. 31, 1916.	Oct. 31, 1915.
First Track	328.50 miles	328.50 miles
Second Track	1.70 "	1.70 "
Yard Track and Sidings	98.31 "	97.96 "
Private Sidings	10.44	12.29 "
	438.95 "	440.45 "
LEASED TO GRAND TRUNK RAILWAY:		
Nipissing Junction Branch	2.10 "	2.10 "
LEASED TO NIPISSING CENTRAL RAILWAY :		—
Main Track	10.45 "	10.45 "
Yard Track and Sidings	1.65	1.14
Private Sidings	1.16 "	1.05
	13.26 "	12.64 "

Details of all track changes are shown in statements included in this report. The equipment owned by the Commission consists of the following:

	Oct. 31, 1916.	Oct. 31, 1915.
Locomotives	43	43
Passenger Cars	66	62
Freight Cars	620	644
Work Cars	89	69

Surveys and Construction.

Surveys for revision of main line were made at several points during the year. In some places these were entirely new surveys, while in others former revision surveys were improved. Of the various lines surveyed, three were chosen for construction during the year, viz:— M.P. 54 to 55, M.P. 63.0 to 66.5 and at M.P. 81, but on account of labor conditions only the grading on the first of these was completed.

The revision between M.P. 54 and 55 is 3920 ft. long. It reduces the distance approximately 30 ft., grades–no change, number of curves by 3, maximum curve from 6° 42′ to a 3° 30′ and curvature 76° 9′.

The diversion, M.P. 63.0 to 66.5 is 3.4 miles long and will reduce the distance 866 ft. Northbound grades from 1 per cent. to 0.4 per cent. and southbound from

1 per cent. to level. Number of curves 6 and the maximum curvature from 7° to 3° and total curvature by 309° 57'.

The diversion at M.P. 81 is 1,300 ft. long and reduces the distance 50 ft., curvature 58° and maximum curve from 6° to 2°.

Additions to Road and Equipment.

ROAD.

During the year, there has been carried on a large amount of work that constitutes a permanent betterment to the Commission's property. The more important of these improvements and additions are:

North Bay Junction:

Extensive enlargements of the locomotive repair shops are now under construction, including:

Brick Extension at east end of Machine Shop 52' 9" x 85' 6".

Brick Extension on north side of Machine Shop 25' x 100'.

New Frame Blacksmith Shop, 30' x 80' with an annex 20' x 37' to house flue-cleaning machines, to replace a smaller Blacksmith Shop torn down to permit the extension to the Machine Shop.

New Frame Wheel Shop—30' x 80'.

This work is all being done by the Bridge and Building Department, except the brickwork, a contract for which was awarded W. A. Martyn, of North Bay. The buildings will be completed about the first of January, 1917, and will provide accommodation for a number of additional machine tools that are required to handle the great increase in repairs to locomotives.

These enlargements in the locomotive shops involved a number of minor track changes and the relocation of track scales, scrap bins, and coach truck drop pit.

M.P. 30.74............Beam culvert replaced by a 36" concrete pipe and embankment.

M.P. 51.5 ....Timber culvert replaced by a 30" concrete pipe.

M.P. 55.94............Beam culvert replaced by a 36" concrete pipe.

Cobalt:

Owing to the difficulty of making satisfactory connections with the town waterworks and sewerage systems, the freight shed and office were without adequate toilet facilities. This has been overcome by the installation of a Kaustine lavatory equipment.

New Liskeard:

An additional spur siding 388 ft. long was laid at the wharf to provide loading accommodation for the increased traffic from Lake Temiskaming.

M.P. 122:

A standard frame shelter 10 ft. x 30 ft. was built for the accommodation of passengers waiting for trains at this flag stop.

Elk Lake:

The freight shed spur siding was extended 155 ft, and made a through siding.

M.P. 139.7 ....Timber culvert replaced by a 30" concrete pipe.

Englehart:

Extensive changes were made in the arrangement of the divisional yard, including new rip and coach tracks and yard sidings and switching leads. These changes will greatly increase the capacity of the yard and the convenience with which it can be operated.

Boston Creek:

A temporary frame building 20 x 30 ft. was built to protect way freight at this promising mining camp.

M.P. 162.3 ....Large timber trestle replaced by a double 19' 0" span rein·
                      forced concrete culvert. Trestle filling not completed.

Ramore:

A spur siding 460 ft. long to provide accommodation for shipments of forest products, etc., under construction at the beginning of the year, was completed.

Matheson:

All of the buildings on the station grounds were destroyed by the forest fire of July 29th last. These included a stone passenger station, frame freight shed, two standard frame section houses and one section tool house. These have all been completely rebuilt by our own forces except the passenger station, which will be completed about February 1st, 1917. In the meantime, the freight shed is used as a passenger station.

The Canadian Stewart Company is building a large dam for the Abitibi Power and Paper Company at Twin Falls on the Abitibi River and all the plant and material required for this work are barged from Matheson. This traffic is switched from the station grounds to the Black River over a spur built by the Canadian Stewart Company under private siding agreement.

Monteith:

Private sidings were built to serve the mill and yards of the Monteith Pulp and Timber Company, which has a very important industry on the Driftwood River at Monteith.

M.P. 214.5 ....Timber culvert replaced by a 30" concrete pipe.

Nushka:

The section house, section tool house and shelter station were destroyed by fire on July 29th. The section house and tool house have been rebuilt by our own forces.

M.P. 224.0 ....Beam culvert, destroyed by fire of July 29th, replaced by a
                      6' x 6' reinforced concrete culvert.

Porquis Junction:

The 100-ton Roberts & Schaeffer Mechanical Coaling Plant and the 41,600-gallon Steel Water Tank under construction at the close of last fiscal year, were completed.

A frame dwelling was built for the operator of the coaling plant and water station.

An Alfalfa Seed Plot on Farm of Jno. McFarlane, near New Liskeard.

A man sitting on a kitchen chair in field of Red Clover. This field yielded three bushels
to the acre of seed. Lot 1, Con. 2, Township Clergue.

Cochrane:

A new frame freight shed 30 x 160 ft. was built to replace the shed destroyed by fire on July 29th. A frame building 14 x 33 ft. was built for the use of the Car Department.

Iroquois Falls:

Two pairs of semi-detached dwelling houses for employees are under construction. These houses will be fitted with all modern conveniences with connections to the town sewers, hot air furnaces, electric lights, etc.

Timmins:

A contract for a new brick passenger station 33 x 126 ft. was awarded Messrs. Henderson and Angus of North Bay.

The building is constructed on 24 in. concrete foundation walls, supporting 13 in. exterior brick walls and 9 in. interior cross walls. The peaked roof is covered with red asbestos shingles to harmonize with the buff pressed brick finish and Indiana limestone trimmings.

The floor plan provides accommodation for waiting rooms, ticket office, telegraph office, baggage room and two express rooms.

The waiting room floors are constructed of reinforced concrete and finished with hardwood. The adjoining lavatories have a Terrazzo flooring.

The floors of the ticket office and telegraph office are of plain concrete and finished with hardwood and in the baggage and express rooms plain concrete is used.

All rooms except baggage and express rooms will be finished in black ash, with walls plastered and painted.

Electric gas-filled pendant fixtures will be installed.

The building will be heated by the Dunham steam vapor system.

It is expected that the station will be completed by the end of the calendar year, when the present frame combined passenger station and freight shed will be used exclusively as a freight shed and office.

Additional shed and team sidings will be provided in the local freight yard.

Porcupine Branch.

M.P.   0.5 ....Two 30" corrugated iron culverts replaced by a 6' x 6'
reinforced concrete culvert.

The above and other additions and betterments are summarized in the annexed statements.

EQUIPMENT.

Additions to the equipment include two all-steel baggage and express, two all-steel first class coaches, eighteen Hart cars, one steel underframe Jordan spreader and two tank cars for fire protection. Delivery of six new " Mikado " type locomotives and six steel underframe vans is expected early in the coming year.

This new equipment and betterments to other equipment is very fully described in the special report of the Master Mechanic, which accompanies this report.

Maintenance of Way.

The safety of the track and structures continues to receive the first consideration of an efficient and faithful staff of officials and employees. Notwithstanding the great scarcity of labor and difficulty in obtaining materials, the standard of maintenance has been well maintained, as is witnessed by the relative freedom from derailments, which is the cause for great thankfulness.

The maintenance programme that is being followed will insure a steady improvement in track conditions. This report includes comparative statements clearly showing this improvement.

General Conditions.

During the past year, the Temiskaming and Northern Ontario Railway has handled the largest traffic in its history, and this under conditions that were exceptionally unfavorable. The conditions included:— a shortage of motive power, an exceptionally severe winter, a great scarcity of labor and material and the disastrous forest fires.

It was anticipated that the through traffic between Cochrane and North Bay following the opening of the Transcontinental Railway, would be handled by the Grand Trunk Railway under its Running Rights' Agreement. The Grand Trunk Railway failed to make this agreement operative, and it was necessary for the Commission to move this traffic with its own power. For the first winter this was overtaxed, but arrangements were made for the purchase of additional locomotives which are now being delivered.

The winter of 1915-16 was exceptionally severe. A very heavy snow fall was accompanied by long periods of very cold weather. This not only restricted train movements but increased operating expenses, as will be seen from the following statement of expenses for Removal of Snow and Ice for the years 1910 to 1916 inclusive:

1910	1911	1912	1913	1914	1915	1916
$14,812.76	$21,137.41	$23,300.74	$24,940.30	$18,322.82	$15,022.37	$36,259.44

The withdrawal of labor due to enlistments for Overseas' Service and the increased demands of the mines and pulp and paper mills served to accentuate in this district the general shortage of labor throughout the Province. It was impossible to obtain a sufficient supply of labor for the Maintenance of Way and Motive Power Departments and the progamme of Maintenance and Betterment work was of necessity considerably modified and curtailed.

The forest fires of July 29th still further complicated the situation by greatly increasing the amount of work to be accomplished through the reconstruction of buildings destroyed.

Wages of Employees.

The machinists in the Motive Power Department and the employees in the Car and Maintenance of Way Departments work under " Rules and Rates of Pay " formally agreed upon between their organizations and the Commission. Applications for " Revised Rules and Increased Rates of Pay " were made by the machinists and the Car Department and Maintenance of Way Department employees. After a series of friendly conferences, new agreements were signed with the machinists and Car Department employees. An agreement with the Maintenance of Way employees has not yet been reached, but it is expected that it will be completed early in the year 1917.

During the year, general increases have been made in the rates of pay of all employees in the Motive Power, Car and Maintenance of Way Departments.

tment
.

n the
.8 per
tes for

e July

ases of
re now
by the

!
cult to
ds that
makes
rolling

n and
ve been
ore the
g from
triously
ochrane
ion and

e track.
t differ-
tanding
he trees
In some
e places
out the
uprooted

t a very
estroyed
brules "
; of the
cost, of

Map Showing Location
of Forest Fires
near the T. & N. O. Rly
1916.

Shaded Portions show Burned Areas.

Motive Power Department:

The increases in rates of pay for machinists in the Motive Power Department that became effective May 1st, 1916, vary from 5.6 per cent. to 9.1 per cent.

The other trades in the Motive Power Department, not included in the schedule, subsequently received very substantial increases, varying from 7.8 per cent. to 32.5 per cent., and now receive the new Canadian Pacific Railway rates for similar trades at North Bay.

Car Department:

The increases in wages of Car Department employees became effective July 1st, 1916, and vary from 6.1 per cent. to 25 per cent.

Maintenance of Way Department:

The employees of the Maintenance of Way Department asked for increases of approximately 18 per cent. to 20 per cent. on their existing schedule, and are now actually receiving various increases. These have not been formally accepted by the organization. It is believed that an early settlement will be reached.

The demands of the munitions factories have made it extremely difficult to obtain deliveries of certain classes of materials. The Munition Board demands that the requirements of plants working on war orders receive preference. This makes it necessary that our orders be reduced, but we are co-operating with the rolling mills as closely as possible.

Forest Fires.

The accompanying map shows the areas in the vicinity of Matheson and Cochrane burned over in the forest fires of July. The fires appear to have been burning for some weeks around the settlers' clearings near the railway before the strong gale of July 29th united them in a huge conflagration extending from Ramore to Nellie Lake and travelling in a southeasterly direction at a rate variously estimated at from 25 to 40 miles an hour. Similar conditions obtained at Cochrane where the front of the fire was about eight miles in a north and south direction and the course was almost due east.

At Nahma the fire travelled north-east but did not extend far beyond the track. While the fire swept over the entire area shown, the damage to the timber in different sections varied greatly. Where there was any slashing or windfalls, the standing trees were entirely destroyed. In places where there is little undergrowth the trees are generally fire killed but not damaged very badly for lumber or pulp. In some thinly timbered areas the larger trees are not even killed, though there are places as at Nushka where even large whitewoods are burned down, and throughout the whole area a great deal of additional loss has occurred through trees being uprooted by the wind after the covering had been burned off the roots.

In any estimate of the damage to the forest it must be noted that on a very large percentage of the area burned over this year, the timber had been destroyed by previous fires, notably by those of 1905 and 1911. And on these old "brules" the conditions for settlement have been greatly improved by the lessening of the labor required to clear the land, and by the removal, though at a deplorable cost, of further danger to life and property by fire.

The villages of Matheson, Nushka and Kelso and a number of smaller settlements were completely destroyed.. Several hundred settlers were rendered homeless and two hundred and twelve people perished.

So intense was the fire that it is marvellous that anything within the area it covered was not consumed. Through good fortune and the strenuous efforts of our employees, who made great use of one of the Commission's tank cars, all the railway buildings at Porquis Junction were saved. This break in the fire saved the greater part of the village of Porquis Junction, the fire burning only a few buildings at its northern end.

The following railway structures were burned:

Location.	Buildings.	Construction.
Belleek	Shelter station	Frame.
Matheson	Station	Stone.
	Freight shed	Frame.
	Section house No. 1	Frame.
	Wood shed No. 1	Frame.
	Section house No. 2	Frame.
	Wood shed No. 2	Frame.
	Tool house	Frame.
Nushka	Tool house	Frame.
	Section house	Frame.
	Wood shed	Frame.
	Shelter station	Frame.
Kelso	Station and freight shed	Frame.
Wicklow	Wood shed	Frame.
	Section house	Frame.
	Tool house	Frame.
Cochrane	Freight shed	Frame.
Iroquois Falls	Tool house	Frame.
	Oil house	Frame.
	Engine shed and bunk house	Frame.

A portion of the deck of the Wataybeag River Bridge and a number of timber culverts were burned and have been renewed.

The Commission also suffered a heavy loss through the destruction of fences, ties, rails and other Maintenance of Way material and tools, including:

Fence—1,600 rods destroyed.
Ties, 8'—11,320 destroyed; 1,775 damaged.
Ties, switch sets—5½ sets destroyed.
Rail—9,533 feet destroyed; 2,033 feet damaged.
Sundry track materials.
Track tools (contents of tool houses burned.)

The loss of rolling stock was as follows:

Location.	Number of cars
Belleek	16
Matheson	6
Nushka	2
Siding, M. P. 216.6	2
Wataybeag pit	1
Kelso	10
Siding, M. P. 226.8	2
Siding, M. P. 245.5	1
Cochrane	2

Iroquois Falls Branch:

M. P. 1.9	3
Onagon	2
Iroquois Falls	62
Total	109

In addition to the above, a steam railway ditcher and a rapid unloader were badly damaged at Kelso.

Of these, 94 were foreign cars, only six of which could be repaired and returned to their owners. Adjustment of losses on foreign cars is now being made with the owners under M.C.B. Rules.

Comparative Statements.

FENCING.

·The following right of way and station grounds fence was repaired and renewed:

		Length—Rods.
Second Division.		
M.P. 223-224 ....Burned July 29th, 1916		640
Iroquois Falls .... " " "		140
Iroquois Falls Branch.		
M.P. 1-4 .... " " "		1,920
Porcupine Branch.		
M.P. 30½-31½		640
Total		3,340 rods
		or 10.4 miles

New standard right of way and station grounds fencing was constructed as follows

		Length—Rods.
North Bay ....Stores and motive power office		95
M.P. 145½ ....Extra land—piling ground		90
M.P. 208 ....Right of way		36
Nushka ....Section house site		27
Monteith ....Station grounds		17
Iroquois Falls ....Section house site		25
M.P. 227 to M.P. 230 ....Right of way		1,000
M.P. 245¼ ....Piling ground		60
Nahma ....Station grounds		215
Elk Lake Branch.		
Leeville ....Right of way		200
Porcupine Branch.		
M.P. 2 to 3 ....Right of way		230
Schumacher ....Station grounds		20
Total		2,015 rods
		or 6.29 miles

The progress in fencing the right of way is indicated in the following statement:

Year.	New fencing Constructed.	Total right of way fenced.
1913	7.77 miles	155.0 miles
1914	21.80 "	165.9 "
1915	10.98 "	171.39 "
1916	6.29	174.54 "

Private Sidings:

The following statement includes all private sidings laid or extended during the year:

Location.	Name.	Length.	Remarks.
Main Line.			
North Bay ......Standard Planing Mills Co.		427 ft.	Second siding. -
Cobalt ....Right of Way Mines		262 "	
North Cobalt ...Northern Lumber Mills		109 "	Extension on existing private siding.
Matheson ....Canadian Stewart Co.		3,254 "	To handle contractors' supplies.
Monteith ......Monteith Pulp & Timber Co.		2,898 "	Three sidings to new mill.
Potter ....Canadian Pulp & Lumber Co. ..		373 "	To load pulpwood.
Porcupine Branch.			
M.P. 12 ....Terry & Gordon................		329 "	To serve sawmill.
Drinkwater Pit...A. C. White		686 "	Extension of railway siding to load pulpwood.
Timmins ......Northern Canada Supply Co		13 "	Extension on existing private siding.
Hollinger Gold Mines		115 "	Extension on existing private siding.
Total		8,466 ft.	

The following includes all private sidings removed or shortened:

Location.	Name.		Remarks.
Main Line.			
Trout Lake......	....	1,267 ft.	
Tomiko	Ferguson & McFadden	3,175 "	Portion of mill yard sidings.
Temagami (M.P.75.7)	Wm. Milne & Sons	784 "	
M.P. 79.6	Black & Wagar	850 "	
Latchford	Empire Lumber Co.	9,074 "	
Gillies Depot	Gillies Bros.	584 "	Siding shortened.
M.P. 110¾	New York Pulp & Paper Co.	340 "	
New Liskeard....	....	595 "	Abandoned brickyard.
M.P. 120	McKnight & Jones	375 "	
Earlton Jct.	McBurney Lumber Co.	613 "	
Porcupine Branch.			
Porcupine	Wm. Milne & Sons	321 "	
S. Porcupine	Dome Mines	270 "	Siding shortened.
Total.................		18,248 ft.	

Meeting, Yard and Loading Sidings:

The following new sidings or extensions to existing sidings have been con-. structed to provide accommodation for loading and unloading freight or for greater convenience in operating terminal yards:

Location.	Description.		Length.
North Bay Jct. ....Spur siding No. 10 ....extended			104 ft.
Spur siding No. 11		"	667 "
Auxiliary siding		"	28 "
Coach track No 1		"	240 "
New Liskeard ....Spur siding at wharf ....new			388 "

Location.	Description.	Length.
Englehart	Coach track .... "	873 "
	Rip tracks No 1 ....:.................. "	767 "
	Rip tracks No. 2 .... "	1,088 "
	Lead north yard ....extended	994 "
	New yard siding No. 2.....................'new	3,502 "
	New yard siding No. 3 .... "	2,151 "
	Cross-overs (3) .... "	528 "
	Engine lead ...."	1,422 "
	Engine lead	377 "
Ramore	Loading spur .... "	460 "
Porquis Jct.	Through siding ....extended	1,155 "
	No. 3 siding ....,....... "	537 "
	Loading spur ....:...new	704 "
	Cross-overs (2) .... "	320 "
	Mechanical coaling station .... "	226 "
Cochrane	Freight shed spur	1,023 "
Elk Lake Branch.		
Elk Lake Branch freight shed ....extended		155 "
	Total.................17,709 ft.	

The following public or railway sidings were taken up or shortened:

Location.	Description.	Length.
North Bay	Rip track—shortened	60
Pit, M. P. 7.75	Pit tracks—shortened	1,431
" 17	" —taken up	2,232
" 25 ....:......	" —taken up	3,951
Jocko	Loading spur—shortened	728
M. P. 81.6	Spur to Pyrite Mine—taken up	5,757
Kerr Lake Jct.	Engine shed siding— "	302
New Liskeard	Loading siding— "	244
Englehart	Cinder pit siding No. 3—shortened	400
	South yard sidings (5)— "	522
	Van siding— "	33
	Cross-over— taken up	176
Charlton	Freight shed siding— shortened......	28
	Total	15,864 ft.

Tie Renewals:

Track ties were renewed as follows:

—	Main Track.	Sidings.	Private Sidings.	Total.
First Division...........................	30,855	5,462	31	36,348
Second Division.........................	41,628	5,558	....	47,186
Kerr Lake Branch.......................	1,931	....	....	1,931
Elk Lake Branch........................	193	....	....	193
Charlton Branch........................	2,533	189	....	2,722
Porcupine Branch .... } Iroquois Falls Branch }	4,427	30	....	4,457
			Total.....	92,837

Sixteen sets of switch ties were also renewed.

The following table gives a comparison of track tie renewals for the last three years:

Fiscal Year.	Main Line.		Branch Lines.		Sidings and Spurs.	
	Total.	Per Mile of Track.	Total.	Per Mile of Track.	Total.	Per Mile of Track.
1914	87,259	346	290	3	9,414	88
1915	87,948	348	3,683	46	11,680	196
1916	72,480	287	9,084	114	11,270	107

Ballasting:

Main track reballasted with gravel ballast during the year:

—	Miles of Track.	Yards Ballast.	Remarks.
First Division :			
M.P. 26–34..............................	8.00	14,570	
M.P. 52–54..............................	2.00	1,200	
Elk Lake Branch :			
M.P. 15–19..............................	4.00	2,700	
Porcupine Branch :			
M.P. 3¼–5..............................	1.75	450	Patching.
Total..............................	15.75	18,920	

Comparing with total miles of track reballasted previous years:

—	1910	1911	1912	1913	1914	1915	1916
Miles Track	44.0	52.5	47.0	22.5	19.0	10.0	15.57
Yards Ballast	51,480	62,370	72,420	29,170	29,720	14,170	18,920

Miscellaneous Betterments:

	1915.	1916.
Timber trestle replaced by embankment..	1,220 lin. ft.	0 feet
Concrete tile used for culverts	1,555 "	1,556 . "
Corrugated iron	496 "	146 "
Tile drain to underdrain roadbed	1.86 miles	0.56 miles
Embankments restored to width by train-filling over a total of	109.75 "	26.5 . "
New right-of-way fences constructed	10.98 "	6.29
Public road crossings constructed	6	7
Private road crossings constructed	4	7

Field of Oats on the Demonstration Farm at Monteith, Walker Township.
South half Lot 12, Con. 2.

A Rural School Fair attracts the kiddies.   School Fair held at Earlton.

ALLEGED ACCIDENTS.

Date. 1916.	Name of Person Injured.	Nature of Employment.	Place of Accident.	Particulars of work at which employee was engaged at time of accident.	Extent of Injury.
Nov. 4	Charles Cadden	Machinist	North Bay	Changing wheels on tender.	Finger sprained.
" 5	Thos. E. Warner	Machinist	North Bay	Stripping engine	Head cut.
Dec. 4	Titus Kecink	Laborer	M.P. No. 2, Charlton Branch		
" 6	John Jenkyn	Car Repairer	North Bay	Handling stone	Finger cut.
" 11	David Leroy	Sectionman	New Liskeard	Handling car wheels	Knee bruised.
				Pulling spikes from ties	Finger bruised.
1916.					
Jan. 21	Joseph Desjardine	Car Repairer	North Bay	Replacing car on track with jack.	Head cut.
" 24	Wilfred Brosseau	Car Repairer	North Bay	Replacing wheels under car.	Finger cut.
" 27	Gio. Barone	Washerout	North Bay	Working on front end of engine, was struck with sledge by fellow employee.	Eye cut.
Feb. 11	Ernest Berard	Sectionman	Heaslip	Riding over section on hand car	Thumb frozen.
Mar. 18	Albert Slater	Laborer	Cochrane	Coaling engine, opening coal chute	Toe bruised.
April 8	J. Delledonne	Sectionman	Porquis Jct.	Opening gate in coal chutes.	Finger cut.
May 12	Daniel Conway	S. S. Repairer	North Bay	Cutting rivets on ballast plow	Head injured.
" 17	Peter Vahey	Laborer	New Liskeard	Loading ties on flat car	Back injured.
" 31	Arthur Houghton	Section Foreman	Bourkes	Unloading ties from flat car.	Toe bruised.
June 12	John Rathkevitch	Laborer	Englehart	Handling track material	Toe bruised.
" 17	Mike Sernak	Sectionman	Gillies Depot	Riding hand car which became derailed	Right forearm broken.
" 17	A. Hoffman	Section Foreman	Gillies Depot	Riding hand car which became derailed	Legs bruised.
" 20	Giovanni Campanille	Section Foreman	Dane	Removing ties from track; assaulted by fellow employee	Right collar bone broken.

ne 20				Closing …
" 27	R.	Cabl man	Engl …	Dressing … planer …
ly 2	Wm. Metcalf	Car Cl …	North By …	
" 5	n. Brown	Secti …	New Iiard	
" 21		Assistant	North Bay	Lifting …
" 29	J. Syesgorak	La …	Nu …	
Aug. 1	M. Bourgare		Iiaд	Driving …
" 3	C.		North Bay	
" 7	W.		North Bay	
" 11	Cli	Car	Nn	
" 29	John …	Machinist	Cochrane	
Sept. 13	Go. W. Bwles		North Bay	
" 26	Thos. Sale		North Bay	
" 7	Ad Smith	Secti	Heaslip	
" 10		Boile	H slip	
"	M. Nelan		N th Bay	Putting …
" 26	Frank		N th Bay	Unloading …

In clusion, I would take this opportunity of expressing appreciation of the faithful and efficient … rendered by the o … and employ a.

… fully limit …

Chief … S. B. …

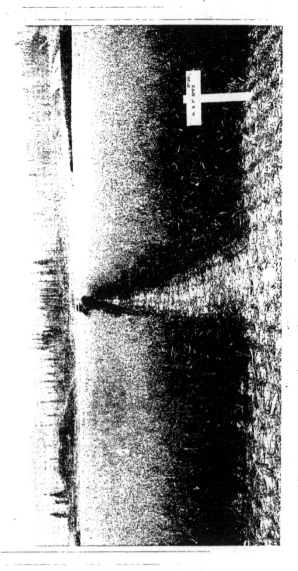

Field of Oats, Monteith Government Farm.

TEMISKAMING AND NORTHERN ONTARIO RAILWAY.

MOTIVE POWER AND CAR DEPARTMENT.

Annual Report for Year ended October 31st, 1916—Thos. Ross, Master Mechanic.

New Locomotives:

In March, 1916, contract was awarded the Canadian Locomotive Company, Kingston, for the construction of six "Mikado" type locomotives, delivery of same to be made in October. Up to the end of October two of these engines have been received, and the following is a general description of same:—

Weight on driving wheels, pounds	197,000
Weight on leading truck, pounds	29,900
Weight on trailing truck, pounds	32,000
Weight, total of engine, pounds	258,900
Weight of tender loaded, pounds	146,000
Wheel base, driving, feet and inches	16-6
Wheel base, total of engine, feet and inches	34-8
Wheel base, total of engine and tender, feet and inches	63-4¾
Cylinder, diameter and stroke, inches	25 by 30
Valves, type and diameter, inches	Piston 14 in.*
Valve gear, type	Walschaert*
Wheels, diameter of driving, inches	63
Wheels, diameter of truck, inches	33
Wheels, diameter of trailing, inches	45
Wheels, diameter of tender, inches	36
Journals, main driving, diameter and length, inches	10 by 13
Journals, other driving, diameter and length, inches	9 by 13
Journals, truck, inches	6½ by 12
Journals, trailing, inches	7 by 14
Journals, tender, inches	5½ by 10
Boiler, type	Extended wagon top
Boiler, pressure, pounds	180
Boiler, outside diameter at front end, inches	71
Boiler, outside diameter at dome course, inches	78
Firebox, length inside sheets, inches	96
Firebox, width inside sheets, inches	75¼
Tubes, number and diameter, inches	202-2
Tubes, length, feet and inches	20-0
Flues, number and diameter, inches	32-5⅜
Arch tubes, number and diameter, inches	4-3
Heating surface, firebox, square feet	208
Heating surface, arch tubes, square feet	28
Heating surface, tubes and flues, square feet	3,016
Heating surface, total, square feet	3,252
Superheating surface, square feet	757
Grate area, square feet	50.1
Water, capacity of tender, U. S. gals.	7,000
Coal, capacity of tender, tons	12
Maximum tractive power, pounds	45,500
Factor of adhesion	4.32

---

*One engine equipped with "Young" valve gear and "Young" piston valves, 12 inches diameter.

Amongst other items the equipment of these locomotives includes the following: Westinghouse E.T. 6 air brake, with 8½ inch, cross compound pump, Pyle National electric headlight equipment type E, Commonwealth Steel Co.'s cast steel rear frame extension and trailing truck, Vanadium steel main frames, these being five inches wide, Vanadium steel springs throughout on engine and tender, Franklin Railway Supply Co.'s No. 8, pneumatic fire doors, Franklin Railway Supply Co.'s power grate shakers, and Franklin Railway Supply Co.'s automatic driving box wedges.

Two of the engines have been equipped with Mudge Slater arrangement on front end and one engine with Oliver Boyer speed recorder.

In the design of these engines, in order to reduce maintenance charges to the minimum, consideration has been given to standardizing as many parts as possible with those of the Consolidation type freight locomotives, which were of about the same tractive power, and which have proven very satisfactory in service.

With the completion of the delivery of the remaining four engines on this contract, the motive power equipment of this railway will be as per the following statement:—

Wheel Arrangement.	Number.	Average Weight on Driving Wheeels.	Average Tractive Power.
Loo00	2	56,500 Lbs.	13,240 Lbs.
Loo000	29	112,270 "	23,600 "
Loo0000o	4	133,375 "	30,400 "
Lo00000o	6	197,000 "	45,500 "
Lo00000	4	182,000 "	42,600 "
L 000	4	123,250 "	28,160 "
		Weight on drivers.	Tractive Power.
Total.........................	49	6,225,330 Lbs.	1,288,520 Lbs.

New Passenger Cars:

In January, two new steel baggage and express cars and two new first class steel coaches were received. These cars were built by the Pullman Co., and are practically duplicates of the all-steel passenger equipment built at a previous date by the Pullman Company for this Railway.

Work Equipment:

In May, eighteen 80,000 lb. capacity Hart cars and one Jordan ballast spreader were received. These are second-hand equipment, purchased through F. H. Hopkins, Montreal, and had been used on the National Transcontinental Railway, but were in very good condition.

Tank Cars:

As a further protection against fires along the railway, two additional second-hand tank cars have been purchased and equipped with pumps, hose, and fire tools.

Electrical Work:

The electric drives for carpenter and machine shops at North Bay Junction have been completed, as also has the re-wiring of the paint shop and the installation of electric lights in the new carpenter shop. Electric lights have been installed in new wheel and blacksmith shop and work in connection with complete installation of power and light service is in hand for all new shops at North Bay Junction. Arrangements are also in progress for installation of electric hoist for use in ice house.

The equipments on all steel cars have been thoroughly overhauled, which includes the dismantling, washing and repairing of all cells.

Headlight equipments on locomotives and snow plows have been maintained in good condition, and in the cases of engines undergoing general repairs, the whole electrical equipment has been completely overhauled and repaired.

The work necessary for the upkeep of lights, etc., at the various stations along the lines where electricity is used has been done and arrangements made for the lighting of buildings now being erected or that have been completed.

Air Brake Equipment:

During the year the air brake running repairs at all divisional points, and all general repairs and renewals to T. & N. O. and N. C. R. air brake equipment have been carried out in accordance with the recommended practice.

In addition to the above the following work has been executed by the Air Brake Department:—

A train air signal testing rack equal to a locomotive and twelve modern passenger cars has been added to the air brake testing equipment. This will enable us to thoroughly test out and adjust all train air signal equipment before being placed in service.

To eliminate moisture from the compressed air and deposit it in the main reservoir on the locomotive, engines 121, 122, 114, 115, 131, 132, 133, 135, 136, 150, 153, have been equipped with between 35 and 45 ft. of $1\frac{1}{4}$ in. cooling pipe, located between the compressor and the main reservoir, and the same amount of equalizing pipe has been placed between the main reservoir.

Records obtained during the past winter of engines thus equipped show freezing took place between the compressor and engineer's brake valve, indicating that efforts to apply proper piping to prevent moisture getting into brake pipe was made in the right direction.

Combination car No. 14 has been equipped with L-N brake, high speed beams, and new foundation brake gear. This completes the installation of high speed brake on all passenger equipment.

New foundation brake gear has been applied to cafe cars " Sesekinika " and " Tetapaga," and the air brake equipment has been rearranged to conform to the Commonwealth steel trucks.

New standard foundation brake gear has been installed on engine 121. This will give more track clearance and uniform shoe wear.

The air appliances for operating snow plows and flangers have been overhauled and put in good condition for the coming winter.

The compressed air water distributing equipment on passenger cars has been maintained in satisfactory condition, and all necessary repairs and renewals made as cars pass through shops for general repairs.

The following car brakes have been cleaned, oiled, tested and stencilled:

139 passenger car brakes.
295 freight car brakes.
 18 van brakes.
 16 miscellaneous car brakes.
115 freight car brakes by T. & N. O. Ry. for foreign lines.
131 T. & N. O. freight car brakes by foreign lines.

A Contented Family of Pigs owned by Mr. A. W. Skinner, Englehart, Ont.

In order to supply sufficient steam to heat long passenger trains, engines Nos. 133, 134, 135, and 136 have been equipped with 1½ in. steam heat throttle and 2 in. regulator. The necessary repairs to steam heat equipment on all locomotives and cars have been made as they pass through the shops for repairs.

All pressure gauges have been tested when necessary and when engines pass through the shops for general repairs. The adjustment of all locomotive safety valves has been maintained at the authorized boiler pressure throughout the year.

Summary of Extensive Repairs to Locomotives:

Since November 1st, 1915, the following locomotives have been through our shops at North Bay Junction, for repairs:

Given General Repair:—114, 115, 116, 121, 122, 124, 132, 136, 150, 153.

Given Heavy Repair:—103, 104, 105, 112, 131, and 135.

Given Light Repair:—101, 103, 106, 113, 140. In addition engines 101, 115, 118, 119, 127, 133, 136, 139 and 140 were in the shop at different times during the year for extensive repairs due to accidents.

Note: The term "Heavy Repair" as applied above refers to cases where an engine has received such repairs as driving tyres turned, driving boxes renewed, valves, piston rings and side rod bushings renewed. "General Repair" refers to cases where an engine has been given a thorough overhauling and rebuilt. "Light Repairs" refers to cases where an engine has received minor repairs such as renewal of side rod bushings, piston rings and valve rings.

Each engine has had the boiler washed out once every two weeks when in regular service. Stay bolts in fire boxes have been regularly tested and renewals made when necessary. Nettings and ash pans and dampers have been examined at the end of each trip during the summer as a precaution against fire. During damp weather, and at such times as the danger from this source is reduced to a minimum, ash pans and dampers have been examined twice a week.

Engine Despatch:

Statement showing the number of engines despatched from different terminal and divisonal points during the year:—

Station.	Number of Engines despatched.
North Bay Junction	5,111
Elk Lake	439
Englehart	4,941
Iroquois Falls	344
Timmins	800
Cochrane	1,888
Total	13,523

The motive power has been generally assigned during the year as follows:—

Class of Service.	Number of Engines.
Passenger	13
Freight	22
Work	3
Switching	5

Locomotive Mileage:

The following statement shows mileage made by locomotives belonging to this railway during the year:—

Engine No.	Miles Run.
101	31,498
103	34,577
104	35,286
105	33,798
106	32,474
107	33,090
108	39,122
109	42,951
110	12,941
111	36,763
112	35,482
113	37,979
114	29,769
115	29,926
116	15,339
117	21,692
118	23,629
119	33,936
120	35,910
121	15,656
122	24,231
123	36,733
124	41,583
125	29,115
126	43,202
127	41,900
128	42,526
129	39,684
130	23,224
131	16,368
132	16,709
133	43,347
134	49,656
135	36,703
136	64,447
137	54,802
138	51,353
139	50,382
140	52,066
150	29,944
151	31,293
152	11,389
153	21,872
	1,464,347

Repairs to Passenger Equipment:

Extensive repairs have been made to passenger equipment at North Bay Junction shops as follows:—

Class of Car.	General Repair.	Light Repair.
First Class	3	9
Second Class	1	4
Baggage and Express	1	3
Mail and Express	..	4
Combination	1	1
Parlor Cafe Cars	..	2

Healthy Cattle owned by Mr. A. W. Skinner, Englehart, Ont.

The term "General Repair" as applied above refers to cases where a coach has had the interior scraped and sanded, sashes removed and refitted, mouldings removed and replaced in interior of car, seats removed and replaced, outside sheathing stripped off, panels removed, side of coach trussed and replanked, piers strengthened, letter board removed and replaced, vestibule ends reinforced with iron plates, trucks rebuilt, transoms and sills and trimmers renewed, journal boxes and brasses renewed and wheels turned.

The term "Light Repair" refers to coaches having seat arms scraped and sanded, interior of car varnished, outside of car washed down and given two coats of varnish, trucks repaired.

While first class coaches were undergoing general repairs the following alterations and betterments were made to the construction of the cars: Two steel sills applied, two extra wooden sills, new friction buffers and draft gear, vestibule curtains and tail gates. The baggage and express cars were equipped with steel sills, new friction buffers and draft gears.

Parlor cafe cars "Sesekinika" and "Tetapaga" have each been equipped with electric lighting system of the Safety Car Heating and Lighting Company's underframe type with Edison storage batteries. In addition these two cars have also been fitted with Commonwealth steel trucks, which is now the railway company's standard truck for all steel and steel underframe passenger equipment.

About the first of the year private car "Sir James" was put in the shop, thoroughly cleaned down and given a coat of varnish. Outside of this no repairs have been necessary with the exception of the ordinary running repairs. Car "Abitibi" was taken into the shop during July of this year and after receiving a thorough cleaning was re-leaded, hard stopped, sandpapered, colored, lettered and varnished.

Coach Cleaning:

Statement showing the number of coaches cleaned at the different stations during the year:—

Station.	Number of Coaches Cleaned.
North Bay Junction	2,818
Englehart	972
Cochrane	2,681
Timmins	1,390
Elk Lake	732
Iroquois Falls	732
Total	9,325

Repairs to Conductors' Vans:

During the year six conductors' vans have been put through the shop and have received a thorough overhauling and repair, including repainting of interior and exterior.

Repairs to Freight and Work Equipment:

During the past year our staff at North Bay Junction have rebuilt two flat cars, applied new sills to forty-seven flat cars, and have redecked fifty flat cars. In addition to this 574 T. & N. O. freight cars, 2538 T. & N. O. coaches and 21,840 foreign freight cars have been repaired on repair track.

Bills have been rendered against foreign roads for repairs to cars which were repaired under rules adopted by the Master Car Builders' Association. In addition to this monthly bills have been rendered against the Grand Trunk covering the cost of repairs to such cars as are governed by the Grand Trunk running rights agreement at actual cost of labor and material, plus 10 per cent.

Snow plows and snow flangers, wrecking cranes, steam shovels, etc., have been overhauled and given such repairs as were necessary. During the forest fire on July 29th, the "American" railroad ditcher was badly damaged by fire, necessitating the rebuilding of all superstructure on the car and extensive repairs to the ditcher itself. The Ledgerwood rapid unloader which was being used in conjunction with the ditcher at the time of the fire was also badly damaged, the car on which the Ledgerwood was built being completely destroyed.

Steel Tyres Turned and Wheels Applied Rolling Stock:

During the year forty pair of driving tyres, one pair of idler wheels, ninety-eight pair of coach wheels, eight pair of new coach tyres, forty pair of tender wheels, twenty-one pair of engine truck wheels and two pair of new engine truck tyres have been turned on wheel lathe at North Bay Junction.

The following tyres were bored out before being applied to wheels: Forty-nine driving wheel tyres, twenty-eight coach wheel tyres, two tender wheel tyres, and fourteen engine truck wheel tyres.

At Englehart 1912 car wheels have been pressed off axles, new wheels bored and remounted on axles.

New wheels have been applied to rolling stock on the T. & N. O. Railway as follows:—

To Locomotives:
      7 pairs 33″ C.I. wheels on 3¾ x 7″ axles.
    44   "   "   "   5 x 9″ "
     1   "   "   ". 5½ x 10″ "
     5   "   Schoen steel tender wheels.
    36 57″ driving tyres.
    14 28″ engine truck tyres.
     2 69″ driving tyres.
     6 63″ driving tyres.

To Passenger Equipment:
    28 36″ steel tyres.
    64 pr. wheels changed and tyres turned.

To Freight Equipment:
    21 pairs new 33″ C.I. wheels on 4¼ x 8″ axles.
     2 " S.H.   "   "   4¼ x 8″ "
     1 " new   "   "   5 x 9″ "
    17 " new   "   "   5½ x 10″ "

To Ballast Cars:
    16 pairs new 33″ C.I. wheels on 4¼ x 8″ axles.
     2 " S.H.   "   "   4¼ x 8″ "
    31 " new   "   "   5 x 9″ "
     1 " S.H.   "   "   5 x 9″ "

To Van, Work and Other Service Equipment:
    17 pairs new 33″ C.I. wheels on 3¾ x 7″ axles.
     1 " S.H.   "   "   3¾ x 7″ "
     5 " new   "   "   4¼ x 8″ "
     3 " new   "   "   5½ x 10″ "

To Foreign Cars:
```
     6 pairs new 33" C.I. wheels on 3¾ x   7" axles.
     5   "     S.H.      "      "    3¾ x   7"   "
 1,418   "     new       "      "    4¼ x   8"  , "
   105   "     S.H.      "      "    4¼ x   8"   "
   348   "     new       .      "    5   x   9"   "
    16   "     S.H.      .      "    5   x   9"   "
   146   "     new       "      "    5½ x  10"   "
     6   "     S.H.      "      "    5½ x  10"   "
```

Rolling Stock Destroyed:

During the destructive fire which swept Northern Ontario during the month of July, 1916, ninety-four cars belonging to foreign roads were burned on the tracks of the T. & N. O. Railway.

In addition to this the following foreign cars were destroyed at different points, along the line: G. T. R. 46935 by wreck at Trout Mills; C. G. R. 19249 by wreck at Latchford; C. G. R. 60550 by wreck at M.P. 212; G.T.R. 61602 and 69081 by wreck at Rabbit Creek Pit; G. T. P. baggage car 422 by fire at Cobalt.

Such trucks and other material from above cars as were in serviceable condition were returned to the owners and balance of cars are being settled for at depreciated value in accordance with regulations laid down by the Master Car Builders' Association.

Of the T. & N. O. freight equipment, ten steel flats and four wooden flats were burned in the fire during July. In addition to this five flat cars and two vans have been destroyed by wreck on our own line, while one stock car, one box car and one flat car have been destroyed on foreign roads. Bills have been rendered against the foreign roads covering depreciated value of cars destroyed on their line, less value of servicable material returned, as per M. C. B. rules.

Work Turned Out of Carpenter Shop:

The following miscellaneous articles have been manufactured and turned out of carpenter shop at North Bay Jct., in addition to material for repairs to rolling stock:

2 tables.	9 conductors' kit boxes.
3 tables repaired.	4 yard limit boards.
2 line posts.	6 step ladders.
6 section posts.	3 ladders.
6 fence posts turned up.	15 gang planks.
3 filing cabinets.	67 mile boards.
2 small cabinets for oil samples.	1 picture frame.
2 stationery cabinets.	1 meter box for ice house.
1 drawing board.	3 signboards.
1 office stool repaired.	2 bulletin boards.
1 case for oil lamp.	2 wheelbarrows repaired.
48 rollers turned up.	150 notice frames.
1 ledger cabinet.	298 transfer cases.
1 cabinet for time sheets.	600 vent plugs for battery boxes.
1 set pigeon holes.	508 bottom blocks for batter boxes.
1 sleigh tongue repaired.	770 rungs for ladders.
3 correspondence trays.	100 flanger boards.
2 extension boxes.	30 wing boards.
1 cupboard for machine shop.	1,000 grade stakes.
1 ice box for Cochrane.	1,000 centre stakes.
25 office chairs repaired.	234 sections cattle guards.
2 barrel skids repaired.	452 slats for repairs to cattle
29 baggage trucks repaired.	guards.
2 new office desks.	229,736 track shims.
4 office desks repaired.	

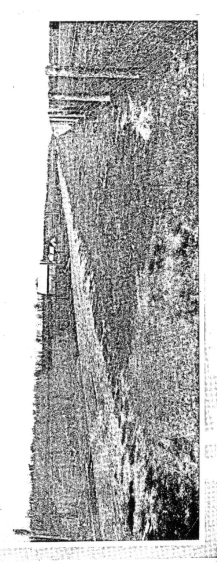

Newly constructed Road through Dack Township.   Farm of Mr. Ed. Wicklun, Brentha, Ont.   South half Lot 6, Con. 3, Township Dack.

Pattern Making:

During the year there have been ninety-three patterns manufactured at the pattern shop at North Bay Jct., for repairs and renewals of different parts of locomotives, cars, work equipment and shop machinery. All patterns are the property of this Railway and a proper record is kept as to location of same.

Equipment Owned:

The Motive Power, Rolling Stock and Equipment of this Railway at present consists of the following:—

39 road locomotives.
4 switching locomotives.
2 private cars.
2 business cars.
14 first-class wooden coaches.
6 first-class steel coaches.
14 second-class wooden coaches.
4 second-class steel coaches.
2 combination wooden second-class and
   baggage cars.
1 combination wooden first-class and
   baggage car.
1 exhibition car.
3 parlor cafe cars.
5 wooden baggage and express cars.
4 steel baggage and express cars.
5 wooden mail and express cars.
3 steel mail and express cars.
1 fish car.
20 conductors' vans.
9 stock cars.
145 box cars.
88 steel underframe flat cars.

358 wooden flat cars.
12 steel drop bottom dump cars.
35 Hart convertible cars.
3 snow plows.
3 snow flangers.
3 right hand ballast plows.
3 left hand ballast plows.
3 centre ballast plows.
2 Jordan ballast spreaders.
1 centre ballast spreader.
2 Ledgerwood rapid unloaders.
1 pile driver.
1 American railroad ditcher.
2 steam wrecking cranes.
3 steam shovels.
2 auxiliary boarding cars.
2 auxiliary tool cars.
2 Road Dept. auxiliary tool cars.
2 crane cabin cars.
2 road cabin cars.
1 pile driver tank car.
8 boarding cars.
6 tank cars for fire protection.

Mechanical Accounting:

During the month of March, the timekeeping for the mechanical department, which had previously been taken care of in the office of the Chief Engineer and Supt. of Maintenance, was transferred to this office, and a little later arrangements were made for the installation of a cost keeping system, for the purpose of keeping accurate record of the different items of cost of repairs to equipment, etc. This system will prove of great assistance in forming estimates on repair work as well as in the work of supervision, inasmuch as it permits the men in charge to keep in close touch with the cost of the work as it progresses.

Haileybury Dock, September 22, 1915.

Piche Point Wharf, October 15, 1916.

ANNUAL REPORT TELEGRAPH AND TELEPHONE DEPARTMENT

W. J. KELLY, S. OF T. & T.

During the fiscal year ending October 31st, 1916, both telegraph and telephone business was exceedingly good.   In order to handle the increased commercial traffic, extensions were made to existing telegraph and telephone circuits as follows:

Telegraph:
                                                                                       Wire miles.
 No. 8 B.W.G. iron wire—New Liskeard to Timmins 140
 No. 8 B.W.G. iron wire—Englehart to Cochrane............................ 115

Telephone:
 Metallic Circuit—No. 12 B.W.G. iron wire, Kenney Siding to Temagami...... 47
 Metallic Circuit—No. 12 B.W.G. iron wire, Gillies Depot to Latchford........ 9
 Metallic Circuit—No. 12 B.W.G. iron wire, Englehart to Boston Creek........ 30
 Metallic Circuit—No. 12 B.W.G. iron wire, Matheson to Ramore............. 20
 Metallic Circuit—No. 12 B.W.G. iron wire, Porquis Junction to Cochrane..... 56

Owing to increased railway message business between North Bay and Cochrane, due to joint G.T.R., T. & N. O. and C.G.R. traffic, telephone train despatching circuit was simplexed, thereby providing another telegraph circuit without necessitating the stringing of any additional wire.

On January 1st telegraph circuit, North Bay to South Porcupine, was leased to Messrs. Kiely, Smith & Amos, stock brokers, under agreement entered into with that firm, and brokers offices opened at Cobalt and South Porcupine.   This was extended to Timmins and office opened at that point on April 1st.

During the year thirty subscriber's telephones were installed and sixteen removed.   On July 29th seven telephones were burned, and of these three have been since re-installed.

During the year public toll offices were opened at Kenney Siding, Krugerdorf, Mindoka, and Monteith, for benefit of settlers and mining camps.

Disastrous bush fires of July 29th destroyed approximately three miles of telegraph poles and line; also station telegraph and telephone equipment as well as the town exchange telephone equipment at Matheson.

Fire at Gowganda, August 7th, destroyed telephone office and exchange equipment at that point.

Outside of those occasioned by fires commercial telegraph and telephone lines have been free from serious interruption throughout the year.

General repairs have been made over the entire system and lines maintained in first-class condition.

Day lettergram service was inaugurated on this railway September 1st, giving patrons the opportunity of sending a fifty-word deferred telegram at greatly reduced rate.

The following statement indicates amount of commercial telegraph and telephone business handled:

 Local messages handled 34,948
 Conjoint messages handled 74,154

  Total 109,102

Cable messages sent 451
Cable messages received 170

     Total 621

Cable words sent 7,682
Cable words received 2,395

     Total 10,077

Telephone calls 29,434

Two hundred and thirty-five telegraph messages were checked free over lines of this railway; account, fire sufferers.

The following is a summary of telegraph and telephone wire in operation at the present time:

Wire.	Gauge.	Service.	Miles.
Iron	No. 8, B.W.G.	Telegraph	1,670
Iron	No. 12, B.W.G.	Long Distance Telephone	167
Iron	No. 12, B.W.G.	Local Exchange and Party Line	231
Copper	No. 9, B. & S.	Telephone Train Despatching	574
Copper	No. 10, N.B.S.	Long Distance Telephone	646
Copper	No. 12, B.& S.	Long Distance Telephone	218
Style B.	Twisted pair	Local Exchange	40,000 feet.

Total wire mileage....... 3,506
Total pole mileage....... 341

Above respectfully submitted.

W. J. KELLY,

Supt of Telegraph and Telephone.

Oats, Farm of Mr. Henry Schafner, Brentha Post Office. North half Lot 1, Con. 1, Back.

ANNUAL REPORT OF SUPERINTENDENT OF TRAFFIC

Year Ended October 31st, 1916.

W. A. GRIFFIN, S. OF T.

Have pleasure in reporting that the fiscal year ended October 31st, 1916, has been the most successful, from traffic standpoint, subsequent to construction of the road, largely due to handling increased traffic to and from Western Canada, via Transcontinental route.

During this period we have been exceptionally free from accidents of serious nature. The only unfortunate occurrence was the fires which passed over the territory adjacent to the T. & N. O. Railway in July and August. Immediately following the fires considerable disorganization occurred handling of traffic. Prompt measures, however, were taken to afford every relief and comfort to fire sufferers, and am thankful to report that practically normal conditions now prevail. In these fires freight shed, Cochrane, station at Kelso and Nushka, and freight shed and station at Matheson were destroyed, together with considerable rolling stock.

Telephone train dispatching (referred to in Annual Report, 1913) is giving every satisfaction.

The Safety First movement, organized March 1st, 1914, for the correction of unsafe conditions and practices, is closely followed up, regular meetings being held monthly.

Necessary time-table changes have been made to meet winter and summer requirements:

Time-table No. 32 made effective November 28th, 1915; time-table No. 33, effective June 25th, 1916. Current time-table No. 34, effective October 8th, shows Trains No. 1 and 2, daily, except Sunday, between North Bay and Cochrane. These trains are equipped with standard C.P.R. sleeper, and inter-line service, via Canadian Pacific Railway to Montreal. Trains No. 46 and 47, daily, except Sunday, between North Bay and Cochrane, with inter-line service, via Grand Trunk Railway to Toronto. These trains are equipped with Pullman cars between North Bay and Cochrane, and parlor-cafe cars between North Bay and Englehart. Trains No. 9 and 10, "The National," tri-weekly, between North Bay and Cochrane, with inter-line service, via Grand Trunk Railway to Toronto, and Canadian Government Railways to Winnipeg. Equipment of these trains consists of Colonist sleeping cars, electric-lighted first-class coaches, Tourist sleeping cars, dining cars, and standard sleeping cars. Dining cars and standard sleeping cars are operated through, without change, between Toronto, Ont., and Winnipeg, Man. Trains No. 50. 51, 52, 53, 54 and 55, daily, except Sunday, between Timmins and Porquis Jct., connecting with main line trains. Trains No. 30, 31, 32 and 33, daily, except Sunday, and Trains No. 34 and 35, Saturdays only, between Iroquois Falls and Porquis Jct., connecting with main line trains. Trains No. 60 and 61, daily except Sunday, and No. 62 and 63, Wednesday only, between Elk Lake and Earlton Jct., connecting with main line trains. Train No. 4, daily, except Saturday and Sunday, Englehart to Cobalt, and Train No. 6, Saturday only, Englehart to Cobalt. Trains No. 23, 24, 25 and 26, daily, except, Sunday, between Englehart and Charlton, connecting with main line trains.

The following derailments and accidents occurred:

1915.

November 2nd, Extra 119, south, passing public road crossing, M.P. 205¾, alleged stuck calf. Owner, W. Monahan, Matheson, Ont.

November 22nd, while Extra 125 east approaching M.P. 36½, Porcupine Sub-Division, alleged struck and killed man named O. P. Taylor, who was walking on track. Railway exonerated from all liability by Coroner's verdict.

November 24th, when Extra 125 west backing into Dome Mines siding, South Porcupine, T. & N. O. 60595 and 100139, loaded with ballast, derailed, due to defective track at this point. Brakeman A. Dorschner, who was riding cars when derailed, jumped, alleged injuring left foot. Resumed duty, Jan. 7th, 1916. Damage to track material account derailment, $28.29.

December 1st, Extra 124 south struck hand car at M.P. 18¾, North Bay sub-division.   Slight damage to engine and hand car.   Responsible employee disciplined.

December 3rd, while switching at Hollinger Compressor Spur, M.P. 32.5, Porcupine Subdivision, engine 125 derailed. No damage to engine. Damage to track, $5.20.

December 13th, 2nd No. 47 struck hand car at M.P.78¾, damaging same to extent of $12.00. Responsible employee disciplined.

December 14th, while Work Extra 114 north passing South Gillies, cars T. & N. O. 60507 and 100157 derailed. Cause, broken wheel on T. & N. O. 60507. Damage to track and labour repairing, $129.01.

1916.

January 19th, while shed gang, North Bay Jct., transferring car of coal at repair track, foreman Samuel Webber alleged injured foot by stepping on nail in board. Resumed duty January 25th.

January 22nd, while brakeman Frank H. Taylor attempting to get on back of tender, engine 132, while in motion, switching in Cochrane yard, snow on which he was standing gave way, and after dragging for a few feet let go his hold and trailing truck of tender, alleged passed over both legs below the knees. Taken to Lady Minto Hospital, New Liskeard, where he succumbed to alleged-injuries January 24th.

February 1st, when fireman J. Yorkton shaking grates on Engine 138 at Thornloe, shaker bar slipped off, alleged injuring little finger.   Resumed duty February 23rd.

February 5th, when Train No. 1, Engine 127, pulling out of Latchford Station side-swiped C.G.R. 19249 on Extra 140 south, which was foul of main line on passing track. Damage to C.G.R. 19249, $300.00; engine 127, $90.00. Responsible employee dismissed.

February 6th, while Extra 140 south, passing M.P. 7, North Bay Subdivision, I.R.C. 81366 derailed, account broken truck on car.   Damage to equipment, $116.00; damage to track and labour repairing and wrecking, $278.09.

February 7th, while Extra 125 west, coming out of Dome siding, Porcupine Subdivision, pony trucks derailed, travelling three hundred feet, striking Dome Extension siding, derailing engine. Auxiliary sent from Englehart. Damage to engine, $65.00. Cause, snow and ice on track.

February 9th, while Train No. 9, "The National," passing South Gillies, fire broke out in baggage car No. 422. Car was detached from train and taken to Cobalt where fire extinguished. Damage to car and contents, $5,474.00. Cause of fire unknown.

February 11th, while switching in North Bay Jct. yard, brakeman Charles Caley was alleged jammed between back of tender, engine 150 and van No. 67. Resumed duty February 22nd.

February 19th, Extra 120 south pitched into rear of Extra 118 south, standing at Matheson water tank, completely demolishing van No. 51 and damaging G.T.P. 304021 and G.T.P. 306877. Total damage to equipment, $810.35. Damage to track, $33.40. Responsible employees dismissed.

February 25th, Extra 137 south, passing through Bushnell yard, car G.T.P. 304198 derailed, also derailing G.T.P. 311957, G.T.P. 301508; I.R.C. 62000 and C.G.R. 60485, loaded with grain. Cause, broken arch bar, east side, leading truck, C.G.R. 60485. Estimated damage to G.T.P. 304198, $125.00. No damage to other four cars. Estimated damage to track, labour and material, $85.00.

February 25th, Extra 129 south pitched into rear of Extra 130 south, standing at Kelso Station. Estimated damage to engine 129, $20.00; G.T.R. 4375, $168.00; G.T.R. 9442, $75.00; C.G.R. 35945, $30.00; D.L. & W. 27394, $35.00, and van No. 58, $25.00. Total, $353.00. Damage to track, nil. Responsible employees dismissed.

March 10th while Extra 104 south passing M.P. 104, John Revard attempted to board train, missing footing and alleged fell beneath train, being instantly killed. Body was discovered by train crew on No. 2 same date.

March 16th, while No. 83 passing Gillies Depot, B.R. & P. 4558 derailed, also derailing T. & N. O. flat 60037 (empty). Damage to track, $289.25. Damage to equipment, $300.00. Cause, fallen brake beam on B.R. & P. 4558.

March 16th, while switching G.T.P. diner 4004 and T. & N. O. mail car No. 203, in North Bay Jct. yard, mail car broke loose running into T. & N. O. coaches 36 and 109, damaging same to extent of $60.00. Responsible employees disciplined.

March 22nd, while Extra 114 south switching at pulp spur M.P. 121.5, brakeman Emile Larocque alleged slipped and fell under car, sustaining serious injuries. Taken to Lady Minto Hospital, New Liskeard, where he succumbed to alleged injuries April 6th.

March 23rd, while switching in North Bay Jct. yard, engine 151 with string of cars, side-swiped G.T.R. Extra 1265, entering yard at No. 20 switch, damaging D.L. & W. 27100, $145.00; A.C.R. 1219, $11.00; B. & S. 3260, $13.00; B. & S. 10850, $7.00; W. of A. 980, $45.00 and M.P. 22618, $35.00. Responsible employees disciplined.

April 4th, Extra 138 south passing M.P. 132 struck hand car. No damage to engine. Hand car damaged to extent of $12.00.

April 5th, No. 97, engine 126, struck hand car at Kenogami Lake. Slight damage to car.

April 16th, Extra 113 south, passing Englehart Jct., alleged struck and killed pig. Owner, Alex. Clark, Englehart, Ont.

April 30th, while Extra 108 south passing twelve poles south, M.P. 212, S.F.R.D. 11331, derailed, also derailing following cars: G.T.R. 10430, G.T.P. 312046, I.R.C. 60550, I.R.C. 61880, G.T.P. 306975, P.R.R. 43261, C.P. 211140, C.P. 135880 and G.T.P. 306860. Total damage to equipment, $1,455.00. Damage to track, material, labour, repairing and wrecking, $666.55. Cause of derailment, excessive speed. Responsible employees dismissed.

Full and Contented.

An abundance of pasture provides good grazing, and thus makes Temiskaming an
ideal sheep country.

May 5th, Extra 112 north, light, struck hand car at Mindoka. Damage to car, $19.50.

May 11th, while Archibald McGillis calling train crew, bicycle on which he was riding struck telegraph pole, alleged throwing him over handle bars, spraining left fore-arm. Resumed duty May 21st.

May 14th, while Train No. 9, " The National," passing through Kenogami yard, alleged struck horse, breaking its leg. Owner, C. Tomlinson, Kenogami Lake, Ont.

May 26th, steer alleged killed M.P. 208.   Train unknown.   Owner, D. Johnson, Matheson, Ont.

June 6th, while Extra 134 north passing four poles south, M.P. 231, alleged struck and killed horse. Owner, Ralph L. Malkin, Nellie Lake, Ont.

June 22nd, Extra 117 east passing M.P. 23½, Porcupine subdivision, alleged struck horse, which was so badly injured it had to be shot. Owner, S. Sulzer, Hoyle, Ont.

June 24th, while switching in Englehart yard, yardman G. Perrault, attempting to open knuckle on car, alleged injured fingers, account slack running out. Resumed duty August 15th.

June 24th, while switching in North Bay Jct. yard, yardman W. L. Treacy fell from top of car, alleged spraining left ankle. Resumed duty July 6th.

June 28th, while Train No. 9, " The National," passing M.P. 51, a child passenger, G. Malo, aged two years, fell out of window, alleged breaking right arm and bruising back, forehead and left leg. · Child taken through on same train.

July 10th, while Extra 103 north switching at Cobalt, Thomas Finton, employee of the O'Brien Mines, Limited, who was working in car B. & M. 47624, was alleged injured. Railway employee responsible for accident disciplined.

July 11th, while Thomas Beverley, trucker, unloading a large steel plate from truck to car at North Bay Jct. shed, same slipped, alleged bruising second knuckle of left thumb. Resumed duty July 18th.

July 12th, while Mrs. William Richards, passenger, detraining from Passenger Extra 138 south at Heaslip, alleged slipped, injuring toes of left foot.

July 14th, while fireman Herbert M. Drury getting down off engine at Bourkes, slipped, alleged injuring foot. Resumed duty August 24th.

September 1st, while fireman Herbert M. Drury working around engine at Matheson, wrench which he was using slipped, causing him to fall against step of engine, alleged fracturing two ribs. Resumed duty September 23rd.

September 2nd, No. 47, passing M.P. 30¾, North Bay Subdivision, alleged struck and killed cow. Owner, J. P. McDougall, North Bay, Ont.

September 2nd, No. 85, and Extra 130 south, collided head on at M.P. 73.7, derailing I.R.C. 80945, N.Y.O. & W. 13881 and G.T.R. 46265 on Extra 140 south. Estimated damage to equipment, $895.00. Damage to track, $14.10. Responsible employees dismissed.

September 19th, Train No. 47, passing public road crossing, M.P. 131¾, alleged struck and killed cow. Owner, A. Houghton, Heaslip, Ont.

September 25th, while Train No. 10, " The National," passing M.P. 189, G.T.P. express car 6009 derailed. No damage to car. Estimated damage to track and labour repairing, $213.00. Cause, class of equipment and bad spot in track.

September 30th, while Train No. 1 approaching Kelso yard struck a horse, alleged killing same. Owner, C. H. Culver, Goldlands, Ont.

October 9th, while Extra 135 north pulling out of Cassidy Pit, derailed B. & O. 148683. Damage to track and labour rerailing, $62.65. Cause, spread track.

October 11th, Train No. 46, passing M.P. 97¼, alleged killed two young cattle and injured a third. Owner, H. Norton, South Gillies, Ont.

October 12th, while foreman Samuel Webber, handling ice at North Bay Jct. ice-house, floor alleged gave way allowing him to drop through, alleged scraping his left knee and spraining left thigh. Resumed duty Nov. 9th.

October 17th, Train No. 2 passing M.P. 140, alleged struck and killed cow. Owner, Angus Cameron, Englehart, Ont.

October 28th, while Extra 136 south passing M.P. 85, P.R.R. 40823 derailed. Cause, fallen brake beam. Damage to car $8.13. Labour repairing track, $93.50.

October 30th, while trucker Frank Gregoire assisting to lift gang plank, North Bay Jct. shed, same slipped, alleged injuring right foot. Resumed duty Nov. 6th.

October 31st, when 2nd No. 85 passing M.P. 84.13, G.T.P. 340125 and T. & N. O. 60681 derailed. Cause, unknown. Estimated damage to equipment and contents, $455.00. Damage to track material and labour, repairing and wrecking, $166.52.

October 31st, Liberato Di Bartolomeo, trucker, North Bay Jct. shed, engaged trucking large casting from car, same overbalanced on truck, alleged rolling on foot. Resumed duty Nov. 6th, 1916.

Herewith reports Dr. A. McMurchy, North Bay; Dr. J. S. McCullough, New Liskeard; Dr. R. C. Lowrey, Englehart and Dr. H. H. Moore, Timmins, covering medical attendance.

REPORT OF DR. A. McMURCHY

I beg to submit my annual report for the year just ended as follows: There have been no accidents involving the loss of life, or causing permanent injury, except one brakeman, who suffered the loss of two fingers. The health of the employees in the offices and on the works has been carefully guarded by the efficient sanitary arrangements made for that purpose, and as a consequence, there have been no cases of communicable diseases among them.

REPORT OF DR. J. S. McCULLOUGH

I beg to submit herewith the medical report for my district for year ended October 31st, 1916:

Office consultations with medicine	305
Town and hospital visits	318
Line visits	18
Surgical cases and operations	14

The medical cases treated were all of a minor nature and none serious—all making good recoveries.

Surgical Cases.—Regret to report two deaths following accident and operation. One case had both legs amputated, the other had one arm amputated, a fractured elbow and dislocated hip. There were two cases of fractured arms and two of fractured ribs.

In addition to this there were several cases of lacerations, broken fingers and other minor injuries, all of which made good recoveries.

REPORT OF DR. R. C. LOWREY

I present herewith annual medical report for this district.

Surgical Cases:
Burns 1
Injured fingers, requiring amputation 1
Blood poisoning 2
Bruised foot 1
Lacerated fingers 1
Injury to back 1

Medical Cases:
Tonsilitis ....
Otitis Medea ....
Cystitis 5

There were also a number of minor surgical cases and medical cases including bronchitis, gastritis, dysentery, etc., which I hardly considered necessary to tabulate.

REPORT OF DR. H. H. MOORE

I beg to report for the year ended October 31st, 1916, the following cases of accident and sickness among the employees of the T. & N. O. Railway, on that part of the line between Iroquois Falls and Timmins:

Boils 6
Baby illnesses 12
Bronchitis 14
Bruised side 1
Bruised foot 1
Colds and la grippe 30
Crushed finger 1
Chicken pox 2
Cut cheek 1
Diarrhoea 1
Debility 2
Eczema 1
Fracture of bones in leg 1
Gastric disorder 3
Hernia 1
Infected glands 1
Mumps 1
Otitis Medea 2
Rheumatism 5
Sprained back 5
Scabies 1
Sprained wrist 1
Tonsilitis 4

Respectfully submitted,

W. A. GRIFFIN,

Supt. of Traffic.

Good crop of Barley on Farm of Mr. Wm. Schell, Englehart.

GENERAL FREIGHT AND PASSENGER DEPARTMENT

Year Ended October 31st, 1916.

A. J. PARR, G. F. & P. A.

Comparison of freight tonnage handled and gross freight receipts for the fiscal year ended October 31st, 1916, as against the year previous, shows following result:

Tonnage, 1916	922,618	Revenue	$1,331,614 31
Tonnage, 1915	676,938	Revenue	$929,650 99
Increase	245,680	Increase	$401,963 32

This increase in tonnage and revenue is due to large extent the opening up of the "Transcontinental Route" and large tonnage of east bound grain, as well as general increase both east and west bound of general commodities. There was, however, decrease in tonnage of lumber, forest products, due to disastrous fires which visited Northern Ontario during latter part of July.

Increase is further accounted for by our participating in the through "Transcontinental Route," resulting in increasing the average distance haul per ton from 140.25 miles in 1915 to 188.42 miles in 1916.

The average gross earnings per ton per mile for 1916 was .77 cents, as compared with .98 cents for 1915.

This decrease in per ton per mile earnings is due to the increase in the average distance haul per ton and lower proportionate rate.

The through "Transcontinental Route" comprised of the Grand Trunk Ry., Temiskaming & Northern Ontario Ry., Canadian Government Rys. and Grand Trunk Pacific Ry., continues in popular favour, and traffic has continued to show gratifying increase.

Number of passengers carried and revenue for 1916, as against 1915, shows as follows:

Passengers carried, 1916	485,759	Revenue	$624,808 12
Passengers carried, 1915	480,995	Revenue	482,349 80
Increase	4,764	Increase	$142,458 32

Trains Nos. 9 and 10, known as the "National," operating between Toronto and Winnipeg, have shown such good results as to indicate that it would be advisable at an early date to run the National daily, instead of tri-weekly as at present.

Temiskaming and Northern Ontario Railway.
GENERAL FREIGHT AND PASSENGER DEPARTMENT

Statement of all Baggage, Corpses and Bicycles Handled during the Fiscal Year Ended October 31st, 1916.

Station	Baggage Forwarded	Baggage Received	Corpses Forwarded	Corpses Received	Bikes Forwarded	Bikes Received	Total 1916	Total 1915	Increase	Decrease
North Bay	1 6254	12,211	1	38		10	29,004	25,395	3,609	
North Bay Junction	5,120	1,088			12	3	6,208	4,984	1,224	
Wild	145	192					337	427		90
diffco	192	337					529	571		42
Diver	12	6					18	564		546
Redwater	70	216					286	Sta. opened	(Station closed) 286	
Temagami	616	1,876					3,492	3,507		15
Latchford	609	733	1				1,343	1,140	203	
Gillies Depot								321	(Station closed)	321
Cobalt	8,240	7,539	8	6			15,815	16,473		658
North Cobalt	831	1,018	10				1,852	1,638	214	
Haileybury	8,284	6,915	10	68	3	5	15,285	14,709	576	
New Liskeard	4,702	4,145	2	6	5	2	8,878	8,943		65
Uno Park	371	478	1	1	10		856	715	141	
Thornloe	425	450	2		2	2	876	729	147	
Earlton	1,411	1,101	2	2		2	2,518	2,482	36	
Elk Lake	1,021	1,133	3				2,157	2,122	35	
Heaslip	244	420					664	648	16	
Englehart	5,240	4,287	1	2	2	2	9,534	7,636	1,898	
Charlton	686	816	1		2		1,504	1,531		27
Dane	484	676					1,161	1,263		102
Swastika	2,002	1,935					3,937	3,309	628	
Matheson	1,809	2,628	11				4,437	3,554	883	
Porquis Junction	2,056	2,433					4,501	4,293	208	
Inis Falls	2,047	3,513			1	1	5,561	4,002	1,559	
Porcupine	358	722	4			2	1,082	1,239		157
South Porcupine	3,512	3,731	2	3	10	13	7,270	6,416	854	
Schumacher	856	984	3			5	1,850	1,407	443	
Ilus	5,479	6,250	1		1	6	11,739	9,058	2,681	
Cochrane	6,068	6,546	1		4	3	12,622	12,128	494	
Total Year, 1915-1916	80,644	74,379	61	124	52	56	155,316		16,135	2,023
" " 1914-1915	73,992	66,984	74	53	51	50	141,204	141,204		
Increase	6,652	7,395		71	1	6	14,112		14,112	
Decrease			13				14,112			

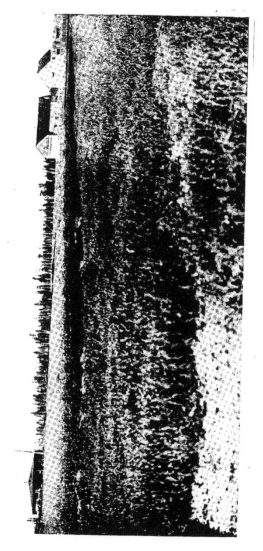

Clover and Potatoes on Farm of Mr. Wm. Nelson. North half Lot 4, Con. 3, Evanturel.

Statement of Baggage Claims.

RECEIVED, PAID, UNDER INVESTIGATION, Etc.

Number of Claims 32.   Amount $6,174 01

Number of Claims Vouchered 24   Amount Claimed $5,444 46   Vouchers for $2,387 10
"   "   Declined, ... 5   "   "   52 50
"   "   Under Investiga'n 3   "   "   677 05

$6,174 01

Credits

Insurance against Fire claims paid.. $2,342 00
Other Credits Nil.

(Year 1915–16)   Net Debit.......... $45 10

Analysis of Baggage Claims—Year 1915-1916

	No.	Paid	Pending	Declined	Remarks
Claims resulting from Baggage Car burning Train No. 9, Feb. 9th 1916	21	20	1	....	J. Spence claim $108.00 waiting surrender duplicate cheque. See detailed list appended.
Claims presented, account alleged loss by fire Matheson Station July 29th, 1916.	2	......	2	....	Under investigation.
Miscellaneous Claims	9	4	....	5	Four Claims paid $45.10. Five declined $52.50.
	32	24	3	5	

Temiskaming and Northern Ontario Railway

GENERAL FREIGHT AND PASSENGER DEPARTMENT

Statement of Claims Received and Vouchered, Account Fire G.T.P. Baggage Car M. 422, Train M. 9, Feby. 9th, 1916

Claim No.	Claimant	Address	Filed Amount	Voucher No.	Date	Vouchered Amount
			$ c.			$ c.
11082	Forbes Hendry	Enid, Sask	59 50	9532	April 18, 1916	59 60
11140	Henri Cusson	..., Man	260 20	9544	" 19, 196	100 00
11141	Mrs. A. Brotherston	" "	310 45	9543		100 00
11142	Clinton Bradbury	Bradwell, Sask	77 30	9542		77 30
11259	Rodger Mosh	Seamans "	102 50	9679		100 00
11269	R. H. Slipp	Trochu, Alta	223 50	9603	May 2, 1916	100 00
11383	Ben S. Elish	Caron, Sask	261 00	9610	" 5,	100 00
11427	Mr. and Mrs. J. N. Walton	Keystone, Sask	400 60	9639	" 23,	200 00
11428	M. John Ross	Kelliher "	135 76	9638		100 00
11458	H. A. Jackson	Edmonton, Alta	1,091 31	9640		300 00
	Mrs. A. L. Jackson					
	Miss Willis Logan					
11468	M. Herbert Bissell	Gilpin, Alta	156 85	9642		100 00
11470	Miss Anna Hall	Winnipeg, Man	151 40	9641		100 00
11491	W. N. Botsford	Edmonton, ...	232 45	9634		100 00
11505	Miss A. C. Lekie	Rivers, Man	333 70	9636		100 00
11520	T. Ben	Yellowgrass, Sask	167 00	9672		100 00
11539	Wm. G. ...	Winnipeg, Man	174 50	9673	June 5,	100 00
11588	Mark Spence		627 05	9677	" 26,	100 00
11731	H. S. Price	Camp Borden, Ont	438 00	9751	July 24,	100 00
11896	Lieut. H. A. McDougal	Asquith, Sask	129 40	9846	Aug. 4,	100 00
12155	Albert ...		340 55	9858	Oct. 13,	205 10
				10280		
			5,386 86			2,342 00

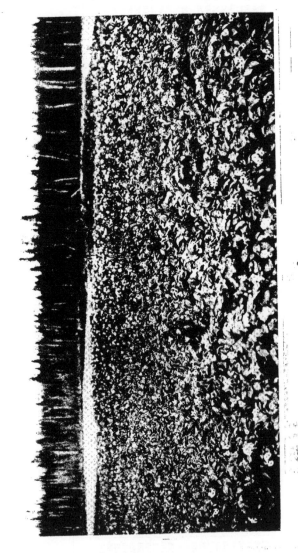

Potatoes on Farm of R. Heaslip. South half Lot 6, Con. 4, Evanturel.

OFFICE OF THE COMMISSIONER

Year Ending October 31st. 1916.

GEO. W. LEE, COMMISSIONER.

The financial year of the Temiskaming and Northern Ontario Railway, ending the 31st day of October, 1916, has been more eventful than any other in the history of the Railway and the territory which it serves.

The beginning of this past year saw the first of the large paper shipments that have been, and are being made, out of the district, from the paper mills at Iroquois Falls, owned and controlled by the Abitibi Pulp and Paper Company. They have four of the largest paper machines in the world in operation there making news print. They are now enlarging their plant so that they will be doubling their capacity in the near future.

The winter of 1915-16 saw the first of the grain haul over our line. Millions of bushels of wheat from the West (on its way to market) were handled. Large shipments of oats and other cereals were also hauled.

During the past year there has been a great increase in the shipments of forest products—logs, lumber, poles, piles, posts, pulp, pulpwood, stove-wood, mine props, et al—and, as a result, our box and flat cars have been taxed to the limit.

The mines have never been so busy, the output never so large or so valuable, as during the past year. Silver, gold, copper and nickel have all been in very active demand and the prices the best ever known. The territory served by the Temiskaming and Northern Ontario Railway being such a source of supply that large and valuable shipments of ore and bullion have been made, enriching those interested in the district as well as the great nation of which we form so important a part.

From an agricultural point of view our district was more favoured this season than almost any other part of Canada, with the result that we had, in the Temiskaming District, a good average crop of hay, grass seeds, potatoes and vegetables. We did not have the excessive spring rains that they had in Old Ontario and which prevented seeding there, instead, we had a moderate rainfall. The excessive drouth that followed the wet spring in Old Ontario, affecting their spring crops and pasturage, did not affect us. Ample growth of grain crops and meadows continued all-season, with the result that pasturage was never better. In the Temiskaming District the fall wheat crop was splendid, hay was never better, grass seeds never so good, potatoes, a good average and better by far than almost any other part of Canada, equal in yield to New Brunswick or British Columbia, and of a superior quality to any, no matter where from.

While the crops did not suffer from drouth still it was dry enough to make large areas of timbered bush in danger of fire. During the haying season, which is generally the end of July, many fires were out and with the high winds that prevailed at this season they spread rapidly until the 29th day of July, when the most unfortunate and regrettable event in our history took place; the great and regrettable loss of life (Cochrane to near New Liskeard) together with the large loss of property—buildings, stock, implements and utensils.

After the fire all that was possible was done to alleviate the loss and sufferings of the survivors. The public, Provincial and Dominion Governments and the Temiskaming and Northern Ontario Ry. came with instant relief to those affected so that none suffered very much from lack of food or clothing. Since the fire nearly all those who were burned out have been re-instated to their farms and holdings.

While we may, and do, deeply deplore the loss of life, the fire, nevertheless, has left a very large territory ready for clearing and at much less cost per acre than before the occurrence. In a few years all the burnt section should be planted and in growing condition and this will be much sooner than it could have been. So, while we suffered greatly it was not without compensation.

Labour has been in great demand during the entire year. Wages have ranged high in order to carry on the industries of the district. Many men have been brought in "under contract" and many more could find remunerative employment.

The enlistments for service overseas have been very large. In some settlements all the eligible men have enlisted and some of them have made the supreme sacrifice, others have suffered injury. Dependent relatives of the soldiers have been well looked after by the various societies that have been organized throughout the district for that purpose.

In common with the rest of Canada we are going through the trials resulting from the war. With increased prosperity there never was a time in our history when we were better off. While the cost of living has increased so has our ability to meet its increases. None should want for the necessaries—few do want for them—many share in the luxuries. All are prosperous and confident for the future.

In all we have had an excellent year and one that the country served by the Temiskaming and Northern Ontario Railway is proud of. All that is required is faith and work combined and the country's future is assured.

Potatoes grown at Englehart, Ont.

Preliminary report on the Mining Industry in that part of Northern Ontario served by the Temiskaming and Northern Ontario Railway, Calendar year 1916

By ARTHUR A. COLE, Mining Engineer.

The mining industry in the Temiskaming district has had another prosperous year. Combined productions of gold and silver will have a gross value this year of twenty-two and a half million dollars. This is an increase of two and a half million dollars over gross value for 1915.

In the gold camps increased activity is very noticeable among the producing mines, and a considerable increase in milling capacity is planned for the near future.

Many promising but unproven prospects are now being opened up. All this development is being made, notwithstanding the increasing prices of supplies and the shortage of skilled labour, which is directly due to the large number of men recruited into the Canadian army for overseas service. Much of the capital available for development now going on is directly traceable to the United States.

In the Cobalt camp the natural falling off in the production of silver due to the gradual depletion of the mines is more than offset this year by the increase in the price of silver. Prospecting has been stimulated and a number of old producers that have been closed down for several years have been re-opened, and once more appear in the list of shippers.

GOLD.

The statistics of Ontario's gold production for the first nine months of the calendar year, issued by the Ontario Bureau of Mines, show a steady increase over previous years. As in 1915 most of the production this year came from Porcupine, but Kirkland Lake and Munroe district also assisted.

GOLD PRODUCTION IN ONTARIO DURING 9 MONTHS ENDING SEPTEMBER 30TH, 1916.

	Ounces.	Value.
First quarter	107,818	$2,210,269 00
Second quarter	127,242	2,612,471 00
Third quarter	127,895	2,690,994 00
Total for 9 months	363,955	$7,513,734 00

Porcupine:

During 1916 the following mines produced gold in the Porcupine district:

Hollinger.	Vipond.
Dome.	Schumacher.
McIntyre.	Dome Lake.
Porcupine Crown.	

The gold production of the Porcupine camp to the end of the calendar year 1916 is shown in the following table:

PORCUPINE GOLD PRODUCTION, 1910-1916.

Year.	Ounces.	Value.
1910	1,947	$35,539 00
1911	765	15,437 00
1912	83,725	1,730,628 00
1913	207,748	4,294,113 00
1914	251,131	5,190,794 00
1915	362,186	7,480,901 00
1916 (estimated)		9,000,000 00

$27,747,412 00

During month of June a merger was completed of the Hollinger Gold Mines, Limited, Acme Gold Mines, Limited, and Millerton Gold Mines, Limited, along with claim 13147 and the plant of the Canadian Mining and Finance Company, Limited. This aggregation is now known as the Hollinger Consolidated Gold Mines, Limited.

The capital of the new company is $25,000,000, and the dividend that is being paid every four weeks is $240,000.

The mill which has a crushing capacity equivalent to 120 stamps handles over 50,000 tons during a four-weekly period. A 100-stamp extension to the mill is now under construction and is expected to be in operation by next spring. .

An amalgamation is also being arranged between the North Thompson and the Porcupine Vipond Mines, and this is likely to be consummated by the end of the year.

Besides considerable addition to the ore reserves of the two larger properties the Hollinger and the Dome, the year has been noteworthy on account of the important ore bodies located on the 1,000 ft. level of the McIntyre Extension, the 100 ft. level of the Schumacher, and between the 7th and 9th levels of the Porcupine Crown, in all cases adding materially to the value of the mines.

Munroe Township:

The Croesus mine was the only producer in this district during the year. On the 29th July, a devastating forest fire swept the district with large loss of life. Besides losing a number of men, all buildings and equipment of this mine were burned and destroyed. Reconstruction was at once started and is now nearing completion.

Bourkes:

Two or three promising gold finds have been located in the vicinity of Bourkes Station and farther east to the north of Wolf Lake.

Sesekinika:

Very little development has been done in this vicinity. A valuable find was reported on the Sullivan claim.

Kirkland Lake:

The year has been a very active one in this district. The only producer has been the Tough Oakes mine which has operated continuously. It is proposed to double the capacity of the mill in 1917.

- The Northern Ontario Light and Power Company is running a power line into the district from Cobalt, a distance of 64 miles. It is expected that power will be available about the first of February, 1917.

On the Teck-Hughes the mill is ready to start as soon as power is received. Mills are also to be erected in 1917 on the Lake Shore and Kirkland Lake mines (Beaver).

Goodfish Lake:

Development at the La Belle Kirkland mine was considered satisfactory and a mill is now contemplated.

Boston Creek:

A number of promising prospects bid fair to become producers in the near future.

Kowkash and Tashota:

East of Lake Nipigon on the National Transcontinental Railway development is proceeding on several gold claims. The principal operating company is the Tash-Orn which has erected a plant on a promising find on the Wells claim near Tashota. This company is also developing the King-Dodds claim near Kowkash, the original find in the district.

SILVER.

The silver production of Ontario is made up for the most part by the mines in the Cobalt district, the small remaining portion is recovered in the gold mills, but this only amounts to .4 per cent. of the whole.

The official returns for nine months of the year are as follows:

SILVER PRODUCTION IN ONTARIO DURING 9 MONTHS ENDING SEPTEMBER 30TH, 1916.

Period 1915.	Ounces.	Value.
First quarter	5,297,831	$3,187,699 00
Second quarter	4,969,912	3,009,570 00
Third quarter	5,935,348	3,561,771 00
	16,203,091	$9,750,040 00

The year 1915 closed with the price of silver gradually rising. Until May the average price per month showed 25 per cent. rise over the average price for 1915. During June and July a partial drop back took place but since that time the increase has been steady and the average price for December will likely be the highest for the year.

The monthly average price of silver in New York and London during the calendar year 1915 and eleven months of 1916 has been as follows:

Month.	1915.		·1916·	
	New York.	London.	New York.	London.
January	48.855	22.731	56.775	26.960
February	48.477	22.753	56.755	26.975
March	50.241	23.708	57.935	27.597
April	50.250	23.709	64.415	30.662
May	49.915	23.570	74.269	35.477
June	49.034	23.267	65.024	31.060
July	47.519	22.597	62.940	30.000
August	47.163	22.780	66.083	31.498
September	48.680	23.591	68.515	32.584
October	49.885	23.925	67.855	32.361
November	51.714	25.094	71.604	34.192
December	54.971	26.373	75.765	36.410
	49.684	23.675	65,661	31.315

The lowest price for year was 55.875 on January 3rd, 1916, and the average price for eleven months of 1916 was 67.147. The year closes with the price of silver higher than at any other time in the history of the Cobalt camp.

The highest point in the silver production of the Cobalt mines was reached in the year 1911, and from that time on we must expect a gradually decreasing production owing to the depletion of the mines. This year will show a falling off in production of about one million ounces. The rise in price of silver not only offsets this decrease but makes the value of the 1916 production nearly two million dollars higher than that of 1915.

The silver production of the Cobalt camp is shown in the following table:—

Year.	Ounces.	Value.
1904..	206,875	$111,887
1905..	2,451,356	1,360,503
1906..	5,401,766	3,667,551
1907..	10,023,311	6,155,391
1908..	19,437,875	9,133,378
1909..	25,897,825	12,461,576
1910..	30,645,181	15,478,047
1911..	31,507,791	15,953,847
1912..	30,243,859	17,408,935
1913..	29,681,975	16,553,981
1914..	25,162,841	12,765,461
1915..	23,730,839	11,742,463
1916 (Estimated)........................	21,500,000	13,500,000
	255,891,494	136,293,020

The adoption of flotation in a number of mills in Cobalt is having a beneficial effect in bettering the extraction and also in making some of the former tailings dumps profitable to re-treat.

SMELTING AND REFINING.

In the early days of the Cobalt camp all shipments of ore had to go out of the country for treatment, most of it going to the United States. Soon Canadian smelters were started which treated high grade ore, and the latest development has been the building of the so-called High Grade Mills at Cobalt, which produce silver bullion by a combination amalgamation-cyanide process.

An examination of the figures for the calendar years 1914 and 1915 shows that the percentage of silver bullion produced from Cobalt ores was in round numbers: ·

	1914. Per cent.	1915. Per cent.
Cobalt Mills Amalgamation and Cyanide	44	39
Southern Ontario Smelters	39	45
United States Smelters	17	16
	100	100

The sixteen per cent. still going to the United States consists of some high grade ore along with all the low grade material both ore and concentrates shipped, as the Canadian smelters are not equipped to handle this low grade material.

Ville Marie Dock, May 21, 1914.

Ville Marie Dock, October 21, 1915.

In the high grade mills at Cobalt the silver only is recovered, the cobalt, nickel and arsenic being left in the residue for future treatment or sold for the cobalt content. The Deloro and Coniagas smelters are equipped with complete refineries so that besides producing silver bullion they also produce and market arsenic, cobalt and nickel.

The cobalt and nickel have been produced mostly as oxides, but as there has recently been a call for the metals they are now also produced in that form.

The output of the Coniagas and Deloro Smelters up to 31st December, 1915, is as follows:

Smelters,	Ore Treated.	Silver—Fine.	Cobalt Oxide.	Nickel Oxide.	White Arsenic.
	Tons.	Oz.	Tons.	Tons.	Tons.
Coniagas	15,520.80	28,388,652	731	423	3,265
Deloro	22,231.	38,327,154	1,246		6,840

HIGH GRADE MILLS, COBALT.

Silver Bullion Production.

Year.	Nipissing.	Buffalo.	Total.
	Ozs.	Ozs.	Ozs.
1911	2,361,845	....	2,361,845
1912	4,244,948	205,302	4,450,250
1913	4,838,215	1,688,763	6,526,978
1914	4,454,180	930,531	5,384,711
1915	3,764,394	751,054	4,515,446
Total........................	19,663,582	3,575,650	23,239,230

Other mills which have adopted cyanide treatment either totally or in part and are now shipping silver bullion are:

> Cobalt Reduction Company.
> Dominion Reduction Company.
> O'Brien Mill.

OPERATING EXPENDITURE.

The gross value of the silver ore shipments for 1915 to the mining companies was $11,703,966. Deduct dividends paid 1915 $4,532,414—$7,171,552.

On the assumption that cash surpluses remained the same at the end of the year as at the beginning it thus costs $7,000,000 to run the producing mines of Cobalt one year. Of this amount we may assume that two-fifths was paid for supplies, or $2,800,000.

The following table gives operating expenditure for thirteen producing mines for 1915:

Mine.	Labour.	Supplies.	Total.
	$	$	$
Beaver	133,317	88,878	222,195
Buffalo	159,723	106,482	266,205
Coniagas	212,869	141,914	354,783
Crown Reserve	177,591	118,394	295,985
Kerr Lake.......................	214,346	142,898	357,244
La Rose.........................	215,541	143,694	359,235
McKinley-Darragh...............	190,830	127,222	318,052
Mining Corporation	809,724	539,817	1,349,541
Nipissing.......................	468,497	312,331	780,828
O'Brien	201,600	134,400	336,000
Penn Canadian...................	125,244	83,496	208,740
Seneca Superior	53,935	35,957	89,892
Temiskaming....................	157,483	104,988	262,471
Total	3,120,700	2,080,470	5,201,170

In the above table an arbitrary division of the total is made into three-fifths for labour and two-fifths for supplies.

Some of the supplies used are given herewith showing quantity, value and origin.

Pebbles.

Cobalt and Porcupine combined use $40,000 per annum; all imported from Europe, mostly from France. Newfoundland formerly had part of this market but lost it through shipments of poor material.

Cyanide.

Cobalt and Porcupine combined use $574,000 per annum. Of this $400,000 comes from the Cassels Cyanide Company of Glasgow, and the remainder has been supplied by a German firm in the United States.

Zinc.

Cobalt and Porcupine combined use 200 tons, value $80,000. This mostly comes from Japan at present, but soon it will be supplied from the United States.

Powder.

Cobalt uses 900 tons per annum, value $450,000, while Porcupine takes an additional 1,650 tons, and other smaller camps a further 80 tons. All this is manufactured in Canada.

Fuse.

Cobalt uses 3,700,000 feet per annum valued at $17,000. Porcupine takes 7,000,000 feet. 56 per cent. is of British and 44 per cent. of United States manufacture. No fuse is made in Canada.

Drill Steel.

Eighty thousand dollars for Cobalt and Porcupine. Formerly this was supplied equally by England and the United States, but now England cannot supply it.

Detonators.

Cobalt uses 740,000, value $22,200.   They are now manufactured at Browns-
burg, Canada.

Oils.

Lubricating oils, etc., $40,000 per annum is used by Cobalt and Porcupine.
All are American oils, but 30 per cent. is refined in Canada.

Casey Township:

Production proceeded at the Casey mine as usual, until the district was swept
by fire on 22nd August, when all buildings and equipment were lost.   At the end
of the year the new plant is nearing completion.

Gowganda:

Interest in this district has been revived to a certain extent by an important
find made on the Miller-Lake-O'Brien mine.   This find was made on the 300 and
350 ft. levels and is one of the best discoveries ever made in the Temiskaming
district.   This mine has shipped regularly during the year and a small shipment
was also made by the Reeves-Dobie.

South Lorraine:

Several companies operated during the year and the Wetlaufer and Bellellen
made shipments.

NICKEL.

The Alexo mine situated three miles from Porquis Junction on the Porcupine
branch of the Temiskaming and Northern Ontario Railway, continued to ship
nickel ore during the year to the Mond Nickel Company's smelter at Coniston,
Ontario.   A statement of shipments for eleven months of 1916 is given herewith:

NICKEL ORE SHIPMENTS OVER T. & N. O. RY., 1916.

	Tons.
January	1,227.60
February	1,026.55
March	1,041.45
April	699.75
May	959.13
June	848.35
July	671.15
August	672.15
September	384.65
October	237.00
November	332.65
December	347.00
	8,447.43

COPPER.

About four miles north of Temagami station near Cedar Lake, a chalcopyrite
prospect was opened up and a test carload of ore was shipped to a United States
smelter.   The property has since been taken over by M. J. O'Brien and more extensive work is now being planned.

A part of the Rahn Company's Apiary, between New Liskeard and Haileybury.

An Apiary Demonstration. Bees and Clover actually go together. Temiskaming can produce more and better clover than any other part of the province; therefore, it is ideal for Bees.

ZINC AND LEAD.

The Dan Smith zinc-lead property is situated to the south-east of Wolf Lake. It is now under working option to some Toronto interests. Camps have been erected and the property is to have some thorough surface prospecting before mining is commenced. The ore is a coarse zinc-blende and galena in a calcite gangue.

MOLYBDENITE.

Several prospects near Amos, Quebec, have had some work done on them during the summer, but so far no shippers have been developed.

ASBESTOS.

In Deloro Township on the Deloro-Shaw road a promising looking asbestos property is being developed. The fibre is fair and colour good, but extent of deposit has yet to be determined.

LIMESTONE.

. Shipments from the Farr Quarry near Haileybury were made regularly to the Abitibi Power and Paper Company's plant at Iroquois Falls.

MINING OPPORTUNITIES IN NORTHERN ONTARIO.

Along the Temiskaming and Northern Ontario Railway from Cobalt to Porquis Junction, a distance of 125 miles, it was noticeable this year that there was hardly a station from which some mining operations were not being carried on. New districts were being reported from time to time and the older districts were looking better as work proceeded.

Anyone who looked over the unbroken forest of Northern Ontario a dozen years ago and predicted that this district would soon be producing over twenty millions in gold and silver annually would have been put down as a fantastic dreamer; but that figure is surpassed to-day by two and-one-half million dollars and the output is continually increasing.

And yet only a small portion of the country has been prospected. Running north-east and north-west from Cobalt and extending to the Arctic Ocean is the great Canadian Pre-Cambrian Shield, the basement formation of the continent. It contains thousands of square miles and offers to prospectors *better chances of locating valuable mineral deposits than can be found in any other country in the world.*

RE STORES DEPARTMENT, PURCHASES AND ISSUES 1915-1916.

Submit herewith statement covering purchases and issues during the year closing October 31st, 1916, which shows a greater volume of business than any previous year.

Shop stock and coal are the main barometers to indicate activities—the former has more than doubled and the latter shows over 50 per cent. increase.

Three elements contribute to the results:

(a) General business activity over the whole country.

6 T.R.

(b) Higher prices attributed to the war.

(c) Replacing property and material destroyed by the lamentable fire at the close of July.

Rails again show a large decrease as it was impossible to get deliveries on outstanding orders, while at the same time stock rail was going out and also a considerable amount of rail was sold that had served its day of usefulness on the railway—a considerable quantity of it realizing twenty-eight dollars per gross ton, which figure had been the base price of rail for many years previous to the commencement of the war.

Nearly all kinds of material show marked increases in price and deliveries slow. Shortage of cars and expanding business in general as well as speeding up manufacture to meet war consumption tended to the slow delivery of material, but notwithstanding, the year's work looms large both in the expenditure of labour and material—the two items, I understand, being almost equal in volume for the year.

Delivery of coal has been a matter of serious concern: labour difficulties, shortage of cars and an abnormal requirement on the American continent is a conjunction of circumstances that we have not had to go into the open market to meet requirements, and many seem to be of the opinion that there is prospect of improvement in conditions in the near future.

We have been able to secure our requirements in lumber thus far at practically same price as last year. A writer in the *Canadian Lumberman* predicts that lumber production will be much below the average this season and that cost of production will fully be twenty-five per cent. above normal.

Ties remained about stationary in price, viz., thirty-two cents average, covering inspection. We expect an increase of three cents average at least as ties are hard to get on account of labour conditions.

Iron and steel products are all high—the rail condition mentioned above may be taken as a measure of the whole line of material except as to scrap. Export of scrap is prohibited which tends to keep prices down as compared with new material.

Scrap disposal has been heavy as a result of the fire and the general depreciation on account of burning shows heavier than what is the result of ordinary wear.

Staff changes during the year have not been excessive, but the heavy demands have meant increased cost for handling material—approximately two thousand dollars. Our payroll for 1915 was .14 of one per cent. of business handled, while this year, nothwithstanding the above increase, the percentage is .08 of one per cent.

I hereby express my thanks to the staff for their effort to meet the abnormal demands of the year and also to all departments for co-operation and assistance. We also feel grateful to the Commission and Toronto office for consideration and courtesies extended in the daily intercourse during the year.

Yours truly,

W. A. GRAHAM,

P. A. & Storekeeper.

Stores Department.

Statement of Purchases and Issues Fiscal Years 1915-1916.

Stock.	1915		1916	
	Purchases.	Issues.	Purchases.	Issues.
	$ c.	$ c.	$ c.	$ c.
Shop	166,125 85	166,159 35	373,985 43	317,216 53
Soft Coal	271,622 07	253,662 97	427,717 32	374,629 07
Hard Coal.....................	10,615 55	10,872 96	9,042 00	10,624 13
Oil and Waste.................	12,172 09	12,190 73	19,347 33	14,685 14
Stationery.....................	10,138 40	10,676 31	17,598 55	15,867 78
Rail	34,345 99	19,520 37	6,322 30	61,093 59
Ties..........................	6,108 37	26,394 98	18,402 35	31,576 80
Ice...........................	2,550 55	3,303 50	3,894 15	5,941 01
Operation of Ballast Pits........	....	20,198 01	....	14,986 75
Nipissing Central Railway	7,390 19	11,107 33	10,177 35	8,935 61
Material for Private Cars	....	37,432 08	....	....
Locomotives—six new..........	....	....	204,851 00	204,851 00
	521,069 06	571,518 59	1,091,336 78	1,060,408 41
Total Issues................		571,518 59		1,060,408 41
Total Purchases		521,069 06		1,091,336 78
		1,092,587 65		2,151,745 19
Pay roll....................		15,300 00		17,374 71

Farm of Mr. Frank Keneah, Brentha, Ont.

FINANCIAL STATEMENTS.

GENERAL BALANCE SHEET.

ASSETS.

Property Owned:—

Cost of Road as of Oct. 31, 1915	$17,913,700 48		
Cost of Road for year ded Oct. 31, 1916	215,314 59	$18,129,015 07	
Cost of Equipment as of Oct. 31, 1915	$2,243,124 88		
Cost of Equipment for year ded Oct. 31, 1916	327,666 83	2,570,791 71	
the Nip' ing ral Rail wy		483,123 31	
the Lumber Plant, Latchf d		6,625 07	

Working Assets:—

Cash—Treasurer	$76,670 92	
Cash—Land ent	17,104 97	
As the	192,928 35	
Balance due on site Sales	37,639 04	
As nd	39,116 64	
Traffic Balances—Freight	2,062 43	
ffic Balances—Tickets	14,252 09	
al and , ties	320,464 11	
As Pit Operati ns	48,790 51	
Other As	1,538 46	750,567 52

Deferred Debit Items:—

Paymaster's i As	$7,000 00	
Treasurer's Advances	100 00	
Ice Paid As	953 81	
M Paid As in Transit	1,573 18	
As in As	7,935 00	17,561 99

	$21,957,684 67

LIABILITIES.

Provincial Loan Account			$21,183,687 59

Working Liabilities:—

ds Payable	$526,353 48	
ffic Balances—Car Mil ge	6,182 30	
Unclaimed Wages	882 55	533,418 33

Deferred Credit Items:—

nal Depr ation—Equipment	$222,193 34	
fits on Sidings	2,198 83	
fits on Contracts	522 40	
War Tax	718 19	
In ofse	642 38	226,275 14

Free Surplus:—

Profit and ss— ; Be		14,303 61

	21,957,684 67

AND LOSS.

ss on retired Road and Equipment	$3,021 36	
ible ants—Cancelled	10,948 88	
Paid Yar of fio	1,000,000 00	
Be Carried Forward	14,303 61	

	$1,028,273 85

By Balance, for 31, 1915 er 31, 1916	$415,664 24	
Revenue of gr ded Central Ry	528,705 46	
ne from ng	20,000 00	
Townsites	2,982 87	
Balances de on wn ss	37,639 04	
nt Stores As to Inventory	23,282 24	

	$1,028,273 85

- STATEMENT OF EXPENDITURE ON CONSTRUCTION.

Fiscal Year Ending October 31st, 1916.

Engineering	2,311 36
Land for transportation purposes	5,520 65
Grading	29,153 61
Bridges, trestles and culverts	28,894 84
Ties	4,170 53
Rails	14,205 76
Other track material	9,533 07
Ballast	3,298 40
Track laying and surfacing	10,038 78
Right-of-way fences	4,982 92
Crossings and signs	1,763 13
Station and office buildings	37,957 20
Roadway buildings	9,313 76
Water stations	2,088 06
Fuel stations	5,356 58
Shops and engine houses	15,294 65
Telegraph and telephone lines	8,255 51
Miscellaneous structures	6,801 49
Shop machinery	2,413 44
Steam locomotives	205,580 09
Freight-train cars ....*Cr.*	1,289 33
Passenger-train cars	82,453 04
Work equipment	40,923 03
Miscellaneous surveys	2,775 17
Revision of line	11,185 68
	$542,981 42

DETAILED STATEMENT OF CHARGES TO CONSTRUCTION.

ROAD.

Filling trestle M.P. 25.71 and installing culvert ....*Cr.*	$40 87
" " " 71.37 " " " ....*,Cr.*	90 17
" " " 163.3 " " . "	593 61
Widening embankments ....*Cr.*	169 94
New siding, Ramore	897 53
Extension siding No. 11, North Bay Jct.	832 39
Hard coal and heater building, Cochrane	565 68
Commercial telephone line, Englehart to Boston Creek	640 94
Telephone exchange, Matheson	432 72
Heating system, agent's house, Cobalt	287 00
Addition to agent's house, Schumacher	437 54
Extension to freight siding, shed, Elk Lake	308 73
Telegraph line, Englehart to Timmins	2,929 00
Telegraph line, New Liskeard to Timmins	1,959 85
New siding, Bourkes	9 00
" " Nahma	9 84
" " Nushka	9 00
" " Mindoka	29 24
New station, Timmins	18,560 06
New siding, Chamberlain	9 00
Public and private road crossings	1,724 34
New fencing	4,695 14
New siding, Heaslip	1,006 78
Additional and improved rail fastenings	1,881 45
Additional yard facilities, Porquis Jct.	23,262 88
Roadbed underdrainage	889 21
Replacing timber trestle, M.P. 181.31, with steel	2,674 43
Filling trestle, M.P. 162.2, and installing concrete slabs	17,576 40
Roadway and spur, New Liskeard wharf	4,961 04
Additional shop machinery, North Bay	2,403 44
Replacing open beam culverts	432 65
Section house, Nushka	2 66
Coaling plant, Porquis Jct.	5,295 30

Addition to coach and carpenter shop, North Bay	239	56
Water service, Porquis Jct.	5,109	42
Passenger train platform, Cochrane	38	30
New siding, mileage 233	437	51
" " " 153.5	253	61
Platform, Rosedale, Porcupine Branch	67	54
Grading, Cochrane terminals	505	98
Roadways, Holland, Nahma, and M.P. 245½	284	04
" Keys, South Porcupine and Iroquois Falls	1,000	45
Culvert, mileage 130	144	98
Main line, revision surveys	2,258	21
Shelter station, M.P. 122	285	14
Telephone line, Swastika to Boston Creek	52	83
" " Matheson to Ramore	321	39
" " Porquis to Nellie Lake	162	11
" " Matheson to Cochrane	784	95
Installation lighting, Matheson Stn.	4	70
" " Iroquois Falls	14	20
Bachelor section house, Kerr Lake Jct.	402	64
Additional yard sidings, Cochrane	2,024	50
" " " Englehart	28,261	21
Alterations, machine shops, North Bay	15,441	35
Pumpmen's dwelling, Porquis Jct.	1,122	93
Installation plumbing, etc., Porquis Jct.	534	97
Culvert, mileage 55.75	468	26
Electric hoist, ice house, North Bay	153	84
Installation track scales, North Bay Jct.	2,526	25
Lavatory accommodation, Cobalt Stn.	251	35
Replacing culvert, M.P. 224-07	2,234	80
Replacing two culverts, M.P. 0.5, Porcupine Branch	3,952	01
Telephone circuit, Kenney's siding to Temagami	971	72
Four semi-detached tenement houses, Iroquois Falls	5,678	56
Two section and tool houses, Matheson	5,451	28
Section and tool house, Nushka	2,097	83
" " " " Nahma	1,333	61
Tool house, Iroquois Falls	21	79
Freight shed, Cochrane	5,062	12
" " Matheson	1,725	35
Station, Matheson	4,361	78
Extra land, Wabewawa	50	00
" " Chamberlain	75	00
" " North Bay	3,513	00
" " Haileybury	1,754	05
North and south half Lot 2, Con. 2, Newmarket	102	00
Completion grading Porcupine Branch	28	15
Coal shed, Iroquois Falls	61	28
Extension siding, Watahbeag	27	76
Private sidings installed and removed	8,617	92
Roadways, Osseo and McCool, Elk Lake Branch ....Cr.	8	19
Water tank, North Bay Jct., removed ....Cr.	3,021	36
Engine shed siding, Kerr Lake, removed ....Cr.	294	43
Auxiliary storage spur, North Bay Jct., shortened ....Cr.	65	67
Siding, Charlton, shortened ....Cr.	14	00
" Jocko, " ....Cr.	530	71

$201,353 74

EQUIPMENT.

Six Mikado locomotives	$205,580	09
Ballast and general service cars	15,190	81
Betterments, passenger train cars	2,319	84
Steel passenger equipment	77,500	58
Conductors' vans	15	85
Lighting equipment, parlor cafe cars	2,632	62
Water tank cars	732	22
Official car Temagami	25,000	00
Additional freight cars	1,600	00
Car 80134 destroyed ....Cr.	1,321	18

327,666 83

SPECIAL ACCOUNTS.

James Bay exploration	$35 15	
Special survey south of North Bay	1,743 03	
Revision of line, mileage 54-55	9,494 11	
" " " " 63	1,666 59	
" " " . " 80.8-81.2	24 98	
Kirkland Lake survey	271 99	
Cobalt Sudbury location	232 87	
Electrification studies	492 13	
		13,960 85

$542,981 42

COMPARATIVE STATEMENT SHOWING EARNINGS AND EXPENDITURES IN OPERATION

PERIOD 1905 TO 1916, INCLUSIVE.

Year.	Freight.	Passenger.	Other Revenue.	Maintenance of Way.	Maintenance of Equipment.	Traffic Expenses.	Transportation Expenses.	Misc. Operations.	General Expenses.	Transportation for Investment. Cr.	Total Revenue.	Total Expenditures.
	$ c.	$ c.	$ c.	$ c.	$ c.	$ c.	$ c.	$ c.	$ c.	$ c.	$ c.	$ c.
1905..	121,530 46	108,681 76	23,508 33	25,072 89	12,533 68		88,312 41		13,823 52		253,720 55	139,772 50
1906..	230,552 63	254,759 33	58,706 89	77,265 87	46,382 65		215,256 08		23,194 61		544,018 85	362,099 21
1907..	390,894 29	388,343 03	74,282 69	112,395 22	88,016 79		412,160 52		32,839 76		853,520 01	645,412 29
1908..	471,203 41	366,504 53	135,357 67	125,563 43	119,563 01	12,499 96	405,907 58		24,863 45		973,065 61	688,397 43
1909..	756,141 66	483,110 89	121,972 33	191,170 18	107,078 96	9,789 99	436,768 41		49,989 34		1,361,224 88	794,796 88
1910..	852,886 46	606,967 91	131,997 65	380,314 75	137,340 46	14,920 04	556,740 45		76,045 66		1,591,852 02	1,165,361 36
1911..	974,678 33	653,063 01	153,223 49	353,918 92	164,145 69	17,705 31	567,316 97		78,911 74		1,780,964 83	1,181,998 63
1912..	929,464 66	599,681 73	178,303 68	346,964 01	249,683 22	17,461 22	676,963 33		93,625 91		1,707,450 07	1,384,697 69
1913..	906,476 16	576,049 37	173,629 32	430,820 04	242,633 93	16,857 36	680,480 08		106,758 60		1,656,154 85	1,477,550 01
1914..	952,090 35	544,820 08	173,988 44	408,046 15	284,935 87	18,872 65	651,687 20		105,032 36		1,670,898 87	1,468,574 23
1915..	925,735 37	482,349 80	143,466 60	325,865 86	262,654 51	18,135 13	625,911 92		95,929 49		1,551,551 77	1,328,496 91
1916..	1,320,569 33	624,808 12	192,744 50	349,024 48	248,702 04	22,465 69	842,058 75	42,562 89	91,317 74	1,954 13	2,138,121 95	1,594,177 46
	8,832,223 11	5,689,139 56	1,561,181 59	3,126,421 80	1,963,670 81	148,707 35	6,159,593 70	42,562 89	792,332 18	1,954 13	16,082,544 26	12,231,334 60

SUMMARY.

Freight Revenue	$8,832,223 11	
Passenger Revenue	5,689,139 56	
Other Revenue	1,561,181 59	
		$16,082,544 26

Maintenance of Way and Structures	$3,126,421 80
Maintenance of Equipment	1,963,670 81
Transportation Expenses	6,159,593 70
Traffic Expenses	148,707 35
Miscellaneous Operations	42,562 89
General Expenses	792,332 18
Taxation for Investment—Cr.	1,954 13
	$12,231,334 60

Total Revenue from Transportation		$16,082,544 26
Total Expenditures		12,231,334 50
		3,851,209 66
Other Income, etc		701,339 11
		4,552,548 77
Paid Treasurer of Ontario		4,538,245 16
Balance Profit and Loss		14,303 61

TEMISKAMING AND NORTHERN
Comparative Statement of Earnings and Expenditures

No.	RECEIPTS.	Per Cent.	1914 November	Per Cent.	1915 November
	I. TRANSPORTATION—RAIL LINE:		$ c.		$ c.
101	Freight		71,316 58	......	97,346 05
102	Passenger		36,977 81	......	43,433 78
103	Excess Baggage		497 53	......	524 23
105	Parlor and Chair Car		82 00	......	62 10
106	Mail		1,787 98	......	1,952 60
107	Express		3,560 57	......	4,337 76
108	Other Passenger Train		....		....
109	Milk		80	......	....
110	Switching		131 00	......	1,065 87
111	Special Service Train		....		....
112	Other Freight Train		....		....
	Total		114,354 27	......	148,722 39
	III. INCIDENTALS:				
131	Dining and Buffet				
133	Station, Train and Boat Privileges		362 49	......	362 49
135	Storage—Freight		75 68	......	131 01
136	Storage—Baggage		50 60	......	42 65
137	Demurrage		678 00	......	492 00
138	Telegraph and Telephone		3,267 34	......	3,659 95
140	Stockyard				
142	Rents of Buildings and other Property		1,534 64	......	1,170 51
143	Miscellaneous		23 64	......	4 25
	Total		5,992 39	......	5,862 86
	IV. JOINT FACILITY:				
151	Joint Facility—Cr.				....
152	Joint Facility—Dr.				118 18
	Total				118 18
	TOTAL REVENUE		120.346 66	......	154.467 07
	EXPENDITURES.				
1	Maintenance of Way and Structures	22.8	27,445 91	23.8	36,819 46
2	Maintenance of Equipment	16.6	19,946 91	15.1	23.272 14
3	Traffic	1.3	1,556 03	1.	1,603 10
4	Transportation—Rail Line	47.1	56,735 10	37.8	58.340 34
5	Transportation—Water Line				
6	Miscellaneous Operations			1.6	2,551 09
7	General	4.5	5,396 59	3.7	5,673 50
8	Transportation for Investment—Cr.		....	.1	201 12
	TOTAL OPERATING EXPENSES	92.3	111,080 54	82.9	128,058 51
	BALANCE		9,266 12	......	26,408 56
	OTHER INCOME:				
	Ore Royalties				Dr.1,572 79
	Rent from Locomotives		2,082 94	......	398 96
	Rent from Work Equipment		533 75	......	83 56
	Rent from Passenger Equipment				....
	Rent from Joint Facilities		25 00	......	1,088 96
	Rent from Lease of Road		837 92	......	1,121 15
	Miscellaneous Income		....	......	112 26
	Outside Operations		247 60	......	....
	Interest		....	......	....
	Total		12,993 33	......	27,640 66
	DEDUCTIONS FROM INCOME:				
	Hire of Equipment—Freight Cars		2,849 50	......	4,067 51
	Hire of Equipment—Passenger Cars		....	......	1,805 15
	Rent for Joint Facilities		....	......	312 00
	Outside Operations		1,085 89	......	....
	Total		3,935 39	......	6,184 66
	NET RESULT		9,057 94	......	21,456 00

ONTARIO RAILWAY
by Months, November, 1914, to October 1916

Per Cent.	1914 December	Per Cent.	1915 December	Per Cent.	1915 January	Per Cent.	1916 January	No.
	$ c.		$ c.		$ c.		$ c.	
......	78,370 76	......	102,238 62	......	87,841 30	,.....	93,137 58	101
......	37,323 71	......	43,943 37	......	30,755 22	......	38,890 21	102
......	209 28	......	230 25	......	315 85	......	288 96	103
......	85 10	......	45 15	......	85 30	......	49 80	105
......	2,029 86	......	2,027 70	......	1,938 04	......	1,952 60	106
......	3,609 54	......	5,319 35	......	8,191 72	......	4,008 47	107
								108
......	18 61			......	50 85			109
......	379 43	......	1,069 33	......	257 81	......	964 15	110
								111
								112
......	122,026 29	......	154,873 77	......	124,436 09	......	139,291 77	
							2,160 52	131
......	362 49	......	362 49	......	362 49	......	362 49	133
......	80 42	......	80 10	......	126 65	......	99 38	135
......	28 75	......	30 90	......	33 05	......	35 65	136
......	1,224 00	......	694 00	......	1,206 00	......	603 00	137
......	3,166 79	......	4,455 19	......	2,709 87	......	5,142 74	138
					57 77			140
......	545 47	......	440 19	......	506 34	......	440 66	142
...... Dr.	3 77	......	42 71	......	26 44	......	37 00	143
......	5,404 15	......	6,105 58	......	5,028 61	......	8,881 44	
								151
		......	63 08	......	24 52	......	55 64	152
		......	63 08	......	24 52	......	55 64	
......	127,430 44	......	160,916 27	......	129,440 18	......	148,117 57	
24.7	31,489 74	18.6	29,981 40	16.8	21,771 15	21.2	31,501 12	1
20.9	26,428 44	13.6	21,829 87	21.1	27,352 15	15.7	23,232 31	2
1.4	1,862 25	1.6	2,536 47	1.5	1,856 28	2.	3,013 91	3
46.8	59,757 59	39.7	63,818 19	47.8	61,916 32	51.5	76,280 49	4
								5
		2.0	3,286 55			3.3	4,975 78	6
5.6	7,093 89	5.7	9,121 10	5.	6,476 63	4.6	6,761 42	7
		.1	136 95			......	35 86	8
99.4	126,627 91	81.1	130,436 69	92.2	119,372 53	98.3	145,729 17	
......	802 53	......	30,479 58	......	10,067 65	......	2,388 40	
......	10,692 53	...... Dr.	375 65	...... Dr.	396 12	......	8,076 37	
......	582 61	......	309 99	......	458 21	......	159 60	
......	19 66	......	113 05	......	17 20	......	Dr. 26 10	
......	25 00	......	1,110 39	......	3,084 53	......	1,116 74	
......	837 92	......	1,140 02	......	1,586 08	......	1,044 42	
		......	81 10	......		......	8 50	
		......	48 09	......		......		
......	12,960 25	......	32,906 57	......	14,817 55	......	12,767 93	
......	5,348 04	......	4,781 29	......	6,694 81	......	7,381 72	
		......	1,239 98			......	1,436 57	
		......	318 00			......	315 00	
......	2,390 01	......		......	2,074 82	......		
......	7,738 05	......	6,339 27	......	8,769 63	......	9,133 29	
......	5,222 20	......	26,567 30	......	6,047 92	......	3,634 64	

Comparative Statement of Earnings and Expenditures by

No.	RECEIPTS.	Per Cent.	1915 February	Per Cent.	1916 February	Per Cent.	1915 March
	I. TRANSPORTATION–RAIL LINE:		$ c.		$ c.		$ c.
101	Freight		81,894 86	......	106,735 47	......	86,006 71
102	Passenger		26,244 94	......	29,940 87	......	34,909 20
103	Excess Baggage		395 33	.....	335 28	.....	288 57
105	Parlor and Chair Car		76 10	......	48 50	.....	81 45
106	Mail		1,788 96	......	1,871 50	.....	1,938 15
107	Express		2,532 93	......	4,047 08	.....	2,771 29
108	Other Passenger Train		....	......	....	.....	....
109	Milk		34 79	......	....	.....	23 09
110	Switching		304 34	......	1,095 54	.....	468 98
111	Special Service Train—		....	.....	226 00	.:...	....
112	Other Freight Train		....	......	....	.....	....
	Total		113,272 25	......	144,300 24	.....	126,487 44
	III. INCIDENTALS :						
131	Dining and Buffet		....	......	1,075 01	.....	....
133	Station,Train and Boat Privileges.	.....	362 49	......	362 56	.....	362 49
135	Storage—Freight		171 19	......	57 03	.....	103 28
136	" —Baggage		22 35	.....	18 10	.....	18 50
137	Demurrage		711 00	......	615 00	.....	885 75
138	Telegraph and Telephone	.....	3,044 28	......	3,457 49	.....	4,502 60
140	Stockyard		....	......	....	.....	Dr. 28 88
142	Rents of Buildings and other Property		2,073 07	......	718 47	.....	177 96
143	Miscellaneous		1 00	......	30 83	.....	15 36
	Total		6,385 38	......	6,334 49	.....	6,037 06
	IV. JOINT FACILITY :						
151	Joint Facility—Cr.		....	......	....	.....	....
152	" " —Dr.		....	......	45 94	.....	62 00
	Total		....	......	45 94	.....	62 00
	TOTAL REVENUE		119,657 63	......	150,588 79	.....	132,462 50
	EXPENDITURES.						
1	Maintenance of Way & Structures.	16.1	19,263 72	23.5	35,310 60	24.1	31,966 15
2	Maintenance of Equipment	20.	23,909 34	16.3	24,491 27	21.8	28,822 57
3	Traffic	1.	1,250 95	1.3	1,902 02	1.2	1,608 79
4	Transportation—Rail Line	49.8	59,556 20	51.5	77,691 60	41.6	55,049 45
5	" —Water Line		....	......	....	.....	....
6	Miscellaneous Operations		....	2.2	3,316 32	.....	....
7	General	5.	5,951 81	4.1	6,233 01	5.3	7,047 66
8	Transportation-for Investment-Cr.		....	......	25 32	.....	....
	TOTAL OPERATING EXPENSES	91.9	109,932 02	98.9	148,919 50	94.	124,494 62
	BALANCE		9,725 61	......	1,669 29	.....	7,967 88
	OTHER INCOME :						
	Ore Royalties		Dr. 356 63	......	Dr. 364 08	.....	10,877 47
	Rent from Locomotives		387 30	......	143 30	.....	150 22
	Rent from Work Equipment		5 50	......	8 80	.....	20 45
	Rent from Passenger Equipment.		16 48	......	....	.....	988 64
	Rent from Joint Facilities		25 00	......	1,046 31	..;	25 00
	Rent from Lease of Road		759 44	......	863 04	.....	749·46
	Miscellaneous Income		....	......	26 24	.....	....
	Outside Operations		....	......	....	.....	....
	Interest		....	......	13 54	.....	....
	Total		10,562 70	......	3,406 44	.....	20,779 12
	DEDUCTIONS FROM INCOME :						
	Hire of Equipment, Freight Cars.		4,941 61	......	9,704 21	.....	5,337 20
	" " Passenger "		....	......	1,322 25	.....	....
	Rent for Joint Facilities		....	......	313 00	.....	304 50
	Outside Operations		2,192 42	......	....	.....	3,582 51
	Total		7,134 03	......	11,339 46	.....	9,224 21
	NET RESULT		3,428 67	......	Dr.7,933 02	—	11,554 91

Months, November. 1914, to October, 1916—Continued

Per Cent.	1916 March	Per Cent.	1915 April	Per Cent.	1916 April	Per Cent.	1915 May	No.
	$ c.		$ c.		$ c.		$ c.	
.....	141,617 65	......	59,581 12	......	173,472 76	......	60,405 95	101
.....	38,263 19	......	36,630 78	......	45,016 03	......	38,875 85	102
.....	440 91	......	495 57	......	347 28	......	438 93	103
.....	68 10	......	97 70	......	74 25	......	103 40	105
.....	2,025 78	......	1,938 04	......	1,877 50	......	1,950 36	106
.....	3,662 41	......	2,977 82	......	4,800 03	......	3,004 22	107
								108
.....	....	......	10 67	......	....	......	1 32	109
.....	1,101 85	......	459 34	......	1,120 51	......	243 81	110
								111
.....	....	......	....	......	....	......	....	112
.....	187,179 89	......	102,191 04	......	226,708 36	......	105,023 84	
								131
.....	963 59	......	....	......	....	......	....	
.....	362 49	......	362 49	......	362 49	......	362 49	133
.....	215 09	......	74 12	......	144 32	......	78 50	135
.....	24 50	......	36 65	......	32 75	......	34 10	136
.....	702 60	......	517 00	......	716 00	......	455 00	137
.....	4,139 80	......	3,299 94	......	5,230 03	......	3,463 94	138
	....							140
.....	351 82	......	729 72	......	328 46	......	451 91	142
.....	16 28	......	16 71	......	26 78	......	33 76	143
.....	6,776 17	......	5,036 63	......	6,840 83	......	4,879 70	
								151
.....	52 46	......	99	......	....	......	58 15	152
.....	52 46	......	99	......	....	......	58 15	
.....	193,903 60	......	107,226 68	......	233,549 19	......	109,845 39	
16.1	31,221 35	27.8	29,850 05	12.2	28,388 98	33.5	36,744 68	1
15.9	30,903 83	24.6	26,354 55	10.7	25,101 54	16.6	18,172 11	2
.7	1,441 97	1.3	1,436 91	.5	1,237 48	1.2	1,321 56	3
48.5	94,015 46	44.2	47,340 38	40.3	94,139 11	38.4	42,227 30	4
								5
2.	3,852 12	12.8	13,739 92	.9	2,091 37	2.1	2,340 88	6
3.4	6,542 81	5.5	5,889 77	2.6	5,977 79	5.5	6,070 74	7
.....	30 88		....		35 95	.1	132 52	8
86.6	167,946 16	116.2	124,611 58	67.2	156,900 32	97.2	106,744 75	
.....	25,957 44	......	Dr. 17,384 90	......	76,648 87	......	3,100 64	
.....	6,016 22		Dr. 357 69		Dr. 364 02	......	Dr. 365 14	
.....	184 72	......	188 93	......	160 72	......	690 80	
.....	16 33	......	29 96	......	24 90	......	236 80	
.....	....	......	4 12	......	....	......	....	
.....	1,329 23	......	3,837 23	......	1,409 19	......	1,242 54	
.....	885 25	......	804 47	......	1,183 34	......	1,728 66	
.....	54 00	......	....	......	65 50	......	....	
.....	45 10	......	....	......	1 97	......	....	
.....	34,488 29	......	Dr. 12,877 88	......	79,130 47	......	6,634 30	
.....	14,869 97	......	2,215 04	......	16,304 03	......	1,677 60	
.....	1,698 55	......	....	......	1,803 88	......	....	
.....	319 00	......	302 00	......	312 50	......	1,515 00	
.....	....	......	Cr. 11,078 05	......	....	......	....	
.....	16,887 52	......	Cr. 8,561 01	......	18,420 41	......	3,192 60	
.....	17,600 77	......	Dr. 4,316 87	......	60,710 06	......	3,441 70	

Comparative Statement of Earnings and Expenditures by

No.	RECEIPTS.	Per Cent	1916 May	Per Cent.	1915 June	Per Cent.	1916 June
	I. TRANSPORTATION—RAIL LINE:		$ c.		$ c.		$ c.
101	Freight		129,688 74		68,099 43		91,969 02
102	Passenger		54,727 06		38,600 15		58,770 50
103	Excess Baggage		474 21		430 75		480 94
105	Parlor and Chair Car		85 45		88 20		105 85
106	Mail		2,025 78		1,952 60		1,952 60
107	Express		4,696 04		3,561 14		4,885 95
108	Other Passenger Train						
109	Milk				88		15
110	Switching		728 59		449 07		678 51
111	Special Service Train						
112	Other Freight Train						
	Total		192,425 87		113,182 22		158,813 52
	III. INCIDENTALS:						
131	Dining and Buffet		1,096 67				
133	Station, Train & Boat Privileges		362 49		362 49		362 50
135	Storage—Freight		173 68		104 03		135 23
136	" —Baggage		32 10		28 40		42 55
137	Demurrage		1,207 00		695 00		562 00
138	Telegraph and Telephone		4,529 42		3,679 77		4,301 79
140	Stockyard						
142	Rents of Buildings & other Property		487 47		789 60		1,096 55
143	Miscellaneous		20 18		3 85		32 35
	Total		7,909 01		5,663 14		6,532 97
	IV. JOINT FACILITY:						
151	Joint Facility—Cr.						
152	" —Dr.						
	Total						
	TOTAL REVENUE		200,334 88		118,845 36		165,346 49
	EXPENDITURES.						
1	Maintenance of Way and Structures	16.5	33,152 63	28.7	34,058 99	22.4	37,065 95
2	Maintenance of Equipment	11.2	22,250 15	16.1	19,166 33	12.9	21,341 88
3	Traffic	.8	1,519 95	1.2	1,485 76	1.	1,691 90
4	Transportation—Rail Line	36.5	73,215 82	36.6	43,454 64	35.4	58,624 87
5	" Water Line						
6	Miscellaneous Operations	1.8	3,784 25	2.2	2,569 77	1.4	2,257 47
7	General	3.2	6,457 00	3.5	4,231 35	4.7	7,709 59
8	Transportation for Invest'nt—Cr.	.2	368 95		94 25	.1	226 53
	TOTAL OPERATING EXPENSES	69.8	140,010 85	88.3	104,872 59	77.7	128,465 13
	BALANCE		60,324 03		13,972 77		36,881 36
	OTHER INCOME:						
	Ore Royalties		Dr. 357 81		Dr. 355 81		Dr. 485 49
	Rent from Locomotives		408 14		429 43		28 01
	Rent from Work Equipment		70 20		132 55		105 31
	Rent from Passenger "						
	Rent from Joint Facilities		904 25		1,118 12		1,081 53
	Rent from Lease of Road		1,382 20		987 78		1,106 84
	Miscellaneous Income		119 84		187 00		62 34
	Outside Operations						
	Interest		365 16				14 37
	Total		63,216 01		16,471 84		38,794 27
	DEDUCTIONS FROM INCOME:						
	Hire of Equipment, Freight Cars		7,019 91		1,232 19		4,004 57
	" Passenger "		2,574 27				2,294 71
	Rent for Joint Facilities		321 00		302 00		318 50
	Outside Operations						
	Total		9,915 18		1,534 19		6,617 78
	NET RESULT		53,300 83		14,937 65		32,176 49

Months, November, 1914, to October, 1916—Continued

Per Cent.	1915 July	Per Cent.	1916 July	Per Cent.	1915 August	Per Cent.	1916 August	No.
	$ c.		$ c.		$ c.		$ c.	
......	68,759 03	......	78,564 32	......	74,112 07	......	94,070 30	101
......	43,895 52	......	64,057 29	......	63,734 68	......	61,493 33	102
......	323 49	......	424 07●	......	321 03	......	335 99	103
......	84 55	......	108 15	......	84 25	......	149 85	105
......	2,027 70	......	1,952 60	......	1,952 60	......	2,025 78	106
......	3,971 90	......	4,642 60	......	4,520 77	......	6,246 78	107
								108
......	2 80	......		......	2 45	......	4 00	109
......	343 83	......	542 08	......	499 22	......	838 61	110
							488 40	111
								112
......	119,408 82	......	150,291 11	......	145,227 07	......	165,653 04	
			774 62				2,531 62	131
......	452 49	......	362 52	......	272 49	......	362 50	133
......	134 53	......	105 60	......	86 37	......	78 54	135
......	33 70	......	38 75	......	25 15	......	30 20	136
......	568 00	......	485 00	......	407 00	......	948 00	137
......	3,667 55	......	5,670 55	......	3,555 38	......	5,125 68	138
								140
......	360 89	......	559 53	......	1,197 33	......	994 74	142
......	21 92	......	16 50	......	38 12	......	12 91	143
......	5,239 08	......	8,013 07	......	5,581 84	......	10,084 19	
								151
......	45 30	......	187 39	......	62 85	......	48 61	152
	45 30	......	187 39	......	62 85	......	48 61	
......	124,602 60	......	158,116 79	......	150,746 06	......	175,688 62	
29.7	37,084 47	13.2	20,808 64	22.7	34,231 99	19.4	33,964 50	1
18.0	22,433 61	8.	12,603 59	16.1	24,339 51	10.0	17,643 29	2
1.2	1,511 46	.9	1,520 49	1.1	1,636 03	2.1	3,758 86	3
38.1	47,481 70	36.5	57,641 04	34.4	51,821 37	35.7	62,658 02	4
								5
1.8	2,392 97	2.	3,209 14	1.6	2,515 73	2.2	3,989 13	6
4.8	5,958 53	4.9	7,770 94	3.6	5,480 34	4.3	7,478 93	7
	135 18	.1	108 84		170 60	.1	220 58	8
93.6	116,727 56	65.4	103,445 00	79.5	119,854 37	73.6	129,222 15	
......	7,875 04	......	54,671 79	......	30,891 69	......	46,466 47	
......	Dr. 364 58	......	Dr. 425 74	......	Dr. 363 02	......	11,741 82	
......	456 88	......	752 17	......	311 64	......	392 74	
......	118 98	......	Dr. 10 15	......	212 65	......	281 50	
......	4 12	......		......		......		
......	1,154 74	......	1,116 74	......	1,064 73	......	1,116 74	
......	984 27	......	1,097 02	......	979 53	......	1,203 13	
......	683 28	......	74 84	......	679 56	......	45 14	
							1,232 54	
......	10,912 73	......	57,276 67	......	33,776 78	......	62,480 08	
......	1,665 95	......	Cr. 1,892 77	......	6,457 91	......	8,894 26	
			1,650 67				Cr. 2,956 94	
......	312 50	......	316 50	......	323 00	......	324 00	
......	1,978 45	......	74 40	......	6,780 91	......	6,261 32	
......	8,934 28	......	57,202 27	......	26,995 87	......	56,218 76	

7 T.R.

Comparative Statement of Earnings and Expenditures by

No.	RECEIPTS.	Per Cent.	1915 September	Per Cent.	1916 September	Per Cent.	1915 October
	I. TRANSPORTATION-RAIL LINE:		$ c.		$ c.		$ c.
101	Freight	.....	90,374 63	.....	96,826 21	.....	97,970 15
102	Passenger	.....	46,901 47	.....	80,469 93	.....	47,500 47
103	Excess Baggage	.....	630 49	.....	373 18	.....	596 00
105	Parlor and Chair Car	.....	81 90	.....	108 95	.....	72 55
106	Mail	.....	1,952 60	.....	1,952 60	.....	1,952 60
107	Express	.....	4,687 32	.....	6,482 33	.....	4,530 33
108	Other Passenger Train	.....	....	.....	....	.....	....
109	Milk	.....	2 40	.....	60	.....	1 18
110	Switching	.....	620 60	.....	824 05	.....	760 97
111	Special Service Train	.....	....	.....	155 00	.....	....
112	Other Freight Train	.....	....	.....	....	.....	....
	Total	.....	145,251 41	.....	187,192 85	.....	153,384 25
	III. INCIDENTALS :						
131	Dining and Buffet	.....	....	.....	2,269 23	.....	....
133	Station, Train and Boat Privileges	.....	362 49	.....	362 50	.....	362 49
135	Storage—Freight	.....	93 05	.....	195 40	.....	70 55
136	'' —Baggage	.....	22 30	.....	27 20	.....	22 20
137	Demurrage	.....	610 00	.....	1,314 00	.....	451 00
138	Telegraph and Telephone	.....	4,271 56	.....	6,077 54	.....	3,857 58
140	Stockyard	.....	....	.....	....	.....	....
142	Rents of Buildings and other Property	.....	543 86	.....	610 81	.....	528 32
143	Miscellaneous	.....	2 75	.....	42 68	.....	34 13
	Total	.....	5,906 01	.....	10,899 36	.....	5,326 27
	IV. JOINT FACILITY :						
151	Joint Facility—Cr	.....	....	.....	....	.....	....
152	'' '' —Dr	.....	1.38	.....	....	.....	66 73
	Total	.....	1.38	.....	....	.....	66 73
	TOTAL REVENUE	.....	151,156 04	.....	198,092 21	.....	158,643 79
	EXPENDITURES						
1	Maintenance of Way & Structures.	12.2	18,409 05	7.9	15,648 55	7.2	11,374 16
2	Maintenance of Equipment	11.3	17,041 62	6.2	12,378 52	10.9	17,368 26
3	Traffic	.9	1,417 17	.5	1,047 35	.9	1,377 47
4	Transportation—Rail Line	34.1	51,464 25	32.8	64,994 19	36.1	57,356 34
5	Transportation—Water Line	.....	....	.....	....	.....	....
6	Miscellaneous Operations	1.6	2,475 19	2.3	4,485 67	1.7	2,666 94
7	General	4.3	6,464 06	5.7	11,358 98	3.1	4,932 78
8	Transportation for Invest'nt-Cr..	.2	275 81	.1	275 80	.2	340 08
	TOTAL OPERATING EXPENSES	64.2	96,995 53	55.3	109,637 46	59.7	94,735 87
	BALANCE	.....	54,160 51	.....	88,454 75	.....	63,907 92
	OTHER INCOME:						
	Ore Royalties	.....	Dr. 371 63	.....	Dr. 404 20	.....	7,629 36
	Rent from Locomotives	.....	338 51	.....	477 02	.....	297 79
	Rent from Work Equipment	.....	90 82	.....	168 90	.....	182 15
	Rent from Passenger ''	.....	Dr. 4 12	.....	....	.....	....
	Rent from Joint Facilities	.....	1,088 95	.....	1,083,33	.....	1,124 42
	Rent from Lease of Road	.....	834 52	.....	1,163 88	.....	5,511 32
	Miscellaneous Income	.....	669 68	.....	166 60	.....	638 46
	Outside Operations	.....	....	.....	....	.....	....
	Interest	.....	....	.....	6 00	.....	....
	Total	.....	56,807 24	.....	91,116 28	.....	79,291 42
	DEDUCTIONS FROM INCOME:						
	Hire of Equipment, Freight Cars..	.....	4,770 27	.....	5,160 03	.....	Cr.2,366 62
	Hire of Equipment, Passenger Cars	.....	....	.....	535 63	.....	7,830 15
	Rent for Joint Facilities	.....	315 50	.....	318 50	.....	315 00
	Outside Operations	.....	....	.....	....	.....	....
	Total	.....	5,085 77	.....	6,014 16	.....	5,778 53
	NET RESULT	.....	51,721 47	.....	85,102 12	.....	73,512 89

Months, November, 1914, to October, 1916—Continued.

Per Cent.	1916 October	Per Cent.	1915 Total	Per Cent.	1916 Total	Increase	Decrease	No.
	$ c.		$ c.		$ c.	$ c.	$ c.	
......	114,932 61	......	924,732 59	.....	1,320,569 33	895,836 74	....	101
......	65,802 56	......	482,349 80	......	624,808 12	142,458 32	....	102
......	543 30	......	4,942 82	......	4,798 60	....	144 22	103
......	78 60	......	1,022 50	......	984 75	....	37 75	105
......	1,952 60	......	23,209 49	......	23,569 64	360 15	....	106
......	5,719 86	......	42,919 55	......	58,848 66	15,929 11	....	107
......	....	......	....	......	....	....	....	108
......		......	149 84	......	4 75	....	145 09	109
......	1,015 89	......	4,918 40	......	11,044 98	6,126 58	....	110
......		......		......	869 40	869 40	....	111
......		......		......			....	112
......	190,045 42	......	1,484,244 99	......	2,045,498 23	561,253 24	....	...
......	1,492 19	......	....	......	12,363 45	12,363 45	....	131
......	362 50	......	4,349 88	......	4,350 02	14	....	133
......	90 58	......	1,198 37	......	1,505 96	307 59	....	135
......	15 75	......	355 75	......	371 10	15 35	....	136
......	1,356 00	......	8,407 75	......	9,694 60	1,286 85	....	137
......	5,007 58	......	42,486 60	......	56,797 76	14,311 16	....	138
......	....	......	28 89	......	....	....	28 89	140
......	670 63	......	9,439 11	......	7,869 84	....	1,569 27	142
......	77 76	......	213 91	......	360 23	146 32	....	143
......	9,072 99	......	66,480 26	......	93,312 96	26,832 70	....	...
......	....	......	....	......	....	....	....	151
......	117 94	......	321 92	......	689 24	367 32	....	152
......	117 94	......	321 92	......	689 24	367 32	....	
......	199,000 47	......	1,550,403 33	......	2,138,121 95	587,718 62	....	
7.6	15,161 24	21.5	333,686 06	16.3	349,024 48	15,338 42	....	1
6.9	13,654 15	17.5	271,335 40	11.6	248,702 04		22,633 36	2
.6	1,192 19	1.2	18,320 66	1.1	22,465 69	4,145 03	....	3
30.5	60,639 62	40.9	634,160 64	39.4	842,058 75	207,898 11	....	4
......	....	......	....	......	....	....	....	5
2.4	4,814 00	1.9	28,701 40	2.	42,562 89	13,861 49	....	6
5.1	10,232 67	4.6	70,994 15	4.3	91,317 74	20,323 59	....	7
.1	287 35	.1	1,148 44	.1	1,954 13	805 69	....	8
53.	105,406 52	87.5	1,356,049 87	74.6	1,594,177 46	238,127 59	....	
......	93,593 95	......	194,353 46	......	543,944 49	349,591 03	....	
......	28,392 99	......	26,268 74	......	49,877 62	23,608 88	....	
......	Dr. 186 05	......	6,875 26	......	3,229 32	....	3,145 94	
......	141 08	......	-1,600 47	......	977 38	....	623 09	
......	....	......	1,009 24	......	....	....	1,009 24	
......	6,217 04	......	13,815 26	......	18,620 45	4,805 19	....	
......	1,156 75	......	16,601 37	......	13,347 04	....	3,254 33	
......	213 42	......	2,857 98	......	1,029 78	....	1,828 20	
......	9 59	......	....	......	1,736 36	1,736 36	....	
......	129,538 77	......	262,881 78	......	632,762 44	369,880 66	....	
......	6,806 85	......	40,823 50	......	87,101 58	46,278 08	....	
......	Cr. 252 32	......	7,830 15	......	13,152 40	5,322 25	....	
......	315 00	......	3,689 50	......	3,803 00	113 50	....	
......	6,869 53	......	52,343 15	......	104,056 98	51,713 83	....	
......	122,669 24	......	210,538 63	......	528,705 46	318,166 83	....	

Comparative Statement of Earnings and Expenditures by

No.	Maintenance of Way and Structures	1914 November.	1915 November.	1914 December.	1915 December.
		$ c.	$ c.	$ c.	$ c.
201	Superintendence....................	2,335 20	1,772 86	2,150 17	1,782 06
202	Roadway Maintenance	7,183 32	6,587 79	6,995 58	4,499 91
208	Bridges, Trestles and Culverts.......	1,571 14	1,316 43	8,314 14	1,705 61
212	Ties	519 11	4,021 35	118 81	3,507 91
214	Rails	941 95	2,125 51	1,089 15	2,296 03
216	Other Track Material...............	1,034 13	4,244 71	1,417 08	Cr. 511 06
218	Ballast...........................	Cr. 167 32	996 19	41 22	886 23
220	Track Laying and Surfacing	8,060 05	10,869 78	5,873 70	7,433 65
221	Right-of-Way Fences	129 31	389 65	....	Cr. 37 04
225	Crossings and Signs...............	240 49	94 99	53 13	205 59
227	Station and Office Buildings	1,234 88	976 49	707 44	753 65
229	Roadway Buildings................	256 63	133 21	240 06	171 59
231	Water Stations	275 25	357 87	167 68	3,238 62
233	Fuel Stations	111 63	12 29	38 69	28 39
235	Shops and Enginehouses	808 98	1,360 92	765 92	1,122 96
247	Telegraph and Telephone Lines......	218 52	319 75	306 01	382 84
249	Signals and Interlockers	3 48	94	....	....
265	Miscellaneous Structures	133 44	98 99	5 24	....
269	Roadway Machines	13 41	36 28	8 70	48 90
271	Small Tools and Supplies	315 49	198 30	505 86	236 07
272	Removing Snow, Ice and Sand.......	1,250 41	541 53	2,089 20	3,735 17
274	Injuries to Persons	....	69 52	75 00	6 27
275	Insurance	954 85	283 90	615 14	239 14
276	Stationery and Printing.............	36 89	29 51	95 05	45 53
277	Other Expenses	....	1 20	....	....
278	Maintaining Joint Tracks, Yards, and other Facilities—Dr..............	118 00	212 00	108 00	218 00
279	Maintaining Joint Tracks, Yards, and other Facilities—Cr..............	133 33	232 50	295 23	2,014 56
	Total.....................	27,445 91	36,819 46	31,485 74	29,981 46
	Maintenance of Equipment.				
301	Superintendence....................	689 41	880 10	734 02	1,037 48
302	Shop Machinery	255 08	553 29	620 30	515 20
308	Steam Locomotives—Repairs........	6,777 54	7,233 64	10,239 59	7,874 93
309	" " —Depreciation ...	1,237 13	1,247 13	1,237 13	1,247 13
314	Freight Train Cars—Repairs	411 83	3,111 61	2,144 40	2,213 53
315	" " "—Depreciation..	1,027 28	1,038 55	1,027 28	1,038 55
316	" " "—Retirements..	....	....	....	....
317	Passenger Train Cars—Repairs......	4,355 17	5,692 90	4,309 90	5,631 30
318	" " "—Depreciation .	1,170 07	1,114 45	1,170 07	1,114 45
319	" " "—Retirements .	....	....	....	....
326	Work Equipment—Repairs..........	3,285 23	1,587 11	3,745 79	514 60
327	" " —Depreciation	278 12	338 41	278 12	338 41
329	Miscellaneous Equipment—Repairs .	....	....	....	....
332	Injuries to Persons	86	37 59	76 68	....
333	Insurance	381 94	563 52	796 27	437 42
334	Stationery and Printing.............	82 52	63 58	56 39	76 92
335	Other Expenses	Cr. 5 27	118 04	Cr. 7 50	118 20
336	Maintaining Joint Equipment at Terminals—Dr...............	....	....	....	....
337	Maintaining Joint Equipment at Terminals—Cr....................	....	307 79	....	328 25
	Total.....................	19,946 91	23,272 14	26,428 44	21,829 87

Months, November, 1914, to October, 1916---Continued.

1915 January.	1916 January.	1915 February.	1916 February.	1915 March.	1916 March.	No.
$ c.	$ c.	$ c.	$ c.	$ c.	$ c.	—
1,806 62	1,519 80	1,806 43	1,623 03	1,894 58	1,870 74	201
4,204 85	4,409 41	. 4,399 79	3,875 16	5,758 91	4,695 69	202
915 41	1,324 19	1,031 58	971 98	2,192 10	793 30	208
48 90	3,465 00	....	3,468 70	4,435 26	3,465 00	212
175 97	705 40	228 16	1,104 18	1,957 81	1,440 75	214
1,159 21	1,207 63	764 41	1,552 13	1,234 42	1,243 26	216
....	1,000 00	6 36	1,047 11	1,500 00	1,000 00	218
5,095 23	5,200 35	4,370 06	6,152 07	8,391 73	7,883 25	220
7 78				118 13	16 89	221
67 28	103 59	8 84	18 70	26 25	37 57	225
1,288 57	839 98	572 83	577 56	616 49	666 61	227
45 33	85 10	63 64	35 91	171 02	Cr. 72 15	229
277 04	Cr. 2,579 38	285 33	318 11	91 06	401 96	231
6 72	20 78	04	36 82	69 80	183 17	233
508 93	420 42	254 95	434 57	498 74	273 64	235
247 26	335 50	228 01	282 45	298 57	422 67	247
20 42	18 26	3 84	Cr. 70	7 48	1 75	249
3 08			1 32	15 45	12 10	265
48 99	101 03	130 52	135 41	116 70	153 00	269
388 62	212 85	318 81	120 16	358 36	86 92	271
5,066 13	11,347 00	4,445 25	13,500 45	1,797 25	6,834 58	272
....			7 84		10 32	274
623 58	239 06	630 37	238 96	547 86	239 98	275
102 13	70 38	45 56	61 32	104 37	44 95	276
....					....	277
104 00	215 00	96 00	213 00	204 50	219 00	278
440 90	Dr. 1,239 77	426 06	465 64	435 69	703 60	279
21,771 15	31,501 12	19,263 72	35,310 60	31,966 15	31,221 35	
856 11	1,085 17	857 99	1,006 31	862 50	950 41	301
562 87	716 17	375 93	533 76	436 81	759 79	302
10,733 76	9,085 43	7,284 68	9,333 03	11,068 76	10,527 22	308
1,287 13	1,247 13	1,287 13	1,247 13	-1,237 13	1,247 13	309
3,002 91	2,658 15	2,487 55	4,194 41	2,378 20	5,947 67	314
1,027 28	1,038 55	1,027 28	1,038 55	1,027 28	1,038 55	315
....					....	316
4,297 35	4,950 79	7,386 85	4,603 09	2,435 64	8,401 45	317
1,170 07	1,114 45	1,170 07	1,114 45	1,170 07	1,114 45	318
....					....	319
3,351 76	808 17	916 97	770 77	7,268 55	396 86	326
278 12	338 41	278 12	338 41	278 12	338 41	327
....					....	329
17			29 25		2 04	332
813 11	423 44	813 11	429 62	813 11	430 82	333
80 51	78 93	82 36	124 79	107 51	118 53	334
Cr. 59 00	118 59	Cr. 8 70	118 44	80 47	117 93	335
....					....	336
....	431 07	....	390 74	341 58	487 43	337
27,352 15	23,232 31	23,909 84	24,491 27	28.822 57	30,903 33	

Comparative Statement of Earnings and Expenditures by

No.	Maintenance of Way and Structures.	1915 April.	1916 April.	1915 May.	1916 May.
		$ c.	$ c.	$ c.	$ c.
201	Superintendence....................	1,980 24	1,982 82	2,017 48	2,276 58
202	Roadway Maintenance..............	7,649 43	8,103 44	7,523 80	7,211 79
208	Bridges, Trestles and Culverts	2,333 39	1,353 51	3,529 15	1,243 43
212	Ties...............................	4,431 03	3,465 00	4,633 69	4,260 80
214	Rails..............................	1,695 36	884 87	3,188 90	1,591 74
216	Other Track Material...............	613 61	1,070 38	97 58	439 51
218	Ballast	1,501 89	1,000 00	1,513 05	1,000 00
220	Track Laying and Surfacing	5,515 06	6,958 32	8,224 61	9,415 07
221	Right-of-Way Fences	280 91	191 57	203 74	466 66
225	Crossings and Signs	82 44	118 19	344 17	97 92
227	Station and Office Buildings........	761 02	988 66	1,929 44	2,396 43
229	Roadway Buildings	128 22	126 92	155 08	129 96
231	Water Stations	158 02	237 11	1,059 57	391 90
233	Fuel Stations	37 46	27 36	42 62	687 02
235	Shops and Enginehouses	1,211 76	342 96	727 17	253 40
247	Telegraph and Telephone Lines	249 95	271 70	203 60	455 21
249	Signals and Interlockers............	....	....	37 50	....
265	Miscellaneous Structures...........	28 93	2 24	8 72	1 03
269	Roadway Machines	164 24	237 22	118 58	611 50
271	Small Tools and Supplies	385 95	440 55	453 43	434 90
272	Removing Snow, Ice and Sand	194 04	390 68	15 92	....
274	Injuries to Persons.................	....	....	....	37 38
275	Insurance	623 59	238 65	639 49	235 42
276	Stationery and Printing	51 05	105 30	48 28	109 82
277	Other Expenses	....	....	....	....
278	Maintaining Joint Tracks, Yards, and other Facilities—Dr...............	202 00	212 50	589 00	221 00
279	Maintaining Joint Tracks, Yards, and other Facilities—Cr...............	429 54	360 97	559 89	815 84
	Total......................	29,850 05	28,388 98	36,744 68	33,152 63
	Maintenance of Equipment.				
301	Superintendence	811 45	1,018 27	860 03	997 85
302	Shop Machinery....................	319 67	548 84	248 49	400 39
308	Steam Locomotives—Repairs.......	9,084 93	8,086 33	4,913 44	7,840 99
309	" " —Depreciation ...	1,237 13	1,247 13	1,237 13	1,247 13
314	Freight Train Cars—Repairs........	1,405 86	5,285 58	738 73	2,305 83
315	" " " —Depreciation.	1,027 28	1,038 55	1,027 28	1,038 55
316	" " " —Retirements.	....	....	....	....
317	Passenger Train Cars—Repairs	3,714 13	4,623 50	3,526 29	3,082 65
318	" " " —Depreciation..	1,170 07	1,114 45	1,170 07	1,114 45
319	" " " —Retirements .	....	....	....	....
326	Work Equipment—Repairs..........	6,755 31	1,609 75	3,646 68	3,595 42
327	" " —Depreciation ...	278 12	338 41	278 12	338 41
329	Miscellaneous Equipment—Repairs .	2 56	....	....	....
332	Injuries to Persons.................	17	....	....	37 53
333	Insurance	813 11	430 79	706 20	428 52
334	Stationery and Printing	55 18	71 70	61 19	94 80
335	Other Expenses	....	117 32	....	126 97
336	Maintaining Joint Equipment at Terminals—Dr.	....	....	....	....
337	Maintaining Joint Equipment at Terminals—Cr......................	320 42	429 08	241 54	399 34
	Total......................	26,354 55	25,101 54	18,172 11	22,250 15

Months, November, 1914, to October, 1916—Continued.

1915 June.	1916 June.	1915 July.	1916 July.	1915 August.	1916 August.	No.
$ c.	$ c.	$ c.	$ c.	$ c.	$ c.	
2,203 93	2,271 73	2,172 17	2,227 29	1,977 28	2,381 41	201
5,358 88	5,923 47	7,282 52	5,564 93	5,378 22	6,273 56	202
2,639 58	676 31	4,133 01	776 50	3,202 39	534 14	208
4,629 47	8,554,46	4,470 52	Cr. 1,516 80	3,126 92	4,107 25	212
1,517 86	1,078 35	1,557 98	Cr. 797 22	1,424 64	21 16	214
433 06	1,379 04	212 76	382 75	511 35	1,091 11	216
1,500 00	994 85	1,782 92	Cr. 589 14	Cr. 645 10	Cr. 580 55	218
11,372 86	11,501 83	11,332 27	10,953 01	13,956 62	13,312 87	220
314 90	300 56	162 18	47 71	1,040 95	267 19	221
235 72	64 93	190 00	84 53	125 55	52 75	225
1,944 65	1,780 76	1,466 94	1,275 25	1,527 34	2,527 60	227
67 69	590 06	100 23	261 69	221 11	81 76	229
195 36	538 25	645 95	127 72	476 29	400 77	231
104 14	162 92	20 29	6 75	18 02	5 25	233
. 380 08	384 77	386 89	256 24	612 85	373 21	235
235 91	389 02	269 22	522 23	298 19	1,084 53	247
Cr. 10 00	3 14	1 45	4 13	....	11 18	249
23		212 46	....	65 13	....	265
38 13	284 10	74 37	318 38	96 90	767 25	269
191 86	348 57	230 23	113 32	255 19	1,140 19	271
176 34	Cr. 90 00	....	....	....	....	272
16 96	12 21	7 11	712 32	....	8 80	274
666 92	242 14	628 54	241 50	635 46	269 02	275
51 43	67 78	34 87	. 54 16	18 16	35 72	276
....	....	....	....	25 00	....	277
202 00	218 50	212 50	216 50	223 00	224 00	278
408 97	611 80	502 91	435 11	339 47	425 67	279
34,058 99	37,065 95	37,084 47	20,808 64	34,231 99	33,964 50	
925 37	961 59	898 27	1,073 78	887 36	1,097 97	301
247 36	325 35	320 81	195 79	478 72	525 22	302
5,397 53	7,579 69	5,937 48	6,805 50	5,466 77	7,307 81	308
1,237 13	1,247 13	1,237 13	1,247 13	1,237 13	1,247 13	309
716 64	2,699 69	2,012 87	1,604 28	1,624 12	3,306 86	314
1,027 28	1,038 55	.1,027 28	1,038 55	1,027 28	1,038 55	315
....	....	....	....	....	418 72	316
3,679 11	4,518 77	3,566 85	4,252 65	4,641 82	5,270 54	317
1,170 07	1,114 45	1,170 07	1,114 45	1,170 07	1,114 45	318
....	....	....	....	....	....	319
, 3,780 05	1,301 97	5,409 18	Cr. 5,487 99	6,898 10	Cr. 4,259 83	326
278 12	338 41	278 12	338 41	278 12	338 41	327
....	....	....	....	....	....	329
8 14	1 55	16 09	169 04	....	34 46	332
721 75	425 48	656 96	425 44	719 77	425 31	333
83 92	70 74	68 30	97 35	49 77	68 49	334
115 74	5 15	115 64	4 70	115 64	12 30	335
....	....	....	....	....	....	336
221 88	286 64	281 44	275 49	255 16	303 10	337
19,166 33	21,341 88	22,433 61	12,603 59	24,339 51	17,643 29	

Comparative Statement of Earnings and Expenditures by

No.	Maintenance of Way and Structures.	1915 September.	1916 September.	1915 October.
		$ c.	$ c.	$ c.
201	Superintendence	2,032 21	2,263 40	2,023 96
202	Roadway Maintenance	Cr. 98 57	4,052 98	826 25
208	Bridges, Trestles and Culverts......	205 51	Cr. 907 53	354 35
212	Ties..............................	4,279 07	Cr. 2,194 01	Cr. 1,847 73
214	Rails..............................	Cr. 3,866 35	Cr. 2,219 92	Cr. 1,185 97
216	Other Track Material	Cr. 198 47	38 22	711 49
218	Ballast............................	Cr. 657 13	Cr. 580 55	Cr. 2,716 56
220	Track Laying and Surfacing........	12,135 23	10,771 93	9,602 22
221	Right-of-Way Fences	801 23	151 45	797 66
225	Crossings and Signs................	126 76	93 62	72 58
227	Station and Office Buildings........	1,243 17	2,283 37	963 64
229	Roadway Buildings.................	193 98	105 40	24 30
231	Water Stations	668 14	176 81	Cr. 23 79
233	Fuel Stations......................	....	7 65	78 26
235	Shops and Enginehouses............	100 94	588 43	729 38
247	Telegraph and Telephone Lines.....	399 99	365 58	333 58
249	Signals and Interlockers...........	....	1 37	Cr. 2 43
265	Miscellaneous Structures...........	....	....	51 59
269	Roadway Machines	124 79	167 27	18 30
271	Small Tools and Supplies	266 98	239 49	131 76
272	Removing Snow, Ice and Sand	....	....	Cr. 12 17
274	Injuries to Persons.................	40 98	18 03	....
275	Insurance	599 66	253 09	654 74
276	Stationery and Printing	94 12	61 28	26 76
277	Other Expenses ...:...............	....	....	1 00
278	Maintaining Joint Tracks, Yards, and other Facilities—Dr.	215 50	218 50	215 00
279	Maintaining Joint Tracks, Yards, and other Facilities—Cr.	298 69	307 31	454 01
	Total......................	18,409 05	15,648 55	11,374 16
	Maintenance of Equipment.			
301	Superintendence	876 07	1,189 27	907 46
302	Shop Machinery.............. ...	384 05	366 10	291 30
308	Steam Locomotives—Repairs	5,618 64	5,098 93	3,746 46
309	" " —Depreciation ...	1,237 13	1,247 13	1,237 13
314	Freight Train Cars—Repairs	749 39	600 16	Cr. 1,463 99
315	" " " —Depreciation ...	1,027 28	1,038 55	1,027 28
316	" " " —Retirements ...	....	....	....
317	Passenger Train Cars—Repairs	4,205 96	5,766 22	1,771 30
318	" " " —Depreciation.	1,170 07·	1,114 45	1,170 07
319	" " " —Retirements.	....	....	....
326	Work Equipment—Repairs..........	811 60	Cr. 4,607 06	7,786 77
327	" " —Depreciation	278 12	338 41	278 12
329	Miscellaneous Equipment Repairs ..	....	....	....
332	Injuries to Persons.................	26 88	27 23	15
333	Insurance	711 66	424 20	733 90
334	Stationery and Printing	88 34	86 71	67 69
335	Other Expenses	115 64	....	115 64
336	Maintaining Joint Equipment at Terminals—Dr.	....	....	....
337	Maintaining Joint Equipment at Terminals—Cr.....................	259 21	306 78	301 02
	Total......................	17,041 62	12,378 52	17,368 26

Months, November, 1914, to October, 1916—Continued.

1916 October.	1915 Total.	1916 Total.	Increase.	Decrease.	No.
$ c.	$ c.	$ c.	$ c.	$ c.	
2,454 78	24,400 27	24,426 50	26 23	....	201
5,038 24	62,462 98	66,236 37	3,773 39	....	202
Cr. 688 47	30,421 75	9,099 40	....	21,322 35	208
Cr. 1,961 24	28,845 05	32,643 42	3,798 37	....	212
Cr. 3,498 01	8,725 46	4,732 84	....	3,992 62	214
679 44	7,990 63	12,817 12	4,826 49	....	216
Cr. 238 51	3,659 33	5,935 63	2,276 30	....	218
9,973 39	103,929 64	110,425 52	6,495 88	....	220
460 48	3,856 79	2,255 12	....	1,601 67	221
95 13	1,572 71	1,067 51	....	505 20	225
1,191 96	14,256 41	16,258 32	2,001 91	....	227
173 71	1,667 29	1,823 16	155 87	....	229
571 85	4,275 90	4,181 59	....	94 31	231
5 60	527 67	1,184 00	656 33	....	233
296 66	6,986 59	6,108 18	....	878 41	235
850 43	3,283 81	5,681 91	2,398 10	....	247
....	61 24	40 07	....	21 17	249
....	524 27	115 68	....	408 59	265
151 25	953 63	3,011 59	2,057 96	....	269
297 14	3,802 54	3,868 46	65 92	....	271
214 30	15,022 37	36,473 71	21,451 34	....	272
25 00	140 05	907 69	767 64	....	274
263 98	7,820 20	2,984 84	....	4,835 36	275 ·
56 89	708 67	742 64	33 97	....	276
....	26 00	1 20	....	24 80	277
165 00	2,489 50	2,553 00	63 50	....	278
1,417 76	4,724 69	6,550 99	1,826 30	....	279
15,161 24	333,686 06	349,024 48	15,338 42	....	
1,271 40	10,166 04	12,569 60	2,403 56	....	301
475 27	4,541 39	5,915 17	1,373 78	....	302
7,167 40	86,269 58	93,935 90	7,666 32	....	308
1,316 16	14,845 56	15,034 59	189 03	....	309
850 92	16,208 51	34,778 69	18,570 18	....	314
1,038 55	12,327 36	12,462 60	135 24	....	315
....	....	418 72	418 72	....	316
– 4,655 48	47,890 37	61,449 35	23,558 98	....	317
1,114 45	14,040 84	13,373 40	....	667 44	318
....	....	....	....	....	319
– Cr. 5,106 06	53,655 99	Cr. 8,876 79	....	62,532 78	326
338 41	3,337 44	4,060 92	723 48	....	327
....	2 56	....	....	2 56	329
327 36	129 14	666 05	536 91	....	332
423 95	8,680 89	5,268 51	....	3,412 38	333
77 51	883 68	1,030 05	146 37	....	334
17 01	578 30	874 65	296 35	....	335
....	....	....	....	....	336
313 66	2,222 25	4,259 37	2,037 12	....	337
13,654 15	271,335 40	248,702 04	....	22,633 36	

Comparative Statement of Earnings and Expenditures by

No.	Traffic.	1914 November.	1915 November.	1914 December.	1915 December.
		$ c.	$ c.	$ c.	$ c.
351	Superintendence	794 47	908 34	876 33	851 48
352	Outside Agencies	10 36	18 19	56 54	3 18
353	Advertising	366 67	284 66	237 63	1,256 94
354	Traffic Associations	36 82	95 73	74 78	34 80
356	Industrial and Immigration Bureaus.	143 00	118 33	130 20	137 46
357	Insurance	54 56	....	11 78	....
358	Stationery and Printing	150 15	177 85	474 99	252 61
359	Other Expenses	....	....	....	....
	Total	1,556 03	1,603 10	1,862 25	2,536 47
	Transportation—Rail Line.				
371	Superintendence	1,142 84	1,209 76	1,415 73	1,404 21
372	Dispatching Trains	1,093 73	1,208 80	1,105 29	1,047 90
373	Station Employees	10,816 69	10,616 80	10,172 59	10,624 79
374	Weighing, Inspection and Demurrage Bureaus	....	21 16	23 55	42 38
376	Station Supplies and Expenses	1,365 08	1,464 97	2,282 37	1,937 78
377	Yardmasters and Yard Clerks	940 00	919 78	950 85	925 27
378	Yard Conductors and Brakemen	1,586 53	1,567 88	1,864 04	1,635 35
379	Yard Switch and Signal Tenders	109 82	60 80	181 64	123 20
380	Yard Enginemen	1,009 24	1,074 54	1,267 97	1,108 62
382	Fuel for Yard Locomotives	3,553 81	1,310 40	2,978 49	1,655 34
385	Water for Yard Locomotives	35 02	41 03	46 11	57 81
386	Lubricants for Yard Locomotives	33 32	24 50	37 95	26 56
387	Other Supplies for Yard Locomotives	16 89	12 81	18 93	15 65
388	Engine-house Expenses—Yard	394 93	324 49	453 56	348 10
389	Yard Supplies and Expenses	72 71	57 56	71 72	70 11
390	Operating Joint Yards & Terminals–Dr.	500 00	100 00	500 00	181 61
391	" " " —Cr.	5,059 21	3,982 64	4,858 71	3,969 55
392	Train Enginemen	6,268 99	7,359 64	6,620 33	7,904 57
394	Fuel for Train Locomotives	14,240 49	17,868 80	16,146 27	20,768 17
397	Water for Train Locomotives	1,861 39	1,193 47	1,756 51	1,217 90
398	Lubricants for Train Locomotives	229 57	252 90	288 12	285 45
399	Other Supplies for Train Locomotives	99 70	118 09	106 56	138 38
400	Engine-house Expenses—Train	3,380 64	2,896 20	3,725 63	3,456 78
401	Trainmen	7,709 92	8,525 28	7,959 40	9,108 48
402	Train Supplies and Expenses	2,921 66	2,359 61	2,001 94	2,230 99
405	Crossing Protection	1 05	....	Cr. 1 16	....
410	Stationery and Printing	917 71	854 06	714 66	826 70
411	Other Expenses	25 85	179 25	19 85	64 41
412	Operating Joint Tracks & Facilities–Dr.	....	....	....	....
413	" " " —Cr.	....	78 85	....	80 81
414	Insurance	1,200 37	164 11	684 39	136 98
415	Clearing Wrecks	24 21	52 39	....	43 50
416	Damage to Property	....	....	528 35	19 25
417	Damage to Live Stock on Right-of-Way.	25 00	100 00	50 00	75 00
418	Loss and Damage—Freight	265 82	377 75	484 58	85 33
419	Loss and Damage—Baggage	8 00	35 00	8 08	13 50
420	Injuries to Persons	33 33	50 00	152 00	288 48
	Total	56,735 10	58,340 34	59,757 59	63,818 19
	Miscellaneous Operations.				
441	Dining and Buffet Service	....	608 32	....	1,230 03
447	Commercial Telegraph Maintenance	....	163 42	....	214 26
448	" " Operation	....	783 15	....	828 39
449	Commercial Telephone Maintenance	....	209 12	....	325 55
450	" " Operation	....	787 08	....	688 32
	Total	....	2,551 09	....	3,286 55

Months, November, 1914, to October, 1916---Continued.

1915 January.	1916 January.	1915 February.	1916 February.	1915 March.	1916 March.	No
$ c.	$ c.	$ c.	$ c.	$ c.	$ c.	
844 13	902 35	856 79	893 79	887 96	874 63	351
5 02	362 03	1 04	35 74	23 78	28 74	352
308 00	1,348 29	36 01	299 54	93 19	141 44	353
56 22	52 24	14 61	36 01	86 06	55 55	354
567 75	154 22	268 67	138 07	231 44	129 29	356
11 78	....	11 78	....	11 78	....	357
63 38	194 78	62 05	498 87	274 58	212 32	358
....	....	....	....	....	....	359
1,856 28	3,013 91	1,250 95	1,902 02	1,608 79	1,441 97	
1,276 06	1,367 59	1,183 38	1,604 19	1,282 21	1,432 37	371
1,149 98	1,090 04	1,082 00	1,053 41	1,078 15	1,059 58	372
10,321 87	10,688 58	10,090 10	11,092 79	9,666 99	11,307 39	373
30 14	....	51 23	53 87	78 09	25 63	374
2,021 97	2,374 49	1,696 26	1,882 77	1,854 76	1,734 69	376
894 26	957 71	954 83	1,004 87	1,001 66	995 67	377
2,003 93	2,314 39	1,670 10	2,584 43	1,834 00	3,026 07	378
151 24	144 40	138 32	140 98	169 86	1€5·30	379
1,242 31	1,538 69	1,146 60	1,742 86	1,215 49	1,951 28	380
1,963 07	2,684 91	1,836 49	2,867 95	1,884 64	3,216 70	382
59 59	50 52	22 68	92 25	60 48	144 49	385
41 45	38 91	37 28	39 43	29 19	-46 21	386
22 32	37 49	21 58	29 05	24 66	30 11	387
444 38	474 84	372 33	497 94	321 06	647 53	388
71 05	66 50	63 09	158 11	81 82	65 37	389
500 00	100 00	500 00	100 00	100 00	100 00	390
4,642 30	4,680 76	3,502 14	4,419 78	4,007 92	4,930 13	391
7,204 96	8,987 83	6,559 77	9,359 90	6,163 81	12,295 61	392
18,233 70	27,264 54	17,967 33	27,410 21	14,853 24	37,634 14	394
1,864 25	1,890 87	1,582 40	2,003 39	1,323 93	2,637 47	397
353 80	327 92	367 64	401 76	297 78	510 60	398
106 65	169 56	107 05	179 71	169 47	232 54	399
4,174 14	3,889 96	3,066 80	3,452 41	3,281 01	3,829 21	400
8,343 46	9,994 69	7,470 68	10,076 87	7,546 66	12,569 68	401
1,953 12	3,185 19	3,148 11	2,344 28	2,554 21	1,596 54	402
....	....	3 93	....	....	....	405
771 04	710 83	586 24	854 01	589 61	869 92	410
353 98	129 26	61 85	126 26	10 35	250 28	411
....	....	....	....	....	....	412
....	61 25	....	89 49	....	25 00	413
692 79	128 04	692 79	133 35	692 79	132 93	414
163 99	73 56	53 30	390 90	29 54	132 28	415
200 00	113 80	325 00	....	....	77 00	416
....	50 00	....	....	....	....	417
Cr. 3 54	170 39	199 18	301 29	859 91	51 86	418
Cr. 50 56	5 00	....	....	....	17 81	419
3 22	2 00	....	221 63	2 00	184 33	420
61,916 32	76,280 49	59,556 20	77,691 60	55,049 45	94,015 46	
....	2,806 22	....	1,446 95	....	1,433 92	441
....	131 03	....	151 38	....	188 08	447
....	816 79	....	707 95	....	874 91	448
....	339 72	....	310 25	....	475 34	449
....	882 02	....	699 79	....	879 87	450
....	4,975 78	....	3,316 32	....	3,852 12	

Comparative Statement of Earnings and Expenditures

No.	Traffic.	1915 April.	1916 April.	1915 May.	1916 May.
		$ c.	$ c.	$ c.	$ c.
351	Superintendence	918 41	858 38	913 18	853 42
352	Outside Agencies	72		52	39 55
353	Advertising	151 77	67 27	122 57	171 63
354	Traffic Associations	45 54		43 02	79 36
356	Industrial and Immigration Bureaus.	202 80	162 97	127 10	132 89
357	Insurance	11 78		12 02	
358	Stationery and Printing	105 89	148 86	103 15	243 10
359	Other Expenses				
	Total	1,436 91	1,237 48	1,321 56	1,519 95
	Transportation—Rail Line.				
371	Superintendence	1,139 93	1,417 66	1,301 46	1,340 86
372	Dispatching Trains	1,008 60	1,080 00	1,104 87	1,065 58
373	Station Employees	9,634 20	11,645 26	9,608 84	11,433 90
374	Weighing, Inspection and Demurrage Bureaus	32 85	25 19	23 42	139 48
376	Station Supplies and Expenses	1,156 13	1,206 23	919 77	939 44
377	Yardmasters and Yard Clerks	940 98	987 52	854 99	1,025 21
378	Yard Conductors and Brakemen	1,416 13	2,805 07	1,150 33	2,291 53.
379	Yard Switch and Signal Tenders	93 10	128 63	97 85	139 00
380	Yard Enginemen	966 52	1,803 41	790 19	1,537 85
382	Fuel for Yard Locomotives	1,265 81	3,640 49	1,054 19	2,354 20
385	Water for Yard Locomotives	13 94	74 14	10 22	81 11
386	Lubricants for Yard Locomotives	23 62	53 36	20 41	37 33
387	Other Supplies for Yard Locomotives	18 83	30 66	21 44	25 65
388	Engine-house Expenses—Yard	331 09	531 92	268 25	427 52
389	Yard Supplies and Expenses	49 96	65 06	27 06	41 10
390	Operating Joint Yards & Terminals—Dr.	100 00	100 00	Cr.1,500 00	100 00
391	" " " " —Cr.	3,894 62	4,795 98	3,628 63	4,633 58
392	Train Enginemen	5,589 04	12,878 21	5,584 44	9,432 42
394	Fuel for Train Locomotives	12,073 62	37,175 09	11,209 87	24,468 84
397	Water for Train Locomotives	1,361 81	1,733 12	928 25	1,457 65
398	Lubricants for Train Locomotives	211 50	530 97	197 11	395 03
399	Other Supplies for Train Locomotives	136 18	241 46	108 85	227 26
400	Engine-house Expenses—Train	2,696 50	3,771 72	2,167 69	2,800 06
401	Trainmen	6,746 86	12,889 59	6,534 05	9,964 07
402	Train Supplies and Expenses	2,571 18	2,196 14	1,512 58	1,947 97
405	Crossing Protection			96 42	
410	Stationery and Printing	488 99	966 22	629 90	1,330 71
411	Other Expenses	277 21	271 26	61 75	278 26
412	Operating Joint Tracks & Facilities—Dr.				
413	" " " " —Cr.	93 61	72 45	25 00	77 29
414	Insurance	692 79	191 62	589 02	132 36
415	Clearing Wrecks	14 84	176 56	Cr. 31	1,422 35
416	Damage to Property				
417	Damage to Live-Stock on Right-of-Way	10 00		10 27	
418	Loss and Damage—Freight	271 40	302 97	497 75	363 87
419	Loss and Damage—Baggage				4 00
420	Injuries to Persons		88 01		722 08
	Total	47,340 38	94,139 11	42,227 30	73,215 82
	Miscellaneous Operations.				
441	Dining and Buffet Service	2,306 23	134 78	681 22	1,338 02
447	Commercial Telegraph Maintenance.		†134 01	60 80	211 11
448	" " Operation		*805 90	758 39	954 10
449	Commercial Telephone Maintenance.	†2,538 84	†227 79	62 53	334 13
450	" " Operation	*8,894 85	*788 89	777 94	946 89
	Total	13,739 92	2,091 37	2,340 88	3,784 25

by Months, November, 1914, to October, 1916.---Continued.

1915 June.	1916 June.	1915 July.	1916 July.	1915 August.	1916 August.	No.
$ c.	$ c.	$ c.	$ c.	$ c.	$ c.	
991 79	829 07	991 05	574 26	943 71	533 12	351
10 01	35 14	....	192 55	1 09	760 53	352
168 20	536 84	206 88	503 32	356 27	2,216 82	353
66 21	35 24	50 24	35 01	40 14	59 04	354
126 27	155 32	125 17	132 45	126 03	103 14	356
12 01	....	12 01	....	12 01	....	357
111 27	100 79	126 11	82 90	156 78	86 21	358
....	....	....	....	....	....	359
1,485 76	1,691 90	1,511 46	1,520 49	1,636 03	3,758 86	
1,273 81	1,380 49	1,161 28	1,431 99	1,150 08	- 1,494 74	371
992 36	1,068 73	1,372 52	1,214 59	1,289 44	1,172 88	372
9,613 27	10,968 35	9,730 14	11,259 49	9,756 12	11,624 10	373
27 59	20 49	20 88	4 50	24 73	48 06	374
665 59	1,026 09	785 04	552 64	628 01	873 67	376
919 67	930 18	971 57	944 58	942 55	989 25	377
1,161 70	1,426 75	1,250 33	1,499 76	1,275 19	1,559 70	378
90 82	133 60	91 20	102 00	75 05	105 21	379
770 43	927 91	816 11	1,043 61	800 50	878 35	380
866 17	1,671 05	1,125 61	1.499 54	1,046 76	1,647 88	382
58 65	42 12	18 41	25 80	28 93	53 02	385
20 73	23 10	Cr. 26 72	Cr. 30 61	24 59	18 73	386
8 10	15 92	10 32	10 29	10 23	15 05	387
256 52	277 99	242 16	253 00	187 61	257 04	388
53 82	48 67	49 30	48 26	48 69	38 71	389
100 00	100 00	100 00	100 00	100 00	100 00	390
3,529 67	3,891 82	3,874 75	3,773 70	3,349 93	4,140 97	391
5,594 05	7,472 18	6,391 22	7,499 24	6,957 45	8,421 14	392
11,356 25	19,108 15	13,086 46	17,370 73	15,393 43	20,465 75	394
1,284 78	1,487 59	1,268 93	1,167 81	967 91	1,100 53	397
205 02	360 71	Cr. 36 24	Cr. 4 33	265 71	314 50	398
85 79	200 34	93 45	137 98	113 75	167 63	399
1,865 42	2,412 06	1,845 51	2,292 28	2,004 94	2,348 49	400
6,593 50	8,663 94	7,463 32	9,006 95	8,088 19	10,027 34	401
1,684 74	1,702 67	1,973 59	2,101 78	2,282 02	1,492 13	402
Cr. 96 42	....	....	....	....	....	405
650 06	701 19	581 55	832 89	786 72	942 38	410
90 79	242 93	61 26	221 67	105 26	....	411
....	....	....	....	....	....	412
110 01	25 00	94 48	105 58	82 66	66 41	413
600 93	135 31	601 20	134 24	601 04	134 47	414
501 25	146 41	44 35	53 89	37 85	188 39	415
....	....	....	....	....	....	416
61 64	3 04	5 88	....	105 65	....	417
Cr. 168 21	Cr. 203 79	249 30	389 22	94 95	260 42	418
Cr. 119 50	....	100 00	50	....	....	419
25 00	47 52	3 00	356 53	60 61	125 84	420
43,454 64	58,624 87	47,481 70	57,641 04	51,821 37	62,658 02	
831 61	Cr. 91 86	678 03	780 12	676 60	879 03	441
148 02	235 28	113 87	274 67	163 08	430 76	447
689 70	917 30	746 67	1,014 23	723 99	1,219 73	448
253 56	371 08	207 70	408 41	283 78	603 10	449
646 88	825 67	646 70	731 71	668 28	806 51	450
2,569 77	2,257 47	2,392 97	3,209 14	2,515 73	3,93 9 13	

Comparative Statement of Earnings and Expenditures by

No.	Traffic.	1915 September.	1916 September.	1915 October.
		$　c.	$　c.	$　c.
351	Superintendence	838 14	544 40	867 05
352	Outside Agencies...................	4 84	134·92	....
353	Advertising.......................	246 09	56 90	268 50
354	Traffic Associations	84 53	53 39	6 39
356	Industrial and Immigration Bureaus..	126 39	101 76	129 95
357	Insurance	12 01	....	12 01
358	Stationery and Printing	105 17	155 98	96 03
359	Other Expenses....................	....	....	Cr.　2 46
	Total	1,417 17	1,047 35	1,377 47
	Transportation—Rail Line..			
371	Superintendence	1,230 15	1,426 99	1,116 33
372	Dispatching Trains	1,237 30	1,125 35	1,283 66
373	Station Employees	9,908 05	12,055 56	10,339 82
374	Weighing, Inspection and Demurrage Bureaus	19 00	24 13	....
376	Station Supplies and Expenses	788 40	961 92	958 21
377	Yardmasters and Yard Clerks	892 08	902 06	900 51
378	Yard Conductors and Brakemen.....	1,432 02	1,660 32	1,404 84
379	Yard Switch and Signal Tenders.....	88 35	102 06	95 00
380	Yard Enginemen...................	984 92	1,087 99	1,002 57
382	Fuel for Yard Locomotives	1,221 22	1,752 46	1,387 38
385	Water for Yard Locomotives........	30 41	30 92	53 33
386	Lubricants for Yard Locomotives	25 55	28 12	27 52
387	Other Supplies for Yard Locomotives.	15 09	17 40	12 39
388	Engine-house Expenses—Yard	293 26	275 79	316 70
389	Yard Supplies and Expenses........	46 59	44 05	41 38
390	Operating Joint Yards & Terminals—Dr.	100 00	100 00	100 00
391	"　　　" 　　　"　—Cr.	3,508 99	4,342 74	3,824 39
392	Train Enginemen	6,937 86	8,407 11	7,547 87
394	Fuel for Train Locomotives·........	15,096 16	21,392 08	19,598 06
397	Water for Train Locomotives	883 48	1,303 34	1,125 43
398	Lubricants for Train Locomotives....	247 55	302 35	227 20
399	Other Supplies for Train Locomotives	147 03	135 61	61 51
400	Engine-house Expenses—Train	2,034 17	2,191 61	2,409 93
401	Trainmen......	8,213 16	9,854 66	8,893 97
402	Train Supplies and Expenses	1,302 14	2,717 02	991 87
405	Crossing Protection	....	....	....
410	Stationery and Printing	758 52	872 04	608 33
411	Other Expenses	61 26	10 40	62 26
412	Operating Joint Tracks & Facilities–Dr.	....	....	....
413	"　　-　"　　　"　—Cr.	71 69	69 89	77 00
414	Insurance	600 19	134 29	600 42
415	Clearing Wrecks	27 61	161 32	Cr.　50 60
416	Damage to Property................	....	....	....
417	Damage to Live Stock on Right-of-Way	78 10	3 84	63 23
418	Loss and Damage—Freight	177 83	196 03	71 34
419	Loss and Damage—Baggage	11 14	....	....
420	Injuries to Persons.................	156 34	130 00	7 27
	Total	51,464 25	64,994.19	57,356 34
	Miscellaneous Operations.			
441	Dining and Buffet Service...........	382 62	2,062 77	631 27
447	Commercial Telegraph Maintenance.	226 73	285 68	198 25
448	"　　　"　　Operation ...	758 00	964 73	789 37
449	Commercial Telephone Maintenance..	365 51	415 57	311 22
450	"　　　"　　Operation.....	742 33	756 92	736 83
	Total	2,475 19	4,485.67	2,666 94

Months, November, 1914, to October, 1916—Continued.

1916 October.	1915 Total.	1916 Total	Increase.	Decrease.	No.
$ c.	$ c.	$ c.	$ c.	$ c.	
559 70	10,723 01	9,182 94	....	1,540 07	351
82 23	113 92	1,692 80	1,578 88		352
172 35	2,561 78	7,055 50	4,493 72	....	353
121 02	604 56	657 39	52 83	....	354
121 51	2,304 77	1,587 41	....	717 36	356
	185 53	....	....	185 53	357
135 38	1,829 55	2,289 65	460 10	....	358
....	Cr. 2 46	....	2 46	....	359
1,192 19	18,320 66	22,465 69	4,145 03	....	
1,530 57	14,673 26	17,041 42	2,368 16	....	371
1,098 43	13,707 90	12,285 29	....	1,422 61	372
12,899 70	119,658 68	136,216 71	16,558 03	....	373
88 20	331 48	493 09	161 61	....	374
1,275 97	15,121 59	16,230 66	1,109 07	....	376
965 34	11,163 95	11,547 44	383 49	....	377
1,901 81	18,049 14	24,273 06	6,223 92	....	378
107 10	1,382 25	1,452 28	70 03	....	379
1,175 45	12,012 85	15,870 56	3,857 71	....	380
1,794 34	20,183 64	26,095 26	5,911 62	....	382
37 91	437 77	731 12	293 35	....	385
34 99	294 89	340 63	45 74	....	386
19 87	195 78	259 95	64 17	....	387
309 95	3,881 85	4,626 11	744 26	....	388
55 71	677 19	759 21	82 02	....	389
150 00	1,200 00	1,331 61	131 61	....	390
11,561 89	47,681 26	59,123 54	11,442 28	....	391
8,707 88	77,419 79	108,725 73	31,305 94	....	392
20,812 59	179,254 88	291,739 09	112,484 21	....	394
1,049 90	16,209 07	18,243 04	2,033 97	....	397
313 29	2,854 76	3,991 15	1,136 39	....	398
236 53	1,335 99	2,185 09	849 10	....	399
3,099 25	32,652 88	37,440 03	4,787 65	....	400
10,384 51	91,563 17	121,066 06	29,502 89	....	401
1,270 98	24,897 16	25,145 30	248 14	....	402
....	3 82	....	....	3 82	405
1,371 62	8,083 33	11,132 57	3,049 24	....	410
62 83	1,191 67	1,836 81	645 14	....	411
....	....	....	....	....	412
71 49	554 45	823 51	269 06	....	413
134 03	8,248 72	1,691 73	....	6,556 99	414
457 78	846 03	3,298 83	2,452 80	....	415
....	1,053 35	210 05	....	843 30	416
50 00	409 77	281 88	....	127 89	417
284 01	3,000 31	2,579 35	....	420 96	418
....	Cr. 42 84	75 81	118 65	....	419
592 46	442 77	2,808 88	2,366 11	....	420
60,639 62	634,160 64	842,058 75	207,898 11	....	
1,768 82	6,187 58	14,397 12	8,209 54	....	441
556 63	....	†2,976 31	....	†2,821 49	447
961 54	†4,933 89	*10,848 72	†2,830 46	....	448
759 01		†4,779 07			449
768 00	*17,579 93	*9,561 67	....	....	450
4,814 00	28,701 40	42,562 89	13,861 49	....	

Comparative Statement of Earnings and Expenditures by

No.	General.	1914 November.	1915 November.	1914 December.	1915 December.
		$ c.	$ c.	$ c.	$ c.
451	Salaries and Expenses of General Officers..........................	1,212 57	1,624 04	2,597 18	2,705 63
452	Salaries and Expenses of Clerks and Attendants	3,058 65	2,854 33	3,522 51	3,166 35
453	General Office Supplies and Expenses	346 92	414 96	284 77	744 07
454	Law Expenses	400 00	400 00	400 50	588 90
455	Insurance	223 01	90	50 29	1 93
457	Pensions...........................	....	183 50	....	1,451 49
458	Stationery and Printing	195 16	192 14	270 18	434 96
459	Valuation Expenses	....	....	....	....
460	Other Expenses.....................	5 60	11 05	11 70	35 05
461	General Joint Facilities—Dr.	....	....	....	....
462	" " " —Cr.	45 32	7 42	43 24	7 28
	Total	5,396 59	5,673 50	7,093 89	9,121 10

Comparative Statement of Earnings and Expenditures by

No.	General.	1915 April.	1916 April.	1915 May.	1916 May.
		$ c.	$ c.	$ c.	$ c.
451	Salaries and Expenses of General Officers..........................	1,443 98	1,465 02	1,728 08	1,503 19
452	Salaries and Expenses of Clerks and Attendants	2,991 71	2,874 43	2,955 02	2,835 40
453	General Office Supplies and Expenses	460 08	469 45	342 55	729 78
454	Law Expenses	400 00	400 00	400 00	425 00
455	Insurance...........................	50 29	78 95	55 80	1 87
457	Pensions............................	320 00	357 46	320 00	569 70
458	Stationery and Printing.............	160 73	328 61	316 97	346 87
459	Valuation Expenses.................	....	....	....	....
460	Other Expenses.....................	110 30	11 05	....	52 50
461	General Joint Facilities—Dr.	....	....	....	....
462	" " " —Cr.	47 32	7 18	47 68	7 31
	Total	5,889 77	5,977 79	6,070 74	6,457 00

Comparative Statement of Earnings and Expenditures by

No.	General.	1915 September.	1916 September.	1915 October.
		$ c.	$ c.	$ c.
451	Salaries and Expenses of General Officers..........................	2,424 06	2,381 00	1,401 00
452	Salaries and Expenses of Clerks and Attendants......................	2,675 25	3,500 85	2,607 04
453	General Office Supplies and Expenses	433 20	498 47	350 89
454	Law Expenses	406 25	400 00	416 49
455	Insurance...........................	55 77	1 87	55 77
457	Pensions............................	165 00	1,175 74	....
458	Stationery and Printing.............	210 96	215 83	97 82
459	Valuation Expenses.................	....	....	....
460	Other Expenses.....................	100 77	3,193 88	11 05
461	General Joint Facilities —Dr........	....	....	....
462	" " " —Cr.........	7 20	8 66	7 28
	Total	6,464 06	11,858 98	4,932 78

Months, November, 1914, to October, 1916---Continued.

1915 January.	1916 January.	1915 February.	1916 February.	1915 March.	1916 March.	No.
$ c.	$ c.	$ c.	$ c.	$ c.	$ c.	
1,408 98	1,606 71	1,336 74	1 520 65	2,445 14	2,575 01	451
3,167 81	2,873 21	3,309 55	2,760 65	2,996 90	2,793 41	452
778 41	438 15	384 40	405 88	426 69	456 93	453
555 00	400 00	400 00	400 00	400 00	400 00	454
50 29	1 87	50 29	1 87	54 99	6 07	455
167 45	1,245 70	295 00	676 55	399 61	112 75	457
389 09	192 37	193 11	463 50	290 27	194 85	458
						459
2 40	11 05	25 00	11 05	80 00	11 05	460
						461
42 80	7 64	42 28	7 14	45 94	7 26	462
6,476 63	6,761 42	5,951 81	6,233 01	7,047 66	6,542 81	

Months, November, 1914, to October, 1916---Continued.

1915 June.	1916 June.	1915 July.	1916 July.	1915 August.	1916 August.	No.
$ c.	$ c.	$ c.	$ c.	$ c.	$ c.	
2,464 74	2,180 55	1,510 60	1,521 31	1,400 27	1,544 39	451
2,565 63	2,903 32	2,532 84	3,042 40	2,654 26	3,339 54	452
544 98	384 50	550 52	410 26	367 22	366 74	453
541 00	650 65	400 00	400 00	400 00	400 00	454
55 77	1 87	55 84	1 87	55 77	1 87	455
545 00	782 98	545 00	1,000 03	165 00	1,100 33	457
185 89	188 24	360 89	495 28	377 66	235 01	458
						459
23 76	624 80	11 05	907 01	67 42	497 34	460
						461
2,695 42	7 32	8 21	7 22	7 26	6 29	462
4,231 35	7,709 59	5,958 53	7,770 94	5,480 34	7,478 93	

Months, November, 1914, to October, 1916---Concluded.

1916 October.	1915 Total.	1916 Total.	Increase.	Decrease.	No.
$ c.	$ c.	$ c.	$ c.	$ c.	
1,481 32	21,373 34	22,108 82	735 48		451
3,550 01	35,037 17	36,493 90	1,456 73		452
809 07	5,270 63	6,128 26	857 63		453
562 89	5,119 24	5,427 44	308 20		454
1 87	813 88	102 81		711 07	455
870 46	2,922 06	9,526 69	6,604 63		457
401 17	3,048 73	3,688 83	640 10		458
					459
2,564 30	449 05	7,930 13	7,481 08		460
					461
8 42	3,089 95	89 14		2,950 81	462
10,232 67	70,994 15	91,317 74	20,323 59		

8 T.R.

Statement Earnings and Expenses—Freight and Passenger—per Train Mile and per Mile of Road

November, 1915

	Total	Freight	Passenger	Per Train Mile Freight	Per Train Mile Passenger	Per Mile of Road Total	Per Mile of Road Freight	Per Mile of Road Passenger
Train Miles	84,030	40,760	43,270					
Car Loaded	768,174	552,109	216,065	13.5	5.0			
" Empty	237,256	237,256		5.8				
Total Car Miles	1,005,430	789,365	216,065	19.3	5.0			
REVENUE.	$ c.	$ c.	$ c.	$ c.	$ c.	$ c.	$ c.	$ c.
Transportation	148,604 21	98,293 74	50,310 47	2 41.1	1 16.3	452 37	299 22	153 15
Total to transportation	5,862 86	3,702 12	2,160 74	09.1	05.0	17 85	11 27	6 58
Total	154,467 07	101,995 86	52,471 21	2 50.2	1 21.3	470 22	310 49	159 73
EXPENDITURES.								
Mtce of Way and Structures	36,819 46	20,508 44	16,311 02	50.3	37.7	112 08	62 43	49 65
" Equipment	23,272 14	10,680 80	12,591 34	26.2	29.1	70 84	32 51	38 33
Traffic Expenses	1,603 10	1,151 28	451 82	02.8	01.0	4 88	3 50	1 38
Transportation Expenses	58,340 34	36,499 63	21,840 71	89.5	50.5	177 60	111 11	66 49
Misc Operations	2,551 09	1,286 11	1,264 98	03.2	02.9	7 77	3 92	3 85
General Expenses	5,673 50	3,245 24	2,428 26	08.0	05.6	17 27	9 88	7 39
Transportation for Investment—Cr.	201 12	201 12		00.5		61	61	
Total Operating Expenses	128,058 51	73,170 38	54,888 13	1 79.5	1 26.8	389 83	222 74	167 09
Hire of Equipment	6,744 31	4,939 16	1,805 15	12.1	04.2	20 53	15 04	5 49
Total Expenses	131,802 82	78,109 54	56,693 28	1 91.6	1 31.0	410 36	237 78	172 58
Balance	19,664 25	23,886 32	Dr. 4,222 07	58.6	Dr. 09.7	59 86	72 71	Dr. 12 85
Income unallocated	1,791 75					5 45		
Net Result	21,456 00					65.31		

Statement Earnings and Expenses—Freight and Passenger—per Train Mile and per Mile of Road.

October, 19.

	Total	Freight	Passenger	Per Train Mile Freight	Per Train Mile Passenger	Per Mile of Road Total	Per Mile of Road Freight	Per Mile of Road Passenger
Train Miles	89,553	44,006	45,547					
Car Miles—Loaded	818,872	584,709	234,163	13.3	5.1			
" Empty	239,327	239,327		5.4				
Total Car Miles	1,068,199	824,036	234,163	18.7	5.1			
REVENUE.	$ c.	$ c.	$ c.	$ c.	$ c.	$ c.	$ c.	$ c.
Transportation	154,810 69	103,244 87	51,565 82	2 34.6	1 13.2	471 26	314 29	156 97
Mail to transportation	6,105 58	3,975 78	2,129 80	09.	04.7	18 59	12 10	6 49
Total	160,916 27	107,220 65	53,695 62	2 43.6	1 17.9	489 85	326 39	163 46
EXPENSES.								
Maintenance of Way and Structures	29,981 46	17,119 41	12,862 05	38.9	28.2	91 27	52 12	39 15
" Equipment	21,829 87	9,611 63	12,218 24	21.8	26.8	66 45	29 26	37 19
Traffic Expenses	2,536 47	1,277 88	1,258 59	02.9	02.8	7 72	3 89	3 83
Transportation Operations	63,818 19	40,671 23	23,146 96	92.4	50.8	194 27	123 81	70 46
Miscellaneous Operations	3,286 55	1,371 01	1,915 54	03.1	04.2	10 01	4 17	5 84
General Expenses	9,121 10	5,262 87	3,858 23	12.0	08.5	27 77	16 02	11 75
" for Investment—Cr.	136 95	136 95		00.3		42	42	
Total Operating Expenses	130,436 09	75,177 08	55,259 61	1 70.8	1 21.3	397 07	228 85	168 22
Hire of Equipment	6,476 22	5,236 24	1,239 98	11.9	02.7	19 71	15 94	3 77
Total Expenses	136,912 91	80,413 32	56,499 59	1 82.7	1 24.0	416 78	244 79	171 99
Balance	24,003 36	26,807 33	Dr. 2,803 97	60.9	Dr. 06.1	73 07	81 60	Dr. 8 53
Income add	2,563 94					7 80		
Net	26,567 30					80 87		

Statement Earnings and Expenses—Freight and Passenger—per Train Mile and per Mile of Road.

January, 1916.

	Total	Freight	Passenger	Per Train Mile Freight	Per Train Mile Passenger	Per Mile of Road Total	Per Mile of Road Freight	Per Mile of Road Passenger
Train Miles	89,263	46,033	43,230					
Car Miles—Loaded	854,240	651,732	202,508	14.2	4.7			
" Empty	227,666	227,666		4.9				
Total Car Miles	1,081,906	879,398	202,508	19.1	4.7			
REVENUE.	$ c.	$ c.	$ c.	$ c.	$ c.	$ c.	$ c.	$ c.
Transportation	139,236 13	94,046 09	45,190 04	2 04	1 05	423 85	286 29	137 56
Total to transportation	8,881 44	4,500 84	4,380 60	10	10	27 04	13 70	13 34
Total	148,117 57	98,546 93	49,570 64	2 14	1 15	450 89	299 99	150 90
EXPENDITURES.								
Office of Way and Structures	31,501 12	18,900 68	12,600 44	41	29	95 89	57 53	38 36
" " Eng.	23,232 31	11,852 12	11,380 19	26	27	70 72	36 08	34 64
Traffic Expenses	3,013 91	1,161 59	1,852 32	03	04	9 18	3 54	5 64
Transportation Expenses	76,280 49	50,743 58	25,536 91	1 10	59	232 21	154 48	77 73
...us Operations	4,975 78	1,475 30	3,500 48	03	08	15 15	4 49	10 66
General Expenses	6,761 42	4,090 66	2,670 76	09	06	20 58	12 45	8 13
Transportation for Investment—Cr.	35 86	35 86				11	11	
Total Operating Expenses	145,729 17	88,188 07	57,541 10	1 92	1 33	443 62	268 46	175 16
Hire of Equipment	8,925 84	7,489 27	1,436 57	16	03	27 17	22 79	4 38
Total Expenses	154,655 01	95,677 34	58,977 67	2 08	1 36	470 79	291 25	179 54
Balance	Dr.6,537 44	2,869 59	Dr.9,407 03	06	Dr. 21	Dr. 19 90	8 74	Dr. 28 64
Income unallocated	10,172 08					30 96		
Net Result	3,634 64					11 06		

Statement Earnings and Expenses—Freight and Passenger—per Train Mile and per Mile of Road.

February, 1916.

	Total	Freight	Passenger	Per Train Mile		Per Mile of Road		
				Freight	Passenger	Total	Freight	Passenger
rfin Miles	89,851	48,664	41,187					
Car Miles—Loaded	946,929	755,748	191,181	15.5	4.6			
" " Empty	233,367	233,367		4.8				
Total Car Miles	1,180,296	989,115	191,181	20.3	4.6			
REVENUE.	$ c.	$ c.	$ c.	$ c.	$ c.	$ c.	$ c.	$ c.
Transportation	144,254 30	107,785 07	36,469 23	2 21	89	439 12	328 11	111 01
al to transportation	6,334 49	3,737 17	2,597 32	08	06	19 29	11 38	7 91
al	150,588 79	111,522 24	39,066 55	2 29	95	458 41	339 49	118 92
EXPENDITURES.								
Maintenance of Way and Structures	35,310 60	22,192 71	13,117 89	45	32	107 49	67 56	39 93
" Equipment	24,491 27	13,465 14	11,026 13	28	27	74 55	40 99	33 56
Traffic Expenses	1,902 02	1,443 61	458 41	03	01	5 79	4 39	1 40
Transportation Expenses	77,691 60	54,514 31	23,177 29	1 12	56	236 50	165 95	70 55
Miscellaneous Operations	3,316 32	1,396 42	1,919 90	03	05	10 10	4 25	5 85
General Expenses	6,233 01	4,063 92	2,169 09	08	05	18 97	12 37	6 60
Transportation for Investment—Cr.	25 32	25 32		08	05	07	07	
al Operating Expenses	148,919 50	97,050 79	51,868 71	1 99	1 26	453 33	295 44	157 89
Hire of Equipment	11,119 16	9,796 91	1,322 25	20	03	33 85	29 82	4 03
Total Expenses	160,038 66	106,847 70	53,190 96	2 19	1 29	487 18	325 26	161 92
Balance	Dr. 9,449 87	4,674 54	Dr.14,124 41	10	Dr. 34	Dr. 28 77	14 23	Dr. 43 00
Ine unallocated	1,516 85					4 62		
Net Result	Dr. 7,933 02					Dr. 24 15		

Statement Earnings and Expenses—Freight and Passenger—per Train Mile and per Mile of Road.

March, 1916.

	Total	Freight	Passenger	Per Train Mile		Per Mile of Road		
				Freight	Passenger	Total	Freight	Passenger
Train Miles	110,881	65,210	45,671					
Car Miles—Loaded	1,328,514	1,113,275	215,239					
" Empty	233,949	233,949						
Total Car Miles	1,562,463	1,347,224	215,239					
Revenue.	$ c.	$ c.	$ c.	$ c.	$ c.	$ c.	$ c.	$ c.
Transportation	187,127 43	142,667 04	44,460 39	2 18.8	97.3	569 64	434 30	135 34
Incidental to transportation	6,776 17	4,328 09	2,448 08	06.6	05.4	20 63	13 18	7 45
Total	193,903 60	146,995 13	46,908 47	2 25.4	1 02.7	590 27	447 48	142 79
Expenditures.				$ c.	$ c.	$ c.	$ c.	$ c.
Maintenance of Way and Structures	31,221 35	21,261 74	9,969 61	32.6	21.8	95 04	64 72	30 32
" Equipment	30,903 33	16,323 12	14,580 21	25	31.9	94 07	49 69	44 38
Traffic Expenses	1,441 97	1,144 31	297 66	01.8	00.7	4 39	3 48	91
Transportation Expenses	94,015 46	70,815 57	23,199 89	1 08.6	50.8	286 20	215 57	70 63
Miscellaneous Operations	3,852 12	1,842 67	2,000 45	02.8	04.4	11 72	5 61	6 11
General Expenses	6,542 81	4,514 54	2,028 27	06.9	04.4	19 92	13 75	6 17
Transportation for Investment—Cr.	30 88	30 88				09		
Total Operating Expenses	167,946 16	115,871 07	52,075 09	1 77.7	1 14	511 25	352 73	158 52
Hire of Equipment	16,690 23	14,991 68	1,698 55	23	03.7	50 81	45 64	5 17
Total Expenses	184,636 39	130,862 75	53,773 64	2 00.7	1 17.7	562 06	398 37	163 69
Balance	9,267 21	16,132 38	Dr. 6,865 17	24.7	Dr. 15	28 21	49 11	Dr. 20 90
Income unallocated	8,333 56					25.37		
Net Result	17,600 77					53.58		

Statement Earnings and Expenses—Freight and Passenger—per Train Mile and per Mile of Road.

April, 916.

	Total	Freight	Passenger	Per Train Mile Freight	Per Train Mile Passenger	Per Mile of Road Total	Per Mile of Road Freight	Per Mile of Road Passenger
Train Miles	120,530	79,627	40,903					
Car Miles—Loaded	1,528,996	1,313,224	215,772	16.5	5.3			
" " Empty	430,975	430,975		5.4				
Total Car Miles	1,959,971	1,744,199	215,772	21.9	5.3			
REVENUE.	$ c.	$ c.	$ c.	$ c.	$ c.	$ c.	$ c.	$ c.
Transportation	226,708 36	174,593 27	52,115 09	2 19.3	1 27.4	690 13	531 49	158 64
Incidental to transportation	6,840 83	5,137 90	1,702 93	06.4	04.2	20 83	15 64	5 19
Total	$233,549 19	179,731 17	53,818 02	2 25.7	1 31.6	710 96	547 13	163 83
EXPENDITURES.								
Maintenance of Way and Structures	28,388 98	19,332 90	9,056 08	24.3	22.1	86 42	58 85	27 57
" " Equipment	25,101 54	14,917 20	10,184 34	18.7	24.9	76 41	45 41	31 00
Traffic Expenses	1,237 48	1,059 91	177 57	01.3	00.4	3 77	3 23	54
Transportation	94,139 11	73,298 87	20,840 24	92.1	51	286 57	223 13	63 44
Miscellaneous	2,091 37	1,506 57	584 80	01.9	01.4	6 37	4 59	1 78
General Expenses	5,977 79	4,357 81	1,619 98	05.4	04	18 20	13 27	4 93
Transportation for Investment—Cr.	35 95	35 95				11	11	
Total Operating Expenses	156,900 32	114,437 31	42,463 01	1 43.7	1 03.8	477 63	348 37	129 26
Hire of Equipment	18,107 91	16,304 03	1,803 88	20.5	04.4	55 12	49 63	5 49
Total Expenses	175,008 23	130,741 34	44,266 89	1 64.2	1 08.2	532 75	398 00	134 75
Balance	58,540 96	48,989 83	9,551 13	61.5	23.4	178 21	149 13	29 08
Income unallocated	2,169 10					6 60		
Net Result	60,710 06					184 81		

Statement Earnings and Expenses—Freight and Passenger—per Train Mile and per Mile of Road.

May, 1916.

	Total	Freight	Passenger	Per Train Mile		Per Mile of Road.		
				Freight.	Passenger.	Total.	Freight.	Passen gr.
Train Ms	100,247	52,817	47,430					
Car Ms—Load	1,039,614	794,237	245,377	15..	5.2			
Car " Empty	329,596	329,596	......	6.3	5.2			
Total Car Miles	1,369,210	1,123,833	245,377	21.3	5.2			
REVENUE.	$ c.	$ c.	$ c.	$ c.	$ c.	$ c.	$ c.	$ c.
Station	192,425 87	130,417 33	62,008 54	2 46.9	1 30.7	585 77	397 01	188 76
Rail to t portation	7,909 01	4,771 12	3,137 89	06.9	06.6	24 08	14 52	9 56
Total	200,334 88	135,188 45	65,146 43	2 55.9	1 37.3	609 85	411 53	198 32
EXPENDITURES.								
Maint. of Way and Structures	33,152 63	20,355 71	12,796 92	38.5	27	100 92	61 96	38 96
" "	22,250 15	12,126 14	10,124 01	23	21.3	67 73	36 91	30 82
......	1,519 95	1,192 74	327 21	02.3	00.7	4 63	3 63	1 00
......	73,215 82	50,670 05	22,545 71	95.9	47.5	222 88	154 25	68 63
Miscellaneous	3,784 25	1,658 54	2,125 71	03.1	04.5	11 52	5 05	6 47
Expenses	6,457 00	4,145 39	2,311 61	07.8	04.9	19 65	12 62	7 03
n for Investment—Cr.	368 95	368 95	......	00.7	......	1 12	1 12	......
Total Operating	140,010 85	89,779 62	50,231 23	1 69.9	1 05.9	426 21	273 30	152 91
Hire of	9,594 18	7,019 91	2,574 27	13.3	65.4	29 21	21 37	7 84
Total Expenses	149,605 03	96,799 53	52,805 50	1 83.2	1 11.3	455 42	294 67	160 75
Balance	50,729 85	38,388 92	12,340 93	72.7	26	154 43	116 86	37 57
Income	2,570 98					7 83		
Net	53,300 83					162 26		

Statement Earnings and Expenses—Freight and Passenger—per Train Mile and per Mile of Road.

June 1916.

	Total	Freight	Passenger	Per Train Mile		Per Mile of Road		
				Freight	Passenger	Total	Freight	Passenger
Train Miles	87,536	42,089	45,447					
Car Miles—Loaded	851,508	601,850	249,658					
" Empty	204,213	204,213						
Total Car Miles	1,055,721	806,063	249,658					
REVENUE.	$ c.	$ c.	$ c.	$ c.	$ c.	$ c.	$ c.	$ c.
Transportation	158,813 52	92,617 53	66,195 99	2 20.1	1 45.6	483 45	281 94	201 51
Incl ... to	6,532 97	3,774 83	2,758 14	08.9	06.1	19 88	11 49	8 39
Total	165,346 49	96,392 36	68,954 13	2 29	1 51.7	503 33	293 43	209 90
EXPENDITURES.								
Maintenance of Way and Structures	37,065 95	18,162 32	18,903 63	43.1	41.6	112 83	55 29	57 54
" " Equipment	21,341 88	9,402 82	11,939 06	22.3	26.3	64 97	28 62	36 35
Traffic Expenses	1,691 90	1,065 53	626 37	02.5	01.4	5 15	3 24	1 91
Transportation Expenses	58,624 87	38,010 63	20,614 24	90.3	45.4	178 46	115 71	62 75
...	2,257 47	1,369 66	887 81	06.3	01.9	6 87	4 17	2 70
General Expenses	7,709 59	4,332 79	3,376 80	10.3	07.4	23 47	13 19	10 28
... on or Investment—Cr.	226 53	226 53		00.5		69	69	
Total of Equipment	128,465 13	72,117 22	56,347 91	1 71.3	1 24	391 06	219 53	171 53
Hire of Equipment	7,417 53	5,122 82	2,294 71	12.2	05	22 58	15 59	6 99
Total	135,882 66	77,240 04	58,642 62	1 83.5	1 29	413 64	235 12	178 52
Balance	29,463 83	19,152 32	10,311 51	45.5	22.7	89 69	58 31	31 38
Income ...	2,712 66					8 25		
Net ...	32,176 49					97 94		

Statement Earnings ad Expenses—Freight ad Passenger— pr Tin Mile ad per Mile of Road.
July, 1916.

	Total	Fht.	sr.	Per Train Freight	Per Train sr.	Per Mile of Road Total	Freight	Passenger
rEin Ms	87,169	41,185	45,984					
Gr Mil Ld Empty	792,322	563,324	228,998	13.7	5.0			
" " Empty	170,057	170,057		4.1				
Tal Gr Miles	962,379	733,381	228,998	17.8	5.0			
REVENUE.	$ c.	$ c.	$ c.	$ c.	$ c.	$ c.	$ c.	$ c.
of in	150,103 72	78,919 01	71,184 71	1 91.6	1 54.8	456 94	240 24	216 70
al to transportat ón	8,013 07	3,891 96	4,121 11	9.5	9.0	24 39	11 85	12 54
Tal	158,116 79	82,810 97	75,305 82	2 01.1	1 63.8	481 33	252 09	229 24
EXPENDITURES.								
M intenance of Way ad Equipment	20,808 64	11,236 67	9,571 97	27.3	20.9	63 34	34 20	29 14
" "	12,603 59	4,703 06	7,900 53	11.4	17.2	38 37	14 32	24 05
Traffic	1,520 49	631 69	888 80	01.5	01.9	4 63	1 92	2 71
ortation	57,641 04	36,321 06	21,319 98	88.2	46.3	175 47	110 57	64 90
al Expenses	3,209 14	1,277 66	1,931 48	03.1	04.2	9 77	3 89	5 88
on or Investment—Cr.	7,770 94	4,398 35	3,372 59	10.7	07.3	23 65	13 39	10 26
	108 84	108 84		00.3		33	33	
Al Operating Expenses	103,445 00	58,459 65	44,985 35	1 41.9	97.8	314 90	177 96	136 94
Hire of	205 65	Cr. 1,445 02	1,650 67	Cr. 03.5	03.6	63	Cr. 4 40	5 03
Tal	103,650 65	57,014 63	46,636 02	1 38.4	1 01.4	315 53	173 56	141 97
Balance	54,466 14	25,796 34	28,669 80	62.7	62.4	165 80	78 53	87 27
e	2,736 13					8 33		
Net Result	57,202 27					174 13		

Sumt Ergs ad Expenses—Freight ad Passenger—per Train Mile ad pr Mile of Rd.

St, 1916.

	Total.	Freight.	Br.	Per Train Mile — Ft.	Pn Mle.	Br.	Per Mile of Rd — Al.	Pn.	Br.
Trn Mles	94,972	46,473	48,499						
Car Miles—Loaded	863,715	562,026	301,689	12.1		6.2			
" " Empty	243,531	243,531		5.2					
Tal Gr Miles	1,107,246	805,557	301,689	17.3		6.2			
	$ c.	$ c.	$ c.	$ c.	$ c.	$ c.	$ c.	$ c.	$ c.
Transportation	165,604 43	94,860 30	70,744 13	2 04.1	1 45.9		504 12	288 77	215 35
to station	10,084 19	4,500 69	5,583 50	9.7	11.5		30 70	13 70	17 00
Total	175,688 62	99,360 99	76,327 63	2 13.8	1 57.4		534 82	302 47	232 35
EXPENDITURES.									
Maintenance of Way ad St uct res	33,964 50	17,899 29	16,05 21	38.5	33.1		103 39	54 49	48 90
"	17,643 29	8,134 57	9,08 72	17.5	19.6		53 71	24 76	28 95
Traffic	3,758 86	751 76	3,007 10	1.6	6.2		11 44	2 29	9 15
	62,658 02	40,511 59	22,46 43	87.2	45.7		190 74	123 32	67 65
	3,939 13	1,753 44	2,85 69	3.8	4.5		11 99	5 34	6 65
for Invest mnt—Cr.	7,478 93	4,233 08	3,245 85	9.1	6.7		22 77	12.89	9 88
	220 58	220 58		.5			67	67	
Hire of	129,222 15	73,063 15	56,159 00	1 57.2	1 15.8		393 37	222 42	170 95
	6,553 37	9,510 31	Cr. 2,956 94	20.5	6.1 Cr.		19 95	28 95	9 00
Total	185,775 52	82,573 46	53,202 06	1 77.7	1 09.7		413 32	251 37	161 95
Ne	39,913 10	16,787 53	23,125 57	36.1	47.7		121 50	51 10	70 40
Md	16,305 66						49 64		
Net alt	56,218 76						171 14		

Statement Earnings and Expenses—Freight and Passenger—per Train Mile and per Mile of Road.

September, 1916.

	Total	Freight	Passenger	Per Train Mile		Per Mile of Road		
				Freight	Passenger	Total	Freight	Passenger
Train Miles	94,202	48,540	45,662					
Car Miles—Loaded	880,962	617,541	263,421	12.7	5.8			
" Empty	255,317	255,317		5.3				
Total Car Miles	1,136,279	872,858	263,421	18.	5.8			
REVENUE.	$ c.	$ c.	$ c.	$ c.	$ c.	$ c.	$ c.	$ c.
Transportation	187,192 85	97,650 26	89,542 59	2 01.2	1 96.1	569 84	297 26	272 58
Incidental to transportation	10,889 36	5,080 66	5,818 70	10.4	12.7	33 18	15 47	17 71
Total	198,092 21	102,730 92	95,361 29	2 11.6	2 08.8	603 02	312 73	290 29
EXPENDITURES.								
Maintenance of Way and Structures	15,648 55	9,123 10	6,525 45	18.8	14.3	47 64	27 77	19 87
" Equipment	12,378 52	3,096 65	9,281 87	06.4	20.3	37 68	9 43	28 25
Traffic Expenses	1,047 35	605 27	442 08	01.2	01	3 19	1 84	1 35
Transportation Expenses	64,994 19	44,404 86	20,589 33	91.5	45.1	197 85	135 17	62 68
Bus Operations	4,485 67	1,264 75	3,220 92	02.6	07	13 65	3 85	9 80
General Expenses	11,358 98	6,747 23	4,611 75	13.9	10.1	34 58	20 54	14 04
Transportation for investment—Cr.	275 80	275 80		.6		84	84	
Total Operating Expenses	109,637 46	64,966 06	44,671 40	1 33.8	97.8	333 75	197 76	135 99
Hire of Equipment	6,254 11	5,718 48	535 63	11.8	01.2	19 04	17 41	1 63
Total Expenses	115,891 57	70,684 54	45,207 03	1 45.6	99	352 79	215 17	137 62
Balance	82,200 64	32,046 38	50,154 26	66	1 09.8	250 23	97 56	152 67
Same	2,901 48					8 83		
Net Result	85,102 12					259 06		

Statement Earnings and Expenses—Freight and Passenger—per Train Mile and per Mile of Road.

...ber, 1916.

	Total	Freight	Passenger	Per Train Mile Freight	Per Train Mile Passenger	Per Mile of Road Total	Per Mile of Road Freight	Per Mile of Road Passenger
Train Miles	97,553	54,120	43,433					
Car Miles—Loaded	952,401	721,045	231,356					
" Empty	213,241	213,241						
Total Car Miles	1,165,642	934,286	231,356					
REVENUE.								
	$ c.	$ c.	$ c.	$ c.	$ c.	$ c.	$ c.	$ c.
Transportation	189,927 48	115,830 56	74,096 92	2 14	1 70.6	578 16	352 60	225 56
Incidental to transportation	9,072 99	4,983 35	4,089 64	09.2	09.4	27 62	15 17	12 45
Total	199,000 47	120,813 91	78,186 56	2 23.2	1 80	605 78	367 77	238 01
EXPENDITURES.								
...ance of Way and Structures	15,161 24	9,142 23	6,019 01	16.9	13.8	46 15	27 83	18 32
" Equipment	13,654 15	4,766 76	8,887 39	08.8	20.5	41 57	14 51	27 06
...fic Expenses	1,192 19	718 70	473 49	01.3	01.1	3 63	2 19	1 44
...in Expenses	60,639 62	40,410 14	20,229 48	74.7	46.6	184 59	123 01	61 58
...ns	4,814 00	1,857 56	2,956 44	03.4	06.8	14 65	5 65	9 00
General Expenses	10,232 67	6,098 67	4,134 00	11.3	09.5	31 15	18 57	12 58
...tion for Investment—Cr.	287 35	287 35		00.5		87	87	
Total ...erating Expenses	105,406 52	62,706 71	42,699 81	1 15.9	98.3	320 87	190 89	129 98
Hire of Equipment	7,152 58	7,404 90	Cr. 252 32	13.6	00.6	21 77	22 54	Cr. 77
Total Expenses	112,559 10	70,111 61	42,447 49	1 29.5	97.7	342 64	213 43	129 21
Balance	86,441 37	50,702 30	35,739 07	93.7	82.3	263 14	154 34	108 80
I...me ...ted	36,227 87					110 28		
Net Result	122,669 24					373 42		

Statement Earnings and E — ▊ight ▊d Passenger—per ▊ain Mile ▊d per Mile of Road

Nov ▊r 1st, 1915, to October 31st, 1916.

	Total	Freight	Passenger	Per Train Mile		Per Mile of Road		
				Freight	Passenger	Total	Freight	Passenger
▊in Mes ▊	1,145,787	600,524	536,263					
Car " ▊led ▊	11,626,247	8,830,820	2,795,427	14.5	5.2			
" " ▊ty ▊	3,018,495	3,018,495		4.9				
▊ Car Miles	14,644,742	11,849,315	2,795,427	19.4	5.2			
REVENUE.	$ c.	$ c.	$ c.	$ c.	$ c.	$ c.	$ c.	$ c.
▊m ▊	2,044,808 99	1,330,925 07	713,883 92	2 18.4	1 33.1	6,224 68	4,051 52	2,173 16
▊al to ▊ansportation	93,312 96	52,384 51	40,928 45	08.6	7.6	284 06	159 47	124 59
▊al	2,138,121 95	1,383,309 58	754,812 37	2 27	1 40.7	6,508 74	4,210 99	2,297 75
EXPENDITURES.								
▊ce of ▊y and Structures	349,024 48	205,235 20	143,789 28	33.7	26.8	1,062 48	624 77	437 71
" " ▊nt	248,702 04	119,080 01	129,622 03	19.5	24.2	757 08	362 49	394 59
▊fic Expenses	22,465 69	12,204 27	10,261 42	02.	01.9	68 39	37 15	31 24
▊h Expenses	842,058 75	576,871 52	265,187 23	94.6	49.4	2,563 35	1,756 08	807 27
Miscellaneous ▊s	42,562 89	18,059 69	24,503 20	03.	04.6	129 57	54 98	74 59
▊h ▊r In ▊ment—Cr.	1,954 13	1,954 13		00.3		5 95	5 95	
▊s	91,317 74	55,490 55	35,827 19	09.1	06.7	277 98	168 92	109 06
Total ▊ating E ▊es	1,594,177 46	984,987 11	609,190 35	1 61.6	1 13.6	4,852 90	2,998 44	1,854 46
Hire of Equipment	105,241 09	92,088 69	13,152 40	15.1	02.4	320 37	280 33	40 04
▊tal Expenses	1,609,418 55	1,077,075 80	622,342 75	1 76.7	1 16	5,173 27	3,278 77	1,894 50
Balance ▊ ▊	438,703 40	306,233 78	132,469 62	50.3	24.7	1,335 47	962 22	403 25
I ▊me ▊ ▊	90,002 06					273 98		
Net ▊ ▊lt	528,705 46					1,609 45		

Freight Traffic Movement—Company's Material Excluded—Year Ending   October 31st, 1916.

Commodity.	Freight originating on T. & N. O.	Freight originating at other stations in Canada.	Freight originating in U.S.	Total Freight.
	Whole Tons.	Whole Tons.	Whole Tons.	Whole Tons.
Products of Agriculture—				
Grain	5,590	209,922	....	215,512
Flour	165	5,881	....	6,046
Other Mill Products	226	1,978	....	2,204
Hay	8,282	1,623	....	9,905
Tobacco	....	124	....	124
Cotton	....	....	....	....
Fruit and Vegetables	2,522	11,472	35	14,029
Other Products of Agriculture	18	271	80	369
Total	16,803	231,271	115	248,189
Products of Animals—				
Live Stock	921	1,503	....	2,424
Dressed Meats	....	697	....	697
Other Packing House Products	....	441	....	441
Poultry, Game and Fish	....	1,626	....	1,626
Wool	....	....	....	....
Hides and Leather	....	1,105	....	1,105
Other Products of Animals	40	1,159	....	1,199
Total	961	6,531	....	7,492
Products of Mines—				
Anthracite Coal	384	9,783	7,585	17,752
Bituminous Coal	1,001	70,047	20,564	91,612
Coke	49	211	735	995
Ores	27,889	....	....	27,889
Stone, Sand and other like articles...	13,969	4,389	195	18,553
Other Products of Mines	389	886	....	1,275
Total	43,681	85,316	29,079	158,076
Products of Forests—				
Lumber	115,856	14,061	....	129,917
Other Products of Forests	142,586	2,301	....	144,887
Total	258,442	16,362	....	274,804
Manufactures—				
Petroleum and other Oils	94	6,202	112	6,408
Sugar	27	1,810	....	1,837
Iron, Pig and Bloom	....	458	65	523
Iron and Steel Rails	136	1,003	27	1,166
Other Castings and Machinery	1,990	13,131	523	15,644
Bar and Sheet Metal	250	3,834	....	4,084
Cement, Brick and Lime	1,521	14,651	119	16,291
Agricultural Implements	37	4,422	....	4,459
Wagons, Carriages, Tools, etc	48	6,080	....	6,128
Wines, Liquors and Beers	68	3,252	114	3,434
Household Goods and Furniture	327	9,585	....	9,912
Other Manufactures	60,211	27,542	1,066	88,819
Total	64,709	91,970	2,026	158,705
Merchandise	21,773	39,259	703	61,735
Miscellaneous—				
Other Commodities not mentioned above	4,213	9,264	140	13,617
Total Tonnage	410,582	479,973	32,063	922,618

Statistics—Temiskaming and Northern Ontario Railway.

Comparative Passenger and Freight Statement.

—	Passengers.	Revenue.
		$ c.
Number of passengers carried during year 1905......	86,648	108,681 76
" " " " 1906......	359,861	254,759 33
" " " " 1907......	518,678	388,343 03
" " " " 1908......	479,005	366,504 53
" " " " 1909......	580,748	483,110 89
" " " " 1910......	670,913	606,967 91
" " " " 1911......	479,102	653,063 01
" " " " 1912......	497,452	599,681 73
" " " " 1913......	508,055	576,049 37
" " " " 1914......	535,869	544,820 08
" " " " 1915......	480,995	482,349 80
" " " " 1916......	485,759	624,808 12
Total	5,683,085	5,689,139 56

Number of passengers carried one mile, period 1905 to 1916, inclusive.......... 236,452,346

—	Tons.	Revenue.
		$ c.
Number of tons of freight carried during year 1905 ...	99,192	121,530 46
" " " " " 1906 ...	273,749	230,552 63
" " " " " 1907 ...	393,589	390,894 29
" " " " " 1908 ...	484,444	471,203 41
" " " " " 1909 ...	498,645	756,141 66
" " " " " 1910 ...	624,820	852,886 46
" " " " " 1911 ...	564,120	974,678 33
" " " " " 1912 ...	562,734	929,464 66
" " " " " 1913 ...	674,942	906,476 16
" " " " " 1914 ...	742,366	952,090 35
" " " " " 1915 ...	676,938	924,732 59
" " " " " 1916 ...	922,618	1,331,614 31
Total..................................	6,518,157	8,842,265 31

Number of tons of freight carried one mile, period 1905 to 1916, inclusive........ 752,164,141

Equipment owned by Temiskaming and Northern Ontario Railway.
October 31st, 1916.

	Total Authorized Equipment.	Available for Service.	Destroyed or Transferred to other classes	Capacity. Tractive Power.	Total Valuation.
STEAM LOCOMOTIVES.					$ c.
Class A 3	4	4	......	112,640	....
Class B 4	4	4	......	170,000	....
Class C 2	2	2	......	26,488	....
Class C 3	30	29	1	680,746	....
Class F 3	4	4	......	121,600	....
Total	44	43	1	....	953,855 81
PASSENGER EQUIPMENT.					
First Class Coaches (wooden.)	14	14	......	......	......
" " " (steel)	6	6	......	......	......
Second " . " (wooden)	21	14	7	......	......
" " " (steel)	4	4	......	......	......
Combination " (wooden)	3	3	......	......	......
- " " (steel)	3	......	3	......	......
Parlor-Cafe	3	3	......	......	......
Baggage and Express (wooden)	7	5	2	......	......
" " (steel)	4	4	......	......	......
Mail and Express (wooden)	6	5	1	......	......
" " (steel)	3	3	......	......	......
Private	2	2	......	......	......
Business	2	2	......	......	......
Total	78	65	13	....	810,887 41
FREIGHT EQUIPMENT.					
Box	150	145	5	......	......
Stock	10	9	1	......	......
Vans	24	20	4	......	......
Flats	502	446	56	......	......
Total	686	620	66	....	621,843 84
MAINTENANCE OF WAY AND STRUCTURES EQUIPMENT.					
Pile Driver	1	1	......	......	......
Snow Plows	4	3	1	......	......
Flangers	3	3	......	......	......
Steam Shovels	3	3	......	......	......
Wrecking Cranes	2	2	......	......	......
Auxiliaries (Complete)	2	2	......	......	......
Road Cabin Cars	2	2	......	......	......
Ledgerwood Unloaders	3	2	1	......	......
Side Ballast Plows	6	6	......	......	......
Centre Ballast Plows	3	3	......	......	......
Jordan Spreaders	2	2	......	......	......
Pile Driver Tank	1	1	......	......	......
Mahoney Ditching Machine	1	1	......	......	......
Centre Ballast Spreader	1	1	......	......	......
American Railroad Ditcher	1	1	......	......	......
Cinder Cars, Steel	12	12	......	......	......
Hart Convertibles	35	35	......	......	......
Exhibition Cars	1	1	......	......	......
Fish Cars (owned by Dept. of Public Works)	1	1	......	......	......
Tank Cars	6	6	......	......	......
Boarding Cars	8	8	......	......	......
Hand Cars	12	108	12	......	......
Push Cars	8	78	8	......	......
Motor Cars	0	3	......	......	......
Velocipedes	20	5	15	......	......
Total	327	290	37	....	184,204 65
Grand Total	......	......	......	....	2,570,791 71

TONNAGE.

Statement of Tons One Mile—Year Ending October 31st, 1916.

Month.	South Bound (Pounds).	North Bound (Pounds).	Total (Pounds).	Whole Tons.	Tons (One Mile).
November 1915....	55,285,326	53,993,987	109,279,313	54,640	9,437,571
December "	62,600,499	61,513,885	124,114,384	62,057	10,830,405
January 1916....	71,440,446	54,134,777	125,575,223	62,787	10,926,224
February "	90,807,369	64,946,021	155,753,390	77,877	14,564,430
March "	164,779,898	70,849,972	235,629,870	117,815	23,550,979
April "	249,784,002	65,017,258	314,801,260	157,400	34,061,092
May "	167,018,965	46,464,665	213,483,630	106,742	22,948,016
June "	59,156,324	43,250,135	102,406,459	51,203	9,227,699
July "	68,952,776	50,209,144	119,161,920	59,581	10,347,823
August "	52,108,646	55,593,133	107,701,779	53,851	8,379,686
September "	38,293,367	66,725,723	105,019,090	52,510	8,456,032
October "	54,871,511	77,437,823	132,309,334	66,155	11,112,562
Total..........	1,135,099,129	710,136,523	1,845,235,652	922,618	173,842,519

FOREST PRODUCTS.

Statement of Tonnage, Tons one mile. Total Revenue, and Revenue per ton per mile, for 12 months November 1st, 1915, to October 31st, 1916, under various headings.

Commodity.	Gross Tonnage. (Pounds).	Whole Tons.	Tons One Mile.	Revenue.	Revenue per ton per mile.
				$ c.	c.
Lumber	184,511,584	92,456	10,067,522	101,967 23	1.0283
Pulpwood.............	222,294,893	111,147	18,102,884	92,917 32	.5133
Pulp	49,602,176	24,801	5,719,085	24,887 68	.4352
Slabwood.............	21,168,976	10,584	446,690	6,507 65	1.4569
Poles	6,268,205	3,134	320,772	3,281 62	1.0227
Posts................	3,017,460	1,509	165,166	1,382 07	.8367
Piling	4,447,500	2,224	87,934	1,604 48	1.8246
Timber	5,425,909	2,713	127,233	2,446 35	1.9227
Logs	33,993,640	16,997	716,102	7,600 44	1.0611
Ties.................	17,705,295	8,853	1,023,424	9,674 59	.9453
Shingles	533,500	267	23,517	334 47	1.4222
Laths ...:...........	438,300	219	32,484	350 71	1.0796
Sawdust	199,700	100	2,124	65 58	3.0876
Total............	549,607,138	274,804	26,834,937	253,020 19	.9429

PASSENGER TRAFFIC.

Statement of Passengers, Revenue. Passengers one Mile and Passenger Revenue per mile, from November 1st, 1915, to October 31st, 1916.

Form of Ticket.	Passengers.	Revenue.	Passengers One Mile.	Passengers, Revenue One Mile.
		$ c.		c.
Commercial	22,524	44,897 10	1,988,145	2.26
Week Ends	16,480	9,309 78	625,759	1.46
Excursion	28,911	54,086 38	3,873,843	1.40
Market	4,991	1,252 20	77,984	1.61
Militia	18,111	43,808 24	3,159,301	1.39
Scholars	2,441	227 10	44,166	.51
Ordinary	392,301	471,277 32	17,202,893	2.74
Total	485,759	624,808 12	26,972,091	2.32

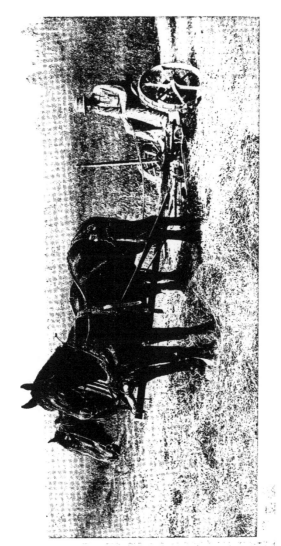

Cutting Oats on Farm of Mr. Joe Brown. South half Lot 2, Con. 2, Chamberlain Township.

Statement of Materials and Supplies on hand October 31st, 1916.

Shop Stock—North Bay.

Class.	Material.	Amount.
1	Air brake material	$1,371 55
2	Wheels, tires and axles	23,698 84
3	Bolts, nuts, etc.	7,106 03
4	Building material	1,617 44
5	Coach fittings	7,961 50
6	Iron castings	7,703 99
7	Couplers and parts	2,021 78
8	Forgings	1,158 89
9	Telegraph and telephone material	1,752 01
10	Electrical material	6,071 81
11	Glass	1,625 00
12	Hardware	1,761 99
13	Brass castings	9,888 25
14	Lamps and parts	967 02
15	Locomotive parts finished	5,819 08
16	Lumber (carpenter shop)	6,208 56
17	" (bridge and building department)	7,434 74
18	Metals	518 09
19	Miscellaneous	3,618 76
21	Water supply service parts	218 64
22	Paints and brushes	2,925 63
23	Pipes, fittings, valves, etc.	5,824 57
26	Hose and rubber	1,567 13
28	Commissary	765 11
29	Springs	2,546 06
30	Iron and steel (bar)	5,773 73
31	Steam shovel, ditcher and ledgerwood parts	504 41
32	Tools, etc.	3,556 18
33	Track material, North Bay	21,190 55
	" , " on line	4,909 78

$148,087 12

Less amount of angle bars and fish plates sold, for which shop stock had
received no debit 187 29

$147,899 83

Shop Stock—Englehart.

Class.	Material.	Amount.
1	Air brake material	$40 19
2	Wheels, tires and axles	11,838 88
3	Bolts, nuts, etc.	567 71
4	Building material	....
5	Coach fittings	33 15
6	Castings	515 62
7	Couplers and parts	333 71
8	Forgings	61 56
9	Telegraph and telephone material	....
10	Electrical material	64 84
11	Glass	70 07
12	Hardware	31 49
13	Brass castings	595 62
14	Lamps and parts	56 23
16	Locomotive parts finished	45 31
16	Lumber (carpenter shop)	....
17	" (bridge and building department)	....
18	Metals	9 11
19	Miscellaneous	222 60
21	Water supply service parts	....
22	Paints and brushes	8 54
23	Pipes, fittings, valves, etc.	394 27
26	Hose and rubber	192 43
28	Commissary	....
29	Springs	226 47
30	Iron and steel (bar)	42 88
31	Steam shovel, ditcher and ledgerwood parts	....

Shop Stock—Englehart.—Continued.

Class.	Material.	Amount.
32	Tools, etc.	$99 19
33	Track material	....
		$15,449 87

Shop Stock—Timmins.

1	Air brake material	$4 41
2	Wheels, tires and axles	86 56
3	Bolts, nuts, etc.	100 85
4	Building material	....
5	Coach fittings	3 30
6	Castings	119 16
7	Couplers and parts	87 85
8	Forgings	44 86
9	Telegraph and telephone material	....
10	Electrical material	10 13
11	Glass	5 42
12	Hardware	2 04
13	Brass castings	....
14	Lamps and parts	11 02
15	Locomotive parts finished	83
16	Lumber (carpenter shop)	....
17 ...	" (bridge and building department)	....
19	Miscellaneous	38 19
21	Water service supply parts	....
22	Paints and brushes	3 86
23	Pipes, fittings and valves	20 84
26	Hose and rubber	58 38
28	Commissary	....
29	Springs	4 34
30	Iron and steel (bar)	....
31	Steam shovel, ditcher and ledgerwood parts	....
32	Tools	10 29
33	Track material	....
		$612 33

Shop Stock—Cochrane.

1	Air brake material	$12 62
2	Wheels, tires and axles	171 52
3	Bolts, nuts, etc.	467 40
4	Building material	08
5	Coach fittings	11 63
6	Castings	144 39
7	Couplers and parts	199 90
8	Forgings	60 48
9	Telegraph and telephone material	....
10	Electrical material	....
11	Glass	1 62
12	Hardware	9 84
13	Brass castings	106 16
14	Lamps and parts	4 74
15	Locomotive parts finished	12 46
16	Lumber (carpenter shop)	....
17	" (bridge and building department)	....
18	Metals	....
19	Miscellaneous	33 23
21	Water supply service parts	7 50
22	Paints and brushes	6 20
23	Pipes, fittings, valves, etc.	52 72
26	Hose and rubber	48 82
28	Commissary	....
29	Springs	47 34
30	Iron and steel (bar)	62
31	Steam shovel, ditcher and ledgerwood parts	....
32	Tools, etc.	27 02
33	Track material	....
		$1,426 29

RECAPITULATION OF SHOP STOCK.

	Amount.
North Bay	$147,899 83
Englehart	15,449 87
Timmins	612 33
Cochrane	1,426 29
	$165,388 32

Less unvouchered material:—

Aikenhead Hardware Co., butts, etc.	$144 00	
Westinghouse Co., air brake material	13 30	
Steel Company of Canada, nuts	11 60	
John Bourke, plaster and lime	9 85	
Lindsay & McCluskey, lime	16 80	
Richardson, J. W., tar paper	48 32	
Begg Bros., cheese cloth and cotton	13 25	
Wagar Furniture Co., mattresses	5 00	
Imperial Oil Company, oil	31 73	
P. McCool, piles	140 00	
		433 85
		$164,954 47

Plus freight and duty paid in October but material not
vouchered until November, 1916:

Northern Electric order No. 2676	$ 65	
Stone & Co., No. 2556	87	
F. Young, Chicago	7 88	
O. F. Jordan	1 97	
R. Ryerson	2 38	
		13 75
		$164,968 22

Stationery Stock.

North Bay		$5,564 45
Less unvouchered material:—		
Form No. 1708	$4 38	
" 1533	1 01	
" 2028	25 30	
2029	25 50	
		56 19
		$5,508 26

Oil and Waste Stock.

North Bay	$4,497 00
Elk Lake	25 98
Englehart	546 06
Timmins	123 06
Cochrane	411 50
	$5,603 60

Tie Stock.

North Bay and on line	$6,475 45

Ice Stock.

North Bay	$419 84
Englehart	22 40
Cochrane	32 00
	$474 24

Anthracite Coal.

	Weight.
North Bay freight office	16,250
" " ice house	5,500
' " " stores shed	99,000
Widdifield	28,500
Tomiko	26,000
Redwater	21,500
Temagami	33,940
Latchford	52,000
Cobalt	94,500
North Cobalt	35,660
Haileybury	102,400
New Liskeard	80,032
Uno Park	6,000
Thornloe	41,000
Earlton	51,360
Elk Lake	30,000
Heaslip	31,000
Englehart	190,760
Charlton	49,000
Dane	36,750
Swastika	35,000
Matheson	2,700
Porquis Jct.	101,280
Iroquois Falls	6,400
Porcupine	32,000
South Porcupine	103,080
Schumacher	69,208
Timmins	11,000
Cochrane	35,632

1,430,432 or 715½ tons

715½ tons at $6.70 per ton $4,791 84

Bituminous Coal.

	Weight.
North Bay	41,500,000
Widdifield	79,000
Tomiko	34,000
Redwater	109,000
Temagami	33,760
Latchford	23,000
New Liskeard	47,820
Elk Lake	40,000
Englehart	773,277
Matheson	17,000
Porquis Junction	682,900
Timmins	56,350
Cochrane	744,000

44,140,107 or 22,070 N.T.

8,471 tons at $4.70 per ton................................... $39,813 70
13,599 "   "   4.60 "   " 62,555 40

22,070 $102,369 10

Less value of confiscated coal less freight and duty.
Car 209996 }
       76658 } $261 74
To advance charges not paid on car 12120 .... 57 75

                                                                319 49

                                                              $102,049 61

Rail Stock.

North Bay and on line $30,592 89

Summary.

Shop stock	$164,968 22
Stationery	5,508 26
Oil and waste	5,603 60
Ties	6,475 45
Ice	474 24
Anthracite coal	4,791 84
Bituminous coal	102,049 61
Rails	30,592 89
Total	$320,464 11

TRAFFIC AND MILEAGE STATISTICS.

Passenger Traffic.

1. Total passengers carried earning revenue	485,759
2. Number of passengers carried one mile	26,972,091
3. Number of passengers carried one mile per mile of road	82,107
4. Average distance carried—miles	55.53
5. Total passenger revenue	$624,808 12
6. Average amount received from each passenger	1 29
7. Average receipts per passenger per mile (cents)	.02.32
8. Total passenger train service revenue	713,883 92
9. Passenger service train revenue per mile of road	2,173 16
10. Passenger service train revenue per train mile	1 33

Freight Traffic.

11. Number of tons carried earning revenue	922,618
12. Number of tons carried earning revenue one mile	173,842,519
13. Number of tons carried earning revenue one mile per mile of road....	529,201
14. Average distance haul of one ton—miles	188.42
15. Total freight revenue	$1,331,614 31
16. Average amount received for each ton	1 44
17. Average amount received per ton per mile (cents)	.00.77
18. Freight revenue per mile of road	4,053 62
19. Freight revenue per train mile	2 18

Total Traffic.

20. Operating revenue	$2,138,121 95
21. Operating revenue per mile of road	6,508 74
22. Operating revenue per train mile	1 97
23. Operating expenses	1,594,177 46
24. Operating expenses per mile of road	4,852 90
25. Operating expenses per train mile	1 47
26. Net operating revenue	543,944 49
27. Net operating revenue per mile of road	1,655 84

Car Mileage.

28. Average number of passengers carried one mile per car mile	9.7
29. Average number of passengers carried one mile per train mile	50
30. Average number of passenger cars per train mile	5.2
31. Mileage of passenger cars	2,795,427
32. Mileage of loaded freight cars—north and east	4,541,996
33. Mileage of loaded freight cars—south and west	4,288,824
34. Mileage of empty freight cars—north and east	1,210,883
35. Mileage of empty, freight cars—south and west	1,807,612
36. Average number of freight cars per train mile	19.4
37. Average number of loaded freight cars per train mile	14.5
38. Average number of empty freight cars per train mile	4.9
39. Average number of tons freight per train mile	285
40. Average number of tons freight per loaded car mile	19.7
41. Average mileage operated during year	328.5

Train Mileage.

42. Mileage of revenue passenger trains	475,833
43. Mileage of revenue mixed trains	60,430
44. Mileage of revenue freight trains	549,094
45. Total revenue train mileage	1,085,357

STATEMENT OF LAND PURCHASED.

November 1st, 1915, to October 31st, 1916.

Simon Henerofsky—north half Lot 1, Con. 5 Chamberlain—1.5 acres........	$75 00
J. Hampden Field—Lot 1, Con. 3 Chamberlain—1 acre	50 00
John Stockdale—Lot 73, North Bay Jct.	1,500 00
Province of Ontario—South Half Lot 2, Con. 2 Newmarket—	
1.24 acres	1 20
North Half Lot 2, Con. 2 Newmarket—.83 acres	80
J. J. Belland—North Half Lot 2, Con. 2 Newmarket—.83 acres	2 00
Chas. P. Scott—South Half Lot 2, Con. 2 Newmarket—1.24 acres	40 00
H. T. Routley—Lots 220´and 221, parcel No. 4675, registered plan M.73	60 00
Haileybury	1,750 00
Imperial Oil Co., Ltd.—Block "F" east side of Gore Street, North Bay ...	2,000 00
Total	$5,477 00

TOWNSITES REPORT.

Statement Receipts and Expenditure—Nov. 1, 1915, to Oct. 31, 1916.

EXPENDITURES.

Latchford.
Donation to Town 200 00

Englehart.
Donation to Town towards installation of Sewerage and Waterworks System 1,318 54

Matheson.
Donation to Town 250 00

Cochrane.
Taxes $151 51
Clearing 100 00
— 251 51

General and miscellaneous expenses 3,247 69
Credit to profit and loss 2,982 87

$8,250 61

RECEIPTS.

Received on lots sold during year.
Englehart	$253 20
Matheson	559 20
Matheson Sub-division	18 75
Monteith	26 25
Porquis Junction ..	37 50
Cochrane	64 00
Cochrane Annex ...	1,286 50
	$2,245 40

Received on deferred payments.
Temagami	$25 00
Cobalt	499 00
Englehart	1,531 18
Dane	37 50
Matheson	338 46
Matheson Sub-division	170 00
Monteith	179 30
Porquis Junction ..	511 80
Cochrane	658 33
Cochrane Annex ...	385 00
	4,335 57

Interest received on deferred payments.
Cobalt	$48 93
Englehart	436 35
Dane	16 79
Matheson	73 54
Matheson Sub-division	39 49
Monteith	18 10
Porquis Junction ..	132 41
Cochrane	233 85
Cochrane Sub-division	109 51
Cochrane Annex ...	23 57
	1,132 54

Interest received on bank deposit 283 10
Hay sold from Englehart Townsite 50 00
Rent lots, Cobalt 179 00
Rent lots, Matheson 25 00

$8,250 61

TOWNSITES ACCOUNTS.

Statement of Lots Sold—Townsites—Nov. 1, 1915, to Oct. 31, 1916.

—	Lots Sold.	Sale Price.		Amount Paid.	Balance due.
		$ c.	$ c.	$ c.	$ c.
Englehart........	1	1 00*			
	1 Parcel (40 Acres)	612 00			
	2 " (37 ")	1,110 00			
	1 " (17 ")	800 00			
	1 " (40 ")	204 00			
			2,727 00	253 20	2,473 80
Matheson	16	975 00			
	1 Parcel (22 Acres)	936 00			
	1 " (121 ")	2,420 00			
			4,331 00	559 20	3,771 80
Matheson—Sub-					
division	1	....	75 00	18 75	56 25
Monteith	2	....	105 00	26 25	78 75
Porquis Junction..	1	....	150 00	37 50	112 50
Cochrane	4	....	320 00	64 00	256 00
Cochrane Annex...	507	5,785 00			
	Block " B "	500 00			
			6,285 00	1,286 50	4,998 50
			13,993 00	2,245 40	11,747 60

*Corporation of the Town of Englehart.

Field of Hay, Farm of Mr. A. Slade, New Liskeard, Ont.

Statement Showing Employees, Total Days Worked, Average Daily Compensation, Etc.

November 1st, 1915, to October 31st, 1916.

Class.	Number.	Total days worked.	Total compensation.	Average daily compensation.
			$ c.	$ c.
I. *General Offices:*				
1. General officers	7	2,562	16,759 92	6 54
2. Chief Clerks	5	1,830	7,340 00	4 01
3. Other Clerks	56	14,518	30,069 27	2 07
4. Stenographers and Typists.	16	4,305	7,814 25	1 81
5. Telegraph and Telephone Operators				
6. Messengers and Attendants				
7. Other General Office Employees	11	3,749	9,744 89	2 60
Total	95	26,964	71,728 33	1 94
II. *Road:*				
11. Officers	6	2,225	13,108 54	5 89
12. Clerks	11	3,628	8,985 06	2 48
13. Shop foremen	1	227	807 04	3 56
14. Structural iron workers..				
15. Machinists				
16. Masons and bricklayers ..				
17. Carpenters	5	5,112	14,536 62	2 84
18. Painters	3	724	1,992 16	2 75
19. Other M. W. S. shopmen ..				
20. Other skilled laborers	1	272	746 46	2 74
21. Section foremen	50	16,251	45,098 46	2 78
22. Watchmen and trackwalkers		186	465 00	2 50
23. Other sectionmen	162	59,689	117,498 81	1 97
24. Unskilled laborers	2	362	871 68	2 41
25. All other M. W. S. employees	14	6,739	15,767 36	2 34
26. Foremen of construction gangs	10	2,759	9,291 71	3 37
27. Other men in construction gangs ....:.......	78	23,018	46,021 77	2 00
Total ......:......	343	121,192	275,190 67	2 27
III. *Equipment:*				
31. Officers..	3	1,081	5,278 75	4 88
32. Clerks and attendants	7	1,700	3,205 88	1 89
33. Shop foremen	6	2,206	8,379 00	3 80
34. Machinists	19	6,088	23,390 62	3 84
35. Carpenters	21	5,900	18,778 36	3 18
36. Painters and upholsterers.	11	3,870	10,960 39	2 83
37. Other shopmen	109	29,227	68,891 83	2 36
38. Car inspectors	9	3,827	10,329 72	2 70
39. Watchmen				
40. All other M. E. employees.	24	7,477	18,293 96	2 45
Total	209	61,376	167,508 51	2 73
IV. *Traffic:*				
51. Officers	1	366	2,400 00	6 56
52. Clerks and attendants	7	3,454	6,118 32	1 77
53. Travelling solicitors				
54. Employees in outside agencies				
55. All other traffic employees.				
Total	8	3,820	8,518 32	2 23

Statement Showing Employees, Total Days Worked, Average Daily
Compensation, Etc.—Continued.

November 1st, 1915, to October 31st, 1916.

Class.	Number.	Total. days worked.	Total compensation.	Average daily compensation.
			$ c.	$ c.
V. *Transportation:*				
71. Officers	3	1,098	7,105 00	6 47
72. Clerks and attendants ...	10	3,201	6,078 61	1 90
73. Despatchers	4	1,624	8,769 58	5 40
74. Station agents	27	10,506	34,829 20	3 32
75. Operators not agents	24	9,269	26,046 50	2 81
76. Other station employees ..	170	47,073	83,478 70	1 77
77. Yardmasters & yard clerks	15	6,057	11,701 98	1 93
78. Yard enginemen..........	8	4,396	15,353 36	3 49
79. Yard conductors and brakemen	12	6,556	24,252 54	3 70
80. Yard switchmen	....	....	....	....
81. Other yard employees	....	....	....	....
82. Enginehouse employees ...	30	12,431	28,041 00	2 26
83. Road enginemen and motormen	50	30,287	114,296 03	3 71
84. Passenger conductors	5	4,600	15,046 75	3 27
85. Freight conductors	17	8,840	37,285 26	4 22
86. Other road trainmen	48	30,177	75,039 03	2 49
87. Operators, interlockers and signals	....	....	....	....
88. Crossing flagmen and gatemen ....·.......	....	....	....	....
89. Drawbridge operators	....	....	....	....
90. Employees on floating equipment	....	....	....	....
91. Employees in express service	....	....	....	....
92. Employees in claim dept..	....	....	....	....
93. All other trans. employees	31	11,564	22,561 37	1 95
Total	454	187,679	509,884 91	2 71
Grand Total	1,109	401,031	1,032,830 74	2 57
Construction	130	34,496	85,707 99	2 48
Total payroll	1,239	435,527	1,118,538 73	2 56
Donations to Employees Enlisted for Overseas Service	....	....	9,347 01	....
Total	....	....	1,127,885 74	....

STATEMENT OF WAGES PAID EMPLOYEES—YEAR ENDED OCTOBER 31st, 1916.

Office of Secretary-Treasurer.

Maund, W. H. .... Secretary-Treasurer	$2,499 96	
Odlum, A. B. .... Chief Clerk	1,020 00	
Pratt, A. B. .... Clerk	1,800 00	
Downing, Miss A. .... Stenographer	900 00	
McNeice, Miss H. .... "	750 00	
Southby, Miss G. .... "	630 00	
Odlum, Miss R. .... "	660 00	
Brocklehurst, Miss H. ...... Clerk	344 52	
Way, Miss K. .... Filing Clerk	369 35	
Whiteside, W. .... Mail Clerk	30 00	
Corbett, G. .... "	50 00	
		$9,053 83

Office of Auditor of Disbursements and Accountant.

Gracey, T. J. .... Auditor of Disbursements and Accountant	$1,920 00	
Hamilton, D. .... Assistant Accountant	1,500 00	
May, E. N. .... Clerk	1,140 00	
Saunderson, G. S. .... "	870 00	
Mack, R. F. .... "	435 00	
Jones, R. V. .... "	240 00	
Robinson, Miss S. .... "	720 00	
Johnson, Miss G. .... Stenographer	250 00	
Henaghan, Miss A. .... "	397 58	
McPhee, Miss K. .... Clerk	367 74	
Harris, Miss I. M. .... "	323 33	
Lennox, Miss V. .... Jr. "	150 00	
Martin, R. .... Jr. "	28 06	$8,341 71

Office of Mining Engineer.

Cole, A. A. .... Mining Engineer	$3,420 00	
Tittensor, Miss E. .... Stenographer	733 87	
Molyneaux, Miss M. .... "	46 13	$4,200 00

Office of Superintendent of Traffic.

Griffin, W. A. .... Supt. Traffic	$3,240 00
Ryan, S. H. .... Trainmaster	2,040 00
Faught, S. J. .... Chief Clerk	1,300 00
Brown, C. F. .... Stenographer and Clerk	598 00
Bain, J. .... Clerk	800 00
Cormack, J. .... "	289 66
Faught, W. F. .... "	25 50
Brockway, W. L. .... "	648 83
Foley, P. S. .... "	340 00
Beaton, W. S. .... "	334 84
Calder, A. .... "	10 64
Newell, M. .... Stenographer	613 47
Gregory, K. E. .... "	645 00
Munns, V. .... "	9 00
Reynolds, E. .... "	22 14
Nugent, P. .... "	218 06
Morgan, P. .... "	72 70
Fitzgerald, H. .... "	25 04
Brewster, L. .... Porter	780 00
Monette, A. P. .... "	780 00
Perry, J. .... "	9 00
Swain, W. .... "	87 99
Swan, R. .... Constable	985 00

Office of Superintendent of Traffic.—Continued.

Hudson, J.	Special Officer	$5 03
Laupret, L.	"	12 34
O'Hare, P.	"	12 34
O'Hare, J.	"	12 34
Daly, J.		12 34
Riddler, C.		10 88
Hudson, J.	"	12 34
Hume, J.	Janitor	840 00
Hume, Mrs. J.	Janitress	7 74
Tompkin, J.	Office Boy	117 16
Martin, R.	"	83
Rayner, E.	Stenographer	7 74

$14,925 95

Office of Paymaster.

Ferguson, C. L.	Paymaster	$2,220 00
Cousineau, L. J.	Chief Clerk	890 00
Amos, H. C.	Clerk	80 00

$3,190 00

Office of Auditor and Car Accountant, Auditor Receipts and Car Accountant, Freight Claims Agent.

Mitchell, R. H.	A. & C. A.'	$1,520 00
Harper, W. J.	A. R. & C. A.	600 00
Teskey, H. W.	C. C. & F. C. A.	1,290 00
McGee, H. H.	Travelling Auditor	1,560 00
Willis, J. B.	" "	1,370 00
Brockway, H.	Clerk	890 00
Brennan, J. B.	"	827 50
Lavery, T. H.	"	820 00
Cartmill, G. H.		760 00
Keeler, S. T.		307 50
Peel, R.		585 73
McCausland, J.	"	455 00
Doidge, M.	"	625 00
Campbell, Mrs. M.	"	505 00
Amos, D.		480 00
Smith, G.		510 00
Sheppard, Mrs. B.	"	319 52
McKeown, J.		190 00
Duncan, H.		166 13
Conroy, P. A.		51 30
McEdwards, W.	"	625 00
Martin, H.	"	259 10
Miller, F.	"	133 06
Cocksedge, G.	"	349 35
Brockway, L.		194 19
Trotter, A. T.	"	272 00
Gallagher, J. A.	"	292 74
Jones, W.		257 50
Rigby, H.		191 94
Freeman, B.		129 84
Harrison, C.		114 03
Knapp, E. A.		157 26
Douglass, M. B.		156 77
Kelly, T. J.		101 83
Osborne, A.		23 71
Hamilton, Mrs. C.	"	10 16
Palmer, G. E.	Claim Inspector	300 00
Fitzgerald, H.	Stenographer	282 50
Ansell, H. V.	"	454 27
Rayner, J. E.	"	249 33
Casey, M.		208 79
Winters, G.		160 00
Wilson, N. R.	"	180 00
Munns, I.	"	16 77

Office of Auditor and Car Accountant, etc.—Continued.

Lefebvre, A. ....Stenographer	$127 74		
Sherman, M. .... "	40 00		
Brockie, P. ....Laborer	1 00		
Fitzsimmons, T. .... ", ...	1 83		
		$19,123 39

Land Department.

Lee, G. W. ....Commissioner and Land Agent...	$2,499 96	
Bauldry, W. J. ....Townsite Inspector	1,300 00	
Palmer, G. E. ....Col. Inspector	900 00	
Gregory, Miss T. ....Stenographer	780 00	
		$5,479 96

Office of General Freight and Passenger Agent.

Parr, A. J. ....G. F. & P. A.	$2,400 00	
Harper, W. J. ....Chief Clerk	1,070 00	
Banks, E. C. .... "	1,070 00	
Jones, W. ....Clerk	495 00	
Kelly, T. J. .... "	311 70	
McLeod, R. C. .... "	505 00	
Gauthier, J. A. .... "	222 50	
Martin, R. M. ....Office Boy and Clerk	122 52	
Aubrey, A. ....·... " "	26 67	
Burritt, W. .... " "	330 00	
Silverthorne, W. G. .... " "	31 45	
Milligan, M. ....Stenographer	306 50	
Crummie, M. A. .... "	200 30	
Casey, M. .... "	243 63	
Anderson, F. R.	570 00	
Jessup, A. L.	366 13	
Wilson, N. R.	85 64	
Winters, G.	60 64	
Munns, I.	7 74	
Taylor, E. L.	92 90	
		$8,518 32

Train Despatchers.

Lamb, R. L. ....Chief Despatcher	$2,220 00	
Chatterton, C. D. ....Despatcher	2,162 47	
Workman, R. .... "	2,161 75	
Trowhill, R.	1,869 12	
Dwyer, J. H. ....Operator and Despatcher	1,140 03	
Clark, M. G. ....Operator	15 83	
Prentice, R. .... "	122 07	
Cattley, B. .... "	292 27	
		$9,983 54

Purchasing and Stores Department.

Graham, W. A. ....P. A. & S. K.	$2,400 00
Alford, G. B. ....Chief Clerk	1,310 00
Freeman, A. ....Clerk	1,125 00
Tarsey, S. G. .... "	860 00
Valliant, E. R. .... "	528 48
Newman, A. C.	193 06
Elston, E.	211 77
Fletcher, D. R. .... "	330 00
Donegan, E. J. ....Stenographer	498 00
Polk, V. K. .... "	18 33
Darling, E. J. ....·...... "	598 40
McGonegal, G.	146 32
Munns, I. .... "	33 55
Sale, T. M. ....Foreman	1,310 00
Dignan, J. C. ....Storeman	786 00
Depledge, F. .... "	786 00
Daly, G. L. .... "	534 71

Purchasing and Stores Department.—Continued.

Bigg, J. E.	Storeman	$600 00
Jones, R. J.	"	19 64
Prue, A.	"	45 29
Cavanagh, A. W.	Inspector	845 16
English, W.	"	1,085 75
McManus, J.	Yard Foreman	903 90
Couch, A.	Laborer	575 70
Labrecque, J.	"	573 65
Watkin, W.	Storekeeper, Englehart	1,056 00

$17,374 71

Freight Office, North Bay.

Baker, C. O.	Agent	$1,800 00
King, A. T.	Chief Clerk	1,014 35
Sullivan, M. J.	Cashier	790 00
Knapp, E. A.	Clerk	436 13
Forrest, W., Sr.	"	805 00
Gibson, R.	"	756 45
Gallagher, J. A.		357 12
Thompson, J. C.		232 42
Prentice, M.		262 58
Forrest, W., Jr.		560 00
Lapointe, H.		530 80
Fetterly, U. A.		76 77
Martin, C.		91 45
Tompkins, J.		18 55
Winters, O.		54 14
Falby, F.		105 89
Beatty, I.		40 00
Biggs, P.		2 58
McNutt, H. M.		400 64
Newman, A. C.		30 35
Samler, W.		44 26
Trotter, A. T.		140 00
Redden, J. B.		47 89
Duncan, A. R.	"	186 29
Lansloot, R.	"	125 84
Fitzsimmons, G.		99 68
Axler, T.	"	186 61
Nugent, P.	Stenographer	408 83
Carr, B.	"	150 97
Devine, M.	"	145 16
Brown, E.	"	44 84
McGillis, A.	Messenger	99 56
Willis, F.	"	322 14
Lariviere, A.	"	41 66
Aubrey, J. N.	"	18 67
Wilson, C. J.		23 59

$10,451.21

Freight Shed, North Bay.

Sharvell, F. W.	Foreman	$1,070 00
Ashford, S.	Timekeeper	761 00
Dugard, W.	Checker	756 00
Rogers, A. E.	"	310 00
Pratt, C.	"	756 00
Smith, A.		232 00
White, R.	"	377 16
Webber, S.	"	751 95
Reddeway, W. H.		808 00
Bird, W. A.		808 00
Sperritt, W.	"	704 00
McNutt, H.	"	244 35
Yorkston, A.		580 00
Pike, F.		727 88
Brigginshaw, W.	"	527 72

10 T.R.

Freight Shed, North Bay.—Continued.

Cox, J. ,	Checker		$706 33
Pugh, A.	"		681 58
Relph, R.	"		246 77
Fitzsimmons, T.			616 67
Barber, W.			540 62
English, J.	"		338 72
Gall, A.	"		649 19
Cockerline, J.			113 06
Childerhose, R.			370 00
Thompson, J. C.			247 21
Brousseau, L.	"		314 68
Connolly, W.			45 00
James, V.			22 37
Truckers and Laborers			8,559 20

$22,865 46

Yard Office, North Bay Junction.

McKerrow, J. O.	Yardmaster		$844 05
Ness, C.	"		1,652 91
Richmond, J. N.	"		768 57
Bradford, J. N.	"		213 75
Treacy, W. L.	"		9 03
Roberts, C. A.	Operator		1,296 25
Cattley, B.	"		274 88
Dwyer, J. H.	"		248 19
Clark, M. G.	"		992 08
Dudley, H. A.	"		160 69
Oulette, A.			226 69
Borthwick, T. D.			98 23
Brasher, S. M.	"		134 12
Knowles, R. T.	"		261 97
Thompson, W. A. S.	Chief Clerk		950 00
Wissler, J. S.	Clerk		815 00
Wright, W. T.	"		661 93
Elston, F.	"		700 00
Chamberlain, S.	"		357 98
Thom, W.	"		229 60
Daly, R.			109 68
Samler, W.			618 40
Donegan, J. C.	"		610 00
Archambault, O.	"		260 64
Archambault, J. O.	"		466 25
Lapointe, E.	"		358 63
Thompson, J. C.	"		49 84
Herbert, E. R.	"		35 48
Prentice, R.	Checker		42 57
Martin, C.	"		10 16
Biggs, P.	"		8 71
Connolly, W.	"		81 29
Edey, J.	Messenger		410 92
Brown, D.	"		456 87
Barnhardt, W. D.	"		80
McGillis, A.			217 33
Harvey, C.			81
Edey, C.	"		20 18
Mallory, B.			80
Gauthier, J.			40
Doyle, R.			1 64
Edwards, E.			40
Patterson, B.	"		2 16
Lensby, J.			158 53
Soule, A.			220 96
Gubb, G.	"		31 45
Hawkins, J.	"		7 26
Lansloot, R.	"		22 22
Barnhardt, W.			63 40
Aubry, J.			2 82

Yard Office, North Bay Junction.—Continued.

Dubois, H. ....Messenger	$48 33	
Peak, W. .... "	83	
Soule, F. .... "	24 64	
Chase, H. F. ....Signalman	1 77	
Prou, A. .... "	257 25	
Cramp, A. .... "	253 71	
Caley, C. .... "	5 32	
Fetterley, W. ....Call Boy	352 06	
Colbon, W. ....Janitor	100 00	
Brousseau, L. T. ....Sanitary Work	1 50	
O'Hara, H. .... "	1 50	
		$16,213 43

Widdifield Station.

Deagle, L. A. ....Agent	$982 26	$982 26

Tomiko Station.

Smith, A. J. ....Agent	$1,154 05	
Vanmeer, A. W. ....Operator	77 66	
Durand, J. B. .... "	2 19	
Dudley, H. A. .... "	742 23	
Marshall, R. S.	35 54	
Noble, S. G.	33 90	
Fisher, C. E.	23 51	
Oulette, A.	23 00	
		$2,092 08

Diver Station.

Baker, T. J. ....Agent	$79 88	$79 88

Redwater Station.

Baker, T. J. ....Agent	$1,142 51	
Valliere, J. L. ....Relieving Agent	44 60	
		$1,187 11

Temagami Station.

Picard, J. W. ....Agent	$979 86	
Clark, M. G. .... "	239 72	
Marshall, R. S. ....Relieving Agent	27 50	
Beaton, W. S. ....Baggageman	8 87	
Calder, A. .... "	62 10	
Purcell, A. D. .... "	67 74	
Bouley, E. ....Cleaning	5 00	
Derosier, T. .... "	5 00	
		$1,395 79

Latchford Station.

Richardson, R. ....Agent	$1,390 18	
Marshall, R. S. ....Relieving Agent	60 75	
Brown, H. G. ....Operator	361 30	
Dudley, H. A. .... "	14 87	
Beemer, F. B.	38 16	
Oulette, A.	50 85	
Durand, J. B.	364 73	
Switzer, H. R. .... "	115 10	
Sullivan, T. W. ....Sanitary Work	5 00	
		$2,400 94

Cobalt Station.

Way, D. H. ....Agent	$1,785 00	
Marshall, R. S. ....Operator	86 85	
Earle, W. R. .... "	1,290 17	

Cobalt Station.—Continued.

Nixon, E. ....Chief Clerk	$940	00
Carter, W. ....Clerk	706	00
Way, V. L. .... "	111	77
Stuckey, H. .... "	130	00
Borland, A.	344	00
Skillicorn, H.	633	87
Downard, F. .... "	229	35
Bywaters, H. ....Checker	773	23
Bell, R. .... "	350	00
Monkhouse, T. .... "	437	00
Whitehead, H. ....Baggageman	840	00
Drew, S. ....Clerk	300	65
Borland, W. .... "	225	00
McLaughlin, J. .... "	159	82
Hyde, S.	85	50
Brewer, W. B.	258	63
Copps, G.	14	76
Brewer, M.	53	71
Clark, R.	138	13
Fitzgerald, Mrs. J.	117	74
Fetterly, U.	21	76
Way, W. K.	73	50
Asseltine, G.	45	82
Renaud, A.	6	00
Sweeney, H. J.	100	00
Gregor, M. .... "	27	26
O'Kelly, A. ....Stenographer	402	58
Lawrence, R. .... "	429	83
Maxwell, V. .... "	23	42
Crummie, M.	100	39
Stewart, M.	46	13
Mayer, M. .... "	143	23
Lafonde, G.	4	84
Bowman, J. H. ....Constable	865	00
Lejambe, W. ....Checker	230	32
Bortimore, E. .... "	79	84
Lavergne, N. .... "	10	64
Forget, E. ....Trucker	14	19
Champagne, A. .... "	15	97
Darbyson, H. .... "	14	19
Perrault, O.	56	00
Perrault, G.	56	00
Lafontesie, A.	10	08
Williams, H. .... "	262	87
Fisher, W. ....Janitor	15	00
St. Pierre, A. .... "	10	00
Bartlett, Mrs. M. .... "	460	00

$13,536 04

North Cobalt Station.

Gibbon, G. ....Agent	$1,000	25
O'Brien, H. ....Sanitary Work...................	6	00

$1,006 25

Haileybury Station.

Shibley, J. H. ....Agent	$1,567	63
Trousdale, F. A. ....Operator	1,071	13
Marshall, R. S. .... "	51	08
White, G. J. ....Clerk ...:	111	29
Copner, J. M. .... "	842	73
Harris, J. B. .... "	606	41
Shibley, E. M.	195	97
Wonch, E. E.	251	94
Wattam, M. J.	317	58
Hunter, H. .... "	41	51
Roach, I. M. ....Stenographer	332	42

Haileybury Station.—Continued.

Duffett, I. S. ....Baggageman	$885 16	
Allingham, J. ....Shed Foreman	11 67	
Edwards, T. .... "	62 42	
Dickson, A. .... "	157 42	
Pinkney, A. ....Trucker	22 58	
Hoolyhan, C. .... "	261 29	
Spence, Mrs. M. E. ....Cleaning	16 00	
		$6,806 23

New Liskeard Station.

Goodman, E. M. ....Agent	$1,426 50	
Milne, W. B. ....C. Clerk and R. Agent	963 33	
Durand, J. B. ....Operator	111 76	
Holt, F. G. .... "	1,049 92	
Murphy, E. M. .... "	771 97	
Dudley, H. A.	49 46	
Valliere, J. L.	51 11	
Hainer, J. R. .... "	15 68	
Wolfe, P. ....Baggageman	220 00	
Herron, F. ....Clerk	420 00	
Ramsay, W. .... "	730 00	
Cragg, F. .... "	176 64	
Brown, R. W.	392 02	
Haggart, W.	24 50	
Brown, W. .... "	46 03	
Wilson, S. ....Checker	315 81	
McRoberts, F. ....Messenger	56 87	
Maloney, M. .... "	41 93	
Davis, E. .... "	40 75	
Brown, K. .... "	21 19	
Stafford, E. I. ....Janitor	245 81	
Hogg, A. .... "	160 00	
McMillan, P. .... " ...,...................	35 00	
		$7,366 28

Uno Park Station.

Doherty, M. R. ....Agent	$967 83	
Marshall, R. S. ....Relieving Agent .:...............	46 53	
O'Brien, H. ....Sanitary Work	6 00	
		$1,020 36

Thornloe Station.

Caldwell, W. H. ....Agent	$939 94	
Murphy, E. M. ....Relieving Agent	43 77	
		$983 71

Earlton Station.

Buchanan, L. ....Agent	$1,132 86	
Brasher, S. M. ....Relieving Agent	128 70	
McMinn, R. ....Clerk	70 97	
McConomy, J. K. .... "	372 13	
Hall, G. W. .... "	9 68	
Brown, R. M.	6 90	
Blanchett, N. J. .... "	135 48	
O'Brien, H. ....Sanitary Work................	12 00	
		$1,868 72

Elk Lake Station.

Belanger, O. ....Agent	$1,380 08	
Murphy, E. M. ....Relieving Agent	50 03	
Aubert, B. ....Clerk	66 13	
Champagne. L, ...Messenger	2 50	
Staniski. Mrs. T. ....Janitress	60 00	
Staniski, T. ....Janitor ....:..	16 00	
		$1,574 74

Heaslip Station.

Chouinard, J. ....Agent ....,	$983 02	
Beemer, J. H. ....Relieving Agent	24 19	
Murphy, E. M. .... "	25 03	
		$1,032 24

Englehart Station.

Murray, F. J. ....Agent	$1,316 45
Brown, A. W. ....Relieving Agent	66 79
Beemer, J. H. ....Operator	29 16
Borthwick, T. D. .... "	166 56
Bruce, G. .... "	1,368 56
Pelkie, J. A.	1,250 51
Prentice, R.	23 87
Oulette, A. .... "	52 58
Errett, F. A. ....Clerk	780 00
Nudds, T. ....·............. "	549 13
Gray, E. .....·............ "	61 29
Plumb, S.	3 06
Soper, W. .... "	351 28
Gray, S. C. ....Shed Foreman	468 58
Monkhouse, T. .... "	331 01
Fox, G. ....Trucker	282 01
Murray, C. .... "	205 32
Haskins, A. .... "	2 01
Phillips, W. H.	73 03
Pullen, C. '.................	1 53
Vreeland, C.	12 82
Graham, J.	6 33
Jarvie, R. .... ··	78 51
Graham, J.	39 84
Merritt, L.	35 60
Vreeland, E.	240 68
Mantha, O. .... ··	6 93
Healy, M. .... ··	6 76
Rowe, J. G.	58 13
Free, W.	80 38
Simpkins, A.	6 71
Stevens, D. R. .... "	45 29
Peden, A. ....Checker	27 10
Wright, V. .... "	48 85
Perrault, G. .... "	30 99
McDonald, A.	145 90
Lennox, S. .... · ··	21 82
Price, A. .... "	320 79
Hough, C. .... "	303 35
Atkinson, H. C. ....Baggageman	130 00
Fennell, J. C. .... "	275 80
Bentley, R. ....Call Boy	119 40
McLean, J. W. .... "	2 42
Preston, G. .... "	19 41
. Ranstead, T.	159 46
Herron, W. .... ··	25 81
Antram, W. .... "	90 33
Price, T. ....Janitor	586 98
Garovitch, M. ....Sanitary Work	12 00
	$10,321 12

Charlton Station.

Price, J. T. ....Agent	$432 39
Brocklebank, C. H. .... " ...., ...	560 51
Prentice, R. ....Relieving Agent	65 59
Marshall, R. S. .... _"	40 19
Kennedy, E. ....Clerk	102 42
Rogers, G. .... "	. 197 58
Moronesky, N. ....Sanitary Work	2 00
	$1,400 68

Dane Station.

Marshall, C.	Agent	$1,094 48	
Valliere, J. L.	Operator	16 20	
Westerbrook, G.	"	23 57	
			$1,134 25

Swastika Station.

Brennan, W. W.	Agent	$1,020 97	
Bates, G. H.	Operator	53 31	
Wright, S.	Clerk	208 06	
Webber, W. S.	"	212 68	
Moore, T.	Checker	3 87	
Furlong, A.	Telephone Operator	425 69	
Wright, G.	"	45 77	
Boisvert, G.	"	21 99	
Boivin, E.	"	94 84	
Gomerick, J.	Sanitary Work	5 00	
			$2,092 18

Bourkes Station.

Valliere, J. L.	Operator	$281 15	
Hainer, J. R.	"	852 26	
Oulette, A.	"	17 35	
			$1,150 76

Matheson Station.

Ackerman, T. R.	Agent	$1,381 22	
Beemer, J. H.	Operator	67 90	
Westbrook, J.	"	26 63	
Westbrook, G.	"	22 89	
Prentice, R.	"	17 14	
Valliere, J. L.	"	7 33	
Bates, G. H.	"	263 86	
Swayne, R.	"	22 84	
Johnston, L.	Clerk	166 45	
Ginn, J. A.	"	553 55	
Whitehead, P. G.	"	241 56	
Wilson, E.	"	436 51	
Leitch, J. M.	"	105 00	
Cameron, R.	Checker	68 00	
Munns, I.	Stenographer	63 35	
Roach, H.	"	21 29	
Cousineau, F.	"	30 16	
Brown, A.	Cleaning	10 00	
Smith, Mrs. K.	"	20 00	
Minter, Mrs. J.	"	5 00	
Kingston, Mrs. J.	"	4 50	
Coyne, J.	"	15 00	
Brown, W.	Messenger	53 55	
			$3,603 73

Porquis Jct. Station.

Beemer, F. B.	Agent	$1,048 86	
Vanmeer, E. W.	Operator	1,059 10	
Pelkie, J. A.	"	114 33	
Oulette, A.	"	50 35	
Bates, G. H.	"	411 44	
Ludford, L.	Telephone Operator	420 00	
Beemer, J. H.	Operator	263 08	
McConomy, J. K.	Clerk	232 42	
Boicey, W. H.	"	154 35	
Leitch, J. M.	"	538 87	
McDonald, G.	"	23 42	
Rowlandson, J.	"	23 83	

Porquis Junction Station.—Continued.

Hess, D.	...................Clerk	$46 13
Hooey, L.	"	17 74
Knapp, F.	...............:.Baggageman	284 17
Switzer, H.	...............Checker	28 98
Hopkins, W.	"	4 84
Clark, H. W.	"	73 73
Beatty, H.	"	363 50
Jensen, A.	"	236 16
Osborne, A.	.................Cleaning	37 50
Nolting, Mrs. C.	............Janitress	70 00
		$5,502 80

Iroquois Falls Station.

Sherlock, G. L.	.............Agent	$1,229 62
Marshall, R. S.	............Operator	17 61
Jardine, A.	"	159 73
Brasher, S. M.	"	198 95
Fisher, E. C.		20 29
Black, W. R.	"	2 90
Emond, E.	...............Clerk	2 66
Hunter, L.	"	869 76
Gregor, M.	"	641 33
Gregor, L.		548 71
Shipley, C. M.		18 33
Johnston, C.		6 66
Critchley, P.		175 12
Beatty, H.		73 57
Carmichael, H. A.		72 21
Lyons, F.		150 21
Hall, G.		138 88
Stewart, J. T.		134 75
Roberts, C. M.		23 71
Libby, H.		52 90
Calder, A.		157 90
Barr, W. B.		92 00
Dufresne, M.	"	20 58
Curtis, J. W.	"	65 81
Rose, K. F.	...............Baggageman	90 75
Anyan, H.	..............Cleaning	5 00
Johnston, Mrs. J.	"	2 00
		$4,981 94

Porcupine Station.

Picard, J. W.	..............Agent	$239 53
Price, J. T.	"	659 03
Bates, G. H.	...........Relv. Agent	42 23
Beemer, J. H.	" "	219 19
Murphy, E. M.	" "	44 19
Hull, J. C.	...............Sanitary Wk.	2 00
		$1,206 17

South Porcupine Station.

Varrett, E. J.	..............Agent	$1,384 71
Cattley, B.	................Operator	490 84
Marshall, R. S.	"	101 24
Brown, H. G.	"	717 06
Humphrey, C. R.	..........Clerk	650 00
Moore, G.	"	60 32
McLeod, R.	"	660 00
Wright, W.		147 26
Audet, E. J.		399 20
Hyde, S.	"	26 61
Hughes, R.	...............Shedman	19 35
Longworth, B.	"	29 03
Palmer, M.	"	23 06
		$4,708 68

Schumacher Station.

Hawkins, J. A. ....Agent	$1,334 96	
Shankman, S. ....Relv. Agent	7 92	
Hawkins, R. ....Clerk	29 03	
McMinn, R. .... "	232 26	
Assad, K. .... "	340 16	
Garovitch, M. ....Sanitary Wk.	10 00	
		$1,954 33

Timmins Station.

Allan, J. D. ....Agent	$1,266 21	
Brown, A. W. ....Relv. Agent	124 70	
Schmallback, J. H. ....Operator	977 29	
Shankman, S. .... "	900 69	
Dudley, H. A. .... "	35 17	
Beatty, E. ....Stenographer	47 68	
Bridger, C. H. ....Clerk	418 70	
Fulton, G. V. .... "	758 17	
Germyn, C. .... "	280 97	
Speirs, J. C.	238 97	
Bardwell, R. .... "	258 19	
McGirr, W. .... "	39 00	
Lett, R.	143 95	
Doher, M.	6 03	
Boicey, W. H.	90 61	
Bernier, J. A. .... "	219 94	
Lacasse, F. B. .... "	224 79	
Lessard, R.	21 29	
Swayne, R.	319 03	
Leitch, J. M.	84 68	
Bergeron, J. S. .... "	100 00	
Hunter, L.	16 94	
Angell, F. .... "	20 32	
Taras, N. ....Checker	5 32	
Nixon, A. .... "	150 97	
McDonald, G. .... "	104 00	
Larocque, A. ....Messenger	206 03	
Vafrquette, P. .... "	1 00	
		$7,060 64

Cochrane Station.

Brown, A. W. ....Agent	$1,198 82	
Daly, R. W. .... "	712 00	
Brasher, S. M. ....Operator	467 24	
Valliere, J. L. .... "	52 50	
Robinson, E. .... "	1,191 76	
Oulette, A.	356 20	
Prentice, R.	24 89	
Westbrook, J. H. .... "	31 31	
Knowles, R. .... "	179 72	
Marshall, R. S.	26 58	
Murphy, E. M.	*40 24	
Cattley, B.	33 41	
Fisher, E. C. .... "	131 41	
Jessup, A. L. ....Stenographer	233 87	
Fitzgerald, H. .... "	260 00	
Lockhart, G. .... "	133 55	
Bernier, J. A. ....Clerk	353 81	
Mortson, R. C. .... "	646 94	
Drinkwater, L. .... "	828 38	
Milligan, B.	308 23	
Murdock, H. .... "	187 72	
Thompson, J. C. .... "	101 69	
Gagnon, A. L.	234 19	
Noble, S. G. .... "	5 32	
Grasser, H. .... "	55 00	
Williams, R. ....Baggageman	508 00	

Cochrane Station.—Continued.

Sproule, R.	Shed Foreman	$235 34
Drinkwater, B.	Trucker	725 69
Belleveau, J.	"	594 34
Dunn, C.	"	73 98
Moore, R.		105 97
Waldron, G. W.		85 50
Cavanagh, J. M.	"	13 06
Millman, H.	Checker	352 86
Hewson, W.	"	405 90
Johnson, F.	"	710 32
Scanlan, W. G.	Heaterman	46 99
Sterritt, S.	"	234 24
Kert, H.	Messenger	195 67
Williams, J.	"	96 00
Waldron, R.	"	10 00
Commanda, A.	Cleaning	2 50
Matheson, G.	Janitor	38 71
Pert, W.	"	427 74
Boyne, B.	"	253 55
Drake, E.	"	110 00
Cummings, A.	Iceman	439 36

$13,460 50

Shelter Stations.

Daly, J.	Attendant	$60 00
Hoffman, Mrs. R.	"	80 00
Fordyce, G.	"	40 00
Schlievert, G.		120 00
Johnston, O.		41 61
Harbridge, Mrs. L.		5 00
Labelle, F.		60 00
Burnett, W.		120 00
Mitchell, J. B.		120 00
Fillmore, J.		113 00
Goodfellow, Mrs. R.		55 00
Bertrand, W.		100 00
Clark, T.		30 00
Bateman, R.		50 00
Tivy, Mrs. K.		20 00
Delledonne. J,		18 39

$1,033 00

Conductors.

Nidd, J. T.	Conductor	$1,450 27
Newell, A.	"	1,645 54
Murray, P. J.	"	1,606 02
Graham, H. F.		1,630 06
Flegg, R.		187 86
McParland, T. J.		1,642 81
Hamilton, T.		1,706 42
Gillespie, J.	"	1,859 66
Sheppard, E. E.	"	1,718 33
Jessup, J. H.		1,794 79
McTavish, R.		1,764 90
Ressor, A. P.	"	1,889 64
McKerrow, G. W.		2,116 79
Cockerline, J.		1,353 18
Miller, A.		2,008 37
Lillie, O.	"	1,662 24
Nixon, W.		1,475 18
Rouble, A.		1,818 00
Sullivan, H.		1,234 15
Thomas, H.	"	1,616 08
McConomy, E. J.	"	1,771 17
Connell, J. S.	"	1,271 27
Beaudet, J. A.	"	1,342 35
Stoughton, N.	"	1,611 39

Conductors.—Continued.

Steinhoff, J. A.	Conductor		$1,741 50
Loney, W.	"		1,395 69
Miller, J. S.	"		1,769 70
Campbell, W. A.	..		731 90
Atkinson, H.			1,445 88
Aubrey, N.			1,550 51
Bradford, J. N.	"		1,093 41
Archer, H. A.	"		1,326 52
Willoughby, J. A.			422 70
Treacy, W. L.			786 60
Kennedy, J.			1,275 25
McCallum, F.	..		653 65
Bourett, J. W.			1,280 12
Leckie, J. W.			1,348 81
Copps, R. W.			13 63
Francis, S. F.			359 37
Kerr, C. D.	..		519 80
Dubois, C. H.			365 20
St. Louis, F.			1,537 04
Richmond, J. N.			152 57
Robinson, E.	.:		1,208 75
Gatacre, G. W.			89 17
Ryan, H.			245 92
Holland, J.			228 21
Lett, W.			316 74'
Doherty, T. J.	..		4 00
King, A. W.			209 96
Sullivan, K.			2 00
Manning, W.			454 76
Pringle, G.	.:		69 72
King, E. J.	-		46 94
Cameron, A.			17 10
McKerrow, J. O.			991 70
Campbell, T. J.			186 20
Castor, D.	..		4 18
Dorschner, A.			31 27
			————— $62,052 94

Brakemen.

Lee, G.	Brakeman		980 83
McQuestion, W. A.	"		955 40
Edwards, A. S.	"		1,039 15
Seguin, J. W.			1,105 55
Downey, M. J.	.:		1,123 49
Coburn, G.	..		1,029 07
Cockerline, A. S.			952 36
Thurlow, J. E.			1,015 97
Aubry, H. J.	.'		1,022 58
Durack, D. B.	"		1,042 98
Winters, R. W.	"		1,218 17
Kilroy, B.			997 38
Biers, B. W.	..		945 53
Thompson, W. G.	.'		535 47
Allan, J.	"		998 72
Barrett, P. J.			567 00
Francis, S. F.	..		1,056 00
Robinson, E.	..		301 77
Holland, J.	.:		1,080 56
Lett, W.	"		1,072 48
Dorschner, A.	..		1,269 86
Ryan, H.	"		960 28
Edwards, W. J.	.:		1,446 09
Manning, W.	"		732 43
Sullivan, K.	"		1,372 92
Ferrier, G.	"		1,277 42
Fleming, R.	.'		1,281 51

Brakemen.—Continued.

Dougherty, T. J. ....Brakeman	....	$1,089 38
Fischer, R. .... "	....	1,189 40
Bailey, J. .... "	....	1,221 33
Copps, R. W.	....	1,481 57
McLeod, J.	....	270 77
Gauthier, A.	....	1,105 78
Clark, C.	....	613 86
Farmer, A.	....	1,031 17
Farmer, W.	....	1,043 29
Pigeau, E. J.	....	1,152 61
McAughey, T. J.	....	841 60
Tetreau, E.	....	1,125 90
Scott, F. J.	....	1,165 51
Kerr, C. D.	....	763 01
Kelly, H.	....	649 72
McCallum, F.	....	569 80
Kennedy, J.	....	399 25
Larone, A. T.	....	1,166 31
Spencer, W. L.	....	1,323 51
Fraser, E.	....	1,135 03
Jewell, J. D.	....	250 59
Gatacre, G. W.	....	648 21
St. Louis, F.	....	257 03
Campbell, W. A.	....	703 17
McMillan, R. J.	....	651 48
Stoughton, F.	....	818 28
James, R.	....	1,242 00
Chambers, W. H.	....	1,041 36
Ryan, W. C.	....	47 40
Wallace, F.	....	1,016 71
Chase, H. F.	....	810 20
Fleury, G.	....	1,096 86
O'Hara, J.	....	1,146 75
Collins, P. H.	....	325 30
O'Toole, G.	....	938 22
Leckie, J. W.	....	290 46
Foster, F.	....	1,271 47
Richmond, J. N.	....	510 73
Treacy, W. L.	....	711 79
Dubois, C. H.	....	1,094 10
King, A. W.	....	1,132 50
King, E. J.	....	1,306 53
Willoughby, J. A.	....	243 00
Pringle, N.	....	1,035 83
Simms, P. .... "	....	1,008 79
Comerford, D. F.	....	1,308 54
Thomas, G.	....	8 12
Taylor, F. H.	....	224 94
Pringle, G.	....	1,383 38
McMillan, N. C.	....	18 13
Moore, W.	....	510 35
Legary, J.	....	45 63
Thomas, H. .... "	....	4 45
Hollands, W. .... "	....	1,011 09
Archer, H. A.	....	3 85
Campbell, T. J.	....	970 90
Aubry, H. H.	....	380 32
Doyle, H. B. J.	....	945 80
Coulthard, L. H.	....	196 01
Venton, W. H.	....	550 97
Gould, A. A.	....	450 89
McEachren, A. .... "	....	1,021 77
Valliere, J.	....	909 06

Brakemen.—Continued.

Hoffbuhr, W.	Brakeman	$125 31
Blair, G. W.	"	161 94
Larocque, E.	"	252 64
Caley, C.	"	871 36
McArthur, N. R.	"	626 97
Comerford, J. ....:......		19 68
Beaudet, J. A.		294 18
Vaillancourt, W.		715 47
Martin, T.	"	61 99
McLeod, R. D.	"	301 35
Harwood, A.		32 17
Cameron, A.		412 82
Belec, D. A.		864 69
McMahon, F.	"	432 33
Croghan, J.		14 70
Perrault, G.		586 02
Castor, D.		340 44
Biglow, E.		870 01
Wall, F. H.	"	705 59
Peters, H.		4 55
Lewis, W. L.		770 32
Guertin, H.		125 47
Denault, W.	"	503 86
Knapp, F.	"	4 46
McCaughan, L.		875 25
Moorehouse, D.		8 88
Irvine, A.		363 01
Connell, R. T.	"	432 40
Thom, W.	"	429 06
Atkinson, H.		93 08
Smith, G. A.		666 33
Demore, P.		66 77
Hickey, W.	"	701 74
Lennox, S.	"	580 70
Childerhose, W. B.	"	293 14
Peden, A.	"	441 07
Sullivan, H.		509 14
Lillie, O.		154 85
Bourett, W. J.	"	507 98
Archer, H.	"	117 60
Nixon, W.		214 52
Saunders, F. A.		15 54
Eheler, E. G.		137 18
Edwards, T.	"	19 96
Fisher, W.		96 35
O'Connell, J.		80 78
Keats, W.		35 57
Sharpe, R. M.		68 75
Biers, J.		19 76
Wagner, H. W.	"	30 35

$92,320 81

Locomotive Engineers.

Morgan, F.	Engineer	$1,922 69
Shaw, L. G.	"	1,893 33
Donohue, J.	"	1,918 48
Smith, D.	"	518 84
Fry, J.	"	1,933 89
McLeod, A.	"	1,979 59
Coomb, G.	"	1,935 55
Thomas, W.	"	1,820 78
Millman, W. C.	"	1,974 91
Wilson, J. T.	"	2,375 75
McKaig, S. J.		1,324 29
McMillan, N.		2,432 09
Currie, N.	"	2,462 93
Johnston, J. C.	"	1,646 12

Locomotive Engineers.—Continued.

Hill, T. H. ....Engineer	....	$2,228 46
Ross, W. .... "	....	2,175 46
Holland, J. .... "	....	1,407 68
Newman, A.	....	1,395 11
Ward, A. .... "	....	1,780 28
McElhaney, H. .... "	....	1,781 99
Thomas, F.	....	2,163 02
Lackie, S.	....	1,161 37
Filiatrault, Z. E.	....	1,825 02
Plaus, W.	....	1,868 83
Nornabell, E. A.	....	1,614 31
Kirk, F. G.	....	1,503 96
Langlois, J.	....	1,555 75
Nolan, P. B.	....	2,421 70
Howard, T.	....	688 98
Durkin, J. T.	....	1,984 24
Johnston, J. A.	....	1,964 57
McKenzie, H. W.	....	1,679 51
McGovern, H. E.	....	2,058 89
Hermeston, H.	....	1,788 63
Morris, J.	....	1,661 22
Bedard, S.	....	1,656 84
McKerrow, J. E.	....	692 22
Reynolds, H.	....	1,721 34
Newman, S. B.	....	1,549 80
Biggs, J.	....	1,714 57
Connell, W. D.	....	1,301 26
Copeland, J. E.	....	1,428 52
Jackson, I.	....	1,726 78
Leishman, E. G.	....	1,618 83
Nudds, G.	....	895 74
McEwen, S.	....	1,030 00
Tripp, G.	....	570 74
Vincent, R.	....	593 61
McMenemy, A.	....	488 20
McKenzie, A. B.	....	41 66
Muldoon, T.	....	46 97
Bear, B.	....	447 18
McElhaney, A.	....	438 98

$80,811 46

Locomotive Firemen.

Connell, W. D. ....Fireman	....	$426 06
Biggs, J. .... "	....	202 15
Newman, S. B. .... "	....	261 96
Jackson, I. .... "	....	355 23
McElhaney, A. .... "	....	890 79
McMenemy,-A.	....	876 44
Vincent, R.	....	735 82
Moore, A.	....	1,060 40
Lewis, H.	....	1,444 33
McEwen, S.	....	745 02
McKenzie, A. B.	....	1,164 71
Biers, G.	....	1,315 48
Beauchamp, H.	....	1,215 06
Muldoon, T.	....	1,322 41
Anyan, G. W.	....	955 91
Yorkston, J.	....	818 06
Woollings, T.	....	1,024 60
Vreeland, C.	....	440 84
McKenney, J. .... "	....	1,288 06
Dods, J.	....	1,474 04
Byers, P.	....	1,468 61
Brooks, G.	....	1,132 16
Smith, D.	....	446 98
Radford, A.	....	777 64

Locomotive Firemen.—Continued.

Gentil, A.	Fireman		$1,116 60
Kelly, H.	"		1,166 23
Hermeston, H.	"		74 07
Tripp, G.			885 16
Nudds, G.			656 30
McLeod, J.			111 49
Thompson, H.			18 11
Leishman, E. G.			224 77
Anderson, J.			1,090 35
Grant, A.			910 78
Vernon, A.			1,065 72
Savard, E.			1,180 46
Merritt, L.			592 22
Logan, P.			85 70
Kay, G. R.	"		38 63
McDonald, M. J.	"		1,129 86
Haman, C.			119 01
Stonehouse, E.			29 05
James, T.			32 41
McKenney, A.			621 91
Brooks, A.			229 86
Thompson, H.			2 90
Leblanc, J.			3 49
Empie, C .H.			791 68
Bebee, T. E.			880 73
Day, E.			245 36
Drury, H. M.			765 44
Lee, M.			125 40
Guitard, O.			344 31
Carmichael, W.			3 01
Colley, A. J.			5 43
Harrington, F.	"		33 37
Chambers, J. W.			899 11
Munro, R.			325 35
Toaze, T. A.			142 44
Gagne, L.	"		42 34
Leduc, E. W.	"		181 81
Brogan, C. R.			374 05
McLennan, E.			705 30
Litterell, A. H.			34 03
Cook, A.			603 16
O'Connell, W.			1,173 85
Romain, D. C.			865 14
Davis, S.			3 28
McDonald, A.			20 51
Vinette, D.	"		787 08
Kehoe, D.			69 03
Gaudette, L.			21 46
Woods, W.			486 84
Gingras, M.			355 43
Guitard, L.	"		289 19
Leblanc, P.			337 31
Davis, S.			3 75
Mann, D.			191 57
Dorey, T.	"		41 26
Tackaberry, J.			260 64
Humphrey, W.			757 70
Gibson, W.			166 59
Leahy, V.			326 62
Quinn, D.	"		621 61
Brunsley, A.			4 03
Reynolds, J. F.			115 49
Belanger, C.			4 64

Locomotive Firemen.—Continued.

Ryan, J. ....Fireman	....	$515 03
Quinn, P. .... "	....	894 02
Gard, W. I. .... "	....	642 43
Leblanc, J. A. .... "	....	4 30
Haskins, G. K.	....	162 28
Fichault, E.	....	114 08
Suffron, J.	....	9 81
Neal, F.	....	24 66
Jowsey, N. T.	....	61 45
Harman, W.	....	68 78
Clark, F. .... "	....	520 45
Mahaffy, A. .... "	....	585 42
Hannan, W.	....	72 63
Lowrey, R. A.	....	71 17
Tignanelli, F.	....	10 52
Lacey, C. F.	....	6 00
Raulston, O.	....	198 81
Leblanc, J.	....	21 55
Floyd, E.	....	52 15
Nevill, S.	....	42 50
Solway, E.	....	3 04
Baker, C.	....	3 23
McKerrow, J. E.	....	**123 34**
McKenzie, H. W.	....	113 28
Arquette, S.	....	81 89
Lind, T. .... "	....	3 22
Britton, L. .... "	....	7 94
		$51,047 16

Telephone and Telegraph Department.

Kelly, W. J. ....S. T. and T.		$1,900 00
Brown, C. A. ....Stenographer		560 00
Ferguson, L. M. ....Inspector		1,100 00
Picard, P. ....Lineman		986 41
Germain, E. .... "	....	7 50
Picard, H. .... "	....	10 00
		$4,563 91

Commercial Telegraph and Telephone Offices.

Cobalt—Elk Lake—Gowganda and Cochrane.

Way, D. H. ....Manager		$15 00
Bunyan, M. ....Opr. and Acct.		827 58
Grace, P. W. ....Operator		503 22
McWilliams, M. .... "	....	19 96
Oulette, A. .... "	....	8 23
Makeen, E. G.	....	60 72
Cattley, B	....	113 19
Jackson, W. .... "	....	83 07
McLaughlin, J. ....Accountant		13 50
Hylands, L. ....Clerk	....	44 72
Asseltine, G. .... "	....	21 94
Simpkins, W. ....Messenger		325 00
Way, W. K. .... "	....	4 35
Maher, E. .... "	....	12 58
Harris, E.	....	4 90
Strickland, A. .... "	....	6 00
Belanger, O. ....Manager		15 **00**
Tremblay, E. ....Operator		410 74
James, M. .... "	....	25 59
Craig, W. H.	....	800 00
Sullivan, N. J. ....Lineman		900 00
Aubert, R. A. .... "	....	14 52
Daly, R. W. ....Manager		15 00
Hann, R. C. ....Operator		868 93

Commercial Telegraph and Telephone Offices.—Continued.

Cobalt—Elk Lake—Gowganda and Cochrane.—Continued.

Stewart, R.	Operator	$3 33	
Kert, A.	Clerk	15 00	
Dunn, A.	"	115 00	
Jamieson, E.	"	80 00	
Williams, D.	Messenger	1 94	
Waldron, R. W.	"	30 00	
Williams, J.	"	90 00	
			$4,949 01

Telephone and Telegraph Linemen, Englehart and Cochrane and Extra Gang.

Simpson, G. M.	Lineman	$542 29	
Loisel, S.	"	974 03	
McLellan, J.	"	616 65	
Ambeault, E.	Foreman	842 00	
Linemen, Groundsmen, etc.		4,127 64	$7,102 61

Office of Chief Engineer and Superintendent of Maintenance.

Clement, S. B.	C. E. & S. M.	$4,140 00	
Dickson, G. H.	Chief Draughtsman	1,705 00	
Angus, G. P.	Draughtsman	111 29	
Scott, C. R.	"	385 00	
Burt, T. K.	"	46 45	
Johnston, W. I.	Chief Clerk	1,525 00	
Young, J.	Clerk	925 00	
McIntosh, R.	"	750 00	
Cavanagh, H. W.	"	185 00	
Huntington, R. S.	Blueprinter	276 67	
McGuire, A.	"	12 00	
Morgan, F.	"	45 50	
Snyder, H. H.	"	84 17	
Armstrong, T.	"	37 50	
Sharpe, H. W.	"	8 00	
Morgan, N. L.	Stenographer	600 16	
Lemieux, G. E.	"	585 00	
Reynolds, E.	"	17 03	
Sherman, M.	"	81 29	
O'Donnell, J. A.	Clerk	137 42	$11,657 48

Greenhouse, Englehart.

Kerrigan, D.	Gardener	$840 00	
Ward, A.	"	720 00	
Price, T.	Laborer	4 60	
Phillips, W.	"	4 40	
Antram, W.	"	54 00	
Druce, P.		5 00	
Cannon, W.		249 92	
Graham, T.		27 40	
Simpkins, W.		300 45	
Danetun, J.	"	8 00	
Stevenson, G.	"	11 00	
Anyan, W.		68 20	
Remus, W.	"	136 00	
Garovitch, M.	Teaming	93 45	
Preston, G.	"	9 00	
Rutledge, W.	"	52 50	$2,583 92

Office of Master Mechanic.

Ross, T.	Master Mechanic	$2,200 00	
Douglass, J. J.	Road Foreman	1,825 00	
Rodgers, H. L.	Mechanical Engineer	1,600 00	
Battley, C.	A. B. Inspector	1,550 00	

11 T R

Office of Master Mechanic.—Continued.

McRoberts, A. A. ....Draughtsman	$1,165 00	
Ellwood, R. E. ....Chief Clerk	1,065 00	
Raymond, J. C. ....Stenographer	695 00	
Leppan, S. ....Clerk	177 10	
Leppan, F. .... "	127 42	
Lye, A. L. .... "	191 94	
Rousseau, E. J.	135 48	
Corbeil, I. .... "	35 48	
Cavanagh, H. W. ....Timekeeper	111 85	
Corbeil, A.	248 06	$11,127 33

Motive Power Department, North Bay.

Black, W. J. ....Foreman ......,.........	$1,610 00	
Machinists	18,779 15	
Carpenters	1,827 74	
Painters	1,268 76	
Other shopmen	50,992 36	$74,478 01

Car Department, North Bay.

Beath, J. ....Foreman	$1,250 00	
Carpenters	3,884 84	
Other employees ...., ...	26,413 73	$31,548 57

Carpenter Shop, North Bay.

Williamson, R. ....Foreman	$1,490 00	
Carpenters	13,524 77	
Painters	9,578 07	
Other shopmen	11,902 35	$36,495 19

Motive Power and Car Departments, Cobalt.

Sibbold, T. ....Car Inspector	$1,090 08	$1,090 08

Motive Power and Car Departments, Elk Lake.

Other shopmen	$1,888 77	$1,888 77

Motive Power and Car Departments, Englehart.

Clarke, R. ....Foreman	$1,490 00	
Machinists	3,458 37	
Other shopmen	21,664 71	$26,613 08

Motive Power and Car Departments, Iroquois Falls.

Other Shopmen	$1,594 20	$1,594 20

Motive Power and Car Departments, Timmins.

Thompson, E. ....Foreman ....."..................	$1,200 00	
Machinists	22 91	
Other shopmen	8,224 92	$9,447 83

Motive Power and Car Departments, Cochrane.

Moth, A. T................Foreman :.........'...........	$1,300 00	
Machinists	859 63	
Other shopmen	14,414 33	$16,573 96

Resident Engineer, Locating Engineer and Assistants.

Boast, R. G. ....Resident Engineer	$1,585 00
Maher, W. R. ....Locating Engineer	1,800 00
Watson, C. G. ....Inst. man	1,045 00

Resident Engineer, Locating Engineer and Assistants.—Continued.

Sinton, J. ....Inst. man	$999 33	
Angus, G. P. .... "	300 00	
Fraser, A. A. .... "	576 58	
Holbrook, B. ....Rodman	21 00	
Allan, H. ....Rodman and Inspector	526 66	
O'Donnell, J. A. ....Rodman	241 50	
Hill, L. ....Chainman	48 00	
Sharpe, H.·W. .... "	40 00	
Samuel, M. .... "	193 33	
Edwards, R.	56 22	
Patterson, E. L.	161 25	
Flannery, W. .... "	44 97	
Morgan, A. ....Axeman	139 36	
Young, C. "	22 00	
Audrey, T. H. .... "	46 67	
McGinnis, C.	9 33	
McGuire, A.	161 67	
Lynch, T. .... "	7 00	
West, C. ....Cook	477 73	
Martin, H. ....Inspector	159 00	
		$8,661 60

Office of B. and B. Master.

Oldham, W. J. ....B. & B. M.	$1,850 00	
Stafford, E. J. .... Clerk	985 00	
		$2,835 00

Water Service.

Day, H. ....Inspector	$1,000 00	
Pumpmen, etc.	8,330 11	
		$9,330 11

B. and B. Department, Extra Gangs.

Carpenters	$35,174 52	
Others	21,044 01	
		$56,218 53

Office of General Roadmaster.

Young, Wm. ....General Roadmaster	$1,980 00	
Jacobs, G. E. .... Stenographer	330 00	
Imeson, W. C. .... "	152 58	
		$2,462 58

Track Supervisors.

Faught, S. J. .... Supervisor	$1,485 00	
Drinkwater, J. .... "	1,620 00	
Switzer, W. .... "	409 35	
Belliveau, J.	39 19	
		$3,553 54

Track Section Gangs.

Section No. 1 ....Foreman	$1,004 71		
Laborers	9,628 14	$10,632 85	
" 2 ....Foreman	858 33		
Laborers	2,037 02	2,895 35	
3 ....Foreman	895 77		
Laborers	2,175 31	3,071 08	
4 ....Foreman	881 45		
Laborers	1,680 88	2,562 33	
5 ....Foreman	883 54		
Laborers	1,933 15	2,816 69	

Track Section Gangs.—Continued.

Section No.	6	Foreman	$883 19	
		Laborers	1,365 35	$2,248 54
"	7	Foreman	881 57	
		Laborers	1,720 83	2,602 40
"	8	Foreman	901 12	
		Laborers	1,792 84	2,693 96
"	9	Foreman	906 69	
		Laborers	1,659 29	2,565 98
"	10	Foreman	886 17	
		Laborers	1,586 74	2,472 91
"	11	Foreman	899 12	
		Laborers	1,731 49	2,630 61
	12	Foreman	882 31	
		Laborers	2,100 96	2,983 27
"	13	Foreman	845 56	
		Laborers	1,969 94	2,815 50
	14	Foreman	879 78	
		Laborers	2,098 35	2,978 13
"	15	Foreman	919 40	
		Laborers	2,015 51	2,934 91
"	16	Foreman	939 78	
		Laborers	1,434 56	2,374 34
"	17	Foreman	903 61	
		Laborers	3,061 94	3,965 55
"	18	Foreman	935 29	
		Laborers	2,856 17	3,791 46
"	19	Foreman	1,034 04	
		Laborers	2,749 24	3,783 28
"	20	Foreman	875 75	
		Laborers	2,173 38	3,049 13
"	21	Foreman	881 45	
		Laborers	2,370 65	3,252 10
	22	Foreman	931 90	
		Laborers	2,129 99	3,061 89
"	23	Foreman	1,094 43	
		Laborers	9,632 52	10,726 95
"	24	Foreman	875 15	
		Laborers	2,077 74	2,952 89
"	25	Foreman	852 07	
		Laborers	2,062 81	2,914 88
"	26	Foreman	886 99	
		Laborers	1,855 21	2,742 20
	27	Foreman	887 84	
		Laborers	2,074 39	2,962 23
"	28	Foreman	876 70	
		Laborers	1,399 71	2,276 41
"	29	Foreman	928 70	
		Laborers	1,257 78	2,186 48
	30	Foreman	873 54	
		Laborers	1,398 23	2,271 77
"	31	Foreman	882 22	
		Laborers	2,507 69	3,389 91
	32	Foreman	867 38	
		Laborers	2,148 12	3,015 50
"	33	Foreman	921 80	
		Laborers	2,132 06	3,053 86
"	34	Foreman	891 35	
		Laborers	2,469 85	3,361 20
"	35	Foreman	949 14	
		Laborers	2,140 70	3,089 84
"	36	Foreman	866 86	
		Laborers	2,016 45	2,883 31
"	37	Foreman	844 62	
		Laborers	1,705 05	2,549 67
"	38	Foreman	861 21	
		Laborers	1,484 05	2,345 26

Track Section Gangs.—Continued.

Section No. 39	Foreman	$1,158 44	
	Laborers	6,970 30	$8,128 74
" 40	Foreman	877 29	
	Laborers	2,362 47	3,239 76
41	Foreman	855 53	
	Laborers	1,593 69	2,449 22
42	Foreman	877 14	
	Laborers	1,897 35	2,774 49
43	Foreman	888 96	
	Laborers	1,800 57	2,689 53
44	Foreman	861 18	
	Laborers	2,153 17	3,014 35
45	Foreman	913 41	
	Laborers	2,108 26	3,021 67
46	Foreman	950 33	
	Laborers	3,310 19	4,260 52
" 47	Foreman	869 89	
	Laborers	1,184 13	2,054 02
48	Foreman	851 27	
	Laborers	1,072 97	1,924 24
49	Foreman	886 89	
	Laborers	1,810 96	2,697 85
50	Foreman	1,005 13	
	Laborers	2,084 35	3,089 48

Road Department, Extra Gangs.

Extra Gang No. 1	Foreman	1,745 00	
	Laborers	13,644 62	15,389 62
" 2	Foreman	1,192 05	
	Laborers	4,868 78	6,060 83
3	Foreman	1,185 70	
	Laborers	8,698 00	9,883 70
4	Foreman	1,824 70	
	Laborers	13,292 79	15,117 49
5	Foreman	958 21	
	Laborers	4,789 45	5,747 66
6	Foreman	1,077 31	
	Laborers	5,812 44	6,889 75
7	Foreman	784 50	
	Laborers	7,328 21	8,112 71
8	Foreman	616 87	
	Laborers	1,780 65	2,397 52
9	Foreman	532 34	
	Laborers	4,023 82	4,556 16
10	Foreman	820 82	
	Laborers	5,007 06	5,827 88
11	Foreman	707 71	
	Laborers	2,192 84	2,900 55
12	Foreman	714 51	
	Laborers	3,104 28	3,818 79
13	Foreman	558 98	
	Laborers	1,249 62	1,808 60
14	Foreman	274 47	
	Laborers	724 65	999 12
15	Foreman	136 87	
	Laborers	970 39	1,107 26

Special Payroll, Donations to Employees Enlisted for Overseas Service.

Mitchell, R. H.	A. & C. A.	$380 00
McCausland, J. H.	Clerk	86 25
Keeler, S. T.	"	183 75
Oulette, T.	"	60 00
Murphy, C. W.	"	45 00
Campbell, K.		75 00

Special Payroll, Donations, etc.—Continued.

Beaton, W. S. ....Clerk	$40 00
Sherman, E. L. .... "	55 00
Giroux, C. A. .... "	55 00
McGill, R.	75 00
Kelly, T. J. .... "	51 66
Johnston, H. G. .... "	40 00
LeGallais, F. G. ....Operator	95 00
Griffiths, G. ....Checker	171 00
James, V. M. .... "	50 00
Relph, E. .... "	150 00
Rogers, A. E.	186 00
Archambault, O.	35 00
Smith, A. R. .... "	58 00
Saunders, L. H. ....Clerk	40 00
Howard, J. E. .... "	52 50
Duncan, G. G. .... "	57 50
Webber, W. S.	50 00
Chamberlain, S.	57 50
Stuckey, H. .... "	62 72
Bell, R. ....Checker	150 00
Borland, A. ....Clerk	57 33
White, G. J. ....Baggageman	214 98
Moore, G. E. ....Clerk	110 00
Brown, R. M. ....Baggageman	82 50
Harris, J. B. ....Shed Foreman	65 00
Ranstead, T. ....Call Boy	25 00
Soper, C. W. ....Checker	55 32
Fox, G. ....Trucker	141 00
Jones, C. S. ....Clerk	130 00
Gray, E. ....Checker	144 60
Knapp, F. ....Baggageman	165 00
Mitchell, A. B. ....Relv. Agt.	92 50
Jardine, A. ....Operator	75 47
Wright, W. A. ....Clerk	50 00
Sproule, R. T. ....Shed Foreman	53 13
Mortson, N. E. ....Clerk	27 50
Saunders, F. A. ....Brakeman	229 50
Ryan, W. C. .... "	68 17
Gatacre, G. W. .... "	279 32
McAughey, T. J.	214 62
Kelly, H.	51 15
McMillan, R. J.	132 27
Shepherd, E. C.	77 87
Clarke, C. .... "	101 06
Yorkston, J. ....Fireman	98 77
Simpson, G. M. ....Lineman	167 86
Huntington, R. S. ....Blueprinter	95 00
Sale, H. ....Draughtsman	85 00
Smith, C. ....Clerk	41 96
English, J. ....Loader	164 91
White, R. M. ....Checker	56 00
Fetterly, G. H. ....Apprentice	50 56
White, J. .... "	59 18
Charnock, W. ....Helper	83 22
Parker, G. M. ....Boilermaker	195 00
Barrand, W. A. ....Helper	75 00
Davis, S. ....Tenderman	227 91
Cadden, C. A. ....Machinist	154 18
McCarthy, L. ....Helper	38 06
Angus, C. ....Repairer	73 18
Rowe, G. .... "	59 80
Atkins, S. J. ....Inspector	232 00
Louden, J. .... "	227 04
Gould, A. G. .... "	57 31
Corbeil, I. ....A. B. Repairer	116 52
Wilson, J. L. ....Painter	90 58

Special Payroll, Donations, etc.—Continued.

McCubbin, M. ....Carpenter	$241 44	
Wicks, H. .... "	227 64	
Webster, J. .... "	189 70	
Newberry, H. ....Painter	140 .94	
Grieve, A. ....Helper	111 48	
Antram, W. H. ....Cleaner	126 50	
Wallace, F. J. .... "	84 82	
Aubert, R. A. ....Stationary Engineer	160 76	
Holbrook, B. ....Rodman	45 00	
Tibbles, A. H. ....Bridgeman	241 44	
Grant, J. W. .... "	66 22	
Kelly, J. ....Cook	45 00	
Jacob, G. E. A. ....Stenographer	60 00	
Donaldson, J. ....Sectionman	150 42	
Papciak, H. .... "	24 95	
Gillespie, C. ....Cook	59 53	
Jones, R. V. ....Clerk	60 00	
Whiteside, W. ....Mail Clerk	30 00	9,347 01

Total payroll $1,127,885 74

Potatoes and Oats on Mr. Wm. Schell's Farm.   North half Lot 1, Con. 4, Dack Township   (Mail received at Englehart.)

TEMISKAMING AND NORTHERN ONTARIO RAILWAY.

EXPENDITURE FOR FISCAL YEAR, 1916.

AMERICAN RAILWAY ASSOCIATION, NEW YORK, N.Y.

56597—Car service and per diem rules	$0 80	
57739—Dues, assessments and copies of proceedings	41 25	
57890—Car service and per diem rules	55	
58586— " " "	1 05	
59143— " . " "	80	
60403—Rule books	4 00	
59992—Assessment No. 51	21 28	
		$69 73

ATCHISON, TOPEKA & SANTA FE RAILWAY COMPANY, TOPEKA, KANSAS.

56615—Car repairs	$13 25	
56814—Car service balance	25 20	
57266—Car repairs	1 22	
58137—Car service balance	31 50	
58038— " "	28 80	
59013—Claim No. 10700—O/c weight silver ore	3 68	
59195—Car service balance	72 90	
59469—Car repairs	4 59	
59016—Claim No. 10635—O/c weight silver ore	3 10	
59222—Car repairs	5 06	
59514—Car service balance	64 80	
60111— " "	97 65	
60371—Ticket balance	46 97	
59930—Car repairs	3 58	
60396—Car service balance	96 75	
61443—Claim No. 11190—Prop'n excess weight silver ore	3 34	
61655—Car service balance	86 40	
61086—Car repairs	4 24	
61306—Claim No. 11610—O/c weight silver ore	3 87	
61836—Car repairs	23 96	
62070—Car service balance	29 25	
62771— " "	30 15	
63390— " . "	15 30	
		$695 56

ASSOCIATION OF FIRE CHIEFS, TORONTO.

56689—Advertising	$10 00	
		$10 00

ALLEN MANUFACTURING CO., LIMITED, TORONTO.

57007—Laundry	$15 89	
57124— "	27 01	
57824— "	7 67	
58098— "	8 31	
60757— "	14 65	
60068— "	7 82	
60786— "	2 14	
		$83 49

S. APPLETON (M. M. DEPT.), COCHRANE, ONT.

57051—Travelling expenses	$0 50	
		$0 50

The Ann Arbor Railroad Company, Toledo, Ohio.

57095—Car repairs and duty on parts	$18	57
58044—**Car service balance**	8	55
59356—Car repairs		98
59522—Car service balance	4	05
59932—Car repairs	2	05
60404—Car service balance	3	60
61359—Car repairs	7	63
61898— "	1	29
62445— "	4	31
63398—Car service balance	18	90
63586—Car repairs	2	68
63732— "		85

$73 46

The Art Metropole, Toronto.

57133—Paints, crayons and erasers	$3	16
57338—Detail paper	3	60
57773—Tacks, pencils and B. P. paper	15	44
58274—Draughtmen's material	98	03
58721—Level Rod cloths, sepia paper	18	39
59002—Draughting supplies	40	22
60467—Paper, pencils, felt	92	68
60296—Tracing paper, tacks and pens	10	49
60672—Pencils, linen	41	44
60864—Erasers	1	28
61563—Vermilion		30
61474—Pencils, paper	54	81
62236—Transit repaired	13	00
63034—Pencils, linen, paper, etc.	84	44

$477 28

American Hoist & Derrick Co., St. Paul, Minn.

57135—Repair parts	$5	70

$5 70

The Acme Machinery Company, Cleveland, Ohio.

57137—Standard caps	$10	20

$10 20

Abitibi Power & Paper Co., Limited, Montreal, P.Q.

57335—Claims Nos. 10528, 10355 and 10198—Refund on construction material, refund of demurrage	$394	36
57024—Claim No. 9344—O/c rate pulpwood	369	73
57036a—Claims Nos. 10310, 10311, 10354, 10535—Rebate on construction material, o/c rate pulpwood	351	32
58009—Claims Nos. 10056 and 10318—Refund of war tax and entry fee collected in error	3	39
57888—Water supplied	70	20
57974—Claims Nos. 10514, 10869, 10534, 10731, 10523, 10055 and 9460—O/c weight lumber, o/c rate on wood pulp	399	75
58883—Claim No. 10440—O/c rate machinery	5	00
58963—Claims. Nos. 10900 and 10521—O/c rate fire brick and clay, woodpulp	61	39
59435—Water supplied	35	10
58820—Claims Nos. 10749 and 11029—Rebate construction material and refund demurrage charges	430	94
59496—Claims	41	77
59787— "	761	21
60439—Claims	12	83
60842—Coal	285	90
60924—Water		90

ABITIBI POWER & PAPER CO., LIMITED, MONTREAL, P.Q.—*Continued.*

60851—Claims Nos. 10304, 10636, 10202—Overcharge weight wood-pulp, fire brick and construction material			244 51
60921—	"	11009—Loss roll felt and overcharge in freight on shipment	10 15
61157—	"	10652, 10681—Damage newsprint papers, overcharge on woodpulp	50 79
61449—	"	11251—Overcharge shipment paper cores	59
61611—	"	11059—Overcharge rate newsprint	6 50
62051A—	"	9951—Rebate on car construction material..	52 93
61308—	"	10147—Overcharge freight woodpulp	33 53
61800—	"	10721 and 12096—Overcharge weight newsprint paper	32 89
62577—	"	9556—Overcharge account weight pulpwood.	155 22
63179—	"	11136 and 12008—Overcharge rate returned newsprint cores	9 86
62878—	"	9747, 9997 and 11995—Overcharge rate pulpwood and car hay	408 70
63220—	"	11637—Overcharge rate car newsprint paper.	4 17

$4,233 63

ALEXO NICKEL MINE, PORQUIS JUNCTION, ONT.

57337—Claim Nó. 9489—Loss account shortage nickel ore			35 17
57976—	"	10843—Demurrage on car ore	1 00

36 17

AMERICAN BRAKE SHOE AND FOUNDRY COMPANY, MAHWAH, N.J.

56548—Brake shoes $563 39

$563 39

ALEXANDER & CABLE LITHOGRAPHING CO., LIMITED, TORONTO.

56650—Passes	$26 50
57126— "	6 00
59848— "	2 00
62790—	6 00

$40 50

ASSOCIATION OF AMERICAN RY. ACCOUNTING OFFICERS, WASHINGTON, D.C.

56710—Passenger synopsis	$1 50
59840—Annual dues	7 00
50976— "	7 00

$15 50

AMERICAN BANK NOTE COMPANY, OTTAWA, ONT.

56712—Engraving passes $30 00

$30 00

AMERICAN RAILWAY ENGINEERING ASSOCIATION, CHICAGO, ILL.

56758—Subscription and dues	$10 50
57779—Vol. 7, Proceedings and Manual	7 50
59990—Binding Manual	50

$18 50

ALGOMA CENTRAL & HUDSON BAY RAILWAY, SAULT STE. MARIE, ONT.

56816—Car service balance		$243 45
58139—	" "	122 85
58040—	" "	171 45
59197—	" "	149 85
59516—	" "	199 80

ALGOMA CENTRAL & HUDSON BAY RAILWAY, ETC.—*Continued.*

59889—Car service balance		$20 06
60113— " "		142 20
60398— " "		46 80
61657— " "		119 25
62072— " "		129 60
62773— " "		134 55
63392— " "		121 50
63828—Car repairs		86 71

$1,688 07

AMERICAN REFRIGERATOR TRANSIT COMPANY, ST. LOUIS, MO.

56818—Car service balance	$1 54
59518— " "	4 51
60115— " "	3 79
60400— " "	1 69
62775— " "	1 69

$13 22

ATLANTIC COAST LINE RAILROAD, WILMINGTON, N.C.

56820—Car service balance	$24 30
58141— " "	22 95
58042— " "	33 75
59199— " "	24 75
59520— " "	55 80
60117— " "	71 10
60402— " "	60 75
61361—Car repairs	37 47
61659—Car service balance	26 10
62074— " "	22 05
62777— " "	51 30
63396— " "	7 65

$437 97

ATLANTA, BIRMINGHAM & ATLANTIC RY. COMPANY, ATLANTA, GA.

56822—Car service balance	$4 50
58865— " repairs	22 84
60119— " service balance	2 25
61715— " "	3 15

$32 74

ALGOMA EASTERN RAILWAY, SAULT STE. MARIE, ONT.

56824—Car service balance	$26 10
58046— " "	30 60
59201— " "	9 00
61663— " "	3 60
62076— " "	10 35
62779— " "	18 45
63400— " "	11 45
63826—Car repairs	1 44
58143—Car service balance	12 15

$123 14

WM. AGAR, THORNLOE, ONT.

57038a—Claim No. 10502—Loss account, bag staples	$0 70

$0 70

AMERICAN ARCH COMPANY, NEW YORK, N.Y.

57334—Fire brick	$29 45
58282— "	26 20
58725— "	16 50
58964— "	36 20
60463—Arch brick	36 40
61001—Bricks	65 60

$210 35

AURORA METAL COMPANY (INCORPORATED), AURORA, ILL.

57336—Packing	$21 87	
58966— "	29 97	
62794— "	40 25	
		$92 09

AMERICAN ASSOCIATION OF GENERAL BAGGAGE AGENTS, TORONTO, ONT.

57525—Annual dues, year 1916, A. J. Parr	$5 00	
62269—Special assessment	5 00	
		$10 00

ASSOCIATION OF TRANSPORTATION & CAR ACCOUNTING OFFICERS, CHICAGO, ILL.

57527—Assessment No. 8	$3 95	
58902—Volume No. 3, minutes, etc.	4 35	
60348—Annual dues, W. J. Harper	10 00	
		$18 30

THE ADAMS & WESTLAKE COMPANY, CHICAGO, ILL.

57771—Sash lifts and holders, locks and hinges	$37 56	
58278—Keys and coach parts	17 01	
58769—Coach fittings	96 18	
58962—Weatherstrip	27 50	
60465—Tail gates, switch locks, etc.	82 74	
61612—Repair parts, lamp shades	243 80	
62671—Locks, holders, etc.	43 56	
62616—Steel coach keys	7 20	
		$555 55

ANCHOR PACKING CO. OF CANADA, LIMITED, MONTREAL, P.Q.

57775—Packing	$7 50	
58723— "	12 66	
58968— "	38 85	
		$59 01

ADVANCE PUMP & COMPRESSOR CO., BATTLE CREEK, MICH.

57777—Repairs for pump	$30 57	
60469—Steam chest cover, spools, etc.	63 00	
		$93 57

A. E. ADSHEAD, HAILEYBURY, ONT.

58011—Claim No. 10305—damage to waggon wheel	$5 80	
		$5 80

ALTON & SOUTHERN RAILROAD, EAST ST. LOUIS, ILL.

58351—Car repairs	$7 79	
		$7 79

THE AMERICAN MUSEUM OF SAFETY, NEW YORK, N.Y.

57692—Annual dues, 1916	$25 00	
		$25 00

THE FRED. ARMSTRONG CO., LIMITED, TORONTO, ONT.

57886—Repairing buzzers and desk buttons	$2 10	
		$2 10

M. A. ATTALLAH, NORTH BAY, ONT.

57992—Claim No. 10787—Account value timber and charge for loading car	$25 00	
		$25 00

AIKENHEAD HARDWARE, LIMITED, TORONTO, ONT.

58276—Drawer pulls	$3 33	
62486—Latches	190 24	
62796—Hook sash, lifts, etc.	19 88	
63262—Lock sets, R. H. door	60	
		$214 05

AHEARN & SOPER, LIMITED, OTTAWA, ONT.

58280—Battery jars	$28 80	
		$28 80

THE ARCADE KEY STORE, TORONTO, ONT.

58687—Key, locks, brass plate	$2 90	
		$2 90

JAMES ANDREWS (M. M. DEPT.), ENGLEHART, ONT.

58774—Expenses—Travelling	$1 80	
59841— " "	45	
		$2 25

PERCY ANDREWS, CANE, P.O.

59754—Ties	$138 42	
		$138 42

ADVERTISING & PUBLISHING AGENCY, TORONTO, ONT.

59727—Advertisement—Directory—S. O. E.	$10 00	
		$10 00

ATLANTIC CITY RAILROAD COMPANY, PHILADELPHIA, PA.

60077—Car repairs	$0 74	
		$0 74

ALBERTA & GREAT WATERWAYS RAILWAY COMPANY, EDMONTON, ALTA.

60121—Car service balance	$16 20	
60406— " "	13 05	
61665— " "	3 60	
		$32 85

LIEUT.-COL. ARMSTRONG, 159TH BATTALION, C.E.F., HAILEYBURY, ONT.

60118—Commission on special train	$133 48	
60158—Donation towards deficit—excursion	40 00	
		$173 48

ARMSTRONG BROS. TOOL COMPANY, CHICAGO, ILL.

60120—Steel	$22 57	
		$22 57

ESTATE OF A. AVERY, NORTH BAY, ONT.

60228—Birch	$299 62	
60230—Birch	2 44	
		$302 06

ALBERTA BROOM & BRUSH SUPPLY COMPANY, ST. THOMAS, ONT.

60294—Brooms	$42 50	
60866— "	42 50	
61889— "	52 50	
		$137 50

AMERICAN RAILWAY MASTER MECHANIC'S ASSOCIATION, CHICAGO, ILL.

61097—Annual dues	$5 00	
		$5 00

AKRON, CANTON, YOUNGSTOWN RY. COMPANY, AKRON, OHIO.

61263—Car repairs	$1 00	
62078—Car service balance	90	
		$1 90

ALABAMA, TENNESSEE & NORTHERN RAILWAY, MOBILE, ALA.

61661—Car service balance	$0 45	
		$0 45

AMERICAN STEEL FOUNDRIES, CHICAGO, ILL.

61891—Wheels	$528 00	
63260—Wheels	720 00	
		$1,248 00

ANNUAL REVIEW PUBLISHING COMPANY, LIMITED, TORONTO, ONT.

61154—Subscription—" Canadian Annual Review "	$10 00	
		$10 00

HUGH ALLAN, ENGINEERING DEPT., NORTH BAY, ONT.

62179—Expenses—Travelling	$20 00	
		$20 00

AMERICAN FOREST PRODUCTS CORPORATION, CARTHAGE, N.Y.

62311—Claim No. 12239—overcharge rate, pulpwood	$25 30	
		$25 30

CHAS. AUGI, COBALT, ONT.

62579—Claim No. 12488—alleged loss, two bottles preserves	$2 95	
		$2 95

AIR BRAKE ASSOCIATION, NEW YORK, N.Y.

62673—Proceedings	$2 00	
		$2 00

AMERICAN TANK LINE, CLEVELAND, O.

62781—Car service balance	$1 90	
63402—Car service balance	1 90	
		$3 80

ADVERTISER JOB PRINTING CO., LIMITED, LONDON, ONT.

63109—Forms...	$44 75	
62798—Receipts	5 11	
		$49 86

ALLITH MANUFACTURING CO., LIMITED, HAMILTON, ONT.

62792—Hangers $18 00

$18 00

AMERICAN NOVELTY COMPANY, NORTH BAY, ONT.

63368—Advertising *re* "sale of lands"—*Booster* $12 75

$12 75

ARMOUR CAR LINE, CHICAGO, ILL.

63394—Car service balance $3 87

$3 87

JAMES ALLAN, BAGGAGEMAN, NORTH BAY, ONT.

63800—Donation, account personal effects, alleged destroyed by
fire $10–00

$10 00

ALABAMA GREAT SOUTHERN RAILROAD COMPANY, CLEVELAND, OHIO.

63824—Car repairs $1 53

$1 53

THE BALTIMORE & OHIO RAILROAD COMPANY, BALTIMORE, MD.

56617—Car repairs		$29 53
56935— " "		6 09
56826— " service balance		49 50
57040—Claim No. 10444—Overcharge on brick		32 16
58145—Car service balance		16 65
58353— " repairs		60 34
58048— " service balance		70 65
59203— " "		60 75
59254— " repairs		31 79
59524— " service balance		50 40
60123— " "		17 55
59934— " repairs		69 93
60032— " "		14 96
60408— " service balance		105 75
61667— " "		10 35
61088— " repairs		8 08
62080— " service balance		31 05
62783— " "		61 35
63404— " "		87 75
63588— " repairs		22 66
63830— " "		23 22

$860 51

M. BROWNSTEIN, COBALT, ONT.

56647—Claim No. 10115—Overcharge on weight potatoes........ $9 38

$9 38

BELL TELEPHONE COMPANY OF CANADA.

56681—Exchange and toll service	$30 60
56713—Toll service	2 50
56833— " service	5 40
56919—Telephone interchange balance	150 51
57083—Toll service	5 65
57085—Changing location of extension set	1 14
56760—Exchange service	9 25
57012— " and toll service	14 80
57122— " service	8 75
57128—Telephone interchange balance	174 95

BELL TELEPHONE COMPANY OF CANADA.—*Continued.*

57218—Exchange and toll service	18	45
57523— " and messenger service	72	14
57659— " and toll service	49	00
58093— " and toll service	13	40
58431—Telephone interchange balance	163	06
57826—Toll service	12	00
58512— "	3	40
58520—Telephone interchange balance	174	07
58485—Toll and messenger service	3	85
58591a—Toll service	2	50
58689—Exchange and toll service	43	65
58691—Toll service		50
59427—Telephone interchange balance	170	16
59437—Exchange and toll service	21	85
58642— " " "	81	49
58924—Toll service	23	40
59452— " and interchange	148	03
59780— " and exchange	13	50
60057— "		45
60079—Telephone interchange balance	170	82
60405—Toll service	3	25
60733— "	7	90
60354—Exchange and toll service	41	00
60464— " "	10	25
60640—Telephone interchange balance	116	40
60978—Exchange service	44	09
60835— " "	47	62
60887— " "	5	00
61099— " and toll service	35	95
61101— " "	11	00
61441—Toll service	8	15
61947—Telephone interchange balance	139	81
62003—Toll service	1	25
62085— "	5	30
61334— "	12	10
62240—Telephone interchange balance and toll service	149	97
62244—Toll service	5	25
63143—Telephone interchange balance	43	10
62490—Toll service	14	60
62492— " and exchange service	41	02
62696—Exchange service	102	29
62700— " and toll service	27	00
62750— " "	8	35
63036— " "	52	22
63154—Telephone interchange balance	99	27
63646—Toll service	8	40

$2,629 81

BEARDMORE BELTING COMPANY, LIMITED, TORONTO.

56697—Belting	$37	04
56982— "	71	50
57348— "	15	00
57587— "	47	63
58292—Star Oak laces	5	25
58729— " "	10	50
58698—Belting	43	75
60676—Laces	5	75
61109— "	4	60
62675—Belting	11	67

$252 69

12 T R

R. G. BOAST, ENGINEERING STAFF, NORTH BAY, ONT.

56715—Travelling expenses			$9 50
57565—	"	"	6 50
57696—	"	"	6 55
58629—	"	"	2 75
59324—	"	"	4 00
59729—	"	"	8 00
61403—	"	"	10 00
61228—	"	"	6 60
62199—	"	"	6 35
62454—	"	"	10 60

$70 85

THE BANK OF OTTAWA.

56767—Unpaid draft	$4 40
57087— "	4,222 58
57222— "	3 15
57228— "	90
57579— "	3 15
57631— "	45
57704—Exchange charges, etc.	319 12
57980—Porcupine Branch, Voucher No. 723, favor A. M. Swenson, account balance special Porcupine Bank account transferred to Bank of Ottawa account	28 15
58797—Unpaid draft	2 25
58734—Advance to cover exchange charges, etc.	50 00
58960—Unpaid draft	95
59711— " "	85
59860—Exchange charges, etc.	32 06
60350— " "	38 24
60791—Unpaid draft	11,085 38
60819— " "	3 50
61047— " "	13 50
61045—Exchange charges, etc.	27 94
62049—Unpaid draft	25
61206—Adjustment of erroneous deposit	3 27
61212—Exchange charges, etc.	23 03
61390—Unpaid draft	21 79
62271 " "	5 79
62387—Exchange charges, etc.	7 93
62586—Unpaid draft	8 80
62690—Exchange charges, etc.	6 43

$15,913 86

BUREAU OF EXPLOSIVES, NEW YORK, N.Y.

56765—Assessment covering membership	$100 47
56762—Bulletins	4 50
57130— "	4 50
58588— "	4 50
59731—Assessment No. 19	91 33
59995—Bulletin No. 31	4 50
61399— "	4 50
63802—Assessment No. 20	57 20
62494—Copies Accident Bulletin No. 33	4 50

$276 00

L. BREWSTER, PORTER, PRIVATE CAR, TORONTO, ONT.

56769—Supplies for private car			$0 80
59450—	"	"	3 10
60207—	"	"	1 20
60759—	"	"	4 25
59994—	"	"	4 30

L. Brewster, Porter, Private Car, Toronto, Ont.—*Continued.*

60979—Supplies for private car	....	$4 25	
61272— " "	....	5 32	
62275— " "	....	4 35	
62972— " "	....	2 00	
			$29 57

E. C. Banks, Claims Investigator, North Bay, Ont.

56771—Travelling expenses	....	$14 25	
56618— "	....	20 00	
57617— "	....	36 25	
57686— "	....	36 05	
58587— "	....	22 25	
			$128 80

The Belt Railway Company of Chicago, Chicago, Ill.

56793—Car repairs	....	$1 19	
56941— "	....	4 34	
59771— "	....	2 51	
			$8 04

Buntin, Gillies & Co., Limited, Hamilton, Ont.

56827—Stationery	....	$102 80	
56612—Paper, pencils and pens	....	30 15	
57489—Stationery	....	153 09	
57648—Stationery and paper	....	62 59	
57806—File folders, forms and paper	....	41 75	
57926—Stationery	....	113 96	
58533—Paper fasteners and file covers	....	2 19	
58745—Stationery	....	92 77	
58696—Fasteners, pencils, etc.	....	53 56	
59004—Stationery	....	196 67	
59961— "	....	49 10	
60108— "	....	60 61	
60638—Erasers, folders, etc.	....	26 39	
61003—Stationery	....	88 40	
61565—Time books	....	1 20	
61466—Stationery	....	25 36	
61566—Stationery	....	240 38	
62345—File backs	....	13 72	
62618—White backing, etc.	....	188 95	
62752—Wire desk baskets	....	5 39	
62762—Ribbons, clips, etc.	....	58 74	
			$1,607 77

Chas. Battley, Air Brake Inspector, North Bay, Ont.

56859—Travelling expenses	....	$3 10	
56736— "	....	1 80	
57567— "	....	7 85	
57706—	....	7 70	
58631—	....	3 20	
58771—	....	69 45	
58848— "	....	4 15	
59322— "	....	7 60	
59697— "	....	4 90	
60176— "	....	5 35	
61401—	....	5 10	
61224—	....	1 25	
62257— "	....	6 25	
			$127 70

J. BEATH, CAR FOREMAN, NORTH BAY, ONT.

56861—Travelling expenses	$1 60	
57726— "	13 15	
58633— "	17 50	
59695—	9 15	
60174—	2 85	
63208— "	55	
		$44 80

J. BRICE, M. M. DEPT., NORTH BAY, ONT.

56863—Travelling expenses	$1 55	
57057—Travelling expenses	1 40	
		$2 95

BUFFALO, ROCHESTER & PITTSBURG RAILWAY CO., ROCHESTER, N.Y.

56937—Car repairs	$4 21	
57274—Car repairs	4 33	
58015—Claim No. 9910—Overcharge weight pulpwood	18 35	
58147—Car service balance	4 05	
59205—Car service balance	31 05	
59228—Car repairs	13 35	
59526—Car service balance	256 05	
60125—Car service balance	197 10	
59938—Car repairs	4 10	
60352—Car repairs	16 06	
60410—Car service balance	214 10	
61669—Car service balance	22 95	
61958—Car repairs	5 42	
62451—Car repairs	2 41	
63406—Car service balance	5 85	
63834—Car repairs	21 97	
		$821 35

BOSTON AND MAINE RALROAD COMPANY, BOSTON, MASS.

56939—Car repairs	$2 33	
56940—Ticket balance	5 49	
57272—Car repairs	56	
58155—Car service balance	28 35	
58307—Ticket balance	24 60	
58365—Car repairs	2 16	
58052—Car service balance	46 80	
59209—Car service balance	22 50	
59397—Ticket balance	51 16	
59226—Car repairs	3 10	
59530—Car service balance	73 35	
59728—Ticket balance	27 56	
60021—Car repairs	8 88	
60129—Car service balance	33 75	
60407—Prop'n expenses, immigrant business	45	
60034—Car repairs	97	
60414—Car service balance	10 80	
61365—Car repairs	24 84	
61673—Car service balance	36 90	
62084—Car service balance	46 35	
62449—Car repairs	13 14	
62787—Car service balance	54 00	
62789—Car service balance	1 80	
62945—Passenger car mileage	40 48	
62949—Ticket balance	2 31	
62951—Ticket balance	11 98	
63225—Interline freight balance	40	
63410—Car service	1 80	
63566—Ticket balance	6 12	
63832—Car repairs	7 03	
		$589 96

BOSTON & ALBANY RAILROAD COMPANY, NEW YORK, N.Y.

56993—Car repairs	$4 36	
58518— "	57	
59224— "	48	
59891— "	1 00	
60019—	61	
61363—	1 59	
63736—	3 06	
		$11 67

C. O. BAKER, AGENT, NORTH BAY, ONT.

57053—Travelling expenses	$11 25	
61332—Travelling expenses	26 95	
		$38 20

ROY BEATTY (M. M. DEPT.), NORTH BAY, ONT.

57055—Travelling expenses	$2 05	
57613— " "	1 25	
		$3 30

WM. BERTRAND, NUSHKA, ONT.

57081—Claim No. 10473—Storage on box butter	$22 33	
		$22 33

BEGG BROS., NORTH BAY, ONT.

57139—Cotton, cheesecloth, etc.	$19 68	
57354—Cotton	9 24	
57791—Roller towels	4 20	
58286—Cottou and cheesecloth	14 70	
58731—Drygoods	55 08	
58970—Oilcloth, cotton, etc.	48 10	
60461—Towelling, cotton, etc.	57 20	
60678—Towelling, oilcloth, etc.	15 45	
60870— " "	19 95	
61893—Cotton, cheesecloth	22 15	
61568—Towels, cheesecloth	12 54	
62677—Oilcloth, towelling, etc.	40 15	
62802—Towelling	1 80	
63040—Grey cotton, cheesecloth	17 43	
		$337 67

BUSINESS SYSTEMS, LIMITED, TORONTO.

57143—Binders and forms	$19 70	
57340—Telegram forms	10 00	
57693—Forms	27 10	
57781— "	10 00	
58100— "	137 05	
58743— "	52 00	
58974— "	28 20	
59006—Stationery	129 99	
60686—Forms, lettergrams, etc.	218 13	
61105—Telegraph forms	13 50	
61468—Forms	28 34	
61560— "	61 31	
62681— "	26 62	
		$761 94

BARBER ELLIS, LIMITED, TORONTO, ONT.

57145—Envelopes	$43 07	
57344— "	2 50	
57789—Way bill pockets	12 45	

BARBER ELLIS, LIMITED, TORONTO, ONT.—*Continued.*

58288—Envelopes, etc.	43 91	
58727— "	22 97	
60477—Forms	69 52	
60300— "	16 76	
60674—Forms, way bill pockets	60 65	
61517—Envelopes	16 95	
61556—Way bill pockets	39 84	
		$328 62

THE BOECKH BROS. COMPANY, LIMITED, TORONTO.

57147—Switch brooms	$21 00	
57785—Brushes	21 00	
58290—Wire switch brooms	21 00	
		$63 00

BENJAMIN ELECTRIC MANUFACTURING CO. OF CANADA, LIMITED, TORONTO.

57233—Street hoods	$7 87	
57356—Lamp sockets	3 60	
		$11 47

BEAVERHOUSE MINING SYNDICATE, HOBONIA MINES, ONT.

57339—Claim No. 9996—Loss account, shortage engine parts	130 00	
		$130 00

BUFFALO & SUSQUEHANNA COAL & COKE CO., BUFFALO, N.Y.

57407—Coal	$2,655 52	
57409— "	2,336 19	
57560— "	1,995 09	
57558—	2,483 70	
58337—	2,547 85	
58339—	2,508 68	
58516— "	2,566 55	
58614—	2,246 64	
58616—	2,147 13	
58907—	2,229 01	
58909— "	2,793 52	
59089—	3,057 40	
58934—	2,838 53	
58936—	2,118 81	
59372— "	2,039 02	
59374—	2,144 81	
59376—	2,093 76	
59428—	2,550 30	
59430— "	2,537 92	
59432—	3,397 22	
60205— "	2,913 70	
60695—	2,793 66	
60751—	2,999 48	
61014—	2,005 74	
61016—	3,270 80	
61018— "	2,080 98	
61020— "	3,011 73	
61407—	2,640 90	
61447—	2,729 23	
61380—	2,605 71	
61382—	2,618 49	
62613— "	3,692 62	
62717—	3,771 75	
62719—	3,744 46	
62970— "	3,046 51	
63038—	3,169 49	
63094—	1,782 22	
		$98,165 12

H. Brockway (Audit Dept.), North Bay, Ont.

56522—Travelling expenses	$6 25	
		$6 25

Beardmore & Company, Toronto.

56578—Leather	$8 98	
56984— "	7 11	
57585— "	7 68	
58549— "	8 36	
61562— "	8 90	
		$41 03

Bessemer & Lake Erie Railroad Company, Pittsburg, Pa.

56828—Car service balance	$4 95	
58149— " "	22 05	
58050— " "	29 25	
59207— " "	92 70	
59528— " \ "	221 40	
60127— " "	512 90	
59936—Car repairs	5 40	
60412—Car service balance	88 20	
61671— " "	28 80	
62082— " "	16 20	
62785— " "	16 20	
63408— " "	36 45	
		$1,074 50

Buffalo & Susquehanna Railway, Buffalo, N.Y.

56830—Car service balance	$58 05	
57270—Car repairs	1 26	
58151—Car service balance	39 60	
		$98 91

Buffalo & Susquehanna Railroad Corporation, Buffalo, N.Y.

56832—Car service balance	$617 40	
57268—Car repairs	7 10	
58153—Car service balance	99 90	
58357—Car repairs	5 65	
58054—Car service balance	240 75	
59211— " "	237 60	
59483—Car repairs	4 64	
59252— "	2 70	
59534—Car service balance	400 95	
60131— " "	949 50	
60416— " "	527 40	
61675— " "	1,090 35	
61956—Car repairs	8 81	
62088—Car service balance	776 25	
62447—Car repairs	20	
62793—Car service balance	633 60	
63522— " "	1,219 50	
		$6,817 30

Berwind-White Coal Mining Company, Philadelphia, Pa.

56834—Car service balance	$3 79	
60133— " "	3 79	
		$7 58

Buffalo Mines, Limited, Cobalt, Ont.

57042—Claim No. 10542—Damage to crucible	$2 00	
59500— " No. 10280—Loss account, damage to lime by rain.	39 05	

BUFFALO MINES, LIMITED, COBALT, ONT.—*Continued.*

61804—Claims Nos. 11849 and 11003—Loss, barrel creosote; over-
    charge freight silver ore 290 85

$331 90

BURROW, STEWART & MILNE CO., LIMITED, HAMILTON, ONT.

57342—Scale cards	$9 63	
58284—Scale cards and lever	13 33	
58741—Platform scales	9 00	
60473—Fireback, grate, ends	4 08	
60684—Scale cards	9 63	
61107— "	8 75	
62679—Trucks, scales, lever, etc.	47 11	
62810—Cards	8 75	

$110 28

R. BUNYAN & COMPANY, NORTH BAY. ONT.

57346—Corn and shorts	$19 20	
57793—Hay	194 40	
58739— "	40 22	
58822—Claim No. 10865—Overcharge weight hay	3 43	
59384— " No. 10871—Loss bag moulee destroyed by fire. ...	1 75	
60298—Grass seed	1 50	
60868—Oats	2 40	

$262 90

JOHN BOURKE & COMPANY, NORTH BAY, ONT.

57350—Coal tar	$12 00	
60680—Paristone, Plaster of Paris	39 45	
61570— " " "	38 90	
62683— " lime, etc.	222 20	
62800— " etc.	235 68	

$548 23

BEAMISH & SMITH, NORTH BAY, ONT.

57352—Braid	$1 25	
61572—Awning duck	9 15	

$10 40

M. BOIVIN, TIMMINS, ONT.

57551—Ties	$2,234 58	
60064— "	48 72	
61500— "	859 86	
62806—	383 68	

$3,526 84

W. BRIMLEY (M. M. DEPT.), NORTH BAY, ONT.

57569—Expenses, travelling $0 75

$0 75

W. J. BAULDRY, COLONIZATION AGENT, COCHRANE, ONT.

57615—Travelling expenses	$9 55	
57730— " "	7 70	
58613— " "	5 35	
58776— " "	10 30	
59763— " "	10 75	
60172— " "	16 25	
61405— " "	9 75	
61226— " "	9 45	
62503— " "	11 60	
62468— " "	10 65	

$101 35

BANNER & OSTROM, NORTH BAY, ONT.

57741—Commissary for "*Abitibi*"	$12 38	
61302—Groceries for private car	15 19	
62246— " "	65 24	
62685— " "	39 85	
62698— " "	12 24	
		$144 90

THE D. W. BOSLEY COMPANY, CHICAGO, ILL.

57783—Weather strip	$24 00	
60471— "	29 00	
60682— "	29 00	
		$82 00

BERLIN FELT BOOT CO., LIMITED, KITCHENER, ONT.

57787—Saddle felt	$12 50	
58735— "	22 50	
		$35 00

L. W. BROWN, SOUTH PORCUPINE, ONT.

58013—Claim No. 10630—Shortage raisins	$0 52	
62030— " No. 12248—Damage and loss, jar olives	1 15	
		$1 67

DR. G. T. BAILEY, COCHRANE, ONT.

58091—Expenses, professional service	$2 00	
		$2 00

BANGOR & AROOSTOOK RAILROAD, BANGOR, ME.

58157—Car service balance	$6 30	
59532— " "	12 60	
62086— " "	5 85	
62791— " "	90	
63412— " "	3 15	
		$28 80

BALTIMORE & OHIO-CHICAGO TERMINAL R. R. COMPANY.

58359—Car repairs	$1 40	
63734— "	2 16	
		$3 56

PETER BENEKE, McCOOL P.O., ONT.

58463—Ties	$107 79	
		$107 79

FRANCIS BURNS, PORQUIS P.O., ONT.

58463—Ties	$37 01	
58593— "	21 40	
59425— "	72 12	
		$130 53

P. BERNARD ICE COMPANY, COCHRANE, ONT.

57618—Ice	$265 60	
		$265 60

J. J. Belland, Nellie Lake P.O., Ont.

57672—.83 acres of land, Township of Newmarket $40 00
                                                                ———————— $40 0

W. Brosseau, North Bay, Ont.

57784—Award, W. C. B., re alleged injuries $13 71
                                                                ———————— $13 7

Burroughs Adding Machine Company, Detroit, Mich.

57830—Attention to adding machine $4 00
61519—   "   "   " 4 00
62687—Stand . . ..·...............   10 00
                                                                ———————— $18 0

Dr. J. A. R. Biron, Cochrane, Ont.

57858—Professional service rendered $5 00
                                                                ———————— $5 0

A. W. Brown (Relieving Agent), Cochrane, Ont.

57924—Expenses, travelling $14 00
58773—   "   " 14 00

58905—   "   " 14 00
                                                                ———————— $42 0

Ernest Berard, Heaslip, Ont.

57962—Award, W. C. B., in full, re alleged injuries received.... $7 84
                                                                ———————— $7 8

S. M. Brasher, Relieving Agent, North Bay, Ont.

57966—Expenses, travelling $14 00
                                                                ———————— $14 0

Chas. Bernstein, Cochrane, Ont.

57978—Claim No. 10367—Loss account, damage to fruit and vege-
           tables $52 44
58965—Claim No. 10647—Loss account, shortage bag onions....   2 16
59498—   "   No. 10887—Overcharge in weight, fruit and vege-
           tables 17 63
                                                                ———————— $72 2

J. L. Bucher, New Liskeard, Ont.

57980—Claim No. 10708—Loss account, damage to whiskey...... $8 82
62581—   "   No. 12494—Loss account, gin 1 75
                                                                ———————— $10 5

Beir, Soudheimer & Company, New York, N.Y.

57982—Claim No. 10244—Overcharge rate on zinc dust $2 59
                                                                ———————— $2 5

Blue Ridge Railway Company, Washington, D.C.

58056—Car service balance .... $3⁻15
                                                                ———————— $3 1

BUMSTEAD BROS., KENABEEK, ONT.

58593—Ties	$87 70	
58593— "	91 61	
59425— "	50 00	
59425—	52 00	
		$281 31

J. H. BUNNELL & COMPANY (INC.), NEW YORK, N.Y.

58733—Relays, keys, sounders	$16 59	
60475—Telegraph keys, springs	38 00	
		$54 59

BROWN BROTHERS, LIMITED, TORONTO, ONT.

58737—Paper, refills, booklets, etc.	$8 69	
		$8 69

CLINTON BRADBURY, BRADWELL, SASK.

59123—Claim No. 11142—Loss, baggage destroyed by fire.........	$77 30	
		$77 30

MRS. ALEX. BROTHERSTON, WINNIPEG, MAN.

59125—Claim No. 11141—Baggage destroyed by fire	100 00	
		$100 00

D. F. BRILL, ST. PAUL, MINN.

59145—Copy " Pacific Northwest Joint Passenger Tariff "......	$0 50	
		$0 50

E. P. BATTLEY, SARNIA, ONT.

58972—Stop watch	$25 00	
		$25 00

T. J. BAKER, REDWATER, ONT.

59448—Board supplied engineering staff	$5 00	
60070— " " " "	23 25	
60636— " " " "	22 50	
62001— " " " "	23 25	
62242— " "	12 50	
		$86 50

BAY TERMINAL RAILROAD COMPANY, TOLEDO, O.

59536—Car service balance	$0 80	
60135— " "	80	
		$1 60

A. C. BAIN (M. M. DEPT.), ENGLEHART, ONT.

59693—Expenses, travelling	$1 75	
		$1 75

E. H. BASTIAN, SHILLINGTON, ONT.

59789—Claim No. 11048—overcharge in rate sleigh	$8 33	
		$8 33

T. BINGHAM (B. & B. DEPT.), NORTH BAY, ONT.

59843—Expenses, travelling	$4 35	
		$4 35

MRS. HERBERT BISSELL, GILPIN, ALTA.

59869—Claim No. 11468—Loss account, baggage burned......... $100 00

$100 00

W. N. BOTSFORD, WINNIPEG, MAN.

59871—Claim No. 11491—Loss account, baggage burned $100 00

$100 00

S. J. BIRD, MATHESON, ONT.

60064—Ties $43 56

$43 56

FRANCIS BROWN, EARLTON P.O., ONT.

60064—Ties $64 05

$64 05

HERMAN BERGER, PORQUIS P.O., ONT.

60064—Ties $62 94

$62 94

D. A. BALFOUR COMPANY, TORONTO, ONT.

60166—Carbon $2 00
61056—   " 12 00
62351—   " 2 00

$16 00

T. BEWLEY, TORONTO, ONT.

60232—Cartage $2 65
62808—   " 2 70

$5 35

BRITISH AMERICAN OIL COMPANY, LIMITED, TIMMINS, ONT.

60855—Claim No. 10796—Loss account, shortage oil $5 00

$5 00

JOHN BROWN, NEW LISKEARD, ONT.

61049—Final award, W. C. B., *re* alleged injuries $18 99

$18 99

J. C. BOGART, THORNLOE, ONT.

61063—Ties $158 10
61063—   " 47 79
61103—Timber 242 82
62347—Lumber 122 50

$571 21

BRANTFORD ROOFING CO., LIMITED, BRANTFORD, ONT.

61111—Asphalt $157 20
61558—   " 192 40

$349 60

THOMAS BEVERLEY, NORTH BAY, ONT.

61445—Award, W. C. B., *re* alleged injuries $5 55

$5 55

BRITISH & COLONIAL PRESS, TORONTO, ONT.

61607—Views on fires, Northern Ontario	$10 00	
		$10 00

J. H. BOWMAN (SPECIAL OFFICER), COBALT, ONT.

61230—Travelling expenses	$3 50	
62488—Amount paid for battery	40	
		$3 90

JOHN L. BUEHIR, NEW LISKEARD, ONT.

61436—Claim No. 11465—Alleged loss, bottle liquor	$0 63	
		$0 63

J. R. BOOTH, OTTAWA, ONT.

61500—Ties	$39 15	
61500— "	4 59	
63222—Claim No. 12838—Loss oil account, leakage	2 76	
		$46 50

BIRD & SON, HAMILTON, ONT.

61564—Waterproof paper	$22 64	
62349—Building paper	25 20	
		$47 84

P. D. BOYER, HAILEYBURY, ONT.

61802—Claim No. 12151—Alleged damage to syrup	$1 01	
		$1 01

C. BERARD, HEASLIP, ONT.

62238—Meals supplied section foreman	$1 75	
		$1 75

M. BOURGARE, LATCHFORD, ONT.

62143—Award, W. C. B., *re* alleged injuries received	$18 03	
		$18 03

A. BRAZEAU, TIMMINS, ONT.

62167—Refund deposit on contract, Timmins Station	$119 50	
		$119 50

EDWARD BROWN, NORTH COBALT P.O., ONT.

62669—Ties	$41 19	
		$41 19

NORMAN BUSS, HOMER P.O., ONT.

62669—Ties	$17 28	
		$17 28

HAROLD BENCH, KENABEEK P.O., ONT.

62669—Ties	$50 49	
		$50 49

BROTHERHOOD OF LOCOMOTIVE ENGINEERS, NORTH BAY, ONT.

62575—Expenses *re* Conference	$10 40	
		$10 40

L. Boïvin, Cochrane, Ont.

62739—Claim No. 12484—Alleged loss, bag rice $2 47
                                                                        $2 47

R. H. Brown Company, Latchford, Ont.

62741—Claim No. 11846—Alleged damage to meat $1 14
                                                                        $1 14

British Hotel, Charlton, Ont.

62743—Claim No. 12322—Alleged loss liquor $9 48
                                                                        $9 48

British Red Cross Society, Toronto, Ont.

62448—Donation $5,000 00
                                                                    $5,000 00

Buffalo Brake Beam Company, New York, N.Y.

62620—Fulcrums $35 00
                                                                        $35 00

Bouvier & Hutchinson, Toronto, Ont.

62702—Linen envelopes $29 69
62804—   "   " 20 39
                                                                        $50 08

F. N. Burt Co., Limited, Toronto, Ont.

62812—Books $55 99
                                                                        $55 99

H. Buckler, Cobalt, Ont.

62880—Claim No. 12646—Alleged loss caddy tobacco $18 48
                                                                        $18 48

Charles Baker, Heaslip, Ont.

63370—Ties $10 42
                                                                        $10 42

Borden Milk Company, Limited, Montreal, Que.

63718—Claim No. 12816—Ten cases milk alleged destroyed by fire $35 88
                                                                        $35 88

A. A. Cole, Mining Engineer, Cobalt, Ont.

56467—Salary, November, 1915	$285 00
56717—Expenses	17 79
56610— . "	20 65
56502—Salary, December, 1915	285 00
57451—Salary, January, 1916	285 00
57555—Expenses	11 20
57580—Salary, February, 1916	285 00
57788—Expenses	9 08
58471—Salary, March, 1916	285 00
58675—Expenses.	5 35
58628—Salary, April, 1916	285 00
58756—Expenses.	9 02
59617—Salary, May, 1916	285 00
59765—Expenses	2 81
59784—Salary, June, 1916	285 00

A. A. COLE, MINING ENGINEER, COBALT, ONT.—*Continued.*

```
60180—Expenses ...........................................      2 27
60801—Salary, July, 1916 ...................................    285 00
61051—Expenses ...........................................     20 04
61038—Salary, August, 1916 ................................    285 00
61232—Expenses ...........................................      2 08
62129—Salary, September, 1916 .............................    285·00
62213—Expenses ...........................................      8 98
62340—Salary, October, 1916 ...............................    285 00
62862—Expenses ...........................................      4 16
                                                            ─────────   $3,533 43
```

CANADIAN PACIFIC RAILWAY COMPANY, MONTREAL, QUE.

```
56487—Freight settlement ..................................  $605 82
56567—     "          "    ...............................  1,013 23
56569—Claims .............................................     96 39
56619—Car repairs ........................................     27 74
56649—Claims .............................................    206 14
56763—Freight settlement ..................................    405 29
57011—Tariffs, fuel, ice, repairs to private car ..........     17 69
57097—Car repairs ........................................     21 42
57445—Terminal charges ...................................    656 45
56526—Freight settlement ..................................  2,051 07
56574—     "          "    ...............................  2,174 60
56836—Car service balance ................................  3,367 51
57036—Claims .............................................     95 27
57166—Interline freight balance ...........................  2,153 61
57230—Car repairs ........................................     48 75
57578—Terminal charges ...................................    695 13
56516—Freight settlement ..................................     55 59
57477—     "          "    ...............................    824 49
57481—     "          "    ...............................    648 02
57535—     "          "    ...............................  1,156 22
57581—     "          "    ...............................  1,854 81
57695—Tariffs, supplies, commissions, etc. ................     20 96
58017—Claims .............................................    151 50
58159—Car service balance ................................  1,918 80
58301—Passenger car mileage ..............................      6 96
58309—Ticket balance .....................................  2,991 34
58341—Interline freight balance ...........................    722 10
58467—Rental joint facilities .............................    640 56
57614—Freight settlement ..................................    853 85
57636—Freight settlement ..................................  1,675 30
57716—     "          "    ...............................  1,762 24
57892—Car repairs, heating cars and tariffs ...............     67 81
58058—Car service balance ................................  1,756 80
58250—Ticket balance .....................................    386 95
58488—Rental terminal facilities ..........................    645 38
58590—Commission on tickets, tariffs ......................     17 49
58487—Freight settlement ..................................  2,144 81
58513—     "          "    ...............................  1,438 47
58517—     "          "    ...............................  2,002 73
58655—     "          "    ...............................  4,527 88
59033—Lead, torpedoes ....................................     14 58
59081—Claims .............................................    159 89
59155—Proportion terminal charges ........................        63
59213—Car service balance ................................  1,679 65
59399—Ticket balance .....................................    888 52
59471—Car repairs ........................................        84
59485—     "          .....................................     44 60
59613—Rent of facilities, etc. ............................    701 84
58646—Freight settlement ..................................  2,489 76
58680—Claims .............................................    105 89
58726—Freight settlement ..................................  3,436 42
58733—     "          "    ...............................    539 48
58852—     "          "    ...............................  2,351 81
```

58930—Tariffs supplied	$0	32
58998—Cylinder head	12	41
59024—Claims	60	33
59538—Car service balance	2,222	10
59730—Ticket balance	1,506	67
59643—Freight settlement	1,538	15
59645— " "	1,846	29
59793—Claims	243	55
60137—Car service balance	1,611	45
60373—Ticket balance	1,370	57
60459—Interline freight settlement	1,529	33
60753—Terminal facilities, etc.	672	53
60755— " "	696	13
59808—Freight settlement	235	54
59850— " "	562	43
59940—Car repairs	53	03
60162—Freight settlement	307	72
60358—Terminal charges on European traffic	1	03
60418—Car service balance	1,253	25
60472—Car repairs	68	49
60612—Passenger car mileage	149	27
61022—Terminal charges, etc.	667	36
61028—Interline freight balance	6,524	80
60923—Claims	35	37
60925— "	9	21
60967—Freight settlement	10	82
61055—Tariffs	4	19
61161—Claim	6	00
61411—Car repairs	2	50
61473—Claims	8	91
61557—Tariffs supplied	1	64
61613—Claim	1	48
61677—Car service balance	942	75
61853—Passenger car mileage	15	18
61859—Ticket balance	2,444	09
61871—Claim	2	48
62051— "	11	07
62109—Terminal charges	670	80
62115—Interline freight balance	2,550	31
61054—Freight settlement	138	31
61090—Steam-heating cars, North Bay	10	00
61060—Freight settlement	2,831	17
61204— " "	1,811	19
61310—Claims	23	93
61418— "	14	41
61806— "		80
61896—Interline freight balance	5,478	69
62090—Car service balance	907	55
62318—Terminal charges	681	16
62324—Ticket balance	4,313	14
62137—Freight settlement	4,091	91
62191— " "	1,751	25
62151— " "	2,629	64
62255— " "	1,932	50
62615—Heating cars, tariffs, etc.	126	42
62795—Car-service balance	1,480	50
62939—Passenger car mileage	42	18
62967—Interline freight balance	3,311	81
63219—Car repairs and tariffs	161	09
63221—Claims	20	36
63223—Terminal facilities	631	67
62362—Freight settlement	358	91
62364— " "	1,240	95
62430— " "	1,242	95
62472— " "	2,297	32
62496—Supplies, private cars	1	85

CANADIAN PACIFIC RAILWAY COMPANY, MONTREAL, QUE.—*Continued.*

62882—Claim	13	73
63042—Fuel, car *Temagami*, tariffs	8	48
63224—Claim	11	34
63320—Fuel supplied private cars	3	34
63442—Car service balance	1,585	10
63568—Ticket balance	2,866	31
63594—Car repairs	45	51
63642—Interline freight balance	9,426	41
63672—Claim	3	73
63798—Terminal charges, etc.	685	56
63808—Ice supplied, etc., car *Temagami*	1	25

$136,353 05

CANADIAN NORTHERN RAILWAY SYSTEM, TORONTO.

56489—Freight settlement	$519	76
56581— " "	623	93
56695— " "	537	78
56775— " "	562	42
56947—Car repairs	3	81
57293—Interline freight balance	74	00
56524—Freight settlement	1,061	55
56528— " "	746	99
56564— " "	1,313	68
56654— " "	1,581	03
56854—Car service balance	28	35
57562—Interline freight balance	293	19
57483—Freight settlement	1,983	24
57537— " "	3,827	64
57635— " "	2,218	69
58177—Car service balance	278	55
57608—Freight settlement	2,640	80
57616— " "	1,163	79
57630— " "	1,161	26
57718— " "	852	35
58108—Car service balance	874	80
58489—Freight settlement	957	58
58507— " "	586	93
58521— " "	965	51
58615— " "	651	42
59079—Claims	88	83
59249—Car service balance	1,096	20
59487—Car repairs		56
59559—Interline freight balance	914	43
58684—Freight settlement	874	70
58730— " "	944	38
58736— " "	1,215	51
58926— " "	368	46
59022—Claim	3	26
59358—Car repairs	4	77
59576—Car service balance	752	45
59633—Freight settlement	957	55
59637— " "	393	44
59651— " "	618	26
59733— " "	300	18
59895—Car repairs	3	91
59937—Interline freight balance	100	65
60177—Car service balance	487	35
59830—Freight settlement	132	14
59852— " "	323	19
59926— " "	309	05
60164— " "	479	08
60450—Car service balance	263	25
61028a—Interline freight balance	867	33
61028b— " " "	1,063	96
60839—Freight settlement	401	27

13 T.R.

Canadian Northern Railway System, Toronto.—*Continued.*

60847—Freight settlement	$108 87	
60965— " "	155 91	
61155— " "	245 05	
61369—Car repairs	1 91	
61409— "	1 86	
62055—Claim	5 71	
61050—Freight settlement	572 86	
61062— " "	250 93	
61064— " "	632 19	
61202— " "	264 45	
62320—Interline freight balance	1,585 03	
62139—Freight settlement	756 19	
62149— " "	245 84	
62189— " "	239 79	
62211— " "	1,396 05	
62215—Car repairs	8 63	
63227—Interline freight balance	2,522 44	
62352—Freight settlement	495 45	
62370— " "	849 85	
62432— " "	1,422 88	
62470— " "	604 13	
62624—Car repairs	10 49	
63436—Car service balance	186 30	
63680—Claim	18 20	
		$51,054 22

The Chesapeake & Ohio Railway Company, Richmond, Va.

56495—Car repairs	$5 75	
56943— "	4 01	
56844—Car service balance	38 40	
58023—Claim No. 8979—Amount charges prepaid on car	127 16	
58167—Car service balance	51 75	
58078— " ".	81 90	
59229— " "	93 15	
59234—Car repairs	7 25	
59554—Car service balance	188 00	
60153— " "	314 80	
59946—Car repairs	7 35	
60036— "	9 49	
60434—Car service balance	86 40	
61691— " "	12 60	
61844—Car repairs	9 96	
62104—Car service balance	110 25	
62807— " "	149 85	
63426— " "	138 50	
63604—Car repairs	76	
63840— "	3 29	
		$1,440 62

Central of Georgia Railway Company, Savannah, Ga.

56497—Car repairs	$33 34	
56842—Car service balance	27 00	
58076— " "	14 85	
59227— " "	27 45	
59552— " "	34 65	
60151— " "	20 25	
60432— " "	5 85	
61689— " "	45	
62102— " "	5 40	
62805— " "	26 55	
63424— " "	13 05	
		$208 84

CHICAGO & NORTH WESTERN RAILWAY CO., CHICAGO, ILL.

56499—Freight charges and car repairs	$54 53	
56942—Ticket balance	1 85	
57288—Car repairs	2 79	
58090—Car service balance	5 05	
59239— " "	58 50	
59564— " "	93 15	
60163— " "	101 70	
59944—Car repairs	18 90	
60444—Car service balance	53 10	
62112— " "	30 60	
62224—Ticket balance	1 85	
62817—Car service balance	35 55	
63598—Car repairs	41 42	
		$498 99

CHICAGO JUNCTION RAILWAY COMPANY, CHICAGO, ILL.

56501—Car repairs	$54 28	
56945— "	13 58	
57284— "	20 95	
58365— "	2 76	
59240— "	87 98	
59897— "	1 94	
59954— "	9 15	
61900— "	5 21	
62461— "	1 85	
		$197 70

CHICAGO, ROCK ISLAND & PACIFIC RAILWAY COMPANY, CHICAGO, ILL.

56503—Car repairs	$8 26	
56995— "	2 38	
58165—Car service balance	12 15	
58361—Car repairs	74 19	
58070—Car service balance	31 50	
58072— " "	4 75	
59223— " "	1 80	
59548— " "	18 00	
59795—Claim	3 18	
60083—Car repairs	51	
60145—Car service balance	60 30	
60428— " "	78 50	
60929—Claim	1 46	
60931— "	3 39	
61269—Car repairs	14 00	
61685—Car service balance	44 10	
61840—Car repairs	53 00	
62018— "	6 02	
62098—Car service balance	38 20	
62797— " "	90	
62554—Claim	6 27	
63746—Car repairs	27 27	
		$490 13

CHICAGO, MILWAUKEE & ST. PAUL RAILWAY COMPANY, CHICAGO, ILL.

56505—Car repairs	$46 10
56955— "	25 19
56997— "	90 01
58405— "	82 16
58062—Car service balance	12 90
59489—Car repairs	7 62
59236— "	58 36
59542—Car service balance	82 70
59893—Car repairs	83 03
60147—Car service balance	85 05

CHICAGO, MILWAUKEE & ST. PAUL RAILWAY, ETC.—*Continued.*

59952—Car repairs	27	39
60042— "	8	40
60422—Car service balance	85	95
60470—Car repairs	44	88
61277— "		55
61681—Car service balance	29	70
61838—Car repairs	8	06
63844— "	12	37

$790 42·

MISS LUCY COLES, MILBERTA, ONT.

56555—Loss account, shortage, suit case, Claim No. 10479 ...... $35 00

$35 00

THE CENTRAL FREIGHT ASSOCIATION, CHICAGO, ILL.

56599—Tariffs	$0	78
57229— "		59
57170— "		57
58095— "		49
57932— "		54
59151— "		73
58938—Group maps	5	00
60211—Tariffs		98
61053— "		46
62277— "		32
63048—Tariffs		22

$10 68

THE CANADIAN FREIGHT ASSOCIATION, MONTREAL, P.Q.

56601—Proportion expenses	$33	15
57017— " "	34	06
57132— " "	34	80
58097— "	35	38
57930— "	36	01
59153— "	35	55
60001— "	33	25
60213— "	35	86
60986— " "	35	24
61117—Freight classification	1	01
61555—Proportion expenses	35	01
61342— " "	34	68
62153—Tariffs and classifications	5	71
62353—Proportion expenses	34	93
62974—Proportion expenses	35	34

$459 98

THE COBALT DAILY NUGGET, LIMITED, COBALT, ONT.

56603—Advertising and forms	$44	52
57227— " "	21	84
57172— " "	30	75
57743— " "	21	00
57934— " "	21	00
59569— " "	23	09
59999— " "	21	69
60411— " "	24	94
60735— " "	10	71
60642— " "	9	00
60926— " "	23	34
61567— " "	21	38
62035— " "	8	40
61614— " "	23	79
62697—Forms	11	10

THE COBALT DAILY NUGGET, LIMITED, COBALT, ONT.—*Continued.*

63151—Advertising	52 89	
62708—Subscription	3 00	
62844—Car cards	3 50	
		$375 94

CHICAGO & EASTERN ILLINOIS RAILROAD, CHICAGO, ILL.

56621—Car repairs	$16 86	
56795— " "	74	
56838— " service balance	16 65	
58363— " repairs	2 16	
58066— " service balance	11 25	
59219— " "	40 95	
59546— " "	10 35	
59899— " repairs	49	
60141— " service balance	24 75	
60048— " repairs	1 48	
60424— " service balance	20 25	
61683— " "	15 75	
62094— " "	8 55	
62801— " "	12 60	
63418— " "	7 65	
63740— " repairs	7 43	
		$197 91

CHICAGO, BURLINGTON & QUINCY RAILROAD COMPANY, CHICAGO, ILL.

56623—Car repairs	$6 83	
56651—Claim	2 66	
56683—Car repairs	35 44	
57048—Claims	6 70	
57232—Car repairs and duty on parts	24 14	
58367— " "	85 66	
58084— " service balance	49 95	
58693—Claims	6 98	
59087— "	57 44	
59235—Car service balance	98 55	
59130—Claim	4 36	
59238—Car repairs	34 31	
59560—Car service balance	104 75	
59791—Claim	3 23	
59903—Car repairs	2 02	
60159— " service balance	59 85	
59948— " repairs	7 17	
60038— " "	14 70	
60440— " service balance	92 70	
60620—Ticket balance	4 35	
60927—Claim	54 56	
61475— "	3 27	
61615— "	3 42	
61697—Car service balance	44 55	
61446—Claim	2 95	
61808— "	2 94	
62020—Car repairs	43 53	
62032—Claim	2 40	
62108—Car service balance	8 10	
62459—Car repairs	18 21	
62635—Claim	3 23	
63181— "	5 50	
62888— "	1 86	
63744—Car repairs	43 25	
		$939 56

A. Cavanagh, Tie Inspector, North Bay, Ont.

56773—Travelling expenses			$13 25
56958—	"	"	3 25
59663—	"	"	27 80
61609—	"	"	4 20
62456—	"	"	8 50
			$57 00

Canadian Pacific Railway Company's Telegraph.

56777—Telegraph service			$4 59
57447—	"	interchange	489 46
56660—	"	service	1 43
56662—	"	"	93
56714—	"	"	3 73
57178—	"	"	4 56
57564—	"	interchange	318 64
58099—	"	service	6 81
58469—	"	interchange	374 51
57894—	"	service	4 16
58532—	"	"	4 88
58592—	"	interchange	427 86
58765—	"	service	6 54
59157—	"	"	15 08
59573—	"	interchange balance	433 40
58928—	"	service	4 18
59454—	"	"	2 13
59758—	"	interchange	493 86
59760—	"	service	18 73
59782—	"	"	13 20
59935—	"	"	3 80
60743—	"	"	3 51
60761—	"	"	8 18 —
60765—	"	interchange	391 38
60928—	"	service	1 40
61024—	"	interchange	525 96
61115—	"	service	5 40
61949—	"	"	14 02
62009—	"	"	1 82
62087—	"	"	28 56
62111—	"	interchange	594 47
62250—	"	service	2 19
62326—	"	interchange	673 96
63147—	"	service	3 66
63231—	"	interchange	464 80
63098—	"	service	27 18
63156—	"	"	20 28
63584—	"	"	43 07
63652—	"	"	3 25
63804—	"	"	25 43
63850—	"	interchange	119 73
			$5,590 73

Canadian Car Service Bureau, Montreal, Que.

56779—Proportion cost operation			$21 16
56656—	"	"	22 14
57174—	"	"	20 24
57750—	"	"	27 17
58528—	"	"	26 70
59159—	"	"	25 63
59756—	"	"	25 19
60215—	"	"	27 90
60980—	"	"	20 49
61274—	"	"	25 23

CANADIAN CAR SERVICE BUREAU, MONTREAL, QUE.—*Continued.*

62248—Proportion cost operation	$22 83	
62355— " "	24 13	
63102— " "	26 50	
		$315 31

CHICAGO GREAT WESTERN RAILROAD COMPANY, CHICAGO, ILL.

56797—Car repairs	$6 83	
57001— " "	3 41	
58171— " service balance	12 15	
58086— " "	16 65	
59237— " "	44 10	
59562— " "	23 60	
60027— " repairs	1 13	
60161— " service balance	19 80	
60442— " "	18 00	
61273— " repairs	1 04	
61699— " service balance	6 75	
61902— " repairs	73	
62110— " service balance	34 20	
62813— " "	4 50	
63430— " "	14 40	
63730— " repairs	3 49	
		$210 78

S. B. CLEMENT, CHIEF ENGINEER AND SUPERINTENDENT OF MAINTENANCE. NORTH BAY, ONT.

56809—Salary, November, 1915	$345 00	
56636— " December, 1915	345 00	
57020—Expenses	24 40	
57619— "	24 25	
57645—Salary, January, 1916	345 00	
57708—Expenses	21 55	
57734—Salary, February, 1916	345 00	
58595—Expenses	33 05	
58659—Salary, March, 1916	345 00	
58810— " April, 1916	345 00	
59699—Expenses	38 25	
59817—Salary, May, 1916	345 00	
60212— " June, 1916	345 00	
60262—Expenses	65 20	
61323—Salary, July, 1916	345 00	
61184— " August, 1916	345 00	
61340—Expenses	31 53	
62243—Salary, September, 1916	345 00	
62600— " October, 1916	345 00	
62756—Expenses	49 38	
		$4,427 61

CHARLES CADDEN, TYRESETTER, NORTH BAY, ONT.

56821—Award, W. C. B., *re* injuries alleged received	$12 59	
		$12 59

CANADIAN CONSOLIDATED RUBBER COMPANY, LIMITED, TORONTO.

56829—Hose and packing	$203 11
56550—Hose and rubber goods	149 88
56614—Rubber bands	20 24
56664—Gaskets and packing	7 45
57491—Hose, packing, boots and bands	134 44
57591—Boots and hose bags	91 04
57663—Hose	198 97
57650—Hose, boots and force cups	124 51
57792—Packing, matting and hose	189 27

Canadian Consolidated Rubber Company, Limited, Toronto.—*Continued.*

58551—Packing, washers and hose	151 27	
58651—Hose and rubber bands	442 91	
58658—Men's Cabot fusion	54 00	
58758—Water hose, packing, etc.	29 67	
58864—Packing, hose and boots	68 87	
58986—Rubber bands	22 54	
59669—Valves	10 19	
59827—Packing, Cabots	39 81	
60124—Packing, hose, etc.	397 08	
60208—Hose, valves, matting	78 26	
60878—Packing, rings	5 16	
61007—Hose, couplings, plugs	27 78	
61901—Cabot, boots	23 40	
61620—Bands, hose, couplings	114 78	
62215—Rubber bands	22 77	
62391—Hose, sprinklers, etc.	296 66	
62689—Hose	38 00	
62384—Fusion	9 95	
62590—Hose	16 64	
63062—Hose	18 82	
		$2,987 47

Thos. Cook & Son, New York, N.Y.

56835—Commission on ticket sales	$0 92	
58522— " "	1 93	
59163— " "	1 23	
62704— " "	6 43	
		$10 51

F. T. Cade, Machinist, North Bay, Ont.

56865—Travelling expenses	$2 15	
58637— " "	2 50	
		$4 65

Cleveland, Cincinnati, Chicago & St. Louis Ry. Co., Cincinnati, Ohio.

56887—Duty and freight on car repair parts	$5 95	
58311—Ticket balance	6 82	
59497—Car repairs	1 10	
59258— " "	11 33	
61373— " "	22	
61842— " "	27 01	
62463— " "	2 71	
63602— " "	11 88	
		$67 02

Canadian Shovel & Tool Company, Limited, Hamilton, Ont.

56891—Shovels	$63 31	
57493— "	42 75	
58555— "	71 25	
58660—	14 25	
58866—	158 27	
59967—	126 62	
60122—	7 92	
61682—	135 66	
62361—	83 09	
		$703 12

Bernard Cairns, Toronto.

56921—Rubber stamps	$0 80	
58324—Steel figures and letters	16 00	
58535—Colonial dater	2 00	
		$18 80

CANADIAN GOVERNMENT RAILWAYS, MONCTON, N.B.

56923—Gas, shifting load, car repairs	$22 48
56700—Freight settlement	342 34
56856—Car service balance	886 17
57044—Claim	1 65
57224—Freight settlement	30 06
57697—Car repairs, commission	36 76
58299—Passenger car mileage	268 18
57782—Rental right of way for pipe line	1 00
57896—Commission on tickets	52
58110—Car service balance	287 55
58246—Passenger car mileage	356 73
58885—Claim	1 33
59251—Car service balance	749 25
59393—Passenger car mileage	308 66
59401—Ticket balance	65 19
59439—Proportion commission paid on tickets	24 22
59561—Interline freight balance	170 85
59018—Claim	5 28
59020—Claims	26 21
59578—Car service balance	1,592 10
59724—Passenger car mileage	488 29
59997—Proportion commission on business	9 42
60023—Car repairs	22 99
60059— " "	96
60109—Claims	19 80
60179—Car service balance	517 92
60365—Passenger car mileage	321 31
60413—Car repairs	23 45
60415—Commission on tickets	26 54
60451—Claims	12 45
59918— "	17 38
59942—Car repairs	5 57
60544— " service balance	47 70
60614—Passenger car mileage	475 64
60977—Claims	82 75
61159— "	1 98
61367—Car repairs	173 58
61851—Passenger car mileage	503 47
62053—Claims	30 63
61096—Car repairs	13 24
61136—Proportion commission paid agents	7 57
61276—Transferring coal, T. & N. O. 60605	1 21
61304—Coal and ice supplied	64
61364—Claims	3 70
61454—Commission paid on tickets	5 35
61666—Claims	26 67
61668— "	46 09
61722— "	30 24
61782— "	40 43
61846—Car repairs	16 13
61892—Claims	54 18
61960—Car repairs	29 58
62034—Claim	1 73
62218—Passenger car mileage	481 17
62228—Ticket balance	842 02
62169—Commission on westbound business	3 40
62715—Claims	65 59
62937—Passenger car mileage	394 11
63093—Claims	10 21
62386—Rental right of way for pipe line	1 00
62760—Freight settlement	2,014 91
62884—Claims	28 38
63372—Fuel supplied car " Sir James "	10 55
63524—Car service balance	273 81
63570—Ticket balance	579 49

CANADIAN GOVERNMENT RAILWAYS, MONCTON, N.B.—*Continued.*

63592—Car repairs	22 63	
63678—Claims	79 25	
63748—Car repairs	3 54	
63806—Supplies, car "Temagami"	6 50	
63836—Car repairs	26 65	
		$13,078 33

ADOLPHE CHARPENTIER, CONNAUGHT, ONT.

56925—Donation, account cow alleged killed	$25 00	
		$25 00

THE CHICAGO & ALTON RAILROAD COMPANY, CHICAGO, ILL.

56949—Car repairs	$2 58	
56959— " "	5 25	
57290— " "	3 42	
58161—Car service balance	4 95	
58060— " "	4 50	
59215— " "	4 90	
59232— " repairs	8 16	
59540— " service balance	7 65	
60139— " "	8 10	
60420— " "	3 15	
61265—Car repairs	62	
62457— " "	9 05	
62799— " service balance	5 85	
63416— "– "	22 95	
63842— " repairs	5 21	
		$96 34

THE CENTRAL RAILROAD COMPANY OF NEW JERSEY, NEW YORK, N.Y.

56951—Car repairs	$0 25	
		$0 25

CINCINNATI, NEW ORLEANS & TEXAS PACIFIC RAILWAY COMPANY, CINCINNATI, OHIO.

56953—Car repairs	$3 44	
56840— " service balance	22 95	
58074— " "	12 00	
59225— " "	14 85	
59230— " repairs	71	
59550— " service balance	43 20	
60025— " repairs	89	
60149— " service balance	19 35	
60430— " "	11 70	
61687— " "	24 30	
62100— " "	90	
62803— " "	22 05	
63422— " "	13 50	
63742— " repairs	19 37	
		$209 21

THE CHICAGO, ROCK ISLAND & GULF RAILWAY COMPANY, FORT WORTH, TEXAS.

56957—Car repairs	$1 17	
59429— " "	41	
61679— " service balance	1 80	
62092— " "	1 35	
63414— " "	12 50	
		$17 23

CINCINNATI, HAMILTON & DAYTON RAILWAY COMPANY, CINCINNATI, OHIO.

56999—Car repairs		$4 03
57286— " "		74
58082— " service balance		16 20
59233— " "		36 90
59558— " "		10 35
60157— " "		21 15
60438— " "		33 75
60468— " repairs		5 49
61267— " "		2 27
61695— " service balance		4 95
62811— " "		4 95
63217— " repairs		1 74
63600— " "		1 95
63750— " "		1 93
		$146 40

COLLECTOR OF CUSTOMS, NORTH BAY, ONT.

57009—Duty on coal, etc.		$3,309 60
56652— " soft coal, etc.		3,091 42
57485— " steel cars		19,149 75
57633— " coal		3,402 24
57626— " electros and half-tones		25 62
57714— " soft coal, etc.		5,126 61
58619— "		5,795 07
58686— "		4,113 35
58728—		4,999 10
58796— "		4,192 81
59635— "		2,739 90
59839— " "		2,367 54
59828— "		2,405 95
59878— "		2,052 89
60827— "		1,272 22
60963— "		1,665 74
61066— " "		522 87
61068— "		940 49
61210— "		1,504 80
62147—		2,261 30
62171— "		2,025 52
62233—		1,625 65
62356— "		1,263 87
62390— "		1,703 13
62770— "		1,369 42
		$78,926 86

COCHRANE STEAM LAUNDRY, COCHRANE, ONT.

57013—Laundry		$45 46
56718— "		19 06
58433— "		19 18
58524—		26 02
58526—		26 00
59567—		28 24
59762— "		23 63
60072—		23 61
60982— "		27 13
62089—		20 12
61616—		20 13
62498— "		23 86
63324—		19 09
		$321 53

THE COURIER PRINTING COMPANY, ENGLEHART, ONT.

57015—Electros $50 00
63322—Advertising 30 08
                                                                        $80 08

THE CHARLTON-ENGLEHART LIGHT & POWER COMPANY, CHARLTON, ONT.

57019—Current supplied $3 30
57413—   " 127 06
56716—   " 3 40
57176—   " 6 20
57566—   " 144 34
58435—   " 141 22
57748—   " 3 20
58530—   " 2 20
58594—   " 141 76
59147—   " 144 65
59458—   " 121 78
59766—   " 3 80
60409—   " 3 20
60741—   " 138 15
60666—   " 155 39
62005—   " 131 50
61338—   " 9 30
62252—   " 108 54
62254—   " 5 20
63145—   " 107 05
62500—   " 4 80
63374—   " 149 81
63650—   " 4 10
                                                                        $1,659 95

B. J. COGHLIN COMPANY, LIMITED, MONTREAL, P.Q.

57141—Springs, tommy bars $6 84
57370—Tail pockets and springs 114 75
58326—Coupling springs 48 13
59031—Chain, bars 50 56
58994—Steel chain, ropes 117 60
60497—Chain 10 20
60302—Wrecking chains, tommy bars 55 19
60694—Brakes, springs, etc. 432 50
60886—Chains 5 71
                                                                        $841 48

CANADIAN FAIRBANKS-MORSE COMPANY, TORONTO.

57149—Pulley, packing, battery supplies, etc. $80 78
57341—Claim No. 10302—Overcharge on steel 3 17
57046—Claims No. 10187 and 10382—Overcharge rate on scales
          and freight on pipe fittings 5 52
57376—Pulley, gears, graphite, etc. 48 04
57398—Packing 11 29
57833—Packing and belt dressing 31 36
58300—Belt, graphite, zinc, soda and oil 219 05
58911—Rivets, plates, etc. 249 08
58992—Pumper, emery powder, etc. 771 50
60493—Graphite, plumbago 10 83
60702—Velocipede cars, graphite 132 00
60872—Water box, castings, etc. 155 52
61009—Scale lever, steam pump 277 80
61129—Vulcan chain, wrench 9 18
61903—Clips 8 16
61504—Tube 3 60
61684—Graphite, plugs, etc. 15 37
62725—Brackets, springs, etc. 19 43
62626—Tube, conductor for motor 9 10

CANADIAN FAIRBANKS-MORSE COMPANY, TORONTO.—*Continued.*

62828—Belt	316 25	
63060—Air cocks, tee handles, etc.	11 16	
63272—Palmetto packing	44 56	
		$2,432 75

CHARCOAL SUPPLY COMPANY, TORONTO.

57151—Jute sacks and charcoal	$18 25	
57390— " "	16 41	
57841— " "	24 00	
58921—	42 15	
60479— " "	19 57	
61897—	20 88	
61512—	31 17	
63064— ..	23 31	
		$195 74

CANADIAN GENERAL ELECTRIC CO., LIMITED, TORONTO.

57153—Electrical material	$47 60	
57366—Lamps, repairing metre	22 39	
57809—Electrical goods	68 63	
58296—Electrical material	28 66	
58995—Switches, cut outs, etc.	12 22	
58978—Electrical material	142 93	
60569—Fish wire, plates, etc.	115 79	
60712—Tape, indicators, torches	21 10	
60930—Holders, alphaduct, etc.	23 37	
61127—Tube	40	
61506—Sockets	73	
61678—Springs, alphaduct	20 25	
63111—Sockets, bushings, etc.	42 75	
62622—Metal shell receptacles	3 66	
62838—Fuses	3 78	
		$554 26

A. D. COOK, LAWRENCEBURG, IND.

57155—Spur gear	$65 00	
		$65 00

THE CANADA PAINT CO., LIMITED, MONTREAL, P.Q.

57157—Paints, putty, turps., etc.	$475 08	
57378— "	55 66	
57801— "	497 76	
58322— " and varnishes	188 50	
58871— " lead, putty, etc.	786 98	
59038— "	142 93	
60483— " etc.	307 05	
60692— " turps, shellac	611 99	
60888— "	156 07	
61013—Turpentine	26 52	
61121—Paint, white lead, putty	259 20	
62699—Paint, white lead, etc.	715 39	
62588—Pumice stone	2 45	
63058—Paint, varnish, etc.	553 31	
		$4,778 89

CANADIAN RAMAPO IRON WORKS, LIMITED, NIAGARA FALLS, ONT.

57159—Compromise splices	$24 00	
57837—Switch stands, braces and slide plates	327 16	
58318—Castings	18 00	
59052—Malleable handles	13 80	
60696—Switch stands	111 00	
61139—Frogs, switches	1,727 25	
61674—Frogs, switches	387 25	
63054—Switch stands, frogs, etc.	1,917 45	
		$4,525 91

THE CLEVELAND-SARNIA SAW MILLS CO., LIMITED, SARNIA, ONT.

57161—Track scales	$350 00	
57393—Claim No. 8646, loss account shortage five bales angle bars	28 75	
		$378 75

THE CANADA METAL CO., LIMITED, TORONTO.

57163—Pig lead	$67 21	
57400—Zinc and copper	87 50	
57817—Metals	150 28	
57928—Metals and lead pipe	56 06	
58314—Zincs, coppers for batteries	250 00	
58747—Metals	120 16	
59044—Metals	144 36	
60501—Zinc, lead, metal	181 18	
61119—Battery coffers	12 50	
61895—Babbitt, solder	90 53	
62703—Babbitt, solder	198 40	
		$1,358 18

THE CARTER'S INK COMPANY, MONTREAL, P.Q.

57165—Ink and mucilage	$108 25	
60495— " "	36 25	
60710— " "	44 38	
61569—Ribbons for typewriter	56 62	
61470—Carbon paper	4 00	
61622—Ink	25 75	
62705—Mucilage	8 50	
		$283 75

CANADIAN CAR & FOUNDRY CO., LIMITED, MONTREAL, P.Q.

57167—Castings, car parts	$44 15	
57380—Brake beams and centre plates	223 00	
57396—Centre plates	5 00	
57803—Bearings and art glass	13 80	
59046—Connecting pins, brake beams	102 50	
61510—Brake beams	123 00	
62727— "	54 00	
62824— "	124 70	
63270—Castings, etc.	47 45	
		$737 60

COWAN & COMPANY OF GALT, LIMITED, GALT. ONT.

57169—Knives	$5 05	
59050—Knives	30 08	
		$35 13

CANADIAN YALE & TOWNE, LTD., ST. CATHARINES, ONT.

57171—Latches	$8 16	
57372—Padlocks and sheaves	44 84	
57825— " latches	36 22	
58917— "	22 59	
59040— " keys	24 09	
60360— "	23 49	
60680—Locks	8 16	
61371—Blanks	99	
61582—Padlocks	8 62	
62389—Latches	19 67	
62628—Padlocks	40 28	
		$237 11

CRUCIBLE STEEL COMPANY OF AMERICA, PITTSBURG, PA.

57173—Steel	$33 80	
		$33 80

CRAIN PRINTERS, LTD., OTTAWA, ONT.

57175—Forms	$51 87	
57827— " and time sheets	11 03	
58809—Time slips, bills of lading	27 25	
59000—Forms	2 47	
60356—Time sheets	17 50	
60714—Forms	57 25	
61201—Binders	3 80	
61472—Forms	13 25	
61618— "	50 63	
62693— "	36 95	
62840—Way bills	13 75	
		$285 75

THE CHAS. CHAPMAN CO., LONDON, ONT.

57177—Books, forms	$75 75	
57358—Account books and forms	172 30	
58320—Forms, memo books and way bills	44 10	
58919— "	88 35	
59008—Stationery	90 75	
60487—Forms	21 00	
61141—Memo. book forms	18 48	
61624—Forms	35 75	
62695— "	17 78	
		$564 26

CANADIAN LOCOMOTIVE COMPANY, LTD., KINGSTON, ONT.

57179—Ash pan guides	$92 00	
57408—Tithe sheet	80 00	
57829—Ash pan guides and slides	86 64	
58316—Ferrules, tubes, guides and slides	184 95	
58873—Rack shafts	23 85	
58982—Engine truck frame	30 38	
60515—Castings, frames, etc.	333 60	
62691—Coupling rod strap	36 75	
62834—Draw bars, etc.	437 52	
63030—Locomotives	100,485 00	
63032— "	67,015 00	
63648—Locomotive and locomotive parts	37,351 00	
		$206,156 69

CANADIAN PNEUMATIC TOOL COMPANY, LTD., MONTREAL, P.Q.

57193—Machine bits	$9 00	
57404—Auger bits	6 94	
58328—Repairing hammer	14 43	
58913— " drill	152 61	
59048—Breast drill	63 00	
60503—Repairs to chipper	12 94	
60708— " "	32 09	
60876— " parts	51 87	
		$342 88

CANADA GRIP NUT COMPANY, LTD., MONTREAL, P.Q.

57195—Grip nuts	$36 01	
57813— " "	13 13	
60481— " "	16 00	
		$65 14

W. H. COE MANUFACTURING COMPANY, PROVIDENCE, R.I., U.S.A.

57197—Gold leaf, etc.	$20 15
57839—Paints	25 42
58332—Gold leaf and aluminum	10 69
58805—Gold leaf	30 70

W. H. Coe Manufactubing Company, Etc.—*Continued.*

60690—Gold ribbon and aluminum	$26 09	
61133— " "	16 66	
61676— " " and aluminum	15 83	
63052— " " etc.	42 15	
		$187 69

Canadian Wm. A. Rogers, Ltd., Toronto, Ont.

57199—Knives and forks	$16 80	
58304—Reflectors replated and refinished	11 50	
58976— " "	43 30	
60505— "	24 73	
61048—E. P. B. M. shield	33 00	
63264—Eudora fruit knives, etc.	18 31	
		$147 64

The Cain Coal Company, North Cobalt, Ont.

57343—Claim No. 10415, damage to doors	$10 35	
		$10 35

Canadian Express Company, North Bay, Ont.

57411—Express charges	$34 31	
57168— " "	22 68	
58437— " "	37 22	
58534— " "	27 75	
59575— " "	28 19	
59456— " "	19 78	
60763— " "	40 48	
60644— " "	28 92	
62007— " "	26 90	
61784— " "	23 40	
62969— " "	36 88	
63852— " "	27 39	
		$353 90

Canadian Westinghouse Company, Ltd., Hamilton, Ont.

57415—Air brake and electrical material	120 60	
57402— " " material	5 06	
57805—Fittings	243 24	
58358— " metre, valves, etc.	242 51	
59133—Air brake material	199 38	
58877— " "	22 42	
59012—Valves, springs, etc.	166 19	
60571—Cases, vents, rings, etc.	396 35	
60704—Rings, cages, bushes	73 80	
60882—Armature, adjuster, etc.	250 36	
61135—Fans, switches, etc.	322 03	
61907—Seat, latch, rings	28 80	
61670—Springs, air brake material	88 17	
61724—Meters, expanders, etc.	218 32	
62971—Air brake material	119 35	
62630— " pistons, etc.	34 12	
62836—Underground reel, bushes, etc.	167 60	
63066—Drain, cocks, keys, etc.	15 32	
		$2,713 62

Canadian Bronze, Ltd., Toronto.

57417—Castings	$427 58	
57419— "	817 01	
57386—Brass castings and bearings	1,661 41	
58302—Castings and journal bearings	1,496 07	
58867— " liners, bearings, etc.	1,649 68	
59042— "	1,210 00	

CANADIAN BRONZE, LTD., TORONTO.—*Continued.*

60517—Castings, bearings, etc.	2,650 77	
61125— "	40 75	
61942—Valves, liners, brasses, etc.	104 12	
63100—Castings, liners, brasses, etc.	1,882 38	
		$11,939 77

COCHRANE HARDWARE, LTD., NORTH BAY, ONT.

57443—Hardware	$171 47	
57394— " and blankets	165 56	
57845— "	79 08	
58298— " snowshoes, crayons, paper	75 74	
58925—Dynamite, twine, etc.	165 17	
59036— " blankets	451 21	
60573— " stock patterns, etc.	608 59	
60304—Alabastine, discs	13 50	
60700—Dynamite, padlocks, keys, etc.	379 21	
61010—Caps, scythes, stones, etc.	154 17	
61011—Traps, dynamite, pails, etc.	.92 06	
61137—Tees, elbows, etc.	8 84	
61571—Crayons, etc.	10 75	
61951—Tea pot, knives, forks, etc.	24 56	
61476—Surprise paper, sulphite, etc.	136 58	
61584—Locks, dynamite, etc.	110 01	
61726—Screen windows, doors, etc.	162 44	
61940—Dynamite, roofing	341 48	
62721—Hardware	346 61	
62372—Overpayment of deposit on contract	8 50	
62764—Sinks, taps, etc.	74 73	
62832—Quebec heater, etc.	41 50	
63046—Galv. ventilators	50 00	
63268—Quebec heater, stove pipe	60 70	
63674—Claim No. 12719, loss glass and hardware	37 52	
		$3,769 98

CANADIAN INDEPENDENT TELEPHONE ASSOCIATION, TORONTO.

56530—Donation	$5 90	
57541—Membership fee	5 00	
		$10 90

W. H. COX COAL CO., LTD., TORONTO.

56620—Coal	$578 71	
57553— "	552 47	
57720— "	402 73	
58617— "	110 50	
59134— "	109 54	
60575— "	122 18	
		$1,876 13

COPELAND-CHATTERSON CO., LTD., TORONTO.

56658—Ledger binders and index	$36 25	
57136—Binder, leaves and index	36 81	
57832—Self locking binder	2 50	
		$75 56

COCHRANE TELEPHONE CO., LTD., COCHRANE, ONT.

56720—Rental of telephone	$15 00	
59735— " "	15 00	
60391— " "	35 00	
60897— " ..	17 50	
		$82 50

14 T.R.

CENTRAL VERMONT RAILWAY, ST. ALBANS, VT.

```
56846—Car service balance .................................    $40 50
58169— "    "      "      .................................     49 95
58080— "    "      "      .................................     31 05
59231— "    "      "      .................................     21 15
59473— "  repairs .........................................      2 40
59495— "    "      .........................................      1 38
59556— "  service balance .................................     25 20
59732—Ticket balance .......................................      1 70
59905—Car repairs .........................................      6 33
60155—Car service balance .................................      2 25
60044— "  repairs .........................................        72
60436— "  service balance .................................      9 00
61279— "  repairs .........................................      4 63
61693— "  service balance .................................     14 85
62014— "  repairs .........................................      1 19
62106— "  service balance .................................     13 05
62809— "    "      "      .................................     30 60
63428— "    "      "      .................................     15 75
63833— "  repairs .........................................        27
                                                               ———————
                                                                $271 97
```

CHARLESTON & WESTERN CAROLINA RAILWAY, WILMINGTON, N.C.

```
56848—Car service balance .................................     $6 75
59241— "    "      "      .................................      3 60
59566— "    "      "      .................................      4 50
60167— "    "      "      .................................        90
60448— "    "      "      .................................      3 60
                                                               ———————
                                                                 $19 35
```

CHICAGO, INDIANAPOLIS & LOUISVILLE RAILWAY, CHICAGO, ILL.

```
56850—Car service balance .................................     $7 65
57278—Car repairs .........................................        20
58094—Car service balance .................................     22 05
59245—Car service balance .................................     10 80
59491—Car repairs .........................................      1 97
59570—Car service balance .................................     31 50
60171—   "      "      .................................     31 95
61703—   "      "      .................................     20 25
62116—   "      "      .................................     22 95
62465—Car repairs .........................................        48
62823—Car service balance .................................        45
63434—   "      "      .................................     15 75
63596—Car repairs .........................................      1 94
                                                               ———————
                                                                $167 94
```

CENTRAL NEW ENGLAND RAILWAY, NEW HAVEN, CONN.

```
56852—Car service balance .................................     $0 45
58096—   "      "      .................................      4 05
59247—   "      "      .................................     13 95
59572—   "      "      .................................      5 85
60173—   "      "      .................................      2 70
61271—Car repairs .........................................        51
61705—Car service balance .................................     15 30
62118—   "      "      .................................      3 60
62825—   "      "      .................................      1 35
63738—Car repairs .........................................        34
                                                               ———————
                                                                 $48 10
```

R. CROGHAN, M.P. DEPT., NORTH BAY, ONT.

```
57030—Expenses—travelling .................................    $14 00
                                                               ———————
                                                                 $14 00
```

A. R. CLARKE & CO., LIMITED, TORONTO, ONT.

57050—Claim No. 10563—damage to trunk $2 50

$2 50

JOHN H. COLE, MATHESON, ONT.

57052—Claim No. 9187—shortage tobacco $50 61

$50 61.

CENTRAL INDIANA RAILWAY COMPANY, ANDERSON, IND.

57276—Car repairs $0 20
62124—Car service balance 5 40

$5 60

CHICAGO, ST. PAUL, MINNEAPOLIS & OMAHA RAILWAY COMPANY, ST. PAUL, MINN.

57280—Car repairs $17 15
58092—Car service balance 8 55
58795—Car repairs 1 15
59493—Car repairs 83
60165—Car service balance 12 40
59950—Car repairs 6 98
60446—Car service balance 9 40
60466—Car repairs 5 95
61275—   " 4 24
61848—   " 3 75
62016—   " 3 68
62819—Car service balance 33 70
63432—Car service balance 10 80
63846—Car repairs 6 38

$124 96

THE CENTRAL RAILROAD COMPANY OF NEW JERSEY, NEW YORK, N.Y.

57282—Car repairs $2 13
58163—Car service balance 1 35
58068—   "   " 50 40
59221—   "   " 64 35
59256—Car repairs 12 10
59901—Car repairs 18 56
60143—Car service balance 50 40
60040—Car repairs 1 47
60426—Car service balance 20 25
61094—Car repairs 4 05
62012—Car repairs 8 92
62096—Car service balance 4 05
63420—Car service balance 33 75

$271 78

CLEVELAND COPPER FERRULE CO., CLEVELAND, O.

57360—Copper ferrules $27 57
57821—   " 22 98
57954—   " 33 13
58553—   " 91 65
59737—   " 183 05
61605—Exchange on cheques 1 29

$359 67

CENTRAL RAILWAY SIGNAL COMPANY, IBERVILLE, QUE.

57362—Fusees $68 00
57646—Fusees and torpedoes 370 93
58557—Torpedoes 208 25
58656—Torpedoes and fusees 580 65
68868—Torpedoes 22 05
62842—Torpedoes 67 50
63050—Fusees, torpedoes 344 00

$1,661 38

CANADIAN STEEL FOUNDRIES, LIMITED, MONTREAL, P.Q.

57364—Tower locks, clevises and pins	$52 30
57799—Couplers and knuckle pins	52 50
58294—Couplers and knuckle lock blocks, etc.	576 68
58915—Couplers and knuckle pins	592 50
58980—Couplers and switch tongues	159 00
60507—Switch points, clamp frogs	628 00
60698—Couplers, knuckles	692 75
60874—Breckett teeth	55 40
61131—Coupler, clevises, etc.	174 60
61909—Express on patterns	90
61574—Switch points	730 00
61672—Coupler, knuckles	101 25
62973—Couplers, steel corners, etc.	215 74
62830—Hub liners and couplers	47 71

$4,078 33

CANADIAN GOLD CAR HEATING & LIGHTING CO., LTD., MONTREAL, P.Q.

57368—Diaphragms	$6 60
57823— "	13 86
58875— "	32 01
62453—Tee traps, trap seats, etc.	64 24
62822—Tee trap bodies, etc.	99 00

$215 71

CANADIAN EXPLOSIVES, LIMITED, OTTAWA, ONT.

57374—Safety fuse	$12 00
58990—Pinions	3 08
60499—Blasting caps	299 81

$314 89

CANADIAN ALLIS-CHALMERS, LIMITED, TORONTO, ONT.

57382—Elbows	$36 26
57831—Castings, fittings and pipes	825 55
58887—Claim No. 10625—overcharge rate shot	1 44
61899—Valves, rods, rings	46 57
62359—Structural steel	2,612 85

$3,522 67

CANADA MACHINERY CORPORATION, LIMITED, GALT, ONT.

57388—Shearing machine	$1,227 00

$1,227 00

THE CARBORUNDUM COMPANY, NIAGARA FALLS, ONT.

57384—Alox wheels	$13 25
60890—Alox wheels	6 63
61005—Emery wheels	18 55
61680—Carbo wheels	3 33

$41 76

CHICAGO CAR HEATING COMPANY, MONTREAL, P.Q.

57392—Stove	$22 00
58801—Steam hose gaskets	12 50
62816—Steam hose gaskets	25 00

$59 50

CANADIAN ASBESTOS COMPANY, MONTREAL, P.Q.

57406—Gaskets	$6 70
57819—Millboard	40 43
57841—Covering	21 37
58869—Asbestos, etc.	14 12

CANADIAN ASBESTOS COMPANY, MONTREAL, P.Q.—*Continued.*

68984—Asbestos, wick, waste	28 25	
59080—Asbestos	3 01	
60706—Magnesia blocks	18 75	
60932—Lagging	75 17	
61123—Air cell	23 40	
62826—Asbestos air cell covering	31 35	
63044—Asbestos air cell covering	12 15	
		$274 70

CORPORATION OF THE TOWN OF HAILEYBURY, HAILEYBURY, ONT.

57531—Water rates	$17 00	
58908— "	17 00	
62512— "	20 40	
60899— "	20 40	
		$74 80

F. CADE, M.P. DEPT.. NORTH BAY, ONT.

57571—Expenses—travelling	$2 40	
		$2 40

CANADA FURNITURE MANUFACTURERS, LIMITED, WOODSTOCK, ONT.

57589—Cabinet and guides	$12 59	
57638—Cards	11 51	
		$24 10

CANADIAN EDGE TOOL COMPANY, GALT. ONT.

57675—Bench axes	$8 73	
59965—Axes	29 11	
		$37 84

COBALT WATER COMMISSION, COBALT, ONT.

57699—Water supplied—locomotives	$2 02	
57898— " "	2 37	
59161— " "	2 03	
59563— " "	9 19	
		$15 61

THE CANADIAN FORESTRY ASSOCIATION, OTTAWA, ONT.

57795—Subscriptions, *Canadian Forestry Journal*	$3 00	
61336— " " " "	1 00	
61938— " " " "	8 00	
		$12 00

L. C. CHASE & COMPANY, BOSTON, MASS.

57797—Plush	$17 99	
58923—Frieze	311 08	
		$329 07

CANADA IRON FOUNDRIES, LIMITED, MONTREAL, QUE.

57807—Castings	$15 48	
62701—Grates	5 40	
62434—Grate castings	21 17	
		$42 05

CANADIAN NATIONAL CARBON COMPANY. LIMITED, TORONTO, ONT.

57811—Columbia regular cells	$31 25	
		$31 25

E. R. CALDWELL & COMPANY, BRADFORD, PA.

57815—Pump bodies $13 00

$13 00

CONSOLIDATED CAR-HEATING COMPANY, ALBANY, N.Y.

57835—Diaphragms	$13 20
57690—Gaskets	33 00
58312— "	66 00
58803— "	33 00
62814—	108 90

$254.10

CHICAGO BRIDGE & IRON WORKS, CHICAGO, ILL.

57955—Steel tower and tank $847 30

$847 30

CLAYBELT PRINTING & PUBLISHING CO., LIMITED, COCHRANE, ONT.

58019—Claim No. 10573—damage to printing press	$5 00
60209—Advertising	4 30
62374— "	8 40
62706— "	21 30

$39 00

CAMPBELL & DEYELL, LIMITED, COBALT, ONT.

58021—Claim No. 8959—overcharge weight silver ore	$157 75
63183—Claim No. 11620—overcharge rate silver ore	28 36

$186 11

CAROLINA, CLINCHFIELD & OHIO RAILWAY. JOHNSTON CITY, TENN.

58173—Car service balance	$15 30
58088— "	"	5 40
62815— "	"	4 05

$24 75

COLORADO & SOUTHERN RAILWAY CO., DENVER, COL.

58175—Car service balance	$3 15
58407—Car repairs	5 29
59243—Car service balance	5 85
59568— "	"	9 25
60169— "	"	6 75
61701— "	"	7 65
61092—Car repairs	2 89
62114—Car service balance	17 55
62821— "	"	13 05

$71 43

CHICAGO, NEW YORK & BOSTON REFRIGERATOR CO., CHICAGO, ILL.

58179—Car service balance	$3 79
58114— "	"	1 93
59255— "	"	1 93
59582— "	"	3 87
60183— "	"	1 90
60454— "	"	86
61709— "	"	1 03
62829— "		1 90
63440— "	"	1 90

$19 11

CANADIAN BROTHERHOOD OF RAILROAD EMPLOYEES, HALIFAX, N.S.

57688—Advertising, *Canadian Railroad Employees' Monthly* $10 00

$10 00

COCHRANE SHEET METAL & CORNISH WORKS, COCHRANE, ONT.

57834—Repairs to heating system $12 60
$12 60

DR. D. R. CAMERON, COCHRANE, ONT.

57860—Professional service rendered $10 00
$10 00

WM. COMRIE, EXTRA GANG FOREMAN, NORTH BAY, ONT.

57968—Travelling expenses $3 70
$3 70

FRANK A. CHILD, COCHRANE, ONT.

57984—Claim No. 10651—loss account, damage to stove $3 70
$3 70

CHICAGO, PEORIA & ST. LOUIS RAILROAD COMPANY, SPRINGFIELD, ILL.

58064—Car service balance	$0 45	
59217— " "	2 25	
59544— " "	5 40	
61962—Car repairs	28	
		$8 38

COTTON BELT ROUTE, TYLER, TEX.

58112—Car service balance	$3 60	
59253— " "	17 10	
59580— " "	17 55	
60181— " "	20 25	
60452— " "	12 15	
61707— " "	90	
62122— " "	15 75	
62827— " "	16 65	
63438— " "	2 70	
		$106 65

CENTRAL WEST VIRGINIA & SOUTHERN RAILROAD COMPANY, HENDRICKS, W. VA.

58166—Car service balance	$0 45	
59257— " . "	4 05	
		$4 50

CANADIAN DETROIT LUBRICATOR COMPANY, LIMITED, WALKERVILLE, ONT.

58306—Lubricator and filing plugs	$82 90	
59054—Lubricator parts	18 20	
62723—Packing, glasses	7 92	
		$109 02

THE CANADIAN BAG COMPANY, LIMITED, MONTREAL, P.Q.

58308—Seamless bags $104 00
$104 00

THE CURTAIN SUPPLY COMPANY, CHICAGO, ILL.

58310—Webbing and gimp	$5 25	
58807—Curtains	54 12	
61686—Tin rollers	7 12	
		$66 49

COLUMBIA GRAPHOPHONE COMPANY, TORONTO, ONT.

58330—Dictaphone cylinders $10 00
$10 00

R. W. Copps, Timmins, Ont.

58596—Livery service $3 00

                  $3 00

W. Connelly, Elk Lake P.O.

58593—Ties $73 80
61063—Ties 42 90

           $116 70

T. Campbell, Car Repairer, North Bay, Ont.

58635—Travelling expenses $2 15

              $2 15

Crouse-Hinds Company of Canada, Limited, Toronto, Ontario.

58749—Galvanized condulets, covers and reducers $17 80
58704—Condulet 2 03
59963—   "   covers, etc. 58 91
61057—   " 2 03
61578—   "   side plate, etc. 13 42

           $94 19

Canadian Pulp and Lumber Company, Limited, Latchford, Ontario.

58967—Claim No. 10701, over-charged rate pulpwood $20 10

           $20 10

Henri Cusson, St. Boniface, Man.

59127—Claim No. 11140, baggage destroyed by fire $100 00

           $100 00

Wm. Cameron. St. Louis. Mo.

59149—Tariffs $15 16
60217—   " 6 42
61559—   " 8 30
63153— 4 40

           $34 28

Colin Cross, Wabun P.O.

59425—Ties $64 97
59754—   " 35 80

           $100 77

S. J. Cherry, North Bay, Ontario.

59571—Plumbing repairs 5 29
62011—Brackets, washers, etc. 4 48
63096—Work performed, general office and freight shed, N. Bay..   19 11
63590—Material supplied and plumbing done 140 00
63654—Pan for Blue Print Room 19 80

           $188 68

Conkey & Murphy, Haileybury, Ontario.

58654—Wood $78 50
63370—Ties 148 68

           $227 18

Canada Cement Company, Limited, Montreal, Quebec.

58850—Cement $284 05
59649—   " 1,136 20
60983—   " 568 10
61576—   " 852 15
62217—   " 284 05
62357— 1,704 30

           $4,828 85

CHAS. CALEY, NORTH BAY, ONTARIO.

58904—Award W.C.B. settlement *re* alleged injuries received $17 23
                                                                         $17 23

CANUCK SUPPLY COMPANY, LIMITED, MONTREAL, QUEBEC.

58988—Front end paint $15 40
                                                                         $15 40

CHICAGO, TERRE HANTE & SOUTH-EASTERN RAILWAY COMPANY, CHICAGO, ILL.

59574—Car service balance   90
60175—   "   ,   "   "   90
62120—   "   "   "   90
                                                                         $2 70

J. E. COPLAND, LOCOMOTIVE ENGINEER, NORTH BAY, ONT.

59725—Advance $100 00
                                                                         $100 00

J. CIPPARONE, M.P. DEPT., NORTH BAY, ONT.

59845—Expenses (travelling) $0 50
                                                                         $00 50

WM. G. COOK, YELLOWGRASS, SASK.

59873—Claim No. 11539, loss account, baggage destroyed $100 00
                                                                         $100 00

CHICAGO RAILROAD ASSOCIATION, CHICAGO, ILL.

60081—Joint passenger tariff, No. 270 .... $2 00
                                                                         $2 00

CINCINNATI, INDIANAPOLIS AND WESTERN RAILROAD CO., INDIANAPOLIS, IND.

60085—Car repairs $85 00
60185— " service balance 7 65
60046— " repairs   42
61711— " service balance 1 35
62126— "   " 19 35
                                                                         29 62

CAMBRIA AND INDIANA RAILROAD COMPANY, PHILADELPHIA, PA.

60187—Car service balance $4 05
60456—   "   "   " 2 70
                                                                         $6 75

B. CATTLEY, RELIEVING AGENT, NORTH BAY, ONT.

60485—Travelling expenses 22 00
60178—   "   " 15 00
63794—   "   " 6 00
                                                                         $43 00

CENTRAL ELECTRIC SUPPLY CO., LIMITED, TORONTO, ONT.

60489—Conduits, elbows and bushings $105 35
60884—Battery charging receptacles, etc. 52 70
                                                                         $158 05

CANADIAN OFFICE AND SCHOOL FURNITURE CO., LIMITED, PRESTON, ONT.

60491—Ticket tubes and hooks $1 37
                                                                         $1 37

COBALT COMET MINES, LIMITED, GIROUX LAKE P.O., ONT.

59832—Rental grounds, Kerr Lake Station $18 00

$18 00

W. C. COLES, THORNLOE P.O.

60064—Ties $15 00
60064— " 16 80
62669— " 42 60

$74 40

THE CLEVELAND STONE COMPANY, CLEVELAND, OHIO.

60148—Grindstone ....:. $7 91

$7 91

CANADIAN H. W. JOHNS MANVILLE COMPANY, TORONTO, ONT.

60366—Asbestos millboard $5 53
62975—Fire felt 6 75

$12 28

COLORADO MIDLAND RAILWAY COMPANY, DENVER, COL.

60458—Car service balance .... - $00 45

$00 45

DENIS CAULEY, TIMMINS, ONT.

60392—Wood $9 88

$9 88

H. V. CARTWRIGHT, MATHESON, ONT.

60880—Groceries $24 48

$24 48

COCHRANE NORTHLAND POST, LIMITED, COCHRANE, ONT.

60984—Advertising $7 40

$7 40

COMMONWEALTH STEEL COMPANY, ST. LOUIS, MO.

60981—Wheel trucks $800 00

$800 00

NOEL CROSLEY, KENABEEK P.O.

61063—Ties $10 80

$10 80

FRANK CIPPARONE, NORTH BAY, ONT.

61553—Award, W. C. B., final payment re.alleged injuries $7 35

$7 35

ARTHUR CAMPBELL, L'ORIGNAL, ONT.

61617—Claim No. 10793, overcharge on drilling outfit $19 32

$19 32

H. JAMES CADWELL, CARTHAGE, N.Y.

61869—Claim No. 11864, overcharge rate pulpwood $41 76

$4: 76

C. Celestine, Labourer, Timmins, Ont.

61270—Award, W. C. B., partial payment re alleged injuries....	$39 05	
62368— " " " "	37 75	
		$76 80

Canadian Cotton & Wool Waste Company, Montreal, Que.

61508—Cotton wipers	$52 30	
		$52 30

Canadian Consolidated Felt Company, Limited, Kitchener, Ont.

61580—Saddle felt	$28 00	
		$28 00

Chicago, West Pullman & Southern Railroad, Chicago, Ill.

61850—Car repairs	$0 70	
		$0 70

Cleveland & Buffalo Transit Company.

62226—Ticket balance	$0 50	
		$0 50

R. Clarke, Locomotive Foreman, Englehart, Ont.

62455—Travelling expenses	$2 80	
		$2 80

John Clarke, Englehart, Ont.

62583—Claim No. 12043, overcharge rate pulpwood	$43 86	
		$43 86

Samuel Clark, Thornloe P.O.

62669—Ties	$25 80	
62806— "	40 00	
		$65 80

Herbert Chapman, McCool P.O.

62669—Ties	$34 93	
		$34 93

Cobalt Miners' Union, Cobalt, Ont.

63149—Commission re excursion	$119 55	
		$119 55

J. J. Corbeill, Dane, Ont.

62886—Claim No. 11381, alleged loss sausages	$3 80	
		$3 80

Carnation Support Company, Connersville, Ind.

63056—Carnation supports	$10 00	
		$10 00

Canadian Ingersoll Rand Company, Limited, Montreal, Que.

63196—Claim No. 12545, alleged loss drills	$1,500 00	
		$1,500 00

CANADIAN INSPECTION & TESTING LABORATORIES, LIMITED, MONTREAL, QUE.

63266—Inspection steelwork $10 87

$10 87

CHARLTON AGRICULTURAL SOCIETY, BRENTHA, ONT.

63364—Donation as prize for best span of horses $10 00

$10 00

EDWARD CAMPBELL, HEASLIP P.O.

63370—Ties $38 67

$38 67

J. E. CHALIFOUR, OTTAWA, ONT.

63450—Atlas of Canada $3 00

$3 00

E. COOK, NORTH BAY, ONT.

63452—Amt. award, W. C. B., partial payment *re* alleged injuries $45 12

$45 12

ANGUS CAMERON, ENGLEHART, ONT.

63582—Donation, cow alleged killed $25 00

$25 00

A. COCKERLINE, NORTH BAY, ONT.

63810—Donation, account personal effects destroyed by fire..... $10 00

$10 00

DELAWARE & HUDSON COMPANY, NEW YORK, N.Y.

56509—Car repairs		$1 33
57099— " "		17
56858— " service balance		9 90
58181— " "		44 55
58369— " repairs		17 30
58116— " service balance		35 10
59259— " "		20 25
59584— " "		35 55
59907— " repairs		2 62
60189— " service balance		68 40
61375— " repairs		1 74
61904— " "		3 02
61964— " "		2 17
62128— " service balance		24 70
62831— " "		14 65
63444— " "		10 95
63606— " repairs		23 08

$315 48

DELAWARE, LACKAWANNA & WESTERN RAILROAD COMPANY, NEW YORK, N.Y.

56507—Car repairs		$13 77
56961— " "		4 99
56860—Car service balance		100 35
58183— " "		33 75
58371— " repairs		2 00
58118— " service balance		110 30
59261— " "		89 55
59501— " repairs		2 89
59242— " "		3 95

DELAWARE, LACKAWANNA & WESTERN RAILROAD COMPANY, ETC.—*Continued.*

59586—Car service balance		$123 75
60029— " repairs		19 03
60191— " service balance		84 15
60052—." repairs		35
60474— " service balance		36 90
61377— " repairs		7 83
61713— " service balance		43 20
62022— " repairs		22 89
62130— " service balance		110 70
62467— " repairs		29
62833— " service balance		126 90
63446— " "		44 49
		$982 03

DULUTH, SOUTH SHORE & ATLANTIC RAILWAY. MARQUETTE, MICH.

56511—Car repairs		$48 49
57003— " "		3 91
58185— " service balance		2 25
58120— " "		1 80
59263— " "		45
59403—Ticket balance		52 17
59588—Car service balance		2 25
60193— " "		1 80
60476— " "		4 50
60622—Ticket balance		11 30
61281—Car repairs		6 02
61717— " service balance		10 80
61966— " repairs		5 83
63752— " "		6 56
		$158 13

MISS B. F. DURHAM, STENOGRAPHER, TORONTO.

56633—Services rendered		$15 00
56691— " "		15 00
56532— " "		15 00
56604— " "		15 00
56572— " "		15 00
56500— " "		15 00
56520— " "		15 00
57465— " "		15 00
57467— " "		15 00
57487— " "		15 00
57543— " "		15 00
		$165 00

DOMINION GLASS COMPANY. LIMITED, MONTREAL, QUE.

56699—Globes		$6 96
56893—Chimneys		14 41
56580—Globes		7 06
57499—Chimneys		13 23
57677— "		12 35
57796— "		6 17
58559—		9 11
58751— " and globes		54 10
58870—Globes		2 67
60130— "		28 51
61486—B. climps		7 20
		$161 77

DUNLOP TIRE & RUBBER GOODS COMPANY LIMITED, TORONTO.

56701—Steam hose bags		$87 58
56652—Air hose bags		75 95

DUNLOP TIRE & RUBBER GOODS COMPANY, LIMITED, TORONTO.—*Continued.*

57497—Hose	....	42 98
57652— "	and couplings	23 81
59671— "	....	13 14
60126— "	and couplings	42 25
61015— " " "	....	43 74
62369— " " "	....	88 20
62856— " " "	....	15 00

$432 65

DOUGALL VARNISH CO., LIMITED, MONTREAL, QUE.

56831—Varnish	....	$93 10
56666— "	....	53 90
57495— "	....	44 10
57595—	....	78 40
57794— ··	....	98 00
58695—	....	68 60
58760—	....	98 00
60110— ··	....	29 40
60128— "	....	98 00
61059—Rubbing	....	58 80
61586—Varnish	....	68 60
62363— "	....	68 60
62766— "	....	137 20

$994 70

JOS. DAJENAIS, CONNAUGHT, ONT.

56837—Donation, account colt alleged killed	....	$30 00

$30 00

DOMINION EXPRESS COMPANY, NORTH BAY, ONT.

56839—Express charges	....	$26 06
56764— " "	....	45 36
57568— " "	....	25 93
58439— " "	....	39 81
58536— " "	....	49 80
59577— " "	....	24 35
60393— " "	....	37 74
60767— " "	....	27 81
60646— " "	....	26 23
62013— " "	....	32 11
61156—Refund telephone rental, Timmins	....	5 10
62256—Express charges	....	27 25
62977— " "	....	25 79
63854— " "	....	27 03

$420 37

J. J. DOUGLASS, ROAD FOREMAN, NORTH BAY, ONT.

56867—Travelling expenses	....	$21 75
56740— " "	....	22 25
57868— " "	....	14 75
58679— ·	....	29 75
58780— " "	....	14 00
59701—	....	20 60
60648— ··	....	22 70
61573—	....	22 00
61238—	....	16 90
62233— ··	....	58 30
63382— ··	....	73 60

$316 60

J. DRINKWATER, SUPERVISOR, COCHRANE, ONT.

56869—Travelling expenses	....	$5 45
56738— " "	....	7 15

J. DRINKWATER, SUPERVISOR, COCHRANE, ONT.—*Continued.*

57665—Travelling expenses	$14 75	
57710— " "	24 45	
57870— " "	14 85	
58677— "	7 20	
59328— "	7 30	
59849—	8 80	
60288— " "	9 85	
61523— "	5 60	
61240— " "	7 75	
62259—	7 55	
62480—	2 75	
		$123 45

H. A. DUDLEY, RELIEVING OPERATOR, TOMIKO, ONT.

56871—Travelling expenses	$14 00	
59858— " "	14 00	
		$28 00

THE DENVER & RIO GRANDE RAILROAD COMPANY, DENVER, COLO.

56963—Car repairs	$1 00	
56862—Car service balance	2 25	
58124— " " "	9 00	
59267— " " "	2 25	
59592— " " "	90	
60195— " " "	11 70	
60478— " " "	17 55	
61721— " " "	18 45	
63462— " " "	90	
		$64 00

DEPT. MILITIA & DEFENCE, OTTAWA, ONT.

57021—Overcharge freight	$27 58	
56766— " "	1 00	
		$28 58

H. DAY, WATER SERVICE INSPECTOR, NORTH BAY, ONT.

57059—Travelling expenses	$12 50	
56742— " "	15 75	
57623— " "	15 80	
57866—	14 30	
58597— " "	12 30	
59326—	12 25	
59847—	14 65	
60264—	12 50	
61521—	12 70	
61234— "	17 00	
62263—	16 90	
62820—	9 65	
		$166 30

DELANY & PETTIT, LIMITED, TORONTO.

57201—Glue	$14 00	
57424—Flint Paper	24 41	
57889— " "	3 54	
58815— " " etc.	49 64	
59066— " " and glue	52 82	
60724—Glue	15 68	
63113—Emery cloth, flint paper	50 60	
63108—Paper	5 88	
		$216 57

HENRY DISSTON & SONS, LIMITED, TORONTO.

57203—Hacksaw blades	$8 60	
57420—Bandsaws	42 24	
57863— "	2 67	
58338—Hacksaws	9 62	
59037— " blades	4 22	
59062— "	13 50	
60525—Sawblades	7 76	
61690—Hand hacks	10 28	
62729—Files	19 12	
62924—Hacksaws	18 90	
63104—Bandsaws, files	20 81	
		$157 72

G. W. DUNCAN, NORTH BAY, ONT.

57205—Groceries	$57 90	
57418—Vegetables and eggs	15 15	
57849—Potatoes	4 50	
58344—Butter, eggs, onions and potatoes	32 95	
59068—Potatoes, onions, etc.	45 30	
60535—Onions, eggs, etc.	107 20	
59870—Claims No. 10976 and 10975—loss fruit	35 96	
60306—Eggs, potatoes, butter	43 80	
60718—Eggs, onions, butter	83 73	
60892—Cabbage	2 00	
61203—Eggs	28 65	
61905—Butter, eggs, etc.	93 79	
61514—Groceries, eggs	26 80	
61786— "	333 75	
61944—Butter	14 56	
62745—Claim No. 12708—loss and damage fruit	37 74	
62989—Butter, potatoes, onions	223 81	
62860—Groceries	187 51	
62890—Claim No. 11638—loss oranges	3 96	
63068—Butter, eggs, potatoes	48 70	
		$1,427 76

DODGE MANUFACTURING CO., LIMITED, TORONTO.

57207—Wood pulley	12 04	
57414—Hanger bearings	2 87	
		$14 91

DOMINION PRINTING & LOOSE LEAF CO., LIMITED, OTTAWA, ONT.

57209—Tariff binders	$19 80	
57430—Fyles and indexes	13 72	
58340—Fyles and indexes	18 90	
57857—Tariff fyles	19 80	
59058— " "	26 62	
60788— " "	37 42	
61490—Tariff binders	19 80	
62735—Fyles and indexes	66 60	
62846—Fyles	16 20	
		$238 86

DOMINION ENVELOPE CO., LIMITED, TORONTO, ONT.

57211—Envelopes	$31 97	
57861— "	40 75	
58336— "	6 75	
59035—	35 75	
60527—	36 50	
61484—	66 88	
62731—	28 80	
62854—	7 00	
		$254 40

DOMINION STEEL FOUNDRY CO., LIMITED, HAMILTON, ONT.

57213—Steel castings	$16 97	
57412—Express on patterns	55	
57851—Castings and freight on patterns	66 88	
58334—Castings	15 67	
58817—Express on patterns	85	
59074—Handrails, castings, etc.	36 06	
60716—Handrail, express charges	4 40	
60936—Iron, express charges	2 53	
61488—Coupler, swivel, etc.	9 48	
61516— "	9 89	
63115—Freight charges on pattern	60	
62632—Swivel joints, etc.	52 60	
62852—Casting	44 78	
		$261 26

DOMINION REDUCTION CO., LIMITED, COBALT, ONT.

57345—Claim No. 9402—overcharge in rate on silver ore	$49 48	
		$49 48

DOMINION WHEEL & FOUNDRIES, LIMITED, TORONTO.

57421—Castings	$655 53	
57410—Castings, wheels, etc.	232 78	
57701—Castings, wheels, grates	1,549 28	
58350—Castings, wheels, grates	2,145 24	
59091—Truck wheels, castings, etc.	2,248 43	
59072—Wheels, castings	3,379 85	
60219—Wheels, castings, etc.	4,768 97	
60728—Castings, grates, etc.	3,318 51	
61205—Castings	243 85	
61911—Castings and express	1 99	
61626—Grate bars, hangers, etc.	80 23	
61946—Wheels	86 52	
52979—Wheels and springs, etc.	312 24	
62864—Supplies	2,646 41	
63070—Wheels, etc.	3,162 90	
63274—Wheels, etc.	2,886 80	
		$27,719 53

FRANK W. DUNCAN, NORTH BAY, ONT.

56546—Uniforms	$583 00	
57859—Uniforms	21 00	
		$604 00

W. J. DAMP, BOILERMAKER, NORTH BAY, ONT.

56558—Travelling expenses	$7 95	
56744— "	3 40	
57621— "	6 10	
57728— "	9 85	
58639— "	5 75	
58798— "	3 05	
59829— "	4 45	
62617— "	3 85	
63326— "	2 35	
		$46 75

DAVIDSON, WAINWRIGHT, ALEXANDER & ELDER, MONTREAL, QUE.

56568—Services—legal	$3 00	
		$3 00

DESPATCH & TRIBUNE, NORTH BAY, ONT.

56768—Advertising and forms	$11 60	
57180—Advertising and printing	35 00	

15 T.R.

DESPATCH & TRIBUNE, NORTH BAY, ONT.—*Continued.*

57855—Forms	11 00	
59167—Forms	5 50	
63376—Advertising	21 60	
63656—Advertising	12 40	
		$97 10

DOMINION OF CANADA GUARANTEE & ACCIDENT COMPANY, TORONTO.

56944—Ticket balance	$2 48	
58313— "	1 04	
58252— "	55	
59405— "	1 51	
59734— "	83	
60375— "	3 58	
60624— "	1 24	
61837— "	2 34	
62230— "	1 65	
62953— "	28	
63572— "	41	
		$15 91

THE DOMINION RADIATOR COMPANY, LIMITED, TORONTO, ONT.

57018—Grates	$43 95	
58662— "	16 26	
62365— "	4 66	
		$64 87

A. DORSCHNER, BRAKEMAN, TIMMINS, ONT.

57022—Award W. C. B., *re* alleged injuries	$90 30	
		$90 30

DRUMMOND, MCCALL & CO., LIMITED, MONTREAL, P.Q.

57038—Claim No. 10333—Overcharge rate, steel plates	$1 94	
57422—Seamless tube	22 41	
57847—Boiler tubes	165 00	
58348—Seamless steel tube	13 65	
58819—Steel tubes	107 19	
59060—Steel tubes	76 19	
60537—Steel tubes, tires, etc.	3,419 30	
60720—Tubes	15 40	
60894—Tubing	27 61	
62059—Claim No. 12320—Refund demurrage	1 00	
61692—Boiler tubes	371 70	
62733—Tubing	55 59	
62850— "	125 75	
63106— "	12 53	
		$4,415 26

R. D. DEVLIN, COBALT, ONT.

57054—Claim No. 10516—loss hair tonic	$3 33	
		$3 33

DOME MINES COMPANY, LIMITED, SOUTH PORCUPINE, ONT.

57056—Claim No. 10628—siding rebate	$182 00	
58025— " Nos. 10175 and 10421—overcharge in weight and damage to mufflers	22 21	
57986—Claims Nos. 10828, 10827, 10222, 10765—siding rebate, etc.	366 00	
58697—Soft coal	521 68	
57347—Claims Nos. 10509 and 10346—siding rebate, etc.	116 98	
57637—Soft coal	94 57	
58889—Claim No. 10959—siding rebate	154 00	
59015— " No. 10724—damage to tube mill	2 29	

DOME MINES COMPANY, LIMITED, ETC.—*Continued.*

59136—Coal	$32 81	
59504—Claim No. 11168—siding rebate.........................	138 00	
59866— " No. 11656— "	168 00	
60913— " No. 11808— "	152 00	
61477— " No. 12006— "	118 00	
62057— " No. 12319— "	82 00	
63189—Claims Nos. 11844 and 12804—siding rebate, etc.........	126 48	
62556—Claim No. 12850—siding rebate ....`..................	120 00	
63170— " No. 12162—damage to castings	261 89	
		$2,658 91

DOME LAKE MINING & MILLING COMPANY, LIMITED, NEW LISKEARD, ONT.

57064—Claim No. 10251—overcharge gold ore....................	$53 25	
59502— " No. 10250— " "	214 71	
59797— " No. 10457— " "	76 49	
59868— " No. 10512— " "	65 93	
60911— " No. 10649— " "	89 13	
62892— " No. 10252— " "	163 95	
		$663 46

DES MOINES UNION RAILWAY COMPANY, DES MOINES, IOWA.

57292—Car repairs	$1 48	
		$1 48

DETROIT, TOLEDO & IRONTON RAILROAD COMPANY, DETROIT, MICH.

57294—Car repairs	$1 44	
58187— " service balance	4 50	
58122— " "	21 15	
59265— " "	7 80	
59244— " repairs	1 85	
59590— " service balance	9 00	
59909— " repairs	9 40	
60050— " "	10 51	
61719— " service balance	2 25	
62132— " "	10 80	
62134— " "	1 35	
62835— " "	3 15	
63448— " "	3 15	
		$86 35

THE DOMINION DISINFECTANT COMPANY, NORTH BAY, ONT.

57416—Carbolacene	$35 20	
57865— "	35 20	
		$70 40

R. E. DIETZ COMPANY, NEW YORK, N.Y.

57426—Lamps	$21 00	
60519— "	23 96	
61143— "	6 00	
		$50 96

DINGLE & ALGER, NORTH BAY, ONT.

57428—Electrical supplies	$2 20	
		$2 20

DOMINION CHAIN COMPANY, LIMITED, MONTREAL, QUE.

57593—Cotters	$22 80	
58700— "	3 74	

DOMINION CHAIN COMPANY, LIMITED, ETC.—*Continued.*

59969—Cotters	$15 15	
62367— "	7 95	
62661— "	13 46	
		$63 10

DOMINION BRAKE SHOE COMPANY, LIMITED, MONTREAL, QUE.

57597—Brake shoes	$580 34	
57654— " truck and car shoes	487 71	
58653— " shoes	739 97	
59056— " "	210 38	
60521— " "	1,136 50	
60934— " "	605 38	
62848— " "	678 80	
		$4,439 08

G. H. DICKSON, CHIEF DRAUGHTSMAN, NORTH BAY, ONT.

57625—Travelling expenses	$3 75	
62261— " "	7 70	
		$11 45

DOMINION PAPER BOX COMPANY, LIMITED, TORONTO, ONT.

57853—Boxes	$8 00	
		$8 00

S. J. DEMPSAY, COCHRANE, ONT.

58027—Claim No. 10620—damage to preserves	$5 00	
		$5 00

DETROIT & MACKINAC RAILWAY COMPANY, DETROIT, MICH.

58189—Car service balance	$1 80	
58128— " "	4 50	
59596— " "	11 25	
60197— " "	45	
59956— " repairs	2 51	
63466— " service balance	3 60	
		$24 11

DULUTH, WINNIPEG & PACIFIC RAILWAY COMPANY, TORONTO, ONT.

58373—Car repairs	$0 74	
58126— " service balance	5 40	
59269— " "	9 00	
59594— " "	13 50	
60480— " "	6 75	
61723— " "	1 80	
62837— " "	2 25	
63464— " "	1 80	
		$41 24

J. DESJARDINE, NORTH BAY, ONT.

57964—Award, W. C. B., in full settlement *re* alleged injuries received	$9 15	
		$9 15

MRS. A. Z. DAKTER, SOUTH PORCUPINE, ONT.

57988—Claim No. 10517—cost repairs to table damaged.........	$2 50	
		$2 50

JAMES DOIG & COMPANY, SWASTIKA, ONT.

57990—Claim No. 10586—loss account damages to turpentine...	$1 75
63185— " No. 11546—overcharge, hay	11 00
	$12 75

THE DEFIANCE MACHINE COMPANY, ROCHESTER, N.Y.

58342—Ink rolls	$2 12
58813— "	1 62
	$3 74

DE SALES MANUFACTURING COMPANY, MONTREAL, QUE.

58346—Selected white wipers	$41 63
59064—White wipers	42 00
60523—Cotton wipers	50 85
61145—Wipers	49 05
	$183 53

ERNEST DOMMETT, McCOOL P.O.

58593—Ties	$104 88
59425— "	126 63
	$231 51

THE THOS. DAVIDSON MANUFACTURING COMPANY, LIMITED, MONTREAL, P.Q.

58811—Torches	$4 70
	$4 70

DR. J. I. DEADMAN, COBALT, ONT.

59165—Professional service	$10 00
	$10 00

JAMES DOUGLAS, FERONIA P.O., ONT.

59425—Ties..	$31 86
59754— "	32 64
	$64 50

DEPARTMENT OF INLAND REVENUE (FEDERAL GOVERNMENT), OTTAWA, ONT.

59433—War tax	$1,407 19
61026— " "	1,989 38
63213— " "	2,608 41
57570— " "	1,768 81
	$7,773 79

THE DENVER & SALT LAKE RAILROAD COMPANY, DENVER, COLO.

59499—Car repairs...	$1 03
60199— " service balance....................................	7 20
61852— " repairs..	5 15
63468— " service balance....................................	90
	$14 28

DEPARTMENT PUBLIC PRINTING AND STATIONERY, OTTAWA, ONT.

58778—Copies "Judgment" Board of Railway Commission......	$6 00
58940— " " " " " "	3 00
60988— " " " " " "	3 00
	$12 00

DOMINION LINENS, LIMITED, GUELPH, ONT.

59070—Roller towels..	$62 00	
61688— " "	27 00	
		$89 00

DUNHAM COMPANY, BEREA, OHIO.

59082—Culte-Packer, Jr.	$11 10	
		$11 10

DAVIE BROS., EARLTON, ONT.

59388—Claim No. 10915, loss account damage to fruit..........	$12 30	
61500—Ties..	332 64	
62806— "	2,958 70	
		$3,303 64

DAY & GORDON, HAILEYBURY, ONT.

59939—Appeal, assessment, Timmins	$25 00	
62273—Service re sanitary conditions, Cobalt	10 00	
62634— " re Haileybury Spur, etc.......................	62 89	
		$97 89

DUSTLESS BRUSH COMPANY, TORONTO, ONT.

59971—Brushes..	$15 30	
		$15 30

DRS. DORSEY & LIPSITT, MATHESON, ONT.

60221—Professional service rendered...........................	$1 50	
		$1 50

DAVIS & HENDERSON, LIMITED, TORONTO, ONT.

60529—Books..	$27 00	
60730— "	12 00	
61492— "	60 00	
		$99 00

THE DAYTON MANUFACTURING COMPANY, DAYTON, OHIO.

60531—Cuspidors	$10 80	
62636—Carpet nails...	3 96	
		$14 76

THE DUFF MANUFACTURING COMPANY, PITTSBURG, PA.

60533—Steel rack, etc..	$2 01	
60722—Levers, springs, etc....................................	4 50	
		$6 51

J. M. DEACON, REGISTRAR, NORTH BAY, ONT.

59996—Searches...	$1 40	
63155— "	50	
		$1 90

DONALD DUFF, THORNLOE P.O.

60064—Ties..	$79 05	
		$79 05

DELTA-STAR ELECTRIC COMPANY, CHICAGO, ILL.

60154—Electric, lighting material............................ $28 80

$28 80

DOMINION WIRE ROPE COMPANY, LIMITED, MONTREAL, QUE.

60224—Cables....................... . ... $65 55

$65 55

DUNLOP'S, TORONTO, ONT.

60896—Flowers......... . ... $12 50

$12 50

DELAWARE, LACKAWANNA & WESTERN COAL & COKE CO.. BUFFALO, N.Y.

60990—Coal.. $2,859 09
61199— " 401 40
61388— " 589 20

$3,849 69

DOMINION BRIDGE COMPANY, LIMITED, MONTREAL, QUE.

60985—Bridge span.. $1,854 87

$1,854 87

J. DEMEIS, REDWATER, ONT.

61413—Meals, extra gang No. 7, bush fires..................... $7 50

$7 50

S. DAVIES, TENDERMAN, NORTH BAY. ONT.

61236—Travelling expenses $3 65

$3 65

B. W. DUNNETT & COMPANY, OTTAWA, ONT.

61422—Claim No. 12157, alleged overcharge weight hay......... $3 13

$3 13

FRANK DARON, CANE P.O.

61500—Ties....................... . ... $116 49

$116 49

DRESSEL RAILWAY LAMP WORKS, NEW YORK. N.Y.

62469—Post lamp and brackets $40 50

$40 50

R. DART, ENGLEHART, ONT.

62737—Bread.............. . ... $6 89

$6 89

DANVILLE & WESTERN RAILWAY COMPANY. WASHINGTON. D.C.

62839—Car service balance.................................. $8 10

$8 10

DUNER COMPANY. CHICAGO. ILL.

62858—Plates and hinge pins................................ $13 80

$13 80

J. L. ENGLEHART, TORONTO, ONT.

—Honorarium	$2,500 00	
—Remuneration	4,999 92	
—Expenses	732 00	
		$8,231 92

THE ERIE RAILROAD COMPANY, NEW YORK, N.Y.

56513—Car repairs	$23 24	
56965— " "	2 42	
56864—Car service balance	19 30	
57296—Car repairs	65 32	
58191—Car service balance	54 00	
58375—Car repairs	40 05	
58130—Car service balance	144 90	
59271— " " "	216 20	
59407—Ticket balance	3 80	
59475—Car repairs	8 70	
59503— " "	23 81	
59598—Car service balance	160 15	
59736—Ticket balance	32 55	
60031—Car repairs	26 16	
60377—Ticket balance	55	
60078—Car repairs	23 88	
60482— " service balance	38 25	
60626—Ticket balance	1 39	
61163—Claim No. 10653, overcharge in rate	36 27	
61379—Car repairs	30 64	
61725— " service balance	61 65	
62061—Claim No. 11709, undercharge, car coal	48 40	
61856—Car repairs	23 20	
61968— " "	71 04	
62136— " service balance	5 85	
62841— " " "	49 50	
63470— " " "	63 25	
		$1,274 47

ELGIN, JOLIET & EASTERN RAILWAY COMPANY, CHICAGO, ILL.

56515—Car repairs	$25 96	
59505— " "	96	
59260— " "	2 90	
59911— " "	94	
60201— " service balance	161 10	
59958— " repairs	15 70	
61854— " "	1 82	
63608— " "	3 73	
		$213 11.

WM. ENGLISH, TIE INSPECTOR, NORTH BAY, ONT.

56781—Travelling expenses	$13 90	
56622— " "	15 95	
57667— " "	25 70	
57790— " "	25 70	
58643— " "	19 25	
58862— " "	26 20	
59741— " "	28 80	
60184— " "	25 15	
61061— " "	27 40	
61244— " "	30 65	
62219— " "	25 45	
63384— " "	31 10	
		$295 25

EASTERN CANADIAN PASSENGER ASSOCIATION, MONTREAL, QUE.

56841—Proportion expenses	$6 77	
57745— " "	11 86	
59169— " "	10 00	
60087— " " and regulation bulletins	10 25	
62868—Rate bulletin	13 20	
		$52 08

ELK LAKE POWER COMPANY, LIMITED, ELK LAKE, ONT.

57023—Current supplied	$4 85	
57752— " "	13 75	
59768— " "	11 30	
63072— " "	6 05	
		$35 95

GEO. EARL, M.M. DEPT., NORTH BAY, ONT.

57061—Travelling expenses	$12 55	
56746— " "	9 44	
57573— " "	5 10	
57872— "	1 75	
58641— " "	6 20	
59703— " "	7 95	
61242— "	13 00	
62335— "	23 60	
63210— "	3 75	
		$83 34

THE E. B. EDDY COMPANY, LIMITED, HULL, P.Q.

57215—Blotting paper and matches	$15 00	
57458—Toilet and wrapping paper	52 21	
58352—Matches, paper and fibre	46 84	
58823—Toilet paper	14 66	
59086— " " blotters	27 49	
60539— " " fixtures	46 72	
60732—Paper	23 00	
61915— "	13 96	
61696—Matches	26 89	
62981— " paper and fibre	50 14	
62638— "	27 66	
		$344 57

EDWARDS, MORGAN & CO., TORONTO, ONT.

56722—Services rendered re audit	$391 88	
		$391 88

EL PASO & SOUTHWESTERN SYSTEMS, EL PASO, TEX.

56866—Car service balance	$0 45	
58193— " " "	45	
58132— " " "	90	
59273— " " "	3 60	
60054— " repairs	83	
61727— " service balance	45	
62138— " " "	1 80	
63472— " " "	1 80	
		$10 28

J. R. EATON & SONS, LIMITED, ORILLIA, ONT.

57058—Claim No. 10307, overcharge on lumber	$2 00	
		$2 00

THE EVENING TELEGRAM, TORONTO, ONT.

58457—Advertising demonstration car	$9 00
59739—Advertisement	1 80
60737— "	3 69
61147— "	3 60
62258—	3 87
63658—	3 78
	$25 74

DR. D. T. EVANS, COCHRANE, ONT.

57862—Professional services rendered	$10 00
	$10 00

EMPIRE COAL COMPANY, LIMITED. MONTREAL, QUE.

58514—Soft coal	$154 77
58971—Claim No. 10940, overcharge in rate coal	6 50
59378—Coal	4,530 63
60697— "	180 45
60844— "	173 03
62589—Claim No. 12470, loss three cars coal by fire	507 38
	$5,552 76

THE ENGLEHART HOTEL, ENGLEHART, ONT.

58544—Meals and lodging furnished passengers account delayed train	$20 00
	$20 00

T. EATON CO., LIMITED, TORONTO, ONT.

58821—Thread	$7 84
59088—Waiter coats, aprons, etc	71 62
61017—Jugs	2 15
61424—Claim No. 12392, loss carload furniture in forest fires	1,110 94
61694—Tapestry, buttons, etc	84 60
62585—Claim No. 12485, loss carload of stoves in forest fires	1,526 76
62866—Counterpanes and towels	14 40
63028—Claim No. 12705, loss sideboard, forest fires	21 50
63244— " No. 12709, loss seven rolls roofing, burned	10 15
	$2,849 96

G. ELIAS & BRO., BUFFALO, N.Y.

58825—Poplar and white wood	$199 52
60150—Oak	383 43
	$582 95

ENERGITE EXPLOSIVES COMPANY, LIMITED. MONTREAL, QUE.

58969—Claim No. 10776, overcharge rate chlorate soda	$80 74
	$80 74

MRS. E. EMBURY, PORQUIS P.O., ONT.

59425—Ties	$37 97
59754— "	79 86
59754— "	20 80
	$138 63

GEORGE EHELER, TOMSTOWN, ONT.

59425—Ties	$82 95
	$82 95

EMPLOYERS' LIABILITY ASSURANCE CORPORATION, LIMITED, TORONTO, ONT.

59034—Renewal premium, collective bond No. 29126 . . . . $142 96

$142 96

B. S. ENGLISH, CARON, SASK.

59661—Claim No. 11383—loss account baggage destroyed by fire. . $100 00

$100 00

H. M. EDWARDS, NEW LISKEARD, ONT.

60453—Claim No. 11434—alleged loss account damage to mill. . . . $0 50
62036—   "   No. 12445—   "   damage to pane glass.   50

$1 00

J. L. ENGLEHART & COMPANY, PETROLIA, ONT.

60541—Iron posts $91 35

$91 35

ENGLEHART & DISTRICT AGRICULTURAL SOCIETY, ENGLEHART, ONT.

59864—Donation. $25 00

$25 00

ERIE & MICHIGAN RAILWAY & NAVIGATION COMPANY, CHICAGO, ILL.

60484—Car service balance. $5 40

$5 40

ELKINS & SINCLAIR, HAILEYBURY, ONT.

61913—Beef. $12 20
61950—   "   pork, fish, etc. 395 15
62983—Meat. 516 83
62502—Beef, pork and trout. 251 03
62976—Meat. 136 22
63110—   " 38 50
63276—Beef, trout 98 03

$1,447 96

ELECTRICAL MAINTENANCE & REPAIRS COMPANY, LIMITED, TORONTO, ONT.

61278—Carbon brushes $0 70

$0 70

EDSON MANUFACTURING COMPANY, BOSTON, MASS.

61698—Hose, couplings, etc. $29 25

$29 25

ELECTRIC SUPPLY COMPANY, NORTH BAY, ONT.

61948—Condulet. $0 70

$0 70

EDMONTON, DUNVEGAN & BRITISH COLUMBIA RY., EDMONTON, ALTA.

62140—Car service balance. $1 35
62843—   "   "   " 3 15
63474—   "   "   "   90

$5 40

W. ERRETT, ENGLEHART, ONT.

62633—Disbursements *re* Northern Ontario fires................ $33 61

$33 61

A. K. EDDY, COBALT, ONT.

62747—Claim No. 11000—damage to stove in transit........... $6 50

$6 50

EMPIRE MANUFACTURING CO., LIMITED, LONDON, ONT.

62985—Traps, basin, supplies, etc............................ $24 21

$24 21

ERIE TOOL WORKS, INC., ERIE, PA.

62987—Vises.................................. . ... $37. 50

$37 50

JOS. G. ELLIES, TIMMÍNS, ONT.

62894—Claim No. 11027—alleged loss underwear............... $18 00

$18 00

J. EYDT, COBALT, ONT.

63682—Claim No. 12695—alleged damage to wash bowl........... $6 25
59579—Plumbing.............................. . ... 1 80

$8 05

L. M. FERGUSON, TELEPHONE INSPECTOR, NORTH BAY, ONT.

56559—Travelling expenses....................................	$35 40	
57067— " "	10 60	
56960— " "	34 60	
57737— " "	11 40	
58775— " "	40 70	
59330— " "	10 20	
59945— ", "	24 65	
60266— " "	2 85	
61525— " "	7 05	
61392— " "	42 80	
62621— " "	12 75	
62772— " "	23 10	

$256 10

C. L. FERGUSON, PAYMASTER, NORTH BAY, ONT.

56719—Passenger refunds $323 91
56817—Payrolls............................. . ....;...... 82,630 87
57091—Expenses *re* safety organizations...................... 4 80
56648—Payrolls............... . ... 81,582 94
56770—Refund of deduction to cover ticket error............; . 43 35
57016—Passenger refunds and petty disbursements 214 49
57182— " " postage, etc. 371 16
57657—Payrolls............... .. .. 84,605 12
57703—Disbursements and postage............................ 121 56
58103—Passenger refunds 153 45
57746—Payrolls............. . ... 86,905 48
57900—Disbursements, postage, etc. 105 61
58538—Passenger refunds ....; 137 25
58657—Payrolls.............................. . ... 92,702 14
58927—Disbursements......... ... .;........... 88 62
59441—Rent, building and license auction sale................. 32 00
58906—Disbursements, postage, etc. 105 71
59434—Passenger refunds.................................... 214 05

C. L. Ferguson, Paymaster, North Bay, Ont.—*Continued.*

59436—Passenger refunds	$220	49
59837—Payrolls	94,777	55
58808—Payrolls	90,824	56
59887—Disbursements, postage, etc.	109	24
60699—Passenger refunds	176	28
60204—Duty on soft coal	963	50
60226—Payrolls	91,887	04
60234—Disbursements for postage, etc.	106	86
61197—Duty on coal, etc.	660	19
61439—Payrolls	92,866	97
61451—Passenger refunds	171	29
61453—Disbursements, stamps, etc.	89	00
62015—Passenger refunds	151	90
61344—Payrolls	96,719	93
61384—Disbursements, stamps, etc.	93	68
61498—Passenger refunds	103	40
62235—Postage, etc.	104	36
62329—Payrolls	97,059	60
62515—Passenger refunds	229	65
62754—Payrolls	100,578	04
62768—Disbursements, postage, etc.	118	32 *
63158—Cash disbursed, account customs charges	345	67
63812—Passenger refunds	221	56

$1,098,921 5

J. Hampden Field, Englehart, Ont.

56823—Lot 1, Con. 3, Tp. Chamberlain, 1 acre	$50	00

$50 0

S. J. Faught, Supervisor, Englehart, Ont.

56873—Travelling expenses	$16	40
56748— " "	11	80
57669— " "	10	95
57922— " "	4	90
58777— " "	18	05
59767— " "	17	35
59851— " "	16	65
60290— " "	16	55

$112 6

Fort Worth & Denver City Railway Co., Fort Worth, Tex.

57005—Car repairs	$1	74
58197— " service balance	4	50
59507— " repairs	1	43
59602— " service balance	9	00
60225— " " "	6	75
61970— " repairs	4	83
62144— " service balance	2	70

$30 9

M. F. Fairlie, Cobalt, Ont.

57349—Claim No. 10365—loss account damage to automobile	$5	45

$5 45

Frothingham & Workman, Limited. Montreal, Que.

56668—Lowmoor iron	$25	17
57503—Spring steel		98
57656—Iron	26	21
58561— "	117	72
59039— "	52	92

Frothingham & Workman, Limited, Etc.—*Continued.*

58762—Iron	$24 76
58872— "	121 05
59973— "	87 73
60236—	52 37
61588—	168 09
61700—	37 92

$714 92

Fruit Growers' Express, Inc., Chicago, Ill.

56868—Car service balance....................................	$3 79
58195— " " "	1 90
59275— " " "	3 79
59600— " " "	2 70
60203— " " "	8 29
60486— " " "	4 15
61729— " " "	1 92
62142— " " "	2 07
62845— " " "	1 54
63476— " " "	1 54

$31 69

Newton L. Forster, Oakville, Ont.

57060—Claim No. 10525—damage, apples........................	$7 50

$7 50

J. Faessler Mfg. Company, Moberly. Mo.

57432—Sectional expanders	$73 44

$73 44

Funk & Wagnalls Company, New York, N.Y.

57434—Dictionary.................................	$2 41

$2 41

Fittings, Limited. Oshawa. Ont.

57501—Fittings................................ . ...:.	$8 20

$8 20

John Fennessy, Haileybury, Ont.

58029—Claim No. 10554—damage to 2 bottles gin	$1 65
58973— " No. 10759— " whiskey	1 09
61312— " No. 11992— " liquor........	8 64
62637— " No. 12123 and 12581—damage to liquor...........	3 74
63172— " No. 12185—damage to liquor	2 23

$17 35

Fort Dodge, Des Moines & Southern R. R. Co., Boone, Ia.

58199—Car service balance.....................................	$2 70
58134— " " "	2 70
59604— " " "	13 95
60227— " " "	23 40
60488— " " "	6 30
61731— " " "	7 20
62146— " " "	4 05
62847— " " "	31 50
63478— " " "	13 50

$105 30

J. FILIATRAULT, PORQUIS JCT.

58463—Ties.. .... $117 40
58593— " 65 60
61500— " 164 94
                                                                        ————————
                                                                        $347 94

FROST WIRE FENCE COMPANY, LIMITED, HAMILTON, ONT.

57594—Wire $740 55
62663—Wire 836 22
                                                                        ————————
                                                                        $1,576 77

O. FRUMKIN, SOUTH PORCUPINE, ONT.

57994—Claim No. 10682—Loss account, shortage one case sausage $27 13
                                                                        ————————
                                                                        $27 13

FLEIGHT CLAIM ASSOCIATION, RICHMOND, VA.

58540—Constitutions and circulars $1 04
60417—Assessment 12 00
                                                                        ————————
                                                                        $13 04

FIREMEN'S ASSOCIATION OF ONTARIO. TORONTO, ONT.

58503—Advertisement—Annual report $10 00
                                                                        ————————
                                                                        $10 00

GEORGE FULTON, KENABEEK P.O.

58593—Ties $111 44
60064—Ties 62 20
                                                                        ————————
                                                                        $173 64

FORSYTH BROS., COMPANY, CHICAGO, ILL.

58827—Sash rackets $57 60
                                                                        ————————
                                                                        $57 60

FORT SMITH & WESTERN RAILROAD, FORT SMITH, ARK.

59277—Car service balance $3 15
61733—Car service balance 2 70
                                                                        ————————
                                                                        $5 85

FLORIDA EAST COAST RAILWAY, ST. AUGUSTINE. FLA.

59279—Car service balance $0 45
59606--- " " 4 05
60229— " " 13 50
60490— 3 15
61735— " " 5 40
61839—Ticket balance 125 70
62148—Car service balance 90
                                                                        ————————
                                                                        $153 15

FERGUSON & McFADDEN. TOMIKO, ONT.

58824—Claim No. 11037—Loss account, shortage, case oranges... $4 50
62593—Claim No. 12536--Overcharge lumber 9 07
62640—Wood 3 00
                                                                        ————————
                                                                        $16 57

A. A. FRASER, INSTRUMENTMAN, NORTH BAY. ONT.

59831—Travelling expenses $10 75
61575— " 31 75
61394— " 14 00
63212— " 44 25
                                                                        ————————
                                                                        $100 75

FRISCO REFRIGERATOR LINE, ST. LOUIS, MO.

60231—Car service balance	$4 99	
60492— " "	80	
61737— " "	3 79	
62849— " "	3 87	
		$13 45

W. J. FIELDING, PORQUIS JCT., ONT.

60441—Claim No. 11173—Overcharge car rental charges	$6 00	
		$6 00

F. FELDMAN, TIMMINS, ONT.

59872—Claim No. 10984—Loss account, potatoes and onions by frost	$13 00	
		$13 00

WILLIAM FLOOD, McCOOL P.O.

60064—Ties	$44 07	
		$44 07

WILLIAM FIELDS, EARLTON P.O.

60064—Ties	$50 40	
60064—Ties	39 87	
		$90 27

FROST STEEL, & WIRE CO., LIMITED, HAMILTON, ONT.

60144—Wire	$933 60	
		$933 60

T. W. FOSTER, KIRKLAND LAKE, P.O.

60915—Claim No. 11112—Overcharge, freight, canoe	$4 08	
		$4 08

CHAS. FRITZ, KENABEEK, ONT.

60163—Ties	$225 90	
		$225 90

FACTORY PRODUCTS, LIMITED, TORONTO, ONT.

61577—Wall brackets, fittings, etc.	$71 15	
		$71 15

GEO. A. FINLEY, CHARLTON, ONT.

61428—Claim No. 10875—Alleged damage, household goods	$50 00	
		$50 00

WILLIAM FARMER, BRAKEMAN, NORTH BAY, ONT.

61198—Award W. C. B. final payment re alleged injuries	$15 89	
		$15 89

WALTER FOWKE, CHARLTON P.O.

61500—Ties	$122 97	
		$122 97

FOSTER POTTERY COMPANY, HAMILTON, ONT.

62393—Flower pots	$13 09	
		$13 09

THOS. FENTON, NORTH BAY, ONT.

62388—Amount paid *re* alleged injuries $100 00

                                                                              $100 00

S. J. FAUGHT, SUPERVISOR, NORTH BAY, ONT.

62482—Travelling expenses $21 05

                                                                              $21 05

A. & F. FISHER, TORONTO, ONT.

63074—Shelving vault, Toronto office $45 65

                                                                              $45 65

T. J. GRACEY, ACCOUNTANT, TORONTO.

56461—Salary, November, 1915 .... $150 00
56593—Additional salary, November and December, 1915....... 20 00
56592—Salary, December, 1915 .... 150 00
57471— "   January, 1916 .... 160 00
57600— "   February, 1916 .... 160 00
58493— "   March, 1916 .... 160 00
58622— "   April, 1916 .... 160 00
59929— "   May, 1916 .... 160 00
59802— "   June, 1916 .... 160 00
60186—Travelling expenses 14 50

                                                                              $1,294 50

GRAND TRUNK RAILWAY SYSTEM, MONTREAL, P.Q.

56481—Freight, settlement $1,908 90
56557—Proportion cost, advertising, Thos Cook & Son tour, New
          York, Prince Rupert, car repairs, rental of cinder
          cars, etc. 412 32
56571—Claims 49 17
56579—Freight settlement 1,041 84
56585—On account interline freight 900 00
56653—Claims 76 84
56685—On account interline freight 1,500 00
56687— "   "   "   " 4,000 00
56929— "   "   "   " 7,000 00
57089—Interline freight, balance 4,906 44
57351—Claim 10 71
57423—Loss, dining car Toronto to Winnipeg 419 22
57425—Proportion expenses parlor cafe cars, Toronto to Englehart 2,599 34
57427—Rental cinder cars, switching, etc. 101 02
56536—Interline freight, account 8,000 00
56566— "   " 3,000 00
56624— "   " 400 00
56776— "   " 1,000 00
56870—Car service balance 8,178 36
57030—Claims 89 93
57234—Car repairs 141 77
57572—Line service, switching and weighing cars 203 14
56518—Freight settlement 1,222 48
57529— "   " 700 00
57539— "   " 506 92
57661—Interline freight balance 6,118 53
57747—On account interline freight 7,000 00
57749—Rent cinder cars, commission on tickets, supplies and
          tariffs 416 65
58031—Claims 71 83
58105—Proportion profit on ice house 1,130 21
58201—Car service balance 2,053 55
58303—Passenger car mileage 1,053 74
58315—Ticket balance 3,724 55
58349—Interline freight balance 10,241 06
58409—Car repairs 682 97

    16 T.R.

GRAND TRUNK RAILWAY SYSTEM, ETC.—*Continued.*

58441—Prop'n adv't Transcontinental train service	1,014 28
58465—Loss parlor cafe cars, weighing cars and switching	872 74
57596—Freight settlement	3,688 84
57612— " "	541 96
57622—On account interline freight	3,000 00
57628—Freight settlement	624 48
57694— " "	1,145 16
57902—Proportion expenses *re* "National"	46 11
57904—Proportion commission adv't and tolls, switching charges	102 27
58136—Car service balance	2,076 73
58248—Passenger car mileage	1,079 84
58254—Ticket balance	64 06
58494—Interline freight balance	18,474 81
58598—Commission, loss dining and parlor, supplies and weigh-	
ing car revenue	524 78
58511—Freight settlement	2,069 17
59083—Claims	44 78
59141—Proportion profit, ice house, North Bay	790 50
59171— " commission, Frank Tourist Co.	3 41
59281—Car service balance	3,375 85
59395—Passenger car mileage	1,013 59
59409—Ticket balance	1,140 79
59515—Car repairs, prop'n exp. pullmans and cars, Toronto to	
Englehart and Cochrane	453 43
59611—Prop'n loss cafe service, weighing cars, etc.	557 62
58648—Freight settlement	1,137 18
58682—Claims	121 02
58694—Freight settlement	825 51
59026—Claims	52 55
59608—Car service balance	5,746 19
59726—Passenger car mileage	1,210 26
59738—Ticket balance	156 39
59629—Freight settlement	386 09
59713—Freight settlement	1,363 13
60107—Claims	8 47
60233—Car service balance	6,757 44
60367—Car service balance	1,474 98
60379—Ticket balance	1,367 16
60513—Claims	140 29
60769—One-third loss operating cafe cars	254 92
59810—Freight settlement	479 10
59846— " "	1,690 20
59880— " "	1,102 06
60160— " "	398 08
60362—Proportion commission outside agents	32 66
60492—Car service balance	3,021 30
60616—Passenger car mileage	1,937 98
60668—G. T. No. 6935 destroyed, car repairs, wheels	1,882 55
60846—Rental cinder cars, supplies private car	128 74
61012—Interline freight balance	18,702 13
60821—Freight settlement	225 06
60841— " "	510 54
60969— " "	1,555 65
60973—Claims	211 73
60975—Claims	170 56
61095—Freight settlement	75 38
61165—Claims	75 73
61381—Cost advertising, car repairs	273 30
61383—Rental cinder cars	389 28
61455—Cost of distributing T. C. L. time-tables	200 36
61457—Proportion operation pullmans, etc.	612 52
61479—Claims	6 70
61529—Inspecting track scales at North Bay	13 71
61621—Claims	33 16
61739—Car service balance	1,658 46
61855—Passenger car mileage	1,768 47
61873—Claims	32 72

GRAND TRUNK RAILWAY SYSTEM, ETC.—*Continued.*

62063—Claims	$228 88	
62117—Interline freight balance	20,158 61	
61046—Freight settlement	881 53	
61058— " "	1,696 48	
61074— " "	1,518 18	
61098—Car repairs	42	
61138—Car repairs and wheels	346 63	
61146—Advertising T. C. R. service	1,340 69	
61208—Freight settlement	4,025 14	
61314—Claims	1 30	
61368— "	20 89	
61430— "	39 03	
61894— "	113 39	
62038—Claim	1 04	
62220—Passenger car mileage	1,159 18	
62260—Claims	1,120 95	
62322—Interline freight balance	5,744 90	
62141—Freight settlement	2,096 19	
62155— " "	2,948 67	
62183— " "	1,998 29	
62209— " "	2,359 86	
62851—Car service balance	1,837 85	
62941—Passenger car mileage	640 36	
62965—Interline freight balance	20,599 72	
63095—Claims	96 56	
63211—Claims	118 10	
62354—Freight settlement	3,319 06	
62366— " "	987 24	
62382— " "	2,080 83	
62476— " "	2,158 61	
62508—Proportion loss operating dining cars, etc.	221 48	
62978—Claims	15 36	
63078—Joint switching, etc.	138 27	
63160—Fifty per cent. charged C. P. R. attending heaters	515 72	
63226—Claims	3 80	
63480—Car service balance	2,039 62	
63612—Proportion amount charged S. J. Gordon, rental of warehouse	27 79	
63614—Proportion expenses cars Toronto to Cochrane	80 07	
63618—Car repairs	64 05	
63708—Claims	65 49	
63754—Car repairs	4 22	
63796—Fifty per cent. amount charged C. N. R. attending heaters, North Bay Junction	2 28	
63848—Supplies for private cars, net loss operating dining cars	168 86	
		$264,741 99

W. A. GRAHAM, PURCHASING AGENT AND STOREKEEPER, NORTH BAY, ONT.

56679—Salary, November, 1915	$200 00	
56640— " December, 1915	200 00	
57649— " January, 1916	200 00	
57738— " February, 1916	200 00	
58663— " March, 1916	200 00	
58812— " April, 1916	200 00	
59821— " May, 1916	200 00	
60216— " June, 1916	200 00	
60790—Travelling expenses	9 50	
61327—Salary, July, 1916	200 00	
61581—Disbursements	2 65	
61184—Salary, August, 1916	200 00	
.62247— " September, 1916	200 00	
62602— " October, 1916	200 00	
		$2,412 15

THE GRAHAM NAIL WORKS, TORONTO.

56703—Wire nails	$31 80	
56986— " "	95 89	

The Graham Nail Works, Toronto.—*Continued.*

57681—Wire nails	$113 63	
57808— " "	112 21	
58565— " "	239 37	
59673— " "	204 97	
60134— " "	138 18	
62371— " "	424 10	
		$1,360 15

Great North Western Telegraph Company of Canada.

56721—Telegraph service	$0 51	
56843— " "	6 31	
57025— " "	56	
57184— " "	5 76	
57711— " "	1 20	
58107— " "	1 24	
57906— " "	1 03	
58498— " "	4 82	
58542— " "	11 76	
59447— " "	1 70	
58942— " "	4 66	
59464— " "	12 16	
59466— " "	76	
59764— " "	25 72	
60003— " "	3 54	
60089—Tariff books	12 00	
60739—Telegraph service	5 95	
60652— " "	4 64	
60938— " "	1 92	
60940— " "	2 71	
60992— " "	4 28	
61459— " "	52	
61953— " "	8 88	
62017— " "	59	
62113— " "	14 05	
61630— " "	4 03	
62264— " "	41	
62504— " "	4 48	
63076— " "	6 53	
63118— " "	3 26	
63580— " "	16 11	
63664— " "	59	
		$172 68

The Globe Printing Company, Toronto.

56723—Advertising	$0 60	
56774— "	56	
57705— "	50 00	
57707— " and subscription	3 80	
58496— "	80	
58782— "	84	
59460— "	33 00	
59998— "	1 64	
61118— "	1 68	
62264— "	1 64	
62506— "	3 36	
		$97 92

Gulf, Colorado & Santa Fe Railway Co., Galveston, Texas.

56799—Car repairs	$7 65	
57300— " "	4 91	
58205— " service balance	1 80	
59477— " repairs	7 87	
59511— " "	1 25	
60082— " "	6 43	

GULF, COLORADO & SANTA FE RAILWAY COMPANY, ETC.—*Continued.*

61285—Car repairs	$6 29	
61858— " "	5 12	
62266— " "	8 66	
63610— " "	8 66	
		$58 64

W. A. GRIFFIN, SUPERINTENDENT OF TRAFFIC, NORTH BAY.

56811—Salary, November, 1915	$270 00	
56638—Salary, December, 1915	270 00	
56962—Travelling expenses	46 60	
57647—Salary, January, 1916	270 00	
57736—Salary, February, 1916	270 00	
57970—Travelling expenses	23 90	
58589—Travelling expenses	13 95	
58661—Salary, March, 1916	270 00	
58814—Salary, April, 1916	270 00	
59250—Travelling expenses	12 05	
59819—Salary, May, 1916	270 00	
60101—Travelling expenses	29 85	
60214—Salary, June, 1916	270 00	
61325— " July, 1916	270 00	
61186— " August, 1916	270 00	
61502—Travelling expenses	35 55	
62245—Salary, September, 1916	270 00	
62604—Salary, October, 1916	270 00	
62612—Travelling expenses	30 70	
		$3,432 60

MISS T. GREGORY, STENOGRAPHER, NORTH BAY, ONT.

56813—Service rendered	$65 00	
56642— " "	65 00	
57651— " "	65 00	
57740— " "	65 00	
58665— " "	65 00	
58816— " "	65 00	
59823— " "	65 00	
60218— " "	65 00	
61329— " "	65 00	
61190— " "	65 00	
62249— " "	65 00	
62606— " "	65 00	
		$780 00

E. M. GOODMAN, AGENT, NEW LISKEARD, ONT.

56815—Remuneration, additional, November, 1915	$10 00	
56644— " " December, 1915	10 00	
57653— " " January, 1916	10 00	
57742— " " February, 1916	10 00	
58667— " " March, 1916	10 00	
58818— " " April, 1916	10 00	
59825— " " May, 1916	10 00	
60220— " " June, 1916	10 00	
61331— " " July, 1916	10 00	
61192— " " August, 1916	10 00	
62251— " " September, 1916	10 00	
62608— " " October, 1916	10 00	
		$120 00

GILL & LONG, TORONTO.

56845—Motor car service	$0 75	
56772—Livery service	75	
62641—Motor car service	75	
		$2 25

The Gurney Foundry Company, Ltd., Toronto.

56895—Van stoves	$36 57
57239—Grates and grate bar	8 10
58035—Claim No. 10481, cost repairs to radiator damaged in transit	.2 40
58362—Grates and grate hangers	7 37
58837—Cook stove	26 18
60308—Copper wire	75 00
61480—Saddle	5 50
62399—Stoves	38 91
63001—Cash drawers	9 00
62874—Coal door, grates, etc.	30 45

$239 48

The B. Greening Wire Company, Limited, Hamilton, Ont.

56897—Wire	$41 99
57505— "	48 48
57658— "	60 91
58835— "	42 78
58702—Cast steel rope	55 22
59675—Steel rope	32 24
59975—Netting, iron, etc.	393 02
60136—Wire	180 44
60238—Wire cloth, wire rope	59 11
60987—Steel rope, copper wire	53 19
61590—Brass riddle cloth	156 07
62395—Wire, rope, etc.	41 45
62592—Ballast rope	563 99

$1,728 89

Great Northern Railway Company, St. Paul, Minn.

57101—Car repairs	$27 20
56872—Car service balance	39 82
57298—Car repairs	1 12
58203—Car service balance	11 30
58305—Passenger car mileage	11 38
58138—Car service balance	.24 45
59283— " " "	8 10
59479— " repairs	6 92
59513— " "	2 66
59262— " "	1 88
59610— " service balance	2 70
60235— " " "	24 30
60369— " " " (passenger)	7 59
60080— " repairs	1 64
60496— " service balance	16 20
60618—Passenger car mileage	11 38
61741—Car service balance	13 50
61857—Passenger car mileage	7 59
61100—Car repairs	21 01
62150—Car service balance	1 80
62853—Car service balance	2 25
62943—Passenger car mileage	41 74
63482—Car service balance	62 32
63574—Ticket balance	5 84

$354 69

The Gourock Ropework Export Co., Limited, Montreal, P.Q.

57217—Rope	$11 00
57867— "	43 31
58833— "	56 55
59090— "	26 37
60742— "	18 00
63117—	108 33

$263 56

GALENA-SIGNAL OIL COMPANY, TORONTO.

57219—Oil and grease	$591 65	
57442—Oil, grease and air brake compound	755 57	
57873—Oil and grease	635 60	
58360— " "	1,027 95	
58829— "	1,014 55	
59096—Oil, and air brake compound	1,067 61	
60549—Oil	1,112 92	
60740— "	1,049 39	
61209— "	666 08	
62991—Oil and grease	814 79	
63112—Oil	942 00	
		$9,678 11

GEO. GORDON & CO., LIMITED, CACHE BAY, ONT.

57235—White pine	$221 03	
57438—White and red pine	505 92	
57869—Lumber	566 27	
61702— "	3,871 96	
62551— "	410 50	
62997—	2,068 67	
63116— "	173 74	
63684—Claim No. 12912—Overcharge rate, car hardware and supplies	26 64	
		$7,844 73

J. R. GORDON, TIMMINS, ONT.

57237—Meat	$11 13	
		$11 13

GUTTA PERCHA & RUBBER, LIMITED, TORONTO.

56554—Hose	$119 07	
57599— "	279 79	
57679— "	84 77	
57798—Hose and valves	303 43	
58649—Hose	93 84	
60132— "	393 96	
60210— "	191 10	
61917—Hose and tubing	97 16	
61478—Hose	43 60	
62397— "	266 72	
62594— "	267 54	
62680— "	114 66	
		$2,255 64

GRAND & TOY, LIMITED. TORONTO.

56778—Stationery and transfer cases, etc.	$99 56	
57936—Stationery	125 07	
59462—Carbon, letter heads, etc.	50 63	
59743—Stationery	106 02	
60005—Stationery	47 74	
60551—Paper	22 50	
61527—Stationery	79 80	
61957—Stationery	163 69	
61628—Index	2 10	
62999—Stationery	82 13	
62918—Stationery	73 60	
		$852 84

GEORGIA RAILROAD, AUGUSTA, GA.

56874—Car service balance	$11 25	
63662—Car service balance	1 35	
		$12 60

ADELARD GRATTON, IROQUOIS FALLS, ONT.

57014—Donation account, horse alleged killed $25 00

$25 00

R. P. GRAHAM, COBALT, ONT.

58033—Claim No. 10618—Loss account, shortage, 1 case meat... $4 80
57072—Claim No. 10617—Loss account, 3 bottles syrup $1 08

$5 88

THE GARLOCK PACKING COMPANY, HAMILTON, ONT.

57436—Spiral packing $28 25
58831—Packing 56 53
60545— "   etc. 58 83
60738— " 18 00
61704— " 70 94
62993— 34 64

$267 19

THE GENERAL SUPPLY CO. OF CANADA, LIMITED, OTTAWA, ONT.

57440—Fittings $50 26
57891— " 20 14
58354— " 33 14
59041— " 127 22
59092—Couplings, valves, etc. 52 59
60543—Bushings, plugs, etc. 14 93
60736—Couplings, bushings, etc. 144 56
60942—Unions, nipples, etc. 51 84
61019—Plugs, tees, flanges 11 39
61955—Bushings, plugs, elbows 20 62
61706—Nipples, elbows, couplings 3 02
62995—Elbows, bushings, etc. 72 13
62872—Street ells, bushings, etc........................ 45 15
63114—Dart unions, nipples, etc. 24 49
63278—Elbows 52

$672 05

A. D. GIBSON, TORONTO, ONT.

57639—Napkins $48 00

$48 00

F. R. GIBSON, HAILEYBURY, ONT.

57709—Installing heating system $258 30
58500—Installing heating system (bal.) 28 70
58993—Claim No. 10763—Loss account, damage to closet tank .. 9 50
59468—Repairs—Englehart station 14 87
59773—Repairs to tap 75
61810—Claim No. 12372—damage, 1 lav. plate 6 15

$318 27

J. GAMMAGE & SONS, LIMITED, LONDON, ONT.

57871—Cuttings $5 50

$5 50

GREEN BAY & WESTERN RAILROAD COMPANY, GREEN BAY, WIS.

58207—Car service balance $0 45
58140— "   " 7 65
60237— "   "   45
60498— "   " 4 05
61283—Car repairs 2 99
61972—Car repairs 1 50
63484—Car service balance 45

$17 54

GILMORE & PITTSBURGH RAILROAD, ORMSTEAD, MONT.

58209—Car service balance	$3 60	
		$3 60

A. GAGNE, SOUTH PORCUPINE, ONT.

57996—Claim No. 10707—Loss account, damage to stove	$3 00	
63097—Claim No. 11536—Damage to glassware	9 97	
		$12 97

R. GARRIOCK, COCHRANE, ONT.

57998—Claim No. 10571—Loss account, shortage bed rails	6 00	
		$6 00

GEORGIA SOUTHERN & FLORIDA RAILWAY COMPANY, MACON, GA.

58142—Car service balance	$1 35	
59285— " "	90	
60241— " "	11 70	
60502— " "	4 95	
61743— " "	5 85	
62152— " "	9 45	
		$34 20

CHAS. S. GILES, COCHRANE, ONT.

58502—Repairing to heating system	$55 71	
59443—Plumbing	7 55	
61207—Plumbing	2 10	
		$65 36

GRAND TRUNK PACIFIC RAILWAY COMPANY, MONTREAL, QUE.

58600—Telegraph charges, account Transcontinental train service	$4 20	
61952—Claims	5 86	
62749—Claims	10 13	
63157—Propn. expenses, Trans. freight bureau	13 46	
62870—Expenses—T. C. freight bureau	73 05	
62980—Claim	66	
63120—Propn. expenses, T. C. R. freight bureau	12 63	
63174—Claim	1 10	
63616—Car repairs	3,236 52	
		$3,357 61

GRAND UNION HOTEL, NEW LISKEARD, ONT.

58602—Breakfast furnished passengers, account delayed train ..	$4 50	
62313—Claim No. 12403—Loss, gin	2 52	
		$7 02

GURNEY SCALE COMPANY, HAMILTON, ONT.

58563—Cash drawers	$5 88	
		$5 88

S. GREENWOOD & SONS. NEW LISKEARD, ONT.

58975—Claim No. 10680—Loss account, shortage, bag bran	$1 15	
59886—Claim No. 9921—Overcharge in weight, shipment potatoes	6 46	
		$7 61

HOTEL GOLDFIELD, TIMMINS, ONT.

59445—Board and lodging furnished	$4 00	
60014— " "	6 00	
62037— " "	84 50	
61120— "	6 00	
62510—	4 00	
62712—	6 00	
63660—	21 00	
		$131 50

GALVESTON, HARRISBURG & SAN ANTONIO RAILWAY COMPANY, HOUSTON, TEXAS.

59509—Car repairs	$1 94	
60500—Car service balance	5 05	
60628—Ticket balance	24 88	
62024—Car repairs	2 64	
		$34 51

R. M. GARROW, PORCUPINE, ONT.

59390—Claim No. 11062—Loss account, shortage sugar	$1 40	
		$1 40

GULF & SHIP ISLAND RAILROAD, GULFPORT, MISS.

60239—Car service balance	1 80	
		$1 80

JOHN GRIEVE (M.P. DEPT.), COCHRANE, ONT.

60509—Travelling expenses	$5 20	
60650— "	2 80	
61579— "	2 40	
61246— "	4 00	
62237— "	2 80	
63214— "	2 40	
		$19 60

GIFFORD-WOOD COMPANY. HUDSON, N.Y.

60547—Chisels, tongs, etc.	$27 01	
		$27 01

GALVESTON WHARF COMPANY, GALVESTON, TEXAS.

59960—Repairs to cars	$2 51	
		$2 51

GRANT-HOLDEN & GRAHAM. LIMITED, OTTAWA, ONT.

60734—Mail bags	$9 60	
		$9 60

GENERAL MANIFOLD & PRINTING COMPANY. FRANKLIN, PA.

60744—Books	$43 52	
62553—Books	46 92	
		$90 44

C. GUITARD, NORTH BAY, ONT.

61481—Claim No. 11574—Shortage, bundles saws	$5 00	
		$5 00

GALT, PRESTON & HESPELER STREET RAILWAY COMPANY, GALT, ONT.

61619—Claim No. 10567—Overcharge, weight, car beer	$7 90	
61366—Claim No. 11958—Overcharge, car beer, Kuntz Brewery ..	9 05	
		$16 95

GILLIES BROS., LIMITED, BRAESIDE, ONT.

62065—Claim No. 11444—Alleged loss spindles	$15 00	
		$15 00

GRIP, LIMITED, TORONTO, ONT.

61280—Printing coloured maps	$33 00	
		$33 00

THE GRILLS COMPANY, NEW LISKEARD, ONT.

62040—Claim No. 12287—alleged loss four bags potatoes........	$6 00	
		$6 00

B. F. GARDINER, THORNLOE, ONT.

62549—Slabs	$36 75	
		$36 75

A. W. GOLDING, COCHRANE, ONT.

62630—Claim No. 12508—alleged loss jam	$16 50	
		$16 50

W. H. GILLARD & COMPANY, HAMILTON, ONT.

62641—Claim No. 12325—alleged loss matches burnt............	$20 38	
		$20 38

W. F. GOOD, WABUN P.O.

62669—Ties	$684 27	
		$684 27

GRASSELLI CHEMICAL COMPANY, LIMITED, CLEVELAND, OHIO.

62855—Car service balance	$1 90	
63486— " "	5 69	
		$7 59

GORDON H. GAUTHIER, SOUTH PORCUPINE, ONT.

62710—Professional services	$5 00	
		$5 00

SIMON HENEROFSKY, ENGLEHART, ONT.

56451—North half Lot 1, Con. 5, Chamberlain, 1.5 acres........	$75 00	
60064—Ties	331 68	
		$406 68

A. O. HOUGHTON, HEASLIP, ONT.

56491—Donation—account cow alleged killed	$20 00	
63258— " " "	25 00	
		$45 00

THE HOTEL CEDRIC, COCHRANE, ONT.

56725—Board and lodging—engineering party	$3 50	
60012— " " "	13 50	
60889— " " "	4 50	
61113— " " "	16 50	
		$38 00

HYDRO-ELECTRIC POWER COMMISSION OF ONTARIO, TORONTO, ONT.

57241—Lamps	$77 43
57448— "	134 03
57877— "	102 08
58374—	59 54
59104— "	164 16
60559—	83 66
60748—	144 55
60898— ··	96 17
61961— ··	51 06

HYDRO-ELECTRIC POWER COMMISSION, ETC.—*Continued.*

61518—Lamps	$15 87	
62268— "	104 64	
63015— "	78 00	
63328—	162 77	
		$1,273 96

HAYES TRACK APPLIANCE COMPANY, RICHMOND, IND.

57243—Operating stands and derails	$111 00	
		$111 00

HAMILTON STAMP & STENCIL WORKS, LIMITED, HAMILTON, ONT.

57245—Rubber stamp	$0 87	
57450— "	3 56	
57893— " and daters	13 90	
58368—Daters, stamps, die and ink	29 39	
58839—Stamps, daters	8 26	
58841— " "	15 95	
59094— " "	4 34	
60310— " "	1 36	
60746—Repairing dater, rubber stamp	1 31	
61217—Daters, etc.	16 74	
61592—Stamp dater	18 62	
61632— "	15 89	
63003— "	15 10	
62922—	1 33	
		$146 62

THE HOLDEN COMPANY, LIMITED, MONTREAL, QUE.

57247—Iron and headlight supplies	$66 92	
57446—Bridge tyres and headlight material	829 33	
57875—Repair parts for headlights	31 23	
58364—Headlight parts	265 82	
58843— " "	239 10	
59102— " "	391 48	
60555—Lamps, carbons, etc.	66 96	
60762—Iron	112 74	
61211—Dynamo doors, complete	63 60	
61919—Iron	19 78	
61728— "	59 67	
63009—Armatures, clutches, etc.	77 91	
		$2,224 54

GEO. H. HEES & CO., LIMITED, TORONTO, ONT.

57249—Shades	$1 06	
57444—Horse hair and shades	31 56	
57881—Shades and nails	10 12	
58370—Shades	2 44	
59098—Canvas	24 82	
60557—Webbing, lining, etc.	9 89	
60900—Twine	6 82	
61732—Shades	2 52	
63005—Thread, canvas	40 66	
		$129 89

F. W. HUTT, HAILEYBURY, ONT.

57353—Claim No. 10331—loss account shortage coal	$4 12	
58006— " No. 10270— " " "	7 85	
		$11 97

HARRIS ABATTOIR COMPANY, LIMITED, TORONTO, ONT.

57355—Claim No. 10474—overcharge, demurrage and detention charges	$4 00	
61814— " No. 11060—loss four cases eggs ....,.....	33 60	
		$37 60

HAMILTON & COMPANY, HAILEYBURY, ONT.

57357—Claim No. 10268—loss account, shortage and damage to whiskey	$14 07	
57074— " No. 10506—loss account, one bottle liquor	1 30	
58039—Claims Nos. 10016, 10624,-6, 10603—shortage and damage to liquor	53 16	
58000— " Nos. 10605, 10619, 10435—loss account, damage to liquor	16 02	
58977— " Nos. 10918 and 10855—loss account, damage to liquor	2 83	
59392—Claim No. 11019—loss, account damage to liquor	1 92	
59799— " No. 10858—loss account, damage to liquor	2 23	
60457—Claims Nos. 11271, 11431, 10881—loss and damage to liquor	7 84	
60859— " Nos. 11018, 11543—loss account, damage to liquor.	1 88	
60933— " Nos. 11595 and 11272—loss of liquor in transit...	7 31	
61167— " Nos. 11017, 11598, 11453—loss three bottles whiskey	7 43	
61483— "	28 55	
61623—Claim No. 11437—loss liquor account, breakage ....:.....	3 47	
61875— " No. 11823—loss, liquor in transit	10 46	
62067— " No. 11987—loss, liquor in transit	70	
61432— " No. 11842—damage and loss of gin	21	
61812—Claims	98	
62042— "	79	
62643— " Nos. 12458, 12371, 12369—loss liquor	34	
62558— " Nos. 12366 and 11996—loss liquor	1 22	
62896—Claim No. 12456—loss liquor	9 76	
63230— " No. 12367—loss account, bottle creme de menthe, broken	75	
63686— " No. 11676—loss account, shortage liquor	2 34	
		$210 56

THE HAMILTON HERALD, HAMILTON, ONT.

56670—Advertising	$20 00	
		$20 00

HOCKING VALLEY RAILWAY COMPANY, COLUMBUS, OHIO.

56876—Car service balance	$7 65	
58211— " " ....:	7 65	
58144— " "	3 60	
59287— " "	37 80	
59264— " repairs	26	
59622— " service balance ....~	26 10	
60243— " "	1 80	
60504— " "	11 25	
61745— "	5 40	
62154— " "	7 65	
62857— " ....-....	24 30	
63488— "	19 80	
		$153 26

C. L. HEATH, SOUTH PORCUPINE, ONT.

57076—Claim No. 10246—loss account, damage to canoe	$5 00	
		$5 00

H. Harrison (M. M. Dept.), North Bay, Ont.

57575—Expenses, travelling	$18 90	
57698— " "	1 20	
		$20 10

F. H. Hopkins & Co., Montreal, Que.

57879—Hoisting chain and cable, wire rope sheaves	$284 50	
58690—Part payment on ballast cars	10,000 00	
58744—Jordan spreader, Hart convertible cars	4,530 00	
59977—Wheelbarrows	84 00	
63011—Woodwork for steam shovel	178 50	
		$15,077 00

Jas. Hylands, Cobalt. Ont.

58037—Claim No. 10597—loss account, damage to fire brick	$0 75	
		$0 75

Mrs. Thos. C. Haley, Wahtaybeag, Ont.

58111—Donation account, pulpwood alleged destroyed	$78 00	
		$78 00

Hamilton Bridge Works Company, Limited, Hamilton, Ont.

58343—Angles	$299 70	
58372—Car sills, rivets and plates	382 90	
59043—Plate and angle	27 44	
59100—Plate	156 98	
60553— "	36 90	
61730—Angles	69 42	
		$973 34

Frank Hartzke, McCool P.O.

58463—Ties	$107 79	
60064— "	124 35	
		$232 14

Max Hartzke, Leeville P.O.

58463—Ties	$83 48	
58593— "	49 23	
58593— "	46 90	
59425— "	50 49	
		$230 10

The Hoyle Lumber Company, Limited, Morrisburg, Ont.

58002—Claim No. 10753—demurrage	$4 00	
61879— " No. 11854—rebate on siding	20 00	
		$24 00

Hogg & Lytle, Limited, Toronto, Ont.

58004—Claim No. 10634—overcharge, weight of oats	$4 22	
60857— " No. 10778—overcharge, weight of peas	6 63	
		$10 85

John Harrison & Sons Company, Limited, Owen Sound, Ont.

58366—Tie plugs	$70 00	
61482— "	70 00	
		$140 00

ROBERT W. HUNT & COMPANY, LIMITED, MONTREAL, QUE.

58376—Inspecting telegraph wire	$15 64	
59045—Wire inspection	2 61	
62270—Inspection structural material	8 48	
63013— " bolts	8 68	
62920—Track bolts (inspection)	2 91	
		$38 32

JAMES HEWLETT, TORONTO, ONT.

58539—Premium on Royal insurance policy No. 271813	$4 20	
		$4 20

JOSEPH HOWE, CAINE P.O., ONT.

58593—Ties	$117 85	
59425— "	149 34	
59425— "	65 60	
59754— "	251 94	
60064— "	82 05	
		$666 78

JOSEPH HARTNEY, CAINE P.O., ONT.

58593—Ties	$164 19	
58593— "	85 38	
59425— "	47 40	
		$296 97

HOWARD HEASLIP, HEASLIP, ONT.

58593—Ties	$61 33	
59754—Ties	33 80	
		$95 13

AMOS HEASLIP, HEASLIP, ONT.

58593—Ties	$99 39	
		$99 39

WILLIAM HAYES, KENABEEK P.O., ONT.

58593—Ties	$61 37	
60064—Ties	36 10	
		$97 47

HOLLINGER GOLD MINES, LIMITED, TIMMINS, ONT.

58699—Soft coal	$569 18	
59380—Soft coal	727 11	
60848—Charges on car coal	29 05	
61221—Coal	117 93	
		$1,443 27

HILL-CLARK-FRANCIS, LIMITED, SCHUMACHER, ONT.

58891—Claim No. 10772—Account, damage to furniture	$1 25	
		$1 25

GEO. D. HAMILTON, SOUTH PORCUPINE, ONT.

58979—Claim No. 10452—Refund demurrage charges	$5 00	
58826—Claim No. 11079—Siding rebate	24 00	
		$29 00

GEO. HAWKINS (M.M. DEPT.), NORTH BAY, ONT.

59025—Expenses—Travelling	$3 50	
61250—Expenses—Travelling	2 10	
		$5 60

FORBES HENDRY, ENID P.O., SASK.

59129—Claim No. 11082—Baggage destroyed by fire	$59 60	
		$59 60

JOHN HUTSON, TROUT MILLS, ONT.

59173—Lighting lamps and rent waiting room	$15 00	
		$15 00

ALBERT HOPKINS, PORQUIS P.O., ONT.

59425—Ties	$141 30	
		$141 30

JOHN HOWARD, HEASLIP, ONT.

59425—Ties	$50 81	
59754—Ties	28 60	
		$79 41

HOUSTON & TEXAS CENTRAL RAILROAD COMPANY, HOUSTON, TEX.

59517—Car repairs	$1 97	
		$1 97

HEATON'S AGENCY, TORONTO, ONT.

58688—Subscription "Heaton's Annual"	1 25	
		$1 25

ADAM HALL, PETERBOROUGH, ONT.

58874—Ranges and reservoirs	$67 65	
		$67 65

S. R. HART & COMPANY, TORONTO, ONT.

58944—Embossed note paper, envelopes	$13 00	
		$13 00

T. E. HICKEY, TIMMINS, ONT.

59394—Claim No. 10093—Loss acount, shortage, boxes poultry	27 09	
		$27 09

HERBERT HOWE, CANE P.O., ONT.

59754—Ties	$194 91	
		$194 91

JOSEPH HEASLIP, HEASLIP, ONT.

59754—Ties	$118 20	
		$118 20

DUGALD HALLIDAY, LEEVILLE P.O., ONT.

59754—Ties	$270 45	
		$270 45

THE HAILEYBURIAN, HAILEYBURY, ONT.

59745—Advertisements, " tenders "	$4 80	
61149— " "	5 10	
61122— " "	4 80	
62758— " " sale of lots "	22 80	
		$37 50

MISS ANNA HALL, VIKING, ALTA.

59875—Claim No. 11470—Loss account, baggage burned	$100 00	
		$100 00

A. W. HAWKSHAW, UNO PARK, ONT.

60223—Meals supplied	$5 75	
		$5 75

HAMILTON & TORONTO SEWER PIPE COMPANY, LIMITED, HAMILTON, ONT.

60561—Pipe	$94 60	
62392—Pipe	105 39	
		$199 99

O. HERMANT & COMPANY, SOUTH PORCUPINE, ONT.

59874—Claim No. 11143—Loss account, damage to potatoes	$6 22	
		$6 22

J. F. HARTZ COMPANY, LIMITED, TORONTO, ONT.

59876—Vials and corks	$0 75	
		$0 75

HUGH HASTINGS, EARLTON P.O., ONT.

60064—Ties	$412 08	
		$412 08

HAUCK MANUFACTURING COMPANY, BROOKLYN, N.Y.

60242—Thawing outfit	$60 00	
		$60 00

HAM & GRANT, ENGLEHART, ONT.

60244—Tea	$4 00	
		$4 00

HARRIMAN & NORTH EASTERN RAILROAD COMPANY, CINCINNATI, O.

60506—Car service balance	$5 40	
61747—Car service balance	2 25	
		$7 65

ARTHUR HOUGHTON, BOURKES, ONT.

60664—Award W. C. B. final payment re injuries alleged sustained	$12 21	
		$12 21

HAILEYBURY SUPPLY STORE, HAILEYBURY, ONT.

60917—Claim No. 11436—Damage to catsup	$0 80	
61485—Claim No. 11592—Loss, gross shoe laces	1 55	
		$2 35

17 T R

HEYWOOD BROS., & WAKEFIELD COMPANY, BUFFALO, N.Y.

61213—Muslin $51 20

$51 20

HORTWELL BROS., LIMITED, WALKERVILLE, ONT.

61215—Pick handles $21 50

$21 50

HAMILTON STOVE & HEATER CO., LIMITED, HAMILTON, ONT.

61219—Key cut to sample $0 30

$0 30

W. J. HARPER, A. R., & C. A., NORTH BAY, ONT.

61415—Travelling expenses $3 75
61248—   " 2 00
62774—   " 1 75

$7 50

F. HEASMAN, NEW LISKEARD, ONT.

61487—Claim No. 11435—Jar olives broken $1 25
61877—   "   12149—Loss account, bottle vinegar 21
61434—   "   12400—Loss, can salmon 36
62595—   "   12035—Loss, jar catsup 80
62898—   "   12140—Loss account, shortage soap 63
63228—   "   12989, 12806—Loss pail candy, chimney broken
                       in transit 3 66

$6 91

R. B. HUNTER, FULTON, N.Y.

61625—Claim No. 11711—Overcharge rate, pulpwood $28 05

$28 05

HENDERSON & ANGUS, NORTH BAY, ONT.

62045—Work performed, Timmins Station $2,550 00
61220—   "   " 3,525 38
62561—   "   " 10,125 62
62674—   "   " 1,224 00

$17,425 00

HOUSTON EAST & WEST TEXAS RAILWAY COMPANY, HOUSTON, TEXAS.

61974—Car repairs $0 12

$0 12

D. HAMILTON, TORONTO, ONT.

62185—Expenses $8 84

$8 84

J. R. HORNER, SHAWVILLE, ONT.

62315—Claim No. 12315—Loss, organ in forest fires $55 00

$55 00

H. S. HENNESSY, HAILEYBURY P.O., ONT.

62669—Ties $183 04

$183 04

A. L. HERBERT, COBALT, ONT.

63099—Claim No. 11414—Alleged loss coal $9 70

$9 70

H. HURWITZ, TIMMINS, ONT.

63187—Claim No. 12010—Alleged damage to glass $8 00
                                                                          $8 00

HERALD PRINTING COMPANY, NEW LISKEARD, ONT.

62514—Advertisement, "sale of lands" $15 20
                                                                          $15 20

INDIANA HARBOR BELT RAILROAD COMPANY, CLEVELAND, OHIO.

56519—Car repairs $9 44
57304—   "   29
59431—   " 2 28
61289—   "   29
61906—   "   50
63756—   " 2 14
                                                                          $14 94

IRISH & MAULSON, LIMITED, TORONTO, ONT.

57231—Premium—Fire insurance $0 90
56626—   "   " 9,744 50
58931—   "   " 1 80
58946— 400 00
61346—   "   " 26 87
62443—   " 10 80
62716—   " 20 03
                                                                          $10,204 90

INTERNATIONAL SEAL & LOCK CO., HAMILTON, MICH.

57251—Tyden seal $56 57
57895—Tyden seal 58 75
58847—Car seals 58 55
60565—Car seals 56 26
62555—Seals 70 58
                                                                          $300 71

THE IMPERIAL OIL CO., LIMITED, TORONTO.

57429—Oil, gasoline, candles $399 81
56878—Car service balance 57 95
57452—Oil, gasoline and cutting compound 277 35
57957—Oil barrels 423 16
58215—Car service balance 28 53
58008—Claim No. 10835—Siding rebate 326 00
58148—Car service balance 64 16
58378—Oil, gasoline and barrels. 676 71
58845—Oil and barrels 312 72
59291—Car service balance 20 14
59106—Oil, gasoline 196 25
59616—Car service balance 31 10
60247—Car service balance 36 20
60563—Gasoline, grease, etc. 408 30
60510—Car service balance 24 37
60760—Gasoline, fuel, oil, etc. 81 62
61021—Gasoline, oil, barrels 203 60
61751—Car service balance 26 59
61921—Oil 87 49
61178—Land—North Bay Jct. 2,000 00
61634—Tank cars 525 00
61636—Oil 36 37
61734—Oil 276 11
62158—Car service balance 15 70
62201—Rental offices, September, 1916 ....   40 97
62597—Claim No. 12481—Loss, oven 2 60
62861—Car service balance 3 50

THE IMPERIAL OIL COMPANY, LIMITED, TORONTO.—*Continued.*

63017—Oil and gasoline	$89 04	
62334—Rental offices, October, 1916	122 92	
62928—Oils ...	267 58	
63122— "	101 06	
63280— "	57 90	
63526—Car service balance	13 54	
58043—Claim No. 10483—Loss, oil	62 66	
		$7,297 00

ILLINOIS CENTRAL RAILROAD COMPANY, CHICAGO, ILL.

57302—Car repairs	$41 49	
58213—Car service balance	7 65	
58317—Ticket balance	7 28	
58377—Car repairs	25 97	
58146—Car service balance	76 00	
58504—Car repairs	3 30	
59289—Car service balance	87 30	
59266—Car repairs	11 05	
59614—Car service balance	81 85	
59913—Car repairs	8 79	
60245—Car service balance	149 85	
59962—Car repairs	4 22	
60508—Car service balance	113 85	
60630—Ticket balance	19 42	
61291—Car repairs	8 74	
61749—Car service balance	48 80	
61841—Ticket balance	17 56	
62156—Car service balance	46 80	
62859—Car service balance	47 60	
63232—Claim No. 11845—Damage to newsprint	1 71	
63490—Car service balance	28 95	
		$838 18

INTERNATIONAL MALLEABLE IRON CO., LIMITED, GUELPH, ONT.

57454—Castings	$77 60	
57883—Castings	19 20	
58380—Castings and express	18 45	
59146—Castings and express on patterns	4 55	
60567—Castings	70 98	
60246—Castings	15 48	
61520—Express on patterns	30	
62926—Express on patterns	30	
63124—Castings	14 70	
		$221 56

ILLINOIS SOUTHERN RAILWAY COMPANY, ST. LOUIS, M.O.

58217—Car service balance	$1 35	
58150— " "	9 00	
59293— " "	4 05	
60251— " "	8 10	
60514— " "	12 60	
61753— " "	2 70	
		$37 80

INTERNATIONAL RAILWAY PUBLISHING CO., LIMITED, MONTREAL, P.Q.

57908—Advertising in "Canadian Official Railw? Guide"	$29 00	
59175— " " " "	27 00	
60654— " " " "	27·00	
62714—	27 00	
		$110 00

INDEPENDENT PACKING COMPANY, CHICAGO, ILL.

58152—Car service balance	$3 87	
59618—Car service balance	3 87	
		$7 74

INDUSTRIAL WORKS, BAY CITY, MICH.

58382—Journal boxes	$34 00	
60758—Hose, grates	91 75	
		$125 75

THOS. INGLIS, ENGLEHART, ONT.

58552—Team work	$107 60	
		$107 60

INTERNATIONAL TIME RECORDING CO. OF CANADA, LIMITED, TORONTO, ONT.

59047—Daily slips	$4 00	
61223—Ribbon	1 25	
61494—Ribbon	1 50	
		$6 75

INTERCOLONIAL RAILWAY OF CANADA, MONCTON, N.B.

59449—Commission on westbound business	$0 54	
60419—Commission on westbound business	1 58	
		$2 12

INTERNATIONAL & GREAT NORTHERN RAILWAY, HOUSTON, TEXAS.

59268—Car repairs	$6 50	
60249— " service balance	7 20	
60084— " repairs	11 92	
60512— " service balance	17 10	
61287— " repairs	10 75	
62863— " service balance	4 05	
63758— " repairs	2 40	
		$59 92

MRS. J. E. IRELAND, SOUTH PORCUPINE, ONT.

59801—Claim No. 8916, loss account damage to mirror	$45 00	
		$45 00

INTERNATIONAL REFINING COMPANY, TULSA, OKLA.

60253—Car service balance	$2 11	
		$2 11

IRON TRADE REVIEW, CLEVELAND, OHIO.

61583—Subscription	$6 00	
		$6 00

IROQUOIS FALLS MERCHANDISE CO., LIMITED, IROQUOIS FALLS, ONT.

61316—Claim No. 12009, alleged loss tomatoes	$0 73	
62044—Claim No. 11443, loss case tea	11 79	
		$12 52

INTERSTATE RAILROAD COMPANY, BIG STONE GAP, VA.

61976—Car repairs	$6 04	
		$6 04

ILLINOIS NORTHERN RAILWAY, CHICAGO, ILL.

61978—Car repairs	$0 46	
		$0 46

I.O.D.E. Provincial Chapter of Manitoba, Winnipeg, Man.

62376—Advertising in "Historical Souvenir"	$35 00	
		$35 00

Irwin Auger Bit Company, Wilmington, Ohio.

63126—Bits	$6 72	
		$6 72

International Harvester Co., Limited, Chicago, Ill.

63176—Claim No. 12440, two pieces waggon alleged destroyed	$13 20	
		$13 20

H. N. Joy, South Porcupine, Ont.

56655—Claim No. 10425, damage to barrel pitch	$0 88	
58045— " " 10541, loss account damage to stove	1 00	
62048— " " 12350 and 11732, damage to washboards	2 52	
		$4 40

D. F. Jones Manufacturing Co., Limited, Gananoque, Ont.

56899—Shovels	$85 01	
56988—Scoops	36 52	
57683—Shovels	36 54	
58753— "	43 84	
58876— "	39 66	
59979— "	47 60	
62373—Scoops	50 16	
		$339 33

The Jackson Press, Kingston, Ont.

57253—Advice books and forms	165 40	
57460—Forms and tags	12 00	
57897— "	133 50	
58384— "	590 28	
59049— "	258 93	
59108—Letterheads, etc.	248 56	
60577—Forms	460 10	
60364—Tags, forms, statements	95 25	
60792—Check sheets, reports, etc.	32 50	
61225—Forms	279 88	
61638— "	161 62	
61640— "	323 45	
63159— "	719 13	
62930—Stationery supplies	306 56	
63128—Form 1543	122 77	
		$3,909 93

D. Johnson, Matheson, Ont.

57359—Claim No. 10,338, loss account shortage tobacco	$22 69	
		$22 69

Don. H. Jacobie, Haileybury, Ont.

57361—Claim No. 10,487, overcharge on tires	$1 66	
60064—Ties	8 00	
		$9 66

The Jamieson Meat Co., Limited, Cobalt, Ont.

57431—Meat	$324 42	
57456—Meat and butter	91 30	
57959—Commissary	96 15	

THE JAMIESON MEAT COMPANY, LIMITED, COBALT, ONT.—*Continued.*

60701—Meat ...	$92 58	
59888—Claim No. 11,063, loss account shortage herring	88	
60756—Meat	96 51	
60994— "	374 53	
61227— "	167 90	
61585— "	290 91	
61963—	15 00	
		$1,550 18

JONES & MOORE ELECTRIC CO., LIMITED, TORONTO, ONT.

56672—Columbia dry cells	$1 75	
		$1 75

JAMES & REID, PERTH, ONT.

57899—Snow scraper	$15 00	
58567—Steel ladder and hooks	71 16	
		$86 16

WILLIAM JUNOR, TORONTO, ONT.

57901—Dishes	$21 40	
60312—Supplies "Temagami"	3 00	
		$24 40

JENCKES MACHINE COMPANY LIMITED, COBALT, ONT.

58047—Claim No. 10694, damage to pump	$4 00	
58010—Claim No. 10600, damage to hoist	270 42	
		$274 42

COLBORN JOHNSON, KENABEEK, ONT.

58463—Ties	$66 90	
58593—Ties	36 60	
		$103 50

JOHN JENKYN, NORTH BAY, ONT.

57632—Award, W. C. B., *re* alleged injuries	$5 27	
		$5 27

JONES & GLASSCO, MONTREAL, QUE.

57938—Chain drive	$207 50	
		$207 50

DR. GORDON F. JACKSON, HAILEYBURY, ONT.

59135—Professional service	$20 00	
		$20 00

C. H. JORDON, KENABEEK P.O., ONT.

59425—Ties	$40 06	
61063— "	21 80	
61500— "	112 35	
		$174 21

H. A. JACKSON, MRS. A. L. JACKSON & PHYLLIS LOGAN, EDMONTON, ALTA.

59877—Claim No. 11458, loss account damage to baggage	$300 00	
		$300 00

ROBERT JARVIS, McCOOL P.O., ONT.

60064—Ties	$80 43	
		$80 43

D. Johnson, Matheson, Ont.

60248—Provisions supplied $67 56

$67 56

O. F. Jordan Company, Chicago, Ill.

60902—Castings.................... .... $2 04

$2 04

Julian Sales Leather Goods Company, Limited, Toronto, Ont.

60849—Pass case $4 00

$4 00

Albert John, Leeville, Ont.

61063—Ties.. $81 42

$81 42

Thomas Johnston, Leeville, Ont.

61063—Ties......... . ... $33 00

$33 00

J. N. Jamieson, Haileybury, Ont.

61881—Claim No. 11901—damages to couch..................... $1 50

$1 50

Joseph Eli, Cochrane. Ont.

62046—Claim No. 11609—loss bottle pineapple.................. $1 17

$1 17

R. W. Johnson. Kenabeek P.O., Ont.

62669—Ties.. $29 82

$29 82

J. G. G. Kerry, Toronto, Ont.

56471—Fee as Consulting Engineer—November, 1915	....	$83 33	
56506— "	"	"	—December, 1915	83 33
57455— "	"	"	—January, 1916	83 33
57584— "	"	"	—February, 1916	83 33
58475— "	"	"	—March, 1916	83 33
58632— "	"	"	—April, 1916	83 33
59623— "	"	"	—May, 1916	83 33
59792— "	"	"	—June, 1916	83 33
60809— "	"	"	—July, 1916	83 33
61030— "	"	"	—August, 1916	83 33
62121— "	"	"	—September, 1916	83 33
62330— "	"	"	—October, 1916	83 33

$999 96

Kansas City Southern Railway Company, Kansas City, Mo.

56521—Car repairs	....	$17 99
57103— " repairs	....	81 53
56880— " service balance	....	1 35
57306— " repairs	....	12 02
59964— " repairs	....	46
60516— " service balance	....	4 05
61293— " repairs	....	12 45
61755— " service balance	....	1 80
62865— " service balance	....	9 00

$140 65

KENTUCKY & INDIANA TERMINAL RAILWAY COMPANY LOUISVILLE, KY.

56625—Car repairs	$1 26	
57308— " "	1 82	
58554— " "	3 03	
		$6 11

KERRY & CHASE, LIMITED, TORONTO, ONT.

56729—Services re Moose Harbour, report and inspection of gas engine	$43 39	
57874—Travelling expenses (J. G. G. Kerry)	4 95	
59451—Service rendered	411 76	
60007— " "	97 65	
62281— " "	131 38	
62516— " "	360 75	
		$1,049 88

W. J. KELLY, SUPERINTENDENT OF TELEGRAPH AND TELEPHONE, NORTH BAY, ONT.

57069—Travelling expenses	$6 55	
56964— " "	14 45	
58266— " "	8 85	
58779—	13 60	
59332— " "	5 65	
59947—	17 05	
60268—	51 35	
61587—	6 50	
61396—	7 70	
62623—	6 30	
62776—	17 25	
		$155 25

REBECCA KENNEDY, NORTH BAY, ONT.

57093—Laundry	$20 49	
57034a— "	20 61	
58109— "	19 86	
57940—	19 56	
59565—	20 58	
59752—	20 46	
60511—	22 17	
60794—	22 45	
62091—	32 30	
61954—	28 38	
63229—	26 58	
62688—	25 11	
		$278 55

KENNEDY BROTHERS, UTICA. N.Y.

57255—Inserts and memo books	$4 00	
59110— " " "	5 00	
62934— " " "	2 00	
		$11 00

H. I. KERT, ENGLEHART, ONT.

57080—Claim No. 10347, loss account one bottle whiskey broken in transit	$0 63	
58012—Claim No. 10666 and 10729, damage to whiskey	10 75	
62609—Claim No. 11915, loss liquor	2 50	
		$13 88

KING EDWARD HOTEL, ENGLEHART, ONT.

57078—Claim No. 10548, loss 1 bottle whiskey	$1 20	
58041—Claim No. 10665, loss 1 bottle whiskey	1 58	
58546—Meals and lodging supplied passengers	55 12	

King Edward Hotel, Englehart, Ont.—*Continued.*

58991—Claim No. 10791—Loss liquor	$1 08
60000—Board supplied engineering party	3 00
60944— " " "	12 00
61318—Claim No. 11916—Loss liquor	1 97
61438—Claims Nos. 12040 and 12202—Loss liquor	5 19
61816—Claim No. 12334—Loss liquor	1 59
62177—Board and lodging supplied engineering party	4 50
63193—Claim No. 12373—Loss liquor	8 00
63378—Claim No. 12497—Loss liquor	18 18

$113 41

The Knechtel Furniture Co., Limited, Hanover, Ont.

57462—Desks and arm chair	$36 75
57685— "	18 13
58621— "	50 50
59981—Office chairs	6 62
61522—Desk	23 00
62221— "	24 50
62401— " and chair	50 71
62682—	24 50

$234 71

King Construction Company, Toronto, Ont.

57464—Grates	$15 92

$15 92

Keuffel & Esser Co. of New York, Montreal, P.Q.

57466—Brushes	$0 56
57903—Brushes	13

$0 69

The Kanawha & Michigan Railway Company, Columbus, O.

58379—Car repairs	$0 21

$0 21

The H. Krug Furniture Co., Limited, Kitchener, Ont.

57800—Chair	$4 56
61925— "	10 40
63021— "	4 40
63282— ". tilter	10 65

$30 01

D. Korman, Englehart, Ont.

57910—Commissary, auxiliary car	$13 69
59177—Supplies to auxiliary car	3 35
59472—Supplies to private car ....,.....	10 10
60368—Commissary	8 19

$35 33

F. G. Kirk, Englehart, Ont.

58490—Award W. C. B., partial settlement account alleged injuries	$123 18
58547—Award W. C. B., partial settlement account alleged injuries	20 53

$143 71

D. Kerrigan, Landscape Gardener, Englehart, Ont.

58645—Expenses	$2 60
59691— "	4 05
60188— "	4 35
61417—	7 55

D. KERRIGAN, LANDSCAPE GARDENER, ENGLEHART, ONT.—*Continued.*

62019—Paris green, hose coupling	$6 08	
61252—Expenses	10 53	
62223— "	4 25	
63386— "	29 45	
		$68 86

TITUS KECINK, COBALT, ONT.

58673—Award W. C. B., *re* alleged injuries	$10 32	
		$10 32

W. K. P. KENNEDY, NORTH BAY, ONT.

58799—Expense *re* Stockdale property	$25 00	
		$25 00

KING'S PRINTER, TORONTO, ONT.

59470—Paper for reports	$29 12	
62563—Mining industry reports	38 76	
		$67 88

KALAMAZOO RAILWAY SUPPLY COMPANY, KALAMAZOO, MICH.

60055—Gauge, levels and drills	$50 00	
60629—Exchange on voucher	50	
61708—Pedestal, etc.	8 20	
		$58 70

M. J. KENNEDY, FERONIA, ONT.

60240—Potatoes	$64 00	
		$64 00

KEYSTONE DRILLER COMPANY, BEAVER FALLS, PA.

61027—Working barrel	$121 00	
		$121 00

A. J. KIRSTIN CANADIAN COMPANY, SAULT STE. MARIE, ONT.

61923—Stump puller	$88 00	
		$88 00

KANSAS CITY, MEXICO & ORIENT RAILROAD, KANSAS CITY, MO.

61980—Car repairs	$33 87	
62160—Car service balance	45	
		$34 32

MRS. A. KING, LATCHFORD, ONT.

62181—Board and lodging supplied	$5 20	
		$5 20

KNIGHT BROS., & McKINNON, LIMITED, COBALT, ONT.

62279—Repairing operating table	$0 50	
62645—Claim No. 12327, loss car flooring and sash in forest fires.	756 63	
63161—Lumber	45	
		$757 58

KENNEDY HARDWARE COMPANY, TORONTO, ONT.

62649—Claim No. 12413, damage to hardware	$5 10	
		$5 10

GEO. F. KRECK, UNO PARK, ONT.

62707—Lumber	$287 48	
		$287 48

KAUSTINE COMPANY, LIMITED, TORONTO, ONT.

63019—Kanstine system models	$123 50	
62932—Kanstine equipment	421 04	
		$544 54

L. KERT, COCHRANE, ONT.

63191—Claim No. 12133, amount realized on meat sold	$19 53	
		$19 53

KENTWOOD & EASTERN RAILWAY COMPANY, KENTWOOD, LA.

63492—Car service balance	$3 60	
		$3 60

G. W. LEE, COMMISSIONER, NORTH BAY, ONT.

56473—Salary as general agent, November, 1915	$208 33	
56576—Expenses	24 70	
56594—Honorarium to December 31, 1915	250 00	
56508—Salary, December, 1915	208 33	
57457—Salary, January, 1916	208 33	
57627—Expenses	10 00	
57586—Salary, February, 1916	208 33	
57676—Expenses	20 30	
58477—Salary, March, 1916	208 33	
58499—Honorarium to March 31, 1916	250 00	
58671—Expenses	25 50	
58634—Salary, April, 1916	208 33	
58752—Expenses	17 00	
59621—Salary, May, 1916	208 33	
59665—Expenses	23 20	
59790—Salary, June, 1916	208 33	
59824—Honorarium to June 30, 1916	250 00	
60190—Expenses	21 70	
60807—Salary, July, 1916	208 33	
61065—Expenses	15 00	
61042—Salary, August, 1916	208 33	
61218—Expenses	20 45	
62133—Salary, September, 1916	208 33	
62161—Honorarium to September 30, 1916	250 00	
62195—Expenses	23 70	
62283—Disbursements *re* Northern Ontario fires	73 15	
62344—Salary, October, 1916	208 33	
62408—Expenses	22 85	
		$3,797 51

THE LADY MINTO HOSPITAL, NEW LISKEARD, ONT.

56561—Annual donation, 1915	100 00	
59137—Service rendered to injured brakeman	16 70	
60825—Donation	500 00	
62718—Treatment Emile Lorócque	30 95	
		$647 65

MRS. J. R. LUSH, JACKS LAKE P.O., ONT.

56573—Loss account damage to H. H. goods in transit, claim No. 10021	$45 00	
		$45 00

THE LABOUR NEWS, HAMILTON, ONT.

56587—Advertising	$15 00	
		$15 00

LEHIGH VALLEY RAILROAD COMPANY, PHILADELPHIA, PA.

56801	Car repairs	$20 93
56780	Commission on tickets	2 56
56882	Car service balance	170 10
57062	Claims	17 48
57236	Car repairs	13 03
58219	Car service balance	80 55
58319	Ticket balance	10 17
58381	Car repairs	6 63
57914	Commission on tickets	92
58154	Car service balance	135 45
59295	" " "	147 60
59301	" " "	25 20
59411	Ticket balance	8 60
59519	Car repairs	2 25
59581	Commission on tickets	1 38
59030	Claim	2 21
59620	Car service balance	252 45
60091	Commission on tickets	1 04
60255	Car service balance	198 45
60086	Car repairs	1 22
60370	Commission on tickets	52
60518	Car service balance	119 25
61151	Commission on tickets	2 00
61297	Car repairs	16 88
61757	Car service balance	76 05
61140	Commission on tickets	2 08
61370	Claims	29 88
61984	Car repairs	18 68
62162	Car service balance	76 50
62222	Passenger car mileage	10 32
62471	Commission on tickets	2 00
62867	Car service balance	104 40
63165	Commission on tickets	78
63209	Claims	54 71
63494	Car service balance	144 90
63760	Car repairs	2 55

$1,759 72

LOUISVILLE & NASHVILLE RAILROAD COMPANY, LOUISVILLE, KY.

56803	Car repairs	$0 46
57105	" repairs	27
56884	" service balance	8 10
57314	" repairs	2 46
58221	" service balance	16 65
58383	" repairs	4 56
58156	" service balance	62 00
59297	" " "	102 60
59305	" " "	7 20
59272	" repairs	2 34
59622	" service balance	116 10
60033	" repairs	1 31
60257	" service balance	128 25
60090	" repairs	28
60520	" service balance	56 70
61295	" repairs	59
61759	" service balance	11 70
61910	" repairs	2 34
61982	" repairs	1 38
62164	" service balance	13 90
63496	" service balance	27 45
63762	" repairs	3 04

$569 68

R. L. LAMB, CHIEF DESPATCHER, NORTH BAY, ONT.

56875	Travelling expenses	$8 30
56968	" "	2 10

R. L. LAMB, CHIEF DESPATCHER, NORTH BAY, QNT.—*Continued.*

57634—Travelling expenses		$2 45
60103— " "		5 95
60870— " "		5 00
62047— " "		1 40
62505— " "		4 00
		$29 20

THE LAKE SIMCOE ICE SUPPLY CO., LIMITED, TORONTO, ONT.

56931—Ice supplied		$2 25
56674— " "		2 25
57838— " "		4 50
59093— " "		2 25
59474— " "		2 25
60061— " "		2 50
60658— " "		2 47
61589— " "		2 47
62272— " "		2 47
62709— " "		1 57
		$24 98

S. LOISEL, LINEMAN, COCHRANE, ONT.

57071—Travelling expenses		$3 50
56966— " "		2 75
57729— " "		4 05
58268— " "		11 55
58781— " "		6 75
59334—		9 80
59949—		7 45
60272— " "		10 10
61531—		9 05
61398—		8 00
62625— "		7 50
62778— "		4 90
		$85 40

R. J. LOVELL CO., LIMITED, TORONTO, ONT.

57257—Order books		$38 85
		$38 85

THE G. R. LOCKER CO., MONTREAL, P.Q.

57259—Gauge glasses		$5 10
57905— " "		6 30
58853— " "		21 12
59112— " "		27 20
60766— " "		33 27
		$92 99

THE LAMBTON CREAMERY CO., LIMITED, PETROLIA, ONT.

57261—Butter		$42 75
57468— "		14 40
60713— "		58 90
60754— "		85 55
61233— "		26 10
61927— "		26 10
61714— "		30 15
63025— "		121 05
62940— "		86 40
63284— "		55 35
		$546 75

LUKENS IRON & STEEL COMPANY, COATSVILLE, PA.

56540—Claim No. 5488—refund of switching charges on steel.... $350 03

$350 03

JOHN W. LECKIE, NORTH BAY, ONT.

56560—Awarded W. C. B., *re* alleged injuries received........... $88 18

$88 18

THE LEADER PRINTING COMPANY, TORONTO, ONT.

56606—Forms..................................	$5 00	
57641— "	10 00	
		$15 00

LOWE-MARTIN COMPANY, LIMITED, TORONTO, ONT.

56676—Pressboard folders	$8 50	
57840—Blue folders	70	
58556—White cards	25	
58706—Folders...................	70	
59438—Blue folders	3 50	
		$13 65

D. LeROY, NEW LISKEARD, ONT.

56628—Award W. C. B., *re* alleged injuries..................... $6 27

$6 27

LOUISIANA RAILWAY & NAVIGATION COMPANY, SHREVEPORT, LA.

56886—Car service balance....................................	$0 90	
58158— " " "	3 15	
59299— " " "	6 30	
59303— " " "	13 05	
62166— " " "	1 80	
62869— " " "	3 60	
63764—Car repairs	4 01	
		$32 81

LEHIGH & NEW ENGLAND RAILROAD COMPANY, SOUTH BETHLEHEM, PA.

36888—Car service balance....................................	$29 25	
58160— " " "	11 25	
59624— " " "	34 65	
60259— " " "	19 20	
60522— " " "	12 60	
61761— " " "	6 30	
62168— " " "	12 60	
62871— " " "	9 40	
63498— " " "	11 70	
		$146 95

DR. R. C. LOWERY, ENGLEHART, ONT.

57082—Claim No. 10519—refund freight charges on construction
material................... .. .. $36 76

$36 76

H. LEEMAN, NORTH COBALT, ONT.

57084—Claim No. 10413—loss account damage to cucumbers.... $3 00

$3 00

LOUISIANA & ARKANSAS RAILWAY COMPANY, TEXARKANA, ARK.

57310—Car repairs	$3 82	
58223—Car service balance	90	
58162— " " "	3 15	
59626— " " "	6 75	
60261— " " "	7 20	
60524— " " "	5 40	
61763— " " "	2 25	
		$29 47

LONDON & PORT STANLEY RAILWAY, LONDON, ONT.

57312—Car repairs	$0 26	
		$0 26

E. LEONARD & SONS, LIMITED, LONDON, ONT.

57470—Grate bars	$70 00	
57907— " "	2 51	
		$72 51

LINDSAY & McCLUSKEY, NORTH BAY, ONT.

57472—Lime and bags	$3 00	
57624—Ice	2,661 12	
60707—Lime	35 00	
63163— "	60 55	
		$2,759 67

R. LAIDLAW & CO., TORONTO, ONT.

57757—Lumber	$828 77	
60314— "	13 50	
60989— "	578 28	
62557— "	810 19	
62942—Freight charges	7 00	
		$2,237 74

LONDON ROLLING MILLS CO., LIMITED, LONDON, ONT.

57909—Swedes iron	$25 95	
		$25 95

WALTER LITTLE, SWASTIKA, ONT.

58115—Hire of team	$21 00	
60656—Staging and livery hire	19 00	
62080—Teaming, with men and tools	10 50	
		$50 50

W. H. LEWIS, HAILEYBURY, ONT.

57722—Searches	$1 20	
58506— "	7 80	
59747— "	1 78	
		$10 78

LONDON GUARANTEE & ACCIDENT CO., LIMITED, TORONTO, ONT.

57912—Premium on collective bond	$91 82	
		$91 82

W. R. LOWERY, COBALT, ONT.

58014—Claim No. 10737—shortage 3 lbs. tobacco	$3 21	
60919— " No. 11260—loss of confectionery	2 80	
		$6 01

P. J. LAFLEUR, EARLTON, ONT.

58386—Slabwood	$51 00	
59993—Cutting old timber	363 25	
61500—Ties	180 00	
		$594 25

MRS. A. LALONDE, NORTH BAY, ONT.

58388—Groceries	$9 94	
58849— "	1 86	
60711— "	17 40	
60904—	2 62	
61591— "	2 35	
62559— "	5 21	
		$39 38

LA BELLE KIRKLAND MINES, LIMITED, KIRKLAND LAKE, ONT.

58558—Meals	$17 50	
		$17 50

L. D. LAMARCH, KENABEEK P.O., ONT.

58593—Ties	$150 12	
60064— "	51 60	
		$201 72

CHAS. LAPORTE, NORTH BAY, ONT.

58609—Ice	$613 80	
60906—Lumber	2 20	
		$616 00

E. LALONDE (M. M. DEPT.), NORTH BAY, ONT.

58783—Travelling expenses	$10 05	
		$10 05

DEXTER P. LILLIE COMPANY, INDIAN ORCHARD, MASS.

58851—Waste	$151 20	
59150— "	226 74	
		$377 94

T. A. LALONDE, NUSHKA, ONT.

58893—Claim No. 10899—ou account demurrage charges	$16 00	
		$16 00

LOCOMOTIVE SUPERHEATER COMPANY, NEW YORK, N.Y.

58997—Damper cylinders	$40 00	
		$40 00

LABOUR DIRECTORY, TORONTO, ONT.

58802—Advertising	$10 00	
		$10 00

LAKE ERIE & WESTERN R. R. COMPANY, INDIANAPOLIS, IND.

59270—Car repairs	$9 18	
60088— " "	18 29	
61860— " "	42	
		$27 89

18 T R

P. LEVINE, SOUTH PORCUPINE, ONT.

59396—Claim No. 10683—loss account shortage cowhide......... $8 78

$8 78

E. LABLANC, TIMMINS, ONT.

59400—Claim No. 10815—loss account 2 bbls. hides destroyed
    by fire ....:................................. $17 28

$17 28

LOUISVILLE, HENDERSON & ST. LOUIS RY. CO., LOUISVILLE, KY.

59628—Car service balance..........·........................... $3 60

$3 60

EDWARD LANSALL, BOURKES P.O., ONT.

59754—Ties............................... .. .. $60 57

$60 57

ONESIME LAROQUE, NORTH BAY, ONT.

59639—Settlement *re* alleged injuries—E. Laroque............. $520 81
59641—Further settlement *re* alleged injuries—E. Laroque......   75 00

$595 81

MISS ANNIE C. LECKIE, EDMONTON, ALTA.

59879—Claim No. 11505—loss, account baggage burned.......... $100 00

$100 00

LUNKENHEIMER COMPANY, CINCINNATI, OHIO.

60631—Relief valve $2 38

$2 38

LONDON ROLLING MILL CO., LIMITED, LONDON, ONT.

60703—Iron.................... .. .. $8 70

$8 70

LAWSON MANUFACTURING COMPANY, CHICAGO, ILL.

60705—Hinges................... .. .. $11 95
63119— " 13 65

$25 60

L'AIR LIQUIDE SOCIETY, TORONTO, ONT.

60709—Oxygen, acetylene, etc. $250 00
60752—Acetylene freight charges 12 04
61231—Oxygen..   15 20
61524—Acetylene.... .. ..,..................   10 82
61712—Oxygen, acetylene 32 85
62274—Freight charges on cylinders..........................   48
63023— "   "   " 1 08
62938—Oxygen, acetylene, etc.................................   56 24
63286— "   " 26 90

$405 61

A. LA FRANCE, NORTH BAY, ONT.

59812—Award W. C. B., final payment *re* alleged injuries........ $12 81

$12 81

W. E. LANE, SILVERDALE, ONT.

59890—Claim No. 11420—overcharge in rate shipment H.H. goods.	$37 76	
		$37 76

LAURENTIDE COMPANY, LIMITED, MONTREAL, QUE.

59892—Claims No. 10960 and 10710—loss account damage to news-print...................................	$5 23	
60863—Claims No. 10800 and 11179—loss account damage to news-print...........	11 17	
		$16 40

GEORGE LAGRAW, CANE P.O., ONT.

60064—Ties.....................................	$249 63	
60064— "	4 29	
		$253 92

JOHN LIBBY, CANE P.O., ONT.

60064—Ties...................	$125 43	
		$125 43

F. X. LAFROMBOISE, NORTH COBALT, ONT.

60064—Ties.....................	$826 77	
		$826 77

LOWE BROTHERS, LIMITED, TORONTO, ONT.

60138—Paints.....................................	$73 01	
60991— "	46 69	
61033— "	249 66	
61929— "	197 44	
61594— "	248 47	
61710— "	61 25	
62276—Freight charges	8 46	
62403—Paint, oil	259 65	
62394—Paint...................................	48 02	
62596— "	123 72	
		$1,316 37

LYMAN TUBE & SUPPLY CO., LIMITED, MONTREAL, P.Q.

60946—Drill...........................	$280 25	
		$280 25

D. LEGAULT, CHARLTON, ONT.

60861—Claim No. 11231—loss account shortage Quaker oats......	$0 47	
61627— " No. 11852—damage to one lounge	3 00	
		$3 47

T. H. LEVERTON, BARBERS BAY, ONT.

61229—Lumber..................	$149 70	
		$149 70

LONDON CONCRETE MACHINERY CO., LIMITED, LONDON, ONT.

61965—Derrick............................	$120 00	
		$120 00

T. H. LAKE, HAILEYBURY, ONT.

62071—Claim No. 10500—alleged loss flour.....................	$1 00	
		$1 00

LIBRARY BUREAU, TORONTO, ONT.

61076—Folders...	$4 52	
62375—Cards...	1 44	
		$5 96

REV. BISHOP LATULIPPE, HAILEYBURY, ONT.

61348—Commission on tickets, excursion........................	$734 75	
		$734 75

LOUISIANA WESTERN RAILROAD COMPANY, NEW ORLEANS, LA.

61908—Car repairs..	$0 37	
63620— " "	5 40	
		$5 77

ALEX. LEE, ENGLEHART, ONT.

62278—Meals supplied extra gang.............................	$8 25	
61350— " " " "	4 00	
		$12 25

LONDON & PETROLIA BARREL CO., LIMITED, LONDON, ONT.

63121—Kegs...	$8 10	
		$8 10

EDGAR LAPOINTE, NORTH BAY, ONT.

62358—Award W. C. B., *re* alleged injuries......................	$3 81	
		$3 81

P. C. LARKIN & COMPANY, TORONTO, ONT.

62560—Claim No. 12625—alleged loss shipment tea..............	$34 19	
		$34 19

A. C. LEWIS COMPANY, TORONTO, ONT.

62936—Repair parts	$24 60	
		$24 60

W. H. MAUND, SECRETARY-TREASURER, TORONTO, ONT.

56463—Salary	$208 33
56465—Payrolls, Toronto staff	870 00
56475— " "	155 00
56595— " "	37 50
56641—Office expenses.....................................	49 95
56544— " "	47 33
56596—Payrolls, Toronto staff	870 00
56598—Salary	208 33
56608—Office expenses	23 10
56510—Payrolls, Toronto staff	187 50
57459—Payrolls, Toronto staff	187 50
57473—Salary	208 33
57475—Payrolls, Toronto staff	857 50
57545—Payrolls, Toronto staff	24 52
57557—Office expenses	41 80
57588—Payrolls, Toronto staff	197 50
57602—Salary	208 33
57604—Payrolls, Toronto staff	812 50
57680—Office expenses	55 48
58479—Payrolls, Toronto staff	275 08

W. H. MAUND, SECRETARY-TREASURER, TORONTO, ONT.—*Continued.*

58495—Salary	$208 33	
58497—Payrolls, Toronto staff	797 50	
58523—Office expenses	45 55	
58624—Salary	208 33	
58626—Payrolls, Toronto staff	797 50	
58636—Payrolls, Toronto staff	364 59	
58754—Office expenses	41 00	
59615—Payrolls, Toronto staff	370 83	
59653—Office expenses	54 55	
59931—Salary	208 33	
59933—Payrolls, Toronto staff	725 00	
59788—Payrolls, Toronto staff	383 95	
59804—Salary	208 33	
59806—Payrolls, Toronto staff	725 00	
60066—Office expenses	45 90	
60799—Payrolls, Toronto staff	1,093 33	
60805—Payrolls, Toronto staff	367 50	
60901—Office expenses	.50 00	
61044—Payrolls, Toronto staff	367 50	
61080—Office expenses	48 96	
61182—Payrolls, Toronto staff	1,093 33	
62135—Payrolls, Toronto staff	367 50	
62165—Payrolls, Toronto staff	1,093 33	
62187—Office expenses	45 18	
62346—Payrolls, Toronto staff	379 11	
62442—Office expenses	49 05	
62450—Payrolls, Toronto staff	1,093 33	$16,758 39

MUNICIPALITY OF MATHESON, TREASURER, MATHESON. ONT.

56483—Donation account, grading and opening up streets in Town Matheson	$250 00	$250 00

MOBILE & OHIO RAILROAD COMPANY, MOBILE, ALA.

56523—Car repairs	$8 85	
56967— " "	7 32	
57240— " "	2 05	
58233— " service balance	16 20	
58391— " repairs	51	
58172— " service balance	28 80	
59317— " "	44 10	
59521— " repairs	1 03	
59284— " "	1 98	
59640— " service balance	39 60	
60273— " "	36 90	
60536— " "	30 15	
61385— " repairs	96	
61771— " service balance	30 60	
61994— " repairs	15 70	
62176— " service balance	7 20	
62879— " "	15 75	
63506— " "	14 40	$302 10

THE MISSOURI PACIFIC RAILWAY COMPANY, ST. LOUIS, MO.

56525—Car repairs	$15 12
56969— " "	4 72
57242— " "	5 20
58387— " "	5 83
59274— " "	20 06

THE MISSOURI PACIFIC RAILWAY COMPANY, ST. LOUIS, MO.—*Continued.*

59632—Car service balance	$61 20	
60035— " repairs	11 98	
60265— " service balance	26 10	
60096— " repairs	3 61	
60528— " service balance	2 25	
61303— " repairs	2 65	
61986— " "	14 33	
62026— " "	14 87	
62873— " service balance	37 80	
63500— " " "	19 05	
		$244 77

THE MINNEAPOLIS & ST. LOUIS RAILROAD COMPANY, MINNEAPOLIS, MINN.

56527—Car repairs	$19 21	
57113—Car repairs	2 80	
57316—Car repairs	65	
58174—Car service balance	2 75	
59319—Car service balance	22 50	
59280—Car repairs	17 06	
59642—Car service balance	8 55	
61307—Car repairs	1 17	
61102— "	1 96	
61914— "	2 21	
		$78 86

MICHIE & COMPANY, LIMITED, TORONTO.

56605—Supplies for private car	$113 54	
56733— " "	4 91	
56847— " "	28 04	
56570— " "	5 82	
58117— " "	30 66	
58574— " "	8 83	
59476— " "	5 32	
60009— " "	16 87	
60004— " "	8 29	
60837— " "	14 17	
60891— " "	20 55	
61282— " "	12 42	
62287— " "	15 80	
62982— " "	27 34	
		$312 56

J. MURPHY, TORONTO.

56643—Subscription to *Telegram, News* and *Star*	$7 50	
		$7 50

MINNEAPOLIS, ST. PAUL & SAULT STE. MARIE RAILWAY COMPANY, MINNEAPOLIS, MINN.

56657—Claims	$22 51
57109—Car repairs	1 41
56890—Car service balance	2 25
57088—Claims	11 32
56946—Ticket balance	76 73
58051—Claim	1 86
58225—Car service balance	5 40
58256—Car service balance	1 15
58901—Claims	3 13
59307—Car service balance	2 25
59282—Car repairs	8 23
59630—Car service balance	27 00
59803—Claims	6 48
60039—Car repairs	3 28
60263—Car service balance	22 50
59896—Claim	3 84
60092—Car repairs	9 93

MINNEAPOLIS, ST. PAUL & SAULT STE. MARIE RAILWAY, ETC.—*Continued.*

60526—Car service balance	$33 30	
60937—Claim	5 50	
61765—Car service balance	5 40	
61990—Car repairs	16 32	
62170—Car service balance	31 05	
63101—Claims	22 11	
62900—Claims	9 73	
63768—Car repairs	5 67	
		$337 35

THOS. J. MEAGHER, HAILEYBURY, ONT.

56731—Registration of lien on contract	$0 15	
		$0 15

A. E. MALLETTE, COCHRANE, ONT.

56783—Repairing typewriter	$3 00	
		$3 00

A. T. MOTH, LOCOMOTIVE FOREMAN, NORTH BAY, ONT.

56877—Travelling expenses	$1 75	
		$1 75

MICHIGAN CENTRAL RAILROAD COMPANY, DETROIT, MICH.

56971—Car repairs	$19 77	
57111— "	5 96	
57220— "	19 66	
58049—Claim No. 10132—Overcharge rate, structural material...	28 45	
58321—Ticket balance	4 33	
58393—Car repairs	7 35	
58258—Car service balance	17 82	
59413—Car service balance	6 66	
59276—Car repairs	74	
60423— "	33 50	
61301— "	2 70	
61862—	34 87	
63622—	169 82	
63766—	82	
		$352 45

MISSOURI, KANSAS & TEXAS RAILWAY, ST. LOUIS, MO.

56973—Car repairs	$0 36	
56892—Car service balance	11 25	
58231—Car service balance	13 95	
58323—Ticket balance	23 86	
58102—Car repairs	7 18	
58170—Car service balance	28 80	
59315— " "	44 55	
59638— " "	18 90	
59740—Ticket balance	23 86	
60271—Car service balance	20 70	
60381— " "	15 24	
60094—Car repairs	25 73	
60534—Car service balance	2 70	
61769— " "	21 15	
61912—Car repairs	91	
62174—Car service balance	31 05	
62877— " "	29 70	
63772—Car repairs	6 92	
		$326 81

The Mail & Empire, Toronto.

57027—Subscription	$3 00	
57956—Advertising	9 00	
58784— "	84	
59749— "	1 64	
		$14 48

W. Meadows, Feronia, Ont.

57183—Wood and car stakes	$23 50	
		$23 50

Maine Central Railroad Company, Portland, Me.

57107—Car repairs	$0 23	
58227—Car service balance	45	
58389—Car repairs	1 15	
58164—Car service balance	18 00	
59309— " "	19 35	
59278—Car repairs	34	
59634—Car service balance	14 40	
60267— " "	3 60	
60530— " "	15 15	
61299—Car repairs	12 19	
61767—Car service balance	33 75	
61372—Claim No. 10745—Overcharge freight, car sulphur	57 78	
61992—Car repairs	2 07	
62172—Car service balance	23 40	
62875— "	78 30	
62520—Depreciated value, M.C. box car 30028	786 41	
63502—Car service balance	4 50	
63770—Car repairs	37	
		$1,071 44

W. L. Mackie,, North Bay, Ont.

57181—Mattresses	$27 00	
57925— "	11 25	
60635— "	254 10	
61971—	2 50	
61736—	10 00	
		$304 85

Geo. Maitland, North Bay, Ont.

57263—Roofing material	$261 40	
		$261 40

Meakins & Sons, Limited, Hamilton, Ont.

57265—Dusters	$8 00	
57480—Brushes, dusters, knives	50 50	
57915—Sash, tools and brushes	25 49	
58394—Knives, brushes, tools, dusters, etc.	37 86	
58855—Dusters and brushes	151 42	
59120—Brushes	15 00	
60637—Brushes, knives, etc.	63 65	
60910—Brushes, dusters	67 59	
60750—Brushes, tools, etc.	58 79	
61931—Brushes, mottlers, etc.	69 97	
63123—Dusters, knives, brushes	112 24	
63294—Dusters, tools, etc.	10 60	
		$671 11

G. P. Murphy, Ottawa, Ont.

57267—Lumber	$271 72	
		$271 72

MINING CORPORATION OF CANADA, LIMITED, COBALT, ONT.

57295—Claim No. 7777—Overcharge on shipment of silver ore ..	$157 08	
58020—Claim No. 10677—Overcharge in rate, wood pipe	43 82	
		$200 9

THE JAMES MORRISON BRASS MANUFACTURING CO., LIMITED, TORONTO.

57269—Fittings ....:...........	$38 67	
57478— "	115 93	
57913— ".	125 30	
58400— " ....:	280 86	
58933—Delivery tubes, valves, etc.	91 13	
59148—Valves, nozzles, tubes, etc.	293 48	
60639—Injector, gauges, etc.	56 77	
60764—Valves, primers, etc.	272 74	
60908—Valves, discs	119 47	
61335—Valves, globes, etc.	132 80	
61969—Valves, nozzles, tubes	108 68	
63127—Discs, valves, tubes, etc.	245 47	
62646—Line checks, steam valves, etc.	43 45	
62946—Valves and radium discs	83 77	
63292—Loco. steam gauge, etc.	27 86	
		$2,036 3

R. C. MILLER OIL SUPPLY CO., MONTREAL, QUE.

57363—Claim No. 10339—Amount realized on shipment refused and sold by agent, Thornloe	$1 90	
		$1 9

MASSEY-HARRIS CO., LIMITED, TORONTO.

57365—Claims Nos. 10429 and 10414—Overcharge rate, sleigh parts	$1 20	
		$1 2

MORROW & BEATTY, LIMITED, IROQUOIS FALLS, ONT.

57367—Claim No. 10360—Loss account, shortage on bundle hyrib	$6 30	
59856—Settlement re alleged damage, engine	950 00	
60865—Claim No. 11447—Overcharge rate, shipment oil	98	
		$957 2

GEO. J. MOORE, HAILEYBURY, ONT.

57369—Claim No. 10433—Loss account, damage to chairs	$1 75	
		$1 7

DENNIS MURPHY, OTTAWA, ONT.

56520a—Honorarium to Dec. 31, 1915	$250 00	
56562—Travelling expenses	114 50	
58501—Honorarium to March 31, 1916	250 00	
59826— " to June 30, 1916	250 00	
62163— " to Sept. 30, 1916	250 00	
		$1,114 5

THE MONETARY TIMES PRINTING CO. OF CANADA, TORONTO.

56678—Subscription	$3 00	
57479—Advertising	50 00	
		$53 0

MIGHT DIRECTORIES, LIMITED, TORONTO.

56680—Press clippings	$0 45	
57678—Directory, 1916	10 00	
58508—Press clippings	20	

MIGHT DIRECTORIES, LIMITED, TORONTO.—*Continued.*

59179—Press clippings	$0 70	
59721— " "	2 17	
60011— " "	35	
60316— " "	75	
62280— " "	45	
63167— " "	10	
63454— " "	10	
		$15 27

MILTON HERSEY CO., LIMITED, MONTREAL, P.Q.

56782—Analysis of coal	$7 50	
58550— " "	15 00	
58929— " "	15 00	
		$37 50

D. MITCHELL, ENGLEHART, ONT.

56784—Cartage	$3 00	
61063—Ties	79 86	
		$82 86

THE MINERAL SPRINGS, LIMITED, TORONTO.

56786—Water	$6 00	
58443— "	2 50	
57842— "	2 50	
59139— "	2 50	
58912—	2 00	
60091—	2 50	
61539—	4 50	
		$22 50

THE MONTREAL STAR PUBLISHING CO., LIMITED, MONTREAL, P.Q.

56788—Advertising	$1 50	
57846— "	1 50	
59453— "	1 59	
		$4 59

METHODIST BOOK & PUBLISHING HOUSE, TORONTO, ONT.

56792—Forms	$16 00	
60063—Printing annual report	40 95	
61456—Printing Mining Industry report	21 80	
		$78 75

MISSOURI & NORTH ARKANSAS RAILROAD, HARRISON, ARK.

56894—Car service balance	$8 55	
58235—Car service balance	4 95	
		$13 50

GEO. E. MARSTERS, BOSTON, MASS.

57186—Proportion commission on tickets	$0 62	
		$0 62

R. L. MALKIN, NELLIE LAKE, ONT.

57188—Slabs	$45 21	
57190—Slabs	68 79	
		$114 00

MUSCATINE NORTH & SOUTH RAILWAY COMPANY, MUSCATINE, IOWA.

57238—Car repairs	$3 12	
58385— " "	6 07	
61305— " "	4 22	
		$13 41

MARSH & TRUMAN LUMBER COMPANY, CHICAGO, ILL.

57474—White oak lumber	$180 26	
58398—Lumber and war tax	275 81	
60579—White oak	94 67	
60796—Oak	346 78	
61738—Lumber	488 29	
		$1,385 81

JOHN MORROW SCREW & NUT COMPANY, LIMITED, INGERSOLL, ONT.

57476—Screws	$2 01	
57923— "	2 76	
58390— "	2 47	
58935— "	1 88	
59118— "	20 08	
61025—	27 57	
61742—	6 23	
		$63 00

R. H. MITCHELL, AUDITOR AND CAR ACCOUNTANT, NORTH BAY, ONT.

57547—Travelling expenses	$16 45	
58681—Travelling expenses	4 00	
58786—Disbursement *re* claim No. 10974, Samuel Reid	85 00	
58806—Travelling expenses	15 20	
59951—Travelling expenses	19 20	
		$139 85

MACLEAN PUBLISHING COMPANY, LIMITED, TORONTO, ONT.

57713—Subscription " Can. Machinery "	$2 00	
62477—Subscription " Can. Machinery "	2 00	
		$4 00.

W. H. MINER, CHICAGO, ILL.

57911—Castings	$148 00	
60581—Vertical thimbles	20 00	
63131—Friction buffer	480 00	
62644—Miner friction gear	80 00	
		$728 00

MORTON, PHILLIPS & CO., MONTREAL, P.Q.

57917—Customs tariff	$1 07	
		$1 07

WILLIAM MANN COMPANY, PHILADELPHIA, PA.

57919—Tissue books	$8 75	
61237—Stationery	11 25	
		$20 00

MASTER CAR BUILDERS' ASSOCIATION, CHICAGO, ILL.

57921—M. C. B. rules	$0 25	
58392—M. C. B. rules	4 90	
59122—Interchange rules	50	
62944—M. C. B. rules	2 90	
		$8 55

METROPOLITAN ENGINEERING COMPANY OF CANADA, TORONTO, ONT.

57927—Electrical goods	$57 00	
		$57 00

MONTEITH PULP & TIMBER COMPANY, LIMITED, TORONTO, ONT.

57953—Claim No. 10633, overcharge weight pulpwood	$16 18	
		$16 18

MONTOUR RAILROAD, PITTSBURG, PA.

58229—Car service balance	$7 65	
58168— " " "	10 80	
59636— " " "	23 40	
60269— " " "	24 30	
63504— " " "	5 40	
		$71 55

HENRY MICHIE, ELK LAKE, P.O.

58463—Ties	$63 55	
60064—Ties	36 20	
		$99 75

E. N. MAY, TORONTO, ONT.

57606—Advance on salary	$45 00	
		$45 00

W. R. MAHER. NORTH BAY, ONT.

57610—Advance on travelling expenses	$200 00	
58505—Travelling expenses	154 90	
59248— " "	155 40	
59833— " "	44 85	
61400—	24 10	
62145—	4 95	
62509—	37 45	
		$621 65

MARSHALL ECCLESTONE, LIMITED, TIMMINS, ONT.

57642—Refund of over-deposit on siding	$73 99	
57644—Refund of over-deposit on siding	41 29	
61171—Claim No. 10387, loss account damage to wall plaster....	55 94	
		$171 22

THE MINES PUBLISHING COMPANY, LIMITED, TORONTO, ONT.

57844—Advertising " Canadian Mining Manual "	$15 00	
58910—Advertising " Canadian Mining Manual "	11 00	
		$26 00

MAP SPECIALTY COMPANY, TORONTO, ONT.

57958—Maps, drawings, etc.	$39 30	
		$39 30

W. MIDDLEDITCH,, SAULT STE. MARIE, ONT.

58016—Claim No. 10715, loss account damage to glass	$4 32	
		$4 32

MATHESON SUPPLY COMPANY, MATHESON, ONT.

58018—Claim No. 10654, loss account shortage 1 case Quaker oats	$3 90	
62050—Claim No. 12012, loss bottle extract	87	
		$4 77

MINNEAPOLIS, ST. PAUL, ROCHESTER & DUBUQUE ELECTRIC TRACTION COMPANY, MINNEAPOLIS, MINN.

58176—Car service balance	$11 25	
59321— " " "	1 35	
60277— " " "	45	
60538— " " "	1 35	
		$14 40

MILLER CHEMICAL ENGINE COMPANY, CHICAGO, ILL.

58396—Recharges for fire extinguishers	$10 50	
61740—Transfers for new Miller No. 8	5 00	
		$15 50

MRS. M. E. MILTON, TIMMINS, ONT.

58895—Claim No. 10656, damage to furniture	$3 60	
		$3 60

MUSSENS, LIMITED, MONTREAL, QUE.

58937—Car replacers	$32 00	
60633—Castings, wheels	31 25	
60948—Parts for drill	4 75	
63133—Drills	18 45	
		$86 45

A. P. MONETTE, TORONTO, ONT.

59027—Deduction in error, for uniforms	$9 45	
		$9 45

MONTOUR RAILROAD, PITTSBURG, PA.

59311—Car service balance	$23 85	
60532—Car service balance	$5 40	
		$29 25

MANISTEE & NORTH EASTERN RAILROAD COMPANY, MANISTEE, MICH.

59523—Car repairs	$0 24	
		$0 24

MACDONALD, SHEPLEY & COMPANY, TORONTO, ONT.

58644—Final settlement re alleged injuries received, E. Kopton- chuk	$600 00	
		$600 00

THE MIDVALE STEEL COMPANY, PHILADELPHIA, PA.

58664—Tires	$1,496 78	
59124—Tires	848 35	
		$2,345 13

THE MONTREAL LOCOMOTIVE WORKS, LIMITED, NEW YORK, N.Y.

59114—Frame foot plates	$124 00	
		$124 00

MORSE TWIST DRILL & MACHINE COMPANY, NEW BEDFORD, MASS.

59116—Staybolt tap	$4 62	
		$4 62

MACKENZIE & COMPANY, TORONTO, ONT.

59478—Framing photo	$2 50	
60168—Mounting and framing honor roll	4 50	
		$7 00

MIDLAND VALLEY RAILROAD, MUSKOGEE, OKLA.

59644—Car service balance	$1 35	
60275—Car service balance	1 80	
		$3 15

Wm. Metcalf (M.P. Dept.), North Bay, Ont.

59853—Travelling expenses	$0 50	
61148—Award W. C. B., *re* alleged injuries	22 20	
		$22 70

Major Milne, O.C. 159th Battalion, North Bay, Ont.

59941—Commission, special train	$117 90	
		$117 80

Missouri, Oklahoma & Gulf Railway Company, Muskogee, Okla.

60037—Car repairs	$3 79	
61988—Car repairs	93	
		$4 72

Arthur Monahan, Matheson, Ont.

60421—Water supplied	$3 50	
		$3 50

Missouri, Kansas & Texas Railway of Texas (Receivers), Dallas, Texas.

60425—Car repairs	$0 79	
62479—Car repairs	3 39	
		$4 18

Walter Matthews, Buffalo, N.Y.

60443—Claim No. 11417—Loss account, damage to suit case	$4 00	
		$4 00

J. P. McVicar, Inwood, Ont.

60583—Hay	$157 65	
60950—Hay	183 09	
		$340 74

Malick & Balon, Timmins, Ont.

59894—Claim No. 11266—Loss account, fruit damaged by frost..	$11 00	
		$11 00

Morgantown & Kingwood Railroad Company, Morgantown, W. Va.

59966—Car repairs	$1 32	
		$1 32

H. Marleau, North Bay, Ont.

60002—Moving building, N. Bay Jct.	$220 00	
		$220 00

William Mills, Heaslip P.O., Ont.

60064—Ties	$32 76	
		$32 76

E. M. Murphy, Relieving Agent, New Liskeard, Ont.

60274--Travelling expenses	$7 00	
61070— "	26 00	
62458— "	14 00	
63388— "	14 00	
		$61 00

MAXWELL'S, LIMITED, ST. MARY'S, ONT.

60372—Lawn mowers	$32 50	
61967—Repairs to lawn mower	1 10	
		$33 60

FRED. MATHIEAU, HAILEYBURY, ONT.

60460—Claim No. 10755—Loss account, shortage case hardware.	$12 00	
		$12 00

JOHN MARSH, CHICAGO, ILL.

60935—Claim No. 10031—Overcharge, freight on cars	$28 50	
		$28 50

W. MIDDLETON, WABUN, ONT.

61063—Ties	$81 96	
61063— "	39 87	
61063— "	19 83	
		$141 66

D. MIDDLETON, WABUN P.O., ONT.

61063—Ties	$140 07	
		$140 07

C. J. MORGAN, HANBURY P.O., ONT.

61063—Ties	$41 25	
		$41 25

R. L. & C. MALKIN, NELLIE LAKE P.O.

61063—Ties	$55 62	
		$55 62

ALBERT MORAN, ASQUITH, SASK.

61461—Claim No. 12155—Loss account, baggage burned	$100 00	
62599—Claim No. 12155—Loss account, baggage burned	105 10	
		$205 10

R. S. MARSHALL, RELIEVING AGENT, NORTH BAY, ONT.

61537—Travelling expenses	$61 00	
61352— "	26 00	
62507— "	26 75	
63456— "	27 00	
		$140 75

MIDDLETOWN, UNIONVILLE RAILROAD, MIDDLETOWN, N.Y.

61773—Car service balance	$0 90	
62881—Car service balance	2 25	
		$3 15

H. H. MacLEAN, NORTH BAY. ONT.

61142—Meals for fire sufferers	$24 50	
		$24 50

J. E. MORIN, COBALT, ONT.

61416—Claim No. 11805—Alleged damage to H. H. goods	$13 75	
		$13 75

WM. MILNE & SON, LIMITED, NORTH BAY, ONT.

61596—Lath	$162 00	
63129— "	27 00	
62948— "	126 00	
		$315 00

A. M. MASON, NEW LISKEARD, ONT.

61642—Wood	$8 00	
62409—Wood	8 00	
		$16 00

J. F. MULLIGAN, NEW LISKEARD, ONT.

61818—Claim No. 12293, alleged damage to suit case	$1 10	
		$1 10

MONONGAHELA RAILWAY COMPANY, PITTSBURG, PA.

61864—Car repairs	$1 52	
61916—Car repairs	8 43	
		$9 95

MACON, DUBLIN & SAVANAH RAILROAD COMPANY, MACON, GA.

61918—Car repairs	$0 12	
		$0 12

HARRY MARTIN, INSPECTOR, NORTH BAY, ONT.

62265—Travelling expenses	$15 50	
62614—Travelling expenses	33 00	
		$48 50

W. A. MARTYN, NORTH BAY, ONT.

62285—Force account *re* machine shop addition	$36 06	
62405—Cert. No. 1, North Bay machine shop	528 02	
63125—Brick	412 50	
63288—Brick	396 00	
		$1,372 58

MASON & CAMPBELL, NORTH BAY, ONT.

62407—Air pipe for blacksmith shop	$97 00	
		$97 00

JAMES MURPHY, NEW LISKEARD, ONT.

62473—Material and labour	$13 50	
		$13 50

MURRAY-KAY, LIMITED, TORONTO.

62518—Polishing floors, Toronto office	$10 85	
		$10 85

THOS. MAGLADERY, ENGLEHART, ONT.

62517—Twine	$0 85	
		$0 85

JOHN MELHUS, KENABEEK P.O., ONT.

62669—Ties	$42 15	
		$42 15

MOUNCE CARTAGE & STORAGE, TORONTO, ONT.

62711—Cartage $26 00
                                                          $26 00

MINERAL RANGE RAILROAD, MARQUETTE, MICH.

62955—Ticket balance $0 84
                                                          $0 84

DR. H. H. MOORE, TIMMINS ONT.

63670—Service rendered C. Celestine $22 41
                                                          $22 4

MISS M. MOLYNEAUX, STENOGRAPHER, COBALT, ONT.

62410—Services rendered $46 13
                                                          $46 1

METHODIST CHURCH, IROQUOIS FALLS, ONT.

62412—Donation towards church and parsonage .... $50·00
                                                          $50 0

HUGH C. MACLEAN, TORONTO, ONT.

62720—Advertising " Contract Record " $6 70
63296—Subscription to " Canada Lumbermen " 4 00
                                                          $10 7

C. C. MILLER, CRANE MAN, ENGLEHART, ONT.

63216—Travelling expenses $3 75
                                                          $3 7

MILTON PRESSED BRICK CO., LIMITED, MILTON, ONT.

63290—Buff pressed brick $167 04
                                                          $167 0

MONTPELIER & WELLS RIVER RAILROAD, BOSTON, MASS.

63624—Car repairs $0 93
                                                          $0 9

H. H. McGEE, TRAVELLING AUDITOR, NORTH BAY, ONT.

56453—Travelling expenses $35 30
56711—   "   " 25 50
57559—   "   " 63 15
58101—   " 9 10
57732—   "   " 34 25
58746—   " 108 30
59953— 19 25
60192—   "   " 38 05
61067—   "   " 27 45
61254—   "   " 35 90
62237—   "   " 50 90
                                                          $447 1

MACDONELL & O'BRIEN, MONTREAL, QUE.

56575—Claim No. 9533, overcharge in weight on machinery...... $13 24
                                                          $13 2

19 T R

MacDonald & Company, Cobalt, Ont.

56659—Claim No. 10149, eggs broken in transit $2 80

$2 80

W. J. McDougall, Cane, Ont.

56737—Donation account heifer alleged killed $25 00
60064—Ties 54 36

$79 36

J. A. McFarlane, Englehart, Ont.

56739—Cartage $5 35

$5 35

J. McLellan, Lineman, Cochrane, Ont.

57073—Travelling expenses	....	$3 00	
56970—	" "	....	6 05
57733—	" "	....	14 35
60276—	" "	....	3 55
61535—	" "	....	17 65
61402—	" "	....	11 65
61404—	" "	....	8 05
62627—	" "	....	16 40
62780—	" "	....	18 20

$98 90

J. D. MacAlpine, Collinwood, Ohio.

57271—Manuals, guides and reference tables $3 90

$3 90

McCord & Company, Incorporated, Chicago, Ill.

57273—Journal boxes	....	$32 10	
58402—	" "	....	122 40
59126—	" "	....	186 00
60589—	" "	....	79 80
60768—	" "	....	155 40

$575 70

McLaren & Dallas, Toronto, Ont.

57371—Claim No. 10508, loss account damage to trunk $3 60

$3 60

J. A. McDonald, K.C., Toronto, Ont.

56682—Services rendered $150 00
59862—Services rendered 247 50

$397 50

J. M. McNamara, K.C., North Bay, Ont.

56790—Legal services $35 90
59583— " " 10 68
60376— " " 14 30

$60 88

McIntyre Porcupine Mines, Limited, Schumacher, Ont.

57090—Claim No. 10538, shortage one dead plate $8 00
59898— " No. 10771, damage to mining machinery 44 41
61169— " No. 12047, 10306, loss gold ore 154 35

$206 76

McCOLL BROTHERS & CO., TORONTO, ONT.

57482—Varnish, soap	$34 65	
60780—Soap	47 90	
61744—Soap	95 40	
		$177 95

J. J. McNEIL, LATCHFORD, ONT.

57484—Slabs	22 13	
61500—Ties	146 07	
59783—Slabs	133 50	
		$301 70

McAUSLAN & ANDERSON, NORTH BAY, ONT.

57715—Plans and descriptions	$10 00	
59480—Services and expenses	36 00	
60016— " rendered	30 00	
62021— " "	34 20	
61124— " "	5 00	
62481—Plans and descriptions, Latchford	5 00	
		$120 20

GEO. W. McDONALD, NORTH BAY, ONT.

57929—Dunnage bag	$1 50	
		$1 50

J. R. McCREA, NEW LISKEARD, ONT.

58053—Claim No. 10648, damage to box ink	$0 68	
		$0 68

JAS. McMANUS, ROAD DEPARTMENT, NORTH BAY, ONT.

57972—Expenses, travelling	$3 30	
		$3 30

McKINLEY-DARRAGH-SAVAGE MINES, COBALT, ONT.

58022—Claim No. 10723, overcharge in weight steel	$2 34	
		$2 34

J. J. McBURNEY, NORTH BAY, ONT.

58404—Birch	$373 79	
58863—Lumber	109 90	
		$483 69

S. McIVOR, M. P. DEPARTMENT, NORTH BAY, ONT.

58599—Travelling expenses	$7 05	
		$7 05

THE R. McDOUGALL CO., LIMITED, GALT, ONT.

58857—Pump valves	$9 00	
60912—Casting	54 40	
61933—Pump	54 40	
61746—Valves, hose, cylinders	79 51	
		$197 31

McCORD MANUFACTURING COMPANY, DETROIT, MICH.

58859—Gaskets	$21 96	
59138— "	9 48	
60585— "	1 75	
60770— "	7 90	
		$41 09

THE McCONWAY & TORLEY CO., PITTSBURG, PA.

58861—Locking pins $5 10
$5 10

GEO. A. McKAY, TORONTO, ONT.

58897—**Claim No.** 10773—Overcharge rate, planing machinery .. $12 00
$12 00

W. McCHRISTIE, MATHESON, ONT.

59181—Services rendered $5 25
$5 25

McWILLIAM & EVERIST, LIMITED, TORONTO.

59131—Claim No. 11011—Damage to fruit $1,080 43
$1,080 43

McGREGOR, BANWELL FENCE CO., LIMITED, WALKERVILLE, ONT.

58878—Railway gates $29 11
$29 11

N. J. McCUBBIN, NORTH BAY, ONT.

59140—Uniforms $581 00
60374— " 115 00
61235— " 44 50
$740 50

A. McLAUGHLIN (M.P. DEPT.), NORTH BAY, ONT.

59336—Expenses—Travelling $7 35
59705— " 9 80
62316— " 10 85
62567— " 16 80
$44 80

RODGER McINTOSH, SEMANS, SASK.

59404—Claim No. 11259—Loss account, baggage destroyed by fire $100 00
$100 00

WESLEY McKNIGHT, NEW LISKEARD, ONT.

59805—Claim No. 11025—Loss account, shortage, 2 pair shoes.... $3 20
62562—Claim No. 12658—Loss, pair shoes 5 00
$8 20

PATRICK McCOOL, NORTH BAY, ONT.

60587—Piles $837 20
61467— " 300 00
61469— " 700 00
61471— " 156 80
62692—Clearance dues deducted 187 20
$2,181 20

HARRY McKNIGHT, TORONTO, ONT.

59794—Services rendered as mail messenger $10 00
60811—   "   "   " 10 00
61032—   "   "   " 10 00
62123—   "   " 10 00
62332—   "   " 10 00
$50 00

ARCHIBALD McGILLIS, NORTH BAY, ONT.

59844—Award W. C. B., final payment *re* alleged injuries $4 71

$4 71

McCLARY MANUFACTURING COMPANY, TORONTO, ONT.

60774—Box stoves $26 82
63135—Soot boxes 2 24
62950—Stoves 42 50

$71 56

JAMES McBRIDE, BRENTWOOD, ONT.

60793—Unclaimed wages $25 75

$25 75

LIEUT. H. A. McDOUGALD, CAMP BORDEN, ONT.

60999—Claim No. 11896—Loss account, baggage destroyed by fire $100 00

$100 00

W. J. McGEATHERS, WIDDIFIELD, ONT.

61419—Clearing station grounds, Widdifield $209 00
62565—   "   "   " 146 30
62678—   "   "   " 207 20

$562 50

WM. McCRACKEN, TIMMINS, ONT.

61489—Claim No. 11263—Account, damage to table $5 00

$5 00

WM. McMILLAN, (M.M. DEPT.), NORTH BAY, ONT.

61533—Expenses—Travelling $16 10
62483—   " 7 00
62676—   " 17 30

$40 40

J. P. McLAUGHLIN, TIMMINS, ONT.

61629—Claim No. 11570—Loss, syrup $0 48

$0 48

MRS. LAURA McKEE, ELK LAKE, ONT.

61284—Rental, telephone lines $5 00
61286—Rental, telephone lines 45 00

$50 00

J. A. McANDREW, TORONTO, ONT.

62052—Claim No. 12200—Damage to boat $10 00

$10 00

GEO. McLOGAN FURNITURE COMPANY, LIMITED, STRATFORD, ONT.

62317—Claim No. 12399—Alleged loss, furniture $1,591 66

$1,591 66

P. McDONELL (M.M. DEPT.), NORTH BAY, ONT.

62339—Travelling expenses $9 75

$9 75

McPHERSON, GLASSCO & COMPANY, HAMILTON, ONT.

62653—Claim No. 12643—Alleged loss soap $48 85

$48 85

McGraw-Hill Book Company, New York, N.Y.

62648—Car Builders' Directory $6 00

$6 00

D. McLellan, New Liskeard, Ont.

62650—Lumber ....:.... $312 01

$312 01

McCormick Mfg. Company, Limited, London, Ont.

63248—Claim No. 12769—Confectionery alleged destroyed $34 08

$34 08

National Life Assurance Co. of Canada, Toronto, Ont.

56477—Rent of offices,		November, 1915	$293 75
56512—	”	December, 1915	293 75
57461—	"	January, 1916	293 75
57590—	"	February, 1916	293 75
58481—	"	March, 1916	293 75
58638—	"	April, 1916	293 75
59625—	"	May, 1916	293 75
59796—	"	June, 1916	293 75
60813—	"	July, 1916	293 75
61034—	"	August, 1916	293 75
62125—	"	September, 1916	293 75
62336—	"	October, 1916	293 75

$3,525 00

Norfolk & Western Railway Company, Roanoke, Va.

56529—Car repairs	....	$5 26
56977—	" ....:	17 40
57119—	"	6 22
58241—Car service balance	....	40 05
58186— "	"	31 05
59331— "	"	14 40
59292— "	repairs	7 06
59654— "	service balance	37 80
60287— "	"	27 00
60102— "	repairs	4 52
60546— "	service balance	16 20
61106— "	repairs	1 51
62002— "	"	4 83
62180— "	service balance	36 00

$249 30

New York, Chicago & St. Louis Railroad Company, Cleveland, Ohio.

56531—Car repairs	....	$11 60
56975— "	"	11 64
57123— "	"	84
56900— "	service balance	9 75
56950—Ticket balance	....	3 70
58237—Car service balance	....	17 10
58183— "	"	23 40
59529— "	repairs	20 64
59286— "	"	2 18
60067— "	"	16 03
60283— "	service balance	49 70
60098— "	repairs	13 38
60542— "	service balance	3 15
61779— "	"	1 80
61104— "	repairs.	3 49
61866— "	"	5 02
62885— "	service balance	27 00
63628— "	repairs	8 15

$228 57

NORTHERN PACIFIC RAILWAY COMPANY, ST. PAUL, MINN.

56533—Car repairs	....	$1 78	
56805— "	"	....	35	
57115— "	"	....	1 58	
57248— "	"	....	1 05	
58239— " service balance	...'..........................	14 85	
58327—Ticket balance	....	6 25	
58399—Car repairs	....	5 50	
58184— " service balance	....	28 80	
59327— " "	....	30 15	
59288— " repairs	...................;	1 91	
59650— " service balance	....	48 70	
60043— " repairs	....	73	
60285— " service balance	....	15 30	
60104— " repairs	....	1 84	
61309— " "	....	79	
61920— " "	....	15 75	
62485— " "	....	1 28	
62957—Ticket balance	....	39	
62566—Claim No. 10315—Overcharge rate, pipe material	....	133 50	

$310 50

NORFOLK SOUTHERN RAILROAD COMPANY, NORFOLK, VA.

56627—Car repairs	....	$0 42	
56906— " service balance	....	15 30	
58249— " "	....	2 70	
58192— " "	....	12 60	
59337— " "	....	7 55	
59658— " "	....	4 05	
60291— " "	....	31 05	
60552— " "	....	18 00	
62182— " "	....	8 10	
62893— " "	....	12 15	
63780— " repairs	....	98	

$112 90

NIPISSING MINING COMPANY, LIMITED, NEW YORK, N.Y.

56661—Claim No. 8414—Overcharge in rate on silver ore	......	$78 09	
57751— " 10395—Loss, acid	....	18 79	
62054— " 12042—Damage to crucible	....	44 60	
62902— " 12252—Overcharge rate, caustic soda	....	43 66	

$185 14

NORTHERN ONTARIO LIGHT & POWER COMPANY, LTD.

56663—Claim No. 10161—Siding rebate	....	$13 00	
56741—Current supplied, Timmins	....................,	19 30	
57029— " " Haileybury	....	5 23	
57031— " " New Liskeard	....	10 66	
57033— " " Porcupine	....	4 81	
57035— " " South Porcupine	....	6 50	
57037— " " Schumacher	...'.....................	6 98	
57039— " " Timmins	....	12 18	
56688— " " Cochrane	....	4 73	
56690— " " Timmins	....	17 94	
56794— " " Cobalt	....	49 79	
56796— " " New Liskeard	....	12 90	
56798— " " Porcupine	....	5 77	
56800— " " South Porcupine	....	8 90	
56802— " " Timmins	....	30 74	
57192— " " Cobalt	...r.........................	56 99	
57194— " " Cochrane	....	6 65	
57196— " " Haileybury	....	9 23	
57198— " " New Liskeard	....	16 90	
57200— " " South Porcupine	....	9 62	
57202— " " Porcupine	....	6 41	

NORTHERN ONTARIO LIGHT & POWER COMPANY, LIMITED.—*Continued.*

57204—Current supplied, Schumacher	$17 96
57206— " " Timmins	13 46
57721— " " Timmins	28 42
57754— " " Haileybury	8 24
57756— " " New Liskeard	14 82
57758— " " South Porcupine	9 14
57760— " " Porcupine	5 77
57762— " " Schumacher	9 14
57764— " " Timmins	16 34
57916— " " Timmins	35 38
58560— " " Cochrane	8 32
58562— " " Haileybury	7 79
58564— " " New Liskeard	12 96
58566— " " South Porcupine	8 18
58568— " " Porcupine	6 01
58604— " " Timmins	41 40
59187— " " Haileybury	5 12
59455— " " Timmins	22 26
59585— " " Cochrane	13 45
59587— " " Porcupine	5 05
59589— " " New Liskeard	10 54
59591— " " South Porcupine	5 85
59593— " " Haileybury	4 88
59595— " " Schumacher	19 56
59597— " " Cobalt	64 16
59599— " " Timmins	10 66
59770— " " South Porcupine	4 90
59772— " " Timmins	8 42
59774— " " Haileybury	4 24
59776— " " Porcupine	3 37
59753— " " Cobalt	56 48
59775— " " Timmins	17 14
60429— " " New Liskeard	8 96
60431— " " Haileybury	3 20
60775— " " Cobalt	46 32
60777— " " Timmins	7 20
60779— " " Schumacher	7 92
60781— " " Cochrane	2 24
60783— " " Timmins	15 14
60785— " " New Liskeard	8 08
60787— " " South Porcupine	4 90
60850— " " Timmins	14 90
60952— " " Porcupine	4 56
60954— " " Haileybury	3 04
60956— " " Timmins	8 24
60996— " " Cochrane	49
60998— " " South Porcupine	4 48
61000— " " New Liskeard	6 08
61002— " " Porcupine	3 69
61004— " " Schumacher	5 84
62041— " " Timmins	17 14
62093— " " Schumacher	4 88
62095— " " Timmins	9 84
62097— " " Porcupine	1 36
62099— " " New Liskeard	4 56
62101— " " South Porcupine	3 68
62103— " " Haileybury	9 03
62105— " " Cobalt	28 64
61354— " " North Cobalt	75 48
61468— " " Cobalt	15 04
62284— " " Timmins	8 40
62286— " " New Liskeard	10 56
62288— " " Timmins	5 60
62290— " " Haileybury	4 00
62289— " " Porcupine	1 92
62291— " " South Porcupine	3 28
63173— " " Timmins	20 56

NORTHERN ONTARIO LIGHT & POWER COMPANY, LIMITED.—*Continued.*

62522—Current supplied, North Cobalt			$6 64
62524— " " Haileybury			4 96
62526— " " Timmins			16 24
62528— " " Porcupine and South Porcupine			6 16
62986— " " Cochrane			1 28
62988— " " Haileybury			6 32
62990— " " Cobalt			27 12
63082— " " New Liskeard			15 68
63084— " " Cobalt			25 20
63086— " " South Porcupine			4 72
63164— " " New Liskeard			11 04
63166— " " Cobalt			4 72
63380— " " Porcupine			2 48
63820— " " Cochrane			2 49

$1,328 94

THE NORTH BAY PROVISION CO., NORTH BAY, ONT.

56743—Supplies for private car	$7 61
56686— " " " "	30 97
58414— " " " "	128 12
63162— " " " "	16 04

$182 74

NIAGARA FRONTIER SUMMER RATE COMMITTEE, MONTREAL, QUE.

56745—Proportion expenses	$21 75

$21 75

NEW ORLEANS, MOBILE & CHICAGO RAILROAD CO., MOBILE, ALA.

56807—Car repairs	$11 17
57121— " repairs	12 30
58255— " service balance	4 95
59664— " " "	12 15
60297— " " "	6 75
59972— " repairs	1 10
60558— " service balance	2 25
61791— " " "	3 60
62188— " " "	1 80

$56 07

NORTH BAY LIGHT, HEAT & POWER CO., LTD., NORTH BAY, ONT.

56849—Current supplied	$0 50
56724— " "	50
57208— " "	50
57933—Lamps "	9 17
58572—Current "	50
58948— " "	50
60065— " "	50
60074— " "	50
60960— " "	50
60829—Bolts	96
61959—Current supplied	50

$14 63

NICHOLSON FILE COMPANY PORT HOPE, ONT.

56901—Files	$25 02
56990— "	58 05
57802— "	47 01
58941—Discount deducted in error	96
59152—Files	37 82
60641— "	75 31
61239— "	89 94
63027—	15 88
63300—	39 39

$389 38

New Orleans & Northeastern R. R. Co., New Orleans, La.

57117—Car repairs	$0 19	
56908— " service balance	45	
57246— " repairs	52	
58251— " service balance	13 50	
58401— " repairs	1 22	
58194— " service balance	29 25	
59339— " service balance	4 50	
59300— " repairs	1 25	
59660— " service balance	13 05	
60293— " service balance	7 65	
59970— " repairs	09	
60554— " service balance	90	
61787— " service balance	1 80	
61998— " repairs	3 11	
62184— " service balance	11 25	
62895— " service balance	1 35	
		$90 08

National Drug & Chemical Co. of Canada, Limited, Toronto, Ont.

57275—Chamois, sponges, chemicals, etc.	$60 40	
57486—Chamois, sal soda	6 36	
57961—First aid supplies and chemicals, etc.	69 25	
58406—Ammon fort, petrolatum, chamois	8 50	
58939—Sponges, cabinet	28 75	
59162—Chemicals, chamois	107 28	
60597—Borax, potash, lime, etc.	69 50	
60798—Chamois, sal soda	10 48	
61598—Castor oil	9 68	
61750—Aid cabinet, chamois, etc.	25 46	
63141—Sal soda, ammonia, etc.	28 31	
62956—First aid material, etc.	9 38	
63298—Sal soda	2 81	
		$436 16

The Nipissing Central Railway Company, Toronto, Ont.

57277—Track spikes, lumber, etc.	$256 87	
59457—Transportation	5 60	
59655—Advance to cover capital account	12,420 47	
63458—Advance to cover capital account	6,024 87	
		$18,707 81

Northern Electric Company, Limited, Toronto, Ont.

57279—Electrical material	$244 87	
57494—Telephone material, gaskets	46 98	
57963—Electrical material	922 78	
58410—Telephone material and wire	3,119 43	
59001—Telephone supplies, etc.	307 30	
59154—Receptacles	2 16	
60591—Staples, wire, cords, etc.	904 81	
59842—Travelling expenses, Spryer	12 50	
60772—Carbon blocks, coils	13 70	
60914—Selectors, wire, etc.	258 47	
61243—Telephone material	41 21	
61593—Panel boards, etc.	79 12	
61937—Clamp, switches, etc.	152 04	
61646—Copper wire, gloves, etc.	50 09	
61748—Receivers, batteries, etc.	418 53	
63137—Wire, lamp, cord, tape, etc.	127 31	
62652—Telephone material	57 94	
62724—Carbon brushes	1 80	
62952—Telephones, batteries, etc.	250 10	
63302—Receptacles, etc.	175 54	
		$7,186 68

NORTHERN CANADA SUPPLY CO., LIMITED, COBALT, ONT.

57373—Claim No. 10469—Siding rebate	$44 93	
57098— " No. 10340—Loss account damage to bbl. turpentine	2 70	
58055— " No. 10569—Loss account shortage to bbl. turpentine	7 90	
60893—Couplings, etc.	1 58	
60939—Claim No. 11572—Damage to pump handle ;.............	77	
61633— " No. 12125—Damage to hoes	65	
62753— " No. 11784—Loss metallic lath	7 26	
		$65 79

NEW ORLEANS COLONIZATION CO., LIMITED, BUFFALO, N.Y.

57375—Claims No. 10295, 10317—Overcharge rate and weight	$92 62	
63252—Claim No. 10632—Overcharge rate	14 57	
		$107 19

NIPISSING POWER CO., LIMITED, NORTH BAY, ONT.

57433—Current supplied	$130 52	
57576— " "	169 14	
58447— " "	150 82	
58606— " "	163 57	
59185— " "	118 57	
59482— " "	106 88	
60789— " "	95 99	
60726— " "	107 48	
62039— " "	110 96	
62282— " "	104 55	
63171— " "	128 13	
		$1,386 61

NATIONAL COUNCIL YOUNG MEN'S CHRISTIAN ASSOCIATION OF CANADA, TORONTO, ONT.

56634—Donation	$25 00	
		$25 00

NIPISSING LAUNDRY CO., LIMITED, NORTH BAY, ONT.

56684—Laundry	$3 21	
57138— "	6 42	
57766— "	5 44	
58570— "	7 90	
58943— "	20 40	
59751— "	2 07	
60771—	8 49	
60773—	1 44	
60018—	6 27	
60250—	6 48	
61006—	2 49	
61421—	5 59	
61290—	2 37	
61292—	4 35	
61644—	2 76	
62292—	1 89	
62530—	1 11	
62992— "	4 73	
63088—	3 60	
63816—	1 23	
63818—	1 98	
		$100 22

NEW YORK CENTRAL RAILROAD CO., NEW YORK, N.Y.

56896—Car service balance	$65 85
56948—Ticket balance	99 70
57094—Claim No. 9794—Overcharge on iron conveyors and fixtures	29 70
57244—Car repairs	99 92

NEW YORK CENTRAL RAILROAD COMPANY, ETC.—*Continued.*

58247—Car service balance		120 90
58325—Ticket balance		59 78
58395—Car repairs		57 17
58178— " service balance		188 74
58260— " " "		24 86
59323— " " "		302 40
59415— " " "		8 18
59525— " repairs		55 93
59296— " "		54 84
59298— " "		3 70
59646— " service balance		561 75
60041— " repairs		39 56
60279— " service balance		551 95
60427— " repairs		82 05
61175—Claim No. 10728—Overcharge weight pulpwood		1 62
61311—Car repairs		58 80
61777— " service balance		299 20
61868— " repairs		42 42
61996— " repairs		63 29
62755—Claim No. 11002—Overcharge rate pulpwood		3 07
62564—Claim No. 12026—Damage paper		18 33
62984—Car repairs		118 89
63626— " "		40 56
63774— " "		2 06
62075—Claim No. 12317—Overcharge rate pulpwood		2 94

$3,058 16

NEW YORK, SUSQUEHANNA & WESTERN RAILROAD COMPANY, NEW YORK, N.Y.

56898—Car service balance		$2 25
59329— " "		10 35
59652— " "		1 80
59968— " repairs		42
61781— " service balance		6 75
62178— " "		18 45
62887— " "		7 20
63510— "		2 25

$49 47

NEW YORK, NEW HAVEN & HARTFORD R.R. COMPANY, NEW HAVEN, CONN.

56902—Car service balance		$23 40
57250— " repairs		31
58243— " service balance		68 40
58397— " repairs		83
58188— " service balance		64 35
59333— " "		28 80
59527— " repairs		65
59302— " "		1 03
59656— " service balance		54 90
60289— " "		77 85
60548— " "		79 20
62000— " repairs		97
62293— " service balance		107 55
62889— " "		50 85
63195—Claim No. 12543—Overcharge rate		9 25
63512—Car service balance		13 95

$582 29

NEW YORK, ONTARIO & WESTERN RAILWAY COMPANY, NEW YORK, N.Y.

56904—Car service balance		$1 80
58245— " "		28 35
58190— " "		45
59335— " "		13 50

NEW YORK, ONTARIO & WESTERN RAILWAY COMPANY, ETC.—*Continued.*

60550—Car service balance	....	$9 45
61785— " "	....	11 70
62891— " "	....	10 80
63514— " "	....	3 15
63630—Value body car and air-brake equipment destroyed		300 15
		$379 35

NASHVILLE, CHATTANOOGA & ST. LOUIS RAILWAY, NASHVILLE, TENN.

56910—Car service balance	....	$11 25
58253— " "	....	1 80
59341— " "	....	18 45
59662— " "	....	31 50
59915— " repairs	....	16
60295— " service balance	....	34 20
60556— " "	....	15 30
61789— " "	....	12 15
62186— " "	....	22 50
62897— " "	....	14 85
63516— " "	....	4 50
		$166 66

NEW ORLEANS GREAT NORTHERN RAILROAD COMPANY, BOGALUSA, LA.

57032a—Car repairs	....	$0 12
58180— " service balance	....	2 25
59325— " "	....	3 15
59010— " repairs	....	5 02
59648— " service balance	....	1 35
60045— " repairs	....	2 30
60281— " service balance	....	90
60540— " "	....	3 15
61775— " "	....	4 05
62883— " "	....	3 15
63508— " "	....	3 60
63778— " repairs	....	10
		$29 14

NORTHERN LUMBER MILLS, LIMITED, NORTH COBALT, ONT.

57068—Claim No. 10192—Siding rebate	....	$132 00
		$132 00

NIAGARA, ST. CATHARINES & TORONTO RAILWAY COMPANY, ST. CATHARINES, ONT.

57096—Claims Nos. 9477 and 9868—Overcharge silver ore	......	$4 10
59085— " Nos. 9956 and 9915— " "	......	4 43
62751—Claim No. 10486— " "	......	5 32
		$13 85

NORTH AMERICAN BENT CHAIR COMPANY, LIMITED, OWEN SOUND, ONT.

57488—Chairs	....	$8 40
58412— "	....	14 00
58996— "	....	8 40
60595— "	....	16 80
63029— "	....	16 80
		$64 40

THE NICHOLS CHEMICAL COMPANY, LIMITED, MONTREAL, QUE.

57490—Sulphuric acid	....	$21 78
60643—Acid, carboys	....	54 72
		$76 50

THE NEW YORK TIMES, NEW YORK, N.Y.

57492—Copies of *New York Times* $0 60

$0 60

NORFOLK & CHESAPEAKE COAL COMPANY, DETROIT, MICH.

57719—Coal	$52 13
58703— "	10 42
59142— "	129 20
60715— "	35 10
60852— "	61 76

$288 61

A. O. NORTON, LIMITED, COATICOOK, QUE.

57931—Repair parts for jacks	$90 40
58408— " "	201 90
61935— " "	3 00

$295 30

NIAGARA FALLS PICKLES, LIMITED, NIAGARA FALLS, ONT.

58057—Claim No. 10067—Loss pickles $16 23

$16 23

NEW ORLEANS, TEXAS & MEXICO R.R., NEW ORLEANS, LA.

58411—Car repairs	$1 31
59294— " "	42
59666— " service balance	3 60
60301— " "	1 80
60562— " "	3 60
62437— " repairs	8 67
63776— " "	1 92

$21 32

NEWS PUBLISHING COMPANY, OF TORONTO, LIMITED, TORONTO, ONT.

58455—Advertising, "Ontario Demonstration Car" $9 00

$9 00

NATIONAL RAILWAY PUBLICATION COMPANY, NEW YORK, N.Y.

57918—Representation in "Official Guide" and subscription.....	$30 50
58742—Subscription, "Official Guide"	7 80
60831—Subscription, "Official Guide"	7 80
61288—Representation, "Official Guide"	30 00

$76 10

NATIONAL SAFETY COUNCIL, CHICAGO, ILL.

58104—Membership fee $20 00

$20 00

THE NATIONAL MALLEABLE CASTINGS COMPANY, CLEVELAND, OHIO.

58416—Hasps	$1 00
59095— "	1 00
63139— "	1 50

$3 50

NIPISSING COCO-COLA BOTTLING WORKS, LIMITED, COCHRANE, ONT.

58903—Claim No. 10466—Shortage, 1 case beer	$2 00
63698— " 12471 " empties	13 05
63702— " 12394 " soft drinks	63 40

NIPISSING COCO-COLA BOTTLING WORKS, LIMITED, ETC.—*Continued.*

63706—Claim No. 12397—Shortage, soft drinks	$12 75	
63710— " 12396 " "	7 65	
63722— " 12398 " "	44 20	
		$143 05

NORTHERN MINER PRESS, LIMITED, COBALT, ONT.

59097—Subscription, *The Northern Miner*	$1 50	
62426—Advertising *re* tenders, sale of land	25 20	
		$26 70

NEW YORK & CUBA MAIL STEAMSHIP CO., NEW YORK, N.Y.

59417—Ticket balance	$84 00	
		$84 00

TOWN OF NEW LISKEARD, NEW LISKEARD, ONT.

59459—Water supplied	$360 00	
59717—Annual sewer charges	542 72	
58492—Water supplied	270 00	
		$1,172 72

NEW ENGLAND PASSENGER ASSOCIATION, BOSTON, MASS.

59601—Propn. cost copies New England and Eastern Summer Rate Proceedings	$10 00	
		$10 00

W. A. NICHOLS, MATHESON, ONT.

58828—Claim No. 10394—Loss account, injuries to cow	$35 00	
		$35 00

G. NAISMITH (M.P. DEPT.), NORTH BAY, ONT.

58854—Expenses, travelling	$5 00	
63218—Expenses, travelling	14 00	
		$19 00

NOVA SCOTIA STEEL & COAL CO., LIMITED, NEW GLASGOW, N.S.

59144—Steel axles	$611 80	
		$611 80

NORTHERN OHIO RAILWAY COMPANY, INDIANAPOLIS, IND.

59290—Car repairs	$0 36	
		$0 36

NORTHERN CANADA POWER CO., LIMITED, TIMMINS, ONT.

59406—Claim No. 10814—Loss account, disconnecting switches destroyed	$64 08	
		$64 08

T. H. NEAL, LEAVILLE P.O., ONT.

59754—Ties	$110 85	
59754—Ties	31 92	
		$142 77

NEWBURGH & SOUTH SHORE RAILWAY COMPANY, CLEVELAND, O.

60299—Car service balance	$3 60	
60560—Car service balance	3 60	
		$7 20

NORTHWESTERN PACIFIC RAILROAD COMPANY, SAN FRANCISCO, CAL.

60383—Ticket balance	$5 53	
61843—Ticket balance	6 47	
		$12 00

NATIONAL-STANDARD COMPANY, NILES, MICH.

60593—Ball bearings	$4 50	
61939—Twist bits	21 60	
		$26 10

NEW ORLEANS TERMINAL COMPANY, NEW ORLEANS, LA.

60100—Car repairs	$0 89	
		$0 89

NORTHLAND STORES, LIMITED, HAILEYBURY, ONT.

61173—Claim No. 11673—Loss account, bottle vinegar broken....	$0 34	
61491— " 11792 " groceries	2 30	
61635— " 11674 " groceries	1 00	
63690— " 11571 " meat	1 80	
59410— " 10973 " groceries ....,.......	6 80	
		$12 24

ROBERT NEELY, THORNLOE P.O., ONT.

61241—Wood	$5 00	
		$5 00

NORFOLK & ROCHESTER HARDWARE CO., LIMITED, HAILEYBURY, ONT.

62073—Claim No. 11986—Damage to lamp glasses	$0 25	
61374—Claim No. 11991 and 12180—Loss of oil, etc.	5 00	
62519—Plyers	6 00	
		$11 25

NIAGARA FRONTIER SUMMER RATE COMMITTEE, MONTREAL, QUE.

61160—Propn. expenses	$24 36	
		$24 36

JOHN NEIL, CANE P.O., ONT.

61500—Ties	$106 77	
		$106 77

C. L. NAMA, HAILEYBURY, ONT.

63197—Claim No. 12601—Alleged loss two pair shoes	$5 00	
		$5 00

NORTH BAY TIMES, NORTH BAY, ONT.

62722—Advertising *re* sale of lands	$18 00	
		$18 00

NORTH BAY MARBLE & GRANITE WORKS, NORTH BAY, ONT.

62954—Sill course	$8 50	
		$8 50

NORTHERN CUSTOMS CONCENTRATORS, LIMITED, COBALT, ONT.

63688—Claim No. 12535—Loss on account, shortage, case liquor.	$16 00	
		$16 00

A. NEWELL, CONDUCTOR, NORTH BAY, ONT.

63814—Donation, personal effects destroyed by fire	$30 00	
		$30 00

THE OLYMPIA COMPANY, LIMITED, WINNIPEG, MAN.

56563—Supplies for private car ....,...............	$26 26	
		$26 26

THE ONTARIO CATHOLIC YEAR BOOK & DIRECTORY, TORONTO.

56635—Advertising	$15 00	
		$15 00

OFFICE SPECIALTY MFG. CO., LIMITED, TORONTO.

56637—Putting on castors	$1 35	
56804—Repairing bookcase door	1 60	
57500—Cards	14 88	
58424—Filing cabinet and boards	24 50	
58705—Transfer cases	38 50	
59051—Filing cards and cabinet	31 75	
58708—Upholstering chair	2 00	
59158—Filing cards, cabinet	3 63	
60599—Cards, file boards, etc.	28 69	
61423—Transfer cases	53 50	
61756—Cabinet	30 00	
63304—Screw top file boards	7 80	
		$238 20

O'BRIEN, MCDOUGALL & O'GORMAN, RENFREW, ONT.

56665—Claim No. 9779, overcharge on weight	$50 39	
58024— " No. 5332, overcharge on rate vans	59 28	
60867— " No. 7127, loss account shortage coal	46 15	
		$155 82

OFFICIAL CLASSIFICATION COMMITTEE, NEW YORK, N.Y.

56747—Classifications	$19 25	
57140—Supplements to classification	1 11	
57753— " "	91	
58914— " "	1 26	
60069—Supplement No. 8, classification No. 43	1 67	
61425—Supplement to off. classification	1 67	
61144—Classifications	1 36	
61162—Supplements to classification	2 41	
62569—Supplements to classification	1 95	
		$31 59

W. M. O'BEIRNE, STRATFORD, ONT.

56749—Advertising Stratford *Beacon*	$0 60	
		$0 60

W. J. OLDHAM, B. & B. MASTER, NORTH BAY, ONT.

56879—Travelling expenses	$12 60	
56750— " "	5 00	
57629— " "	17 00	
57876— " "	14 25	
58601— " "	17 20	
59338— " "	14 25	
59855— " "	10 50	
60194— " "	23 35	
61541— " "	12 00	
61256— " "	17 85	
62267— " "	13 95	
62818— " "	11 50	
		$169 45

ONTARIO REFORMATORY INDUSTRIES, GUELPH, ONT.

57281—Brooms	$45 00	
57496— "	42 50	
57935— "	27 00	
58422— "	90 00	

20 T R

ONTARIO REFORMATORY INDUSTRIES, GUELPH, ONT.—*Continued.*

59160—Brooms	$50 00	
60645— "	56 25	
		$310 75

THE O'BRIEN MINE, COBALT, ONT.

57377—Claim No. 9883, overcharge on silver ore	$186 05	
62056—Claim No. 12323, damage and loss 7 carboys acid	35 00	
		$221 05

MR. J. J. O'HANDLEY, NORTH COBALT, ONT.

57379—Claim No. 10241, loss account shortage household goods..	$10 78	
		$10 78

JAS. A. OGILVY & SONS, MONTREAL, QUE.

57498—Flags	$44 28	
58420— "	10 98	
58945— "	17 46	
59156—Linoleum.	20 00	
60778—Flags	110 88	
61941— "	45 00	
		$248 60

O'BRIEN & MARTIN, MONTREAL, QUE.

58061—Claim No. 10552, overcharge freight on coal	$5 76	
58065—Claim No. 10552, overcharge freight on coal	40	
		$6 16

OFFICIAL ANNUAL LABOUR REVIEW, TORONTO, ONT.

58707—Advertising	$25 00	
		$25 00

OTLEY PAINT MFG. CO., CHICAGO, ILL.

58947—Cement	$15 90	
60605— "	17 10	
63031— "	17 25	
		$50 25

J. A. O'DONNELL, ENGINEERING DEPT., NORTH BAY, ONT.

58800—Travelling expenses	$22 00	
61164—Travelling expenses	7 55	
		$29 55

ONTARIO WIND ENGINE & PUMP CO., LIMITED, TORONTO.

59014—Flag poles	$648 00	
		$648 00

OKLAHOMA, NEW MEXICO & PACIFIC RAILWAY CO., ARDMORE, OKLA.

59304—Car repairs	$1 41	
		$1 41

THOMAS W. OFFEN, RIVERS, MAN.

59881—Claim No. 11520, loss account baggage burned	$100 00	
		$100 00

ONEIDA NATIONAL CHUCK COMPANY, ONEIDA, N.Y.

60601—Drill chuck repairs	$2 33	
		$2 33

THE OSTER MANUFACTURING COMPANY, CLEVELAND, OHIO.

60603—Dies	$2 81	
		$2 81

OREGON SHORT LINE RAILROAD COMPANY, SALT LAKE CITY, UTAH.

60106—Car repairs	$0 87	
		$0 87

OFFICIAL LIST OF OPEN & PREPAY STATIONS, ST. LOUIS, MO.

60378—Supplements to list No. 15	$1 33	
61427—Supplements to list No. 16	3 30	
62295—Tariffs	1 58	
		$6 21

OWEN SOUND WIRE FENCE COMPANY, LIMITED, OWEN SOUND, ONT.

60776—Wire, staples, fence	$817 36	
61754—Fence gates	2,826 00	
62411—Fence wire	964 84	
		$4,608 20

OTIS FENSOM ELEVATOR COMPANY, LIMITED, TORONTO, ONT.

61600—Hand wheel, drum, screw	$21 65	
62958—Hand wheel, pinion	12 00	
		$33 65

ONTARIO SPRING BED & MATTRESS CO., LIMITED, LONDON, ONT.

61752—Brooms	$3 35	
62521— "	33 50	
62726— "	33 50	
		$70 35

OREGON-WASHINGTON RAILROAD & NAVIGATION COMPANY, PORTLAND, ORE.

61870—Car repairs	$2 73	
		$2 73

E. O'BLIN, COBALT, ONT.

62904—Claim No. 11569, alleged loss scrap brass	$22 08	
		$22 08

THE PENNSYLVANIA RAILROAD COMPANY, PHILADELPHIA, PA.

56537—Car repairs	$59 82	
56629— " "	17 33	
56616— " . "	58 67	
56914— " service balance	21 95	
57252— " repairs	31 10	
58263— " service balance	81 00	
58413— " repairs	31 18	
58202— " service balance	220 70	
59349— " service balance	297 70	
59533— " repairs	38 01	
59308— " "	60 70	
59310— " "	10 49	
59312— " "	3 28	
59360— " "	1 87	
59674— " " service balance	468 00	

The Pennsylvania Railroad Company, Etc.—*Continued.*

59865—Ticket balance	15	10
59919—Car repairs	3	61
60047— " repairs	6	21
60309— " service balance	744	70
60433— " repairs	12	28
60445—Claim	124	48
59820—Two first class fares, Philadelphia to Atlantic City and return	2	50
59974—Car repairs	16	13
60056— "　"	79	82
60380— "　"		87
60570— " service balance	294	10
61177—Claim	4	98
61387—Car repairs	59	00
61797— " service balance	199	35
61108— " repairs	93.	00
61110— " repairs	30	88
61822—Claim	6	15
61874—Car repairs	26	71
61926— "　"	31	30
62004— "　"	28	90
62028— "　"	1	70
62194— " service balance	56	30
62903— "　"	168	35
63103—Claims	4	40
63199— "	2	38
63528—Car service balance	258	75
63634— " repairs	51	17
63782— " repairs	44	64

$3,751 56

Pittsburgh & Lake Erie Railroad Company, Pittsburgh, Pa.

56539—Car repairs	$11	17
56981— "　"		28
59531— "　"	19	42
60049— "　"	22	93
60058— "　"	6	60
61313— "　"	16	51
61637—Claim No. 10987, loss two steel rails	1	15
62006—Car repairs	29	09

$107 15

Pere Marquette Railroad Company, Detroit, Mich.

56541—Car repairs	$3	23
56667—Claim No. 10257, overcharge on latches, etc.	2	10
57127—Car repairs	2	81
56912— " service balance	1	80
57258— " repairs	2	70
58071—Claim No. 10206, damage to sugar	1	10
58259—Car service balance	34	20
58415— " repairs	2	54
58198— " service balance	50	80
59345— " service balance	77.	80
59314— " repairs	2	22
59670— " service balance	74	25
59921— " repairs	5	66
60305— " service balance	83	70
59976— " repairs	3	51
60568— " service balance	34	65
61463— " repairs	55	55
61795— " service balance	56	90
61876— " repairs	6	34
61924— " repairs	18	33

PERE MARQUETTE RAILROAD COMPANY, DETROIT, MICH.—*Continued.*

62192—Car service balance	$25 65	
62899— " " "	50 40	
63518— " "	45 00	
		$641 24

PENNSYLVANIA COMPANY, PITTSBURGH, PA.

56577—Claims	$12 43	
58069—Claim	4 84	
58329—Ticket balance	3 86	
		$21 13

THE PINTSCH COMPRESSING COMPANY, NEW YORK, N.Y.

56851—Gas	$220 95	
56692— "	113 41	
58449— "	119 12	
59029— "	250 40	
59603— "	134 22	
60789a— "	229 61	
60660— "	100 50	
62043— "	90 95	
61796— "	91 30	
63636— "	158 61	
		$1,509 07

PILKINGTON BROTHERS. LIMITED, TORONTO.

56903—Glass	$121 90	
56994— "	24 34	
57507— " and resilvering mirrors	14 94	
57605—	163 68	
57660—	113 51	
57810—	16 53	
58569—	152 75	
58591—	61 81	
58757—	408 03	
58710—	69 15	
58884—	2 23	
60112—	14 41	
61075— "	429 43	
62377—	93 32	
		$1,686 03

THE THOMAS PINK COMPANY. PEMBROKE, ONT.

56905—Peaveys, etc.	$18 52	
58755— "	13 01	
61945— "	7 44	
62225— "	14 89	
		$53 86

PEORIA & PEKIN UNION RAILWAY COMPANY, PEORIA, ILL.

56979—Car repairs	$0 29	
57256— "	1 90	
61872— "	7 84	
		$10 03

P. PICARD, LINEMAN, NORTH BAY, ONT.

57075—Travelling expenses	$12 25	
56972— "	9 65	
57735— "	3 80	
58270— "	5 35	
58785— "	6 65	
59340— "	5 10	

P. Picard, Lineman, North Bay, Ont.—*Continued.*

59955—Travelling expenses	$10 30	
60278— "	6 70	
61543— "	6 60	
62629— "	7 90	
62782— "	12 30	
		$86 60

Philadelphia & Reading Railway Company, Philadelphia, Pa.

57125—Car repairs	$5 70	
57100—Claim No. 10285—Loss account, damage to gear guards..	2 63	
57254—Car repairs	1 83	
58257— " service balance	23 40	
58403— " repairs	76	
58196— " service balance	71 10	
59343— " "	16 65	
59306— " repairs	2 10	
59668— " service balance	43 65	
59777— " repairs	45 66	
59917— " "	9 23	
60303— " service balance	54 45	
60382— " repairs	2 87	
60564— " service balance	37 80	
61315— " repairs	11 54	
61793— " service balance	52 20	
61922— " repairs	1 81	
62190— " service balance	31 50	
62489— " repairs	1 90	
63632— " "	23 70	
		$440 48

Wm. Pollock & Son, Englehart, Ont.

57185—Spruce	$4 80	
58463—Fence posts	13 12	
		$17 92

The Hiram L. Piper Co., Limited, Montreal, P.Q.

57187—Burners for heaters and freight car heaters	$53 50	
57510—Railway supplies	243 05	
57937—Signal burners	11 40	
55436—Wicks	1 00	
58955—Switch lamps	57 40	
63007—Founts, burners, wick	12 73	
		$379 08

Pearce Meat Company, Limited, North Bay, Ont.

57283—Meat	$77 06	
57504— "	20 15	
57965— "	212 09	
58426— "	36 88	
59005— "	35 00	
60609— "	46 08	
60784— "	27 28	
62656— "	4 46	
		$459 00

Power Specialty Company, New York, N.Y.

57189—Pump parts	$39 50	
58623—Gate valve	52 47	
		$91 97

PRATT & WHITNEY CO. OF CANADA, LIMITED, DUNDAS, ONT.

57285—Drill chuck cap and arbor	$6 46	
58432—Taps and drills	7 70	
60649—Taps and drills	12 54	
60318—Sleeves	6 84	
60782—Drills, taps	16 85	
60916—Sleeves	5 71	
61247—Drills, etc.	46 42	
61602—Drills	2 49	
61794—Drills and taps	33 78	
63039—Taps, drills, dies, etc.	69 59	
62654—M. T. S. drills	2 19	
62962—Drills and taps	4 55	
63308—Shank drills	127 50	
		$342 62

THE N. L. PIPER RAILWAY SUPPLY CO., LIMITED, TORONTO.

57287—Oil feeders, mop rags, supplies, etc.	$140 29	
57508—Railway supplies	50 28	
57941—Lanterns, cans, mop rags, etc.	74 83	
58428—Supplies	155 48	
59009—Lamp fonts, burners, etc.	139 57	
59099—Oil cans, wicks, etc.	84 30	
59168—Wicks, burners	307 34	
60611—Oil feeders, lamp hoods, etc.	97 30	
60320—Lenses	26 40	
60802—Oil feeders, squirt cans	131 95	
61943—Lamps, headlights	193 67	
61526—Pail, cans, globes, etc.	77 75	
63035—Globes, brackets, lanterns	160 70	
62994—Mop rags, sticks, etc.	40 30	
		$1,680 16

PITTSBURG SPRING STEEL CO., PITTSBURG, PA.

57289—Driving springs	$54 70	
58438— "	50 32	
68856— "	551 33	
58932— "	217 44	
60613— "	320 44	
61029— "	217 15	
61251— "	15 51	
62525— "	348 25	
62660— "	157 69	
		$1,932 83

THE PLANET, CHATHAM, ONT.

57291—Forms	$15 38	
57506— "	8 50	
57939— "	28 70	
58434— "	208 60	
59003— "	47 50	
59166— "	163 62	
60615— "	131 08	
60800— "	6 00	
61249— "	13 50	
61716— "	265 14	
63037— "	35 75	
62658— "	11 50	
62964— "	46 25	
63306— "	27 53	
		$1,009 05

PATERSON MFG. COMPANY, LIMITED, TORONTO.

56588—Felt, pitch and coal tar	$149 12	
57601—Building paper	42 07	
58666—Tarred felt and roofing	68 48	
58882—Roofing	180 80	
59677— "	51 45	
60140— " felt, etc.	107 07	
61073— "	277 18	
61788—Spruce, sheathing	25 40	
62413—Felt, roofing, etc.	165 07	
		$1,066 64

GEO. PORTER, HEASLIP, ONT.

56806—Donation account—pulpwood alleged destroyed by fire ..	$19 25	
		$19 25

PITTSBURG, SHAWMUTT & NORTHERN RAILROAD, ST. MARY'S, PA.

56916—Car service balance	$19 35	
57142—Refund per diem	45	
58261—Car service balance	5 40	
58200— " "	14 40	
59347— " "	2 70	
59672— " "	7 65	
60307— " "	8 55	
60568— " "	45	
62901— " "	5 85	
63520— " "	27 90	
		$92 70

PEERLESS TRANSIT LINE, CLEVELAND, O.

56918—Car service Balance	$3 79	
58206— " "	3 79	
59353— " "	1 90	
59678— " "	1 90	
60574— " "	7 59	
61801— " "	7 59	
62198— " "	4 83	
62907— " "	14 14	
63532— " "	17 08	
		$62 61

PAGE-HERSEY IRON TUBE & LEAD CO., LIMITED, TORONTO.

56992—Pipe	$78 32	
57603— "	117 19	
57804— "	78 45	
58571— "	148 09	
58880— "	6 73	
59983— "	22 87	
60647— "	93 15	
60146— "	241 73	
61071— "	147 53	
62227— "	126 87	
62415— "	110 99	
62665— "	239 83	
63206— "	17 19	
		$1,428 94

PITTSBURG, CHARTIERS & YOUGHIOGHENY RY. COMPANY, PITTSBURG, PA.

57102—Claim No. 9391—Overcharge on silver ore	$2 04	
		$2 04

F. C. Preston, Ltd., Haileybury, Ont.

57104—Claim No. 10507—Loss account, damage to 3 lbs. butter..	$0 96	
58981— " 10403—Loss account, shortage case matches..	4 50	
59902— " 10856—Loss account, shortage box butter	15 30	
61414— " 11993—Loss, tin syrup	75	
62236— " 12977—Loss, coffee, account damage	54	
		$22 05

Porter & Company, Elk Lake, Ont.

57106—Claim No. 10402—Loss account, shortage, raisins	$0 90	
58073—Claim No. 10576—Loss account, shortage, grapes	1 00	
		$1 90

Pomeroy & Fischer, New York, N.Y.

57502—Paints	$26 10	
		$26 10

The Pullman Company, Chicago, Ill.

57512—Steel bulkheads and freight charges	$214 66	
57620—Steel coaches and cars	51,060 00	
58510—Lighting pullmans	72 29	
		$51,346 95

Wm. Potter & Son, Tottenham, Ont.

57032—Claim No. 10692—Siding rebate	$79 05	
57034—Claim No. 10692—Siding rebate	44 00	
		$123 05

A. J. Parr (G. F. & P. A.), North Bay, Ont.

57561—Travelling expenses	$19 20	
58603— " "	41 40	
58764— " "	23 85	
59857— " "	49 25	
60196— " "	25 90	
61069— " "	42 40	
61258— " "	15 95	
62239— " "	9 00	
62444— " "	14 85	
56751— " "	32 75	
56630— " "	15 90	
57700— " "	23 40	
		$313 85

Peerless Carbon & Ribbon Manufacturing Company, Limited, Toronto, Ont.

57943—Carbon paper	$79 50	
58430— "	32 00	
58951— "	20 00	
60617— "	57 25	
61245—Pencils, etc.	45 25	
63033—Carbon	34 00	
62960—Stationery	58 50	
		$326 50

Hugh Park, Cobalt, Ont.

58067—Claim No. 10540—loss account, damage to bottle water..	$1 43	
		$1 43

A. H. Porter, Elk Lake, Ont.

58119—Rent telephone office—Elk Lake	60 00	
61429— " "	70 00	
		$130 00

Pacific Fruit Express, San Francisco, Cal.

58265—Car service balance	$7 17	
58204— " "	1 90	
59351— " "	11 57	
59676— "	3 83	
60572— "	7 62	
61799— "	5 56	
62196— "	6 80	
62905— "	18 27	
63530— "	18 50	
		$81 22

Porcupine Telephone Lines, Limited, South Porcupine, Ont.

57768—Telephone rental—Timmins	$33 00	
60903— " " —South Porcupine	48 45	
61294— " " —Schumacher and Timmins	75 45	
		$156 90

L. Pelkie, Section Foreman, Thornloe, Ont.

57878—Travelling expenses	$1 00	
		$1 00

H. Pilling, Machinist, North Bay, Ont.

57880—Travelling expenses	$7 50	
58605— " "	2 75	
		$10 25

Polar Refrigerator Line, Chicago, Ill.

58208—Car service balance	$3 79	
		$3 79

The Pedlar People, Limited, Oshawa, Ont.

58949—Galvanized iron	$41 63	
61604—Iron	48 18	
		$89 81

H. Picard, North Bay, Ont.

58953—Bacon and tomatoes	$3 63	
62523—Groceries	1 06	
		$4 69

Preston Car & Coach Company, Limited, Preston, Ont.

58804—Iron forgings, equalizers, etc.	$466 72	
62193—Hangers	325 24	
		$791 96

A. Pullan, Englehart, Ont.

58846—Claim No. 10709—loss account, damage to furniture	$3 00	
62319— " No. 11456—damage to marble table top	5 90	
		$8 90

THE PANTASOTE COMPANY, NEW YORK, N.Y.

59164—Upholstery, agasote	$57 46	
60619—Agasote boards and war tax	9 60	
62529— " " "	21 01	
62966—War tax on material	1 43	
		$89 5

PRATT & LITCHWORTH COMPANY, LIMITED, BRANTFORD, ONT.

59170—Pins	$1 47	
61973—Castings	5 25	
61792— "	6 58	
		$13 3

ANDREW PRATT (M. P. DEPT.), NORTH BAY, ONT.

59342—Travelling expenses	$7 35	
59707— " "	9 80	
		$17 1

ROBT. PRENTICE, RELIEVING AGENT, NORTH BAY, ONT.

59882—Travelling expenses	$10 75	
59884— " "	3 25	
		$14 0

A. PLANT, COBALT, ONT.

59412—Claim No. 10296—overcharge, fare, man in charge horses	$2 85	
		$2 8

PERKINS, INCE & COMPANY, TORONTO.

59506—Claim No. 11081—refund storage charges on pickles	$2 02	
		$2 0

PIEDMONT & NORTHERN RAILWAY COMPANY, CHARLOTTE, N.C.

59680—Car service balance	$0 90	
60311— " "	1 35	
		$2 2

G. E. PALMER, CLAIMS DEPARTMENT, NORTH BAY, ONT.

59723—Travelling expenses	$14 30	
61465— " "	12 50	
61648— " "	21 35	
62203— " "	29 15	
62464— " "	38 10	
		$115 4

PORCUPINE ADVANCE, TIMMINS, ONT.

59755—Advertisement	$3 20	
61128— "	8 50	
		$11 7

PRESSED PRISM PLATE GLASS COMPANY, MORGANTOWN, W. VA.

60607—Glass	$18 00	
		$18 0

CHAS. PIERCE & SONS, LIMITED, TIMMINS, ONT.

59900—Claims Nos. 11030, 11114—damage to onions and fruit by frost	$15 35	
60871—Claim No. 11077—loss account, shortage apricots	55	
60941— " No. 11152—loss account, lamp chimney in transit..	4 15	
		$20 05

THOMAS POTTER, McCOOL P.O., ONT.

60064—Ties	$130 38	
		$130 38

H. S. PRICE, WINNIPEG, MAN.

60346—Claim No. 11731—Loss account, baggage burned	$100 00	
		$100 00

W. J. PARSONS, NORTH BAY, ONT.

60962—Glasses	$0 50	
		$0 50

HERBERT PETERS, COBALT, ONT.

60943—Claim No. 10063—o/c in freight, potatoes	$16 94	
63184— " No. 10058—o/c weight, 13 cars potatoes	95 12	
		$112 06

E. PETERS, EARLTON P.O., ONT.

61063—Ties	$47 70	
		$47 70

PIPE & PRESLEY, COBALT, ONT.

61179—Claim No. 11635—loss, case soap	$3 85	
		$3 85

TAYLOR PIPE, COBALT, ONT.

61493—Claim No. 11624—loss account, syrup	$9 06	
61643— " No. 11633—damage to pickle equipment	3 50	
62077— " No. 11634—loss sugar in transit	8 31	
61820— " 12278—loss bottle olives, pickles and lime juice	1 80	
		$22 67

GUSTAVE PERRAULT, YARDMAN, ENGLEHART, ONT.

62025—Award W. C. B. *re* alleged injuries	$46 20	
61200— " " " " "	57 75	
62436— " " " " "	377 70	
		$481 65

E. H. PARMELEE, NORTH BAY, ONT.

61758—Electrical fixtures	$16 44	
62296—Porc. tubes	5 76	
		$22 20

PEASE FOUNDRY CO., LIMITED, TORONTO, ONT.

61790—Set grates	$22 60	
		$22 60

C. H. POWELL, ENGLEHART, ONT.

62300—Meat and groceries	$39 60	
62968—Provisions	7 65	
		$47 25

PITTSBURG METER COMPANY, EAST PITTSBURG, PA.

62417—Register, studs, etc.	$28-50	
		$28 50

PUBLIC SERVICE CUP CO. OF CANADA, LIMITED, OTTAWA, CAN.

62527—Cups	$11 00	
		$11 00

GEO. W. POWLES, MACHINIST, NORTH BAY, ONT.

62378—Award W. C. B. *re* alleged injuries received	$46 23	
62414—Award W. C. B. *re* alleged injuries received	11 01	
		$57 24

PALMER & SMITH, EARLTON, ONT.

62906—Claim No. 12718, alleged loss sugar	$1 72	
		$1 72

P. PASTENE & COMPANY, INC., MONTREAL, QUE.

62996—Claim No. 12624, alleged loss, olives and canned goods....	$29 00	
63180—Claim No. 12580—Loss groceries, fire, Cochrane	111 55	
		$140 55

MRS. W. E. PICARD, GANANOQUE, ONT.

63234—Claim No. 11781, alleged loss lumber in transit	$3 00	
		$3 00

PREST-O-LITE COMPANY, MERRITTON, ONT.

63310—Acetylene	$36 51	
		$36 51

QUEEN'S HOTEL, COCHRANE, ONT.

56727—Board and lodging	$7 50	
59461— "	11 50	
60020— " and lodging	3 00	
		$22 00

G. W. QUANTZ, CANE P.O., ONT.

57226—Donation account loss cow alleged killed	$50 00	
		$50 00

QUEBEC CENTRAL RAILWAY COMPANY, SHERBROOKE, QUE.

57260—Car repairs	$1 62	
60315— " service balance	4 50	
61112— " repairs	2 45	
62908—Claim No. 10363, outstanding account, error billing	2 00	
		$10 57

QUEBEC, MONTREAL & SOUTHERN RY. COMPANY, NEW YORK, N.Y.

57332—Car service balance	$0 45	
58267— " " "	9 90	
58210— " " "	14 40	

QUÉBEC, MONTREAL & SOUTHERN RAILWAY COMPANY, ETC.—*Continued.*

59355—Car service balance	$0 90	
59535— " repairs	66	
59682— " service balance	17 55	
60313— " " "	19 80	
60576— " " "	17 55	
62909— " " "	1 35	
63534— " " "	7 65	
		$90 21

QUEBEC RAILWAY, LIGHT & POWER COMPANY, QUEBEC, QUE.

62232—Ticket balance	$201 00	
		$201 00

McGIVEN QUIRT, NIPISSING JCT., ONT.

62806—Ties	$9 00	
		$9 00

QUEEN VICTORIA MEMORIAL HOSPITAL, NORTH BAY, ONT.

63366—Donation	$100 00	
		$100 00

RAILWAY MAIL CLERKS ASSOCIATION, TORONTO.

56457—Advertising in Railway Mail Clerks Review, 1915	$15 00	
61168—Advertising in Railway Mail Clerks Review, 1916	15 00	
		$30 00

S. H. RYAN, TRAINMASTER, NORTH BAY, ONT.

56609—Travelling expenses	$13 20	
56881— " "	18 10	
56974— " "	20 10	
57885— " "	32 55	
58418— " "	30 65	
58787— " "	40 85	
59346— " "	23 65	
60105—	14 05	
60280—	20 65	
61865— "	13 70	
62511—	25 60	
62460—	17 60	
		$270 70

M. ROTHSCHILD, COCHRANE, ONT.

56669—Claim No. 9654, damage to furniture	$15 50	
58983— " No. 8811, " "	17 50	
63201— " No. 12620, loss liquor	2 06	
		$35 06

THE JAMES ROBERTSON COMPANY, LIMITED, MONTREAL, P.Q.

56705—Sinks	$10 98
56907—Plates	75 55
56584—Steel plates	55 78
57662—Iron	10 82
58573—Plates	56 71
59176—Grey fuller balls	64
59681—Seneca steel	39 98
59985—Plates	155 27
60114—Iron	12 47
60142—Plates	213 34
61077— "	155 00
61977— "	126 22

THE JAMES ROBERTSON COMPANY, LIMITED, ETC.—*Continued.*

62419—Plates	$63 22	
62423—Hardware	78 95	
63398—Iron plates	45 66	
62684—Steel plates	110 88	
63006—Buffer plates	82 62	
		$1,294 09

J. W. RICHARDSON, NORTH BAY, ONT.

56909—Door hangers, etc.	$18 91	
56998—Globe valves	1 16	
57607—Mattresses	21 82	
57664— " and springs	45 10	
57812— "	14 55	
58709— "	14 55	
59679— "	14 55	
59987—Alabastine	3 88	
60252—Alabastine	4 37	
61606—Mattresses, hinges, etc.	80 22	
62598—Washboard, spoons, etc.	5 04	
63204—Blankets	19 69	
		$243 84

THE RATCLIFF PAPER CO., LIMITED, TORONTO.

56911—Twine	$15 44	
57509— "	7 42	
58444— "	5 25	
58541—Wrapping paper and holder	4 61	
59076—Twine	24 50	
61496— "	37 70	
		$94 92

RUTLAND RAILROAD COMPANY, NEW YORK, N.Y.

56983—Car repairs	$0 36	
56920—Car service balance	50	
56952—Ticket balance	258 79	
57262—Car·repairs	2 79	
58331—Ticket balance	49 83	
58417—Car repairs	49	
58212—Car service balance	5 40	
58262— " " "	90 60	
59357— " " "	7 20	
59419— " " "	6 76	
59537— " repairs	57	
59684— " service balance	14 40	
60317— " " "	11 70	
60385—Ticket balance	14 96	
60578—Car service balance	5 85	
61389—Car repairs	56	
61845—Ticket balance	14 01	
61878—Car repairs	5 27	
62959—Ticket balance	57 89	
63576—Ticket balance	4 67	
		$552 60

H. L. RODGERS, MECHANICAL ENGINEER, NORTH BAY, ONT.

57063—Travelling expenses	$92 20	
57671— " "	79 05	
59667— " "	70 45	
61595— " "	95 80	
62157— " "	45 00	
62396— " "	70 65	
		$453 15

RICHARDSON, BOND & WRIGHT, LIMITED, OWEN SOUND, ONT.

57301—Ledgers, registers and forms	$68 65	
57518—Accounting books and forms	72 50	
57945—Accounting books and forms	116 90	
58440—Binders and forms	133 60	
59101—Forms	115 45	
59103—Forms	26 95	
60627—Rule books	13 60	
60717—Stationery	188 90	
60856—Forms	78 20	
61597—Forms	25 45	
61608—Cards and forms	100 70	
61650—Forms	14 25	
63041—Forms	74 40	
63004—Transfer cards	388 15	
63314—Forms	21 05	
		$1,438 75

ROYAL POLISHES CO., MONTREAL, QUE.

57303—Metal polish	$16 20	
57514— " "	16 20	
57967— " "	16 20	
57828— " "	16 20	
58448— " "	8 10	
59053— " "	12 15	
59178— " "	12 15	
60324— " "	16 20	
60804— " "	12 15	
61530— " "	16 20	
61760— " "	16 20	
63047— " "	8 10	
		$166 05

RICE LEWIS & SON, LIMITED, TORONTO, ONT.

57305—Screw drivers and glass cutters	$14 05	
57522—Steel and emery dresser	273 46	
58446—Hardware	34 70	
58999—Springs, washers, etc.	9 93	
59172—Steel, pliers, etc.	221 85	
60621—Augers, steel, roofing, etc.	50 64	
60854—Steel, gouges, etc.	40 11	
60918—Spring steel, pipe cutter	30 83	
61253—Post	12 75	
61975—Stocks, dies	23 00	
61528—Steel	566 28	
61764—Die, nuts, tape lines	25 50	
62535—Level glasses	1 47	
63043—Hardware	22 72	
62416—Steel	333 75	
63002—Hardware supplies	49 50	
63312—Latches	9 30	
		$1,719 84

I. RICE, IROQUOIS FALLS, ONT.

57381—Claim No. 10335, loss account damage to fruit in transit..	$1 20	
58075— " " 10463 " " damage to building paper..	1 01	
58830— " " 10864 " " case Epsom salts	1 60	
59510— " " 10690 " " damage to sausages	2 20	
62655— " " 12468 " " rice	24 25	
62570— " " 12144 " " salt	94	
62910— " " 12186 " " meat	1 64	
63714— " " 12154 " " groceries	2 68	
		$35 52

W. D. RODGERS, CHARLTON, ONT.

57383—Claim No. 10154—loss account, shortage barrel H.H. goods $5 00
                                                                              $5 00

WILLIAM T. ROBSON COMPANY, MONTREAL, QUE.

56538—Time-tables, folders, maps, engravings, etc. .... $1,184 01.
                                                                              $1,184 01

RUSSIA CEMENT COMPANY, GLOUCESTER, MASS.

56582—Liquid glue $25 09
57687—   " 12 54
61762—   " 27 20
62421—   " 13 33
                                                                              $78 16

RAILWAY AGE GAZETTE, NEW YORK, N.Y.

56694—Subscriptions $14 00
57210—   " 6 00
58545—   " 6 00
59757—   " 6 00
62533—   " 6 00
                                                                              $38 00

REMINGTON TYPEWRITER COMPANY, LIMITED, TORONTO, ONT.

56726—Typewriter and inspection $62 00
58451—Repairing typewriter 12 20
57848—Carbon paper 7 49
58543—   " 2 00
59486—   " 7 50
                                                                              $91 19

RAILWAY EQUIPMENT & PUBLICATION COMPANY, NEW YORK, N.Y.

56808—Registration rolling stock equipment $96 00
57770—Representation in "Railway Line Clearance" 10 00
                                                                              $106 00

THOMAS ROBERTSON & COMPANY, LIMITED, MONTREAL, QUE.

56996—Copper $6 93
58575—Wash basins 5 88
                                                                              $12 81

RAILWAY MECHANICAL COMPUTING TABLES, LAKEWOOD, OHIO.

57516—Computing tables $2 00
                                                                              $2 00

THE RENFREW MACHINERY COMPANY, LIMITED, RENFREW, ONT.

57520—Truck scale $25 20
                                                                              $25 20

M. J. ROCHE, TIMMINS, ONT.

57533—Repairing clocks $2 75
62538—   "   " 2 00
                                                                              $4 75

21 T R

RYRIE BROS., LIMITED, TORONTO, ONT.

57947—"Safety First" buttons	$17 15	
58442— " "	35	
		$17 50

RAILWAY AND MARINE WORLD, TORONTO, ONT.

58121—Subscriptions	$28 00	
		$28 00

MRS. HENRY ROSE, HOMER P.O., ONT.

58463—Ties	$31 14	
		$31 14

THE ROCK ISLAND EMPLOYEES' MAGAZINE, CHICAGO, ILL.

57850—Subscription	$1 50	
		$1 50

THOMAS ROSS, MASTER MECHANIC, NORTH BAY, ONT.

57882—Expenses—travelling	$9 80	
		$9 80

ROBERTS & SCHAEFER COMPANY, CHICAGO, ILL.

58106—Equipment for coaling plant	$197 00	
59055—Time and expense re coaling plant	104 47	
		$301 47

BLAIR RUSHTON, BEAUCHAMP, ONT.

58593—Ties	$117 01	
61500— . "	63 06	
61500— "	65 90	
		$245 97

T. RANSON, M. P. DEPT., NORTH BAY, ONT.

58607—Travelling expenses	$7 05	
		$7 05

RAND AVERY SUPPLY COMPANY, BOSTON, MASS.

58957—Punches	$30 00	
		$30 00

THE RATHBUN MATCH COMPANY, LIMITED, DESERONTO, ONT.

59007—Matches	$3 80	
60623— . "	3 80	
		$7 60

WM. RENNIE COMPANY, LIMITED, TORONTO, ONT.

59011—Seeds	$31 74	
59174—Lawn seeder	4 25	
63000—Tulips	13 38	
		$49 37

H. T. ROUTLEY, HUNTINGTON, QUE.

58678—Purchase price house and lot, Town of Haileybury	$1,750 00	
		$1,750 00

ROUS & MANN, LIMITED, TORONTO, ONT.

58712—Prints of maps	$11 00	
59814—Folders	111 00	
60006— "	125 00	
61296— "	487 50	
62536—Slips re passes	10 75	
62728—Composition for changes on folders	7 60	
		$752 85

RAILWAY SIGNAL ASSOCIATION, BETHLEHEM, PA.

58788—Additions and revisions, one set	$1 00	
		$1 00

ROOFERS' SUPPLY COMPANY, LIMITED, TORONTO, ONT.

58832—Claim No. 10303—overcharge in weight shipment iron....	$4 94	
		$4 94

ALFRED ROGERS, LIMITED, TORONTO, ONT.

59508—Claim No. 9897—loss account, shortage cement sacks...	$5 26	
		$5 26

MRS. JOHN ROSS, KELLIHER, SASK.

59883—Claim No. 11428—loss account, baggage burned	$100 00	
		$100 00

RICHMOND, FREDERICKSBURG & POTOMAC R.R. COMPANY, RICHMOND, VA.

60319—Car service balance	$7 65	
		$7 65

A. C. ROBABECK, NORTH BAY, ONT.

60625—Tartaric acid	$1 75	
63045—Bedbug poison	1 50	
63316—Oxalic acid	7 50	
		$10 75

RAILWAY & LOCOMOTIVE ENGINEERING, NEW YORK, N.Y.

60022—Subscription	$2 00	
63638— "	2 00	
		$4 00

REDFIELD-KENDRICK-ODELL COMPANY, INC., NEW YORK, N.Y.

60322—Corrections in T. & N. O. map	$14 00	
		$14 00

STEVEN ROBINSON, FERONIA, ONT.

60905—Clearing Lot No. 7, Con. 1, Widdifield	$25 00	
		$25 00

RAILWAY STEEL SPRING COMPANY, NEW YORK, N.Y.

60993—Tires	$3,360 24	
61652— "	2,278 06	
		$5,638 30

MRS. E. RIGBY, NORTH BAY, ONT.

61079—Disbursement, account telegrams	$1 32	
		$1 32

Rodd & Deacon, Cobalt, Ont.

61495—Claim No. 11457—loss account, boots $4 20

                                                                        $4 20

Mrs. F. Richardson, Porquis Jct., Ont.

62027—Rental stumper $9 00

                                                                        $9 00

Wm. Riddler (Carpenter), North Bay, Ont.

61150—Award W. C. B., *re* alleged injuries $16 09
62205—Award W. C. B., *re* alleged injuries 26 12

                                                                        $42 21

John Rathevich (Labourer), North Bay, Ont.

61166—Award W. C. B., *re* alleged injuries $8 80

                                                                        $8 80

Chas. Reckin & Sons, Cobalt, Ont.

61412—Claim No. 11471—Alleged loss coffee $2 50
62058—   "   12231—Damage and loss, wine jars 3 77
62601—   "   12281—Loss, cocoa squares 3 22
62568—   "   12230—Loss, cornmeal 2 00

                                                                        $11 49

Rock Island Southern Railway, Manmouth, Ill.

61928—Car repairs $0 46

                                                                        $0 46

Mrs. Sophia Richards, Heaslip, Ont.

62331—Settlement *re* alleged injuries $100 00

                                                                        $100 00

Rand, McNally & Company, Chicago, Ill.

62531—Atlas $15 00

                                                                        $15 00

Reliable Printing Company, Haileybury, Ont.

62757—Claim No. 12454—Alleged damage to glass $6 10

                                                                        $6 10

J. Frank Raw, Toronto, Ont.

62350—Reglazing picture frames $2 45

                                                                        $2 45

Ritchie, Ludwig & Ballantyne, Toronto, Ont.

62380—Fee *re* suit—A. R. MacDonell vs. T. & N. O. $100 00

                                                                        $100 00

Bert Riches (M.P. Dept.), North Bay, Ont.

62478—Travelling expenses $3 85

                                                                        $3 85

James Redpath, New Liskeard, Ont.

62534—Repairing clock, New Liskeard Station $2 00

                                                                        $2 00

RITCHIE CUT-STONE CO., LIMITED, HAMILTON, ONT.

62662—Stone $281 00

$281 00

ROUTLEY & SUMMERS, HAILEYBURY, ONT.

62730—Building walk, agent's house, Timmins $10 71

$10 71

H. ROBINSON, KENABEEK P.O.

62806—Ties $67 08

$67 08

RAYMOND & WHITCOMB COMPANY, BOSTON, MASS.

63008—Commission on tickets $1 30
63332—   "   " 1 48
63334—   "   " 1 09

$3 87

REVILLION FRERES TRADING CO., LIMITED, COCHRANE, ONT.

63238—Claim No. 12585—Alleged damage to canned meat $1 70

$1 70

SCHOOL SECTION NO. 3, CLERGUE, FRED. BROWN, SEC.-TREAS., PORQUIS JCT., ONT.

56485—Donation $50 00

$50 00

SEABOARD AIR LINE RAILWAY, PORTSMOUTH, VA.

56543—Car repairs	$6 58	
57129— " "	8 48	
57028— " "	4 08	
57320— " "	1 42	
58275— " service balance	4 95	
59363— " "	25 65	
59545— " repairs	2 23	
59690— " service balance	25 65	
60325— " "	6 30	
60584— " "	3 15	
61805— " "	26 10	
61930— " repairs	1 57	
62913— " service balance	2 20	
63538— " "	6 75	
63784— " repairs	2 58	

$127 69

SOUTHERN RAILWAY COMPANY, WASHINGTON, D.C.

56545—Car repairs	$49 66	
56985— " "	2 74	
57264— " "	11 66	
58273— " service balance	90	
58421— " repairs	6 53	
59361— " service balance	13 50	
59543— " repairs	4 20	
59688— " service balance	52 15	
60051— " repairs	72	
60323— " service balance	18 90	
60582— " "	22 05	
61391— " repairs	10 44	
61882— " "	11 05	
61932— " "	3 56	
63786— " "	6 22	

$214 28

JOSEPH SEBREAU, NORTH BAY, ONT.

56565—Award W. C. B., *re* injuries alleged received $21 42

$21 42

ANTONIO SCHIARONE, NORTH BAY, ONT.

56591—Award W. C. B., *re* injuries alleged received $23 10

$23 10

R. SWAN, SPECIAL OFFICER, NORTH BAY, ONT.

56611—Travelling expenses	$37 65	
56883— "	33 80	
56976— "	32 95	
57887— "	32 10	
57942— "	32 65	
58789— "	35 35	
59348— "	31 25	
60282— "	38 15	
61863— "	41 75	
61867— "	33 25	
61356— "	37 10	
62513— "	41 20	
63090— "	40 30	

$467 50

SOUTHAM PRESS, LIMITED, TORONTO.

56613—Forms	$44 25
56755—Hat checks	20 00
57041—Folders, time tables, etc.	53 00
57191—Tickets	27 50
56696—Time tables	78 00
56728—Tariffs	23 25
56730—Tickets	13 35
57152—Tariffs	93 75
57154—Labels	25 00
57761—Tariffs	31 50
57763—Passes	22 50
58123—Tariffs	45 25
57772—Tariffs	49 75
58454—Tickets, passes, checks	107 35
58711—Tickets	36 20
59189—Tariffs	11 75
58916—Loc. freight tariff No. 80	11 00
59184—Baggage checks, duplex tickets	260 00
60071—Ticket tariffs	293 40
60073—Tariffs F. D. 162	54 00
59816—Supplement 4 to F. D. 127	6 50
60384—Tariffs, time tables, etc.	115 00
60390—Time table	99 00
61433—Tariffs F. D. No. 170	8 00
61298—Circulars	12 00
62302—Tickets	170 14
62537—Checks, cards	44 76
63067—Tickets	13 22
63175—Tariffs, etc.	46 50
62542—Copies embargo notices, etc.	98 00
62734—Copies folders and time tables	54 75
63020—Cards	33 00
63022—Forms, books, tickets	99 85
63340—Forms, etc.	133 81
63666—Circulars No. 108	3 75

$2,239 08

THE SOCIETY OF RAILWAY FINANCIAL OFFICERS, RIVERSIDE, ILL.

56639—Annual dues, 1915-1916	$10 00
59759—Annual dues, 1916-1917	10 00

$20 00

SAUNDERS & PETCHERSKY, TIMMINS, ONT.

56671—Claim No. 10293—Damage to flour by wet	$35 49

$35 49

SWIFT CANADIAN COMPANY, LIMITED, TORONTO.

56673—Claim No.	10428—Realized on damaged meat	$7 00
57385— "	10248—Loss account, shortage, 1 basket bacon	9 75
58834— "	10866—Loss account, shortage, sausage	2 31
62603— "	12216—Loss, meat by deterioration in transit.	11 98

$31 04

SHEET METAL PRODUCTS CO. OF CANADA, LIMITED, TORONTO.

56707—Stove pipes	$7 43
56915—Oil cans, shovels, etc.	26 98
56556—Gal. iron	56 49
57006—Pails and iron	32 10
57519—Stove pipes and elbows, sheet metal	26 57
57609—Iron and pails	31 84
57689—Rivets and iron	74 27
57670—Oilers and can screws	1 44
57816—Iron, plates and oil cans	81 84
58583—Pails and plate	18 85
58759—Cups	4 28
59061—Apollo, iron	42 03
58672—Screws, pipes, elbows, etc.	39 36
58718—Wash basins, etc.	8 87
58888—Iron, etc.	79 07
60075—Oil cans, shovels, dampers, etc.	71 46
60653—Measures, funnels	2 37
60326—Canada plate, pails	61 98
61035—Pipes, elbows	22 49
61536—Cups	8 91
62231—Pails, hods	59 58
62379—Iron, elbows	69 37
62431—Plate, cans, etc.	55 99
63198—Iron	10 54

$894 11

THE STEEL COMPANY OF CANADA, LIMITED, HAMILTON, ONT.

56709—Bolts, nuts, screws, etc.	$480 26
56917—Tacks, etc.	6 86
57221—Tacks and iron	72 44
57223—Iron and steel plates	173 43
57000—Rivets, nuts, bolts, screws	343 47
57532—Common iron	29 40
57534—Iron and steel	257 38
57515—Washers	20 14
57517—Rivets, nuts, tacks	152 80
57611—Bolts	58 64
57691—Washers	12 14
57951—Bolts and screws	213 09
57971—Bolts, nuts and steel	138 39
57666—Nuts, rivets, nails, screws and tacks	240 96
57820—Washers	22 86
57822—Bolts, screws, nails, washers and tacks	394 34
58450—Iron and steel	37 57
58452—Iron, steel, bolts, nuts, rivets	421 52
58577—Nuts, rivets and tacks	23 74
58761—Nuts, rivets and tacks	463 29
59067—Iron	11 85
59105—Iron, nuts, rivets, spikes	1,255 43
58668—Iron, nuts, rivets, bolts	197 31
58674—Screws, nuts, rivets, bolts	257 03
58720—Screws, bolts	42 28

THE STEEL COMPANY OF CANADA, LIMITED, ETC.—*Continued.*

58722—Rivets	27 15
58770—Spikes, bolts, etc.	1,169 45
58892—Machine bolts	163 25
59188—Steel bolts, nuts, etc.	2,322 70
59214—Iron and steel	402 71
59687—Washers, nuts and bolts	31 06
59689—Rivets, nuts, etc.	50 63
59719—Screws, rivets	190 24
60665—Bars, steel	24 64
60671—Iron	154 91
60152—Nuts, rivets, screws	1,760 16
60156—Washers	40 03
60256—Rivets, nuts, bolts, etc.	718 59
60330—Iron	8 09
60662—Screws, rivets, spikes, etc.	890 83
60806—Iron	115 72
60995—Nuts	203 72
61031—Bolts, screws	186 90
61043—Iron, nuts, washers, etc.	79 97
61981—Steel, iron	291 90
61532—Iron	14 60
61534—Iron	4 90
61658—Steel bars	12 04
61766—Iron	27 35
61798—Bolts, screws and rivets	1,965 99
62435—Bolts, screws, nuts	528 40
62437—Nuts, washers	56 75
63047—Iron	139 13
63049—Bolts, spikes, nuts, etc.	1,651 32
62686—Nuts, iron, steel	35 23
63014—Iron	53 64
63202—Iron and tracks	13 63
63348—Steel	12 54
	$18,674 79

T. W. SQUIRE, TORONTO, ONT.

56753—Supplies for private car	$2 62
56853— " " " "	25 88
57043— " " " "	21 78
56734— " " " "	39 39
57212— " " " "	46 72
57920— " " " "	28 86
58531— " " " "	29 49
59488— " " " "	11 72
60008— " " " "	16 53
60026— " " " "	21 53
60997— " " " "	14 90
61078— " " " "	18 53
62297— " " " "	14 95
	$292 90

J. H. STILL MANUFACTURING CO., LTD., ST. THOMAS, ONT.

56913—Handles	$19 27
57528—Flag-staffs	2 10
57513—Handles	42 79
57640— "	17 23
57814— "	41 07
58670—Peavies	2 47
58894—Handles	16 44
59190—Flag-staffs	3 50
59685—Handles	153 48
59989—Handles	73 15
60657—Flag-staffs	3 50
60254—Handles	35 24
62229— "	23 16
62400— "	63 98
	$497 38

JAS. SINTON, ENGINEERING DEPT., NORTH BAY, ONT.

56933—Travelling expenses		$9 30
58647— " "		7 20
59352— " "		12 65
59835— " . "		18 60
60198—		14 00
61431—		20 35
61260—		5 60
62207—		21 50
62462—		10 05

$119 25

G. M. SIMPSON, LINEMAN, ENGLEHART, ONT.

57077—Travelling expenses		$8 80
56980— " "		8 05
57731— " "		3 65
58272— " "		12 05
58612—Disbursement account drill		75
58791—Travelling expenses		8 80
59647— " "		21 60

$63 70

N. J. SULLIVAN, LINEMAN, ELK LAKE, ONT.

57079—Travelling expenses		$18 50
56978— " "		1 40
58793— " "		31 40
59350—		3 35
59957—		12 85
60284— "		2 50
61545—		12 95
61406—		26 00
62631—		2 25
62788—		24 35

$135 55

J. STOCKDALE, NORTH BAY, ONT.

57297—Lot No. 73, North Bay Junction	$1,500 00

$1,500 00

STANDARD PLANING MILLS, LIMITED, NORTH BAY, ONT.

57307—Picture moulding	$2 62
56812—Wood, building material, etc.	123 67
58125—Lumber, sash, doors and frames	45 05
58515— "	513 63
60651— "	408 99
60328—Lath	42 00
61983—Lumber, doors	671 12
61540—Wicket and grill, casings	35 00
62304—Lumber	123 27
62425—Frames, lumber, etc.	330 60
62539—Flooring, moulding, etc.	17 19
63018—Lumber	394 75
63344—Lumber	59 65

$2,767 54

W. J. STEVENSON, THORNLOE, ONT.

57309—Slabs	$84 00
60386—Slabs	120 00
61039—Lumber	120 00
61654—Slabs	168 00

$492 00

SMITH'S FALLS MALLEABLE CASTINGS CO., LIMITED, SMITH'S FALLS, ONT.

57311—Castings	$1 58	
57977— "	25 54	
59063— "	25 42	
60818—Express on patterns	70	
61538—Freight on patterns	40	
61772—Castings	22 19	
63045— "	3 99	
62664— "	51 01	
63336—	10 35	
		$141 18

WILLIAM SCULLY, MONTREAL, P.Q.

57313—Uniform caps	$4 50	
58464— " "	2 25	
59192— " "	76 25	
60812— " buttons	2 10	
63089— " buttons	70 10	
63132— " caps	60 75	
		$215 95

THE SAFETY CAR HEATING & LIGHTING CO., NEW YORK, N.Y.

57315—Lighting equipment	$1,468 00	
57530—Fittings	58 61	
57973—Fittings and mantles	146 10	
58456—Mantles and opal bowls	84 30	
60667—Brush, fasteners, etc.	218 85	
60822—Fuses, fuse holders	6 10	
61337—Mantles, etc.	117 00	
61979—Lamps, brackets	507 37	
62433—Lighting equipment	1,290 00	
63012—Keys, pulley, cover, etc.	126 56	
63318—Screws, lead, washers, etc.	22 26	
		$4,045 15

SCYTHES & COMPANY, LIMITED, TORONTO, ONT.

57317—Waste	$315 42	
56586—Duck	77 66	
57002—Duck	57 49	
57524—Waste	194 98	
57975—Waste	390 56	
58579—Duck	161 88	
59057—Waste	759 21	
58890—Duck	77 42	
59180—Waste	437 19	
60824— "	712 35	
61770— "	995 53	
63049— ..	232 85	
62666—	586 80	
63010— "	223 64	
63200—Duck	83 97	
		$5,306 95

J. STONÉ & COMPANY, LIMITED, DEPTFORD, LONDON, S.E., ENGLAND.

57437—Belting, etc.	$195 22	
56810—Belting, etc.	83 24	
58466—Dynamos and electrical goods	1,588 93	
58650—Tonum accumulators, etc.	1,482 81	
59182—Resistancé covers, springs	7 17	
60669—Ebonite sheets, floats, etc.	92 82	
60388—Ammeter repaired	6 85	

J. STONE & COMPANY, LIMITED, ETC.—*Continued.*

60816—Electrical supplies	....	219 43	
60920—Switchboard	....	23 54	
61033—Belting, side sheets	....	122 82	
61985—Repairing armature	....	30 15	
62784—Belt fasteners, etc.	....	152 12	
63016—Electrical fixtures	....	30 57	
63338—Belt fasteners, etc.	....	40 86	$4,076 53

T. M. STEPHENSON, TORONTO.

56698—Canadian Almanac	....	$1 00	$1 00

STODDART BROS., NORTH BAY, ONT.

56732—Supplies furnished private car	....	$17 93	
57765—Supplies furnished private car	....	16 54	$34 47

ST. LOUIS & SAN FRANCISCO RAILROAD CO., ST. LOUIS, MO.

56922—Car service balance	....	$5 30	
57318— " repairs	....	2 36	
58269— " service balance	....	12 10	
58423— " repairs	....	2 21	
58214— " service balance	....	12 60	
59359— " service balance	....	27 00	
59539— " repairs	....	1 96	
59362— " repairs	....	10 84	
59686— " service balance	....	28 80	
60095— " repairs	....	71	
60321— " service balance	....	35 50	
60580— " " "	....	27 45	
61803— " " "	....	6 45	
61114— " repairs	....	1 22	
61884— " repairs	....	1 14	
62911— " service balance	....	10 70	
63536— " service balance	....	6 15	$192 49

SOUTHERN PACIFIC COMPANY, PACIFIC SYSTEM, SAN FRANCISCO, CAL.

56924—Car service balance	....	$13 50	
57322— " repairs	....	1 88	
58271— " service balance	....	24 30	
58216— " " "	....	29 25	
59365— " " "	....	34 60	
59364— " repairs	....	52	
59692— " service balance	....	40 50	
60327— " " "	....	37 35	
60586— " " "	....	24 75	
61807— " " "	....	49 10	
61880— " repairs	....	2 31	
62200— " service balance	....	9 45	
62915— " " "	....	4 05	
63540— " " "	....	27 90	$299 46

ST. LOUIS, BROWNSVILLE & MEXICO RAILWAY COMPANY, KINGSVILLE, TEX.

56926—Car service balance	....	$8 10	
58279— " "	....	11 25	
58220— "	....	.6 75	
59369—	....	9 00	
59696— "	....	2 70	

St. Louis, Brownsville & Mexico Railway Company, Etc.—*Continued.*

60331—Car service balance	$9 45	
60333— "	3 60	
61811— · "	45	
		$51 30

Santa Fe Refrigerator Despatch Company, Topeka, Kan.

56928—Car service balance	$1 90	
58281— "	1 90	
59698— "	2 30	
60335—	21 63	
60588—	20 71	
61813—	3 79	
62917—	17 52	
63544—	10 20	
		$79 95

The James Smart Mfg. Co., Brockville, Limited, Brockville, Ont.

57004—Hammers	$3 43	
57521—Cylinders	36 69	
57818—Pressure plate	5 39	
58581—Tools	14 44	
58766—Hammers	15 22	
59683—Lawn mower	4 36	
59991—Hasps, staples, etc.	14 09	
61542—Wrenches	48 30	
61768—Copying presses, fulcrums, etc.	73 35	
62429—Hammers	3 67	
62402—Hinges, gate hooks, etc.	8 47	
		$227 41

Shurly-Dietrich Company, Limited, Galt, Ont.

57008—Saws	$6 85	
57668— "	8 08	
58714— "	32 34	
58768— "	3 80	
59128— "	16 50	
60661— " handles	17 50	
60808— "	8 48	
61257— "	9 10	
63051—	33 84	
		$136 49

Station List Publishing Company, St. Louis, Mo.

57144—Supplements to station lists	$1 19	
57759—Station lists	3 20	
58610—Supplements to station lists	1 31	
		$5 70

The Stratford Daily Herald, Stratford, Ont.

57148—Advertising	$0 50	
57723— "	1 00	
58576— "	50	
60749— "	3 00	
61259— "	1 10	
62298— "	1 09	
63668— "	1 12	
		$8 31

The Spectator Printing Co., Limited, Hamilton, Ont:

57150—Advertising	$20 00	
60028— "	2 46	
61132— "	2 52	
62540— " ·	2 52	
		$27 50

SOUTHERN CLASSIFICATION COMMITTEE, ATLANTA, GA.

57156—Supplements to tariffs	$0 66	
59605— " "	54	
60397— " "	23	
62301—Tariffs	42	
		$1 85

SWEDISH STEEL & IMPORTING CO., LIMITED, MONTREAL, QUE.

57526—Steel	$8 32	
57987— "	3 88	
59071— "	48 28	
60659—	56 83	
63130—	2 55	
		$119 86

SUNBEAM SPECIALTY COMPANY, LIMITED, TORONTO, ONT.

57511—Lanterns	$12 74	
58716— "	12 74	
58886— "	25 48	
		$50 96

STRATFORD DAILY & WEEKLY BEACON, STRATFORD, ONT.

57725—Advertising	$1 15	
58713— "	70	
59779— "	1 20	
60030— "	1 05	
61130— "	1 50	
62532— "	1 23	
		$6 83

SLAGHT & SLAGHT, HAILEYBURY, ONT.

57755—Donation to H. Robinson *re* cow alleged struck	$50 00	
		$50 00

SAMSON CORDAGE WORKS, BOSTON, MASS.

57969—Signal cords	$21 05	
60810—Signal cords	96 00	
		$117 05

JOHN B. SMITH & SONS, LIMITED, TORONTO, ONT.

57979—Lumber	$356 40	
63043—Lumber	38 85	
		$395 25

SHEA, SMITH & CO., CHICAGO, ILL.

57981—Books	$45 00	
58458—Memo tablets	3 87	
59059—Binding cases	30 75	
60655—Fillers	2 07	
61660—Waybill tissue	33 49	
		$115 18

THE STEEL EQUIPMENT COMPANY, LIMITED, PEMBROKE, ONT.

57983—Binding cases	$24 00	
60663—Binding cases	12 00	
61339—Transfer cases	25 50	
61656—Files, binding cases	24 00	
		$85 50

SUPERINTENDENT OF DOCUMENTS, WASHINGTON, D.C.

57985 —Report on deep waters $3 50

       $3 50

SCHUMACHER GOLD MINES, LIMITED, SCHUMACHER, ONT.

58077—Claim No. 10391—Loss account, damage furnace $30 00
60873—Claim No. 10176—Loss account, damage to machinery ..   12 85

       $42 85

SAN ANTONIO & ARANSAS PASS RAILWAY COMPANY, SAN ANTONIO, TEX.

58277—Car service balance $4 50
58218—"   " 9 45
63542— "   " 4 50

       $18 45

SANDY VALLEY & ELKHORN RAILWAY, BALTIMORE, MD.

58283—Car service balance $4 50
58222— "   " 13 05
59371— "   " 13 05
59700— "   " 12 15
60337— "   " 6 75
60590— "   "   90
61815— "   " 10 35
62204— "   "   45

       $61 20

SAN ANTONIO, UALDE & GULF RAILROAD COMPANY, ST. LOUIS, MO.

58419—Car repairs $0 98

       $0 98

SAMUEL STAYMAN, ENGLEHART P.O.

58463—Ties $275 85

       $275 85

RICHARD SOMERVILLE, NORTH BAY P.O.

58463—Ties $81 54

       $81 54

CHAS. P. SCOTT, NELLIE LAKE P.O., ONT.

57674—1.24 acres of land $60 00

       $60 00

MRS. AMBROSE SMALL, 208TH IRISH FUSILIERS BATTALION, TORONTO.

57682—Advertising in programme $25 00

       $25 00

M. SILVERSTONE, COCHRANE, ONT.

58026—Claim No. 10572—Loss account, damage to shoes $48 97

       $48 97

SAN PEDRO, LOS ANGELES & SALT LAKE RAILROAD COMPANY, LOS ANGELES, CAL.

58224—Car service balance $0 90
59373—Car service balance 1 80
59744—Ticket balance   82
60060—Car repairs   34
62919— "   service balance 7 20
63546— "   "   90

       $11 96

SWIFT REFRIGERATOR TRANSPORTATION COMPANY, CHICAGO, ILL.

58226—Car service balance	$2 56	
59375— " "	3 83	
59702— " "	10 60	
60339— " "	4 90	
59854— " repairs	12	
60592— " service balance	1 93	
61817— " "	5 80	
62921— " "	3 87	
		$33 61

W. C. STAHLE COMPANY, PITTSBURG, PA.

58460—Computing tables	$5 17	
59196—Computing tables	5 17	
		$10 84

STOWELL MANUFACTURING & FOUNDRY COMPANY, SOUTH MILWAUKEE, WIS.

58462—Door hangers	$15 00	
		$15 00

EDWARD SOWBY, CANE P.O.

58593—Ties	$89 60	
59754—Ties	49 90	
		$139 50

SKINNER CHUCK COMPANY, NEW BRITAIN, CONN.

58625—Universal chuck and face plate	$49 20	
		$49 20

MESSRS. SULLIVAN & SHILLINGTON, COBALT, ONT.

58899—Claim No. 10672—Overcharge, weight apples	$12 38	
		$12 38

SMITH, FASSETT & COMPANY, CHARLTON, ONT.

58985—Claim No. 10985—Refund, demurrage charges	$1 00	
		$1 00

STANDARD CHEMICAL IRON & LUMBER COMPANY OF CANADA, LIMITED, TORONTO, ONT.

59065—Shellac spirits	$39 20	
63346— " and barrel	39 97	
		$79 17

THE STEVENSON BOILER & ENGINE WORKS, PETROLIA, ONT.

59069—Chemical bottles	$12 00	
63061—Cages and stoppers	10 20	
		$22 20

ST. JOSEPH & GRAND ISLAND RAILROAD COMPANY, ST. JOSEPH, MO.

59367—Car service balance	$5 85	
59694— " "	90	
60329— " "	3 60	
61809— " "	2 70	
62202— " "	5 85	
		$18 90

ST. LOUIS SOUTHWESTERN RAILWAY COMPANY OF TEXAS, TYLER, TEXAS.

59541—Car repairs	$1 54	
59316— " "	2 19	
		$3 73

STANDARD STEEL WORKS COMPANY, PHILADELPHIA, PA.

58652—Tires	$556 47	
		$556 47

STEEL & RADIATION, LIMITED, TORONTO, ONT.

58896—Grates	$5 85	
62427—Steel sash	1,269 15	
		$1,275 00

THE SMART-TURNER MACHINE COMPANY, LIMITED, HAMILTON, ONT.

59194—Cylinder levers for duplex pump	$42 00	
60719—Pump parts	72 66	
		$114 66

SENECA COAL MINING COMPANY, BUFFALO, N.Y.

59382—Coal	$1,742 89	
60858— "	41 55	
		$1,784 44

A. SHAHEN, GOWGANDA, ONT.

59416—Claim No. 10897—loss box junk destroyed by fire	$23 10	
		$23 10

GEORGE SASSEVILLE, WIDDIFIELD, ONT.

59420—Claim No. 10873—loss account, cowhide destroyed by fire	$8 80	
		$8 80

R. H. SLIPP, TROCHU, ALTA.

59512—Claim No. 11269—loss account, baggage destroyed by fire.	$100 00	
		$100 00

SPOKANE, PORTLAND & SEATTLE RAILWAY COMPANY, PORTLAND, ORE.

59742—Ticket balance	$0 87	
		$0 87

A. SKJONSBYE, SESEKINIKA P.O.

59754—Ties	$109 41	
		$109 41

THOS. M. SALE, STORES DEPT., NORTH BAY, ONT.

59769—Travelling expenses	$14 30	
60200— " "	25 40	
61081— " "	21 00	
		$60 70

ST. LOUIS SOUTHWESTERN RAILWAY COMPANY, ST. LOUIS, MO.

59923—Car repairs	$0 31	
		$0 31

A. W. SKINNER, ENGLEHART, ONT.

60097—Load straw and bags	$2 65	
		$2 65

ARTHUR STEVENS, ENGLEHART, ONT.

60395—Lunches to passengers, Train No. 1	$3 50	
63203—Claim No. 11807—alleged loss three gals. orangeade	8 38	
62572— " No. 11911—loss cigarettes	52	
		$12 40

SUDBURY STAR PUBLISHERS, LIMITED, SUDBURY, ONT.

60435—Advertising	$4 05	
		$4 05

STEPHENSON & SON, "NEW LISKEARD SPEAKER," NEW LISKEARD, ONT.

60747—Advertising	$4 00	
61255— "	4 70	
61134— "	4 80	
62732— "	25 80	
		$39 30

MARK SPENCE, WINNIPEG, MAN.

59838—Claim No. 11588—loss account, baggage destroyed by fire	$100 00	
		$100 00

HENRY SMITH, PORQUIS JUNCTION, ONT.

60064—Ties	$31 14	
		$31 14

G. G. SMITH, EARLTON, ONT.

60064—Ties	$117 72	
		$117 72

STAR GROCERY, NORTH BAY, ONT.

60076—Supplies, private car	$23 19	
		$23 19

SAFETY PRESS, NEW YORK, N.Y.

60814—Safety standards	$3 16	
		$3 16

STEELE, BRIGGS SEED COMPANY, LIMITED, TORONTO, ONT.

60820—Supplies	$4 50	
60922—Seeds	30 35	
		$34 85

ERNEST STRAND, BOURKES, ONT.

60795—Award, W. C. B., alleged accident	$550 00	
		$550 00

MIKE SERUAK, GILLIES DEPOT, ONT.

60823—Award, W. C. B., partial payment re alleged injuries	$19 29	
61083— " " " "	7 50	
		$26 79

22 T R

JOSEPH STARK, NORTH BAY, ONT.

60833—Award, W. C. B., partial payment *re* alleged injuries....	$18 26	
60971— " " " " ...	18 26	
61052— " " " "	16 74	
62786— final ·· ··	200 00	
		$253 26

P. SEDUCKO, NORTH BAY, ONT.

61085—Unclaimed wages	$4 60	
		$4 60

O. SCHAFFER, ST. PAUL, MINN.

61087—Tariffs	$1 00	
62299— "	1˙ 00	
		$2 00

STRONG DRUG COMPANY, LIMITED, HAILEYBURY, ONT.

61181—Claim No. 11573—loss account, wine in transit	$0 71	
63186—Claims Nos. 12979 and 12978—loss bottle wine broken in transit	1 42	
		$2 13

ANGUS SINCLAIR, C.E., TORONTO, ONT.

61341—Harness	$25 00	
63065—Carts	36 00	
		$61 00

MRS. C. R. SELLAR, COBALT, ONT.

61497—Claim No. 10912—loss account, damage to tea	$1 90	
		$1 90

W. SWITZER (RELIEVING SUPERVISOR), NORTH BAY, ONT.

61547—Travelling expenses	$11 45	
61262— " "	6 10	
62341— " "	5 15	
		$22 70

M. SITEMAN, COBALT, ONT.

61639—Claim No. 11472—loss gallon lemonade	˙$2 00	
		$2 00

MRS. J. H. SUMBLER, COBALT, ONT.

61641—Claim No. 12027—damage to umbrellas	$0 50	
		$0 50

CHAS. R. SCOTT, ENGINEERING DEPT., NORTH BAY, ONT.

61170—Travelling expenses	$6 90	
		$6 90

STENSON BROS., SOUTH PORCUPINE, ONT.

61824—Claim No. 12171—alleged loss, Scott's Emulsion.........	$1 80	
63694— " No. 12172—loss account, damage to barrel drugs ..	34 46	
		$36 26

W. J. STOTHERS, PORQUIS JUNCTION, ONT.

62541—Groceries, butter $14 30
$14 30

ALBERT SMITH PRINTING COMPANY, TORONTO, ONT.

62571—Statements, forms $29 50
$29 50

J. A. SIMMERS, LIMITED, TORONTO, ONT.

63063—Glass catcher $4 75
$4 75

THOMAS STEEL, NORTH BAY, ONT.

62404—Award, W. C. B., *re* alleged injuries $20 14
$20 14

SHANKMAN BROS., TIMMINS, ONT.

62912—Claim No. 12037—alleged loss two bottles syrup $0 60
$0 60

STANDARD SANITARY MANUFACTURING COMPANY, LIMITED, TORONTO, ONT.

63342—Sinks and traps $55 46
$55 46

MISS E. FITTENSOR, STENOGRAPHER, COBALT, ONT.

56469—Salary,	November, 1915	$65 00
56504— "	December, 1915	65 00
57453— "	January, 1916	65 00
57582— "	February, 1916	65 00
58473— "	March, 1916	65 00
58630— "	April, 1916	65 00
59619— "	May, 1916	65 00
59786— "	June, 1916	65 00
60803— "	July, 1916	65 00
61040— "	August, 1916	65 00
62131— "	September, 1916	65 00
62342— "	October, 1916	18 87

$733 87

MISS E. TITTENSOR, STENOGRAPHER, COBALT, ONT.

56479—Fee as Counsel,	November, 1915		$400 00
56514— " "	December, 1915		400 00
57463— " "	January, 1916		400 00
57592— " "	February, 1916		400 00
58483— " "	March, 1916		400 00
58640— " "	April, 1916		400 00
59627— " "	May, 1916		400 00
59798— " "	June, 1916		400 00
60815— " "	July, 1916		400 00
61036— " "	August, 1916		400 00
62127— " "	September, 1916		400 00
62338— " "	October, 1916		400 00

$4,800 00

TORONTO, HAMILTON & BUFFALO RAILWAY COMPANY, DETROIT, MICH.

56547—Car repairs $8 55
56954—Ticket balance 10 95
57328—Car repairs 1 85
58333—Ticket balance 4 48

TORONTO, HAMILTON & BUFFALO RAILWAY COMPANY, ETC.—*Continued.*

59421—Ticket balance	6 58	
59549—Car repairs	1 60	
59746—Ticket balance	3 30	
60053—Car repairs	2 08	
60387—Ticket balance	3 44	
60632— " "	2 20	
61847— " "	2 20	
61888—Car repairs	3 01	
62963—Ticket balance	3 51	
63578— " "	3 85	
63788—Car repairs	11 09	
		$68 69

THE TOLEDO & OHIO CENTRAL RAILWAY COMPANY, CLEVELAND, OHIO.

56549—Car repairs	$2 05	
57324— " "	42	
59547— " "	42	
58958—Car service balance	7 20	
		$10 09

TOWN OF COBALT, COBALT, ONT.

56583—Grant towards general purposes of town	$1,200 00	
		$1,200 00

THE TREASURER OF ONTARIO, TORONTO, ONT.

56589—Account fire ranging	$7,909 50	
57643— " fire ranging	5,000 00	
58129— " land required for piling ground purposes	2 00	
58509— " fire ranging	1,464 50	
58676— " " "	5,000 00	
60099— " " "	5,000 00	
61172— " " "	5,000 00	
62438—Proceeds from operation	1,000,000 00	
		$1,029,376 00

TOUGH-OAKES GOLD MINES, LIMITED, SWASTIKA, ONT.

56675—Claim No. 10088, carboy acid broken in transit	$6 02	
58715—Coal	340 75	
61185—Claim No. 11813, damage to slate	12 50	
		$359 27

THE TORONTO ELECTRIC LIGHT COMPANY, LIMITED, TORONTO, ONT.

56757—Current supplied	$5 06	
56704— " "	7 86	
58345— " "	7 82	
57854— " "	4 82	
59107— " "	3 29	
59084— " "	3 02	
59867— " "	2 20	
60170— " "	1 96	
61089— " "	1 92	
61152— " "	3 02	
62694— " "	2 60	
		$43 57

TIME-TABLE DISTRIBUTING CO. OF CANADA, ST. JOHN, N.B.

56759—Distributing time-tables	$15 00	
57767— " "	15 00	
57950— " "	15 00	
58920— "	15 00	

TIME-TABLE DISTRIBUTING CO. OF CANADA, ETC.—*Continued.*

59078—Distributing time-tables	....	$31 27	
60013— " "	....	15 00	
60010— " "	....	15 00	
61153— "	....	15 00	
62308— "	....	15 00	
62493— ::	....	15 00	
62738—	....	15 00	
			$181 27

TEMISKAMING & NORTHERN ONTARIO RAILWAY AGENT, ENGLEHART, ONT.

56761—Clearance of outstanding	$0 50	
57112—Claim No. 9822, outstanding	35	
57769—Expenses re lecture on explosives	31 75	
59398—Claim No. 10683, outstanding	35	
62307—Board and lodging, freight shed employees	15 45	
		$48 40

TEMISKAMING TELEPHONE CO., LIMITED, NEW LISKEARD, ONT.

56785—Telephone rental	$28 50	
56702—Telephone rental	5 00	
57991—Wire	66 28	
58453—Telephone rentals	28 50	
57776— " "	35 00	
59607— " "	17 50	
58922— " "	22 50	
59761— " "	25 00	
60401— " "	39 00	
60907— " "	28 50	
60909— " "	35 00	
61174— " "	15 00	
61386— " "	17 50	
63024— " "	15 00	
63138— " "	28 50	
63168— " "	22 50	
		$429 28

TUDHOPE LUMBER COMPANY, ELK LAKE, ONT.

56787—Wood supplied agent	$7 50	
57321—Lumber	205 96	
57010— "	429 84	
58627— "	429 98	
61610— "	80 64	
63370—Ties	179 18	
		$1,333 10

P. TAUPIN, LINEMAN, NORTH BAY, ONT.

61549—Expenses, travelling	$1 35	
		$1 35

TRANS-CONTINENTAL FREIGHT BUREAU, CHICAGO, ILL.

56855—Tariffs supplied	$1 83	
57158— " "	2 18	
57778— " "	1 08	
58580— " "	3 49	
58950— " "	1 66	
59943— " "	1 27	
60399— " "	1 52	
59818— " "	3 02	
61093— " "	4 34	
62303— " "	3 20	
62740—Supplements supplied	3 19	
		$26 78

TEMISKAMING & NORTHERN ONTARIO RY. TELEGRAPH, NORTH BAY, ONT.

56857—Telegraph service		$1 77
57160—	" "	88
57216—	" "	3 37
57780—	" "	1 50
57944—	" "	3 02
58582—	" "	2 97
58767—	" "	2 96
59463—	" "	32
59609—	" "	72
59490—	" "	21
59778—	" "	26
60670—	" "	64
61008—	" "	79
62029—	" "	33
61462—	" "	33
62310—	" "	48
62546—	" "	28
63350—	" "	35

$31 18

TOWN OF ENGLEHART, ENGLEHART, ONT.

56927—Donation towards installation of sewage and waterworks
plant $1,318 54

$1,318 54

TORONTO SANITARY TOWEL SUPPLY CO., TORONTO, ONT.

57045—Rent of towel supply		$1 00
56706—	" " " "	1 00
57948—	" " " "	1 00
59320—	" " " "	3 00
60015—	" " " "	1 00
60260—	" " " "	1 00
61091—	" " " "	1 00
61300—	" " " "	1 00
62439—	" " " "	2 65
62742—	" " " "	4 80

$17 45

TEMISKAMING & NORTHERN ONTARIO RY. AGENT, NEW LISKEARD, ONT.

57047—Supplies for private car $1 43
61216—Disbursements *re* bush fires 68 40
57864—Transportation issued account alleged fatal injuries, brakeman 40 65

$110 48

TERMINAL RAILROAD ASSOCIATION OF ST. LOUIS, ST. LOUIS, MO.

57131—Car repairs		$1 40
58425—	" "	1 29
59366—	" "	4 11
59704—	" service balance	2 70
60437—	" repairs	2 68
61317—	" "	4 11
61886—	" "	5 09
63640—	" "	2 37

$23 75

J. J. TAYLOR, LIMITED, TORONTO.

57319—Repairing key $0 50
63071—Safe 185 00

$185 50

JAS. R. TODD, SCHUMACHER, ONT.

57387—Claim No. 10442, loss turps. account damage to container.. $4 80

$4 80

TRAFFIC SERVICE BUREAU, CHICAGO, ILL.

61561—Subscription $10 00

$10 00

TEMISKAMING & NORTHERN ONTARIO RAILWAY, AGENT, DIVER, ONT.

57391—Claim No. 8646—Outstanding account, shipment short .. $3 50

$3 50

TEMISKAMING & NORTHERN ONTARIO RAILWAY, AGENT, HEASLIP, ONT.

57395—Claim No. 10476—Outstanding account, shortage, barrel
apples $0 84

$0 84

CORPORATION OF THE TOWN OF NORTH BAY, NORTH BAY, ONT.

56607—Water supplied		$12 75
57435—	"	211 75
57574—	"	305 83
57717—	"	12 75
58445—		268 10
58608—		284 48
59183—		345 87
58740—	"	12 75
59484—	"	248 64
60745—		331 66
60958—		281 75
62023—	"	221 48
61126—		12 75
62294—	"	346 36
63167—		204 82
63330—	"	269 57

$3,371 31

TEMISKAMING & NORTHERN ONTARIO RAILWAY (OPERATION), TORONTO, ONT.

57439—Potatoes				$35 00
57026—Claim No. 9344—Undercharge, weight woodpulp				32
57066—Claim No. 10251—Undercharge, weight on gold ore				2 56
57214—Stove pipe				2 40
57536—Pickles				13 23
58085—Claim No. 7899—Undercharge on cheese box stock				3 52
59028—Claim No. 9344—Undercharge, wood pulp				1 37
59414—Claim No. 10296—Undercharge, passenger rate				10
59797a—	"	10457	" silver ore	1 15
59807—	"	10784	" silver ore	11 31
60447—	"	11024	" lumber	1 10
60853—	"	10304	" pulpwood	50
60875—	"	6483	" pork	15 78
61515—	"	11467	" H. H. goods	1 39
62605—	"	12375	" lumber	2 14
62651—	"	12413—Outstanding		1 20
62767—	"	12222—Undercharge, paint		19
63075—Oil, iron, steel from lockup				147 18
63136—Potatoes				7 00
63242—Claim No. 12709—Outstanding				1 77
63246—	"	12769	"	1 51
63250—	"	10632—Undercharge, pulpwood		31 65
63362—Potatoes				47 58
63460—Claim No. 12780—Loss, coal in transit				33 25
63700—	"	12394—Outstanding		1 20
63704—	"	12397	"	38

TEMISKAMING & NORTHERN ONTARIO RAILWAY, ETC.—*Continued.*

63712—Claim No. 12396—Outstanding	$0 35	
63716— " 12856 "	2 80	
63720— " 12398 "	1 01	
		$368 94

TEMISKAMING & NORTHERN ONTARIO RAILWAY, AGENT, NORTH COBALT.

57086—Claim No. 10413—Outstanding account, undercharge on shipment cucumbers	$0 69	
61513— " 11912—Outstanding	84	
		$1 53

TOWN OF COCHRANE, COCHRANE, ONT.

56534—Taxes on lot No. 206	$64 10	
56542—Taxes on lot No. 269	$7 41	
57836—Water supplied	36 96	
		$188 47

THE TORONTO WORLD, TORONTO, ONT.

56708—Subscription	$3 00	
58459—Advertising demonstration car	9 00	
		$12 00

TOLEDO, ST. LOUIS & WESTERN RAILROAD, TOLEDO, O.

56930—Car service balance	$14 40	
58287— " "	6 30	
58230— " "	5 80	
59377— " "	2 70	
59370— " repairs	4 66	
59708— " service balance	4 50	
60343— " "	8 55	
59980— " repairs	71	
61821— " service balance	8 55	
61849—Ticket balance	1 79	
62206—Car service balance	8 55	
63550— " "	5 40	
		$71 91

TRAVELERS INSURANCE COMPANY, HARTFORD, CONN.

56956—Ticket balance	$3 44	
58335— "	96	
58264— "	69	
59423— "	1 93	
59748— "	1 24	
60389— "	1 72	
60634— "	1 38	
62234— "	49	
62961— "	2 34	
		$14 19

GEORGE TAYLOR HARDWARE CO., LIMITED, COBALT, ONT.

57070—Claim No. 10558—Overcharge, rate on steel rails	$127 21	
57946—Galv. casing and iron pipe, etc.	16 45	
58028—Claim No. 10789—Loss account, damage to wheel	10 35	
58836— " 10972—Loss account, damage to stove	3 56	
59908— " 10848—Damage, closet bowl	4 30	
60951— " 10847—Damage, cook stove	5 95	
61645— " 12138—Loss, churn lid	1 28	
61885— " 12039—Loss, stone	6 95	
61320— " 11806—Loss, acid	8 93	
62321— " 12443—Damage, cauldron	3 70	

GEORGE TAYLOR HARDWARE COMPANY, LIMITED, ETC.—*Continued.*

62495—Fire clay, glasses and gauges	7 03	
63188—Claim No. 12706 and 12707—Damage, hardware	68 49	
63726—Claim No. 12697—Loss, acid	12 54	
		$276 74

TEMISKAMING & NORTHERN ONTARIO RAILWAY, AGENT, TEMAGAMI, ONT.

57116—Claim No. 10545—Outstanding	$1 60	
60877— " 6483 "	145 55	
		$147 15

THE TOWN OF CHARLTON, CHARLTON, ONT.

57134—Lighting street, rear station	$14 50	
		$14 50

THE THOMAS COMPANY, NORTH BAY, ONT.

57146—Repairing clocks	$10 50	
57538—Clocks	5 50	
58578—Repairs to air brake clock	2 00	
61460— " clock at Latchford	5 00	
62544— " clock	9 50	
		$32 50

TEXAS & NEW ORLEANS RAILROAD COMPANY, HOUSTON, TEXAS.

57326—Car repairs	$0 33	
		$0 33

TALLMAN BRASS & METAL COMPANY, HAMILTON, ONT.

57540—Brass rod	$27 22	
58127—Brass and copper	31 13	
58468—Copper	30 10	
59075—Copper tubes	23 82	
59198—Brass and copper rods	61 83	
60830—Brass rod	51 13	
61546—Brass and copper	11 40	
61774—Brass rod	4 08	
63142—Copper tube	8 93	
		$249 64

JOHN TAYLOR & CO., LIMITED, TORONTO, ONT.

57542—Soap	$22 00	
57989— "	52 50	
59113— "	49 70	
59206— "	37 30	
60675— "	13 50	
60826— "	30 50	
61544— "	42 90	
63069— "	66 61	
		$315 01

TAYLOR & ARNOLD, LIMITED, MONTREAL, P.Q.

57544—Lock blocks	$49 80	
59115—Knuckles, lock blocks, etc.	71 10	
59204—Lock blocks	13 50	
60721—Lock blocks	52 50	
60828—Knuckles, lock blocks	48 00	
61989—Glasses and gaskets	7 92	
63073—Lock blocks, knuckles	44 50	
		$287 32

TORONTO & YORK COUNTY PATRIOTIC FUND ASSOCIATION, TORONTO, ONT.

57583—Donation $5,000 00

                                                 $5,000 00

TEMISKAMING & NORTHERN ONTARIO RAILWAY, AGENT, NORTH BAY, ONT.

58059—Claim No.	10067—Outstanding			$0 76
59386—	"	10871	"	35
59402—	"	10815	"	40
59408—	"	10814	"	40
59422—	"	10873	"	35
59426—	"	10872	"	2 70
60947—	"	11212	"	8 39
61183—	"	10225	"	4 00
61511—	"	11721	"	86
61631—	"	12215 & 10893."		7 71
61883—	"	10371	"	14 16
61444—	"	11840	"	51
62062—	"	10910	"	15 61
62759—	"	12622 & 12621 "		42
63205—	"	12764	"	46
63240—	"	11886	"	106 10
57397—	"	10536 & 10520 "		4 80
57114—	"	10594, 10488 and 10537—Outstanding		8 66

                                                 $176 64

TEMISKAMING & NORTHERN ONTARIO RAILWAY, AGENT, COCHRANE, ONT.

56789—One drawer lock			$0 65
57110—Claim No.	9862—Overcharge, weight apples		15 84
58063—	"	10552—Shortage on shipment	5 70
58079—	"	10652 and 10716—Shortage on shipment	1 12
59017—	"	10678—Outstanding	5 00
58842—	"	10798—	3 36
58954—Express charges on typewriter			1 10
61505—Claim No.	7933—Outstanding		4 30
63105—	"	11853 "	96
62998—	"	12624 "	2 13
63182—	"	12580 "	9 36
63190—	"	12707 "	2 00
63676—	"	12719 "	1 86
63696—	"	12471 "	38
63724—	"	12161 "	5 80

                                                 $59 56

TEMISKAMING & NORTHERN ONTARIO RAILWAY, AGENT, SOUTH PORCUPINE, ONT.

58081—Claim No.	10345—Outstanding account, shipment short ..		$4 27
58844—	"	11014 and 10682—Outstanding	2 96
59910—	"	11382—Outstanding	10 00

                                                 $17 23

THE TEMISKAMING & NORTHERN ONTARIO RAILWAY AGENT, THORNLOE, ONT.

58083—Claim No. 10314—outstanding account, damage to H.H.
         goods $10 00

                                                 $10 00

J. G. TURNEY, WAHTAYBEAG, ONT.

58113—Donation account, pulpwood alleged destroyed $30 00

                                                 $30 00

TEMISKAMING & NORTHERN ONTARIO RAILWAY AGENT, COBALT, ONT.

57389—Claims Nos. 10324 and 5861—outstanding	$198 40
57108—Claim No. 10575—outstanding	3 ·15
58131—Board of Trade dues—D. Hway.	5 00
57774—Water rates—Cobalt Water Commission	18 00
58790—Claim No. 11028—outstanding	2 00
58792— " No. 10073— "	1 41
58860—Water rates, Cobalt Water Commission	18 00
59912—Claim No. 11410—outstanding	2 00
60895—Water rates, Cobalt Water Commission	18 00
61507—Claim No. 10777—outstanding	1 65
61214—Disbursements *re* bush fires	6 00
61322—Claim No. 10482—outstanding	76
61358—Inspection scales	3 00
61420—Claim No. 12377—outstanding	1 00
61826— " No. 11712— "	46
62306—Copies by-law	1 50
62548—Water rates, Cobalt Water Commission	18 00
62736—Travelling expenses	5 60
59073—Typewriter ribbons, *Cobalt Telegraph*	1 50
	$305 43

TOLEDO, PEORIA & WESTERN RAILWAY COMPANY, PEORIA, ILL.

58285—Car service balance	$6 30
58228— " "	15 75
59706— " "	10 80
60341— "	8 55
60594— "	8 10
61819— "	1 80
63548— "	45
	$51 75

THE TEXAS & PACIFIC RAILWAY COMPANY, DALLAS, TEXAS.

58427—Car repairs	$3 24
59551— " "	3 42
59246— " "	84
60345— " service balance	1 35
60596— " "	9 00
61823— " "	90
62208— " "	11 70
62923— "	4 95
	$35 40

TEMISKAMING & NORTHERN ONTARIO RAILWAY AGENT, HAILEYBURY, ONT.

57852—Phone rental (Tem. Telephone Company)	$15 00
61509—Claim No. 11964—outstanding	17 03
61376— " No. 12326— "	4 58
62576— " No. 12423— "	4 80
63192— " No. 12379— "	84
	$42 25

TEMISKAMING & NORTHERN ONTARIO RAILWAY AGENT, PORQUIS JUNCTION, ONT.

58030—Claim No. 10833—outstanding, demurrage, 2 cars pulpwood	$16 00
59021— " No. 10525—outstanding	1 88
	$17 88

TORONTO DISINFECTANT COMPANY, TORONTO, ONT.

58356—Carbolacene	$30 10
58717— " and blockettes	47 80

TORONTO DISINFECTANT COMPANY, TORONTO, ONT.—*Continued.*

58898—Blockettes	17 00	
60017—Carbolacene	37 41	
60462— "	37 41	
61718— "	37 41	
62619— "	38 28	
62876— "	38 28	
		$283 69

MRS. NELLIE E. TAYLOR, COCHRANE, ONT.

58525—Award, W. C. B., *re* alleged injuries, F. H. Taylor......	$63 14	
58724— " " " " "	30 00	
59631— " " " " "	30 00	
59834— " " " " "	30 00	
60843— " " " " "	30 00	
61072— " " " " "	30 00	
62173— " " " " "	30 00	
62348— " " " " "	30 00	
		$273 14

THORPE BROS., NEW LISKEARD, ONT.

58527—Services *re* injuries to F. H. Taylor	$59 22	
58987—Claims Nos. 10963, 4, 5, 1 and 2—damage to furniture....	2 50	
58692—Service *re* injuries to F. H. Taylor	40 78	
59418—Claim No. 10999—damage to bookcase	50	
59904— " No. 11161—damage to chairs	25	
61499—Claims Nos. 11174, 11540—damage to chairs	6 65	
61324—Claim No. 12232—damage to china cabinet	75	
61448— " No. 12245—damage to chairs	50	
61828—Claims Nos. 12275 and 12243—damage to furniture......	11 15	
62060—Claims Nos. 12242 and 12417—damage to furniture.......	1 75	
		$124 05

CHAS. TAYLOR, CACHE BAY, ONT.

58529—Services *re* alleged injuries to F. H. Taylor	$4 74	
		$4 74

THE THIEL DETECTIVE SERVICE COMPANY OF CANADA, LIMITED, TORONTO, ONT.

58959—Services and expenses of operatives	$240 22	
58918— " " "	212 65	
59781— " " "	233 15	
60258— " " "	221 65	
61435— " " "	185 40	
		$1,093 07

TEMISKAMING & NORTHERN ONTARIO RAILWAY AGENT, DANE, ONT.

59019—Claim No. 10719—outstanding account, shipment short...	$0 35	
		$0 35

J. J. TURNER & SONS, PETERBOROUGH, ONT.

59109—Tarpaulins	$67 20	
59200—Union Jack, tent	29 13	
60964— " sash cord	143 78	
61343—Pulley awning	95 55	
		$335 66

TAYLOR INSTRUMENT COMPANIES, ROCHESTER, N.Y.

59111—Thermometer	$5 53	
		$5 53

TEMISKAMING & NORTHERN ONTARIO RAILWAY AGENT, MATHESON, ONT.

59191—Water supplied		$5 00	
61426—Claim No. 12392—outstanding		47 00	
62587— " No. 12485— "		91 01	
62591— " No. 12470— "		309 08	
62611— " No. 12446— "		130 94	
62647— " No. 12327— "		64 15	
62657— " No. 12468— "		1 90	
63026— " No. 12705— "		1 34	
63194— " No. 12545— "		6 01	
			$656 43

TRINITY & BRAZOS VALLEY RAILWAY COMPANY, HOUSTON, TEX.

59379—Car service balance	$3 60	
		$3 60

A. C. TEED, McCOOL P.O., ONT.

59425—Ties	$72 94	
59754— "	40 40	
		$113 34

TOMSTOWN LUMBER COMPANY, TOMSTOWN P.O., ONT.

59425—Ties	$295 25	
60064— "	237 15	
		$532 40

TOWN OF TIMMINS, TIMMINS, ONT.

59465—Water supplied	$359 85	
60966— " "	188 85	
63177— " "	171 90	
57727— " "	220 35	
		$940 95

G. TANCREDI, M. P. DEPT., NORTH BAY, ONT.

58748—Travelling expenses	$8 55	
		$8 55

TRANSCONTINENTAL RAILWAY, MONCTON, N.B.

58858—Freight settlement	$207 91	
59750—Ticket balance	581 71	
		$789 62

TORONTO WEEKLY RAILWAY & STEAMBOAT GUIDE, LIMITED, TORONTO, ONT.

58952—Subscription	$2 60	
62381—Subscription	2 60	
		$5 20

TERRY & GORDON, TORONTO, ONT.

59132—Claim No. 10152—Overcharge, weight lumber	$61 90	
61268—Overpayment *re* siding at M. P. No. 12, Porcupine	5 56	
		$67 46

J. H. A. TAYLOR, NORTH BAY, ONT.

59202—Bread	$1 08	
62543—Bread	1 92	
		$3 00

Templeton, Kenly & Co., Limited, Toronto, Ont.

59208—Pawls, indicator, disk	$7 00	
60677—Handles	50	
		$7 50

Tremont & Gulf Railway Company, Winnfield, La.

59368—Car repairs	$1 40	
		$1 40

Transit Company, Limited, Toronto, Ont.

59710—Car service balance	$10 52	
60347— " "	5 69	
62210— " "	87	
		$17 08

Telegraph & Telephone Age, New York, N.Y.

59657—Subscription	$2 00	
		$2 00

Temiskaming & Northern Ontario Railway, Agent, Timmins, Ont.

59809—Claim No. 10137—Undercharge, weight, silver ore	$15 15	
62305—Duty paid on goods	1 50	
63822—Ice supplied	2 00	
56791—Board supplied relief staff	1 75	
57399—Claims No. 10353, 10491, 10549—Outstanding	332 31	
		$352 71

Tennessee Central Railroad Company, Nashville, Tenn.

59925—Repairs to cars	$2 14	
63790—Repairs to cars	46	
		$2 60

Toronto Salt Works, Toronto, Ont.

60673—Salt	$40 00	
61987—Salt	100 00	
		$140 00

G. S. Tatham, New Liskeard, Ont.

59906—Claim No. 11288—Loss account, damage to iron tonic ...	$2 03	
60869—Claim No. 11286—Damage to cough medicine	1 10	
		$3 13

Town of Latchford, Latchford, Ont.

59928—Donation—General purposes	$200 00	
		$200 00

Toledo Terminal Railroad Company, Toledo, Ohio.

59978—Car repairs	$0 54	
61393—Car repairs	2 72	
		$3 26

E. A. Tilley (M.M. Dept.), North Bay, Ont.

60202—Expenses, travelling	$1 00	
63352—Expenses, travelling	2 50	
		$3 50

Tuckett Tobacco Co., Limited, Hamilton, Ont.

60860—Stems	$10 00	
		$10 00

M. M. THIBEAULT, CHARLTON, ONT.

60949—Claim No. 11663—Damage to castings	$1 80	
		$1 80

WM. TAYLOR, EARLTON P.O., ONT.

61063—Ties	$187 41	
		$187 41

TIMES PRINTING COMPANY, HAMILTON, ONT.

61345—Forms	$31 75	
61599— "	11 25	
63077— "	61 25	
63134— "	38 70	
		$142 95

WM. L. TRACEY, NORTH BAY, ONT.

61551—Award W. C. B., re alleged injuries	$24 78	
		$24 78

TEMISKAMING L.O.L. No. 60, NEW LISKEARD, ONT.

62107—Commission on sales—"Excursion"	$105 05	
		$105 05

TORONTO DISTRICT LABOR COUNCIL, TORONTO, ONT.

61082—Advertising in "Official Labor Day Souvenir"	$15 00	
		$15 00

TEMISKAMING & NORTHERN ONTARIO RAILWAY, AGENT, IROQUOIS FALLS.

61442—Claim No. 12439—Outstanding account, shipment short..	$1 26	
63107—Claims Nos. 12101, 12090, 12093—Outstanding account, rate paper cores	11 07	
62574—Claim No. 12378—Outstanding account, shipment short ..	96	
		$13 29

TRACK NECESSITIES COMPANY, CHICAGO, ILL.

61776—Tongs	$9 25	
		$9 25

TEMISKAMING & NORTHERN ONTARIO RY. AGENT, SCHUMACHER.

62323—Claim No. 11806, outstanding account, carboy acid broken	$1. 71	
		$1 71

TORONTO CARPET CLEANING COMPANY, TORONTO, ONT.

62491—Rugs cleaned	$7 50	
		$7 50

TEMAGAMI STEAMBOAT & HOTEL COMPANY, TEMAGAMI, ONT.

62545—Groceries, fruit	$3 34	
		$3 34

TALLULAH FALLS RAILWAY, WASHINGTON, D.C.

62925—Car service balance	$0 90	
63552—Car service balance	2 25	
		$3 15

TEMISKAMING DISTRICT POULTRY ASSOCIATION, ENGLEHART, ONT.

62406—Donation *re* 5th annual show $5 00

$5 00

TEMISKAMING & NORTHERN ONTARIO RY. AGENT, WIDDIFIELD, ONT.

63140—Outstanding amount paid messenger calling steam shovel $1 00

$1 00

JAMES THOMPSON, OSSEO, ONT.

63370—Ties $144 21

$144 21

TEXAS MIDLAND RAILROAD, TERRELL, TEX.

63792—Car repairs $1 08

$1 08

UNION PACIFIC RAILROAD COMPANY, OMAHA, NEB.

56677—Claims	$5 86
56987—Car repairs	8 40
56934— " service balance	21 15
57120—Claims	12 96
57330—Car repairs	1 11
58291— " service balance	24 75
58429— " repairs	20
58234— " service balance	87 75
59381— " " "	150 75
59714— " " "	54 45
60351— " " "	68 85
59914—Claims	9 09
60600—Car service balance	44 55
61827—Car service balance	36 90
61326—Claims	3 20
61450—Claims	2 00
62214—Car service balance	48 60
62325—Claim	35 06
62497—Car repairs	9 95
62761—Claim	3 91
62927—Car service balance	34 65
63554—Car service balance	32 55

$696 69

UNITED STATES STEEL PRODUCTS CO., NEW YORK, N.Y.

56825—Steel channels	$11 97
60723—Beams, Z-Ees, channels, angles	89 60

$101 57

UNITED TYPEWRITER COMPANY, LIMITED, TORONTO, ONT.

57049—Inspection, rental of machine, etc.	$22 60
57323—Stencils, ribbons, note-books, etc.	36 44
57162—Type Bar and letter "E"	60
57546—Repairing machine, stencil paper, keys	23 95
57993—Typewriter and stationery	219 72
57856— " supplies and repairs	113 20
58470— " supplies	216 38
58879—Inspection and overhauling machines	28 05
59117—Stencil paper, ribbons	162 69
59467—Repairing typewriter	9 35
59210—Ribbons, stencil paper	91 67
60679—Typewriter repairs and supplies	180 17
60332—Note-books	3 50
60832—Typewriter, pencil sharpener	140 79

UNITED TYPEWRITER COMPANY, LIMITED, TORONTO, ONT.—*Continued.*

61347—Stationery	7 69	
61601—Extension phone rack and desk	36 50	
61991—Typewriter	115 42	
61662—Note-books and keys	7 60	
62713—Inspection of typewriters	18 00	
63079—Ribbons, repairs, etc.	6 19	
62360—Cleaning. repairs typewriter	8 35	
62550—Repairing, etc., typewriter	5 45	
62744—Desk basket, repairs to typewriter	13 10	
63144—Typewriter and supplies	127 67	
63354—Supplies	10 55	
		$1,605 63

UNION LUMBER CO., LIMITED, TORONTO, ONT.

57299—Claim No. 10312, overcharge in rate on spruce	$8 85	
61548—Lumber	423 22	
		$432 07

UNITED COAL SALES COMPANY, DETROIT, MICH.

57325—Smithing coal	$47 25	
58611— " "	203 50	
61037— " "	50 75	
		$301 50

UNION RAILROAD COMPANY, PITTSBURG, PA.

56932—Car service balance	$9 90	
58289— " " "	5 00	
58232— " " "	1 35	
59440— " repairs	11	
59712— " service balance	99 00	
60349— " " "	212 85	
60062— " repairs	57	
60598— " service balance	48 15	
60945—Claim No. 9751, outstanding weight silver ore	3 83	
61825— " service balance	69 75	
62008— " repairs	20	
62212— " service balance	9 45	
63178—Claim No. 12819, outstanding weight and rate silver ore..	39 55	
63692—Claim Nos. 12467, 11678, 12638, overcharge weight silver ore	39 59	
		$539 30

UNION TANK LINE, NEW YORK, N.Y.

56936—Car service balance	$14 98	
58293— " " "	1 62	
58236— " " "	1 60	
60353— " " "	1 60	
60602— " " "	5 34	
61829— " " "	7 59	
62216— " " "	3 44	
62929— " " "	8 14	
63556— " " "	6 11	
		$50 42

UNIVERSAL IRON & SUPPLY COMPANY, ST. LOUIS, MO.

57949—Chalk	$4 50	
59119—Chalk	4 50	
		$9 00

23 T R

UNION REFRIGERATOR TRANSIT COMPANY, MILWAUKEE, WIS.

59716—Car service balance	$1 54	
60604— " " "	3 87	
63560— " . " "	1 90	
		$7 31

THE UNION MEAT MARKET, SCHUMACHER, ONT.

60455—Claim No. 10818, loss account shortage one hog	$14 55	
		$14 55

DAVID UFLAND, ELK LAKE, ONT.

60206—Clearing station grounds, Elk Lake	$243 20	
62031— " " " "	243 20	
61222— " " " "	235 60	
62552— " " " "	135 52	
		$857 52

UNION CHURCH OF MATHESON, MATHESON, ONT.

61176—Donation to rebuild church	$50 00	
		$50 00

UNIVERSITY OF CHICAGO PRESS, CHICAGO, ILL.

61360—Journal, Political Economy	$0 38	
		$0 38

UNITED COAL SALES COMPANY, DETROIT, MICH.

61778—Coal	$51 63	
		$51 63

H. L. USBORNE, COBALT, ONT.

61830—Claim No. 11282, alleged loss drill steel	$40 56	
		$40 56

VAN TUYL & FAIRBANK, PETROLIA, ONT.

57225—Oil well cups	$8 00	
57995—Valves	50 00	
		$58 00

A. VANSTONE, M. M. DEPT., NORTH BAY, ONT.

56752—Expenses, travelling	$8 40	
		$8 40

VOLUNTEER FIRE DEPARTMENT, COBALT, ONT.

57724—Service *re* fire baggage car	$35 00	
		$35 00

VENDOME HOTEL COMPANY, LIMITED, HAILEYBURY, ONT.

58548—Board and lodging—engineering party	$18 00	
58794— " " "	6 00	
59492— " " "	12 50	
60968—	3 00	
61261—	7 00	
62499—	6 00	
		$52 50

Dr. E. G. VERNON, COCHRANE, ONT.

59032—Amount deducted from wages of S. Sotiroff, Section No. 38	$5 00	
59715—Professional services rendered *re* F. Cassi	20 00	
		$25 00

VERONA TOOL WORKS, PITTSBURG, PA.

60725—Lining and claw bars, spike mauls and wrenches......	$97 02	
63081—Chisels, gauges, etc.	79 81	
		$176 83

PETER VAHEY, NEW LISKEARD, ONT.

60817—Award, W. C. B., *re* alleged injuries	$10 53	
		$10 53

HENRY VERNON & SON, HAMILTON, ONT.

61084—North Bay Directory	$2 50	
61464—Copies North Bay Directory	5 00	
		$7 50

W. G. VERNER (RELIEVING FOREMAN), ENGLEHART, ONT.

62501—Expenses travelling	$18 20	
62446— " "	23 45	
		$41 65

HARRY VISSERING & COMPANY, CHICAGO, ILL.

62547—Bell ringers	$13 35	
		$13 35

VIRGINIA CAROLINA RAILWAY, ABINGDON, VA.

62931—Car service balance	$6 30	
		$6 30

VIRGINIA RAILWAY COMPANY, NORFOLK, VA.

62933—Car service balance	$3 60	
		$3 60

A. VALLEE, COCHRANE, ONT.

62578—Claim No. 12487—alleged loss shingles	$14 70	
		$14 70

VIRGINIA & SOUTHWESTERN RAILWAY COMPANY, BRISTOL, VA., TENN.

63558—Car service balance	$1 35	
		$1 35

JAMES B. WILLIS, TRAVELLING AUDITOR, NORTH BAY, ONT.

56455—Travelling expenses	$68 20
56889— " "	26 25
56632— " "	27 25
57563— " "	48 75
57712— " "	47 95
58683— " "	57 65
58750— " "	46 35
59959— " "	45 80
60286— " "	43 30

JAMES B. WILLIS, TRAVELLING AUDITOR, ETC.—*Continued.*

61861—Travelling expenses		$68 75
61408— " "		40 00
62241— " "		39 75
62466— " "		53 50
		$613 50

THE WESTERN MARYLAND RAILWAY COMPANY, BALTIMORE, MD.

56551—Car repairs		$8 49
56991— " "		5 35
56938— " service balance		90
58295— " "		9 90
58242— " "		18 45
59387— " "		6 30
59444— " repairs		5 33
59720— " service balance		90
60359— " "		9 45
61833— " "		45
61934— " repairs		1 89
		$67 41

THE WHEELING & LAKE ERIE RAILROAD COMPANY, CLEVELAND, OHIO.

56553—Car repairs		$14 49
58240— " service balance		9 45
59385— " "		1 35
59442— " repairs		92
60357— " service balance		11 25
59986— " repairs		55
61395— " "		5 80
61936— " "		14 54
		$58 35

THE WABASH RAILROAD COMPANY, ST. LOUIS, MO.

56631—Car repairs		$73 94
58461—Interline freight balance		95 29
58238—Car service balance		6 75
59383— " "		22 05
59481— " repairs		2 71
59553— " "		39 92
59718— " service balance		17 45
59811—Claim		13 20
60355—Car service balance		57 15
59982— " repairs		22 13
60606— " service balance		57 15
61321— " repairs		30 99
61831— " service balance		35 55
61116— " repairs		3 85
62010— " "		47 17
62947—Passenger car mileage		10 32
62580—Claim		4 05
63564—Car service balance		3 60
		$543 27

WASHINGTON SOUTHERN RAILWAY COMPANY, RICHMOND, VA.

56989—Car repairs		$15 70
58135— " "		57
59555— " "		2 58
59785— " "		2 64
59984— " "		39
61397— " "		1 23
63644— " "		27
		$23 38

WARWICK BROS. & RUTTER, LIMITED, TORONTO, ONT.

57327—Books	$34 50
57164—Journal	13 50
57554—Telegraph ledgers	19 00
57997—Receipt book	12 00
58472—Envelopes and pay cheques	105 00
58763—Pens	7 35
59218—Forms	50 00
60693— " envelopes	445 00
60336—Despatchers' books	21 00
61349—Stationery	77 50
61720—Forms	103 60
62441—Oil	2 20
63085—Forms, claims register, etc.	420 50
63146—Despatch trains order books	21 00

$1,332 15

WOOD, VALLANCE & COMPANY, HAMILTON, ONT.

57329—Nails	$4 12
57550—Augers	7 80
58003—Locks	6 15
60685—Pulleys	1 00
60840—Handles, springs, rakes, etc.	28 38
61041—Hooks and eyes, locks	19 21
59216—Steel spring wire	75
60338—Grain scoops	8 00
60970—Wood blocks	4 56
61355—School bells	32 10
61993—Shears, hose, rakes	16 85

$128 92

JACK WATSON & COMPANY, LIMITED, MONTREAL, QUE.

57331—Bluestone	$81 00
58480—Telegraph crystals	58 50
60729—Bluestone and cartage	144 40
61351— "	117 00
61550— " crystals	117 00
63087— "	47 25

$565 15

THE WHITMAN & BARNES MANUFACTURING CO., ST. CATHARINES, ONT.

57333—Drills	$31 38
58001—Wrenches, hammers and cotters	31 35
58476—Drills, keys, cotters and wrenches	16 93
58961—Drills, wrenches, etc.	69 13
59212—Wrenches, cotters, keys	63 77
60691—Wrenches, hammers	25 47
60334—Wrenches	11 88
60838—Cotters	28 63
61353—Cotters	23 15
61780—Wrenches, hammers	40 72
62668—Wrenches, hammers	39 63
62746—Wrenches, drills and keys	70 09

$452 13

WABI IRON WORKS, LIMITED, NEW LISKEARD, ONT.

57401—Claims Nos. 10590 and 10553—Siding rebate	$207 00
58584—Repairing scales	1 95
59121—Castings	60 42
58838—Claim No. 11107, siding rebate	42 90

WABI IRON WORKS, LIMITED, ETC.—*Continued.*

59494—Repairs to ditcher	4 65	
59920—Claims No. 11448 and 11398—Loss account, shortage iron	3 53	
63356—Castings	1 00	
		$321 45

WHELAN & NEWTON, COBALT, ONT.

57403—Claim No. 9709—Loss account, shortage, coal	$16 00	
		$16 00

J. T. WELBOURN, UNO PARK, ONT.

57405—Claim No. 10498—Loss account, shortage bag shorts	$1 52	
58087— " 10588—Loss account, damage to eggs	1 20	
61187— " 11147—Loss, one bag whole beans	9 02	
		$11 74

C. G. WATSON, ENGINEERING DEPT., NORTH BAY, ONT.

57065—Travelling expenses	$6 35	
56754—Travelling expenses	4 00	
		$10 35

WHITE STAR DOMINION LINE, MONTREAL, QUE.

56600—Refund of amount over remitted on B-C. 25690	$0 40	
		$0 40

GUSTAV WIEDEKE & CO., DAYTON, OHIO.

57548—Expanders	$26 96	
58133—Mandrels for expanders	8 40	
		$35 36

E. T. WRIGHT CO., LIMITED, HAMILTON, ONT.

57552—Lanterns	$21 75	
59077— " and founts	48 30	
60689— " and founts, etc.	48 30	
		$118 35

T. E. WARNER, MACHINIST, NORTH BAY, ONT.

57577—Travelling expenses	$0 75	
		$0 75

THE WORLD'S ONLY DUSTLESS BRUSH COMPANY, NORTH BAY, ONT.

57999—Brush	$3 75	
62748—Brooms	7 50	
		$11 25

WELLSVILLE & BUFFALO R. R. CORPORATION, BUFFALO, N.Y.

58297—Car service balance	$15 30	
58244— " "	99 45	
59389— " "	58 05	
59446— " repairs	2 34	
59722— " service balance	94 95	
60361— " "	138 60	
60610— " "	78 30	
62935— " "	4 95	
63562— "	45	
		$492 39

WEAVER COAL COMPANY, BUFFALO, N.Y.

58347—Coal	$100 38	
58719— "	213 49	
58956— "	49 43	
59186— "	78 66	
60727— "	235 20	
60953—Claim No. 11523—Overcharge, freight	1 00	
		$678 16

ARTHUR WILSON, KENEBEEK, ONT.

58463—Ties	$126 00	
		$126 00

THE WESTERN CLASSIFICATION COMMITTEE, CHICAGO, ILL.

57702—Subscription of "Western Classification Renewal"	$1 00	
59193—Subscription of "Western Classification Renewal"	1 00	
		$2 00

THE WESTERN TRUNK LINE COMMITTEE, CHICAGO, ILL.

57952—Tariffs and supplements	$1 04	
62309—Tariffs and supplements	3 06	
		$4 10

A. C. WHITE, PORCUPINE, ONT.

58032—Claim No. 10754—Overcharge in rate, pulpwood	$10 48	
62175—Refund, deposit on siding	68 53	
		$79 01

A. T. WILEY & CO., LIMITED, MONTREAL, QUE.

58474—Dishes	$57 16	
		$57 16

J. B. WILSON, TORONTO, ONT.

58478—Track sanders	$48 00	
60687—Track sanders	48 00	
		$96 00

F. H. WHITTELSEY COMPANY, WINDSOR LOCKS, CONN.

58482—Yellow copy paper	$25 50	
		$25 50

WARDEN KING, LIMITED, MONTREAL, QUE.

58585—Grate bars	$5 33	
62383—Grate bars	10 66	
		$15 99

WESTERN CANADA FLOUR MILLS CO., LIMITED, TORONTO, ONT.

58989—Claim No. 10874, account cars over-carried	$8 00	
		$8 00

WICHITA FALLS & NORTHWESTERN RAILWAY CO., WICHITA FALLS, TEX.

59313—Car service balance	$1 35	
59988—Car repairs	96	
		$2 31

WABASH PITTSBURG TERMINAL RAILWAY CO., PITTSBURG, PA.

59391—Car service balance	$10 35	
59557— " repairs	1 65	
60363— " service balance	8 55	
61319— " repairs	36	
		$20 91

FREDERICK WILSON, McCOOL P.O., ONT.

59425—Ties	$24 73	
59754—Ties	13 40	
		$38 13

WELLAND VALE MANUFACTURING CO., LIMITED.

58900—Scythes and snaths	$68 21	
		$68 21

THE WILLIAMS PIANO COMPANY, LIMITED, OSHAWA, ONT.

59424—Claim No. 10872, loss account piano destroyed by fire	$450 00	
		$450 00

WABI KON CAMP, LAKE TEMAGAMI, ONT.

59709—Advertising in folder	$50 00	
		$50 00

WORK & FRETZ, DETROIT, MICH,

59813—Claims, overcharge in freight	$12 38	
59922— " " " "	111 20	
60879— " " " "	20 70	
60955—	2 00	
61189—	34 05	
61501—	24 45	
61651—	7 28	
62079—	50 31	
61378— "	10 55	
61452— "	33 95	
62066— " " " "	9 88	
62763— "	44 60	
62765—	39 54	
63207—	40 96	
62582—	30 65	
		$472 50

WORKMEN'S COMPENSATION BOARD, TORONTO, ONT.

59863—Assessment	149 53	
		$149 53

MR. & MRS. J. N. WALTON, KEYSTOWN, SASK.

59885—Claim No. 11427, loss account baggage burned	$200 00	
		$200 00

WALTER F. WULLAN, HEASLIP, ONT.

60449—Claim No. 11109, overcharge in weight cattle	$7 25	
		$7 25

WAGAR & GRIFFITH FURNITURE COMPANY, NORTH BAY, ONT.

60731—Mattresses	$19 20	
61437— "	14 40	
63083—Tables	17 75	
		$51 35

Isaac Walle, Cochrane, Ont.

59836—Clearing bush, Cochrane townsite	$100 00	
62033— " station grounds, Kelso, certificate No. 1	160 00	
62573— " station grounds, Kelso, certificate No. 2	240 00	
62474— " station grounds, Kelso, certificate No. 3	160 00	
		$660 00

F. W. Woolworth Co., Limited, Toronto, Ont.

59916—Claim No. 11115, loss account damage to tumblers, etc....	$1 17	
60881— " " 11440, 11438, damage to glass tumblers	1 13	
62081— " " 12136, damage to chinaware	1 02	
61410— " " 11591 and 11687, loss skin foods and cleanser..	50	
62607— " " 12424, damage to cups and saucers	78	
62914— " " 12785, damage to pictures	58	
63256— " " 12879, loss and damage to gloves	40	
		$5 58

J. Webster, M. P. Dept., North Bay, Ont.

59924—Travelling expenses	$1 60	
		$1 60

Walter Walstrom, Monteith P.O., Ont.

60064—Ties	$149 19	
		$149 19

S. West, McCool, Ont.

60340—Butter	$6 00	
60342—Carrots, beets, potatoes	82 10	
		$88 10

Western Railway of Alabama, Toronto.

60608—Car service balance	$2 25	
61835—Car service balance	4 50	
		$6 75

West Disinfecting Company, Toronto.

60834—Protectus fluid	$26 25	
		$26 25

C. L. Williams, Connaught Station, Ont.

60836—Lumber	$349 75	
61995—Lumber	240 67	
61328—Claim No. 11855, loss pike poles	7 14	
61552—Lumber	308 00	
		$905 56

J. J. Walsh, Temagami, Ont.

60845—Donation re advertising Lake Temagami	$100 00	
61196—Donation re advertising Lake Temagami	100 00	
		$200 00

Watson Company, Limited, New Liskeard, Ont.

60883—Claim No. 11285, loss account syrup destroyed	$0 95	
61647— " " 11826, damage to seven jars	52	
62916— " " 12808, loss tins peas	26	
		$1 73

. MRS. S. D. WALKER, HUNTSVILLE, ONT.

60957—Claim No. 10893, loss H.H. goods in transit $160 00

$160 00

R. W. WOODS, HAILEYBURY, ONT.

61649—Claim No. 11672, alleged loss two quarts Luxo $2 50

$2 50

W. WARD, GARDENER, ENGLEHART, ONT.

61264—Travelling expenses $4 50

$4 50

PHILIP WENNERSHEIMER, McCOOL, P.O.

61500—Ties $15 60
61500—Ties 7 98

$23 58

E. B. WHORLEY, HAILEYBURY, ONT.

62064—Claim No. 11538, alleged loss bag carrots $1 00

$1 00

WEST DOME CONSOLIDATED MINES, LIMITED, SOUTH PORCUPINE, ONT.

62609—Claim No. 12446, loss car coal by fire $174 87

$174 87

WARRELL & YATES, COCHRANE, ONT.

62659—Claim No. 12486, alleged loss oats $42 20
63254—Claim No. 11038, damage to potatoes by frost 54 65

$96 85

W. J. WILSON, TORONTO, ONT.

62428—Repairing chair $1 00

$1 00

WATERLOO MANUFACTURING CO., LIMITED, WATERLOO, ONT.

62584—Claim No. 12544, damage to threshing machine $1,328 88

$1,328 88

M. P. WASHBURN, LOUISVILLE, KY.

63092—Tariffs $5 47

$5 47

R. B. WATSON, COBALT, ONT.

63728—Claim No. 12674, bottle water alleged broken $1 48

$1 48

WM. YOUNG, GENERAL ROADMASTER, NORTH BAY, ONT.

56885—Travelling expenses $8 50
56756—   "   " 10 40
57673—   "   " 4 60
57884—   " 8 30
58685—   " 42 50
59354— .   " 2 80
59859—   ..   " 2 50
60292—   " 9 60

WM. YOUNG, GENERAL ROADMASTER, NORTH BAY, ONT.—*Continued.*

61603—Travelling expenses		$8 05
61266— " "		2 85
62343— " "		8 20
62484—		10 00
		$118 30

YOUNG COMPANY, LIMITED, NORTH BAY, ONT.

57441—Groceries	$191 76
57556—Groceries	103 05
58005—Bon Ami and lye	10 75
58089—Claims No. 10401 and 10527, shortage 1 case milk	6 90
58034—Claim No. 10627, shortage 2 bags potatoes	2 10
58484—Groceries, Bon Ami and lye	54 92
58881—Hay	144 72
59220—Hay, blankets, groceries	586 47
60681—Groceries	499 59
60344—Groceries, etc.	257 62
60862—Commissary	580 03
60972—Commissary	16 15
60959—Claim No. 11710, loss barrel pork	31 36
61357—Grocery supplies	181 76
61997—Groceries	517 53
61554—Sugar, flour, etc.	113 63
62312—Groceries	721 31
63091— "	1,170 66
62670— "	389 08
63148—Switching charges on car hay	1 50
63150—Groceries	124 94
63358— "	213 01
63462— "	228 68
	$6,147 52

YE TOGGERY SHOP, COCHRANE, ONT.

57118—Claim No. 10436, loss 2 dozen pair sox	$5 14
61193— " 11502, loss boots	8 70
61832— " 11501, loss caps	2 55
	$16 39

FREDERICK YOUNG, CHICAGO, ILL.

58007—Burners	$6 00
	$6 00

JOHN YORKSTON, NORTH BAY, ONT.

57786—Award W. C. B. *re* alleged injuries	$45 30
	$45 30

W. J. YATES, NEW LISKEARD, ONT.

58036—Claims, loss and damage to liquor	$6 94
59023— " " " " " "	79 70
58840— " " " " " "	3 58
59815— " " " " " "	5 19
60885— " " " " " "	12 37
60961— " " " " " "	1 11
61191— " " " " " "	1 09
61503— " " " " " "	5 93
61653— " " " " " "	95
61887— " " " " " "	94
62083— " " " " " "	59
61330— " " " " " "	3 77
61440— " " " " " "	14 57

W. J. Yates, New Liskeard, Ont.—*Continued.*

61834—Claims, loss and damage to liquor	$7 03	
62068— " " " " " . "	1 01	
62327— " " " " " "	19 02	
62769— " " " " " "	18 96	
		$182 75

The Yale & Towne Manufacturing Company, Stamford, Conn.

58486—Door closers	$26 25	
62314—Differential block	11 55	
		$37 80

The Young Lumber Company, North Bay, Ont.

58772—Lumber	$519 54	
60683— "	268 24	
60116— "	226 60	
60974—Freight deducted in error	7 28	
61999—Lumber	378 65	
61664—Roofing	457 65	
62667—Lumber	1,518 32	
62672— "	949 75	
63152— "	2,142 68	
63360—Freight deducted in error	4 00	
		$6,472 71

York Springs, Limited, Toronto, Ont.

60394—Water	$2 00	
61362— "	4 00	
62385— "	50	
		$6 50

Zanesville & Western Railway Company.

61890—Car repairs :...	$2 45	
		$2 45

RECAPITULATION ACCOUNTS PAYABLE.

November 1st, 1915, to October 31st, 1916.

General Ledger Balance, Accounts Payable as of November 1st, 1915		$432,815 65
Disbursements for year, November 1st, 1915, to October 31st, 1916, as per detailed statement		3,651,507 28
Cash payments by Treasurer during year $3,557,969 45		
General Ledger Balance, Accounts payable as of October 31st, 1916	526,353 48	
	$4,084,322 93	$4,084,322 93

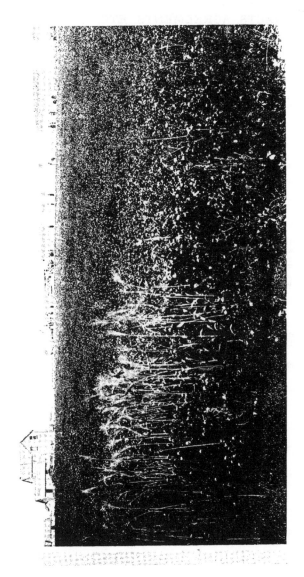

Red Clover; three tons yield per acre. Monteith Government Farm, year 1915.

CONTRACTS, AGREEMENTS, ETC.

RE INSTALLATION HEATING AND PLUMBING SYSTEM, PASSENGER STATION, TIMMINS.

Tenders received as follows:

A. Brazeau, Timmins, Ont.	$2,390 00
S. J. Cherry, North Bay, Ont.	2,472 00
F. R. Gibson, Haileybury, Ont.	2,700 00
Cochrane Hardware, Ltd., North Bay	2,649 00

Contract awarded A. Brazeau, Timmins, Ont., lowest tenderer.

RE ADDITIONS TO MACHINE SHOP, NORTH BAY JUNCTION, ONT.

Tenders received as follows:

Henderson & Angus	$1,600 00
Jeffrey & Stevens	2,191 00
W. A. Martyn	1,430 00

Contract awarded W. A. Martyn, lowest tenderer.

RE INSTALLATION HEATING AND PLUMBING SYSTEMS IN FOUR SEMI-DETACHED TENEMENT HOUSES, IROQUOIS FALLS, ONT.

Tenders received as follows:

F. R. Gibson, Haileybury, Ont.	$1,440 00
Cochrane Hardware, Ltd., North Bay, Ont.	1,496 00
A. Brazeau, Timmins	1,640 00

Contract awarded F. R. Gibson, lowest tenderer.

RE ELECTRIC WIRING, FOUR TENEMENT HOUSES, IROQUOIS FALLS, ONT.

Tenders received as follows:

E. M. Allworth, Timmins, Ont.	$240 00
Electric Supply Co., North Bay	375 00
D. Clutchey, Haileybury, Ont.	285 93

Contract awarded E. M. Allworth, lowest tenderer.

INSTALLATION, PLUMBING AND DRAINAGE SYSTEM No. 10 PASSENGER STATION, IROQUOIS FALLS.

Tenders received as follows:

—	Completion.	Plumbing System.	Tile Drain per lin. ft.	Tile Drain Complete.	Total.
		$ c.	$ c.	$ c.	$ c.
A. Brazeau, Timmins.......	5 weeks	475 00	1 95	1,365 00	1,840 00
Cochrane Hdwe. Ltd., North Bay.....................	6 "	550 00	65	455 00	1,005 00
S. J. Cherry, North Bay	6 "	508 00	80	560 00	1,068 00
F. R. Gibson, Haileybury....	6 "	435 00	1 25	875 00	1,310 00
J. Murphy, New Liskeard ..	4 "	610 00	90	630 00	1,240 00

Contract awarded Cochrane Hardware, Ltd., lowest tenderer.

CONTRACTS EXTENDED

Canada Railway News Co.

Contract for train privileges extended for period one year from January 1st, 1916 to January 1st 1917, same terms and conditions.

Canada Railway News Co.

Contract for lease of space in Cobalt Station for purpose selling books, newspapers, etc., extended for period one year from August 1st, 1916 to July 31st, 1917, same terms and conditions.

NEW LISKEARD WHARF.

LAND TITLES ACT.

TEMISKAMING & NORTHERN ONTARIO RAILWAY COMMISSION registered owner of the freehold land registered in the office of Land Titles at Haileybury as parcel No. 5152 in the register for the District of Nipissing, North Division in consideration of the sum of one dollar ($1.00) and other good and valuable consideration paid to it transfers to His Majesty the King represented herein by The Honourable The Minister of Public Works for Canada, the lands hereinafter particularly described, namely:

Part of Lot 9 in the First Concession of the Township of Dymond in the District of Temiskaming and Province of Ontario, more particularly described as follows:

COMMENCING at the north-west corner of Lot 9, at the intersection between the line dividing Lots 8 and 9 and the line between Concessions 1 and 2, in a direction due east along the said concession line for a distance of fifteen hundred and twenty-eight (1,528) and fifty-six hundredths (56/100) feet to its intersection with the east line of Boulevard Street produced; then in a direction south, twenty-one (21) degrees and sixteen (16) minutes west, along the said east line of Boulevard Street for a distance of one hundred and eighty-six (186) feet and nine (9) inches; then in a direction due east for a distance of two hundred and thirty-nine (239) feet and four (4) inches, to the starting point of the land required and hereinafter described as follows:

FROM the starting point, as above indicated, in a direction due east for a distance of one hundred and twenty (120) feet and eleven (11) inches; then south, fifty-six (56) degrees and fifty-seven (57) minutes east, for a distance of two hundred and sixty-two (262) feet and eight (8) inches (this last line and the preceding one being boundaries of the land sold lately by K. Farah to the Dominion Government); then south thirty-four (34) degrees and thirty-eight (38) minutes west, for a distance of sixty-six (66) feet; then north fifty-six (56) degrees and fifty-seven (57) minutes west for a distance of three hundred and sixty-two (362) feet and three (3) inches, the starting point as shown tinted red on annexed plan, comprising an area of twenty thousand six hundred and twenty-five (20,625) square feet, or forty-seven hundredths (47/100) of an acre, as shown on the plan hereto annexed.

The bearings given are astronomic, being part of said parcel.

AND His Majesty the King represented herein by The Honourable The Minister of Public Works for Canada to the intent that the burden of these covenants may run with the land aforesaid for himself, his successors and assigns, hereby covenants and agrees with the Temiskaming and Northern Ontario Railway Commission, its successors and assigns:

(1) To keep the wharf at present situate and being upon the said lands at all times hereafter in good repair and condition.

(2) To permit the Temiskaming and Northern Ontario Railway Commission at all times hereafter to make such reasonable use of the said wharf as may be necessary for the purpose of conveying any traffic required to be conveyed between the said wharf and the railway of the said Temiskaming and Northern Ontario Railway Commission.

The true intent and meaning of this covenant being that no obstruction shall be placed by or on behalf of His Majesty the King, represented herein by the Honourable the Minister of Public Works for Canada, to the transhipping of freight from or to said wharf to or from the cars standing on the spur line of the Temiskaming and Northern Ontario Railway Commission on the lands adjoining the lands hereby transferred.

DATED the 7th day of June A.D. 1916.

WITNESS:
SIGNED, SEALED AND DELIVERED
by the Acting Minister of Public Works
and countersigned by the Secretary this
7th day of June, A.D. 1916, in my
presence:

T. A. CHASSE, *Law Clerk.*

A. B. ODLUM.

J. D. REID, Acting Minister of
Public Works.
R. C. DESROCHERS.

TEMISKAMING   AND   NORTHERN
ONTARIO RY. COM'N.
J. L. ENGLEHART,
                Chairman.
W. H. MAUND,
                Secretary-Treasurer.

THIS AGREEMENT made and entered into this first day. of April, A.D. 1916.

BETWEEN:

THE TEMISKAMING AND NORTHERN ONTARIO RAILWAY COMMISSION hereinafter called the Commission.

                ＼   —and—

PHILIP G. KIELY, WILLIAM E. SMITH AND ALFRED A. AMOS, carrying on business under the firm name and style of KIELY, SMITH AND AMOS hereinafter called the Lessees.

WITNESSETH that for and in consideration of the covenants and agreements herein contained the parties hereto have agreed as follows:

1. The Commission agrees to furnish during every week day from and after the date hereof until the 31st day of December, 1916, from nine o'clock a.m. to five

o'clock p.m. for the use of the Lessees a telegraph wire between the offices of the Lessees at Timmins, South Porcupine and Cobalt and the telegraph office of the Canadian Pacific Railway Company at North Bay, and also to furnish instruments and local batteries and material to maintain such batteries at said offices, and the necessary main batteries for the operation of said wire; said wire shall be connected at North Bay with the wire leased by the Canadian Pacific Railway Company. The Commission agrees to keep said wire in good working order and repair, it being understood and agreed that in the event of the interruption of said wire the Lessees shall immediately notify the Commission of such interruption and the said Commission shall repair said wire without unnecessary delay. It being further understood and agreed that the Commission shall not be held responsible for any defects or delays in the working of said wire except when a continued interruption for one day or more occurs, in which event a *pro rata* abatement of the rental of said wire shall be made for each day of continued interruption, computation being made on the basis of thirty days to the month.

2. It is understood and agreed that the Commission retains the right to use said wire except and otherwise than during the hours in which same is set apart for the use of the Lessees as herein specified, PROVIDED ALWAYS and it is hereby agreed between the parties hereto that the Commission shall have the right to use said wire at any time when in its judgment the necessities of the service to the general public so require.

3. The Lessees for the use of said wire for the period as hereinbefore specified agree to pay the Commission the sum of four thousand six hundred and thirty-five dollars ($4,635.00) in three equal, consecutive, quarterly payments of one thousand five hundred and forty-five dollars ($1,545) each in advance; the first of such payments to become due and to be made on the date hereof.

4. The Lessees agree with the Commission to provide at their own expense the necessary operators who shall be satisfactory to the Commission, and also to provide office room for the operation of said wire and instruments at the offices of the said Lessees in the Town of Cobalt, Timmins and South Porcupine respectively.

5. It is understood and agreed that said wire herein provided for to be set apart for the benefit of the Lessees as aforesaid shall be used by the Lessees and their employees only in the transmission of messages concerning the business and affairs of the said Lessees, and that said wire shall not be used in any manner for the transmission of messages for the public or for any person or persons other than the Lessees.

6. It is further understood and agreed that no other office or place shall be connected with said wire either directly or indirectly without the consent in writing of the Commission.

7. It is further understood and agreed that in the event of the failure of the Lessees to pay the rental herein agreed upon the days and times herein specified or of any violation of this agreement by the Lessees or any of their employees, the Commission may forthwith terminate this agreement and the Lessees shall pay to the Commission any damage that may accrue from such violation of this agreement.

24 T R

8. It is further understood and agreed that such wire, instruments and batteries shall at all times be and remain the property of the Commission, and shall be accessible to its employees and that nothing herein contained shall have or be construed as having the effect of vesting in the Lessees any right, title or interest to or in the same except in the manner and during the term and upon the conditions herein provided, and further that the Commission shall in no wise be responsible for errors or delays or for defaults or mishaps in messages which may be transmitted by the operators of the Lessees over the wire provided for herein.

9. This agreement shall be and continue in force until the 31st day of December, 1916, and thereafter until the expiration of thirty days written notice given by either party hereto to the other of its or their intention to terminate the same (unless sooner terminated by the Commission as provided in paragraph 7 hereof), save and except that the rental from and after said 31st day of December, 1916, shall be payable in advance in monthly instalments of $515.00 each instead of in quarterly instalments of $1,545 as hereinbefore provided.

10. This agreement shall not be assigned or transferred by the Lessees without the written consent of the Commission first had and obtained.

11. If during the currency of this agreement the Lessees shall require any additional connections which the Commission is willing to make the Lessees shall pay for each drop or extra office at the rate of $500 per annum, payable in advance in equal monthly instalments.

12. Where the word " wire " is used in this agreement it means telegraph circuit.

13. The agreement dated the first day of January, 1916, made between the parties hereto is hereby declared to be cancelled and at an end.

IN WITNESS WHEREOF the said Commission has caused these presents to be executed under its corporate seal and under the hands of its proper officers in that behalf, and the said Lessees have set their hands and seals the day and year first above written.

SIGNED, SEALED AND DELIVERED
   in the presence of:

   A. B. ODLUM.

   E. B. THAUBURN.

TEMISKAMING AND NORTHERN ONTARIO RY. COM'N.

   J. L. ENGLEHART,   (Seal.)
                   Chairman.

   W. H. MAUND,
       Secretary-Treasurer.
   PHILIP G. KIELY.   (Seal.)
   W. E. SMITH.   (Seal.)
   ALFRED A. AMOS.   (Seal.)

Crop of Barley; 35 bushels per acre.   Farm of Mr. W. Mulverill, Armstrong Township.

THIS AGREEMENT made in duplicate this 31st day of October, A.D. 1916.
BETWEEN:

DOMINION WHEEL AND FOUNDRIES, LIMITED, hereinafter called
the Contractor,   —and—

THE TEMISKAMING AND NORTHERN ONTARIO RAILWAY
COMMISSION, hereinafter called the Commission.

WITNESSETH that in consideration of the mutual covenants and agreements
herein contained and other good and valuable consideration the parties hereto have
mutually agreed and do each agree with the other as follows:

1. The Contractor agrees to sell and deliver to the Commission as and when
ordered all the cast iron car wheels required by the Commission for the period of
one year commencing the first day of November, 1916, such cast iron car wheels to
be constructed in strict compliance with the Master Car Builders' rules and regulations and to the complete satisfaction of the Chief Engineer and Superintendent of
Maintenance of the Commission, and the Commission agrees to purchase and pay
for the said cast iron car wheels at the rate or price of one dollar and eighty cents
($1.80) per hundred pounds.

2. The said cast iron car wheels shall be delivered to the Commission free on
board the Commission's tracks at the Town of North Bay.

3. The Contractor further agrees to sell and deliver to the Commission as and
when ordered all the gray iron castings required by the Commission during the said
period of one year, such iron castings to be constructed to the complete satisfaction
of the Chief Engineer of the Commission, and the Commission agrees to purchase
and pay for such gray iron castings at the rate or price of two dollars and fifty
cents ($2.50) per hundred pounds.

4. The said gray iron castings shall be delivered to the Commission free on
board the Commission's tracks at the Town of North Bay.

5. In consideration of the premises the Contractor agrees to purchase and the
Commission agrees to sell, for the period above mentioned, all the Commission's
used cast iron car wheels, and the Contractor agrees to pay for such used cast iron
car wheels at the rate or price of fifteen dollars and ninety cents ($15.90) per gross
ton, such used cast iron car wheels to be delivered to the Contractor free on board
the Commission's tracks at the Town of North Bay, and the Contractor further
agrees to purchase and the Commission to sell all the Commission's cast scrap and
malleable scrap iron at the rate or price of thirteen dollars and seventy-five cents
($13.75) per gross ton, such cast and malleable scrap iron to be delivered to the
Contractor free on board the Commission's tracks at the Town of North Bay.

This agreement and everything herein contained shall enure to the benefit of
and be binding upon the parties hereto, their successors and assigns respectively.

IN WITNESS WHEREOF the parties hereto have hereunto set their respective corporate seals under the hands of the proper officers in that behalf.

	DOMINION WHEEL AND FOUNDRIES,
SIGNED, SEALED AND DELIVERED.	LIMITED.
in the presence of: .	F. J. NEALE, (Seal.)
	Secretary-Treasurer.
	J. A. KILPATRICK, *President.*
G. S. GARDINER.	TEMISKAMING AND NORTHERN
	ONTARIO RY. COM'N.
A. B. ODLUM.	J. L. ENGLEHART, (Seal.)
	Chairman.
	W. H. MAUND, *Secretary-Treasurer.*

MEMORANDUM OF AGREEMENT made this fifteenth day of September, one thousand nine hundred and fifteen.

BETWEEN:

THE GRAND TRUNK PACIFIC TELEGRAPH COMPANY, hereinafter called the Company

Of the First Part

—and—

THE TEMISKAMING AND NORTHERN ONTARIO RAILWAY COMMISSION, hereinafter called the Commission

Of the Second Part.

1. WHEREAS the Commission own and operate a system of telegraph lines for the public as well as for its own business. and the Company propose to operate lines on its line of telegraph for similar purposes IT IS MUTUALLY AGREED between the Company and the Commission, as hereinafter set forth, that in consideration of the Commission acting as Agents for the Company at Cochrane, Ont.

2. The Company will put its wire or wires into the Commission's office at Cochrane and provide all necessary instruments for the same. The Commission will provide operator and messenger.

3. The Company will maintain its own lines and instruments and furnish all supplies in connection therewith.

4. The through telegraph rates shall be made up as follows:

Company's tolls plus Commission's and connecting lines tolls, as per published tariffs.

5. DIVISION OF RATES:

The Company will retain its rates as per tariff and pay to the Commission local rates plus connection lines rates as per tariffs, and in addition, the Company will pay to the Commission 20 per cent. of Company's tolls on all messages handled by Commission's Agent at Cochrane for messages to and from the Company's lines.

6. Each party shall be responsible to the other for any errors, delays, non-delivery, or any act or omission resulting in claims for damages that may occur on its lines in the case of messages received by the other for transmission over its lines, and each party shall be responsible for any delays, errors, or omissions in the case of joint business received by it for points on the lines of the other, which delays, errors or omissions have resulted before delivery to the other.

7. This agreement shall remain in force for a period of one year from its date and thereafter until terminated by three month's notice in writing from either party to the other, which notice may be either delivered or mailed, postage prepaid and registered, addressed to the Superintendent of Telegraphs of the Commission at North Bay, or Manager of Telegraphs of the Company at Montreal.

WITNESS the corporate seals of the parties hereto under the hands of their proper officers.

SIGNED, SEALED AND DELIVERED
in the presence of:

E. B. WAY.

Recommended:
H. HULATT.

A. B. ODLUM.

THE GRAND TRUNK PACIFIC TELE-
GRAPH COMPANY.

E. J. CHAMBERLIN,
President.

HENRY PHILLIP,
Secretary.

TEMISKAMING AND NORTHERN
ONTARIO RY. COM'N.
In the presence of:

J. L. ENGLEHART,
Chairman.

W. H. MAUND,
Secretary-Treasurer.

MEMORANDUM OF AGREEMENT made this 17th day of February in the year of our Lord, one thousand nine hundred and sixteen.

BETWEEN:

BUFFALO AND SUSQUEHANNA COAL AND COKE COMPANY of Buffalo, N.Y., hereinafter called the Contractors

—and—

THE TEMISKAMING AND NORTHERN ONTARIO RAILWAY COMMISSION, hereinafter called the Commission.

1. Subject of the terms hereof the Contractors agree to sell to the Commission, and the Commission agrees to buy from the Contractors, one hundred thousand net tons three-quarter lump coal of Sagamore Mine at the price of two dollars and thirty-seven cents per net ton (two thousand pounds) on board cars, International Bridge, Black Rock, N.Y. Delivery as required up to May 1st, 1917, and subject to the provisions hereinafter stated.

2. The Contractors absolutely guarantee (*a*) that all coal to be delivered under this contract shall be suitable for the purposes of the railway of the Commission, and (*b*) shall on analysis, in manner hereinafter provided, prove to be at least equal to the following which is agreed to be the standard analysis:

Moisture	1.25
Hydro Carbons	32.75
Fixed Carbons	58.25
Ash	7.75
	100.00
Sulphur	1.65

3. Samples for purpose of analysis may be taken (so far as deemed necessary by the Commission) from each carload of coal on or at any time after the arrival thereof at 'North Bay, and may be so taken at any point on the railway of the Commission, and such sample consist of not less than twenty-five pounds of lump and slack in the same relative proportion as appears in the shipment, to be taken from carload by the Superintendent, the Master Mechanic, or the Storekeeper of the Commission, and any sample so taken shall be conclusively presumed to be a fair sample for purposes of analysis of such carload and the certificate of Milton L. Hersey, analyst and chemist of Montreal, as to whether such sample answers the aforesaid guarantee (*b*) of the Contractors shall be absolutely final, binding and conclusive upon both parties as to whether the carload from which such sample has been taken answers such guarantee.

4. In case of analysis as aforesaid if any carload of coal delivered under this contract shall be found below standard quality as shown by analyst's certificate as aforesaid, the Commission shall be at liberty to reject such carload or the portion of it not used, notwithstanding that delivery of same may theretofore have been taken; notwithstanding that the necessary entry for passing same through the customs may have been made, and notwithstanding that same may have been unloaded or stored or wholly or partly paid for or otherwise dealt with, and thereupon the same shall be at the risk of and shall be deemed for all purposes to be the property of the Contractors, who shall forthwith remove and take delivery of same and repay to the Commission all moneys which the Commission may have paid in respect thereof, whether for freight, duties, cost of analysis, storage, unloading or any other charges or expenses, and if the Commission shall theretofore have paid the price or any part thereof, the Contractor shall forthwith repay the same. IT BEING HOWEVER EXPRESSLY AGREED THAT the aforesaid right of the Commission to reject any coal so delivered shall be in addition to all its other legal rights and remedies in the premises and not in the substitution for same or any of them.

5. Should coal at any time delivered under this Contract whether analyzed as aforesaid or not and irrespective of the result of such analysis prove in the opinion of the Master Mechanic or Superintendent of the Commission unsuitable for the purposes of the railway of the Commission, the Commission may at its option by notice in writing to the Contractors cancel and annul this contract as to any coal not theretofore shipped without prejudice to the liability of the Contractors for any breaches of this contract.

6. Beginning with the first day of May, 1916, there shall be shipped by the Contractors from the mines, properly consigned to the Commission at North Bay Junction, and with all freight and other charges prepaid to International Bridge, Black Rock, N.Y., or at mines at the option of the Commission approximately seven cars per day, subject to the increase or diminution from time to time of the daily shipments as shall be required by written notice, by letter or telegram from the Storekeeper of the Commission at North Bay to the Contractors at Buffalo, such notice to be duly sent from North Bay at least one week prior to the week to the shipments of which such notice shall apply. Coal will be sold at initial manifest weights which shall be binding and no claim shall be allowed for short weights except in the case of unusual loss by reason of defective cars. Provided and required that twenty-five per cent. of daily shipments of said coal be delivered in flat bottom cars.

7. The Commission shall further have the right at any time to cancel its purchase hereunder to the extent of not more than ten per cent. of the quantity of coal covered by this contract, in which case such ten per cent. or less proportion as the case may be, shall be taken from the last deliveries herein agreed upon.

8. If, during the continuance of this contract, the Commission is unable to make use of the said coal by reason of strike, destruction or disability of its railway or any part thereof, the Commission shall have the right during the continuance of such disability at its option to discontinue taking coal in quantities herein specified.

It is also understood that should Contractors encounter strikes, accidents, shut-downs at the mines, from reasons beyond their control, they shall not be expected to deliver on this contract during the period of suspension.

9. At the time of each shipment the Contractors shall send to the Storekeeper of the Commission at North Bay five correct copies of invoices of the coal covered by such consignment charges at the price of one dollar and twenty-seven cents per ton "being the purchase price for said coal at the mines less freight charges of $1.10 per ton to International Bridge, Black Rock," two of which copies shall be duly certified as required by the Canadian Customs Law.

10. Payments shall be made by the Commission to the Contractors in Toronto funds, for all coal delivered to the Commission at North Bay in any one month, on or before the 20th day of the following month.

11. This contract shall inure to the benefit of and be binding upon the successors and assigns of the parties respectively.

AS WITNESS the corporate seals of the said parties under the hands of the proper officers in that behalf.

WITNESS:

M. W. DRULLARD.

A. B. ODLUM.

W. A. GRAHAM,
    P. A. and S. K.

BUFFALO AND SUSQUEHANNA COAL
AND COKE CO.
    J. W. TROUNCE,
        General Sales Agent.
TEMISKAMING AND NORTHERN
ONTARIO RY. COM'N.
    J. L. ENGLEHART,
        Chairman.
    W. H. MAUND,
        Secretary-Treasurer.

Boundary line between Chamberlain and Pacaud Townships, looking west, showing Farm of Mr. Harry Bedford, Lot 1, south half, Con. 1, Pacaud.

MEMORANDUM OF AGREEMENT made this 25th day of February, in the year of our Lord, one thousand nine hundred and sixteen.

BETWEEN:

> THE ALGOMA STEEL CORPORATION, LIMITED, hereinafter called the Contractor,   —and—
> THE TEMISKAMING AND NORTHERN ONTARIO RAILWAY COMMISSION, hereinafter called the Commission.

WITNESSETH:

1. The Contractor agrees to furnish and deliver to the Commission free of all charges on cars at North Bay, Ontario, as hereinafter specified, twelve hundred and seventy-five gross tons open hearth steel rails, A.R.A. (90) ninety pounds A. section, in strict compliance with American Railway Association's standard specifications for carbon steel rails as found in 1915 specifications attached, and forming part of this agreement, boring for said rails to be in compliance with attached blue print, showing boring of T. & N. O. Ry. standard angle-bar, and of date February 28th, 1916, for the price of thirty-six dollars per gross ton of 2,240 pounds, f.o.b. cars North Bay, delivery to be made between the first and fifteenth days of September, 1916, time being agreed to be material and the essence of this contract.

2. In the event of stoppage or partial stoppage of the works of the Contractor, of shipments being delayed through strikes, accidents, breakage of machinery, or other cause beyond the Contractor's control (of which the Commission shall be promptly notified), or in case any shipment or any part thereof shall be lost in transit, the Contractor shall be entitled to such additional time in respect of the whole or any part of such delivery as the Chief Engineer of the Commission for the time being shall decide, and certify in writing to be fair and reasonable, having reference to the character and duration of such stoppage, delay, or loss, and such Engineer shall be the sole and final judge as to the additional time to be allowed and as to what part of such delivery the same shall extend to, and his decision in every such case shall be absolutely final and binding upon both parties. The last preceding clause of these presents shall be construed as far as relates to any portion of such deliveries or any of them affected by such extension of time as if the time fixed by the Engineer were time fixed in such clause.

3. The Contractor shall give written notice to the Commission at its office in Toronto of the commencement of rolling at least eight days in advance of such commencement, and shall similarly give written notice to the Commission at its office in Toronto of the resuming of the work after its temporary suspension at least two clear days before such resuming.

4. The written certificate of the Inspector of the Commission provided for by said specifications certifying that the rails have been manufactured to his satisfaction in accordance with this contract, and the said specifications shall be a condition precedent to the right of the Contractor to receive and be paid the price herein agreed to be paid for the same.

5. In case default shall be made by the Contractor in delivery of any of the said rails in accordance with the terms of this contract and the continuance of such default for thirty days, the Commission may, at its option, cancel this contract, but the Contractor shall nevertheless remain liable for all loss which may be suffered by the Commission by reason of the non-completion by the Contractor of this contract, PROVIDED, HOWEVER, that credit shall be given to the Con-

tractor notwithstanding such cancellation of the price of all rails which shall have been delivered by the Contractor in accordance with this contract and said specifications.

6. The cost of inspection provided for by the specifications shall be borne by the Commission.

7. The Commission in consideration of the premises agrees to pay in Toronto funds for each shipment of said rails upon delivery thereof on the tracks of the Commission at North Bay on presentation of invoices and certificate of the Inspector of the Commission at the Commission's office in Toronto.

IN WITNESS WHEREOF the said parties have caused these presents to be executed under their respective corporate seals and the hands of the proper officers in that behalf.

WITNESS:

A. B. PRATT.

ALGOMA   STEEL   CORPORATION,
LIMITED.
W. C. FRANZ,
Vice-President.
JAMES HEWSON,
Assistant Secretary.
TEMISKAMING   AND   NORTHERN
ONTARIO RY. COM'N.
J. L. ENGLEHART,
Chairman.
W. H. MAUND,
Secretary-Treasurer.

MEMORANDUM OF AGREEMENT made this 19th day of May, in the year of our Lord, one thousand nine hundred and sixteen.

BETWEEN:

THE ALGOMA STEEL CORPORATION, LIMITED, hereinafter called the Contractor

—and—

THE TEMISKAMING AND NORTHERN ONTARIO RAILWAY COMMISSION, hereinafter called the Commission.

WITNESSETH:

1. The Contractor agrees to furnish and deliver to the Commission free of all charges on cars at North Bay, Ontario, as hereinafter specified, two thousand gross tons open hearth steel rails, A.R.A. (90) ninety pound A. section, in strict compliance with American Railway Association's standard specifications for carbon steel rails as found in 1915 specifications attached, and forming part of this agreement, boring for said rails to be in compliance with attached blue print, showing boring of T. & N. O. Ry. standard angle-bar, and of date February 28th, 1916, for

the price of thirty-seven dollars and fifty cents per gross ton of 2,240 lbs., f.o.b. cars North Bay, delivery to be made between the first and fifteenth day of May, 1917, time being agreed to be material and the essence of this contract.

2. In the event of stoppage or partial stoppage of the works of the Contractor, of shipments being delayed through strikes, accidents, breakage of machinery, or other cause beyond the Contractor's control (of which the Commission shall be promptly notified), or in case any shipment or any part thereof shall be lost in transit, the Contractor shall be entitled to such additional time in respect of the whole or any part of such delivery as the Chief Engineer of the Commission for the time being shall decide, and certify in writing to be fair and reasonable having reference to the character and duration of such stoppage, delay, or loss, and such Engineer shall be the sole and final judge as to the additional time to be allowed and as to what part of such delivery the same shall extend to, and his decision in every such case shall be absolutely final and binding upon both parties. The last preceding clause of these presents shall be construed so far as relates to any portion of such deliveries or any of them affected by such extension of time as if the time fixed by the Engineer were time fixed in such clause.

3. The Contractor shall give written notice to the Commission at its office in Toronto of the commencement of rolling at least eight days in advance of such commencement, and shall similarly give written notice to the Commission at its office in Toronto of the resuming of the work after its temporary suspension at least two clear days before such resuming.

4. The written certificate of the Inspector of the Commission provided for by said specifications certifying that the rails have been manufactured to his satisfaction in accordance with this contract, and the said specifications shall be a condition precedent to the right of the Contractor to receive and be paid the price herein agreed to be paid for the same.

5. In case default shall be made by the Contractor in delivery of any of the said rails in accordance with the terms of this contract and the continuance of such default for thirty days, the Commission may, at its option, cancel this contract, but the Contractor shall nevertheless remain liable for all loss which may be suffered by the Commission by reason of the non-completion by the Contractor of this contract, PROVIDED, HOWEVER, that credit shall be given to the Contractor notwithstanding such cancellation for the price of all rails which shall have been delivered by the Contractor in accordance with this contract and said specifications.

6. The cost of inspection provided for by the specifications shall be borne by the Commission.

7. The Commission in consideration of the premises agrees to pay in Toronto funds for each shipment of said rails upon delivery thereof on the tracks of the Commission at North Bay on presentation of invoices and certificate of the Inspector of the Commission at the Commission's office in Toronto.

IN WITNESS WHEREOF the said parties have caused these presents to be executed under their respective corporate seals and the hands of the proper officers in that behalf.

ALGOMA   STEEL   CORPORATION,
LIMITED.

WITNESS:

HARRY A. WORKMAN.

A. B. ODLUM.

W. C. FRANZ,
Vice-President.

JAMES HEWSON,
Assistant Secretary.

TEMISKAMING   AND   NORTHERN
ONTARIO RY. COM'N.

J. L. ENGLEHART,
Chairman.

W. H. MAUND,
Secretary-Treasurer.

MONTREAL, PROVINCE QUEBEC, CANADA, APRIL 17th, 1916.

To the Commissioners of the Temiskaming and Northern Ontario Railway.

GENTLEMEN,—The Dominion Brake Shoe Company, Limited (hereinafter called the " Brake Shoe Company "), proposes to furnish to the Temiskaming and Northern Ontario Railway Commission (hereinafter called the " Purchaser "), and the Purchaser agrees to purchase from the Brake Shoe Company all brake shoes used by it, and by any other lines of railroad it may purchase, control or operate, for locomotive and car equipment, including any new equipment that may be built or ordered, upon the following terms:—

TYPES AND PRICES—
Locomotive Driver Brake shoes: Per net ton.
   " Perfecto " type, with crucible steel inserts and full plate steel back... $66 00

Brake Shoes for Locomotive Tender and Passenger Car Equipment:
   " Diamond S " type, flanged with full plate steel back and wrought lug.   61 00
   " Diamond S" type, unflanged with full plate steel back and wrought lug   56 00

Freight Car Brake Shoes:
   " Diamond T " type, unflanged with full plate steel back and wrought lug   40 00

DELIVERY: F.O.B. cars at St. Thomas, Ontario.

PAYMENT: Net cash thirty (30) days from date of invoice.

STOCK OF BRAKE SHOES: To insure prompt deliveries. the Brake Shoe Company will carry in stock such a quantity of brake shoes, of each type and pattern as the purchaser may request, which, upon the termination of this agreement, the purchaser agrees to immediately purchase from the Brake Shoe Company at the above-named prices.

INSPECTION: The Brake Shoe Company will, upon request of, and without charge to the purchaser, furnish an experienced inspector to assist and instruct its employees in the economical use of brake shoes and in the inspection of same in stock and in scrap. This inspector shall make such reports to the purchaser as it may require; duplicates of which will be furnished to the Brake Shoe Company.

TERM OF AGREEMENT: The term of this agreement is three (3) years from date of its acceptance and it shall continue thereafted from year to year unless terminated by either party by sixty (60) days' written notice to the other prior to its expiration, or prior to the expiration of any succeeding yearly period.

An acceptance of this proposition shall constitute an agreement between the Purchaser and the Brake Shoe Company, their successors and assigns, in accordance with the terms and conditions herein set forth.

Accepted this 1st day of May, 1916, Temiskaming and Northern Ontario Railway Commission.	DOMINION BRAKE SHOE COMPANY, LIMITED. THE HOLDEN COMPANY, LIMITED, AGENTS.
	D. M. BROWN.
	TEMISKAMING AND NORTHERN ONTARIO RY. COM'N.
WITNESS:	J. L. ENGLEHART, Chairman.
A. B. PRATT.	W. H. MAUND, Secretary-Treasurer.

Rates of Pay and Rules Governing Service of Machinists in Motive Power Department.

Effective May 1st, 1916.

GENERAL RULES.

ARTICLE 1.

Duration:

The rules and rates hereafter specified will supersede all others in effect, and will remain in force until April 30th, 1917, and from year to year thereafter, unless 30 days' notice is given prior to that date in each respective year of a desire to change.

ARTICLE 2.

Hours:

(a) Work hours for shop work are as follows:

For day work, excepting Saturdays and Sundays, 7 a.m. to noon, and 1 p.m. to 5 p.m.; Saturdays 7 a.m. to noon.

For night work, 9½ hours between 7 p.m. and 6 a.m. on the day following. When shops are on full time, men will be worked 10½ hours each night, five nights a week.

(b) Work hours for running work in locomotive department are as follows:

For day work, excepting Saturdays and Sundays, 7 a.m. to noon, and 1 p.m. to 6 - p.m.; Saturdays, 7 a.m. to noon.

For night work, excepting Sundays, 7 p.m. to 6 a.m. on the day following, one-half hour to be allowed for meals between 11 p.m. and 2 a.m.

(c) The assignment of men to running work is determined by their service being required in connection with train service and will be arranged by the Railway. They will be permanently employed on one class or the other and will not be transferred for periods of less than one week.

NOTE.—This clause is not intended to change existing conditions except as justified by increasing business.

(d) So far as consistent with the proper maintenance of the train service, men assigned to running work will be allowed alternate Saturday afternoons and either Sunday or one other day in seven.

ARTICLE 3.

Overtime:

(a) Overtime at the rate of time and a half will be paid for as follows:

For all time worked outside of work hours.

For all time worked between 7 a.m. on the following Dominion public holidays, and 7 a.m. on the following days: New Year's Day, Good Friday, Victoria Day, King's Birthday, Dominion Day, Civic Holiday, Labor Day, Thanksgiving Day and Christmas Day.

Should any of the above-mentioned holidays fall on Sunday, the day observed by the Provincial or Federal Government will be observed.

As far as possible, overtime will be distributed equally among the machinists and

Farm of Mr. Hughey Anderson. South half Lot 1, Con. 3, Chamberlain Township.

they will not be laid off during working hours to equalize their time on account of working overtime.

(b) When men permanently on day or night shift are transferred from one to the other and are required to work on two successive shifts, the second shift will be considered as overtime.

(c) Men assigned to shop work if called out to work after work hours will receive in all not less than 4½ hours straight time. - .

Men assigned to running work, if called out to work after work hours will receive in all not less than one and one-half hours straight time if called out within three hours after working hours; if called out after three hours after work hours they will receive not less than five hours straight time.

Men who, while working, are told to continue to work after work hours, or who are told to return to work overtime, commencing not over one hour after work hours, will not be considered as having been called out.

(d) Machinists shall not be expected to work overtime more than one night per week, except in emergencies.

ARTICLE 4.

Travelling: .

(a) Men sent from their regular place of employment to work temporarily, or returning thereto, will receive work time for the first eight hours and straight time for the remaining time while travelling or waiting trains, until arrival at destination. Work hours will govern while working, and reasonable expenses will be allowed.

NOTE.—Arrangements will be made that men should, as far as possible, be notified in advance.

NOTE.—Arrangements will be made to supply men with food, when sent out to work at points where it cannot be obtained.

(d) Men will be paid straight time when travelling to and from wrecks from the time called for (except between midnight and midnight on Sundays and holidays specified in article 3, clause A, when time and one-half will be paid), and time and one-half while working at wrecks, and to a man left in charge of a wrecking gang or wrecked engine. No time will be allowed when laid up for rest. Straight time will be allowed while waiting for the movement of wrecking trains.

ARTICLE 5.

Reduction:

(a) Before any general reduction is made in men who have been engaged for six months or over, shop working hours will be reduced to eight hours per day, five days per week. If further reduction is necessary, men having others dependent upon them for support will be given preference of employment, seniority and efficiency governing.

(b) When working hours have been shortened as above, force will not be increased until full working hours are restored. Men laid off on account of reduction of force, if competent and available, will, when force is increased be given preference over new men.

(c) Men who are discharged or resigned will be given certificates as quickly as possible, stating term of service, capacity in which employed and if discharged, the reason.

(d) Men leaving the service will receive their wages in full within two working days.

NOTE.—Men underpaid on account of errors, will, on application to their foreman, have their case referred to their superior officers for decision as to whether immediate payment can be allowed.

ARTICLE 6.

Committees:

(a) Employees having grievances either specific or of a general nature, may present their case to the proper officer. If investigation is desired, the aggrieved party, another employee representing him, or a committee of employees representing him, may, during working hours arrange with his foreman for same, investigation to be held within forty-eight hours after such application, and in case a satisfactory adjustment cannot be made, the case may be referred to the next higher officer of the department until the commission is approached. If, after investigation, the employee is found to be unjustly dealt with, he will be reinstated and paid for all time lost. In order that the committee may be properly constituted and entitled to formal recognition, it must have applied to adjust the case with the foreman before applying to the higher officer who will not unduly delay his investigation.

(b) Applicants for employment as machinists for the Commission shall only be expected to file the address of relatives, and prove that they are of good moral character.

(c) Leave of absence and free transportation to points on the Temiskaming and Northern Ontario Railway will be granted to members of committees properly constituted for the adjustment of matters in dispute with the Railway after receipt of written application to the proper officer.

Note.—Members of committees will not be discriminated against on account of serving on committees.

(d) Men will be subject to the general rules of the Commission with regard to leave of absence and free or reduced transportation.

Article 7.

Seniority:

(a) When a man accepts transfer to another station he thereby loses his seniority at the station he leaves, but the seniority rights at the station he goes to date from the time he entered the service.

(b) Promotion or advancement to more desirable work will be based on seniority and efficiency.

Article 8.

Classification:

(a) Machinists, who, while paid by the hour, permanently direct and are responsible for the work of others are designated as leading hands.

(b) Men will not be employed as improvers and helpers will not be advanced to the detriment of machinists or apprentices unless committee has been unable to furnish men after one week's notification. Helpers or improvers advanced to machinist's work will be paid the schedule rate of pay.

(c) Machinists being hired by this Railway shall be started at the standard rate of pay and if retained in the service of the Commission thirty days, their ability 'as a machinist shall have been established.

Article 9.

Apprentices:

(a) Machinist's apprentices when engaged must be between the ages of fifteen and eighteen years and will serve five years. Their number will be limited to one for the shop and one for every four tradesmen engaged therein.

(b) Apprentices when engaged must be able to read and write and know the first four rules of arithmetic.

(c) Apprentices who have served twelve months or less showing no aptitude to acquire the trade may be dismissed or transferred.

Note.—The Commission will furnish all opportunity possible for the apprentice to secure a complete knowledge of the trade during his apprenticeship. So far as possible, he shall serve three years on the different machines and special jobs, air brake work included, not serving more than six months on any one machine or any special job, and two years on the floor, the last six months in the roundhouse.

(d) Apprentices will not be worked overtime or at night unless necessary and only under the supervision of a machinist.

(e) Apprentices if retained in the employ of the Commission after finishing their apprenticeship shall receive machinist pay.

Article 10.

Machinists:

(a) Men who have served an apprenticeship or had four years' varied experience and are competent to operate lathes, planing, slotting, milling, shaping and tire boring machines or other machine tools requiring skilled operation, and are capable of repairing and assembling the various parts of locomotives or any kind of machinery whatsoever, will be designated as machinists.

Note.—The fitting, adjusting, shaping, boring, turning, finishing the disassembling of metal of locomotives or other machines, dry and steam pipe work, and brake riggings, shall be considered as machinist work; all laying off, building and mechanical work on repairs of engine trucks are also-included.

(b) Boys serving an apprenticeship to learn the trade are designated as machinists' apprentices.

Article 11.

Working Conditions:

So far as possible shop and roundhouse will be kept warm and comfortable.

Any part of engine requiring repairs will be cleaned on request.

The sanitary arrangements in shops and roundhouses will be given regular attention, such as wash basins, closets, drainage, plentiful supply of good drinking water, smoke jacks and leaky steam pipes.

25 T R

When it can be avoided, men will not be required to work out of doors in inclement weather, nor under engines until same have been placed over pit.

Machinists wishing to be absent two days or more from the service must obtain leave of absence from the foreman.

All machinists and apprentices must be treated with due respect and shown gentlemanly courtesy. When found necessary to interview any machinist he must be called into the office and interview as privately as possible.

ARTICLE 12.

Rates of Pay—Machinists:

(a) The minimum rate of pay for machinists will be forty cents per hour.

(b) Charge hands will receive not less than three cents above the highest minimum rate paid the men under their charge.

ARTICLE 13.

Rates of Pay—Apprentices:

(a) For the apprentices serving five years, rates of pay will be as follows:—

First year .... 13 cents.
Second year .... 15 cents.
Third year .... 16 cents.
Fourth year .... 19 cents.
Fifth year .... 24 cents.

Witness:

R. E. ELLWOOD.

A. B. ODLUM.

Signed for Machinists:
W. C. CRIPPS.
GEO. HAWKINS.
F. T. CADE.

Signed for Commission:
J. L. ENGLEHART,
Chairman.
W. H. MAUND,
Secretary-Treasurer.
S. B. CLEMENT,
C. E. & S. of M.
F. R. ROSS,
Master Mechanic.

Proposed Rates of Pay and Rules Governing Service in Car Department.

GENERAL RULES.

ARTICLE 1.

Duration:

The rules and rates hereinafter specified will supersede all others in effect and will reman in force until June 30th, 1917, and from year to year thereafter, unless 30 days' notice is given prior to that date, in each respective vear of a desire to change.

ARTICLE 2.

(a) Work hours for shop work are as follows: for day work, excepting Saturdays and Sundays, 7 a.m. to noon, and 1 p.m. to 6 p.m., Saturdays, 7 a.m. to noon. For night work, 9½ hours between 7 p.m. to 6 a.m. on the following day. When shops are on full time men will be worked 10½ hours each night, five nights a week.

(b) Work hours for running work in Car Department are as follows:

For day work excepting Sundays, ten hours out of eleven consecutive hours, between 7 a.m. and 7 p.m., 1 hour for meals between noon and 2 p.m.

For night work, excepting Sundays, eleven consecutive hours between 7 p.m. and 7 a.m. on the day following half hours for meals to be allowed between 11 p.m. and 2 a.m.

(c) The assignment of men to running work is determined by their service being required in connection with train service, and will be arranged by the railway. They will be permanently employed on one class or the other and will not be transferred for periods of less than one week. This does not include men relieving.

NOTE.—This clause is not intended to change existing conditions except as justified by increasing business.

(d) So far as consistent with the proper maintenance of train service, men assigned to running work will be allowed alternate Saturday afternoons and either Sunday or one other day in seven.

(e) When working hours are reduced for any portion of shops, such shortened hours will constitute work hours for that portion of the shop, 24 hours' notice will be bulletined of any such change. At all other points work hours will be shortened as deemed advisable by the railway without affecting the work hours as defined above.

NOTE.—So far as possible, full time worked will be divided between men employed, and they will be notified in advance.

(f) Men with duties of Car Inspectors at points where only one carman is employed will be allowed 330 hours per month, without overtime. This does not apply to men employed at outside points on work trains.

ARTICLE 3.

Overtime:

(a) Overtime at the rate of time and a half will be paid for as follows:
For all time worked outside of work hours.
For all time worked between 7 a.m. on the following Dominion public holidays and 7 a.m. on the following days:
New Year's Day, Good Friday, Victoria Day, King's Birthday, Dominion Day, Civic Holiday, Labour Day, Thanksgiving Day and Christmas Day.
Should any of the above-mentioned holidays fall on Sunday, the day observed by the Federal or Provincial Government will be observed.

(b) When men permanently on day or night shift are transferred from one to the other and are required to work on two successive shifts, the second shift will be considered as overtime.

(c) men assigned to shop work, if called out to work after work hours, will receive in all not less than four and a half hours' straight time.

Men assigned to running work, if called out to work after work hours will receive in all not less that one and a half hours' straight time, if called out within three hours after work hours; if called out after three hours after work hours they will receive not less than five hours' straight time.

Men who, while working, are told to continue work after work hours, or who are told to return to work overtime commencing not over one hour after work hours, will not be considered as having been called out.

ARTICLE 4.

(a) Men sent from their regular place of employment to work temporarily, or returning thereto, will receive work time for the first eight hours' and straight time for the remaining time while travelling or waiting trains, until arrival at destination. Work hours will govern while working and reasonable expenses will be allowed.
Arrangements will be made that men should as far as possible, be notified in advance.

(b) Men will be paid straight time when travelling to and from wreck from the time called for (except between midnight and midnight on Sundays and holidays specified in article 3, clause A, when time and one-half will be paid) and time and a half while working at wrecks, and to a man left in charge of a wrecking gang or wrecked engine. No time will be allowed while laid up for rest. Straight time will be allowed while waiting for movement of wrecking trains.

ARTICLE 5.

Reduction:

(a) Before any general reduction is made in men who have been engaged for six months or over, shop working hours will be reduced to nine hours per day, five days per week. If further reduction is necessary, men having others dependent on them for support will be given preference of employment, seniority and efficiency governing.

(b) When working hours have been shortened, as above, force will not be increased until full working hours are restored. Men laid off on account of reduction of force, if competent and available, will, when force is increased, be given preference over new men.

(c) Men who are discharged or resign will be given certificate as quickly as possible, stating term of service, capacity in which employed and if discharged, the reason.

(d) Men leaving the service will receive their wages in full within two working days.

NOTE.—Men underpaid on account of errors, will on application to their foremen, have their case referred to their Superior Officer for decision as to whether immediate payment can be allowed.

ARTICLE 6.

Committee:

(a) Employees having grievances either specific or of a general nature, may present their case to their proper officer. If investigation is desired, the aggrieved party, another employee representing him, or a committee of employees, may, during working hours, arrange with his foreman, for same, investigation to be held within forty-eight hours after such application, and in case a satisfactory adjustment cannot be made, the case may be referred to the next higher officer of the Department, until the Commission is approached. If, after investigation, the employee is found to be unjustly dealt with, he will be paid for all time lost. In order that the Committee may be properly constituted and entitled to formal recognition, it must have applied to adjust the case with the foreman, before applying to the higher officer.

(b) For men discharged within thirty days of engagement, on account of past record, with the railway, Section A above will not apply.

(c) Leave of absence and free transportation to points on the Temiskaming & Northern Ontario Railway will be granted to members of committees properly constituted for the adjustment of matters in dispute with the railway after receipt of written application to the proper officer.

(d) Men will be subjected to the general rules of the Commission with regard to leave of absence, and free or reduced transportation.

ARTICLE 7.

Seniority:

(a) When a man accepts transfer to another station, he thereby loses his seniority rights at the station he leaves, but the seniority rights at the station he goes to date from the time he entered the service.

ARTICLE 8.

Classification:

(a) Men who while paid by the hour, permanently direct and are responsible for the work of others, are designated as leading hands.

(b) Promotion will be governed by efficiency and seniority.

NOTE.—So far as possible vacancies occurring will be bulletined for forty-eight hours to afford men opportunity to apply if they desire.

ARTICLE 9.

Carmen:

(a) Car repairers required to furnish and regularly use carpenters' tools will be classed as freight car carpenters.

Carmen with duties of Car Inspectors, on work trains, will be classed as Inspectors.

Carpenters on coach, bench and cab work, will be classed as coach carpenters.

Carpenters on truck, tender, pilot and coach platform work will be classed as general carpenters.

(b) Carmen who have worked overtime will not be required to lay off to equalize their time to straight time. Overtime will, as far as possible, be equalized between qualified men.

(c) Unless agreed otherwise, carmen on running staff working night and day relays, will work alternate weeks day and night.

(d) So far as possible, two men will be sent out on the road when work requires their services.

(e) When carmen are sent from home stations on such notice as to prevent them from obtaining funds to defray living expenses, the railway will provide them with meals, or means for obtaining same, and when possible, sleeping accommodation.

(f) When consistent with good service and provided the railway is not put to additional expense thereby, free transportation will be given the carmen to enable them to get to their places of residences at week·end.

ARTICLE 10.

Pipefitters:

(a) Men who have served four years at the trade, and are capable of making and fitting up engine, car or general pipe work, or plumbing will be designated as pipefitters or plumbers.

ARTICLE 11.

Carmen:

(a) The rates of pay will be as follows:

	Shop.	Running.
Pattern Maker	$0.39	
Carpenters—Coach	.36½	$0.35½
" Locomotive Cab	.35	
" General	.33½	.31½
" Freight Car	.31½	
Wood Machinist	.36½	
" " Helper	.25½	
Pipe Fitters	.35½	
Car Inspectors		.29
Car Repairers	.27½	.26½
Air Brake Cleaners	.28½	.27
Triple Tester	.32½	
Coach Truck Repairers	.27½	
Car Cleaners—Sleeping and Diners		.25½
Car Cleaners, others		.24½
Painters—Decorator and Letterers	.34½	.33½
" First Class Brush Hands and Varnishers	.32½	.31½
" First Class Helpers	.27½	.26½
" General Helpers	.25	.24

Car repairers promoted to car carpenters will receive two cents less than minimum rate of pay for the first six months.

(b) Above rates of pay apply to permanent carmen or those who have been in the service of the car department continually for six months or more, or who have had six months' cumulative service during the year immediately preceding. Other carmen may be employed at a rate of two cents below those shown.

(c) Leading hands will receive not less than three cents above the highest minimum rate paid the men under their charge.

Signed for Car Department Employees
    H. J. TIPLER, *Past President.*
    L. SHEA, *President.*
    R. STENNING, *Vice-President.*
    (Seal)

    T. J. G.

Signed for Commission:
    T. R. Ross, *Master Mechanic.*
    S. B. CLEMENT, *C. E. & S. of M.*

TEMISKAMING & NORTHERN ONTARIO RAIL-
WAY COMMISSION.
    J. L. ENGLEHART, ·*Chairman.*
    W. H. MAUND, *Sec.-Treasurer.*

RE PURCHASE SIX MIKADO TYPE LOCOMOTIVES.

Tenders received as follows:

Canadian Locomotive Co., Kingston	$33,495 00 each
Montreal Locomotive Works, Montreal	39,334 50 each
Lima Locomotive Corporation, Lima, Ohio	38,796 88 each
Baldwin Locomotive Works, Philadelphia, Pa.	40,400 00 each

Contract awarded Canadian Locomotive Co., Ltd., Kingston, lowest tenderer.

Wm. Agar's Apiary near Thornloe.

Fall Wheat which yielded thirty bushels to the acre. Walker Tp., Con. 2, Lot 11.

ARTICLES OF AGREEMENT made this 11th day of May, in the year of our Lord one thousand nine hundred and sixteen.

'BETWEEN:

> CANADIAN LOCOMOTIVE COMPANY, LIMITED, hereinafter called the Contractor.

—and—

> TEMISKAMING AND NORTHERN ONTARIO RAILWAY COM-MISSION, hereinafter called the Commission.

WITNESSETH:

1. In this contract the words "Mechanical Engineer" shall mean the Mechanical Engineer for the time being of the Commission, and the word "Inspector" shall mean the Inspector for the time being appointed by the Mechanical Engineer to represent and act for the Commission in the supervision and in the inspection and certification of the locomotive engines hereinafter referred to.

2. The Contractor will supply and provide all and every kind of labor, work, materials, articles and things whatsoever necessary for the due construction and completion, and will well and duly build and complete in a perfect and workmanlike manner six Mikado type locomotive engines, with all necessary appliances, for use on the line of railway of the Commission, in strict compliance with the specifications and plans hereunto annexed and to the complete satisfaction of the Mechanical Engineer, and will deliver the same complete to the Commission f.o.b. on the Commission's tracks at North Bay, Ontario, as follows: Three of said locomotive engines on or before the 7th day of September, 1916, and the balance on or before the 14th day of September, 1916, time being agreed to be material and of the essence of this contract, and in default of such delivery within the times aforesaid the Contractor will pay to the Commission by way of liquidated damages the sum of ten dollars ($10.00) in respect of each of the said locomotive engines for each day which may elapse after the dates fixed for delivery of said locomotive engines respectively, which sum the Commission is authorized to deduct from the price hereinafter mentioned: PROVIDED, HOWEVER, that such damages shall not be recoverable in respect of any delays caused wholly by strikes, fires, accidents or other unavoidable occurrences wholly beyond the control of the Contractor.

3. The Contractor shall submit all drawings and detail plans for the approval of the Mechanical Engineer of the Commission before material is ordered or work commenced.

4. The Mechanical Engineer shall be the sole judge of all work and material done and supplied under this contract, and his decision on all questions in dispute with regard to any such work or material shall be final, and the whole work shall be executed to his satisfaction as evidenced by his certificate in writing, which certificate shall be a condition precedent to the right of the Contractor to be paid therefor.

5. The Mechanical Engineer or Inspector or any person deputed by them or either of them to represent them or either of them in their absence shall have free entry and access to the works of the Contractor at all times while this contract is being performed, and shall have all reasonable facilities afforded to them and their representatives as aforesaid to satisfy them that the same is being carried out and performed in accordance with this contract.

6. The acceptance of and payment for said locomotive engines or any of them by the Commission shall not be considered as any waiver of the obligations of the Contractor hereunder.

7. The Commission, in consideration of the premises, covenants with the Contractor that the Contractor from time to time and in all respects having fulfilled and performed the conditions of this contract (except the fulfillment of the guarantee which is to continue as set out in the specifications) on the Contractor's part intended to be fulfilled and performed shall be paid for each of said locomotive engines the sum of thirty-three thousand four hundred and ninety-five dollars ($33,495.00) within thirty days after delivery of said locomotive engines, respectively, as aforesaid, the above price per locomotive being made up as follows:

Base price (including Vaughan vestibule cab)	$32,000 00
Extra for Commonwealth cast steel cradle	200 00
Extra for Vanadium cast steel main frames	350 00
Extra for Mansell retaining rings on driving wheels	125 00
Extra for heat treated Vanadium heat-treated engine and tender springs	600 00
Extra for Franklin grate shakers	250 00
Extra for radial buffer between engine and tender	70 00
	$33,595 00
Credit to T. & N. O. Ry., *re* substituting Russian type of vestibule cab instead of the Vaughan cab	100 00
Total	**$33,495 00**

In addition to the above the Contractor agrees to furnish and equip two (2) of the locomotives with Mudge-Slater smoke box arrangement at an extra cost of twenty-five dollars ($25.00) per engine, and one (1) locomotive with Boyer speed recorder at an extra cost of one hundred and forty-five dollars ($145.00).

The Contractor also will furnish and supply with the first engine delivered the following extra parts mentioned in paragraph 77, page No. 20 of specification No. 16 attached at prices set opposite same below:—

Eight driving springs—Vanadium heat treated steel Two tender springs—Vanadium heat treated steel Two trailing truck springs—Vanadium heat treated steel .... Four engine truck springs—Vanadium heat treated steel	$840 00
One pair of engine truck wheels with cast steel centres, Standard Steel Co., O.H. steel tires and Mansell retaining rings	200 00
One pair of engine truck brasses	11 00
Six sets each of piston rod metallic packing rings, extension rod metallic packing rings and valve rod metallic packing rings	110 00
One complete set of general and detail blue prints	25 00

8. It is understood that the price payable for each of said locomotive engines as aforesaid is based on the material therefor being imported into Canada under the present tariff of duties now in force, namely, seven per cent. (7%), and the Commission hereby agrees with the Contractor that in the event of any increase in the customs duties affecting the materials required in the construction of said locomotive engines the price hereby agreed to be paid for each of said locomotive engines shall be increased proportionately to the increase in said customs duties.

IN WITNESS WHEREOF the said parties have caused these presents to be executed under their respective corporate seals and under the hands of the proper officers in that behalf.

SIGNED, SEALED AND DELIVERED
 in the presence of
  A. GRADY.

JNO. J. HARTY,
Vice-President and Sales Manager.

TEMISKAMING AND NORTHERN
ONTARIO RY. COM'N.
J. L. ENGLEHART,
Chairman.
W. H. MAUND,
Secretary-Treasurer.

A. B. ODLUM.

RE PURCHASE SIX CONDUCTORS' VANS.

Tenders received as follows:
    National Steel Car Company, Ltd., Hamilton.... $3,725 00 f.o.b. North Bay
    Preston Car & Coach Company, Ltd., Preston ..   3,420 00 f.o.b. North Bay
    Canadian Car & Foundry Company, Montreal...   3,675 00 f.o.b. North Bay
Contract awarded Preston Car & Coach Co., Ltd., lowest tenderer.

ARTICLES OF AGREEMENT made this 16th day of June, one thousand nine hundred and sixteen.

BETWEEN:

THE PRESTON CAR AND COACH COMPANY, LIMITED, hereinafter called the Contractor.
—and—

TEMISKAMING AND NORTHERN ONTARIO RAILWAY COMMISSION, hereinafter called the Commission.

WITNESSETH:

1. In this contract the word "Inspector" shall mean the Inspector for the time being appointed by the Commission to represent and act for the Commission in the supervision of the construction and in the inspection and certification of the caboose cars hereinafter referred to.

2. The Contractor will supply and provide all and every kind of work, labor, materials, articles and things whatsoever for the due construction and completion, and will well and duly built and complete in a perfect and workmanlike manner

six standard twenty-nine foot caboose cars with all necessary appliances for use on the line of railway of the Commission in strict compliance with the specifications hereto annexed and the plans relating thereto, to the complete satisfaction of the Inspector, and the Contractor will deliver the said caboose cars, completed, to the Commission, free on the railway tracks of the Commission at North Bay Junction on or before the 15th day of November, 1916, time being agreed to be material and of the essence of this contract, and in default of such delivery within the time aforesaid the Contractor will pay to the Commission, by way of liquidated damages, the sum of ten ($10) dollars in respect of each caboose car for each day which shall elapse after the date aforesaid before delivery of such caboose cars respectively, which sums the Commission is authorized to deduct from the purchase price hereinafter mentioned. It is understood and agreed between the parties hereto that in the event of strikes, labor troubles, fire, delay in transmission or inability beyond the Contractor's control to obtain delivery of necessary materials, or failure to receive necessary working details from the Commission, or from any other cause beyond the control of the Contractor, the said Contractor shall be exempted from strict compliance with the provisions of this agreement as to the time of delivery.

3. The Contractor will furnish and deliver to the Commission at Toronto, without extra charge, two complete sets of blue prints of all detailed plans of said caboose cars, and until delivery of such blue prints the Contractor shall not, be deemed for the purpose of this contract to have delivered said caboose cars or to be entitled to payment therefor.

4. The Inspector shall be the sole judge of all work and material done and supplied under this contract, and his decision on all questions in dispute with regard to any such work or material shall be final, and the whole work shall be executed to his satisfaction as evidenced by his certificate in writing which shall be given before he allows the cars to leave the Contractor's works, and which certificate shall be a condition precedent to the right of the Contractor to be paid therefor.

5. The Inspector and all persons from time to time authorized by him in that behalf shall have free entry and access to the works of the Contractor at all times while this contract is being performed, and shall have all reasonable facilities afforded to him and his representatives as aforesaid to satisfy him that same is being carried out and performed in accordance with this contract.

6. The acceptance and payment for one of said caboose cars shall not be considered as any waiver of the obligation of the contract with reference to the other of said caboose cars.

7. The Contractors guarantee all parts, and particularly the following, the enumeration of which is not in any way to limit the extent of this guarantee: steel underframe, wood superstructure framing, wheels, axles, truck springs; not to show signs of defect or weakness within three years' service under fair usage. The books or other records of the Commission shall be taken as final and conclusive evidence of the times said steel underframe, wood superstructure framing, wheels, axles, truck springs have lasted in service.

8. The Commission, in consideration of the premises, covenants with the Contractor that the Contractor from time to time, and in all respects having fulfilled

and performed the provisions of this contract (except the fulfillment of the guarantee which is to continue for three years) on the Contractors' part intended to be fulfilled and performed shall be paid for each of the said caboose cars the sum of three thousand four hundred and twenty dollars ($3,420.00) within thirty days after delivery of each caboose car f.o.b. tracks of the Commission at North Bay Junction as aforesaid.

IN WITNESS WHEREOF the said parties have caused these presents to be executed under their respective corporate seals under the hands of the proper officers in that behalf.

SIGNED, SEALED AND DELIVERED

in the presence of

Roy V. Bullock.

A. B. Pratt.

THE PRESTON CAR AND COACH CO., LTD.
CHAS. S. WRIGHT,
General Manager.
F. CLARE,
President.
(Seal.)

TEMISKAMING AND NORTHERN ONTARIO RY. COM'N.
J. L. ENGLEHART,
Chairman.
W. H. MAUND,
Secretary-Treasurer.
(Seal.)

CONSTRUCTION OF PASSENGER STATION, TIMMINS, ONT.

. Contract awarded Messrs. Henderson & Angus, North Bay, lowest tenderer.

ARTICLES OF AGREEMENT made in triplicate this 19th day of June, in the year of our Lord one thousand nine hundred and sixteen.

BETWEEN:

LEONARD W. HENDERSON and HENRY W. ANGUS, both of the Town of North Bay in the District of Nipissing, Contractors, carrying on business under the firm name and style of HENDERSON & ANGUS, hereinafter called the Contractors.

—and—

TEMISKAMING AND NORTHERN ONTARIO RAILWAY COMMISSION, hereinafter called the Commission.

WITNESSETH:

1. In this contract the word "work" or "works" shall, unless the context requires a different meaning, mean the whole of the work and materials, matters and things required to be done, furnished and performed under this contract. The

Cutting O. A. C. No. 3 Oats, August 5th, on farm, Clergue Township. Sown on May 5th.
Yield, 60 bushels per acre.   South half Lot 1, Con. 2.

A field of Alsike Clover on Mr. Johnston's Farm near McCool.   A field like this will
yield 9 bushels of seed per acre.

word " Engineer " or " Chief Engineer " shall mean the Chief Engineer of the Temiskaming and Northern Ontario Railway Commission for the time being acting as such either directly or through the Assistant Chief Engineer, Division Engineer, Assistant Engineer, Resident Engineer or Inspector having immediate charge of the work or of that portion thereof limited by the particular duties entrusted to him. All instructions and directions, or certificates given, or decisions made, by anyone acting under the authority of the Chief Engineer shall be subject to his approval and may be cancelled, altered, modified and changed as he may see fit. In all cases where the Contractors are dissatisfied with the decision of the Engineer or Inspector in immediate charge of the work, an appeal to the Chief Engineer may be made. It is declared and agreed that it shall not be in the power of the Chief Engineer or of any Engineer or Inspector to waive any of the provisions of this agreement and no waiver of any such shall on any pretence be claimed by the Contractors.

2. The Contractors will at their own expense provide all and every kind of work, labor, materials, articles and things whatsoever necessary for the due construction and completion, and will well and truly build and complete in perfect and workmanlike manner a brick and concrete passenger station at Timmins, Ontario, in strict compliance with the general conditions and specifications annexed hereto and which, for the purpose of identification, have been signed by the Chief Engineer and the Contractors and form part of this agreement, and to the plans, profiles and drawings in the office of the Chief Engineer and any further plans or drawings in addition thereto which the Chief Engineer may find necessary to provide from time to time for the full and complete performance of the work, and will deliver the said passenger station complete to the Commission on or before the 31st day of October, 1916; time being agreed to be material and of the essence of this contract.

3. The Contractors shall forthwith commence work and shall proceed diligently therewith at the rate required by the Chief Engineer, and shall complete the work, including extras and alterations, and notwithstanding any delay or hindrance by the Commission, to the satisfaction of the Chief Engineer by the date set out in the last preceding paragraph, or by such other date as on the written application of the Contractors for an extension of time the Chief Engineer may in writing substitute, and in default shall pay to the Commission by way of liquidated damages the sum of ten ($10) dollars for each day which shall or may elapse after the date mentioned in the last preceding paragraph or the date expressly substituted therefor in manner aforesaid by the Chief Engineer until the whole work shall be so completed and delivered.

4. The Chief Engineer shall be at liberty at any time either before the commencement or during construction of the works or any portion thereof to order any extra work to be done and to make any changes which he may deem expedient in the dimensions, character, nature, location or position of the works or any part or parts thereof or in any other things connected with the works, whether or not such changes increase or diminish the work to be done or the cost of doing the same, and the Contractors shall immediately comply with all requisitions of the Chief Engineer in that behalf, and shall commence and complete the work so ordered to be done within the time specified by the Chief Engineer, but the Contractors shall not

make any change in or addition to or omission or deviation from the work and shall not be entitled to any payment for any change, addition, deviation or any extra work unless such change, addition, omission, deviation or extra work shall have been first directed in writing by the Chief Engineer and notified to the Contractors, and the decision of the Chief Engineer as to whether any such change or deviation increases or diminishes the work and as to the allowance (under the Contractors' schedule of prices hereinafter referred to) to be made to the Contractors or deducted from the Contractors in respect of any such increase or diminution shall be final, and all the provisions of this contract shall apply to any changes, addition, deviations or extra work in like manner and to the same extent as to the work tendered for, and no changes, additions, deviations or extra work shall annul or invalidate this contract and no compensation shall be claimable by the Contractors for any loss of anticipated profits in respect of or in consequence of any change or deviation in or omission from the works.

5. The Chief Engineer shall be the sole judge of the work and material in respect of both quantity and quality, and his decision on all matters in dispute in respect to work and material shall be final, and no works or extra or additional works or changes shall be deemed to have been executed nor shall the Contractors be entitled to payment for the same unless the same shall have been directed in writing as hereinbefore provided and executed to the satisfaction of the Chief Engineer as evidenced by his certificate in writing, which certificate shall be a condition precedent to the right of the Contractors to be paid therefor.

6. The Contractors shall be at the risk of and shall bear all loss or damage whatsoever which may occur to the works or any of them until the same be fully and finally completed and delivered up to and accepted by the Commission, and if any such loss or damage occur before such completion, delivery and acceptance the Contractors shall immediately, at their own expense, repair, restore and re-execute the work so damaged so that the whole works or the respective parts thereof will be completed within the time hereby limited or such further time as shall be expressly substituted therefor in the manner aforesaid by the Chief Engineer.

7. The Contractors shall not at any time, in connection with the said work or any matter arising out of or connected with this contract, employ any person or persons in contravention of the Alien Labor Act or the provisions of the Railway Act of Ontario respecting the employment of alien labor, and shall pay to all workmen, laborers and servants employed in or about the work such rates of wages as shall or may be currently payable to workmen, laborers and servants engaged in similar occupations in the district in which said work shall be performed, and shall be responsible for the observance by all sub-contractors on their part of the provisions of this clause, and in the event of the Commission, who shall be the sole, absolute and final judge of these matters, being satisfied at any time that the Contractors or any sub-contractors have been guilty of any violation of any of the provisions of this clause the Commission shall have the right from time to time, and as often as it shall be satisfied that any such violation has taken place, to withhold all payments from the Contractors until any such violation of any of the provisions of this clause shall, in the opinion of the Commission, have ceased, and until such amends as the Commission shall require shall have been made for all such violation, and on being notified by the Commission of any such violation it shall be the duty

of the Chief Engineer to withhold all certificates from the Contractors until the Commission shall be satisfied that such violation has ceased and until amends shall have been made to the satisfaction of the Commission as aforesaid.

8. A competent superintendent or foreman shall be kept on the ground by the Contractors during all the working hours to receive the orders of the Chief Engineer, and should the person so appointed be deemed by the Chief Engineer incompetent or conduct himself improperly he may be discharged by the Chief Engineer and another shall be at once appointed in his stead; such superintendent or foreman shall be considered as the lawful representative of the Contractors and shall have full power to carry out all requisitions and instructions of the Chief Engineer.

9. In case any materials, or other things in the opinion of the Chief Engineer which are not in accordance with the several parts of this agreement or are not sufficiently sound or are otherwise unsuitable for the respective work, shall be used for or brought to the intended works or any part thereof, or in case any work shall be improperly executed the Chief Engineer may require the Contractors to remove the same and to provide proper materials or other things or to properly re-execute the work, as the case may be; and thereupon the Contractors shall and will immediately comply with the said requisition, and if twenty-four hours shall elapse and such requisition shall not have been complied with, the Chief Engineer may cause such materials or other things, or such work, to be removed, and, in any such case, the Contractors shall pay to the Commission all such damages and expenses as shall be incurred in the removal of such materials or other things or of such work, or the Commission may, in its discretion, retain and deduct such damages and expenses from any amounts payable to the Contractors.

10. All machinery and other plant, materials and things whatsoever provided by the Contractors for the works hereby contracted for, and not rejected under the provisions of the last preceding clause, shall, from time of their being so provided, become, and, until the final completion of the said work shall be the property of the Commission for the purpose of the said works, and the same shall on no account be taken away or used or disposed of except for the purposes of the said works without the consent in writing of the Chief Engineer, and the Commission shall not be answerable for any loss or damage whatsoever which may happen to such machinery or other plant, materials or things, provided always that upon the completion of · the works and upon payment by the Contractors of all such moneys, if any, as shall be due from them to the Commission, such of the said machinery and other plant, materials and things as shall not have been used and converted in the works and shall remain undisposed of, shall upon demand be delivered up to the Contractors.

11. In case the Contractors shall make default or delay in diligently continuing to execute or advance the works to the satisfaction of the Chief Engineer, and such default or delay shall continue for six days after notice in writing shall have been given by the Chief Engineer to the Contractors requiring them to put an end to such default or delay, or in case the Contractors shall become insolvent or make an assignment for the benefit of creditors, or neglect either personally or - by skilful and competent agent to superintend the works, or if any winding-up order is made against the Contractors under the provisions of the Winding-Up Act or any Act of a similar character applicable to the Contractors, or in

case the Contractors do not give access to and allow inspection of and the making of extracts from payrolls, books and vouchers, from time to time to the Chief Engineer or the Commission, or to any person or persons from time to time instructed by the Chief Engineer or by the Commission in that behalf, so that the said Chief Engineer may satisfy himself of the due observance by the Contractors and all sub-contractors of all the provisions of this contract, and especially of the provisions of clause 13 hereof, and that the Commission may satisfy itself from time to time of the due observance by the Contractors and by all sub-contractors of the provisions of clause 7 of this contract, or if the Contractors or any sub-contractors are, in the opinion of the Chief Engineer, who shall be the sole and final judge thereof, guilty of any violation of any of the provisions of clause 13 hereof, or if the Contractors or any sub-contractors are, in the opinion of the Commission, who shall be the sole and final judge thereof, guilty of any violation of any of the provisions of clause 7 hereof, then in any of such cases the Commission may take the work out of the hands of the Contractors and employ such means as it may see fit to complete the work, and the Contractors shall have no claim for damages or for any further payment in respect of the work performed, but shall nevertheless remain liable for all loss or damage which may be suffered by reason of the non-completion by them of the works; and all materials and things whatsoever and all horses, machinery and other plant provided by them for the purposes of the works shall remain and be considered as the property of the Commission for the purposes and according to the provisions and conditions contained in paragraph 14 hereof.

12. If the work to be done under this agreement shall be abandoned or be assigned by the Contractors without the consent of the Commission, or if the Contractors shall lose control of the work for any cause, excepting the acts of God or of the public enemy, or if at any time the Chief Engineer shall be of the opinion, and shall so certify in writing to the Commission, that the Contractors are wilfully and persistently violating any of the conditions or covenants of this agreement or are not executing said works in good faith, the Commission may take the work out of the hands of the Contractors and may employ such means as it may see fit to complete the work, and all the provisions of section 11 of the agreement shall thereupon apply and the Commission shall have in regard to the said work all the powers therein provided.

13. In case any sum due for the labor of any foreman, workman or laborer, or for the use of any horse or other animals or wagons or other plant employed upon or in respect of the said works or any of them, or the price of any materials or supplies purchased for the said work remains unpaid, the Chief Engineer may notify the Contractors to pay such sum and if two days elapse and the same be not paid the Commission may pay such sum and the Contractors covenant with the Commission to repay at once any and every sum so paid, and if the Contractors do not repay the same within two days the Commission may deduct the amount or amounts so paid by it from any sum that may then or thereafter be or become due by the Commission to the Contractors.

14. If the Chief Engineer shall at any time consider that the number of workmen, horses or quantity of machinery or other plant, or the quantity of proper materials respectively employed, provided or supplied by the Contractors on or for the said works is insufficient for the advancement thereof towards completion within the limited time, or that the works are, or some part thereof is, not being carried

on with due diligence, then in every such case the Chief Engineer may, by written notice to the Contractors, require them to employ or provide such additional workmen, horses, machinery or other plant or materials as the Chief Engineer may think necessary, and in case the Contractors shall not thereupon within seven days, or such other longer period as may be fixed by any such notice, in all respects comply therewith the Chief Engineer may, either on behalf of the Commission, or, if he sees fit, may as the agent of and on account of the Contractors, but in either case at the expense of the Contractors, provide and employ such additional workmen, horses, machinery and other plant or any portion thereof or such additional materials, respectively as he may think proper, and may pay such additional workmen such wages and for such additional horses, machinery or other plant and materials respectively such prices as he may think proper, and all such wages and prices respectively shall thereupon at once be repaid by the Contractors or the same may be retained and deducted out of any sum that may then or thereafter be or become due from the Commission to the Contractors, and the Commission may use in the execution or advancement of the said works not only the horses, machinery and other plant and materials so in any case provided by anyone on its behalf, but also all such as may have been or may be provided by or on behalf of the said Contractors.

15. Neither the acceptance of nor the payment for the said passenger station by the Commission shall be construed as any waiver of the obligations of the Contractors hereunder with reference thereto.

16. The Contractors shall furnish the Commission with a bond of the United States Fidelity and Guaranty Company as security for the performance of this contract, such bond being hereto annexed.

17. Approximate estimates of the work done, made up from returns of progress measurements and computed at the prices determined or agreed upon under the provisions of this agreement are to be made by the Engineer at the end of each calender month, and on or about the twentieth day of the next ensuing month payments equal to about eighty-five per cent. of the value of the work done, as shown by such approximate monthly estimate, shall be made to the Contractors upon presentation of the written certificate of the Chief Engineer that the work for or on account of which the certificate is granted has been duly performed and executed to his satisfaction and stating the value of such work computed as mentioned, and upon approval of such certificate by the Commission and the said certificate and such approval thereto shall be a condition precedent to the right of the Contractors to be paid the said eighty-five per cent. or any part thereof. The remaining fifteen per cent. shall be retained by the Commission until the final completion of the whole work as an additional security for the performance of this agreement by the Contractors, and when, in the opinion of the Chief Engineer, this agreement has been completely performed in accordance with the provisions thereof and until the Chief Engineer shall be satisfied that all wages of all workmen, laborers and servants' of the Contractors and of all sub-contractors under them as well as the price of all materials and supplies made, procured or provided for the Contractors or for any of the sub-contractors have been duly paid he shall certify the same accordingly in writing under his hand with a final estimate of the work done by the Contractors and with a statement of the work due and unpaid, and within two months after the granting of such certificate the amount so found due and unpaid

26 T R

shall be paid to the Contractors upon delivery to the Commission of a good and valid release and discharge of and from any and all claims and demands for and in respect of all matters and things growing out of or connected with this agreement or the subject matter thereof. The written certificates of the Chief Engineer certifying to the final completion of the work to his entire satisfaction and of the evidence called for by this clause having been furnished to him shall be a condition precedent to the right of the Contractors to receive or be paid the amount certified by the Chief Engineer as due and unpaid or any part thereof, and the certificate of the Chief Engineer shall be conclusive as to the amount to be paid to the Contractor.

18. The Commission in consideration of the premises covenants with the Contractors that the Contractors from time and in all respects having fulfilled and performed the provisions of this contract on the Contractors' part intended to be fulfilled and performed will be paid for and in respect of the said work the sum of twenty-three thousand eight hundred and twenty-five dollars ($23,825.00) subject to such deductions and additions as shall be certified by the Chief Engineer in accordance with the terms of this contract; said deductions or additions to be based on the Contractors' schedule of prices hereto annexed being the schedule of prices called for by said general conditions; payments to be made from time to time on the progress estimates of the Chief Engineer and the final payment to be made within sixty days after the date of the Chief Engineer's final certificate of the completion of the said work.

19. In addition to the foregoing contract price the Commission will pay to the Contractors for extra work done under written orders of the Chief Engineer, not covered by this agreement but done in the proper execution of this agreement and for which prices are not named herein, the actual cost of such work with an additional fifteen per cent. on the cost of labor and materials for the use of tools, contractors' plant, superintendence and profit, but such actual cost shall not exceed the reasonable market value of such labor and materials as the case may be.

20. Where, in the opinion of the Chief Engineer, the work done or materials furnished is not, having regard to the nature and character of the work remaining to be performed or the materials remaining to be furnished, of sufficient value to justify computation at the prices agreed upon and determined under the provisions of this agreement, it shall be competent for the Chief Engineer in certifying the value of the work done or materials furnished for the purpose of such payment to disregard the prices so agreed upon or determined and to compute and certify its relative and proportionate value, having regard to the nature and character of the work remaining to be performed or materials remaining to be furnished in which case the Contractor shall only be entitled to receive eighty-five per cent. of the value of the work done or materials furnished as stated in such certificate, and he shall not be paid the difference between eighty-five per cent. of the value of the work done or materials furnished as so ascertained and certified, and eighty-five per cent. of the value of such work or materials according to the prices stipulated therefor under the provisions of this agreement until such time as the Chief Engineer, by reason of the performance of additional work or materials of greater relative value, shall certify that the Contractors are entitled to receive the same.

21. It is distinctly agreed that no implied contract of any kind whatsoever by or on behalf of the Commission shall arise or be implied from anything contained in this contract, including the said general conditions, specifications, plans and drawings, or the tender of the said Contractors for the said work or from any position or situation of the parties at any time; it being clearly understood and agreed that the express contracts, covenants, agreements and stipulations contained in these presents and in the said general conditions, specifications, plan and drawings are and shall be the only contracts, covenants, agreements and stipulations upon which any right of action against the Commission is to be founded; it being further expressly agreed that the said general conditions and specifications and these presents are to be read together, and in case of any discrepancy between these presents and anything contained in the said specifications the provisions of these presents shall govern. In case of any discrepancy appearing at any time between the specifications, profiles, plans, drawings and detailed drawings or any of them the Contractors shall follow such one of them as the Chief Engineer shall in writing direct.

AS WITNESS the hands and seals of the said Contractors and the Corporate seal of the said Commission under the hands of its proper officers in that behalf.

SIGNED, SEALED AND DELIVERED
in the presence of
JEANETTE M. ANGUS.

A. B. ODLUM.

HENDERSON AND ANGUS.
G. W. HENDERSON.
H. W. ANGUS.

TEMISKAMING AND NORTHERN ONTARIO RY. COM'N.
J. L. ENGLEHART,
Chairman.
W. H. MAUND,
Secretary-Treasurer.

BOND No. 402267-16.

Issued in duplicate.

KNOW ALL MEN BY THESE PRESENTS that we, LEONARD W. HENDERSON and HENRY W. ANGUS, both of the Town of North Bay, in District of Nipissing, Contractors, carrying on business under the firm name and style of HENDERSON AND ANGUS, hereinafter called the Principals, and the UNITED STATES FIDELITY AND GUARANTY COMPANY, a corporation created and existing under the laws of the State of Maryland, and whose principal office is located in Baltimore City, Maryland, duly registered under the laws of the Dominion of Canada and entitled to transact business therein, hereinafter called the Surety, are held and firmly bound unto the Temiskaming and Northern Ontario Railway Commission, hereinafter called the Commission, in the full and just sum of two thousand three hundred and eighty-two dollars and fifty cents ($2,382.50) for the payment of which sum well and truly to be made the said Principals and the said Surety bind themselves and their respective heirs, executors, administrators, successors and assigns jointly and severally firmly by these presents.

Horse owned by Mr. Frank Hunter, Englehart, Ont.

SIGNED, SEALED AND DELIVERED by the Principals at North Bay, Ontario, this 19th day of June, 1916, and by the said Surety at Toronto, Canada, this 28th day of June, 1916.

WHEREAS the said Principals have entered into a written contract hereto annexed with the Commission for the building of a brick and concrete passenger station at Timmins, Ontario.

NOW THEREFORE the condition of the foregoing obligation is such that if the said Principals, their heirs, executors, administrators, successors or assigns do or shall well and faithfully do all the work and furnish all the materials and observe and perform all the matters and things required to be done, furnished, observed and performed by them under the said contract hereto annexed within the times and in the manner and according to the true intent and meaning of the said contract, then this obligation shall be void otherwise the same shall remain in full force and virtue.

PROVIDED, HOWEVER, that this bond is issued subject to the following conditions and provisions:

1. That no liability shall attach to the Surety hereunder unless in the event of any default on the part of the Principals in the performance of any of the terms, covenants and conditions of the said contract the Commission shall promptly upon knowledge thereof by its Secretary, and in any event not later than thirty days after such knowledge of default by its Secretary, deliver to the Canadian Manager or Assistant Manager of the said Surety at its office in the City of Toronto, written notice thereof, with a statement of the principal facts showing such default and the date thereof nor unless the said Commission shall deliver written notice to the said Manager or Assistant Manager of the Surety at its office aforesaid, and the consent of the Surety or its Manager or Assistant Manager aforesaid thereto obtained before making to the Principals the final payment provided for under said contract.

2. That in case of such default on the part of the Principals the Surety shall have the right, if it so desires, to assume and complete or procure the completion of said contract, and in case of such default the Surety shall be subrogated and entitled to all the rights of the Principals arising out of the said contract and otherwise including all securities and indemnities, if any, heretofore received by the Commission, and all deferred payments retained, percentages and credits due to the Principals at the time when the Surety shall have assumed said contract or to become due thereafter by the terms and dates of said contract.

3. That in no event shall the Surety be liable for any greater sum than the penalty of this bond or subject to any suit, action or proceeding which is instituted later than the 31st day of October, 1917.

IN WITNESS WHEREOF the Principals have executed these presents under their hands and seals, and the said Surety has caused these presents to be executed by its attorney in fact, sealed with its corporate seal, the day and the year first above written.

HENDERSON AND ANGUS. L. W. HENDERSON. H. W. ANGUS. (Seal.) WITNESS: JEANETTE M. ANGUS.	UNITED STATES FIDELITY AND GUARANTY CO. W. E. KIRKPATRICK.

ARTICLES OF AGREEMENT made in duplicate this 7th day of October, in the year of our Lord one thousand nine hundred and sixteen.

BETWEEN:

F. R. GIBSON, of the Town of Haileybury, in the District of Timiskaming, hereinafter called the " Contractor."

Of the First Part.

—and—

TEMISKAMING AND NORTHERN ONTARIO RAILWAY COMMIS-SION, hereinafter called the " Commission."

Of the Second Part.

WITNESSETH:

1. In this contract the word " work " or " works " shall, unless the context requires different meaning, mean the whole of the work and materials, matters and things required to be done, furnished and performed under this contract. The word " Engineer " shall mean the Chief Engineer for the time being appointed by the Commission and having control over the work.

2. The Contractor will at his own expense provide all and every kind of work, labor, materials, articles and things whatsoever for the due construction and completion, and will well and duly build, install and complete in a perfect and work-manlike manner heating and plumbing systems in four semi-detached tenement houses of the Commission at Iroquois Falls, Ontario, in strict compliance with the specifications hereto annexed and with the plans and drawings relating thereto to the complete satisfaction of the Engineer, and will deliver said heating and plumbing systems in each of said tenement houses complete to the Commission on or before the 16th day of November, 1916; time being agreed to be material and of the essence of this contract.

3. The Contractor shall forthwith commence work and shall proceed diligently therewith at the rate required by the Engineer, and shall complete the work, including extras and alterations, and notwithstanding any delay or hindrance by the Commission to the satisfaction of the Engineer by the date set out in the last preceding paragraph or by such other date as on the written application of the contractor for an extension of time the Engineer may in writing substitute, and in default shall pay to the Commission by way of liquidated damages the sum of five dollars ($5.00) for each day which shall or may elapse after the date mentioned in the last preceding paragraph for the completion of the heating and plumbing system in each of said tenement houses, or the date or dates expressly substituted therefor in manner aforesaid by the Engineer until the whole work in respect of each of said tenement houses shall be so completed and delivered.

4. The Engineer shall be at liberty at any time either before the commencement or during the construction of the works or any portion thereof to order any extra work to be done and to make any changes which he may deem expedient in the dimensions, character, nature, location or position of the works or any part or parts

thereof, or in any other things connected with the works whether or not such changes increase or diminish the work to be done or the cost of doing the same; and the Contractor shall immediately comply with all requisitions of the Engineer in that behalf and shall commence and complete the work so ordered to be done within the time specified by the Engineer, but the Contractor shall not make any change in or addition to or omission or deviation from the work, and shall not be entitled to any payment for any change, addition, deviation or any extra work unless such change, addition, omission, deviation or extra work shall have been first directed in writing by the Engineer and notified to the Contractor, and the decision of the Engineer as to whether any such change or deviation increases or diminishes the work and as to the allowance to be made to the Contractor or deducted from the Contractor in respect of any such increase or diminution shall be final, and all the provisions of this contract shall apply to any changes, additions, deviations or extra work in like manner and to the same extent as to the work tendered for, and no changes, additions, deviations or extra work shall annul or invalidate this contract, and no compensation shall be claimable by the Contractor for any loss of anticipated profits in respect of or in consequence of any change or deviation in or omission from the works.

5. The Engineer shall be the sole judge of the work and material in respect of both quantity and quality, and his decision on all matters in dispute in respect to work and material shall be final, and no works or extra or additional works or changes shall be deemed to have been executed, nor shall the Contractor be entitled to payment for the same unless the same shall have been directed in writing as hereinbefore provided and executed to the satisfaction of the Engineer as evidenced by his certificate in writing, which certificate shall be a condition precedent to the right of the Contractor to be paid therefor.

6. The Contractor shall be at the risk of and shall bear all loss or damage whatsoever which may occur to the works or any of them until the same be fully and finally completed and delivered up to and accepted by the Commission, and if any such loss or damage occur before such time for completion, delivery and acceptance the Contractor shall immediately, at his own expense, repair, restore and re-execute the work so damaged so that the whole works or the respective parts thereof will be completed within the time hereby limited.

7. In case the Contractor shall make default or delay in diligently continuing to execute or advance any of the works to be performed under this contract to the satisfaction of the Engineer, or shall make default in commencing any portion or portions of the work or complete same within the periods specified by the Engineer as provided for in section 3 of this contract, and such default and delay shall continue for six days after notice in writing shall have been given by the Engineer to the Contractor requiring him to put an end to such default or delay, or in case the Contractor shall become insolvent or shall, without the written consent of the Commission, make an assignment of this contract, or shall, without the written consent of the Engineer, make any sub-contract, or neglect personally to superintend the works, then and in any of such cases the Commission may take all the work under this contract off the Contractor's hands and employ such means as it may see fit to complete the work embraced in the contract, and in such case the Contractor shall have no claim for any further payment in respect of the work per-

formed, but all things done and means employed under this section by the Commission shall be as binding on the Contractor as if the things done and means employed had been done and employed by him under this contract, but the Contractor shall nevertheless remain liable for all loss or damage which shall be suffered by the Commission by reason of the non-completion by the Contractor of the works, and no question or claim shall be raised or made by the Contractor by reason of or on account of the ultimate cost of the work so taken over proving greater than in the opinion of the Contractor it should have been, and all materials, articles and things whatsoever, and all machinery and other plant provided by the Contractor for the purposes of the works shall remain and be considered as the property of the Commission for the purposes of the said works, and the Commission may at its option sell or otherwise dispose of the whole or a portion of such materials, articles and things whatsoever, machinery and other plant, and may retain the proceeds of such sale or disposition or a sufficient part thereof on account of or in satisfaction of any loss which it may have sustained by reason aforesaid.

8. Neither the acceptance nor the payment for the said heating and plumbing systems or any part thereof by the Commission shall be construed as any waiver of the obligations of the Contractor with reference thereto.

9. The Commission in consideration of the premises covenants with the Contractor that the Contractor from time to time in all respects having fulfilled and performed the provisions of this contract on the Contractor's part intended to be fulfilled and performed will be paid for and in respect of the said heating and plumbing systems so completed as aforesaid the sum of fourteen hundred and forty dollars ($1,440) subject to such deductions or additions as shall be certified by the Engineer; payments to be made from time to time on progress certificates of the Engineer and the final payment to be made within forty (40) days after the date of the Engineer's final certificate of the completion of said work.

10. In addition to the foregoing contract price the Commission will pay to the Contractor for extra work done under written orders of the Chief Engineer not covered by this agreement but done in the proper execution of this agreement and for which prices are not named herein the actual cost of such work with an additional fifteen per cent. on the cost of labor. This percentage shall include all overhead charges for offices, superintendence, general expenses, use of tools, equipment, profit, etc., but such actual cost shall not exceed the reasonable market value of such labor.

11. As security for the due performance, execution, and completion of this contract by the Contractor the Contractor shall upon the execution hereof deposit with the Commission the sum of one hundred and forty-four dollars in cash, or in lieu of such deposit furnish the Commission with a bond of the United States Fidelity and Guaranty Company or such other guarantee company as the Commission shall approve for a like amount.

12. It is distinctly agreed that no implied contract of any kind whatsoever by or on behalf of the Commission shall arise or be implied from anything contained in this contract including the said specifications and the plans and drawings or the tender of the said Contractor for said work or from any position or situation of the

parties at any time, it being clearly understood and agreed that the express contracts, covenants, agreements and stipulations contained in these presents and in the said specifications, plans and drawings are and shall be the only contracts, covenants, agreements and stipulations upon which any right of action against the Commission is to be founded; it being further expressly agreed that the said specifications and these presents are to be read together, and in case of any discrepancy between these presents and anything contained in such specifications the provisions of these presents shall govern, and in case of any discrepancy appearing at any time between the specifications, plans and drawings or any of them the Contractor shall follow such one of them as the Engineer shall in writing direct.

IN WITNESS WHEREOF the Contractor has hereunto set his hand and seal and the Commission has affixed its corporate seal under the hands of its proper officers in that behalf.

SIGNED, SEALED AND DELIVERED
   in the presence of: F. R. GIBSON.
     KATHLEEN MASON.

                           TEMISKAMING   AND   NORTHERN
                             ONTARIO RY. COM'N.
                             J. L. ENGLEHART,
     A. B. ODLUM.   *Chairman.*
                                    (Seal.)
                           W. H. MAUND,
                              Secretary-Treasurer.

SPECIFICATIONS FOR HEATING AND PLUMBING SYSTEMS IN SEMI-DETACHED TENEMENT HOUSES AT IROQUOIS FALLS.

GENERAL.

Work to be Done.

The work to be governed by these specifications consists in the furnishing of all materials, tools, labor and equipment necessary for the complete installation of hot air heating systems and complete plumbing systems in four (4) tenement houses at Iroquois Falls, Ont., for the Temiskaming and Northern Ontario Railway Commission.

Terms Employed.

Wherever the word " Commission " is employed in these specifications it refers to the Temiskaming and Northern Ontario Railway Commission.

Wherever the word " Contractor " is employed in these specifications it refers to the Contractor for the work governed by these specifications.

Wherever the word " Engineer " is employed in these specifications it refers to the Chief Engineer of the Temiskaming and Northern Ontario Railway or his regularly appointed Assistant or Inspector.

Labor and Materials.

The Contractor shall furnish all labor, tools and materials necessary for the complete and substantial installation of everything described or implied for the work.

Work Done by Commission.

The Commission is now erecting the four (4) tenement houses at Iroquois Falls and will also install all soil drains in basement floors and will leave all drains with elbow ends so that this Contractor can make proper connections with soil stacks.

The Commission will further have the water supply pipe brought into basement of each building.

HOT AIR HEATING SYSTEM.

Furnace.

Furnish and set up in basement of each house one No. 308 Pease " Economy " hot air furnace having a capacity of 14,000 cu. ft., a full set of five tools shall be installed with each furnace.   Furnaces to be located as shown on plans.

Smoke Pipe.

Connect furnace to chimney flues with No. 20 gauge galvanized iron smoke pipe to be the same size as opening on top of furnace and have a proper damper in same.

Bends.

All bends and turns in all pipes to be made with three-piece elbows; all pipes to be firmly supported.

Cold Air Ducts.

Run two cold air ducts in basement from furnace to register faces as shown in plans.

Hot Air Pipes.

Furnish and set up to the furnace and register faces pipes and ducts to be made air and gas proof of 1 x tin.   All pipes in partitions to be wrapped with asbestos paper and all turns and bends in leaders to be made as above specified under " Bends."

Registers.

All registers to be of cast iron, japanned, of approved design and installed according to sizes and locations shown on plans.   All register boxes to be made double.

Basement Pipes.

All horizontal pipes in basement to be round and according to sizes shown as plans.   All basement pipes to be firmly supported, and where passing through partitions, etc., are to have suitable collars.

New Liskeard Dock, January 22, 1915.

New Liskeard Harbour, March 10, 1915.

Dampers and Regulators.

All pipes to be provided with full dampers and place a regulator where directed on ground floor.

Protect Woodwork.

Wherever pipes are in close contact with woodwork the wood is to be properly covered with tin and protected from any danger by fire.

Testing and Final Acceptance.

When all work or works have been completed each heating system shall be thoroughly tested by and at the expense of the Contractor. Each system shall be tested for a period of ten (10) hours working the boiler to its capacity. All tests shall be carried on in the presence of and subject to the approval of the Engineer. After the above test has been completed the Commission requires a test on each system for a period of thirty (30) days, operating under working conditions, after which time, if satisfactory and approved by the Engineer, shall issue final certificate as acceptance of all works. The full expense for the 30 days' test will be borne by the Commission.

PLUMBING SYSTEM.

General.

The Contractor shall supply and install in each of the four (4) tenement houses all plumbing fixtures and materials necessary in accordance with the following specifications and plans and to the entire satisfaction of the Engineer.

Fixtures.

Supply and install the following fixtures selected from Empire Mfg. Coy., Ltd., catalogue " A."

Bath-room.

One (1) enamelled iron lavatory, plate A-1556.P with soap cups attached supported on concealed wall hanger, D pattern bowl fitted with A-429 faucets, nickel plated with $2\frac{1}{2}$-inch shank, $1\frac{1}{2}$-inch P trap and $\frac{1}{2}$-inch angle supplies with stops.

One (1) porcelain enamelled bath, plate A-1427, length $5\frac{1}{2}$ ft. with $\frac{1}{2}$-inch supply pipes and compression double bath cocks, complete with waste and overflow, chain and rubber stopper.

One (1) low down water closet, plate A-10.B complete with all fittings.

One (1) porcelain enamelled sink, size 20 in. x 30 in. with apron and back in one piece, plate A-1631, complete with bibs, strainer and $1\frac{1}{2}$-inch P trap.

Soil-Pipes.

All cast iron pipes must be sound, smooth and cylindrical, free from cracks, sand holes or other defects, of a uniform thickness 4 inches diameter and of a grade known as " extra heavy." All joints must be made with picked oakum and molten lead, thoroughly caulked and gas tight. All vertical runs of cast iron pipe shall be firmly secured in position with strong pipe placed under each hub and all horizontal runs with strong iron hangers not more than five feet apart. The soil pipe shall be carried up through the roof and made water tight by heavy sheet lead flashing. All waste connections are to be made with " Y's " and bends.

Vent Pipes.

All traps in the building shall be ventilated by running 2-inch iron vent pipe connected to the traps by a short length of lead pipe of the full size of the waste on which the trap is located; these vent pipes to be run into the soil or waste pipe above the highest fixtures or extended independently through the roof.

Waste Pipes.

Waste pipes from wash basin and bath shall be 1½-inch medium lead pipe. All connections of lead to iron pipe shall be made with brass ferrules with neatly wiped joints and caulked into iron hubs. All connections of lead pipe to fixtures to be made with brass couplings neatly wiped to lead pipe.

Range Boiler.

Supply and install in kitchen a 30 gallon galvanized iron range boiler mounted on cast iron stand, boiler to be left so that connection can be made to stove when required.

Painting.

All plumbing pipes shall be decorated in two coat work (one of white and one of bronze) as directed by the Engineer.

Water Supply.

Water supply pipes will be brought into the basement of each house by the Commission, but this Contractor will supply all labor and materials to connect up all fixtures specified above.

Ceiling and Floor Plates.

All pipes passing through walls, floors and ceilings to be cased with suitable floor and ceiling plates and left in a neat and workmanlike condition.

Payments.

Monthly payments will be made to the extent of 85 per cent. of value of the work done, as estimated by the Engineer, the balance after system has had a thirty days' test.

No payment except the final one shall be construed as accepting any part of the work as satisfactory.

Completion.

All heating work must be carried on during the construction of the buildings and this contract must be completed on or before the 1st of November, 1916.

(Sgd.) F. R. GIBSON.

CARTAGE—COBALT.

MEMORANDUM OF AGREEMENT made this 5th day of March, A.D. 1916.

BETWEEN:

JOSEPH SIMMS and D. McKAY, both of the Town of Cobalt, Cartage Agents, carrying on business under the firm name and style of THE SIMMS CARTAGE COMPANY, hereinafter called the Contractor.

—and—

TEMISKAMING AND NORTHERN ONTARIO RAILWAY COMMIS-SION, hereinafter called the Commission.

WHEREAS the Contractor proposes to establish a cartage service business in and adjoining Cobalt and elsewhere, and has requested the Commission to enter into the following agreement for cartage service of freight in and adjoining Cobalt:

NOW THESE PRESENTS WITNESS that the agreement between the parties in the premises is as follows:

1. The Contractor agrees to immediately provide a sufficient equipment of horses, vehicles and all necessary appliances, and a sufficient force of men to effi-ciently and promptly handle the cartage business of merchandise to and from the Cobalt Station of the Commission for receipt and delivery in Cobalt and vicinity and that it will promptly and efficiently during the continuance of this agreement deliver freight received from and for the Commission in Cobalt and the vicinity at the rates and on the terms hereinafter provided.

2. The Commission, so far as entitled to control the same, will during the currency of this agreement, hand over to the Contractor all freight included in the Canadian Freight Association's cartage classification which shall require to be carted for delivery or shipment in Cobalt and vicinity, due regard being had to the right of consignees or shippers to take delivery direct or to ship through carters designated by them.

3. The Contractor shall be entitled to charge for its services in the premises not exceeding the following rates: For car loads to any one point within the Town of Cobalt—four cents per one hundred pounds, and for freight in less than car loads to any one point within the Town of Cobalt, five cents per one hundred pounds, provided these rates shall not include "smalls" (being consignments weighing three hundred pounds or less) or any freight not covered by the Canadian Freight Association's cartage classification; and for "smalls" fifteen cents per "small."

4. For freight not covered by the Canadian Freight Association's cartage classification and for all freight, for delivery outside the limits of the Town of Cobalt the Contractor shall make its own terms with the consignees and shall be entitled to charge accordingly.

5. The Commission, so far as bound to make delivery to the Contractor hereunder, shall deliver to, and the Contractor shall take delivery of all freight from the Commission at the freight shed door or car door as .the case may be, and the Commission agrees to keep the freight shed doors open from seven-thirty a.m. to five p.m. each lawful day, and from the first of May to the first of November in each year from seven a.m. to five p.m.

6. The Contractor (except where the Commission shall have otherwise directed in writing) shall before delivery of any freight collect all railway and other charges against same including cartage, and if the contractor shall in any case fail so to collect the charges he will in all respects be responsible therefor as if same had been collected, and the Contractor will pay over to the Commission in cash within twenty-four hours all moneys collected or which should have been collected as aforesaid during each day, including both railway and other charges and cartage.

7. All goods taken out of which delivery shall be refused shall be promptly returned by the Contractor to the Commission free of charge in respect of either delivery or return, and all freight charges on shipments charged by the Commission to the Contractor shall, when delivery is not accepted, be credited back by the Commission to the Contractor upon the return to the Commission such goods, but in that case the cartage shall be added to the freight and when delivery is subsequently made by the Contractor, the Contractor shall be credited with cartage at the aforesaid rate on any such freight.

8. The Commission shall provide desk room for one representative of the Contractor in the Commission's Cobalt station building, free of charge, and will at all times keep a competent clerk in charge of the accounts of the freight delivered to the Contractor and to check over the Contractor's collections daily and to duly receipt for same.

9. The Commission will pay over to the Contractor cartage charges received by the Commission for or on behalf of the Contractor on statements showing weight and "smalls" made upon the seventh, fourteenth, twenty-first and end of each month, such payments to be made from the Toronto office of the Commission forthwith on the accounts being vouched by the local agent of the Commission at Cobalt, and the Traffic Accountant of the Commission, subject to errors, if any, being corrected in subsequent statements.

10. This agreement shall continue in force for two years from the date hereof, subject to the right of either party to terminate same at an earlier date on giving to the other party not less than six months' notice in writing of the desire to terminate the agreement, such notice, if given by the Commission, to be given by the Superintendent of Traffic thereof for the time being and may be given by delivery thereof to any representative of the Contractor or to the Contractor's representative at the Commission's Cobalt Station or to any grown person in the Contractor's office at Cobalt, and if given by the Contractor may be given by delivery thereof to the Chairman, Secretary or Superintendent of Traffic of the Commission, and in case of the giving of any such notice the agreement shall terminate on the date fixed by such notice.

11. It is expressly agreed that if the Contractor is unable to fully carry out at any time any of the terms of this agreement by reason of workmen's strikes,

storms or impassable roads, or by any other matter wholly beyond its control such inability in any such case shall not be considered a breach of this agreement and the Contractor shall not be liable in damages in respect of any failure occurring by reason of any of the causes aforesaid.

12. The Contractor shall not assign or sublet this contract without the consent in writing of the Commission first had and obtained.

13. If the Contractor shall assign or sublet this contract without the consent in writing of the Commission as aforesaid, or if the goods or chattels of the Contractor shall at any time be taken in execution or in attachment by any creditor of the Contractor, or if the said Contractor shall make an assignment for the benefit of creditors, or shall take the benefit or shall be put into liquidation under any Act which may be in force for bankrupt or insolvent debtors or companies, or if the Contractor shall remove its business from the Town of Cobalt, or shall not promptly and faithfully and to the satisfaction of the Superintendent of Traffic for the time being of the Commission do and carry on the cartage business hereby required to be done in accordance with the terms of this agreement, this agreement shall, at the option of the Commission become and be forfeited and void without notice; it being further agreed that waiver, if any, by the Commission of any cause of forfeiture shall apply only to the cause of forfeiture so waived and shall not affect the right of the Commission in respect of any future or other cause of forfeiture.

14. The Contractor shall upon the execution hereof furnish and deliver to the Commission a bond in the penal sum of one thousand dollars in form satisfactory to the Commission, with a surety or sureties approved by the Commission, conditioned for the due performance and observance by the Contractor of this contract.

15. The Contractor will deliver all goods received from the Commission for delivery to the proper consignees and will indemnify the Commission in respect of all misdeliveries.

AS WITNESS the hands and seals of the Contractor and the Corporate seal of the Commission under the hands of the proper officers in that behalf the day and year first above written.

SIGNED, SEALED AND DELIVERED

In the presence of:
  D. H. WAY.

Jos. SIMMS.
D. McKAY.

TEMISKAMING AND NORTHERN ONTARIO RY. COM'N.
  J. L. ENGLHEART,
          Chairman.
                (Seal.)

A. B. PRATT.

W. H. MAUND,
          Secretary-Treasurer.

Coiling Pure Red Clover Hay; yield, 3 tons per acre. Lot 1, Con. 2, Tp. Clergue.

Mixed Timothy, Alsike and Red Clover. Lot 1, Con. 2, Township Clergue.

27 T R

LEASE LAND, LATCHFORD, AND SALE OF OLD BUILDINGS, EMPIRE LUMBER COMPANY.

THIS INDENTURE made the 11th day of July in the year of our Lord one thousand nine hundred and sixteen.

IN PURSUANCE OF THE SHORT FORMS OF LEASES ACT.

BETWEEN:

TEMISKAMING AND NORTHERN ONTARIO RAILWAY COMMIS-SION, hereinafter called the Commission.

Of the First Part.

—and—

M. J. CONKEY and A. J. MURPHY, of the Town of Latchford, in the District of Timiskaming, carrying on business under the firm name and style of CONKEY AND MURPHY, hereinafter called the Lessees.

Of the Second Part.

WHEREAS the Lessees intend to erect a lumber mill and to carry on a lumbering and milling business at or near Latchford Station, in the District of Temiskaming, and to take advantage of the transportation facilities afforded by the railway of the Commission.

AND WHEREAS the Lessees desire a lease of the lands hereinafter described for use as a lumber yard and mill site in carrying on their business, and desire also to purchase from the Commission the buildings hereinafter mentioned at present situate on said lands, and to have a railway siding built connecting said lands with the said railway on the terms hereinafter mentioned.

NOW THIS INDENTURE WITNESSETH that in consideration of the premises and of the rents, covenants and agreements hereinafter respectively reserved and contained on the part of the said Lessees their executors, administrators, successors and assigns to be respectively paid, observed and performed the said Commission doth hereby demise and lease unto the Lessees, their executors, administrators, successors and assigns ALL AND SINGULAR that certain parcel or tract of land and premises, situate, lying and being in the Township of Coleman, in the District of Temiskaming, and Province of Ontario, and being composed of a portion of the station grounds of the Temiskaming and Northern Ontario Railway Commission at Latchford Station, and which parcel may be more particularly described as follows, that is to say: COMMENCING at a point in the easterly limit of the right-of-way of the Temiskaming and Northern Ontario Railway, the position of which point may be definitely located as follows: beginning at the B.C. (in the centre line of the said right-of-way) of a curve whose degree of curvature is 3° 57' and whose central angle is 54° 03' and on which curve occurs the original 94th mile post and the chainage of which B.C. is 368-02.4; thence northerly along the said centre line 250 feet; thence south-easterly and at right angles to the said centre line 49.5 feet to the said point which is the place of commencement; thence

-·still south-easterly and at right angles to the said centre line 150 feet more or less to the high water mark on the westerly shore of the Montreal· River; thence southerly and westerly following the said high water mark to the intersection with the aforementioned easterly limit of the said right-of-way; thence in a north-easterly, northerly and north-westerly direction following the said limit of said right-of-way to the place of commencement and containing by admeasurement 9.5 acres, more or less, as shown on plan of survey prepared by H. M. Anderson, O.L.S., and dated at North Bay, Ont., June 7th, 1915, the same hereto attached.

TO HAVE AND TO HOLD the said demised premises for and during the term of six years to be computed from the date hereof and thenceforth next ensuing and fully to be complete and ended.

YIELDING AND PAYING therefor yearly and every year during the said term unto the said Commission, its successors or assigns, the sum of one hundred dollars ($100) of lawful money of Canada without any deduction, defalcation or abatement whatsoever to be payable on the following days and times, that is to say, in advance on the 11th day of July. in each and every year during the currency of this lease, the first of such payments to become due and to be made on the date of the execution of these presents and the last payment to become due and to be paid on the 11th day of July, 1921.

The Commission hereby agrees to sell and the Lessees hereby agree to purchase the following buildings at present situate upon the lands hereby demised, namely, blacksmith shop, stable, planing mill, storehouse and the framework of·mill as it at present stands, all of said buildings being shown outlined in red on the plan hereto annexed. The purchase price for said buildings shall be the sum of five hundred dollars ($500) payable as follows: $100 in cash (the receipt whereof is hereby acknowledged) and the balance amounting to $400 in four equal consecutive annual payments of $100 each, payable on the 11th days of July in the years 1917, 1918, 1919, and 1920, with interest on said purchase price or so much thereof as shall from time to time remain unpaid at the rate of six per cent. per annum computed from the date hereof payable on the 11th days of July in each of the years 1917, 1918, 1919 and 1920, PROVIDED that the Lessees may, while not in default here-under, pay off the whole of said purchase money at any time without notice or bonus upon paying therewith interest thereon at the rate aforesaid up to the date of such payment.

The Lessees hereby covenant with the Commission that until the purchase price for said buildings has been paid in full they will insure and keep the same insured up to their full insurable value in dollars currency with loss if any payable to the said Commission, and will forthwith upon demand deliver to the Commission the insurance policy or policies covering said buildings and all renewal receipts therefor.

The said Lessees hereby covenant and agree with the Commission that in con-sideration of the premises and of the leasing and letting by the said Commission to the Lessees of the lands and premises above mentioned for the term hereby created (and it is upon that express understanding that these presents are entered into), that notwithstanding anything contained in Section thirty of Chapter one hundred and fifty-five of the Revised Statutes of Ontario, 1914, or in any other section of the said Act, or any other Statute which may hereafter be passed to take the place of said Act or to amend the same, that none of the goods or chattels of the said Lessees at any time during the continuance of the term hereby created, on said demised premises, shall be exempt from levy by distress for rent in arrear by said Lessees as provided for by section or sections of the said Act above named, or any amendment or amendments thereto, and that upon any claim being made for such exemption by said Lessees or on distress being made by the said Commission this covenant and agreement may be pleaded as an estoppel against said Lessees in any action brought to test the right of the levying upon any such goods as are named as exempted in said section or sections or amendment or amendments thereto. Said Lessees waiving as they hereby do all and every benefit that could or might have accrued to them under and by virtue of the said section or sections of said Act or any amendment or amendments thereto but for the above covenant.

The said Lessees covenant with the said Commission to pay rent.

AND to pay taxes and will not assign or sublet without leave.

AND ALSO that if the term hereby created shall be at any time seized or taken in execution or in attachment by any creditors of the said Lessees, or if the said Lessees shall make any assignment for the benefit of creditors or becoming bankrupt or insolvent shall take the benefit of any Act that may be in force for bankrupt or insolvent debtors, the said term shall immediately become forfeited and void, and in such case it shall be lawful for the Commission at any time hereafter into and upon the said demised premises or any part thereof in the name of the whole to re-enter and the same to have again, re-possess and enjoy as of former estate anything herein contained to the contrary notwithstanding.

PROVISO for re-entry by the said Commission on non-payment of rent or non-performance of covenants.

The said Commission covenants with the said Lessees for quiet enjoyment.

The said Lessees may construct a siding connecting the Lessees' mill and other buildings with the railway of the Commission, the location of such siding to be approved by the Chief Engineer of the Commission before any work on the construction of the same shall commence, it being understood and agreed between the parties hereto that upon the approval of the location of the said siding by the said Chief Engineer as aforesaid the said Lessees shall execute a siding agreement upon the terms and in the form hereto annexed, it being further understood and agreed between the parties hereto that notwithstanding anything herein or in said siding agreement contained the Commission, in the event of its leasing other mill sites north of the lands hereby demised to other parties, shall have the right to provide such other parties with railway siding accommodation through the lands hereby demised to the Lessees, PROVIDED that the use of such railway siding accommodation by such other parties shall not unreasonably interfere with the business of the Lessees.

It is agreed that on the termination of this lease the Lessees may within three months thereafter remove all plant, machinery, buildings and erections built or placed upon the said lands otherwise the same shall become the property of the Commission.

IN WITNESS WHEREOF the Commission has hereunto affixed its corporate seal under the hands of its proper officers in that behalf and the Lessees have hereunto set their hands and seals.

' SIGNED, SEALED AND DELIVERED

In the presence of:
    FRED. A. DAY.

    M. J. CONKEY.
    W. J. MURPHY.

    TEMISKAMING AND NORTHERN ONTARIO RY. COM'N.

A. B. ODLUM.

    J. L. ENGLEHART,
        Chairman.
        (Seal.)

    W. H. MAUND,
        Secretary-Treasurer.

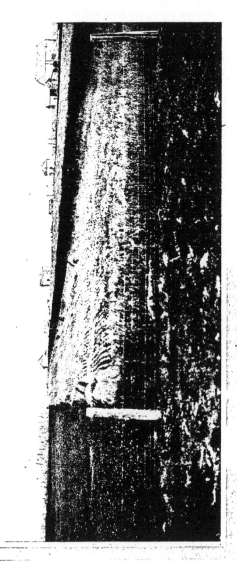

Farm of Mr. Wm. Carr, Township of Armstrong.

NIPISSING CENTRAL RAILWAY

ANNUAL REPORT CHIEF ENGINEER AND SUPERINTENDENT OF MAINTENANCE, NIPISSING CENTRAL RAILWAY,

Year ended October 31st, 1916,

NORTH BAY, ONTARIO, December 7th, 1916.

W. H. MAUND, ESQ.,

Secretary-Treasurer,

Toronto, Ontario.

DEAR SIR,—I beg to submit my annual report, as Chief Engineer and Superintendent of Maintenance, for the fiscal year ended October 31st, 1916.

Mileage.

The mileage now operated is as follows:—

Main Track:

Owned and maintained by Company	4.92 miles	
Lease from T. & N. O. Rly. Commission: .		
Maintained by Company	5.28 miles	
Maintained by Commission	5.17 miles	
		15.37 miles

Sidings and Spurs:

Sidings on that part of the line owned by T. & N. O. Commission:		
Yard Tracks and Sidings	1.65 miles	
Private Sidings	1.16 miles	
		2.81 miles

Sidings on that part of the line owned by N. C. Rly.:		
Company Spurs		2.00 miles
Total Track		20.18 miles

Equipment.

Rolling equipment consists of the following:

8 Electric Motor Passenger Cars.
1 Combination Switching Locomotive, Express Car and Snow Plow.
2 Freight Cars.

Additions to Road and Equipment.

During the year a spur track was laid on to the new Government dock at Haileybury 500 feet long and a private siding was installed for the Right-of-Way Mines at Cobalt 262 feet long.

No additions to the rolling stock during the year.

Maintenance.

The property of the railway, including roadbed, track, buildings, electrical equipment and rolling stock has all been maintained in good condition.

Accidents.

The only accident occurring on the Nipissing Central Railway during the year was:

January 30th, 1916. Harry Andrews, line foreman, North Cobalt, while operating snow plow caught the thumb of his left hand in piston of plow and it was necessary to amputate it at the first joint.

Respectfully submitted,

S. B. Clement.

GENERAL BALANCE SHEET

ASSETS.

Property Owned:				
Cost of Road as of Oct. 31, 1915	$298,815 70			
" " for year ended Oct. 31, 1916....	7,522 42	$3838 12		
Cost of Equipment as of Oct. 31, 1915....	$74,290 98			
" " for year ended Oct. 31, 1916....		74,290 98		
Townsite Property—North Cobalt		242,700 20		
Working Assets:				
Cash	$25,316 72			
Accounts Collectible	6,957 06			
Balance due on Townsite Sales......	8,777 82			
Bills	157 36			
Balance due from Agents and Conductors ...	158 91			
Material on hand	4,015 66	45,383 53		
Deferred Debit Items:				
Insurance paid in advance......	$35 39			
Accounts in Suspense......	2,028 74	2,064 13		
Other Assets				
Franchise......		141,383 32		
		$812,160 28		

LIABILITIES.

Capital Stock......			$530,000 00
T. & N. O. Ry. Advance......			247,639 50
Working Liabilities:			
Accounts Payable		$32,974 84	
Unclaimed Wages		126 51	33,101 35
Deferred Credit Items:			
War Tax			4 30
Free Surplus:			
Profit and Loss Balance			1,415 13
			$812,160 28

PROFIT AND LOSS.

Townsites	$2,659 35	By Balance—October 31, 1915	$1,877 03
Paid T. N. O. Ry. Commission	20,000 00	Revenue for year ended October 31, 1916	22,197 45
Balance carried forward......	1,415 13		
	$24,074 48		$24,074 48

NIPISSING CENTRAL

Comparative Statement of Earnings and Expenditures

No.	RECEIPTS·	Per cent.	1914 November	Per cent.	1915 November
	I. REVENUE FROM TRANSPORTATION—		$ c.		$ c.
101	Passenger Revenue		7,516 90		6,830 10
102	Baggage Revenue		35 05		17 25
103	Parlor, Sleeping, Dining, and Special Car Revenue		21 00		10 00
104	Mail Revenue				
105	Express Revenue				
106	Milk Revenue		27 30		23 55
107	Freight Revenue		420 38		315 71
108	Switching Revenue		580 29		783 96
109	Miscellaneous Transportation Revenue				
	Total		8,600 92		7,980 57
	II. REVENUE FROM OTHER RAILWAY OPERATIONS—				
110	Station and Car Privileges				
111	Parcel Room Receipts				
112	Storage				
113	Demurrage		49 00		15 00
114	Telephone and Telegraph Service				
115	Rent of Tracks and Facilities				
116	Rent of Equipment				
117	Rent of Buildings and other Property				128 00
118	Power				
119	Miscellaneous				
	Total		49 00		143 00
	TOTAL REVENUE		8,649 92		8,123 57
	EXPENDITURES				
1	Way and Structures	15.2	1,314 31	11.6	943 02
2	Equipment	4.8	414 04	3.6	294 87
3	Power	18.5	1,599 50	18.	1,462 16
4	Conaucting Transportation	26.4	2,282 59	29.5	2,392 43
5	Traffic	.6	48 80	.3	28 00
6	General and Miscellaneous	15.2	1,318 62	6.8	552 21
7	Transportation for Investment—Cr.				
	TOTAL OPERATING EXPENSES	80.7	6,977 86	69.8	5,672 69
	BALANCE		1,672 06		2,450 88
	OTHER INCOME— Interes				55 60
	Total		1,672 06		2,506 48
	DEDUCTIONS FROM INCOME— Rent for Leased Road				1,205 33
	Taxes		27 19		
	NET RESULT		1,644 87		1,301 15

RAILWAY

by Months, November, 1914' to October, 1916.

Per Cent.	1914 December	Per Cent.	1915 December	Per cent.	1915 January	Per Cent.	1916 January	No.
	$ c.		$ c.		$ c.		$ c.	
......	7,775 75	......	7,239 05	......	7,121 33	......	6,435 50	101
......	31 25	......	19 25	......	24 25	......	16 00	102
......	39 00	......	10 00	......	25 00	......	55 00	103
......	....	......	....	......	....	......	....	104
								105
......	27 10	......	28 13	......	14 06	......	18 04	106
......	398 48	......	465 57	......	731 12	......	....	107
......	555 30	......	791 12	......	394 01	......	1,382 43	108
......	....	......	....	......	....	......	....	109
......	8,826 88	......	8,553 12	......	8,309 77	......	7,906 97	
......	....	......	44 86	......	65 83	......	25	110
......	....	......	....	......	....	......	....	111
......	....	......	....	......	....	......	....	112
......	84 00	......	34 00	......	42 00	......	17 00	113
......	....	......	....	......	....	......	....	114
......	....	......	....	......	186 00	......	....	115
......	....	......	....	......	....	......	....	116
......	....	......	35 00	......	....	......	....	117
......	....	......	....	......	....	......	....	118
......	....	......	....	......	....	......	....	119
......	84 00	......	113 83	......	293 83	......	17 25	
......	8,910 88	......	8,666 98	......	8,603 60	......	7,924 22	
1 .3	1,362 67	8.9	773 59	8.5	732 16	12.3	973 32	1
.6	587 12	5.2	445 82	8.1	699 19	6.2	488 62	2
29.8	1,855 48	17.8	1,542 57	23.	1,975 60	23.2	1,840 56	3
29.4	2,618 29	28.8	2,498 70	26.5	2,278 43	27.1	2,150 09	4
.7	65 60	.4	33 60	.5	43 20	.6	44 80	5
Cr.2.1	Cr. 184 72	7.2	626 22	5.1	435 76	7.3	582 90	6
......	....		....		....		....	7
70.7	6,304 44	68.3	5,920 50	71.7	6,164 34	76.7	6,080 29	
......	2,606 44	......	2,746 48	......	2,439 26	......	1,843 93	
......	....	......	41 85	......	....	......	55 90	
......	2,606 44	......	2,788 33	......	2,439 26	......	1,899 83	
......	1,209 18	......	1,143 82	......	604 58	......	1,156 80	
......	....	......	....	......	....	......	....	
......	1,397 26	......	1,644 51	......	1,834 68	......	743 03	

NIPISSING CENTRAL

Comparative Statement of Earnings and Expenditures

No.	RECEIPTS.	Per cent.	1915 February	Per cent.	1916 February	Per cent.	1915 March
	I. REVENUE FROM TRANSPORTATION—		$ c.		$ c.		$ c.
101	Passenger Revenue	......	6,537 20	......	6,084 00	......	7,484 25
102	Baggage Revenue	......	23 00	......	22 75	......	25 75
103	Parlor, Sleeping, Dining and Special Car Revenue	......	65 00	......	40 00	......	20 00
104	Mail Revenue	......	....	......	....	......	....
105	Express Revenue	......	....	......	....	......	....
106	Milk Revenue	......	08	......	5 17	......	53
107	Freight Revenue	......	617 08	......		......	655 32
108	Switching Revenue	......	195 59	......	1,590 95	......	401 37
109	Miscellaneous Transportation Revenue	......	....	......	....	......	....
	Total	......	7,437 95	......	7,742 87	......	8,587 22
	II. REVENUE FROM OTHER RAILWAY OPERATIONS—						
110	Station and Car Privileges	......	65 84	......	....	......	46 10
111	Parcel Room Receipts	......	....	......	....	......	....
112	Storage	......	....	......	....	......	....
113	Demurrage	......	57 00	......	49 00	......	142 00
114	Telephone and Telegraph Service	......	....	......	....	......	....
115	Rent of Tracks and Facilities	......	....	......	....	......	....
116	Rent of Equipment	......	....	......	....	......	....
117	Rent of Buildings and other Property	......	....	......	....	......	....
118	Power	......	....	......	....	......	....
119	Miscellaneous	......	....	......	....	......	....
	Total	......	122 84	......	49 00	......	188 10
	TOTAL REVENUE	......	7,560 79	......	7,791 87	......	8,775 32

	EXPENDITURES.						
1	Way and Structures	16.2	1,227 25	12.4	969 84	14.3	1,251 81
2	Equipment	8.6	649 86	4.9	379 54	6.8	595 30
3	Power	25.2	1,901 15	23.5	1,827 89	19.2	1,683 22
4	Conducting Transportation	32.5	2,459 14	25.2	1,960 56	26.3	2,308 76
5	Traffic	.2	11 20	.2	13 96	......	....
6	General and Miscellaneous	8.0	608 52	7.1	556 37	8.1	715 40
7	Transportation for Investment—Cr.	......	....	......	....	......	....
	TOTAL OPERATING EXPENSES.	90.7	6,857 12	73.3	5,708 16	74.7	6,554 49
	BALANCE	......	703 67	......	2,083 71	......	2,220 83
	OTHER INCOME— Interest	......	....	......	45 85	......	....
	Total	......	703 67	......	2,129 56	......	2,220 83
	DEDUCTIONS FROM INCOME— Rent for Leased Road	......	604 58	......	1,155 25	......	604 58
	Taxes	......	....	......	....	......	....
	NET RESULT	......	99 09	......	974 31	......	1,616 25

RAILWAY.

by months, November, 1914, to October, 1916.—Continued.

Per cent.	1916 March	Per cent.	1915 April	Per cent.	1916 April	Per cent.	1915 May	No.
	$ c.		$ c.		$ c.		$ c.	
......	7,379 81	......	7,739 65	......	8,218 90	......	8,006 00	101
......	14 90	......	36 75	......	46 75	......	57 25	102
......	55 00	......	60 00	......	10 00	......	30 00	103
......	....	......	....	......	....	......	....	104
......	....	......	....	......	....	......	....	105
......	4 49	......	23 03	......	20 49	......	34 43	106
......	....	......	364 04	......	....	......	302 88	107
......	1,464 38	......	523 12	......	1,251 92	......	552 53	108
......	....	......	....	......	....	......	....	109
......	8,918 58	......	8,746 59	......	9,548 06	......	8,983 09	
......	250 00	......	59 25	......		......	6 38	110
......	....	......	....	......	....	......	....	111
......	....	......	....	......	....	......	....	112
......	176 00	......	76 00	......	48 00	......	45 00	113
......	....	......	....	......	....	......	....	114
......	....	......	Dr. 46 00	......	....	......	....	115
......	....	......	....	......	....	......	....	116
......	....	......	....	......	....	......	.	117
......	....	......	....	......	....	......	....	118
......	....	......	....	......	....	......	....	119
......	426 00	......	89 25	......	48 00	......	51 38	
......	9,344 58	......	8,835 84	......	9,596 06	......	9,034 47	
11.4	1,060 43	11.3	996 06	7.	720 79	9.1	821 15	1
5.8	543 11	6.1	540 74	3.5	338 19	6.8	613 13	2
18.2	1,702 18	16.2	1,433 26	15.	1,436 75	15.6	1,408 66	3
27.6	2,582 89	29.7	2,622 72	28.4	2,727 04	24.	2,172 15	4
1.	92 28	.7	57 40	.6	53 08	.8	75 79	5
10.2	955 19	9.2	814 98	10.4	1,002 68	12.9	1,162 47	6
......	....	......	....	......	....	......	....	7
74.2	6,936 08	73.2	6,465 16	65.4	6,278 53	69.2	6,253 35	
......	2,408 50	......	2,370 68	......	3,317 53	......	2,781 12	
......	19 35	......	....	......	....	......	....	
......	2,427 85	......	2,370 68	......	3,317 53	......	2,781 12	
......	1,150 88	......	604 58	......	1,179 04	......	604 58	
......	....	......	....	......	....	......	....	
......	1,276 97	......	1,766 10	......	2,138 49	......	2,176 54	

NIPISSING CENTRAL

Comparative Statement of Earnings and Expenditures

No.	RECEIPTS	Per cent.	1916 May	Per cent.	1915 June	Per cent.	1916 June
	I. REVENUE FROM TRANSPORTATION—		$ c.		$ c.		$ c.
101	Passenger Revenue	......	8,597 30	......	8,029 27	......	8,959 55
102	Baggage Revenue	......	42 00	......	53 25	......	58 75
103	Parlor, Sleeping, Dining, and Special Car Revenue	......	70 00	......	60 00	......	40 00
104	Mail Revenue	......	....	......	....	......	....
105	Express Revenue.............	......	....	......	....	......	....
106	Milk Revenue	......	9 75	......	9 15	......	5 64
107	Freight Revenue ....:.......	......	....	......	259 27	......	....
108	Switching Revenue	......	852 89	......	680 30	......	886 60
109	Miscellaneous Transportation Revenue	......	....	......	....	......	....
	Total.................	......	9,571 94	......	9,091 24	......	9,950 54
	II. REVENUE FROM OTHER RAILWAY OPERATIONS—						
110	Station and Car Privileges...'	......	....	......	29 07	......	....
111	Parcel Room Receipts........	......	....	......	....	......	....
112	Storage.....................	......	....	......	....	......	....
113	Demurrage	......	68 00	......	58 00	......	16 00
114	Telephone and Telegraph Service	......	....	......	....	......	....
115	Rent of Tracks and Facilities.	......	....	......	....	......	....
116	Rent of Equipment	......	....	......	....	......	....
117	Rent of Buildings and other Property	......	....	......	....	......	....
118	Power......................	......	....	......	....	......	....
119	Miscellaneous	......	....	......	....	......	....
	Total...................	......	68 00	......	87 07	......	16 00
	TOTAL REVENUE........	......	9,639 94	......	9,178 31	......	9,966 54
	EXPENDITURES						
1	Way and Structures	9.8	945 86	9.9	907 30	9.4	937 55
2	Equipment..................	4.5	432 15	2.8	261 64	4.6	460 72
3	Power......................	15.8	1,522 55	15.5	1,420 65	14.4	1,435 80
4	Conducting Transportation ..	24.1	2,323 31	23.4	2,143 68	23.3	2,323 17
5	Traffic	.6	57 63	.4	33 60	.5	51 73
6	General and Miscellaneous ...	9.3	898 99	7.7	713 99	11.6	1,155 89
7	Transportation for Investment—Cr. ..:.........	......	....	......	....	......	....
	TOTAL OPERATING EXPENSES	64.1	6,180 49	59.7	5,480 86	63.8	6,364 86
	BALANCE..................	......	3,459 45	......	3,697 45	......	3,601 68
	OTHER INCOME— Interest	......	79 60	......	....	......	....
		......	3,539 05	......	3,697 45	......	3,601 68
	DEDUCTIONS FROM INCOME— Rent for Leased Road......	......	1,144 52	......	604 58	......	1,150 58
	Taxes...................	......	....	......	....	......	....
	NET RESULT............	......	2,394 53	......	3,092 87	......	2,451 10

RAILWAY.

by Months, November, 1914, to October, 1916.—Continued.

Per cent.	1915 July	Per cent.	1916 July	Per cent.	1915 August	Per cent.	1916 August	No.
	$ c.		$ c.		$ c.		$ c.	
......	8,965 10	......	9,374 25	......	7,992 92	......	9,538 20	101
......	77 50	......	81 75	......	49 50	......	92 50	102
......	40 00	......	30 00	......	35 00	......	135 00	103
......	....	......	....	......	....	......	....	104
......		......		......		......		105
......	16	......	4 60	......	38	......	6 05	106
......	188 02	......		......	323 16	......		107
......	1,009 61	......	896 96	......	1,041 29	......	895 26	108
......	....	......	....	......	....	......	....	109
......	10,280 39	......	10,337 56	......	9,442 25	......	10,667 01	
......	14 28	......	125 00	......	42 38	......	....	110
......	....	......	....	......	....	......	....	111
......	....	......	....	......	....	......	....	112
......	1 00	......	45 00	......	2 00	......	94 50	113
......	....	......	....	......	....	......	....	114
......	....	......	....	......	....	......	....	115
......	....	......	....	......	....	......	....	116
......	....	......	....	......	....	......	....	117
......	....	......	....	......	....	......	....	118
......	....	......	....	......	....	......	....	119
......	15 28	......	170 00	......	44 38	......	94 50	
......	10,295 67	......	10,557 56	......	9,486 63	......	10,761 51	
9.8	1,006 73	10.5	1,113 46	10.5	996 02	7.9	856 81	1
2.9	302 34	3.2	333 75	2.7	256 81	3.6	377 55	2
14.1	1,447 50	13.9	1,470 25	15.8	1,499 65	14.0	1,507 70	3
22.9	2,360 53	22.5	2,371 91	22.2	2,108 73	22.4	2,421 73	4
.3	28 00	.4	47 48	.5	49 20	.1	13 88	5
6.4	665 60	8.7	914 15	8.7	820 62	10.4	1,127 51	6
......	....	......	....	......	....	......	....	7
56.4	5,810 70	59.2	6,251 00	60.4	5,731 03	58.5	6,305 18	
......	4,484 97	......	4,306 56	......	3,755 60	......	4,456 33	
......	....	......	57 55	......	16 45	......	42 25	
......	4,484 97	......	4,364 11	......	3,772 05	......	4,498 58	
......	604.58	......	1,176 35	......	604 58	......	1,187 50	
......	....	......	....	......	....	......	....	
......	3,880 39	......	3,187 76	......	3,167 47	......	3,311 08	

NIPISSING CENTRAL
Comparative Statement of Earnings and Expenditures

No.	RECEIPTS	Per cent.	1915 September	Per cent.	1916 September	Per cent.	1915 October
	I. REVENUE FROM TRANSPORTATION—		$ c.		$ c.		$ c.
101	Passenger Revenue	......	7,160 85	......	8,617 07	......	7,293 30
102	Baggage Revenue	......	40 50	......	49. 00	......	28 00
103	Parlor, Sleeping, Dining and Special Car Revenue	......	30 00	......	35 00	......	45 00
104	Mail Revenue	......	....	......	....	......	....
105	Express Revenue	......	....	......	....	......	....
106	Milk Revenue	......	3 00	......	7 24	......	9 00
107	Freight Revenue	......	353 47	......	....	......	261 01
108	Switching Revenue	......	961 63	......	1,019 30	......	966 43
109	Miscellaneous Transportation Revenue	......	....	......	....	......	....
	Total	......	8,549 45	......	9,727 61	......	8,602 74
	II. REVENUE FROM OTHER RAILWAY OPERATIONS—						
110	Station and Car Privileges	......	18 00	......	125 00	......	152 00
111	Parcel Room Receipts	......	....	......	....	......	....
112	Storage	......	....	......	....	......	....
113	Demurrage	......	42 00	......	86 00	......	15 00
114	Telephone and Telegraph Service	......	....	......	....	......	....
115	Rent of Tracks and Facilities	......	....	......	....	......	....
116	Rent of Equipment	......	....	......	....	......	....
117	Rent of Buildings and other Property	......	....	......	....	......	....
118	Power	......	....	......	....	......	....
119	Miscellaneous	......	....	......	....	......	....
	Total	......	60 00	......	211 00	......	167 00
	TOTAL REVENUE	......	8,609 45	......	9,938 61	......	8,769 74
	EXPENDITURES						
1	Way and Structures	9.9	855 83	9.1	907 34	10.3	905 92
2	Equipment	5.2	443 76	4.1	406 88	1.7	145 21
3	Power	17.2	1,475 25	1".9	1,683 88	28.3	2,484 43
4	Conducting Transportation	24.	2,065 44	23.7	2,250 45	23.9	2,096 10
5	Traffic	.3	28 00	.4	41 88	.4	33 60
6	General and Miscellaneous	8.8	760 20	9.1	900 66	7.5	658 37
7	Transportation for Investment—Cr.	......	....	......	....	......	....
	TOTAL OPERATING EXPENSES	65.4	5,628 48	62.3	6,191 09	72.1	6,323 63
	BALANCE	......	2,980 97	......	3,747 52	......	2,446 11
	OTHER INCOME— Interest	......	92 90	......	45 67	......	108 65
	Total	......	3,073 87	......	3,793 19	......	2,554 76
	DEDUCTIONS FROM INCOME— Rent for Leased Road	......	604 58	......	1,170 46	......	604 58
	Taxes	......	....	......	....	......	....
	NET RESULT	......	2,469 29	......	2,622 73	......	1,950 18

RAILWAY.

by Months, November, 1914, to October, 1916—Continued.

Per cent.	1916 October	Per cent.	1915 Total	Per cent.	1916 Total	Increase	Decrease	No.
	$ c.		$ c.		$ c.	$ c.	$ c.	
......	6,981 71	......	91,622 52	......	94,255 44	2,632 92	....	101
......	33 75	......	482 05	......	494 65	12 60	....	102
......	20 00	......	470 00	......	510 00	40 00	....	103
......	....	......	....	......	....	....	....	104
								105
......	24 02	......	148 22	......	157 17	8 95	....	106
......	....	......	4,874 23	......	781 28	....	4,092 95	107
......	923 03	......	7,861 47	......	12,738 80	4,877 33	....	108
......	....	......	....	......	....	....	....	109
......	7,982 51	......	105,458 49	......	108,937 34	3,478 85	......	
......	....	......	499 13	......	545 11	45 98	....	110
......	....	......	....	......	....	....	....	111
......	....	......	....	......	....	....	....	112
......	71 00	......	613 00	......	719 50	106 50	....	113
								114
......	33 00	......	140 00	......	33 00	....	107 00	115
......	....	......	....	......	....	....	....	116
......	....	......	....	......	163 00	163 00	....	117
......	....	......	....	......	....	....	....	118
......	....	......	....	......	....	....	....	119
......	104 00	......	1,252 13	......	1,460 61	208 48	....	
......	8,086 51	......	106,710 62	......	110,397 95	3,687 33	....	
12.9	1,046 73	11.6	12,377 21	10.2	11,248 74	....	1,128 47	1
6.1	496 91	5.2	5,509 14	4.5	4,998 11	....	511 03	2
13.9	1,123 78	18.9	20,184 35	16.8	18,556 07	....	1,628 28	3
34.9	2,819 27	25.8	27,516 56	26.1	28,821 55	1,304 99	....	4
.7	53 08	.4	474 39	.5	531 40	57 01	....	5
16.2	1,305 99	8.	8,489 81	9.6	10,578 76	2,088 95	....	6
......	....	......	....	......	....	....	....	7
84.7	6,845 76	69.9	74,551 46	67.7	74,734 63	183 17	....	
......	1,240 75	......	32,159 16	......	35,663 32	3,504 16	....	
......	56 33	......	218 00	......	499 95	281 95	....	
......	1,297 08	......	32,377 16	......	36,163 27	3,786 11	....	
......	1,145 29	......	7,254 98	......	13,965 82	6,710 84	....	
......	....	......	27 19	......	....	....	27 19	
......	151 79	......	25,094 99	......	22,197 45	....	2,897 54	

28 T Ŕ

NIPISSING CENTRAL

Comparative Statement of Earnings and Expenditures, by

№	MAINTENANCE OF WAY AND STRUCTURES.	1914 November	1915 November	1914 December	1915 December
		$ c.	$ c.	$ c.	$ c.
1	Superintendence of way and structures	32 00	16 00	32 00	16 00
2	Ballast	15 22	14 00	28 00	14 00
3	Ties		231 67	79 34	39 67
4	Rails		51 33	102 66	51 33
5	Rail fastenings and joints		9 37	9 34	4 67
6	Special work	22 39	4 67	9 34	4 67
7	Underground construction				
8	Track and roadway labor	450 88	352 49	506 15	178 60
9	Miscellaneous track and roadway expenses	2 87	6 40	11 55	3 37
10	Paving	22 79	25 57		
11	Cleaning and sanding track	17 10	15 48	14 25	2 58
12	Removal of snow and ice	51 81	64 38	279 15	321 76
13	Tunnels and subways				
14	Elevated structures and foundations				
15	Bridges, trestles and culverts				
16	Crossings, fences and signs	24 86	25 89	7 97	1 94
17	Signal and interlocking apparatus				
18	Telephone and telegraph lines	28 00	25 00	24 49	25 00
19	Miscellaneous way expenses				
20	Poles and fixtures	130 50	49 00	65 00	52 00
21	Underground conduits				
22	Distribution system	160 40	49 00	111 39	58 00
23	Miscellaneous electric line expenses				
24	Buildings, fixtures and grounds	355 49	2 77	82 04	
25	Depreciation of way and structures				
26	Other operations—Dr.				
27	Other operations—Cr.				
28	Equalization—way and structures				
	Total	1,314 31	943 02	1,362 67	773 59

№	MAINTENANCE OF EQUIPMENT.				
29	Superintendence of equipment	32 00	20 50	36 50	16 00
30	Passenger and combination cars	179 40	209 54	304 32	373 86
31	Freight, express and mail cars				
32	Service equipment				
33	Electric equipment of cars	199 77	51 51	226 33	42 89
34	Locomotives				
35	Floating equipment				
36	Shop equipment				
37	Shop expenses	2 87	13 32	19 97	13 07
38	Vehicles and horses				
39	Miscellaneous equipment expenses				
40	Depreciation of equipment				
41	Equipment retired				
42	Other operations—Dr.				
43	Other operations—Cr.				
44	Equalization—equipment				
	Total	414 04	294 87	587 12	445 82

RAILWAY.

Months, November, 1914, to October, 1916—Continued.

1915 January	1916 January	1915 February	1916 February	1915 March	1916 March	No.
$ c.	$ c.	$ c.	$ c.	$ c.	$ c.	
32 00	17 00	16 00	36 48	16 00	36 44	1
14 00	134 19	14 00	14 00	14 00	14 00	2
39 67	39 67	39 67	39 67	39 67	39 67	3
51 33	51 33	51 33	51 33	51 33	51 33	4
4 67	4 67	4 67	4 67	21 49	4 67	5
4 67	4 67	4 67	4 67	117 31	4 67	6
						7
238 72	147 80	270 01	148 94	330 94	181 83	8
6 18	3 37	4 57	3 13	8 58	3 13	9
						10
				6 65		11
354 59	478 68	323 02	600 20	211 99	642 59	12
						13
						14
		137 44				15
						16
						17
34 00	28 50	21 00	18 75	18 00	10 00	18
						19
67 87	25 85	59 16	24 00	75 00	21 25	20
						21
124 00	37 34	77 00	24 00	174 17	50 50	22
						23
Cr. 239 54	25	204 71		171 68	35	24
						25
						26
						27
						28
732 16	973 82	1,227 25	969 84	1,251 81	1,060 43	
58 10	17 00	16 00	22 60	16 00	22 55	29
488 69	351 06	481 42	221 89	492 58	319 37	30
						31
						32
127 31	110 70	131 18	131 63	74 71	193 79	33
						34
						35
						36
25 09	9 86	21 26	3 42	12 01	7 40	37
						38
						39
						40
						41
						42
						43
						44
699 19	488 62	649 86	379 54	595 30	543 11	

NIPISSING CENTRAL

Comparative Statement of Earnings and Expenditures,

No.	MAINTENANCE OF WAY AND STRUCTURES.	1915 April	1916 April	1915 May	1916 May
		$ c.	$ c.	$ c.	$ c.
1	Superintendence of way and structures	16 00	36 44	16 00	36 44
2	Ballast	14 00	14 00	14 00	14 00
3	Ties	39 67	39 67	39 67	39 67
4	Rails	51 33	51 33	51 33	51 33
5	Rail fastenings and joints	4 67	4 67	11 69	4 67
6	Special work	4 67	4 67	4 67	95 42
7	Underground construction	....	....	....	....
8	Track and roadway labor	407 01	367 67	489 02	498 51
9	Miscellaneous track and roadway expenses	3 77	4 79	3 13	3 13
10	Paving	....	....	....	....
11	Cleaning and sanding track	18 05	....	24 57	16 44
12	Removal of snow and ice	32 81	88 81	....	1 66
13	Tunnels and subways	....	....	....	....
14	Elevated structures and foundations	....	....	....	....
15	Bridges, trestles and culverts	173 72	....	....	....
16	Crossings, fences and signs	11 57	2 58	....	....
17	Signal and interlocking apparatus	....	....	....	....
18	Telephone and telegraph lines	15 25	9 00	25 00	25 75
19	Miscellaneous way expenses	....	....	....	....
20	Poles and fixtures	15 25	15 00	25 00	72 75
21	Underground conduits	....	....	....	....
22	Distribution system	72 25	18 00	29 00	74 13
23	Miscellaneous electric line expenses	....	....	....	....
24	Buildings, fixtures and grounds	116 04	64 16	88 07	11 96
25	Depreciation of way and structures	....	....	....	....
26	Other operations—Dr.	....	....	....	....
27	Other operations—Cr.	....	....	....	....
28	Equalization—way and structures	....	....	....	....
	Total	996 06	720 79	821 15	945 86

No.	MAINTENANCE OF EQUIPMENT.				
29	Superintendence of equipment	16 00	22 55	16 00	22 55
30	Passenger and combination cars	373 20	161 42	466 38	267 95
31	Freight, express and mail cars	....	....	....	....
32	Service equipment	....	....	....	....
33	Electric equipment of cars	150 18	148 24	129 01	124 81
34	Locomotives	....	....	....	....
35	Floating equipment	....	....	....	....
36	Shop equipment	....	....	....	....
37	Shop expenses	1 36	5 98	1 74	16 84
38	Vehicles and horses	....	....	....	....
39	Miscellaneous equipment expenses	....	....	....	....
40	Depreciation of equipment	....	....	....	....
41	Equipment retired	....	....	....	....
42	Other operations—Dr.	....	....	....	....
43	Other operations—Cr.	....	....	....	....
44	Equalization—equipment	....	....	....	....
	Total	540 74	338 19	613 13	432 15

RAILWAY.

by Months, November, 1914, to October, 1916—Continued.

1915 June	1916 June	1915 July	1916 July	1915 August	1916 August	No.
$ c.	$ c.	$ c.	$ c.	$ c.	$ c.	
16 00	36 44	16 00	33 69	16.00	40 94	1
14 00	14 00	14 00	14 00	14 00	14 00	2
39 67	39 67	238 71	39 67	115 51	63 67	3
51 33	51 33	51 33	51 33	119 83	51 33	4
4 67	4 67	4 67	4 67	4 67	4 67	5
4 67	4 67	4 67	4 67	34 69	4 67	6
						7
588 76	487 67	477 94	654 61	493 87	478 29	8
6 40	11 58	5 65	33 96	6 92	7 26	9
		5 65		5 01		10
26 72	27 20	34 71	42 92	25 46	30 17	11
						12
						13
						14
					36 00	15
2 96					3 50	16
						17
25 00	27 83	25 00	33 25	31 08	14 68	18
						19
34 00	36 50	35 29	27 50	25 00	13 00	20
						21
35 80	195 99	34 00	110 58	47 05	26 99	22
						23
57 32		59 11	62 61	56 93	67 64	24
						25
						26
						27
						28
907 30	937 55	1,006 73	1,113 46	996 02	856 81	
16 00	22 55	20 50	22 55	16 00	22 55	29
136 69	242 47	143 51	185 35	118 40	205 23	30
						31
						32
108 38	188 60	136 29	109 97	115 18	128 23	33
						34
						35
						36
57	7 10	2 04	15 88	7 23	21 54	37
						38
						39
						40
						41
						42
						43
						44
261 64	460 72	302 34	333 75	256 81	377 55	

NIPISSING CENTRAL

Comparative Statement of Earnings and Expenditures by

No.	MAINTENANCE OF WAY AND STRUCTURES.	1915 September	1916 September	1915 October
		$ c.	$ c.	$ c.
1	Superintendence of way and structures	16 00	36 44	16 00
2	Ballast	14 00	14 00	14 00
3	Ties	39 67	113 59	39 67
4	Rails	51 33	51 33	48 93
5	Rail fastenings and joints	4 67	4 67	4 67
6	Special work	4 67	4 67	4 67
7	Underground construction			
8	Track and roadway labor	483 81	595 73	477 18
9	Miscellaneous track and roadway expenses	2 73	2 81	5 40
10	Paving	4 78		4 40
11	Cleaning and sanding track	37 66	18 32	33 54
12	Removal of snow and ice			
13	Tunnels and subways			
14	Elevated structures and foundations			
15	Bridges, trestles and culverts			
16	Crossings, fences and signs			
17	Signal and interlocking apparatus			
18	Telephone and telegraph lines	25 00	13 00	25 00
19	Miscellaneous way expenses			2 00
20	Poles and fixtures	46 00	13 00	60 75
21	Underground conduits			
22	Distribution system	46 00	39 00	113 25
23	Miscellaneous electric line expenses			
24	Buildings, fixtures and grounds	79 51	78	56 46
25	Depreciation of way and structures			
26	Other operations—Dr.			
27	Other operations—Cr.			
28	Equalization—way and structures			
	Total	855 83	907 34	905 92
	MAINTENANCE OF EQUIPMENT.			
29	Superintendence of equipment	16 00	22 55	16 00
30	Passenger and combination cars	144 46	76 67	108 76
31	Freight, express and mail cars		69 14	
32	Service equipment			
33	Electric equipment of cars	47 96	233 16	15 43
34	Locomotives			
35	Floating equipment			
36	Shop equipment			
37	Shop expenses	235 34	5 36	5 02
38	Vehicles and horses			
39	Miscellaneous equipment expenses			
40	Depreciation of equipment			
41	Equipment retired			
42	Other operations—Dr.			
43	Other operations—Cr.			
44	Equalization—equipment			
	Total	443 76	406 88	145 21

RAILWAY.

✔ Months, November, 1914, to October, 1916—Continued.

1916 October	1915 Total	1916 Total	Increase	Decrease	No.
$ c.	$ c.	$ c.	$ c.	$ c.	
36 44	240 00	378 75	138 75	....	1
14 00	183 22	288 19	104 97	....	2
252 47	750 92	978 76	227 84	....	3
51 33	682 06	615 96	....	66 10	4
4 67	79 88	60 74	....	19 14	5
4 67	221 09	146 79	....	74 30	6
....	....	....	....	....	7
482 02	5,214 29	4,574 16	....	640 13	8
5 89	62 75	88 82	26 07	....	9
31 85	42 63	57 42	14 79	....	10
13 48	238 71	166 59	....	72 12	11
24 76	1,253 37	2,222 84	969 47	....	12
....	....	....	....	....	13
....	....	....	....	....	14
....	311 16	36 00	....	275 16	15
7 39	47 36	41 30	....	6 06	16
....	....	....	....	....	17
30 58	296 82	261 34	....	35 48	18
....	2 00	....	....	2 00	19
22 00	638 82	371 85	....	266 97	20
....	....	....	....	....	21
59 90	1,024 31	743 43	....	280 88	22
....	....	....	....	....	23
5 28	1,087 82	215 80	....	872 02	24
....	....	....	....	....	25
....	....	....	....	....	26
....	....	....	....	....	27
....	....	....	....	....	28
1,046 73	12,377 21	11,248 74	....	1,128 47	
22 55	275 10	256 50	....	18 60	29
336 43	3,437 81	2,951 24	....	486 57	30
28 36	....	97 50	97 50	....	31
....	....	....	....	....	32
104 55	1,461 73	1,568 08	106 35	....	33
....	....	....	....	....	34
....	....	....	....	....	35
....	....	....	....	....	36
5 02	334 50	124 79	....	209 71	37
....	....	....	....	....	38
....	....	....	....	....	39
....	....	....	....	....	40
....	....	....	....	....	41
....	....	....	....	....	42
....	....	....	....	....	43
....	....	....	....	....	44
496 91	5,509 14	4,998 11	....	511 03	

NIPISSING CENTRAL

Comparative Statement of Earnings and Expenditures by

No.	POWER.	1914 November	1915 November	1914 December	1915 December
		$ c.	$ c.	$ c.	$ c.
45	Superintendence of power	32 00	16 00	41 38	16 00
46	Power plant buildings, fixtures,grounds	....	....	....	....
47	Power plant equipment	....	....	....	....
48	Substation equipment	....	....	....	....
49	Transmission system	33 00	25 00	40 85	25 00
50	Depreciation of power plant buildings and equipment	....	....	....	....
51	Equalization—power	....	....	....	....
52	Power plant employees..	....	....	....	....
53	Fuel for power....................	....	....	....	....
54	Water for power...................	....	....	....	....
55	Lubricants for power..............	....	....	....	....
56	Miscellaneous power plant supplies and expenses	....	....	....	....
57	Substation employees	157 50	160 00	160 00	160 00
58	Substation supplies and expenses....	....	3 41	....	7 32
59	Power purchased	1,377 00	1,257 75	1,613 25	1,334 25
60	Power exchanged—balance	....	....	....	....
61	Power transferred—credit	....	....	....	....
62	Other operations—credit	....	....	....	....
	Total	1,599 50	1,462 16	1,855 48	1,542 57
	CONDUCTING TRANSPORTATION.				
63	Superintendence of transportation....	32 00	112 00	32 00	112 00
64	Passenger conductors, motormen and trainmen	1,586 30	1,435 76	1,593 37	1,482 48
65	Freight and express conductors, motormen and trainmen	273 00	320 06	279 40	288 40
66	Miscellaneous car service employees..	6 08	6 46	10 26	....
67	Miscellaneous car service expenses...	85 71	300 83	368 33	462 16
68	Station employees	25 50	....	95 50	....
69	Station expenses	63 46	7 32	21 93	90
70	Carhouse employees	210 00	210 00	217 50	150 00
71	Carhouse expenses	....	....	....	....
72	Operation of signal and interlocking apparatus	....	....	....	....
73	Operation of telephone and telegraph lines	54	....	....	1 40
74	Operation of floating equipment.....	....	....	....	....
75	Operation of steam locomotives	....	....	....	....
76	Freight and express collection and delivery	....	....	....	....
77	Loss and damage	....	....	....	....
78	Other transportation expenses	....	....	....	1 36
	Total	2,282 59	2,392 43	2,618 29	2,498 70
	TRAFFIC.				
79	Superintendence and solicitation	32 00	....	32 00	....
80	Advertising	16 80	28 00	33 60	33 60
81	Parks, resorts and attractions.......	....	....	....	....
82	Miscellaneous traffic expenses	....	....	....	....
	Total	48 80	28 00	65 60	33 60

RAILWAY.

Months, November, 1914, to October, 1916—Continued.

1915 January	1916 January	1915 February	1916 February	1915 March	1916 March	No.
$ c.	$ c.	$ c.	$ c.	$ c.	$ · c.	
32 00	.17 00	23 30	22 60	16 00	22 55	45
....	....	....	....	....	....	46
....	....	....	....	....	....	47
119 10	79 70	173 75	18 75	....	....	48
31 00	25 00	89 60	41 25	51 47	....	49
....	....	....	....	....	....	50
....	....	....	....	....	....	51
....	....	....	....	....	....	52
....	....	....	....	....	....	53
....	....	....	....	....	....	54
....	....	....	....	....	....	55
....	....	....	....	....	....	56
160 00	168 40	165 50	160 00	160 00	160 00	57
....	2 46	....	1 29	....	3 13	58
1,633 50	1,548 00	1,449 00	1,584 00	1,455 75	1,516 50	59
....	....	....	....	....	....	60
....	....	....	....	....	....	61
....	....	....	....	....	....	62
1,975 60	1,840 56	1,901 15	1,827 89	1,683 22	1,702 18	
32 00	119 00	112 00	132 96	112 00	132 88	63
1,646 16	1,525 18	1,507 72	1,501 64	1,660 10	1,590 59	64
276 40	293 84	251 20	269 68	279 40	368 10	65
6 84	6 84	6 08	5 70	6 84	6 84	66
31 27	29 33	79 58	Cr. 154 87	40 53	277 91	67
58 00	....	37 50	....	3 00	....	68
1 15	9 82	17 29	5 45	17 78	6 57	69
208 91	166 08	210 00	200 00	185 00	200 00	70
17 70	....	233 35	....	4 11	....	71
....	....	....	....	....	....	72
....	....	....	....	....	....	73
....	....	....	....	....	....	74
....	....	....	....	....	....	75
....	....	....	....	....	....	76
....	....	4 42	....	....	....	77
....	....	....	....	....	....	78
2,278 43	2,150 09	2,459 14	1,960 56	˗2,308 76	2,582 89	
32 00	....	....	13 96	....	13 88	79
11 20	44 80	11 20	....	....	78 40	80
....	....	....	....	....	....	81
....	....	....	....	....	....	82
43 20	44 80	11 20	13 96	....	92 28	

NIPISSING CENTRAL

Comparative Statement of Earnings and Expenditures by

No.	POWER.	1915 April	1916 April	1915 May	1916 May
		$ c.	$ c.	$ c.	$ c.
45	Superintendence of power	16 00	22 55	16 00	22 55
46	Power plant buildings, fixtures and grounds	1 51	....	1 91	....
47	Power plant equipment	....	....	....	....
48	Substation equipment	21 00	....	2 00	30 00
49	Transmission system	33 25	....	25 00	34 00
50	Depreciation of power plant buildings and equipment	....	....	....	....
51	Equalization—power	....	....	....	....
52	Power plant employees.............	....	....	....	....
53	Fuel for power....................	....	....	....	....
54	Water for power....................	....	....	....	....
55	Lubricants for power................	....	....	....	....
56	Miscellaneous power plant supplies and expenses	160 00	160 00	160 00	160 00
57	Substation employees	160 00	160 00	160 00	160.00
58	Substation supplies and expenses....	....	95	....	25
59	Power purchased	1,201 50	1,253 25	1,203 75	1,275 75
60	Power exchanged—balance	....	....	....	....
61	Power transferred—credit	....	....	....	....
62	Other operations—credit	....	....	....	....
	Total	1,433 26	1,436 75	1,408 66	1,522 55
	CONDUCTING TRANSPORTATION.				
63	Superintendence of transportation....	241 95	132 88	112 00	132 88
64	Passenger conductors, motormen and trainmen	1,560 54	1,551 92	1,540 58	1,679 07
65	Freight and express conductors, motormen and trainmen	270 00	268 10	273 50	265 90
66	Miscellaneous car service employees..	6 46	6 46	6 84	6 56
67	Miscellaneous car service expenses...	331 61	369 24	27 46	65 90
68	Station employees	....	....	....	....
69	Station expenses	2 16	4 68	1 77	Cr. 55
70	Carhouse employees	210 00	189 67	210 00	173 55
71	Carhouse expenses	....	204 09	....	....
72	Operation of signal and interlocking apparatus	....	....	....	....
73	Operation of telephone and telegraph lines	....	....	....	....
74	Operation of floating equipment......	....	....	....	....
75	Operation of steam locomotives	....	....	....	....
76	Freight and express collection and delivery	....	....	....	....
77	Loss and damage	....	....	....	....
78	Other transportation expenses	....	....	....	....
	Total	2,622 72	2,727 04	2,172 15	2,323 31
	TRAFFIC.				
79	Superintendence and solicitation	....	13 88	....	13 88
80	Advertising	57 40	39 20	75 79	43 75
81	Parks, resorts and attractions........	....	....	....	....
82	Miscellaneous traffic expenses	....	....	....	....
	Total	57 40	53 08	75 79	57 63

RAILWAY.

Months, November, 1914, to October, 1916—Continued.

1915 June	1916 June	1915 July	1916 July	1915 August	1916 August	No.
$ c.	$ c.	$ c.	$ c.	$ c.	$ c.	
16 00	22 55	16 00	22 55	16 00	22 55	45
						46
						47
36 15	22 50		47	25 15		48
25 00		25 00	14 90	25 00	13 00	49
						50
						51
						52
						53
						54
						55
						56
160 00	160 00	160 00	160 00	160 00	160 00	57
			1 08		40	58
1,183 50	1,230 75	1,246 50	1,271 25	1,273 50	1,311 75	59
						60
						61
						62
1,420 65	1,435 80	1,447 50	1,470 25	1,499 65	1,507 70	
112 00	132 88	112 00	132 88	112 00	132 88	63
1,525 01	1,646 44	1,596 65	1,649 71	1,426 82	1,621 93	64
272 40	263 00	279 40	263 40	278 00	267 50	65
6 99		6 99	7 20	6 46	6 30	66
18 93	3 33	147 05	106 17	9 00	29 44	67
						68
	18 17	8 44	90	66 45	120 92	69
210 00	259 35	210 00	211 65	210 00	210 00	70
						71
						72
						73
						74
						75
						76
Cr. 1 65						77
					32 76	78
2,143 68	2,323 17	2,360 53	2,371 91	2,108 73	2,421 73	
	18 13		13 88		13 88	79
33 60	33 60	28 00	33 60	49 20		80
						81
						82
33 60	51 73	28 00	47 48	49 20	13 88	

- NIPISSING CENTRAL

Comparative Statement of Earnings and Expenditures by

No.	POWER.	1915 September	1916 September	1915 October
		$ c.	$ c.	$ c.
45	Superintendence of power	16 00	22 55	16 00
46	Power plant buildings, fixtures and grounds..	....	....	....
47	Power plant equipment	....	60 60	....
48	Substation equipment	75	157 27	953 68
49	Transmission system	25 00	13 00	25 00
50	Depreciation of power plant buildings and equipment			
51	Equalization—power	....	....	....
52	Power plant employees	....	....	....
53	Fuel for power	....	....	....
54	Water for power	....	....	....
55	Lubricants for power .... ?......	....	....	....
56	Miscellaneous power plant supplies and expenses	....	....	....
57	Substation employees	160 00	160 00	160 00
58	Substation supplies and expenses	....	1 46	....
59	Power purchased	1,273 50	1,269 00	1,329 75
60	Power exchanged—balance	....	....	....
61	Power transferred—credit	....	....	....
62	Other operations—credit	....	....	....
	Total	1,475 25	1,683 88	2,484 43

	CONDUCTING TRANSPORTATION.			
63	Superintendence of transportation	112 00	132 88	112 00
64	Passenger conductors, motormen and trainmen	1,430 76	1,596 71	1,469 13
65	Freight and express conductors, motormen and trainmen	261 60	257 00	270 40
66	Miscellaneous car service employees	6 46	7 14	6 84
67	Miscellaneous car service expenses	23 85	82 72	14 10
68	Station employees	....	....	....
69	Station expenses	2 56	2 03	13 63
70	Carhouse employees	210 00	210 00	210 00
71	Carhouse expenses	18 21		
72	Operation of signal and interlocking apparatus	....	....	....
73	Operation of telephone and telegraph lines....	....	....	....
74	Operation of floating equipment	....	....	....
75	Operation of steam locomotives	....	....	....
76	Freight and express collection and delivery...	....	....	....
77	Loss and damage	....	....	....
78	Other transportation expenses	....	Cr. 38 03	....
	Total	2,065 44	2,250 45	2,096 10

	TRAFFIC.			
79	Superintendence and solicitation	....	13 88	....
80	Advertising	28 00	28 00	33 60
81	Parks, resorts and attractions...............	....	....	....
82	Miscellaneous traffic expenses	....	....	....
	Total	28 00	41 88	33 60

RAILWAY.

Months, November, 1914, to October, 1916—Continued.

1916 October	1915 Total	1916 Total	Increase	Decrease	No.
$ c.	$ c.	$ c.	$ c.	$ c.	
22 55	256 68	252 00	....	4 68	45
....	3 42	....	....	3 42	46
....	....	60 60	60 60	....	47
Cr. 379 00	1,331 58	Cr. 70 31	....	1,401 89	48
5 40	429 17	196 55	....	232 62	49
....	....	....	....	....	50
....	....	....	....	....	51
....	....	....	....	....	52
....	....	....	....	....	53
....	....	....	....	....	54
....	....	....	....	....	55
....	....	....	....	....	56
217 60	1,923 00	1,986 00	63 00	....	57
1 73	....	23 48	23 48	....	58
1,255 50	16,240 50	16,107 75	....	132 75	59
....	....	....	....	....	60
....	....	....	....	....	61
....	....	....	....	....	62
1,123 78	20,184 35	18,556 07	....	1,628 28	
132 88	1,233 95	1,539 00	305 05	....	63
1,573 52	18,543 14	18,854 95	311 81	....	64
263 40	3,264 70	3,388 38	123 68	....	65
6 72	83 14	66 22	....	16 92	66
539 49	1,177 42	2,111 65	934 23	....	67
36 25	219 50	36 25	....	183 25	68
9 40	216 62	185 61	....	31 01	69
210 00	2,501 41	2,390 30	....	111 11	70
....	273 37	204 09	....	69 28	71
....	....	....	....	....	72
....	54	1 40	86	....	73
....	....	....	....	....	74
....	....	....	....	....	75
....	....	....	....	....	76
....	2 77	....	....	2 77	77
47 61	....	43 70	43 70	....	78
2,819 27	27,516 56	28,821 55	1,304 99	....	
13 88	96 00	129 25	33 25	....	79
39 20	378 39	402 15	23 76	....	80
....	....	....	....	....	81
....	....	....	....	....	82
53 08	474 39	531 40	57 01	....	

Comparative Statement of Earnings and Expenditures by

No.	GENERAL AND MISCELLANEOUS.	1914 November.	1915 November.	1914 December.
		$ c.	$ c.	$ c.
83	Salaries and expenses of general officers	....	....	....
84	Salaries and expenses of general office clerks	155 00	155 00	155 00
85	General office supplies and expenses	84 49	10 00	41 27
86	Law expenses	....	....	....
87	Relief department expenses	....	....	....
88	Pensions and gratuities	....	....	....
89	Miscellaneous general expenses	7 85	3 90	90
90	Valuation expenses	....	....	....
91	Amortization of franchises	....	....	....
92	Injuries and damages	....	....	....
93	Insurance	132 96	48 20	119 63
94	Stationery and printing	....	233 11	37 50
95	Store expenses	....	....	....
96	Garage and stable expenses	....	....	....
97	Rent of tracks and facilities	862 92	102 00	Cr. 812 92
98	Rent of equipment	75 90	....	273 90
99	Other operations—Dr.	....	....	....
100	Other operations—Cr.	....	....	....
	Total	1,318 62	552 21	Cr. 184 72

Comparative Statement of Earnings and Expenditures by

No.	GENERAL AND MISCELLANEOUS.	1915 March.	1916 March.	1915 April.
		$ c.	$ c.	$ c.
83	Salaries and expenses of general officers ...	....	248 33	....
84	Salaries and expenses of general office clerks	155 00	186 66	155 00
85	General office supplies and expenses	5 84	5 00	7 33
86	Law expenses	....	....	....
87	Relief department expenses	....	....	....
88	Pensions and gratuities	....	....	....
89	Miscellaneous general expenses	12 50	3 50	1 75
90	Valuation expenses	....	....	....
91	Amortization of franchises	....	....	....
92	Injuries and damages	....	104 00	....
93	Insurance	114 12	35 39	113 77
94	Stationery and printing	84 69	28 01	5 00
95	Store expenses	....	....	....
96	Garage and stable expenses	....	....	....
97	Rent of tracks and facilities	50 00	50 00	249 68
98	Rent of equipment	293 25	294 30	282 45
99	Other operations—Dr.	....	....	....
100	Other operations—Cr.	....	....	....
	Total	715 40	955 19	814 98

Months, November, 1914, to October, 1916.—Continued.

1915 December.	1915 January.	1916 January.	1915 February.	1916 February.	No.
$ c.	$ c.	$ c.	$ c.	$ c.	
....	....	....	....	248 36	83
155 00	155 00	160 00	155 00	186 72	84
5 00	3 75	11 40	4 45	5 00	85
....	....	....	....	....	86
....	....	....	....	....	87
....	....	....	....	....	88
3 00	5 50	3 35	2 25	2 40	89
....	....	....	....	....	90
....	....	....	....	....	91
....	....	....	....	25 00	92
32 77	112 91	35 41	112 91	35 39	93
32 60	58 60	13 73	6 21	3 50	94
....	....	....	....	....	95
....	....	....	....	....	96
50 00	25 00	159 66	25 00	50 00	97
347 85	75 00	199 35	302 70	....	98
....	....	....	....	....	99
....	....	....	....	....	100
626 22	435 76	582 90	608 52	556 37	

Months, November, 1914, to October, 1916.—Continued.

1916 April.	1915 May.	1916 May.	1915 June.	1916 June.	No.
$ c.	$ c.	$ c.	$ c.	$ c.	
248 33	....	248 33	....	248 33	83
186 66	155 00	186 66	155 00	186 66	84
5 00	4 50	5 00	4 25	5 00	85
....	....	3 00	....	....	86
....	....	....	....	....	87
....	....	....	....	....	88
1 20	40	....	....	2 90	89
....	....	....	....	....	90
....	....	....	....	....	91
39 66	....	32 11	100 00	400 00	92
35 39	113 77	35 39	94 09	44 14	93
....	6 00	12 50	10 20	15 91	94
....	....	....	....	....	95
....	....	....	....	....	96
150 74	50 00	97 45	50 00	50 00	97
335 70	832 80	278 55	300 45	202 95	98
....	....	....	....	....	99
....	....	....	....	....	100
1,002 68	1,162 47	898 99	713 99	1,155 89	

Comparative Statement of Earnings and Expenditures

No.	GENERAL AND MISCELLANEOUS.	1915 July.	1916 July.	1915 August.
		$ c.	$ c.	$ c.
83	Salaries and expenses of general officers	8 39	248 33	....
84	Salaries and expenses of general office clerks	155 00	191 66	155 00
85	General office supplies and expenses....	5 00	5 05	5 00
86	Law expenses	....	....	....
87	Relief department expenses	....	....	....
88	Pensions and gratuities	....	....	....
89	Miscellaneous general expenses	30	....	29 90
90	Valuation expenses	....	....	....
91	Amortization of franchises	....	....	....
92	Injuries and damages	....	....	....
93	Insurance	65 95	35 39	48 20
94	Stationery and printing	....	165 02	193 37
95	Store expenses	....	....	....
96	Garage and stable expenses............	....	....	....
97	Rent of tracks and facilities............	135 01	50 00	50 00
98	Rent of equipment	295 95	218 70	339 15
99	Other operations—Dr...................	....	....	....
100	Other operations—Cr.	....	....	....
	Total	665 60	914 15	820 62

No.	GENERAL AND MISCELLANEOUS.	Total, 1915.
		$ c.
83	Salaries and expenses of general officers.................	8 39
84	Salaries and expenses of general office clerks............	1,860 00
85	General office supplies and expenses.....................	175 63
86	Law expenses	10 00
87	Relief department expenses	....
88	Pensions and gratuities	....
89	Miscellaneous general expenses	63 75
90	Valuation expenses	....
91	Amortization of franchises	....
92	Injuries and damages	100 00
93	Insurance	1,119 88
94	Stationery and printing	437 49
95	Store expenses	....
96	Garage and stable expenses...........................	....
97	Rent of tracks and facilities...........................	958 52
98	Rent of equipment	3,756 15
99	Other operations—Dr.	....
100	Other operations—Cr.	....
	Total	8,489 81

by Months, November, 1914, to October, 1916.—Continued.

1916 August.	1915 September.	1916 September.	1915 October.	1916 October.	No.
$ c.	$ c.	$ c.	$ c.	$ c.	
248 33	....	248 33	....	248 33	83
191 66	155 00	191 66	155 00	191 66	84
9 91	5 00	5 00	4 75	5 00	85
....	10 00	....	....	....	86
					87
....	....	....	....	....	88
5 85	2 00	18 40	90	45	89
....					90
....					91
....	48 20	....	....	461 00	92
35 39	48 20	35 39	43 37	35 39	93
195 68	8 41	5 35	27 51	19 86	94
					95
....	....	....	....	....	96
102 29	177 14	130 58	96 69	50 00	97
338 40	354 45	265 95	- 330 15	294 30	98
....	....	....	....	....	99
					100
1,127 51	760 20	900 66	658 37	1,305 99	

Total, 1916.	Increase.	Decrease.	No.
$ c.	$ c.	$ c	
2,235 00	2,226 61	....	83
2,170 00	310 00	....	84
76 36	....	99 27	85
3 00	....	7 00	86
			87
....	....	....	88
44 95	....	18 80	89
			90
....	....	....	91
1,061 77	961 77	....	92
443 64	....	676 24	93
725 27	287 78	....	94
			95
....	....	....	96
1,042 72	84 20	....	97
2,776 05	....	980 10	98
....	....	....	99
			100
10,578 76	2,088-95	....	

Comparative Statement of Earnings and Expenditures

No.	MISCELLANEOUS STATISTICS.	1914 November.	1915 November.	1914 December.	1915 December.
101	Passenger Car Hours	2,318	2,120	2,408	2,184
102	Passenger Car Miles	24,042	21,707	24,658	22,362
103	Total Passengers Carried	110,990	106,851	117,571	112,446
104	Average Daily Receipts	$286 69	$266 02	$284 73.8	$275 90.7
105	Average Receipts per Car Hour—Passenger	3 27	3 23.5	3 25.8	3 32.8
106	Average Receipts per Car Mile—Passenger	31.5	31.6	31.8	32.5
107	Earnings per Passenger	06.8	06.4	06.6	06.4

Comparative Statement of Earnings and

No.	MISCELLANEOUS STATISTICS.	1915 April.	1916 April.	1915 May.	1916 May.
101	Passenger Car Hours	2,290	2,174	2,275	2,348
102	Passenger Car Miles	23,376	22,261	23,390	24,043
103	Total Passengers Carried	113,460	120,750	118,138	132,417
104	Average Daily Receipts	$291 55.3	$318 26.9	$293 23	$308 77
105	Average Receipts per Car Hour—Passenger	3 42.2	3 60.5	3 60	3 70.9
106	Average Receipts per Car Mile—Passenger	33.5	37.2	34	36.2
107	Earnings per Passenger	06.9	06.8	06.8	06.5

Comparative Statement of Earnings and

No.	MISCELLANEOUS STATISTICS.	1915 September.	1916 September.	1915 October.	1916 October.
101	Passenger Car Hours	2,123	2,300	2,171	2,311
102	Passenger Car Miles	21,743	23,552	22,230	23,663
103	Total Passengers Carried	108,827	129,985	111,412	109,269
104	Average Daily Receipts	$284 98	$324 25	$277 51	$257 50
105	Average Receipts per Car Hour—Passenger	3 40.8	3 78.3	3 39.3	3 04.4
106	Average Receipts per Car Mile—Passenger	33.3	36.9	33.1	29.7
107	Earnings per Passenger	06.6	06.7	06.6	06.4

by Months, November, 1914, to October, 1916.—Continued.

1915 January.	1916 January.	1915 February.	1916 February.	1915 March.	1916 March.	No.
2,423	2,138	2,185	1,986	2,411	2,215	101
24,813	21,892	22,373	20,313	24,690	22,681	102
110,436	98,164	100,479	97,047	111,989	115,991	103
$268 05.7	$255 06.4	$265 64.1	$266 99.6	$277 00.7	$287 69.6	104
2 95.9	3 04.3	3 03.2	3 09.5	3 12.3	3 36.3	105
28.9	29.7	29.6	30.3	30.5	32.9	106
06.5	06.6	06.5	06.3	06.7	06.4	107

Expenditures by Months, etc.—Continued.

1915 June.	1916 June.	1915 July.	1916 July.	1915 August.	1916 August.	No.
2,239	2,284	2,344	2,346	2,139	2,379	101
22,932	23,383	24,002	24,023	21,908	24,361	102
117,211	135,454	130,877	138,709	116,512	142,813	103
$303 04	$331 68	$331 62	$335 08	$304 59	$344 10	104
3 64	3 96.6	3 87.5	4 04.3	3 77.6	4 10.5	105
35.5	38.7	37.8	39.5	36.9	40.1	106
06.9	06.8	06.9	06.8	06.9	06.7	107

Expenditures by Months, etc.—Concluded.

1915 Total.	1916 Total.	Increase.	Decrease.	No.
27,326	26,785	....	541	101
280,157	274,241	....	5,916	102
1,367,902	1,439,896	71,994	....	103
$288 92.7	$297 64.3	$8 71.6	....	104
3 38.8	3 55.6	16.8	....	105
33	34.7	1.7	....	106
06.7	06.6	....	$0 00.1	107

Crop of Clover. Farm of Mr. E. Lamb. South half Lot 7, Con. 3, Township Dack.

NIPISSING CENTRAL RAILWAY

Statement Showing Investment in Road and Equipment. November 1st, 1915, to October 31st, 1916.

Grading	$5,865 63	
Ballast	84 09	
Ties	32 04	
Rails, Fastenings and Joints	904 05	
Paving	600 00	
Poles and Fixtures ....Cr.	6 00	
Distribution System	42 61	
		$7,522 42

Detail of Charges.

Paving Whitewood Avenue, New Liskeard	$600 00	
Sidings—Northern Customs Concentrators, Limited	1,217 19	
Market spur, Haileybury	28 14	
Siding, Right-of-Way Mines	417 19	
Spur to loading dock, Haileybury	5,259 90	
		$7,522 42

NIPISSING CENTRAL RAILWAY COMPANY

Statement of Wages paid Employees for Year ending October 31st, 1916

McDonald, K.	Superintendent		$2,020 00
Crouch, R. J.	Cashier		1,310 00
Miller, N. A.	Stenographer		620 00
Stewart, W. F.	Land Agent		900 00
Brooks, Mrs. A.	Cleaning		27 50
Duval, Mrs. T.	"		5 00
Andrews, Mrs. H.	"		32 50
Mercier, A.	Sanitary Work		3 00
Montgomery, A.	Conductor		1,001 76
Murray, D. R.	"		997 92
Holden, E.	"		1,150 88
McAuley, A.	"		794 08
Anderson, G.	"		729 12
McDonald, A. A.	"		1,186 90
Curry, T. W.	"		1,142 81
Presley, W.	"		726 27
Noble, J.			1,091 73
Normandy, B.			377 65
Mills, J. G.			384 42
Kilgour, A. H.	"		5 00
Doughty, J.	"		184 25
McRae, A. J.	Motorman		1,124 64
Quinn, P.	"		1,190 24
Finlay, F.	"		1,195 52
Morrel, J. A.	"		432 64
Lyons, H. G.	"		1,104 32
Parks, W.			1,168 28
Richardson, R.			976 02
Garrison, T.	"		986 98
McIsaac, N.	"		823 18
Carmichael, W.	"		108 30
Hoppins, G.	"		636 64
Lemieux, P.	"		584 80
Beer, F.	"		498 47
Johnston, W.	"		225 75
Nickason, G.			202 74

STATEMENT OF WAGES PAID EMPLOYEES, ETC.—*Continued.*

Moodie, F.	Switchman	530	54
Brooks, A. W.	"	254	00
Peterson, C.	"	280	49
Dennison, S.	"	180	62
Decker, E.	Laborer	6	40

$27,201 36

MAINTENANCE.

Andrews, H.	Line Foreman	$532	26
Forrest, D.	Barn Foreman	540	00
McDonald, R.	"	493	55
Davies, J. H.	S.S. Operator	960	00
Warner, J.	"	730	32
Christefolo, H.	"	60	00
McQuaig, J.	"	777	42
Draper, J.	Barnman	1,078	14
Hoppins, G.	"	54	04
Quinn, G.	"	50	00
Moodie, F.	Arm. Winder	538	50
Stewart, L.	"	54	45
Carmichael, W.	Lineman	303	90
Gagnon, L.	"	279	90
Mills, J. G.	"	80	87
Hagar, W.	"	97	50
Harper, E. A.	Cleaner	370	00
Curry, W. J.	"	172	26
Dunn, G.	"	101	35
Brett, F.	Carpenter	33	58
Viau, J.	Painter	26	00
Lansloot, R.	"	26	00
Lato, G.	"	19	20
Montgomery, P.	Blacksmith	817	45
Finlay, W.	Teaming	42	00
Thomas, W.	"	10	00
Decker, J.	Laborer	6	40

8,255 09

SECTION No. 1.

Foreman	$855	96
Laborers	1,384	10

2,240 06

SECTION No. 2.

Foreman	$1,039	56
Laborers	2,338	31

3,377 87

Total $41,074 38

Detail of Nipissing Central Railway Accounts for Fiscal Year,
ending October 31st, 1916.

ALEXANDER & CABLE LITHOGRAPHING CO., LIMITED, TORONTO, ONT.

1257—Embossing and printing passes	$2 35	
1460—Letterheads	14 00	
		$16 35

H. ANDREWS, NORTH COBALT.

1343—Award W. C. B., *re* alleged injuries	$104 00	
1338— " " "	39 66	
1379— " " "	32 11	
1394— " " "	400 00	
		$575 77

ADAMS & WESTLAKE CO., CHICAGO, ILL.

1462—Hinges, window lifts	$8 04	
		$8 04

MUNICIPAL CORPORATION OF BUCKE.

1253—Taxes, 1915	$1,633 29	
1351—Statutory charges on lots	7 06	
		$1,640 35

BARBER ELLIS, LTD., TORONTO, ONT.

1244—Envelopes	$3 25	
1291—Envelopes	7 73	
		$10 98

COBALT DAILY NUGGET, COBALT, ONT.

1254—Subscription and forms	$15 00	
1397—Time tables	15 75	
1398—Advertising *re* lots	39 00	
1420—Time sheets	6 00	
1464—Tickets, slips	9 25	
1526—Time cards	6 75	
		$91 75

B. J. COGHLIN CO., LTD., MONTREAL, QUE.

1250—Springs	$1 60	
1311—Springs	1 60	
		$3 20

CHAS. COURTMARCHE, POSTMASTER, NORTH COBALT, ONT.

1470—Rent P.O. drawer	$3 00	
		$3 00

COLEMAN FARE BOX CO., TORONTO.

1443—Repairing portable boxes	$39 43	
1483—Boxes	63 00	
		$102 43

CANADIAN GENERAL ELECTRIC CO., LIMITED, TORONTO, ONT.

1313—Brushes	$11 10
1355—Switches, etc.	10 34
1342—Snap switches	10 50
1372—Armature coils, etc.	180 45
1409—Electrical material	684 00

CANADIAN GENERAL ELECTRIC CÓ., LIMITED, TORONTO, ONT.—*Continued.*

1408—Segments, fingers	23 01	
1468—Carbon brushes	10 00	
1498—Imperial compound	2 55	
1485—Commutator rings	12 50	
1564—Switches	9 26	
		$953 71

CANADIAN WESTINGHOUSE CO., LIMITED, HAMILTON, ONT.

1370—Lightning arresters	$24 90	
1406—Sockets	3 13	
1425—Cocks	6 27	
1481—Brushes, coils	120 19	
1566—Sets mica " V " rings for motor	9 00	
		$163 49

R. J. CROUCH, CASHIER, NORTH COBALT, ONT.

1248—Commission on advertising	$5 39	
1400—Expenses, travelling	4 25	
		$9 64

BERNARD CAIRNS, TORONTO, ONT.

1402—Stamp	$0 80	
		$0 80

COCHRANE HARDWARE, LTD., NORTH BAY, ONT.

1261—Extension ladder	$6 50	
1309—Wrench and jaw	2 13	
1312—H. & C. hooks	58	
1381—Screws, brush	55	
1479—Wrenches	3 20	
		$12 96

CANADA PAINT CO., LTD., MONTREAL, P.Q.

1423—Shellac	$10 25	
1524—Paint	7 05	
		$17 30

CROUSE, HINDS CO., OF CANADA, LTD., TORONTO.

1344—Headlight globes	$10 00	
1441—Carbon, clamps, etc.	63 60	
		$73 60

CANADIAN CONSOLIDATED RUBBER CO., LTD., TORONTO, ONT.

1407—Hose	$6 14	
1466—Hose bags	8 00	
		$14 14

CANADIAN EXPRESS CO., NORTH BAY, ONT.

1259—Express charges	$1 00	
1246— "	55	
1390— "	1 70	
1438— "	3 60	
1461— "	3 20	
1477— "	2 50	
1540— "	1 75	
		$14 30

PAUL COLLINS, HAILEYBURY, ONT.

1252—Fare box covers	$7 20	
		$7 20

CURTAIN SUPPLY CO., CHICAGO, ILL.

1293—Curtains $77 96
                                                              ————
                                                              $77 96

S. B. CLEMENT, C. E. & S. OF M., NORTH BAY, ONT.

1290—Honorarium $150 00
                                                              ————
                                                              $150 00

DAWSON & CO., LTD., MONTREAL, P.Q.

1295—Trolley wheels $9 00
1346—Brass connectors 5 58
1383—Wire, trolley parts 40 62
1422—Trolley wheels, carbons, etc. 208 92
1487—Lockwashers, bushings, etc. 261 21
1528—Springs, controllers, etc. 14 92
                                                              ————
                                                              $540 25

DAY & GORDON, HAILEYBURY, ONT.

1411—Services re Forrest $3 00
1522—Settlement re injuries, Mr. and Mrs. J. Sweeney and Mrs.
        Badour 450 00
1542—Services rendered 11 00
                                                              ————
                                                              $464 00

DOMINION EXPRESS CO., NORTH BAY, ONT.

1315—Express charges $0 40
1395—   " 2 45
1463—   " 1 30
1500—   " 2 90
1544—   "   65
                                                              ————
                                                              $7 70

H. DISSTON & SONS, LTD., TORONTO, ONT.

1568—Chromat hacks $3 78
                                                              ————
                                                              $3 78

FRANK W. DUNCAN, NORTH BAY, ONT.

1256—Uniforms $399 00
                                                              ————
                                                              $399 00

EMPLOYERS LIABILITY ASSURANCE CORPN., LTD., TORONTO, ONT.

1396—Renewal premium on No. 29251 .... $8 75
                                                              ————
                                                              $8 75

ELECTRIC RAILWAY JOURNAL, NEW YORK, N.Y.

1263—Subscription $4 50
1445—   " 6 50
1502—   " 4 50
                                                              ————
                                                              $15 50

J. L. ENGLEHART, PRESIDENT, TORONTO, ONT.

1282—Honorarium $500 00
                                                              ————
                                                              $500 00

C. L. FERGUSON, PAYMASTER, NORTH BAY, ONT.

1251—Pay rolls $3,135 67
1242—   " 3,190 44
1289—   " 3,457 14

C. L. FERGUSON, PAYMASTER, NORTH BAY, ONT.—*Continued.*

1300—Honorarium	115 00	
1310—Pay rolls	3,497 14	
1347— "	3,754 13	
1340— "	3,214 14	
1377— ..	3,560 54	
1404—	3,582 83	
1439—	3,421 23	
1490— ..	3,303 03	
1475—	3,431 83	
1538—	3,526 26	
		$41,189 38

F. F. FINDLAY, NORTH COBALT, ONT.

1330—Donation account, alleged injuries $25 00

$25 00

MRS. ALEX. FISHER, NORTH COBALT, ONT.

1349—Refund deposit on lots $10 00

$10 00

F. R. GIBSON, HAILEYBURY, ONT.

1258—Installing heating system $110 62

.$110 62

W. A. GRIFFIN, SUPERINTENDENT OF TRAFFIC, NORTH BAY, ONT.

1292—Honorarium $125 00

$125 00

GENERAL SUPPLY COMPANY OF CANADA, LIMITED, OTTAWA, ONT.

1570—Close R. & L. rad. nipples $1 44

$1 44

B. GREENING WIRE COMPANY, LIMITED, HAMILTON, ONT.

1374—Galvanized strand $36 76

$36 76

W. A. GRAHAM, PURCHASING AGENT AND STOREKEEPER, NORTH BAY, ONT.

1298—Honorarium $125 00

$125 00

T. J. GRACEY, AUDITOR OF DISBURSEMENTS AND ACCOUNTANT, TORONTO, ONT.

1302—Honorarium $125 00

$125 00

CORPORATION OF TOWN OF HAILEYBURY, ONT.

1492—Taxes, 1914, 1915, 1916 .... $1,528 74

$1,528 74

"THE HAILEYBURIAN," HAILEYBURY, ONT.

1424—Advertising lots for sale $12 25

$12 25

HYDRO-ELECTRIC POWER COMMISSION OF ONTARIO, TORONTO, ONT.

1260—Laco lamps	$40 00	
1348—Lamps	40 00	
1376—Laco lamps ....e............	40 00	
1504—Lamps	39 00	
		$159 0

D. HAMILTON, ASSISTANT ACCOUNTANT, TORONTO, ONT.

1304—Honorarium	$75 00	
		$75 0

IMPERIAL OIL COMPANY, LIMITED, TORONTO, ONT.

1265—Engine oil	$13 16	
1317— "	14 51	
1350— "	15 38	
1378— "	14 35	
1415—Curve grease	11 46	
1427—Grease	11 55	
1472—Oil	12 80	
1506— "	18 90	
1489—Grease and oil	27 73	
1572—Curve grease	11 43	
		$151 2

INTERNATIONAL REGISTER COMPANY, CHICAGO, ILL.

1413—Register repairs	$4 47	
		$4 4

JACKSON PRESS, KINGSTON, ONT.

1262—Certificates	$10 50	
1319—Car order slips	6 00	
1314—Accident reports	3 50	
1359—Letter paper	16 50	
1417—Time slips	7 50	
1426—Detention reports	1 50	
1447—Stationery, etc.	63 50	
		$109 0

G. C. KUHLMAN CAR COMPANY, CLEVELAND, OHIO.

1574—Wide canvas lined seat, rattan	$130 00	
		$130 0

KERRY & CHACE, LIMITED, TORONTO, ONT.

1316—Services rendered	$41 25	
1491— " "	157 27	
		$198 5

GEO. W. LEE, DIRECTOR, NORTH BAY, ONT.

1280—Honorarium	$500 00	
1286— " additional	175 00	
		$675 0

W. H. LEWIS, HAILEYBURY, ONT.

1440—Tax deeds	$9 10	
		$9 1

FRANK D. LYMAN, MONTREAL, QUE.

1321—Trolley bushings $52 50

         $52 50

LYMAN TUBE & SUPPLY COMPANY, LIMITED, MONTREAL, QUE.

1352—Trolley poles $21 00
1410—Intermediate No. 2 .... 57 90
1428—Tubes 8 54
1429—Wheels 9 00
1508—Harps, poles 42 60

         $139 04

JOHN MILLEN & SON, LIMITED, MONTREAL, QUE.

1267—Drums for Earl Letriever $33 00
1266—Trolley harps 21 60
1299—Automotoneers and trolley wheels 47 40

         $102 00

THE MUIR CAP COMPANY, TORONTO, ONT.

1576—Conductors' and motormen's caps $44 00

         $44 00

R. H. MITCHELL, AUDITOR AND CAR ACCOUNTANT, NORTH BAY, ONT.

1294—Honorarium $150 00

         $150 00

MINISTER OF INLAND REVENUE, OTTAWA, ONT.

1264—War tax $12 65
1357—   " 13 10
1454—   " 14 40
1503—   " 15 15

         $55 30

MIDVALE STEEL COMPANY, PHILADELPHIA, PA.

1297—Tires $41 90

         $41 90

JAMES MORRISON BRASS MANUFACTURING COMPANY, LIMITED, TORONTO, ONT.

1323—Brackets and sash stops $3 64
1361—Sockets 10 80
1442—Valves 6 30
1474—Brass stops 8 96

         $29 70

DENIS MURPHY, DIRECTOR, OTTAWA, ONT.

1284—Honorarium $500 00

         $500 00

W. H. MAUND, SECRETARY-TREASURER, TORONTO, ONT.

1288—Honorarium $160 00

         $160 00

JNO. MORROW SCREW & NUT COMPANY, LIMITED, INGERSOLL, ONT.

1380—Rivets $2 69

         $2 69

J. G. MILLS, CONDUCTOR, NORTH COBALT, ONT.

1494—Alteration to uniform	$2 50	
		$2 50

WESLEY McKNIGHT, NEW LISKEARD, ONT.

1354—Uniforms	$528 00	
1431— "	24 00	
1578— "	682 40	
		$1,234 40

H. H. McGEE, TRAVELLING AUDITOR, NORTH BAY, ONT.

1308—Honorarium	$50 00	
		$50 00

NORTHERN ONTARIO LIGHT & POWER COMPANY, LIMITED, COBALT, ONT.

1269—Current for power and lighting	$1,265 37	
1268— " power	1,334 25	
1301— " lighting	3 77	
1327— " power and lighting	1,551 93	
1320— " power and lighting	1,587 45	
1365— " power	1,516 50	
1356— " lighting	2 65	
1382— " power	1,253 25	
1388— " lighting	2 73	
1403— " power	1,275 75	
1444— " power	1,230 75	
1465— " power	1,271 25	
1476— " lighting	6 42	
1512— " power	1,311 75	
1495— " lighting	1 25	
1509— " power	1,269 00	
1546— " power	1,255 50	
		$16,139 57

NORTHERN ELECTRIC & MFG. CO., LTD., TORONTO, ONT.

1318—Fuse wire and plugs	$1 79	
1363—Friction tape	7 50	
1449—Friction tape	7 50	
1493—Tape	13 25	
1532—Duncan plugs	1 13	
1580—Telephone wire, etc.	24 26	
		$55 43

NORTHERN LUMBER MILLS, LTD., NORTH COBALT, ONT.

1325—Lumber	$4 55	
1510— " pickets	18 01	
1530— "	4 75	
		$27 31

NIPISSING MINING CO., LTD., COBALT, ONT.

1255—Rental property	$3 00	
		$3 00

NICHOLSON FILE CO., PORT HOPE, ONT.

1584—Slim taper files	$1 28	
		$1 28

NATIONAL DRUG & CHEMICAL CO. OF CANADA, LTD., TORONTO, ONT.

1582—Yellow petrolatum	$0 60	
		$0 6

NORTHERN CUSTOMS CONCENTRATORS, LTD., COBALT, ONT.

1307—Siding rebate	$615 00	
1328— " "	119 00	
1353— " "	112 00	
1430— " "	371 19	
		$1,217 1

OHIO BRASS CO., MANSFIELD, O.

1432—Rail bonds	$73 14	
		$73 1

PRESTON CAR & COACH CO., LTD., PRESTON, ONT.

1271—Car seat springs	$9 02	
1345—Castings	11 00	
1419—Castings	25 80	
		$45 8

PILKINGTON BROS., LIMITED, TORONTO, ONT.

1329—Glass	$43 42	
1478—Glass	4 46	
		$47 8

N. L. PIPER RAILWAY SUPPLY CO., LTD., TORONTO, ONT.

1385—Oil tank with pump	$12 00	
		$12 0

A. J. PARR, G. F. & P. A., NORTH BAY, ONT.

1296—Honorarium	$125 00	
		$125 0

PRATT & WHITNEY CO. OF CANADA, LTD., DUNDAS, ONT.

1480—Drills	$4 59	
		$4 5

RICE LEWIS & SON, LTD., TORONTO, ONT.

1412—Postage, invoice August 6th, 1916	$0 30	
1446—Shears, snips, etc.	3 20	
1482—Dies	10 31	
		$13 8

W. F. STEWART, LAND AGENT, NORTH COBALT, ONT.

1331—Commission on land sales	$24 50	
1332— " " "	7 50	
1360— " " "	27 50	
1401— " " "	36 .75	
1458— " "	43 75	
1499— " "	2 00	
1548— " " "	12 85	
		$154 8

STEEL COMPANY OF CANADA, LTD., HAMILTON, ONT.

1287—Screws	$7 86	
1358—Steel	2 28	
1453—Bolts, screws	3 61	
		$13 75

SOUTHAM PRESS, LIMITED, TORONTO, ONT.

1273—Tickets	$230 00	
1467—Certificates	21 75	
1469—Tariffs	9 25	
		$261 00

SOUTHAM PRESS, LIMITED, MONTREAL, P.Q.

1451—School tickets	$55 00	
1484—Forms	167 50	
		$222 50

—SAMSON CORDAGE WORKS, BOSTON, MASS.

1414—Signal cord	$9 43	
		$9 43

WILLIAM SCULLY, MONTREAL, P.Q.

1275—Caps	$42 75	
1387—Caps	45 00	
1497—Buttons	2 75	
		$90 50

SCYTHES & CO., LTD., TORONTO, ONT.

1416—Duck	$6 50	
		$6 50

PETER SMITH HEATER CO., DETROIT, MICH.

1322—Lubricant	$1 25	
		$1 25

STANDARD STEEL WORKS CO., PHILADELPHIA, PA.

1336—Tires	$311 19	
		$311 19

STANDARD PLANING MILLS, NORTH BAY, ONT.

1433—Lumber	$13 25	
		$13 25

TEMISKAMING & NORTHERN ONTARIO RY., TORONTO, ONT.

1279—Rental Kerr Lake Branch, Aug. 1, 1914 to Oct. 31, 1915....	$4,591 57
1281—Rails, oil, etc.	1,284 61
1285—Rent for lease of road, etc.	1,022 10
1270—Per diem	347 85
1272—Duty, express, stationery, etc.	38 69
1278—Insurance	392 58
1278a—Rent for lease of road, etc.	1,052 16
1335—Work performed, material and per diem	5,218 73
1337—Insurance	29 50
1341—Rent for lease of road, etc.	1,065 14
1334—Rent for lease of road, etc.	1,063 59
1369—Freight charges, hard coal, oil, stationery, etc.	368 96

TEMISKAMING & NORTHERN ONTARIO RY., TORONTO, ONT.—*Continued.*

1371—Per diem, water for locomotives, etc.	310	30
1375—Rent for lease of road, etc.	1,059	22
1362—Repairing air brakes, etc.	47	89
1364—Duty on tires .... ̈	23	33
1384—Per diem, soft coal, constables' time and lighting Cobalt station .... ̈	604	28
1392—Rent for lease of road, etc.	1,087	38
1389—Stationery, freight charges, etc. ....:...................	148	74
1399—Per diem, constables' time and lighting Cobalt station....	326	00
1405—Rent for lease of road, etc.	1,052	86
1421—Freight charges, waste, supplies	47	28
1434—Per diem, repairs to air brakes	214	59
1452—Rent for lease of road, etc.	1,058	92
1448—Duty, stationery	9	37
1435—Express charges, labour	207	48
1455—Freight charges	8	23
1457—Oil, wax, nuts, etc. ....,...............	72	61
1471—Rent for lease of road, etc.	1,084	69
1473—Per diem	218	70
1456—Per diem	338	40
1488—Ties	32	04
1496—Loading stones,.etc.	88	29
1514—Labour and material supplied in construction of Right of Way Mines siding, Cobalt, and construction service, etc., at station landing, M.P. 104	687	89
1520—Rent for lease of road, etc.	1,095	84
1501—Per diem, ties, etc.	420	45
1507—Patterns	10	29
1511—Rent for lease of road, etc.	1,078	80
1534—Freight charges, duty on seat rattan	58	18
1550—Labour and material supplied cars	28	36
1552—Car service	294	30
1554—Revenue year ended Oct. 31, 1916	20,000	00
1558—Rent for lease of road, etc.	1,053	63
1560—Constables' time, lighting Cobalt station	41	41
1588—Hard coal, stationery, etc.	879	57

$50,164 80

TEMISKAMING TELEPHONE CO., NEW LISKEARD, ONT.

1277—Telephone service	$3	90
1303— " "	3	35
1324— " "	2	40
1367— " "	3	50
1386— " "	1	20
1450— " "	2	90
1486— " "	2	85
1505—Toll service and phone rent	18	40
1556—Telephone service		45
1562— " " ....:................................	1	45

$40 40

TALLMAN BRASS & METAL CO., HAMILTON, ONT.

1333—Brass rod ....,....	$2	30

$2 30

WABI IRON WORKS, LTD., NEW LISKEARD, ONT.

1283—Brake shoes	$37	66
1274—Brake shoes, grate and bar	33	00
1305—Trolley wheels and labour	76	30
1339—Brake shoes	52	03
1326—Trolley wheels	7	50

WABI IRON WORKS, NEW LISKEARD, ONT.—*Continued.*

1373—Coal grates, brake shoes	37 25
1366—Brake shoes	172 75
1391—Brake shoes	47 25
1418—Repairing motor bearings	9 00
1436—Brake shoes	30 13
1437— " "	27 68
1459— " "	28 05
1516— " "	14 70
1536— " "	85 00
1586— " "	197 65

$855 95

WORLD'S ONLY DUSTLESS BRUSH CO., NORTH BAY, ONT.

1276—Brushes	$3 75

$3 75

YOUNG CO., LTD., NORTH BAY, ONT.

1368—Dutch Cleanser	$1 00
1393—Bon Ami	3 60
1518—Dutch Cleanser	3 60

$8 20

WM. YOUNG, GENERAL ROADMASTER, NORTH BAY, ONT.

1306—Honorarium	$125 00

$125 00

Total $123,301 77

RECAPITULATION ACCOUNTS PAYABLE.

Nov. 1st, 1915 to Oct. 31st, 1916.

General ledger balance, accounts payable as of Nov. 1st, 1915	....	$60,124 93
Disbursements for year Nov. 1st, 1915 to Oct. 31st, 1916, as per detailed statement	....	123,301 77
Cash payments by Treasurer during year	$150,451 86	....
General ledger balance, accounts payable, as of Oct. 31st, 1916	32,974 84	....
	$183,426 70	$183,426 70

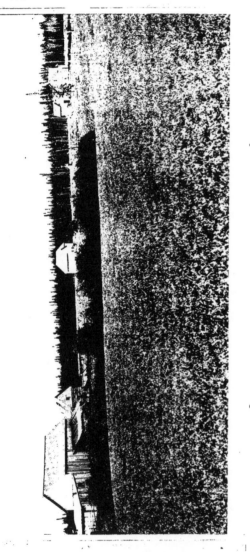

Farm of Mr. H. Netherton, Brentha, Ont.   South half Lot 1, Con. 3, Dack.   Prize grain exhibited at Ottawa grown on this farm.

INDEX.

	PAGE
Officials of T. & N. O· Railway	6
General Remarks	7
Auditor's Report	14
Insurance—Fire	17
Counsel's Report	19
Report of Chief Engineer and Superintendent of Maintenance	21
Mileage and Equipment	21
Surveys and Construction	21
Additions to Road and Equipment	22
Maintenance of Way	25
General Conditions	26
Wages of Employees	26
Forest Fires	27
Fencing	29
Private Sidings laid and extended	30
Private Sidings removed and shortened	30
Meeting Yard and Loading Sidings	30
Public or Railway Sidings taken up or shortened	31
Tie Renewals	31
Ballasting	32
Miscellaneous Betterments	32
Alleged accidents	34
Motive Power and Car Department	37
New Locomotives	37
New Passenger Cars	38
Work Equipment	38
Additional Tank Cars	38
Electrical Work	38
Air Brake Equipment	39
Repairs to Locomotives	41
Engine Despatch	41
Locomotive Mileage	42
Repairs to Passenger Equipment	42
Coach Cleaning	44
Repairs to Freight and Work Equipment	44
Tyres turned and Wheels applied Rolling Stock	45
Rolling Stock Destroyed	46
Work turned out of Carpenter Shops	46
Equipment Owned	48
Mechanical Accounting	48
Report of Telegraph and Telephone Department	50
Commercial Telegraph and Telephone business handled	50
Free Telegraph Messages account Fire Sufferers	51
Telegraph and Telephone wire in operation	51
Report of Superintendent of Traffic	53
Alleged Accidents	54
Physician's Report	58
Report of General Freight and Passenger Agent	61
Statement of Baggage, Corpses and Bicycles handled	62
Statement Baggage Claims	64
Report of the Commissioner—Land Department	67
Mining Engineer—Preliminary Report	70
Stores Department—Purchases and Issues	79
Financial Statements	83
General Balance Sheet	84
Expenditure on Construction	85
Detailed Statement of Charges to Construction	85
Comparative Statement, Earnings and Expenditures in operation 1905 to 1916	88
Comparative Statement of Earnings and Expenditures by Months	90
Statement Earnings and Expenses, Freight and Passenger, per Train Mile per Mile of Road	112
Freight Traffic Movement	125

PAGE

Statistics, Comparative Passenger and Freight Statement   126
Equipment Owned   127
Tonnage Statement   128
Forest Products   128
Passenger Traffic—Revenue—One Mile   128
Materials and Supplies on Hand   130
Traffic and Mileage Statistics   134
Statement of Land Purchased   135
Townsite Report   135
Townsite Accounts   136
Statement Employees—total days worked—average daily compensation ......   13?
Detailed Statement of Wages paid Employees   140
Detailed Statement of Expenditure   167
Contracts—Agreements   364
Contracts Extended   365
New Liskeard Wharf   365
Leased Through Telegraph Wire—Kiely, Smith and Amos   366
Wheels and Castings—Dominion Wheel and Foundries, Ltd.   370
Telegraph Connection—Cochrane—Grand Trunk Pacific Telegraph Co.   371
Coal Contract—Buffalo and Susquehanna Coal and Coke Co.   372
Rail Contract—Algoma Steel Corporation, Ltd. ....376 and   377
Dominion Brake Shoe Co., Ltd.   379
Machinists' Schedule—Effective May 1st, 1916   380
Car Department Schedule   384
New Locomotives—Canadian Locomotive Company, Ltd.   387
Conductors' Vans—Preston Car and Coach Co., Ltd.   391
New Station—Timmins, Henderson and Angus   393
Plumbing Tenement Houses, Iroquois Falls, F. R. Gibson   404
Cartage—Cobalt—The Simms Cartage Co.   412
Lease Land, Latchford—Sale of Old Buildings—Conkey and Murphy   416
Nipissing Central Railway   421
Report of Chief Engineer and Superintendent of Maintenance   421
General Balance Sheet   423
Comparative statement of Earnings and Expenditures by Months   424
Investment in Road and Equipment   451
Statement of Wages paid Employees   451
Details of Expenditures   453

THE

MINING INDUSTRY

IN THAT PART OF

NORTHERN ONTARIO

SERVED BY THE

Temiskaming and Northern Ontario Railway

ONTARIO GOVERNMENT RAILWAY

SIR WILLIAM H. HEARST, PREMIER

COMMISSION:

J. L. ENGLEHART, Chairman

DENIS MURPHY GEO. W. LEE

W. H. MAUND, Sec.-Treas.

(Appendix to Annual Report Temiskaming and Northern Ontario
Railway Commission)

CALENDAR YEAR 1916

By ARTHUR A. COLE

Mining Engineer

PRINTED BY ORDER OF

THE LEGISLATIVE ASSEMBLY OF ONTARIO

TORONTO:

Printed and Published by A. T. WILGRESS, Printer to the King's Most Excellent Majesty

1917

Printed by
WILLIAM BRIGGS
Corner Queen and John Streets
Toronto

To His Honour Sir John Strathearn Hendrie, K.C.M.G., C.V.O., a Colonel in the Militia of Canada, etc., etc.

Lieutenant-Governor of the Province of Ontario.

May it Please Your Honour:

The undersigned has the honour to present to Your Honour Report of the Mining Engineer of the Mining Industry in that part of Northern Ontario served by the Temiskaming and Northern Ontario Railway for the calendar year 1916.

Respectfully submitted,

F. G. Macdiarmid,
Minister of Public Works and Highways.

HON. FINLAY G. MACDIARMID,

   Minister of Public Works and Highways,

         Toronto.

   SIR,—I have the honour, by direction, to submit to you Report of the Mining Engineer on the Mining Industry, in that part of Northern Ontario served by the Temiskaming and Northern Ontario Railway, for the calendar year 1916.

         I have the honour to be,

            Sir,

      Your obedient servant,

                  W. H. MAUND,
                        Secretary-Treasurer.

TEMISKAMING AND NORTHERN ONTARIO
RAILWAY COMMISSION

J. L. ENGLEHART, Chairman.

DENIS MURPHY, Commissioner.

GEO. W. LEE, Commissioner.

W. H. MAUND, Secretary-Treasurer.

A. A. COLE, Mining Engineer.

Teck-Hughes Mine and Mill, Kirkland Lake, Ontario.

INTRODUCTION

Northern Ontario has just completed another prosperous mining year. The combined production of gold and silver for 1916 amounts to twenty-three million dollars, which is an increase of two and one-quarter millions over the previous year. This result was accomplished in the face of a shortage of men, slow delivery of supplies, particularly machinery, and towards the end of the year to what almost amounted to a famine in coal.

A marked revival in prospecting was noted and many new prospects opened and old ones reopened. Diamond drilling activity was particularly noticeable in Porcupine where every available drill was working to its full capacity. The result has been the extension of the already known deposits, as well as the discovery of new ore fields.

In the preceding report to the Commission a comparative table of prices was given for supplies used in mining and milling previous to the war and on March, 1916. At the end of the year several changes are to be noted. Zinc dust has dropped back from 27 cents to 18 cents.

The cyanide situation was for some time unsettled but the year closed with most of the difficulties overcome. The gold and silver mines of Northern Ontario consume over 100 tons of cyanide per month. This was supplied in about the following proportions:

(1) Two-thirds by the Cassel Cyanide Company of Glasgow, Scotland.

(2) One-third by the Roessler & Hasslacher Company, of New York.

In October, word was received from the Cassel Company that owing to the shortage of men and dearth of raw materials it was possible they would have to cut down their shipments to Canada. These difficulties were overcome by the British War Office. Then, in December, the Roessler & Hasslacher Company gave notice to their Canadian customers that after January 1st, 1917, they would have to discontinue shipments of cyanide to Canada owing to the withdrawal of power from the Chemical Company at Niagara which makes the metallic sodium used in the manufacture of cyanide. This power was required by the Hydro-Electric Power Commission of Ontario, and though generated on the Canadian side of Niagara was previously exported and sold in the United States. The companies depending on this cyanide supply are now being supplied temporarily by the Cassel Company.

Progress in the gold and silver mining may be judged to a certain extent by the dividends paid.

—	Amount of Dividends and Bonuses paid during 1916.	Total Amount of Dividends paid to December 31st, 1916.
	$ c.	$ c.
Cobalt	4,958,650 84	67,459,852 41
Porcupine	4,166,000 00	9,168,000 00
Kirkland Lake	260,750 00	325,937 50
	9,385,400 84	76,953,789 91

[7]

THE GOLD CAMPS

The statistics of Ontario's gold production for 1916 issued by the Ontario Bureau of Mines, show a steady increase over previous years. As in 1915, most of the production this year came from Porcupine, but Kirkland Lake and Munroe district also assisted.

Porcupine

The following mines produced gold in the Porcupine district during the year:

Hollinger, Dome, McIntyre, Porcupine Crown, Vipond, Schumacher, Dome Lake.

The gold production of the Porcupine camp to the end of the calendar year 1916 is shown in the following table:

PORCUPINE GOLD PRODUCTION, 1910-1916.

Year.	Ounces.	Value.
		$
1910	1,947	35,539
1911	765	15,437
1912	83,725	1,730,628
1913	207,748	4,294,113
1914	251,131	5,190,794
1915	362,186	7,480,901
1916	452,095	9,397,536
	1,359,597	28,144,948

This year has been one of amalgamations or proposed amalgamations, and the greatest of these was the consolidation of the Hollinger group.

During June a merger was completed of the Hollinger Gold Mines, Limited, Acme Gold Mines, Limited, and Millerton Gold Mines, Limited, along with claim 13147, and the plant of the Canadian Mining & Finance Company, Limited. This aggregation is now known as the Hollinger Consolidated Gold Mines, Limited. The capital of the new company is $25,000,000 and the dividend that was paid every four weeks during the year was $240,000, or a total of $3,126,000 for the year.

An amalgamation was also arranged between the North Thompson and the Porcupine-Vipond mines and this was consummated early in 1917.

A third amalgamation which was also ratified early in 1917 was that of the McIntyre with the McIntyre extension and the Jupiter.

All of these amalgamations will allow for a better and more economic handling of the ore and cutting down of overhead expenses.

The general development in the Porcupine camp has been very satisfactory. Besides considerable additions to the ore reserves of the two larger properties, the Hollinger and the Dome, the year has been noteworthy on account of the important ore bodies located on the 1,000-foot level of the McIntyre Extension, the 100-foot level of the Schumacher, and between the 7th and 9th levels of the Porcupine Crown, in all cases adding materially to the value of the mines.

Around the regular producers a considerable number of promising prospects are being tested out by diamond drill or mining, and besides these many others are operating both in Deloro and Shaw, and some activity is also shown to the north of Porcupine Lake.

Considering present war conditions, it is remarkable that so much activity is being shown in this district, and if the times were normal this would soon assume the proportions of a boom.

HOLLINGER.

The Hollinger Consolidated Company has a milling capacity equivalent to 120 stamps, but an extension to the mill, which is now under progress, will add another 100 stamps.

The Company in 1916 milled 601,584 tons of ore and recovered values of $5,073,401, and paid out $3,126,000 in dividends.

Managing Director Robbins estimates that he has 3,988,000 tons of ore of an average value of $8.68 per ton. The estimated gross value of the ore reserves on December 31st, 1916, was $34,185,000 as against $33,837,000 on December 31st, 1915.

A continual advance in the cost of supplies, and the growing shortage and the lowering quality of labour has increased the costs of operation, until they are approximately 50 cents per ton above normal, which means a reduction in profits of from $900 to $1,000 per day.

Actual costs of mining and milling are shown below.

Account.	Labour.	Stores.	Total.	Per ton Ore Milled.
	$ c.	$ c.	$ c.	
Mining	804,083 34	513,372 20	1,317,455 54	2.188
Milling	187,880 18	395,580 52	583,460 70	0.969

Grand total of costs amounted to $2,428,601.72 or $4.033 per ton of ore milled.

The record of production of the Hollinger and Acme mines is shown in the following tabulation:

HOLLINGER GOLD MINES, LTD. AND ACME GOLD MINES, LTD.

Year.	Tons of Ore Milled.	Values Recovered.	Dividends Paid.
		$ c.	$
1911	1,000	46,082 52	
1912	45,195	933,682 00	270,000
1913	140,131	2,488,022 58	1,170,000
1914	211,846	2,719,354 47	1,170,000
1915	441,236	4,205,901 69	1,720,000
Totals......................	839,408	10,393,043 26	4,330,000

HOLLINGER CONSOLIDATED GOLD MINES, LTD.

1916	601,854	5,037,401 05	3,126,000
Grand Totals	1,441,982	15,430,444 31	7,456,000

DOME.

The main or No. 3 shaft has been completed to the 8th level (850 feet) and development has been prosecuted on the 7th, 6th and 5th levels. Shortage of men greatly curtailed development. The production record for 1916 was as follows:—

The production record for the year was as follows:

1916	Tons Milled.	Bullion Produced.	Value per ton.	Total Cost per ton.
		$	$	$
January	31,600	175,639	5,558	2.772
February	32,040	164,027	5,119	2.716
March	34,300	173,725	5,064	2.640
April	37,300	177,624	4,762	2.402
May	39,400	190,230	4,828	2.447
June	36,700	179,245	4,883	2.667
July	38,150	179,370	4,701	2.571
August	40,010	179,531	4,487	2.553
September	38,300	184,505	4,817	2.627
October	40,200	181,946	4,526	2.654
November	37,900	181,172	4,780	2.895
December	39,000	186,724	4,788	2.782
	444,900	2,153,738	4,841	2.634

MᴄIɴᴛʏʀᴇ-Pᴏʀᴄᴜᴘɪɴᴇ.

MILLING RECORD FOR 1916.

1916.	Tons Milled.	Average Value.	Production.	Ton Costs.	Profit Operating.
		$ c.	$ c.	$ c.	$ c.
1st Quarter	27,248	7 74	201,110 00	3 85	97,128 00
2nd Quarter	*30,452	8 29	241,650 05	4 23	122,064 00
3rd Quarter	*35,810	9 08	250,744 69	4·93	136,083 00
4th Quarter	*39,369	10 62	340,194 22	4 51	208,990 41

*The above tonnage figures include ore milled for subsidiary companies.

To the above operating profit must be added the profits earned by milling Jupiter ore, which, under the terms of the late amalgamation, become the property of the McIntyre Company. For the last quarter these amounted to $23,081.60, so that it is certain that the operating profit for the year with these profits included will exceed $600,000 or 20 per cent. on the original capital.

The outstanding feature in the development of this property during the year has been the opening up of an important high grade ore body on the 1,000-foot level of the McIntyre Extension or old Pearl Lake property. This ore which has been followed for about 320 feet, will average about 15 feet in width and carry an average value of $14.00.

The new aerial tram across the Lake from the central shaft to the mill is now ready. It has a capacity several times the present mill capacity, which is 450 tons per day. With the completion of the new shaft the mine will be ready to materially increase production as fast as enlargements are added to the mill.

Pᴏʀᴄᴜᴘɪɴᴇ-Cʀᴏᴡɴ.

At the end of 1915 the deepest working in this mine was 700 feet, but the deepest ore developed was on the 600-foot level. During 1916 the 900-foot level was reached. The main shaft is down to the 500-foot level, but the 600, 700, 800 and 900-foot levels are reached by a winze. Good ore was encountered in the winze from 750 feet to 920 feet and this ore has not yet been bottomed.

The mill continues to handle about 140 tons per day and during the year treated 51,273 tons which yielded 27,877 ounces gold of a gross value of $574,604.

Dividends were continued at the rate of 12 per cent. on the capital.

The following is a statement of the operating figures for the past three years:

—	■1914	1915	1916
	$	$	$
Production	691,394	615,537	574,604
Expenses	386,319	316,421	304,174
Profit	305,075	299,116	270,430
Interest	2,330	5,069	4,574
Total Revenue	307,405	304,185	275,004
Less—			
Dividends.............................	240,000	240,000	240,000
Bonus—Employees	5,854	6,333	4,563
Deductions............................	245,854	246,333	244,563
Balance	61,551	57,852	30,441
Previous Balance	150,572	212,124	267,440
Surplus	212,123	269,976	297,881
War Taxes	....	....	20,797
Net Surplus			277,084

PORCUPINE-VIPOND-NORTH THOMPSON GOLD MINES.

A basis for amalgamation was completed between the Porcupine-Vipond and the North Thompson properties, and this has been ratified by the shareholders. Operations commenced under the new administration on December 16th, 1916.

The plan of operation as at present projected is to make the North Thompson shaft the permanent working shaft for the combined properties. The Vipond mill will be used and, for the present, ore from the North Thompson shaft will be brought over the surface. It is planned to sink the North Thompson shaft, which is down 500 feet, to the 600-foot level and then drive on this level to connect with the Vipond. The corresponding level in the Vipond will be 640 feet.

During the year the Porcupine-Vipond mill treated 43,041 tons of ore which yielded 8,508 ounces gold, valued at $175,874.

SCHUMACHER.

During the year this property produced and milled 46,463 tons of ore which yielded 10,844 ounces gold valued at $224,157. The mill has a capacity of about 130 tons per day, but it is proposed to double this in 1917. The first four levels supplied the ore milled, very little development work having yet been done on the 5th and 6th levels.

Most of the workings are north of the shaft, but an important high grade vein was found on the 100-foot level about 200 feet south of the shaft.

Power.

The Northern Canada Power Company, Limited, supplies electrical power to all the mines in the Porcupine district.

This Company has two developments on the Mattagami River, namely, Wawaiten Falls, 12 miles south-west, and Sandy Falls, 6 miles north-west from the town of Timmins.)

Wawaiten Falls plant is located in the Township of Thornloe, at the foot of Lake Kenogamisee. A concrete dam 1,000 feet long at this point diverts the water into a 1,200-foot canal. From intake at foot of canal water is carried by two 9-foot wooden stave pipes, each 1,500 feet long, to two 40-foot diameter surge tanks on top of the hill overlooking the power house. Two 8-foot iron pipes 1,300 feet long, lead from this surge tank down the side of hill direct to the wheels in the power house. The power house is of reinforced concrete and contains two 3,300 h.p. Morgan Smith water-wheels under head of 125 feet, direct connected to two 2,500 k.v.a., 3-phase, 12,000-volt Canadian Westinghouse alternators; two 70 k.w. exciter sets driven by independent water-wheels and Westinghouse switching and switch-board apparatus. The original construction had one 12-foot iron pipe 1,500 feet long, from intake at foot of canal to the surge tank, but this was replaced during the season of 1913-14 by two 9-foot wooden stave pipes of 3-inch Oregon fir, erected by the Pacific Coast Pipe Co., of Seattle, Wash., under the personal supervision of their engineer. There is in course of construction at this point a 4,000 h.p. unit, driven by a 4,750 h.p. turbine. The generator is manufactured by the Canadian Westinghouse Co., and the turbine by the Morgan Smith Co. Another 4,000 h.p. unit is being contemplated.

Sandy Falls plant is located in the Township of Mountjoy. A solid concrete dam and intake, approximately 1,500 feet long, diverts the water into one 8-foot steel pipe direct connected to water-wheel with surge tank to protect; and one 8-foot wooden stave pipe, direct connected to water-wheel with surge tank also to protect. The power house is of wood covered on outside and roof with corrugated iron, and on inside completely sheeted with asbestos board, and contains two 1,200 h.p. Morgan-Smith wheels under a head of 33 feet, direct connected to two 950 k.v.a., 3-phase, 12,000-volt, Canadian Westinghouse alternators, with exciters on the same shaft. Switching and switchboard apparatus is of Canadian Westinghouse manufacture.

In addition to the above the Company has just completed the installation of a 2,500 h.p. Canadian General Electric generator, driven by a 3,000 h.p. turbine, manufactured by the I. P. Morris Co., Philadelphia.

The Power Company has thirty-five miles of main and branch transmission lines now operating in the district. There are two separate transmission lines from Wawaiten Falls to the Hollinger and Dome, and one transmission line with two circuits from Sandy Falls to the Dome via the Hollinger, complete with switching towers so that the two plants work continually in parallel.

Conservation dams for supply of water have been erected on the Grassy River, and two dams are now in the course of construction at the head waters of the Mattagami River, on Lakes Minniesiniqua and Mesomekenda, so as to give continuously 20,000 h.p. for the Porcupine camp.)

Kirkland Lake.

Next to Porcupine the Kirkland Lake camp holds a prominent position in the public eye.

Gold was first discovered in this district on the Wright-Hargraves property early in 1912, but little general interest was shown till after a high grade shipment was made in 1913 from the Tough-Oakes property. Slowly but steadily the district was developed. A small hydro-electric power development, at Charlton delivered electric power to the Tough-Oakes Mine from June, 1914, to March, 1917, but even at high water this plant could only generate 670 h.p., while at low water a much smaller amount was available. The Northern Ontario Light and Power Company, of Cobalt, have now completed a power line into the Kirkland Lake camp and started the delivery of power at the beginning of March, 1917. One thousand five hundred h.p. is now being delivered at the Kirkland Lake substation and this can be increased as required. This installation should prove a large factor in the early and more economical development of this district.

The principal working properties in the district are:

1. Tough-Oakes Gold Mines, Limited.
2. Teck-Hughes Gold Mines, Limited.
3. Wright-Hargraves Mines, Limited.
4. Lake Shore Mines, Limited.
5. Kirkland Lake Gold Mines, Limited.
6. Sylvanite Gold Mines, Limited.
7. LaBelle Kirkland Mines, Limited.
8. Elliott Kirkland Gold Mines, Limited.

1. TOUGH-OAKES GOLD MINES, LIMITED.

This was the first property working in the district, is the farthest advanced with its development, and up to the end of 1916 was the only producer. Nine veins have been located in an area of about 35 acres. The total acreage of the property is 183. Most of the ore produced to date has been taken from Nos. 2, 3 and 6 veins. Other veins containing pay ore are Nos. 7, 9 and 11. Underground development to the end of 1916 totalled 9,347 feet.

The power plant consists of 2 motor-driven compressors (motors being 250 h.p. and 225 h.p.) giving a total of 3,000 cubic feet of free air per minute. Number of drills working is 28 (March, 1917). Total power now used, supplied by the Northern Ontario Light & Power Company, amounts to 880 h.p.

Total men employed 225, of whom 170 are working underground.

The mill has a daily capacity of about 110 tons.

Milled in 1916	39,865 tons
Value	$702,761

Total value recovered to end of 1916, $1,458,320.

2. TECK-HUGHES GOLD MINES, LIMITED.

This property has underground development as follows:

Shaft sinking	796 feet
Drifting	2,600 "
Crosscutting	1,031 "
Deepest level	400 "
Men employed—Mining	37
Surface and construction	19
Mill	9
Total	65
Compressing capacity	10 drill
Total electric installation	440 h.p.

The mill has a daily capacity of from 80 to 100 tons. Four machines are now working, two of which are on development of the 400-foot level. During the coming season it is proposed to sink to the 600-foot level, putting on more machines as ore is required for the mill. Development is on three veins, and a crosscut is now being driven north on the 400-foot level to tap a fourth.

3. Wright-Hargraves Mines, Limited.

The first gold discovery in the Kirkland Lake district was on this property, but the present company has only been operating since August 1st, 1916. Since that date about 1,000 feet of trenching has been done and two shafts sunk. No. 3 to 100 feet and No. 2 to 70 feet. Sampling is said to show a high grade of milling ore in both shafts. In connection with this work about sixty acres of the property has been cleared. No. 1 shaft was sunk on No. 1 vein, about three years ago by the previous management, and some high grade ore taken out. No. 2 and No. 3 shafts are 750 feet apart on this lead. Present plans are to sink to a depth of 300 feet in No. 2 and No. 3 shafts and connect them at the level. One 4-drill compressor is now running by steam, but it is proposed to install a 10-drill during the coming summer to be run by a 175 h.p. motor.

4. Lake Shore Mines, Limited.

The underground development on this property for 1916 consisted of 1,200 feet of drifting and 100 feet of raising. Deepest working is 300-foot level. Power is supplied by a 7-drill compressor. The ore chute has a length of about 300 feet at the 300-foot level and 150 feet at the 100-foot level. A small mill is to be erected this summer, work to be started April 1st. Crushing capacity of the mill is to be 60 tons per day, but this can be increased at any time to 100 tons, which is to be the capacity of the cyanide end of the mill.

Men now employed, 30; drills, 3.

All development so far is on one vein, but a prospecting crosscut is to be started north to prospect for further veins under Kirkland Lake.

5. Kirkland Lake Gold Mines, Limited.

A summary of development on this property to the end of February, 1917:

Drifting	916.0	feet
Crosscutting	617.5	"
Shaft sinking	410.0	"
Total	1,943.5	"
Station cutting	149.0	cubic yards
Sump cutting	95.0	" "
Total	244.0	'

Development to the 500-foot level has been extended and sinking to the 6th level is soon to be consummated. The property was formerly equipped with a small plant consisting of two small boilers, locomotive type, three drill compressors and a small hoist, to this has recently been added: one Jenckes' boiler, 125 h.p.; one 10-drill compressor, an electric light plant, and a hoist capable of working to a depth of 800 or 900 feet.

6. Sylvanite Gold Mines, Limited.

This property is equipped with a 4-drill air compressor, electrically driven. It is proposed to sink and crosscut on a vein which carries fair values over a small width. Sinking is being done with two machines on contract.

7. LaBelle Kirkland Mines, Limited.

This property is situated two miles due north of the Tough-Oakes Mine. It is now well equipped with buildings and a steam driven plant, with an air compressor of 460-foot capacity. The property is being developed at three levels, the deepest being 330 feet.

8. Elliott Kirkland Gold Mines, Limited.

This company started operations on December 1st, 1916, and now has a shaft down 65 feet. A small plant has been installed and it is hoped to have it in operation by April 1st, 1917.

Munro Township

The Croesus Mine was the only producer in this district during the year. From the 477 tons ore milled from this property a yield of 2,495 ounces gold was obtained, valued at $51,578. On the 29th July a devastating forest fire swept the district with large loss of life. Besides losing a number of men, all buildings and equipment of this mine were burned and destroyed. Reconstruction was at once started and the mine is again running with a full force.

Boston Creek

A number of promising prospects bid fair to yield some gold producers with continued development. The Boston Creek Mining Company has installed a new fuel-oil engine-driven compressor plant in two units, each of which will have a capacity of 400 cubic feet. The plant was built by the Chicago Pneumatic Tool Company. This installation is the first of its kind in this district and its working will be watched with interest by managers who are opening up other properties that are not conveniently situated to obtain hydro-electric power.

The advantages of such an installation are:

(1) Small room required for installation.
(2) Easily installed.
(3) Can be added to unit by unit as further power is required.

Kowkash and Tashota

East of Lake Nipigon on the National Transcontinental Railway development is proceeding on several gold claims. The principal operating company is the Tash-Orn, which has erected a plant on a promising find on the Wells claim near Tashota. This company is also developing the King Dodds claim near Kowkash, the original discovery in the district.

Other Gold Camps

Several promising gold finds have been located in the vicinity of Bourkes Station and farther east to the north of Wolf Lake, and during the past summer a good discovery was reported on the Sullivan claim, at *Sesekinika*. Reports of valuable gold finds were also received from *Gauthier* and *Benoit* Townships and at the end of the year quite a staking rush took place into *Powell* and *Cairo* Townships just south of Matachewan.

DIVIDENDS PAID BY THE PORCUPINE GOLD MINES.

To December 31st, 1916.

Mine.	Percentage paid during 1916.	Amt. of Dividends and Bonuses paid during 1916.	Total percentage paid to Dec. 31st, 1916.	Total amount of Dividends paid to Dec. 31st, 1916.
		$ c.		$ c.
Dome Mines......................	20	800,000 00	30	1,200,000 00
Hollinger Gold Mines,...........	13	3,126,000 00	47¾	7,456,000 00
Porcupine Crown Mines	12	240,000 00	33 ·	660,000 00
Rea Mines.....................			6	12,000 00
Total................		4,166,000 00		9,328,000 00

DIVIDENDS PAID BY KIRKLAND LAKE GOLD MINES.

Tough–Oakes	10	260,750 00	12½	325,987 50

THE SILVER CAMPS

The silver production of Ontario is made up for the most part by the mines in the Cobalt district; the small remaining portion is recovered in the gold mills, but this only amounts to .4 per cent. of the whole.

THE SILVER PRODUCTION OF THE COBALT CAMP.

Year.	Ounces.	Value.
		$
1904...	206,875	111,887
1905...	2,451,356	1,360,503
1906...	5,401,766	3,667,551
1907...	10,023,811	6,155,391
1908...	19,437,875	9,133,378
1909...	25,897,825	12,461,576
1910...	30,645,181	15,478,047
1911...	31,507,791	15,953,847
1912...	30,243,859	17,408,935
1913...	29,681,975	16,553,981
1914...	25,162,841	12,765,461
1915...	23,730,839	11,742,463
1916 (Estimated)	20,000,000	13,000,000
	254,391,494	$135,793,020

Cobalt's production reached its zenith in 1911 and from that year on we may expect a gradual decline owing to the depletion of the mines. This year, however, although there is actually a falling in production of nearly three million ounces, there is an increase in value of over one million dollars. This is due to the phenomenal rise in the price of silver.

The average price during 1915 was 49.7 cents per ounce. Towards the end of that year a rise set in which has continued during 1916 as is shown in the following table:

Month.	New York.		London.	
	1915	1916	1915	1916
January	48.855	56.775	22.731	26.960
February	48.477	56.755	22.753	26.975
March	50.241	57.935	23.708	27.597
April...........................	50.250	64.415	23.709	30.662
May............................	49.915	74.269	23.570	35.477
June	49.034	65.024	23.267	31.060
July	47.519	62.940	22.597	30.000
August	47.163	66.083	22.780	31.498
September.......................	48.680	68.515	23.591	32.584
October.........................	49.385	67.855	23.925	32.361
November	51.714	71.604	25.094	34.192
December.......................	54.971	75.765	26.373	36.410
Year	49.684	65.661	23.675	31.315

New York Quotations—Cents per ounce troy, fine silver.
London—Pence per ounce, sterling silver, 0.925 fine.

The lowest price for the year 1916 was 55.875 on January 3rd, and the highest 76.75 on December 15th. The year closed with the price of silver higher than at any other time in the history of the Cobalt camp.

The war is doubtless accountable for this rise in price. The belligerent countries all have the gold standard, so when hostilities broke out gold vanished from general circulation, being either conserved by the Governments or hoarded by individuals. Then came large orders for silver from the different Governments to take the place, to a certain extent, of the gold, and the rise in value started. Under normal conditions Mexico is the largest silver producer in the world, but owing to the present unsettled state of the country and difficulty in securing supplies, her production is much curtailed and this undoubtedly is another important factor in the price of silver.

The better returns being received by the mines for their ore is already having its effect in increased activity in and around the silver camps, not only are old prospects being given a better trying out than ever before, but some of the old mines that have been closed down for a number of years have been re-opened and again appear on the list of shippers. The results of this new movement should be still more apparent in 1917.

The above are outside influences affecting the silver industry, but there are also internal developments that are of much importance.

On the 1,600-foot level of the Beaver Mine (the deepest working in the district) an interesting development has taken place.

The following quotation taken from the annual report of the company refers to this find. "In No. 2 crosscut to the west, a large vein of from six to eight inches in width was recently cut. This vein shows native silver, and leaf silver is scattered through the wall rock for a distance of about four feet on both sides of the vein." This discovery may have far-reaching effects and will undoubtedly stimulate further exploratory work in this part of the district.

From a metallurgical standpoint the greatest recent development is the introduction of oil-flotation and its application in the concentration of low grade silver ores. It is not at all likely that this method of concentration will supersede the standard methods of concentration already in use in the camp, but in many cases it can be made a valuable addition to the existing plants and the extraction bettered with only a small additional cost.

Concentration by Flotation.

The Buffalo Mine was the first property to install a flotation plant in the Cobalt Camp. A 50-ton unit was run for eight months, and in that time demonstrated the applicability of oil flotation for the concentration of cobalt ores. Then this was replaced by the present plant of 600 tons daily capacity. The following is a list of the mills that have added flotation plants to their equipment, while several others are still experimenting and are likely to put in plants in the future.

Flotation Plants Installed in Cobalt.

Mill.	Daily Capacity. Tons.
Beaver	30
Buffalo	600
Coniagas	200
Dominion Reduction	200
McKinley-Darragh	200
National Mines (King Edward)	100
Nipissing	300
Northern Customs	200
Total capacity	1,830

Concentration by oil flotation will not only make available for treatment large tonnages of tailings now being produced by the mills, but many tailings-dumps will also be re-treated at a profit. The tonnage of such old tailings-dumps will amount to about two and one-half million tons. If we assume that at least four ounces per ton can be saved at a cost of two ounces, we have a profit on this material alone of three and three-quarter million dollars. Another important phase of the situation is that oil flotation will be additional help to make lower grade material treatable at a profit, and so the available tonnage is increased and the life of the camp is materially prolonged.

Flotation Oils.

Oils used in the flotation of ores may be roughly divided into two classes (1) collectors, (2) frothers. Many different oils may be used as collectors which will give good results, but in the choice of a frother it has been found that at least a small proportion of pine oil is necessary to give the best results. The demand for pine oil for flotation purposes during the last two years has grown so rapidly that the supply is totally inadequate to meet the market. The price has doubled and the material now obtained is much less pure than formerly. All the pine oil used on this continent is obtained from the southern United States, so that Canadian consumers are dependent on this foreign supply. These facts were laid before the Dominion Government with the result that an investigation was started by the Forest Products Laboratories of the Forestry Department, working in conjunction with the Mines Branch, Department of Mines, Ottawa, to see if pine oil or a suitable substitute could not be produced from Canadian woods. The investigation has already met with considerable encouragement and important results are anticipated.

MILLING IN COBALT DURING 1916.

Mills and Mines.	Tons Milled.	Concentrates.	Concentration. Ratio.
1 Beaver	37,594	393	96–1
2 Buffalo	12,155	126	96–1
3 Casey-Cobalt	13,237	239	55–1
4 Cobalt Lake	16,374	506	32–1
5 Cobalt Reduction	97,255	998	97–1
6 Coniagas	58,127	643	90–1
7 McKinley-Darragh	62,696	1,391	45–1
8 Northern Customs—			
La Rose	54,229	1,242	44–1
Right-of-Way	8,048	198	41–1
Seneca Superior	3,399	124	27–1
Chambers-Ferland	58	4	15–1
9 Penn-Canadian	33,095	472	70–1
10 Seneca Superior	2,459	216	11–1
11 Timiskaming	32,897	349	94–1
12 Trethewey	18,541	286	65–1
Total	450,164	7,187	65–1

Cyanide Mills.	Tons Milled.	Bullion Produced Oz.
13 Dominion Reduction—		
Crown Reserve Mining Co., Ltd.	14,739	
Silver Leaf	164	
Kerr Lake Mining Co	36,417	
Peterson Lake Mining Co	582	
Cobalt Comet Mines, Ltd.	6,945	
Glen Lake Mines	1,452	1,615,386
Dominion Mines	408	
Drummond Fraction	955	
Chambers-Ferland Mining Co	949	
Silver Queen Mines, Ltd.	76	
Hargraves Silver Mines, Ltd.	420	
14 Nipissing, Low Grade	76,851	2,133,681
15 O'Brien	45,000	590,000
Total	184,958	4,339,067

Total tons milled by water concentrating mills	450,164
Total tons milled by Cyanide Mills	184,958
Total	635,122

Total tons milled,	1916	635,122
"	1915	693,782
"	1914	743,531
"	1913	664,845
"	1912	455,517
"	1911	381,871
"	1910	305,513
"	1909	126,421
"	1908	49,424
Grand Total		4,056,026

NOTE.—The preceding tables do not include the tailings that are being re-treated.

BUFFALO.

The new installation for the treatment of ore in Callow Pneumatic Flotation Machines, at the property of The Buffalo Mines is now in operation.

The plant is for the treatment of the tailing resulting from the concentrating tables; 150 tons per day from the mine and 450 tons per day from the tailing piles will be treated. The ore from the mine is run through the mill as usual and the tailing from the tables sent to the flotation plant. The sand from the tailings piles is loaded to belt conveyors, delivering to the sand storage bin by a 12-ton locomotive crane, handling a 1¼-yard clam shell bucket.

The additional grinding necessary is done in four 5 ft. 6 in x 20 ft. tube mills in closed circuit with Dorr classifiers.

The flotation plant proper consists of four, two-compartment, treble length, rougher cells, and four two-compartment, cleaner cells. Each rougher cell in conjunction with one cleaner cell, has a capacity of 150 tons per 24 hours. The plant makes available as ore all the tailing which has accumulated in years past as well as much mine rock of low grade.

The cleaner cell makes two products, the concentrate and a tailing or "flotation middling." The concentrate is pumped direct to the high grade plant for treatment, while the cleaner tailing is sent to the low grade cyanide plant.

In the high grade plant, the concentrate first has added to it thirty pounds of lime per ton. It is then thickened in a Dorr thickener and dewatered on an Oliver filter. Salt is added partly as a brine wash and partly as a solid.

The concentrate is then dried and after adding further salt and sulphur, is then roasted in a reverberatory roaster.

The calcines are then given an acid wash with a 13 per cent. hydrochloric acid solution. The solution resulting from this acid wash which at times carries as high as twenty-five per cent., is sent to scrap iron precipitation boxes for the recovery of the copper.

After washing the pulp, it is agitated with cyanide solution of fifteen pounds per ton strength. The silver chloride present enters the solution almost instantly. The silver in the pregnant cyanide solution is precipitated by means of sodium sulphide.

The final refining of the silver is accomplished in an oil-fired reverberatory furnace.

A 7-ft. x 9-ft. Holt-Dern roasting furnace is soon to take the place of the present roaster, from which certain economics are expected to result.

FLOTATION RECORD, BUFFALO MILL.

Week Ending December 10th, 1916.

Date	December 4		December 5		December 6		December 7		December 8		December 9		December 10	
Shift	Day	Night	Day	Night	Day	Night	Day	Night	Day	Night	Day	Night	Day	Night
Assay Heads, Ozs	7.0	100	10.2	13.2	14.0	11.2	8.4	9.0	8.2	8.6	8.8	8.4		8.6
Tails	0.8	0.9	1.4	1.7	1.5	1.5	1.1	0.8	0.8	0.8	0.8	0.8		0.8
...gs	.2.4	5.6	5.8	9.0	6.8	7.2	4.8	6.4	4.2	6.8	7.0	4.0		8.0
Concentrates	631.5	598.0	550.0	1,017.0	915.0	541.5	558.5	700.0	660.0	530.0	467.5	580.0		585.0
lbs ...ed		95		86		56		100		58		66		32
Extraction	88.6	910	86.2	87.1	89.3	86.6	86.9	91.1	90.2	90.7	90.9	90.5		90.7

Week Ending February, 11th, 1917.

Date	February 5		February 6		February 7		February 8		February 9		February 10		February 11	
Shift	Day	Night	Day	Night	Day	Night	Day	Night	Day	Night	Day	Night	Day	Night
Assay Heads, Ozs	9.4	7.6	8.6	100	8.4	7.8	10.0	9.0	10.0	9.8	8.4	8.8		7.6
Tails	1.3	0.8	0.9	1.2	1.2	1.1	1.2	1.1	1.4	1.1	1.5	1.7		1.2
Middlings	22.0	18.0	17.6	30.6	14.0	24.0	16.6	59.0	34.0	24.6	23.6	36.0		12.0
...s	462.0	499.0	520.5	740.0	688.5	1,013.5	760.0	775.0	975.0	1,085.0	842.5	740.0		603.0
Tons Treated		336		306		352		308		307		316		180
Extraction	86.2	90.0	90.0	88.0	85.7	86.0	88.0	87.8	86.0	88.8	82.1	80.7		84.2

COBALT LAKE MILL.

This mill was closed down on June 11th, 1916, after which any ore produced by the Cobalt Lake Mine was treated in the Cobalt Reduction Mill.

COBALT REDUCTION COMPANY MILL.

This mill is now cyaniding tailings, and during the year treated 51,172 tons, producing therefrom 573,013 ounces silver bullion.

McKINLEY-DARRAGH.*

The feed to the flotation plant consists of slimes resulting from mining operations and primary crushing, which are separated in the jigging plant, and mill slimes resulting from crushing in stamps and one pebble mill. The mill treats 200 tons per day, approximately 50 per cent. of which reaches and is treated in the flotation plant; 93 per cent. of the feed to the flotation plant is finer than 200 mesh. The chief economic minerals recovered by flotation are argentite, proustite, pyrargyrite and metallic silver.

The plant consists of two triple length Callow roughers, operating in parallel and two standard length Callow cleaners, operating in series, the tailing from cleaner No. 1 being recleaned in cleaner No. 2.

The following table gives a summary of typical results:

FLOTATION RESULTS AT THE McKINLEY-DARRAGH-SAVAGE MINES, LTD. AVERAGES BY WEEKS

Month.	Week.	Heads. Oz.	Tails. Oz.	Concentrates.	Per cent. Extraction.
June	2nd	8.04	2.01	310	75.00
"	3rd	8.91	1.75	386	80.30
"	4th	7.74	1.64	363	78.80
July	1st	8.65	1.90	334	78.00
"	2nd	8.03	2.10	231	73.80
"	3rd	5.86	1.40	172	76.10
"	4th	6.10	1.41	233	77.00
August	1st	6.20	1.48	309	76.10
"	2nd	6.43	1.71	269	73.40
"	3rd	5.88	1.66	233	71.70
"	4th	6.71	1.53	260	73.20
September	1st	7.68	2.55	349	66.80
"	2nd	6.55	2.16	272	67.00
"	3rd	5.30	1.35	206	74.50
"	4th	6.29	1.91	211	69.60
October	1st	8.05	2.35	238	70.80
"	2nd	10.05	3.74	331	62.78
"	3rd	8.03	2.60	279	67.62
"	4th	8.07	3.04	177	62.30
November	1st	5.64	2.13	309	62.20
"	2nd	4.71	1.38	248	70.70
"	3rd	4.73	1.53	204	67.60
"	4th	4.65	1.70	178	64.00
December	1st	5.36	1.60	220	70.70
"	2nd	6.92	1.08	217	84.50
Average		6.78	1.909	262	71.37

*Notes on Flotation—1916. J. M. Callow. Transactions, A.I.M.E.

NIPISSING.

HIGH GRADE MILL.

The high grade mill ran at full capacity throughout the year, and treated 1,064 tons of Nipissing ore and metallics, assaying 1,800 ounces per ton, and 598 tons of custom ore and metallics, with an average assay of 3,113 ounces per ton.

The precipitate from the low grade mill containing over two million ounces was also refined at the high grade plant.

Shipments of bullion amounted to 192 tons, averaging 998 fine and contained 5,578,162 fine ounces.

The treatment cost was higher on account of the largely increased cost of mercury and cyanide. The active demand for cobalt enabled the company to sell the entire stock of cobalt residue and to contract for the whole of the 1917 output.

Shipments of cobalt residue in 1916 amounted to 2,506 tons, compared with 326 tons in 1915.

LOW GRADE MILL.

—	Tons.	Contents, Ounces.
Ore Treated	76,851 106	2,275,833 183,508
	76,957	2,459,341

Recovered from above in Cyanide Plant.................................. 2,133,681
Extraction by Cyanide.. 86.76%

The ore coming from the lower levels of the mine is more difficult to treat and consumes more cyanide. This, together with rapid rise in prices of all chemicals and supplies and the advance in wages brought the mill costs up to $4.60 per ton, compared with $3.91 in 1915; of this increase $.34 is due to cyanide and $.15 to wages.

The high cost of aluminum dust necessitated the adoption of some other method of precipitation, and after exhaustive experiments, precipitation by sodium sulphide was substituted. A solution of caustic soda is added to the precipitate, which is then desulphurized by circulating it through a small tube mill filled with aluminum ingots. The precipitate is then melted down to fine silver. The new practice is very satisfactory, and is cheaper even should the prices of all supplies drop to the pre-war basis.

Experiments with the flotation of the tailing from the cyanide plant have been carried on throughout the year; the results are not yet satisfactory. The extraction is low, notwithstanding many variations in the method of applying the flotation treatment. By supplementing the treatment with concentration, either before or after flotation, much better results can probably be obtained, and experiments are now being conducted along this line.

CONSUMPTION OF SUPPLIES AT LOW GRADE MILL.

—	Total Pounds.	Cost per Pound	Total Cost.	Pounds per Ton.	Cost per Ton.
		$	$ c.		$
Sodium Cyanide........	390,256	.2547	99,411 81	5.078	1.2986
Lime.................	524,245	.0040	2,091 40	6.822	.0272
Caustic Soda	138,799	.0509	7,062 60	1.806	.0919
Aluminum Dust........	20,400	.4576	9,335 40	0.265	.1215
Aluminum Plates	1,800	.2364	425 52	0.023	.0056
Aluminum Ingots	11,946	.4994	5,965 86	0.155	.0776
Pebbles...............	425,500	.0100	4,265 06	5.537	.0555
Coal	2,479,940	.0032	7,978 81	32.269	.1038
Borax	8,890	.0823	731 95	0.116	.0095
Sodium Sulphide	150,479	.0215	3,241 30	1.958	.0422
Soda Ash	100,200	.0377	3,773 86	1.304	.0491
Power K.W.H..........	4,532,280	.01023	49,016 97	58.975	.6378
			193,300 54		2.5153

SUMMARY OF ORE RESERVES, DECEMBER 31, 1916.

—	Tons.	Assay.	Ounces.
High Grade Ore.........................	3,673	1,370	5,031,232
Mill Ore..............................	163,721	25.2	4,121,907
Total	167,394	55	9,153,139

Insurance on bullion to London has risen from $.50 before the war to $22.50 per $1,000. The cost of mining has increased to $12.53 per ton, compared with $10.02 in the year previous; the cost of producing silver was 24.13 cents compared with 19.06 cents per ounce.

O'BRIEN.

The O'Brien mill is partly water concentration and partly cyanide. Total production included in concentrates and bullion from cyanidation reached a total of 1,030,000 fine ounces.

The concentrates are treated at the Deloro Smelter.

DIVIDENDS PAID BY COBALT SILVER MINES TO DECEMBER 31, 1916.

Mining Company.	Percentage Paid During 1916	Amount of Dividends and Bonuses Paid During 1916	Total Percentage Paid to 31st Dec., 1915	Total amount of Dividends Paid to 31st Dec., 1916
		$ c.		$ c.
Beaver	3	60,000 00	32.5	650,000 00
Buffalo..................			282	2,787,000 00
Caribou-Cobalt (Drummond)			22.5	225,000 00
Casey-Cobalt.............			25	203,249 33
City of Cobalt............			23	189,231 42
Cobalt Central			4	192,845 00
Cobalt Lake.............			15.5	465,000 00
Cobalt Silver Queen			21	315,000 00
Cobalt Townsite...........			97.5	966,726 31
Coniagas.................	15	600,000 00	211	8,440,000 00
Crown Reserve............			345	6,102,399 30
Foster			5	45,774 00
Hudson Bay (T. & H. B.)..			26,000	1,940,250 00
Kerr Lake (Holding Co.)...	20	600,000 00	224	6,720,000 00
La Rose (Holding Co.).....	4	299,725 40	78.5	6,882,707 87
Mining Corporation........	27½	570,615 00	65	1,348,740 00
McKinley-Darragh-Savage .	12	269,723 04	217	4,876,474 30
Nipissing Mines Co. (Holding Co.)............	25	1,500,000 00	249	15,340,000 00
Peterson Lake............	7	168,127 40	17.5	420,318 50
Right-of-Way Mines	1	16,855 00	14	235,965 00
Right-of-Way Mining Co....			65	324,643 93
Seneca Superior...........	125	598,605 00	330	1,579,817 20
Temiskaming	9	225,000 00	68	1,684,156 25
Trethewey	5	50,000 00	113	1,111,998 50
Wettlaufer			45	637,465 50
Private Corporations (Estimated)...............			175	3,825,000 00
Totals...............		4,958,650 84		67,459,852 41

Casey Township

Production proceeded at the Casey Mine as usual, until the district was swept by fire on 22nd August, when all buildings and equipment were lost. At the end of the year the new plant is nearing completion.

South Lorrain

Several companies operated during the year, and the Wettlaufer and Bellellen made shipments.

Gowganda

Interest in this District has been revived to a certain extent by an important find made on the Miller-Lake-O'Brien Mine. This find was made on the 300 and 350-foot levels, and is one of the best discoveries ever made in the Timiskaming District. The ore will average 25 inches wide and the ore chute is 120 feet long, but the vertical limits have not yet been determined. The grade of the ore is about 4,000 ounces per ton, with considerable mill rock in the adjoining walls.

The mill ran six and one-half months on double shift, and five and one-half months on single shift (12 hours per day), and treated 8,258 tons of ore, producing therefrom 128 tons concentrate.

The mine has shipped 168 tons during the year. A small shipment was also made by the Reeves-Dobie property on Gowganda Lake.

STATEMENT SHOWING SHIPMENTS FROM COBALT DISTRICT, INCLUDING GOWGANDA, ELK LAKE AND SOUTH LORRAIN.

(In tons of 2,000 lbs.)

Year.	Cobalt.	Gowganda.	Elk Lake.	S. Lorrain.	Totals.
1904	158.55				158.55
1905	2,336.01				2,336.01
1906	5,836.59				5,836.59
1907	14,851.34				14,851.34
1908	25,362.10			43.25	25,405.35
1909	29,942.99	2.00		112.59	30,057.58
1910	33,976.97	486.68	20.00	226.64	34,710.29
1911	24,921.71	267.00	4.00	530.51	25,733.22
1912	21,631.79	333.10		478.00	22,442.89
1913	20,916.16	192.90		120.00	21,229.06
1914	18,220.71	138.80	10.86	49.46	18,419.83
1915	15,944.82	119.41			16,064.23
1916	15,594.88	174.55		64.48	15,813.01
Totals ...	229,694.62	1,714.44	34.86	1,624.93	233,057.95

ORE SHIPMENTS FROM COBALT SILVER DISTRICT FOR CALENDAR YEAR 1916.

Mine.	Jan.	Feb.	March.	April	May	June	July	Aug.	Sept.	Oct.	Nov.	Dec.	Totals.
1. Alladin	57.26		23.25	38.54	16.62	26.77	23.33	25.20		20.50		22.30	118.02
2. Beaver	93.80	33.73	73.55	62.55	31.28	47.87	70.55	52.61	35.11	40.77		69.08	488.47
3. Buffalo—By Dom. Red.		-.00	62.64								31.69	32.47	422.67
4. Colt Comet—By Dom. Red. Co.	44.00	55.00	54.00	84.37	54.75	82.38	61.53	52.47	31.25	64.38	49.13	61.88	695.14
5. Coniagas	60.76	84.21	30.64	86.37	110.83	68.29	70.12	71.23	9.72	74.20	104.70	56.40	897.47
6. Crown Reserve—By Dom. Red. Co.	65.12	81.40	119.89	124.88	103.61	121.91	91.07	77.66	46.25	95.27	72.70	91.57	1,091.33
7. Hudson Bay									30.31		70.98	30.52	131.81
8. Kerr Lake—By Dom. Red. Co.	66.88	83.60	112.46	128.25	113.50	155.48	93.53	110.00	47.50	97.85	74.67	94.05	1,177.77
9. Kerr Lake Mining Co.										30.23			30.23
10. La Rose	135.90	87.09	152.94	87.59	96.02	130.75	135.15	160.88	91.18	126.98	87.32	43.70	1,305.50
11. Mining Corp. of Canada	121.19	207.10	225.53	288.07	159.07	298.42	107.31	183.20	38.09	36.96	94.20	107.25	1,866.39
12. McKinley-Darragh	76.47	207.86	163.80	163.09	333.34	195.54	201.39	214.68	130.89	167.53	166.64	165.37	2,176.60
13. Nipissing	196.11	65.52	130.25		64.69		131.95	539.66	615.27	649.18	535.70		2,928.33
14. O'Brien			36.59		42.99	31.00	31.77		33.00	64.91	33.00		273.26
15. Penn-Canadian	90.58	35.99	48.95		76.45	85.76	43.74		83.22		54.10	41.75	560.54
16. Peterson Lake	115.98	123.08	110.55	46.96	41.77	79.11							517.44
17. Right-of-Way			47.82		46.58		60.62	43.71	20.00	42.03			200.14
18. Temiskaming	63.60	38.92	30.50	39.68	68.44	42.04	41.94	38.28	41.55	42.01	81.54		466.79
19. Trethewey									44.85		41.67	38.23	246.98
Totals	1,187.65	1,141.19	1,413.36	1,150.34	1,359.94	1,365.32	1,120.16	1,583.32	1,368.19	1,552.80	1,498.04	854.57	15,594.88

ORE SHIPMENTS FROM THE COBALT DISTRICT TO END OF 1916.

(In tons of 2,000 lbs.)

Mine.	Totals to 1916.	1916	Totals.
1. Alladin		118.02	118.02
2. Badger	27.10		27.10
3. Bailey	388.07		388.07
4. Beaver	2,691.13	488.47	3,179.60
5. Buffalo	7,966.96	422.67	8,389.63
6. Casey-Cobalt	1,829.80		1,829.80
7. Chambers-Ferland	3,610.24		3,610.24
8. City of Cobalt	2,820.02		2,820.02
9. Cobalt Lake	5,930.12		5,930.12
10. Cobalt Townsite	8,020.82		8,020.82
11. Cobalt Comet	7,997.73	695.14	8,692.87
12. Colonial	456.12		456.12
13. Coniagas	13,264.30	897.47	14,161.77
14. Crown Reserve	10,992.38	1,091.33	12,083.71
15. Foster	822.58		822.58
16. Green-Meehan	251.36		251.36
17. Hargrave	491.92		491.92
18. Hudson Bay	5,098.25	131.81	5,230.06
19. Imperial Cobalt	14.61		14.61
20. Kerr Lake	12,178.27	1,208.00	13,386.27
21. King Edward	776.22		776.22
22. La Rose	34,646.04	1,305.50	35,951.54
23. Lawson	75.73		75.73
24. Lost and Found	74.00		74.00
25. Lumsden	20.00		20.00
26. McKinley-Darragh	20,008.28	2,176.60	22,184.88
27. Mining Corporation :—			
Cobalt Lake Mine	1,445.24 ⎫	1,866.39	6,408.32
Townsite City Mine	3,096.69 ⎭		
28. Nancy Helen	347.74		347.74
29. Nipissing	30,562.88	2,928.33	33,491.21
30. North Cobalt	9.87		9.87
31. Nova Scotia	778.90		778.90
32. O'Brien	10,081.93	273.26	10,355.19
33. Penn-Canadian	2,516.71	560.54	3,077.25
34. Petersen Lake (Leases)	122.52	517.44	639.96
Gould	59.65		59.65
Little Nipissing	422.50		422.50
Nova Scotia	121.15		121.15
Seneca Superior	2,298.66		2,298.66
35. Provincial	250.65		250.65
36. Princess	3.93		3.93
37. Red Rock	45.71		45.71
38. Right-of-Way	4,881.07	200.14	5,081.21
39. Rochester	28.30		28.30
40. Silver Bar	43.30		43.30
41. Silver Cliff	606.69		606.69
42. Silver Leaf	252.39		252.39
43. Silver Queen	2,214.92		2,214.92
44. Temiskaming	6,169.94	466.79	6,636.73
45. Trethewey	6,858.66	246.98	7,105.64
46. University	231.51		231.51
47. Victoria	.47		.47
48. Violet	36.00		36.00
49. Waldman	38.81		38.81
50. Wyandoh	24.15		24.15
51. Temiskaming Cobalt	88.45		88.45
Totals	214,091.44	15,594.88	229,686.32

Power.

The following review covers the power situation in the Cobalt District, no new powers having been developed recently. There are four water-power plants owned and operated by the Northern Ontario Light & Power Company, Limited.

Station.	H.P. Capacity.
1. Matabitchouan	10,000
2. Hound Chutes	4,500
3. Fountain Falls	3,300
4. Ragged Chutes	5,000

1. Matabitchouan Hydro-Electric Plant is located on the Matabitchouan River about 25 miles south-east of Cobalt. The equipment consists of 1875 K.V.A. generating units, operating under a nominal head of 312 feet, with a total capacity of 10,000 h.p., 44,000 volts. The transmission lines consist of two circuits on separate poles extending from the power house to South Lorrain and Cobalt. This plant operates in parallel with the Hound Chutes and Fountain Falls plants. In Cobalt, four electrically driven air compressors convert 3,500 h.p. of this power into compressed air.

2. Hound Chutes Hydro-Electric Plant is located on the Montreal River about six miles south of Cobalt. Its equipment consists of four 375 K.V.A. generators, developing 4,500 h.p., at 11,000 volts. It operates under a nominal head of 33 feet.

3. Fountain Falls Hydro-Electric Plant is located about five miles below Hound Chutes on the Montreal River. The equipment consists of two 1,500 h.p. vertical I.P. Morris turbines directly connected to two 1250 K.V.A., 11,000 volt generators operating under a nominal head of 30 feet.

4. Ragged Chutes Hydraulic Air Compressor Plant is located on the Montreal River three miles south of the Hound Chutes plant. It has a capacity of about 5,000 h.p. compressed air produced by the Taylor system. The air is transmitted in pipes approximately nine miles to the mines in the Cobalt District. The main distributing system consists of 20-inch steel pipes with secondary and service lines of from 12-inch to pipes of smaller diameter.

The Northern Ontario Light & Power Company sells most of the above power in the Cobalt Mining District at $50.00 per h.p. per year.

In order to find a market for the surplus power a transmission line has been constructed north approximately 65 miles from the Cobalt sub-station to a sub-station in the Kirkland Lake Mining District, and the first power was delivered 1st March, 1917.

The equipment of the transmission line consists of thirty-five and forty-foot standard cedar poles, spaced 150 feet between centres, supporting a three-phase copper power line attached to most up-to-date insulators, surmounted by a standard galvanized iron guard wire grounded every tenth pole as a protection against lightning. The poles also hold the company's private telephone circuit. The line is equipped with three standard switch towers spaced at equal distances, or about every fifteen miles, installed to facilitate the location of line trouble.

The sub-station at Kirkland Lake is a substantial concrete structure of ample size to take care of 15,000 h.p. The present line and equipment is designed to transmit 5,000 h.p. at 44,000 volts, 60 cycles. It will be transformed at the Kirkland Lake sub-station to 2,200 volts for distribution over service lines to customers. The initial load runs from 1,500 to 2,000 H.P.

The principal undeveloped water power now available in the District is located near the head of Lake Timiskaming on the Des Quinzes River, a part of the Ottawa River, about 25 miles north-east of Cobalt. An approximation made from several estimates of this power credits it with 150,000 H.P.

Smelting and Refining.

In the early years of the Cobalt camp all shipments of ore had to go out of the country for treatment, most of it going to the United States. Soon Canadian smelters were started which treated high grade ore; and the latest development has been the building of the so-called High Grade Mills at Cobalt, which produce silver bullion by a combination amalgamation-cyanide process.

An examination of the figures for the calendar years 1914 and 1915 shows that the percentage of the silver bullion produced from Cobalt ores was in round numbers:

—	1914 %	1915 %
Cobalt Mills Amalgamation and Cyanide	44	39
Southern Ontario Smelters	39	45
United States Smelters	17	16
	100	100

The sixteen per cent. still going to the United States consists of some high grade ore along with all the low grade material both ore and concentrates shipped, as the Canadian smelters are not equipped to handle this low grade material.

In the high grade mills at Cobalt the silver only is recovered, the cobalt, nickel and arsenic being left in the residue for future treatment or sold for the cobalt content. The Deloro and Coniagas smelters are equipped with complete refineries so that besides producing silver bullion they also produce and market arsenic, cobalt and nickel.

The cobalt and nickel have been produced mostly as oxides, but as there has recently been a call for the metals they are now also produced in that form.

DELORO SMELTING AND REFINING COMPANY, LIMITED.

The Deloro smelter is situated at Deloro, Hastings County, Ontario, one and one-quarter miles by road from Marmora Station, and connected by a railway spur with the Canadian Northern Ontario Railway.

PRODUCTION OF DELORO SMELTER, 1908–1916.

Year.	Ore Treated Tons.	Silver, Fine Oz.	Cobalt and Mixed Oxides Tons.	Refined Arsenic Tons.
Previous to 1913	11,065	20,339,860	500	3,275
1913	2,920	6,350,500	190	893
1914	3,612	5,207,000	300	1,038
1915	4,634	6,429,794	256	1,634
1916	3,834	5,234,620	272	1,627
Totals	26,065	43,561,774	1,518	8,467

CONIAGAS REDUCTION COMPANY.

The smelter of the Coniagas Reduction Company is situated at Thorold, Ontario, six miles west of Niagara Falls. The output of the smelter up to the 31st December, 1916, is as follows:

Year.	Ore Treated Tons.	Silver Fine Oz.	Cobalt Oxide Tons.	Nickel Oxide Tons.	White Arsenic Tons.
1908...................	266.80	360,683	5.5	1.5	13.5
1909...................	1,116.90	1,659,604	.9	....	100.0
1910...................	2,017.25	3,485,243	53.8	13.2	557.7
1911...................	2,821.50	5,770,271	60.5	17.3	766.1
1912...................	2,288.77	4,824,632	129.0	50.7	636.7
1913...................	2,509.80	4,977,012	250.6	115.6	319.4
1914.........	1,968.78	3,865,546	171.9	124.9	399.2
1915...................	2,541.00	3,445,661	59.0	99.8	472.8
1916................ ...	2,718.87	4.428,913	190.4	67.6	420.8
Total...........	18,249.67	32,817,565	921.6	490.6 .	3,686.2

During 1915 and 1916 this company also produced 85,350 lbs. metallic arsenic and 174,032 lbs. metallic cobalt. Nickel metal is also produced in shot form.

A considerable quantity of metallic cobalt is now absorbed in the manufacture of the alloy known as Stellite.

The binary alloy of cobalt and chromium was discovered by Elwood Haynes, of Kokomo, Indiana, in 1899. A patent was obtained on it in 1907, but it was not developed till 1910.

Stellite is essentially an alloy of cobalt and chromium. When the chromium does not exceed twenty-five per cent. the alloy is malleable at a bright red heat, and may be forged with proper care into flat or square bars, and easily worked into knife blades and other utensils. This alloy is suitable for tableware, such as knives, forks and spoons. It is practically immune to all chemical solutions excepting aqua regia.

When once polished it holds its lustre indefinitely, and on account of its star-like appearance has been named stellite.

If tungsten is added to the cobalt-chromium alloy it increases its hardness, and when the tungsten content reaches about 10 per cent. the alloy becomes sufficiently hard for lathe tools, and is used for such in the cast form. It turns both steel and iron on the lathe much faster than any tool steel yet known. When the tungsten content reaches 20 per cent. the alloy is harder than any steel yet made, though more brittle than the 10 per cent. alloy.

The use of stellite is of great value to munition work shops as may be judged from the following tests. A stellite tool was tested in a Toronto munition factory where 18-pound shells were being manufactured. A tool of high speed tool steel will ordinarily make the first cut on from 25 to 30 of these shells without regrinding. The stellite tool made 250 cuts before requiring regrinding. In certain instances as many as 300 shells have been roughed before regrinding. Then the steel tool regularly takes two minutes to make this first cut, to run it faster would make it lose its temper. Stellite has no temper to lose and it was found that it could be speeded up till it made the cut in thirty seconds without any loss of efficiency in other ways. The value of stellite in such work is therefore very great, and yet it is sold at a price only slightly above the price of the best high speed tool steels.

Stellite is made in Canada by the Deloro Smelting and Refining Company, at Deloro, Ontario, and in the United States by the Haynes Stellite Company, of Kokomo, Indiana. It is made up mostly in bars but also in special shapes, such as reamers, dies, etc.

The average monthly consumption of metallic cobalt for this use alone now amounts to about twelve tons.

NICKEL

The Alexo Mine situated three miles from Porquis Junction on the Porcupine branch of the Temiskaming and Northern Ontario Railway, continued to ship nickel ore during the year to the Mond Nickel Company's smelter at Coniston, Ontario. A statement of shipments for 1916 is given herewith.

NICKEL ORE SHIPMENTS OVER THE T. & N. O. RY. 1916.

——	Tons.
January	1,227.60
February	1,026.55
March	1,041.45
April	699.75
May	959.13
June	848.35
July	671.15
August	672.15
September	384.65
October	237.00
November	332.65
December	847.00
	8,447.43

For some years the Mond Nickel Company has purchased at a uniform rate all nickel ore offered in car load lots, and will probably continue to do so if of suitable composition for their work.

COPPER

A copper property has been opened up by a Mr. A. Fallahay, at Cedar Lake, about four miles north of Temagami Station. The ore is chalcopyrite. A trial shipment of 20.7 tons was made in September from an open cut on the vein to United States Metals Refining Company, at Chrome, N.J. An analysis of this ore gave the following results:

Gold	.005	Ounces.
Silver	1.96	ˮ
Copper	7.95	%
Iron	20.13	%
Insoluble	37.31	%
Lime	1.92	%
Sulphur	15.76	%
Arsenic	.07	%

No nickel is reported in this analysis but similar ore from this property was found to contain half as much nickel as copper.

The property is now under option to Mr. M. J. O'Brien, of the O'Brien Mine, and development work is to start early in 1917.

ZINC AND LEAD

The Dan Smith zinc-lead property is situated to the south-east of Wolf Lake. It is now under working option to some Toronto interests. Camps have been erected and the property is to have some thorough surface prospecting before mining is commenced. The ore is a coarse zinc-blende and galena in a calcite gangue.

MOLYBDENITE

Several prospects near Amos, Quebec, have had some work done on them during the summer, but so far no shippers have been developed.

ASBESTOS

In Deloro Township on the Deloro-Shaw road a promising looking asbestos property is being developed. The fibre is fair and colour good, but extent of deposit has yet to be determined.

LIMESTONE

Shipments from the Farr quarry near Haileybury were made regularly to the Abitibi Power and Paper Company's plant at Iroquois Falls. They totalled during the year 2,968 tons.

IRON

The following excerpt is from an article by Mr. Thomas Cantley in the Bulletin of the Canadian Mining Institute for January, 1917:

"In the section of country lying in close proximity to Lake Temagami on the Temiskaming and Northern Ontario Railway, are deposits of stratified magnetites—large quantities of which having been exposed by glacial action lie on the surface to be loaded in cars and only require to be conveyed to a concentrating plant. This ore would probably furnish half its volume in concentrates, running fifty per cent. or more in iron, with no pronounced deleterious elements, while a further very large quantity could be won by open quarry work. Another interesting feature is presented by this district, namely the possibility or even probability, that deeper mining would disclose the presence of large areas of secondary enrichment deposits containing a very large tonnage of really high grade ores. To prove conclusively the existence of such secondary deposits would require a very considerable expenditure of capital under the supervision of competent mining engineers; and this matter is of sufficient importance to warrant the Government of Ontario in giving substantial aid and encouragement to those who control these properties on which large expenditures have already been made without return."

BARITE

The Langmuir Premier Barite property is situated in Langmuir Township about one half mile from Night Hawk Lake. It is reached by water from Connaught Station on the Porcupine branch of the T. & N. O. Ry. Machinery was brought to this point last summer, but owing to low water could not be transported to the property. In the meantime a small amount of development is being accomplished by hand and a tunnel is being driven on the vein. The vein carries fair silver values in the barite.

LOGS OF WELLS IN THE DISTRICT

For several years it has been the policy to publish, whenever obtainable, the results of deep well drilling in the hope that in this way information would be put in a permanent form that might be of value in the future development of the country. In this way time and money may at times be saved. Already the logs published have answered a valuable purpose and it is hoped that in future those drilling wells will keep and turn in for publication logs of all wells drilled.

The most important well drilled recently is that from which the Town of New Liskeard draws its auxiliary water supply. At 310 feet the first big flow was struck, but it increased somewhat later. At present the natural flow is approximately 45,000 gallons per day. This is on a head of about 2½ feet.

A pumping test was made with a pump working at the rate of 250,000 gallons per day with the working barrel lowered 12 feet from the top and did not suck air.

A sample of the water on analysis was pronounced very satisfactory.

Samples of drillings taken at different depths were as follows:

100 feet—Clay.

200 feet—Soft white Niagara Dolomite.

230 feet—Still soft material of mostly white to dark gray angular fragments, but with a little in flat dark flakes suggesting shaly limestone.

260 feet—Evidence of banding of light and dark layers shown.

280 feet—Similar to 260 sample with the addition of a few fine grains of transparent quartz.

300 feet—Very fine and of brownish colour. Likely corresponds to sandstone horizon of the Niagara as found at Dawson's Point, where it is 2 ft. thick.

325 feet—Fragments of gray and white colour like typical Niagara but with brown material also present.

350 feet—Soft dolomite similar to last.

370 feet—Deeper brown colour than last. A little quartz in transparent grains.

385 feet—Colour is greenish. Also has grains of quartz. Cataract?

400 feet—Greenish colour, more light coloured material. Selenite present.

430 feet—Dark greenish brown. Tendency to be shaly. Selenite present.

449 feet—Same as previous sample.

MINING OPPORTUNITIES IN NORTHERN ONTARIO

Along the Temiskaming and Northern Ontario Railway from Cobalt to Porquis Junction, a distance of 125 miles, it was noticeable this year that there was hardly a station from which some mining operations were not being carried on. New districts were being reported from time to time and the older districts were looking better as work proceeded.

Anyone who looked over the unbroken forest of Northern Ontario a dozen years ago and predicted that this district would soon be producing over twenty millions in gold and silver annually would have been put down as a fantastic dreamer; but that figure is surpassed to-day by three million dollars, and the output is continually increasing.

And yet only a small portion of the country has been prospected. Running north-east and north-west from Cobalt and extending to the Arctic Ocean is the great pre-Cambrian shield, the basement formation of the Continent. It contains thousands of square miles and offers to prospectors *Better Chances of Locating Valuable Mineral Deposits Than Can Be Found in Any Other Country in the World.*

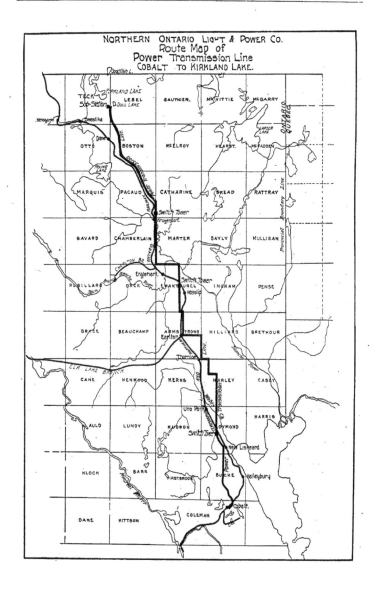

NORTHERN ONTARIO LIGHT & POWER CO.
Route Map of
Power Transmission Line
COBALT TO KIRKLAND LAKE.

INDEX

	PAGE
General	7
The Gold Camps	8
Porcupine	8
Hollinger	9
Dome	9
McIntyre-Porcupine	10
Porcupine Crown	10
Porcupine-Vipond-North Thompson	11
Schumacher	11
Power	11
Kirkland Lake	12
Tough-Oakes	13
Teck-Hughes	13
Wright-Hargraves	14
Lake Shore	14
Kirkland Lake	14
Sylvanite	15
LaBelle Kirkland	15
Elliott	15
Munro Township	15
Boston Creek	15
Kowkash and Tashota	15
Other Gold Camps	15
The Silver Camps	16
Cobalt	16
Concentration by Flotation	18
General Milling	19
Buffalo	20
Cobalt Lake	22
Cobalt Reduction	22
McKinley-Darragh	22
Nipissing	23
Dividends	25
Casey Township	25
South Lorrain	25
Gowganda	25
Power	29
Smelting and Refining	30
Deloro Smelter	30
Coniagas Smelter	31
Stellite	31
Nickel	32
Copper	32
Zinc and Lead	33
Molybdenite	33
Asbestos	33
Limestone	33
Iron	33
Barite	33
Deep Wells	34
Mining Opportunities in Northern Ontario	34

Ninth Annual Report

OF THE

HYDRO-ELECTRIC POWER COMMISSION

OF THE

PROVINCE OF ONTARIO

FOR THE YEAR ENDED OCTOBER 31st

1916

VOLUME I.

PRINTED BY ORDER OF
THE LEGISLATIVE ASSEMBLY OF ONTARIO

TORONTO:
Printed and Published by A. T. WILGRESS, Printer to the King's Most Excellent Majesty
1 9 1 7   .

Printed by
WILLIAM BRIGGS
Corner Queen and John Streets
TORONTO

To His Honour, COLONEL SIR JOHN HENDRIE, K.C.M.G., C.V.O.,

Lieutenant-Governor of Ontario.

MAY IT PLEASE YOUR HONOUR:

The undersigned has the honour to present to Your Honour the Ninth Annual Report of the Hydro-Electric Power Commission of Ontario for the fiscal year ending October 31st, 1916.

Respectfully submitted,

ADAM BECK,

Chairman.

TORONTO, ONT., February 17th, 1917.

COLONEL SIR ADAM BECK, K.B., LL.D.,

Chairman, Hydro-Electric Power Commission,

Toronto, Ont.

SIR,—I have the honour to transmit herewith the Ninth Annual Report of the Hydro-Electric Power Commission of Ontario for the fiscal year ending October 31st, 1916.

I have the honour to be,

Sir,

Your obedient servant,

W. W. POPE,

Secretary.

HYDRO-ELECTRIC POWER COMMISSION
OF ONTARIO

COLONEL SIR ADAM BECK, K.B., LL.D., London, Chairman.

HON. I. B. LUCAS, M.P.P., Markdale, Commissioner.

COL. W. K. McNAUGHT, C.M.G., Toronto, Commissioner.

W. W. POPE, Secretary.

F. A. GABY, Chief Engineer.

CONTENTS

Section.   Page

I. Legal Proceedings 1
    A. Acts 1
    B. Right of Way 94
    C. Crossings 94
    D. Agreements 94

II. Transmission Systems 95
    A. Steel Tower Transmission Lines 95
    B. Station Equipment and Building Department 95
    C. Low Tension Transmission Lines 123

III. Operation of the Systems 140
    A. Niagara System 140
    B. Severn System 146
    C. Eugenia System 148
    D. Wasdell System 150
    E. Parallel Operation of the Severn, Eugenia and Wasdell Systems..... 151
    F. Central Ontario System 151
    G. Muskoka System 153
    H. Port Arthur System 154
    I. St. Lawrence System 155
    J. Capital Cost 156
    K. Provincial Expenditures 158
    L. Balance Sheet 159

IV. Municipal Work 160
    A. Municipal Advices 160
    B. Municipal Electrical Inspection 184
    C. Municipal Purchases and Sales 185
    D. Rural Power 187
    E. Ornamental Street Lighting 189
    F. Municipal Underground Construction 191
    G. Electric Railway Projects 191
    H. Testing and Research Laboratories 194
    I. General Engineering 201

ILLUSTRATIONS

Eugenia Falls ....*Frontispiece*

FACING PAGE

Main Entrance Hall—Administration Building 96

Interior of Board Room—Administration Building 96

Diagram of Stations—Niagara System 98

Diagram of Stations—Central Ontario System 100

Diagram of Stations—Severn, Eugenia, Wasdell and St. Lawrence Systems 112

Curve Showing Monthly Increase of Power Load of Municipalities—Niagara System 140

Typical Daily Load Curves—Severn, Eugenia and Wasdell Generating Stations
Operating in Parellel—October, 1916 150

Curve Showing Weekly System Peaks—Central Ontario System, 1916 152

St. Thomas—Street Lighting System 190

Hydro-Electric Radial Railway Map ......:................................... 192

Cement and Sand Testing Equipment at the Laboratory 194

18″ Integrating Sphere Photometer, Lamp Testing Laboratory 194

Curves of Candle Power Distribution of a Gas Filled Lamp Equipped with Prismatic Refractor 196

Curves Showing Variation of Candle Power and Efficiency of a Tungsten Lamp with
Life ....:... 196

Electrical Standards Laboratory 198

High Tension Test—Transformer Flashing over String of Four Suspension
Insulators—Voltage 260,000 198

Testing Machines—Strength of Materials Laboratory 198

Gasoline Driven Standby Fire Pump, Stratford Municipal Waterworks 202

Elevated Water Tower at Stratford Municipal Waterworks ......:............... 204

Eugenia Falls

NINTH ANNUAL REPORT

OF THE

Hydro-Electric Power Commission

SECTION I

LEGAL PROCEEDINGS

ACTS

The following Act to amend *The Power Commission Act* and to confirm certain by-laws and contracts was passed by the Legislature of the Province of Ontario during the Session of 1916.

An Act to amend *The Power Commission Act* and to confirm Certain By-laws and Contracts.

Assented to 27th April, 1916.

H IS MAJESTY, by and with the advice and consent of the Legislative Assembly of the Province of Ontario, enacts as follows:—

1. This Act may be cited as "*The Power Commission Act; 1916.*" Short title.

2. Subsection 2 of section 6 of *The Power Commission Act* is amended Rev. Stat. by striking out all the words therein after the words "Lieutenant-Gov- c. 39, s. 6, subs. 2, ernor in Council" in the third line. amended.

3. Section 6 of *The Power Commission Act* is amended by adding Rev. Stat. thereto the following subsections:— c. 39, s. 6, amended.

(3) Such salaries and remuneration and the travelling and other Apportion- expenses of the persons appointed or employed by the Com- ment of salaries and mission, as well as any other expenses of the Commission, expenses of officers. shall be apportioned by the Commission among, and shall be chargeable to the various works and undertakings carried on by the Commission upon which such persons are employed, but any portion of such salaries or other remuneration and travelling and other expenses which are not properly chargeable to such works or undertakings and which are earned or incurred in the performance of work or services other than those rendered in respect of works or undertakings of the Commission under contract with municipal corporations shall be chargeable and payable out of such moneys as may be appropriated for that purpose by the Legislature.

n-   (4) The apportionment by the Commission of such salaries or
             other remuneration and travelling and other expenses shall
             be final.

ce-   (5) The provisions of this section shall take effect as from the 1st
             day of January, 1910.

t.   **4**. *The Power Commission Act* is amended by adding the following
     section:—

ller.   6a.—(1) The Lieutenant-Governor in Council may appoint an
             officer to be known as the Comptroller of the Commission
             who shall hold office during the pleasure of the Lieutenant-
             Governor in Council and shall countersign every cheque
             issued by the Commission, but before countersigning shall
             satisfy himself that the issue of the cheque is authorized.

nd   (2) The Comptroller shall give such directions as he may deem
s.   proper as to the books of account kept by the Commission and
             shall cause to be kept and entered therein regular accounts
             according to a system and method approved of from time to
             time by the Lieutenant-Governor in Council of all sums of
             money received and paid out by the Commission and of the
             several purposes for which the same are received and paid,
             and such books shall be at all times open to the inspection of
             any person appointed by the Lieutenant-Governor in Council
             for that purpose, and any such person may take copies or
             extracts from such books.

,   (3) The Commission, through the Comptroller, shall, before the
             15th day of February in each year, make to the Treasurer of
             Ontario an annual report for the information of the Lieu-
             tenant-Governor in Council and for the information of the
             Assembly, and such report shall contain, among other things,
             clear and comprehensive statements disclosing and exhibit-
             ing—

                (a) The actual condition as to the amount and character of
                     the assets and liabilities (direct and indirect) of the
                     undertakings conducted by it as on 31st December last
                     preceding;

                (b) The cash transactions, including receipts and disburse-
                     ments for the year ending on 31st December last pre-
                     ceding;

                (c) The revenues, income and interest earned and the
                     amount of the costs, expenses and other items charge-
                     able there against in connection with the operation,
                     maintenance, administration and conduct of the under-

takings controlled by it for the year ending 31st December last preceding; ·

(d) The amounts, with the expected sources of the same, which it is estimated will be received in cash or its equivalent and the payments, loans and advances with the purpose of the same, which it is contemplated shall be made in cash or otherwise, in the next succeeding year;

(e) The amounts and particulars of the obligations and liabilities which it is contemplated shall be incurred in the next succeeding year;

(f) The securities or evidence of indebtedness which it is contemplated shall be created, issued, sold or otherwise disposed of, together with the method of dealing with the same in the next succeeding year;

and such other matters as may appear to be of public interest in relation to the said Commission or its works, as the Lieutenant-Governor in Council may direct, and such statements shall be in form approved of by the Treasurer of Ontario, and shall contain such information and particulars as he shall require, and shall be certified by the chairman or vice-chairman as true and correct in all particulars.

(4) The Comptroller shall make such other and further reports, Other returns by and prepare and furnish such other statements to the Comptroller. Treasurer of Ontario as he shall from time to time request or direct.

(5) In case of the illness or absence of the Comptroller or a vacancy in the office, the Lieutenant-Governor in Council ·may appoint some other person to act as Comptroller, and the person so appointed shall, during such absence or vacancy, possess the powers and perform the duties of the Comptroller.

(6) The accounts of the Commission shall, upon the direction of the Lieutenant-Governor in Council, be from time to time, and at least once every year; audited either by the Auditor for Ontario, or by other auditor or auditors.

(7) The salary of the Comptroller and the expenses of such audits shall be fixed by the Lieutenant-Governor in Council and shall be payable out of such moneys as may be appropriated for the purposes of the Commission by the Legislature, as part of the costs of the administration.

Appointment of sole arbitrator in lieu of Rev. Stat. cc. 35, 39 and 4 Geo. V. c. 31.

5. —(1) In lieu of the provisions contained in *The Ontario Public Works Act, The Power Commission Act,* and *The Hydro-Electric Railway Act, 1914,* with respect to the appointment of arbitrators where land or other property is taken or injured by the Commission in the doing of any work under the authority of any of the said Acts, the Chief Justice of the Supreme Court of Ontario, upon the request of the Lieutenant-Governor in Council, may nominate some person who, in his opinion, is skilled in the valuing of real property, and upon such nomination being approved by the Lieutenant-Governor in Council and until such approval is revoked the person so nominated shall become and be the sole arbitrator for the purpose of any arbitration proceedings taken under any of the said Acts to which the Commission is a party, but in all other respects the provisions of the said Acts, including those relating to appeals, shall apply.

Determining compensation before sole arbitrator is appointed.

(2) Until such nomination is made and approved and after such approval is revoked and until another nomination has been made and approved, the compensation to be paid to any person whose property may be taken or injured by the Commission, shall be determined in the same manner as heretofore.

Rev. Stat. c. 39, amended.

6. *The Power Commission Act* is amended by adding thereto the following sections:—

Payment over to Commission of moneys appropriated.

14a. Where the Legislature has appropriated money for the purposes of the Commission, such money shall be payable out of such appropriation to the Commission from time to time, upon the requisition of the Chairman of the Commission and the direction of the Lieutenant-Governor in Council, in such amounts and at such times as shall be stated in the requisition and direction, and this section shall have effect notwithstanding that there may be sums due from the Commission to the Province and notwithstanding anything in

Rev. Stat. c. 23.

The Audit Act contained.

Reserve fund.

14b. The Commission may set apart out of the moneys coming to its hands from time to time from any municipal corporation, railway company, or distributing company such sums as may be sufficient in the opinion of the Commission to provide for the renewal, reconstruction, alteration and repair of the works constructed and operated by the Commission, and to meet any unforeseen expenditure caused by the destruction or injury of any such works.

Rev. Stat. c. 39, s. 15, amended.

7.—(1) Section 15 of *The Power Commission Act* is amended by inserting after the word " Commission " in the first line the words " on account of sinking fund or interest."

(2) Section 15 of the said Act is amended by adding thereto the following subsection:—

(2) The income of the Commission shall be applied to the necessary operating expenses, to the preservation, improvement, supervision, renewal, repairs, maintenance and insurance of its works, and to the payment of the remuneration and expenses of the Commissioners, and the salaries of officers and others employed by the Commission, and to other incidental expenses. *Rev. Stat. c. 39, s. 15, amended. Application of income of Commission.*

8. *The Power Commission Act* is amended by adding thereto the following section :— *Rev. Stat. c. 39, amended.*

15a.—(1) The Commission may, out of any funds in its hands, from time to time purchase such electrical, hydraulic or other machinery, appliances, apparatus and furnishings as may be used in the transmission, distribution, supply or use of electrical power or energy, and may dispose of the same from time to time to municipal corporations and commissions. *Commission may purchase and sell supplies.*

(2) The Commission may undertake and carry out the installation, construction, erection or purchase of supplies for any plant, machinery, wires, poles and other things for the transmission, distribution, supply or use of electrical power or energy for light, heat or power purposes, by a municipal corporation or commission which has entered into a contract with the Commission for the supply of electrical power or energy, and the Commission may charge and collect from such corporation or commission the cost of any work done or service rendered by the Commission, its officers, servants or workmen under this subsection. *Doing work for contracting municipalities.*

(3) This section shall take effect as from the 31st day of October, 1910. *Commencement of section.*

9. Section 18 of *The Power Commission Act* is amended by adding thereto the following subsection :— *Rev. Stat. c. 39, sub. 8, amended.*

(8) Where a corporation has entered into a contract with the Commission for the supply of electrical power or energy, the debentures issued for any works for the distribution and supply of such electrical power or energy by the corporation, shall not be included in ascertaining the limit of the borrowing powers of the corporation as prescribed by *The Municipal Act.* *Debentures of contracting municipalities not included in ascertaining limit of borrowing powers. Rev. Stat. c. 192.*

10. Section 37 of *The Power Commission Act,* as enacted by section 12 of *The Power Commission Act, 1915,* is repealed and the following substituted therefor :— *5 Geo. V. c. 19, s. 12, amended.*

37.—(1) The Commission may, with the approval of the Lieutenant-Governor in Council, make-regulations as to the design, construction, installation, protection, operation, maintenance and inspection of works, plant, machinery, apparatus, *Regulations as to electrical works.*

2 H

appliances, devices, material and equipment for the generation, transmission, distribution, connection and use of electrical power or energy by any municipal corporation or
commission and by any railway, street railway, electric light,
power or transmission company, or by any other company
or individual generating, transmitting, distributing or using
electric power or energy, or whose undertaking, works or
premises are electrically connected with any plant for the
generation, transmission or distribution of electric power or
energy, and the Commission may impose penalties for the
breach of any such regulations.

(2) The Commission may, at any time, order such work to be done
in the installation, removal, alteration or protection of any
of the works mentioned in subsection 1, as the Commission
may deem necessary for the safety of the public, or of workmen, or for the protection of the property damaged by fire
or otherwise, and pending the performance of such work, or
in case of noncompliance with the regulations or with any
order of the Commission, may order the supply of electrical
power or energy to be cut off from such works.

(3) The Commission may appoint inspectors for the purpose of
seeing that the regulations and orders of the Commission,
made under the authority of this section, or any other provision of this Act, are carried out and may collect the
fees to be paid by any municipal corporation or commission,
or by any company, firm, or individual under the regulations
or by order of the Commission, and may provide for the payment of the remuneration, travelling and other expenses of
the Inspector out of the fines and fees so collected or out of
the funds appropriated for carrying on the work of the
Commission.

(4) Every Inspector so appointed may, during any reasonable hour,
enter upon, pass over or through any land, buildings or
premises for the purpose of carrying out the regulations and
orders of the Commission, and perform the duties assigned
to him; and every municipal corporation or commission, company, firm, or individual, molesting, hindering, disturbing or
interfering with an inspector in the performance of his duty,
shall be guilty of an offence, and shall incur the penalty
provided by subsection 7.

(5) Every municipal corporation or commission, and every company, firm or individual, upon receiving notice in writing
by the Commission to remedy any defect or to make any
alteration, or carry out any work, or comply with such notice
within the time thereby prescribed, and in default, shall
incur the penalty provided by subsection 7.

(6) Every municipal corporation or commission, and every company, firm or individual, supplying electrical power or energy for use in any electric works, plant, machinery, apparatus, appliance or equipment before the same have been inspected and such supply authorized by the certificate of the Commission, and after notice from the Commission of the unauthorized supply or use, shall incur a penalty of not less than $300 nor more than $500. *Penalty for supplying electricity before works approved.*

(7) Every municipal corporation or commission, and every company, firm and individual, refusing or neglecting to disconnect or discontinue the supply of electricity to any electric works, plant, machinery, apparatus, appliance, or equipment, upon due notice in writing from the Commission so to do, shall incur a penalty of not less than $300 nor more than $500. *Penalty for disobeying order to discontinue supply.*

(8) Nothing in this Act shall affect the liability of any municipal corporation or commission, or of any company, firm, or individual, for damages caused to any person or property by reason of any defect in any electric works, plant, machinery, apparatus, appliance, device, material, or equipment, or in the installation or protection thereof, nor shall the Commission or any inspector incur any liability by reason of any inspection or the issue of any certificate or on account of any loss occasioned by the cutting off of the supply of electrical power or energy in accordance with the orders of the Commission. *Other liability not affected.*

(9) Every municipal corporation or commission, and every company, firm or individual, disobeying the provisions of this Act, or of the regulations, or any order of the Commission, shall incur a penalty of not less than $10 nor more than $50, and in the event of continuing the offence, of not less than $10 nor more than $50 for every day during which such offence continues. *Penalty for disobeying regulations.*

(10) The penalties imposed by or under the authority of this section shall be recoverable under *The Ontario Summary Convictions Act* and shall be paid over to the Commission. *Recovery of penalties under Rev. Stat. c. 56.*

11. Section 48 of *The Power Commission Act,* as enacted by section 15 of *The Power Commission Act 1915,* is amended by adding thereto the following subsection :— *5 Geo. V. c 19, s. 15, amended.*

(4) Every member or officer of a municipal commission who contravenes any of the provisions of this section shall forfeit his office, and shall be disqualified and incapable of being elected or appointed to any such municipal commission or to any other municipal office for a period of two years, and the like *Disqualification of member of municipal commission dealing in electrical supplies.*

proceedings may be taken by the commission or by a ratepayer against any such member or officer to remove him
from his office or declare his disqualification, as may be
taken by a ratepayer for the removal or disqualification of a
member of a municipal council who has become disqualified
from sitting and voting therein, but the Commission shall
not be required to furnish security for costs.

Relieving
-municipality
from sink-
ing fund
-charges.

12. Notwithstanding anything in *The Power Commission Act* contained the Commission, with the approval of the Lieutenant-Governor in
Council, may relieve any municipal corporation which has entered into
a contract with the Commission from the payment of any sum in the
sinking fund account during the first five years of such contract, and the
amount required from the corporation for sinking fund shall be payable
only during the remainder of the term of the contract.

By-laws
confirmed.

13. By-laws Nos. 716 and 718 of the Corporation of the City of
Niagara Falls; By-laws Nos. 486 and 491 of the Corporation of the Town
of Blenheim; By-laws Nos. 10 and 11 of 1914, Nos. 7 and 11 of 1915,
and No. 3 of 1916, of the Corporation of the Town of Bothwell; By-laws
Nos. 576 and 612 of the Corporation of the Town of Chesley; By-laws
Nos. 653 and 654 of the Corporation of the Town of Durham; By-laws
Nos. P-19 and P-20 of the Corporation of the Town of Gravenhurst; By-
laws Nos. 498 and 499 of the Corporation of the Town of Harriston; By-
laws Nos. 658 and 659 of the Corporation of the Town of Listowel; By-
laws Nos. 265 and 266 of the Corporation of the Town of Markdale; By-
laws Nos. 654 and 659 of the Corporation of the Town of Mount Forest;
By-laws Nos. 1,169 and 1,178 of the Corporation of the Town of Orangeville; By-laws Nos. 474 and 476 of the Corporation of the Town of
Palmerston; By-laws Nos. 1,033 and 1,034 of the Corporation of the
Town of Petrolia; By-laws Nos. 602, 603 and 615 of the Corporation of
the Town of Ridgetown; By-laws Nos. 207 and 222 of the Corporation
of the Village of Ailsa Craig; By-laws Nos. 8 and 9 of 1914 as amended
by By-law No. 3 of 1916, and No. 8 of 1915, of the Corporation of the
Village of Chatsworth; By-laws Nos. 292 and 294 of the Corporation of
the Village of Dutton; By-laws Nos. 254 and 257 of the Corporation
of the Village of Dundalk; By-laws Nos. 21 and 14 of the Corporation
of the Village of Exeter; By-laws Nos. 29 and 30 of the Corporation of
the Village of Flesherton; By-laws Nos. 165 and 166 of the Corporation
of the Village of Milverton; By-laws Nos. 318 and 321 of the Corporation of the Village of Shelburne; By-laws Nos. 320, 321 and 327 of the
Corporation of the Village of Thamesville; By-laws Nos. 59 and 60 of
the Corporation of the Village of Tavistock; By-laws Nos. 83 and 84
of the Corporation of the Village of Victoria Harbor; By-laws Nos. 25,
243 and 259 of the Corporation of the Township of Tilbury West; By-
laws Nos. 657 and 658 of the Corporation of the Township of Delaware;
By-laws Nos. 304 and 305 of the Corporation of the Township of Egre-
mont; By-laws Nos. 723, 724 and 745 of the Corporation of the Township of Westminster; By-laws Nos. 596 and 597 of the Corporation of
the Township of Beverly; By-law No. 592 of the Corporation of the

Township of Ancaster; By-laws Nos. 532 and 542 of the Corporation of the Township of Caradoc; By-laws Nos. 553 and 585 of the Corporation of the Township of South Dumfries; By-law No. 631 of the Corporation of the Township of Tay; By-laws Nos. 811, 849 and 851 of the Corporation of the Township of Toronto are confirmed and declared to be legal, valid and binding upon such corporations and the ratepayers thereof, respectively, and shall not be open to question upon any ground whatsoever, notwithstanding the requirements of *The Power Commission Act,* Rev. Stat. or the amendments thereto or of any other statute.

14. The Municipal Corporation of the City of Niagara Falls, the Certain corpora-tions added Municipal Corporation of the Town of Blenheim, the Municipal Corporation of the Town of Bothwell, the Municipal Corporation of the as parties to contract Town of Harriston, the Municipal Corporation of the Town of Listowel, with Commission. the Municipal Corporation of the Town of Palmerston, the Municipal Corporation of the Town of Petrolia, the Municipal Corporation of the Town of Ridgetown, the Municipal Corporation of the Village of Ailsa Craig, the Municipal Corporation of the Village of Dutton, the Municipal Corporation of the Village of Exeter, the Municipal Corporation of the Village of Milverton, the Municipal Corporation of the Village of Thamesville, the Municipal Corporation of the Village of Tavistock, the Municipal Corporation of the Police Village of Delaware, the Municipal Corporation of the Police Village of Lambeth, the Municipal Corporation of the Police Village of Lynden, the Municipal Corporation of the Police Village of St. George, the Municipal Corporation of the Township of Toronto are added as parties of the second part to the contract set out in Schedule "A" to *The Power Commission Act 1909,* as varied, confirmed and amended by the said Act, and as further varied, confirmed and amended by the Act passed in the tenth year of the reign of His late Majesty King Edward VII, chaptered 16, and by subsequent Acts and by this Act, and the said contract shall be binding upon the parties thereto, respectively, as to the City of Niagara Falls, from the Time from 15th day of December, 1915; as to the Town of Blenheim, from the 15th which contract to be day of June, 1915; as to the Town of Bothwell, from the 21st day of binding on June, 1915; as to the Town of Harriston, from the 27th day of August, tions added. 1915; as to the Town of Listowel, from the 23rd day of August, 1915; as to the Town of Palmerston, from the 23rd day of August, 1915; as to the Town of Petrolia, from the 11th day of August, 1915; as to the Town of Ridgetown, from the 16th day of June, 1915; as to the Village of Ailsa Craig, from the 5th day of July, 1915; as to the Village of Dutton, from the 29th day of March, 1915; as to the Village of Exeter, from the 5th day of August, 1915; as to the Village of Milverton, from the 30th day of September, 1915; as to the Village of Thamesville, from the 15th day of June, 1915; as to the Village of Tavistock, from the 22nd day of September, 1914; as to the Police Village of Delaware, from the 1st day of April, 1915; as to the Police Village of Lambeth, from the 18th day of February, 1915; as to the Police Village of Lynden, from the 28th day of June, 1915; as to the Police Village of St. George, from the 14th day of June, 1915; as to the Township of Toronto, from the 10th day of June, 1913.

Amendment
of schedule
to contract.

15. The names of the said municipal corporations are added to Schedule " B " of the said contract, and such schedule shall be read as containing the particulars set out in Schedule "A" to this Act.

Certain
other
contracts
confirmed.

16. The contracts set out as Schedules "A," " B," " C," " D," " E," " F," " G," " H," " I," " J," " K," " L," and " M " hereto between the Hydro-Electric Power Commission of Ontario and the Corporations of the Town of Chesley, the Town of Durham, the Town of Gravenhurst, the Town of Huntsville, the Town of Markdale, the Town of Mount Forest, the Village of Chatsworth, the Village of Dundalk, the Village of Flesherton, the Village of Shelburne, the Village of Victoria Harbor, the Police Village of Holstein, and the Police Village of Williamsburg are hereby confirmed and declared to be legal, valid and binding upon the parties thereto respectively, and shall not be open to question upon

Rev. Stat
c. 39.

any grounds whatsoever, notwithstanding the requirements of *The Power Commission Act,* or the amendments thereto or any other statute.

SCHEDULE "A."

Column 1	2	3	4	5	6	7
Name of Municipal Corporation.	Quantity of Power applied for in H.P.	Maximum Price of Power at Niagara Falls.	*No. of Volts.	Estimate maximum cost of power ready for distribution in Municipality.	Estimate proportionate part of costs to construct transmission line, transormer stations and works for nominally 30,000 H.P., with total capacity of 60,000 H.P.	Estimate proportionate part of line loss and of part cost to operate, maintain, repair, renew and insure transmission line, transformer stations and works for nominally 30,000 H.P., with total capacity of 60,000 H.P.
				$ c.	$ c.	$ c.
Niagara Falls	2,000	....	....	11 50	17,500 00	1,185 00
Blenheim	250	....	....	43 70	74,901 00	4,122 00
Bothwell	150	....	....	59 26	70,905 00	3,427 00
Harriston	200	....	....	46 62	64,706 00	3,440 00
Listowel	300	....	....	37 41	74,565 00	3,927 00
Palmerston	200	....	....	40 82	55,208 00	2,926 00
Petrolia	500	....	....	36 26	117,295 00	6,512 00
Ridgetown	200	....	....	47 17	65,016 00	3,645 00
Ailsa Craig	100	....	....	49 67	32,784 00	2,063 00
Dutton	50	....	....	43 53	15,130 00	849 00
Exeter	200	....	....	43 70	59,550 00	3,247 00
Milverton	200	....	....	35 63	46,986 00	2,446 00
Thamesville	125	....	....	45 40	38,779 00	3,183 10
Tavistock	100	....	....	49 50	35,173 00	2,010 00
Delaware	25	....	....	46 56	8,704 00	434 17
Lambeth	25	....	....	46 56	8,704 00	434 17
Lynden	120	....	....	33 00	21,714 00	1,621 00
St. George	100	....	....	38 78	24,384 00	1,456 00
Toronto Township	100	....	....	25 00	13,680 00	807 00

*Number required by each Corporation.

SCHEDULE " B."

This indenture made the 6th day of October, 1915,

Between

>   The Hydro-Electric Power Commission of Ontario, hereinafter called
>   the " Commission," party of the first part;

>   'and

>   The Municipal Corporation of the Town of Chesley, hereinafter called
>   the " Corporation," party of the second part.

Whereas the Corporation under the provisions of the *Power Commission
Act* and amendments thereto, Revised Statutes of Ontario Chapter 39, has
applied to the Commission for a supply of power, and has passed a by-law
No. 612, passed the eighteenth day of October, 1915, to authorize the execution of an agreement therefor.

Now therefore this indenture witnesseth, that in consideration of the
premises and of the agreement of the Corporation herein set forth, subject
to the provisions of the said Act and amendments thereto, the parties hereto
agree each with the other as follows:—

1. The Commission agrees:

(*a*) To reserve and deliver at the earliest possible date four hundred
(400) h.p., or more, of electrical power to the Corporation.

(*b*) At the expiration of reasonable notice, in writing, which may be
given by the Corporation from time to time during the continuance of this
agreement, to reserve and deliver to the Corporation additional electric
power when called for.

(*c*) To use at all times first-class, modern, standard commercial apparatus and plant, and to exercise all due skill and diligence so as to secure
satisfactory operation of the plant and apparatus of the Corporation.

(*d*) To deliver commercially continuous twenty-four (24) hour power
every day in the year to the Corporation at the distribution bus bars in the
Commission's sub-station within the Corporation's limits.

2. The Corporation agrees:

(*a*) To use all diligence by every lawful means in its power to prepare for
the receipt and use of the power dealt with by this agreement so as to be
able to receive power when the Commission is ready to deliver same.

(*b*) To pay annually in twelve (12) equal monthly instalments interest
upon its proportionate part, (based on the quantity of electrical energy or
power taken) of all moneys expended by the Commission on capital account
for the acquiring of properties and rights, and acquiring and construction of
generating plants, transformer stations, transmission lines, distributing
stations and other works necessary for the delivery of said electrical energy
or power to the Corporation under the terms of this contract.

To pay an annual sum for its proportionate part of all moneys expended by the Commission on capital account for the acquiring of the said properties and rights, and the cost of the said construction, so as to form in thirty (30) years a sinking fund-for the retirement of securities issued by the Province of Ontario.

Also to bear its proportionate part of the line loss, and pay its proportionate part of the cost to operate, maintain, repair, renew and insure the said generating plants, transformer stations, transmission lines, distributing stations, and other necessary works.

All payments under this clause shall be subject to adjustment under paragraph 6.

(c) The amounts payable in accordance with clause 2 (b) shall be paid in gold coin of the present standard of weight and fineness, at the offices of the Commission at Toronto. Bills shall be rendered by the Commission on or before the 5th day and paid by the Corporation on or before the 15th day of each month. If any bills remain unpaid for fifteen days, the Commission may, in addition to all other remedies, and without notice, discontinue the supply of power to the Corporation until said bill is paid. No such discontinuance shall relieve the Corporation from the performance of the covenants, provisoes, and conditions herein contained. All payments in arrears shall bear interest at the legal rate.

(d) To take electric power exclusively from the Commission during the continuance of this agreement.

(e) To pay for three-fourths of the power ordered from time to time by the Corporation, and held in reserve for it, as herein provided, whether it takes the same or not. When the highest average amount of power taken for any twenty (20) consecutive minutes during any month exceeds during the twenty consecutive minutes three-fourths of the amount ordered by the Corporation and held in reserve, then the Corporation shall pay for this greater amount during the entire month.

If the Corporation during any month takes more than the amount of power ordered and held in reserve for it, as determined by an integrated peak, or the highest average, for a period of twenty consecutive minutes, the taking of such excess shall thereafter constitute an obligation on the part of the Corporation to pay for, and on the part of the Commission to hold in reserve, such increased quantity of power in accordance with the terms and conditions of this contract.

When the power factor of the highest average amount of power taken for said twenty consecutive minutes falls below 90 per cent., the Corporation shall pay for 90 per cent. of said power divided by the power factor.

(f) To use at all times first-class, modern standard commercial apparatus and plant, to be approved by the Commission, and to exercise all due skill and diligence so as to secure satisfactory operation of the plant and apparatus of the Commission and of the Corporation.

(g) To co-operate by all means in its power at all times with the Commission to increase the quantity of power required from the Commission, and in all other respects to carry out the objects of this agreement, and of the said Act.

3. This agreement shall remain in force for thirty (30) years from the date of the first delivery of power under this contract.

4. The power shall be alternating, three-phase, having a periodicity of approximately 60 cycles per second, and shall be delivered as aforesaid at a voltage suitable for local distribution.

5. The engineers of the Commission, or one or more of them, or any other person or persons appointed for this purpose by the Commission, shall have the right from time to time during the continuance of this agreement to inspect the apparatus, plant and property of the Commission, and to take records at all reasonable hours.

6. The Commission shall at least annually, adjust and apportion the amount or amounts payable by the Municipal Corporation or Corporations, for such power and such interest, sinking fund, cost of lost power, and cost of generating, operating, maintaining, repairing, renewing and insuring said works.

7. It is hereby declared that the Commission is to be a trustee of all property held by the Commission under this agreement for the Corporation and other Municipal Corporations supplied by the Commission, but the Commission shall be entitled to a lien upon said property for all moneys expended by the Commission under this agreement and not repaid. At the expiration of this agreement the Commission shall determine and adjust the rights of the Corporations and other Municipal Corporations, supplied by the Commission, having regard to the amounts paid by them respectively, under the terms of this agreement, and such other considerations as may appear equitable to the Commission, and are approved by the Lieutenant-Governor in Council.

8. If at any time any other Municipal Corporation, or pursuant to said Act, any railway or distributing company, or any other corporation, or person, applies to the Commission for a supply of power, the Commission shall notify the applicant and the Corporation, in writing, of a time and place to hear all representations that may be made as to the terms and conditions for such supply.

Without discrimination in favour of the applicants, as to the price to be paid for equal quantities of power, the Commission may supply power upon such terms and conditions as may, having regard to the risk and expense incurred and paid, and to be paid by the Corporation, appear equitable to the Commission, and are approved by the Lieutenant-Governor in Council.

No such application shall be granted if the said works or any part thereof are not adequate for such supply, or if the supply of the Corporation will be thereby injuriously affected, and no power shall be supplied within the limits of a municipal corporation taking power from the Commission at the time of such application without the written consent of such corporation.

In determining the quantity of power supplied to a municipal corporation, the quantity supplied by the Commission within the limits of the Corporation to any applicant, other than a municipal corporation, shall be computed as part of the quantity supplied to such corporation, but such corporation shall not be liable for payment for any portion of the power supplied. No power shall be supplied by the municipal corporation to any railway or distributing company without the written consent of the Commission, but the Corporation may sell power to any person or manufacturing companies within the limits of the Corporation, but such power shall not be sold for less than cost, neither shall there be any discrimination as regards price and quantity.

9. If differences arise between corporations to which the Commission is supplying power, the Commission may, upon application, fix a time and place and hear all representations that may be made by the parties, and the Commission shall, in a summary manner, when possible, adjust such differences, and such adjustment shall be final. The Commission shall have all the powers that may be conferred upon a commissioner appointed under the *Act respecting Enquiries concerning Public Matters.*

10. This agreement shall extend to, be binding upon, and enure to the benefit of the successors and assigns of the parties hereto.

In witness whereof, the Commission and the Corporation have, respectively, affixed their corporate seals and the hands of their proper officers.

HYDRO-ELECTRIC POWER COMMISSION OF ONTARIO.

A. Beck, *Chairman.*

W. W. Pope, *Secretary.*

MUNICIPAL CORPORATION OF THE TOWN OF CHESLEY.

C. J. Halliday, *Mayor.*

H. S. Sanderson, *Clerk.*

———

SCHEDULE " C."

This indenture made in duplicate the   day of   .
in the year of our Lord,

Between

The Hydro-Electric Power Commission of Ontario, hereinafter called the " Commission," party of the first part;

and

The Municipal Corporation of the Town of Durham hereinafter called the " Corporation," party of the second part.

Whereas, pursuant to an Act to provide for the transmission of electrical power to municipalities known as the *Power Commission Act* and amendments thereto, the Corporation applied to the Commission for supply of power, and the Commission furnished the Corporation with estimates of the total cost of such power, ready for distribution within the limits of the

Corporation (and the electors of the Corporation assented to the by-laws authorizing the Corporation to enter into a contract with the Commission for such power).

1. Now therefore this indenture witnesseth that in consideration of the premises and of the agreement of the Corporation herein set forth, subject to the provisions of the said Act and amendments thereto, the Commission agrees with the Corporation.

(a) To reserve and deliver at the earliest possible date 100 h.p. or more of electrical power to the Corporation.

(b) At the expiration of reasonable notice in writing which may be given by the Corporation from time to time during the continuance of this agreement, to reserve and deliver to the Corporation additional electric power when called for.

(c) To use at all times first-class, modern, standard, commercial apparatus and plant, and to exercise all due skill and diligence so as to secure satisfactory operation of the plant and apparatus of the Corporation.

(d) To deliver commercially continuously 24-hour power every day in the year to the Corporation at the distribution bus bars in the Commission's substation within the Corporation's limits.

2. In consideration of the premises and of the agreements herein set forth, the Corporation agrees with the Commission.

(a) To use all diligence by every lawful means in its power to prepare for the receipt and use of the power dealt with by this agreement so as to be able to receive power when the Commission is ready to deliver same.

(b) To pay annually, interest at rate payable by the Commission upon the Corporation's proportionate part (based on the quantity of electrical energy or power taken) of all moneys expended by the Commission on capital account for the acquiring of properties and rights, the acquiring and construction of generating plants, transformer stations, transmission lines, distributing stations, and other works necessary for the delivery of said electrical energy or power to the Corporation under the terms of this contract.

Also to pay an annual sinking fund instalment of such amount as to form at the end of 30 years, with accrued interest, a sinking fund sufficient to repay the Corporation's proportionate part, based as aforesaid, of all moneys advanced by the Province of Ontario, for the acquiring of properties and rights, the acquiring and construction of generating plants, transformer stations, transmission lines, distributing stations and other work necessary for the delivery of said electrical energy or power, delivered to the Corporation under the terms of this contract. Also to pay the Corporation's proportionate part, based as aforesaid, of the cost of lost power and of the cost of operating, maintaining, repairing, renewing and insuring said generating plants, transformer stations, transmission lines, distributing stations and other necessary work. Subject to adjustment under Clause 6 of this agreement.

(c) The amounts payable under this contract shall be paid in twelve monthly payments, in gold coin of the present standard of weight and fineness, at the offices of the Commission at Toronto. Bills shall be rendered by the Commission on or before the 5th day and paid by the Corporation on or before the 15th day of each month. If any bill remains unpaid for fifteen days, the Commission may, in addition to all other remedies and without notice, discontinue the supply of power to the Corporation until said bill is paid. No such discontinuance shall relieve the Corporation from the performance of the covenants, provisoes and conditions herein contained. All payments in arrears shall bear interest at the legal rate;

(d) To take electric power exclusively from the Commission during the continuance of this agreement.

(e) To co-operate by all means in its power at all times with the Commission to increase the quantity of power required from the Commission, and in all other respects to carry out the objects of this agreement, and of the said Act.

(f) To pay for three-fourths of the power ordered from time to time by the Corporation and held in reserve for it as herein provided whether it takes the same or not. When the highest average amount of power taken for any twenty consecutive minutes during any month shall exceed during the twenty consecutive minutes three-fourths of the amount ordered by the Corporation and held in reserve, then the Corporation shall pay for this greater amount during the entire month.

(g) If the Corporation during any month takes more than the amount of power ordered and held in reserve for it, as determined by an integrated peak, or the highest average, for a period of twenty consecutive minutes, the taking of such excess shall thereafter constitute an obligation on the part of the Corporation to pay for, and on the part of the Commission to hold in reserve, such increased quantity of power in accordance with the terms and conditions of this contract.

(h) When the power factor of the highest average amount of power taken for said twenty consecutive minutes falls below 90 per cent. the Corporation. shall pay for 90 per cent. of said power divided by the power factor.

(i) To use at all times first-class, modern, standard commercial apparatus and plant, to be approved by the Commission.

(j) To exercise all due skill and diligence so as to secure satisfactory operation of the plant and apparatus of the Commission and of the Corporation.

3. This agreement shall remain in force for thirty years from date of the first delivery of power under this contract.

4. The power shall be alternating, three phase, having a periodicity of approximately 60 cycles per second and shall be delivered as aforesaid at a voltage suitable for local distribution.

(a) That the meters with their series and potential transformers shall be connected at the point of delivery.

(b) The maintenance by the Commission of approximately the agreed voltage at approximately the agreed frequency at the substation in the limits of the Corporation shall constitute the supply of all power involved herein and the fulfilment of all operating obligations hereunder, and when voltage and frequency are so maintained, the amount of power, its fluctuations, load factor, power factor, distribution as to phases and all other electric characteristics and qualities, are under the sole control of the Corporation, their agents, customers, apparatus, appliances and circuits.

5. The engineers of the Commission, or one or more of them, or any other person or persons appointed for this purpose by the Commission shall have the right from time to time during the continuance of this agreement to inspect the apparatus, plant and property of the Corporation and take records at all reasonable hours.

6. The Commission shall at least annually adjust and apportion the amount or amounts payable by the Municipal Corporation or Corporations for such power and such interest, sinking fund, cost of lost power and cost of generating, operating, maintaining, repairing, renewing and insuring said works.

If at any time any other Municipal Corporation, or pursuant to said Act, any railway or distributing company, or any other Corporations or person, applies to the Commission for a supply of power, the Commission shall notify the applicant and the involved Corporation or Corporations in writing, of a time and place to hear all representations that may be made as to the terms and conditions for such supply.

Without discrimination in favour of the applicants as to the price to be paid, for equal quantities of power, the Commission may supply power upon such terms and conditions as may, having regard to the risk and expense incurred, and paid and to be paid by the Corporation, appear equitable to the Commission, and are approved by the Lieutenant-Governor in Council.

No such application shall be granted if the said works or any part thereof are not adequate for such supply, or if the supply of the Corporation will be thereby injuriously affected, and no power shall be supplied within the limits of a Municipal Corporation taking power from the Commission at the time of such application without the written consent of such Corporation.

In determining the quantity of power supplied to a Municipal Corporation, the quantity supplied by the Commission within the limits of the Corporation to any applicant, other than a Municipal Corporation shall be computed as part of the quantity supplied to such Corporation, but such Corporation shall not be liable for payment for any portion of the power so supplied. No power shall be supplied by the Municipal Corporation to any railway or distributing company without the written consent of the Commission. Power shall not be sold for less than the cost and there shall be no discrimination as regards price and quantity.

7. It is hereby declared that the Commission is to be a trustee of all property held by the Commission under this agreement for the Corporation or Corporations supplied by the Commission but the Commission shall be entitled to a lien upon said property for all moneys expended by the Com-

mission under this agreement and not repaid.   At the expiration of this agreement the Commission shall determine and adjust the rights of the Corporation and any other (if any) supplied by the Commission, having regard to the amounts paid by them respectively under the terms of this agreement, and such other consideration as may appear equitable to the Commission and are approved by the Lieutenant-Governor in Council.

8. If differences arise between Corporations to which the Commission is supplying power, the Commission may upon application fix a time and place and hear all representations that may be made by the parties and the Commission, shall, in a summary manner, when possible, adjust such differences and such adjustment shall be final.   The Commission shall have all the powers that may be conferred upon a Commissioner appointed under the *Act respecting Enquiries concerning Public Matters.*

9. This agreement shall extend to, be binding upon, and enure to the benefit of the successors and assigns of the parties hereto.

In witness whereof the Commission and the Corporation have respectively affixed their corporate seals and the hands of their proper officers.

THE HYDRO-ELECTRIC POWER COMMISSION OF ONTARIO.

A. Beck, *Chairman.*
W. W. Pope, *Secretary.*

(Seal.)

MUNICIPAL CORPORATION OF THE TOWN OF DURHAM.

A. S. Hunter, *Mayor.*
Wm. B. Vollet, *Clerk.*

(Seal.)

SCHEDULE " D."

This indenture made in duplicate the Twenty-fifth day of October, in the year of our Lord, One Thousand Nine Hundred and Fifteen.

Between

The Hydro-Electric Power Commission of Ontario, hereinafter called " The Commission," party of the first part;

and

The Municipal Corporation of the Town of Gravenhurst, hereinafter called " The Corporation," party of the second part.

Whereas pursuant to an Act to provide for the transmission of electric power to municipalities, known as *The Power Commission Act,* and amendments thereto, the Corporation applied to the Commission for a supply of power, and the Commission furnished the Corporation with estimates of the total cost of such power, ready for distribution within the limits of the

Corporation (and the electors of the Corporation assented to the by-laws authorizing the Corporation to enter into a contract with the Commission for such power).

1. Now therefore this indenture witnesseth that in consideration of the premises and of the agreements of the Corporation herein set forth, subject to the provisions of the said Act and amendments hereto, the Commission agrees with the Corporation:

(a) To reserve and deliver at the earliest possible date 300 h.p., or more, of electrical power to the Corporation.

(b) At the expiration of reasonable notice in writing, which may be given by the Corporation from time to time during the continuance of this agreement, to reserve and deliver to the Corporation when called for any additional electrical power then available.

(c) To use at all times first-class, modern, standard, commercial apparatus and plant, and to exercise all due skill and diligence so as to secure satisfactory operation of the plant and apparatus of the Corporation.

(d) To deliver commercially continuous 24-hour power every day in the year to the Corporation at the outgoing line bracket on the Commission's generating station at South Falls on the south branch of the Muskoka River.

2. In consideration of the premises and of the agreements herein set forth, the Corporation agrees with the Commission:

(a) To use all diligence by every lawful means in its power to prepare for the receipt and use of the power dealt with by this agreement so as to be able to receive power when the Commission is ready to deliver same.

(b) To pay annually to the Commission the Corporation's proportionate part of interest and sinking fund (based on the quantity of electrical energy or power taken) on all moneys expended by the Commission on capital account for the acquiring of properties and rights and acquiring and construction of generating plant and other works necessary for the delivery of said electrical power or energy to the Corporation under the terms of this agreement.

Also to pay annually to the Commission the Corporation's proportionate part (based as above) of the cost of lost power and operating, maintaining, repairing, renewing and insuring the generating plant and other necessary works.

(c) The amounts payable under this contract shall be paid in twelve monthly payments, in gold coin of the present standard of weight and fineness, at the offices of the Commission at Toronto. Bills shall be rendered by the Commission on or before the 5th day and paid by the Corporation on or before the 15th day of each month. If any bill remains unpaid for fifteen days, the Commission may, in addition to all other remedies and without notice discontinue the supply of power to the Corporation until the said bill is paid. No such discontinuance shall relieve the Corporation from the performance of the covenants, provisoes and conditions herein contained. All payments in arrears shall bear interest at the legal rate.

(d) To co-operate by all means in its power at all times with the Commission to increase the quantity of power required from the Commission, and in all other respects to carry out the objects of this agreement and of the said Acts.

(e) To take electric power exclusively from the Commission during the continuance of this agreement.

(f) To pay for three-fourths of the power ordered from time to time by the Corporation and held in reserve for it as herein provided whether it takes the same or not. When the greatest average amount of power taken for any twenty consecutive minutes during any month shall exceed during the twenty consecutive minutes three-fourths of the amount ordered by the Corporation and held in reserve, then the Corporation shall pay for this greater amount during the entire month.

(g) If the Corporation during any month takes more than the amount of power ordered and held in reserve for it, for twenty consecutive minutes, the taking of such excess shall thereafter constitute an obligation on the part of the Corporation to pay for, and on the part of the Commission to hold in reserve such increased quantity of power in accordance with the terms and conditions of this contract.

(h) When the power factor of the greatest amount of power taken for said twenty consecutive minutes falls below 90%, the Corporation shall pay for 90% of said power divided by the power factor.

(i) To use at all times first-class, modern, standard, commercial apparatus and plant approved by the Commission.

(j) To exercise all due skill and diligence so as to secure satisfactory operation of the plant and apparatus of the Commission and the Corporation.

3. This agreement shall remain in force for 16 years from the date of the first delivery of power under this contract.

4. The power shall be alternating, three-phase, having a periodicity of approximately 60 cycles per second, and shall be delivered as aforesaid at approximately 6,600 volts.

(a) The metres, with their series and potential transformers, shall be connected at the point of delivery as near as practicable.

(b) The maintenance by the Commission of approximately the agreed voltage at approximately the agreed frequency at the generating station at South Falls on the Muskoka River shall constitute the supply of all power involved herein, and the fulfilment of all operating obligations hereunder, and when the voltage and frequency are so maintained, the amount of the power, its fluctuations, load factor, power factor, distribution as to phases, and all other electrical characteristics and qualities are under the sole control of the Corporation, their agents, customers, apparatus, appliances and circuits.

5. The engineers of the Commission, or one or more of them, or any person or persons appointed for this purpose by the Commission, shall have

3 H

the right from time to time during the continuance of this agreement to inspect the apparatus, plant and property of the Corporation and take records at all reasonable hours.

6. The Commission shall at least annually adjust and apportion the amount or amounts payable by the Municipal Corporation or Corporations for such power and such interest, sinking fund, cost of lost power, and cost of generating, operating, maintaining, repairing, renewing and insuring said works.

If at any time any other municipal corporation, or, pursuant to said Act, any railway or distributing company, or any other corporation or person, applies to the Commission for a supply of power, the Commission shall notify the applicant and involved corporation or corporations in writing of a time and place to hear all representations that may be made as to the terms and conditions for such supply.

Without discrimination in favour of the applicants as to the price to be paid for equal quantities of power, the Commission may supply power upon such terms and conditions as may, having regard to the risk and expense incurred, and paid, and to be paid by the Corporation, appear equitable to the Commission and are approved by the Lieutenant-Governor in Council.

No such application shall be granted if the said works or any part thereof are not adequate for such supply, or if the supply of said Corporation will be thereby injuriously affected, and no power shall be supplied within the limits of said Municipal Corporation taking power from the Commission at the time of such application without the written consent of such Corporation.

In determining the quantity of power supplied to a Municipal Corporation, the quantity supplied by the Commission within the limits of the Corporation to any applicant other than a Municipal Corporation shall be computed as a part of the quantity supplied to such Corporation, but such Corporation shall not be liable for payment for any portion of the power so supplied. No power shall be supplied by the Municipal Corporation to any railway or distributing company without the written consent of the Commission. Power shall not be sold for less than the cost, and there shall be no discrimination as regards price and quantity.

7. At the expiration of this agreement the Commission shall determine and adjust the rights of the Corporation and any other (if any) supplied by the Commission.

8. If differences arise between Corporations to which the Commission is supplying power, the Commission may, upon application, fix a time and place and hear all representations that may be made by the parties, and the Commission shall in a summary manner, when possible, adjust such differences, and such adjustment shall be final. The Commission shall have all the powers that may be conferred upon a Commissioner appointed under *The Act Respecting Inquiries Concerning Public Matters.*

9. This agreement shall extend to, be binding upon, and enure to the benefit of the successors and assigns of the parties hereto.

In witness whereof the "Commission" and the "Corporation" have respectively affixed their corporate seals and the hand of their proper officers.

Signed, sealed and delivered this twenty-fifth day of October, 1915, A.D., in the presence of

HYDRO-ELECTRIC POWER COMMISSION.

A. BECK, *Chairman.*
W. W. POPE, *Secretary.*

(Seal)

MUNICIPAL CORPORATION OF THE TOWN OF GRAVENHURST.

ARCHY. SLOAN, *Mayor.*
W. H. BUTTERWORTH, *Town Clerk.*

(Seal)

SCHEDULE "E."

This Indenture, made in Duplicate the 10th day of March, in the year of our Lord one thousand nine hundred and fifteen (1915).

Between

The Hydro-Electric Power Commission of Ontario, hereinafter called "The Commission," party of the first part;

and

The Municipal Corporation of the Town of Huntsville, hereinafter called "The Corporation," party of the second part.

Whereas pursuant to an Act to provide for the transmission of electric power to municipalities known as *The Power Commission Act* and amendments thereto, the Corporation applied to the Commission for a supply of power, and the Commission furnished the Corporation with estimates of the total cost of such power, ready for distribution within the limits of the Corporation (and the electors of the Corporation assented to the By-laws, authorizing the Corporation to enter into a contract with the Commission for such power).

1. Now therefore this indenture witnesseth that in consideration of the premises and of the agreement of the Corporation herein set forth, subject to the provisions of the said Act and amendments thereto, the Commission agrees with the Corporation:

(a) To reserve and deliver at the earliest possible date 800 h.p. or more of electrical power to the Corporation.

(*b*) At the expiration of reasonable notice in writing, which may be given by the Corporation from time to time during the continuance of this agreement, to reserve and deliver to the Corporation additional electrical power when called for.

(*c*) To use at all times first-class, modern, standard commercial apparatus and plant, and to exercise all due skill and diligence so as to secure satisfactory operation of the plant and apparatus of the Corporation.

(*d*) To deliver commercially continuous twenty-four-hour power every day in the year to the Corporation at the distribution bus bars in the Commission's substation within the Corporation's limits.

2. In consideration of the premises and of the agreements herein set forth, the Corporation agrees with the Commission:

(*a*) To use all diligence by every lawful means in its power to prepare for the receipt and use of the power dealt with by this agreement so as to be able to receive power when the Commission is ready to deliver the same.

(*b*) To pay annually interest at 4% to 4½% per annum upon the Corporation's proportionate part (based on the quantity of electrical energy or power taken) of all moneys expended by the Commission on capital account for the acquiring of properties and rights, and acquiring the construction of generating plants, transformer stations, transmission lines, distributing stations, and other works necessary for the delivery of the said electrical power or energy to the Corporation under the terms of this contract.

Also to pay an annual sinking fund instalment of such amount as to form at the end of sixteen years, with accrued interest, a sinking fund sufficient to repay the Corporation's proportionate part, based as aforesaid, of all moneys advanced by the Province of Ontario for the acquiring of the properties and rights, the acquiring and construction of generating plants, transformer stations, transmission lines, distributing stations, and other work necessary for the delivery of electrical energy or power, delivered to the Corporation under the terms of this contract. Also to pay the Corporation's proportionate part, based as aforesaid, on the cost of lost power, and the cost of operating, maintaining, repairing, renewing and insuring said generating plants, transformer stations, transmission lines, distributing stations, and other necessary works.

(*c*) The amounts payable under this contract shall be paid in twelve monthly payments, in gold coin of the present standard of weight and fineness, at the offices of the Commission at Toronto. Bills shall be rendered by the Commission on or before the 5th day and paid by the Corporation on or before the 15th day of each month. If any bill remains unpaid for fifteen days, the Commission may, in addition to all other remedies and without notice, discontinue the supply of power to the Corporation until the said bill is paid. No such discontinuance shall relieve the Corporation from the performance of the covenants, provisoes and conditions herein contained. All payments in arrears shall bear interest at the legal rate.

(*d*) To take electric power exclusively from the Commission during the continuance of this agreement.

(e) To co-operate by all means in its power at all times with the Commission to increase the quantity of power required from the Commission, and in all other respects to carry out the objects of this agreement, and of the said Act.

(f) To pay for three-fourths of the power ordered from time to time by the Corporation and held in reserve for it as herein provided, whether it takes the same or not. When the highest amount of power taken for any twenty consecutive minutes during any month shall exceed during the twenty consecutive minutes three-fourths of the amount ordered by the Corporation and held in reserve, then the Corporation shall pay for this greater amount during the entire month.

(g) If the Corporation during any month takes more than the amount of power ordered and held in reserve for it for twenty consecutive minutes, the taking of such excess shall thereafter constitute an obligation on the part of the Corporation to pay for, and on the part of the Commission to hold in reserve such increased quantity of power in accordance with the terms and conditions of this contract.

(h) When the power factor of the highest amount of power taken for said twenty consecutive minutes falls below 90% the Corporation shall pay for 90% of said power divided by the power factor.

(i) To use at all times first-class modern, standard, commercial apparatus and plant approved by the Commission.

(j) To exercise all due skill and diligence so as to secure satisfactory operation of the plant and apparatus of the Commission and the Corporation.

3. This agreement shall remain in force sixteen years from the date of the first delivery of power under this contract.

4. The power shall be alternating, three phase, having a periodicity of approximately sixty cycles per second, and shall be delivered as aforesaid at a voltage suitable for local distribution.

(a) That the meters with their series and potential transformers shall be connected at the point of delivery.

(b) That the maintenance by the Commission of approximately the agreed voltage, at approximately the agreed frequency at the substation in the limits of the Corporation shall constitute the supply of all power involved herein, and the fulfilment of all operating obligations hereunder, and when the voltage and frequency are so maintained, the amount of the power, its fluctuations, load factor, power factor, distribution as to phases, and all other electrical characteristics and qualities are under the sole control of the Corporation, their agents, customers, apparatus, appliances and circuits.

5. The engineers of the Commission, or one or more of them, or any person or persons appointed for this purpose by the Commission shall have the right from time to time during the continuance of this agreement to inspect the apparatus, plant, property of the Corporation and take records at all reasonable hours.

6. The Commission shall at least annually adjust and apportion the amount or amounts payable by the municipal corporation or corporations for such power and such interest, sinking fund, cost of lost power, and cost of generating, operating, maintaining, repairing, renewing, and insuring said works.

If at any time any other municipal corporation, or pursuant to said Act, any railway or distributing company, or any other corporation or person, applies to the Commission for a supply of power, the Commission shall notify the applicant and involved corporation or corporations in writing of a time and place to hear all representations that may be made as to the terms and conditions for such supply.

Without discrimination in favour of the applicants as to the price to be paid, for equal quantities of power, the Commission may supply power upon such terms and conditions as may, having regard to the risk and expense incurred, and paid, and to be paid by the Corporation, appear equitable to the Commission, and are approved by the Lieutenant-Governor in Council.

No such application shall be granted if the said works or any part thereof are not adequate for such supply, or if the supply of said Corporation will be thereby injuriously affected, and no power shall be supplied within the limits of said municipal corporation taking power from the Commission at the time of such application without the written consent of such corporation.

In determining the quantity of power supplied to a municipal corporation the quantity supplied by the Commission within the limits of the corporation to any applicant other than a municipal corporation shall be computed as a part of the quantity supplied to such corporation, but such corporation shall not be liable for payment for any portion of the power so supplied. No power shall be supplied by the municipal corporation to any railway or distributing company without the written consent of the Commission. Power shall not be sold for less than the cost, and there shall be no discrimination as regards price and quantity.

7. It is hereby declared the Commission is to be a trustee of all property held by the Commission under this agreement for the corporation or corporations supplied by the Commission, but the Commission shall be entitled to a lien upon said property for all moneys expended by the Commission under this agreement and not repaid. At the expiration of this agreement the Commission shall determine and adjust the rights of the Corporation and any other (if any) supplied by the Commission, taking regard to the amounts paid by them respectively under the terms of this agreement, and such other considerations as may appear equitable to the Commission and are approved by the Lieutenant-Governor in Council.

8. If differences arise between corporations to which the Commission is supplying power, the Commission may, upon application, fix a time and place, and hear all representations that may be made by the parties, and the Commission shall in a summary manner, when possible, adjust such differences, and such adjustment shall be final. The Commission shall have all the powers that may be conferred upon a Commissioner appointed under *The Act respecting Enquiries Concerning Public Matters.*

9. This agreement shall extend to, be binding upon, and enure to the benefit of the successors and assigns of the parties hereto.

In witness whereof the "Commission" and the "Corporation" have respectively affixed their corporate seals and the hand of their proper officers.

HYDRO-ELECTRIC POWER COMMISSION.

A. BECK, *Chairman.*
W. W. POPE, *Secretary.*

(Seal)

MUNICIPALITY OF THE TOWN OF HUNTSVILLE.

H. E. RISE, *Mayor.*
J. M. CULLON, *Clerk.*

(Seal.)

SCHEDULE "F."

This Indenture, made the 11th day of September, 1915.

Between .

The Hydro-Electric Power Commission of Ontario, hereinafter called the "Commission," party of the first part;

and

The Municipal Corporation of the Town of Markdale, hereinafter called the "Corporation," party of the second part.

Whereas the Corporation, under the provisions of *The Power Commission Act* and amendments thereto, Revised Statutes of Ontario, Chapter 39, has applied to the Commission for a supply of power and has passed a By-law No. 265, passed the 30th day of July, 1915, to authorize the execution of an agreement therefor.

Now therefore this indenture witnesseth that in consideration of the premises and of the agreement of the Corporation herein set forth, subject to the provisions of the said Act and amendments thereto, the parties hereto agree each with the other as follows:

1. The Commission agrees:

(a) To reserve and deliver at the earliest possible date one hundred and fifty (150) horse power, or more, of electrical power to the Corporation.

(b) At the expiration of reasonable notice, in writing, which may be given by the Corporation from time to time during the continuance of this agreement, to reserve and deliver to the Corporation additional electric power when called for.

(c) To use at all times first-class, modern, standard commercial apparatus and plant, and to exercise all due skill and diligence so as to secure satisfactory operation of the plant and apparatus of the Corporation.

(d) To deliver commercially continuous twenty-four (24) hour power every day in the year to the Corporation at the distribution bus bars in the Commission's substation within the Corporation's limits.

2. The Corporation agrees:

(a) To use all diligence by every lawful means in its power to prepare for the receipt and use of the power dealt with by this agreement so as to be able to receive power when the Commission is ready to deliver same.

(b) To pay annually in twelve (12) equal monthly instalments, interest upon its proportionate part (based on the quantity of electrical energy or power taken) of all moneys expended by the Commission on capital account for the acquiring of properties and rights, the acquiring and construction of generating plants, transformer stations, transmission lines, distributing stations, and other works necessary for the delivery of said electrical energy or power to the Corporation under the terms of this contract.

To pay an annual sum for its proportionate part of all moneys expended by the Commission on capital account for the acquiring of the said properties and rights, and the cost of the said construction, so as to form in thirty (30) years a sinking fund for the retirement of securities issued by the Province of Ontario.

Also to bear its proportionate part of the line loss and pay its proportionate part of the cost to operate, maintain, repair, renew, and insure the said generating plants, transformer stations, transmission lines, distributing stations, and other necessary works.

All payments under this clause shall be subject to adjustment under paragraph 6.

(c) The amounts payable in accordance with clause 2 (b) shall be paid in gold coin of the present standard of weight and fineness, at the offices of the Commission at Toronto. Bills shall be rendered by the Commission on or before the 5th day and paid by the Corporation on or before the 15th day of each month. If any bills remain unpaid for fifteen days the Commission may, in addition to all other remedies and without notice, discontinue the supply of power to the Corporation until said bill is paid. No such discontinuance shall relieve the corporation from the performance of the covenants, provisoes and conditions herein contained. All payments in arrears shall bear interest at the legal rate.

(d) To take electric power exclusively from the Commission during the continuance of this agreement.

(e) To pay for three-fourths of the power ordered from time to time by the Corporation and held in reserve for it as herein provided, whether it takes the same or not. When the highest average amount of power taken for any twenty consecutive minutes during any month exceeds during the twenty consecutive minutes three-fourths of the amount ordered by the

Corporation and held in reserve, then the Corporation shall pay for this greater amount during the entire month.

If the Corporation during any month takes more than the amount of power ordered and held in reserve for it, as determined by an integrated peak, or the highest average, for a period of twenty consecutive minutes, the taking of such excess shall thereafter constitute an obligation on the part of the Corporation to pay for, and on the part of the Commission to hold in reserve, such increased quantity of power in accordance with the terms and conditions of this contract.

When the power factor of the highest average amount of power taken for said twenty consecutive minutes falls below 90 per cent., the Corporation shall pay for 90 per cent. of said power divided by the power factor.

(*f*) To use at all times first-class, modern, standard commercial apparatus and plant, to be approved by the Commission, and to exercise all due skill and diligence so as to secure satisfactory operation of the plant and apparatus of the Commission and of the Corporation.

(*g*) To co-operate by all means in its power at all times with the Commission to increase the quantity of power required from the Commission, and in all other respects to carry out the objects of this agreement, and of the said Act.

3. This agreement shall remain in force for thirty (30) years from the date of the first delivery of power under this contract.

4. The power shall be alternating, three-phase, having a periodicity of approximately 60 cycles per second, and shall be delivered as aforesaid at a voltage suitable for local distribution.

5. The engineers of the Commission, or one or more of them, or any other person or persons appointed for this purpose by the Commission, shall have the right from time to time, during the continuance of this agreement, to inspect the apparatus, plant, and property of the Corporation, and take records at all reasonable hours.

6. The Commission shall at least annually adjust and apportion the amount or amounts payable by the Municipal Corporation or Corporations for such power and such interest, sinking fund, cost of lost power and cost of generating, operating, maintaining, repairing, renewing and insuring said works.

7. It is hereby declared that the Commission is to be a trustee of all property held by the Commission under this agreement for the Corporations and other municipal corporations supplied by the Commission, but the Commission shall be entitled to a lien upon said property for all moneys expended by the Commission under this agreement and not repaid. At the expiration of this agreement the Commission shall determine and adjust the rights of the Corporations and other municipal corporations, supplied by the Commission, having regard to the amounts paid by them, respectively, under the terms of this agreement, and such other considerations as may appear equitable to the Commission and are approved by the Lieutenant-Governor in Council.

8. If at any time any other municipal corporation, or pursuant to said Act, any railway or distributing company, or any other corporation or person, applies to the Commission for a supply of power, the Commission shall notify the applicant and the Corporation, in writing, of a time and .place to hear all representations that may be made as to the terms and conditions for such supply.

Without discrimination in favour of the applicants as to the price to be paid, for equal quantities of power, the Commission may supply power upon such terms and conditions as may, having regard to the risk and expense incurred, and paid, and to be paid by the Corporation, appear equitable to the Commission, and are approved by the Lieutenant-Governor in Council.

No such application shall be granted if the said works, or any part thereof, are not adequate for such supply, or if the supply of the Corporation will be thereby injuriously affected, and no power shall be supplied within the limits of a municipal corporation taking power from the Commission at the time of such application, without the written consent of such Corporation.

In determining the quantity of power supplied to a municipal corporation, the quantity supplied by the Commission within the limits of the Corporation to any applicant, other than a municipal corporation, shall be computed as part of the quantity supplied to such Corporation, but such Corporation shall not be liable for payment for any portion of the power so supplied. No power shall be supplied by the municipal corporation to any railway or distributing company, without the written consent of the Commission, but the Corporation may sell power to any person or persons, or manufacturing companies within the limits of the Corporation, but such power shall not be sold for less than cost; neither shall there be any discrimination as regards price and quantity.

9. If differences arise between corporations to which the Commission is supplying power, the Commission may, upon application, fix a time and place and hear all representations that may be made by the parties, and the Commission shall, in a summary manner, when possible, adjust such differences, and such adjustment shall be final. The Commission shall have all the powers that may be conferred upon a commissioner appointed under the *Act respecting Enquiries concerning Public Matters.*

10. This agreement shall extend to, be binding upon, and enure to the benefit of the successors and assigns of the parties hereto.

In witness whereof, the Commission and the Corporation have respectively affixed their Corporate Seals and the hands of their proper officers.

HYDRO-ELECTRIC POWER COMMISSION OF ONTARIO.

A. BECK, *Chairman,*
W. W. POPE, *Secretary.*

(SEAL.)

MUNICIPAL CORPORATION OF THE TOWN OF MARKDALE.

R. W. EMIER, *Reeve.*
R. GILFILLAN, *Clerk.*

(SEAL.)

SCHEDULE "G."

This Indenture made in duplicate the 15th day of March, in the year of our Lord, 1915.

Between

    The Hydro-Electric Power Commission of Ontario, hereinafter called the "Commission," party of the first part;

and

    The Municipal Corporation of the Town of Mount Forest, hereinafter called the "Corporation," party of the second part.

Whereas, pursuant to an Act to provide for the transmission of electrical power to municipalities known as the *Power Commission Act* and amendments thereto, the Corporation applied to the Commission for a supply of power, and the Commission furnished the Corporation with estimates of the total cost of such power, ready for distribution within the limits of the Corporation (and the electors of the Corporation assented to the by-laws authorizing the Corporation to enter into a contract with the Commission for such power).

1. Now therefore this indenture witnesseth that in consideration of the premises and of the agreement of the Corporation herein set forth, subject to the provisions of the said Act and amendments thereto, the Commission agrees with the Corporation:

(a) To reserve and deliver at the earliest possible date 400 h.p. or more of electrical power to the Corporation.

(b) At the expiration of reasonable notice in writing which may be given by the Corporation from time to time during the continuance of this agreement, to reserve and deliver to the Corporation additional electric power when called for.

(c) To use at all times first-class, modern, standard commercial apparatus and plant, and to exercise all due skill and diligence so as to secure satisfactory operation of the plant and apparatus of the Corporation.

(d) To deliver commercially continuous 24-hour power every day of the year to the Corporation at the distribution bus bars in the Commission's sub-station within the Corporation's limits.

2. In consideration of the premises and of the agreement herein set forth, the Corporation agrees with the Commission:

(a) To use all diligence by every lawful means in its power to prepare for the receipt and use of the power dealt with by this agreement, so as to be able to receive power when the Commission is ready to deliver same.

(b). To pay annually, interest at rate payable by the Commission upon the Corporation's proportionate part (based on the quantity of electrical energy or power taken) of all moneys expended by the Commission on capital account for the acquiring of properties and rights, the acquiring and construction of generating plants, transformer stations, transmission lines, distributing stations, and other works necessary for the delivery of said electrical energy or power to the Corporation under the terms of this contract.

Also to pay an annual sinking fund instalment of such amount as to form at the end of 30 years, with accrued interest, a sinking fund sufficient to repay the Corporation's proportionate part, based as aforesaid, of all moneys advanced by the Province of Ontario for the acquiring of properties and rights, the acquiring and construction of generating plants, transformer stations, transmission lines, distributing stations and other work necessary for the delivery of said electrical energy or power, delivered to the Corporation under the terms of this contract. Also to pay the Corporation's proportionate part, based as aforesaid, of the cost of lost power and of the cost of operating, maintaining, repairing, renewing and insuring said generating plants, transformer stations, transmission lines, distributing stations and other necessary works. Subject to adjustment under Clause 6 of this agreement.

(c) The amount payable under this contract shall be paid in twelve monthly payments, in gold coin of the present standard of weight and fineness, at the offices of the Commission at Toronto. Bills shall be rendered by the Commission on or before the 5th day and paid by the Corporation on or before the 15th day of each month. If any bill remains unpaid for fifteen days, the Commission may, in addition to all other remedies and without notice, discontinue the supply of power to the Corporation until said bill is paid. No such discontinuance shall relieve the Corporation from the performance of the covenants, provisoes and conditions herein contained. All payments in arrears shall bear interest at the legal rate.

(d) To take electric power exclusively from the Commission during the continuance of this agreement.

(e) To co-operate by all means in its power at all times with the Commission to increase the quantity of power required from the Commission, and in all other respects to carry out the objects of this agreement, and of the said Act.

(f) To pay for three-fourths of the power ordered from time to time by the Corporation and held in reserve for its as herein provided, whether it takes the same or not. When the highest average amount of power taken for any twenty consecutive minutes during any month shall exceed during the twenty consecutive minutes three-fourths of the amount ordered by the Corporation and held in reserve, then the Corporation shall pay for this greater amount during the entire month.

(g) If the Corporation during any month takes more than the amount of power ordered and held in reserve for it, as determined by an integrated peak, or the highest average, for a period of twenty consecutive minutes, the taking of such excess shall thereafter constitute an obligation on the part of the Corporation to pay for, and on the part of the Commission to hold in reserve, such increased quantity of power in accordance with the terms and conditions of this contract.

(*h*) When the power factor of the highest average amount of power taken for said twenty consecutive minutes falls below 90 per cent., the Corporation shall. pay for 90 per cent. of said power divided by the power factor.

(*i*) To use at all times first-class, modern, standard commercial apparatus and plant, to be approved by the Commission.

(*j*) To exercise all due skill and diligence so as to secure satisfactory operation of the plant and apparatus of the Commission and of the Corporation.

3. This agreement shall remain in force for thirty years from date of the first delivery of power under this contract.

4. The power shall be alternating, three-phase, having a periodicity of approximately 60 cycles per second and shall be delivered as aforesaid at a voltage suitable for local distribution.

(*a*) That the meters, with their series and potential transformers, shall be connected at the point of delivery.

(*b*) The maintenance by the Commission of approximately the agreed voltage at approximately the agreed frequency at the sub-station in the limits of the Corporation shall constitute the supply of all power involved herein and the fulfilment of all operating obligations hereunder, and when voltage and frequency are so maintained, the amount of power, its fluctuations, load factor, power factor, distribution as to phases and all other electric characteristics and qualities, are under the sole control of the Corporation, their agents, customers, apparatus, appliances and circuits.

5. The engineers of the Commission, or one or more of them, or any other person or persons appointed for this purpose by the Commission, shall have the right from time to time during the continuance of this agreement, to inspect the apparatus, plant and property of the Corporation, and take records at all reasonable hours.

6. The Commission shall at least .annually adjust and apportion the amount or amounts payable by the Municipal Corporation or Corporations for such power and such interest, sinking fund, cost of lost power and cost of generating, operating, maintaining, repairing, renewing and insuring said works.

If at any time any other Municipal Corporation, or pursuant to said Act, any railway or distributing company, or any other Corporations or person, applies to the Commission for a supply of power, the Commission shall notify the applicant and the involved Corporation or Corporations, in writing, of a time and place to hear all representations that may be made as to the terms and conditions for such supply.

Without discrimination in favour of the applicants as to the price to be paid, for equal quantities of power, the Commission may supply power upon such terms and conditions, as may, having regard to the risk and expense incurred, and paid, and to be paid by the Corporation, appear equitable to the Commission, and are approved by the Lieutenant-Governor in Council.

No such application shall be granted if the said works or any part thereof are not adequate for such supply, or if the supply of the Corpora. tion will be thereby injuriously affected, and no power shall be supplied within the limits of a Municipal Corporation taking power from the Com. mission at the time of such application, without the written consent of such corporation.

In determining the quantity of power supplied to a Municipal Corpora. tion, the quantity supplied by the Commission within the limits of the Cor. poration to any applicant, other than a Municipal Corporation, shall be computed as part of the quantity supplied to such Corporation, but such Corporation shall not be liable for payment for any portion of the power so supplied. No power shall be supplied by the Municipal Corporation to any railway or distributing company, without the written consent of the Commission. Power shall not be sold for less than the cost, and there shall be no discrimination as regards price and quantity.

7. It is hereby declared that the Commission is to be a trustee of all property held by the Commission under this agreement for the Corporation or Corporations supplied by the Commission, but the Commission shall be entitled to a lien upon said property for all moneys expended by the Commission under this agreement and not repaid. At the expiration of this agreement the Commission shall determine and adjust the rights of the Corporation and any other (if any), supplied by the Commission, having regard to the amounts paid by them respectively under the terms of this agreement, and such other considerations as may appear equitable to the Commission and are approved by the Lieutenant-Governor in Council.

8. If differences arise between Corporations to which the Commission is supplying power, the Commission may upon application fix a time and place, and hear all representations that may be made by the parties, and the Commission shall, in a summary manner, when possible, adjust such differences and such adjustment shall be final. The Commission shall have all the powers that may be conferred upon a Commissioner appointed under the Act respecting Enquiries Concerning Public Matters.

9. This agreement shall extend to, be binding upon, and enure to the benefit of the successors and assigns of the parties hereto.

In witness whereof the Commission and the Corporation have respectively affixed their corporate seals and the hands of their proper officers.

HYDRO-ELECTRIC POWER COMMISSION OF ONTARIO.

     A. BECK, Chairman,
     W. W. POPE, Secretary.
       (SEAL.)

MUNICIPAL CORPORATION OF THE TOWN OF MARKDALE.

     T. CLARK, Mayor.
     W. C. PERRY, Clerk.
       (SEAL.)

SCHEDULE "H."

This Indenture made in duplicate the   day of
in the year of our Lord,

Between

The Hydro-Electric Power Commission of Ontario, hereinafter called the " Commission," party of the first part;

and

The Municipal Corporation of the Village of Chatsworth, hereinafter called the " Corporation," party of the second part.

Whereas, pursuant to an Act to provide for the transmission of electrical power to municipalities known as *The Power Commission Act* and amendments thereto, the Corporation applied to the Commission for a supply of power, and the Commission furnished the Corporation with estimates of the total cost of such power, ready for distribution within the limits of the Corporation (and the electors of the Corporation assented to the' by-laws authorizing the Corporation to enter into a contract with the Commission for such power).

1. Now therefore this indenture witnesseth that in consideration of the premises and of the agreement of the Corporation herein set forth, subject to the provisions of the said Act and amendments thereto, the Commission agrees with the Corporation:

(*a*) To reserve and deliver at the earliest possible date 75 h.p. or more of electrical power to the Corporation.

(*b*) At the expiration of reasonable notice in writing which may be given by the Corporation from time to time during the continuance of this agreement, to reserve and deliver to the Corporation additional electric power when called for.

(*c*) To use at all times first-class, modern, standard commercial apparatus and plant, and to exercise all due skill and diligence so as to secure satisfactory operation of the plant and apparatus of the Corporation.

(*d*) To deliver commercially continuous 24-hour power every day in the year to the Corporation at the distribution bus bars in the Commission's sub-station within the Corporation's limits.

2. In consideration of the premises and of the agreements herein set forth, the Corporation agrees with the Commission:

(*a*) To use all diligence by every lawful means in its power to prepare for the receipt and use of the power dealt with by this agreement, so as to be able to receive power when the Commission is ready to deliver same.

(*b*) To pay annually interest at rate payable by the Commission upon the Corporation's proportionate part (based on the quantity of electrical energy or power taken) of all moneys expended by the Commission on capital account for the acquiring of properties and rights, the acquiring and construction of generating plants, transformer stations, transmission lines, distributing stations and other works necessary for the delivery of said electrical energy or power to the Corporation under the terms of this contract.

Also to pay an annual sinking fund instalment of such amount as to form at the end of 30 years, with accrued interest, a sinking fund sufficient to repay the Corporation's proportionate part, based as aforesaid, of all moneys advanced by the Province of Ontario for the acquiring of properties and rights, the acquiring and construction of generating plants, transformer stations, transmission lines, distributing stations, and other work necessary for the delivery of said electrical energy or power delivered to the Corporation under the terms of this contract. Also to pay the Corporation's proportionate part, based as aforesaid, of the cost of lost power and of the cost of operating, maintaining, repairing, renewing and insuring said generating plants, transformer stations, transmission lines, distributing stations and other necessary works. Subject to adjustment under clause 6 of this agreement.

(c) The amounts payable under this contract shall be paid in twelve monthly payments, in gold coin of the present standard of weight and fineness, at the offices of the Commission at Toronto. Bills shall be rendered by the Commission on or before the 5th day and paid by the Corporation on or before the 15th day of each month. If any bill remains unpaid for fifteen days, the Commission may, in addition to all other remedies, and without notice, discontinue the supply of power to the Corporation until said bill is paid. No such discontinuance shall relieve the Corporation from the performance of the covenants, provisoes and conditions herein contained. All payments in arrears shall bear interest at the legal rate.

(d) To take electric power exclusively from the Commission during the continuance of this agreement.

(e) To co-operate by all means in its power at all times with the Commission to increase the quantity of power required from the Commission, and in all other respects to carry out the objects of this agreement and of the said Act.

(f) To pay for three-fourths of the power ordered from time to time by the Corporation and held in reserve for it as herein provided, whether it takes the same or not. When the highest average amount of power taken for any twenty consecutive minutes during any month shall exceed during the twenty consecutive minutes three-fourths of the amount ordered by the Corporation and held in reserve, then the Corporation shall pay for this greater amount during the entire month.

(g) If the Corporation during any month takes more than the amount of power ordered and held in reserve for it, as determined by an integrated peak, or highest average, for a period of twenty consecutive minutes, the taking of such excess shall thereafter constitute an obligation on the part of the Corporation to pay for, and on the part of the Commission to hold in reserve, such increased quantity of power, in accordance with the terms and conditions of this contract.

(*h*) When the power factor of the highest average amount of power taken for said twenty consecutive minutes falls below 90 per cent., the Corporation shall pay for 90 per cent. of said power divided by the power factor.

(*i*) To use at all times first-class, modern, standard commercial apparatus and plant, to be approved by the Commission.

(*j*) To exercise all due skill and diligence, so as to secure satisfactory operation of the plant and apparatus of the Commission and of the Corporation.

3. This agreement shall remain in force for thirty years from date of the first delivery of power under this contract.

4. The power shall be alternating, three-phase, having a periodicity of approximately 60 cycles per second, and shall be delivered as aforesaid at a voltage suitable for local distribution.

(*a*) That the meters, with their series and potential transformers, shall be connected at the point of delivery.

(*b*) The maintenance by the Commission of approximately the agreed voltage at approximately the agreed frequency at the sub-station in the limits of the Corporation shall constitute the supply of all power involved herein and the fulfilment of all operating obligations hereunder, and when voltage and frequency are so maintained, the amount of power, its fluctuations, load factor, power factor, distribution as to phases and all other electric characteristics and qualities, are under the sole control of the Corporation, their agents, customers, apparatus, appliances and circuits.

5. The engineers of the Commission, or one or more of them, or any other person or persons appointed for this purpose by the Commission, shall have the right from time to time during the continuance of this agreement to inspect the apparatus, plant and property of the Corporation and take records at all reasonable hours.

6. The Commission shall at least annually adjust and apportion the amount or amounts payable by the Municipal Corporation or Corporations for such power, and such interest, sinking fund, cost of lost power and cost of generating, operating, maintaining, repairing, renewing and insuring said works.

If at any time any other Municipal Corporation, or, pursuant to said Act, any railway or distributing company, or any other Corporations or person applies to the Commission for a supply of power, the Commission shall notify the applicant and the involved Corporation or Corporations in writing of a time and place to hear all representations that may be made as to the terms and conditions for such supply.

Without discrimination in favour of the applicants as to the price to be paid for equal quantities of power, the Commission may supply power upon such terms and conditions as may, having regard to the risk and expense incurred and paid and to be paid by the Corporation, appear equitable to the Commission and are approved by the Lieutenant-Governor in Council.

4 H

No such application shall be granted if the said works, or any part thereof, are not adequate for such supply, or if the supply of the Corporation will be thereby injuriously affected, and no power shall be supplied within the limits of a Municipal Corporation taking power from the Commission at the time of such application, without the written consent of such Corporation.

In determining the quantity of power supplied to a Municipal Corporation, the quantity supplied by the Commission within the limits of the Corporation to any applicant, other than a Municipal Corporation, shall be computed as part of the quantity supplied to such Corporation, but such Corporation shall not be liable for payment for any portion of the power so supplied. No power shall be supplied by the Municipal Corporation to any railway or distributing company without the written consent of the Commission. Power shall not be sold for less than the cost, and there shall be no discrimination as regards price and quantity.

7. It is hereby declared that the Commission is to be a trustee of all property held by the Commission under this agreement for the Corporation or Corporations supplied by the Commission, but the Commission shall be entitled to a lien upon said property for all moneys expended by the Commission under this agreement and not repaid. At the expiration of this agreement the Commission shall determine and adjust the rights of the Corporation and any other (if any) supplied by the Commission, having regard to the amounts paid by them respectively under the terms of this agreement, and such other considerations as may appear equitable to the Commission and are approved by the Lieutenant-Governor in Council.

8. If differences arise between Corporations to which the Commission is supplying power, the Commission may, upon application, fix a time and place and hear all representations that may be made by the parties, and the Commission shall, in a summary manner, when possible, adjust such differences, and such adjustment shall be final. The Commission shall have all the powers that may be conferred upon a Commissioner appointed under *The Act Respecting Enquiries Concerning Public Matters*.

9. This agreement shall extend to, be binding upon, and enure to the benefit of the successors and assigns of the parties hereto.

In witness whereof the Commission and the Corporation have respectively affixed their corporate seals and the hands of their proper officers.

HYDRO-ELECTRIC POWER COMMISSION OF ONTARIO.

> J. B. Lucas, *Vice-Chairman.*
> W. W. Pope, *Secretary.*

(Seal)

THE CORPORATION OF THE VILLAGE OF CHATSWORTH.

> Wm. Breese, *Reeve.*
> W. G. Reilly, *Clerk.*

(Seal)

SCHEDULE "I.'"

This Indenture made in duplicate the 1st day of March in the year of our Lord, 1915,

Between

The Hydro-Electric Power Commission of Ontario, hereinafter called the "Commission," party of the first part;

and

The Municipal Corporation of the Village of Dundalk, hereinafter called the "Corporation," party of the second part.

Whereas, pursuant to an Act to provide for the transmission of electrical power to municipalities, known as the *Power Commission Act* and amendments thereto, the Corporation applied to the Commission for a supply of power, and the Commission furnished the Corporation with estimates of the total cost of such power, ready for distribution within the limits of the Corporation (and the electors of the Corporation assented to the by-laws authorizing the Corporation to enter into a contract with the Commission for such power).

1. Now therefore this indenture witnesseth that in consideration of the premises and of the agreement of the Corporation herein set forth, subject to the provisions of the said Act and Amendments thereto, the Commission agrees with the Corporation:

(*a*) To reserve and deliver at the earliest possible date 200 h.p. or more of electrical power to the Corporation.

(*b*) At the expiration of reasonable notice in writing, which may be given by the Corporation from time to time during the continuance of this agreement, to reserve and deliver to the Corporation additional electric power when called for.

(*c*) To use at all times first-class, modern, standard, commercial apparatus and plant, and to exercise all due skill and diligence so as to secure satisfactory operation of the plant and apparatus of the Corporation.

(*d*) To deliver commercially continuous 24-hour power every day in the year to the Corporation at the distribution bus bars in the Commission's sub-station within the Corporation's limits.

2. In consideration of the premises and of the agreements herein set forth the Corporation agrees with the Commission:

(*a*) To use all diligence by every lawful means in its power to prepare for the receipt and use of the power dealt with by this agreement so as to be able to receive power when the Commission is ready to deliver same.

(*b*) To pay annually, interest at rate payable by the Commission upon the Corporation's proportionate part (based on the quantity of electrical energy or power taken) of all moneys expended by the Commission on capital account for the acquiring of properties and rights, the acquiring and construction of generating plants, transformer stations, transmission lines, distributing stations, and other works necessary for the delivery of said electrical energy or power to the Corporation under the terms of this contract;

Also to pay an annual sinking fund instalment of such amount as to form at the end of 30 years, with accrued interest, a sinking fund sufficient to repay the Corporation's proportionate part, based as aforesaid, of all moneys advanced by the Province of Ontario for the acquiring of properties and rights, the acquiring and construction of generating plants, transformer stations, transmission lines, distributing stations and other work necessary for the delivery of said electrical energy or power, delivered to the Corporation under the terms of this contract. Also to pay the Corporation's proportionate part, based as aforesaid, of the cost of lost power and of the cost of operating, maintaining, repairing, renewing and insuring said generating plants, transformer stations, transmission lines, distributing stations and other necessary works. Subject to adjustment under clause 6 of this agreement.

(c) The amounts payable under this contract shall be paid in twelve monthly payments, in gold coin of the present standard of weight and fineness, at the offices of the Commission at Toronto. Bills shall be rendered by the Commission on or before the 5th day and paid by the Corporation on or before the 15th day of each month. If any bill remains unpaid for fifteen days, the Commission may, in addition to all other remedies and without notice, discontinue the supply of power to the Corporation until said bill is paid. No such discontinuance shall relieve the Corporation from the performance of the covenants, provisoes and conditions herein contained. All payments in arrears shall bear interest at the legal rate.

(d) To take electric power exclusively from the Commission during the continuance of this agreement.

(e) To co-operate by all means in its power at all times with the Commission to increase the quantity of power required from the Commission, and in all other respects to carry out the objects of this agreement and of the said Act.

(f) To pay for three-fourths of the power ordered from time to time by the Corporation and held in reserve for it as herein provided whether it takes the same or not. When the highest average amount of power taken for any twenty consecutive minutes during any month shall exceed during the twenty consecutive minutes three-fourths of the amount ordered by the Corporation and held in reserve, then the Corporation shall pay for this greater amount during the entire month;

(g) If the Corporation during any month takes more than the amount of power ordered and held in reserve for it, as determined by an integrated peak, or the highest average, for a period of twenty consecutive minutes, the taking of such excess shall thereafter constitute an obligation on the part of the Corporation to pay for, and on the part of the Commission to hold in reserve, such increased quantity of power in accordance with the terms and conditions of this contract.

(h) When the power factor of the highest average amount of power taken for said twenty consecutive minutes falls below 90 per cent., the Corporation shall pay for 90 per cent. of said power divided by the power factor.

(*i*) To use at all times first-class, modern, standard commercial apparatus and plant, to be approved by the Commission.

(*j*) To exercise all due skill and diligence so as to secure satisfactory operation of the plant and apparatus of the Commission and of the Corporation.

3. This agreement shall remain in force for thirty years from date of the first delivery of power under this contract.

4. The power shall be alternating, three-phase, having a periodicity of approximately 60 cycles per second and shall be delivered as aforesaid at a voltage suitable for local distribution.

(*a*) That the meters with their series and potential transformers shall be connected at the point of delivery.

(*b*) The maintenance by the Commission of approximately the agreed voltage at approximately the agreed frequency at the sub-station in the limits of the Corporation shall constitute the supply of all power involved herein and the fulfilment of all operating obligations hereunder. and when voltage and frequency are so maintained, the amount of power, its fluctuations, load factor, power factor, distribution as to phases and all other electric characteristics and qualities, are under the sole control of the Corporation, their agents, customers, apparatus, appliances and circuits.

5. The engineers of the Commission, or one or more of them, or any other person or persons appointed for this purpose by the Commission, shall have the right from time to time during the continuance of this agreement to inspect the apparatus, plant, and property of the Corporation and take records at all reasonable hours.

6. The Commission shall at least annually adjust and apportion the amount or amounts payable by the Municipal Corporation or corporations for such power and such interest, sinking fund, cost of lost power and cost of generating, operating, maintaining, repairing, renewing and insuring said works.

If at any time any other municipal corporation, or pursuant to said Act, any railway or distributing company, or any other corporations or person, applies to the Commission for a supply of power, the Commission shall notify the applicant and the involved Corporation or corporations in writing of a time and place to hear all representations that may be made as to the terms and conditions for such supply.

Without discrimination in favour of the applicants as to the price to be paid, for equal quantities of power, the Commission may supply power upon such terms and conditions as may, having regard to the risk and expense incurred, and paid, and to be paid by the Corporation, appear equitable to the Commission, and are approved by the Lieutenant-Governor in Council.

No such application shall be granted if the said works or any part thereof are not adequate for such supply, or if the supply of the Corporation will be thereby injuriously affected, and no power shall be supplied within the limits of a municipal corporation taking power from the Commission at the time of such application without the written consent of such corporation.

In determining the quantity of power supplied to a municipal corporation, the quantity supplied by the Commission within the limits of the Corporation to any applicant, other than a municipal corporation, shall be computed as part of the quantity supplied to such corporation, but such corporation shall not be liable for payment for any portion of the power supplied. No power shall be supplied by the municipal corporation to any railway or distributing company without the written consent of the Commission. Power shall not be sold for less than the cost, and there shall be no discrimination as regards price and quantity.

7. It is hereby declared that the Commission is to be a trustee of all property held by the Commission under this agreement for the Corporation or corporations supplied by the Commission, but the Commission shall be entitled to a lien upon the said property for all moneys expended by the Commission under this agreement and not repaid. At the expiration of this agreement the Commission shall determine and adjust the rights of the Corporation and any other (if any) supplied by the Commission, having regard to the amounts paid by them respectively under the terms of this agreement, and such other considerations as may appear equitable to the Commission and are approved by the Lieutenant-Governor in Council.

8. If differences arise between corporations to which the Commission is supplying power, the Commission may upon application fix a time and place and hear all representations that may be made by the parties and the Commission shall, in a summary manner, when possible, adjust such differences and such adjustment shall be final. The Commission shall have all the powers that may be conferred upon a commissioner appointed under the *Act respecting Enquiries concerning Public Matters*.

9. This agreement shall extend to, be binding upon, and enure to the benefit of the successors and assigns of the parties hereto.

In witness whereof the Commission and the Corporation have respectively affixed their corporate seals and the hands of their proper officers.

HYDRO-ELECTRIC POWER COMMISSION OF ONTARIO.

A. BECK, *Chairman.*
W. W. POPE, *Secretary.*

(Seal)

THE MUNICIPAL CORPORATION OF THE VILLAGE OF DUNDALK.

JOHN SINCLAIR, *Reeve.*
M. N. RINLEY, *Clerk.*

(Seal)

SCHEDULE " J."

This Indenture made in duplicate the   day of   , in the year of
our Lord

Between

The Hydro-Electric Power Commission of Ontario, hereinafter called the
" Commission," party of the first part;

and

The Municipal Corporation of the Village of Flesherton, hereinafter
called the " Corporation," party of the second part.

Whereas, pursuant to an Act to provide for the transmission of electrical
power to municipalities, known as *The Power Commission Act* and amendments thereto, the Corporation applied to the Commission for a supply of
power, and the Commission furnished the Corporation with estimates of the
total cost of such power, ready for distribution within the limits of the
Corporation (and the electors of the Corporation assented to the by-laws
authorizing the Corporation to enter into a contract with the Commission
for such power).

1. Now therefore this indenture witnesseth that in consideration of the
premises and of the agreement of the Corporation herein set forth, subject
to the provisions of the said Act and amendments thereto, the Commission
agrees with the Corporation:

(a) To reserve and deliver at the earliest possible date 75 h.p. or more
of electrical power to the Corporation.

(b) At the expiration of reasonable notice in writing which may be given
by the Corporation from time to time during the continuance of this agreement, to reserve and deliver to the Corporation additional electric power
when called for.

(c) To use at all times first-class, modern, standard commercial apparatus and plant, and to exercise all due skill and diligence so as to secure
satisfactory operation of the plant and apparatus of the Corporation..

(d) To deliver commercially continuous twenty-four hour power every
day in the year to the Corporation at the distribution bus bars in the Commission's sub-station within the Corporation's limits.

2. In consideration of the premises and of the agreements herein set
forth, the Corporation agrees with the Commission:—

(a) To use all diligence by every lawful means within its power to
prepare for the receipt and use of the power dealt with by this agreement
so as to be able to receive power when the Commission is ready to deliver
the same.

(b) To pay annually interest at rate payable by the Commission upon
the Corporation's proportionate part (based on the quantity of electrical
energy or power taken), of all moneys expended by the Commission on

capital account for the acquiring of properties and rights, the acquiring and construction of generating plants, transformer stations, transmission lines, distributing stations, and other works necessary for the delivery of said electrical energy or power to the Corporation under the terms of this contract.

Also to pay an annual sinking fund instalment of such amount as to form at the end of thirty years, with accrued interest, a sinking fund sufficient to repay the Corporation's proportionate part, based as aforesaid, of all moneys advanced by the Province of Ontario for the acquiring of properties and rights, the acquiring and construction of generating plants, transformer stations, transmission lines, distributing stations and other work necessary for the delivery of said electrical energy or power delivered to the Corporation under the terms of this contract. Also to pay the Corporation's proportionate part, based as aforesaid, of the cost of lost power and of the cost of operating, maintaining, repairing, renewing and insuring said generating plants, transformer stations, transmission lines, distributing stations and other necessary works. Subject to adjustment under Clause 6 of this agreement.

(c) The amounts payable under this contract shall be paid in twelve monthly instalments, in gold coin of the present standard of weight and fineness, at the offices of the Commission at Toronto. Bills shall be rendered by the Commission on or before the 5th day and paid by the Corporation on or before the 15th day of each month. If any bill remains unpaid for fifteen days the Commission may, in addition to all other remedies and without notice, discontinue the supply of power to the Corporation until said bill is paid. No such discontinuance shall relieve the Corporation from the performance of the covenants, provisoes and conditions herein contained. All payments in arrears shall bear interest at the legal rate.

(d) To take electric power exclusively from the Commission during the continuance of this agreement.

(e) To co-operate by all means in its power at all times with the Commission to increase the quantity of power required from the Commission, and in all other respects to carry out the objects of this agreement and of the said Act.

(f) To pay for three-fourths of the power ordered from time to time by the Corporation and held in reserve for it as herein provided whether it takes the same or not. When the highest average amount of power taken for any twenty consecutive minutes during any month shall exceed during the twenty consecutive minutes three-fourths of the amount ordered by the Corporation and held in reserve, then the Corporation shall pay for this greater amount during the entire month;

(g) If the Corporation during any month takes more than the amount of power ordered and held in reserve for it, as determined by an integrated peak, or the highest average, for a period of twenty consecutive minutes, the taking of such excess shall thereafter constitute an obligation on the part of the Corporation to pay for, and on the part of the Commission to hold in reserve, such increased quantity of power in accordance with the terms and conditions of this contract.

(h) When the power factor of the highest average amount of power taken for said twenty consecutive minutes falls below 90%, the Corporation shall pay for 90% of said power divided by the power factor.

(i) To use at all times first-class, modern, standard commercial appara-tus and plant, to be approved by the Commission.

(j) To exercise all due skill and diligence so as to secure satisfactory operation of the plant and apparatus of the Commission and of the Corpora-tion.

3. This agreement shall remain in force for thirty years from date of the first delivery of power under this contract.

4. The power shall be alternating, three phase, having a periodicity of approximately sixty cycles per second and shall be delivered as aforesaid at a voltage suitable for local distribution.

(a) That the meters with their series and potential transformers shall be connected at the point of delivery.

(b) The maintenance by the Commission of approximately the agreed voltage at approximately the agreed frequency at the sub-station in the limits of the Corporation shall constitute the supply of all power involved herein and the fulfilment of all operating obligations hereunder, and when voltage and frequency are so maintained, the amount of power, its fluctua-tions, load factor, power factor, distribution as to phases and all other electric characteristics and qualities, are under the sole control of the Cor-poration, their agents, customers, apparatus, appliances and circuits.

5. The engineers of the Commission, or one or more of them, or any other person or persons appointed for this purpose by the Commission, shall have the right from time to time during the continuance of this agreement to inspect the apparatus, plant and property of the Corporation and take records at all reasonable hours.

6. The Commission shall at least annually adjust and apportion the amount or amounts payable by the municipal corporation or corporations for such power and such interest, sinking fund, cost of lost power and cost of generating, operating, maintaining, repairing, renewing and insuring said works.

If at any time any other municipal corporation, or pursuant to said Act, any railway or distributing company, or any other corporations or person, applies to the Commission for a supply of power, the Commission shall notify the applicant and the involved corporation or corporations in writing, of a time and place to hear all representations that may be made as to the terms and conditions for such supply.

Without discrimination in favour of the applicants as to the price to be paid, for equal quantities of power, the Commission may supply power upon such terms and conditions as may, having regard to the risk and expense incurred, and paid, and to be paid by the Corporation, appear equitable to the Commission, and are approved by the Lieutenant-Governor in Council.

No such application shall be granted if the said works or any part thereof are not adequate for such supply, or if the supply of the Corporation will be thereby injuriously affected, and no power shall be supplied within the limits of a municipal corporation taking power from the Commission at the time of such application without the written consent of such Corporation.

In determining the quantity of power supplied to a municipal corporation, the quantity supplied by the Commission within the limits of the Corporation to any applicant other than a municipal corporation, shall be computed as part of the quantity supplied to such corporation, but such corporation shall not be liable for payment for any portion of the power so supplied. No power shall be supplied by the municipal corporation to any railway or distributing company without the written consent of the Commission. Power shall not be sold for less than the cost and there shall be no discrimination as regards price and quantity.

7. It is hereby declared that the Commission is to be a trustee of all property held by the Commission under this agreement for the corporation or corporations supplied by the Commission, but the Commission shall be entitled to a lien upon said property for all moneys expended by the Commission under this agreement and not repaid. At the expiration of this agreement the Commission shall determine and adjust the rights of the Corporation and any other (if any) supplied by the Commission, having regard to the amounts paid by them respectively under the terms of this agreement, and such other consideration as may appear equitable to the Commission and are approved by the Lieutenant-Governor in Council.

8. If differences arise between Corporations to which the Commission is supplying power, the Commission may upon application fix a time and place and hear all representations that may be made by the parties, and the Commission shall, in a summary manner, when possible, adjust such differences, and such adjustment shall be final. The Commission shall have all the powers that may be conferred upon a commissioner appointed under *The Act respecting Enquiries Concerning Public Matters.*

9. This agreement shall extend to, be binding upon, and enure to the benefit of the successors and assigns of the parties hereto.

In witness whereof the Commission and the Corporation have respectively affixed their corporate seals and the hands of their proper officers.

     HYDRO-ELECTRIC POWER COMMISSION OF ONTARIO.

                 A. BECK, *Chairman.*
                 W. W. POPE, *Secretary.*

   MUNICIPAL CORPORATION OF THE VILLAGE OF FLESHERTON.

                 D. McTAVISH, *Reeve.*
                 W. J. BELLAMY, *Village Clerk.*

SCHEDULE "K."

This Indenture made in duplicate the   day of
in the year of our Lord,

Between

The Hydro-Electric Power Commission of Ontario, hereinafter called the " Commission," party of the first part,

and

The Municipal Corporation of the Village of Shelburne, hereinafter called the " Corporation," party of the second part.

Whereas, pursuant to an Act to provide for the transmission of electrical power to municipalities known as the *Power Commission Act*, and amendments thereto, the Corporation applied to the Commission for a supply of power, and the Commission furnished the Corporation with estimates of the total cost of such power, ready for distribution within the limits of the Corporation (and the electors of the Corporation assented to the by-laws authorizing the Corporation to enter into a contract with the Commission for such power).

1. Now therefore this indenture witnesseth that in consideration of the premises and of the agreement of the Corporation herein set forth, subject to the provisions of the said Act and Amendments thereto, the Commission agrees with the Corporation:

(*a*) To reserve and deliver at the earliest possible date 300 h.p. or more of electrical power to the Corporation.

(*b*) At the expiration of reasonable notice in writing which may be given by the Corporation from time to time during the continuance of this agreement, to reserve and deliver to the Corporation additional electric power when called for.

(*c*) To use at all times first-class, modern, standard commercial apparatus and plant, and to exercise all due skill and diligence so as to secure satisfactory operation of the plant and apparatus of the Corporation.

(*d*) To deliver commercially continuous 24-hour power every day in the year to the Corporation at the distribution bus bars in the Commission's sub-station within the Corporation's limits.

2. In consideration of the premises and of the agreement herein set forth, the Corporation agrees with the Commission:

(*a*) To use all diligence by every lawful means in its power to prepare for the receipt and use of the power dealt with by this agreement, so as to be able to receive power when the Commission is ready to deliver same.

(*b*) To pay annually, interest at rate payable by the Commission upon the Corporation's proportionate part (based on the quantity of electrical energy or power taken) of all moneys expended by the Commission on capital account for the acquiring of properties and rights, the acquiring and construction of generating plants, transformer stations, transmission lines, distributing stations, and other works necessary for the delivery of said electrical energy or power to the Corporation under the terms of this contract. -

Also to pay an annual sinking fund instalment of such amount as to form at the end of 30 years, with accrued interest, a sinking fund sufficient to repay the Corporation's proportionate part, based, as aforesaid, on all moneys advanced by the Province of Ontario, for the acquiring of properties and rights, the acquiring and construction of generating plants, transformer stations, transmission lines, distributing stations and other work necessary for the delivery of said electrical energy or power, delivered to the Corporation under the terms of this contract. Also to pay the Corporation's proportionate part, based as aforesaid, of the cost of lost power, and the cost of operating, maintaining, repairing, renewing and insuring said generating plants, transformer stations, transmission lines, distributing stations and other necessary works. Subject to adjustment under Clause 6 of this agreement.

(c) The amounts payable under this contract shall be paid in twelve monthly payments, in gold coin of the present standard of weight and fineness, at the offices of the Commission at Toronto. Bills shall be rendered by the Commission on or before the 5th day and paid by the Corporation on or before the 15th day of each month. If any bill remains unpaid for fifteen days, the Commission may, in addition to all other remedies and without notice, discontinue the supply of power to the Corporation until said bill is paid. No such discontinuance shall relieve the Corporation from the performance of the covenants, provisoes and conditions herein contained. All payments in arrears shall bear interest at the legal rate.

(d) To take electric power exclusively from the Commission during the continuance of this agreement.

(e) To co-operate by all means in its power at all times with the Commission to increase the quantity of power required from the Commission, and in all other respects to carry out the objects of this agreement, and of the said Act.

(f) To pay for three-fourths of the power ordered from time to time by the Corporation and held in reserve for it as herein provided, whether it takes the same or not. When the highest average amount of power taken for any twenty consecutive minutes during any month shall exceed during the twenty consecutive minutes three-fourths of the amount ordered by the Corporation and held in reserve, then the Corporation shall pay for this greater amount during the entire month.

(g) If the Corporation during any month takes more than the amount of power ordered and held in reserve for it, as determined by an integrated peak, or highest average, for a period of twenty consecutive minutes, the taking of such excess shall thereafter constitute an obligation on the part of the Corporation to pay for, and on the part of the Commission to hold in reserve such increased quantity of power, in accordance with the terms and conditions of this contract.

(*h*) When the power factor of the highest average amount of power taken for said twenty consecutive minutes falls below 90 per cent., the Corporation shall pay for 90 per cent. of said power divided by the power factor.

(*i*) To use at all times first-class, modern, standard commercial apparatus and plant, to be approved by the Commission.

(*j*) To exercise all due skill and diligence, so as to secure satisfactory operation of the plant and apparatus of the Commission and of the Corporation.

3. This agreement shall remain in force for thirty years from date of the first delivery of power under this contract.

4. The power shall be alternating, three-phase, having a periodicity of approximately 60 cycles per second, and shall be delivered as aforesaid at a voltage suitable for local distribution.

(*a*) That the meters, with their series and potential transformers, shall be connected at the point of delivery.

(*b*) The maintenance by the Commission of approximately the agreed voltage at approximately the agreed frequency at the sub-station in the limits of the Corporation shall constitute the supply of all power involved herein and the fulfilment of all operating obligations hereunder, and when voltage and frequency are so maintained the amount of power, its fluctuations, load factor, power factor, distribution as to phases and all other electric characteristics and qualities, are under the sole control of the Corporation, their agents, customers, apparatus, appliances and circuits.

5. The engineers of the Commission, or one or more of them, or any other person or persons appointed for this purpose by the Commision, shall have the right from time to time during the continuance of this agreement to inspect the apparatus, plant and property of the Corporation, and take records at all reasonable hours.

6. The Commission shall at least annually adjust and apportion the amount or amounts payable by the Municipal Corporation or Corporations for such power and such interest, sinking fund, cost of lost power and cost of generating, operating, maintaining, repairing, renewing and insuring said works.

If at any time any other Municipal Corporation, or pursuant to said Act, any railway or distributing company, or any other Corporations or person, applies to the Commission for a supply of power, the Commission shall notify the applicant and the involved Corporation or Corporations in writing, of a time and place to hear all representations that may be made as to the terms and conditions for such supply.

Without discrimination in favour of the applicants as to the price to be paid, for equal quantities of power, the Commission may supply power upon such terms and conditions as may, having regard to the risk and expense incurred, and paid, and to be paid by the Corporation, appear equitable to the Commission, and are approved by the Lieutenant-Governor in Council.

No such application shall be granted if the said works or any part thereof are not adequate for such supply, or if the supply of the Corpora. tion will be thereby injuriously affected, and no power shall be supplied within the limits of a Municipal Corporation taking power from the Com. mission at the time of such application, without the written consent of such Corporation.

In determining the quantity of power supplied to a Municipal Corpora. tion, the quantity supplied by the Commission within the limits of the Corporation to any applicant, other than a Municipal Corporation, shall be computed as part of the quantity supplied to such Corporation, but such Corporation shall not be liable for payment for any portion of the power so supplied. No power shall be supplied by the Municipal Corporation to any railway or distributing company without the written consent of the Commission. Power shall not be sold for less than the cost and there shall be no discrimination as regards price and quantity.

7. It is hereby declared that the Commission is to be a trustee of all property held by the Commission under this agreement for the Corporation or Corporations supplied by the Commission, but the Commission shall be entitled to a lien upon said property for all moneys expended by the Commission under this agreement and not repaid. At the expiration of this agreement the Commission shall determine and adjust the rights of the Corporation and any other (if any), supplied by the Commission, having regard to the amounts paid by them respectively under the terms of this agreement, and such other considerations as may appear equitable to the Commission and are approved by the Lieutenant-Governor in Council.

8. If differences arise between Corporations to which Commission is supplying power, the Commission may, upon application, fix a time and place and hear all representations that may be made by the parties, and the Commission shall, in a summary manner, when possible, adjust such differences and such adjustment shall be final. The Commission shall have all the powers that may be conferred upon a Commissioner under the *Act respecting Enquiries concerning Public Matters.*

9. This agreement shall extend to, be binding upon, and enure to the benefit of the successors and assigns of the parties hereto.

In witness whereof the Commission and the Corporation have respectively affixed their corporate seals and the hands of their proper officers.

THE HYDRO-ELECTRIC POWER COMMISSION OF ONTARIO.

> A. BECK, *Chairman.*
> W. W. POPE, *Secretary.*

MUNICIPAL CORPORATION OF THE VILLAGE OF SHELBURNE.

> HUGH FALCONER, *Reeve.*

Witness:
THOS. WHALLEY, *Clerk.*

SCHEDULE "L."

This Indenture made (in duplicate) the twenty-sixth day of August, in the year of our Lord one thousand nine hundred and fifteen.

Between

    The Hydro-Electric Power Commission of Ontario, hereinafter called the " Commission," party of the first part;

        and

    The Municipal Corporation of the Village of Victoria Harbour, hereinafter called the " Corporation," party of the second part.

Whereas, pursuant to *An Act to provide for transmission of Electrical Power to Municipalities,* the Corporation applied to the Commission for a supply of power, and the electors of the Corporation assented to a by-law authorizing the Corporation to enter into a contract with the Commission for such power.

1. Now therefore this indenture witnesseth that in consideration of the premises and of the agreements of the Corporation herein set forth, subject to the provisions of said Act and of the said contract, the Commission agrees with the Corporation:

(a) To reserve and deliver at the earliest possible date 50 h.p. or more of electric power to the Corporation.

(b) At the expiration of thirty days' notice in writing which may be given by the Corporation from time to time, during the continuance of this agreement, to reserve and deliver to the Corporation additional electric power when called for in blocks of 25 h.p. each up to the limit of the capacity of the Big Chute's Power Development.

(c) To use at all times first-class, modern, standard commercial apparatus and plant, and to exercise all due skill and diligence, so as to secure satisfactory operation of the plant and apparatus of the Corporation.

(d) The power shall be delivered to the Corporation at approximately 2,200 volts and at approximately sixty cycles per second.

2. In consideration of the premises and of the agreements herein set forth, the Corporation agrees with the Commission:

(a) To use all diligence by every lawful means in its power to prepare for the receipt and use of the power dealt with by this agreement so as to be able to receive power when the Commission is ready to deliver same.

(b) Subject to the provisions of paragraph 2 (f) hereof, to pay the Commission sixteen dollars and fifty cents ($16.50) per h.p. per annum for all power taken by the Corporation at the interswitching structure located on the Commission's transmission lines at the Village of Waubaushene.

Nothing herein contained shall bind the Commission to supply power on the demand of the Corporation after the capacity of the Big Chute's plant has been reached, unless the Commission has power available or capable of development.

(c) To pay in addition annually, interest (at the same rate as paid by the Commission) upon the moneys expended by the Commission on capital account for the construction of transmission lines, the transformer station and equipment, and all other necessary works required for the delivery of power and transforming it from 22,000 to 2,200 volts.

Also to pay an annual part of the cost of the construction of said line, station and works so as to form in thirty years a sinking fund for the repayment of the moneys advanced by the Province of Ontario, in connection with this work.

Also to pay the Corporation's proportionate part of the cost of lost power, of operating, maintaining, repairing, renewing and insuring the said line, station and works.

(d) The amounts payable under this contract shall be paid in twelve monthly payments, in gold coin of the present standard of weight and fineness, at the office of the Commission at Toronto, and bills shall be rendered by the Commission on or before the 5th day and paid by the Corporation on or before the 15th day of each month. If any bill remains unpaid for fifteen days, the Commission may, in addition to all other remedies and without notice, discontinue the supply of power to the Corporation until said bill is paid. No such discontinuance shall relieve the Corporation from the performance of the covenants, provisoes and conditions herein contained. All payments in arrears shall bear interest at the legal rate.

(e) To take electric power exclusively from the Commission during the continuance of this agreement.

(f) To pay for three-fourths of the power ordered from time to time by the Corporation and held in reserve for it as herein provided, whether it takes the same or not. When the greatest average amount of power taken for any twenty consecutive minutes during any month shall exceed during the twenty consecutive minutes three-fourths of the amount ordered by the Corporation and held in reserve, then the Corporation shall pay for this greater amount during the entire month.

If the Corporation during any month takes more than the amount of power ordered and held in reserve for it for twenty consecutive minutes, the taking of such excess shall thereafter constitute an obligation on the part of the Corporation to pay for, and on the part of the Commission to hold in reserve an additional block of power in accordance with the terms and conditions of this contract.

When the power factor of the greatest amount of power taken for said twenty consecutive minutes falls below 90%, the Corporation shall pay for 90% of said power divided by the power factor.

(g) To use at all times first-class, modern, standard commercial apparatus and plant, approved by the Commission.

(h) To exercise all due skill and diligence so as to secure satisfactory operation of the plant and apparatus of the Commission and the Corporation.

3. This agreement shall remain in force until the date of expiration of the lease to the water rights on the Severn River of the Big Chute development, that is to say, until the tenth (10th) day of September in the year nineteen hundred and twenty-nine; providing the said lease is renewed by the Commission, then this agreement shall remain in force for thirty (30) years from the date of the first delivery of power thereunder.

4. The power shall be approximately 2,200 volts, 60 cycle, 3 phase, alternating commercially continuous twenty-four hour power every day in the year except as provided herewith, and shall be delivered by the Commission to the Corporation at the 2,200 volt terminals of the step-down transformers in the substation in the Corporation limits.

(a) That the meters with their series or potential transformers may be connected to the high tension side or low tension side of the transformers, or some connected to one side and some connected to the other, as the Commission may elect. That whenever connected at other than the point of measurement, their reading shall be subject to a correction and shall be corrected to give a reading such as would be obtained by instruments as if connected at the point of measurement. That such corrections shall be based upon tests made upon the step-down transformers and transmission lines by the Commission, or any other tests upon them acceptable to the Commission as to the efficiency, regulation, or any other constants of the transformers and transmission lines necessary for said correction, but that such tests, when made by the Commission, are to be made in the presence of the representatives or representative of the customer if it so desires.

(b) The maintenance by the Commission of approximately the agreed voltage at approximately the agreed frequency at the substation in the limits of the Corporation shall constitute the supply of all power involved herein and the fulfilment of all operating obligations hereunder; and when voltage and frequency are so maintained, the amount of the power, its fluctuations, load factor, power factor, distribution as to phases, and all other electric characteristics and qualities are under the sole control of the Corporation, their agents, customers, apparatus, appliances and circuits.

5. The engineers of the Commission, or one or more of them, or any other person or persons appointed for this purpose by the Commission, shall have the right from time to time during the continuance of this agreement to inspect the apparatus, plant and property of the Corporation and take records at all reasonable hours.

6. In case the Commission should at any time or times be prevented from supplying said power, or any part thereof, or in case the Corporation shall at any time be prevented from taking said power, or any part thereof, by strike, lock-out, fire, invasion, explosion, act of God, or the King's enemies, or any other cause reasonably beyond their control, then the Commission shall not be bound to deliver such power during such times, and the Corporation shall not be bound to pay the price of said power during such time, but as soon as the cause of such interruption is removed, the Commission shall without any delay supply said power as aforesaid, and the Corporation shall take the same and shall be prompt and diligent in removing and overcoming such cause or causes of interruption.

7. If at any time any other municipal corporation, or pursuant to said Act, any railway or distributing company, or any other corporation or person,

5 H

applies to the Commission for a supply of power, the Commission shall notify the applicant and the Corporation in writing, of a time and place, and hear all representations that may be made as to the terms and conditions for such supply.

Without discrimination in favour of the applicants as to the price to be paid, for equal quantity of power, the Commission may supply power upon such terms and conditions as may, having regard to the risk and expense incurred, and paid, and to be paid by the Corporation, appear equitable to the Commission, and are approved by the Lieutenant-Governor in Council.

No such application shall be granted if the said line is not adequate for such supply, or if the supply of the Corporation will be thereby injuriously affected, and no power shall be supplied within the limits of a municipal corporation taking power from the Commission at the time of such application without the written consent of such corporation.

In determining the quantity of power supplied to a municipal corporation, the quantity supplied by the Commission within the limits of the Corporation to any applicant other than a municipal corporation, shall be computed as part of the quantity supplied to such corporation, but such corporation shall not be liable to pay for the power so supplied, or otherwise in respect thereof. In order to prevent discrimination by the municipal corporation, no power shall be supplied by the municipal corporation to any railway or distributing company or person outside the corporation without the written consent of the Commission, but the Corporation may sell power to any person or persons or manufacturing companies inside the limits of the corporation, but such power shall not be sold for less than the cost and without discrimination as regards price and quantity.

8. If differences arise between corporations to whom the Commission is supplying power, the Commission may upon application fix a time and place to hear all representations that may be made by the parties, and the Commission shall, in a summary manner, when possible, adjust such differences, and such adjustment shall be final. The Commission shall have all the power that may be conferred upon a commissioner appointed under *The Act respecting Enquiries Concerning Public Matters.*

9. If differences arise between the Corporation and the Commission, the Lieutenant-Governor in Council may, upon application, fix a time and place to hear all representations that may be made by the parties, and the Lieutenant-Governor in Council shall, in a summary manner, when possible, adjust such differences, and such adjustment shall be final. The Lieutenant-Governor in Council shall have all the powers that may be conferred upon a commission appointed under *The Act respecting Enquiries Concerning Public Matters.*

10. This agreement shall extend to, be binding upon, and enure to the benefit of the successors and assigns of the parties hereto.

In witness whereof the Commission and the Corporation have respectively affixed their corporate seals and the hands of their proper officers.

HYDRO-ELECTRIC POWER COMMISSION OF ONTARIO.

A. BECK, *Chairman.*
W. W. POPE, *Secretary.*

THE MUNICIPAL CORPORATION OF THE VILLAGE OF VICTORIA HARBOUR.

JEROME DUCKWORTH, *Reeve.*
E. B. BROWNE, *Clerk.*

(Seal.)

SCHEDULE " M."

This indenture made this eleventh day of October, one thousand nine hundred and fifteen.

Between

The Hydro-Electric Power Commission of Ontario, hereinafter called the " Commission," party of the first part;

and

The Municipal Corporation of the Police Village of Holstein, hereinafter called the " Corporation," party of the second part.

Whereas the Corporation under the provisions of the *Power Commission Act* and amendments thereto, Revised Statutes of Ontario, Chapter 39 has applied to the Commission for a supply of power, and has passed a by-law No. 304, passed the 10th day of August, 1915, to authorize the execution of an agreement therefor.

Now therefore this indenture witnesseth that in consideration of the premises and of the agreement of the Corporation herein set forth, subject to the provisions of the said Act and amendments thereto, the parties hereto agree each with the other as follows:

1. The Commission agrees:

(*a*) To reserve and deliver at the earliest possible date fifty (50) h.p., or more, of electrical power to the Corporation.

(*b*) At the expiration of reasonable notice, in writing, which may be given by the Corporation from time to time during the continuance of this agreement, to reserve and deliver to the Corporation additional electric power when called for;

(*c*) To use at all times first-class modern, standard commercial apparatus and plant, and to exercise all due skill and diligence so as to secure satisfactory operation of the plant and apparatus of the Corporation.

(*d*) To deliver commercially continuous twenty-four (24) hour power every day in the year to the Corporation at the distribution bus bars in the Commission's sub-station within the Corporation's limits.

2. The Corporation agrees:

(*a*) To use all diligence by every lawful means in its power to prepare for the receipt and use of the power dealt with by this agreement so as to be able to receive power when the Commission is ready to deliver same.

(*b*) To pay annually in twelve (12) equal monthly instalments, interest upon its proportionate part (based on the quantity of electrical energy or power taken) of all moneys expended by the Commission on capital account for the acquiring of properties and rights, the acquiring and construction of generating plants, transformer stations, transmission lines, distributing stations, and other works necessary for the delivery of said electrical energy or power to the Corporation under the terms of this contract.

To pay an annual sum for its proportionate part of all moneys expended by the Commission on capital account for the acquiring of the said properties and rights, and the cost of the said construction, so as to form in thirty (30) years a sinking fund for the retirement of securities issued by the Province of Ontario.

Also to bear its proportionate part of the line loss, and pay its proportionate part of the cost to operate, maintain, repair, renew, and insure the said generating plants, transformer stations, transmission lines, distributing stations, and other necessary works.

All payments under this clause shall be subject to adjustment under paragraph 6.

(*c*) The amounts payable in accordance with clause 2 (*b*) shall be paid in gold coin of the present standard of weight and fineness, at the offices of the Commission at Toronto. Bills shall be rendered by the Commission on or before the 5th day, and paid by the Corporation on or before the 15th day of each month. If any bills remain unpaid for fifteen days, the Commission may, in addition to all other remedies, and without notice, discontinue the supply of power to the Corporation until said bill is paid. No such discontinuance shall relieve the Corporation from the performance of the covenants, provisoes and conditions herein contained. All payments in arrears shall bear interest at the legal rate.

(*d*) To take electrical power exclusively from the Commission during the continuance of this agreement.

(*e*) To pay for three-fourths of the power ordered from time to time by the Corporation, and held in reserve for it, as herein provided; whether it takes the same or not. When the highest average amount of power taken for any twenty (20) consecutive minutes during any month exceeds during the twenty consecutive minutes three-fourths of the amount ordered by the Corporation and held in reserve, then the Corporation shall pay for this greater amount during the entire month.

If the Corporation during any month takes more than the amount of power ordered and held in reserve for it, as determined by an integrated peak, or the highest average, for a period of twenty consecutive minutes, the taking of such excess shall thereafter constitute an obligation on the part of the Corporation to pay for, and on the part of the Commission to hold in reserve, such increased quantity of power in accordance with the terms and conditions of this contract.

When the power factor of the highest average amount of power taken for said twenty consecutive minutes falls below 90 per cent. the Corporation shall pay for 90 per cent. of said power divided by the power factor.

(*f*) To use at all times first-class, modern standard commercial apparatus and plant, to be approved by the Commission, and to exercise all due skill and diligence so as to secure satisfactory operation of the plant and apparatus of the Commission and of the Corporation.

(*g*) To co-operate by all means in its power at all times with the Commission to increase the quantity of power required from the Commission, and in all other respects to carry out the objects of this agreement, and of the said Act.

3. This agreement shall remain in force for thirty (30) years from the date of the first delivery of power under this contract.

4. The power shall be alternating, three-phase, having a periodicity of approximately 60 cycles per second, and shall be delivered as aforesaid at a voltage suitable for local distribution.

5. The engineers of the Commission, or one or more of them, or any other person or persons appointed for this purpose by the Commission, shall have the right from time to time during the continuance of this agreement to inspect the apparatus, plant, and property of the Corporation, and take records at all reasonable hours.

6. The Commission shall, at least annually, adjust and apportion the amount or amounts payable by the Municipal Corporation, or corporations, for such power and such interest, sinking fund, cost of lost power, and cost of generating, operating, maintaining, repairing, renewing, and insuring said works.

7. It is hereby declared that the Commission is to be a trustee of all property held by the Commission under this agreement for the Corporations and other municipal corporations supplied by the Commission, but the Commission shall be entitled to a lien upon said property for all moneys expended by the Commission under this agreement and not repaid. At the expiration of this agreement the Commission shall determine and adjust the rights of the Corporations and other municipal corporations, supplied by the Commission, having regard to the amounts paid by them, respectively, under the terms of this agreement, and such other considerations as may appear equitable to the Commission, and are approved by the Lieutenant-Governor in Council.

8. If at any time any other municipal corporation, or pursuant to said Act, any railway or distributing company, or any other corporation, or person, applies to the Commission for a supply of power, the Commission shall notify the applicant and the Corporation, in writing, of a time and place to hear all representations that may be made as to the terms and conditions for such supply.

Without discrimination in favour of the applicants as to the price to be paid for equal quantities of power, the Commission may supply power upon such terms and conditions as may, having regard to the risk and expense incurred and paid, and to be paid by the Corporation, appear equitable to the Commission, and are approved by the Lieutenant-Governor in Council.

No such application shall be granted if the said works, or any part thereof, are not adequate for such supply, or if the supply of the Corporation will be thereby injuriously affected, and no power shall be supplied within the limits of a municipal corporation taking power from the Commission at the time of such application without the written consent of such Corporation.

In determining the quantity of power supplied to a municipal corporation, the quantity supplied by the Commission within the limits of the Corporation to any applicant, other than a municipal corporation shall be computed as part of the quantity supplied to such corporation, but such corporation shall not be liable for payment for any portion of the power supplied. No power shall be supplied by the municipal corporation to any railway or distributing company without the written consent of the Commission, but the Corporation may sell power to any person or persons, or manufacturing companies within the limits of the Corporation, but such power shall not be sold for less than cost, neither shall there be any discrimination as regards price and quantity.

9. If differences arise between corporations to which the Commission is supplying power, the Commission may, upon application, fix a time and place and hear all representations that may be made by the parties, and the Commission shall, in a summary manner, when possible, adjust such differences, and such adjustment shall be final. The Commission shall have all the powers that may be conferred upon a commissioner appointed under the *Act respecting Enquiries concerning Public Matters.*

10. This agreement shall extend to, be binding upon, and enure to the benefit of the successors and assigns of the parties hereto.

In witness whereof the Commission and the Corporation have, respectively, affixed their corporate seals, and the hands of their proper officers.

HYDRO-ELECTRIC POWER COMMISSION OF ONTARIO.

A. BECK, *Chairman.*
W. W. POPE, *Secretary.*

(Seal.)

MUNICIPAL CORPORATION OF THE POLICE VILLAGE OF HOLSTEIN.

RICHARD IRWIN, *Chairman.*
R. M. TRIBE, *Inspecting Trustee.*
L. B. NICHOLSON, *Secretary.*

(Seal.)

"SCHEDULE "N."

This indenture made this first day of November, A.D. one thousand nine hundred and fourteen.

Between

The Hydro-Electric Power Commission of Ontario, acting herein on its own behalf and with the approval of the Lieutenant-Governor in Council (hereinafter called the Commission), party of the first part;

and

The Municipal Corporation of the Police Village of Williamsburg (hereinafter called the Corporation), party of the second part.

Whereas pursuant to *An Act to Provide for Transmission of Electrical Power to Municipalities,* and the amendments thereto, the Corporation applied to the Commission to transmit and supply such power, and the Commission has entered into contracts with a company or companies for the supply of such power at the prices set forth in the schedule, hereto attached, and the Commission has furnished the Corporation with estimates, as shown in the schedule of the total cost of such power, and the electors of the Corporation assented to by-laws authorizing the Corporation to enter into a contract with the Commission for such power, and the Commission have estimated the line loss and the cost to construct, operate, maintain, repair, renew and insure a line to transmit such power to the Corporation, and have apportioned the part of such cost to be paid by each Corporation as shown in said schedule.

Now therefore this indenture witnesseth that in consideration of the premises and of the agreements of the Corporation herein set forth, subject to the provisions of said Act and the amendments thereto, and of the said contracts subject to any variations thereof by the Corporation, the Commission agrees with the Corporation respectively:

1. (*a*) To construct a line to transmit the quantities of electric power, shown in column 2 of the said schedule, to the Corporation shown in column 1 respectively.

(*b*) On the 15th day of May, 1915, or on any earlier day on which the Commission shall be prepared to supply said power in quantities set forth in column 2 of said schedule, to the Corporation within the limits thereof, ready for distribution at approximately the number of volts set forth in column 4 of the said schedule, and approximately 60 cycles per second frequency.

(*c*) At the expiration of three months' written notice, which may be given by the Corporation from time to time during the continuance of this agreement, to supply from time to time to the Corporation in blocks of not less than 10 h.p. each, additional power until the total amount so supplied shall amount to 15,000 horse power, or such further amount as the Commission may be able and willing to supply.

(*d*) To use at all times first-class, modern, standard commercial apparatus and plant and to exercise all due skill and diligence so as to secure the most perfect operation of the plant and apparatus of the Corporation.

In consideration of the premises and of the agreements herein set forth each of the Corporations for itself, and not one for the other, agrees with the Commission:

2. (a) Subject to the provisions of paragraph 2 (g) hereof, to pay to the Commission for the quantities of power shown in column 2 of said schedule to be supplied as aforesaid from the date when the Commission notifies the Corporation that it is ready to supply such power, and for all additional power held in reserve upon any of the above mentioned notices from the respective dates thereof until the termination of this agreement, the price set forth in column 3 of said schedule in twelve monthly payments, in gold coin of the present standard of weight and fineness, and bills shall be rendered by the Commission on or before the fourth and paid by the Corporation on or before the fifteenth of each month. If any bill remains unpaid for fifteen days, the Commission may, in addition to all other remedies and without notice, discontinue the supply of such power to the Corporation in default until said bill is paid. No such discontinuance shall relieve the Corporation in default from the performance of the covenants, provisoes, and conditions herein contained. All payments in arrears shall bear interest at the legal rate.

(b) To take electric power exclusively from the Commission during the continuance of this agreement; provided, if the Commission is unable to supply the said power as quickly as required, the Corporation may obtain the supply otherwise until the Commission has provided such supply, thereupon the Corporation shall immediately take from the Commission; and the Corporation may generate, store or accumulate electric power for emergencies, or to keep down the peak load of the power taken from the Commission; and nothing herein contained shall affect existing contracts between the Corporation and other parties for a supply of electric power, but the Corporation shall determine said contracts at the earliest possible date.

(c) To pay, annually, interest at four per cent. per annum upon its proportionate part of the moneys expended by the Commission on capital account for the construction of the said line, transformer stations and other necessary works, shown, respectively, in column 6 of said schedule, subject to adjustment under paragraph 9.

(d) To pay an annual sum for its proportionate part of the cost of the construction of said line, stations, and works, shown, respectively, in column 6 of said schedule, subject to adjustment under paragraph 9, so as to form in thirty years a sinking fund for the retirement of the securities to be issued by the Province of Ontario.

(e) To bear its proportionate part of the line loss and pay its proportionate part of the cost to operate, maintain, repair, renew and insure the said lines, stations and work, shown, respectively, in column 7 of said schedule subject to adjustment under paragraph 9.

(f) To keep, observe and perform the covenants, provisoes and conditions set forth in said contracts, intended by the Commission and the company to be kept and observed and performed.

(g) To pay as a minimum for three-fourths of the power to be supplied at said date or of the power held in reserve upon any of the said notices, whether the said power is taken or not; and when the greatest amount of power taken for twenty consecutive minutes in any month shall exceed during such twenty minutes three-fourths of the amount to be supplied and held in reserve to pay for this greater amount during that entire month; the amount payable for a month being one-twelfth part of the annual rate applicable to the horse power in question. When the power factor of the greatest amount of power taken for said twenty minutes falls below 90 per cent., the Corporation shall pay for 90 per cent. of said power divided by the power factor.

(*h*) To take no more power than the amount to be supplied and held in reserve at said date and upon said notices, as per paragraph 1 (*c*).

(*i*) To use at all times first-class, modern, standard commercial apparatus and plant to be approved by the Commission.

(*j*) To exercise all due skill and diligence so as to secure the most perfect operation of the plant and apparatus of the Commission and the company.

3. If, as herein provided, the said contracts are continued until nineteen hundred and forty-two (1942), this agreement shall remain in force until that date.

4. (*a*) Said power shall be three-phase, alternating, commercial continuous twenty-four hour power every day of the year, except as provided in paragraph 6 hereof, and shall be measured by curve-drawing meters, subject to test as to accuracy by either party hereto.

(*b*) The maintenance by the Commission of approximately the agreed voltage at approximately the agreed frequency at the point of delivery to the Corporation shall constitute the supply and the holding in reserve of all power involved herein, and the fulfilment of all operating obligations hereunder; the amount of the power, its fluctuations, load factor, power factor, distribution as to phases, and all other electric characteristics and qualities being under the sole control of the Corporation, its agents, customers, apparatus, appliances and circuits.

5. The engineers of the Commission, or one or more of them, or any other person or persons appointed for this purpose by the Commission, shall have the right from time to time during the continuance of this agreement to inspect the apparatus, plant and property of the Corporation, and take records at all reasonable times on giving to the Corporation six hours' notice of the intention to make such inspection. The Corporation shall have a like right, on giving a like notice, to inspect the apparatus, plant and property of the Commission.

6. In case the Commission or the Company shall at any time or times be prevented from supplying said power, or any part thereof, or in case the Corporation shall at any time be prevented from taking said power, or any part thereof, by strike, lock-out, riot, fire, invasions, explosion, act of God, or the King's enemies, or any other cause reasonably beyond their control, then the Commission shall not be bound to deliver such power during such time, and the Corporation shall not be bound to pay the price of said power at the point of delivery by the Company during such time, but the Corporation shall continue to make all other payments, but as soon as

the cause of such interruption is removed the Commission shall without any delay supply said power as aforesaid, and the Corporation shall take the same, and each of the parties hereto shall be prompt and diligent in removing and overcoming such cause or causes of interruption.

7. If, and so often as, any interruption shall occur in the service of the Company, due to any cause or causes other than those provided for by the next preceding paragraph hereof, the Commission shall pay to the Corporation as liquidated and ascertained damages, and not by way of penalty, their respective proportionate shares of whatever sum is payable to the Commission by reason of such interruption; and when the amount thereof has been settled, such sum may be deducted from any moneys payable by the Corporation to the Commission, but such right of deduction shall not in any case delay the said monthly payments, nor shall the Commission be subject to any other liability for any non-delivery.

8. In case any municipal corporation, or any person, firm or corporation which shall contract with the Commission or with any municipal corporation for a supply of power furnished to the Commission by the Company shall suffer damages by the act or neglect of the Company, and such municipal corporation, person, firm or corporation would, if the Company had made the said contracts directly with them, have had a right to recover such damages or commence any proceedings or any other remedy, the Commission shall be entitled to commence any such proceedings or bring such action for or on behalf of such municipal corporation, person, firm or corporation, and notwithstanding any Statute, decision or rule of law to the contrary, the Commission shall be entitled to all the rights and remedies of such municipal corporation, person, firm or corporation, including the right to recover such damages, but no action shall be brought by the Commission until such municipal corporation, person, firm or corporation shall have agreed with the Commission to pay any costs that may be adjudged to be paid if such proceedings or action is unsuccessful. The rights and remedies of any such municipal corporation, person, firm or corporation shall not be hereby prejudiced.

9. The Commission shall at least annually adjust and apportion the amounts payable by municipal corporations for such power and such interest, sinking fund, line loss, and cost of operating, maintaining, repairing, renewing and insuring the line and works.

10. (a) If at any time, any other municipal corporation, or, pursuant to said Act, any railway or distributing company or any other corporation or person, applies to the Commission for a supply of power, the Commission shall notify the applicant and the corporation, party hereto, in writing, of a time and place, and hear all representations that may be made as to the terms and conditions for such supply.

(b) Without discrimination in favour of the applicants as to the price to be paid, for equal quantities of power, the Commission may supply power upon such terms and conditions as may, having regard to the risk and expense incurred, and paid, and to be paid by the Corporation, party hereto, appear equitable to the Commission, and are approved by the Lieutenant-Governor in Council.

(c) No such application shall be granted if the said line is not adequate for such supply, or if the supply of the Corporation, party hereto, will be thereby injuriously affected, and no power shall be supplied within the limits of a municipal corporation taking power from the Commission at the time of such application, without the written consent of such corporation.

(d) In determining the quantity of power supplied to a municipal corporation, the quantity supplied by the Commission within the limits of the Corporation to any applicant, other than a municipal corporation, shall be computed as part of the quantity supplied to such corporation, but such corporation shall not be liable to pay for the power so supplied, by any municipal corporation, to any railway or distributing company, without the written consent of the Commission.

11. It is hereby declared that the Commission is to be a trustée of all property held by the Commission under this agreement, for the Corporation and other municipal corporations supplied by the Commission, but the Commission shall be entitled to a lien upon said property for all moneys expended by the Commission under this agreement and not repaid. At the expiration of this agreement, the Commission shall determine and adjust the rights of the Corporation and other municipal corporations, supplied by the Commission, having regard to the amounts paid by them, respectively, under the terms of this agreement, and such other considerations as may appear equitable to the Commission and are approved by the Lieutenant-Governor in Council.

12. Each of the Corporations agree with the other:

(a) To take electric power exclusively from the Commission during the continuance of this agreement, subject to the provisoes above set forth in paragraph 2 (b).

(b) To co-operate, by all means in its power, at all times with the Commission, to increase the quantity of power required from the Commission, and in all other respects to carry out the objects of this agreement and of the said Act.

13. If differences arise between the Corporations, the Commission may, upon application, fix a time and place to hear all representations that may be made by the parties, and the Commission shall, in a summary manner, when possible, adjust such differences, and such adjustments shall be final. The Commission shall have all the powers that may be conferred upon a commissioner appointed under the *Act respecting Enquiries concerning Public Matters.*

14. This agreement shall extend to, be binding upon, and enure to the benefit of the successors and assigns of the parties hereto.

In witness whereof the Commission and the Corporation have respectively affixed their corporate seals and the hands of their proper officers.

THE HYDRO-ELECTRIC POWER COMMISSION OF ONTARIO.

> A. BECK, *Chairman.*
> W. W. POPE, *Secretary.*

POLICE VILLAGE OF WILLIAMSBURG.

> OBLIN BECKER, *Secretary.*
> P. E. BECKSTEAD, *Chairman.*
> E. C. MERKLEY, *Inspecting Trustee.*

SCHEDULE

Column 1	2	3	4	5	6	7
Name of Municipal Corporation ...ity of Power applied for in H.P.	Cost of Power at point of ...ery to Commission.	M. of Volts.	Estimate maximum cost of power ...ly for distribution in ...ly.	Estimate proportionate part of cost to construct trans. line, transformer station and works for nominally ...........H.P., with total capacity of	Estimate proportionate part of line loss and of part cost of to operate, maintain, ..., renew and insure transmission line, trans...er station ...ks for ...ly for ...ly of ..........H.P., with a .............H.P.	
Brockville	1,000 360 H.P.	Then for all taken up to 10,000 H.P. or over, $...0 per H.P.	13,200	$24 04	$76,950 00	$7,077 00
Prescott..........	H.P.		13,200	24 54	30,594 00	1,838 00
Chesterville.......	H.P.		4,400	35 00	10,224 00	487 00
Winchester	1 H.P.		4,400	24 00	7,280 00	638 00
Williamsburg	: H.P.		4,000	34 66	3,522 00	272 00
				(without Sinking Fund)		

$14.00 for not less than 2,000 H.P.
Then for all power taken up to 1,000 H.P., $13.40 per H.P.
Then for all power taken up to 6,000 H.P., $12.50 per H.P.
Then for all power taken up to 8,000 H.P., $12.00 per H.P.
Then for all power taken up to 10,000 H.P., $11.50 per H.P.

The Legislature also passed the Act set out hereafter with reference to the "Public Development of Water Power at Niagara Falls."

An Act respecting the Public Development of Water Power in the vicinity of Niagara Falls.

Assented to 27th April, 1916.

WHEREAS the demand for the supply of electrical power or energy Preamble. in the district which may be served by power from the vicinity of Niagara Falls has so greatly increased that in order to obtain an adequate supply to meet the present and future demands of the municipalities interested or that may be interested, it is necessary that new sources of power should be developed; and whereas the existing development works at Niagara Falls are inadequate for the development and supply of the required amount of power, the quantity of power now generated by them and available for use in Canada being exhausted; and whereas it is desirable that the work of development should be carried on upon an adequate scale in order to utilize to the fullest possible extent the available supply of water which may be diverted from the Niagara River under the terms of the treaty between the United States of America and His Majesty, the King; and whereas the Hydro-Electric Power Commission of Ontario, after investigation by its engineers, has reported to the Government upon a scheme for the development of a supply of power from the Niagara River and its tributaries, and has prepared estimates of the cost thereof; and whereas there has been a general demand upon the part of the inhabitants of the said municipalities that the Government of Ontario should develop, through the Commission, power sufficient to meet the present and future requirements of the municipalities which it is possible to serve from the neighborhood of Niagara Falls, and that in the meantime the Commission should procure on the best terms available such additional power as may be necessary to supply the requirements of the municipalities and furnish the same to the municipalities at the average cost of all the power supplied to the municipalities under Contract with the Commission; and whereas it is desirable that the said work of development should be undertaken and carried out as economically, efficiently, and expeditiously as possible, taking into consideration the financial and other conditions arising out of the present war, and to this end that it should be conducted by the Commission, and under the authority and direction of the Government of Ontario, acting for and on behalf of the municipalities which may be supplied with power from such development;

Therefore His Majesty, by and with the advice and consent of the Legislative Assembly of the Province of Ontario enacts as follows:—

1. This Act may be cited as *The Ontario Niagara Development Act.* Short title.

2. In this Act—   Interpretation.

(a) " Commission " shall mean Hydro-Electric Power Commission "Commission." of Ontario;

"Government."

(b) "Government" shall mean Lieutenant-Governor in Council acting for and on behalf of the Province of Ontario;

Powers which the Crown may confer upon the Commission.
Entering on and laying out land.

3. The Government may authorize the Commission to—

(a) Enter upon, survey and lay out, all such lands, water, water privileges and water powers as may be required for the construction of the works hereinafter mentioned;

Acquiring options and making contracts for purchase of lands.

(b) Acquire options upon and enter into preliminary contracts for the purchase of land for sites, right-of-way, the location of buildings, plant, works, machinery and appliances required for the works herinafter mentioned;

Constructing works, etc.

(c) Construct, erect, maintain and operate works for the purpose of diverting the waters of the Niagara River, Welland River, and tributary waters, or any of them, and conveying the same by aqueduct, conduit or canal, or in any other manner, from any point on the Welland River, or on the Niagara River, above the Cataract, and discharging such waters into the Niagara River;

Development works.

(d) Construct, erect, maintain and operate at or in the vicinity of such place of discharge, works, plant, machinery and appliances for the use of the waters so taken and diverted in the development of a water power for the production of electrical or pneumatic power or energy;

General powers.

Rev. Stat. c. 39.

(e) For such purposes, exercise all powers and enforce all rights which may be exercised and enforced by the Commission when taking land or other property in the exercise of powers conferred by or under *The Power Commission Act*.

Cost to be defrayed out of appropriation.

4.—(1) The cost of the construction and maintenance of the works authorized by this Act shall be defrayed out of such money as may, from time to time, be appropriated by the Legislature for that purpose, and the works which may be authorized under section 3 shall be carried out and constructed as far as possible in such a manner that an appropriation made in any one fiscal year shall not be exceeded by the cost of the work to be carried out in that year.

Payments to Commission.

(2) The Government may direct the Treasurer of Ontario from time to time to pay over to the Commission out of such sums, any sums which may be required to defray the cost of the works carried on by the Commission under this Act, and all such sums shall be duly accounted for as hereinafter provided.

Special account to be opened.

5.—(1) Upon receiving the authority provided for by section 4, the Commission shall open an account to be styled "The Niagara Power Development Works Account," and such account shall contain an accurate and detailed statement:—

(*a*) Of all sums received by the Commission from the Government, for the purposes of the works hereby authorized; and

(*b*) An accurate and detailed statement of the cost of the work, including the services of the engineers, surveyors, and other officers of the Commission, and such proportion of the expenses of the administration of the Commission as may be fixed by Order-in-Council as fairly chargeable to the works undertaken and operated under the provisions of this Act.

(2) The Government may appoint an auditor whose duty it shall Auditors. be, by himself or his deputy, to examine, check and audit all accounts chargeable against the account mentioned in subsection 1, and certify them before payment thereof, and the auditor, or his deputy, shall countersign all cheques issued against the said account.

(3) The account shall be examined and audited at least once in and Annual audit. for every fiscal year by a chartered accountant nominated by the Government, who shall make his report to the Government thereon.

(4) The Government shall cause a full and detailed statement of the Annual statement to operations carried on under the authority of this Act, and of all the Assembly. receipts and expenditures on account thereof, during the last preceding fiscal year, together with the report mentioned in subsection 3, to be laid before the Assembly within fifteen days after the opening of each session.

   6.—(1) Until an adequate supply of power from the works author- Provisional ized by this Act can be developed and transmitted to the municipalities. ments for the Commission, with the approval of the Government, may procure supply. upon the best terms available a supply of such additional power as may be necessary to meet the requirements of the municipalities over and above the 100,000 h.p. supplied under the terms of the contract heretofore entered into between the municipalities and the Commission, and such additional power shall be furnished to the municipalities at the average cost of all the power supplied to the municipalities under contract with the Commission for the supply of power from Niagara Falls and the vicinity.

(2) The additional cost to the municipalities of the power procured Additional cost—ad- under the authority of section 1, shall be included in the price per h.p. justment of. payable by a municipal corporation under the terms of the contract entered into with the Commission, and shall be annually adjusted and apportioned by the Commission as provided by *The Power Commission* Rev. Stat. *Act.* c. 39.

   7. The exercise of the powers, which may be conferred by or under Extent of the authority of this Act, or of any of them, shall not be deemed to be a operation of Act. making use of the waters of the Niagara River to generate electric or pneumatic power within the meaning of any stipulation or condition contained in any agreement entered into by the Commissioners for the Queen Victoria Niagara Falls Park.

An Act was also passed to regulate the use of the waters of the Province of Ontario for power development purposes.

An Act to regulate the use of the Waters of the Province of Ontario for Power Development Purposes.

Assented to 27th April, 1916.

H IS MAJESTY, by and with the advice and consent of the Legislative Assembly of the Province of Ontario, enacts as follows:—

Short title.   **1.** This Act may be cited as *The Water Powers Regulation Act, 1916.*

Interpretation.   **2.** In this Act,

"Power."   (*a*) " Power " shall mean and include hydraulic, electrical, or pneumatic power or energy;

"Owner of a water power."   (*b*) " Owner of a water power " shall mean and include every municipal corporation, company, firm or individual being or claiming to be the owner, lessee, licensee, occupant, tenant, or assignee of a right to use any of the waters of Ontario for the purpose of generating hydraulic, electrical, or pneumatic power or energy under any grant, lease or license from the Crown, or any person, or under contract with, or franchise from any public body representing the Crown or the Province of Ontario or under the general law or any special Act of this Legislature or otherwise; '

"Inspector."   (*c*) " Inspector " shall mean a commission, public body, or person designated by the Lieutenant-Governor in Council to act as Inspector under this Act, and shall include the officers, agents and servants of the Inspector employed and acting under the authority and direction of such Inspector;

"Works."   (*d*) " Works " shall mean and include every dam, wing dam, forebay, gate, rack, canal, conduit, pipe, aqueduct, penstock, tunnel, and every other work which has been or may be constructed or used for or in connection with the control or diversion of water and the conveying of it to a power house or other place at which power may be generated; and all buildings, structures, plant, machinery, appliances and other works and things now or hereafter used for or appurtenant to the production and generation of power;

"Regulations."   (*e*) " Regulations " shall mean regulations made by the Lieutenant-Governor in Council under the authority of this Act.

Duty of owner as to use of water.   **3.** It shall be the duty of every owner of a water power to ensure as far as possible the economical and efficient use of the water used by him.

4. The Lieutenant-Governor in Council may appoint an Inspector or Inspectors who may, in addition to the powers hereinafter mentioned when required by the Lieutenant-Governor in Council so to do, Appointment of Inspector.

(a) At all reasonable times enter upon any works, and examine and inspect the same; Inspection.

(b) Take such measurements and tests as may be necessary from time to time in order to determine or to fix, as the case may be, in respect of the owner of any water power: Measurements and tests.

   (i) The quantity of water used, permitted to be used or available for use;

   (ii) Operating head and head losses;

   (iii) Electrical and hydraulic efficiency of main or auxiliary machinery or of any other portion of the works, or of the works as a whole;

   (iv) The amount of power developed, permitted to be developed, or available for development;

   (v) Fix in terms of cubic feet per second the amount of water necessary to use in order to develop or generate any amount of horse-power or to exercise any water rights for any purpose;

(c) Require the production of books, records, charts, readings, maps, plans, load curves and all other documents and records pertaining to the matters to be investigated, enquired into or determined under the provisions of this Act; Production of records, etc.

(d) If it appears to him that the water permitted to be used is not being utilized with a proper degree of efficiency or economy, or that the works or any part of the works are so constructed, or are of such a type, or have so depreciated that the water cannot be used with a proper degree of efficiency or economy, after giving the interested parties a reasonable opportunity to be heard, order the water to be used, or the machinery or the works or any part of them, to be replaced or removed, altered, or reconstructed as the case may be, in such manner or to such an extent as may be necessary to secure the proper degree of efficient and economical use of the water; and Ordering alterations in works, etc.

(e) If any order so made is not carried out within a reasonable time, enter upon the works and, at the expense of the owner of a water power, shut off or reduce the supply of water or close the works or any part thereof in such a manner as to prevent further use until such order has been obeyed. Shutting off water or closing works.

6 H

Appeal to
Lieutenant-
Governor
in Council.

5.—(1) Where an order made by the Inspector calls for alterations, repairs or improvements in the works there may be an appeal from the order of the Inspector to the Lieutenant-Governor in Council, and the Lieutenant-Governor in Council may make such order in the premises as may be deemed meet, which order shall be final.

Reference
to deter-
mine com-
pensation
where owner
not com-
mercially
benefited
by altera-
tions, etc.

(2) Upon such appeal, if the Lieutenant-Governor in Council is of the opinion that the additions, alterations or improvements required to be made in the works will be of material public advantage, by reason of the more efficient or economical use of the water, and that the owner of the water power will not presently receive a corresponding commercial advantage from such alterations or improvements, the Lieutenant-Governor in Council may direct a reference to determine what compensation, if any, should be made to the owner of the water power by reason of his being compelled to make such additions, alterations or improvements; and upon such reference all the circumstances shall be taken into account and if the referee is of opinion that the owner is entitled to compensation the referee may fix the amount thereof at such sum as he may deem just and reasonable, and upon the owner carrying out the order of the Inspector or of the Lieutenant-Governor in Council, the amount so awarded shall be payable to the owner in the same manner as a judgment recovered against the Crown in any court in Ontario.

Duty of
owner as to
inspection.

6. It shall be the duty of the owner of a water power, subject to the right of appeal hereinbefore given, to obey at all times the orders of the Inspector and to afford every facility for carrying out this Act and the regulations, and every owner of a water power who neglects or refuses to carry out any such order, or who obstructs or hinders or delays the Inspector or refuses to furnish him with such information and records

Penalty.

as he may require, shall incur a penalty of not less than $300 nor more than $2,000, and each and every day on which such offence is committed or continued shall be deemed to create a separate offence.

Fixing
quantity of
water to
be taken
in exercise
of rights.

7. Where any lease, license, Order-in-Council or other instrument or any general or special statutory provision confers or purports to confer the right to develop or generate power measured expressly or impliedly in horsepower, or where any such instrument or provision confers or purports to confer a right of division or use of water defined wholly or in part by the character, location or dimensions of works, the Inspector may fix in terms of cubic feet per second the amount of water which it is necessary to use in order to develop or generate such power or to exercise such right, having regard to the location of the works and to all the circumstances of the case, and to the degree of efficiency which the owner of the water power should be required to maintain in the premises.　　　　—

Submission
and
approval
of plans.

8. Every owner of a water power, before proceeding with the construction of any works or any alteration or extension of existing works or with the purchase or installation of new works, shall submit to an Inspector plans and specifications showing the details of the proposed construction, alteration or extension or of the new works proposed to be purchased or installed, and he shall not proceed therewith or let contracts therefor until such plans and specifications have been approved by the Inspector.

9.—(1) Where the rights of the owner of a water power to use water Limitation and defini-for the purpose of generating power do not appear to be expressly or tion of rights by impliedly limited by any stipulation as to the quantity of water to be Lieutenant-used or as to the amount of horsepower which may be generated or Governor in Council. otherwise, and the Lieutenant-Governor in Council deems it desirable in the public interest that such rights should be specifically limited and defined, he may direct the Inspector to enquire and report as to (1) the amount of power which the owner of a water power is authorized to generate under any contract, lease, license or other instrument, or under any general or special Act of this Legislature or otherwise, and (2) as to the quantity of water which it is necessary, having due regard to efficiency and economy in development, to use for the purpose of generating such amount of power, and upon such report the Lieutenant-Governor in Council may fix and determine, in horsepower, the amount of power which the owner shall generate and in terms of cubic feet per second the amount of water which it is necessary to use in order to develop or generate such power.

(2) If the owner is dissatisfied with the construction so placed upon Reference to ascertain his rights, or with such limitation and definition, the Lieutenant-Gov- rights ernor in Council may, upon the application of the owner, direct a refer- affected. ence to ascertain what rights, if any, have been restricted or impaired by such limitation and definition, and if it is found that such rights exist, and that they are so restricted or impaired, to ascertain the compensation that should be paid to such owner for such restriction or impairment.

(3) The amount of the compensation awarded to the owner upon Payment of com-such reference shall be paid to him in the same manner as the amount pensation. of a judgment recovered against the Crown.

10.—(1) Where the Lieutenant-Governor in Council deems that the Limitation of rights public interest requires that any rights heretofore conferred upon the of owner owner of a water power should be restricted or limited in any particular, by Order-in-Council. he may by Order-in-Council limit, define or restrict such rights to the construction, operation and use of such works only as may be deemed expedient in the public interest.

(2) If the owner deems himself aggrieved by any such limitation, Reference definition or restriction, the Lieutenant-Governor in Council may direct to deter-mine com-a reference to determine what compensation, if any, should be paid to pensation. the owner, and the referee shall have the like powers and shall proceed in the same manner, and the amount awarded shall be payable in the same way as in the case of a reference under section 9.

Matters to
be con-
sidered on
reference.

11.—(1) Upon any reference under this Act, the referee shall take into consideration

> (a) The conditions under which any rights to generate or develop power were originally obtained;
>
> (b) The consideration paid or agreed to therefor;
>
> (c) The capital invested in any works by the owner of a water power;
>
> (d) The circumstances which render any limitation or restriction of such rights necessary and desirable in the public interest.

Powers of
Commis-
sioner

Rev. Stat.
c. 18.

(2) The referee, upon any inquiry under this Act directed by the Lieutenant-Governor in Council, shall have all the powers which may be conferred upon a commissioner under *The Public Inquiries Act.*

Regula-
tions by
Lieutenant-
Governor
in Council.

Rev. Stat.
c. 18.

12. The Lieutenant-Governor in Council may make regulations respecting

> (a) The procedure to be followed by the Inspector and for conferring upon him the powers of a commissioner under *The Public Inquiries Act;*
>
> (b) The form and term of notices to be given by the Inspector and the enforcement of his orders;
>
> (c) The appointment of officers, servants and agents by the Inspector and their duties and powers;
>
> (d) The procedure to be followed upon any appeal from an order of the Inspector;
>
> (e) Any returns to be made by the owner of a water power and the particulars to be stated in such returns;
>
> (f). The better carrying out of the provisions of this Act in general.

And the following Act was also passed by the Legislature of the Province of Ontario, during the Session of 1916, being "An Act to Amend *The Hydro-Electric Railway Act*, and to Confirm Certain By-laws and Contracts," as set out therein.

An Act to amend *The Hydro-Electric Railway Act* and to confirm certain By-laws and Contracts.

Assented to 27th April, 1916.

HIS MAJESTY, by and with the advice and consent of the Legislative Assembly of the Province of Ontario, enacts as follows:—

1. This Act may be cited as *The Hydro-Electric Railway Act, 1916.* Short title.

2. Subsections 4 and 5 of section 4 of *The Hydro-Electric Railway Act, 1914,* are repealed and the following substituted therefor:— 4 Geo. V., c. 31, s. 4, subs. 4, 5, repealed.

(4) The agreement shall not be submitted to the electors nor shall any by-law for that purpose be proceeded with by the council of the corporation until the terms of the agreement have been submitted to and have received the sanction of the Lieutenant-Governor in Council. By-law and agreement to be first approved by Lieutenant-Governor in Council.

(5) After such sanction shall have been obtained the council of the municipal corporation, or of each of the municipal corporations interested, may submit to the vote of the municipal electors authorized to vote on money by-laws, a by-law approving of the agreement and directing its execution, and if a majority of such electors vote in favour of the by-law, the council shall pass the same and the agreement shall be executed as directed by the by-law. Submission of by-law

(a) The by-law shall not be voted upon by the electors until at least three months have expired since the date of the sanctioning of the agreement by the Lieutenant-Governor in Council nor until the by-law and agreement have been published in the manner provided by *The Municipal Act* in the case of money by-laws, at least once a week for four successive weeks. Rev. Stat. c. 192.

3. Subsection 6 of section 4 of *The Hydro-Electric Railway Act, 1914,* as enacted by section 3 of *The Hydro-Electric Railway Act, 1915,* is repealed, and the following substituted therefore:— 4 Geo. V., c. 31, s. 4, subs. 6, amended. 5 Geo. V., c. 32,

6. The agreement may include in its terms the purchase or leasing or obtaining running rights over any steam railway, electrical railway, or street railway or any part thereof, as part of the line of railway to be constructed and operated by the Commission. Acquiring running rights, etc.

Municipal
corporation
not to sell,
etc., any
railway
without
assent of
electors.

4. Notwithstanding anything contained in any general or special Act heretofore passed by this Legislature, a municipal corporation shall not sell or otherwise dispose of any steam railway, electrical railway or street railway owned by it or of which it has acquired control by foreclosure or other proceedings or under the provisions of any special Act, unless and until a by-law authorizing such sale or other disposal has been submitted to and has received the assent of the municipal electors qualified to vote on money by-laws according to the provisions of *The Municipal Act.*

Rev. Stat.
c. 192.

By-law
approved.

5.—(1) The by-law, the form of which is set out in Schedule "A" to this Act, and which has been heretofore submitted to the vote of the municipal electors of the municipalities named in Schedule "B" to the said by-law is declared to have been so submitted in due compliance with the provisions of *The Hydro-Electric Railway Act, 1914,* and when finally passed by the council of any of the municipalities named in the contract appended to the by-law shall be legal, valid and binding upon the corporation and the ratepayers thereof, anything in any general or special Act of this Legislature to the contrary notwithstanding.

4 Geo. V.,
c. 31.

Council to
pass by-law
when
assented to.

(2) It shall be the duty of the council of every municipality in which such by-law has been approved, or shall hereafter be approved by the electors, to finally pass the by-law and give effect to the same.

By-laws
heretofore
passed con-
firmed.

(3) The by-laws enumerated in Schedule "B" to this Act are confirmed and declared to be legal, valid and binding upon the respective corporations named in Schedule "B" and the ratepayers thereof, anything in any general or special Act relating to such corporation to the contrary notwithstanding.

Agreement
confirmed.

6. Subject to the provisions hereinafter contained, the contract set out in Schedule "A" to this Act, and purporting to be made between the Hydro-Electric Power Commission of Ontario, of the first part, and certain municipal corporations shall be deemed to have been made in pursuance of *The Hydro-Electric Railway Act, 1914,* and to comply with the provisions thereof, and the said contract shall be legal, valid and binding upon the Commission and upon every municipal corporation a party thereto and executing the same, anything in the said Act or in any other general or special Act of this Legislature to the contrary notwithstanding.

Execution
of agree-
ment.

7. It shall be the duty of the head and the clerk or treasurer of each of the said municipal corporations to sign the said contract and affix the seal of the corporation thereto within three weeks after the passing of the by-law approving of the same, whether the same shall have been so submitted before or after the passing of this Act.

8. Notwithstanding anything in *The Municipal Act* contained, debentures issued or purporting to be issued by a municipal corporation under the authority of *The Hydro-Electric Railway Act, 1914,* for the purpose of carrying out any contract entered into with the Commission under the authority of the said Act shall not be included in ascertaining the limit of the borrowing powers of the Corporation as prescribed by *The Municipal Act.* *Debentures issued under 4 Geo. V., c. 31, not to be included in municipal debt for certain purposes.*

9. Notwithstanding anything in this Act, or in *The Hydro-Electric Railway Act, 1914,* or the amendments thereto:— *4 Geo. V., c. 31, when work under contract may be proceeded with.*

    (*a*) No bonds shall be issued for, nor shall any work be undertaken, or expense incurred upon the railways provided for in the contract mentioned in Section 6, until after the close of the present war; and

    (*b*) No such bonds shall be issued, or work undertaken, or expense incurred thereafter, except at such times and to such amount or extent, and within such periods as may be authorized from from time to time by the Lieutenant-Governor in Council;

but the Lieutenant-Governor in Council may, at any time after the passing of this Act, authorize the Commission to enter into agreements for the purchase of the right-of-way for any part of such railways, or for the procuring of options therefor.

SCHEDULE "A."

MUNICIPALITY OF THE   OF   BY-LAW No.

A By-law to authorize a certain agreement made between The Hydro-Electric Power Commission of Ontario and the Municipal Corporation of
the   of   , and other municipal corporations,
for the construction, equipment and operation of an Electric Railway
under *The Hydro-Electric Railway Act, 1914*, and amendments thereto.

Whereas it is expedient that the Corporation of the
of   , and other municipal corporations should enter into an
agreement under *The Hydro-Electric Railway Act, 1914*, and amendments
thereto, with the Hydro-Electric Power Commission of Ontario, hereinafter
called the Commission, for the construction, equipment and operation of an
electric railway in and through the Municipality of the
of   , and certain other municipalities, upon the terms and
conditions and subject to the provisions set forth and contained in the
agreement set out in this by-law, and according to the routes set forth in
Schedule "A" to the said agreement;

And whereas the estimated cost of the work under the said agreement
is $13,734,155; and whereas the portion of the cost of the construction and
equipment of the line to be borne by the Corporation of the Municipality
of the   of   is estimated at $, as set out
in Schedule "B" to the said agreement, subject to adjustments and apportionment between the Corporations by the Commission from time to time,
as provided by the said agreement;

And whereas the total amount estimated to be required for the maintenance of the railway, apart from operating expenses, is $214,583 (the
operating revenue being estimated at $1,692,175, and operation and main-
tenance at $817,025);

And whereas the total annual amount estimated to be required, for the
period of ten years immediately following the date of the issue of the
bonds to be issued under the said agreement, for interest on the said bonds,
is $686,708; and thereafter, for the next ensuing forty years, the annual
amount estimated to be required for sinking fund charges for the retirement of the said bonds is $137,342, and for interest on the said bonds
$686,708;

And whereas the portion to be borne by the Municipality of the
            of   of the said annual amounts estimated to be
required for maintenance, sinking fund charges and interest is estimated at
$ for the first ten years, as aforesaid, and thereafter at $
on the same basis as the portion of the cost of construction and equipment,
as aforesaid, subject to adjustments and apportionment between the Corporations by the Commission from time to time as provided by the said
agreement;

And whereas the amount of the whole rateable property of the Corporation according to the last revised assessment roll is $, and the
amount of the debenture debt of the Corporation is $, of which
neither principal nor interest is in arrear;

And whereas only a portion of the Municipality of the of   as enumerated in Schedule "C" to the said agreement, is served by said railway;

Therefore the Municipal Council of the Corporation of the of   enacts as follows:—

1. It shall be lawful for the Corporation of the   of   , and the said Corporation is hereby authorized to enter into the following agreement with the Hydro-Electric Power Commission of Ontario and other corporations, the said agreement being hereby incorporated into and forming a part of this by-law, and the   and Clerk of the Corporation are hereby authorized and directed to execute the said agreement upon behalf of this Corporation and to attach the Seal of the Corporation thereto.

2. Only those duly qualified electors residing in the   of   , in the district enumerated in Schedule "C" of said agreement shall be entitled to vote on the By-law, and any rate required to be levied for payment of debentures or interest thereon shall be raised, levied and collected from the rateable property in such district only.

Agreement Hereinbefore Referred to.

This indenture made the   day of   in the year of our Lord, one thousand nine hundred and

Between

The Hydro-Electric Power Commission of Ontario (hereinafter called the "Commission") of the first part;

and

The Municipal Corporations of the Township of London, the Township of Trafalgar, the Township of Waterloo, the Township of Blanshard, the Township of Wilmot, the Township of Downie, the Township of South Easthope, the Township of Toronto, the Township of Nassagaweya, the Township of Guelph, the Township of Etobicoke, the Township of North Easthope, the Township of Biddulph, the Township of Esquesing, the Township of Puslinch, the Township of Eramosa, the Township of Nelson, the Township of Ellice, the Township of East Zorra, the City of Toronto, the City of London, the City of Berlin, the City of Guelph, the City of Stratford, the Town of Waterloo, the Town of St. Mary's, the Town of Milton, the Village of Mimico, the Village of New Toronto, the Village of Port Credit, and the Village of New Hamburg (hereinafter called the "Corporations"), of the second part.

Whereas pursuant to the *Hydro-Electric Railway Act, 1914*, and amendments thereto, the Commission was requested to enquire into, examine, investigate and report upon the cost of construction and operation of an electric railway or railways to be constructed through certain districts in which the Corporations are situated, together with the probable revenue that would result from the operation of such railway or railways;

And whereas the Commission has furnished the Corporations with such a report showing (1) the total estimated cost, operating revenue and expenses of the railway or railways, and (2) the proportion of the capital cost to be borne by each of the Corporations as set forth in Schedule "B" attached hereto;

And whereas on receipt of the said report the Corporations requested the Commission to construct, equip and operate a system of electric railways (hereinafter called the railway) over the routes laid down in Schedule "A" attached hereto, upon the terms and conditions and in the manner herein set forth;

And whereas the Commission has agreed with the Corporations on behalf of the Corporations to construct, equip and operate the railway upon the terms and conditions and in the manner herein set forth; but upon the express conditions that the Commission shall not in any way be liable by reason of any error or omission in any estimates, plans or specifications for any financial or other obligation or loss whatsoever by virtue of this agreement or arising out of the performance of the terms thereof;

And whereas the electors of each of the Corporations have assented to by-laws authorizing the Corporations to enter into this agreement with the Commission for the construction, equipment and operation of the railway as laid down in the said schedules, subject to the following terms and conditions;

And whereas the Corporations have each issued debentures for the amounts set forth in Schedule "B" attached hereto, and have deposited the said debentures with the Commission;

Now, therefore, this indenture witnesseth:—

1. In consideration of the premises and of the agreements of the Corporations herein contained, and subject to the provisions of the said Act and amendments thereto, the Commission agrees with the Corporations respectively:—

(a) To construct, equip and operate the railway through the districts in which the Corporations are situate on behalf of the Corporations;

(b) To construct and operate the railway over the routes laid down in Schedule "A";

(c) To issue bonds, as provided in paragraph 3 of this agreement, to cover the cost of constructing and equipping the railway;

(d) To furnish as far as possible first-class modern and standard equipment for use on the railway, to operate this equipment so as to give the best service and accommodation possible, having regard to the district served, the type of construction and equipment adopted and all other equitable conditions, and to exercise all due skill and diligence so as to secure the most effective operation and service of the railway consistent with good management;

(e) To regulate and fix the fares and rates of toll to be collected by the railway for all classes of service;

(*f*) To utilize the routes and property of the railway for all purposes from which it is possible to obtain a profit;

(*g*) To combine the property and works of the railway and the power lines of the Commission where such combination is feasible and may prove economical to both the railway and the users of the power lines;

(*h*) To permit and obtain interchange of traffic with other railways wherever possible and profitable;

(*i*) To supply electrical power or energy for operation of the railway at rates consistent with those charged to municipal corporations;

(*j*) To apportion annually the capital costs and operating expenses of all works, apparatus and plant used by the railway in common with the Commission's transmission lines in a fair manner, having regard to the service furnished by the expenditure under consideration;

(*k*) To apply the revenue derived from operation of the railway and any other revenue derived from the undertaking to the payment of operating expenses (including electrical power), the cost of administration, and annual charges for interest and sinking fund on the money invested, and such other deductions as are herein provided for;

(*l*) To set aside from any revenue thereafter remaining an annual sum for the renewal of any works belonging in whole or in part to the undertaking;

(*m*) To pay over annually to the Corporations, if deemed advisable by the Commission in the interests of the undertaking, any surplus that may remain after providing for the items above mentioned. The division of such surplus between the Corporations to be fixed by the Commission on an equitable basis, having regard in the case of each Corporation to the capital invested, the service rendered, the comparative benefits derived, and all other like conditions;

(*n*) To take active steps for the purpose of constructing, equipping and operating the railway at the earliest possible date after the execution of this agreement by the Corporations and the deposit of the debentures as called for under clause 2 (*b*) hereof and to commence operation of each section as soon as possible after its completion;

(*o*) To make such extensions of the railway described in Schedule " A " as may appear advantageous and profitable from time to time.

2. In consideration of the premises and of the agreements herein set forth, each of the Corporations, for itself, and not one for the other, agrees with the Commission:

(*a*) To bear its share of the cost of constructing, equipping, operating, maintaining, repairing, renewing and insuring the railway and its property and works as established by the Commission, subject to adjustments and apportionment between the Corporations by the Commission from time to time;

(b) To issue debentures for the amounts set forth in Schedule "B" maturing in fifty years from the date of issue thereof, and payable yearly at the   Bank, at Toronto, Ontario. Such debentures shall be deposited with the Commission previous to the issuing of the bonds mentioned above, and may be held or disposed of from time to time by the Commission, as provided for in clause 4 hereof, in such amounts, at such rates of discount or premium, and on such terms and conditions as the Commission in its sole discretion shall deem to be in the interests of the railway, the proceeds of such debentures being used solely for the purposes herein contained. The amount of debentures of each Corporation sold or disposed of from time to time shall be such proportion as may be fixed by the Commission of the total amount of debentures, due regard being given to the capital invested, the service rendered, the comparative revenue derived, and all other equitable conditions;

(c) To make no agreement or arrangement with, and to grant no bonus, license or other inducement to any other railway or transportation company without the written consent of the Commission;

(d) To keep, observe and perform the covenants, provisoes and conditions set forth in this agreement intended to be kept and observed and performed by the Corporations, and to execute such further or other documents and to pass such by-laws as may be requested by the Commission for the purpose of fully effectuating the objects and intent of this agreement;

(e) To furnish a free right of way for the railway and for the power lines of the Commission over any property of the Corporations upon being so requested by the Commission, and to execute such conveyance thereof or agreement with regard thereto as may be desired by the Commission.

3. It shall be lawful and the Commission is hereby authorized to create or cause to be created an issue of bonds, and to sell or dispose of the same on behalf of the Corporations. Such bonds to be charged upon and secured by the railway, and all the assets, rights, privileges, revenues, works, property and effects belonging thereto or held or used in connection with the railway constructed, acquired, operated and maintained by the Commission under this agreement, and to be for the total amounts mentioned in Schedule "B" hereto attached; provided that the Commission may, upon obtaining the consent as herein defined of the majority of the Corporations, increase the said bond issue by any amount necessary to cover the capital cost of extending the railway, and may also without such consent increase the said bond issue to cover the cost of additional works or equipment of any kind for use on the railway to an extent not exceeding ten per cent. (10%) of the bonds issued from time to time. In order to meet and pay such bonds and interest as the same becomes due and payable the Commission shall in each year after the expiration of ten years from the date of the issue of the bonds out of the revenue of the railway after payments of operating expenses (including electrical power) and the cost of administration set aside a sufficient sum to provide a sinking fund for the purpose of redeeming the same at maturity. Debentures issued by the Corporations in compliance with clause 2 (b) hereof, shall, to the extent of the par value of any bonds outstanding from time to time, be held or disposed of by the Commission in trust for the holders of such bonds as collateral security for payment thereof, it being understood and agreed that in the event of any increase of the said bond issue each Corporation shall, upon the request of the Commission, deposit with the Commission additional

debentures as described in clause 2 (*b*) hereof, to be held or disposed of by the Commission as collateral security for such increase of the said bond issue, and that any debentures held by the Commission in excess of the par value of the outstanding bonds from time to time may be held or disposed of by the Commission to secure payment of any deficit arising from the operation of the railway.

4. In the event of the revenue derived from the operation of the undertaking being insufficient in any year to meet the operating expenses (including electrical power), the cost of administration and the annual charges for interest and sinking fund on the bonds, and for the renewal of any works belonging in whole or in part to the railway, such deficit shall be paid to the Commission by the Corporations upon demand of and in the proportion adjusted by the Commission. In the event of the failure of any corporation to pay its share of such a deficit as adjusted by the Commission, it shall be lawful for the Commission in the manner provided in clause 2 (*b*) to dispose of debentures held by the Commission as security for any such deficit. Any arrears by any Corporation shall bear interest at the legal rate.

5. Should any Corporation fail to perform any of the obligations to the Commission under this agreement, the Commission may, in addition to all other remedies and without notice, discontinue the service of the railway to such Corporation in default until the said obligation has been fulfilled, and no such discontinuance of service shall relieve the Corporation in default from the performance of the covenants, provisoes and conditions herein contained.

6. In case the Commission shall at any time or times be prevented from operating the railway or any part thereof by strike, lockout, riot, fire, invasion, explosion, act of God, or the King's enemies, or any other cause reasonably beyond its control, then the Commission shall not be bound to operate the railway or such part thereof during such time; but the Corporations shall not be relieved from any liability or payment under this agreement, and as soon as the cause of such interruption is removed the Commission shall, without any delay, continue full operation of the railway, and each of the Corporations shall be prompt and diligent in doing everything in its power to remove and overcome any such cause or causes of interruption.

7. It shall be lawful for, and the Corporations hereby authorize the Commission to unite, the business of the railway with that of any other railway system operated in whole or in part by the Commission, and to exchange equipment and operators from one system to the other, proper provision being made so that each system shall pay its proportionate share of the cost of any equipment used in common.

8. If at any time any other municpal corporation applies to the Commission for an extension of the railway into its municipality, the Commission shall notify the applicant and the Corporations, in writing, of a time and place to hear all the representations that may be made as to the terms and conditions relating to such proposed extension. If, on the recommendation of the Commission, such extension shall be authorized, without discrimination in favour of the applicant, as to the cost incurred or to be incurred for or by reason of any such extension, the Commission may extend the railway upon such terms and conditions as may appear equitable to the Commission.

No such application for an extension of the railway into any municipality the Corporation of which is not a party to this agreement shall be granted if it is estimated by the Commission that the cost of service of the railway to the Corporations parties hereto will be thereby increased or the revenue and accommodation be injuriously affected without the written consent of the majority of the Corporations parties hereto.

9. The consent of any Corporation required under this agreement shall mean the consent of the council of such Corporations, such consent being in the form of a municipal by-law duly passed by the council of the Corporation.

10. The Commission shall, at least annually, adjust and apportion between the Corporations the cost of construction, equipment operation, interest, sinking fund, and also the cost of renewing the property of the railway.

11. Every railway and all the works, property and effects held and used in connection therewith, constructed, acquired, operated and maintained by the Commission under this agreement and the said Act shall be vested in the Commission on behalf of the Corporations; but the Commission shall be entitled to a lien upon the same for all money expended by the Commission under this agreement and not repaid.

12. Each of the Corporations covenants and agrees with the other:

(a) To carry out the agreements and provisions herein contained.

(b) To co-operate by all means in its power at all times with the Commission to create the most favourable conditions for the carrying out of the objects of the agreement and of the said Act, and to increase the revenue of the railway and ensure its success.

13. In the event of any difference between the Corporations, the Commission may, upon application, fix a time and place to hear all representations that may be made by the parties, and the Commission shall adjust such differences, and such adjustments shall be final. The Commission shall have all the powers that may be conferred upon a commissioner appointed under *The Act Respecting Enquiries Concerning Public Matters.*

14. This agreement shall continue and extend for a period of fifty years from the date hereof, and at the expiration thereof be subject to renewal, with the consent of the Corporations from time to time for like periods of fifty years, subject to adjustment and re-apportionment as herein provided for the purposes of this agreement as though the terms hereof had not expired. At the expiration of this agreement the Commission shall determine and adjust the rights of the Corporations, having regard to the amounts paid or assumed by them respectively under the terms of this agreement, and such other considerations as may appear equitable to the Commission and are approved by the Lieutenant-Governor in Council.

15. It is understood and agreed that the rates imposed for the share of the cost to be borne by those municipalities listed in Schedule "C" attached hereto, shall be imposed upon the rateable property set forth respectively in the said schedule.

16. This agreement shall not come into effect until it has been sanctioned by the Lieutenant-Governor in Council.

In witness whereof the Commission and the Corporations have respectively affixed their corporate seals and the hands of their proper officers.

SCHEDULE " A."

ROUTES:

Toronto Terminal-Humber River Section:

From the passenger terminal located near the foot of Yonge Street the line will run westerly to Sunnyside, using Harbour Board property and private right-of-way wherever possible; thence to the Humber River the line will parallel the G.T.R. as at present constructed.

Humber River-Port Credit Section:

From the west limits of the City of Toronto at the Humber River, the line runs westerly parallel to the G.T.R. main line. It crosses the Credit River at a point between the Lake Shore Road and the G.T.R.

Port Credit-Milton Section:

Leaving Port Credit the line crosses the G.T.R. about one mile west, running thence to a point north of Sheridan P.O., and from there directly to Milton.

Milton-Guelph Section:

Crossing the C.P.R. west of the C.P.R. station at Milton, location runs to Township of Esquesing, thence to Township of Nassagaweya, thence to Township of Puslinch, and thence in the general direction of the Eramosa River to Guelph.

Guelph-Berlin Section:

From Guelph the line continues to Berlin, leaving Guelph in a westerly direction and entering Berlin from the northeast. The location lies north of the present G.T.R. between Guelph and Berlin.

Berlin-Stratford Section:

From Berlin the line runs to the G.T.R. main line, which it parallels to a point near Baden, and thence south of the G.T.R. to a point east of Stratford, where it will cross the G.T.R. and enter the city.

Stratford-St. Mary's Section:

From Stratford the line runs in a westerly direction parallel to the old main line of the G.T.R. to a point north of St. Mary's.

St. Mary's-London Section:

The line runs in a south-westerly direction through St. Mary's and thence westerly, crossing the Canadian Pacific Railway at grade, and over the Thames River, running thence parallel to the old main line of the Grand Trunk Railway to a point near Granton; thence in a southerly direction through Biddulph Township to the northern boundary of London Township; thence in a southeasterly direction from concessions 14 to 10, inclusive, in London Township. From this point the line runs in a southerly direction through concessions 9 to 4, inclusive; thence following the Thames River through concessions 3 to 1, inclusive, in London Township, to a point between the Sarnia road and the Thames River, a short distance west of the Warncliffe road, outside of the northwesterly boundary line of the City of London. Thence the roads runs in a southeasterly direction over private property and city streets, crossing over the Thames River in the City of London, to a point on Bathurst Street; thence easterly along Bathurst Street to the London & Port Stanley Railway, which at present terminates on Bathurst Street, immediately east of Richmond Street.

SCHEDULE "B."

Total amount of debentures to be issued by respective municipalities for deposit with the Commission under clause 2 (b).

Name of Municipal Corporation:

Township of London	$630,389
Township of Trafalgar	578,921
Township of Waterloo	521,903
Township of Blanshard	402,909
Township of Wilmot	479,065
Township of Downie	418,735
Township of South Easthope	316,262
Township of Toronto	345,355
Township of Nassagaweya	343,147
Township of Guelph	361,025
Township of Etobicoke	401,335
Township of North Easthope	248,585
Township of Biddulph	142,166
Township of Esquesing	91,922
Township of Puslinch	70,300
Township of Eramosa	42,180
Township of Nelson	31,130
Township of Ellice	33,100
Township of East Zorra	39,000
City of Toronto	4,240,196
City of London	1,109,303
City of Berlin	774,040
City of Guelph	734,862
City of Stratford	651,735
Town of Waterloo	193,900
Town of St. Mary's	153,940
Town of Milton	65,000
Village of Mimico	111,200
Village of New Toronto	82,250
Village of Port Credit	54,050
Village of New Hamburg	66,250

Total amount of bonds to be issued, mentioned in clause 3 ....$13,734,155

SCHEDULE "C."

Districts, rateable prop-
erty of which shall bear
rate levied against the
Corporation:

Name of Municipal
Corporation:

———

Made, passed and entered this   day of   191 .

....Reeve (Mayor).

....Clerk.

———

SCHEDULE "B."

By-law No.   , of the Municipal Corporation of the Township of
London, to authorize a certain agreement made between the Hydro-Electric
Power Commission of Ontario and the Municipal Corporation of the Town-
ship of London and other Municipal Corporations, for the construction,
equipment and operation of an electric railway under *The Hydro-Electric
Railway Act, 1914*, and amendments thereto.

———

By-law No.   , of the Municipal Corporation of the Township of
Trafalgar, to authorize a certain agreement made between the Hydro-Elec-
tric Power Commission of Ontario and the Municipal Corporation of the
Township of Trafalgar, and other Municipal Corporations, for the construc-
tion, equipment and operation of an electric railway under *The Hydro-
Electric Railway Act, 1914*, and amendments thereto.

———

By-law No.   , of the Municipal Corporation of the Township of
Wilmot, to authorize a certain agreement made between the Hydro-Electric
Power Commission of Ontario and the Municipal Corporation of the Town-
ship of Wilmot and other Municipal Corporations, for the construction,
equipment and operation of an electric railway under *The Hydro-Electric
Railway Act, 1914*, and amendments thereto.

———

By-law No.   , of the Municipal Corporation of the Township of
Downie, to authorize a certain agreement made between the Hydro-Electric
Power Commission of Ontario and the Municipal Corporation of the Town-

7 H

ship of Downie and other Municipal Corporations, for the construction, equipment and operation of an electric railway under *The Hydro-Electric Railway Act, 1914*, and amendments thereto.

———

By-law No.   , of the Municipal Corporation of the Township of Toronto, to authorize a cerain agreement made between the Hydro-Electric Power Commission of Ontario and the Municipal Corporation of the Township of Toronto and other Municipal Corporations, for the construction, equipment and operation of an electric railway under *The Hydro-Electric Railway Act, 1914*, and amendments thereto.

———

By-law No.   , of the Municipal Corporation of the Township of Nassagaweya, to authorize a certain agreement made between the Hydro-Electric Power Commission of Ontario and the Municipal Corporation of the Township of Nassagaweya and other Municipal Corporations, for the construction, equipment and operation of an electric railway under *The Hydro-Electric Railway Act, 1914*, and amendments thereto.

———

By-law No.   , of the Municipal Corporation of the Township of Guelph, to authorize a certain agreement made between the Hydro-Electric Power Commission of Ontario and the Municipal Corporation of the Township of Guelph and other Municipal Corporations, for the construction equipment and operation of an electric railway under *The Hydro-Electric Railway Act, 1914*, and amendments thereto.

———

By-law No.   , of the Municipal Corporation of the Township of Etobicoke, to authorize a certain agreement made between the Hydro-Electric Power Commission of Ontario and the Municipal Corporation of the Township of Etobicoke and other Municipal Corporations, for the construction, equipment and operation of an electric railway under *The Hydro-Electric Railway Act, 1914*, and amendments thereto.

———

By-law No.   , of the Municipal Corporation of the Township of Biddulph, to authorize a certain agreement made between the Hydro-Electric Power Commission of Ontario and the Municipal Corporation of the Township of Biddulph and other Municipal Corporations, for the construction, equipment and operation of an electric railway under *The Hydro-Electric Railway Act, 1914*, and amendments thereto.

———

By-law No.   , of the Municipal Corporation of the Township of Esquesing, to authorize a certain agreement made between the Hydro-Electric Power Commission of Ontario and the Municipal Corporation of the Township of Esquesing and other Municipal Corporations, for the construction, equipment and operation of an electric railway under *The Hydro-Electric Railway Act, 1914,* and amendments thereto.

By-law No.   , of the Municipal Corporation of the City of Toronto, to authorize a certain agreement made between the Hydro-Electric Power Commission of Ontario and the Municipal Corporation of the City of Toronto and other Municipal Corporations, for the construction, equipment and operation of an electric railway under *The Hydro-Electric Railway Act, 1914,* and amendments thereto.

By-law No.   , of the Municipal Corporation of the City of London, to authorize a certain agreement made between the Hydro-Electric Power Commission of Ontario and the Municipal Corporation of the City of London and other Municipal Corporations, for the construction, equipment and operation of an electric railway under *The Hydro-Electric Railway Act, 1914,* and amendments thereto.

By-law No.   , of the Municipal Corporation of the City of Berlin, to authorize a certain agreement made between the Hydro-Electric Power Commission of Ontario and the Municipal Corporation of the City of Berlin and other Municipal Corporations, for the construction, equipment and operation of an electric railway under *The Hydro-Electric Railway Act, 1914,* and amendments thereto.

By-law No.   , of the Municipal Corporation of the City of Guelph, to authorize a certain agreement made between the Hydro-Electric Power Commission of Ontario and the Municipal Corporation of the City of Guelph and other Municipal Corporations, for the construction, equipment and operation of an electric railway under *The Hydro-Electric Railway Act, 1914,* and amendments thereto.

By-law No.   , of the Municipal Corporation of the City of Stratford, to authorize a certain agreement made between the Hydro-Electric Power Commission of Ontario and the Municipal Corporation of the City of Stratford and other Municipal Corporations, for the construction, equipment and operation of an electric railway under *The Hydro-Electric Railway Act, 1914,* and amendments thereto.

By-law No.   , of the Municipal Corporation of the Town of Waterloo, to authorize a certain agreement made between the Hydro-Electric Power Commission of Ontario and the Municipal Corporation of the Town of Waterloo and other Municipal Corporations, for the construction, equipment and operation of an electric railway under *The Hydro-Electric Railway Act, 1914,* and amendments thereto.

By-law No.   , of the Municipal Corporation of the Town of St. Mary's, to authorize a certain agreement made between the Hydro-Electric Power Commission of Ontario and the Municipal Corporation of the Town of

St. Mary's and other Municipal Corporations, for the construction, equipment and operation of an electric railway under *The Hydro-Electric Railway Act, 1914*, and amendments thereto.

By-law No.   , of the Municipal Corporation of the Town of Milton, to authorize a certain agreement made between the Hydro-Electric Power Commission- of Ontario and the Municipal Corporation of the Town of Milton and other Municipal Corporations, for the construction, equipment and operation of an electric railway under *The Hydro-Electric Railway Act, 1914*, and amendments thereto.

By-law No.   , of the Municipal Corporation of the Village of Mimico, to authorize a certain agreement made between the Hydro-Electric Power Commission of Ontario and the Municipal Corporation of the Village of Mimico and other Municipal Corporations, for the construction, equipment and operation of an electric railway under *The Hydro-Electric Railway Act, 1914*, and amendments thereto.

By-law No.   , of the Municipal Corporation of the Village of New Toronto, to authorize a certain agreement made between the Hydro-Electric Power Commission of Ontario and the Municipal Corporation of the Village of New Toronto and other Municipal Corporations, for the construction, equipment and operation of an electric railway under *The Hydro-Electric Railway Act, 1914*, and amendments thereto.

By-law No.   , of the Municipal Corporation of the Village of Port Credit, to authorize a certain agreement made between the Hydro-Electric Power Commission of Ontario and the Municipal Corporation of the Village of Port Credit and other Municipal Corporations, for the construction, equipment and operation of an electric railway under *The Hydro-Electric Railway Act, 1914*, and amendments thereto.

By-law No.   , of the Municipal Corporation of the Village of New Hamburg, to authorize a certain agreement made between the Hydro-Electric Power Commission of Ontario and the Municipal Corporation of the Village of New Hamburg and other Municipal Corporations, for the construction, equipment and operation of an electric railway under *The Hydro-Electric Railway Act, 1914*, and amendments thereto.

Electric Power Company Agreement

An Act to confirm An Agreement between the Electric Power Company, Limited, and His Majesty the King, was passed at the previous Session of the Legislature.

An Act to confirm an Agreement between the Electric Power Company Limited, and His Majesty, the King.

Assented to 27th April, 1916.

WHEREAS the Electric Power Company is the owner of or con-Preamble. trols the shares of the capital stock of the corporations named in the first recital of the agreement hereinafter mentioned; and whereas the said Electric Power Company, Limited, and the said Companies so controlled by it are the owners of or control, among other properties, assets, rights, contracts, licenses, privileges and franchises, a number of water powers and water privileges in the central portion of Ontario; and whereas it is desirable in the public interest that such water powers and privileges, and the development, transmission and distribution of electrical power or energy therefrom should be owned or controlled as public utilities; and whereas His Majesty, the King, represented therein by the Honourable George Howard Ferguson, Minister of Lands, Forests and Mines, has entered into a contract with the Electric Power Company, a copy of which is set out in Schedule "A" to this Act, providing for the purchase of all the assets and undertakings of every kind and nature whatsoever, of the Electric Power Company, Limited, and the said twenty-two companies mentioned in Schedule "A" to the said contract; and whereas it is expedient that the said contract should be confirmed, and the Government of Ontario should be empowered to complete the said purchase, and to deal with, manage and dispose of the property acquired under the said contract, or any part thereof;

Therefore His Majesty, by and with the advice and consent of the Legislative Assembly. of the Province of Ontario, enacts as follows:—

1. This Act may be cited as *The Central Ontario Power Act, 1916.*   Short title.

2. The agreement, dated the 10th day of March, 1916, between the Agreement between Electric Power Company, Limited, and His Majesty the King, repre-Crown and sented therein by the Honourable George Howard Ferguson, Minister Electric Power Co. of Lands, Forests and Mines, which agreement is set out in Schedule confirmed. "A" to this Act, is hereby confirmed and declared to be legal, valid and binding upon the parties thereto.

3. All and every part of the property, assets, rights, contracts, pri-Property vested in vileges, licenses, franchises, undertakings and businesses dealt with or Crown. purporting to be dealt with, or agreed to be purchased or sold under the terms of the said contract set out in Schedule "A" are hereby vested in His Majesty the King, as representing the Province of Ontario, free from all liens, charges and encumbrances, save as provided in the said contract of purchase.

Crown.
authorized
to carry out
contract.

4. The Lieutenant-Governor in Council is hereby authorized and empowered to do all and every act, matter and thing requisite or necessary, or deemed advisable to be done in order to complete and carry out the said contract, and all and every proviso and stipulation therein contained purporting to be made by or on behalf of His Majesty the King.

Issue of
bonds for
purchase
money.

5.—(1) The Treasurer of Ontario is authorized to issue debentures of the Province of Ontario to the amount of $8,350,000, payable at the office of the Treasurer of Ontario, Toronto, Canada, or the agency of the Bank of Montreal in the City of New York, United States of America, or at the agency of the said bank in the City of London, England, at the holder's option in debentures of $1,000 each, bearing date the first day of March, 1916, and payable in gold coin on the first day of March, A.D. 1926, and with coupons to be attached for payment of interest at the rate of 4 per cent. per annum, payable in gold coin half-yearly at the office of the Treasurer of Ontario, Toronto, Canada, or at the agency of the Bank of Montreal in the City of New York, United States of America, or at the agency of the said bank in the City of London, England, at the option of the holder of the debentures, on the first day of March and the first day of September in each year until the principal falls due.

Registra-
tion of
bonds.

(2) The Treasurer of Ontario is authorized at the request of the holders of the said debentures from time to time, or any of them, to have the same registered in the office of the Treasurer of Ontario.

Delivery of
bonds to
vendor
company.

(3) The said debentures, upon their issue, shall be delivered to the Electric Power Company, Limited, in full discharge of the purchase money agreed to be paid by the Crown under the contract of Purchase, Schedule "A" to this Act, and neither His Majesty, or the Treasurer of Ontario, or any member of the Government of Ontario shall be bound to see to the application of the said debentures or of the proceeds thereof.

Bonds
charged on
Consolidated
Revenue.

(4) The said debentures, and the interest thereon, shall be a charge upon, and shall be payable out of the Consolidated Revenue Fund of Ontario.

Order-in-
Council
vesting
property in
Commission,
etc.

6. The Lieutenant-Governor in Council may at any time, or from time to time by Order-in-Council vest in any commission, municipal corporation, municipal commission, company, corporation, firm or individual, the ownership or control, or power of administration and management of all or any of the undertakings, properties, rights, contracts, licenses, privileges, franchises and businesses of all or any of the twenty-two companies named in the first recital in the said agreement, to such extent, and in such manner and for such purposes, for such periods and on such terms and conditions and for such estate as such Order-in-Council may provide, and thereupon such commission, municipal corporation, municipal commission, company, corporation, firm or individual shall be clothed with and have, hold, exercise, enforce and enjoy all the rights, powers and privileges in respect of such undertakings, properties, rights, contracts, licenses, privileges, franchises and businesses as shall be granted by such order-in-council and, subject to any limitations or restriction in such order-in-council, shall have, hold exercise, enforce and enjoy in respect of such undertakings, properties, rights, contracts, licenses, privileges, franchises and businesses all the rights, powers and privileges which the company, whose undertakings, properties, rights, contracts, licenses, privileges, franchises and businesses is or are vested as aforesaid had therein before the passing of the Act.

7. Until the Lieutenant-Governor in Council shall in manner herein provided otherwise direct, the said undertakings, properties, rights, contracts, licenses, privileges, franchises and businesses, and every part thereof shall be under the management and control of some person nominated by the Lieutenant-Governor in Council who shall control, manage and administer the same for the benefit of His Majesty, either in the name of His Majesty, or in the name of the company now owning, controlling, or administering the same, and such person shall have, hold, exercise, enjoy and enforce all rights, powers and privileges in respect of the management, control or administration of the same as shall be granted or conferred by such order-in-council and, subject to any limitations and restrictions contained in such order-in-council, shall have, hold, enjoy, exercise and enforce all the rights, powers and privileges in respect of the property under his control, which such company or companies had before the passing of this Act. *Management of property until disposed of.*

8. A copy of this Act shall be deposited, copied and registered in the General Register of every Registry Office and Land Titles Office in which is registered or recorded the title to any lands affected by the terms of this Act, and every Registrar of Deeds, or Master of Titles as the case may be, shall, upon the request of the solicitors for the Crown, enter in the abstract index of each parcel or tract of land, the title to which is in any way affected by this Act, a note, entry or memorandum showing that the title thereto has been changed or affected by this Act, and referring to the date and registration number in the General Index where this Act has been recorded or registered as aforesaid. *Registration of Act.*

SCHEDULE " A."

AGREEMENT made this tenth day of March, 1916,

Between:

THE ELECTRIC POWER COMPANY, LIMITED,

hereinafter called the vendor,

Of the first part,

and

HIS MAJESTY THE KING, herein represented by the Honourable George Howard Ferguson, Minister of Lands, Forests and Mines,

hereinafter called the purchaser,

Of the second part.

WHEREAS the vendor owns or controls the capital stock of the following companies carrying on business in the Province of Ontario, that is to say:

1. Auburn Power Company, Limited.
2. Central Ontario Power Company, Limited.
3. City Gas Company of Oshawa, Limited.
4. Cobourg Utilities Corporation, Limited.
5. Cobourg Water and Electric Company.
6. Cobourg Gas, Light and Water Company.
7. Eastern Power Company, Limited.
8. Light, Heat and Power Company of Lindsay.
9. Napanee Gas Company, Limited.
10. Napanee Water and Electric Company.
11. Nipissing Power Company, Limited.
12. Northumberland Pulp Company, Limited.
13. Oshawa Electric Light Company.
14. Otonabee Power Company, Limited.
15. North Bay Light, Heat and Power Company.
16. Peterborough Light and Power Company, Limited.
17. Peterborough Radial Railway Company.
18. Port Hope Electric Light and Power Company.
19. Seymour Power and Electric Company, Limited.
20. Sidney Electric Power Company, Limited.
21. Trenton Electric and Water Company, Limited.
22. Tweed Electric Light and Power Company, Limited.

And whereas the vendor has agreed to sell, and the purchaser has agreed to purchase, all the assets and undertakings of the said companies of every kind and nature, excepting such assets as are hereinafter specifically excepted, for the considerations hereinafter mentioned.

Now this agreement witnesseth as follows:

1. The vendor shall sell, and the purchaser shall purchase, as they existed on the first day of March, 1916, all the assets and undertakings of every kind and nature whatsoever of the vendor and of the said companies as follows:

1. All freehold and leasehold lands, tenements and hereditaments of the said company.

2. All plant, machinery, furniture, licenses, franchises, stock-in-trade, stores and all other chattels to which the said companies or any of them are or is entitled in connection with the businesses carried on by them respectively.

3. All pending contracts and engagements of the said companies or any of them in connection with any business so carried on.

4. All other property to which the said companies or any of them are or is entitled except, however, all cash and all bills and notes and all book and other debts due to the vendor or any of the said companies.

2. The consideration for the sale shall be the sum of Eight Million Three Hundred and Fifty Thousand dollars ($8,350,000), which shall be paid and satisfied by the issue and delivery to the vendor of Ontario Government Debentures bearing date March 1st, 1916, and payable March 1st, 1926, and bearing interest at the rate of four per cent., payable half-yearly in Toronto, New York and London.

3. The assets and undertakings are sold free of all encumbrances, but as regards leaseholds subject to all the rents and covenants contained in any leases or agreements for leases under which the same are held, all of which are known to the purchaser. The vendor undertakes to pay and discharge all existing debts and liabilities of the said Companies.

4. The purchaser agrees to assume all contracts and engagements of the Vendor or any of the said Companies and to indemnify them against any claims in respect thereof, which arise hereafter.

5. The purchaser accepts the title of the vendor and the said Companies to all the said premises; it being understood that the purchaser shall obtain at his own expense the requisite consents for the assignments of any lease-holds.

6. From and after the first day of March, 1916, the vendor and the said Companies shall carry on the respective businesses and maintain the same as going concerns, but they shall from the said date be deemed to be carrying on such businesses on behalf of the purchaser, and shall account and be entitled to be indemnified accordingly, and all income and receipts shall be adjusted and divided as of the first day of March, 1916.

Should any difference arise as to said adjustments these shall be referred to G. T. Clarkson, Esquire, of Toronto, as an Expert and not as an arbitrator, and his decision shall be final and binding on the parties.

7. Taxes and rents and insurance shall be adjusted as of the first day of March, 1916.

The purchase shall be completed before the first day of May, 1916.

In Witness whereof the parties have executed this agreement the day and year above mentioned.

(Sgd.) THE ELECTRIC POWER COMPANY, LIMITED,

STRACHAN JOHNSTON,

President.

(Sgd.) SAMUEL D. FOWLER,

Asst. Sec'y.

(Seal of Co.)

(Sgd.) G. H. FERGUSON,

Minister Lands, Forests and Mines.

Witness: (Sgd.) C. C. HELE.

RIGHT-OF-WAY

High Tension Lines

The work of the staff during the early part of the year was devoted to completing the purchase of the right-of-way for the second High Tension Transmission Line rom Niagara Falls to Dundas, and this work is practically completed.

Work was commenced in September on the purchase of lands necessary for the Chippawa-Queenston Development. Owing to the route of this work passing through lands in the Township of Stamford, which have been largely devoted to fruit growing and gardening, the holdings in the majority of cases being small and quite valuable, the work of acquiring these lands has necessarily been rather slow, but considerable progress has been made, and it is anticipated that the work will be completed before spring. In all it will be necessary to acquire about one hundred and twenty-five parcels of land owned by different parties for this right-of-way.

Plans have been completed and the work of purchasing the right-of-way commenced on the duplicate line from Dundas to Toronto. An additional purchasing agent, who will devote his time to this work during the coming winter, has been added to the staff, in order that delay in acquiring the needed lands in this case may be avoided.

The Commission now owns its own right-of-way through twenty-two townships and five urban municipalities, and in no case has it been necessary to resort to arbitration in order to acquire the lands desired. The Department has endeavoured to maintain a policy of uniform prices, and has met with comparatively little opposition from the owners of the lands sought to be purchased.

Low Tension Lines

On account of the large mileage of Low Tension Lines constructed during the past season, the whole time of one member of the staff, and at times of two, has been required to secure the necessary tree trimming and pole rights for this work.

CROSSINGS

The construction of high-tension and low-tension lines during the year has made it necessary to obtain the permission of various steam and electric railways, telegraph, telephone and power companies for crossings, to the extent of 300. In each case it was necessary to prepare applications and blue prints and forward the same to the different companies for approval and consent. Where consent is not given the matter is placed before the Board of Railway Commissioners for a ruling, all of which necessarily entails a considerable amount of work.

AGREEMENTS

During the fiscal year agreements for a supply of power have been made with the Cities of Sarnia and Kingston; the Towns of Dunnville and Forest; the Villages of Point Edward, Tara, Watford, Arthur, West Lorne, Milverton, Wyoming, Oil Springs, Rodney, Grand Valley and Omemee, and the Police Villages of Burgessville, Dashwood, Dublin, Highgate, Otterville, Springfield, St. Jacobs, Alton, and Zurich, and the Townships of York, Scarboro, Brant, Bentinck and Artemesia.

SECTION II

TRANSMISSION SYSTEM

STEEL TOWER TRANSMISSION LINES

Surveys

DUNDAS-TORONTO

During the early part of 1916, a great deal of reconnaissance work was done in the district between Dundas and Toronto, in order that the most suitable location possible might be found for a second steel tower line.

On June 10th, 1916, a survey party commenced work at Dundas, and made a very complete survey from there to the Humber river. This location survey was completed late in October, and the party is now engaged in taking levels for a profile of the entire line.

STATION EQUIPMENT AND BUILDING DEPARTMENT

GENERAL

Station Construction

During the year just closed the following stations which were referred to in the last report as having been authorized have been completed and placed in service: Linden, Listowel, Milverton, Harriston, Palmerston, Ridgetown, Blenheim, Petrolia, Exeter, Eugenia, Owen Sound, Chatsworth, Chesley, Durham, Dundalk, Mount Forest, South Falls, Huntsville.

The construction of stations was authorized during the year at Tavistock, Hanover, York, Etobicoke, West Lorne, Kilsyth, Orangeville, Port McNicoll (C.P.R.), Forest.

Changes for addition of transformers or switching equipment or both have been made, or authorized, for several of the transformer and distributing stations, these being necessitated by increase of load on the station in the majority of cases and by additional feeders being required in others. These alterations and additions are described later in this report.

The progress on design and construction of stations has not been as satisfactory as in past years, owing to conditions arising from war. At the time of writing, promises of delivery of equipment of six to eight months (where formerly two to three months were promised) are the rule. Furthermore, the high cost of materials and equipment is unprecedented. At the present time, contracts are placed for certain pieces of apparatus at double the prices that we were able to purchase same for two or three years ago.

Administration Building

The Administration Building described as being constructed in previous report was completed and the transfer of offices from the Continental Life Building was effected as conditions in the new building would permit, the executive offices moving in on April 1st.

It was thought that the Administration Building would provide sufficient quarters for several years. When the layout was prepared, each department was provided with at least three times the floor space which it had at that time in the Continental Life Building. However, the phenomenal growth of the Commission and the addition of the Central Ontario System has necessitated increasing the staff to such an extent that some of the departments are now utilizing all the space available.

A garage, with accommodation for three motor cars, was constructed on the property to the rear of the building to house motor cars for office use.

Toronto Storehouse Extension

The Stores Department, Laboratory and garage have all outgrown their quarters, and it was decided to proceed with the construction of an addition to the Toronto Storehouse and Laboratory. The extension is being made 132 feet deep, the full length of the present building. Reinforced concrete, flat slab construction, with brick curtain walls is being used. The extension will provide for a garage approximately 108 feet long by 66 feet wide, providing accommodation for about 24 motor cars. A machine and repair shop, the same dimensions as the garage, immediately over same, will be provided. The top story of this portion of the building will be used as a carpenter and paint shop. The interior portion of the building, 66 feet by 108 feet with basement and three floors, will be used exclusively for stores.

The entire basement, first and second floors of the present building will be remodelled and converted into laboratory accommodation.

Tenders were called for the construction of the building extension and the contract awarded to Messrs. Witchall & Sons, in the early fall. At the time of writing, excavation has been completed and the majority of the concrete footings have been poured.

Central Ontario System

When the Electric Power Company's interests were acquired, all drawings and designs available were transferred to this Department for use in connection with any extensions which might be decided upon.

Niagara Development

Several conferences were held with representatives of the electrical manufacturing companies with regard to the special features of the plant. Preliminary specifications for the main generators and transformers were issued to the different manufacturers and at the present time they are engaged in preparing designs which will enable them to more intelligently prepare tenders when our detailed specifications are issued. Conferences have also been held regarding special mechanical features of the generating station.

Public Utilities Commission of Peterboro

Preliminary designs were prepared for a proposed transformer station for the municipality. However, it was decided that this work be held up for the time being, at least.

Main Entrance Hall, Administration Building

Interior of Board Room, Administration Building

Cobden Municipal Generating Station

Plans and specifications were prepared for the electrical equipment for a generating station for the village of Cobden. The contract for the generator and exciter was placed with the Canadian General Electric Company, who also furnished the 3-k.w. station service transformer, and for the switchboard and connecting material with the Northern Electric Company.

The generator is rated at 100 kv-a., 2,300-volt, 3-phase, 60-cycle, 720 r.p.m., and is direct connected to a turbine. The belt-driven exciter is of 5-k.w. capacity at 125 volts.

The switchboard consists of one panel with automatic oil switch and full compliment of meters, including one Westinghouse type "RO" watthour meter for measuring the output of the plant.

The contracts were awarded in May, and it is expected that equipment will be placed in operation in a short time.

NIAGARA SYSTEM

NIAGARA FALLS TRANSFORMER STATION

Building Extension

In order to provide improved facilities for handling equipment such as has been contracted for for this station, an extension to the erection room was authorized. This extension will also provide space for the equipment required for supplying 12,000 volt power to local municipalities and office space for different departments having duties in or around the station. This new addition will be approximately 30 feet wide by 84 feet long by 33 feet high. The work is being done by Messrs. Wells and Gray, the contracting firm which built the recent extension.

12,000 Volt Feeders

The two feeders, each composed of two 300,000 C.M. 3-conductor, lead-covered and steel-tape armored cables, referred to in the last report, were installed during the past summer. These connect our station with that of the Ontario Power Company. They will be utilized as spare feeders, and are designated No. 10 and No. 11.

For the purpose of receiving power from the Canadian Niagara Power Company a cable system consisting of eight 350,000 C.M. 3-conductor, lead-covered and steel-tape armored cables will be provided. This line will run on a private right of way from our station in a south-easterly direction to the brow of the hill overlooking the river near Falls View Station of the Michigan Central Railway, thence across this railway right of way and through the Queen Victoria Niagara Falls Park to a manhole at the south-western corner of the Generating Station of the Canadian Niagara Power Company. The cables for this system will be supplied and installed by the Standard Underground Cable Company. Two cables will comprise a feeder, and each feeder will be capable of delivering 12,500 horse power. The cables will be laid directly in the earth with creosoted plank above to prevent mechanical injury. Where cables cross highways they will be drawn into cast-iron soil pipe arranged with ventilators. It is expected to have at least one of these feeders in service early in December, 1916, installation work having already been started.

Additional Electrical Equipment

No. 7 bank of 110,000-volt transformers, consisting of three 3,500-kv-a. units, was installed and made ready for service in September. This equipment is similar to that installed for No. 5 bank and No. 6 bank, and was mentioned in previous report.

No. 3 bank of 45,700-volt transformers, consisting of three 3,500-kv-a. units, was contracted for with the Canadian General Electric Company. Two of these have been shipped, and work is progressing on the installation. The Canadian Westinghouse Company are supplying the switching equipment for this bank, and installation work is proceeding. This equipment is similar to that previously installed for banks No. 1 and No. 2.

Owing to additional capacity being required to meet the increasing loads, tenders were asked for and the Canadian Westinghouse Company were awarded the contract for three 7,500-kv-a. 12,000/63,500-volt transformers, forming No. 8 bank of transformers on the 110,000-volt bus, together with the necessary 12,000-volt and 110,000-volt switching equipment. These were the largest size units that could be placed in the space available in the building. When this bank is installed, the total capacity in this station in 110,000-volt transformers will be 96,000-kv-a. with one spare 3,500-kv-a. unit extra. It is expected that this No. 8 bank will be completed early in 1917.

Switching Equipment

In addition to the switching equipment above referred to as being supplied by the Canadian Westinghouse Company, this company will also supply the 12,000-volt and other equipment required for handling the four feeders from the Canadian Niagara Power Company, and the two spare armored cable feeders from the Ontario Power Company.

Bus and Switch Cell Structures

The contract for the construction of the necessary concrete cell work for the 12,000-volt oil switches and bus bars on above equipment was awarded to Messrs. Wells and Gray and this work is being proceeded with.

Water System

A contract was awarded to Messrs. Wells and Gray for the construction of a third sprinkling tank to take care of the increased amount of cooling water necessitated by the increase in the number of transformers in this station. The work on this tank has been started, and it is expected will be completed before the severe winter weather commences.

Additional pumping capacity was deemed advisable and an order was placed with the Storey Pump and Equipment Company for an additional (No. 5) pump, same to have capacity of 600 Imperial gallons per minute.

A 6-inch main running along Dixon St. to connect to the city water mains for emergency supply of water was installed by the Operating Department.

Protection of Service

Further studies are being made of possible methods of protecting and bettering the service. The incoming feeders from the Canadian Niagara Power Company

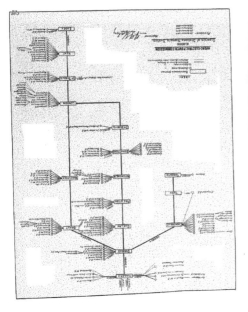

will be arranged so that at a later date we will be able to operate with two independent busses, that is, with duplicate feeder and transformer switches. The installation of power limiting reactors is also being investigated.

Niagara Falls Distributing Station

It was decided to designate equipment required for supplying 12,000-volt power
locally as "Distributing Station," although it is housed in the same building with
Transforming Equipment. It is desirable for accounting purposes to keep them
separate.

Equipment, consisting of three 100-kv-a. Westinghouse transformers with oil
switch and meters, was temporarily installed to supply the Niagara Falls waterworks with 2,200-volt power for pumping purposes. Also work is under way on
outgoing feeder equipment for supplying 12,000-volt power to the City of Niagara
Falls, also to the Township of Stamford, by the date when their present contract
expires. The permanent equipment for this service will be placed in the building
extension referred to above.

Welland Municipal Station

Three Canadian Westinghouse Company's 150-kv-a., 13,200/2,300-volt, single-
phase transformers were purchased from the St. Thomas Light, Heat and Power
Commission. These transformers were received at Welland early in October. The
switching equipment for these transformers was purchased and installed by the
Welland Hydro-Electric Power Commission and the transformer bank was placed
in service on October 30th.

Port Robinson Distributing Station

The Standard Steel Construction Company at Port Robinson have been receiving 12,000-volt power from the Commission at their sub-station, which contained
three 60-kv-a., 13,200/220-volt single-phase transformers and switching equipment for two incoming 12,000-volt lines, for the above transformers and for the
220-volt feeders to their steel plant. This station and equipment was purchased by
the Commission.

An additional bank of transformers and two 2,300-volt feeders have since been
installed in this station. These transformers were purchased from the Dundas
Hydro-Electric System, and consist of three 75-kv-a., 13,200/2,300-volt, 25-cycle,
single-phase, self-cooled transformers. The new switching equipment was purchased
from the Canadian General Electric Company. One feeder is used for feeding
2,300-volt, 3-phase power to the Standard Steel Construction Company and the
other feeder for 2,300-volt, 3-phase local distribution service for the Welland Hydro-
Electric Commission.

One of the 12,000-volt incoming lines has been disconnected from the station
and arrangements have been made to tie these two lines together outside the station
by means of a horn gap 3-pole disconnecting switch in each line.

This station was placed in service on October 13th.

Niagara-on-the-Lake Municipal Station

The corporation of the town of Niagara-on-the-Lake, built under the supervision of the Commission's construction men a new galvanized iron building for
housing equipment necessary to enable them to receive power at 12,000 volts from

8 H

the Commission. This equipment was removed by the Commission's staff from the then existing power and pump house and erected in the new station, together with the connecting material and station entrances which had to be purchased. This station was placed in service about August 10th.

TORONTO TRANSFORMER STATION

Erection Room

The transformer erection room in this station is being enlarged to accommo-date 5,000-kv-a. transformers, and a pit is being made in order to obtain necessary headroom. A new transformer truck is also being ordered.

Water Main

A 6-inch connection to the city of Toronto water main on Exhibition Road was made to the water system in this station in order to assure water supply for cooling the transformers during progress of work by the Toronto Harbor Commission, which is expected to interfere with the intake to the present pump house on the Lake Shore.

Drain

A connection is being made between the storm sewer on Strachan Avenue and the Toronto Hydro-Electric System's cable duct line manhole, which is a few feet north of the station. A tap will be taken off this connection and connected to the transformer water-cooling system and also to the storehouse.

No. 5 Transformer Bank

On December 16th, a contract was placed with the Canadian General Electric Company for three 5,000-kv-a.; 63,500/13,200 volts, 25-cycle, oil-insulated, water-cooled, single-phase transformers, together with the 110,000-volt and 13,200-volt switching equipment for connecting this bank of transformers to the existing busses. The layout of the switching equipment is similar to that for the existing 2,500-kv-a. transformers, except that the 13,200-volt equipment was of heavier carrying capacity. These 5,000-kv-a. units were the largest that could be placed in the space available in the building and will be installed during the winter.

Changes to Transformer Banks No. 3 and No. 4

On August 15th a contract was placed with the Canadian General Electric Company for six 5,000-kv-a., 63,500/13,200-volt, 25-cycle, oil-insulated, water-cooled, single-phase transformers. Three of these are promised for shipment in August, 1917, and the other three in October, 1917. The contract will be placed within a short time for the necessary 13,200-volt switching equipment and connect-ing material to change or replace the existing equipment to control the additional transformer capacity. The above transformers will be used to replace the existing 2,500-kv-a. transformers on bank No. 3 and 4. This will make a total station capacity of 60,000-kv-a. with one 2,500-kv-a. spare unit extra.

ce was given

nection with

1's car barns
is room is 15
ree 200-kv-a.
c Company's
ers. All this
iission.

n connection
rchase of two
disconnecting
more flexible
ise Company,

adian General
tly connected
s. The order

der the super-

cember. The
13,200/2,300-
e and for one
tric Company.
May 4th. In
npany for one
r for an addi-
o Hensall was
t, and will be

stributing Sta-
nel and equip-
the Canadian
operation on

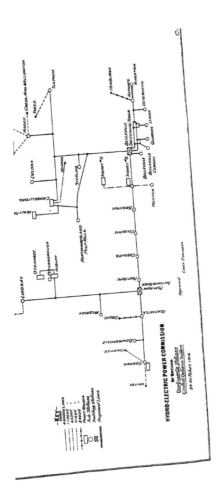

HYDRO-ELECTRIC POWER COMMISSION
of Ontario
Diagram of Stations
Central Ontario System
24 October 1916.

Approved
Chief Engineer

Key
4000 V Lines
110000 "
66000 "
44000 "
24000 "
Power-Houses
Sub-Stations
Switching Stations
Proposed Lines

LONDON TRANSFORMER STATION

London Utilities Commission

Office Building

At the request of the Public Utilities Commission, some assistance was given them in connection with an office building which is proposed.

Copies of specifications for different classes of work as used in connection with the construction of the Administration Buildings were given them.

Car Barn Sub-Station

Plans for a sub-station room in the London Railway Commission's car barns were prepared and submitted to the Public Utilities Commission. This room is 15 feet 6 inches by 17 feet 0 inches, and is designed to accommodate three 200-kv.-a. single-phase, self-cooled 13,200/2,300-volt, 25-cycle, Moloney Electric Company's transformers, with necessary switching equipment and lightning arresters. All this electrical equipment was supplied and installed by the Utilities Commission.

Horton Street Station Railway Equipment

Engineering assistance was given to the Utilities Commission in connection with repairs on rotary converters and also in connection with the purchase of two 1,000-ampere S.P.D.T. and one 1,000-ampere S.P.S.T. 1,500-volt disconnecting switches for installing in the 1,500-volt D.C. feeders to provide a more flexible arrangement. These were purchased from the Canadian Westinghouse Company, and installed by the Utilities Commission at the end of July.

The Utilities Commission authorized the purchase from the Canadian General Electric Company of two 1,500-volt electrolytic arresters to be directly connected across the commutators of the 500-k.w., 1,500-volt rotary converters. The order for these was placed in September.

London Railway Commission

The car barns referred to in the last report were completed under the supervision of this Commission.

Exeter Distributing Station

The contractor, Mr. P. Bawden, finished the building early in December. The contract for the electrical equipment, consisting of three 100-kv.-a., 13,200/2,300-volt, single-phase transformers, with switching equipment for same and for one 210-kv.-a., 4,000-volt feeder was awarded to the Canadian General Electric Company. The installation was finished and the station was placed in service May 4th. In August an order was placed with the Canadian General Electric Company for one 13,200-volt electrolytic lightning arrester for this station. The order for an additional feeder panel and equipment controlling a 4,000-volt feeder to Hensall was awarded to the Canadian General Electric Company on July 5th, and will be installed this fall.

Lucan Distributing Station—Granton Feeder

The installation of a 4,000-volt feeder equipment in Lucan Distributing Station to supply the municipality of Granton was authorized, and a panel and equipment was taken from stock equipment previously ordered from the Canadian Westinghouse Company. This panel was installed and put into operation on July 27th.

GUELPH TRANSFORMER STATION

Board of Light and Heat Commissioners of Guelph

Engineering assistance was given to the Board of Light and Heat Commissioners of Guelph in connection with the purchase and testing of one 550-kv-a., 3-phase, 25-cycle, O.I.S.C., 13,200/2,300/575-volt transformer. Contract was placed with the Canadian General Electric Company, Limited, for this unit in March, and tests at the factory were witnessed and reported in August.

Prices were also obtained on 50-kv-a. and 100-kv-a., 3-phase automatic voltage regulators for the above Board.

Central Prison Farm Sub-Station

It was decided to replace the 13,200-volt condenser-type lightning arrester in this station by an electrolytic type of arrester and a Canadian Westinghouse 13,200-volt, 3-phase arrester was purchased. This will be installed and put into service by the Commission's maintenance department.

PRESTON TRANSFORMER STATION

1916 Extension

Plans and specifications have been prepared and tenders called for the construction of a 33 feet by 56 feet extension to the north end of the present building for the accommodation of an additional bank of three 750-kv-a., 63,500/13,200-volt transformers with necessary switching equipment, this additional bank of transformers to be comprised of the former spare unit and two 750-kv-a. units to be transferred from Stratford Transformer Station.

The secondary voltage of this station will be changed from the present 6,600 volts to 13,200 volts, and all oil switches will be made electrically operated requiring a rearrangement of apparatus, plans for which are now being prepared. This change will necessitate changing the voltage of all stations fed from this station, including Preston, Hespeler, Galt and Breslau Stations, and the Galt, Preston & Hespeler Railway feeder to 13,200 volts, for which the necessary changes are now being considered.

Galt Waterworks Commission

In order to provide a more flexible arrangement and to obtain greater power factor corrective capacity from the motors, it was decided by the Galt Waterworks Commission to divide the motor-driven pumping unit in the waterworks station into two separate units, by adding another 250-kv-a. synchronous motor and connecting it to the south 800-gallon pump, leaving the 250-kv-a. motor first supplied on the north pump. Accordingly the Hydro-Electric Power Commission of Ontario were requested to prepare specifications and obtain tenders on the new motor and switching equipment required.

Tenders were obtained and submitted to the Waterworks Commission and the contract for one 250-kv-a., 3-phase, 25-cycle, 750 r.p.m. synchronous motor with exciter and control panel and necessary wiring material was placed with the Canadian Westinghouse Company, Limited, in February.

The manufacture of this equipment was followed up in the factory by frequent inspections and witness tests were made when the motor was completed. This motor and other equipment was placed in operation in October.

KITCHENER TRANSFORMER STATION

No work was done in this station during the year by this Department. The erection of the sheet steel storehouse mentioned in last report was completed.

Baden Distributing Station Extension

Transformers

It has been arranged to increase the transformer capacity of this station by removing the present bank of 75-kv-a. transformers and replacing them by a bank of 150-kv-a. capacity, purchased from the municipality of Seaforth.

Wellesley Feeder

An additional 4,000-volt feeder equipment, to supply the village of Wellesley, has been bought from Canadian Westinghouse Company and installed in this station by the construction staff of the S. E. & B. Department. In service on October 23rd.

STRATFORD TRANSFORMER STATION

Plans are under consideration for the removal of the 750-kv-a. transformers in this station to Preston Transformer Station and for a rearrangement of the outgoing feeders, making all feeders out of this station operate at 26,400 volts. This will involve changes to the municipal stations at Stratford, Seaforth and Mitchell, which are noted below.

Stratford Municipal Station

Owing to arrangements which have been made to supply power at 26,400 volts instead of 13,200 volts to the Stratford Utilities Commission, it was decided to construct a new sub-station.

At the request of the Utilities Commission, specifications and drawings have been prepared by the Commission covering a new two-storey building with basement to form an extension measuring 53 feet 9 inches by 29 feet 5 inches by 42 feet 9 inches high, to their existing station. This new building will accommodate four 750-kv-a., 26,400/2,300-volt, 3-phase, 25-cycle O.I.W.C. transformers, together with switching equipment for same and for two incoming 26,400-volt, 3-phase lines and the low-tension circuits.

The 26,400-volt switching equipment will be located on the second floor, the transformers and low-tension switching equipment, street lighting transformers, etc., on the main floor, while the potential regulator, water pumps, etc., will be located in the basement.

Drawings and specifications have also been made up and tenders requested for the switching equipment to control the two incoming lines, three 750-kv-a., 3-phase transformers, three 2,300-volt commercial lighting feeders, one 100-kv-a. potential regulator, one street lighting bus and one station service bank of transformers with 110 and 220-volt station feeders. The present four power and lighting feeder panels together with the eight constant current street lighting transformers and their panels will be moved to the new station. The present 110-k.w., 2,300-volt, 3-phase synchronous motor which is now driving a 220-volt D.C. generator will be moved to the basement of the new station, and the control panel will be placed in the main switchboard on the main floor. This motor will then be used for power factor correction.

Seaforth Municipal Station

This station which is now operating at 13,200 volts high tension with three 150-kv-a., 13,200/2,200-volt, single-phase Canadian Crocker Wheeler Company's transformers will be rearranged to be fed from two 26,400-volt lines tied together through horn gap disconnecting switch outside the station. Three 150-kv-a. 26,400/2,300-volt transformers have been purchased from the Canadian General Electric Company and should be ready for shipment in November. The necessary switching equipment required on account of the change to 26,400 volts has been ordered.

As soon as the existing 13,200-volt transformers are released, they will be transferred to the Baden Distributing Station, and the remaining 13,200-volt equipment will be used elsewhere on the System.

Mitchell Municipal Station

Owing to the arrangements to transmit power to Mitchell at 26,400 volts instead of 13,200 volts, three 75-kv-a., 26,400/575-volt, single-phase transformers have been purchased from the Canadian General Electric Company, and the switching equipment required has been purchased. At present the 13,200-volt equipment is located in a building, part of which is used for other purposes. The corporation of Mitchell are considering the advisability of building a new and separate brick station for housing the 26,400-volt equipment and transformers.

As soon as the new 26,400-volt equipment and transformers are installed and placed in service, the existing 13,200-volt equipment and transformers will be removed for use elsewhere on the System.

Tavistock Distributing Station

For the purpose of distributing power to Tavistock, a standard type " H " station layout equipment is being installed in a part of the existing pump house at Tavistock. On August 30th three 75-kv-a., 26,400/2,300-volt, single-phase, Canadian Crocker Wheeler Company's transformers were purchased for this station and are due for shipment in November. The 2,300-volt feeder panel, the 26,400-volt fuses and the insulators and connecting materials were supplied by the Canadian Westinghouse Company. Standard outdoor horn gap switch and a choke coil made up in the Commission's machine shop are being installed on the incoming line.

In order to give service from the station as soon as possible it was arranged to transmit power to same at 13,200 volts temporarily and install therein three 25-kv-a. 13,200/2,300-volt, single-phase Canadian Moloney Electric transformers which were in stock. This work is now under construction, and it is expected that the station will be placed in service at 13,200 volts early in November.

Listowel Distributing Station

The equipment for this station, as listed in last year's report, was furnished by the Canadian Westinghouse Company. A 26,400-volt ungrounded neutral aluminum cell lightning arrester was ordered from the Canadian General Electric Company. The Canadian Westinghouse Company were notified May 5th, to make shipment of the 100-kv-a. transformers and switching equipment, and same was installed and power furnished on May 27th. The lightning arrester referred to above was installed and put into service June 3rd.

Milverton Distributing Station

The type " H " building referred to in last annual report was completed in the early part of January. The contract for the three 75-kv-a., 26,400/4,000-volt transformers and switching equipment as mentioned in last report was awarded to the Canadian General Electric Company in January. The work of installation was completed about the middle of May. The station was placed in service on May 22nd.

Harriston Distributing Station

The contract for the type " H " station building referred to in last year's report was awarded to Mr. W. N. Hutchison in November, and the building was completed first week of January. The contract for the three 75-kv-a., 26,400/4,000-volt transformers and switching equipment was awarded to the Canadian General Electric Company. The installation of this equipment was finished about the middle of June, and the apparatus tested out and put into service June 30th.

This station also accommodates the 12-k.w. constant current street lighting transformer and panel belonging to the municipality, which equipment was transferred from the old station to the new distributing station by the Commission's construction staff.

Palmerston Distributing Station

The type " H " building referred to in last year's report was finished the latter part of January. Contract for the three 75-kv-a., 26,400/4,000-volt transformers and switching equipment was awarded to the Canadian General Electric Company, and installation was completed the latter part of May. The station was tested out and placed in service on June 6th.

There is also installed in this station a 12-k.w. constant current transformer and panel, the property of the municipality.

Municipality of Palmerston

At the request of the municipality tenders were obtained on a street lighting transformer and panel for same. The orders were placed in February with the Canadian General Electric Company for the panel, and with A. H. Winter Joyner, Limited, for one 12-k.w., 6.6-ampere, 2,300-volt Adams Bagnall constant current transformer. The equipment was installed by the Commission's construction staff.

ST. MARY'S TRANSFORMER STATION

The corrugated sheet steel shed referred to in last report was completed. No other work was done at this station.

St. Mary's Portland Cement Company Distributing Station Extension

Owing to the increased load at this station it was considered advisable to increase the transformer capacity and it was decided to have three 150-kv-a., 13,200/550-volt Packard Electric Company's transformers now in use in the Stratford Municipal Station transferred to this station, when released from Stratford.

Plans were prepared showing necessary changes in the original arrangement, and additions for this second transformer bank and the necessary additional apparatus was ordered from the Canadian Westinghouse Company, and will be installed by the Commission's Construction Department.

The 550-volt leads from this second bank of transformers will run to a new feeder panel to be supplied by the St. Mary's Portland Cement Company.

WOODSTOCK TRANSFORMER STATION

The corrugated sheet steel shed referred to in last report was completed. Plans are being considered for extending this station to accommodate equipment for a second 110,000-volt line.

ST. THOMAS TRANSFORMER STATION

No. 2 Bank of Transformers

A contract was placed with the Canadian Westinghouse Company in April for the 110,000-volt and 13,200-volt switching and metering equipment for the second bank of three 750-kv-a., 63,500/13,200-volt transformers. This second bank comprises two transformers from Guelph Transformer Station, which were delivered and installed in this station by the Maintenance Department in March, and the original spare transformer in this station.

The installation work was completed by the Commission's Construction Department and the second bank was placed in service July 30th.

Additional Feeder Equipment

A contract was placed with the Canadian Westinghouse Company, April 6th for complete switching and metering equipment for two additional 13,200-volt feeders, including lightning arresters. One of these feeders will be in the old station and one in the new extension. The switchboard panel in the old station will line up as far as possible with the present Canadian General Electric switchboard. The installation work will be done by the Commission's Construction Department when material is received.

Railway Supply Eqipment

Considerable time has been spent in obtaining data and studying the operation of 1,500-volt D.C. rotary converters on railway work, and this is being continued.

In order to better sectionalize the feeder system, three 1,000-ampere S.P.D.T. and one 1,000-ampere S.P.S.T. 1,500-volt disconnecting switches were purchased from the Canadian Westinghouse Company, Limited, and installed in 1,500-volt feeders. This work was completed early in August.

Two electrolytic lightning arresters were purchased in August from the Canadian General Electric Company, and it is the intention to connect these directly across the commutators of the two 500-kw. rotary converters in this station to give increased protection to the windings.

St. Thomas Municipal Station

Building

At the request of the St. Thomas Hydro-Electric Commission, plans and specifications were prepared for the construction of a combined office and sub-station. Tenders were called for and submitted to the local Commission, who awarded the contract to Mr. A. E. Ponsford, of St. Thomas, in February.

The building, which is 40 feet by 80 feet, is located on the south-west corner of St. Catharine and Gas Streets. It is built of red pressed brick with buff-colored Indiana limestone trim. Steel window sash, reinforced concrete floors, and steel beam construction were used throughout, making an entirely fireproof building. The front part of the building is partitioned off for offices on all floors, the space occupied being 37 feet wide by 20 feet 1 inch deep inside. The building will be completed early in December.

Electrical Equipment

The electrical equipment is located at the rear of the offices, occupying a space of approximately 37 feet by 55 feet 6 inches on each floor. The 13,200-volt apparatus is located on the second floor, the main transformers, constant current transformers, rotary convertor and switchboard on the main floor, and the cables and service transformers in the basement, which will also be used for storage purposes.

The station is fed by two 13,200-volt incoming lines and has one 13,200-volt outgoing feeder with provision for a second outgoing feeder, all these being equipped with Canadian Westinghouse electrolytic lightning arresters. These feeders are connected through choke coils, disconnecting switches and oil switches to a sectionalized bus, and from this bus leads are taken through oil-switches to three 100-kv-a. 13,200/375-volt, single-phase Canadian Westinghouse transformers and two new 750-kv-a., 13,200/2,300-volt, three-phase, Canadian General Electric transformers. Provision was also made for a future three-phase transformer. From the 100-kv-a. transformers the 375-volt leads are taken in conduit to a 200-k.w., 600-volt D.C. rotary convertor, which feeds the local street railway circuit.

From the 750-kv-a. transformer, leads are carried in conduit to the 2,300-volt busses back to the main switchboard on the main floor from which the following feeders are taken out in conduits underground, three commercial lighting, one 2,300-volt power, two 550-volt power feeders and five series street lighting feeders with provision for several future feeders. The 550-volt power is obtained from three 30-kv-a., 2,300/550-volt, single-phase Packard Electric Company's transformers installed in the basement. Three 28-k w. Adams Bagnall, and two 22-k w. Canadian Westinghouse constant current transformers are used for the series lighting feeders. The main 2,300-volt busses are sectionalized to allow for the future installation of a regulator if found necessary.

Three 25-kv-a., 2,300/220/110-volt transformers located in the basement and connected to the 2,300-volt busses through expulsion fuses supply light, heat and power for the station and office.

As much as possible of the electrical equipment from the old station was used in the new station, but in addition to the new 750-kv-a. transformers and the 25-kv-a. service transformers mentioned above, it was found necessary to purchase a number of new switchboard panels, meters and relays from the Canadian Westinghouse Company.

The equipment in the new station is being installed by the Commission's construction staff in conjunction with the local Commission's staff in such a way that no serious interruption of service is necessary. One 750-kv-a. transformer was installed in the old station and put in service temporarily on September 20th, releasing one old bank of three 150-kv-a. single-phase transformers which were disposed of to the Welland Hydro-Electric Commission for use in the Welland Municipal Station. It is expected that the installation will be entirely completed early next year, the progress not being as rapid as expected, owing to slow deliveries of material and the necessity for maintaining service during the transfer to the new building.

West Lorne Distributing Station

A type " E-2 " station was authorized for West Lorne to supply power to West Lorne and to Rodney. The contract was awarded for the building to Messrs. Horton Bros., of St. Thomas, on October 14th. This station is to contain three 75-kv-a., 13,200/2,300-volt transformers with two outgoing 4,000-volt feeders, each of 100-kv-a. capacity, one to supply West Lorne and the other Rodney. The contract for the electrical apparatus was given to the Canadian Westinghouse Company. It is expected that this station will be placed in operation before January 1st, 1917.

COOKSVILLE TRANSFORMER STATION

The corrugated sheet steel shed referred to in previous report was erected. Plans are being considered extending this station to accommodate equipment for a second 110,000-volt line.

Mimico Distributing Station

Owing to increasing demand for power, it was found necessary to put in additional transformer capacity in the Mimico Distributing Station. As the plans under consideration for this district contemplated the erection of a new larger station, it was decided to install the additional transformers required in a temporary extension to the existing building.

Three 300-kv-a., 13,200/2,300-volt, 25-cycle, single-phase transformers of Johnson and Phillips make were purchased from Chapman and Walker (in liquidation) for this station, but, owing to the necessity for overhauling them, they could not be made ready for service in time, and arrangements were finally made to purchase from the corporation of Brampton three 150-kv-a., 13,200/2,200-volt Crocker Wheeler Company's transformers. The temporary building extension was erected and the 150-kv-a. transformers installed and the necessary wiring changes made by the Commission's construction staff. These additional transformers were placed in service on October 15th.

Etobicoke Distributing Station

This station will be constructed in New Toronto village and will be used for supplying power to Mimico, New Toronto and the Provincial Institutions in the neighborhood. Tenders have been called for the supply of two 1,500-kv-a., 3-phase transformers for this station. This station will be supplied from Cooksville Transformer Station at 13,200 volts, but is so designed that it can later be fed from the proposed York Transformer Station at 26,400 volts.

In a former report " Etobicoke Distributing Station " was mentioned. This, however, referred to a proposed station in the vicinity of Mimico Asylum, which was never constructed, and the switching equipment ordered for same was used elsewhere, partly at Port Robinson Distributing Station and partly at Paris Municipal Station (McFarlane Engineering Company).

Pending construction of the above new station, a temporary station will be erected to take care of the immediate requirements for a supply of power to Brown's Copper and Brass Rolling Mills at New Toronto. It is proposed to use here the three 300-kv-a. Johnson and Phillips transformers referred to above under Mimico Distributing Station.

Brampton Municipal Station

At the request of the corporation of Brampton, tenders on three 300-kv-a., 13,200/2,300/575-volt transformers were obtained and submitted to the Brampton Commission. The contract for these was awarded to the Moloney Electric Company of Canada. Witness tests on these were made at the manufacturer's factory and the results reported to Brampton. These transformers were installed in the latter part of August.

The 150-kv-a. transformers which were replaced by the 300-kv-a. units, were purchased by the Commission for use at Mimico Distributing Station.

Corporation of Weston

The Commission have purchased for the Weston Hydro-Electric Commission three 150-kv-a. transformers 13,200/2,200/550-volt from the Stratford Utilities Commission to take care of the load of Canada Cycle and Motor Works at Weston.

The transformers will be installed in the company's own building by the Commission's construction staff.

The Commission will also take care of the necessary changes in the Weston Municipal Station to take care of this additional load. This will consist of the purchase and installation of one 13,200-volt oil-switch with panel and necessary metering equipment. It is expected that this equipment will be ready in December.

BRANT TRANSFORMER STATION

No work was undertaken in the Brant Transformer Station during the year, but plans are being considered for extending this station to accommodate equipment for a second 110,000-volt line.

Paris Municipal Station (McFarlane·Engineering Company)

With authority from the corporation of the town of Paris, the Commission purchased electrical equipment for a second municipal sub-station to be installed in a brick building, the property of the McFarlane Engineering Company for the purpose of supplying this company with power. The equipment consists of three 150-kv-a., 26,400/2,300-volt Moloney Electric Company's transformers, protected by expulsion type fuses; choke coils and air-break switch.

One 2,300-volt, 3-phase feeder panel purchased from Canadian General Electric Company is erected equipped with metering apparatus and oil switch for controlling the power to the company's factory.

The equipment is being installed by the Commission's construction staff. This station will be completed ready for service in November.

KENT TRANSFORMER STATION

No work was undertaken in this station during the year.

Ridgetown Distributing Station

The building referred to in last annual report was completed early in November and the electrical equipment installed and placed in service November 24th.

Blenheim Distributing Station

The installation of the 22-k.w. constant current transformer and panel for same mentioned in the last report was completed and this equipment was placed in service in December.

Petrolia Distributing Station

The building for this station was completed in December. The contract for the electrical equipment was awarded to the Canadian General Electric Company and included two 4,000-volt feeder panels and two street lighting feeder panels for the local Commission. The contract also included one 4,000-volt feeder panel for supplying the municipality of Wyoming.

The two 16-kw. constant current transformers purchased previously by the Commission for the municipality were installed, and the entire station, excepting the Wyoming feeder, was placed in service on April 25th. · The Wyoming feeder was completed later and placed in service October 4th.

Forest Distributing Station

The corporation of Forest decided to take power from the Commission instead of generating same by steam. · It was arranged to use a part of their present building to house the necessary electrical material.

On September 5th a contract was placed with the Canadian Westinghouse Company for a standard type " H " station equipment which will be installed by them and which will consist of three 75-kv-a., 26,400/2,300-volt, single-phase transformers together with the switching equipment and connecting material for one incoming 26,400-volt line and one 2,300-volt feeder. The Westinghouse equipment is due for shipment early in December.

Sarnia Municipal Station

It has been arranged to supply the corporation of Sarnia with power over two 26,400-volt, 3-phase lines from the Kent Transformer Station. This equipment will consist of three 750-kv-a., 3-phase, 26,400/4,000-volt water-cooled transformers, with provision for one future transformer, four 28-k.w., 6.6-ampere constant current street lighting transformers, three 25-kv-a. station service transformers and one 75-kv-a., 4,000-volt feeder potential regulator, together with switching equipment for two incoming 26,400-volt lines, three 26,400-volt commercial lighting feeders, four 4,000-volt power feeders, one 4,000-volt feeder to railway bus, and one 4,000-volt feeder to the constant current transformer bus. The contract for the three 750-kv-a. transformers was placed with the Canadian General Electric Company on May 9th.

Five of the existing switchboard panels will be used in the new switchboard. All the remaining switching equipment, together with the 75-kv-a. potential regulator and the service transformers were purchased from the Canadian General Electric Company on August 14th, and are due for shipment on December 29th, 1916, excepting the 26,400-volt oil switches, which are due on March 14th, 1917.

The 28-k.w. street lighting transformers were purchased from A. H. Winter Joyner, Toronto, on May 23rd. One of these transformers was shipped to the Commission's Testing Laboratory for special tests.

Arrangements are being made to transfer a 26,400-volt oil switch from the Commission's Essex Station and to have the Canadian General Electric Company ship some 26,400-volt disconnecting switches in order to make temporary connections to place two of the 750-kv-a. transformers in service early in November.

This equipment will be installed by the Hydro-Electric Power Commission's Construction Department, in the existing steam generating station formerly owned by the Sarnia Gas and Electric Company. Power to this station will be metered at the incoming 26,400-volt lines.

On September 7th, a contract was placed with the Canadian General Electric Company to supply and install one 410-kv-a., 4,000-volt, 3-phase, 25-cycle synchronous motor and base to replace an existing 450-h.p., 23,000-volt, 3-phase, 60-cycle induction motor which is direct connected to a 300 kw. D.C. 600-volt railway generator. This motor is due for shipment on February 21st, 1917.

ESSEX TRANSFORMER STATION

In order to provide temporary switching equipment at Sarnia Municipal Station, one spare 26,400-volt oil switch with current transformers was removed from Essex Transformer Station and shipped to Sarnia. This will be returned to Essex Station and re-installed at a later date.

Walkerville Municipal Sub-Station

Engineering assistance was given to Walkerville Hydro-Electric System in connection with transformer repairs, also in connection with preparation of plans and specifications for the switching equipment required for controlling one 400-kv-a. 3-phase, O.I.W.C., 25-cycle, 26,400/2,300-volt transformer of Moloney Electric Company's manufacture, to supply the 400-kv-a. 2,300-volt feeder to the Canadian Bridge Company.

YORK TRANSFORMER STATION

It was decided to construct a transformer and interswitching station near the western limits of the City of Toronto, same to be used as a transformer station to relieve Toronto Transformer Station, and to supply power in New Toronto and the vicinity, and for interswitching between the two present and two new lines from Dundas and the two present lines into Toronto. It is the intention to ultimately deliver power from this station at 26,400 volts, but for the present it is intended to install the two banks of 2,500-kv-a. transformers now in Toronto Station, but which will be replaced next summer by 5,000-kv-a. units and operate at 13,200 volts.

WASDELL'S FALLS SYSTEM

WASDELL'S FALLS GENERATING STATION

It was decided to use one of the two 22,000-volt lines out of the Wasdell's Falls Generating Station as a tie line to the Severn System, and as a feeder to the Corporation of Orillia Station and to instal the necessary metering equipment to measure the power supplied over this line.

Plans were prepared showing the necessary changes in the original arrangement. The material was ordered by the Operating Department. The necessary changes, except the metering equipment, were completed on July 23rd, 1916, and the metering equipment will be completed when the new meters arrive at the station, all the installation work being done by the Operating Department.

Beaverton Distributing Station

There will be installed in the Beaverton Distributing Station the Canadian Westinghouse 22,000-volt, low equivalent lightning arrester, which will be moved from Cannington Distributing Station.

Cannington Distributing Station

An order was placed with the Canadian General Electric Company for one 22,000-volt electrolytic lightning arrester, to be installed in the Cannington Distributing Station. This arrester will replace the Canadian Westinghouse low equivalent 22,000-volt arrester now installed in this station and which will then be moved to Beaverton Distributing Station.

SEVERN SYSTEM

BIG CHUTE POWER HOUSE

In December estimates were prepared covering additional electrical equipment and superstructure for contemplated increased generator capacity.

Collingwood Distributing Station

Owing to the increase of the load at this station, it was found necessary to increase the transformer capacity, and on December 22nd, the contract was awarded to the Canadian General Electric Company for three 400-kv-a. 22,000/2,300-volt 60-cycle, single-phase transformers to replace the three 250-kv-a. Canadian General Electric transformers originally installed.

Plans showing the changes in the station were prepared and the necessary additional material was ordered. The installation was made by the Commission's Construction Department and was completed and put into service on May 1st. A 24-inch roof ventilator, purchased from the A. B. Ormsby Company, was also installed to obtain better ventilation for this station, required on account of the larger size of the transformers.

The 250-kv-a. transformers were shipped to Port McNicoll for installation in the distributing station at Canadian Pacific Railway Company's Terminal.

Port McNicoll (Canadian Pacific Railway) Distributing Station

Owing to the Canadian Pacific Railway Company having signed a contract for power for use in the elevator at Port McNicoll, a modified type "G" station was authorized. Plans were prepared and arrangements made with the Railway Company to install the Commission's equipment in their steam generating station. The necessary changes in the building were made by the Railway Company and the Commission installed the three 250-kv-a. 22,000/2,200/550-volt transformers which were transferred from Collingwood Distributing Station. A General Electric 22,000-volt K-21 oil switch, and an electrolytic lightning arrester was obtained from the Walkerville Hydro-Electric Commission and the remaining material required was purchased from Canadian General Electric Company and the Canadian Westinghouse Company, the latter supplying the metering equipment. Two incoming 22,000-volt, 60-cycle, 3-phase feeders supply this station and power is sold to the Railway Company at the low tension side of the transformers.

All the equipment in this station was installed by the Commission's Construction staff and the station was placed in operation on July 15th.

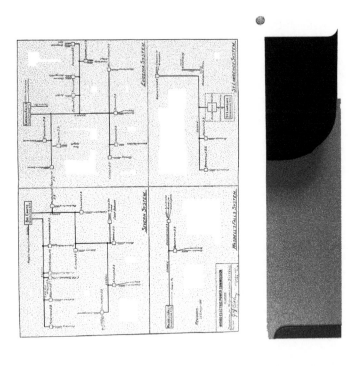

Camp Borden Municipal Station

Owing to the Commission having contracted to supply the Department of Militia and Defence with power for Camp Borden, a distributing station was authorized. Drawings were immediately prepared for a combined type " G " distributing station and pump house. The pump house which was 40 feet by 45 feet, and the distributing station, were built of brick by the Department of Militia and Defence, according to the plans prepared by the Commission.

The switching equipment was purchased by the Commission from the Canadian Westinghouse Company and consisted of one 22,000-volt type " E " oil switch with the necessary high-tension material, and two 2,200-volt feeders, with meter equipment for measuring the power on the 2,200-volt side of the transformers. The transformers were of Canadian Westinghouse Company's make, rated at 125-kv-a. 22,000/2,200-volt, 60 cycle, single-phase, and were purchased from the Pine River Power Company. There was also installed one 22,000-volt electrolytic light-ning arrester, purchased from the Canadian General Electric Company. All of this equipment was installed in the distributing station.

In the pump house the installation consisted of two 150-h.p. 2,200-volt induc-tion motors with starting compensators and relays to drive two belt-driven water pumps.

Foundations for this building were started about June 9th, and by June 21st work on the building was advanced sufficiently for the electrical construction work to commence. Work was started at once by the Commission's construction staff on the erection of all the electrical equipment for the distributing station and the pump house, and on June 29th this station was put into service, and one motor made ready for pumping. The second motor was ready for service on July 21st.

Coldwater Distributing Station

As the load at Coldwater Distributing Station did not warrant the trans-former capacity installed, consisting of three 75 kv-a. Canadian General Electric Company's transformers and as use could be made of same at Grand Valley Dis-tributing Station, it was decided to purchase two 25 kv-a. units and install them in place of the 75 kv-a. units. It was also decided to remove the 22,000 volt oil switch from this station and substitute fuses for same.

Accordingly two 25 kv-a. 22,000/2,300 volt transformers were purchased from the Moloney Electric Company and as soon as they are installed, the 75 kv-a. units with the oil switch will be removed and shipped to Grand Valley, and 22,000 volt " S & C." fuses installed to protect the transformers. This work was done by the Commission's construction staff.

EUGENIA SYSTEM

EUGENIA FALLS GENERATING STATION

Electrical Equipment

The characteristic tests on the generating equipment were completed early in November and the switching equipment tested out and the station was formally placed in service on November 19th.

Operators' Cottages

Owing to the isolated location of the Eugenia Generating Station it was found necessary to provide living accommodation for the operating staff. A single house and a pair of semi-detached houses were constructed in the vicinity of the Generating Station.

1916 Extension

It was decided to put in an additional 22,000 volt line with lightning arresters and metering equipment to be used as a tie line to Collingwood Station.

Plans were prepared showing necessary changes in the electrical equipment using the present transformer oil switch for the new line. The additional 22,000 volt apparatus and the switchboard panel with graphic wattmeters was purchased from the Canadian Westinghouse Company; three Weston ammeters were purchased from A. H. Winter Joyner.

The tie line was connected temporarily by the Commission's Construction Department on October 18th, and will be completed by them when all apparatus arrives at the station.

Markdale Municipal Station

The switchboard panel and constant current transformer referred to in last annual report to supply the street lighting system was installed and placed in service the early part of February.

Owen Sound Distributing Station

This station, described in last annual report, was placed in temporary service on November 18th, and equipment was permanently completed on January 30th. The electrical equipment was installed in this station by the construction staff of the Commission, and consists of three 550 kv-a. 22,000/2,300 volt, Canadian Westinghouse transformers fed from two 22,000 volt lines and protected with Canadian Westinghouse type " E " oil switches and choke coils and Canadian General Electric Company electrolytic lightning arresters. Provision is made for installation of a second similar bank of transformers at a later date.

Power is supplied at 2,300 volts to the Municipality's switching equipment consisting of one main oil switch between transformers and bus and two power feeders, one commercial lighting feeder, and one street lighting feeder. The two panels controlling the two steam driven units have been moved into the new building and arrangements made to synchronize one or both units with the Commission's system.

Chatsworth Distributing Station

The distributing station at Chatsworth as described in previous report was completed and placed in service on November 18th.

Chesley Distributing Station

The distributing station at Chesley was completed early in March and placed in operation on June 18th.

A 16 kw., 6.6 ampere, 2,300 volt, 60 cycle, Canadian Westinghouse constant current transformer, purchased from the Municipality of Palmerston was installed in this station by the Commission's construction staff for the Municipality of Chesley, for street lighting service.

Durham Distributing Station

The distributing station at Durham was completed and placed in service on November 18th.

The 100 kv-a. 4,000 volt feeder to supply the Village of Holstein was installed by the Canadian General Electric Company, and was placed in service April 3rd.

Dundalk Distributing Station

The distributing station at Dundalk was completed and placed in service on November 18th.

Mount Forest Distributing Station

The installation of the electrical equipment was completed by the Canadian General Electric Company, and station was placed in service on November 18th.

A 20 kw. constant current transformer, the property of the Municipality, is installed in this station for street lighting service.

Hanover Distributing Station

Arrangements were made to supply power to the flour mills of Wm. Knechtel at Hanover. A temporary wooden building was erected on his property and two 40 kv-a. 22,000/2,200 volt Canadian Westinghouse Company transformers were transferred from Hornings' Mills Power House to Hanover and there installed. These transformers are protected on the 22,000 volt side by " S. & C." fuses and on the secondary side by a Canadian General Electric " K-3 " 2,300 volt oil switch, obtained from the Commission's stores.

This station was put in service in September.

Shelburne Distributing Station

The original station was part of the property purchased from the Pine River Light and Power Company. The building was of brick with gable tin roof and contained three 50 kv-a. Allis Chalmers 22,000/2,200 volt transformers, one electrolytic 22,000 volt lightning arrester manufactured by the Canadian Westinghouse Company, and one small switchboard panel with voltmeter and ammeters.

The original electrical apparatus was removed to a temporary building along side of the old building and a contract was let to Messrs. Wells and Gray to remodel the building to resemble our standard type " H " station building.

New high tension switching equipment was ordered from the Canadian Westinghouse Company and a 2,000 volt feeder panel was transferred from the Pine River Power Company's power house. The temporary building was destroyed by fire before the apparatus was moved into the remodelled building and practically all the equipment was lost. In order to restore service two transformers of 25 kv-a. capacity, which had just been completed by the Moloney Electric Company for Coldwater Distributing Station, were rushed immediately to Shelburne by express, and installed temporarily in the remodelled brick building thus giving service to Shelburne after a very short interruption. New transformers for Shelburne Distributing Station were necessary and a contract was let to the Moloney Electric Company for three 50 kv-a. 22,000/2,300 volt transformers. These will be delivered in January, 1917. The new permanent switching equipment has been installed.

9 H

The Police Village of Hornings Mills is supplied from this station by a 4,000 volt feeder, the load on this feeder being measured on Canadian Westinghouse Company Type "RO" maximum demand meter mounted on the Shelburne feeder panel.

On the authority of the Corporation of Shelburne, a 12 kw. 6.6 ampere constant current Adams Bagnall transformer and a panel for same was ordered from the Northern Electric Company. This was installed temporarily in the Town Hall in April, by the Commission's construction staff. It will be transferred in a short time to the remodelled distributing station.

Orangeville Distributing Station

The old station of the Pine River Light and Power Company was deemed unsuitable and the construction of a new type " G " station building was authorized. The contract was awarded to Messrs. Wells and Gray of Toronto, at the end of July, for the construction of this building, but construction was not started for some time. A 22,000 volt type " K-21 " Canadian General Electric Company oil switch was transferred from Coldwater Distributing Station and re-arranged and installed in this new building, with new 22,000 volt wiring and connecting material ordered from the Canadian Westinghouse Company. A 22,000 volt electrolytic lightning arrester of the latter company's make was transferred from the Pine River Light and Power Company's station at Hornings' Mills and installed.

The two 125 kv-a. 22,000/2,200 volt single phase transformers, one of Allis-Chalmers Bullock Company's make, the other of Canadian Westinghouse Company's make, which were purchased with the Pine River Light and Power Company's station at Orangeville will be overhauled and installed in the new building. A third 125 kv-a. transformer, to complete the bank, will be ordered in a short time. Two 4,000 volt feeder panels were transferred from Midland Distributing Station to Orangeville and remodelled to suit the requirements.

The old station will be kept in service until the equipment, excepting the transformers, is installed in the new building, and when this work is completed, the transformers will be moved.

On the authority of the Municipality of Orangeville, a contract was placed in September with A. H. Winter Joyner, Limited, for two 10 kw., 6.6 ampere, 2,300 volt, Adams Bagnall constant current transformers with two switchboard panels for same. When these are delivered, they will be installed in the new station by the Commission's construction staff, who are doing all the installation work in the new building.

The new station will receive power over one 22,000 volt line from the Eugenia transmission system.

Grand Valley Distributing Station

A type " H " station was authorized for Grand Valley and the contract was let in August for the construction of the building to Mr. H. G. Wynne, of Collingwood. This building was completed in September. The contract for the switching equipment was let to the Canadian General Electric Company. Three 75 kv-a. transformers of Canadian General Electric Company's make will be transferred from Coldwater Distributing Station. There will be two 4,000 volt feeders, one to supply the Municipality of Grand Valley, and the other to supply the Municipality of Arthur. In addition to the standard equipment, there will be installed one 3 phase 20 kv-a. automatic voltage regulator on the Arthur 4,000 volt feeder and one 3' phase 10 kv-a. voltage regulator on the Grand Valley feeder. These regulators were purchased from the Canadian General Electric Company. Temporary service will be given these municipalities in November.

Kilsyth Distributing Station

The construction of a pole type distributing station near Kilsyth, to supply power to Kilsyth and to Tara has been authorized. This station will be equipped with one 75 kv-a. 3 phase 22,000/4,000 volt 60 cycle outdoor type transformer, and with two feeder circuits with metering equipment. A careful study of designs for pole type stations is being made, before proceeding with this station, in order to develop a satisfactory standard design of pole type stations for similar requirements.

SOUTH FALLS SYSTEM

SOUTH FALLS GENERATING STATION

The specifications for the building, transformers and switching equipment were completed and contracts were awarded to Messrs. Witchall & Sons, of Toronto, for the construction of the building, and to the Canadian General Electric Company, Limited, for all the electrical equipment, excepting meters and direct current circuit breakers. The indicating meters were ordered from the Weston Electrical Instrument Company through A. H. Winter Joyner, Limited, Toronto, and the recording meters were obtained from the Canadian Westinghouse Company. The direct current circuit breakers on the exciters were ordered from the Cutter Company.

The electrical apparatus supplied by the Canadian General Electric Company consists of one 750 kv-a. 3 phase, 60 cycle, 6,600 volt, 720 r.p.m. waterwheel type generator; one 20 kw. 125 volt, 1,200 r.p.m. compound wound exciter direct connected to a 35 h.p. 3 phase, 60 cycle, 220 volt induction motor; three 400 kv-a. single phase 60 cycle, 25,000/22,000—6.900/6,600/2,300 volt O.I.S.C. transformers; three 30 kv-a. 6,600/220/110 volt station service transformers; two 22,000 volt feeder equipments and four 6,600 volt feeder equipments. The old switchboard was dismantled and the old connecting cables removed and new equipment used to replace them.

The building extension is of pressed brick and steel construction with concrete floors and roof. A concrete roof was built over the older part of the station and a new concrete floor was also laid in this part of the building.

Owing to the difficulties in carrying on construction work, incident to the war conditions, this plant was not completed as early as had been expected.

The installation was completed and the new equipment placed in service in September. During the installation of this new equipment, the operation of the 450 kv-a. generator originally in this station and the service on the feeder to Gravenhurst was not interfered with.

One of the 22,000 volt electrolytic arresters supplied for this station was transferred to Camp Borden sub-station in August in order to complete the installation of protective equipment at that station. This will not be replaced at South Falls until the second 22,000 volt line is to be placed in service.

The 22,000 volt feeder to Huntsville was placed in service on August 24th, with temporary connections.

Plans are being considered at present for installation of a new belt driven exciter for this station.

Huntsville Distributing Station

The contract for the distributing station building at Huntsville mentioned in last annual report was awarded to Mr. F. Beston and a modified type " G " station building was constructed. The contract for electrical equipment required was placed with the Canadian General Electric Company. This equipment consists of one incoming 22,000 volt feeder with lightning arresters, three 300 kv-a. single phase 60 cycle, 22,000/2,300/575 volt transformers, and two 2,300 volt 3 phase feeders.

The building is of standard type with pressed brick walls, concrete floor and roof and is designed to accommodate transformers of 500 kv-a. size as well as a second incoming line. Provision was made for the future installation of additional 2,300 volt feeders.

The Corporation of Huntsville has installed in this station one 12 kw. 6.6 ampere constant current transformer, Adams Bagnall Company's make, also a control panel for same furnished by the Canadian General Electric Company.

Corporation of Huntsville

Constant Current Transformers

At the request of the Corporation of Huntsville, tenders were obtained and orders placed in February for one 12 kw. 6.6 ampere, 60 cycle constant current transformer and for the control panel and wiring for same. The transformer was purchased from the Northern Electric Company and is of Adams Bagnall Company's manufacture. The panel is of Canadian General Electric make.

Anglo Canadian Leather Company

Engineering assistance was given to the Anglo Canadian Leather Company in making witness tests at factory of Moloney Electric Company of Canada, Limited, at Windsor, on three 250 kv-a. 2,200/550 volt single phase 60 cycle O.I.S.C. transformers. A report of the tests was made to this company.

NORTHERN ONTARIO SYSTEM

Powassan Distributing Station

Lightning arrester equipment has been ordered for the Powassan sub-station from the Moloney Electric Company, which will be installed at an early date.

CENTRAL ONTARIO SYSTEM

Kingston Municipal Station

Three 75 kv-a. 13,200/2,300 volt transformers which the Canadian Westinghouse Company were holding to the order of the Commission, were loaned to the Kingston Utilities Commission and shipped the end of October. When released from Kingston, these will be used at Niagara Falls Transformer Station.

Table No. 1

CAPACITIES OF TRANSFORMERS INSTALLED OR ORDERED FOR COMMISSI ... STATIONS*

Total Capacity, 310,530 Kv-a.

Station	Voltage	Transformers		...rs Ordered		Total Station Capacity Kv-a.	System Capacity Kv-a.
		Mfr.	Kv-a.	Mfr.	Kv-a.		
NIAGARA SYSTEM.							
1. Niagara Transformer Station	12,000—110,000	C.W.Co.	77,000	C.W.Co.	22,500	134,500	
2. ...hs Transformer Station	12,000—45,700	C.G.E.Co.	24,500	C.G.E.Co.	10,500	7,500	
...lia Dist. Station	110,000—13,200	C.G.E.Co.	7,500			450	
Waterdown	13,200—2,300	P.T.Co.	450			225	
Hagersville	13,200—4,000	C.W.Co.	225			225	
Lynden	13,200—4,000	C.W.Co.	225			225	
3. Toronto Transformer Station	110,000—13,200	C.G.E.Co.	32,500†	C.G.E.Co.	45,000	67,500	
4. London Transformer Station	110,000—13,200	C.G.E.Co.	8,750			8,750	
Dorchester Dist. Station	13,200—4,000	C.W.Co.	225			225	
Lucan	13,200—4,000	C.G.E.Co.	225			225	
Delaware	13,200—4,000	P.E.Co.	75			75	
Exeter	13,200—4,000	C.G.E.Co.	300			300	
5. ...her Station	110,000—13,200	C.W.Co.	3,000			3,000	
Acton Dist. Station	13,200—2,300	S.Co. of C.	225			225	
Georgetown Dist. Station	13,200—4,000	C.G.E.Co.	450			450	
Rockwood	13,200—2,300	C.G.E.Co.	75			75	
Cheltenham	13,200—575	C.G.E.Co.	225			225	
Fergus	13,200—2,300	C.G.E.Co.	225			225	
Elora	13,200—4,000	C.W.Co.	225			225	
6. Preston Transformer Station	110,000—6,600	C.G.E.Co.	3,000			3,000	
Breslau Dist. Station	6,600—2,300	C.W.Co.	225			225	
7. Kitchener Transformer Station	110,000—13,200	C.G.E.Co.	6,000			6,000	
New Hamburg Dist. Station	13,200—2,200	P.E.Co.	225			225	
Baden	13,200—4,000	P.E.Co.	225			225	
Elmira	13,200—4,000	C.W.Co.	225			225	
8. Stratford Transformer Station	110,000—13,200	C.G.E.Co.	3,000†			8,000	
...el Dist. Station	110,000—26,400	C.W.Co.	5,000				
Harriston	26,400—4,000	C.W.Co.	300			300	
Tavistock	26,400—4,000	C.G.E.Co.	225			225	

* Spare transformers are ... d.   † Transformers to be transferred to another station.

Table No. 1—Continued

CAPACITIES OF TRANSFORMERS INSTALLED OR ORDERED FOR COMMISSION'S STATIONS*—Continued

Total Capacity, 310,630 Kv-a.

Station	Voltage	Transformers Installed		Transformers Ordered		Total Capacity Kv-a.	System Capacity Kv-a.
		Mfr.	Kv-a.	Mfr.	Kv-a.		
...ton Dist. Station	26,400— 4,000	C.G.E.Co.	225			225	
Palmerston "	26,400— 4,000	C.G.E.Co.	225			225	
9. St. Mary's : ...er ...n	110,000—13,200	C.G.E.Co.	3,000			3,000	
St. ...s ...nt Dist. Station	110,000— 575	C.G.E.Co.	1,500			1,500	
10. Woodstock ...er Station	110,000—13,200	C.G.E.Co.	3,000			3,000	
Beachville Dist. Station	13,200— 2,300	S.Co. of C.	150			150	
Norwich " "	13,200— 2,300	S.Co. of C.	150			150	
Embro " "	13,200— 4,000	C.G.E.Co.	225			225	
11. St. Thomas ...er Station	110,000—13,200	C.G.E.Co.	3,000			3,000	4,110
	13,200— 920	C.W.Co.	1,110			1,110	
Port-Stanley Dist. Station	13,200— 2,300	S.Co. of C.	150			150	
Dutton Dist. Station	13,200— 4,000	C.W.Co.	225			225	
West Lorne Dist. Station	13,200— 4,000	C.W.Co.	225			225	
12. Cooksville Transformer Station	110,000—13,200	C.C.W.Co.	5,000			5,000	5,000
Mimico Dist. ...n	13,200— 2,300	C.G.E.Co.	900			900	
Port Credit Dist. Station	13,200— 2,300	C.G.E.Co.	225			225	
Cooksville " "	13,200— 2,300	P.E.Co.	40			40	
...le " "	13,200— 4,000	C.G.E.Co.	225			225	
Woodbridge " "	13,200— 4,000	C.G.E.Co.	225			225	
13. Brant ...er Station	110,000—26,400	C.W.Co.	5,000			5,000	5,000
Waterford ...t. Station	26,400— 4,000	C.W.Co.	225			225	
Drumbo " "	26,400— 4,000	C.G.E.Co.	225			225	
Ayr " "	26,400— 4,000	C.G.E.Co.	225			225	
St. George " "	220— 4,000	C.C.W.Co.	150			150	
Burford " "	26,400— 4,000	C.W.Co.	225			225	
14. Kent ...er Station	110,000—26,400	C.W.Co.	5,000			5,000	5,000
...ng Dist. Station	26,400— 4,000	C.G.E.Co.	450			450	
Dresden " "	26,400— 4,000	C.W.	300			300	
Bothwell " "	26,400— 4,000	C.W.Co.	225			225	
Thamesville " "	26,400— 4,000	C.W.Co.	225			225	
Ridgetown " "	26,400— 4,000	C.W.Co.	225			225	
Blenheim " "	26,400— 4,000	C.W.Co.	225			225	

Station	Ratio	Make	Capacity	Make	No.	Capacity	No.	Total
Forest Dist. Station	26,400— 4,000							
15. Essex Transformer Station	110,000—26,400	C.W.Co.	10,000	C.C.W.Co.	225	10,000	225	286,225
EUGENIA SYSTEM.								
Eugenia Generating Station	60-Cycle							6,080
Owen [Sound] Dist. Station	4,000— 2,300	C.W.Co.	2,700			2,700		
Chatsworth	22,000— 2,300	C.W.Co.	650			1,650		
Chesley	22,000— 4,000	C.G.E.Co.	75			75		
Durham	22,000— 4,000	C.G.E.Co.	300			300		
Dundalk	22,000— 4,000	C.G.E.Co.	150			150		
Mount Forest	22,000— 4,000	C.G.E.Co.	300			300		
Hanover	22,000— 2,200	C.G.E.Co.	80			80		
Shelburne	22,000— 4,000	C.W.Co.	50†			200		
Grand Valley	22,000— 4,000	M.E.Co.		M.E.Co.	150		150	
Orangeville	22,000— 4,000	A.C.&C.W.Co.	250	C.G.E.Co.	225	250	225	
SEVERN SYSTEM.								
Big Chute Power House	60-Cycle							8,125
Penetanguishene Dist. Station	2,300—22,000	C.W.Co.	3,600			3,600		
Barrie	22,000— 2,300	C.C.W.Co.	600			600		
Collingwood	22,000— 2,300	C.G.E.Co.	700			700		
Coldwater Distributing Station	22,000— 2,300	C.G.E.Co.	1,200	M.E.Co.		1,200		
[...]le	22,000— 2,300	C.W.Co.	150			200		
Port McNicoll	22,000— 4,000	C.W.Co.	225		50	225	50	
[...]le	22,000— 2,300	C.G.E.Co.	300			300		
Midland	22,000— 2,300	M.E.Co.	50			50		
	22,000— 2,300		50			50		
C.P.R. Pt. McNicoll Dist. Station	22,000— 575	C.G.E.Co.	450			450		
			750			750		
[...]L'S FALLS SYSTEM.								
Generating Station	60-Cycle							1,650
Beaverton Dist. Station	2,300—22,000	C.W.Co.	1,050			1,050		
Cannington	22,000— 2,300	C.W.Co.	300			300		
	22,000— 4,000	C.W.Co.	300			300		
ST. LAWRENCE SYSTEM.								
Prescott Dist. Station	60-Cycle							1,200
Winchester	26,400— 2,300	C.G.E.Co.	450			450		
Brockville	26,400— 2,300	C.G.E.Co.	150			150		
	26,400— 2,300	C.G.E.Co.	600			600		
PORT ARTHUR SYSTEM.								
Port Arthur Dist. Station	[60-Cyc]le	S.Co. of C.	5,250			5,250		5,250
[SOUTH] FALLS SYSTEM.								
[Sou]th Falls Generating Station	6,600—22,000	C.G.E.Co.	1,200			1,200		2,100
Huntsville Dist. Station	22,000— 2,300	C.G.E.Co.	900			900		

* Spare transformers are idle.   † Transformers to be transferred to another station.

Table No. 2

STATION TRANSFORMERS ORDERED FOR MUNICIPALITIES AND COMMISSION DURING FISCAL YEAR ENDING OCTOBER 31st, 1916

Station	Cycles	Voltage	Mfr.	No.	Kv-a. each	Total Kv-a.
Niagara Falls Trans. Station.....	25	12,000–45,700	G.E.Co.	3	3,500	10,500
	25	12,000–63,500	.W.Co.	3	7,500	22,500
Welland Municipal Station......	25	13,200– 2,300	.W.Co.	3	150	450†
Port Robinson Dist. Station.....	25	13,200– 2,300	C.E.Co.	3	75	225†
Toronto Transformer Station......	25	63,500–13,200	B.G.E.Co.	9	5,000	45,000
London Transformer Station—						
Exeter Dist. Station............	25	13,200– 2,300	C.G.E.Co.	3	100	300
Guelph Transformer Station—						
Guelph Municipal Station......	25	13,200– 2,300	C.G.E.C.	1	550	550
Preston Transformer Station.....	25	63,500–13,200	C.G.E.Co.	2	750	1,500†
Stratford Transformer Station—						
Stratford Municipal Station....	25	26,400– 2,300	G.E.Co.	3	750	2,250
Seaforth Municipal Station.....	25	26,400– 2,300	G.E.Co.	3	150	450
Mitchell Municipal Station.....	25	26,400– 575	G.E.Co.	3	75	225
Tavistock Dist. Station.........	25	26,400– 2,300	C.W.Co.	3	75	225
Milverton Dist. Station.........	25	26,400– 4,000	G.E.Co.	3	75	225
Harriston Dist. Station.........	25	26,400– 4,000	G.E.Co.	3	75	225
Palmerston Dist. Station........	25	26,400– 4,000	G.E.Co.	3	75	225
St. Thomas Transformer Station..	25	63,500–13,200	G.E.Co.	2	750	1,500†
St. Thomas Municipal Station..	25	13,200– 2,300	C.G.E.Co.	2	750	1,500
West Lorne Dist. Station.......	25	13,200– 2,300	C.W.Co.	3	75	225
Cooksville Transformer Station—						
Mimico Distributing Station....	25	13,200– 2,300	& P.Co.	3	300	900
	25	13,200– 2,200	C.W.Co.	3	150	450†
Brampton Municipal Station....	25	13,200– 575	J.E.Co.	3	300	900
Corporation of Weston..........	25	13,200– 550	C.B.Co.	3	150	450†
Brant Transformer Station—						
Paris Municipal Station........	25	26,400– 2,300	M.E.Co.	3	150	450
Kent Transformer Station—						
Petrolia Distributing Station...	25	26,400– 2,300	C.G.E.Co.	3	150	450
Forest Distributing Station.....	25	26,400– 2,300	C.W.Co.	3	75	225
Sarnia Municipal Station.......	25	26,400– 4,000	C.G.E.Co.	3	750	2,250
Big Chute Power House—						
Collingwood Dist. Station.......	60	22,000– 2,300	G.E. o.	3	400	1,200
Port McNicoll Dist. Station.....	60	22,000– 550	G.E. o.	3	250	750†
Camp Borden Municipal Station.	60	22,000– 2,200	C.W.C.	3	125	375†
Coldwater Dist. Station.........	60	22,000– 2,500	M.E.Co.	2	25	50
Eugenia Falls Generating Station—						
Hanover Dist. Station..........	60	22,000– 2,200	C.W.Co.	2	40	80†
Shelburne Dist. Station.........	60	22,000– 2,300	M.E.Co.	3	50	150
Orangeville Dist. Station........	60	22,000– 2,200	C.W.C	1	125	
			A.C.B. o.	1	125	250†
South Falls Generating Station—	60	25,000– 2,300	C.G.E. o.	3	400	1,200
		6,600– 110	C.G.E. o.	3	30	90
Huntsville Dist. Station........	60	22,000– 2,300	C.G.E.Co.	3	300	900

† Transformers transferred from other stations.   Total Kv-a., 99,1

LOW-TENSION TRANSMISSION LINES

On October 31st, 1916, there were completed and under construction 1,321 miles of low tension transmission lines, of voltages varying from 46,000 volts to 2,200 volts.

The mileage of these lines is distributed among the various systems as follows:

Niagara System—840.32 miles.

St. Lawrence System—66.35 miles.

Severn System—102.94 miles.

Wasdell's Falls System—65.85 miles.

Eugenia Falls System—219.41 miles.

Muskoka System—26.32 miles.

In the construction of these lines, 8,960 miles of wire, weighing 5,513,923 lbs., and 54,372 wood poles were used.

On the transmission line poles 1,126 miles of single circuit telephone line has been erected for use in operating the system.

During the year 10 gangs were employed, 2 of which, under the direction of a forestry expert were employed solely in trimming trees. These gangs constructed 229 miles of transmission lines as well as distributing systems in 7 towns and villages, and rural lines in 5 townships.

For the above lines 230 crossing plans were prepared and submitted to telephone and railway companies for approval.

The low tension distributing systems were constructed by the commission in the towns and villages of Chesley, Shelbourne, Victoria Harbour, Markdale, Holstein, Orangeville, Grand Valley, and rural lines in the townships of Toronto, Etobicoke, Vaughan, Grantham and Zone.

Although handicapped by a scarcity of labour, and difficulty in obtaining material, some important lines were successfully constructed in record time, to the great satisfaction of the communities benefitted thereby. Among these are Barrie Tap to Camp Borden, Eugenia Falls to Collingwood, and Niagara Falls to Ontario Power Company's Line.

Description

NIAGARA

Sec. No.	From	To	Length of pole	Span	Miles	No. of Poles
L.T.			feet	feet		
1	Dundas Sub. H.E.P.C....	Junction Pole No. 134:...	40	120	2.84	134
2	Junction Pole No. 134....	Beach Pump House......	40	120	6.34	323
3	'' '' No. 134....	Asylum	50	120	1.13	67
× 4	Berlin Sub. H.E.P.C....	Junction Pole No. 10	40	....	.18	10
∫ 5	Junction Pole No. 10.....	Waterloo	40	120	1.64	78
6	'' '' No. 10.....	Berlin Corp. Station.....	45	120	.76	35
7	Berlin Sub. H.E.P.C.....	New Hamburg..........	40	120	12.27	556
8	Woodstock ''	Ingersoll	40	120	9.90	455
9	'' ''	Junction Pole No. 508....	40	120	11.12	508
10	Junction Pole No. 508....	Tillsonburg.............	40	120	10.30	467
11	'' '' No. 508....	Norwich................	40	120	4.59	207
12	St. Thomas Sub. H.E.P.C.	St. Thomas Corp. Station	40 & 45	120	1.13	50
13	Stratford '' ''	Stratford '' ; .	40 & 45	120	1.75	78
14	Preston '' ''	Junction Pole No. 99.....	45	120	2.04	99
15	Junction Pole No. 99....	Hespeler...............	40	120	2.08	99
16	'' '' No. 99...	Galt...................	40	120	3.75	173
17	Preston Sub. H.E.P.C....	Preston Corp. Station....	35	120	.14	11
			These poles also carry Section L.T. 35			
18	London Sub.............	Junction Pole No. 38.....	40	120	.79	38
19	Junction Pole No. 38.....	Asylum, London	45	120	1.54	70
20	'' '' No. 38.....	Junction Pole No. 93....	40	120	1.22	55
21	London Sub. H.E.P.C....	London Sub. No. 1.......	40	120	3.56	178
22	Junction Pole No. 93.....	'' '' No. 1......	40	120	1.71	96
23	'' '' No. 93.....	'' '' No. 2......	40	120	.31	20
24	London Sub. No. 1.......	Springbank	40	120	3.55	156
25	Dundas Sub. H.E.P.C....	Dundas Town...........	40 & 45	120	.98	58
26	Cooksville Sub. H.E.P.C.	Port Credit L.S. Road ...	40	120	2.74	129
26a	Pt. Credit L.S. Road....	Port Credit Brick Works	45	120	.24	14
27	Cooksville Sub. H.E.P.C.	Brampton	40	120	11.24	510
			These poles also carry Section L.T. 34 Circuits			
28	Junction Pole No. 1547...	Clinton...............	40	120	1.27	78
29	'' '' No. 1152...	Seaforth...............	40	120	1.50	74
30	'' '' No. 648...	Mitchell	40	120	1.27	63
31	Guelph Sub. H.E.P.C.....	O. A. College...........	40	120	1.56	77
32	'' H.E.P.C. Sub. Pro- perty:.......... }	....	40	120	.09	8 {
			18 poles on Station			
34	Cooksville Sub. H.E.P.C..	Weston................	40	120	14.07	551
			These Circuits carried on			
35	Preston Sub. H.E.P.C....	G. P. & H. Ry..........	40	120	.12	6
			These Circuits carried on			
36	Junction Pole No. 84, Port Credit...............	Mimico (New Toronto)...	45	120	5.75	266
38	Dundas Sub. H.E.P.C....	Dom. Sewer Pipe Works.	40	120	7.35	350
39	Hamilton Asylum P.H...	Hamilton Asylum.......	35	120	.63	30
40	Junction Pole No. 260....	Waterdown	35	120	1.50	72
40a	Dom. Sewer Pipe Works.	Junction Pole No. 260....	....	....	1.92	....
41	St. Thomas Sub. H.E.P.C.	Port Stanley...........	35	120	12.27	573
42	Junction Pole,No.290,LT.8	Standard White Lime Co.	....	....	1.00	2
			These circuits carried on Section			
43	Dundas Sub. H.E.P.C....	Jno. Bertram & Son.....	40	120	1.21	10
			These Circuits carried on Section			
44	Baden Sub.............	Wellesley	30	150	7.92	316
45	Junct. Pole No. 240 L.T. 8	Beachville	~40	120	.09	3
46	St. Mary's Sub..........	St. Mary's Cement Works	40	120	2.22	80

of Lines.

SYSTEM.

Voltage	No. of Circuits	Power Cables B.& S. Gauge	Telephone Wires, B.&S & B.W.G. Gauge	Ground Wire	Work Commenced	Work Completed	In Operation
13,200	2	No. 1/0 Alum	10 Copper	¼" Gal. Steel	July 13, 1910	Jan. 2, 1911	
" "	2	1/0 " "	10 " "	¼" " "	July 13, " "	Jan. 2, " "	
" "	1	2 " "	10 " "	¼" " "	Dec. 5, " "	Feb. 8, " "	
" "	2	1/0 " "	10 " "	¼" " "	Aug. 25, " "	Sept.11, 1910	
" "	2	1/0 " "	10 " "	¼" " "	Sept.11, " "	Nov. 25, " "	
" "	2	1/0 " "	10 " "	¼" " "	Aug. 25, " "	Sept.11, " "	
" "	2	2 " "	10 " "	¼" " "	Sept.11, " "	Jan. 2, 1911	Feb. 3, 1911
" "	2	1/0 " "	10 " "	¼" " "	Nov. 14, " "	Mar. 28, " "	
" "	2	1/0 " "	10 " "	¼" " "	Jan. 2, 1911	Apr. 29, " "	
" "	2	1/0 " "	10 " "	¼" " "	Jan. 2, " "	Apr. 29, " "	
" "	1	2 " "	10 " "	¼" " "	Feb. 13, " "	Mar. 30 " "	
" "	2	1/0 " "	10 " "	¼" " "	Dec. 14, 1910	Dec. 30, 1910	
" "	1	2 Copper	10 " "	¼" " "	Built by Corporation		
6,600	3	{ 1-2 Alum 2-4/0 " "	10 – " "	¼" " "	Oct. 8, 1910	Jan. 19, 1911	
" "	1	2 Alum	10 " "	¼" " "	Oct. 8, " "	Dec. 30, 1910	
" "	2	4/0 " "	10 " "	¼" " "	Oct. 8, " "	Jan. 19, 1911	
" "	1	2 Copper	10 " "	¼" " "	Built by Corporation.		

circuits to G. P. H. Railway Sub.

Voltage	No. of Circuits	Power Cables B.& S. Gauge	Telephone Wires, B.&S & B.W.G. Gauge	Ground Wire	Work Commenced	Work Completed	In Operation
13,200	2	{ 1-3/0 Alum 1-2	} 10 Copper	¼"	Oct. 26, 1910	Jan. 10, 1911	
" "	2	2 " "	10 " "	¼"	Oct. 26, " "	Jan. 19. " "	
" "	1	3/0 " "	10 " "	¼"	Oct. 24, " "	Jan. 21, " "	
" "	1	3/0 " "	10 " "	¼"	Oct. 20, " "	Jan. 20, " "	
" "	2	{ 1-3/0 " " 1-1/0 " "	10 " "	¼"	Dec. 23, " "	Jan. 20, " "	
" "	1	1/0 " "	10 " "	¼"	Dec. 23, " "	Jan. 20, " "	
" "	1	1/0 " "	10 " "	¼"	Jan. 1, 1911	Jan, 7, " "	
2,200	1	{ 400,000c.m. 250,000c.m.	Alum } Copper }	....	Dec. 1, 1910	Jan. 1, " "	
13,200	2	2 Alum	10 Copper	¼" Gal. Steel	Feb. 24, 1911	July 10, " "	
" "	2	2 " "	10 " "	¼" " "	Apr. 5, " "	July 23 " "	
" "	2	2 " "	10 " "	¼" " "	Feb. 15, " "	May 6, " "	

from poles No. 1 to 89—1.94 miles

Voltage	No. of Circuits	Power Cables B.& S. Gauge	Telephone Wires, B.&S & B.W.G. Gauge	Ground Wire	Work Commenced	Work Completed	In Operation
26,400	2	3/0 Alum	10 Copper	¼" " "	Apr. 6, " "	Aug. 4, " "	
" "	2	2 Alum	10 " "	¼" " "	Mar. 25, " "	Sept.13, " "	
" "	2	2 " "	10 " "	¼" " "	Mar. 24, " "	Aug. 3, " "	
13,200	1	1/0 " "	10 " "	¼" " "	July 21, " "	Nov. 9, " "	
550d.c. 2,200a.c.	1 4	} Municipal lines					
13,200a.c.	3	1/0 Alum	10 Copper	¼" " "	Aug. 7, 1911	Sept. 3, 1911	Sept. 4, 1911

Property in all.

Voltage	No. of Circuits	Power Cables B.& S. Gauge	Telephone Wires, B.&S & B.W.G. Gauge	Ground Wire	Work Commenced	Work Completed	In Operation
13,200	2	2 Alum	8 Copper	¼" " "	Apr. 19. " "	July 24, " "	

Section L.T. 27 poles, 1 to 89, inclusive

Voltage	No. of Circuits	Power Cables B.& S. Gauge	Telephone Wires, B.&S & B.W.G. Gauge	Ground Wire	Work Commenced	Work Completed	In Operation
6,600	1	1/0 Alum	10 Copper	¼" " "	Mar. 13, " "	Mar. 21, " "	

Section L.T. 17 poles, 1 to 11, inclusive

Voltage	No. of Circuits	Power Cables B.& S. Gauge	Telephone Wires, B.&S & B.W.G. Gauge	Ground Wire	Work Commenced	Work Completed	In Operation
13,200	1	2 Alum	8 Copper	¼" " "	Apr. 26, " "	Feb. 29, 1912	
" "	1	2 " "	8 " "	¼" " "	July 21, " "	Dec. 19, 1911	Apr. 6,1912
2,200	2	4 Copper	10 " "	....	Sept. 6, " "	Oct, 27, " "	Apr. 6 " "
13,200	1	2 Alum	8 " "	¼" Gal.Steel	Sept.30, " "	Oct. 10, " "	Apr. 6 " "
" "	1	2 " "	8 " "	¼" " "	Sept.30, " "	Oct. 7, " "	Mar. 1 " "
" "	1	2 " "	8 " "	¼" " "	Oct. 16, " "	Mar. 8, 1912	Mar. 9 " "
2,200	1	2 " "		....	....	....	....

L.T. 8 poles. from Beachville pole 290 to pole 240.

Voltage	No. of Circuits	Power Cables B.& S. Gauge	Telephone Wires, B.&S & B.W.G. Gauge	Ground Wire	Work Commenced	Work Completed	In Operation
13,200	1	2 Alum	10 Copper	¼" Gal.Steel	Dec. 1, 1911	Dec. 19, 1911	Dec. 21,1911

L.T. 25 poles, 1 to 58 inclusive.—.98 miles

Voltage	No. of Circuits	Power Cables B.& S. Gauge	Telephone Wires, B.&S & B.W.G. Gauge	Ground Wire	Work Commenced	Work Completed	In Operation
4,000	1	4 Copper	....	6 B.W.G.Iron	May 16, 1916	Aug.11, 1916	Oct. 23,1916
13,200	1	1/0 Alum	8 Copper	¼" Gal. Steel	June 1, 1912	June 29, 1912	July 17,1912
" "	1	3/0 " "	8 " "	¼" " "	July 15, " "	Aug. 19, " "	Sep. 7, " "

Description of

NIAGARA

Sec. No.	From	To	Length of Pole	Span	Miles	No. of Poles
			feet	feet		
47	Dundas Sub	Caledonia..............	40	120	14.36	674
47a	Caledonia	Paris Alabastine Co.....	.....	.....	.22	....
					These Circuits carried on	
48	Caledonia	Junction Pole No. 940....	40	120	5.87	267
49	Junction Pole No. 940....	Hagersville	40	120	3.79	176
50	‘‘ No. 940....	Lythmore...............	40	120	4.98	230
55	St. Thomas Sub. H.E.P.C.	L.L.E. Ry. Sub..........	40	120	1.68	88
56	Port Credit.............	Toronto Golf Club.......	30	120	3.24	11
56a	Extension from Sect. L.T.				Carried on Section	
	56 on T.G.C. property..	....	.....	.....	.90	37
57	O. A. College...........	Guelph Prison Farm. Pole 156............	40	120	1.93	86
57a	Guelph Prison Farm	Property	40	120	.08	4
58	Guelph Prison Farm, Pole 156.................	Junction Pole No. 454....	40	120	6.42	297
59	Junction Pole No. 454....	Acton	40	120	5.82	268
60	St. Catharines	Port Dalhousie	30	120	3.18	142
61	Caledonia Sub..........	Caledonia	.....	.....	.30	....
					Carried on	
62	Junction Pole No.230 L.T.27	Milton..................	40	120	16.65	740
63	Preston Sub	Doon Twine Mill	35	120	4.18	208
					Carried on Section	
64	Mimico Sub.............	Mimico Asylum.........	.....	.....	1.51	17
					Carried on Section	
65	Acton	Georgetown	40	120	9.03	411
66	Junction Pole No. 454....	Rockwood	35	120	1.64	77
68	Brant Station	Paris	40	120	3.21	152
69	‘‘ ‘‘	Brantford	40	120	6.66	320
71	Waterloo	Elmira	40	120	10.93	518
72	Preston	Breslau	40	120	6.48	293
73	Niagara Falls..........	Junction Pole 113........	48	250	5.00	113
74	Junction Pole 113........	Union Carbide Co........	48	250	10.50	235
75	‘‘ 303........	Electric Steel & Metal Co	48	250	1.93	45
76	Junction Pole No.38,L.T.18	Crumlin Junction........	35	132	5.31	218
77	Crumlin Junction........	Thorndale .;...........	35	132	7.91	310
78	‘‘ ‘‘	Thamesford	35	132	6.85	281
79	Jct. Pole No. 381 L.T. 62	Streetsville............	45	120	.43	19
81	Essex Station	Jct. Pole No. 55	45	120	1.10	55
82	Jct. Pole No. 55.........	Windsor...............	45	120	2.27	102
83	Jct. Pole No. 55.........	Walkerville.............	40	120	1.30	61
84	Kent Station............	Chatham	40	132	1.93	99
85	Jct. Pole No. 118 L.T 57 .	Jct. Pole No. 776, L.T. 85	40	120	14.61	658
86	‘‘ ‘‘ 776 ‘‘ 85.	Elora	40	120	1.18	58
87	‘‘ ‘‘ 776 ‘‘ 85.	Fergus	35	120	1.96	94
88	Paris	Junction Pole No. 313....	35-40	132	7.41	312
89	Jct. Pole No. 313 L.T. 88	Ayr	40	120	1.20	58
90	Jct. Pole No. 313 L.T. 88	Drumbo	35	132	6.83	284
91	Drumbo	Princeton	35	132	5.65	233
92	Drumbo	Plattsville.............	35	132	7.35	299
					1.00 miles carried	
93	Jct. Pole No. 388 L.T. 77	Deller Bros	30	132	.89	48
94	Jct. Pole No. 1005 L.T. 65	I. P. B. Co.............	35	132	5.08	221
95	London	Lambeth (Pole No. 462)..	40	120	10.15	463
96	Lambeth (Pole No. 462) ..	Komoka Jct. (Pole No. 759)	40	120	6.58	298
97	Komoka Jct. (Pole No. 759)	Mt. Brydges (Pole No. 943)	40	120	4.00	184
98	Mt. Brydges (Pole No. 943)	Strathroy (Pole No. 1,368)	40	120	9.27	424
99	London	Lucan	35-40	132	19.18	783
99c	London	Lucan	.....	.....	21.51	....
					These circuits carr ed	
100	Niagara Falls	Elect. Devel. Co	45	100	1.25	52

Lines—Continued

SYSTEM

Voltage	No. of Circuits	Power Cables B. & S. Gauge	Telephone Wires, B. & S. & B. W. G. Gauge	Ground Wires.	Work Commenced	Work Completed	In Operation
13,200	1	3/0 Alum	8 Copper.	¼" Gal. Steel	May 10,1912	Sept. 18,1912	Sep. 20,1912
2,200	1	2/0 Copper	....	....	Sept. 5, "	Sept. 18, "	" 20, "
Section L.T. 49 poles.							
13,200	1	3/0 Alum	8 Copper	¼" Gal. Steel	June 22, "	Sept. 18, "	Sep. 20 "
"	1	2 "	10 "	¼" "	Feb. 28, 1913	May 2,1913	Aug. 15,1913
"	1	3/0 "	8 "	¼" "	June 15, 1912	Sept. 18,1912	Sep. 20 "
"	1	2 "	8 "	¼" "	Aug. 9, "	Oct. 11, "	Oct. 27,1912
2,200	1	6 D.B.W.P. Copper		....	June 10, "	Aug. 3, "	Aug. 6 "
L.T. 36 poles							
2,200	1	6 "	....	....	Nov. 22, "	Jan. 3, 1913	Dec. 24 "
13,200	1	2 Alum	8 Copper	¼" Gal. Steel	Aug. 19, "	Dec. 14, 1912	Dec. 14 "
"	1	2 "	10 "	¼" "	May 14, 1913	May 19,1913	Sep. 4 "
"	1	2 "	8 "	¼" "	Aug. 19, 1912	Dec. 14, 1912	Dec. 14,1912
"	1	2 "	8 "	¼" "	" 19, 1912	Dec. 14, 1912	Dec. 14 "
2,200	1	1/0 "	....	....	Oct. 16, 1912	Nov. 21, "	Nov.17 "
"	1	4 D.B.W.P. Copper ...		....	Nov. 20, 1912	Nov. 30, "	Nov. 30 "
Section L.T. 47 poles.							
13,200	1	3/0 Alum	10	¼" Gal. Steel	Nov. 25, 1912	Mar. 13, 1913	Mar.13,1913
6,600	1	2 "	....		Dec. 2, 1912	Apl. 11, "	Apl. 1 "
L.T. 17 poles, No. 1 to 11, inclusive. L.T. 35 from 11 to 17 inclusive.							
2,200	1	2 Copper	....		Mar. 30, 1912	Feb. 3, "	Apl. 26 "
L.T., 36 poles							
13,200	1	3/0 Alum	10 Copper	¼" Gal. Steel	Mar. 11, 1913	Aug. 1, "	Aug. 1 "
"	1	2 "	10 "	¼" "	May 6,1913	July 3, "	Aug. 1 "
26,400	2	3/0 Alum	10 "	¼" "	Nov. 11, 1913	Jan. 2,1914	Jan. 3, 1914
26,400	2	3/0 "	10 "	¼" "	Dec. 15, 1913	Jan. 17, "	Jan. 17 "
13,200	1	2 "	10 "	¼" "	May 17, 1913	Oct. 14, 1913	Oct. 25,1913
6,600	1	2 "	10 "	¼" "	Apr. 4, 1913	Dec. 23, 1913	Dec. 23,1913
46,000	3	4/0 Copper	8 "	¼" "	Mar. 15, 1914		
46,000	3	4/0 "	8 "	¼" "	Mar. 15, 1914	Steel Towers.	Aug. 20,1914
46,000	1	2/0 "	8 "	¼" "	July 11, 1914		Aug. 20,1914
							Oct. 17,1914
13,200	1	2 Alum	....	¼" "	Sept.18, 1913	May 8, 1914	Jan. 27,1914
"	1	2 "	....	¼" "	Oct. 10, 1913	Feb. 6,1914	Feb. 6 "
"	1	2 "	....	¼" "	Oct. 13, 1913	Jan. 19, "	Jan. 27 "
"	1	2 "	10 Copper	¼" "	Nov. 1, 1913	Nov. 24,1913	Nov.24,1913
26,400	4	3/0 "	10 "	¼" "	July 28, 1914	Sept. 6, 1914	Sep. 6, 1914
"	2	3/0 "	10 "	¼" "	July 31, 1914	Sept.18, 1914	Sep. 18 "
"	2	3/0 "	10 "	¼" "	June 2, 1914	Aug. 1, 1914	Sep. 6 "
"	2	2/0 "	10 "	¼" "	Oct. 21, 1914	Feb. 22, 1915	Feb 1,1915
13,200	1	3/0 "	10 "	¼" "	June 3, 1914	Oct. 17, 1914	Oct.22,1914
"	1	3/0 "	10 "	¼" "	Aug. 18, 1914	Oct. 28, 1914	Oct. 22 "
26,400	1	3/0 "	10 "	¼" "	Aug. 1, 1914	Oct. 13, 1914	Oct. 22 "
"	1	1/0 "	10 "	¼" "	July 21, 1914	Nov. 30, 1914	Dec. 1 "
"	1	1/0 "	10 "	¼" "	Sept.15, 1914	Nov. 30, 1914	Dec. 1 "
"	1	1/0 "	10 "	¼" "	July 13, 1914	Nov. 30, 1914	Dec. 1 "
4,000	1	6 Copper	....	¼" "	Aug. 17, 1914	Nov. 30, 1914	Dec. 18 "
"	1	4 "	....	¼" "	Aug. 17, 1914	Nov. 30, 1914	Dec. 1 "
on L.T. 90 Poles							
4,000	1	6 "	....	¼" "	Mar. 19, 1914	Mar. 19, 1915	Mar. 19,1915
13,200	1	1/0 Alum	10 Copper	¼" "	June 10, 1914	June 31, 1914	July 3,1914
"	1	3/0 "	10 "	¼" "	Sept. 1, 1914	Nov. 30, 1914	Nov. 30 "
"	1	3/0 "	10 "	¼" "	Oct. 15, 1914	Nov. 30, 1914	Nov. 30 "
"	1	3/0 "	10 "	¼" "	Sept.29, 1914	Nov. 30, 1914	Nov. 30 "
"	1	2 S.R. "	10BWG Iron	¼" "	Sept.14, 1914	Nov. 30, 1914	Nov. 30 "
"	1	2 S.R. "		¼" "	Oct. 23, 1914	Jan. 20, 1915	Jan. 21,1915
					July 3, 1916	....	....
on L.T. 18 poles 1 to 38, L.T. 19poles 38 to 100 and L.T. 99.							
12,000	2	4/0 Copper	9BWGIron	¼" Gal. Steel	Oct. 27, 1915	Oct. 31, 1915	Oct. 31 "

Description of

NIAGARA

Sec. No.	From	To	Length of Pole.	Span.	Miles	No. of Poles
			feet	feet		
101	Kent Sta. Pole No. 40....	Tilbury	30	132	16.91	85
					15.00 miles carried	
102	Kent Station............	Junction No. 68	40	120	1.48	68
102a	"	Junction No. 68			1.48	
102b	"	Junction Pole No. 68....			1.48	......
103	Junction Pole 68, L.T. 102	Junction Pole No. 519....	40	120	9.98	451
103a	" " 68 L.T. 102	Junction Pole No. 519....			9.98	
104	" " 519 L.T. 103	Wallaceburg	40	120	8.50	386
105	" " 519 L.T. 103	Dresden................	40	120	7.40	309
106	" " 289 L.T. 8	Embro................	35	132	6.10	254
107	" " 564 L.T. 34	Woodbridge'............	35	132	6.44	277
108	Woodbridge	Bolton................	35–40	132	13.03	540
109	Junction Pole............	W. T. & I.Ry............			.02	2
110	Mimico Sub-Station	Prison Brick Yard.......	30	125	.71	32
111	Brant Sub-Station	Junction Pole 249........	35–40	132	5.84	249
112	Junction Pole 249 L.T. 111	Burford................	35	132	3.48	142
113	" " 249 L.T. 111	Waterford	35–40	132	14.20	616
114	Waterford............	Simcoe	35	132	8.90	366
115	Tilbury	Comber................	30	132	7.26	306
116	Delaware Sub-Station ...	Lambeth	40	120	6.58	
					Carried on	
117	" Junc. Pole 759,.	Mount Brydges	40	120	4.00	
					Carried on	
118	Bertram's Sub-Station, Pole No. 69-L.T. 43....	Dundas	55	....	.37	21
119	Junction Pole 759 L.T. 96	Delaware Sub-Station ...	55	120	.09	5
					Lambeth & Mt. Brydges	
121	St. Thomas............	Dutton	30	132	18.50	756
122	Ridgetown............	Highgate	....		6.18	9
					These circuit carried on	
123	Junction Pole 68 L.T. 102	Thamesville	35	132	14.60	683
124	Junction Pole 676 L.T. 123	Bothwell	35	132	9.83	410
125	Stratford............	Tavistock	35	132	9.72	398
126	Junction Pole 68 L.T. 102	Blenheim	35	132	9.52	390
127	Junction Pole 469 L.T. 123	Ridgetown............	35	132	8.02	333
128	Brant	St. George	30	132	9.09	369
					4.50 miles carried	
129	Dundas	Lynden	35	132	12.75	430
130	Lucan	Ailsa Craig	30	132	10.14	410
131	Dresden	Petrolia	35–40	125	21.78	947
132	Petrolia	Wyoming Jct. Pole 220 ..	35	125	4.85	220
133	Wyoming Jct. Pole 220 ..	Perch Jct. Pole 562......	35	125	7.92	343
134	Lucan	Granton	30	132	6.95	246
135	Perch Jct. Pole 562......	Sarnia................	35	125	7.73	332
136	Lucan	Exeter	35	132	13.24	552
137	Petrolia	Wyoming	25	132	e 7.50	e 25
138	Sebringville Junction Pole 311 L.T. 67	Milverton Jct. Pole 802..	35	132	11.90	491
139	Milverton Jct. Pole 802..	Milverton	35	132	.96	40
140	" " 802..	Listowel Jct. Pole 1313 ..	35	132	12.65	512
141	Listowel Jct. Pole 1313..	Listowell................	35	132	2.77	122
142	" " 1313..	Palmerston	35	132	10.48	431
143	Palmerston	Harriston	35	132	6.11	259
145	Wyoming Jct. Pole 1963.	Forest................	35–40	132	e20.50	817
146	Stratford Sub	Jt. Pole 311 (Sebringville)	40	120	6.81	311
147	Jct. Pole 311(Sebringville)	Jct. Pole 648 (Mitchell)..	40	120	7.61	337
148	Jct. Pole 648 (Mitchell)..	Jct. Pole 1152 (Seaforth).	40	120	11.36	505
149	Jct. Pole 1152 (Seaforth)	Jct. Pole 1547 (Clinton)..	40	120	8.84	395
150	Jct. Pole 1547 (Clinton)..	Goderich	40	120	13.61	612
151	Exeter	Hensall	30	132	e 5.04	e 205
152	Niagara Falls Sub	Ont. Power Co. Line.....	40	125	.31	17

Lines—Continued

SYSTEM

Voltage.	No. of Circuits	Power Cable B. & S. Gauge	Telephone Wires, B. & S. & B. W. G. Gauge	Ground Wire	Work Commenced	Work Completed	In Operation
26,400	1	2 S.R. Alum	10 BWG Iron	¼" Gal. Steel	Jan. 13, 1915	May 12, 1915	Mar. 3,1915
on H.T. Telephone Poles							
26,400	1	1/0 "	10 "	¼" "	Oct. 28, 1914	Feb. 3, "	Feb. 3, "
"	1	3/0 "	....	....	June 22, 1915	June 29, "	June 29 "
"	1	3/0 "	....	....	Oct. 7, "	Oct. 13, "	Oct. 13 "
"	1	1/0 "	10 BWG Iron	¼" Gal. Steel	Oct. 30, 1914	Feb. 3, "	Feb. 3 "
"	2	3/0 "	....	....	Oct. 12, 1915	Mar. 15, 1916	Mar. 15,1916
"	1	1/0 "	10 BWG Iron	¼" Gal. Steel	Nov. 6, 1914	Feb. 3, 1915	Feb. 3 1915
"	2	3/0 "	10 "	¼" "	Nov. 3, "	May 1, "	Mar. 30 "
13,200	1	1/0 "	10 "	¼" "	Oct. 1, "	Dec. 24, 1914	Dec. 22,1914
"	1	1/0 "	10 "	¼" "	Sept. 25, "	Oct. 21, "	Dec. 2 "
"	1	1/0 "	10 "	¼" "	Oct. 20, "	Nov. 26, "	Jan. 26,1915
"	1	2 "	10 "	....	Sep. 12, "	Sep. 12, "	Sep. 13,1914
2,200	1	2/0 Copper	....	....	Oct. 24, "	Feb. 17, 1915	Feb. 17,1915
26,400	1	2 S.R. Alum	10 BWG Iron	¼" Gal. Steel	Nov. 6, "	May 4, "	May 6 "
"	1	2 S.R. "	10 "	¼" "	Nov. 21, "	May 28, "	May 6 "
"	1	2 S.R. "	10 "	¼" "	Nov. 21, "	May 5, "	May 10 "
"	1	2 S.R. "	10 "	¼" "	Nov. 26, "	May 7, "	May 9 "
4,000	1	1/0 Copper	....	¼" "	Jan. 14, 1915	May 8, "	Apr. 20 "
"	1	6 Copper	....	¼" "	Jan. 25, "	Mar. 12, "	Mar. 15 "
L.T. 96 poles							
4,000	1	6 M.H.D.	....	¼" "	Jan. 7, "	Jan. 23, "	Mar. 1 "
L.T. 97 poles							
13,200	1	1/0 Alum	10 BGW Iron	¼" "	Feb. 25. "	Mar. 15, "	Mar. 15 "
"	1	3/0 "	10 "	¼" "	Jan. 27, "	Mar. 9, "	Feb. 1 "
4,000 v. circuit carried on L.T. 119 poles							
13,200	1	1/0 Alum	....	¼" "	May 3, "	Aug. 21, "	Aug. 27 "
4,000	1	6 B.W.G.Iron	....	6 B.W.G.Iron	Oct. 3, 1916	Nov. 4, 1916	Nov. 6,1916
H.T. relay poles.							
26,400	1	1/0 Alum	9 BWG. Iron	¼" Galv Steel	May 18, 1915	July 14, 1915	Sep. 14,1915
"	1	2 S.R. "	9 "	¼" "	June 26, "	Aug. 17, "	Aug. 17 "
"	1	6 B.W.G.Iron	9 "	6 B.W.G.Iron	Sept. 9, "	Sep. 5, 1916	Oct. 26,1916
"	1	2 S. R. Alum	9 "	¼" Gal. Steel	July 2, "	Oct. 7, 1915	Oct. 20,1915
"	1	2 "	9 "	¼" "	June 24, "	Sept. 7, "	Nov. 24 "
4,000	1	2 "	9 "	¼" "	July 1, "	Aug. 17, "	Aug. 17 "
On H.T. Tel. and Relay line							
13,200	1	2 S.R. Alum	9 BWG. Iron	¼" "	July 24, "	Oct. 15, "	Oct. 22 "
4,000	1	2 S.R. "	....	¼" "	July 28, "	Dec. 11, "	Dec. 15 "
26,400	2	3/0 "	9 BWG Iron	¼" "	Aug. 30, "	Feb. 18, 1916	Apl. 6,1916
"	2	3/0 "	9 "	¼" "	Mar 1, 1916	Sep. 12, "	Nov. 10 "
"	2	3/0 "	9 "	¼" "	Apl. 6, "	Sep. 29, "	Nov. 10 "
4,000	1	6 Copper	....	6 B.W.G.Iron	Apl. 6, "	May 27, "	June 29 "
26,400	2	3/0 Alum	9 B.WG. Iron	¼" Galv. Steel	May 9, "	Nov. 4, "	Nov. 10 "
13,200	1	3/0 "	9 "	¼" "	Nov. 26, 1915	May 4, "	May 4 "
4,000	1	6 Copper	9 "	....	Sept. 1, "	Oct. 4, "	Oct. 4 "
26,400	1	1/0 S.R. Alum	9 BWG. Iron	¼" Gal. Steel	Sept. 20, "	May 15, "	May 18 "
"	1	2 "	9 "	¼" "	Oct. 15, "	May 18, "	May 18 "
"	1	1/0 "	9 "	¼" "	Oct. 13, "	May 22, "	May 27 "
"	1	2 "	9 "	¼" "	Oct. 28, "	May 22, "	May 27 "
"	1	1/0 "	9 "	¼" "	Oct. 14 "	June 6, "	June 6 "
"	1	1/0 "	9 "	¼" "	Dec. 10, "	June 30, "	June 30 "
"	1	6 B.W.G Iron	9 "	¼" "	June 26, "	....	....
"	2	3/0 Alum	10 Copper	¼" "	Apl. 23, 1913	June 4, 1914	Dec. 23, 1914
"	2	3/0 "	10 "	¼" "	Apl. 23, "	June 4, "	Dec. 23 "
"	2	3/0 "	10 "	¼" "	Apl. 23, "	June 4, "	Dec. 23 "
"	2	3/0 "	10 "	¼" "	Apl. 23, "	June 4, "	Dec. 23 "
"	2	3/0 "	10 "	¼" "	Apl. 23, "	June 4, "	Dec. 23 "
4,000	1	6 Copper	....	6 B.WG. Iron	Sept. 11, 1916	....	....
12,000	2	2/0 "	....	....	Oct. 24, "	Nov. 1, 1916	Nov. 5, 1916

Description of

SEVERN

Sec. No.	From	To	Length of pole	Span	Miles	No. of Poles
S.L.			feet	feet		
1	Waubaushene............	Jct. Pole 193 (Coldwater).	40	120	4.29	193
2	Jct. Pole 193 (Coldwater).	Coldwater.............	40	120	1.16	55
3	" " 193 "	Jct. Pole 903 (Elmvale)..	40	120	15.86	710
4	" " 903 (Elmvale)..	Elmvale	40	120	.42	19
5	" " 903 " ..	Jct. Pole 1110 (Phelpston)	40	120	4.55	207
6	" " 1110 (Phelpston).	Barrie...............	40	120	12.27	550
7	" " 1110 " .	Jct. Pole 1785 (Stayner)..	40	120	15.07	675
8	" " 1785 (Stayner)...	Stayner	40	120	1.50	68
9	" " 1785 " ..	Collingwood............	40	120	11.86	530
10	Stayner	Creemore	35	120	7.67	348
12a	Waubaushene Pole 540 ..∴	Victoria Harbor Jct. 730.	35	100	8.59	190
14a	Victoria Harbor Jct. 730 .	Port McNicholl Jct. 969..	35	100	4.02	213
15	Port McNicholl Jct. 969 .	Port McNicholl	35	120	.50	35
17	Midland	Penetang	40	120	4.50	223
20	Port McNicholl Jct. 943 .	C.P.R. Elevators........	35	125	1.34	58
21	Jct. Pole 1590 S.L 6	Camp Bordon..........	35	132	14.34	604

ST.L.   ST. LAWRENCE

1	Morrisburg	Prescott...............	40	120	22.96	1,083
2	"	Winchester	40	120	16.29	747
3	Winchester	Chesterville	40	120	6.52	294
5	Prescott	Brockville	40	120	14.08	639
6	Morrisburg	North Williamsburg....			6.50	....

This circuit carried on St. L. 2 poles

WASDELL'S FALLS

W.L.						
1	Wasdell's Falls	Jct. No. 1 Pole 1203	40	120	25.50	1,203
1a	" "	Junction Pole 183.......	40	120	3.94	....
	Carried on W.L. 1 Poles					
2	Jct. No. 1 Pole 1203.....	Beaverton	40	120	1.47	70
3	Jct. No. 1 " 1203......	Cannington	40	120	9.67	442
4	Beaverton	Gamebridge			6.50	....
	Carried on Sec. W.L. 1 & 2 poles					
5	Gamebridge	Brechin			3.75	....
	Carried on Sec. W.L. 1 poles					
6	Cannington	Woodville	30	120	5.15	147
7	Cannington	Sunderland	30	120	7.40	335
8	Jct. Pole 183 W.L. 1	Longford	35	132	6.41	269

EUGENIA FALLS

EFL			feet	feet		
1	Eugenia Falls Pwr. House	Chatsworth Sub-Station.	40	125	22.15	972
2	Chatsworth Sub-Station.	Owen Sound	40	125	9.22	394
3	Eugenia Falls..........	Flesherton ....∴..	40	125	6.78	296
4	Flesherton Jct. Pole 296.	Durham Jct. Pole 964 ...	40	125	15.97	687
5	Durham Jct. Pole 964....	Mount Forest..........	40	125	15.70	692
6	Laurel Jct..............	Grand Valley	35	132	e8.50	357
7	Durham Jct. Pole 964....	Hanover Jct. Pole 1491 ..	40	125	12.09	526
8	Hanover Jct Pole 1491 ..	Chesley	40	125	11.06	473
9	Flesherton Jct. Pole 296.	Dundalk...............	40	125	11.73	500
10	Dundalk...............	Shelbourne ....∴.	40	125	13.16	562

Lines.—Continued.

SYSTEM

Voltage	No. of Circuits	Power Cable B. & S. Gauge	Telephone Wires, B.&S. & B.W.G. Gauge	Ground Wire	Work Commenced	Work Completed	In Operation
22,000	2	4/0 Alum	10 Copper	¼" Gal. Steel	Sep. 20, 1912	Feb. 18, 1913	Feb. 24, 1913
''	1	2 ''	''	¼" ''	Sep. 20, ''	Feb. 18, ''	Feb. 24 ''
''	2	4/0 ''	''	¼" ''	Sep. 25, ''	Feb. 18, ''	Feb. 24 ''
''	1	2 ''	''	¼" ''	Feb. 1, 1913	May 17, ''	May 27 ''
''	2	4/0 ''	''	¼" ''	Oct. 20, 1912	Feb. 18, ''	Feb. 24 ''
''	2	2/0 ''	''	¼" ''	Nov. 6, ''	Apl. 5, ''	April 6 ''
''	2	3/0 ''	''	¼" ''	Oct. 23, ''	Feb. 18, ''	Feb. 24 ''
''	1	2 ''	''	¼" ''	Jan. 24, 1913	Apl. 26, ''	Sep. 25 ''
''	2	3/0 ''	''	¼" ''	Nov. 1, 1912	Feb. 18, ''	Feb. 24 ''
4,000	1	1/0 ''	....	¼" ''	Aug. 15, 1914	Oct. 25, 1914	Oct. 21, 1914
22,000	2	1/0 ''	10 Copper	¼" ''	Apl. 1, 1916	May 5, 1916	July 24, 1916
''	2	1/0 ''	''	¼" ''	Mar. 7 ''	May 5 ''	July 24 ''
4,000	1	1/0 ''	''	¼" ''	Oct. 15, 1914	Dec. 25, 1914	Dec. 24, 1914
22,000	1	2 ''	''	¼" ''	June 7, 1911	July 18, 1911	July 18, 1911
''	2	1/0 ''	9 B.W.G. Iron	¼" ''	Feb. 29, 1916	Apl. 14, 1916	July 24, 1916
''	1	6 Copper	9 '' ''	6 B.W.G. Iron	May 30 ''	July 11, 1916	June 29 ''

SYSTEM

26,400	1	3/0 Alum	10 Copper	¼" Gal. Steel	Oct. 29, 1912	June 14, 1913	Oct. 23, 1913
''	1	3/0 ''	''	¼" ''	June 4, ''	Dec. 15, 1913	Dec. 18 ''
''	1	3/0 ''	''	¼" ''	Sept. 6, 1913	Feb. 17, 1914	Feb. 7, 1914
''	1	3/0 ''	''	¼" ''	Oct. 16, 1914	Mar. 20, 1915	Apr. 4, 1915
2,200	1	6 Copper	....	....	Feb. 22, 1915	Mar. 20, ''	Mar. 20, 1915

SYSTEM

22,000	1	1/0 Alum	10 Copper	¼" Gal. Steel	Jan. 17, 1914	Sept. 28, 1914	Sep. 28, 1914
''	1	1/0 ''	....	....	July 6, 1916	July 23, 1916	July 23, 1916
''	1	1/0 ''	10 Copper	¼" Gal. Steel	Mar. 30, 1914	Sep. 28, 1914	Sep. 28, 1914
''	1	1/0 ''	''	¼" ''	Feb. 18, ''	Sep. 28 ''	Sep 28 ''
4,000	1	1/0 ''	....	....	May 2, ''	....	Oct. 6 ''
4,000	1	1/0 ''	....	....	July 25, ''	....	Oct. 6 ''
4,000	1	1/0 ''	....	¼" Galv. Steel	May 19, ''	....	Oct. 19 ''
4,000	1	1/0 ''	....	¼" ''	June 1, ''	July 10, 1914	Oct. 19 ''
22,000	1	1/0 ''	9 B.W.G. Iron	¼" ''	Feb. 17, 1916	May 27, 1916	June 4, 1916

SYSTEM

22,000	2	3/0 Alum	9 BWG. Iron	¼" Galv. Steel	Mar. 17, 1915	July 7, 1915	Nov. 18, 1915
''	2	3/0 ''	9 ''	¼" ''	Apr. 7, ''	Sept. 24. ''	Nov. 18 ''
''	2	3/0 ''	9 ''	¼" ''	Apr. 10, ''	July 21, ''	Nov. 18 ''
''	2	3/0 ''	9 ''	¼" ''	Apr. 13, ''	July 11, ''	Nov. 18 ''
''	2	3/0 ''	9 ''	¼" ''	Apr. 26, ''	Aug. 25, ''	Nov. 18 ''
''	1	6 Copper	9 ''	¼" ''	July 21, 1916	....	....
''	1	3/0 Alum	9 ''	¼" ''	Oct. 19, 1915	Aug. 19, 1916	June 18, 1916
''	1	3/0 ''	9 ''	¼" ''	Dec. 4 ''	June 10, ''	June 18 ''
''	1	1/0 ''	9 ''	¼" ''	May 20 ''	Aug. 14, 1915	Nov. 18, 1915
''	1	1/0 ''	9 ''	¼" ''	June 9 ''	Aug. 24, ''	Nov. 18 ''

Description of

EUGENIA FALLS

Sec. No.	From	To	Length of pole	Span	Miles	No. of poles
11	Hanover Jct. Pole 1491..	Hanover	40	125	.76	34
12	Eugenia Falls..........	Markdale............... Car'd on Sec. EFL 1, poles	....	....	6.50	....
13	Eugenia Falls	Flesherton............. Car'd on Sec. EFL 3, poles	....	....	7.50	....
14	Durham Jct. 1326 E.F.L.5	Holstein................ Car'd on Sec. EFL 5, poles	30	130	2.63	107
15	Junction Pole 1190	Kilsyth Sta.............	40	125	e 6.25	244
16	Kilsyth Station.........	Tara...................	40	125	e 7.25	311
17	Shelbourne	Orangeville	30	130	e14.61	e614
18	" "	Horning's Mills	30	130	e 5.13	e215
19	Eugenia Falls	Meaford Jct. Pole 186...	35-40	132	4.00	186
20	Meaford Jct. Pole 186...	Collingwood	35-40	132	20.17	885
21	Orangeville.............	Alton	30	132	e 5.75	e253
22	Grand Valley	Arthur	30	120	e12.50	e539

MUSKOKA

M L.						
1	South Falls.............	Huntsville	35	132	26.32	1,142

CENTRAL ONTARIO

C.O.S.						
1607 (e)	Napanee................	Newburgh (Houpt Paper Mills)...............	30	132	(e)8.25	....

(e) Estimated

Lines.—Continued

SYSTEM.—Continued

Voltage	No. of Circuits	Power Cable B. & S. Gauge	Telephone Wires, B.&S. & B.W.G. Gauge	Ground Wire	Work Commenced	Work Completed	In Operation
22,000	1	1/0 S.R Alum	9 B.W.G. iron	¼" Galv.Steel	Aug. 18, 1916	Sep. 16, 1916	Sep. 16,1916
4,000	1	2 S.R ''	....	....	Dec. 28, 1915	Jan. 17 ''	Feb. 8 ''
4,000	1	2 S.R ''	....	....	June 4 ''	Aug. 16, 1915	Nov.18,1915
4,000	1	2 S.R. ''	....	....	Dec. 10 ''	Apl. 3, 1916	Apl. 3, 1916
22,000	1	6 B.W.G.iron	9 B.W.G.iron	¼"Galv.Steel	Oct. 12, 1916	....	....
4,000	1	6 Copper....9	''	¼" ''	Oct. 12 ''	....	....
22,000	1	6 '' 10	''	¼" ''	June 13 ''	June. 15,1916	June13,1916
22,000	1	6 '' 10	''	¼" ''	June 13 ''	June 13 ''	June13 ''
''	1	1/0 '' 9	''	½' ''	Aug. 21 ''	Oct. 5 ''	Oct. 6 ''
''	1	1/0 '' 9	''	¼" ''	Aug. 14 ''	Oct. 5 ''	Oct. 6 ''
4,000	1	4 ''	....	6 B.W.G.iron	Oct. 17 ''	Nov. 22 ''	Nov.27 ''
4,000	1	4 ''	 6	''	Oct. 30 ''	....	....

SYSTEM

Voltage	No. of Circuits	Power Cable B. & S. Gauge	Telephone Wires, B.&S. & B.W.G. Gauge	Ground Wire	Work Commenced	Work Completed	In Operation
22,000	1	2 S.R. Alum	Galv. 9 BWG. Iron	¼"Galv. Steel	Aug. 6, 1915	Apl. 29, 1915	Aug.15,1916

SYSTEM

Voltage	No. of Circuits	Power Cable B. & S. Gauge	Telephone Wires, B.&S. & B.W.G. Gauge	Ground Wire	Work Commenced	Work Completed	In Operation
4,000	1	6 Copper..	....	6 B.W.G.iron	Nov. 23, 1916		

The Mileage of Lines Tabulated According to Voltage and Number of Circuits

Transmission Lines

Voltage	Single Circuit Totals			Double Circuit Totals			Three Circuit Totals			Four Circuit Totals			1-2-3-4-Circuit Totals			
	Completed Oct. 31, 1915	Completed Oct. 31, 1915 to Oct. 31, 1916	Under Construction Oct. 31, 1916	Completed Oct. 31, 1915	Completed Oct. 31, 1915 to Oct. 31, 1916	Under Construction Oct. 31, 1916	Completed Oct. 31, 1915	Completed Oct. 31, 1915 to Oct. 31, 1916	Under Construction Oct. 31, 1916	Completed Oct. 31, 1915	Completed Oct. 31, 1915 to Oct. 31, 1916	Under Construction Oct. 31, 1916	Completed Oct. 31, 1915	Completed Oct. 31, 1915 to Oct. 31, 1916	Under Construction Oct. 31, 1916	Completed Oct. 31, 1915 to Oct. 31, 1916
46,000..	1.93	....	....	....	....	....	15.50	....	....	....	....	....	17.43	....	....	17.43
26,400..	182.29	54.59	20.50	95.55	12.77	7.73	11.46	....	....	1.10	....	....	290.40	67.36	28.23	357.76
22,000..	76.78	114.89	14.75	133.72	8.95	....	....	....	....	....	....	....	210.50	123.84	14.75	334.34
13,200..	277.31	13.24	....	88.54	....	....	.09	....	....	....	....	....	365.94	13.24	....	379.18
12,000..	....	....	....	1.25	....	.31	....	....	....	....	....	....	1.25	....	.31	1.25
6,600..	13.00	....	....	3.75	....	....	2.04	....	....	....	....	....	18.79	....	....	18.79
4,000..	71.62	41.64	36.72	....	....	....	....	....	....	....	....	....	71.62	41.64	36.72	113.26
2,200..	18.54	....	....	.63	....	....	....	....	....	....	....	....	19.17	....	....	19.17
Total.	....	....	....	....	....	....	....	....	....	....	....	....	....	....	....	1,241.18

Total Mileage of Lines and Number of Poles

—	To Oct. 31st, 1915	Oct. 31st, 1915, to Oct. 31st, 1916	Total to Oct. 31st, 1916
Total mileage low tension lines................	1,092.13	229.06	1,321.19
Total mileage low tension lines completed	995.10	246.08	1,241.18
Total mileage low tension lines under construction..	97.03	80.01	80.01
Total mileage single circuit lines................	738.50	199.30	937.80
Total mileage double circuit lines..............	323.44	29.76	353.20
Total mileage three circuit lines...............	29.09	....	29.09
Total mileage four circuit lines...............	1.10	....	1.10
Total mileage telephone lines complete...........	864.11	211.94	1,076.05
Total mileage telephone lines under construction..	86.89	50.23	50.23
Number of poles	41,203	13,169	54,372

NOTE.—Under total mileage low tension lines completed Oct. 31st, 1915, to Oct. 1916. 246.08 includes total mileage low tension under construction to Oct. 31st, 1915. 97.03.

Total Weights and Mileages of Cable and Wire
TRANSMISSION AND TELEPHONE LINES

Cable and Wire	Wire Miles				Weight in Pounds			
	Completed to Oct. 31st, 1915	Completed Oct. 31st, 1915 to Oct. 31st, 1916	Under construction to Oct. 31st, 1916	Completed and under construction to Oct. 31st, 1916	Completed to Oct. 31st, 1915	Completed Oct. 31st, 1915 to Oct. 31st, 1916	Under construction to Oct. 31st, 1916	Completed and under construction to Oct. 31st, 1916
Aluminum	3,630.69	375.49	24.34	4,030.52	2,507,234	254,367	20,250	2,781,851
Steel Reinforced Aluminum...	394.44	214.09	....	608.53	191,697	115,210	....	306,907
Copper Wire.....	313.96	253.93	123.93	691.82	651,296	208,606	67,653	927,555
Copper Clad Steel Wire...	1,123.82	15.62	....	1,139.44	191,952	2,405	....	194,357
Galv. Iron Wire..	606.94	426.69	209.21	1,242.84	171,705	249,944	91,608	513,257
Galv. Steel Cable...	983.70	212.91	50.23	1,246.84	623,272	134,899	31,825	789,996
Totals......	7,053.55	1,498.73	407.71	8,959.99	4,337,156	965,431	211,336	5,513,923

Gauge, Length and Weight of Copper Clad Steel and Galvanized Iron Wire

TELEPHONE LINES

Gauge	Wire Miles				Weight in Pounds				Single Circuit Mileage			
	Completed to Oct. 31st, 1915	Completed Oct. 31st, 1915 to Oct. 31st, 1916	Under construction to Oct. 31st, 1916	Completed and under construction to Oct. 31st, 1916	Completed to Oct. 31st, 1915	Completed Oct. 31st, 1915 to Oct. 31st, 1916	Under construction to Oct. 31st, 1916	Completed and under construction to Oct. 31st, 1916	Completed to Oct. 31st, 1915	Completed Oct. 31st, 1915 to Oct. 31st, 1916	Under construction to Oct. 31st, 1916	Completed and under construction to Oct. 31st, 1916
No. 8 B. & S., C.C. steel	207.52	......	......	207.52	50,842	......	......	50,842	103.76	......	......	103.76
No. 10 " "	913.76	15.62	......	929.38	143,124	2,405	......	145,529	456.88	7.61	......	464.49
No. 9 B.W.G., iron	363.10	369.18	100.46	831.07	110,745	112,599	30,640	253,984	181.55	184.59	50.23	416.37
No. 10 " "	243.84	33.48	......	282.32	60,960	9,620	......	70,580	121.92	19.74	......	141.66
Totals...	1,728.22	423.28	100.46	2,250.29	365,671	124,624	30,640	520,935	864.11	211.94	50.23	1,126.28

Size, Length and Weight of TRANSMISSION LINES

Brown & Sharpe Gauge	Wire Miles Completed to Oct. 31, 1915	Total Oct. 1915, to Oct. 1916	Under construction to Oct. 31, 1916	Weight Pounds to Oct. 31, 1915	Total Oct. 31, 1915, to Oct. 31, 1916	Under construction to Oct. 31, 1916	Miles completed to Oct. 31, 1915	Total Oct. 1915, to Oct. 1916	Under construction to Oct. 1916	Circuit Lines completed to Oct. 31, 1915	Total Oct. 1915 to Oct. 1916	Under construction to Oct. 31, 1916	Total Single Circuit and Double Circuit Lines Oct. 31, 1916
400,000 c.m. Alum.	1.54			3,032			.49						.49
4/0	43.85	45.07		243,049			.49	30.49	36.39	30.49	12.77	7.73	30.49
3/0	1,356.3	45.07	24.34	1,536,229	162,298	20,250	181.11	201.3	36.39	201.3	12.77	7.73	431.70
2/0	89.46			58,954				14.20		14.20			14.20
0	36.33	68.68		458,320	88,219		189.51	44.30	35.65	44.30	8.95		278.41
2	63.08	11.74		207,650	3,850		114.12	43.43	3.73	43.43			161.28
2 S.R	94.44	14.22		191,697	84,670		125.22		55.31				180.53
1/0 S.R		39.87			30,540				12.66				12.66
250,000 c.m. Copper	1.54			6,246			.49						.49
4/0	44.35			520,931				16.75		16.75			16.75
2/0	9.00		.97	19,107		2,059	2.86					.31	2.86
0	22.86	76.13		38,473	1,128,126		7.26		24.17				31.43
2	10.71			11,331			3.40						3.40
4	28.06	24.94	57.48	18,659	16,585	38,224	7.65	.63	7.92	.63			16.20
6	87.44	152.86	65.48	36,549	63,896	27,370	27.76		48.53				76.29
6 B.W.G. rln			103.73			59,698			32.93				
Totals	4,339.09	843.51	252.00	3,350,227	560,677	147,601	687	351.23	224.36	351.23	21.72	8.04	1,257.18

NOTE.—A total of 16.00 miles occurs twice in the total mileage, due to there being circuits of different conductor on the same line.

Total Mileage by the Tel ... le Lines

COMPLETED AND UNDER CONSTRUCTION TO OCTOBER 31, 1916

Sect. No.	Miles	Set. No.	Miles	Sect. No.	Miles	Sect. No.	Miles	Sect. No.	Miles	Sect. No.	Miles	Sect. No.	Miles
L.T. 1	2.84	L.T. 26A	.24	L.T. 58	6.42	L.T. 96	6.58	L.T. 128	9.09	S.L. 1	4.29	E.F.L. 1	22.15
2	6.34	27	11.24	59	5.82	97	4.00	129	12.75	2	1.16	2	9.21
3	1.13	28	1.27	62	16.65	98	9.27	131	21.78	3	15.86	3	6.78
4	.18	29	1.50	65	9.03	99	19.18	132	4.85	4	.42	4	15.97
5	1.64	30	1.27	66	1.64	100	1.25	133	7.92	5	4.55	5	15.70
6	.76	31	1.56	68	3.21	101	16.91	135	7.73	6	12.27	6	E 8.50
7	12.27	32	.09	69	6.66	102	1.48	136	13.24	7	15.07	7	12.09
8	9.90	33	14.07	71	10.93	103	9.98	137	7.50	8	1.50	8	11.06
9	11.12	34	.12	72	6.48	104	8.50	138	11.90	9	1.86	9	11.73
10	10.30	35	5.75	73	5.00	105	7.40	139	.96	12 A	3.59	10	13.16
11	4.59	36	7.35	74	10.50	106	6.10	140	2.77	4 A	4.02	11	.76
12	1.13	37	.63	75	1.93	107	6.14	141	E 2.65	15	.50		
13	1.75	38	1.50	79	.43	108	13.03	142	6.11	17	4.50	15	E 6.25
14	2.04	39	1.92	81	1.10	109	3.02	143	10.48	20	1.34	16	E 7.25
15	2.08	40	1.21	82	2.27	111	5.84	145	20.50	21	14.34	17	E14.61
16	3.75	40A	12.27	83	1.30	112	3.48	146	6.81	St. L. 1	22.96	18	E 5.13
17	.14	41	1.21	85	1.93	113	14.20	147	7.61	2	16.29	19	4.00
18	.29	43	.09	86	14.61	114	8.90	148	11.36	3	6.52	20	20.17
19	1.54	45	2.22	87	1.18	118	.37	149	8.84	5	14.08		
20	1.22	46	14.36	88	1.96	119	.09	150	13.61	W.L.	25.50		
21	3.56	47	5.87	89	7.11	123	14.60				1.47		
22	1.71	48	3.79	90	1.20	124	9.83				9.67		
23	.31	49	4.98	94	6.83	125	9.72				6.41		
24	3.55	50	1.68	95	5.08	126	9.52			M.L. 1	26.32		
26	2.74	55	1.93		10.15	127	8.02						
		57	.08										
		57A											

"E"

Total 1,126.28

Size of Telephone Wire used on Telephone Lines
COMPLETED OCT. 31, 1915–OCT. 31, 1916

Section No.	Mileage	Gauge	Section No.	Mileage	Gauge	Section No.	Mileage	Gauge
L.T. 125	9.72	No. 9 B.W.G. Iron	S.L. 12 A	3.59	No. 10 B.&S.C.C.Steel	E.F.L. 17	14.61	No. 10 B.W.G. Iron
" 132	4.85	" "	" 14 A	4.02	"	" 18	5.13	" "
" 133	7.92	" "						
" 136	13.24	" "						
" 137	7.50	" "						
" 138	11.90	" "						
" 139	.96	" "						
" 140	12.65	" "						
" 141	2.77	" "						
" 142	10.48	" "						
" 143	6.11	" "						
E.F.L. 7	12.09	" "						
" 8	11.06	" "						
" 11	.76	" "						
" 19	4.00	" "						
" 20	20.17	" "						
W.L. 8	6.41	" "						
M.L. 1	26.82	" "						
S.L. 20	1.34	" "						
" 21	14.34	" "						
Total	184.59	....	Total.	7.61	....	Total.	19.74	

Size of Telephone Wire used on Telephone Lines
UNDER CONSTRUCTION OCT. 31, 1916

Section No.	Mileage	Gauge	Section No.	Mileage	Gauge
L.T. 135....	7.73	No. 9 B.W.G. Iron.	E.F.L. 6...	8.50	No. 9 B.W.G. Iron.
" 145....	20.50	" "	" 15...	6.25	" "
			" 16...	7.25	" "
Total......	28.23		Total.....	50.23	

SECTION III

OPERATION OF THE SYSTEMS

NIAGARA SYSTEM

The operation of the Niagara System for the year 1916, was attended with gratifying success. In no other year, and especially since the war commenced, have the lines and apparatus of this system been called upon for such extraordinary duty. This condition was occasioned by the rapid recovery of industry together with the enormous development of the manufacture of war munitions in Canada.

During the months of November to April, inclusive, and from July to October, power was purchased for transformation and transmission from two, and indirectly three sources, the supplying plants being linked together by the Commission's Transforming Station at Niagara Falls. On April 30th, the temporary contract with the Toronto Power Company expired, and from this date until July 26th, when the first generating unit from the Canadian Niagara Power Company was connected, the total load of the Niagara System was carried by the Ontario Power Company. On August 21st, a second unit at the Canadian Niagara Power Company's Plant was parallelled with the first, and from this date until the end of October, the amount of power available from this company amounted to approximately 25,000 horse-power. As these generating stations were operating at maximum capacity, extreme caution was necessarily exercised in the operation of the system in order to preserve equilibrium at all times. Due credit is extended to the Ontario Power Company for the satisfactory service received during the year.

Electrical storms during the past year were much more frequent and severe than in previous years. The Niagara System was subjected to these storms on sixty different days. On eight days these storms traversed practically the entire system, and were particularly severe. The balance of the storms traversed only portions of the system, mainly in the Niagara Peninsula, Preston, Stratford and Chatham Districts, and were more or less severe. No total system interruption occurred from lightning causes during the summer, and when it is considered that the Commission has in operation approximately 1,200 miles of high and low tension lines overstreching a strip of Ontario approximately 215 miles long and averaging 60 miles wide, all lines being subjected to the accumulation of electrical discharges, which must be dissipated by passage to ground, the efficiency of the protective apparatus is strikingly evident.

Work of a special nature carried out by the Line Maintenance Department, and required by reason of the rapid increase of load, included the erection of a temporary 12,000 volt double circuit pole line of No. 4/0 copper conductor between the power house of the Canadian Niagara Company's station and a point (on the present line between the Hydro and Toronto Power Company Transforming Stations) approximately 1,800 feet south of the Commission's station. Both circuits of this pole line are still in service pending the installation of the balance of the underground feeders to the Canadian Niagara Power Company's plant.

The erection of a fourth No. 4/0 copper, three-phase circuit 15.5 miles long, on the 46,000 volt tower line between Niagara Falls and Welland was completed and placed in operation.

The single or three-phase circuit of No. 2 aluminum between the High Tension station and the Municipal Station at Dundas was replaced with a double circuit of No. 4 copper. Two 13,200 volt air break switches were erected in these

r the
iden.
·hich
. and

pply
and
work
ition

and
lines
trat-
:d to.
end
pre-
were
The
the

.tion
con-
ided

feet
new
ctric
e to

Iigh
with
ʹ on
the
hort
bove
tion
.sfer

·erts
the
om-

to

vith
:red
ents
lard
of

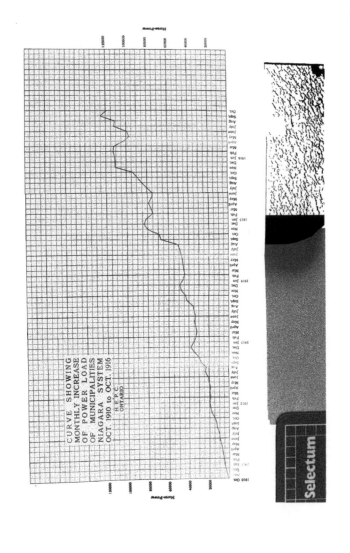

CURVE SHOWING
MONTHLY INCREASE
OF POWER LOAD
OF MUNICIPALITIES
NIAGARA SYSTEM
OCT. 1910 to OCT. 1916

H.E.P.C.
ONTARIO

lines at the entrance to the John Bertram and Sons Foundry, and also near the Dundas Municipal Station for the control of the line of the village of Lynden. The wood pole line from the Dundas High Tension to the City of Hamilton, which was replaced by a steel tower line during the summer of 1915, was taken down, and the material placed in stock.

Short stretches of single circuit 26,400 volt lines were constructed to supply the Lake Erie and Northern Railway Company's sub-stations at Brantford and Simcoe, from the outgoing circuits of Brant High Tension Station. This work also included the erection of telephone lines and instruments, and the installation of an air break switch at the Company's Simcoe sub-station.

The wood pole Low Tension Line entrances at London and St. Thomas, and at the Weston Municipal sub-station were remodeled to accommodate new lines erected in these districts. In view of the many new customers added in the Stratford District, and the length of line necessary to serve them, it has been decided to raise the transmission voltage in this district from 13,200 to 26,400. To this end considerable re-arranging of the power and telephone lines was carried out in preparation for this change. For sectionalizing purposes two air break switches were erected at Mitchell in the double circuit line between Stratford and Seaforth. The telephone line between Stratford and Sebringville Junction was doubled by the erection of a circuit of No. 9 iron wire.

Some re-location of the 13,200 volt line feeding the Mimico Distribution Station from the Cooksville High Tension Station was necessary, due to the construction of the Toronto-Hamilton Highway. The portion of line affected extended from Port Credit to New Toronto.

A twenty-five "pair" lead covered telephone cable approximately 13,500 feet long, was installed between the High Tension Station and the Commission's new office building at Toronto. The cable was laid in the Toronto Hydro-Electric System duct line to the corner of Queen and William Streets and from thence to the office building on the concrete poles.

Few failures of any of the electrical or mechanical equipment of the High Tension stations occurred during the year. As the Commission, in common with other enterprises in Canada, was severely handicapped in obtaining delivery on additional apparatus required to cope with the abnormal demand for power, the present equipment in some of the stations was subjected to overload for short periods, but without any depreciating results. The difficulty, mentioned above was partially met by the transfer, where feasible, of transformers from one station to another. One of the more important changes of this nature was the transfer of two 750 kv-a transformers from Guelph to the St. Thomas station.

The Commission now employs a staff of nine highly trained meter experts whose regular duties consist of the periodic calibration and adjustment of the various types of graphic recording and indicating instruments located in the Commission's stations.

These men also attend to the setting and adjustment of all relays used to protect the Commission's lines and equipment.

Considerable time has been spent in perfecting refinements in connection with the measurement of power, which has been to a great extent apparently considered unnecessary heretofore by the majority of other organizations. These refinements extend from the periodic comparison of the Commission's portable standard meters with ultimate standards to the determination of the characteristics of instrument transformers of various types.

The services of the meter inspectors may also be requisitioned by any of the Commission's customers to inspect or adjust metering and relay equipment, or to conduct special measurements of any loads with regard to which the customer is desirous of obtaining particular information.

A long felt want was realized in the erection of the storehouses on the High Tension Station ground during the summer. These buildings will accommodate maintenance materials of a bulky nature. This work, together with the building of suitable approaches, was done under the supervision of the operators. Outside lights surmounting concrete poles were installed at Dundas, London and Kent High Tension Stations, with pleasing effect. Considerable improvement in appearance was accomplished in grading the grounds surrounding the High Tension Stations, and re-surfacing of the roads through the grounds from the highway.

A concrete roadway approximately 300 feet long and 6 inches thick, was laid across the flats at Preston, from the fair grounds to the Hydro-Electric Power Commission's Property. It is expected that this roadway will be unaffected by the heavy spring floods in this vicinity, which previously rendered impassable the original gravel topped roadway. An increase was made in the supply of cooling water for this station by the sinking of a well just outside the station, and the installation of a deep well pump for pumping the water directly into the cooling system. The supply originally obtained from the small creek in the flats had latterly become inadequate.

The tables given below show the load demands of the various municipalities as well as the increase during the year.

The plotted curve on another page shows the monthly increase in the load supplied from October, 1910, to October, 1916.

NIAGARA SYSTEM

Capital Investments of the Niagara System in operation at October 31st, 1916:

Right-of-Way	$1,034,920 58
Steel Tower Transmission Lines	3,403,585 05
Telephone Lines	129,706 69
Relay System Lines	54,537 32
Conduit System (Ontario Power Co. to Niagara Station)	96,698 64
Wood Pole Lines	1,785,208 01
Transformer Stations	2,797,209 61
Distributing Stations	221,130 02
Total Operating Capital	$9,522,995 92

Total expenditures in connection with the operation and maintenance of Niagara System for the Fiscal year 1915-16:

Operators' Salaries and Expenses, including Supplies	$92,521 66
Maintenance of Steel Tower Lines	68,792 04
" Telephone and Relay Lines	15,422 41
" Low Tension Lines	20,350 09
Transformer Stations	68,883 54
" Distributing Stations	7,514 28
Administration	44,811 77
	$318,295 79

Interest on Invested Capital	$371,404 94	
Cost of Power at Niagara Falls	997,257 60	
		1,368,662 54

Summary of Financial Statement of the Niagara System operation for fiscal year 1915-16:

Receipts

Power delivered, including charges for Administration, General Expense, Operation, Maintenance and Interest	$2,038,792 32

Disbursements

Power purchased, including losses in Transmission and Transformation, Administration, General Expense, Operation, Maintenance and Interest	1,686,958 33
Surplus applicable to Sinking Fund and Depreciation Reserve Account	$351,833 99

Municipality	Load in H.P. Oct., 1915.	Load in H.P. Oct., 1916.	Increase in H.P.
Toronto	32,748	38,465	5,717
Dundas	362	548	186
Hamilton	7,694.5	8,562	867.5
Waterdown	63	71	8
Caledonia	40.2	55	14.8
Hagersville	106	97.8	....
London	5,971.5	7,359	1,377.5
Thorndale	28.4	34.8	6.4
Thamesford	19.3	26.5	7.2
Guelph	1,954.5	2,549.5	595
Ontario Agricultural College	153	160	7
Central Prison Farm	203.5	203.5	....
Rockwood	34.2	11.9	....
Georgetown	266.5	300	33.5
Acton	84.5	70.3	....
Preston	973	1,149	166
Galt	1,602	2,285.5	683.5
Hespeler	368.5	450.4	81.9
Breslau	21.5	30	8.5
Kitchener	2,285.5	3,262	976.5
Waterloo	717	815	98
Elmira	91	109.9	18.9
New Hamburg	84.5	76.4	....
Baden	157	196.5	39.5
Stratford	1,179.5	1,448	268.5
Mitchell	123.5	148.8	25.3
Seaforth	275	387.4	112.4
Clinton	98	101.8	3.8
Goderich	217	214.5	....
St. Mary's	339	434.3	95.3
Woodstock	1,048	1,170	122
Ingersoll	740	792	52
Tillsonburg	233	242.6	9.6
Norwich	100.5	171.6	71.1
Beachville	132.5	96.5	....
St. Thomas	1,658.5	2,011	352.5
Port Stanley	68.5	75	6.5
Brantford	1,552.5	1,783	230.5
Paris	381	398	17
Port Credit	57.5	59.6	2.1
Weston	178.5	197	16.5
Brampton	539	656.8	117.8
Milton	287	355	68
Mimico	127.5	156.1	28.6
Mimico Asylum	35	31.5	....
Prov. Brick Yard	171	136	....
New Toronto	80.5	291	210.5
Toronto Township	62.5	99.1	36.6
Cooksville }	23	22.7	....
Dixie }			
Windsor	216	1,502.6	286.6
Walkerville	777.5	1,576.5	799
Elora	51.6	77.7	26.1
Fergus	68.5	92.5	24
Welland	3,038.5	5,626	2,587.5
St. Catharines	2,158.5	2,433	274.5
Port Dalhousie	104.5	79	....
Strathroy	143.5	203.7	60.2
Drumbo	18	10.9	....
Plattsville	32.2	57.6	25.4
Woodbridge	32.2	76.4	44.2
Ayr	35.5	36.2	.7
Princeton	9.8	10.4	.6
Embro	25	28.1	3.1
Chatham	431.5	509.4	67.9

Municipality.	Load in H.P. Oct., 1915.	Load in H.P. Oct., 1916.	Increase in H.P.
Lucan	33.5	30.2	....
Bolton	34.8	95.2	60.4
Mount Brydges	26	26.8	.8
Wallaceburg	177	277.5	100.5
Delaware	7.2	8.9	1.7
Tilbury	60.3	63	2.7
Simcoe	114	103.2	....
Waterford	35	97.8	62.8
Lambeth	50.9	17.9	....
Grantham Township	12.3	17.4	5.1
Dresden	70	68.3	....
Dorchester	20.7	16	....
Comber	19.5	21.4	1.9
Burford	45.6	31.5	....
Bothwell	28	28.1	....
St. George	45.6	38.2	....
Dutton	47	44.9	....
Thamesville	52.9	45	....
Blenheim	53.6	77.7	24
Lynden	6.7	79.7	73.1

A list of the municipalities connected to the Niagara System during the last year is given below.

Municipality.	Date connected	Initial Load in H.P.	Load in H.P. Oct., 1916	Increase in H.P.
Ailsa Craig	Dec. 15th, 1915	15.3	16	.7
Niagara Falls	Dec. 19th, 1915	371.3	2,364.5	1,993.2
Otterville	Jan. 15th, 1916	10	11.7	1.7
Petrolea	Apr. 25th, 1916	134	146	12
Exeter	May 4th. 1916	57	77.7	20.7
Milverton	May 18th 1916	26.5	33.5	7.
Listowel	May 27th, 1916	90.3	117.9	27.6
Palmerston	June 6th, 1916	83.7	93	9.3
Granton	June 29th, 1916	10	12.4	2.4
Harriston	June 30th, 1916	56.3	52.9	....
Wyoming	Oct. 4th, 1916	22.7	22.7	....
Wellesley	Oct. 23rd, 1916	13.4	13.4	....
Burgessville	Oct. 26th, 1916	8	8	....
Tavistock	Oct. 26th, 1916	28	28	....

SEVERN SYSTEM

The Commission's generating station at the Big Chute on the Severn River was overtaxed toward the middle of the fiscal year by the relatively large increase of the power demand of this district, as on the Niagara System, the increase in load resulting from the same cause. The steps taken to remedy this condition will be mentioned later.

The operation of the generating station, sub-stations and transmission lines was very satisfactory and the increased load was taken care of in a very creditable manner. The Trent Valley Canal contractors completed certain work on the canal scheme in the vicinity of the generating station which greatly benefited the control of the head and tail water at this plant. Other special maintenance work was carried out by which the hydraulic regulation was improved.

A slight change was effected in the construction of the power and telephone lines of the Power House-Waubaushene Section where these lines cross Matcheash Bay, by the erection of an "A" frame structure with rock-crib foundation to shorten this long span. This has eliminated trouble which was previously experienced at this point during very severe wind storms.

The temporary 22,000-volt pole type interswitching station at Waubaushene was moved to a new location on the Commission's property and altered slightly in design. The change was made to accommodate additional lines built from this point and for more efficient control of all lines from this operating centre.

The work commenced in October, 1915, on the stringing of a second telephone circuit between Waubaushene and the power house was completed and placed in operation in the late fall. The additional rod of right-of-way acquired on each side of the line from Midland to Penetang was cleared of trees through the bush section of that line.

Two new customers were connected to the Severn System lines during the year. Camp Borden, the new military training grounds prepared by the Department of Militia and Defence, was first supplied with power on June 29th, when the water pumps and the camp lighting was put in operation. The camp sub-station is fed over a single circuit of No. 6 copper tapped by means of airbreak switches on to the main transmission lines near the Barrie sub-station.

The elevator of the Canadian Pacific Railway at Port McNicoll was first supplied with Hydro power on July 25th. The Company's station is fed from a double circuit of No. 1/0 aluminum from the Midland-Penetang main line, which -was double circuited from Waubaushene to this point during the summer. This company is being supplied with approximately 1,000 h.p. of off peak power at 575 volts during the season of navigation, in addition to approximately 250 h.p. for the operation of wharf machinery, lighting, etc., which will be utilized throughout the entire year. Below will be found a list of the demands of the various municipalities in October, 1915 and 1916, and the increase during the year.

SEVERN SYSTEM

Municipality	Load in H.P. Oct., 1915	Load in H.P. Oct., 1916.	Increase in H.P.
Midland	500	815	315
Penetang	415.5	495	79.5
Collingwood	572.4	888.7	316.3
Barrie	368.6	541.5	72.9
Coldwater	37.5	34.8	....
Elmvale	34.8	36.2	1.4
Stayner	81.7	56.3	....
Creemore	48.2	38.8	....
Orillia	1239.9	1414	174.1
Waubaushene	18.1	16.8	....
Port McNicoll	23.4	19.3	....
Victoria Harbor	29.5	26.8	....

New Stations on Severn System

Customer	Date connected	Initial load in H.P.	Present load in H.P.	Increase in H.P.
Camp Borden,	June 29th, 1916	225	325.7	100.7
C.P.R. Elevator	July 25th, 1916	600	1176.6	576.6

OPERATING STATEMENT, FISCAL YEAR 1915-16.

Capital Investment as at October 31st, 1916:

Big Chute Power Development, including Generating and Transformer Station	$349,787 46
Transmission Lines	335,497 20
Distributing Stations	78,451 08
Total Operating Capital	$763,735 74

Revenue as per details below

Midland Power Accounts	$10,856 88	
Penetang "	11,983 47	
Collingwood "	23,613 38	
Barrie "	13,970 30	
Coldwater "	1,007 77	
Elmvale "	1,335 50	
Stayner "	2,800 01	
Creemore "	2,254 47	
Orillia	13,229 32	
Waubaushene "	640 19	
Port McNichol "	698 22	
Victoria Harbor "	1,762 98	
Camp Borden "	3,592 45	
C.P.R. Elevator "	6,949 99	
		$94,694 93

Expenditures

Operators' and Patrolmen's Salaries and Expenses and proportion of Administration and General Office Expense	$18,152 30	
Cost of Power purchased from Wasdell and Eugenia Systems	6,366 26	
Interest on Capital Investment	29,920 27	
		$54,438 83

Surplus applicable to Sinking Fund and Depreciation Reserve Accounts		$40,256 10

11 H

EUGENIA SYSTEM

The second generating station which the Commission has constructed was placed in official operation by Sir Adam Beck on November 18th when the municipalities of the Eugenia System received Hydro power for the first time. The service supplied on this system has quite fulfilled the Commission's expectations in every way.

The hydraulic and electrical features of the generating station have been given detailed description in previous reports.

The transmission system now comprises 195 miles of 22,000-volt and 24 miles of 4,000-volt lines. The municipalities now served on this system are Owen Sound, Mount Forest, Durham, Dundalk, Flesherton, Chatsworth, Markdale, Holstein and Chesley.

On June 13th a part of the Pine River System which was acquired by the Commission was connected to the Eugenia System by means of a thirty mile tie line built between Dundalk and Shelburne. The municipalities thus supplied were Orangeville, Shelburne and Horning's Mills. While satisfactory service was delivered since the acquisition of this system, the Commission is taking steps to place it on a par with the operating condition of the balance of the Eugenia System. This will consist of the erection of new sub-stations at Shelburne and Orangeville and complete renovation of the 22,000-volt lines between these points. The future outlook for this portion of the Eugenia System is very bright.

The actual operation and maintenance of the Eugenia System is carried on jointly by co-operation with the municipalities supplied. The success of this scheme was no exception to that enjoyed on the other northern systems.

Below will be found a tabulation showing the date of connection, initial load and load taken in October, 1916, of the municipalities on this system.

Eugenia System

Municipality	Date connected	ni tial load in H.P.	Load in H.P. Oct. 1916	Increase in H.P.
Owen Sound.......	November 18th, 1915.	899.5	992.	92.5
Flesherton	" "	29.5	36.2	6.7
Dundalk..........	" "	50.9	50.2	....
Durham	" "	81.7	63.9	....
Mt. Forest	" "	156	98.5	....
Chatsworth........	December 17th, 1915.	8	25.4	17.4
Markdale..........	November 18th, 1915.	67	60	....
Holstein	April 3rd, 1916......	6.8	16.9	10.1
Chesley	June 18th, 1916	87	80.4	....
Shelburne.........	" 13th "	45	51.2	6.2
Orangeville........	" 13th "	60	128.7	68.7
Horning's Mills....	" 13th "	5	5	....

EUGENIA SYSTEM

OPERATING STATEMENT, FISCAL YEAR 1915-16.

Capital Investment as at October 31st, 1916:

Eugenia Falls Power Development and Generating Plant	$638,854 14
Eugenia Distributing Stations	51,944 33
Eugenia Transmission Lines	409,355 93
Total Operating Capital	$1,100,154 40

Revenue as per details below

Owen Sound Power Accounts, December to October..			$22,536 94	
Flesherton	"	"	" ..	733 13
Dundalk	"	"	"	1,232 32
Durham				1,825 00
Mount Forest	"	"	" ...	3,226 07
Chatsworth	"	January	" ..	662 70
Markdale	"	March		933 36
Holstein	"	May	..	185 96
Chesley		July	.. ..	1,076 01
Orangeville	"	"	...	979 12
Shelburne		"	" ..	500 50
Hanover	..	September 16 to October 31	183 12	
Severn System	"	October 6 to October 31	2,520 13	
Hornings Mills	"	....	70 17	
				36,669 53

Expenditures

Operators' and Patrolmen's Salaries and Expenses and proportion of Administration and General Office Expenses	$14,584 03	
Interest on Capital Investment	34,205 94	
		48,789 97
Deficit on operation		12,120 44

WASDELLS SYSTEM

While the power demand of the municipalities fed from the Wasdells System does not indicate the same growth which characterized the operation of some of the other systems, very satisfactory progress was maintained. A thoroughly reliable and continuous service was provided. The power house, transmission lines, and sub-stations required no extensive repairs and are in first-class operating condition.

The excess capacity available at the power house over what was required for serving the Wasdells System was very conveniently and economically utilized to take care of the increased power demand of the municipalities of the Severn System.

A tie line between the power house and the Orillia substation at Longford, constructed during the summer, made this arrangement possible, and after parallel operation was commenced on July 24th, the Wasdells power house supplied an average load of 750 h.p. continuously throughout the balance of the year without difficulty. Thus the Big Chute generating station was relieved of the greater part of the power demand of the municipality of Orillia, at Orillia and at Longford.

Wasdells System

Municipality	Load in Oct., 1915 H.P.	Load in Oct., 1916 H.P.	Increase in H.P.
Beaverton	54.9	56.3	1.4
Brechin	37.5	36.2	....
Cannington	46.9	57.6	10.7
Sunderland	20.1	52.2	32.1
Woodville	49.6	48.2	....

OPERATING STATEMENT, FISCAL YEAR 1915-16.

Capital Investment as at October 31st, 1916:

Wasdell Power Development and Generating Plant	$136,658 47
Wasdell Distributing Stations	13,616 24
Wasdell Transmission Lines	114,406 03
Total Operating Capital	$264,680 74

Revenue as per details below

Beaverton Power Accounts	$3,156 97	
Brechin "	2,615 77	
Cannington "	3,163 11	
Sunderland "	2,018 92	
Woodville "	3,354 15	
Severn System "	3,846 13	
		$18,155 05

Expenditures

Operators' and Patrolmen's Salaries and Expenses, including supplies	$3,461 02	
Administration and General Office Expenses	1,010 19	
Interest on Capital Investment	9,114 66	
		13,585 87
Surplus applicable to Sinking Fund and Depreciation Reserve Account		$4,569 18

PARALLEL OPERATION OF THE SEVERN, EUGENIA
AND WASDELLS SYSTEMS

Kilowatts

T|

ditions
emand

ine of
nd the
nce of
Orillia
e tele-
llia to
rd.
h, the
from
of the
asdells
Chute

rallel-
by the
ircuit,
d dis-
e and
ctober
id the

with

; con-

actory
points
om, if
ilures

djust-
pe to
int of
inter-
. At
more

e was

force. Careful studies of the lines were made and whenever it was profitable the amount of conductor material was reduced to the most economical point. The material recovered in this way enabled almost all extensions necessary to be taken care of without delay and without the purchase of additional conductor.

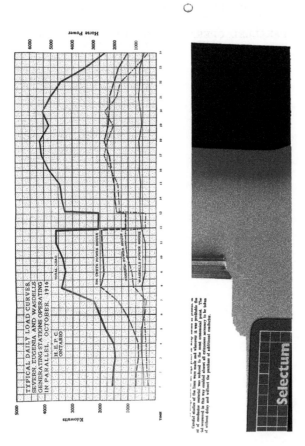

TYPICAL DAILY LOAD CURVES,
SEVERN, EUGENIA AND WASDELLS
GENERATING STATIONS OPERATING
IN PARALLEL, OCTOBER, 1916

H.E.P.C.
ONTARIO

Horse Power

Kilowatts

Careful studies of the lines were made and whenever it was profitable the
... of .. combustion material was reduced to the most economical point. The
... recovered in this way enabled almost all extensions necessary to be taken
of without delay and without the purchase of additional conductor.

PARALLEL OPERATION OF THE SEVERN, EUGENIA AND WASDELLS SYSTEMS

As mentioned above, some action became necessary to relieve the load conditions at the Big Chute generating station caused by the increase of the power demand of the municipalities fed from this plant.

The first step in this direction was the erection of a 22,000-volt tie line of No. 1/0 aluminum, seven miles long, between the Wasdells power house and the sub-station belonging to the Municipality of Orillia at Longford. The balance of the circuit was completed by the existing Orillia 22,000-volt lines via the Orillia transforming and switching stations and the Big Chute plant. To complete telephone communication between the plant arrangements were made with Orillia to erect a telephone circuit on the power line poles between Orillia and Longford.

The two plants were placed in normal parallel operation on July 24th, the Wasdells plant supplying practically all the load previously taken by Orillia from the Big Chute plant in addition to the load taken by the municipalities of the Wasdells System. Thus the primary object was gained of loading the Wasdells plant to a degree of economical operation and reducing the load on the Big Chute plant.

The power supply for the Severn System was further augmented by the paralleling of the Eugenia plant with the Big Chute plant. This was accomplished by the erection of a 22,000-volt tie line of No. 1/0 copper and No. 9 iron telephone circuit, twenty-four miles long, between the Eugenia power house and the Collingwood distribution station. The tie line was built in an incredibly short space of time and power from the Eugenia plant was first supplied to the Severn System on October 6th. Temporary metering equipment was installed at both the Wasdells and the Eugenia plants to measure the interchange of power.

The parallel operation of these systems has been entirely satisfactory, with added security of service to all customers supplied therefrom.

On another page will be found curves showing typical fall operating conditions for twenty-four hours with the three systems in synchronism.

CENTRAL ONTARIO SYSTEM

The operation of the Central Ontario System has been entirely satisfactory since passing into the hands of the Commission. On account of the various points of supply total interruptions to service are almost impossible and have seldom, if ever, occurred. The operation of equipment has been most successful, no failures of any importance having taken place.

The steadily growing load at various points has necessitated some readjustment of equipment. One 750 k.v.a. transformer was moved from Port Hope to Oshawa, bringing the capacity of that point up to 2,250 k.w., and on account of the construction of the Government arsenal at Lindsay it was necessary to interchange two 300 k.w. units at Lindsay for two 750 k.w. units from Cobourg. At other points equipment of less importance has been replaced by apparatus more suitable to existing load conditions than that formerly used.

Practically all equipment which had become obsolete or unfit for service was scrapped and advantage taken of the high prices for scrap metals at present in force. Careful studies of the lines were made and whenever it was profitable the amount of conductor material was reduced to the most economical point. The material recovered in this way enabled almost all extensions necessary to be taken care of without delay and without the purchase of additional conductor.

While the growing load will undoubtedly soon overtake the present capacity of generating plants it has been possible to carry all load this year without taxing equipment and with a conservative amount of reserve apparatus available.

Loads at the various towns are shown in the table below and the curve of the weekly peaks shows the growth of load since this property has been under the control of the Commission. Another table shows the total output of the system for the current year and comparison of operation for the year 1915.

Power Generated, Central Ontario System

Month	Peak Load, 1915	Peak Load, 1916	Increase in H.P.
November	15,100	17,800	2700
December	13,400	18,190	4790
January, 1916	13,300	16,150	2850
February	12,560	13,700	1140
March	11,500	13,750	2250
April	11,610	12,640	1030
May	11,100	12,650	1550
June	10,600	15,300	4700
July	11,980	15,600	3020
August	14,570	15,850	1280
September	14,550	16,500	1950
October	16,200	18,600	2400
Peak for year	16,200	18,600	1800

Municipality	Load in H.P. October, 1916
Whitby	217
Bowmanville	1247
Oshawa	1568
Newcastle	20
Orono	20
Port Hope	375
Cobourg	502
Colborne	75
Brighton	72
Trenton	670
Belleville	1434
Napanee	315
Deseronto	302
Stirling	75
Tweed	87
Lindsay	1062
Peterboro	3067
Millbrook	38

MUSKOKA SYSTEM

The power development on the south branch of the Muskoka River at Muskoka Village which had been taken over from the Municipality of Gravenhurst was formally under operation by the Commission on November 1st. The purchase comprised the power site which had been partially developed by the municipality and the existing generating station and hydraulic works on the property. On November 1st power was being supplied to Gravenhurst at 6,600 volts and a small amount to Muskoka Village at 120 volts.

The Commission immediately proceeded with the extension and remodelling of the generating station to place it in first-class operating condition and to deliver the power covered by contract with the Municipality of Huntsville. A detailed description of the new hydraulic and electrical equipment of the plant will be found in another section of the report. Every effort was exerted by the Commission to supply uninterrupted service during the alterations to the station.

On August the 15th a 26 mile, 22,000-volt, No. 2 S.R. aluminum line to Huntsville distribution station was made alive for test. The sub-station was placed in operation permanently on August 25th.

All construction details at the power house were not completed at the end of October, which was due to the difficulty in obtaining reasonable delivery of materials.

The peak load demands of the Municipalities of Gravenhurst and Huntsville for the month of October were 235 and 580 h.p. respectively. The Commission will be in a position to supply standard service and anticipates a very successful future for the Muskoka System.

PORT ARTHUR SYSTEM

Steady progress was made in the operation of the Port Arthur System during the past year. The increase in load was taken care of by loading the Current River Hydraulic Plant of the City of Port Arthur to its full capacity. Thus the Commission was not obliged to increase the present reserve demand of 2,600 h.p. from the Kaministquia Power Company. The Company's power supply to the Commission during the year was of the usual high standard.

The total demand from both sources is approximately 5,100 horse-power at the present with indications of a very material increase in the near future.

The more uniform routine of operation established in 1915 whereby the load control of the Current River station was placed in the hands of the Commission's operators has proved very economical in every respect.

The Hydro transforming sub-station is in excellent condition, and no failures were reported during the year.

Plans and specifications were prepared and material ordered for the erection of a wood pole line entrance and switching structure, at the transformer station to provide a means of sectionalizing the two 22,000 volt outgoing circuits to the grain elevators and to the waterworks station. This work will be carried out in conjunction with the Port Arthur Commission. Five air break switches will be installed on this structure. The Port Arthur Commission is proceeding with the erection of two air break switches on each of the lines built to the elevators and to the waterworks station. When these installations are completed it will be possible to feed any one of the four elevator stations from either of the two outgoing 22,000 volt lines from the sub-station and will greatly increase the flexibility and security of the service on the high tension portion of the system.

Capital Investments for the Port Arthur System to October 31st, 1916:

Transmission Lines	$21,303 12
Transformer Stations	86,089 91
Total Operating Capital	$107,393 03

The Operating and Maintenance Expenses for the fiscal year ending October 1916, are as follows:—

Operators' Salaries and Expenses, including Operating supplies, and proportion of Administration and General Office Expenses	$5,721 88	
Interest at 4% per annum	4,325 00	
Sinking Fund at 1.8% per annum	1,946 25	
Cost of Power	37,365 00	
		$49,358 13

A Financial Statement of Operation for the fiscal year ending October 31st, 1916 is given below:—

Sum of monthly loads delivered and value, including charges for Administration, General Expenses, Operation, Interest, Sinking Fund and Depreciation	28,080 h.p.	$54,322 11
Sum of monthly loads purchased and value, including Administration, General Expense, Operation, Interest and Sinking Fund	28,080 h.p.	49,358 13
Surplus applicable to Depreciation Reserve		$4,963 98

THE ST. LAWRENCE SYSTEM

The operation of the Commission's system on the St. Lawrence River for the past year proved very successful. The service received from the hydraulic plant at Iroquois was thoroughly reliable and practically no interruptions occurred. A recent inspection of the Commission's sub-stations and lines shows that so far the depreciation of this system is quite negligible.

The total load demand of the municipalities during the year increased to 1,000 h.p., an amount considerably above the capacity of the generating station at Iroquois. This difficulty was temporarily solved by paralleling the municipal auxilliary steam plant at Brockville with the Commission's power supply purchased at Iroquois.

The transpositions in the transmission line between Morrisburg and Prescott are being rearranged to remove the inductive effect which has interfered with the proper operation of the Bell Telephone Company's line paralleling this line. A series of very interesting tests from an engineering standpoint are being made in connection with this work.

Municipality.	Load in Oct., 1915. H.P.	Load in Oct., 1916. H.P.	Increase in H.P.
Brockville	335	348.5	13.5
Prescott	205	217	12
Winchester	60.3	58.9	...
Chesterville	40.2	48.2	8.
Williamsburg	29.5	17.4	...

ST. LAWRENCE SYSTEM OPERATING STATEMENT, FISCAL YEAR 1915-16.

Capital Investments as at October 31st, 1916:
St. Lawrence Distributing Stations	$23,063 25	
St. Lawrence Transmission Lines	147,013 62	
Total Operating Capital		$170,076 87

Revenue as per details below

Prescott Power Accounts ..	$4,462 11	
Chesterville "	1,838 69	
Winchester "	2,321 42	
Williamsburg "	563 21	
Brockville "	8,340 86	
		17,526 29

Expenditures

Operators' and Patrolmen's Salaries and Expenses proportion of Administration and General Office Expense	$1,559 66	
Interest on Capital Investment	6,783 35	
Cost of Power purchased	5,513 89	
		13,856 90
Surplus applicable to Sinking Fund and Depreciation Reserve Accounts		$3,669 39

TOTAL CAPITAL INVESTMENT TO OCTOBER 31st, 1916

Following is a statement of expenditures on Capital Account, including Niagara, Severn, St. Lawrence, Wasdell, Eugenia, Muskoka, Port Arthur, Renfrew and Ottawa Systems, Stock on Hand, Tools and Equipment, Municipal Construction.

Niagara System—Transmission Lines

Right-of-Way	$1,034,920 58	
Steel Tower Lines	3,403,585 05	
Telephone Lines	129,706 69	
Relay System Lines	54,537 32	
Conduit System (Ont. Power Co. to Niagara Station)	96,698 64	
		$4,719,448 28
Right-of-Way (Dundas-Toronto), in course of construction	$6,366 37	
Steel Tower Lines, in course of construction	8,631 74	
Conduit System, in course of construction	22,157 54	
Telephone Line (Section A), in course of construction	1,297 70	
		38,453 35
Wood Pole Lines	$1,785,208 01	
Wood Pole Lines, in course of construction	189,094 42	
		1,974,302 43
Welland and St. Catharines District Lines	$16,445 63	
		16,445 63
Rural Line Construction	$324,168 44	
		324,168 44
Power Development, Right-of-Way and Preliminary Engineering	$33,512 91	
		33,512 91

Transformer Stations

Stations	$2,797,209 61	
Stations and Extensions to same, in course of construction	34,415 66	
		2,831,625 27
Distributing Stations	$221,130 02	
Distributing Stations, in course of construction	10,634 26	
		231,764 28

Severn System

Big Chute Power Development, including Generating and Transformer Stations	$349,787 46	
Transmission Lines	335,497 20	
Distributing Stations	78,451 08	
Distributing Stations Extensions in course of construction	1,409 83	
		765,145 57

St. Lawrence System

Transmission Lines	$147,228 58	
Distributing Stations	23,063 25	
Distributing Stations in course of construction	6,366 07	
		176,657 90

Wasdell System

Power Development, including Generating and Transformer Station	$136,658 47	
Transmission Lines	114,406 03	
Distributing Stations	13,637 00	
		264,701 50

Eugenia System

Power Development, including Generating and Transformer Station	$638,854 14	
Transmission Lines	409,355 93	
Distributing Stations	51,944 33	
Distributing Stations in course of construction	1,249 29	
Transmission Lines in course of construction	36,276 66	
Operation	12,120 44	
		1,149,800 79

Muskoka System

South Falls Power Development, including Generating and Transformer Station	$78,707 61	
Transmission Line	52,626 47	
Distributing Station	8,923 95	
Operation	912 26	
		141,170 29

Port Arthur System

Transmission Lines	$21,303 12	
Transformer Station	86,089 91	
		107,393 03

Renfrew System

Round Lake Storage Dam	$20,168 86	
Power Development (repayable)	717 41	
		20,886 27

Ottawa System

Meter Equipment	$432 39	
		432 39

General Accounts (Chargeable)

Municipal and Rural Construction Work repayable ..	$290,247 62	
Sales to Municipalities	159,226 01	
Renfrew District Operating Charges	2,519 82	
		451,993 45

General Accounts (Capitalized)

Office Furniture, Equipment, Stationery, Unexpired Insurance, etc.	$36,531 78	
Office Furniture and Equipment, Electrical Inspection Dept.	3,863 60	
Toronto Storehouse, Testing Laboratory, Garage and Machine Shop	117,883 72	
Dundas Storehouse	1,586 04	
Automobiles and Trucks (Depreciated value)	27,480 29	
Office Building	335,866 60	
		523,212 03

Stock and Tools

Stock on hand for construction purposes and sale to Municipalities	$163,673 72	
Line Maintenance Stock for all Systems	59,905 07	
Operating Department's Testing and Metering Equipment for all Systems	2,609 76	
		226,188 55
Line and Station Construction Tools and Equipment ..	$4,000 32	
Line and Station Maintenance Tools	6,666 08	
Hydraulic Construction Tools	1,402 88	
		12,069 28
Laboratory Operation	$9,482 04	
Machine Shop Operation (Stock)	520 35	
		10,002 39
		$14,019,374 03

PROVINCIAL EXPENDITURES

Fiscal Year 1915-16

Engineering assistance to non-operating Municipalities for the gathering of data throughout the Province for statistical purposes; reports on Municipal operation	$19,897 74	
Municipal estimates for power supply non-operating Municipalities and also rates investigations	4,058 45	
Hydrographic surveys, storage surveys, reports and investigations on power sites and stream flow for the Province......	31,366 77	
Reports and statistical data on overhead and underground construction for Municipalities; investigations relative supply of power to rural districts and gathering information with respect to the use of electricity along lines not at present operated by the use of such	8,625 85	
Engineering investigations, surveys and reports on proposed Municipal Electric Railways	38,675 66	
Administration and general office expense over all above expenditures	28,140 55	
	$130,765 02	

Less:

Credits:—Various supplies, equipment and capital expenditures charged Province former years, now capitalized in Commission's books, sold, or placed in stock	38,391 49	
		$92,373 53
Electrical Inspection—Balance of operating expenses for the year, not including capital investment, such as furniture, typewriters, etc., which is carried forward		31,345 53
Special Hydrographic Investigations—Lake-of-the-Woods Districts for the Department of Lands and Mines		1,972 02
Equipment on hand purchased for Hydrographic work		1,353 28
		$127,044 36

BALANCE SHEET

OCTOBER 31st, 1916.

Assets

Sundry Expenditures, per list	$14,019,374	03
Warrantable Advances	35,118	16
Unpaid Power Bills, October 31st, 1916	375,579	20
Cash on hand	297,140	80
	$14,727,212	**19**

Liabilities

Provincial Treasurer	$13,588,667	72
Niagara System, Surplus applicable to Sinking Fund and Depreciation Reserve Account	939,814	38
Wasdell System, Surplus applicable to Sinking Fund and Depreciation Reserve Account	4,569	18
Severn System, Surplus applicable to Sinking Fund and Depreciation Reserve Account	57,030	56
St. Lawrence System, Surplus applicable to Sinking Fund and Depreciation Reserve Account	4,345	93
Welland System, Surplus applicable to Sinking Fund and Depreciation Reserve Account	1,449	24
Port Arthur System, Surplus applicable to Sinking Fund and Depreciation Reserve Account	27,151	56
Ottawa, applicable to unpaid Power	1,204	00
Interest Account	54,061	38
Cable Reels	210	85
Central Ontario System Balance	38,536	29
Storehouse Operation, Surplus	6,697	03
Garage Operation, Surplus	533	25
Administrative Office Building, applicable to Sinking Fund	2,940	82
	$14,727,212	**19**

SECTION IV

MUNICIPAL WORK

MUNICIPAL ADVICES

Niagara System

The Hydro-Electric enabling and money by-laws were submitted in:—
Dashwood, Dublin, New Dundee, Forest, Hensall, Rodney, West Lorne, Springfield, St. Jacobs and Zurich.

Estimates of the cost of supplying power to these municipalities have been forwarded by the Commission at their request.

The work of building and remodelling the distribution systems in these municipalities is being arranged for, and contracts with the Commission for power have been forwarded for signature.

At the request of these municipalities arrangements are being made by the Commission to have their engineers supervise the construction and remodelling of distribution systems for these municipalities, and, as soon as the necessary transmission lines and distribution systems are completed, power will be supplied.

Hydro-Electric enabling and money by-laws were submitted in:
Burgessville, Exeter, Harriston, Highgate, Listowell, Milverton, Otterville, Palmerston, Wellesley and Wyoming.

All of these by-laws carried by large majorities, and distribution systems were constructed under the supervision of the Commission's engineers, and power was turned on early in the year. All of these systems are now operating satisfactorily.

Engineering advice was given and rates were forwarded to the following municipalities in connection with proposed extensions to rural customers, outlining the necessary procedure to be followed under which power could be supplied to petitioners in these townships:

Ancaster Township, Barton Township, Biddulph Township, Blandford Township, Blenheim Township, Brantford Township, Burford Township, Chinguacousy Township, Dover Township, East Flamboro' Township, Esquesing Township, Etobicoke Township, Enniskillen Township, Guelph Township, London Township, Raleigh Township, Sandwich East Township, South Dumfries Township, Southeast Hope Township, Thorold Township, Tilbury Township, Tilbury East Township, Toronto Township, Townsend Township, Vaughan Township, Waterloo Township, Wilmot Township, West Nissouri Township, West Oxford Township, Woodhouse Township, Yarmouth Township, York Township, Zone Township.

The auditor's annual report shows that the operation of the systems in Ancaster, Blenheim, Comber, Dresden, Dundas, Ford City, Pt. Dalhousie, Sandwich and Thamesville has been very satisfactory, each of these systems showing a fair margin of profit for the year's operation.

During the year engineering assistance, in connection with extensions to distribution system and the taking on of new power customers, was given to the following municipalities:

Ailsa Craig, Ayr, Baden, Beachville, Brantford, Caledonia, Delaware, Dorchester, Dutton, Elmira, Elora, Embro, Fergus, Goderich, Hagersville, Lambeth, Lucan, Lynden, Mt. Brydges, New Hamburg, Paris, Pt. Stanley, Rockwood, Simcoe, Seaforth, St. George, Tilbury, Walkerville, Watford, Woodstock.

The auditor's report shows that all of these municipalities have operated for the year with a margin of profit, the number of lighting customers having been materially increased during the year, and the power consumption considerably increased, especially in those towns that are manufacturing large quantities of war munitions.

During the year estimates were forwarded to the following municipalities: Agincourt, Amherstburg, Atwood, Brigden, Brownsville, Burlington, Chippawa, Crediton, Drayton, Essex, Harrow, Humberstone, Kerrwood, Kingston, Leamington, Moorefield, Pt. Colborne, Scarborough Township.

Acton

During the year the Department assisted in obtaining two large additional power loads which will greatly increase the business done by this municipality. Engineering advice was also given in connection with necessary changes to the distribution to take care of the increased load and of altered conditions in connection with the streets.

Amherstburg

During the year engineering assistance was given to the Municipality of Amherstburg in designing and supervising the remodelling of their street lighting system.

This system is now operating satisfactorily.

Bothwell

The Bothwell system shows a very satisfactory operating report for the year and in December a small oil pumping load was taken on. It is expected that a considerable amount of power will be sold in Bothwell district in the near future for oil pumping purposes.

Brampton

Owing to the marked increase in the power load it became necessary to increase the capacity of the municipal station, and at request of the local Commission assistance was given in the purchase of larger transformers to take care of the increased load. Assistance was also given from time to time in connection with various matters connected with the business.

Burford

The operating report for Burford for the year is very satisfactory and in September a considerable number of customers were taken on the system, owing to the fact that the local companies decided to discontinue service in Burford.

Chatham

The number of "Commercial" and "Domestic" customers in Chatham shows a large increase for the year, and approximately 500 h.p. in motor loads has been connected to the system. The municipality has installed 120 h.p. in pumping motors at the municipal pumping plant.

Clinton

The Light and Power Department of the Utilities Commission reports a very favourable year with some additional lighting load and also extra power load.

When the Hydro was first introduced at Clinton, a privately owned plant had contracts with various customers, which did not expire until 1916. One of these contracts necessitated the operation of the old steam plant at a considerable loss to the Department. This has now been changed over to Hydro power and the system is operating at a much higher point of efficiency.

Dereham Township

A large number of rural petitions were received from the ratepayers in this township in the district between Tillsonburg and Brownsville, and also between Tillsonburg and Springford, and during the year a systematic canvass was made in these districts and sufficient contracts signed at the approved rates to warrant the Commission proceeding with the construction of the necessary lines to supply this power.

Dunnville

In September the Hydro-Electric enabling by-law and a money by-law for $53,000.00 were voted on by the ratepayers and passed by large majorities.

At the request of the municipality a valuation was made of the local plant and distribution system belonging to the Dunnville Electric Light Company, and negotiations were entered into by the municipality through the Commission which resulted in the purchase of the company's plant by the municipality for $16,500.00.

A contract with the Commission has been signed at the following rate:

H.P.	Delivered volts.	Cost per H.P. per year.
300	45,700	$27.77

Galt

The municipality has approved of the Commission supplying power at 12,200 volts, instead of 6,600 volts, as at present, and arrangements will be made by the local Commission during the coming year to install additional transformer equipment to take care of the large increase in load.

Grantham Township

During the year engineering advice was given at various times in connection with extensions to the Grantham Township system. The operation of this system is being handled by the St. Catharines Commission.

Hamilton.

A detailed report was prepared by the Commission's engineers at the request of the municipality, in connection with the matter of placing the wires of all crossings in the business district under ground on the main streets.

Arrangements have been made whereby the municipality will pay for and take over the 13,000 volt lines within the limits of the municipality, which lines were originally installed by the Commission to supply the waterworks with power direct.

Hespeler

Owing to the large increase in loads in the various municipalities in this district, after receiving the approval of the municipalities, the Commission has decided to supply power to Hespeler and other municipalities in this district at 13,200 volts instead of 6,600 volts as at present.

A full report in connection with this change was made by the Commission's engineers and submitted to the municipality.

Ingersoll

The Commission, at the request of the municipality, has given engineering assistance in connection with the installation of an ornamental street lighting system on the Main Street, as well as engineering assistance in connection with other matters regarding the operation of the system.

London

At the request of the municipality the Commission's engineers investigated the matter of interference between the lines of the Public Utilities Commission and the lines of the London Electric Company. A full report in connection with this matter was made and submitted.

London Township

On requests for petitions from the proof line district and that adjacent to Ettrick, arrangements were made and meetings held at which committees were elected to go on with the propaganda work in the districts referred to.

Mitchell

Arrangements are being made by the Commission to supply this municipality with power at 26,400 volts instead of 13,200 volts as formerly, and while this change is being made the municipality is advised to erect a new sub-station building in which this equipment will be installed.

The municipality has decided to discontinue the use of the 60-cycle steam plant, which will mean a considerable saving to the power and lighting users.

New Toronto

Contracts for large amounts of power have been made and assistance given by the Municipal Department in laying out extensions to the local system to serve these loads.

The greatly increased demand will necessitate extensive additions to the transmission line supplying that municipality and will also necessitate the building of a new and much larger transformer station. To meet the immediate demands, arrangements have been made and work commenced on the erection of temporary lines and stations, while engineering has been done on the permanent work.

Niagara Falls

Hydro rates were put into force in the municipality at the first of the year.

In November the municipality's contract with the Ontario Power Company expired and from that date power was supplied by this Commission. The lines connecting the municipal station with the Commission's high tension station, were in the most part purchased from the Ontario Power Co. Arrangements were

12 H.

also made whereby the municipality purchased the sub-station equipment in the municipal station, which was the property of the Ontario Power Company. A number of estimates were prepared *re* cost of power to several large customers who were considering locating in the neighbourhood of this city.

Niagara-on-the-Lake

At the request of the municipality the Commission's engineers supervised the installation of new electrically operated pumps, as well as a new sub-station building for same.

Norwich

During the year assistance was given to the municipality in connection with the installation of an ornamental street-lighting system for the business section of the village. The operation of the system for the year shows a substantial increase in load and a considerable surplus.

North Norwich Township

At the beginning of the year forty-eight rural customers were being supplied with power, and during the year extensions have been made to Burgessville and also an extension to supply a number of farmers south of Newark. The township having signed a standard township contract with the Commission for power, arrangements have been made to extend the township lines south from Newark and west from Burgessville.

Hydro-Electric power for rural purposes in this township has proved a great success, as is shown by the number of farmers who have signed contracts during the year.

South Norwich Township

A large number of petitions have been received from petitioners in the Springford district in this township, and during the year sufficient contracts were signed at the standard rural rates for the construction of a line running south of Newark, and arrangements are now being made for the construction of extensions to supply the consumers who have signed contracts for power.

Petrolia

The distribution system in Petrolia, which was purchased from the Petrolia Utilities Company, was remodelled under the direction of the Commission's engineers and Hydro-Electric power was first supplied to the municipality in the month of April.

A considerable number of extensions were made to the system during the year, to supply power to various companies for oil-pumping purposes, and there is every indication that practically all of the oil pumping in this district will be done by Hydro-Electric power in the very near future.

A complete street lighting system was put into operation, as well as an ornamental lighting system on the main street, consisting of ornamental cast iron standards of the shepherd's crook type, equipped with 600 c.p. lamps.

Port Arthur

Municipal operations in this city ran smoothly during the year and with little assistance from this office. Late in the year, however, the Commission was waited upon by a deputation composed of the Mayor and several of the Commissioners, who urged that Dog Lake be developed for Port Arthur. Many facts and figures were presented, showing the necessity for providing another source of power supply by the time the present Kam power contract expires in the spring of 1920.

The deputation departed to follow out the suggestion made to them, namely, to submit a written petition to the Commission setting forth the facts in the case. Such a petition will doubtless be received within the coming year.

Preston

At the request of the municipality the Commission's engineers prepared and submitted a complete report in connection with the waterworks situation in the municipality.

Engineering assistance and advice were also given in connection with various matters relating to the operation of the system.

Ridgetown

Arrangements were made whereby the municipality installed electric-driven pumps to operate some new wells in connection with its municipal pumping plant. These pumps were put into operation in November, 1916.

Sarnia

The Hydro enabling by-law and also a money by-law were passed by large majority at the municipal elections.

The enabling by-law was for an amount of $120,000, which is the amount necessary to cover the first payment for the plant purchased from the Sarnia Gas and Electric Light Co., and also take care of the cost of remodelling that system. The plant purchased is being remodelled under the direction of the Commission's engineers and a complete street lighting system is being installed. Ornamental lamps are being installed on the main streets. A combination steel trolley pole and ornamental brackets being used. Lamps in the main street will be 20 ampere lamps of 1,000 candle power capacity. It is expected that the full amount of power contracted for will be required within the first year's operation of the system.

Scarboro Township

Acting on petitions received from the township, an investigation was made as to the possibility of supplying residents in the south-western portion of the township with an electric lighting and power service, and estimates, together with rates for such service, were submitted. A number of public meetings were held and the Council appointed representatives to canvass the districts in question. As a result of this canvass some 215 contracts were secured.

At the end of the fiscal year the Township Council was preparing to enter into an agreement with the Commission for the building of lines and the supply of electric power.

St. Catharines

Arrangements were made whereby the Ontario Power Company has agreed to supply additional power to the municipality for a period of three years. Power to be supplied from the Ontario Power Company's transformer lines in the St. Catharines district.

Approximately 1,000 customers have been added to the system during the year and arrangements have been made to supply power to a number of very important munition plants.

St. Mary's

The revision of the street lighting system and also the power plant, which were under way last year, have been completed.

New power customers have been obtained and the operation during the year has been quite satisfactory.

St. Thomas

Owing to the large increase in loads on the system the municipality requested the Commission to prepare and submit specifications and drawings to the local commission for a new sub-station building, and additional equipment to be installed therein.

At the request of the municipality the Commission's engineers supervised the erection of this building and the installation of the electrical equipment.

Stamford Township

At the request of the Township of Stamford the Commission negotiated with the Ontario Distributing Company and purchased for the municipality the Company's lines, plant and system in the township outside of the limits of the City of Niagara Falls for the sum of $29,500.00, and the township submitted to the ratepayers the Hydro-Electric enabling by-law and a money by-law for an amount to cover the purchase of this system.

The Commission is at present operating this system for the township until such time as legislation has been passed whereby the township can sell debentures and operate this system; after which time the plant will be turned over to the township and the Commission reimbursed for the purchase amount.

Stratford

The load at Stratford station has increased to such an extent that it was decided to erect a new sub-station and contracts for the station and equipment have been let. The station when complete will be one of the most modern on our system and will have a capacity for a nominal load of 3,000 h.p.

In the Water Works Department the year's business shows the completion of the revisions which were being carried out in the pumping plant and also the completion of the new water tower. These additions are working out very satisfactorily to the city.

The installation of gasoline driven pumps in place of steam as auxiliary to Hydro pumping shows a net saving of over $3,000 per year.

Strathroy

During the year the local Hydro-Electric System and the waterworks system were placed under the management of a Utilities Commission, and the old steam pumps have been replaced with electrically operated centrifugal pumps for the domestic water supply, and a gasoline engine operated unit has been installed as a stand-by for fire purposes.

Tavistock

During the year the Commission's engineers looked over the incorporated village's requirements for a distribution system and estimates were prepared showing the cost and submitted to the council. Estimates showing the cost of 4,000-volt power were also submitted and a contract was signed with this Commission for 50 h.p.

At the municipality's request the Commission's engineers supervised the installation of the system, all labour being employed locally.

A small automatic domestic pump, driven by a single-phase motor, was installed in the waterworks station to handle the pumping electrically.

The local system was put into operation October the 26th.

Tillsonburg

During the year the municipality authorized the Commission to change its distribution system from 2,200 volts to 4,000 volts operation, in order that the surrounding rural districts might be supplied more advantageously at this voltage.

Engineering assistance was also given by the Commission in connection with various matters regarding the operation of the system.

Toronto

During the year negotiations have been in progress in connection with the purchase of the lines and system of the Interurban Power Company lying east of the Humber, and it is expected that negotiations for the purchase of these lines will be completed early in the coming year.

The auditor's report shows that in spite of the large cut in rates at the beginning of the year the system shows a good margin of profit for the year's operation, and the large increase in the number of power and lighting customers shows that the ratepayers in Toronto appreciate and patronize their own utility.

Toronto Township

During the year a number of extensions were made to the distribution system to serve additional customers, while sufficient new customers came on the existing lines to warrant a cut of 25 per cent. in the service charge.

Wallaceburg

During the year electrically operated pumps were installed and put into operation in the new waterworks station, and also small sewage pumps to take care of the necessary sewage pumping in the municipality.

The auditor's report for the year shows a substantial surplus for the year, and a number of large important power customers have been added to the system.

Waterloo

The auditor's report for the year 1916 shows that the Waterloo Hydro-Electric System is operating very successfully from a financial standpoint, and arrangements are being made to have this municipality supply power to a rural line extending north from the limits of the municipality in Waterloo Township.

Waterloo Township

Various petitions have been received from farmers in the township for a supply of Hydro power and an extension from the Waterloo system is being constructed on King St. North and the Lexington Road, to supply some twelve farmers who have signed contracts with the township.

Watford

The Hydro-Electric enabling by-law and a money by-law for $10,000.00 were submitted to the ratepayers in August and passed by large majorities, and a contract was signed with the Commission for power at the following rate:

H.P.	Delivered volts.	Cost per H.P. per year.
100	4,000	$59 45

Arrangements have been made to purchase the local distribution system for $2,500.00, and the municipality has requested the Commission to superintend the remodelling of this system to make it suitable for the distribution of Hydro-Electric power.

Welland

Arrangements were made to construct a new sub-station in the municipality according to plans prepared by the Commission's engineers. This station will be made so that power will be supplied at 2,200 or 13,200 volts, and station will have an ultimate capacity of approximately 10,000 h.p. The load on the Welland station has increased from 1,200 to approximately 2,100 h.p. during the year. Several very large munition plants are supplied from the Welland system.

A number of estimates were prepared by the Commission's engineers *re* cost of power to large power customers who proposed locating in the Welland district.

Weston

Assistance was given the local Commission in various matters, particularly in securing a large power contract, while engineering advice was given in laying out and erecting the necessary additions to the system to provide for this load.

Windsor

During the year an extension was made to the system to supply the Municipality of Ojibway, where a large steel plant is being constructed. It is expected that considerable power load will be obtained in Ojibway in the near future.

York Township

Many applications for electric lighting and power services were received during the year and estimates made on the costs of supplying these applications, while numerous extensions and additions were made to the distribution system.

In order to place the business on a better basis and to relieve the Toronto Hydro System from a portion of the responsibility of supplying such service in the township, an effort was made to have the township enter into an agreement with the Commission for the necessary supply of power and the financing of transmission lines. This proved unsuccessful and as a result a number of applicants have been unable to secure the service.

EUGENIA AND SEVERN SYSTEMS,

Distribution systems, inclusive of street lighting, were designed, constructed and extended during the year in the following municipalities, under the supervision of the engineers of the Department, and Hydro service given for the first time to such systems from the transmission lines of the Commission:

Chatsworth, Chesley, Grand Valley, Holstein, Markdale, Orangeville, Shelburne.

Distribution systems, construction work on which was begun during the latter part of 1915, were completed and placed in operation and given Hydro power for the first time in the following municipalities:

Dundalk, Durham, Flesherton, Mount Forest.

Valuations were made under the supervision of and by the engineers of the Department of privately owned electric light and power plants, distribution systems and transmission lines at the request of various municipalities.

Valuations were made with the idea of purchasing the privately owned properties for the purpose of incorporating same into the local Hydro-Electric Systems. These valuations were supplemented with estimates showing cost of power to the municipalities concerned, and also by special investigations for each locality in connection with load conditions.

Alton: A valuation of distribution system.

Grand Valley and Arthur: A valuation of steam generating plant, distribution systems and transmission lines connecting the municipalities.

Chesley, Hanover, Meaford, Markdale, Port Elgin, and Southhampton: A valuation of hydraulic generating plants, transmission lines and distribution systems.

Assistance was given by engineers of the Department in the nature of addressing public meetings prior to voting on money and enabling by-laws in the following municipalities:

Arthur, Chesley, Grand Valley, Holstein, Markdale, Tara.

Estimates covering the cost of power and cost of installation of Hydro service were made and submitted to the following municipalities:

Alliston, Alton, Arthur, Beeton, Caledon, Erin, Horning's Mills, Hepworth, Grand Valley, Kincardine, Lucknow, Meaford, Paisley, Port Elgin, Priceville, Southampton, Tottenham, Teeswater, Tara, Wingham, Wiarton.

Petitions were received and estimates made up and submitted, covering the cost of power to various townships. Investigations were made as to load possibilities, public meetings were held, the Township Councils addressed by engineers of the Department and local committees appointed and rates submitted to these various townships as follows:

Artemesia Township, Amabel Township, Brant Township, Bentinck Township, Derby Township, Essa Township, Euphrasia Township, Floss Township, Nottawasaga Township, Proton Township, Sunnidale Township, Tiny Township, Tay Township, Vespra Township.

Investigations were made and information and engineering advice given *re* the installation of electric motor driven pumps for the purpose of operating waterworks systems in various municipalities. Estimates were made up and submitted covering the cost of operation and installation of such equipment in the following municipalities:

Barrie, Collingwood, Chesley, Mount Forest, Shelburne.

Installations of electric driven pumps were made and completed in the Towns of Collingwood and Mount Forest, and the installations in the other municipalities will be installed and completed early in the new year.

Engineering assistance and advice was given to the following municipalities, in the nature of rate application, soliciting of power loads and new consumers, and other matters pertaining to the management and general operation of the utility, and an engineer of the Department visited each town and village from time to time for such purposes:

Severn System—

Barrie, Collingwood, Coldwater, Creemore, Elmvale, Midland, Penetang, Pt. McNichol, Stayner, Victoria Harbor, Waubaushene.

Eugenia System—

Chatsworth, Chesley, Durham, Flesherton, Holstein, Markdale, Mount Forest, Orangeville, Owen Sound, Shelburne.

Notes on engineering assistance rendered other municipalities are given in the following:

Alton

During the year investigations were made and estimates prepared and submitted covering the delivery of power to the Village of Alton and adjacent villages in the district.

Estimates were also prepared covering the construction of a transmission line from Orangeville to Alton, to supply the Alton Foundry Company with power for the purpose of manufacturing munitions. An agreement was made with the Company, the line constructed and power delivered for the purposes mentioned above.

The Village is making preparations for submitting enabling and money by-laws to the ratepayers early in the new year, with the intention of taking over the transmission line and the Alton Foundry Company's load.

Artemesia Township

An agreement was made between the Township Council and the Commission covering Hydro service for farms and for the rural communities of Eugenia and·

Ceylon. Power was delivered to a large stock farm near Markdale under this agreement and from requests already received and investigations made the indications are that a large and important rural load will develop in the township and the surrounding district.

Camp Borden

Advice and information was given to the Department of Militia and Defence in connection with Hydro service for lighting, power, and waterworks systems at Camp Borden.

An agreement was drawn up and submitted for supplying this power.

A transmission line was constructed from a point near the Town of Barrie to the Camp site.

A sub-station building and waterworks pumping plant were also designed and constructed for the Department of Militia and Defence, and power delivered for the operation of the Camp System in the month of June.

East Luther Township

Estimates were prepared and submitted covering the delivery of from 1,000 to 2,000 h.p. to a point in the township near the Village of Grand Valley, for the purpose of manufacturing peat, large deposits of which exist in paying quantities in that locality.

The industrial growth in this district will be greatly stimulated by the use of Hydro power in such an industry.

Hanover

Valuations were made, at the request of the municipality, of the Hanover Electric Light Company's property, including the distribution system within the limits of the municipality and the transmission lines to the hamlets of Carlsruhe and Neustadt, and the generating plant at Maple Hill.

The municipality was given advice and assistance by engineers of the Department in the purchase negotiations for this property, prior to voting on a money by-law to provide debentures for such purpose.

Estimates were made up and submitted to the municipality covering the cost of rebuilding the distribution system, which it was proposed to purchase from the private company, and also covering the construction of an entirely new and separate system.

Estimates were made up covering the cost of supplying a large flour and milling company's property with power, independent of the municipality. An agreement was made between this company and the Commission, the transmission line and sub-station constructed and power delivered during the month of October. This line, station and contract will be taken over by the municipality as soon as the service can be given to same after by-laws have been submitted to the rate-payers for approval.

Owen Sound

Very creditable results from a financial standpoint were made by the operation of the Hydro utility in this municipality during the year, so much so in fact that during the first six months of operation it was found possible to make a reduction of 10 per cent. in rates charged to the consumers for lighting and power service.

The new sub-station building and office building were completed and placed in service during the year.

Orillia

Negotiations were carried on between the municipality and the Commission, covering the sale of power from the Orillia-Swift Rapids Development, for use on the Commission's Severn system, and also covering the interchange of electric power and energy between the Commission's development at Big Chute, Eugenia Falls and Wasdell's Falls and the Orillia system.

A short term agreement was also entered into between the Water and Light Commission of the Town of Orillia and the Hydro-Electric Power Commission of Ontario, covering the purchase by the town of 2,000 h.p. required for the use of munition plants in the municipality prior to the completion of the Swift Rapids Development. This agreement also provided for the joint use of transmission lines by both parties.

Port McNichol

An agreement was made between the Canadian Pacific Railway Company and the Commission covering the supply of power for the operation of the Company's terminal and grain elevator at Port McNichol, and power was delivered under the agreement during the latter part of the month of July.

The transmission line was constructed and sub-station equipment installed in the Company's power house to take care of this load.

At the present time the Company's peak load exceeds 1,000 h.p. and preparations are already being made for installing new equipment to take care of increased loads during the coming year.

Eugenia System—

This system was placed in operation for the first time during the year, power for which being supplied from the Eugenia Falls hydraulic development.

Power was first delivered to 5 municipalities when the development was placed in service on November 1st. Since that date service has been given to 6 additional towns and villages, making a total of 11 municipalities connected to the system at the close of the fiscal year on October 31, 1916.

By-laws were submitted to the ratepayers and carried in four additional municipalities and construction of distribution systems begun and were in progress at the close of the year.

Assistance was also given to two municipalities, which will submit enabling and money by-laws during the early part of the coming year.

The loads and revenue in the municipalities connected to the system during the year have greatly increased since connection to the system and the first delivery of Hydro power, and the development at Eugenia Falls has been delivering its surplus capacity to the adjacent towns in Simcoe County and the Severn system.

Plans are now progressing for an extension to the Eugenia plant to take care of these growing loads.

The negotiations begun during the year 1915, covering the purchase of the transmission system, sub-stations and distribution systems of the Pine River Light and Power Company, were completed and this Company's properties taken over by the Commission and merged into the Eugenia system on May 1st, the following properties comprising this transaction being taken over:

Orangeville distribution system and auxiliary steam plant by the municipality.
Shelburne distribution system by the municipality.

Twenty-five miles of 22,000-volt, single-circuit transmission line from Horning's Mills power house at Orangeville by the Commission.

Horning's Mills distribution system and sub-station buildings and equipment at Shelburne and Orangeville by the Commission.

The transformers, lightning arresters and other transmission equipment at the development by the Commission.

Severn System—

A remarkable growth in the load and revenue produced from same has been made by the Severn system during the past year.

The capacity of the Big Chute development serving the district was reached during the month of July, and connections were made to both the Wasdell's Falls and Eugenia Falls developments, in order that the demands for power in the Severn district might be taken care of satisfactorily. Practically all of the surplus power available in both of the latter generating plants is now needed to satisfy the power requirements of the district, and plans are being prepared for increasing the capacity of the Big Chute and Eugenia Falls plants, and also for new developments to take care of the increased and growing loads in the district.

ST. LAWRENCE, EASTERN, WASDELLS, MUSKOKA, NORTH BAY AND PARRY SOUND SYSTEMS

Numerous requests were received for a representative to investigate the requirements of a Hydro-Electric System and, in such cases, an engineer visited the municipalities and obtained the necessary information. Estimates, showing the figure at which power could be supplied to the municipalities, were forwarded by the Commission. A number of valuations and investigations, in connection with utilities have also been made for municipalities.

Engineering assistance has also been given to a great many of the operating towns, on matters pertaining to rate application, economical operation of their local systems, and increasing the light and power business.

During the year, work of the foregoing nature was taken care of by the department in the following municipalities:—Alexander, Arnprior, Aultsville, Bath, Billings Bridge, Brechin, Brock Tp., Carleton Place, Carp, Casselman, Cedarhurst, Dysart, Emily Tp., Ernestown, Faraar Point, Harrowsmith, Kinbourne, Kinmount, Lanark, Lyn, Rear Leeds and Lansdowne, Manotick, Maple Grove, Mattawa, Monck Tp., Moscow, Newboro, Nipissing, North Gower, Perth, Powassan, Richmond, Roblins Mills, South Crosby, Sturgeon Point, Sydenham, Westport, Winchester Springs, Woodville.

Notes on engineering assistance rendered other municipalities are given in the reports following:

Almonte

Work on the remodelling of the municipal power plant and distribution system was begun in July, 1916. An addition was made to the power station, to accommodate a 250 K.V.A., 2,200-volt, generator and belted-exciter, and the existing penstocks, turbines, etc., were thoroughly overhauled, and altered. The water wheel units were re-set, the main shaft extended, and the whole arrangement strengthened by special castings and braces.

The distribution system, which before had been direct-current, was remodelled for 2'200-volt, three-phase distribution, and an efficient system of series street lighting is being installed. The current from the new unit was turned on on October 14th.

Aultsville

Requests were received for estimates on a supply of power to Aultsville, Faraar Point, and the surrounding rural district. The municipality was advised that when the St. Lawrence system was extended as far as this district, it might be feasible to supply them with power.

Beaverton

The distributing station was repaired and put into first-class operating condition, and a set of 22,000-volt lightning arresters installed. Negotiations are under way for a supply of power to be delivered to the surrounding farming district.

Bracebridge

On request from the town officials, estimates were prepared on the cost of power to be delivered to the municipality from the Commission's South Falls plant. It is expected that the municipality will be in a position for further negotiations in the near future.

Township of Brock

Arrangements are being completed for a supply of power to the farms in the townships,—same to be distributed from the substation at Gamebridge.

Brockville

Requisitions have been received from several rural communities, for a supply of light and power, and some of these are being served by the municipality. Negotiations are at present under way for a further supply of power to the St. Lawrence system, and it is expected that load conditions in Brockville will shortly be much improved.

Cannington

The laying of the substation floor was completed, and the interior of the station painted. A set of electrolytic lightning arresters was installed, to replace the former multigap arresters. Negotiations are in progress leading to the supply of light and power to farmers in the surrounding district.

Cobden

At the request of the municipality, estimates were submitted on the cost of building and equipping a local Hydro-Electric plant and distributing system. The money by-law was submitted to the people and passed on January 1, and work was commenced early in May. An efficient storage system was supplied by constructing a conservation dam some distance above the site of the power house. The old regulating dam at the power house site was repaired and new head works, penstock and power house built,—the power house having adjoined to it a dwelling house for the operator.

The power was first turned on on November 24th. The plant is operating very satisfactorily with a load of about 65 K.W. This development enjoys the distinction of being the smallest isolated development yet built by the Commission.

A 135 h.p. Boving re-action turbine is direct-connected to a Canadian General Electric Company 100 K.V.A., 2,300-volt generator. A flywheel was supplied to improve regulation on the outgoing lines.

Cornwall

Exhaustive reports and estimates on the cost of a satisfactory supply of power to the town have been under consideration. . Several requests have been received from residents and manufacturers for a supply of power to the town and surrounding district. Investigations are at present under way, with a view to supplying this district from the Commission's St. Lawrence system, in the near future.

Gamebridge

Following the request from residents of this hamlet, estimates were prepared and submitted on the cost of the supply of light and power. Individual contracts were obtained from several residents. The distribution system will be built in the near future, as soon as the requisite by-laws are executed by the township officials.

Gravenhurst

The Commission has acquired from Gravenhurst all rights and titles to that town's generating system at South Falls on the South Branch of the Muskoka River, and also has made a contract with Gravenhurst for a supply of power therefrom. The South Falls power house was remodelled and enlarged to serve Gravenhurst and Huntsville—the former, at 6,600 volts; the latter, at 22,000 volts. The plant was taken over and first operated by the Commission on November 1, 1915— the 6,600-volt transmission line to Gravenhurst being owned and maintained by the municipality.

In August, the accounts of the Corporation were revised to conform with the standards of the Commission.

Booster transformers have been installed on the municipality's incoming lines, to improve the regulation of the distribution system throughout the town.

Huntsville

Following the requests of the town officials, estimates were submitted on the cost of a supply of power to the municipality, and also on the cost of remodelling the distribution system, which, formerly, had been single-phase. In March, an agreement was executed for the supply of 800 h.p. from the Commission's plant at South Falls. Work on the transmission line was begun early in the Spring, and this was carried on concurrently with the erection of a brick substation, and the renovation of the town distribution system. An up-to-date system of series street lighting was also installed. Power was first delivered on August 24, 1916, being carried over the line from the Commission's South Falls plant, at a pressure of 22,000 volts and stepped down to 2,200 volts at the new town substation, for distribution.

Iroquois

Requests were received from the village Council for estimates on the cost of a supply of power to the municipality. After investigation, they were advised that it would be more feasible for them to remodel and operate their present plant, and this work has been undertaken by the municipality.

Kemptville

Estimates on the cost of supplying power to the Corporation of Kemptville, from a source of supply in Merrickville, were prepared and submitted, and a comprehensive survey made of the requirements in the village and surrounding district.

Kingston

In January, the Utilities Commission of Kingston sent in a request for estimates on the cost of power to the city. These were prepared and submitted, based on a supply of 1,500 h.p. On June 19th, in order that the urgency of the situation might be met, the ratepayers voted to ratify an agreement for a limited supply of power to be brought in over an existing pole-line from Kingston Mills. On December 2nd, a contract for the supply of 1,200 h.p., to be delivered from the Commission's Ontario System, at a price of $28 per h.p., was ratified by the local Commission, and later passed by the Council. The transmission lines for the supply of this power are now in course of erection.

During the year, the Municipal Accounting System of the city was, by request of the Utilities Commission, revised to conform with the standards of the Commission.

Merrickville

Early in the year, the Commission was requested for information as to the advisability of entering into a contract with the Rideau Power Company, for a supply of power to the municipality. After investigation, the village Council was advised against this action, as at that time proposed. A by-law was, however, passed, on submission to the ratepayers, and the village is now being supplied from the Rideau Power Company's generating station.

A study of the water conditions on the Rideau River, is at present being made by the Commission's engineers, with a view to using power from this river for a comprehensive distribution system to supply the surrounding district.

Mille Roches

An industrial survey was made in the village, to ascertain the probable requirements of power and light for residents in the village and outlying district.

Morrisburg

Negotiations have been under way during the year, with a view to leasing the municipal generating plant, for use in supplying power to the St. Lawrence system. Detailed reports have been made, with a view to ascertaining the cost of the necessary repairs before the plant could be connected with the system.

North Bay

The Nipissing Power Company, which supplies power tb North Bay, was, in March, 1916, taken over by the Ontario Government and handed over to the Commission for operation in trust. This system is supplied from a generating station on the South River, near Nipissing Village. The power plant is equipped with two (2) three-phase, 450 K.W., direct-connected 2,200-volt units, with direct-connected exciters. The voltage is stepped up at the generating station to a pressure of 22,000 volts, and transmitted at this voltage to North Bay, Callander and Powassan, where it is, in each case, stepped down to 2,200 volts for distribution throughout the respective municipalities. In addition to the above, a 2,200 volt single-phase transmission line supplies light and power to the village of Nipissing.

Estimates were prepared and submitted on the cost of installing a duplicate feeder to supply power to the Trout Lake pumping station for North Bay Waterworks Department.

Omemee

Following requests received from the village officials, estimates were submitted on the cost of a supply of power to be supplied from the Central Ontario System. An enabling by-law was presented to the people on January 1, 1917, and passed by a large majority. The proposed scheme includes the purchase and utilization of the present distributing system. An up-to-date series street lighting system will be installed. The distribution will be at a pressure of 4,000 volts, which provides for the extension of the lines into the surrounding rural districts without further transformation.

Ottawa

In February, the City Commission executed a contract with the Ottawa & Hull Power & Manufacturing Company, for a temporary supply of 750 h.p. Investigations are now being undertaken to ascertain the cost of developing 4,000 additional horse-power capacity, at the Queen street station, to generate power for the proposed pumping plant at Lemieux Island.

Parry Sound

On request from the town officials, estimates were prepared on the cost of a supply of power to the municipality to be transmitted from Chaudiere Falls on the French River. Requests were also received for estimates on the cost of further developing the present town plant and conservation system, and for the supply of power to the Canadian Explosives Company, located at Noebel. Negotiations with this in view are at present under way.

Engineering assistance has also been given to this municipality, in regard to the failure of certain apparatus.

Prescott

Exhaustive investigations have been made, to ascertain the probable future requirements of light and power for the town.

Renfrew

In November, 1915, the local Commission entered into a contract with the O'Brien Munitions Company, whereby they agreed to deliver to the Munitions Company a supply of 900 h.p. This, added to the existing load, made it imperative that a further supply of power be secured. A timber dam was constructed at Golden Lake, on the Bonnechere River, for conservation purposes, which, owing to the excessively high water in the Spring of 1916, had to be partly blown out. The Commission was approached *re* a further supply of power and, after investigating conditions, proposed an addition to the present plant, by adding a new turbine and generator. This the local Commision decided not to do, and asked for estimates on the cost of a separate supply of power. Accordingly, estimates were prepared on a supply to be transmitted from either the first and fourth chutes on the Bonnechere River and, after consideration of the same, the scheme of developing the first chute was recommended. As a temporary source of supply, a second-hand generator was procured by the Commission and belted to the standby steam engine in the municipal generating station. The by-law to enable the town to raise debentures of the first chute development was defeated on September 2nd, by a small majority. In November, the town Council, with the approval of the Commission, purchased the holdings of the Renfrew Electric Company,—the same comprising a distribution system supplying light and power throughout the town.

Smith's Falls

Estimates are at present being completed with a view to procuring a satisfactory system to supply Smith's Falls and surrounding district with light and power. Exhaustive surveys were made in the town and district, to ascertain industrial conditions and probable present and future loads.

Sunderland

The township of Brock is arranging for a supply of power to be distributed from the substation at Sunderland.

Wasdell's System

The No. 1/0 aluminium wire at present supplying this system is being removed and steel wire installed in its place, thereby affecting a very appreciable decrease in the cost of power to municipalities connected with the system.

Washago

Negotiations have been carried on throughout the year for a supply of light and power to the village. After industrial surveys were made and estimates prepared, it was decided that the load is as yet too small to warrant the building of a necessary transmission line distribution system.

Winchester

Repairs and improvements have been completed in connection with the Winchester substation. A satisfactory increase in power load has been procured for this section of the St. Lawrence system by the addition of the new condensed milk plant in the village of Chesterville.

CENTRAL ONTARIO SYSTEM

The generating stations, transmission lines and distributing systems formerly controlled and operated by the Electric Power Company, Limited, and its subsidiary companies are comprised in the system now known as the "Central Ontario System." The territory served extends from Whitby to Napanee on the south and from Lindsay to Sulphide on the north.

All the holdings of the Electric Power Company were purchased by the Province of Ontario, as of March 1st, 1916; the purchase being confirmed by Act of Legislature, known as the Central Ontario Power Act, which is reproduced in its entirety on page 89.

As provided in the Act, the system was operated for several months by the staff of the Electric Power Company, as agents for the Province. By Order-in-Council, dated May 5th, 1916, the Hydro-Electric Power Commission of Ontario was charged with the operation of the property, and this obligation was assumed by the Commission on June 1st, 1916.

The electrical system is briefly described in the following pages, and in addition to this the property purchased by the Province, and now administered by the Commission, includes a number of gas-plants and waterworks systems, and one electric railway, all of which will receive further mention on succeeding pages.

Generating Stations

Power is obtained from six generating stations on the Trent river, which are operated by the Commission, and which have the capacities indicated in the accompanying table. In most cases the concrete dams constructed by the Department of Railways and Canals in connection with the Trent Valley Canal are utilized for the power developments, and future developments to be made on the river will also utilize other similar dams located at various points between Trenton and Fenelon Falls.

In addition to the generating stations operated by the Commission, further supplies of power are obtained from the generating station of the Corporation of the Town of Campbellford at Dam No. 12, to the extent of 1,250 K.W., and from the Peterborough Hydraulic Power Company, from whose station at Dam No. 17, 1,120 K. W. is obtained.

13 H.

DEVELOPED AND UNDEVELOPED WATER POWERS ON TRENT RIVER

Power Site	Present developed normal capacity kilowatts	Total normal power which can be developed kilowatts
Dam No. 1 Trenton		2,500
" No. 2 Trenton	3,000	3,000
" No. 3 } Combined.............................		4,200
" No. 4		
" No. 5 Frankford............................	2,600	2,600
" No. 8 Meyersburg		4,800
" No. 9 Meyersburg		3,200
" No. 10 Ranney's Falls		6,100
" No. 11 Campbellford........................	3,000	3,000
" No. 14 Healey's Falls.......................	6,000	9,000
" No. 18 Peterborough........................	1,500	1,500
" No. 21 } Combined		2,000
" No. 22		
" No. 27 Burleigh Falls		1,800
" No. 28 Buckhorn............................		500
" No. 30 Fenelon Falls........................	725	1,000
	16,825	45,200
Power purchased from Corporation of Campbellford at Dam No. 12	1,250	
Power purchased from Peterborough Hydraulic Power Co., Peterborough	1,120	
Total developed power available	19,195	

The control of the flow of the river is being constantly improved, and it is hoped that still greater success will attend the efforts being made, to utilize to the fullest extent, the natural storage basins in the Trent Valley, thus securing a uniform and unfailing supply of electric power at all seasons of the year.

Transmission Lines

The diagram on another page will indicate clearly the extent and nature of the transmission system. Operation is conducted at 44,000 volts on most of the network, the exceptions being the line between Fenelon Falls and Lindsay, which operates at 11,000 volts, and the line connecting Dam No. 2 and Dam No. 5, which operates at 6,600 volts. All future developments at and in the neighbourhood of Trenton, will operate at this voltage, and will all feed into a switching and transformer station at Dam No. 2, where the voltage is stepped up to 44,000 volts for transmission. The total length of transmission lines is 285 miles. Additional lines will be constructed for the improvement of voltage regulation, and the duplication of service to safeguard against interruptions. Wooden poles are used throughout.

Substations

The following substations are connected to the transmission system and step-down the voltage to distribution or utilization voltage. Three-phase transformers are used entirely for capacities of 300 K.V.A. or larger.

The substation at Oshawa contains, in addition to transforming equipment, a stand-by unit consisting of a 400 K.W. generator, direct connected to a 615 H.P. Diesel oil engine. This unit is not used except when necessary in case of interruptions, but is kept in readiness at all times, and can be placed in operation in a very few minutes.

SUBSTATIONS

Location of Substation	Total transformer Capacity, K.V.A.
Belleville	2,250
Bowmanville	1,500
Brighton	300
Canada Cement Co., Lehigh Mill	3,000
Canada Cement Co., Belleville Mill	2,250
Cobourg	600
Colborne	100
Deloro	750
Deseronto	600
Lindsay	3,060
Madoc	480
Millbrook	100
Napanee	600
Newcastle	100
Oshawa	2,230
Peterboro	5,250
Port Hope	750
Point Ann Quarries	600
Pulp Mill, Campbellford	2,250
Sulphide	780
Treaton	1,350
Total	28,920

Municipalities Served

The distributing systems, instead of being owned and operated by the Municipalities as on the Niagara and other systems, are operated directly by the Commission, until such times as the Municipalities may desire to purchase and operate them under Local Commissions. The Corporations of Whitby, Madoc and Stirling are exceptions, and these Municipalities already control their own distributing systems, obtaining their supply of power through the agency of the Commission.

The complete list of Municipalities served is as below:—Belleville, Bowmanville, Brighton, Cedardale, Cobourg, Colborne, Deseronto, Lindsay, Madoc, Millbrook, Napanee, Newcastle, Newburgh, Oshawa, Orono, Peterborough, Port Hope, Stirling, Trenton, Tweed, Whitby.

Rates

The rates used by the former owners of the property have been continued in force pending the compilation of sufficient operating data to permit the determination of the cost of power delivered at the various Municipalities. It is expected that this will be completed early enough to permit of placing in effect a new schedule of rates in the Commission's standard form at the beginning of the year 1917. All flat rates will be extinguished as quickly as possible, and power contracts as they mature will be altered to conform to the Commission's standard form of contract.

Future Developments

The demand for power throughout the district is increasing very rapidly, and in order to meet this demand, additional transmission lines will be constructed next year, and additional generating units will be installed at Healey Falls. It is also expected that new generating stations will be built at a number of the dams on the Trent river.

Gas and Water Plants

In addition to the electric properties, the Gas Plants at Oshawa, Peterborough, Cobourg and Napanee, and the Waterworks Systems at Cobourg and Trenton are operated by the Commission at present, although it is expected that the Municipalities will desire to purchase these properties and operate them as municipal enterprises. Improvements have been made to most of these plants to cope with increased demand and to secure higher operating efficiency.

Peterborough Radial Railway

This property is at present operated by the Commission, but as the City of Peterborough have signified that they would prefer to operate it, it is likely that the road will be purchased by the city during the coming year.

Northumberland Pulp Mill

This mill is situated at Campbellford, and manufactures ground wood pulp. Supplies of raw material are obtained in the northern townships of the Counties of Hastings and Haliburton, and negotiations have been carried on with a view to the purchase of timber limits, which would assure a supply of pulpwood for many years, in addition to a large number of cedar poles. As the operation of this mill is outside the scope of the usual activities of the Commission, it is probable that negotiations now under way will result in the sale of the mill.

Cobourg

For some years the waterworks intake pipe had been of insufficient capacity, and in a precarious condition from exposure to ice pressure and storms, and contracts were let in July to John E. Russell for the installation, and to The Thor Iron Works for the material, of a steel intake pipe 25½-inch diameter and 900 feet long, to be laid in a trench excavated in the rock bottom of Lake Ontario; together with a large suction well housed in an annex to the present pump house. This work has been completed with steel intake box, screens, new suction main and reservoir connections, at a cost of about $36,000.

At the same time the four motor-driven turbine pumps have had all the interior parts renewed, including impellers of larger diameter, to meet the demand for increased pressure.

Estimates have been prepared for the installation of gasoline-driven turbine pumps to replace the present steam standby plant, and for a sewerage disposal system to serve the pumping station and the engineer's residence.

At the gas works the old bench of 4 S has been replaced by a modern half depth bench of 4 S complete with hydraulic main and tar regulator. This bench meets the demand for gas except during the summer season, when the bench of 6 S is in use.

Peterboro

Increased service given by The Peterborough Radial Railway has rendered necessary additional pit accommodation in the car barns, and a new pit to take three cars, with pockets for the convenient removal of wheels and axles, has been built.

The track within the paved area on the Jackson Park line has been fitted with continuous rail joints, with the result that car maintenance has decreased and the operation of this section of the railway has been considerably improved.

At the gas works, a small annex has been built at the rear of the boiler house, and a new oxide room and general storehouse is being built adjacent to the present workshop.

A new generator has been installed as a spare in order to enable the present generator to be properly repaired from time to time, and consideration has been given to the completion of a second carbureted water-gas unit with modern condensing and scrubbing equipment, also to the completion of the purifier plant, half of which was installed in 1913.

Valuations of the physical assets of the Radial Railway and the Gas Works commenced by the Electric Power Company have been completed.

Oshawa

The rapid increase in demand for gas within the last few years has resulted in serious deficiency of holder capacity. The present holder was designed for the addition of a flying lift, and is of English manufacture. Owing to British Government restrictions, it has not been possible to obtain a quotation from the makers on the completion of this holder. The installation of a complete coal-gas plant has been under consideration, and additional land has been purchased adjoining the gas works property to accommodate such a plant, which would be of capacity sufficient to meet all demands for gas, except peak loads in summer, and these would be taken by the present water-gas units.

Northumberland Pulp Company

Owing to certain changes in the wiring of one of the grinder motors, and the installation of an additional wet machine, to meet the heavy demand for pulp, the three hydraulic presses are now deficient in capacity and a fourth press is being built by the Boomer Boschert Company, of Montreal, to give 300 tons with the hydraulic pressure now in use in the mill, and an ultimate pressure of 600 tons with a capacity of 15 tons per day and reduction to 60 per cent. air dry.

In connection with these presses a triplex pump of comparatively low pressure is being added, which will accelerate the speed of the presses during the major part of the stroke, leaving the final heavy pressure to the present hydraulic pumps.

Nipissing

Estimates and drawings have been made for a new building adjacent to the old gas house at North Bay, for storage and garage purposes, but it was decided that the work should not be proceeded with this year.

A sewage disposal plant was laid out, and is being built in connection with the power house at Nipissing, and in accordance with the requirements of the Public Health authorities.

Arrangements have been made and orders placed for the remodelling of the gate mechanism of one hydraulic turbine, the existing devices being insufficiently rigid to allow of proper control of the unit by the governor. The other unit in this station was treated some years ago in a similar manner with marked success.

MUNICIPAL ELECTRICAL INSPECTION

During the past year great activity has characterized the work of the department through the Province. The introduction of new legislation has placed the control of electrical installations in the hands of the Commission in a much more effective manner than existed before the Act of 1916.

At the present time there is some confusion between the Power Commission Act, the Cinematograph Act and the Mining Act, which should be adjusted. Experience during the past year has also disclosed the necessity for the introduction of some further amendments to the present regulations, but the present Act, together with the rules and regulations, has been very effective and tended to improve conditions greatly.

The introduction of compulsory permits has been very effective, and through its introduction the irresponsible wiremen, amateurs, and unskilled persons are now obliged to notify the department before they undertake to do any electric wiring for light or power, so that under a rigid enforcement of this clause promiscuous work will be reduced to a minimum. In order to enforce this law it has been necessary to subpoena a number of offenders to court, and in all cases the magistrates have at once seen the necessity and wisdom of the law, and fines have been imposed as required by the Act. This is creating a very marked respect for the Act, and is very highly commended by the better and responsible wiring firms throughout the Province.

In many large factories and other buildings where a local electrician or engineer has been in the habit of doing the wiring, making alterations and repairs, much very defective wiring and the mutilation of what was once good wiring was a common practice, and a method of controlling this has been formulated by the adoption of a system of monthly inspection at a nominal annual inspection fee. Under this system any concerns thus employing their own electrician are at liberty to proceed with such alterations or repairs to their wiring without the formality of obtaining a permit for each and every job. Upon payment of a small annual fee of from $10 to $100, according to the extent and proportion of the place to be thus inspected, the electrical inspector makes a monthly visit to each factory or building, going over all work done during that month, and reporting any defects to the owner, who is obliged under the Act to see that the defective work is corrected. Owners will then, in their own interest, see that their electricians, or others entrusted with this work, are competent. The introduction of this method is only being commenced now, and promises to develop to very large and profitable proportions.

During the past year we have been able to place trained inspectors in charge of all districts in the Province, rather than depend upon the services of local superintendents of supply companies, as was done in some districts. By a judicious distribution of inspection offices throughout the Province, there is hardly, with the exception of one small section in the extreme north of New Ontario, a municipality or community without electrical inspection.

Under a re-arrangement of the inspection districts we have in some places been able to relieve two or more inspectors, and place the districts they once controlled under other inspectors. This has been accomplished by consolidating the several small districts into one, and with the service of a small runabout the inspector is able to handle all the work to a much better advantage.

During the year there has been recorded 100,787 actual inspections made throughout the Province. This figure represents actual visits of an inspector to an electrical installation, and does not include a vast number of inspections on old work, which are made during the inspectors' rounds, of which no record is kept.

There is a marked increase in building activity, and a consequent increase in the work, and the prospects are that, with the introduction of the monthly factory inspection, the coming year will be an extremely busy one.

The new edition of Rules and Regulations has been published and largely distributed. This edition contains amendments to take care of new conditions which are ever presenting themselves in the way of evolutions and improvements in electrical construction work, and also contains under the same cover a copy of the Act.

We have enjoyed the good will and hearty co-operation of the best electrical firms in the Province, as well as that of the Fire Marshal, who has been active in probing the cause of alleged electric fires, and the Electrical Inspection Department has rendered him all the assistance possible.

All district inspectors report daily to the Chief Electrical Inspector at Toronto, who reports to the Chief Engineer.

A supervising inspector is constantly employed on the road visiting the various districts and checking up the work of the district inspectors, and generally assisting the Chief Inspector in the administration and general supervision of the department.

A number of new municipalities have been added to the large list contained in last year's report, and the wiring in many municipalities has been carefully gone over, and recommendations made by our inspectors towards eliminating dangerous wiring, with good effect. While a great deal has been accomplished in this respect, much more could be done if it were not for the scarcity of skilled labour. We have found owners of buildings, as a general rule, ready to heed the warnings of inspectors, and to proceed with such changes and overhauling as required by our inspectors, just so soon as labour and material could be found.

MUNICIPAL PURCHASES AND SALES

The municipal electrical enterprises in Ontario require in the aggregate large quantities of poles, line wire, cross arms, insulators, transformers, house service meters and of everything needed for the construction and maintenance of their various projects.

This demand can, in a measure, be filled by individual municipal purchase, but this is not always satisfactory. Owing to the wide range in the variety of materials and in the requirements, the municipal officials may lack the equipment necessary to properly safeguard their interests, and may not know exactly what should be used and where it can be obtained to the best advantage. The requirements of an individual town are comparatively limited. It cannot always afford large quantities and accordingly has to pay higher prices. At times rush orders may be placed for urgently needed material, which through lack of provision, may not be in stock. For these and other reasons individual effort of this kind often means through lack of co-operation the more or less indiscriminate purchase of smaller quantities at higher prices, and the absence of an effective means of control which would tend to standardize quality and efficiency.

If the large requirements of the municipalities as a whole were combined and centralized, there would be created a purchasing agency which could control the various commercial conditions so that each municipality could obtain, its comparatively smaller requirements under the favorable conditions attending competitive wholesale purchase.

To give practical effect to this centralized purchasing idea the Commission maintains a Purchasing Department whose services are offered to any municipality or Provincial institution in Ontario, whether connected with the Hydro system or not.

During the past year we have been buying for one hundred and fifty-three municipalities. Their total requirements, of over $700,000, have enabled us to obtain for them at prices lower than those previously available all of the many items required in the extension of their various projects. On transformers, lamps, watt-hour meters and rubber covered wire we have been able to effect savings of from five to fifty per cent. over the prices previously paid. These are only a few of the economies effected, but will serve to show what can be done by co-operation.

A feature of this centralized service to which attention should be directed is the possibility of intelligent discrimination. Low cost is important, but it should not be the only consideration. It is necessary to know that the article purchased represents good value for the money. We have on our staff men who are experts on the many materials and processes which enter into the make-up of the various items used. In addition, we have complete equipment for standardizing and testing. Full use of these resources is made by our Purchasing Department, so that it is in a position to know that the materials recommended represent the best values obtainable. We call attention to this as we have appreciated that such complete facilities are seldom available to the individual towns, and we want to make it perfectly clear that this service has been organized for their benefit and is available for the asking.

The reduction in Hydro rates has greatly enlarged the possibilities of electric service in the household and on the farm, and the sales of irons, air heaters, motors, and all of the many other utilities, have been greatly increased.

To assist the municipal officials in the promotion of this revenue producing business the Sales Department made a careful investigation of the merchandising conditions, and as a guide in formulating campaigns complete data was secured of the methods adopted by the leading electrical companies. This information has been condensed and is available for municipal use. A number of the municipalities have availed themselves of this service and have found that the broad gauged, progressive policies outlined have enabled them to show a very substantial increase in their sales of utilities.

In building up this business they have been further assisted by definite advertising campaigns, from which gratifying results have already been derived.

The services of the Sales and Advertising Department are freely offered to any of the municipalities in Ontario, and information in connection with this subject will be gladly given upon request.

RURAL POWER

USES ON A GROUP OF FARMS IN WATERLOO TOWNSHIP

A further report of the operation of Syndicate No. 1 is submitted for the year 1916, for purposes of comparison with the report on same Syndicate as submitted in the 1915 report.

As a result of the satisfactory operation of the outfit of this syndicate, 12 new farm contracts were signed on the Waterloo-St. Jacobs road, and two more syndicates formed.

Waterloo Township Syndicate

WORK DONE JANUARY 1st, 1916, TO JANUARY 1st, 1917

No. 1 Farm, E. C. Hallman

Silo filling ....   30 ft. in 12 ft. x 42 ft. silo.
Threshing ....   960 bushels wheat.
                         1,800   "   mixed grain and oats.
Chopping   1,900   "
Sawing wood ....   15 cords.

No. 2 Farm, I. C. Hallman

Silo filling ....   24 ft. in 14 x 39 ft. silo.
Threshing ....   1,000 bushels wheat.
                         1,950   "   oats.
Chopping   2,000   "
Sawing wood ....   18 cords.

No. 3 Farm, J. S. Stauffer

Silo filling ....30 ft. in 12 ft. x 40 ft. silo.
Threshing ....   900 bushels wheat.
                         1,500   "   oats.
                         800   "   mixed.
Chopping   2,200   "
Sawing wood ......:...   10 cords.

No. 4 Farm, Noah Snyder

Silo filling ....   15 ft. in 10 ft. x 22 ft. silo.
Threshing ....   250 bushels wheat.
                         1,100   "   oats.
Chopping   1,200   "
Sawing wood ....   15 cords.

No. 5 Farm, Uriah Snyder

Silo filling ....   14 ft. in 11 ft. x 30 ft. silo.
Threshing ....   500 bushels wheat.
                         1,000   "   mixed.
Chopping   700   "
Sawing wood ....   15 cords.

No. 6 Farm, Alvin Schieffle

Silo filling ....   15 ft. in 14 ft. x 40 ft. silo.
Threshing ....   600 bushels wheat.
                         550   "   oats.
                         1,200   "   mixed.

G. Shanty

Threshed ....   300 bushels.
                         1,000   "

Waterloo Township.—Syndicate No. 1

Uses January 1st, 1916 to January 1st, 1917

Rate—Service Charge $30.00; Power 4c. per K.W.H. Discount 10% from power only

No.	Jan.	Feb.	Mar.	April	May	June	July	Aug.	Sept.	Oct.	Nov.	Dec.	Total	Total K.W.H.	Domestic	Power	Service Charge	Total
													K.W.H. Domestic Uses					
1	90	47	43	34	35	29	24	32	40	53	72	73	572	1,646	20.59	38.66	35.00	94.25
2	77	49	48	41	37	33	34	44	48	54	77	62	604	2,102	21.74	53.92	30.00	105.66
3	53	34	22	21	25	17	16	22	25	25	49	41	350	1,562	12.60	43.63	30.00	86.23
4	74	46	48	42	38	37	30	33	35	46	66	65	560	1,125	20.16	20.34	35.00	75.50
5	43	21	14	11	15	7	8	12	12	21	35	31	230	777	8.28	19.69	30.00	57.97
6	25	26	22	16	13	8	8	14	19	26	32	41	250	1,508	9.00	45.29	30.00	84.29
													2,566	8,720	92.37	221.53	190.00	503.90
													K.W.H. Power Uses					
1		91	73					362	110		438		1,074					
2	120		128	170	87	35		331	579			48	1,498					
3	36	91	83	141	43	26		317	82	45	348		1,212					
4	80			65	61				28	37	294		565					
5	32			62				129	22	30		272	547					
6		78	68	65	63	14		59	20	34	563	294	1,258					
7	264									62			326	326		11.74	9.00	20.74
													6,480	9,046	92.37	233.27	199.00	524.64

See Record of Detail of work done on page 187.

ORNAMENTAL STREET LIGHTING

REVIEW

The installations of "White Way" systems made in many Hydro municipalities during the past few years have been received with approbation by the public in general.

The success of such installations has encouraged engineers engaged in their design and construction to make further investigations, resulting in the production of lighting units of improved appearance, and more effective in the utilization of light. Economy in first cost and in maintenance has also resulted and equipment has been devised which will render the continuous operation of street lighting circuits more secure, and provide additional safe guards against accidents to employees.

As might be expected, the "White Way" system has attracted more attention than what is usually designated as the "ordinary" street lighting system, which is generally installed in residential districts. However, the equipment for the "ordinary" lighting units has been the subject of much thought, and the improvements which have been made are noteworthy. Improvements in this system of lighting are the more important as by far the greater area of streets illuminated comes within this class.

The gas-filled incandescent lamp has become firmly established, and is now being installed in all new "series" systems to the total exclusion of the arc lamp, as well as the evacuated incandescent lamp. The Commission's engineers have made special investigations concerning gas-filled lamps, which will be supplied in the near future to the Commission's specifications, resulting in a great saving to the municipalities.

Heretofore the use of the "series" system of street lighting has not been considered feasible except in cities and larger towns, where a considerable number of lighting units is required. Hence, the smaller municipalities have been debarred from obtaining the benefits of the "series" system, which is, in many ways, ideal for street lighting service. Due to recent developments in the regulating apparatus, which is required for the satisfactory operation of the "series" system, the latter is now available for even the smallest village.

INSTALLATIONS

Almonte

A complete new street lighting system is now being constructed in this municipality under the supervision of the Commission. The existing D.C. arc lamps will be taken out of service.

Blenheim

A "White Way" system of ornamental standards fed by underground cable has been installed; the lights were put into operation during the week ending January 8th, 1916.

Cobden

A street lighting system is being constructed in Cobden under the Commission's supervision.

Cobourg

At the request of the municipality the Commission has submitted plans and estimates for a new street lighting system to replace the present system of enclosed arc lamps.

Ingersoll

The Commission's engineers, on the request of the municipality, made recommendations concerning the installation of a "White Way" system on Thames Street. This system is now being constructed by the local authorities, and all the equipment has been supplied by this Commission.

Norwich

This municipality has been advised regarding the installation of a "White Way" system, and has constructed the same, the equipment being purchased through this Commission.

Sarnia

A new system of street lighting is now under construction, planned and installed under the supervision of the Commission. Some 650-100 watt units are required for the residential streets, and 76-500 watt units in the commercial district. Combination railway and lighting poles of tubular steel are being erected and the "White Way" units will be mounted on them. The circuits will be carried overhead, except at the Square in front of the City Hall, and in the park at the Public Library.

Petrolia

A "White Way" system according to recommendations from the Commission has been constructed in Petrolia. Lights were put into operation on April 25th, 1916.

Ridgetown

A "White Way" system fed by underground cable was installed in Ridgetown and placed in service during the last week in December, 1915.

GENERAL

Special equipment for Ornamental Lighting has been supplied to a number of municipalities; others have been provided with estimates or recommendations regarding existing or proposed installations; these municipalities include Amherstburg, Chatham, Dunnville, Exeter, Guelph, Huntsville, Kingston, North Bay, St. Catharines, Stratford, and Windsor.

St. Thomas White Way
Note the combination railway and lighting poles

St. Thomas White Way
Note the several lines of wooden poles on both sides of the street. These have been removed

MUNICIPAL UNDERGROUND CONSTRUCTION

There has been but little activity in underground construction during the past year, in accordance with the general policy of eliminating expenditures for all works not absolutely necessary at the present time.

Hamilton

Cables have been installed in the Joint Underground Conduit System, and are now being operated by the Hamilton Hydro-Electric Department and the Great North Western and Canadian Pacific Railway Telegraph Companies.

St. Thomas

In connection with the new municipal sub-station, manholes and conduits have been installed to carry the distribution feeders underground from the sub-station to the overhead pole lines.

Owen Sound

A twelve-duct underground run with manholes was constructed leading from the new municipal sub-station to the overhead distribution system. The cables were placed in operation in January, 1916.

ELECTRIC RAILWAY PROJECTS

A number of resolutions from Municipal Councils asking for reports on additional electric railway projects were received during the year. In some cases these resolutions were from Municipalities who had already requested to be considered in one or more lines in their particular district. No attempt has been made to keep track of these duplicate applications, but to date resolutions have been received from 15 cities, 47 towns, 51 villages, 8 police villages, 172 townships and from 7 counties or other similar governing bodies. A total of 300 resolutions has, therefore, been received since the passing of the first railway act. In response to these resolutions the Commission has made preliminary surveys on 2639.46 miles of line, and has gathered traffic statistics for approximately three-quarters of the district affected by such surveys.

The map of south-western Ontario as found on the following page shows in black the routes covered by the principal surveys that have been made in that section of the Province, and also in green the lines upon which reports have been made. The projects which have been voted upon and carried by the ratepayers are indicated in red. Other surveys not shown on the map were made as follows:—

1. Gravenhurst to Baysville and Hollow Lake.
2. Kingston to Cornwall.
3. Ottawa to Morrisburg.
4. Various lines in Prince Edward County.

In addition to engineering and traffic surveys considerable work was done during the year on preparation of standard drawings and specifications for construction and equipment of the proposed lines. This work is being carried on in a very careful way, as it is felt that considerable savings in cost of construction

14 H.

and operating of the various lines will be possible if they are all built to conform to the same specifications.

The most outsanding events of the year as related to the proposed system of municipally-owned electric railways were:—

1st. The voting on the Toronto-London Line.

2nd. The commencement of the campaign for the Port Credit-St. Catharines and Welland-Bridgeburg Lines.

3rd. The remarkable success achieved by the London-Port Stanley Railway during their first year of service.

Proposed Toronto-London Line

A report on the Toronto-London Line was given to the municipalities interested in the Fall of 1915, and voting on the By-laws took place at the annual elections in January, 1916. The report covered a 137-mile line extending from the foot of Yonge Street, Toronto, westward along the new Harbor Board property, under the Exhibition grounds and parallel and south of the G.T.R. to one mile west of Port Credit, where the G.T.R. is crossed. From this point the line proceeds in a westerly direction through Milton, Guelph, Kitchener, Stratford and St. Marys to London, where connection would be made with the London and Port Stanley Railway at the corner of Richmond and Bathurst Streets. The estimated cost of construction and equipment was placed at $13,734,155. Further details of the route and distribution of the guarantee can be obtained from the form of agreement as contained in the *Railway Act* for 1916, which Act will be found in this report under the heading of " Legal Proceedings."

A number of Public Meetings were held in the Municipalities voting on the By-law, at which representatives of the Hydro-Electric Railway Association and the Commission were present. Considerable opposition to the scheme developed, chiefly in the City of Toronto, where the Board of Trade opposed the scheme very strenuously both at the Public Meetings and in the daily papers. The opposition seemed to assist rather than retard the interest in the project, and the By-laws were carried by very large majorities in the 5 cities, 3 towns, 4 villages and 11 out of 14 townships interested. Some 5 townships that were assessed very small amounts for the guarantee, due to the line passing only close to or through a corner of the municipality, did not vote upon their By-laws.

The agreements with the municipalities that carried their By-laws were duly signed and were ratified by Act of Parliament in the Spring of 1916, but this Act, while legalizing the agreement, expressly states that no construction can be undertaken during the period of the war. Provision is made, however, for the carrying on of location surveys and the purchase of property for the right-of-way.

Proposed Niagara District Lines

A report on a 60-mile line from Port Credit through Hamilton to St. Catharines was presented to delegates from the municipalities in that district at Hamilton on September 1st, 1916. The feeling of the meeting was so unanimously in favour of proceeding with the scheme that representatives of the Hydro-Electric Railway Association and engineers of this Commission were sent to the Council of the Municipalities with full details and resolutions were then passed asking the Commission to secure the necessary sanction of an agreement to provide for the construction and operation of the line and to secure such sanction in sufficient time so that voting on the proposition might take place on January 1st, 1917.

HYDRO - ELECTRIC POWER COMMISSION
of
Western Ontario

The ratepayers in the Welland-Port Colborne-Bridgeburg district have been desirous for a number of years of securing electric railway service through that district, and although the Commission was not prepared to give final decision on a through route to the Niagara Frontier, still they found from the traffic surveys that there was sufficient local business to make the construction of a local line a splendid proposition, irrespective of the location of the through line. A general report was at once presented to the Councils of the municipalities interested and they passed resolutions requesting the Commission to procure the sanction of the agreement so that voting on the proposition may take place at the annual elections in January, 1917.

Two lines will, therefore, be voted upon in January next, the first 60 miles in length extending from Port Credit westerly through Oakville, Burlington, Hamilton, Grimsby and Beamsville to St. Catharines, and the second line 28 miles in length extending southward from Welland to Port Colborne on the east side of the canal, and from thence easterly through Ridgeway, Crystal Beach and Fort Erie to Bridgeburg. The estimated cost of the Port Credit-St. Catharines line is placed at $11,360,363 and the Welland-Bridgeburg line at $2,208,716. The construction and equipment proposed for these lines would be of a very high standard and would be similar to that found on the London and Port Stanley Railway. A large proportion of the revenue will be received from the transportation of freight. The route through the City of Hamilton involves a high level bridge across the ravine at Valley Inn at the northern limit of the city, and the construction of a double-track line through the city, passing along the edge of Dundurn Park and hence on private right-of-way through the manufacturing district to the easterly boundary of the city. There would only be one or two minor highway crossings at grade within the city limits.

London-Port Stanley Railway

This electric railway reconstructed and electrified under the Commissions' standard specifications, finished its first year of operation under municipal management on June 30th, 1916. Previous reports of this Commission contain information showing the manner in which this railway was assisted in the reconstruction and electrification and consequently the results achieved by this line may be used to illustrate the service that will be given over the various lines that have been favorably reported upon by the Commission. The report that has just been issued, covering this first year of operation indicates that the line after meeting all charges, including taxes, interest, rentals, etc., and full sinking fund charges on the new investment, yielded a surplus of some $24,000. This is considered a remarkable success, as sufficient rolling stock was not available to carry all the business that was offered, and also the first few months of operation were not profitable because many of the side tracks were not electrified and the Michigan Central freight business was withdrawn and given to a competing line.

Officials of the line were assisted at various times during the year with engineering advice on the location of new tracks and other similar matters. Designs were also worked up for a 70-foot motor car which would become a standard of the Commissions. These new specifications are now being used by the L. & P. S. railway to secure tenders on two of such cars for their own use. These cars will be of the three-compartment type and will be very similar to the 60-foot cars now operating on this railway. The same high standards of interior finish, such as mahogany trim, bronzed fittings, plush seats, etc., as found on the earlier cars are also to be used for these new cars.

15 H.

During the year this railway constructed a modern car barn, and in this work were assisted by the Commission from time to time, and the design of this building and equipment will probably be used on the various lines that have been reported upon by the Commission.   Engineers were loaned the railway company for the purpose of assisting them in working out details of maintenance of equipment and instructing the employees connected with such work.

TESTING AND RESEARCH LABORATORIES

The activities of the laboratories have been extended in several directions during the past year.   One of the most important extensions of the work has been the undertaking of comprehensive investigations of conditions on the high tension transmission lines; these include a theoretical study of voltage and current conditions at all stations, with a view to improvement in voltage regulation, a study of relay protection, of high tension insulators, of current and power supplied under short-circuit conditions at various points on the system, of the possibility of using steel for transmission line conductors and of many other subjects suggested by those mentioned above.   These investigations are the result of the endeavors which are continually being made by the Commission, as well as by all large power companies, to perfect the transmission of power at high voltages. .Their importance will be appreciated by the layman when the object in view is stated—to make it possible to supply electric power to the consumer without interruption and at constant supply voltage.

Reference should also be made to the label service operated by the laboratories in conjunction with the Electrical Inspection Department; further reference to this is made below.

During the year the handling of used apparatus by the Commission has been taken up systematically and a suitable method of carrying on this work was adopted; this is described in the November issue of the Hydro Bulletin.   The inspection of this class of apparatus is done by the laboratories.

The number of mechanical and other non-electrical tests has so increased that it was considered sufficient to occupy the attention of a specialist in this line. Accordingly the Structural Materials Laboratory was organized and additional equipment for this class of work has been placed on order.

The following equipment has been added during the year:

An exciter for the 60-cycle alternator, a 33,000-volt transformer for testing oil and other insulation, a set of laboratory standard ammeters, voltmeters and wattmeters, a large number of portable and laboratory type meters, an integrating sphere photometer 84 inches in diameter, a 40,000-lb. Universal testing machine, a 200,000-lb. hydraulic compression machine, besides numerous smaller pieces of apparatus.

The extension of the test work has rendered the present space entirely inadequate to our needs and additions are at present being made which will make available for the laboratories about 20,000 sq. ft.   When this space has been added the present testing equipment will be rearranged to suit the requirements of the laboratories.

High Tension Testing Laboratory

Previous reports have indicated the general purpose and development of this laboratory and in harmony with the increased scope and activity of the Com-

Cement and Sand Testing Equipment

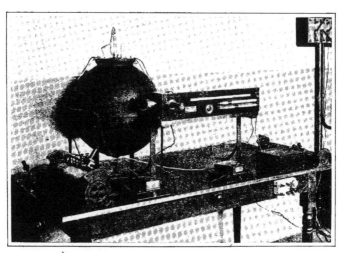

18" Integrating Sphere Photometer, Lamp Testing Laboratory

mission as a whole, this department is continually widening its sphere of usefulness.

Routine tests are made on samples of all classes of apparatus purchased by the Commission from the high voltage tests on the insulators for the 110,000-volt lines and stations to small motors and switches for the small consumer. Apparatus is available from which any single-phase 25-cycle voltage up to 200,000 volts or 60-cycle voltage of 400,000 volts may be obtained and a great deal of work is done at 100,000 volts and higher.

One routine test which has an important value in the operation of the system is the testing of three hundred and fifty samples of oil each month, sent in from the high-tension stations on the system and taken from the 110,000-volt transformers and oil circuit breakers. In addition to the regular samples from twenty to fifty special samples per month are received from municipal stations. These are all tested for dielectric strength and records kept of the condition of this insulating medium are of inestimable value in forestalling failure of the apparatus due to faulty oil. Apparatus is under development which reduces the time and cost of these tests to a minimum and ensures very accurate results. Insulator testing also has a very important value to the system, and with the proposed extension of space available for the high-tension testing it is expected that high voltages and high frequency oscillations may be used that under previous conditions have been more or less unsatisfactory.

Special tests are made on apparatus purchased under guarantee by the Commission, either for its own direct use or for the use of municipalities for which it is acting in an advisory capacity. During the past year complete tests have been run on constant-current transformers, constant-potential transformers, motors, motor-starters, circuit-breakers, lightning arresters, fuses, rubber gloves and various other protective devices and apparatus. The result has been most beneficial in bringing the manufacturer and consumer to terms, sometimes by proving the good points of the article in question, at other times by noting the weaknesses and encouraging and advising the manufacturer as to the changes to be made in design or process of manufacture. The honest manufacturer invariably appreciates the fact that the laboratories exist for his benefit as well as for that of the general public and harmonious relations are the result.

Used apparatus, sold by one municipality to another, as the result of change in service supply, is sent for inspection to this laboratory, and the tests given to this apparatus are such as to test its ability to operate satisfactorily under any reasonable condition of service. Although the arrangements of this scheme were made quite recently, a considerable amount of material has already been transferred in this way.

The testing and approval of fittings and other apparatus has become an integral part of the work of this department, and activity among the manufacturers and dealers of this Province is evident from the amount of material inspected and the urgent need for its return as soon as approved. The laboratory co-operates in this work with the Inspection Department and operates a label service, by means of which approved apparatus is labelled. The utmost care is taken to approve no apparatus which would become hazardous when in or out of service, and suggestions are made as to the alterations necessary to meet with the approval of the Commission. In addition to approval tests in the laboratory periodical inspection is made in the factories with the object of seeing that no apparatus which does not comply with our requirements is placed on the market.

The scope of this department, as outlined in previous reports, includes general tests on mechanical strength, quality of building materials, etc. The work of both electrical and mechanical sections has grown to such an extent as to warrant the formation of two separate departments, hence the general tests on strength of materials are not included in the work of the High-Tension Laboratory.

Meter and Standards Laboratory

The increase in the amount of energy transmitted and distributed has reacted in several ways upon the activities of the Meter and Standards Department. The large volume of power handled necessitates an ever increasing degree of precision in its measurement; and the greater number of consumers means a greater number of metering units to be maintained in accuracy. These and similar conditions have resulted in this Department now handling approximately twice the volume of work of a year ago.

A complete set of Weston long scale standard indicating instruments has been placed in the laboratory, and pending further extensions to the building, temporarily installed; so that calibrations may be made on ammeters, voltmeters and wattmeters. By means of standard cells and standard resistances it is possible at any time to compare the accuracy of these laboratory instruments with the standards at Ottawa and at Washington. With the improved standardization equipment frequent checks are possible on the large number of portable meters used by the Laboratory and by the Operating Department. Meters are also being sent in by the municipalities and by electrical manufacturers in the Province for calibration.

The work of investigating various types of new apparatus as to suitability for installation upon the Commission's circuits has been energetically followed out. Complete comparative tests have been made on several improved types of watthour meters which have recently appeared on the market; and their high standing, according to the specifications indicates that the art of meter manufacture has advanced to a point where a revision of many of the ratings in the meter specifications is desirable, to give a useful value to the results. This revision is now under consideration. The investigation of demand indicators and other special types of metering apparatus has given much valuable information regarding the approach of the readings of various types to the true value of maximum demand, under loads of widely differing peak characteristics.

With a view to determining the most suitable indicating instruments for the switchboards, as the power systems are extended, a detailed comparative test was made on the meters of a number of manufacturers. These were submitted to practically every condition, normal or abnormal, under which such instruments might be expected to operate, and careful records made of their performance. The results so obtained contain much valuable information to guide in the selection of switchboard meters.

The problem of better protection of the great network of transmission lines against interruptions due to short circuits, grounds and other accidental conditions is being taken up by the Laboratory, and it has fallen to the lot of the Meter Department to make examinations and tests of a number of types of protective relays supplied for such work. Though these tests are not complete some very interesting results have been collected to show the comparative operation, as regards selective and other features under widely diverse conditions of load, temperature and location.

Considerable design work has been undertaken. This includes relays for motor protection, mechanical refinements to demand and other special meters, as

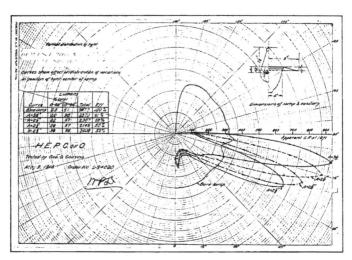

Curves of candle power distribution of a gas filled lamp equipped with prismatic refractor

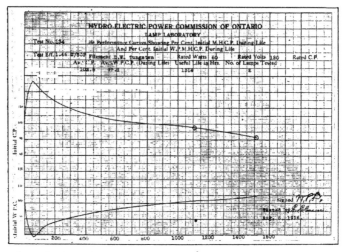

Curves showing variation of Candle power and efficiency of a tungsten lamp with life

well as such auxiliary apparatus as may be required by the Laboratory for its own use. The construction of special meters, and the alteration of others to suit special conditions has occupied much time, the principal work of this class being the conversion of a number of polyphase wattmeters into "wattless component" meters. This consists in a simple modification of the resistances and connections so that by throwing a switch the converted meter may be made to read the reactive volt-amperes of a polyphase circuit. With a graphic "wattless" meter installed beside a wattmeter it is a simple matter to determine at any time the true power factor of the load, no matter how badly unbalanced the currents may be; while by throwing over the switch the instrument reads the power component and may be made to duplicate or replace the wattmeter in the circuit.

A large amount of repair work has been done in the meter shop for the municipalities. This has included watthour meters, defective, disputed or damaged through overloads or other causes, demand indicators, graphic and indicating instruments. In addition to this a systematic overhauling and adjusting of the meggers used by the Operating Department is carried on. By the nature of their work on insulator testing these meggers receive very heavy service and without periodic attention they would soon lose their usefulness.

The work which has shown the greatest increase is that of handling used apparatus. Old watthour meters in batches of from half a dozen to several hundred have poured in from all points. These are sorted out, the manifestly obsolete ones set aside and the others put through a schedule of cleaning, adjustment and recalibration. They are then either returned to the original owners or taken into stock to supply the great demand for used meters. Among those coming are many, some fifteen or more years of age, which because of obsolescense or inherently bad characteristics are immediately relegated to the scrap heap, where they are later joined by others which fail to show the required accuracy on the test board. For these an allowance is made to the owner for the value of the metal contained. About a thousand meters have in this way passed through the Laboratory.

The variety of meters carried in the storehouse stock demands supervision so that meters sent out on order will be suited to the requirements of the service. The Meter Department in doing this is often able to adapt to a special need meters which might otherwise lie unused on the shelves. Meters for Government inspection are taken into the test room where a representative of the Inland Revenue Department inspects them and applies the seal of the Department.

With a view to establishing a suitable basis of billing certain classes of power and lighting loads, several extended tests have been made on services of various classes. These include determination of demand by means of a graphic meter and a general consideration of all existing conditions. The loads so investigated include beside a variety of lighting services, printing offices, elevators, incline railways, metal works, woollen mills, electric signs and amusement parks.

A wide use has been made of the oscillograph, and by its use some very knotty problems made possible of solution. Early in the year the complete outfit was set up in the power house at Eugenia Falls and a complete examination made, with particular attention to special transformer connections. Photographic records were obtained of practically every electrical quantity in the plant; and an analysis of the oscillograms soon led to a decision as to connections best suited to the case in hand. Oscillographic records have also been obtained of currents flowing through the resistances used between ground and the neutral of the star connected 110,000-volt transmission lines.

A problem confronting the engineers of to-day is to design auxiliary apparatus to effectually prevent " flashing over " of high voltage rotary converters; and with this in view a number of oscillograms were obtained from the machines supplying the London and Port Stanley Railway. Records were obtained of operation under widely varying conditions of load and data obtained from these, which should result in great strides toward the elimination of flashovers and other troublesome features of machines of this type.

In addition to the special work described above the Meter Laboratory has been many times called into service to perform special tests for the Inspection Department, and to pass approval on relays and other apparatus manufactured either in the Commission's shops or elsewhere for use on the numerous lines and services throughout the Province.

Lamp Testing Laboratory

During the year just closed the lamp laboratory has continued the routine testing of lamps for stock. Such tests include tests for vacuum, rating and life tests, as well as inspection for mechanical defects. The volume of routine testing has been fully up to that of previous years, while the number of tests for parties outside the Commission has been considerably increased. These include complete tests on new types of lamps and life tests on manufacturers' samples.

A notable departure in our method of testing gas-filled lamps and vacuum lamps with concentrated filaments has been necessary. Candle power values for lamps of these types are no longer given in terms of horizontal candle power; the mean spherical candle power is the unit which is now used by the Commission to express the light intensity of such lamps, and the light output of the lamps is expressed in terms of lumens. This change is necessary because of certain inherent features of gas-filled lamps and because of different spherical reduction factors of concentrated filament vacuum lamps. These measurements are all made in an integrating sphere photometer. An 18-inch sphere was fitted up in the lamp laboratory and has been in use for the testing of the smaller sizes. An 84-inch sphere is being constructed of reinforced concrete for the testing of the largest sizes. This sphere is nearing completion. Specifications have been issued for the purchase of gas-filled lamps, embodying the changes in rating made necessary by the new methods of testing. This new method of test is in keeping with similar changes taking place in all lamp testing laboratories in America. All gas-filled lamps are now rated by most laboratories according to their lumens output or to their mean spherical candle power, the efficiency being expressed as mean spherical candle power per watt or as lumens per watt.

A new size of series lamp has been standardized by the Commission to consume 100 watts regardless of changes of efficiency that may occur due to improved methods of manufacture. The new 50 watt vacuum lamp recently placed on the market is being tested. Lamp frosting methods are being investigated and the laboratory is now in a position to frost all such lamps as may be required for the Commission's business.

A large number of tests have been made for various municipal managers. The Commission's policy of buying lamps in the open market for testing has been followed, thereby enabling us to keep in close touch with the output of many factories.

The work of this laboratory has been of value in detecting defective shipments of lamps, several cases of which have occurred within the past year.

Electrical Standards Laboratory

Testing Machine—Strength of Materials Laboratory

High Tension Test—Transformer Flashing Over String of Four
Suspension Insulators—Voltage 260,000

Illumination Laboratory

As the science of illumination advances new types of apparatus are produced and the Commission, through the illumination laboratory, is enabled to obtain first-hand data on new appliances as they appear. Several new types of street lighting fixtures were investigated during the past year as well as the modified application of older types. One of the problems arising out of the use of gas-filled lamps for street lighting is glare. The effect of bowl frosted lamps on the reduction of glare and their effects on the distribution of illumination when used in common fixtures were fully investigated. A very extended investigation of standard street lighting fixtures of the latest types was made. Representative samples of the product of several manufacturers were sent to the laboratory and were subjected to the most rigid tests to determine their optical, mechanical and operating characteristics. These tests included light distribution and efficiency, flashover tests on the insulators, puncture tests on film cutouts, accessibility of parts, general design and appearance and the effects of the various features on operation. For the first time in the history of the Commission diffusing globes were purchased on specification. A number of samples of various makes were tested and the make to be purchased was decided upon. On completion of the order the globes were tested to insure compliance with the specifications. The effect of different positions of the light-centre of lamps relative to the reflectors was studied with standard fixtures.

Illumination surveys were made of new installations of street lighting.

A number of fixtures and illumination tests were made for outside parties.

On the 84-inch integrating sphere being constructed in the laboratory provision is made for making efficiency tests on lighting units of all kinds. This feature is of particular value in making acceptance tests on globes and reflectors.

This department planned the lighting installations of the various departments of the storehouse extension.

Structural Materials Laboratory

During the past year it became advisable to further subdivide the work of the laboratory and create a new department to take care of the testing of structural materials. This work had formerly been performed by the High-Tension and General Testing Laboratory, but since it was not related to the regular work of this department, being largely on a non-electrical nature, and as in the immediate future the demands of the Commission for this class of testing were expected to be considerable, it was decided that specialization in this field was warranted and a new department, called the Structural Materials Laboratory, was organized.

This new department is to take care of all tests and questions relating to the purely physical properties of the various materials of engineering, such as cement, aggregates and concrete, steel, iron and other metals, woods, oils, paints, etc., also all mechanical tests of clamps, wire, cable and various transmission line materials, tests of galvanizing and other rust-proofing, tests of water-proofing, heat insulating materials, wood preservatives and allied work. To this end the necessary equipment is being installed or will be installed in the near future.

Formerly the laboratory was equipped for the physical testing of cement and partially for the testing of sand and gravel. Since the creation of the new department additional apparatus is being intalled and the laboratory will shortly have a very full and complete equipment for both the above classes of tests. With the additional apparatus soon to be-installed the Commission will have one of the most completely equipped laboratories in this field in the Province, prepared to undertake all classes of physical testing and investigations on cement, concrete and concrete materials.

Since its inception this department has been mainly concerned with the studies of equipment and methods of testing for the work previously outlined. Besides this a certain amount of testing has been undertaken in connection with the present storehouse extension, the purchase of the Commission's transmission line hardware and other routine test work.

A preliminary report has been prepared covering the methods of testing, equipment and operation of a field laboratory to handle the necessary testing in connection with the large amount of concrete work involved in the New Niagara Power Development. The proposed field laboratory will be operated in connection with the permanent laboratory under the direction of this department and will involve the testing and inspection of the cement, sand, concrete, steel and other materials for this large undertaking. Preliminary to this work it is proposed to experiment extensively with a view of evolving the most suitable and economical methods of testing possible with the attainment of the object in view, also to make a complete study of the available concrete materials, their possibilities, limitations and drawbacks.

Photographic Laboratory

The equipment of this department and the scope of its work have been described in a previous report.

The work handled by the Department has so increased during the past year that an increase of staff has been necessary. During the year about 400 orders passed through the laboratory, adding over 500 new negatives to the files and over 20,000 prints of various sizes were made for the different departments of the Commission. A considerable amount of field work was done by the official photographer necessitating several trips to various points on the system. These trips covered such subjects as electric railway development, rural distribution of power, surveys for power sites, etc.

GENERAL ENGINEERING

WATERWORKS

Stratford

Gasoline Driven Centrifugal Pumps for Standby Purposes

During 1914 the question of providing pumping equipment to act as a stand-by to electric pumps in case of fire, as required by the Fire Underwriters,· was taken up, and the Commission agreed to act as engineers for this work.

High speed gasoline engines for direct coupling to centrifugal pumps having been (at that time) recently tried in several places, their merits were investigated and it was decided that if a suitable reliable engine of this type could be found it would form an àlmost ideal standby, because of the small space occupied, comparatively light weight, low first cost, ease and readiness with which it could be started up, and the small amount of labour required.

After having settled on the capacity and head which the required pump should give, the Commission communicated with many manufacturers of high speed gasoline engines, or their representatives, in Great Britain and various European countries, as well as in Canada and the United States, and later issued specifications covering a complete pumping unit comprising a centrifugal pump mounted on a common bed-plate with, and direct connected to, a gasoline engine, some latitude being given with regard to pump capacity, head and speed.

Most of the firms, both in Europe and on this continent, which were asked to tender, expressed their inability to provide a suitable engine, owing either to the high speed asked for (1,200-1,500 r.p.m.) or horse power required (130-150 h.p.) or both.

The tender of the Storey Pump and Equipment Company, was finally recommended to the Waterworks' Commission of Stratford. This tender was for a bronze fitted, 3 stage, 8-inch horizontal centrifugal pump with horizontally-split casing, direct coupled to a 6 cylinder gasoline engine made by the Van Blerck Motor Company, of Munroe, Mich. The pump at a speed of 1,500 r.p.m. was guaranteed to be capable of delivering 1,000 Imp. g.p.m. of fresh water against a total head of 292 feet. The engine was guaranteed to develop 136 h.p. at a speed of 1,500 r.p.m., and to be capable of running continuously for not less than 10 hours at that speed, and at a speed of 1,700 r.p.m. for 2 hours continuously.

A governor was to be provided which would hold the speed steady to within plus or minus 3 per cent. between no load and full load, and which would prevent "hunting."

The consumption of gasoline was guaranteed not to exceed 0.66 Imp. pint per brake horse-power hour.

The Stratford Waterworks' Commissioners decided to purchase two of these pumps, and an order was placed for this number.

When the gasoline engines were ready at the maker's works, one of the Commission's engineers went over to witness the tests, which proved quite satisfactory, the guarantees being more than fulfilled. ·

The pumps also underwent rigid tests at the maker's works, and finally the completed units were tested.

Both pumping sets were then shipped to Stratford and erected. During this stage of the work air-starters were fitted on to the engines, operated by compressed

16 H.

air. These starters comprise a small air compressor driven by the engine, an air tank and a selector valve.

The compressor fills the tank with air to a pressure of about 250 lbs. per square inch, and on starting the engine this compressed air is admitted in proper sequence to the cylinders, along with gasoline, by means of the selector valve; the engine is then started by the combined effect of the compressed air, and the combustion of the gasoline in the usual manner.

In connection with the provision of gasoline engines, the matter was taken up with the Canadian Fire Underwriters Association, and their views obtained as to the precautions required in view of the risk of fire; plans were later prepared and submitted to them; these received their approval, except in one or two minor features which were altered to comply with their wishes.

After erection these pumping units were submitted to further severe tests in Stratford, and found to fulfil the guarantees in all respects within the allowable limits of variation of plus or minus 2 per cent.

Since completion, the pumps have been utilized on several occasions in emergencies for giving domestic supply, and within a few months of installation had been found so satisfactory that the Stratford authorities entirely discarded their steam plant by taking it out altogether, and installed a small heating plant for use in winter.

There has been received from the Secretary of the Public Utility Commission of Stratford the following estimated comparison of standby service for steam and gasoline for one year, based on actual experience with the latter for about nine months.

	Steam	Gasoline	Saving
Fuel and Supplies	$2,432.82	$400.00	....
Labour	2,460.00	1,800.00	....
Repairs (estimated)	365.00	50.00	....
	$5,257.82	$2,250.00	$3,007.82

The actual saving is probably a little less than that shown, as it is understood that the steam pumps were employed in pumping for domestic purposes to a greater extent than is the case with the gasoline pumps.

However, since the total cost of this plant will not much exceed $10,000, it is evident that it forms a good investment for the city.

The two pumping sets, each of 1,000 Imp. g.p.m. capacity at 292 feet total head, occupy rather less space than that originally taken up by 1-1,750 Imp. g.p.m. steam pump together with its condenser, and the space occupied by the boilers, firing floor, coal storage space and smoke stack is available for other uses. Investigation shows that gasoline driven units such as these take up about one-tenth to one-fifteenth of the floor space required for equivalent steam plant. The extreme height of these sets does not exceed 3 feet 6 inches.

Since the pumps are required for standby purposes only, the wear and tear on them will be very small, and they should therefore last a long time; ordinarily they are only run about one hour or so a week each to make sure that everything is in good working condition.

For the same reason the fact that gasoline is very expensive compared with coal is of not great importance, as very little is actually used normally, and the high cost of operating merely during emergency does not therefore matter.

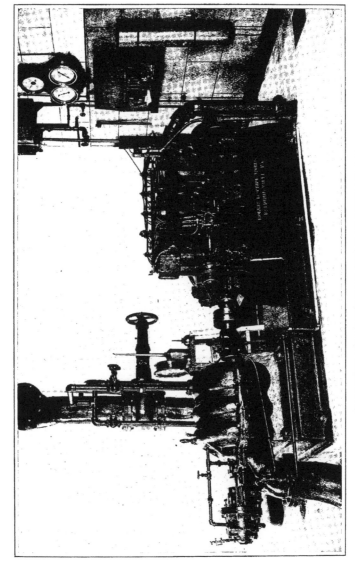

Gasoline Driven Standby Fire Pump, Stratford Municipal Waterworks

Elevated Steel Water Tank

During 1914 the question of conserving electric power by storing water, especially on peak load, came up for consideration and was referred to this Commission. The matter was gone into carefully, the final decision being that a tank of 500,000 Imperial gallons, elevated so as to give a pressure of 80 lbs. in the pump house, would make suitable provision for this purpose.

A site near the pump house was then chosen, investigation being made as to the suitability of the ground to carry so heavy a weight, that of the water alone being 2,500 tons.

Specifications for an elevated tank of steel, with alternatives for reinforced concrete, were then issued and tenders called for the work, eleven being received; eight of these were for steel and three for reinforced concrete structures.

Very careful attention was given to these tenders from the point of view of design, construction and appearance, as well as from that of the extent of the experience which the various tenderers had had in building such large structures.

After eliminating all other tenders for one reason or another, those of the Canadian Bridge and Iron Works and the Pittsburg DesMoines Steel Company, were the last two between whose bids a decision had to be made; the first named being actually awarded the contract on September 17th, 1915, for the erection of a 500,000 Imperial gallon steel tank, 39 feet 9 inches deep and 54 feet in diameter, elevated so that when full the water level would be 155 feet above the ground; the supports to consist of 8 legs constructed of steel, and the riser drum to be 6 feet in diameter.

This tank for its size is very shallow, having the special elliptical bottom designed by the Chicago Bridge and Iron Works, one advantage, of course, being that the water pressure varies only between small limits, while another is that the flat bottom acts as a diaphragm and takes care of the expansion and contraction of the riser drum. The large diameter of the riser drum obviates the need for a frost casing. The weight of steel in the whole of this structure is 250 tons, making a total weight on the foundations, when full of water, of 2,750 tons.

Special precautions were taken to insure that the fabrication of this structure should be carried out in Canada, and that Canadian labour should be employed to the fullest extent possible.

Specifications were also drawn up covering the concrete foundations. Tenders were called for on this work, and a contract was finally made with a local firm in Stratford for the construction of the foundations, and a valve chamber which was located at the foot of the tower.

These foundations had to be very massive, in the 8 footings for the tower legs and the footings for the 6-foot riser drum over 300 cubic yards of concrete were used.

At the foot of the tower it was necessary to build a large valve chamber to accommodate an electro-hydraulic valve and two ordinary gate valves. These three are all 16-inch valves.

The first named is operated from the pump house by turning a switch, which closes an electric circuit, thus actuating a small control valve which admits the water to one side or the other of a hydraulic piston, connected with the main valve, according to whether this valve is to be opened or closed. On receiving an alarm of fire the operator in the pump house can close the valve in the manner described, thereby shutting off the tank, when the water pressure can be immediately raised to that required for fire purposes. The two hand operated gate valves are located one on either side of the electro-hydraulic valve for use in case of emergency or in the event of the last named valve needing repairs.

Drainage, ventilation and lighting of the valve chamber were also provided for.

The level of water in the tank is indicated on the side of the tank on a large vertical scale, marked in feet, the slider being actuated by a float in the tank. In the pump house the water level is read on the pressure gauge.

The tank has a balcony with a stout iron railing all around it, and access to this is gained by an iron ladder, which extends from the balcony to about 7 feet from the ground.

The whole structure received one shop coat and one field coat of graphite paint.

The tank is roofed over and may be entered by ascending the ladder (which reaches from the balcony to the roof) and climbing through a man-hole. This ladder is arranged to revolve around the whole tank, so as to give access to every portion of the sides and roof for inspection and painting.

Inside the tank at the bottom, in order to guard against the possibility of anyone falling down the riser drum, during construction, or at any future time, an iron grid is provided over the opening.

The total cost of this work amounted to about $30,000.

The advantages of such an elevated tank are several:—

1. There is available at all times for domestic supply a considerable quantity of water at a pressure ranging from 80 to 63 lbs. per square inch.

2. Water at this pressure can be used in case of fire for a few minutes until proper fire pressure is available or possibly altogether for small fires.

3. It is possible to do all the pumping outside of peak load hours, thereby effecting considerable economy.

4. The pumping conditions generally, and the pressure at services are rendered more uniform, thereby permitting the use of smaller units, as otherwise the available pumping capacity must be at least equal to that of the water peak.

Niagara-on-the-Lake

At the beginning of 1916, the Commission was approached by the authorities of the town of Niagara-on-the-Lake, with a view to obtaining engineering advice in connection with their waterworks' pumping.

This work was taken up and after careful consideration of local conditions, specifications were issued and tenders called for two electrically driven centrifugal pumps.

Various tenders were received for these, the order finally going to the Storey Pump and Equipment Company, for 2 6-inch, 2-stage, bronze-fitted, centrifugal pumps, each capable of delivering 600 Imp. g.p.m. of fresh water against a total head of 180 feet, and each direct coupled to a Crocker Wheeler, 50 h.p., three-phase, 25-cycle, 2,200-volt, 1,500 r.p.m., squirrel cage induction motor.

The pumps when ready at the maker's works were tested in the presence of one of the Commission's engineers, but failed to fulfil the guarantees regarding efficiency, and the Commission therefore refused to accept them. It was then arranged that the makers should build two new pumps of a somewhat different pattern. This was done very expeditiously, and the new pumps, having proved satisfactory under test at the maker's works, were accepted.

Elevated Water Tower at Stratford Municipal Waterworks

Very careful tests were also witnessed at the maker's works on the motors, which were found to properly meet the guarantees.

The completed units were then erected at Niagara-on-the-Lake, and have been running satisfactorily ever since, i.e. about six months.

Camp Borden

During the negotiations for the supply of electric power to Camp Borden, the matter of pumping plant was taken up with the Commission by the Military Authorities, as such plant was required very urgently.

The conditions having been looked into, steps were immediately taken to secure the necessary pumps, motors and auxiliary equipment. It was found possible to obtain from the Storey Pump and Equipment Company, two centrifugal pumps which they had in stock, and which would be suitable if driven at a speed of about 1,800 r.p.m.

Two 150 h.p., 2,200-volt, three-phase, 25-cycle, 750 r.p.m. motors were also procured, one from the Canadian General Electric Company, and the other from the Canadian Westinghouse Company.

The essential feature of this work was that it be carried out in the shortest possible time, and although it would have been preferable to use motors direct coupled to the pumps, it was impossible to do so, owing to the limited time available, the pumps were therefore arranged to be belt driven.

The necessary outboard bearings and pulleys were on this account obtained from the pump makers; suitable valves and pipe fittings were purchased, and the equipment was all shipped to Camp Borden and erected there.

This plant was put into operation within one month of the date on which the Commission took the matter up.

Palmerston

At the request of the town authorities, specifications were issued in July for a vertical electrically driven centrifugal pump, capable of delivering 300 Imp. g.p.m. of fresh water against a total head of 150 feet. The pump was to be suspended about 14 feet below the motor in a steel framework.

After consideration of the various tenders received, an order for this equipment was placed with the Canadian Fairbanks-Morse Company, by the town officials on the recommendations of the Commission. It has already been tested and found satisfactory at the maker's works, and instructions have been given for immediate delivery to Palmerston. The pump will be erected in a well about 6 feet diameter and 35 feet deep, close to the pump house.

Tavistock

During August of this year, the subject of pumping was brought before the Commission's engineers by the Reeve, asking for prices on an electrically driven pump for domestic purposes.

After having ascertained the local requirements, and upon instructions from the town, a 4-inch x 4-inch 60 Imp. g.p.m. Luitwieler pump to discharge against a head of from 65 to 104 lbs. per square inch, geared to a single-phase, 220-volt, 25-cycle motor, was purchased from the General Machinery Company; the motor was equipped with an automatic device, whereby the motor is started and stopped automatically according to whether the tank is empty or full.

Ridgetown

At the request of the Waterworks' Commission in Ridgetown, one of the Commission's engineers witnessed a test carried out on two triplex 6-inch x 8-inch single acting pumps supplied by the Canadian Fairbanks-Morse Company, and designed to deliver 104 Imp. g.p.m. at a speed of 43 r.p.m. against a head of 125 lbs. These pumps are geared and each is belt driven from a 15 h.p. 750 r.p.m. 550 volt, three-phase, 25-cycle motor.

The test results were only approximate owing to the character of the testing equipment available, but were sufficient to enable the Commission to inform the town authorities that the plant as a whole was quite satisfactory, and that it was capable of doing the work required of it.

Kingston, Chesley, Listowel, etc.

Estimates, reports and preliminary engineering work have also been carried out in connection with Waterworks' pumping problems for the following:—

Kingston, Chesley, Listowel, Preston, Lindsay, Exeter.

Progress has also been made in connection with work at Goderich and Galt, where certain revisions of existing plant were necessary. A contract for a motor for Galt has been arranged, and this has been installed. At Goderich a contract for a new pump has been let, which it is expected will be running early in 1917.

INSPECTION OF MATERIALS

A good deal of inspection work has been carried out during the year.

Insulators for voltages of from 4,000 to 110,000 volts, and for telephone work, numbering nearly 100,000 have been inspected.

Two carloads each of insulator pins and hardware, as well as various sizes of copper, steel and aluminum wire and cable exceeding a total weight of 320 tons, were also inspected within the period.

NITROGEN FIXATION

A considerable amount of investigation has been made during the year in regard to the fixation of atmospheric nitrogen, more especially by electrical processes, with a view to ascertaining the possibilities of developing a useful "off-peak" load.

Nitrogen is required in enormous quantities, in particular, for two purposes, viz:—as a fertilizing agent for crops and plant life generally, and also for the manufacture of explosives.

The largest natural source of nitrogen in a useful form is the great nitrate beds of Chili, and as an indication of the extent to which the demand throughout the world has grown, it is of interest to note that, while in the year 1830 about 1,000 tons of nitrate were exported from Chili, the quantity exported in 1912 was in the neighbourhood of 2½ million tons.

There are some other sources of nitrogen naturally available in the world, but the total visible supplies are comparatively limited, and scientists have for several years been anxious to find some source whence the element nitrogen could be made commercially available.

Electrical methods of obtaining this element in a useful chemically-combined form, while not the only ones which have been developed, have been brought to a point where they are of great commercial importance, as the cost of thus producing nitrogen compounds is competitive with the cost of Chilean nitrate, this latter, up to the present, controlling the market prices.

Plants for the fixation of atmospheric nitrogen, on a large scale, by electric methods, are in operation, under construction, or projected, in Norway, Switzerland, Spain, Germany, Italy, India, the United States, Canada, Japan, and possibly some other countries.

In all the countries named water power is, or will be, the source of energy for this rapidly growing industry, with the exception of Germany, where poor grade coal is to be used in generating electric power. It is probable that there are now some half million or more horse-power in use throughout the world for obtaining nitrate from the air electrically, the bulk of this being in Norway, which is favourably situated in respect both of cheap water power and available markets.

The electric methods which have been devised so far for obtaining nitrogen may be classified under two main headings, viz:—the electric arc process and the cyanamide process.

The former, comparatively, takes a good deal of energy, and since the cost of water power in Canada is relatively high, it is hardly probable that any of the arc processes would be a commercial success in this country, unless the production per unit quantity of combined nitrogen per kilowatt hour can be appreciably increased over and above what has hitherto been realized.

The cyanamide process, which is that in use at Niagara Falls, Ontario, has proved financially practicable there, and probably can be made so in other parts of Canada; since the raw materials are the air we breathe, coke, and lime, there are doubtless a number of points in Ontario where the obtaining of these essentials in sufficient quantity would be comparatively easy.

The chief points to be considered in connection with the commercial production of nitrogen compounds are—

1. The cost of electric power at the point where it is to be used.

2. The cost of transportation for the raw materials.

3. The size and availability of the markets.

The Canadian market for these compounds in normal times, at least, will be practically limited to the demand for fertilizer products, at present this is of limited dimensions, but is likely to grow at an increasingly rapid rate.

A good deal of activity has been evident in the United States in recent months in connection with nitrogen fixation. During the summer a number of meetings were held in Washington, D.C., in connection with nitrogen fixation and water power development. Some of these meetings were attended by a representative of the Commission. A great many records were examined at the same time.

Owing to the war, and the great shortage of power now being experienced, it is not possible to do more than keep in touch with the trend of events regarding this subject.

ELECTRIC FURNACES

During the year the Commission has been investigating modern electric furnace practice, and the possibilities of this load in Ontario. The results of investigation so far show that where power is plentiful and reasonable in price the electric steel furnace is entirely practical.

The increasing number of these furnaces in the Province confirms this belief, and it is anticipated that the electric furnace will not only be applied to the production of fine steels, but that it will even compete with the open hearth furnace.

There is also every indication that electric smelting for iron, copper and other ores will be an important factor in the mining districts of the Province.

The high prices ruling for coke and coal and for steel products during this year, makes the electric furnace very attractive, and there is every indication that electric steel production in this Province will grow rapidly during the next year or two.

The electrical production of such products as calcium carbide, carborundum and other substances requiring high heat, is growing, and in this Province such production will undoubtedly take an increasing share of the surplus water powers.

RULES AND REGULATIONS

The drafting of rules and regulations governing outside overhead work has been in hand during the year, considerable progress having been made. These are now at a stage where they are being considered in detail by the Commission's engineers in conference, and it is intended later to submit a revised draft to electrical engineers outside the Commission's staff, for criticism and such further revision as may appear to be necessary.

INDEX

A

Page

Acton—Municipal Work 161
Acts 1
Administration Building 95
Agreements 94
Almonte—Municipal Work 173
Almonte—Ornamental Street Lighting 189
Alton—Municipal Work 169-170
Amherstburg—Ornamental Street Lighting 190
Arthur—Municipal Work 169
Artemesia Township—Municipal Work 170
Aultsville—Municipal Work 174

B

Baden—Distributing Station 103
Beaverton—Distributing Station ... 112
Beaverton—Municipal Work 174
Big Chute—Power House 112
Blenheim—Distributing Station 110
Blenheim—Ornamental Street Lighting 189
Bothwell—Municipal Work 161
Brampton—Municipal Station 109
Brampton—Municipal Work 161
Bracebridge—Municipal Work 174
Brant—Transformer Station 109
Brock Township—Municipal Work.. 174
Brockville—Municipal Work 174
Brownsville—Municipal Work 162
Burford—Municipal Work 161

C

Camp Borden—Municipal Station .. 113
Camp Borden—Municipal Work 171
Camp Borden—Waterworks Pumping 205
Cannington—Distributing Station .. 112
Cannington—Municipal Work 174
Central Ontario Power Act 89
Central Ontario System—Operation. 151
Central Ontario System—Description of Lines 132-133
Central Prison Farm, Substation ... 102
Chatham—Ornamental Street Lighting 190
Chatham—Municipal Work ...:.. 161
Chatsworth—Distributing Station .. 114
Chesley—Distributing Station 114
Chesley—Municipal Work 169
Chesley—Waterworks Pumping 206
Clinton—Municipal Work 161
Cobden—Municipal Generating Station 97
Cobden—Municipal Work 174
Cobden—Ornamental Street Lighting 189
Cobourg—Municipal Work 182
Cobourg—Ornamental Street Lighting 190

Page

Coldwater—Distributing Station ... 113
Collingwood—Distributing Station '. 112
Cooksville—Transformer Station ... 108
Cornwall—Municipal Work 175
Crossings 94

D

Dereham Township—Municipal Work 162
Dundalk—Distributing Station 115
Dundas-Toronto—Surveys 95
Dunnville—Municipal Work 162
Dunnville—Ornamental Street Lighting 190
Durham—Distributing Station 115

E

East Luther Township—Municipal Work 171
Essex—Transformer Station 111
Etobicoke—Distributing Station 108
Eugenia—Generating Station 113
Eugenia—Operation 148
Eugenia—Description of Lines 130-31
Exeter—Distributing Station ....
Exeter—Ornamental Street Lighting 190
Exeter—Waterworks Pumping 206

F

Forest—Distributing Station 110

G

Galt—Waterworks Commission 102
Galt—Municipal Work 162
Galt—Waterworks Pumping 206
Gamebridge—Municipal Work 175
Goderich—Waterworks Pumping ... 206
Grand Valley—Distributing Station . 116
Grand Valley—Municipal Work 169
Grantham Township—Municipal Work 162
Granton—Feeder 101
Gravenhurst—Municipal Work 175
Guelph—Transformer Station 102
Guelph—Ornamental Street Lighting 190

H

Hamilton—Municipal Work 162
Hamilton—Municipal Underground Construction 191
Hanover—Distributing Station .:... 115
Hanover—Municipal Work 169-171
Harriston—Distributing Station ... 105
Hespeler—Municipal Work 162
Huntsville—Distributing Station ... 118
Huntsville—Municipal Work 175
Huntsville—Ornamental Street Lighting 190
Hydro-Electric Railway Act .:..... 73

Page

Ingersoll—Municipal Work 163
Ingersoll—Ornamental Street Lighting 190
Iroquois—Municipal Work 276

K

Kemptville—Municipal Work 176
Kent—Transformer Station 109
Kilsyth—Distributing Station 117
Kingston—Municipal Station 118
Kingston—Municipal Work 176
Kingston—Ornamental Street Lighting 190
Kingston—Waterworks Pumping 206
Kitchener—Transformer Station ... 103

L

Lindsay—Waterworks Pumping 206
Listowel—Distributing Station 104
Listowel—Waterworks Pumping 206
London—Utilities Commission 101
London—Railway Commission 101
London—Municipal Work 163
London Township—Municipal Work 163
Lucan—Distributing Station 101

M

Markdale—Municipal Station 114
Markdale—Municipal Work 169
Meaford—Municipal Work 169
Merricksville—Municipal Work 176
Mille Roches—Municipal Work 176
Milverton—Distributing Station 105
Mimico—Distributing Station 108
Mitchell—Municipal Station 104
Mitchell—Municipal Work 163
Mount Forest—Distributing Station 115
Morrisburg—Municipal Work 176
Muskoka System—Operation 153
Muskoka System—Description of
Lines 132-33

N

New Toronto—Municipal Work 163
Niagara—Development 96
Niagara Falls—Transformer Station 97
Niagara Falls—Distributing Station. 99
Niagara-on-the-Lake—Municipal Station 99
Niagara-on-the-Lake—Municipal Work 164
Niagara-on-the-Lake — Waterworks
Pumping 204-5
Niagara System—Operation 140
Niagara System—Description of
Lines 124-25-26-27-28-29
Niagara Falls—Municipal Work 163
Nipissing—Municipal Work 183
North Bay—Ornamental Street Lighting 190
North Bay—Municipal Work 177
North Norwich Township—Municipal Work 164
Northumberland Pulp Mill 182-83

Page

Norwich—Ornamental Street Lighting 190
Norwich—Municipal Work 164

O

Ontario Niagara Development Act .. 65
Omemee—Municipal Work 177
Ornamental Street Lighting 189
Orangeville—Distributing Station .. 116
Orillia—Municipal Work 172
Oshawa—Municipal Work 183
Ottawa—Municipal Work 177
Owen Sound—Distributing Station . 114
Owen Sound—Municipal Work 171
Owen Sound—Municipal Underground Construction 191

P

Palmerston—Distributing Station. .. 105
Palmerston—Waterworks Pumping.. 205
Paris—Municipal Station 109
Parry Sound—Municipal Work ... 177
Peterborough—Public Utilities Commission 96
Petrolia—Municipal Work 164
Peterborough—Municipal Work 183
Peterborough Radial Railway 182
Petrolia—Distributing Station 110
Petrolia—Ornamental Street Lighting 190
Port Arthur System—Operation ... 154
Port Arthur—Municipal Work 165
Port Elgin—Municipal Work 169
Port McNichol—Distributing Station 112
Port McNichol—Municipal Work ... 172
Port Robinson—Distributing Station 99
Powassan—Distributing Station 113
Power Commission Act 1
Prescott—Municipal Work 177
Preston—Municipal Work 165
Preston—Transformer Station 102
Preston—Waterworks Pumping 206

R

Railway Act—Hydro-Electric 73
Renfrew—Municipal Work 177
Ridgetown—Distributing Station ... 109
Ridgetown—Municipal Work 165
Ridgetown—Ornamental Street Lighting 190
Ridgetown—Waterworks Pumping . 206
Right of Way—High Tension Lines. 94
Right of Way—Low Tension Lines.. 94
Rural Power—Municipal Work 187-88

S

Sarnia—Municipal Station 110
Sarnia—Municipal Work 165
Sarnia—Ornamental Street Lighting. 190
Scarboro Township—Municipal Work 165
Seaforth—Municipal Station 104
Severn System—Description of Lines
130-31
Severn System—Operation 146

Page

Shelbourne—Distributing Station .. 115
Smith's Falls—Municipal Work ... 178
South Falls—Generating Station ... 117
Southampton—Municipal Work 169
South Norwich Township—Municipal
Work 164
Springford—Municipal Work 162
Stamford Township—Municipal
Work ....᷒............ 166
Storehouse, Toronto—Extension 96
Stratford—Municipal Station 103
Stratford—Municipal Work 166
Stratford—Transformer Station 103
Stratford—Waterworks Pumping
201-2-3-4
St. Catharines—Municipal Work . 166
St. Catharines—Ornamental Street
Lighting 190
St. Lawrence System—Description
of Lines 130-31
St. Lawrence System—Operation .. 155
St. Mary's—Municipal Work 166
St. Mary's—Transformer Station .. 105
St. Mary's—Portland Cement Co.—
Distributing Station 105
St. Thomas—Municipal Station 106
St. Thomas—Municipal Underground
Construction 191
St. Thomas—Municipal Work 166
St. Thomas—Transformer Station .. 106
Sunderland—Municipal Work 178

T

Tavistock—Distributing Station 104
Tavistock—Municipal Work 167
Tavistock—Waterworks Pumping .. 205
Toronto-Dundas—Surveys 95
Toronto—Municipal Work 167
Toronto Township—Municipal Work 167
Tillsonburg—Municipal Work .. 162-167

Page

Transformers—Capacities installed
or ordered for Commission's Stations 119-120-21
Transformers—Station transformers
ordered for municipalities and
Commission during 1916 122
Transmission Lines—Low Tension.. 123

U

Underground Construction 191

W

Walkerville—Municipal Substation.. 111
Wallaceburg—Municipal Work 167
Wasdell Falls—Generating Station .111
Wasdell Falls—Description of Lines
130-31
Wasdell Falls—Parallel operation
with Eugenia and Severn 151
Wasdell System—Operation 150
Washago—Municipal Work 178
Watford—Municipal Work 168
Water Powers Regulation Act 68
Waterloo—Municipal Work 168
Waterloo Township—Municipal Work 168
Welland—Municipal Station 99
Welland—Municipal Work 168
West Lorne—Distributing Station .. 108
Weston—Municipal Station 109
Weston—Municipal Work 168
Windsor—Municipal Work 168
Windsor—Ornamental Street Light-
ing 190
Woodstock—Transformer Station ... 106
Winchester—Municipal Work 178

Y

York—Transformer Station 111
York Township—Municipal Work .. 168

Ninth Annual Report

. OF .THE

HYDRO-ELECTRIC POWER COMMISSION

OF THE

PROVINCE OF ONTARIO

FOR THE YEAR ENDED OCTOBER 31st

1916

VOLUME II.

PRINTED BY ORDER OF

THE LEGISLATIVE ASSEMBLY OF ONTARIO

TORONTO:

Printed and Published by A. T. WILGRESS, Printer to the King's Most Excellent Majesty

1917

Printed by
WILLIAM BRIGGS
Corner Queen and John Streets
Toronto

To His Honour, COLONEL SIR JOHN HENDRIE, K.C.M.G., C.V.O.,

Lieutenant-Governor of Ontario.

MAY IT PLEASE YOUR HONOUR:

The undersigned has the honour to present to Your Honour the second volume of the Ninth Annual Report of the Hydro-Electric Power Commission of Ontario for the fiscal year ending October 31st, 1916.

Respectfully submitted,

ADAM BECK,

Chairman.

TORONTO, ONT., February 17th, 1917.

COLONEL SIR ADAM BECK, K.B., LL.D.,

      Chairman, Hydro-Electric Power Commission,

                Toronto, Ont.

SIR,—I have the honour to transmit herewith the second volume of the Ninth Annual Report of the Hydro-Electric Power Commission of Ontario for the fiscal year ending October 31st, 1916.

      I have the honour to be,

          Sir,

        Your obedient servant,

                W. W. POPE,

                    Secretary.

HYDRO-ELECTRIC POWER COMMISSION OF ONTARIO

CONTENTS

OPERATION OF THE SYSTEMS.

Niagara System: Page

Notes on Operation 1
Curve Showing Monthly Increase of Power Loads of Municipalities 1
Capital Investment 4
Expenditures 4
Receipts and Disbursements 4
Comparative Load Records of Municipalities 5
Municipalities Connected to Niagara System during the past year 6

Severn System:

Notes on Operation 7
Comparative Load Records of Municipalities 8
Municipalities Connected to Severn System during the past year 8
Capital Investment 8
Revenue and Expenditures 8

Eugenia System:

Notes on Operation 9
Comparative Load Records of Municipalities 9
Capital Investment 10
Revenue and Expenditures 10

Wasdells System:

Notes on Operation 11
Comparative Load Records of Municipalities 11
Capital Investment 11
Revenue and Expenditures 11
Typical Daily Load Curves, Severn, Eugenia and Wasdells Generating Stations
    Operating in Parallel, October, 1916 11
Parallel Operation of the Severn, Eugenia and Wasdells Systems 12

Central Ontario System:

Notes on Operation 12
Power Generated 13
Load Records of Municipalities, October, 1916 13
Curve Showing Weekly System Peaks 13

Muskoka System:

Notes on Operation 14

Port Arthur System:

Notes on Operation 15
Capital Investment 15
Operation and Maintenance Expenses 15
Financial Statement of Operation 15

ix

St. Lawrence System: Page
    Notes on Operation   16
    Comparative Load Records of Municipalities   16
    Capital Investment   16
    Revenue and Expenditures   16
    Total Capital Investment   17
    Provincial Expenditures   19
    Balance Sheet   20

Municipal Accounts
    Outline of work of Municipal Accounts Department, with comparative consoli-
        dated balance sheets and comparative consolidated operating reports for
        years 1912, 1913, 1914, 1915 and 1916   21

Statement:
    A. Comparative Balance Sheets, 1914 and 1915   26
            Total Plant Cost.
            Total Investment.
            Debt Balance.
            Reserves.
            Percentage of Net Debt to Total Assets.

    B. Condensed Operating or Revenue and Expense Reports for 1916   61
            Population.
            Plant Cost.
            Balance Construction Debt.
            Operation, Maintenance and Administration.
            Fixed Charges, Debenture Payments and Interest.
            Total Operation.
            Total Revenue.
            Surplus.
            Depreciation Charge.
            Surplus, Less Depreciation Charge.
            Number of Consumers.
            Percentage of Consumers to Population.
            Horsepower Peak Taken in December, 1916.
    C. Comparative Detailed Operating Reports for 1913, 1914, 1915 and 1916   68
    D. Comparative Statement of Revenue, Number of Consumers, Total Consump-
        tion, Average Monthly Consumption per Consumer, Average Monthly Bill
        and Net Cost per kw-hr for years 1912, 1913, 1914, 1915 and 1916 113
    E. Street Light Installations 124
    F. Cost of Power and Selling Rates ....Folders
    G. Lighting Rates in Effect in all Municipalities in 1912, 1913, 1914, 1915, 1916
        and Suggested Rates for 1917 ....Folders

OPERATION OF THE SYSTEMS

NIAGARA SYSTEM

The operation of the Niagara System for the year 1916, was attended with gratifying success. In no other year, and especially since the war commenced, have the lines and apparatus of this system been called upon for such extraordinary duty. This condition was occasioned by the rapid recovery of industry together with the enormous development of the manufacture of war munitions in Canada.

During the months of November to April, inclusive, and from July to October, power was purchased for transformation and transmission from two, and indirectly three sources, the supplying plants being linked together by the Commission's Transforming Station at Niagara Falls. On April 30th, the temporary contract with the Toronto Power Company expired, and from this date until July 26th, when the first generating unit from the Canadian Niagara Power Company was connected, the total load of the Niagara System was carried by the Ontario Power Company. On August 21st, a second unit at the Canadian Niagara Power Company's Plant was paralleled with the first, and from this date until the end of October, the amount of power available from this company amounted to approximately 25,000 horse-power. As these generating stations were operating at maximum capacity, extreme caution was necessarily exercised in the operation of the system in order to preserve equilibrium at all times. Due credit is extended to the Ontario Power Company for the satisfactory service received during the year.

Electrical storms during the past year were much more frequent and severe than in previous years. The Niagara System was subjected to these storms on sixty different days. On eight days these storms traversed practically the entire system, and were particularly severe. The balance of the storms traversed only portions of the system, mainly in the Niagara Peninsula, Preston, Stratford and Chatham Districts, and were more or less severe. No total system interruption occurred from lightning causes during the summer, and when it is considered that the Commission has in operation approximately 1,200 miles of high and low tension lines overstreching a strip of Ontario approximately 215 miles long and averaging 60 miles wide, all lines being subjected to the accumulation of electrical discharges, which must be dissipated by passage to ground, the efficiency of the protective apparatus is strikingly evident.

Work of a special nature carried out by the Line Maintenance Department, and required by reason of the rapid increase of load, included the erection of a temporary 12,000 volt double circuit pole line of No. 4/0 copper conductor between the power house of the Canadian Niagara Company's station and a point (on the present line between the Hydro and Toronto Power Company Transforming Stations) approximately 1,800 feet south of the Commission's station. Both circuits of this pole line are still in service pending the installation of the balance of the underground feeders to the Canadian Niagara Power Company's plant.

The erection of a fourth No. 4/0 copper, three-phase circuit 15.5 miles long, on the 46,000 volt tower line between Niagara Falls and Welland was completed and placed in operation.

The single or three-phase circuit of No. 2 aluminum between the High Tension station and the Municipal Station at Dundas was replaced with a double circuit of No. 4 copper. Two 13,200 volt air break switches were erected in these lines at the entrance to the John Bertram and Sons Foundry, and also near the Dundas Municipal Station for the control of the line of the village of Lynden. The wood pole line from the Dundas High Tension to the City of Hamilton, which was replaced by a steel tower line during the summer of 1915, was taken down, and the material placed in stock.

Short stretches of single circuit 26,400 volt lines were constructed to supply the Lake Erie and Northern Railway Company's sub-stations at Brantford and Simcoe, from the outgoing circuits of Brant High Tension Station. This work also included the erection of telephone lines and instruments, and the installation of an air break switch at the Company's Simcoe sub-station.

The wood pole Low Tension Line entrances at London and St. Thomas, and at the Weston Municipal sub-station were remodeled to accommodate new lines erected in these districts. In view of the many new customers added in the Stratford District, and the length of line necessary to serve them, it has been decided to raise the transmission voltage in this district from 13,200 to 26,400. To this end considerable re-arranging of the power and telephone lines was carried out in preparation for this change. For sectionalizing purposes two air break switches were erected at Mitchell in the double circuit line between Stratford and Seaforth. The telephone line between Stratford and Sebringville Junction was doubled by the erection of a circuit of No. 9 iron wire.

Some re-location of the 13,200 volt line feeding the Mimico Distribution Station from the Cooksville High Tension Station was necessary, due to the construction of the Toronto-Hamilton Highway. The portion of line affected extended from Port Credit to New Toronto.

A twenty-five "pair" lead covered telephone cable approximately 13,500 feet long, was installed between the High Tension Station and the Commission's new office building at Toronto. The cable was laid in the Toronto Hydro-Electric System duct line to the corner of Queen and William Streets and from thence to the office building on the concrete poles.

Few failures of any of the electrical or mechanical equipment of the High Tension stations occurred during the year. As the Commission, in common with other enterprises in Canada, was severely handicapped in obtaining delivery on additional apparatus required to cope with the abnormal demand for power, the present equipment in some of the stations was subjected to overload for short periods, but without any depreciating results. The difficulty, mentioned above was partially met by the transfer, where feasible, of transformers from one station to another. One of the more important changes of this nature was the transfer of two 750 kv-a transformers from Guelph to the St. Thomas station.

The Commission now employs a staff of nine highly trained meter experts whose regular duties consist of the periodic calibration and adjustment of the various types of graphic recording and indicating instruments located in the Commission's stations.

These men also attend to the setting and adjustment of all relays used to protect the Commission's lines and equipment.

Considerable time has been spent in perfecting refinements in connection with the measurement of power, which has been to a great extent apparently considered unnecessary heretofore by the majority of other organizations. These refinements extend from the periodic comparison of the Commission's portable standard meters with ultimate standards to the determination of the characteristics of instrument transformers of various types.

of the
or to
mer is

-High
aodate
ilding
'utside
Kent
nt in
High
·m the

as laid
Power
by the
le the
cooling
nd the
cooling
ts had

palities

ıe load

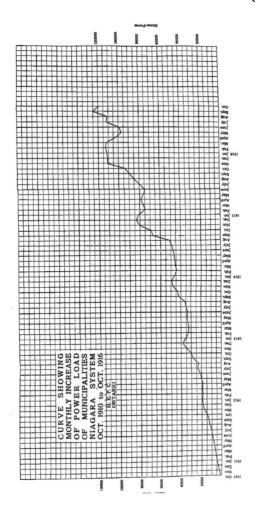

CURVE SHOWING
MONTHLY INCREASE
OF POWER LOAD
OF MUNICIPALITIES
NIAGARA SYSTEM
OCT. 1910 to OCT. 1916

H.E.P.C.
ONTARIO

The services of the meter inspectors may also be requisitioned by any of the Commission's customers to inspect or adjust metering and relay equipment, or to conduct special measurements of any loads with regard to which the customer is desirous of obtaining particular information.

A long felt want was realized in the erection of the storehouses on the High Tension Station ground during the summer. These buildings will accommodate maintenance materials of a bulky nature. This work, together with the building of suitable approaches, was done under the supervision of the operators. Outside lights surmounting concrete poles were installed at Dundas, London and Kent High Tension Stations, with pleasing effect. Considerable improvement in appearance was accomplished in grading the grounds surrounding the High Tension Stations, and re-surfacing of the roads through the grounds from the highway.

A concrete roadway approximately 300 feet long and 6 inches thick, was laid across the flats at Preston, from the fair grounds to the Hydro-Electric Power Commission's Property. It is expected that this roadway will be unaffected by the heavy spring floods in this vicinity, which previously rendered impassable the original gravel topped roadway. An increase was made in the supply of cooling water for this station by the sinking of a well just outside the station, and the installation of a deep well pump for pumping the water directly into the cooling system. The supply originally obtained from the small creek in the flats had latterly become inadequate.

The tables given below show the load demands of the various municipalities as well as the increase during the year.

The plotted curve on another page shows the monthly increase in the load supplied from October, 1910, to October, 1916.

NIAGARA SYSTEM

Capital Investments of the Niagara System in operation at October 31st, 1916:

Right-of-Way	$1,034,920 58
Steel Tower Transmission Lines	3,403,535 05
Telephone Lines	129,706 69
Relay System Lines	54,537 32
Conduit System (Ontario Power Co. to Niagara Station)	96,698 64
Wood Pole Lines	1,785,208 01
Transformer Stations	2,797,209 61
Distributing Stations	221,130 02
Total Operating Capital	$9,522,995 92

Total expenditures in connection with the operation and maintenance of Niagara System for the Fiscal year 1915-16:

Operators' Salaries and Expenses, including Supplies		$92,521 66
Maintenance of Steel Tower Lines		68,792 04
" Telephone and Relay Lines		15,422 41
" Low Tension Lines		20,350 09
" Transformer Stations		68,883 54
" Distributing Stations		7,514 28
Administration		44,811 77
		$318,295 79
Interest on Invested Capital	$371,404 94	
Cost of Power at Niagara Falls	997,257 60	
		1,368,662 54

Summary of Financial Statement of the Niagara System operation for fiscal year 1915-16:

Receipts

Power delivered, including charges for Administration, General Expense, Operation, Maintenance and Interest	$2,038,792 32

Disbursements

Power purchased, including losses in Transmission and Transformation, Administration, General Expense, Operation, Maintenance and Interest	1,686,958 33
Surplus applicable to Sinking Fund and Depreciation Reserve Account	$351,833 99

Municipality	Load in H.P. Oct., 1915.	Load in H.P. Oct., 1916.	Increase in H.P.
Toronto	32,748	38,465	5,717
Dundas	362	548	186
Hamilton	7,694.5	8,562	867.5
Waterdown	63	71	8
Caledonia	40.2	55	14.8
Hagersville	106	97.8	....
London	5,971.5	7,359	1,377.5
Thorndale	28.4	34.8	6.4
Thamesford	19.3	26.5	7.2
Guelph	1,954.5	2,549.5	595
Ontario Agricultural College	153	160	7
Central Prison Farm	203.5	203.5	....
Rockwood	34.2	11.9	....
Georgetown	266.5	300	33.5
Acton	84.5	70.3	....
Preston	973	1,149	166
Galt	1,602	2,285.5	683.5
Hespeler	368.5	450.4	81.9
Breslau	21.5	30	8.5
Kitchener	2,285.5	3,262	976.5
Waterloo	717	815	98
Elmira	91	109.9	18.9
New Hamburg	84.5	76.4	....
Baden	157	196.5	39.5
Stratford	1,179.5	1,448	268.5
Mitchell	123.5	148.8	25.3
Seaforth	275	387.4	112.4
Clinton	98	101.8	3.8
Goderich	217	214.5	....
St. Mary's	339	434.3	95.3
Woodstock	1,048	1,170	122
Ingersoll	740	792	52
Tillsonburg	233	242.6	9.6
Norwich	100.5	171.6	71.1
Beachville	132.5	96.5	....
St. Thomas	1,658.5	2,011	352.5
Port Stanley	68.5	75	6.5
Brantford	1,552.5	1,783	230.5
Paris	381	398	17
Port Credit	57.5	59.6	2.1
Weston	178.5	197	16.5
Brampton	539	656.8	117.8
Milton	287	355	68
Mimico	127.5	156.1	28.6
Mimico Asylum	35	31.5	....
Prov. Brick Yard	171	136	....
New Toronto	80.5	291	210.5
Toronto Township	62.5	99.1	36.6
Cooksville }Dixie }	23	22.7	....
Windsor	216	1,502.6	286.6
Walkerville	777.5	1,576.5	799
Elora	51.6	77.7	26.1
Fergus	68.5	92.5	24
Welland	3,038.5	5,626	2,587.5
St. Catharines	2,158.5	2,433	274.5
Port Dalhousie	104.5	79	....
Strathroy	143.5	203.7	60.2
Drumbo	18	10.9	....
Plattsville	32.2	57.6	25.4
Woodbridge	32.2	76.4	44.2
Ayr	35.5	36.2	.7
Princeton	9.8	10.4	.6
Embro	25	28.1	3.1
Chatham	431.5	509.4	67.9

Municipality.	Load in H.P. Oct., 1915.	Load in H.P. Oct., 1916.	Increase in H.P.
Lucan	33.5	30.2	....
Bolton	34.8	95.2	60.4
Mount Brydges	26	26.8	.8
Wallaceburg	177	277.5	100.5
Delaware	7.2	8.9	1.7
Tilbury	60.3	63	2.7
Simcoe	114	103.2	....
Waterford	35	97.8	62.8
Lambeth	50.9	17.9	....
Grantham Township	12.3	17.4	5.1
Dresden	70	68.3	....
Dorchester	20.7	16	....
Comber	19.5	21.4	1.9
Burford	45.6	31.5	....
Bothwell	28	28.1	....
St. George	45.6	38.2	....
Dutton	47	44.9	....
Thamesville	52.9	45	....
Blenheim	53.6	77.7	24
Lynden	6.7	79.7	73.1

A list of the municipalities connected to the Niagara System during the last year is given below.

Municipality.	Date connected	Initial Load in H.P.	Load in H.P. Oct., 1916	Increase in H.P.
Ailsa Craig	Dec. 15th, 1915	15.3	16	.7
Niagara Falls	Dec. 19th, 1915	371.3	2,364.5	1,993.2
Otterville	Jan. 15th, 1916	10	11.7	1.7
Petrolea	Apr. 25th, 1916	134	146	12
Exeter	May 4th. 1916	57	77.7	20.7
Milverton	May 18th 1916	26.5	33.5	7.
Listowel	May 27th, 1916	90.3	117.9	27.6
Palmerston	June 6th, 1916	83.7	93	9.3
Granton	June 29th, 1916	10	12.4	2.4
Harriston	June 30th 1916	56.3	52.9	....
Wyoming	Oct. 4th, 1916	22.7	22.7	....
Wellesley	Oct. 23rd, 1916	13.4	13.4	....
Burgessville	Oct. 26th, 1916	8	8	....
Tavistock	Oct. 26th, 1916	28	28	....

SEVERN SYSTEM

The Commission's generating station at the Big Chute on the Severn River was overtaxed toward the middle of the fiscal year by the relatively large increase of the power demand of this district, as on the Niagara System, the increase in load resulting from the same cause. The steps taken to remedy this condition will be mentioned later.

The operation of the generating station, sub-stations and transmission lines was very satisfactory and the increased load was taken care of in a very creditable manner. The Trent Valley Canal contractors completed certain work on the canal scheme in the vicinity of the generating station which greatly benefited the control of the head and tail water at this plant. Other special maintenance work was carried out by which the hydraulic regulation was improved.

A slight change was effected in the construction of the power and telephone lines of the Power House-Waubaushene Section where these lines cross Matcheash Bay, by the erection of an "A" frame structure with rock crib foundation to shorten this long span. This has eliminated trouble which was previously experienced at this point during very severe wind storms.

The temporary 22,000-volt pole type interswitching station at Waubaushene was moved to a new location on the Commission's property and altered slightly in design. The change was made to accommodate additional lines built from this point and for more efficient control of all lines from this operating centre.

The work commenced in October, 1915, on the stringing of a second telephone circuit between Waubaushene and the power house was completed and placed in operation in the late fall. The additional rod of right-of-way acquired on each side of the line from Midland to Penetang was cleared of trees through the bush section of that line.

Two new customers were connected to the Severn System lines during the year. Camp Borden, the new military training grounds prepared by the Department of Militia and Defence, was first supplied with power on June 29th, when the water pumps and the camp lighting was put in operation. The camp sub-station is fed over a single circuit of No. 6 copper tapped by means of airbreak switches on to the main transmission lines near the Barrie sub-station.

The elevator of the Canadian Pacific Railway at Port McNicoll was first supplied with Hydro power on July 25th. The Company's station is fed from a double circuit of No. 1/0 aluminum from the Midland-Penetang main line, which was double circuited from Waubaushene to this point during the summer. This company is being supplied with approximately 1,000 h.p. of off peak power at 575 volts during the season of navigation, in addition to approximately 250 h.p. for the operation of wharf machinery, lighting, etc., which will be utilized throughout the entire year. Below will be found a list of the demands of the various municipalities in October, 1915 and 1916, and the increase during the year.

SEVERN SYSTEM

Municipality	Load in H.P. Oct., 1915	Load in H.P. Oct., 1916.	Increase in H.P.
Midland	500	815	315
Penetang	415.5	495	79.5
Collingwood	572.4	888.7	316.3
Barrie	368.6	541.5	72.9
Coldwater	37.5	34.8	....
Elmvale	34.8	36.2	1.4
Stayner	81.7	56.3	....
Creemore	48.2	38.8	....
Orillia................................	1239.9	1414	174.1
Waubaushene	18.1	16.8	....
Port McNicoll	23.4	19.3	....
Victoria Harbor	29.5	26.8	....

New Stations on Severn System

Customer	Date connected	Initial load in H.P.	Present load in H.P.	Increase in H.P.
Camp Borden, ...	June 29th,1916......	225	325.7	100.7
C.P.R. Elevator....	July 25th, 1916.....	600	1176.6	576.6

OPERATING STATEMENT, FISCAL YEAR 1915-16.

Capital Investment as at October 31st, 1916:

Big Chute Power Development, including Generating and Transformer Station	$349,787 46
Transmission Lines	335,497 20
Distributing Stations	78,451 08
Total Operating Capital	$763,735 74

Revenue as per details below

Midland Power Accounts	$10,856 88	
Penetang "	11,983 47	
Collingwood "	23,613 38	
Barrie	13,970 30	
Coldwater "	1,007 77	
Elmvale "	1,335 50	
Stayner "	2,800 01	
Creemore "	2,254 47	
Orillia	13,229 32	
Waubaushene "	640 19	
Port McNichol "	698 22	
Victoria Harbor "	1,762 98	
Camp Borden "	3,592 45	
C.P.R. Elevator "	6,949 99	
		$94,694 93

Expenditures

Operators' and Patrolmen's Salaries and Expenses and proportion of Administration and General Office Expense	$18,152 30	
Cost of Power purchased from Wasdell and Eugenia Systems	6,366 26	
Interest on Capital Investment	29,920 27	
		$54,438 83
Surplus applicable to Sinking Fund and Depreciation Reserve Accounts		$40,256 10

EUGENIA SYSTEM

The second generating station which the Commission has constructed was placed in official operation by Sir Adam Beck on November 18th when the municipalities of the Eugenia System received Hydro power for the first time. The service supplied on this system has quite fulfilled the Commission's expectations in every way.

The hydraulic and electrical features of the generating station have been given detailed description in previous reports.

The transmission system now comprises 195 miles of 22,000-volt and 24 miles of 4,000-volt lines. The municipalities now served on this system are Owen Sound, Mount Forest, Durham, Dundalk, Flesherton, Chatsworth, Markdale, Holstein and Chesley.

On June 13th a part of the Pine River System which was acquired by the Commission was connected to the Eugenia System by means of a thirty mile tie line built between Dundalk and Shelburne. The municipalities thus supplied were Orangeville, Shelburne and Horning's Mills. While satisfactory service was delivered since the acquisition of this system, the Commission is taking steps to place it on a par with the operating condition of the balance of the Eugenia System. This will consist of the erection of new sub-stations at Shelburne and Orangeville and complete renovation of the 22,000-volt lines between these points. The future outlook for this portion of the Eugenia System is very bright.

The actual operation and maintenance of the Eugenia System is carried on jointly by co-operation with the municipalities supplied. The success of this scheme was no exception to that enjoyed on the other northern systems.

Below will be found a tabulation showing the date of connection, initial load and load taken in October, 1916, of the municipalities on this system.

Eugenia System

Municipality	Date connected	Initial load in H.P.	Load in H.P. Oct. 1916	Increase in H.P.
Owen Sound	November 18th, 1915.	899.5	992.	92.5
Flesherton	" "	29.5	36.2	6.7
Dundalk	" "	50.9	50.2	....
Durham	" "	81.7	63.9	....
Mt. Forest	" "	156	98.5	....
Chatsworth	December 17th, 1915.	8	25.4	17.4
Markdale	November 18th, 1915.	67	60	....
Holstein	April 3rd, 1916	6.8	16.9	10.1
Chesley	June 18th, 1916	87	80.4	....
Shelburne	" 13th "	45	51.2	6.2
Orangeville	" 13th "	60	128.7	68.7
Horning's Mills	" 13th "	5	5	....

EUGENIA SYSTEM

OPERATING STATEMENT, FISCAL YEAR 1915-16.

Capital Investment as at October 31st, 1916:

Eugenia Falls Power Development and Generating Plant	$638,854 14
Eugenia Distributing Stations	51,944 33
Eugenia Transmission Lines	409,355 93
Total Operating Capital	$1,100,154 40

Revenue as per details below

Owen Sound Power Accounts, December to October..				$22,536 94
Flesherton	"	"	" ..	733 13
Dundalk	"	"	" ..	1,232 32
Durham			..	1,825 00
Mount Forest	"	"	..	3,226 07
Chatsworth	"	January	" ..	662 70
Markdale	"	March	" ..	933 36
Holstein	"..	May	" ..	185 96
Chesley		July	" ..	·1,076 01
Orangeville	"	"	.. ..	979 12
Shelburne	"..	"	" ..	500 50
Hanover		September 16 to October 31		183 12
Severn System	"	October 6 to October 31		2,520 13
Hornings Mills	"	....		70 17
				36,669 .53

Expenditures

Operators' and Patrolmen's Salaries and Expenses and proportion of Administration and General Office Expenses	$14,584 03	
Interest on Capital Investment	34,205 94	
		48,789 97
Deficit on operation		12,120 44

WASDELLS SYSTEM

While the power demand of the municipalities fed from the Wasdells System does not indicate the same growth which characterized the operation of some of the other systems, very satisfactory progress was maintained.　A thoroughly reliable and continuous service was provided.　The power house, transmission lines, and sub-stations required no extensive repairs and are in first-class operating condition.

The excess capacity available at the power house over what was required for serving the Wasdells System was very conveniently and economically utilized to take care of the increased power demand of the municipalities of the Severn System.

A tie line between the power house and the Orillia substation at Longford, constructed during the summer, made this arrangement possible, and after parallel operation was commenced on July 24th, the Wasdells power house supplied an average load of 750 h.p. continuously throughout the balance of the year without difficulty.　Thus the Big Chute generating station was relieved of the greater part of the power demand of the municipality of Orillia, at Orillia and at Longford.

Wasdells System

Municipality	Load in Oct., 1915 H.P.	Load in Oct., 1916 H.P.	Increase in H.P.
Beaverton	54.9	56.3	1.4
Brechin	37.5	36.2	....
Cannington	46.9	57.6	10.7
Sunderland	20.1	52.2	32.1
Woodville	49.6	48.2	....

OPERATING STATEMENT, FISCAL YEAR 1915-16.

Capital Investment as at October 31st, 1916:

Wasdells Power Development and Generating Plant	$136,658 47
Wasdells Distributing Stations	13,616 24
Wasdells Transmission Lines	114,406 03
Total Operating Capital	$264,680 74

Revenue as per details below

Beaverton Power Accounts	$3,156 97	
Brechin "	2,615 77	
Cannington "	3,163 11	
Sunderland "	2,018 92	
Woodville "	3,354 15	
Severn System "	3,846 13	
		$18,155 05

Expenditures

Operators' and Patrolmen's Salaries and Expenses, including supplies	$3,461 02	
Administration and General Office Expenses	1,010 19	
Interest on Capital Investment	9,114 66	
		13,585 87
Surplus applicable to Sinking Fund and Depreciation Reserve Account		$4,569 18

PARALLEL OPERATION OF THE SEVERN, EUGENIA AND WASDELLS SYSTEMS

As mentioned above, some action became necessary to relieve the load conditions at the Big Chute generating station caused by the increase of the power demand of the municipalities fed from this plant.

The first step in this direction was the erection of a 22,000-volt tie line of No. 1/0 aluminum, seven miles long, between the Wasdells power house and the sub-station belonging to the Municipality of Orillia at Longford. The balance of the circuit was completed by the existing Orillia 22,000-volt lines via the Orillia transforming and switching stations and the Big Chute plant. To complete telephone communication between the plant arrangements were made with Orillia to erect a telephone circuit on the power line poles between Orillia and Longford.

The two plants were placed in normal parallel operation on July 24th, the Wasdells plant supplying practically all the load previously taken by Orillia from the Big Chute plant in addition to the load taken by the municipalities of the Wasdells System. Thus the primary object was gained of loading the Wasdells plant to a degree of economical operation and reducing the load on the Big Chute plant.

The power supply for the Severn System was further augmented by the paralleling of the Eugenia plant with the Big Chute plant. This was accomplished by the erection of a 22,000-volt tie line of No. 1/0 copper and No. 9 iron telephone circuit, twenty-four miles long, between the Eugenia power house and the Collingwood distribution station. The tie line was built in an incredibly short space of time and power from the Eugenia plant was first supplied to the Severn System on October 6th. Temporary metering equipment was installed at both the Wasdells and the Eugenia plants to measure the interchange of power.

The parallel operation of these systems has been entirely satisfactory, with added security of service to all customers supplied therefrom.

On another page will be found curves showing typical fall operating conditions for twenty-four hours with the three systems in synchronism.

CENTRAL ONTARIO SYSTEM

The operation of the Central Ontario System has been entirely satisfactory since passing into the hands of the Commission. On account of the various points of supply total interruptions to service are almost impossible and have seldom, if ever, occurred. The operation of equipment has been most successful, no failures of any importance having taken place.

The steadily growing load at various points has necessitated some readjustment of equipment. One 750 k.v.a. transformer was moved from Port Hope to Oshawa, bringing the capacity of that point up to 2,250 k.w., and on account of the construction of the Government arsenal at Lindsay it was necessary to interchange two 300 k.w. units at Lindsay for two 750 k.w. units from Cobourg. At other points equipment of less importance has been replaced by apparatus more suitable to existing load conditions than that formerly used.

Practically all equipment which had become obsolete or unfit for service was scrapped and advantage taken of the high prices for scrap metals at present in force. Careful studies of the lines were made and whenever it was profitable the amount of conductor material was reduced to the most economical point. The material recovered in this way enabled almost all extensions necessary to be taken care of without delay and without the purchase of additional conductor.

present capacity of
ar without taxing
available.
d the curve of the
as been under the
put of the system
1915.

Kilowatts

1916	Increase in H.P.
	2700
	4790
	2850
	1140
	2250
	1030
	1550
	4700
	3020
	1280
	1950
	2400
	1800

	Load in H.P. October, 1916
.....	217
.....	1247
.....	1568
.....	20
.....	20
.....	375
.....	502
.....	75
.....	72
.....	670
.....	1434
.....	315
......	302
......	75
......	87
......	1062
......	3067
......	38

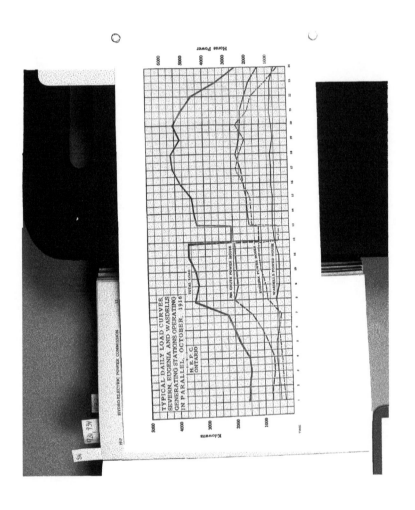

Horse Power

Kilowatts

TYPICAL DAILY LOAD CURVES.
SEVERN, EUGENIA AND WASDELLS
GENERATING STATIONS OPERATING
IN PARALLEL. OCTOBER. 1916

H. E. P. C.
ONTARIO

TOTAL LOAD

BIG CHUTE POWER HOUSE

EUGENIA POWER HOUSE

WASDELLS POWER HOUSE

While the growing load will undoubtedly soon overtake the present capacity of generating plants it has been possible to carry all load this year without taxing equipment and with a conservative amount of reserve apparatus available.

Loads at the various towns are shown in the table below and the curve of the weekly peaks shows the growth of load since this property has been under the control of the Commission. Another table shows the total output of the system for the current year and comparison of operation for the year 1915.

Power Generated, Central Ontario System

Month	Peak Load, 1915	Peak Load, 1916	Increase in H.P.
November	15,100	17,800	2700
December	13,400	18,190	4790
January, 1916	13,300	16,150	2850
February	12,560	13,700	1140
March	11,500	13,750	2250
April	11,610	12,640	1030
May	11,100	12,650	1550
June	10,600	15,300	4700
July	11,980	15,600	3020
August	14,570	15,850	1280
September	14,550	16,500	1950
October	16,200	18,600	2400
Peak for year	16,200	18,600	1800

Municipality	Load in H.P. October, 1916
Whitby	217
Bowmanville	1247
Oshawa	1568
Newcastle	20
Orono	20
Port Hope	375
Cobourg	502
Colborne	75
Brighton	72
Trenton	670
Belleville	1434
Napanee	315
Deseronto	302
Stirling	75
Tweed	87
Lindsay	1062
Peterboro	3067
Millbrook	38

MUSKOKA SYSTEM

The power development on the south branch of the Muskoka River at Muskoka Village which had been taken over from the Municipality of Gravenhurst was formally under operation by the Commission on November 1st. The purchase comprised the power site which had been partially developed by the municipality and the existing generating station and hydraulic works on the property. On November 1st power was being supplied to Gravenhurst at 6,600 volts and a small amount to Muskoka Village at 120 volts.

The Commission immediately proceeded with the extension and remodelling of the generating station to place it in first-class operating condition and to deliver the power covered by contract with the Municipality of Huntsville. A detailed description of the new hydraulic and electrical equipment of the plant will be found in another section of the report. Every effort was exerted by the Commission to supply uninterrupted service during the alterations to the station.

On August the 15th a 26 mile, 22,000-volt, No. 2 S.R. aluminum line to Huntsville distribution station was made alive for test. The sub-station was placed in operation permanently on August 25th.

All construction details at the power house were not completed at the end of October, which was due to the difficulty in obtaining reasonable delivery of materials.

The peak load demands of the Municipalities of Gravenhurst and Huntsville for the month of October were 235 and 580 h.p. respectively. The Commission will be in a position to supply standard service and anticipates a very successful future for the Muskoka System.

System
ling the
capacity.
demand
's power
dard.
ower at
.ture.
:eby the
' he Com-

and no

erection
·station
s to the
:ied out
hes will
ng with
elevators
it will
the two
:ase the
system.

3 03

ber 1916,

8 13

st, 1916

2 11

8 13

3 98

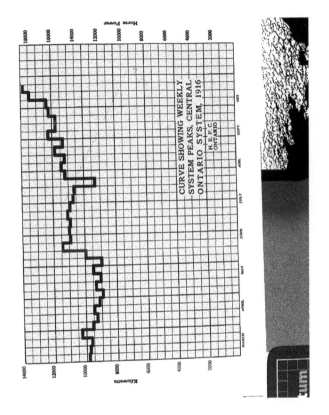

CURVE SHOWING WEEKLY
SYSTEM PEAKS, CENTRAL
ONTARIO SYSTEM, 1916

H. E. P. C.
ONTARIO

PORT ARTHUR SYSTEM

Steady progress was made in the operation of the Port Arthur System during the past year. The increase in load was taken care of by loading the Current River Hydraulic Plant of the City of Port Arthur to its full capacity. Thus the Commission was not obliged to increase the present reserve demand of 2,600 h.p. from the Kaministquia Power Company. The Company's power supply to the Commission during the year was of the usual high standard.

The total demand from both sources is approximately 5,100 horse-power at the present with indications of a very material increase in the near future.

The more uniform routine of operation established in 1915 whereby the load control of the Current River station was placed in the hands of the Commission's operators has proved very economical in every respect.

The Hydro transforming sub-station is in excellent condition, and no failures were reported during the year.

Plans and specifications were prepared and material ordered for the erection of a wood pole line entrance and switching structure, at the transformer station to provide a means of sectionalizing the two 22,000 volt outgoing circuits to the grain elevators and to the waterworks station. This work will be carried out in conjunction with the Port Arthur Commission. Five air break switches will be installed on this structure. The Port Arthur Commission is proceeding with the erection of two air break switches on each of the lines built to the elevators and to the waterworks station. When these installations are completed it will be possible to feed any one of the four elevator stations from either of the two outgoing 22,000 volt lines from the sub-station and will greatly increase the flexibility and security of the service on the high tension portion of the system.

Capital Investments for the Port Arthur System to October 31st, 1916:

Transmission Lines	$21,303 12
Transformer Stations	86,089 91
Total Operating Capital	$107,393 03

The Operating and Maintenance Expenses for the fiscal year ending October 1916, are as follows:—

Operators' Salaries and Expenses, including Operating supplies, and proportion of Administration and General Office Expenses	$5,721 88
Interest at 4% per annum	4,325 00
Sinking Fund at 1.8% per annum	1,946 25
Cost of Power	37,365 00
	$49,358 13

A Financial Statement of Operation for the fiscal year ending October 31st, 1916 is given below:—

Sum of monthly loads delivered and value, including charges for Administration, General Expenses, Operation, Interest, Sinking Fund and Depreciation	28,080 h.p.	$54,322 11
Sum of monthly loads purchased and value, including Administration, General Expense, Operation, Interest and Sinking Fund	28,080 h.p.	49,358 13
Surplus applicable to Depreciation Reserve		$4,963 98

THE ST. LAWRENCE SYSTEM

The operation of the Commission's system on the St. Lawrence River for the past year proved very successful. The service received from the hydraulic plant at Iroquois was thoroughly reliable and practically no interruptions occurred. A recent inspection of the Commission's sub-stations and lines shows that so far the depreciation of this system is quite negligible.

The total load demand of the municipalities during the year increased to 1,000 h.p., an amount considerably above the capacity of the generating station at Iroquois. This difficulty was temporarily solved by paralleling the municipal auxiliary steam plant at Brockville with the Commission's power supply purchased at Iroquois.

- The transpositions in the transmission line between Morrisburg and Prescott are being rearranged to remove the inductive effect which has interfered with the proper operation of the Bell Telephone Company's line paralleling this line. A series of very interesting tests from an engineering standpoint are being made in connection with this work.

Municipality.	Load in Oct., 1915. H.P.	Load in Oct., 1916. H.P.	Increase in H.P.
Brockville	335	348.5	13.5
Prescott	205	217	12
Winchester	60.3	58.9	...
Chesterville	40.2	48.2	8.
Williamsburg	29.5	17.4	...

ST. LAWRENCE SYSTEM OPERATING STATEMENT, FISCAL YEAR 1915-16.

Capital Investments as at October 31st, 1916:

St. Lawrence Distributing Stations	$23,063 25	
St. Lawrence Transmission Lines	147,013 62	
Total Operating Capital		$170,076 87

Revenue as per details below

Prescott Power Accounts ..	$4,462 11	
Chesterville "	1,838 69	
Winchester "	2,321 42	
Williamsburg "	563 21	
Brockville "	8,340 86	
		17,526 29

Expenditures

Operators' and Patrolmen's Salaries and Expenses proportion of Administration and General Office Expense	$1,559 66	
Interest on Capital Investment	6,783 35	
Cost of Power purchased	5,513 89	
		13,856 90

Surplus applicable to Sinking Fund and Depreciation Reserve Accounts	$3,669 39

TOTAL CAPITAL INVESTMENT TO OCTOBER 31st, 1916

Following is a statement of expenditures on Capital Account, including Niagara, Severn, St. Lawrence, Wasdells, Eugenia, Muskoka, Port Arthur, Renfrew and Ottawa Systems, Stock on Hand, Tools and Equipment, Municipal Construction.

Niagara System—Transmission Lines

Right-of-Way	$1,034,920 58	
Steel Tower Lines	3,403,585 05	
Telephone Lines	129,706 69	
Relay System Lines	54,537 32	
Conduit System (Ont. Power Co. to Niagara Station)..	96,698 64	
		$4,719,448 28
Right-of-Way (Dundas-Toronto), in course of construction	$6,366 37	
Steel Tower Lines, in course of construction	8,631 74	
Conduit System, in course of construction	22,157 54	
Telephone Line (Section A), in course of construction	1,297 70	
		38,453 35
Wood Pole Lines	$1,785,208 01	
Wood Pole Lines, in course of construction	189,094 42	
		1,974,302 43
Welland and St. Catharines District Lines	$16,445 63	
		16,445 63
Rural Line Construction	$324,168 44	
		324,168 44
Power Development, Right-of-Way and Preliminary Engineering	$33,512 91	
		33,512 91

Transformer Stations

Stations	$2,797,209 61	
Stations and Extensions to same, in course of construction	34,415 66	
		2,831,625 27
Distributing Stations	$221,130 02	
Distributing Stations, in course of construction	10,634 26	
		231,764 28

Severn System

Big Chute Power Development, including Generating and Transformer Stations	$349,787 46	
Transmission Lines	335,497 20	
Distributing Stations	78,451 08	
Distributing Stations Extensions in course of construction	1,409 83	
		765,145 57

St. Lawrence System

Transmission Lines	$147,228 58	
Distributing Stations	23,063 25	
Distributing Stations in course of construction	6,366 07	
		176,657 90

Wasdells System

Power Development, including Generating and Transformer Station	$136,658 47	
Transmission Lines	114,406 03	
Distributing Stations	13,637 00	
		264,701 50

Eugenia System

Power Development, including Generating and Transformer Station	$638,854 14	
Transmission Lines	409,355 93	
Distributing Stations	51,944 33	
Distributing Stations in course of construction	1,249 29	
Transmission Lines in course of construction	36,276 66	
Operation	12,120 44	
		1,149,800 79

Muskoka System

South Falls Power Development, including Generating and Transformer Station	$78,707 61	
Transmission Line	52,626 47	
Distributing Station	8,923 95	
Operation	912 26	
		141,170 29

Port Arthur System

Transmission Lines	$21,303 12	
Transformer Station	86,089 91	
		107,393 03

Renfrew System

Round Lake Storage Dam	$20,168 86	
Power Development (repayable)	717 41	
		20,886 27

Ottawa System

Meter Equipment	$432 39	
		432 39

General Accounts (Chargeable)

Municipal and Rural Construction Work repayable	$290,247 62	
Sales to Municipalities	159,226 01	
Renfrew District Operating Charges	2,519 82	
		451,993 45

General Accounts (Capitalized)

Office Furniture, Equipment, Stationery, Unexpired Insurance, etc.	$36,531 78	
Office Furniture and Equipment, Electrical Inspection Dept.	3,863 60	
Toronto Storehouse, Testing Laboratory, Garage and Machine Shop	117,883 72	
Dundas Storehouse	1,586 04	
Automobiles and Trucks (Depreciated value)	27,480 29	
Office Building	335,866 60	
		523,212 03

Stock and Tools

Stock on hand for construction purposes and sale to Municipalities	$163,673 72	
Line Maintenance Stock for all Systems	59,905 07	
Operating Department's Testing and Metering Equipment for all Systems	2,609 76	
		226,188 55
Line and Station Construction Tools and Equipment ..	$4,000 32	
Line and Station Maintenance Tools	6,666 08	
Hydraulic Construction Tools	1,402 88	
		12,069 28
Laboratory Operation	$9,482 04	
Machine Shop Operation (Stock)	520 35	
		10,002 39
		$14,019,374 03

PROVINCIAL EXPENDITURES

Fiscal Year 1915-16

Engineering assistance to non-operating Municipalities for the gathering of data throughout the Province for statistical purposes; reports on Municipal operation	$19,897 74	
Municipal estimates for power supply non-operating Municipalities and also rates investigations	4,058 45	
Hydrographic surveys, storage surveys, reports and investigations on power sites and stream flow for the Province	31,366 77	
Reports and statistical data on overhead and underground construction for Municipalities; investigations relative supply of power to rural districts and gathering information with respect to the use of electricity along lines not at present operated by the use of such	8,625 85	
Engineering investigations, surveys and reports on proposed Municipal Electric Railways	38,675 66	
Administration and general office expense over all above expenditures	28,140 55	
	$130,765 02	
Less:		
Credits:—Various supplies, equipment and capital expenditures charged Province former years, now capitalized in Commission's books, sold, or placed in stock	38,391 49	
		$92,373 53
Electrical Inspection—Balance of operating expenses for the year, not including capital investment, such as furniture, typewriters, etc., which is carried forward		31,345 53
Special Hydrographic Investigations—Lake-of-the-Woods Districts for the Department of Lands and Mines		1,972 02
Equipment on hand purchased for Hydrographic work		1,353 28
		$127,044 36

BALANCE SHEET

OCTOBER 31st, 1916.

Assets

Sundry Expenditures, per list	$14,019,374 03
Warrantable Advances	35,118 16
Unpaid Power Bills, October 31st, 1916	375,579 20
Cash on hand	297,140 80
	$14,727,212 19

Liabilities

Provincial Treasurer	$13,588,667 72
Niagara System, Surplus applicable to Sinking Fund and Depreciation Reserve Account	939,814 38
Wasdells System, Surplus applicable to Sinking Fund and Depreciation Reserve Account	4,569 18
Severn System, Surplus applicable to Sinking Fund and Depreciation Reserve Account	57,030 56
St. Lawrence System, Surplus applicable to Sinking Fund and Depreciation Reserve Account	4,345 93
Welland System, Surplus applicable to Sinking Fund and Depreciation Reserve Account	1,449 24
Port Arthur System, Surplus applicable to Sinking Fund and Depreciation Reserve Account	27,151 56
Ottawa, applicable to unpaid Power	1,204 00
Interest Account	54,061 38
Cable Reels	210 85
Central Ontario System Balance	38,536 29
Storehouse Operation, Surplus	6,697 03
Garage Operation, Surplus	533 25
Administrative Office Building, applicable to Sinking Fund	2,940 82
	$14,727,212 19

MUNICIPAL ACCOUNTS

The results from municipal distribution of Hydro power are shown in the tables submitted in this section. In accordance with the requirements of the Ontario Government the municipal year ends on December 31st. The tables which follow under " Municipal Accounts " cover the calendar year ending December 31st, while all other sections of the annual report deal with the fiscal year ending October 31st.

The work of standardizing the electrical accounts of the Hydro-Electric municipalities, commenced in 1912, has been continued. During the year accounting systems were established in Ailsa Craig, Blenheim, Brockville, Chesley, Chatsworth, Dundalk, Durham, Exeter, Flesherton, Grantham Township, Gravenhurst, Granton, Harriston, Holstein, Listowel, Markdale, Milverton, Mount Forest, Niagara Falls, Orangeville, Otterville, Owen Sound, Palmerston, Petrolia, Ridgetown, Stamford Township, Sarnia and Shelburne, and the local officers instructed in the proper handling of the books.

A periodical inspection has been made of the electrical accounts of all Hydro-Electric municipalities, our accountants assisting the local officers by suggesting improved methods of office routine, and in the case of smaller towns and villages, where the utility is in charge of men of little bookkeeping experience, actually doing most of the accounting.

The system of monthly balance sheets and operating reports enables the Provincial Commission to keep in close touch with local conditions, and from the reports and other data collected and worked up by the auditors, the capital expenditure and operating expenses are periodically divided into the principal revenue accounts, lighting, commercial power, municipal power and street light, these in turn being set against the respective revenues for the purpose of rate adjustment.

This data enables this Commission to authorize and enforce a schedule of selling rates in each municipality which makes each of the above-named revenue departments self-supporting, so that an excessively high rate in one does not take care of a deficit in another.

The seven statistical reports which follow show the result of operation and the present status of the electric utilities in the one hundred and twenty-eight municipalities in which the service has been installed long enough to justify a report.

The municipalities have been listed in the order of their size according to Municipal Bulletin No. 10, Bureau of Industries of the Ontario Department of Agriculture; the populations are shown and the statistics permit an intelligent comparison of operating results in municipalities where conditions are similar. This is resulting in a friendly rivalry between the municipalities for an increased load, an efficient and economical administration, and an intelligent effort to improve the load factor, which is so essential to low selling rates.

Statement " A " is a comparative condensed balance sheet of each municipality as at December 31st, 1915, and December 31st, 1916, showing the plant cost in logical subdivisions, and other items making up the total assets. The true or quick liabilities, such as debenture balance, bank overdraft and accounts payable, are totalled separately before including such reserve accounts as debentures paid, sinking fund reserve, depreciation reserve and surplus. In this way the relative increase in plant value and net debt during the year in any municipality can be quickly determined.

The percentage of net debt to plant cost at the end of each year has been worked out, and shows a marked decrease. Special attention is called to this very interesting and gratifying feature.

All of the accounts appearing in the balance sheet under " Reserves," such as " Debentures Paid," " Sinking Fund Reserve," " Depreciation Reserve," and " Surplus," might properly be called surplus and represent the gross profit from operation.

While a proper depreciation charge has been included in the operating expenses from the beginning, the plant extensions resulting from the growth of the service have in most cases absorbed most of the depreciation funds. A proper accounting has been kept of this, and interest credited the Depreciation Reserve on the funds so used. A characteristic feature of the operation during the past two years has been a steady increase in the cash balances, which in some cases now amount to more than 25 per cent. of the total plant cost, notwithstanding the constant reductions in selling rates. Many commissions have loaned cash to the municipalities, and some have invested largely in Canadian War Loans, an innovation unique in the operation of civic utilities.

Statement "B" is a condensed operating report for the year ending December 31st, 1916, showing the result in each municipality. The population and the number of consumers in each class is also given to facilitate comparisons. In some cases where the power was turned on subsequent to January 1st, the proportion of the annual fixed charges corresponding to the period of operation has been used, and in other municipalities where the operation covers a very short period, and no actual payment has been made, the fixed charges have been omitted entirely to simplify the accounting in future years and avoid the necessity for annual adjustments.

The cost of the service, which is the basis on which service is billed to the consumers includes every possible loading, i.e., cost of power, operation, maintenance, administration, interest and sinking fund payments on debenture debt, and in addition the sinking fund equivalent of a 5 per cent. straight line depreciation charge. No utility is considered to be on a satisfactory basis until the revenue is sufficient to meet this burden. The rate of depreciation, however, is subject to modification to meet unusual conditions such as large investments for land or perpetual water rights—concrete construction, unusual types of overhead or underground construction or short term debentures.

A study of Statement " B " will show that of the 128 municipalities reported, the revenue in 111 was sufficient to take care of all operating and fixed charges and depreciation, in 11 others all charges except full depreciation were met, and in six only was there an actual loss, due to local conditions, which will correct themselves. The net credit balance of surplus from the year's operation in 128 municipalities, amounted to $357,393.72, and the systems are now serving 148,732 customers, and a population of approximately 1,155,000.

Statement "C" shows in detail the comparative revenue and expenses in each municipality for the past four years. This shows graphically the increase in business year by year and the gradual decrease in the proportion of revenue contributed by the municipal utilities. In comparing the cost of power purchased, the varying price paid per horse-power must be taken into consideration. This schedule will be found in Statement " F."

Statement "D" shows for each municipality for each year of operation, the number of consumers served with light and power, the average monthly kw. hr. consumption, the average net cost per kw. hr., and the average net monthly bill. This is a tabulation of data never before attempted, so far as can be determined, and while built up on information not originally obtained for this purpose, and subject to errors, the averages are substantially correct and show the constantly increasing monthly consumption and decreasing net cost per kw. hr. and average monthly bill, and reflects the satisfactory nature of the service from the standpoint of the consumer.

Statement "E" shows the approximate installation and annual cost per lamp of the street lighting service in cities, towns and villages where Hydro service has been installed. An interesting feature is the annual cost per capita based on the total populations.

Statements "F" and "G" show comparatively the cost of power to the municipalities, the selling rates for power and light in 1912, 1913, 1914, 1915 and 1916 and the recommended rates for 1917.

In order that the effect of the Hydro co-operative scheme on the Hydro municipalities as a whole may be clearly shown, the operation for the past five years of all municipalities has been consolidated into one report, likewise the balance sheets for four years. These consolidated reports show the sound financial condition of the enterprise from the municipal standpoint and meet every criticism against municipal ownership and operation of electric utilities as carried on under the control of the Commission. Particular attention is called to the steady decrease in the percentage which the net debt balance bears to the total assets each year.

CONSOLIDATED OPERATING REPORTS

	1912	1913	1914	1915	1916
Number of Municipalities included	28	45	69	99	128
EARNINGS					
Domestic Light		$ 572,154 38	$ 789,130 81	$ 944,271 08	$ 1,172,878 96
Commercial Light		525,438 16	673,803 92	720,209 26	812,130 78
Power		905,378 17	1,214,825 31	1,501,797 78	1,921,152 31
Street Light		560,925 56	698,409 71	835,970 87	930,057 48
Miscellaneous		53,543 24	57,482 41	68,046 29	147,381 50
Total	$ 1,617,674 00	$ 2,617,439 51	$ 3,433,656 16	$ 4,070,295 28	$ 4,983,601 03
EXPENSES					
Power Purchased		$ 789,632 87	$ 1,045,752 65	$ 1,485,614 73	$ 1,959,446 83
Sub-Stn. Operation		78,394 81	97,658 90	107,607 31	153,761 08
Maintenance		38,698 46	31,790 99	25,935 56	46,131 53
Dist. System, Operation and Maintenance		104,114 51	130,998 65	154,409 71	154,247 17
Line Transformer Maintenance		8,547 61	11,764 32	11,508 92	14,528 17
Meter		5,222 19	9,536 07	12,899 14	24,218 48
Consumers' Premises—Expenses		53,108 38	65,192 23	47,494 26	52,602 01
Street Light System, Operation and Maintenance		84,902 76	113,047 80	136,983 38	145,471 50
Promotion of Business		72,303 51	86,683 02	74,402 55	79,324 85
Billing and Collecting		77,351 76	106,560 71	131,541 27	154,508 58
General Office, Salary and Expenses		154,932 69	230,899 75	236,777 86	306,709 35
Undistributed Expenses		64,538 69	81,261 28	94,978 89	88,646 65
Interest and Debenture Payments		528,549 21	662,092 34	817,978 89	951,781 99
Miscellaneous Expenses		884 95	8,089 63	34,230 26	8,687 44
Total Expenses	$ 1,377,168 00	$ 2,041,183 40	$ 2,678,328 34	$ 3,371,414 00	$ 4,140,065 51
Surplus	$ 240,506 00	$ 576,256 11	$ 755,327 82	$ 698,881 28	$ 843,535 52
Depreciation Charge	$ 124,992 47	$ 262,675 24	$ 357,883 31	$ 414,506 99	$ 486,141 80
Surplus Less Depreciation Charge	$ 115,513 53	$ 313,580 87	$ 397,444 51	$ 284,374 29	$ 357,393 72

Note.—Details of 1912 Revenue and Expenses not now available.

CONSOLIDATED BALANCE SHEETS

Year ending December 31st	1913	1914	1915	1916
ASSETS—Number of Municipalities included	45	69	99	128
Lands and Buildings	$ 626,707 34	$ 791,732 20	$ 873,838 18	$ 1,335,936 33
Sub-Station Equipment	1,090,875 69	1,476,087 84	1,582,062 56	1,934,626 12
Distribution System, Overhead	2,690,834 74	3,422,763 93	4,234,626 05	4,832,353 27
" " Underground	644,514 24	807,153 53	928,420 77	1,095,709 62
Line Transformers	615,546 20	787,613 52	981,754 70	1,179,132 07
Meters	840,606 64	1,172,475 11	1,418,165 08	1,711,299 49
Street Lighting Equipment, Regular	900,614 80	1,071,255 37	1,309,628 49	1,251,057 13
" " Ornamental	62,765 34	270,386 55	197,644 82	306,388 95
Miscellaneous Equipment and Const. Exp.	866,551 89	2,062,035 90	1,701,182 66	2,059,263 42
Steam or Hydraulic Plant	1,401,175 28	420,108 33	461,651 60	864,500 01
Old Plant	341,277 00	478,881 56	415,518 23	689,272 67
Other Miscellaneous		140,631 56	768,854 63	70,475 99
Total Plant	$10,081,469 16	$12,901,125 40	$14,873,347 77	$17,330,015 07
Bank and Cash Balance	450,887 97	422,350 12	284,653 96	1,061,029 90
Inventories	344,487 95	561,873 08	602,920 69	695,152 23
Accounts Receivable	540,274 58	615,226 76	726,556 76	764,504 59
Sinking Fund	431,747 27	625,217 03	868,983 78	1,166,017 73
Other	58,959 93	123,410 97	326,801 11	342,215 87
Total	$11,907,826 86	$15,249,203 36	$17,683,264 07	$21,358,935 39
LIABILITIES—Debenture Balance	$ 8,711,308 37	$10,678,078 36	$11,831,811 03	$15,058,641 57
Accounts Payable	1,553,711 45	1,682,150 29	2,040,038 01	969,187 75
Bank Overdraft	160,919 16	228,622 50	292,106 44	178,413 26
Other Liabilities	42,412 81	113,838 66	37,388 31	491,874 90
Total Liabilities	$10,468,351 79	$12,702,689 81	$14,201,343 79	$16,698,117 48
RESERVES—Debentures Paid	$ 202,751 26	$ 320,129 10	$ 394,466 22	$ 549,778 59
Sinking Fund Reserve	431,747 27	625,217 07	868,983 78	1,165,785 94
Depreciation Reserve	478,145 88	850,618 07	1,337,739 73	1,843,804 68
Surplus	326,830 66	750,549 35	880,730 55	1,101,448,70
Total Reserves	$ 1,439,475 07	$ 2,546,513 55	$ 3,481,920 28	$ 4,660,817 91
Total Liabilities and Reserves	$11,907,826 86	$15,249,203 36	$17,683,264 07	$21,358,935 39
Percentage of Net Debt to Total Assets	88.0%	83.0%	80.3%	78.4%

STATE

Comparative Condensed Balance Sheets of Electric Departments

Municipality Population	Toronto 463,705		Hamilton 100,461	
—	1915	1916	1915	1916
ASSETS	$ c.	$ c.	$ c.	$ c.
Lands and Buildings	373,733 08	703,215 79	59,020 10	72,609 20
Sub-Station Equipment	729,143 69	946,400 28	89,694 10	89,713 89
Distribution System, Overhead.....	1,554,253 98	1,703,286 32	287,116 34	300,134 25
" " Underground..	685,557 44	852,317 09	156,569 93	157,415 41
Line Transformers................	394,525 78	394,432 05	88,927 58	102,299 20
Meters..........................	564,238 32	638,229 41	125,792 86	146,947 41
Street Light Equipment, Regular...	795,750 64	700,908 22	92,520 48	92,882 82
" " Ornamental.				
Miscel. Equip. and Construction Exp.	1,231,753 03	1,528,054 43	118,426 02	120,189 97
Steam or Hydraulic Plant.........	e 50,106 14	e 34,343 18	....	....
Old Plant.......................	f 505,646 83	....	2,000 00	2,000 00
Total Plant....................	6,884,708 93	7,501,186 77	1,020,067 41	1,084,192 15
Bank and Cash Balance...........	84,220 22	710,141 95	....	....
Inventories.....................	440,845 89	425,259 74	34,450 25	32,300 98
Accounts Receivable..............	344,828 27	241,461 01	95,138 39	104,485 43
Sinking Fund....................	480,949 94	590,195 03	50,189 06	72,887 60
Other Assets....................	73,657 99	4,122 20	3,217 39	6,071 12
Total Assets...................	8,309,211 24	9,472,366 70	1,203,062 50	1,299,937 28
LIABILITIES AND RESERVES				
Liabilities				
Debenture Balance...............	6,300,000 00	7,898,000 00	840,000 00	840,000 00
Accounts Payable................	848,851 48	166,789 53	63,298 69	75,881 85
Bank Overdraft..................	....	....	110,745 32	101,022 98
Other Liabilities................	....	17,184 46	23,607 37	23,944 75
Total Liabilities...............	7,148,851 48	8,081,973 99	1,037,651 38	1,040,849 58
Reserves				
Debentures Paid.................				
Sinking Fund Reserve............	480,949,94	590,195 03	50,189 06	72,887 60
Depreciation Reserve.............	....	736,807 23	55,893 88	92,777 42
Surplus.........................	679,409 82	63,390 45	59,328 18	93,422 68
Total Liabilities and Reserves....	8,309,211 24	9,472,366 70	1,203,062 50	1,299,937 28
Percentage of Net Debt to Total Assets	86.0	79.2	86.3	89.0

"e"   Exhibition construction.
"f"   Work orders in progress.

MENT "A"

of Hydro Municipalities as at December 31st, 1915 and 1916

	Ottawa 100,163		London 58,055		Brantford 25,420		Windsor 24,162	
	1915	1916	1915	1916	1915	1916	1915	1916
	$ c.	$ c.	$ c.	$ c.	$ c.	$ c.	$ c.	$ c.
	83,084 17	88,344 15	68,220 17	70,728 19	11,069 21	11,753 82	11,605 94	11,629 09
	102,612 38	108,988 09	144,439 34	168,395 04	38,710 52	89,521 99	30,862 05	35,569 56
	318,704 90	318,229 86	279,633 40	329,206 48	100,808 23	105,373 04	112,368 72	133,385 25
	77,771 77	77,897 39	352 43	352 43	....	....		
	89,194 77	92,663 05	35,324 59	41,516 23	18,750 49	22,384 67	14,516 02	15,567 06
	100,689 89	109,891 07	110,487 46	123,342 88	18,837 13	24,735 95	17,839 38	34,904 43
	55,895 88	57,433 54	38,441 58	41,191 09	15,909 64	15,920 77	119,163 76	121,476 80
	29,957 84	29,957 84	....	....	33,053 38	31,068 29	33,621 09	35,404 07
	29,293 13	29,847 05	47,031 27	50,627 34	21,357 12	23,919 96	42,499 88	50,445 21
	....	....						
	....	....					6,548 02	....
	887,204 23	913,252 04	723,980 24	825,359 68	257,995 72	274,678 49	389,024 86	438,380 97
	66,323 19	51,110 55	24,567 86	4,072 54	1,413 88	2,051 95	3,858 52	3,689 43
	8,274 30	22,481 62	36,561 72	37,841 57	552 51	1,386 39	8,019 99	14,747 82
	16,320 77	17,658 60	47,573 16	78,958 90	1,252 91	3,553 21	720 96	3,164 66
	99,389 59	114,201 16	30,900 36	42,681 40	10,229 50	17,859 68	2,791 18	5,666 09
	....	1,186 12	210,000 00	185,000 00	....	....	....	88 77
	1,077,512 08	1,119,840 09	1,073,533 34	1,173,914 09	271,444 52	299,529 72	404,415 51	465,737 24
	700,000 00	700,000 00	661,010 13	706,897 55	222,500 00	237,500 00	343,477 40	219,928 72
	12,665 18	4,713 68	168,450 68	139,342 16	....	3,544 29	50,664 05	10,000 00
	....	....	....	....	16,452 58	....	....	....
	....	....	1,571 00	2,086 50	....	2,276 50	375 00	213,884 09
	712,665 18	704,713 68	831,031 81	848,326 21	238,952 58	243,320 79	394,516 45	443,812 81
	....	....	30,889 87	35,002 45	....	....	1,788 01	5,071 31
	99,389 59	114,201 16	30,900 36	42,681 40	10,229 50	17,859 68	2,791 18	5,666 09
	222,378 30	254,553 30	98,604 15	124,896 06	15,408 22	22,908 22	....	5,157 50
	43,079 01	46,371 95	82,107 15	123,507 97	6,854 22	15,441 03	5,324 87	6,029 53
	1,077,512 08	1,119,840 09	1,073,533 34	1,173,914 09	271,444 52	299,529 72	404,415 51	465,737 24
	66.1	62.9	77.3	72.3	88.1	81.3	97.5	94.1

STATEMENT

Comparative Condensed Balance Sheets of Electric Departments .

Municipality Population	Peterborough 20,426		Kitchener 19,266	
—	1915	1916	1915	1916
ASSETS	$ c.	$ c.	$ c.	$ c.
Lands and Buildings	15,198 33	8,248 17	31,068 71	31,423 12
Sub-Station Equipment	....	12,824 50	72,450 20	70,216 45
Distribution System, Overhead.....	1,354 73	70,605 90	84,877 71	94,801 23
"　　　"　　Underground..	....	....	6,785 40	6,864 35
Line Transformers................	3,051 94	28,622 94	29,079 41	34,074 57
Meters...........................	12,365 76	32,876 43	38,768 09	45,067 49
Street Light Equipment, Regular...	32 72	5,334 91	20,242 17	20,521 23
"　　　"　　Ornamental.	....	26,107 68	....	....
Miscel. Equip. and Construction Exp.	5,266 12	32,251 12	6,016 95	6,834 96
Steam or Hydraulic Plant..........	....	....	....	....
Old Plant........................	136,050 95	11,789 42	56,879 74	55,952 40
Total Plant.....................	173,320 55	228,661 07	346,168 38	365,755 80
Bank and Cash Balance............	....	850 26	11,617 59	8,583 96
Inventories......................	....	2,898 98	6,371 06	5,960 22
Accounts Receivable..............	5,810 98	5,692 47	17,613 09	8,106 14
Sinking Fund.....................	4,364 80	7,795 08	....	....
Other Assets.....................	....	....	....	17,730 42
Total Assets....................	183,496 33	245,897 86	381,770 12	406,136 54
LIABILITIES AND RESERVES				
Liabilities				
Debenture Balance................	120,000 00	120,000 00	243,675 27	236,220 14
Accounts Payable.................	27,302 24	78,619 25	10,125 09	11,343 22
Bank Overdraft...................	10,665 48	....	....	....
Other Liabilities................	5,500 00	8,487 96	....	....
Total Liabilities................	163,467 72	207,107 21	253,800 36	247,563 36
Reserves				
Debentures Paid..................	....	....	56,474 73	63,929 86
Sinking Fund Reserve.............	4,364 80	7,795 08	....	....
Depreciation Reserve.............	7,500 00	13,750 00	34,803 24	49,441 49
Surplus..........................	8,163 81	17,245 57	36,691 79	45,201 83
Total Liabilities and Reserves....	183,496 33	245,897 86	381,770 12	406,136 54
Percentage of Net Debt to Total Assets	90.0	84.2	66.5	60.9

"A"—Continued

of Hydro Municipalities as at December 31st, 1915 and 1916

	St. Catharines 17,880		St. Thomas 17,174		Stratford 17,081		Guelph 16,735	
	1915	1916	1915	1916	1915	1916	1915	1916
	$ c.	$ c.	$ c.	$ c.	$ c.	$ c.	$ c.	$ c.
	1,492 42	1,492 42	12,351 59	29,463 54	23,597 29	23,977 25	19,400 41	19,547 56
	5,276 84	11,407 86	35,337 54	41,382 42	21,409 13	21,180 71	40,571 05	59,022 65
	68,349 25	99,137 55	67,507 25	69,620 45	85,523 21	90,347 88	56,657 84	48,565 40
	1,383 80	....	....	862 95	....	....	....	....
	9,245 24	26,101 39	13,373 59	13,984 50	14,726 43	15,357 80	9,966 00	12,687 97
	11,031 05	22,828 57	24,058 50	27,151 73	23,722 21	27,791 74	22,836 82	31,279 81
	6,501 94	7,625 55	12,030 48	12,234 32	5,971 43	5,980 95	25,553 60	25,350 34
	....	....	6,749 83	6,767 16	22,175 22	22,725 24	....	....
	19,896 25	22,773 94	6,423 66	7,023 16	7,848 12	7,848 12	6,777 76	6,919 76
	....	....	....	....	....	....	a36,301 89	a36,132 81
	75,554 13	41,351 25	4,289 96	2,795 84	11,187 00	10,927 00	....	....
	198,730 92	232,718 53	182,122 40	211,286 07	216,160 04	226,136 69	218,065 37	239,506 80
	25 00	10,513 39	22,597 51	32,627 98	408 17	8,244 03	17,752 16	11,793 31
	986 60	1,840 26	1,879 27	3,275 27	2,759 65	2,199 76	12,374 40	17,559 32
	2,821 50	2,752 90	10,960 39	9,086 15	13,178 01	479 93	7,646 42	7,655 01
	4,219 31	6,667 03	....	....	13,553 36	17,751 59	15,741 28	18,619 72
	....	....	86 25	138 57	3,243 74	....	....	....
	206,783 34	254,492 11	217,645 82	256,414 04	249,302 97	254,812 00	271,579 63	295,133 66
	116,000 00	207,022 83	109,146 67	120,810 52	161,710 00	142,000 00	125,355 51	123,201 16
	74,239 94	8,964 32	8,888 40	9,398 24	20,255 48	33.091 41	5,868 23	7,437 01
	1,288 82	....	....	....	7,319 21	....	....	....
	....	....	....	....	....	....	....	....
	191,528 76	215,987 15	118,035 07	130,208 76	189,284 69	175,091 41	131,223 74	130,638 17
	....	....	23,937 76	27,273 91	24,090 00	28,470 00	19,644 48	21,798 83
	4,219 31	6,667 03	....	....	13,553 36	17,751 59	15,741 28	18,619 72
	8,100 00	18,600 00	56,662 04	66,462 04	22,374 92	29,874 92	58,546 12	69,279 03
	2,935 27	13,287 93	19,010 95	32,469 33	....	3,624 08	46,424 01	54,797 91
	206,783 34	254,492 11	217,645 82	256,414 04	249,302 97	254,812 00	271,579 64	295,133 66
	92.6	84.8	54.2	50.7	75.9	69.1	48.3	44.2

"a" Motors rented to consumers.

STATEMENT

Comparative Condensed Balance Sheets of Electric Departments

Municipality Population	Port Arthur 14,307		Chatham 12,863	
—	1915	1916	1915	1916
ASSETS	$ c.	$ c.	$ c.	$ c.
Lands and Buildings	....	....	18,320 18	22,144 44
Sub-Station Equipment	1,056 49	....	6,055 12	13,856 63
Distribution System, Overhead....	201,080 80	....	45,955 34	50,362 48
" " Underground	....	....	....	....
Line Transformers..............	10,848 93	a	9,810 16	12,727 18
Meters.........................	42,714 41	....	9,522 19	15,561 50
Street Light Equipment, Regular.	27,000 00	....	6,282 21	7,517 98
" " Ornamental	....	....	20,208 57	26,907 19
Miscel. Equip. and Construct'n Exp.	8,803 41	....	13,627 39	14,154 87
Steam or Hydraulic Plant........	378,798 55	675,641 74	....	....
Old Plant......................	....	....	....	....
Total Plant...................	670,302 59	675,641 74	129,781 16	163,232 27
Bank and Cash Balance..........	13,363 06	6,834 64	691 84	25 00
Inventories.....................	240 22	12,194 06	7,307 45	21,712 28
Accounts Receivable.............	26,178 99	98,690 26	1,308 20	3,797 92
Sinking Fund...................	68,476 51	81,537 46	....	....
Other Assets...................	164 62	9,765 00	b 721 47	b 119 81
Total Assets...................	778,726 01	884,663 16	139,810 12	188,887 28
LIABILITIES AND RESERVES Liabilities				
Debenture Balance..............	568,758 70	559,403 71	88,861 60	87,654 90
Accounts Payable...............	....	34,170 24	26,147 08	62,712 49
Bank Overdraft.................	....	....	22,853 04	7,137 59
Other Liabilities................	10,031 67	70,412 25	810 00	29,037 20
Total Liabilities...............	578,790 37	663,986 20	138,671 72	186,542 18
Reserves				
Debentures Paid................	58,823 83	66,696 29	1,138 40	2,345 10
Sinking Fund Reserve...........	68,476 51	81,537 46	....	....
Depreciation Reserve............	....	12,283 82	....	....
Surplus........................	72,635 30	60,159 89	....	....
Total Liabilities and Reserves.	778,726 01	884,663 16	139,810 12	188,887 28
Percent'ge of Net Debt to Total Assets	....	....	....	98.8

"a" All plant included in total.
"b" Operating losses shown in italics.

" A "—Continued

of Hydro Municipalities as at December 31st, 1915 and 1916

Owen Sound 11,910	Galt 11,852		Sarnia 11,676	Niagara Falls 11,147	Brockville 9,428
1916	1915	1916	1916	1916	1916
$ c.	$ c.	$ c.	$ c.	$ c.	$ c.
24,446 80	12,201 05	12,286 30	96 06	14,183 10	27,079 01
9,626 38	22,082 47	26,104 06	5,900 11	22,165 31	....
46,266 12	105,277 47	115,954 39	33,562 61	51,385 71	37,671 14
....	....	....	....	....	....
11,001 65	17,795 56	19,488 11	10,253 97	28,952 40	10,258 61
20,853 60	28,938 43	31,975 55	1,446 43	30,107 74	12,778 36
6,788 66	8,484 27	8,501 57	2,281 53	9,542 43	11,448 52
500 00	50,697 06	50,703 11	410 06	16,000 00	....
1,202 04	11,192 06	12,104 91	557 39	1,943 49	3,763 23
33,282 00	....	....	169,063 55	....	51,948 00
....	....	....	....	7,772 00	....
153,967 25	256,668 37	277,118 00	223,571 71	182,052 18	154,946 87
16,883 65	....	....	45,784 84	50 00	200 00
4,845 02	1,591 89	3,138 81	31 29	....	3,484 08
2,062 43	....	....	....	7,386 00	34,707 55
58,733 81	20,459 43	26,666 56	....	....	20,778 13
139 40	....	....	....	973 41	1,367 94
236,631 56	278,719 69	306,923 37	269,387 84	190,461 59	215,484 57
141,000 00	165,999 55	178,902 34	244,737 85	98,809 07	153,375 35
4,830 18	....	....	10,462 15	1,522 41	1,672 48
....	39,483 55	40,001 97	....	9,704 36	11,024 49
....	....	....	....	923 17	....
145,830 18	205,483 10	218,904 31	255,200 00	110,959 01	166,072 32
....	20,459 43	26,666 56	3,262 15	43,948 98	3,977 99
58,733 81	35,500 00	44,000 00	....	....	20,778 13
3,307 80	17,277 16	17,352 50	....	7,945 00	7,000 00
28,759 77	....	....	10,925 69	27,608 65	17,656 13
236,631 56	278,719 69	306,923 37	269,387 84	190,461 59	215,484 57
61.6	73.7	71.3	94.6	58.2	77.2

STATEMENT

Comparative Condensed Balance Sheets of Electric Departments

Municipality	Woodstock		Welland	
Population	10,084		7,243	
—	1915	1916	1915	1916
	$ c.	$ c.	$ c.	$ c.
ASSETS				
Lands and Buildings	7,331 95	7,331 95	6,503 78	6,550 39
Sub-Station Equipment	27,685 13	27,685 13	15,846 88	16,185 58
Distribution System, Overhead	36,335 71	38,264 67	43,624 07	47,636 88
" " Underground				
Line Transformers	20,173 06	20,635 31	11,743 46	12,605 44
Meters	16,994 24	18,492 45	8,549 11	8,755 87
Street Light Equipment, Regular	10,328 77	10,450 67	2,269 59	2,305 19
" " Ornamental				
Miscel. Equip. and Construction Exp.			7,348 74	7,348 74
Steam or Hydraulic Plant	15,743 62	15,835 26		
Old Plant	15,835 26	15,743 62		
Total Plant	150,427 74	154,439 06	95,885 63	101,388 09
Bank and Cash Balance	13,953 07	1,796 60	1,803 40	3,630 67
Inventories	113 12	525 33		2,753 28
Accounts Receivable			16,936 34	33,899 06
Sinking Fund	36,347 74	40,296 29	3,566 00	5,170 70
Other Assets	1,500 00	23,000 00		
Total Assets	202,341 17	220,057 28	118,191 37	146,841 80
LIABILITIES AND RESERVES				
Liabilities				
Debenture Balance	107,385 63	107,385 63	90,000 00	90,000 00
Accounts Payable			16,322 18	32,852 15
Bank Overdraft				
Other Liabilities				
Total Liabilities	107,385 63	107,385 63	106,322 18	122,852 15
Reserves				
Debentures Paid			3,566 00	5,170 70
Sinking Fund Reserve	36,347 24	40,296 29		
Depreciation Reserve	22,483 98	29,414 18	4,425 00	8,425 00
Surplus	36,124 32	42,961 18	3,878 19	10,393 95
Total Liabilities and Reserves	202,341 17	220,057 28	118,191 37	146,841 80
Percentage of Net Debt to Total Assets	53.1	48.8	90.0	83.7

" A "—Continued

of Hydro Municipalities as at December 31st, 1915 and 1916

	Barrie 6,453		Collingwood 6,361		Midland 6,258		Ingersoll 5,176	
	1915	1916	1915	1916	1915	1916	1915	1916
	$ c.	$ c.	$ c.	$ c.	$ c.	$ c.	$ c.	$ c.
	12,034 61	12,034 61	4,343 60	4,343 60	4,780 69	4,780 69	3,057 57	3,057 57
	20,540 44	4,553 77	4,352 80	4,368 39	8,407 78	8,407 78	10,232 56	10,302 31
	19,824 30	21,641 41	25,104 34	26,364 70	31,627 90	34,013 89	31,051 22	31,785 67
	3,617 24	4,646 63	5,219 75	6,740 60	8,640 06	10,759 05	7,898 75	8,025 25
	15,208 25	15,487 93	9,648 56	11,098 00	11,236 62	12,188 33	10,542 34	11,538 95
	3,789 52	3,357 02	2,446 35	2,446 35	3,421 85	3,860 32	2,336 01	2,336 01
								4,597 59
	757 49	757 49	5,069 51	5,208 02	3,500 58	3,500 58	8,253 30	8,631 30
	31,062 48	46,491 57						
			4,415 17	3,519 17	7,057 84	7,057 84	22,334 21	22,334 21
	106,834 33	108,970 43	60,600 08	64,088 83	78,673 32	84,568 48	95,705 96	102,608 86
	2,923 18	9,125 32	2,643 45	9,575 32	10,455 21	12,833 55		4,008 65
	5,257 50	5,850 42	175 13	45.30	311 87	902 25	404 29	1,093 84
	5,072 17	4,835 56	7,412 52	7,369 37	4,373 10		7,757 02	6,326 75
							8,388 82	10,304 50
	120,087 18	128,781 73	70,831 18	81,078 82	93,813 50	98,304 28	112,256 09	124,342 60
	48,437 13	44,547 24	33,295 21	31,171 45	38,562 52	36,304 07	79,800 00	79,800 00
	1,434 21	1,659 72	2,689 50	3,404 50	800 00	1,300 00	1,824 74	1,837 50
							2,130 08	
								4,597 59
	49,871 34	46,206 96	35,984 71	34,575 95	39,362 52	37,604 07	83,754 82	86,235 09
	38,562 87	42,452 76	6,115 08	8,238 84	15,187 48	17,445 93		
							8,388 82	10,304 50
	10,350 00	12,925 00	7,390 00	9,540 00	12,400 00	15,500 00	9,230 00	11,880 00
	21,302 97	27,197 01	21,341 39	28,724 03	26,863 50	27,754 28	10,882 45	15,923 01
	120,087 18	128,781 73	70,831 18	81,078 82	93,813 50	98,304 28	112,256 09	124,342 60
	41.5	35.9	50.5	42.6	42.0	38.2	76.8	69.4

STATEMENT

Comparative Condensed Balance Sheets of Electric Departments

Municipality	Walkerville		Waterloo	
Population	5,096		4,956	
—	1915	1916	1915	1916
	$ c.	$ c.	$ c.	$ c.
ASSETS				
Lands and Buildings	16,837 66	16,917 78	4,740 85	5,142 20
Sub-Station Equipment	18,154 62	19,133 82	18,146 58	19,502 40
Distribution System, Overhead......	17,078 32	18,979 67	35,280 24	36,959 55
" " Underground..	....	....		
Line Transformers.................	14,002 76	14,182 87	8,992 44	9,240 38
Meters...........................	15,990 97	14,891 76	9,566 70	10,823 75
Street Light Equipment, Regular...	d	45,876 33	5,191 76	5,229 63
" " Ornamental.	d	....	....	....
Miscel. Equip. and Construction Exp.	15,403 42	16,272 91	1,266 56	2,933 16
Steam or Hydraulic Plant..........	....	18,556 21	2,483 64	2,483 64
Old Plant........................	39,753 34	18,509 77	9,666 15	9,666 15
Total Plant.....................	137,221 09	183,321 12	95,334 92	101,980 86
Bank and Cash Balance...........	590 60	50 00	37 27	....
Inventories......................	....	10,418 98	1,559 42	2,583 41
Accounts Receivable...............	7,717 87	14,880 78	5,206 24	3,401 83
Sinking Fund.....................	....	....	1,728 00	2,016 00
Other Assets.....................	....	....	....	2,137 05
Total Assets....................	145,529 56	208,670 88	103,865 85	112,119 15
LIABILITIES AND RESERVES				
Liabilities				
Debenture Balance.................	93,156 89	90,907 37	62,915 67	61,838 48
Accounts Payable..................	43,362 27	39,029 53	1,440 00	1,656 29
Bank Overdraft...................	....	4,639 37	....	2,144 89
Other Liabilities.................	266 78	m 50,639 41	....	....
Total Liabilities.................	136,785 94	185,215 68	64,355 67	65,639 66
Reserves				
Debentures Paid..................	3,102 11	5,351 63	3,084 33	4,161 52
Sinking Fund Reserve.............	....	....	1,728 00	2,016,00
Depreciation Reserve..............	....	3,773 06	15,450 00	19,150,00
Surplus..........................	5,641 51	14,330 51	19,247 85	21,151,97
Total Liabilities and Reserves....	145,529 56	208,670 88	103,865 85	112,119 15
Percentage of Net Debt to Total Assets	94.0	88.8	63.5	58.5

"A"—Continued

of Hydro Municipalities as at December 31st, 1915 and 1916

	Goderich 4,655		Dundas 4,652		Preston 4,643		Paris 4,370	
	1915	1916	1915	1916	1915	1916	1915	1916
	$ c.	$ c.	$ c.	$ c.	$ c.	$ c.	$ c.	$ c.
	12,915 81	12,915 81	2,803 50	8,227 20	....	....	7,626 26	7,626 26
	7,266 83	9,943 24	6,527 27	4,741 17	13,667 48	13,676 42	10,944 83	10,944 83
	24,131 48	28,440 55	38,889 98	39,519 25	36,090 52	39,573 54	30,608 45	31,517 91
	....	....	....	....	....	....	....	....
	6,587 57	6,581 72	7,851 91	9,556 93	12,800 35	13,501 69	4,491 51	5,258 11
	9,970 58	10.327 51	7,226 28	8,522 81	11,085 14	12,301 42	6,467 62	7,289 88
	4,495 29	4,915 52	1,708 67	1,740 34	2,561 53	2,743 78	2,114 05	2,114 05
	1,967 26	3,990 81	5,984 67	5,840 41	5,255 35	6,294 12	210 04	210 04
							15,000 00	
	9,230 65	8,231 05	2,110 38	1,960 38	23,549 22	23,549 22	19,275 66	19,271 46
	76,565 47	85,346 21	73,102 66	80,108 49	105,009 59	111,640 19	96,738 42	84,232 04
	161 43	8,053 02	....	....	....	....	....	....
	232 87	375 81	1,810 49	1,250 09	812 11	1,472 60	41 32	22,13
	7,375 10	2,929 34	....	2,834 68	5,139 61	4,603 14	....	75,12
	2,767 40	2,883 30	....	....	....	....	4,353 17	6,857 22
	....	....	....	....	....	183 80	....	....
	87,102 27	99,587 68	74,913 15	84,193 26	110,961 31	117,899 73	101,132 91	91,186 51
	52,925 75	51,233 87	50,905 67	50,039 67	67,984 96	64,769 69	62,588 88	55,049 42
	....	8,130 24	....	....	2,073 75	1,575 44	....	....
	....	....	11,155 46	13,764 99	8,735 25	13,813 32	160 70	2,219 66
	....	....	....	....	....	....	4,196 87	....
	52,925 75	59,364 11	62,061 13	63,804 66	78,793 96	80,158 45	66,946 45	57,269 08
	3,162 30	4,854 18	2,094 33	2,960 33	9,880 55	13,095 82	29,411 12	21,950 58
	2,767 40	2,883 30	....	....	....	....	4,353 17	6,857 22
	6,670 00	9,270 00	7,083 00	9,149 00	13,548 34	17,048 34	....	2,000 00
	21,576 82	23,216 09	3,674 69	8,279 27	8,738 46	7,597 12	422 17	3,109 63
	87,102 27	99,587 68	74,913 13	84,193 26	110,961 31	117,899 73	101,132 91	91,186 51
	60.7	59.6	82.3	75.8	71.0	68.0	66.3	62.8

STATEMENT

Comparative Condensed Balance Sheets of Electric Departments

	Wallaceburg		Simcoe	
Municipality	4,107		4,061	
Population				
—	1915	1916	1915	1916
ASSETS	$ c.	$ c.	$ c.	$ c.
Lands and Buildings	1,753 84	3,876 29	1,486 55	1,496 75
Sub-Station Equipment		760 50	3,668 01	5,851 99
Distribution System, Overhead......	10,401 94	18,935 55	17,194 16	17,330 44
" " Underground..	1,799 07	3,687 92	1,786 07	2,270 87
Line Transformers.................	2,931 10	6,574 53	1,117 47	1,534 55
Meters............................	70 55	1,568 81	1,478 85	1,478 85
Street Light Equipment, Regular...			1,181 83	1,181 83
" " Ornamental.	2,302 41	3,229 32	3,140 28	3,662 16
Miscel. Equip. and Construction Exp.				
Steam or Hydraulic Plant..........			931 92	927 92
Old Plant........................	26,017 56	23,884 42		
Total Plant....................	45,276 47	62 517 34	31,985 14	35,735 36
Bank and Cash Balance...........			4,636 00	5,222 56
Inventories.......................	784 15	3,515 34	395 45	86 00
Accounts Receivable...............	1,276 81	2,874 81	789 90	789 90
Sinking Fund.....................				
Other Assets.....................				
Total Assets....................	47,337 43	68,907 49	37,806 49	41,833 82
LIABILITIES AND RESERVES				
Liabilities				
Debenture Balance................	44,389 16	43,744 15	35,434 90	35,434 90
Accounts Payable.................	1,229 34	21,362 02	281 46	866 14
Bank Overdraft......	569 54	1,223 19		
Other Liabilities..................	450 00	100 00		3,500 00
Total Liabilities.................	46,638 04	66,429 36	35,716 36	39,801 04
Reserves				
Debentures Paid..................	610 84	1,255 85		
Sinking Fund Reserve.............				
Depreciation Reserve.............		1,038 00		1,350 00
Surplus..........................	88.55	184 28	2,090 13	682 78
Total Liabilities and Reserves....	47,337 43	68,907 49	37,806 49	41,833 82
Percentage of Net Debt to Total Assets	98.5	96.4	94.4	95.1

"A"—Continued

of Hydro Municipalities as at December 31st, 1915 and 1916

	Brampton 4,041		St. Mary's 3,960		Penetanguishene 3,928		Petrolia 3,891
	1915	1916	1915	1916	1915	1916	1916
	$ c.	$ c.	$ c.	$ c.	$ c.	$ c.	$ c.
	3,808 08	3,808 08	13,674 27	13,674 27	2,151 00	2,151 00	....
	5,200 25	8,995 62	13,002 74	11,837 64	3,507 71	3,507 71	2,360 59
	31,951 88	31,947 38	22,025 40	23,365 50	24,333 58	24,811 72	14,897 59
	....	....	....	....	....	....	....
	9,141 24	10,039 24	10,695 83	11,907 19	3,846 07	4,535 87	3,824 69
	9,403 89	9,651 13	12,709 33	13,311 59	5,191 76	5,408 94	4,143 66
	1,799 02	1,805 73	5,049 39	5,888 52	1,721 95	1,721 95	818 01
	....	....	....	....	....	....	3,864 07
	2,904 61	2,904 61	1,713 53	2,084 77	278 93	278 93	3,903 29
	....	....	....	....	....	....	....
	15,000 00	15,000 00	....	....	2,874 00	2,874 00	8,740 44
	79,208 97	84,151 79	78,870 49	82,069 48	43,905 00	45,290 12	42,552 34
	5,663 24	1,800 14	3,430 53	4,033 61	....	....	....
	129 84	360 33	1,207 66	1,598 94	513 50	533 09	1,746 96
	....	3,552 08	1,685 00	1,685 00	3,659 27	2,932 05	....
	....	....	1,594 91	2,140 51	....	....	....
	....	....	....	....	....	....	....
	85,002 05	89,864 34	86,788 59	91,527 54	48,077 77	48,755 26	44,299 30
	63,070 87	61,180 02	42,635 27	40,275 79	28,197 45	27,505 90	34,516 80
	....	....	5,980 63	7,526 39	....	....	7,573 21
	....	....	....	....	1,712 04	215 16	1,655 26
	....	....	....	....	....	300 00	....
	63,070 87	61,180 02	48,615 90	47,802 18	29,909 49	28,021 06	43,745 27
	5,979 77	7,870 62	20,611 75	22,971 23	2,802 55	3,494 10	483 20
	....	....	1,594 91	2,140 51	....	....	....
	11,200 00	14,200 00	6,940 00	9,840 00	7,445 00	9,225 00	....
	4,751 41	6,613 70	9,026 03	8,773 62	7,920 73	8,015 10	70 83
	85,002 05	89,864 34	86,788 59	91,527 54	48,077 77	48,755 26	44,299 30
	74.2	68.1	56.0	52.2	62.2	57.5	98.8

STATEMENT

Comparative Condensed Balance Sheets of Electric Departments

Municipality	Tillsonburg		Strathroy	
Population	3,084		2,998	
—	1915	1916	1915	1916
ASSETS	$ c.	$ c.	$ c.	$ c.
Lands and Buildings	1,974 27	1,974 27	1,070 00	1,070 00
Sub-Station Equipment	6,818 47	6,818 47	4,175 40	4,691 16
Distribution System, Overhead.....	18,252 15	19,135 69	15,841 42	16,649 55
" " Underground..	....	....	....	....
Line Transformers.................	4,041 90	3,408 92	3,211 14	3,460 85
Meters..........................	4,638 91	5,016 13	3,534 75	4,731 00
Street Light Equipment, Regular...	1,762 50	1,762 50	1,463 28	1,499 14
" " Ornamental.	....	....	....	....
Miscel. Equip. and Construction Exp.	918 83	918 83	555 15	578 15
Steam or Hydraulic Plant..........	....	....	....	....
Old Plant........................	....	....	12,824 13	12,343 15
Total Plant.....................	38,407 03	39,034 81	42,675.27	45,023 00
Bank and Cash Balance...........	3,804 89	5,587 50	3,496 96	3,602 89
Inventories.......................	1,271 84	3,104 63	152 66	4,523 64
Accounts Receivable...............	3,331 74	1,584 87	....	....
Sinking Fund.....................	880 26	1,337 49	....	....
Other Assets.....................	....	....	....	....
Total Assets....................	47,695 76	50,649 30	46,324 89	53,149 53
LIABILITIES AND RESERVES				
Liabilities				
Debenture Balance.................	33,605 10	32,895 86	15,486 92	44,698 73
Accounts Payable..................	700 00	727 12	26,941 40	536 95
Bank Overdraft....................	....	....	....	....
Other Liabilities..................	....	....	....	....
Total Liabilities.................	34,305 10	33,622 98	42,428 32	45,235 68
Reserves				
Debentures Paid...................	2,394 90	3,104 14	745 08	1,533 27
Sinking Fund Reserve.............	880 26	1,337 49	....	....
Depreciation Reserve..............	6,311 50	7,911 50	1,500 00	2,550 00
Surplus..........................	3,804 00	4,673 19	1,651 49	3,830 58
Total Liabilities and Reserves....	47,695 76	50,649 30	46,324 89	53,149 53
Percentage of Net Debt to Total Assets	71.9	66.4	91.6	84.7

"A"—Continued

of Hydro Municipalities as at December 31st, 1915 and 1916

	Hespeler 2,740		Prescott 2,740		Orange-ville 2,493	Listowel 2,326	Ridge-town 2,329	Elmira 2,270	
	1915	1916	1915	1916	1916	1916	1916	1915	1916
	$ c.	$ c.	$ c.	$ c.	$ c.	$ c.	$ c.	$ c.	$ c.
	3,499 23	3,499 23	2,753 04	2,761 54	100 00	....	....	....	....
	8,471 64	8,502 78	....	....	....	....	889 26	....	....
	6,686 61	7,171 70	23,886 23	24,405 64	13,330 35	3,582 31	8,780 65	9,009 28	9,747 18
	4,880 87	4,886 87	5,028 61	5,468 06	707 67	2,123 63	1,789 62	2,317 42	2,396 92
	4,175 69	4,583 14	7,354 45	7,523 11	919 46	2,698 72	1,949 33	2,550 46	2,686 73
	815 07	1,009 68	1,288 30	1,316 52	784 65	1,686 20	823 17	578 29	607 84
	93 08	93 08	1,118 53	1,127 53	431 39	897 33	1,030 89	2,076 74	2,076 74
	....	....	12,108 35	12,108 35	....	20,261 59	373 35	....	....
	3,000 00	3,000 00	....	....	11,849 50	....	8,066 14	2,296 27	2,295 52
	31,622 19	32,746 48	53,537 51	54,710 75	28,123 02	31,249 78	23,702 41	18,828 46	19,810 93
	2,522 35	3,835 89	....	296 25	....	1,695 16	3,064 20	5,000 25	6,196 10
	....	....	....	....	974 16	2,501 94	989 55	96 03	123 28
	184 33	246 68	441 53	588 72	730 53	1,108 05	341 00	139 85	61 32
	....	....	460 00	617 92	....	....	....	....	....
	b 1108 06	....	....	....	....	4,925 89	....	....	....
	35,436 93	36,829 05	54,439 04	56,213 64	29,827 71	41,480 82	28,097 16	24,064 59	26,191 63
	26,720 76	24,909 72	22,548 34	21,862 15	28,286 12	34,178 52	18,759 89	19,494 04	19,241 06
	141 42	838 19	350 00	....	1,296 91	442 68	....	....	....
	....	....	115 78	....	....	....	1,225 12	....	....
	....	....	....	....	....	1,348 66	1,319 10	....	....
	26,862 18	25,747 91	23,014 12	21,862 15	29,583 03	35,969 86	21,304 11	19,494 04	19,241 06
	5,849 75	7,660 79	1,431 00	2,117 19	....	1,411 37	696 10	505 96	758 94
	....	....	460 00	617 92	....	....	....	....	....
	2,725 00	3,403 56	1,950 00	5,830 00	....	....	425 00	1,400 00	2,020 00
	....	16 79	27,583 92	25,786 38	244 68	4,099 59	5,671 95	2,664 59	4,171 63
	35,436 93	36,829 05	54,439 04	56,213 64	29,827 71	41,480 82	28,097 16	24,064 59	26,191 63
	75.7	69.9	42.3	38.9	99.2	86.7	75.8	81.0	73.4

STATEMENT

Comparative Condensed Balance Sheets of Electric Departments

Municipality	Clinton		Weston		Milton	
Population	2,177		2,156		2,072	
—	1915	1916	1915	1916	1915	1916
ASSETS	$ c.	$ c.	$ c.	$ c.	$ c.	$ c.
Lands and Buildings			3,230 94	3,230 94		
Sub-Station Equipment ..	7,738 47	7,738 47	4,985 23	5,450 72	5,550 19	5,550 19
Dist. System, Overhead...	10,391 70	10,719 10	11,875 08	13,525 06	10,354 52	10,354 52
" Underground..						
Line Transformers......	2,139 79	2,496 79	4,871 82	5,680 72	1,881 05	1,966 05
Meters.................	2,683 27	2,865 04	3,848 68	4,260 69	3,126 86	3,282 59
Street Light Equip.Regular	206 41	206 41	1,914 16	1,936 66	935 43	935 43
" Ornamental.						
Miscel. Equip. and Con.Exp.	3,310 45	3,310 45	2,831 67	2,833 77	2,486 23	2,486 23
Steam or Hydraulic Plant						
Old Plant..............	13,456 00	12,085 32			4,344 48	4,065 85
Total Plant...........	39,926 09	39,421 58	33,557 58	36,918 56	28,678 76	28,640 86
Bank and Cash Balance..	392 93	1,329 56		878 60	1,171 63	3,553 37
Inventories.............	736 86	1,697 68	117 23	72 89	1,882 83	2,468 43
Accounts Receivable......	71 67	71 67	1,344 16	4,689 88	2,737·21	3,924 16
Sinking Fund...........	1,584 80	2,557 29	2,096 65			
Other Assets...........						
Total Assets..........	42,712 35	45,077 78	37,175 62	42,559 93	34,470 43	38,586 82
LIABILITIES AND RESERVES						
Liabilities						
Debenture Balance......	40,500 00	40,500 00	17,234 76	16,492 60	21,274 54	19,982 95
Accounts Payable.......	247 35		1,449 79	3,181 50		
Bank Overdraft.........						
Other Liabilities........			1,350 57			300 00
Total Liabilities.......	40,747 35	40,500 00	20,035 12	19,674 10	21,274 54	20,282 95
Reserves						
Debentures Paid........			2,733 12	3,475,28	3,438 44	4,730 03
Sinking Fund Reserve...	1,584 80	2,557 29				
Depreciation Reserve.....	380 20	1,200 00	5,620 00	7,220 00	3,240 00	4,140 00
Surplus................		820 49	8,787 38	12,190 55	6,517 45	9,433 84
Total Liabilities and Reserves....	42,712 35	45,077 78	37,175 62	42,559 93	34,470 43	38,586 82
Percentage of Net Debt to Total Assets	95.4	89.9	53.9	46.2	61.7	52.5

"A"—Continued

of Hydro Municipalities as at December 31st, 1915 and 1916

Mimico 1,976		Chesley 1,975	Seaforth 1,964		Mount Forest 1941	Georgetown 1,905	
1915	1916	1916	1915	1916	1916	1915	1916
$ c.	$ c.	$ c.	$ c.	$ c.	$ c.	$ c.	$ c.
98 30	98 30	....	1,203 25	1,204 53	3,725 00	12 00	12 00
....	....	585 17	6,031 75	6,031 75	686 75	....	....
16,958 20	18,953 45	13,872 32	14,700 33	14,987 19	13,817 62	13,646 65	15,996 12
1,592 62	2,210 37	1,312 85	3,212 30	4,086 58	1,926 64	5,233 91	6,471 35
4,953 01	5,935 62	1,864 28	3,642 67	3,992 92	2,307 58	3,564 24	4,104 95
1,022 20	1,022 20	816 26	797 34	805 25	1,655 77	956 14	956 14
1,355 99	1,308 49	2,612 12	355.98	355 98	876 07	1,184 25	1,193 20
....	....	5,509 60	....	....	4,059 92	2,209 80	2,209 80
25,980 32	29,528 43	26,572 60	29,943 62	31,464 20	29,055 85	26,806 99	30,943 56
459 59	1,207 29	....	628 68	1,396 83	1,335 00	994 45	1,049 53
133 03	20 00	350 00	2,686 32	2,744 57	509 42	608 73	824 87
531 59	656 29	780 57	130 57	132 95	669 83	457 38	432 92
....	....	....	1,892 86	2,414 32	....	....	....
....	....	....	....	....	....	....	....
27,104 53	31,412 01	27,703 17	35,282 05	38,152 87	31,569 60	28,867 55	33,250 88
16,858 35	18,368 36	21,854 71	25,000 00	25,000 00	17,576 36	19,478 86	19,194 59
3,458 89	3,608 40	4,429 51	....	....	7,307 02	306 80	....
....	....	179 96	....	....	....	....	....
....	....	....	....	....	....	....	....
20,317 24	21,976 76	26,464 18	25,000 00	25,000 00	24,883 38	19,785 66	19,194 59
1,141 65	1,631 64	645 29	....	....	4,423 64	512 14	805 41
....	....	....	1,892 86	2,414 32	....	....	....
2,860 00	3,860,00	....	4,150 00	5,375 00	615 00	2,430 00	3,640.00
2,785 64	3,943,61	593 70	4,239 19	5,363 55	1,647 58	6,130 75	9,610.88
27,104 53	31,412 01	27,703 17	35,282 05	38,152 87	31,569 60	28,867 55	33,250 88
74.9	70.0	95.5	70.8	65.5	78.5	68.5	57.7

STATEMENT

Comparative Condensed Balance Sheets of Electric Departments

Municipality	Palmerston	Fergus		Tilbury	
Population	1,843	1,776		1,740	
—	1916	1915	1916	1915	1916
ASSETS	$ c.	$ c.	$ c.	$ c.	$ c.
Lands and Buildings					`957 46
Sub-Station Equipment	691 88				
Distribution System, Overhead	5,611 28	8,144 42	8,988 86	5,268 42	5,303 84
" " Underground					
Line Transformers	1,620 66	2,074 38	2,434 47	1,057 60	1,177 10
Meters	1,435 43	2,109 83	2,515 02	1,563 05	1,735 21
Street Light Equipment, Regular	489 49	826 27	826 27	176 35	194 49
" " Ornamental					
Miscel. Equip. and Construction Exp.	672 47	543 57	562 37	893 10	1,159 48
Steam or Hydraulic Plant	12,429 55				
Old Plant		2,546 59	2,440 33	4,244 20	3,644 20
Total Plant	22,950 76	16,245 06	17,767 32	13,202 72	14,171 78
Bank and Cash Balance				218 47	509 19
Inventories	1,985 05	2,750 83	2,546 59	129 87	40 91
Accounts Receivable	5,741 25		313 03	2,065 75	4 17
Sinking Fund					
Other Assets					
Total Assets	30,677 06	18,995 89	20,626 99	15,616 81	14,726 05
LIABILITIES AND RESERVES					
Liabilities					
Debenture Balance	14,736 87	15,779 11	15,546 07	9,873 52	13,739 44
Accounts Payable	5,225 48		357 50	5,350 46	
Bank Overdraft	207 71	1,483 32	8 31		
Other Liabilities					
Total Liabilities	20,170 06	17,262 43	15,911 88	15,223 98	13,739 44
Reserves					
Debentures Paid	7,263 13	220 89	453 93	126 48	260 56
Sinking Fund Reserve					
Depreciation Reserve	295 00	650 00	1,150 00		275 00
Surplus	2,948 87	862 57	3,111 18	266 35	451 05
Total Liabilities and Reserves	30,677 06	18,995 89	20,626 99	15,616 81	14,726 05
Percentage of Net Debt to Total Assets	65.8	90.8	77.1	97.6	93.3

" A "—Continued

of Hydro Municipalities as at December 31st, 1915 and 1916

Acton 1,735		Gravenhurst 1,702	Mitchell 1,687		Durham 1,600	Exeter 1,572
1915	1916	1916	1915	1916	1916	1916
$ c.	$ c.	$ c.	$ c.	$ c.	$ c.	$ c.
1,500 00	,1,500 00	12,258 29	4,550 44	4,796 10	....	....
597 62	597 62	11,074 20	9,034 86	9,034 86	584 88	....
4,839 74	5,142 52	25,870 73	7,631 03	8,119 67	11,917 19	11,693 79
....	....	....	....	....	....	....
1,696 50	2,164 50	578 25	1,113 82	1,113 82	971 92	1,494 04
2,109 15	2,391 48	3,632 16	2,564 87	2,827 43	1,059 18	2,276 12
896 21	896 21	....	978 00	1,063 55	699 56	721 38
....	....	....	....	....	....	....
777 99	777 99	1,542 00	....	....	547 24	1,451 48
....	....	....	1,500 00	1,500 00	....	....
3,510 85	3,510 85	....	....	....	2,800 00	....
15,928 06	16,981 17	54,955 63	27,373 02	28,455 43	18,079 97	17,636 81
2,200 50	2,726 25	590 79	1,354 31	....	213 04	....
276 03	· 654 33	1,173 19	800 00	945 38	....	546 70
....	....	2,374 24	˙337 97	2,385 79	....	457 20
4,156 00	4,358 00	·· 2,569 73	....	....	....	....
....	....	81,952 92	....	....	b 103 41	....
22,560 59	24,719 75	143,616 50	29,865 30	31,786 60	18,396 42	18,640 71
13,973 03	13,689 62	95,853 05	8,816 25	˙9,919 45	12,646 61	17,240 08
322 00	322 00	379 73	993 33	450 00	5,396 42	378 87
....	....	....	....	986 85	....	65 92
....	....	25,093 20	....	....	....	....
14,295 03	14,011 62	121,325 98	9,809 58	11,356 30	˙18,043 03	17,684 87
526 97	810 38	17,596 21	6,036 53	˙7,375 77	353 39	419 05
4,156 00	4,358 00	2,337 94	....	....	....	....
1,500 00	2,000 00	1,650 00	4,377 21	5,377 21	....	....
2,082 59	3,539 75	706 37	9,641 98	7,677 32	....	536 79
22,560 59	24,719 75	143,616 50	29,865 30	31,786 60	18,396 42	18,640 71
63.4	56.6	84.5	82.8	35.7	....	95.4

" b "   Operating losses shown in italics.

STATEMENT

Comparative Condensed Balance Sheets of Electric Departments

Municipality Population	New Hamburg 1,548		Dresden 1,521		Victoria Harbor 1,477
—	1915	1916	1915	1916	1915
ASSETS	$ c.	$ c.	$ c.	$ c.	$ c.
Lands and Buildings	2,257 59	2,257 59	....	....	....
Sub-Station Equipment	1,083 10	1,083 10	523 00	523 00	....
Distribution System, Overhead.....	8,114 35	8,281 57	5,999 51	6,011 99	134 49
" " Underground..	....	....	....	....	....
Line Transformers................	2,664 75	2,664 75	1,418 21	1,418 21	....
Meters..........................	3,127 07	3,257 25	2,605 72	2,743 76	265 85
Street Light Equipment, Regular...	1,149 43	1,149 43	715 38	715 38	....
" " Ornamental.	....	....	....	....	....
Miscel. Equip. and Construction Exp.	958 48	958 48	398 43	404 24	21 34
Steam or Hydraulic Plant.........	....	....	....	....	....
Old Plant.......................	5,242 56	5,242 56	6,026 59	5,766 54	4,800 00
Total Plant..................	24,597 33	24,894 73	17,686 84	17,583 12	5,221 68
Bank and Cash Balance...........	202 24	789 57	644 67	814 27	1,680 05
Inventories......................	4,511 38	4,246 78	542 22	610 46	....
Accounts Receivable..............	1,083 13	646 13	....	....	....
Sinking Fund....................	....	....	....	....	....
Other Assets....................	....	....	....	....	....
Total Assets..................	30,394 08	30,577 21	18,873 73	19,007 85	6,901 73
LIABILITIES AND RESERVES Liabilities					
Debenture Balance...............	16,509 00	16,163 22	15,950 94	15,340 47	6,500 00
Accounts Payable.................	1,217 86	242 67	2,503 99	2,433 84	211 83
Bank Overdraft....................	....	....	....	....	....
Other Liabilities.................	....	....	....	....	45 97
Total Liabilities...............	17,726 86	16,405 89	18,454 93	17,774 31	6,757 80
Reserves					
Debentures Paid...:..............	1,220 08	1,565 86	287 31	897 78	....
Sinking Fund Reserve.............	....	....	....	....	....
Depreciation Reserve..............	3,845 00	4,675 00	....	314 74	....
Surplus.........................	7,602 14	7,930 46	131 49	21 02	143 93
Total Liabilities and Reserves....	30,394 08	30,577 21	18,873 73	19,007 85	6,901 73
Percentage of Net Debt to Total Assets	58.1	53.7	98.0	92.0	97.9

"A"—Continued

of Hydro Municipalities as at December 31st, 1915 and 1916

Victoria Harbor 1,477	Blenheim 1,424	Harriston 1,404	Pt. Dalhousie 1,318		Caledonia 1,217		Norwich 1,189	
1916	1916	1916	1915	1916	1915	1916	1915	1916
$ c.	$ c.	$ c.	$ c.	$ c.	$ c.	$ c.	$ c.	$ c.
....	909 64	600 00	....	....	....	....	910 40	910 40
4,727 86	9,543 23	6,948 25	3,273 52	3,658 63	4,651 20	4,881 97	6,504 04	6,708 36
600 00	1,330 76	1,740 00	1,792 00	2,541 43	391 65	565 65	1,149 41	1,541 12
1,154 47	2,085 93	1,915 66	2,124 13	3,647 85	761 27	947 44	2,293 66	2,476 93
127 81	823 67	350 00	268 67	268 67	349 62	441 49	546 06	546 06
....	1,475 64	....	....	....	....	....	....	1,811 96
642 64	568 06	413 73	1,081 66	1,093 66	473 20	473 20	963 17	969 34
....	....	2,062 15	6,325 50	6,325 50	....	....	3,509 82	3,509 82
7,252,78	16,736 93	14,029 79	14,865 48	17,535 74	6,626 94	7,309 75	15,876 56	18,473 99
208 74	836 08	122 98	....	50 03	217 29	419 20	2,261 99	494 65
....	....	671 00	385 50	89 76	....	....	2,038 83	1,903 54
....	151 78	966 00	· 712 08	181 21	....	....	672 30	1,755 04
....	....	b 23 35	....	....	....	....	455 90	....
7,461 52	17,724 79	15,818 12	15,963 06	17,856 74	6,844 23	7,728 95	21,805 58	22,627 22
6,313 59	13,822 92	12,846 89	12,500 00	12,121 97	4,539 72	4,450 40	12,963 89	12,717 24
....	1,737 78	2,155 09	1,953 12	1,913 12	50 05	90 05	901 19	1,333 64
....	....	....	42 20	2,060 00	....	....	....	....
6,313 59	15,560 70	15,001 98	14,495 32	16,095 09	4,589 77	4,540 45	13,865 08	14,050 88
186 41	177 08	· 471 14	....	378 03	84 28	173 60	792 11	1,038 76
190 00	440 00	345 00	1,279 02	1,279 02	810 00	1,070 00	2,225 00	3,595 00
771 52	1,547 01	....	188 72	104 60	1,360 18	1,944 90	4,423 39	3,942 58
7,461 52	17,724 79	15,818 12	15,963 06	17,856 74	6,844 23	7,728 95	21,805 58	22,627 22
84.6	87.9	94.8	90.8	90.1	67.6	58.8	65.1	62.1

STATEMENT

Comparative Condensed Balance Sheets of Electric Departments

Municipality	New Toronto		Waterford		Shelburne
Population	1,186		1,134		1,115
—	1915	1916	1915	1916	1916
ASSETS:	$ c.	$ c.	$ c.	$ c.	$ c.
Lands and Buildings					
Sub-Station Equipment					566 60
Distribution System, Overhead......	6,541 85	11,167 80	783 65	2,116 17	9,137 23
" " Underground..					
Line Transformers.................	1,474 23	2,964 38	....	914 36	399 01
Meters............................	1,502 25	2,319 68	73 80	1,331 10	391 75
Street Light Equipment, Regular...	271 18	310 30	....	81 26	921 65
" " Ornamental.					
Miscel. Equip. and Construction Exp.	1,200 37	1,200 37	156 11	352 77	2,102 07
Steam or Hydraulic Plant..........					
Old Plant.........................			6,789 32	5,151 53	3,779 40
Total Plant..................	10,989 88	17,962 53	7,802 88	9,947 19	17,297 71
Bank and Cash Balance............	....	1,717 13	81 60	277 97	2,346 82
Inventories.......................	124 77	124 77			12 20
Accounts Receivable..............	223 08	97 92	205 79	205 79	....
Sinking Fund.....................					
Other Assets.....................					
Total Assets..................	11,337 73	19,902 35	8,090 27	10,430 95	19,656 73
LIABILITIES AND RESERVES					
Liabilities					
Debenture Balance.................	7,753 14	7,620 39	6,803 44	5,811 26	14,468 79
Accounts Payable.................	1,371 76	6,218 49	217 90	2,325 82	4,180 99
Bank Overdraft...................	119 59				
Other Liabilities.................			40 58	97 98	....
Total Liabilities.................	9,244 49	13,838 88	7,061 92	8,235 06	18,649 78
Reserves					
Debentures Paid..................	246 86	379 61	942 09	1,934 27	451 21
Sinking Fund Reserve.............					
Depreciation Reserve..............	750 00	1,200 00			
Surplus..........................	1,096 38	4,483 86	86 26	261 62	555 74
Total Liabilities and Reserves....	11,337 73	19,902 35	8,090 27	10,430 95	19,656 73
Percentage of Net Debt to Total Assets	81.5	69.6	83.5	79.0	94.9

"A"—Continued

of Hydro Municipalities as at December 31st, 1915 and 1916

	Elora 1,115			Hagersville 1,105		Winchester 1,065		Port Credit 944	
	1914	1915	1916	1915	1916	1915	1916	1915	1916
	$ c.	$ c.	$ c.	$ c.	$ c.	$ c.	$ c.	$ c.	$ c.
	....	....	....	....	....	224 15	224 15	675 00	675 00
	6,138 53	7,189 83	7,539 37	6,493 43	6,678 90	7,225 62	7,319 95	7,613 47	8,313 48
	803 21	1,250 05	1,791 53	1,078 27	1,203 27	481 86	665 86	722 48	812 48
	1,068 18	1,391 03	1,564 27	1,865 83	2,021 32	1,014 44	1,241 04	1,826 78	1,851 63
	438 33	438 33	438 33	415 55	435 35	564 98	564 98	294 99	324 63
	839 00	908 18	926 18	101 80	101 80	264 14	275 54	614 26	626 31
	2,100 00	1,482 85	1,408 35	....	....	1,100 00	1,100 00	....	....
	11,387 25	12,661 27	13,668 03	9,954 88	10,440 64	10,875 19	11,391 52	11,746 98	12,603 53
	10 34	30 21	642 51	1,066 60	2,829 55	1,621 20	1,236 43	986 91	645 28
	342 12	576 62	1,034 54	165 71	67 77	881 74	1,476 81	....	....
	....	....	42 21	....	....	....	....	180 00	180 00
	11,739 71	13,268 10	15,387 29	11,187 19	13,337 96	13,378 13	14,104 76	12,913 89	13,428 81
	9,790 48	9,570 48	12,839 48	7,754 37	7,591 30	10,515 30	10,372 52	7,013 89	7,876 16
	1,709 52	2,639 52	584 52	....	....	200 00	....	1,495 16	226 02
	11,500 00	12,210 00	12,874 00	7,754 37	7,591 30	10,715 30	10,372 52	8,508 55	8,102 18
	209 52	429 52	660 52	245 63	408 70	134 70	277 48	486 61	623 84
	....	460 00	835 00	925 00	1,305 00	965 00	1,335 00	1,581 00	2,051 00
	30 19	168 58	1,017 77	2,262 19	4,032 96	1,563 13	2,119 76	2,337 73	2,651 79
	11,739 71	13,268 10	15,387 29	11,187 19	13,337 96	13,378 13	14,104 76	12,913 89	13,428 81
	97.1	92.0	83.7	69.0	56.9	80.1	73.5	66.0	60.3

STATEMENT

Comparative Condensed Balance Sheets of Electric Departments

Municipality	Beaverton		Markdale	Stayner	
Population	1,015		989	972	
—	1915	1916	1916	1915	1916
ASSETS	$ c.	$ c.	$ c.	$ c.	$ c.
Lands and Buildings	250 00	250 00	....	....	....
Sub-Station Equipment ...	....	....	780 80	200 00	200 00
Dist. System, Overhead....	5,912 64	5,901 74	5,983 31	3,467 35	7,530 29
" " Underground.	....	....	....	....	....
Line Transformers	470 75	470 75	378 50	959 03	1,350 14
Meters	1,720 22	1,836 96	841 94	875 08	1,224 79
Street Light Equip., Regular	453 44	453 44	522 62	386 31	478 16
" " " Ornamental	....	....	....	....	....
Miscel. Equip. and Con. Exp.	1,141 32	1,141 32	549 06	128 40	287 77
Steam or Hydraulic Plant.	....	....	....	....	....
Old Plant	3,787 92	3,787 92	2,080 65	4,490 15	4,213 01
Total Plant	13,736 29	13,842 13	11,136 88	10,506 32	15,284 16
Bank and Cash Balance ...	865 12	441 27	72 44	641 00	861 70
Inventories	403 42	213 40	2,230 68	66 44	51 19
Accounts Receivable	....	....	....	....	416 47
Sinking Fund	....	....	....	....	....
Other Assets	....	....	....	....	....
Total Assets	15,004 83	14,496 80	13,440 00	11,213 76	16,613 52
LIABILITIES AND RESERVES					
Liabilities					
Debenture Balance	9,691 45	9,525 51	8,886 16	8,221 10	12,929 70
Accounts Payable	5,004 83	4,496 80	3,236 98	1,072 16	1,009 66
Bank Overdraft	....	....	....	....	....
Other Liabilities	....	....	....	....	....
Total Liabilities	14,696 28	14,022 31	12,123 14	9,293 26	13,939 36
Reserves					
Debentures Paid	308 55	474 49	113 84	778 90	1,070 30
Sinking Fund Reserve	....	....	....	....	....
Depreciation Reserve	....	....	....	415 00	695 00
Surplus	....	....	1,203 02	726 60	908 86
Total Liabilities and Reserves	15,004 83	14,496 80	13,440 00	11,213 76	16,613 52
Percentage of Net Debt to Total Assets		100.0	90.2	82.7	83.9

"A"—Continued

of Hydro Municipalities as at December 31st, 1915 and 1916

Cannington 903		Milverton 893	Dutton 870		Port Stanley 849		Chesterville 854	
1915	1916	1916	1915	1916	1915	1916	1915	1916
$ c.	$ c.	$ c.	$ c.	$ c.	$ c.	$ c.	$ c.	$ c.
....	....	206 00	....	....	1,505 37	1,505 38	....	....
6,112 21	6,227 12	5,266 42	5,086 66	5,124 93	9,322 94	9,509 81	5,058 44	4,958 20
930 38	1,017 63	783 10	617 24	778 24	1,495 56	1,495 56	401 48	1,002 48
1,533 22	1,797 14	773 09	1,377 84	1,599 88	1,960 26	1,960 26	977 19	1,082 96
492 98	533 48	505 36	441 01	441 01	570 60	570 60	306 46	506 46
367 58	367 58	161 84	258 88	256 99	5,517 16	5,517 16	552 68	552 68
3,699 37	3,609 37	....	....	....	1,000 00	975 00	....	....
13,135 74	13,552 32	7,695 81	7,781 63	8,201 05	21,371 90	21,533 77	7,296 25	7,902 78
1,034 58	355 01	102 54	427 02	1,766 37	4,495 30	5,551 04	383 85	100 25
649 78	668 00	141 30	394 74	79 50	....	....	578 75	671 31
170 62	247 40	2,000 00	....	....	....	....	....	128 97
....	....	....	....	....	....	....	b *54 47*	....
14,990 72	14,822 83	9,939 65	8,603 39	10,046 92	25,867 20	27,084 81	8,313 32	8,803 31
11,834 35	11,659 58	9,227 50	8,407 49	8,407 49	17,487 16	17,128 79	4,858 20	4,781 40
2,991 72	2,822 73	405 93	....	....	20 00	30 00	2,807 38	2,382 49
....	....	....	....	....	....	....	....	334 94
....	....	....	....	....	....	....	258 44	120 00
14,826 07	14,482 31	9,633 43	8,407 49	8,407 49	17,507 16	17,158 79	7,924 02	7,618 83
165 65	340 42	272 50	....	....	1,462 84	1,821 21	141 80	.218 60
....	....	....	....	240 00	3,078 08	3,743 08	247 50	622 50
....	....	83 72	195 90	1,399 43	3,819 12	4,361 73	....	343 38
14,990 72	14,822 73	9,939 65	8,603 39	10,046 92	25,867 20	27,084 81	8,313 32	8,803 31
	100.0	.96.9	97.7	83.6	67.7	63.4	95.4	86.5

"b" Operating loss shown in italics.

STATEMENT

Comparative Condensed Balance Sheets of Electric Departments

Municipality Population	Ayr 800		Waterdown 785		Thamesville 769	
—	1915	1916	1915	1916	1915	1916
ASSETS	$ c.	$ c.	$ c.	$ c.	$ c.	$ c.
Lands and Buildings	125 00	125 00	....	....	....	....
Sub-Station Equipment	....	....	....	....	....	....
Dist System, Overhead.....	2,934 89	2,985 40	7,024 71	7,083 27	3,418 12	3,600 40
" Underground.	....	....	••••••••	••••••••	....	....
Line Transformers.........	694 05	983 09	1,663 58	1,751 00	879 01	977 26
Meters....................	814 67	979 60	1,319 36	1,624 23	800 96	1,318 49
Street Light Equip., Regular	360 27	360 27	156 65	156 65	305 70	318 10
" " Ornamental	....	....	....	....	....	....
Miscel. Equip. and Con. Exp.	785 49	785 49	100 34	100 34	392 35	561 75
Steam or Hydraulic Plant...	....	....	....	....	....	....
Old Plant..................	3,959 68	6,635 73	....	....	4,893 80	4,703 40
Total Plant..............	9,674 05	12 854 58	10,264 64	10,715 49	10,689 44	11 479 40
Bank and Cash Balance.....	....	....	1,273 49	1,767 75	....	689 33
Inventories................	115 24	58 84	4 44	....	....	240 00
Accounts Receivable........	91 50	91 00	••••••••	....	917 65	988 96
Sinking Fund..............	....	.. ....	....	••••••••	....	....
Other Assets..............	....	....	....	••••••••	....	....
Total Assets.............	9,880 79	13,004 42	11,542 57	12,483 24	11,607 09	13 397 69
LIABILITIES AND RESERVES						
Liabilities						
Debenture Balance..........	9,346 58	11,067 91	7,430 16	7,038 74	4,937 80	10,930 33
Accounts Payable...........	133 70	....	....	....	1,463 42	1,081 64
Bank Overdraft............	27 81	55 70	....	....	4,985 59	....
Other Liabilities...........	....	....	....	....	....	....
Total Liabilities.........	9,508 09	11,123 61	7,430 16	7,038 24	11,386 81	12,011 97
Reserves						
Debentures Paid............	....	993.67	569 84	961 26	....	257 47
Sinking Fund Reserve......	....	....	....	....	....	....
Depreciation Reserve........	250 00	510 00	1,785 00	2,672 00	....	190 00
Surplus....................	122 70	377 14	1,757 57	1,811 24	220 28	938 25
Total Liabilities and Reserves....	9,880 79	13,004 42	11,542 57	12,483 24	11,607 09	13,397 69
Percentage of Net Debt to Total Assets	96.2	85.6	64.4	56.4	96.0	89.5

"A"—Continued

of Hydro Municipalities as at December 31st, 1915 and 1916

Bolton 727		Dundalk 721	Bothwell 707		Lucan 662		Woodbridge 639	
1915	1916	1916	1915	1916	1915	1916	1915	1916
$ c.	$ c.	$ c.	$ c.	$ c.	$ c.	$ c.	$ c.	$ c.
6,442 50	7,220 79	5,008 22	3,153 38	3,069 94	5,327 10	5,749 94	5,278 03	5,924 17
998 38	2,039 11	551 73	432 00	499 55	811 56	1,442 57	1,667 57	1,945 29
875 60	967 72	479 20	879 40	969 30	1,191 31	1,431 76	787 58	1,008 59
561 14	561 14	510 82	316 75	326 10	372 54	372 54	314 81	319 61
681 75	811 17	228 69	297 15	392 94	369 01	373 49	471 26	515 86
2,236 60	1,582 85	937 90	534 19	172 82	3,204 10	2,860 45	....	....
11,795 97	13,182 77	7,716 56	5,612 87	5,430 65	11,275 62	12,230 75	8,519 25	9,713 52
167 06	76 71	288 61	266 82	247 86	414 07	47 62	752 97	744 66
248 90	364 76	36 76	....	....	799 05	731 09	15 93	....
73 75	148 75	....	155 00	585 75	....	....	118 91	91 41
....	....	....	....	....	b *21 08*	....	....	....
12,285 68	13,772 99	8,041 93	6,034 69	6,264 26	12,509 82	13,009 46	9,407 06	10,549 59
9,357 01	9,206 88	5,879 12	534 19	5,345 15	11,213 62	10,766 47	8,499 97	8,382 63
2,694 24	2,730 35	827 21	508 79	....	1,296 20	1,205 09	....	369 88
....	....	....	4,832 16	....	....	....	....	....
12,051 25	11,937 23	6,706 33	5,875 14	5,345 15	12,509 82	11,971 56	8,499 97	8,752 51
142 99	293 12	457 78	....	189 04	....	447 15	....	117 34
....	321.00	200 00	....	135 00	....	270 00	425 00	725 00
91 44	1,221.64	677 82	159 55	595 07	....	320 75	482 09	954 74
12,285 68	13,772 99	8,041 93	6,034 69	6,264 26	12,509 82	13,009 46	9,407 06	10,549 59
98.0	86.7	83.4	97.0	85.3	100.0	92.1	89.0	82.9

"b" Operating loss shown in italics.

STATEMENT

Comparative Condensed Balance Sheets of Electric Departments

Municipality Population	Ailsa Craig 586	Creemore 585		Coldwater 579		Wyoming 544
—	1916	1915	1916	1915	1916	1916
ASSETS	$ c.	$ c.	$ c.	$ c.	$ c.	$ c.
Lands and Buildings	....	....	....	275 00	275 00	....
Sub-Station Equipment						
Dist System, Overhead.....	4,406 27	4,150 11	4,181 44	5,278 18	5,295 16	5,105 92
" " Underground.	....					
Line Transformers	657 46	681 39	681 39	1,010 77	1,010 77	471 17
Meters	547 49	738 56	844 47	1,114 04	1,193 44	607 77
Street Light Equip., Regular	362 97	272 07	272 07	354 20	354 20	342 72
" " " Ornamental	....					
Miscel. Equip. and Con. Exp.	229 97	185 41	185 41	132 53	132 53	544 50
Steam or Hydraulic Plant.	....					
Old Plant	....	2,651 15	2,651 15	....	....	....
Total Plant	6,204 16	8,678 69	8,815 93	8,164 72	8,261 10	7,072 08
Bank and Cash Balance ...	534 57	326 56	739 69	117 78	1,177 47	305 89
Inventories	162 44	214 94	210 22	724 86	538 71	....
Accounts Receivable	....	73 31	74 65	354 25	....	128 00
Sinking Fund	....	....	....	....	....	....
Other Assets	....	....	....	....	....	....
Total Assets	6,901 17	9,293 50	9,840 49	9,361 61	9,977 28	7,505 97
LIABILITIES AND RESERVES						
Liabilities						
Debenture Balance	6,426 65	6,323 31	6,136 01	6,801 40	6,693 83	6,313 77
Accounts Payable	140 79	2,655 76	2,637 36	90 00	90 00	915 11
Bank Overdraft	....	....	....	....	....	....
Other Liabilities	....	....	....	....	....	....
Total Liabilities	6,567.44	8,979 07	8,773 37	6,891 40	6,783 83	7,228 88
Reserves						
Debentures Paid	....	176 69	363 99	198 60	306 17	186 23
Sinking Fund Reserve ...	....	....	....	....	....	....
Depreciation Reserve	180 00	....	200 00	1,135 00	1,460 00	....
Surplus	153 73	137 74	503 13	1,136 61	1,427 28	90 86
Total Liabilities and Reserves	6,901 17	9,293 50	9,840 49	9,361 61	9,977 28	7,505 97
Percentage of Net Debt to Total Assets	95.2	91.5	89.2	73.6	68.9	96.4

" A "—Continued

of Hydro Municipalities as at December 31st, 1915 and 1916

Embro 483		Flesherton 428	Woodville 388		Chatsworth 374	Baden k	
1915	1916	1916	1915	1916	1916	1915	1916
$ c.	$ c.	$ c.	$ c.	$ c.	$ c.	$ c.	$ c.
....	....	....	....	....	65 00	660 64	660 64
5,298 84	5,415 37	3,910 09	1,397 49	1,597 02	3,502 90	3,869 75	3,997 98
480 79	657 79	206 83	550 50	700 96	546 92	1,035 14	1,285 14
811 24	902 16	482 48	543 43	765 20	418 03	786 78	877 53
209 29	209 29	384 61	91 57	95 67	207 29	370 02	370 02
249 84	249 84	814 11	88 96	88 96	283 12	....	....
426 25	426 25	....	2,250 00	2,250 00	....	....	....
7,476 25	7,860 70	5,798 12	4,921 95	5,497 81	5,023 26	6,722 33	7,191 31
223 80	489 68	1,705 24	....	149 35	....	1,984 76	2,128 12
....	....	433 80	648 75	315 16	....	....	....
....	57 96	54 23	....	35 65	150 00	....	....
....	....	....	....	....	175 00	....	....
7.700 05	8,408 34	7,991 39	5,570 70	5,997 97	5,348 26	8,707 09	9,319 43
....	....	5,417 22	3,944 36	3,885 65	4,000 00	4,672 31	4,581 66
....	7,520 95	2,097 41	1,527 79	1,997 97	892 33	740 69	586 67
7,399 78	....	....	42 91	....	200 57	....	....
4 95	....	....	....	....	....	....	2 79
7,404 73	7,520 95	7,514 63	5,515 06	5,883 62	5,092 90	5,413 00	5,171 12
....	94 82	82 78	55 64	114 35	....	327 69	418 34
....	....	....	....	....	175 00	....	....
250 00	485 00	150 00	....	....	....	857 00	1,132 00
45 32	307 57	243 98	....	....	80 36	2,109 40	2,597 97
7,700 05	8,408 34	7,991 39	5,570 70	5,997 97	5,348 26	8,707 09	9,319 43
96.0	89.4	94.1	....	98.0	95.2	62.2	55.7

"k" Population figures not published by the Department of Agriculture.

STATEMENT

Comparative Condensed Balance Sheets of Electric Departments

Municipality / Population	Bréchin k		Beachville k		Burford k	
—	1915	1916	1915	1916	1915	1916
ASSETS	$ c.	$ c.	$ c.	$ c.	$ c.	$ c.
Lands and Buildings	....	....	161 03	161 03	202 00	202 00
Sub-Station Equipment ...						
Dist System, Overhead....	1,330 29	1,330 29	6,376 73	6,310 36	3,119 31	3,470 99
" " Underground.						
Line Transformers	366 43	366 43	810 45	1,736 69	868 50	983 23
Meters	315 62	315 62	807 66	873 72	401 42	879 88
Street Light Equip., Regular	69 89	69 89	237 03	237 03	147 40	147 40
" " " Ornamental						
Miscel. Equip. and Con. Exp.	215 77	215 77	540 36	540 36	654 70	659 20
Steam or Hydraulic Plant.						
Old Plant						
Total Plant	2,298 00	2,298 00	8,933 26	9,859 19	5,393 33	6,342 70
Bank and Cash Balance ...	296 45	693 89	764 67	360 90	....	248 36
Inventories	....	....	250 00	42 24	....	....
Accounts Receivable	9 75	45 91	580 00	1,176 02	....	....
Sinking Fund						
Other Assets	....	....	....	....	b 46.63	....
Total Assets	2,604 20	3,037 80	10,527 93	11,438 35	5,439 96	6,591 06
LIABILITIES AND RESERVES Liabilities						
Debenture Balance	1,750 00	1,713 66	5,013 93	4,904 99	4,848 79	4,690 01
Accounts Payable	1,854 20	1,287 80	77 97	679 50	280 46	1,300 45
Bank Overdraft	....	....	....	....	104 60	....
Other Liabilities	....	....	....	....	54 90	....
Total Liabilities	2,604 20	3,001 46	5,091 70	5,584 49	5,288 75	5,990 46
Reserves						
Debentures Paid	....	36 34	346 07	455 01	151 21	309 99
Sinking Fund Reserve ...	....	....	....	....	....	....
Depreciation Reserve	....	....	1,345 00	1,720 00	....	165 00
Surplus	....	....	3,744 96	3,678 85	....	125 61
Total Liabilities and Reserves	2,604 20	3,037 80	10,527 93	11,438 35	5,439 96	6,591 06
Percentage of Net Debt to Total Assets	....	....	49.1	40.1	97.4	90.9

" b " Operating loss shown in italics.

"A"—Continued

of Hydro Municipalities as at December 31st, 1915 and 1916

Comber k		Drumbo k		Delaware k		Dorchester 'k		Elmvale k	
1915	1916	1915	1916	1915	1916	1915	1916	1915	1916
$ c.	$ c.	$ c.	$ c.	$ c.	$ c.	$ c.	$ c.	$ c.	$ c.
....	....	....	....	....	....	....	....	106 25	106 25
3,328 22	3,622 99	60 58	2,582 58	2,020 90	2,101 21	2,531 45	2,889 39	5,687 64	5,799 59
420 25	420 25	....	316 55	216 75	216 75	694 32	694 32	755 41	755 41
487 13	631 13	18 60	614 51	316 06	316 06	641 79	659 71	1,003 45	1,050 50
199 55	199 55	....	129 89	89 76	106 93	183 13	212 34	317 98	317 98
929 11	929 11	....	201 16	227 81	227 81	267 41	326 54	455 93	455 93
....	....	3,675 29	....	....	....	....	....	....	....
5,364 26	5,803 03	3,754 47	3,844 69	2,871 28	2,968 76	4,318 00	4,782 30	8,326 66	8,485 66
24 73	114 66	819 43	926 68	1,235 11	262 71	-443 20	206 94	....	154 40
....	....	6 35	63 41	....	985 64	....	430 10	,251 86	548 55
....	....	....	....	....	....	....	....	95 11	140 11
5,388 99	5,917 69	4,580 25	4,834 78	4,106 39	4,217 11	4,761 30	5,419 34	8,673 63	9,328 72
4,363 91	4,221 02	4,432 27	4,361 15	4,000 00	3,989 79	4,300 00	4,235 28	6,667 85	6,545 88
831 71	1,217 33	....	42 77	....	42 29	....	....	169 22	150 00
....	....	....	....	....	....	....	....	192 46	....
48 47	....	....	....	24 00	24 00	....	....	....	....
5,244 09	5,438 35	4,432 27	4,403 92	4,024 00	4,006 08	4,300 00	4,235 28	7,029 53	6,695 88
136 09	278 98	67 73	138 89	....	60 21	....	64 72	332 15	454 12
....	145 00	....	,110 00	....	80 00	200 00	350 00	735 00	1,025 00
8 81	55 36	80 25	182 01	82 39	70 82	261 30	769 34	576 95	1,153 72
5,388 99	5,917 69	4,580 25	4,834 78	4,106 39	4,217 11	4,761 30	5,419 34	8,673 63	9,328 72
97.6	91.9	96.8	91.1	98.0	95.0	89.5	78.1	81.0	71.8

STATEMENT

Comparative Condensed Balance Sheets of Electric Departments

Municipality Population	Granton k	Grantham Township	Holstein k	Lambeth k	
—	1916	1916	1916	1915	1916
ASSETS	$ c.	$ c.	$ c.	$ c.	$ c.
Lands and Buildings	....	....	....	....	
Sub-Station Equipment					
Distribution System, Overhead	2,671 73	2,190 60	1,649 25	2,503 51	2,606,19
" " Underground..	....	....	....	621 01	621 01
Line Transformers	221 22	1,005 62	305 33	621 01	621 01
Meters	445 47	626 06	192 42	639 78	639 78
Street Light Equipment, Regular ...	149 27	....	141 25	134 37	169 37
" " Ornamental	....	....	....	....	....
Miscel. Equip. and Construction Exp.	110 28	78 19	164 71	312 68	204 73
Steam or Hydraulic Plant	....	....	....	....	....
Old Plant	....	....	....	....	....
Total Plant	3,597 97	3,900 47	2,452 96	4,211 35	4,241 08
Bank and Cash Balance	262 28	3,195 78	142 49	1,184 06	107 07
Inventories			83 71	....	
Accounts Receivable	....		51 16	102 03	63.10
Sinking Fund	....	279 12			
Other Assets	....	b 1,581 49	b 57 73	b 218 54	....
Total Assets	3,860 25	8,956 86	2,788 05	5,715 98	4,411 25
LIABILITIES AND RESERVES Liabilities					
Debenture Balance	3,455 73	7,500 00	2,676 01	....	3,939 79
Accounts Payable	254 27	1,177,74	26 00	5,715 98	98 47
Bank Overdraft	....	....	....	....	....
Other Liabilities	....	....	....	....	....
Total Liabilities	3,710 00	8,677 74	2,702 01	5,715 98	4,038 26
Reserves					
Debentures Paid	44 27	279 12	86 04	....	60 21
Sinking Fund Reserve	....	....	....	....	
Depreciation Reserve	....	....	....	....	100 00
Surplus	105 98	....	....	....	212 78
Total Liabilities and Reserves ...	3,860 25	8,956 86	2,788 05	5,715 98	4,411 25
Percentage of Net Debt to Total Assets	96.1	....	100.0	100.0	91.5

" b " Operating loss shown in italics.

" A "—Continued

of Hydro Municipalities as at December 31st, 19[5 and 1916

	Lynden k		Mount Brydges k		Plattsville k		Otterville k	Princeton k	
	1915	1916	1915	1916	1915	1916	1916	1915	1916
	$ c.	$ c.	$ c.	$ c.	$ c.	$ c.	$ c.	$ c.	$ c.
	100 00	241 18	....	....	....	....	....	....	....
	2,297 50	2,489 73	2,646 79	2,650 77	2,478 44	2,482 86	2,546 60	1,671 68	1,910 44
	336 18	942 37	609 50	673 25	662 94	1,270 58	479 75	297 70	680 74
	344 06	424 91	668 71	691 83	862 36	891 11	473 40	342 96	479 00
	137 90	137 90	120 09	120 09	133 65	133 65	193 37	116 30	116 30
	144 37	200 32	143 82	143 82	504 42	504 42	142 00	27 85	32 85
	3,360 01	4,436 41	4,188 91	4,279 76	4,641 81	5,282 62	3,835 12	2,456 49	3,219 33
	1,934 64	213 24	1 19	743 06	367 22	221 66	163 69	1,163 08	908 69
	....	....	20 05	20 00	12 96	11 24	59 50	....	....
	67 50	304 57	171 09	52 88	372 60	713 27	516 30	....	5 72
	....	....	b *129 13*	....	....	....	....	....	b *18 33*
	5,362 15	4,954 22	4,510 37	5,095 70	5,394 59	6,228 79	4,574 61	3,619 57	4,152 07
	4,495 00	4,432 95	4,161 73	4,100 27	5,158 18	5,075 41	4,377 67	3,496 57	3,440 46
	766 66	220 00	290 37	672 69	19 14	217 19	60 00	....	506 07
	....	....	....	....	....	....	....	....	....
	5,261 66	4,652 95	4,452 10	4,772 96	5,177 32	5,292 60	4,437 67	3,496 57	3,946 53
	....	62 05	58 27	119 73	78 82	161 59	122 33	53 48	109 54
	....	120 00	....	125 00	....	145 00	....	....	96 00
	100 49	119 22	....	78 01	138 45	629 60	14 61	69 57	....
	5,362 15	4,954 22	4,510 37	5,095 70	5,394 59	6,228 79	4,574 61	3,619 57	4,152 07
	98.1	93.9	98.5	93.7	96.1	85.0	97.0	96.5	....

" b "   Operating loss shown in italics.

STATEMENT

Comparative Condensed Balance Sheets of Electric Departments

Municipality Population	Pt. McNicoll k		Rockwood k		Sunderland k	
—	1915	1916	1915	1916	1915	1916
ASSETS	$ c.	$ c.	$ c.	$ c.	$ c.	$ c.
Lands and Buildings	202 60	202 60	79 00	79 00	....	....
Sub-Station Equipment						
Distribution System, Overhead	3,156 54	3,259 63	3,866 93	4,150 53	2,731 81	2,826 66
" " Underground..	....	....	....	....	....	....
Line Transformers	250 35	305 60	972 93	1,211 93	470 00	731 75
Meters	593 61	714 81	781 60	979 45	639 40	788 68
Street Light Equipment, Regular ...	103 40	103 40	254 58	257 50	190 82	190 82
" " Ornamental	....	....	....	....	....	....
Miscel. Equip. and Construction Exp.	396 44	396 44	277 01	308 05	147 22	147 22
Steam or Hydraulic Plant	....	....	....	....	....	....
Old Plant ..../.	....	....	....	....	2,030 00	2,030 00
Total Plant	4,502 94	4,982 48	6,232 05	6,986 46	6,209 25	6,715 13
Bank and Cash Balance	127 27	....				
Inventories	59 86	57 86	80 56	73 45	148 27	94 93
Accounts Receivable	129 12	....	....	....	607 85	720 44
Sinking Fund	....	....	....	....	....	....
Other Assets	....	b 271 26	....	....	....	....
Total Assets	4,819 19	5,311 60	6,312 61	7,059 91	6,965 37	7,530 50
LIABILITIES AND RESERVES Liabilities						
Debenture Balance	4,769 07	4,377 67	1,427 82	1,217 71	5,635 45	5,546 32
Accounts Payable	....	56 29	....	....	320 00	....
Bank Overdraft	....	625 31	2,118 28	1,796 60	845 37	1,730 50
Other Liabilities	....	....	....	....	....	....
Total Liabilities	4,769 07	5,059 27	3,546 10	3,014 31	6,800 82	7,276 82
Reserves						
Debentures Paid	....	122 83	572 18	782 29	164 55	253 68
Sinking Fund Reserve	....	....	....	....	....	....
Depreciation Reserve	....	130 00	575 00	815 00	....	....
Surplus	50 12	....	1,618 33	2,448 31	....	....
Total Liabilities and Reserves ...	4,819 19	5,311 60	6,312 61	7,059 91	6,965 37	7,530 50
Percentage of Net Debt to Total Assets	99.0	....	56.2	42.7	100	....

"k" Population, under 500.
"b" Operating loss shown in italics.

"A"—Continued

of Hydro Municipalities as at December 31st, 1915 and 1916

St. George k		Stamford Tp.	Thorndale k		Thamesford k		Toronto Township	
1915	1916	1916	1915	1916	1915	1916	1915	1916
$ c.	$ c.	$ c.	$ c.	$ c.	$ c.	$ c.	$ c.	$ c.
2,759 81	2,838 77	....	1,863 71	1,893 29	2,955 44	3,490 27	1,555 50	7,204 65
851 31	851 31	....	381 71	381 71	937 05	953 88	214 91	5,309 85
739 43	868 73	....	466 53	534 23	918 91	1,017 56	355 15	2,908 68
218 11	218 11	....	59 40	59 40	176 85	176 85	....	....
374 18	374 18	....	273 95	273 95	260 05	158 25	....	258 16
....	....	29,671 12	....	....	....	....	....	....
4,942 84	5,151 10	29,671 12	3,045 30	3,142 58	5,248 30	5,796 81	2,125 66	15,681 34
593 44	1,959 09	....	61 50	77 73	246 10	186 96	1,910 90	2,828 86
87 69	22 61	....	13 76	45 39	....	20 00	....	....
814 32	....	1,070 48	294 00	131 00	....	113 01	914 56	914 56
....	....	....	....	....	....	....	....	....
6,438 29	7,132 80	30,741 60	3,414 56	3,396 70	5,494 40	6,116 78	4,951 02	19,424 76
5,917 17	5,829 78	....	2,500 00	2,462 37	2,975 73	2,923 08	....	11,673 78
229 55	330 33	29,381 21	222 30	688 68	1,281 81	1,686 75	1,314 54	1,349 56
....	....	....	....	....	7 62	....	....	....
6,146 72	6,160 11	29,381 21	2,722 30	3,151 05	4,265 16	4,609 83	1,314 54	13,023 34
82 83	170 22	....	....	37 63	82 27	134 92	....	326 22
....	150 00	....	265 00	100 66	500 00	735 00	1,800 00	3,734 00
208 74	652 47	1,360 39	427 26	107 36	646 97	637 03	1,836 48	2,341 20
6,438 29	7,132 80	30,741 60	3,414 56	3,396 70	5,494 40	6,116 78	4,951 02	19,424 76
95.6	86.3	....	79.8	92.8	77.6	75.3	26.6	67.1

"k" Population, under 500.

STATEMENT "A"—Concluded.

Comparative Condensed Balance Sheets of Electric Departments of Hydro Municipalities as at December 31st, 1915 and 1916

Municipality Population	Williamsburg k		Waubaushene k	
—	1915	1916	1915	1916
ASSETS	$ c.	$ c.	$ c.	$ c.
Lands and Buildings				
Sub-Station Equipment				
Distribution System, Overhead	1,478 83	1,478 83	2,637 80	2,755 95
" " Underground..				
Line Transformers	297 89	297 89	239 66	239 66
Meters	427 57	427 57	532 86	664 13
Street Light Equipment, Regular ...	66 16	66 16	142 22	142 22
" " Ornamental				
Miscel. Equip. and Construction Exp.	4 00	4 00	257 66	257 66
Steam or Hydraulic Plant				
Old Plant				
Total Plant	2,274 45	2,274 45	3,810 20	4,059 62
Bank and Cash Balance	636 27	827 76	365 41	3 00
Inventories	168 91	121 70	62 23	3 28
Accounts Receivable			99 64	387 90
Sinking Fund				
Other Assets				
Total Assets	3,079 63	3,223 91	4,337 48	4,453 80
LIABILITIES AND RESERVES Liabilities				
Debenture Balance	2,666 83	2,579 50		3,891 26
Accounts Payable	52 39	41 75	4,164 57	49 00
Bank Overdraft	220 67			
Other Liabilities				
Total Liabilities	2,939 89	2,621 25	4,164 57	3,940 26
Reserves				
Debentures Paid	83 17	170 50		108 74
Sinking Fund Reserve				
Depreciation Reserve		70 00		115 00
Surplus	56 57	362 16	172 91	289 80
Total Liabilities and Reserves ...	3,079 63	3,223 91	4,337 48	4,453 80
Percentage of Net Debt to Total Assets	95.5	81.3	96.0	86.5

CONDENSED
REVENUE AND EXPENSE

OR

OPERATING REPORT

FOR

1 9 1 6

STATE

Report Showing Operation of Municipalities

Municipality	Months Covered by Report	Population	Plant Cost	Debenture Debt and Overdraft	Operation and Maintenance	Fixed Charges	Total Operation
			$ c.	$ c.	$ c.	$ c.	$ c.
Toronto......	12	463,705	7,501,186 77	6,097,731 80	1,063,778 95	400,434 57	1,464,213 52
Hamilton	12	100,461	1,084,192 15	825,104 45	197,843 10	61,266 73	259,109 83
Ottawa......	12	100,163	913,252 04	498,125 63	141,041 02	42,371 44	183,412 46
London	12	58,055	825,359 68	499,771 80	230,230 75	40,099 60	270,330 35
Brantford	12	25,420	274,678 49	218,469 56	46,734 70	17,221 00	63,955 70
Windsor.....	12	24,162	438,380 97	416,545 31	76,682 19	17,258 16	93,940 35
Peterborough.	12	20,426	228,661 07	189,870 42	79,050 39	11,981 33	91,031 72
Kitchener ...	12	19,266	365,755 80	207,182 62	80,063 85	18,474 43	98,538 28
St. Catharines	12	17,880	232,718 53	194,213 57	45,479 47	12,411 67	57,891 14
St. Thomas..	12	17,174	211,286 07	85,080 79	64,559 75	8,314 07	72,873 82
Stratford	12	17,081	226,136 69	146,416 10	48,533 08	14,794 02	63,327 10
Guelph	12	16,785	239,506 80	75,010 81	62,184 49	10,273 28	72,457 77
Port Arthur .	12	14,307	675,641 74	388,735 82	80,232 38	47,428 64	127,661 02
Chatham.....	12	12,863	163,232 27	161,006 98	25,457 35	8,855 45	34,312 80
Owen Sound .	12	11,910	153,967 25	63,165 87	41,889 31	11,281 56	53,170 87
Galt.........	12	11,852	277,118 00	189,098 94	55,209 42	15,303 85	70,513 27
Sarnia.......	6	11,676	223,571 71	209,383 87	14,954 32	7,738 92	22,693 24
Niagara Falls	12	11,147	182,052 18	102,549 60	34,161 50	9,078 40	43,239 90
Woodstock ...	12	10,084	154,489 06	41,767 41	36,312 92	7,241 71	43,554 63
Brockville ...	12	9,428	154,946 87	105,534 62	34,907 77	15,535 74	50,443 51
Welland	12	7,243	101,388 09	77,398 44	72,489 20	8,199 77	80,688 97
Barrie.......	12	6,453	108,970 43	26,395 66	20,687 73	6,052 29	26,740 02
Collingwood..	12	6,361	64,088 83	17,585 96	28,701 65	3,393 33	32,094 98
Midland	12	6,258	84,568 48	23,868 27	16,812 34	3,955 47	20,767 81
Ingersoll.....	12	5,176	102,608 86	64,501 35	25,594 07	4,905 00	30,499 07
Walkerville..	12	5,096	183,321 12	159,865 92	91,766 04	11,092 60	102,858 64
Waterloo	12	4,956	101,980 86	55,501 87	25,664 44	3,475 25	29,139 69
Goderich	12	4,655	85,346 21	45,122 64	13,593 88	5,302 27	18,896 15
Dundas	12	4,652	80,108 49	59,719 89	13,103 58	5,565 39	18,668 97
Preston	12	4,643	111,640 19	73,898 91	26,900 28	7,258 79	34,159 07
Paris........	12	4,370	84,232 04	50,314 61	11,881 72	6,665 00	18,546 72
Wallaceburg .	12	4,107	62,517 34	60,039 21	13,811 43	3,701 50	17,512 93
Simcoe	12	4,061	35,735 36	33,702 58	4,819 71	1,948 91	6,768 62
Brampton	12	4,041	84,151 79	55,467 47	18,526 63	4,739 19	23,265 82
St. Marys ...	12	3,958	82,069 48	38,344 12	14,585 97	4,775 42	19,361 39
Penetang	12	3,928	45,290 12	24,555 92	14,859 07	2,050 40	16,909 47
Petrolea	7	3,891	42,552 34	41,998 31	4,508 25	1,486 24	5,994 49
Tillsonburg...	12	3,084	39,034 81	22,008 49	11,762 50	2,594 83	14,357 33
Strathroy....	12	2,998	45,023 00	37,109 15	9,669 81	2,188 26	11,857 57
Hespeler	12	2,740	32,746 48	21,665 34	13,039 83	3,144 84	16,183 67
Prescott.....	12	2,740	54,710 75	20,359 26	10,492 35	1,983 39	12,475 74
Orangeville ..	5	2,493	28,123 02	27,878 34	2,233 77	610 88	2,844 65
Listowel.....	12	2,326	31,249 78	24,390 16	7,126 50	2,928 48	10,054 98
Ridgetown ..	12	2,326	23,702 41	16,909 86	5,303 48	1,840 86	7,144 34
Elmira	12	2,270	19,810 93	12,860 36	4,765 69	1,377 58	6,143 27
Clinton	12	2,177	39,421 58	34,843 80	5,918 41	3,089 21	9,007 62
Weston., ...	12.	2,156	36,918 56	14,032 73	8,740 21	2,096 09	10,836 30
Milton.......	13	2,072	28,640 86	10,336 99	11,420 84	2,178 67	13,599 51
Mimico	12	1,976	29,528 43	20,093 18	6,267 82	2,580 10	8,847 92
Chesley......	4	1,975	26,572 60	25,333 61	1,512 63	482 05	1,994 68
Seaforth.....	12	1,964	31,464 20	18,311 33	13,583 03	1,695 75	15,279 7 8
Mount Forest	12	1,941	29,055 35	22,369 13	4,904 35	1,622 33	6,526 68
Georgetown..	12	1,905	30,943 56	16,887 27	11,442 26	1,963 05	13,405 31
Palmerston ..	12	1,843	22,950 76	12,443 76	3,768 63	1,840 00	5,608 68
Fergus	12	1,776	17,767 32	13,052 21	4,320 60	1,148 74	5,469 34

MENT "B"

for Period ending December 31st, 1916

Revenue	Surplus	Depreciation	Surplus less Depreciation	Domestic	Com'l	Power	Total	PerCent of Consumers to Population	H. P. taken in Dec. 1916
$ c.	$ c.	$ c.	$ c.						
1,690,998 42	226,784 90	208,388 09	18,396 81	34,347	7,406	1,707	43,460	† 9.4	47,165
343,330 63	84,220 80	32,110 54	52,110 26	12,423	1,546	464	14,433	† 14.4	10,482
219,480 40	86,067 94	32,775 00	3,292 94	7,912	1,107	188	9,207	† 9.2	5,484
340,791 79	70,461 44	29,060 62	41,400 82	8,282	1,129	295	9,706	† 16.7	9,256
80,042 51	16,086 81	7,500 00	8,586 81	2,056	334	26	2,416	† 9.5	2,393
99,802 51	5,862 16	5,157 50	704 66	3,180	439	66	3,685	† 14.9	1,696
107,279 07	16,247 35	6,250 00	9,997 35	3,401	602	117	4,120	20.2	3,794
121,686 57	23,148 29	14,638 25	8,510 04	2,407	543	147	3,097	16.1	3,702
78,814 24	20,923 10	10,500 00	10,423 10	2,410	247	48	2,705	† 15.1	3,020
98,159 08	25,285 26	9,800 00	15,485 26	2,241	464	107	2,812	16.4	2,121
74,931 86	11,604 76	7,500 00	4,104 76	1,993	463	103	2,559	14.9	1,655
91,531 67	19,073 90	10,700 00	8,373 90	2,033	490	86	2,609	15.6	3,003
170,982 98	43,321 96	....	43,321 96	2,701	481	46	3,228	22.6	2,355
34,914 46	601 66	....	601 66	1,171	215	25	1,411	† 11.0	660
61,201 13	8,030 26	3,307 80	4,722 46	1,376	435	83	1,894	15.9	812
79,088 61	8,575 34	8,500 00	75 34	2,236	386	79	2,701	22.8	2,673
83,618 93	10,925 69	....	10,925 69	1,888	418	54	2,360	20.2	......
57,465 87	14,225 97	8,315 00	5,910 97	2,050	400	80	2,530	22.7	2,543
56,627 61	13,072 98	6,930 20	6,142 78	1,224	372	72	1,668	16.5	1,185
59,719 76	9,276 25	7,000 00	2,276 25	965	312	31	1,308	13.9	303
93,646 11	12,957 14	4,000 00	8,957 14	536	75	24	635	† 8.8	5,963
35,021 86	8,281 84	2,575 00	5,706 84	896	257	18	1,171	16.6	591
41,627 62	9,532 64	2,150 00	7,382 64	714	242	33	989	15.5	1,064
27,477 04	6,709 23	3,100 00	3,609 23	732	184	31	947	15.1	824
38,189 63	7,690 56	2,650 00	5,040 56	590	206	51	847	16.4	882
112,465 90	9,607 26	3,773 06	5,834 20	1,513	216	75	1,804	*	1,765
34,743 81	5,604 12	3,700 00	1,904 12	592	150	50	792	16.0	874
23,135 42	4,239 27	2,600 00	1,639 27	511	159	9	679	14.6	221
26,103 55	7,434 58	2,830 00	4,604 58	673	168	35	876	† 18.8	612
37,790 20	3,631 13	3,500 00	131 13	785	182	34	1,001	21.6	1,249
23,234 18	4,687 46	2,000 00	2,687 46	552	150	4	706	16.2	413
18,645 63	1,132 70	1,038 00	94 70	484	154	5	593	14.4	312
8,165 21	1,396 59	1,350 00	46 59	57	84	12	153	3.8	113
28,128 11	4,862 29	3,000 00	1,862 29	722	175	24	921	22.8	815
22,838 66	3,477 27	2,900 00	577 27	563	161	28	752	18.8	489
18,783 84	1,874 37	1,780 00	94 37	189	95	16	300	7.7	460
6,065 32	70 83	....	70 83	257	155	14	426	10.9	224
17,227 88	2,870 55	1,600 00	1,270 55	375	158	17	550	17.8	249
15,086 66	3,229 09	1,050 00	2,179 09	314	152	8	474	15.8	231
18,033 52	1,849 85	1,075 00	774 85	277	84	12	383	14.0	651
14,558 20	2,082 46	1,880 00	202 46	380	133	12	525	19.2	243
3,089 33	244 68	....	244 68	120	77	4	201	8.1	185
10,464 38	409 40	....	409 40	225	117	7	349	15.0	177
8,999 72	1,855 38	425 00	1,430 38	174	101	3	278	12.0	88
8,270 31	2,127 04	620 00	1,507 04	233	93	12	338	14.9	125
10,647 91	1,640 29	1,200 00	440 29	211	112	7	330	15.2	138
15,797 35	4,961 05	1,600 00	3,361 05	475	88	11	574	26.6	267
16,815 90	3,216 39	900 00	2,316 39	197	84	6	287	13.9	361
11,515 64	2,667 72	1,000 00	1,667 72	621	31	8	660	*	186
2,588 38	593 70	....	593 70	157	70	4	231	11.7	100
17,629 14	2,349 36	1,225 00	1,124 36	280	110	12	402	20.5	472
8,613 58	2,086 90	615 00	1,471 90	164	106	2	272	......	111
18,095 44	4,690 13	1,210 00	3,480 13	306	99	21	426	22.8	295
7,927 15	2,318 47	295 00	2,023 47	151	63	1	215	11.7	91
8,217 95	2,748 61	500 00	2,248 61	149	92	7	248	14.0	114

STATEMENT

Report Showing Operation of Municipalities

Municipality	Months Covered by Report	Popu- lation	Plant Cost	Debenture Debt and Overdraft	Operation and Maintenance	Fixed Charges	Total Operation
			$ c.	$ c.	$ c.	$ c.	$ c.
Tilbury......	12	1,740	14,171 78	13,185 17	3,356 62	864 00	4,220 62
Acton	12	1,735	16,981 17	6,273 04	3,675 50	1,101 41	4,776 91
Gravenhurst .	12	1,702	54,955 63	32,665 11	5,930 06	3,483 41	9,413 47
Mitchell	12	1,687	28,455 43	8,025 13	7,210 74	1,808 33	9,019 07
Durham	12	1,600	18,079 97	17,829 99	2,470 18	1,277 28	3,747 46
Exeter	6	1,572	17,636 81	16,680 97	2,089 74	665 47	2,755 21
New Hamburg	12	1,543	24,894 73	10,723 41	4,573 25	1,170 92	5,744 17
Dresden	12	1,521	17,583 12	16,349 58	4,110 62	1,492 65	5,603 27
Vict. Harbor.	12	1,477	7,252 78	6,104 85	1,218 11	497 96	1,716 07
Blenheim	13	1,424	16,736 93	14,572 84	4,271 82	897 08	5,168 90
Harriston	12	1,404	14,029 79	13,242 00	3,278 64	992 61	4,271 25
Pt. Dalhousie.	12	1,318	17,535 74	15,774 09	3,659 39	1,264 89	4,924 28
Caledonia....	12	1,217	7,309 75	4,121 25	1,114 15	361 72	1,475 87
Norwich	12	1,189	18,473 99	9,897 65	7,703 17	2,452 31	10,155 48
New Toronto.	12	1,186	17,962 53	11,899 06	7,536 87	922 31	8,459 18
Waterford ...	12	1,133	9,947 19	7,751 30	2,549 61	1,366 87	3,915 98
Shelburne ...	5	1,115	17,297 71	16,290 76	888 83	34 33	923 16
Elora........	12	1,115	13,668 03	11,154 74	2,961 90	875 17	3,837 07
Hagersville ..	12	1,105	10,440 64	4,693 98	3,976 97	550 80	4,527 77
Winchester...	12	1,065	11,391 52	7,659 28	3,243 81	773 70	4,017 01
Pt. Credit ...	12	1,046	12,603 53	7,276 00	2,190 80	568 95	2,759 75
Beaverton ...	12	1,015	13,842 13	13,367 64	2,996 11	855 20	3,851 31
Markdale	9	989	11,136 88	9,820 02	1,451 13	657 86	2,108 99
Stayner	12	972	15,284 16	12,610 00	3,238 41	753 16	3,991 57
Cannington ..	12	903	13,552 32	13,211 90	3,089 79	898 52	3,988 31
Milverton....	7	893	7,695 81	7,389 59	640 35	690 86	1,331 21
Dutton	12	870	8,201 05	6,561 62	2,110 32	476 04	2,586 36
Pt. Stanley..	12	849	21,583 77	11,577 75	5,981 88	1,232 82	7,214 60
Chesterville..	12	854	7,902 78	6,718 30	2,498 91	435 34	2,934 25
Ayr	12	800	12,854 58	10,973 77	1,782 59	1,076 82	2,859 41
Waterdown ..	12	785	10,715 49	5,270 99	2,791 53	1,482 95	4,274 48
Thamesville .	12	769	11,479 40	10,093 68	2,157 76	740 65	2,898 41
Bolton	12	727	13,182 77	11,347 01	4,518 83	866 16	5,384 99
Dundalk	12	721	7,716 56	6,380 96	1,551 02	818 56	2,369 58
Bothwell	12	708	5,430 65	4,511 54	1,746 30	565 99	2,312 29
Lucan	12	662	12,230 75	10,992 85	1,879 34	873 49	2,752 83
Woodbridge ..	12	639	9,713 52	7,916 44	2,838 72	636 88	3,475 60
Ailsa Craig ..	12	586	6,204 16	5,870 43	893 39	401 10	1,294 49
Creemore	12	585	8,815 93	7,748 81	2,714 05	689 52	3,403 57
Coldwater .	12	579	8,261 10	5,067 65	1,505 04	481 64	1,986 68
Wyoming	2	544	7,072 08	6,794 99	116 32	103 04	219 36
Embro.......	12	483	7,860 70	6,973 31	1,243 70	390 30	1,634 00
Flesherton ...	12	428	5,798 12	5,321 36	1,017 27	85 34	1,102 61
Woodville....	12	388	5,497 81	5,383 46	2,287 11	330 46	2,617 57
Chatsworth..	11	374	5,023 26	4,767 90	884 13	310 81	1,194 94
Baden	12	....	7,191 31	3,043 00	5,462 16	325 28	5,787 44
Brechin	12	....	2,298 00	2,261 66	1,826 35	171 09	1,997 44
Beachville ...	12	....	9,859 19	4,565 33	5,808 74	369 82	6,178 56
Burford	12	....	6,342 70	5,742 10	1,299 36	413 25	1,712 61
Comber......	12	....	5,803 03	5,323 69	1,426 85	378 26	1,805 11
Drumbo	12	....	3,844 69	3,413 83	671 88	271 11	942 99
Delaware....	12	....	2,968 76	2,757 73	439 96	229 35	669 31
Dorchester...	12	....	4,782 30	3,598 24	943 93	281 55	1,225 48
Elmvale	12	....	8,485 66	5,852 82	1,855 84	498 83	2,354 67
Granton	5	....	3,597 97	3,447 72	277 24	108 53	385 77

"B."—Continued

for Period ending December 31st, 1916

Revenue	Surplus	Depreciation	Surplus less Depreciation	Number of Consumers				Per Cent. of Consumers to Population	H. P. taken in Dec. 1916
				Domestic	Com'l	Power	Total		
$ c.	$ c.	$ c.	$ c.						
4,680 32	459 70	275 00	184 70	127	79	2	208	12.0	60
6,734 07	1,957 16	500 00	1,457 16	185	60	7	252	14.5	82
11,769 84	2,356 37	1,650 00	706 37	285	63	10	358	21.0	241
10,330 45	1,311 88	1,000 00	311 38	218	103	21	342	20.3	145
3,644 05	103 41	....	103 41	155	67	......	222	13.9	60
3,292 00	536 79	....	536 79	140	81	2	223	14.3	91
6,902 49	1,158 32	830 00	328 32	196	70	4	270	17.5	91
5,918 01	314 74	314 74	....	197	106	......	303	19.9	66
2,533 66	817 59	190 00	627 59	65	31	......	96	6.5	29
7,155 91	1,987 01	440 00	1,547 01	208	85	......	293	20.6	75
4,587 90	316 65	345 00	28 35	113	58	. 1	172	12.3	48
4,840 16	84 12	....	84 12	330	32	8	370	*	71
2,320 59	844 72	260 00	484 72	27	37	3	67	5.5	43
11,044 67	889 19	1,370 00	480 81	297	87	6	390	*	190
12,296 66	3,837 48	450 00	3,387 48	210	12	4	226	19.1	429
4,091 34	175 86	....	175 86	99	42	2	143	12.6	114
1,478 90	555 74	....	555 74	112	72	......	184	16.5	49
5,061 26	1,224 19	375 00	849 19	105	63	2	170	15.2	95
6,678 54	2,150 77	380 00	1,770 77	127	69	4	200	18.1	96
4,943 64	926 62	370 00	556 63	135	46	1	182	17.1	67
3,535 91	776 16	470 00	306 16	145	32	3	180	17.2	60
3,851 31	....	....	....	131	60	6	197	19.4	54
2,735 94	626 95	....	626 95	106	68	3	177	18.0	56
4,453 83	462 26	280 00	182 26	115	65	3	183	18.8	56
3,988 31	....	....	....	137	57	7	201	22.3	58
1,364 93	33 72	....	33 72	56	50	......	106	11.9	40
4,029 89	1,443 53	240 00	1,203 53	112	52	1	165	19.0	44
8,422 26	1,207 61	665 00	542 61	308	72	11	391	*	59
3,707 10	772 85	375 00	397 85	89	47	1	137	16.0	61
3,373 85	514 44	260 00	254 44	83	48	2	133	16 6	39
5,215 15	940 67	887 00	53 67	93	32	6	131	*	48
3,806 38	907 97	190 00	717 97	137	59	......	196	25.5	40
6,836 19	1,451 20	321 00	1,130 20	70	36	4	110	15.1	99
3,247 40	877 82	200 00	677 82	88	63	2	153	21.2	70
2,882 81	570 52	135 00	435 52	78	52	......	130	18.5	28
3,256 56	503 73	270 00	233 73	98	42	7	147	22.2	50
4,248 25	772 65	300 00	472 65	58	33	7	98	15.3	78
1,628 22	333 73	180 00	153 73	51	11	1	63	10.8	18
3,996 85	593 28	200 00	393 28	78	44	2	124	21.2	41
2,602 35	615 67	325 00	290 67	70	39	2	111	19.2	37
310 22	90 86	....	90 86	45	28	......	73	13.4	27
2,131 25	497 25	235 00	262 25	58	29	2	89	....	27
1,496 59	393 98	150 00	243 98	73	30	......	103	....	33
2,617 57	....	....	....	41	24	3	68	....	46
1,275 30	80 36	....	80 36	36	23	1	60	....	30
6,551 01	763 57	275 00	488 57	84	......	5	89	....	220
1,997 44	....	....	....	16	20	1	37	....	33
6,207 45	28 89	375 00	346 11	42	12	3	57	....	188
2,049 85	337 24	165 00	172 24	64	30	1	95	....	27
1,996 66	191 55	145 00	46 55	37	37	......	74	....	21
1,154 75	211 76	110 00	101 76	35	22	......	57	....	15
737 74	68 43	80 00	11 57	23	12	......	35	....	8
1,883 52	658 04	150 00	508 04	61	16	2	79	....	11
3,221 44	866 77	290 00	576 77	81	62	3	146	....	70
491 75	105 98	....	105 98	41	16	......	57	....	1

STATEMENT

Report Showing Operation of Municipalities

Municipality	Mon hs Coveved by Report	Popu-lation	Plant Cost	Debenture Debt and Overdraft	Operation and Maintenance	Fixed Charges	Total Operation
			$ c.	$ c.	$ c.	$ c.	$ c.
Grantham Tp.	12	....	3,900 47	5,202 84	1,614 28	2,997 93	4,612 21
Holstein	8	....	2,452 96	2,424 65	263 99	229 17	493 16
Lambeth	12	....	4,241 08	3,868 09	951 60	382 49	1,334 09
Lynden......	12	....	4,436 41	4,135 14	1,038 66	315 32	1,353 98
Mt. Brydges .	12	....	4,279 76	3,957 02	1,479 45	296 20	1,775 65
Otterville ...	10	...:....	3,835 12	3,641 53	517 84	346 74	864 58
Plattsville...	12	....	5,282 62	4,346 43	2,235 22	346 17	2,581 39
Princeton....	12	....	3,219 33	3,082 12	1,077 47	239 57	1,317 04
Pt. McNicoll .	12	....	4,982 48	5,001 41	972 85	482 51	1,455 36
Rockwood....	12	....	6,986 46	2,940 86	1,065 53	395 77	1,461 30
Sunderland ..	12	....	6,715 13	6,461 35	1,677 81	399 07	2,076 88
St. George ...	12	....	5,151 10	4,178 41	1,358 57	412 83	1,771 40
Stamford Tp.	12	....	29,671 12	28,310 73	2,964 95	737 19	3,702 14
Thorndale ...	12	....	3,142 58	2,896 93	1,383 40	205 60	1,589 00
Thamesford..	12	....	5,796 81	4,289 86	1,221 72	477 08	1,698 80
Toronto Twp.	12	....	15,681 34	9,279 92	3,081 97	3,253 87	6,285 84
Williamsburg.	12	....	2,274 45	1,671 79	703 09	220 67	923 76
Waubashene .	12	....	4,059 62	3,546 08	883 12	425 56	1,308 68
Total		1.155,000	17,330,015 07	12,580,845 40	3,188,283 52	951,781 99	4,140,065 51

NOTE—Population in Villages estimated at 400

† Competitive territory.
* Rural or Summer populations create abnormal condition.

" B " —Continued

for Period ending 31st December, 1916

Revenue	Surplus	Depreciation	Surplus less Depreciation	Number of Consumers				Per Cent. of Consumers to Population	H. P. taken in Dec. 1916
				Domestic	Com'l	Power	Total		
$ c.	$ c.	$ c.	$ c.						
3,030 72	1,581 49	....	1,581 49	130	.....	......	130	....	19
435 43	57 73	....	57 73	26	14	......	40	....	8
1,453 97	119 88	100 00	19 88	54	13	1	68	....	18
1,492 71	138 73	120 00	18 73	24	10	1	35	....	86
2,107 79	332 14	125 00	207 14	55	15	2	72	....	25
879 19	14 61	....	14 61	40	24	1	65	....	15
3,217 54	636 15	145 00	491 15	60	22	3	85	....	53
1,325 14	8 10	96 00	87 90	44	11	.....	55	....	10
1,264 11	101-25	130 00	321 25	66	21	1	88	....	21
2,531 28	1,069 98	240 00	829 98	72	11	4	87	....	15
2,076 88	....	....	463 73	61	37	1	99	....	52
2,385 13	613 73	150 00	463 73	56	24	2	82	....	56
5,062 53	1,360 39	....	1,360 39	160	.....	15	175	....	...
1,485 93	103 07	85 00	188 07	33	12	1	46	....	42
1,923 86	225 06	235 00	9 94	64	29	2	95	....	32
8,369 78	2,083 94	1,934 00	149 94	213	.....	......	213	....	88
1,299 35	375 59	70 00	305 59	41	9	1	51	....	17
1,540 57	231 89	115 00	116 89	58	20	1	79	....	19
4,983,601 03	843,535 52	486,141 80	357,393 72	118,849	25,230	4,653	148,732	....	......

STATE

Comparative Detailed Operating Reports of Electric Departments of Hydro

Municipality Population	Toronto				Hamilton
	xa		463,705		100,461 xa
—	1913	1914	1915	1916	1913
EARNINGS	$ c.	$ c.	$ c.	$ c.	$ c.
Domestic Light	190,376 89	289,645 45	331 807 18	335,181 19	34,451 95
Commercial Light	233,799 04	305,534 31	291,907 92	272,243 06	25,453 99
Power	347,708 88	483,681 15	575,239 17	612,918 32	47,415 58
Street Light	344,933 79	364,214 17	350,085 97	361,920 32	2,250 89
Miscellaneous	29,891 21	39,651 98	40,076 70	108,735 53	9,841 52
Total	1,146,709 81	1,482,727 06	1,589,116 94	1,690,998 42	119,413 93
EXPENSES					
Power Purchased	255,986 26	323,586 97	430,830 00	529,180 54	47,307 65
Sub-Stn. Operation	32,216 66	42,667 33	42,890 24	44,866 07	3,240 97
" " Maint'ce. ..	11,510 69	23,560 14	17,243 40	35,187 08	94 01
Dist. System, Operation and Maintenance	50,693 34	59,013 81	59,782 15	53,175 4ᴜ	3,168 21
Line Transformer M't'c'e.	3,396 98	5,218 22	6,768 29	4,976 03	1,216 21
Meter Maintenance.......	1,648 28	3,072 21	3,856 44	7,085 21	16 39
Consumers' Premises–Exp.	36,536 64	52,893 31	37,821 37	44,278 89	2,693 70
Street Light Sys., Opera- tion and Maintenance..	45,801 72	48,674 18	63,981 72	61,202 90	1,375 46
Promotion of Business...	60,256 03	71,477 64	54,128 73	53,416 92	4,391 01
Billing and Collecting...	43,581 71	50,028 39	64,825 42	72,579 07	6,270 38
Gen. Office, Sal. and Exp.	85,957 58	125,972 92	93,332 31	124,068 67	3,623 22
Undistributed Expenses .	44,304 25	54,191 98	57,693 43	33,762 17	1,289 35
Int. and Deb. Payments.	274,285 24	325,551 67	362,337 99	400,434 57	30,201 49
Miscellaneous Expenses .	....	b 4,335 80	b 23,330 01	....	....
Total Expenses	946,175 38	1,190,244 57	1,318,821 50	1,464,213 52	104,888 05
Surplus	200,534 43	292,482 49	270,295 44	226,784 90	14,525 88
Loss	....	.	....	....	....
Depreciation Charge..	115,236 80	147,181 40	173,862 95	208,388 09	9,031 35
Surp. Less Depr. Chg.	85,297 63	145,301 09	96,432 49	18,396 81	5,494 53

"b"   Patriotic Fund contributions.
xa   Hydro Department operated separately.
xb   Hydro and Water Departments operated jointly.
xc   Hydro and Gas Departments operated jointly.
xd   Hydro and Railway Departments operated jointly.
xe   Hydro, Railway and Gas Departments operated jointly.
xf   Hydro, Water and Gas Departments operated jointly.
xg   Hydro, Water, Telephone and Railway Departments operated jointly.
xh   Hydro Department handled by municipal officials.

MENT "C"

Municipalities for the years ending December 31st, 1913, 1914, 1915 and 1916

xa	Hamilton 100,461			xa	Ottawa 100,163			
	1914	1915	1916		1913	1914	1915	1916
	$ c.	$ c.	$ c.		$ c.	$ c.	$ c.	$ c.
	74,668 38	92,723 71	108,137 22		68,032 27	68,767 48	67,441 19	72,875 12
	35,125 57	34,754 72	36,126 03		53,438 04	51,769 72	46,636 99	42,569 96
	70,665 43	83,990 38	115 224 78		26,978 76	31,748 23	32,126 50	42,996 89
	51,154 36	86,244 98	80,815 73		49,199 57	50,439 29	56,813 66	60,632 48
	2,564 82	2,619 70	3,026 87		....	183 11	225 48	- 406 45
	234,178 56	300,333 49	343,330 63		197,648 64	202,910 83	203,243 82	219,480 40
	78,968 72	103,922 98	121,982 71		50,750 00	55,512 39	53,018 54	60.859 15
	5,741 24	7,226 49	9,107 51		3,127 63	3,321 20	3,989 78	4,341 42
	653 61	1,644 78	2,012 08		107 58	300 81	588 81	132 82
	6,504 84	14,090 13	6,847 26		13,694 44	17,041 58	18,193 82	17,787 91
	505 26	921 70	1,067 67		245 82	1,996 40	635 82	683 36
	143 97	1,172 88	886 05		1,537 17	2,390 11	3,444 25	3,241 68
	2,782 23	4,061 03	3,556 22		10,572 43	6,082 30	2,534 80	....
	13,380 35	10,394 16	10,735 03		15,465 59	15,318 91	19,712 71	15,147 81
	8,999 76	3,443 77	3,752 54		1,008 50	1,060 00	3,118 79	8,277 56
	10,825 27	13,832 80	15,780 73		6,417 69	7,481 30	8,915 38	13,722 50
	12,894 66	17,083 98	17,740 82		6,941 68	9,604 33	11,699 46	11,470 18
	3,407 34	4,972 47	4,374 48		1,458 47	2,350 91	3,671 03	4.660 34
	46,398 68	60,759 61	61,266 73		30,961 54	38,002 88	40,365 58	42,371 44
	....				....	....		b - 716 29
	186,205 93	243,526 78	259,109 83		142,283 54	160,463 12	169,888 77	183,412 46
	47,972 63	56,806 71	84,220 80		55,365 10	42,447 71	33,355 05	36,067 94
	....	....			....	....		
	21,053 66	25,808 87	32,110 54		24,000 00	52,650 00	33,000 00	32,775 00
	26,918 97	30,997 84	52,110 26		31,365 10	9,797 71	355 05	3,292 94

"b" Patriotic Fund Contributions.
xa See page 68.

STATEMENT

Comparative Detailed Operating Reports of Electric Departments of Hydro

Municipality Population	xb	London 58,055			Brantford 25,420 xd
—	1913	1914	1915	1916	1914
					1
EARNINGS	$ c.	$ c.	$ c.	$ c.	$ c.
Domestic Light	41,172 64	57,473 08	57,184 75	71,146 90	7,103 77
Commercial Light	39,256 07	47,593 44	43,751 37	48,747 74	5,392 87
Power	79,659 78	130,936 35	148,567 23	180,204 33	647 69
Street Light	28,372 20	30,535 83	31,168 87	31,719 17	21,724 64
Miscellaneous	3,763 78	3,313 10	4,958 29	8,973 65	627 57
Total	192,224 47	269,851 80	285,630 51	340,791 79	35,496 54
EXPENSES					
Power Purchased	72,676 41	97,404 63	122,893 29	155,208 55	12,999 65
Sub-Stn. Operation	5,816 18	9,925 89	8,671 25	11,260 87	1,069 43
" " Maint'ce...	519 81	767 40	135 79	329 76	7 84
Dist. System, Operation and Maintenance	5,342 67	3,850 78	5,220 69	6,069 41	376 83
Line Transformer M't'c'e.	1,674 88	760 87	94 82	839 69	65 26
Meter Maintenance.......	138 23	95 60	372 13	3,169 66	10 08
Consumers' Premises–Exp..	1,827 71	2,119 53	2,455 20	3,217 49	40
Street Light Sys., Operation and Maintenance..	5,278 72	8,511 05	6,303 42	7,577 61	1,460 00
Promotion of Business ..	5,833 84	5,840 01	6,902 59	7,853 28	1,608 37
Billing and Collecting ...	6,738 13	9,126 81	10,762 84	10,560 10	994 63
Gen. Office, Sal. and Exp..	14,180 20	16,845 61	15,042 13	12,777 04	1,089 66
Undistributed Expenses .	6,297 08	6,687 31	4,943 05	6,866 73	215 98
Int. and Deb. Payments..	29,488 97	35,127 20	38,493 89	40,099 60	7,444 31
Miscellaneous Expenses ..	....	....	b 2,776 28	4,500 56	....
Total Expenses	155,812 83	197,062 69	225,067 37	270,330 35	27,322 44
Surplus	36,411 64	72,789 11	60,563 14	70,461 44	8,174 10
Loss	....	....	....		....
Depreciation Charge .	21,058 82	27,588 39	32,734 97	29,060 62	6,000 00
Surp. Less Depr. Chg.	15,352 82	45,200 72	27,828 17	41,400 82	2,174 10

"b" Patriotic Fund contributions.
"1" 9 months' operation.
xb, xd See page 68.

"C"—Continued

Municipalities for the years ending December 31st, 1913, 1914, 1915 and 1916

xd	Brantford 25,420		xa	Windsor 24,162			xc	Kitchener 19,266	
	1915	1916		1914	1915	1916		1913	1914
				f				p	
	$ c.	$ c.		$ c.	$ c.	$ c.		$ c.	$ c.
	13,629 36	17,504 44		3,143 41	23,161 57	35,565 59		16,558 82	17,757 08
	10,746 67	10,530 19		1,107 38	12,009 99	16,831 60		20,985 35	19,549 45
	12,901 29	24,213 00		9 77	3,734 81	7,370 82		38,368 34	49,173 17
	28,691 05	27,500 83		3,997 85	31,947 11	37,266 17		17,373 81	16,544 11
	327 94	294 05		....	961 07	2,768 13		1,268 87	1,726 92
	66,296 31	80,042 51		8,258 41	71,814 55	99,802 51		94,555 19	104,750 73
	24,661 13	33,566 59		4,330 41	38,849 61	51,655 51		33,359 47	40,275 75
	2,111 85	2,975 10		408 67	2,588 72	2,466 76		4,892 72	4,282 95
	177 02	114 98		....	236 47	282 77		1,175 64	294 68
	684 06	814 74		240 41	629 41	816 44		1,575 15	4,411 10
	160 65	267 97		....	48 49	157 84		205 39	20 35
	199 00	167 27		....	11 70	131 68		326 51	564 97
	3 53	3 19		....	222 87	750 40		101 97	75 83
	3,420 03	3,110 37		....	1,667 97	6,647 83		2,803 88	3,884 76
	1,644 50	1,813 05		....	1,455 58	1,301 56		452 28	630 50
	1,625 66	1,819 63		441 36	2,416 24	4,661 77		1,901 40	2,259 54
	1,443 91	1,371 24		2,170 90	3,821 74	4,922 46		2,532 25	2,615 07
	798 48	1,210 57		....	1,502 25	2,887 17		1,966 04	1,966 38
	14,686 37	17,221 00		666 66	13,038 53	17,258 16		17,897 45	18,719 43
	....				....	....		....	b 619 00
	81,616 19	63,955 70		8,258 41	66,489 68	93,940 35		69,190 15	80,620 31
	14,680 12	16,086 81		....	5,324 87	5,862 16		25,365 04	24,130 42
	....	....		....	....	....		....	....
	10,000 00	7,500 00		....	....	5,157 50		10,980 79	12,884 05
	4,680 12	8,586 81		....	5,324 87	704 66		14,384 25	11,246 37

"f"　4 months' operation.
"p"　13 months' operation.
xa, xd, xe　See page 68.

6 H. (ii)

STATEMENT

Comparative Detailed Operating Reports of Electric Departments of Hydro

Municipality Population	Kitchener xe 19,266		Peterboro' xb 20,426		
—	1915	1916	1914	1915	1916
			e		
EARNINGS	$ c.	$ c.	$ c.	$ c.	$ c.
Domestic Light	19,108 60	20,876 63	8,661 71	27,991 24	31,020 72
Commercial Light	16,807 15	17,323 67	7,749 91	27,563 41	26,403 82
Power	54,732 50	62,436 31	7,013 23	30,185 83	36,597 04
Street Light	17,017 43	18,621 19	3,081 59	12,294 64	13,257 49
Miscellaneous	2,714 76	2,428 77	....	....	....
·Total	110,380 44	121,686 57	26,506 44	98,035 12	107,279 07
EXPENSES					
Power Purchased	47,644 33	59,814 81	11,920 90	45,240 12	48,888 66
Sub-Stn. Operation	3,727 21	3,888 64	840 05	3,269 50	2,498 52
" " Maint'ce...	465 16	621 93	9 08	313 85	464 58
Dist. System, Operation and Maintenance	4,193 45	4,392 79	996 31	4,632 71	7,963 09
Line Transformer M't'c'e.	21 76	28 05	26 35	178 43	387 43
Meter Maintenance.......	384 57	442 18	6 52	1,326 47	1,242 59
Consumers' Premises–Exp.	127 92	24 07	....	....	....
Street Light Sys., Operation and Maintenance..	1,699 89	1,976 07	1,465 01	6,000 91	5,367 18
Promotion of Business ..'	169 29	118 17	....	....	....
Billing and Collecting ...	2,569 37	2,809 95	242 70	2,125 05	2,865 07
Gen. Office, Sal. and Exp..	2,686 19	2,603 33	3,777 45	9,542 34	7,617 20
Undistributed Expenses ..'	2,427 57	2,099 02	214 94	821 47	1,756 07
Int. and Deb. Payments..'	18,436 93	18,474 43	2,026 21	13,372 97	11,981 33
Miscellaneous Expenses ..	b 1,265 63	b 1,244 84	....	....	....
Total Expenses	85,819 27	98,538 28	21,525 52	86,823 82	91,031 72
Surplus	24,561 17	23,148 29	4,980 92	11,211 30	16,247 35
Loss	....	....	....	....	....
Depreciation Charge .	13,500 00	14,638 25	....	7,500 00	6,250 00
Surp. Less Depr. Chg.	11,061 17	8,510 04	4,980 92	3,711 30	9,997 35

"b" Patriotic Fund contribution.
"e" 3 months' operation.
xb, xe See page 68.

" C "—Continued

Municipalities for the years ending December 31st, 1913, 1914, 1915 and 1916

xa	St. Catharines 17,880			xc	St. Thomas 17,174		
	1914	1915	1916	1913	1914	1915	1916
e		·	-				
$ c.	$ c.	$ c.	$ c.	$ c.	$ c.	.$ c.	$ c.
	2,013 49	9,540 70	16,419 57	11,125 50	13,221 00	16,517 37	20,210 52
	412 75	3,810 11	5,925 49	16,097 41	13,480 75	13,422 48	15,145 47
	12,742 98	25,193 30	40,688 67	36,550 26	44,247 13	44,780 45	46,698 91
	944 63	11,579 42	15,261 33	10,989 22	11,025 36	14,199 64	14,690 24
	44 28	522 83	519 18	361 15	869 76	984 54	1,413 94
	16,158 13	50,646 36	78,814 24	75,124 04	82,844 00	89,904 48	98,159 08
	9,328 14	19,191 12	29,827 81	31,435 85	38,279 18	44,655 44	47,539 96
	579 90	1,617 35	2,235 46	2,452 25	2,571 06	2,567 38	2,575 16
	46 19	237 97	53 27	913 99	80 40	107 33	603 07
	249 06	2,069 73	1,994 66	1,580 22	2,989 04	5,392 80	3,621 55
	640 56	242 25	1,290 92	47 57	77 64	154 75	47 02
	152 97	254 38	221 07	53 40	183 34	170 35	77 42
							75 77
	443 16	1,281 13	1,693 72	2,405 21	3,023 53	2,454 54	2,834 07
	981 77	1,459 99	1,238 73	....	....	1,224 10	707 81
	107 00	984 37	871 98	339 43	1,604 98	1,393 43	1,593 06
	607 53	4,213 82	5,496 64	1,593 77	2,733 80	3,037 32	2,949 91
	....	250 93	555 21	739 67	967 72	2,248 54	1,934 95
	1,105 87	9,724 03	12,411 67	7,402 65	7,406 14	8,359 74	8,314 07
	....	....					
	14,242 15	41,527 07	57,891 14	48,964 01	59,915 83	71,765 72	72,873 82
	1,915 98	9,119 29	20,923 10	26,160 03	22,927 17	18,138 76	25,285 26
	....	....	....	....	....	....	....
	850 00	7,250 00	10,500 00	6,900 00	7,350 00	8,735 00	9,800 00
	1,065 98	1,869 29	10,423 10	19,260 03	15,577 17	9,403 76	15,485 26

" e "—3 months' operation.
xa, xc See page 68.

· STATEMENT

Comparative Detailed Operating Reports of Electric Departments of Hydro

Municipality Population	xb	Stratford 17,081			Guelph 16,735 xc
—	1913	1914	1915	1916	1913 .
EARNINGS	$ c.	$ c.	$ c.	$ c.	$ c.
Domestic Light	11,636 59	15,180 91	16,967 58	20,108 76	11,528 09
Commercial Light	17,033 98	16,336 30	14,766 75	14,803 08	15,075 61
Power	15,123 78	16,519 24	18,178 84	23,506 12	42,091 34
Street Light	12,120 00	12,120 00	15,466 32	15,753 20	9,500 04
Miscellaneous	69 33	1,319 04	1,449 46	760 70	2,531 74
Total	55,983 68	61,475 49	66,828 95	74,931 86	80,726 82
EXPENSES					
Power Purchased	22,028 75	25,875 69	31,081 79	37,453 45	32,473 66
Sub-Stn. Operation	1,651 06	1,557 16	1,752 93	1,615 03	1,700 14
" " Maint'ce...'	200 54	16 70	71·99	391 78	1,076 44
Dist. System, Operation and Maintenance	1,630 72	2,515 22	1,985 74	1,896 78	3,004 51
Line Transformer M't'c'e.	148 48	1 56	44 37	19 20	179 90
Meter Maintenance.......	261 33	37 34	153 44	76 04	585 91
Consumers' Premises–Exp.	501 90	....	....	....	206 39
Street Light Sys., Opera- tion and Maintenance..	1,509 91	926-11	1,627 04	1,056 63	1,566 58
Promotion of Business ..	....	62 45	15 37	....	....
Billing and Collecting ...	1,325 47	1,647 47	2,007 92	1,948 60	430 35
Gen. Office, Sal. and Exp..	2,339 27	1,918 44	1,900 16	1,577 91	3,424 77
Undistributed Expenses ..	211 15	1,211 78	1,984 03	2,497 66	1,750 98
Int. and Deb. Payments..	10,536 75	12,989 75	14,398 80	14,794 02	10,273 27
Miscellaneous Expenses ..	....	b 1,750 00	b 3,752 52	....	x 884 95
Total Expenses	42,345 33	· 50,724 89	60,726 10	63,327 10	57,567 85
Surplus	13,638 35	10,750 60	6,102 95	11,604 76	23,158 97
Loss	....	....	....	....	....
Depreciation Charge .	3,420 00	4,631 50	5,250 00	7,500 00	8,000 00
Surp. Less Depr. Chg.	10,218 35	·6,119 10	852· 86	4,104 76	15,158 97

"b"   Patriotic Fund contributions.
"x"   Motor repairs.
xb, xc See page 68.

"C"—Continued

Municipalities for the years ending December 31st, 1913, 1914, 1915 and 1916

xc	Guelph 16,735			xg	Port Arthur 14,307		
1914	1915	1916	1913	1914	1915	1916
$ c.	$ c.	$ c.	$ c.	$ c.	$ c.	$ c.
16,920 54	15,514 10	17,221 76	81,830 66	38,097 65	32,048 37	31,152 52
15,923 51	12,692 86	13,710 72	h	32,933 91	28,662 58	27,439 63
38,148 46	38,404 28	48,369 83	78,193 51	92,804 49	85,060 78	96,913 51
9,590 66	9,298 95	9,518 72	14,709 41	15,458 88	15,514 61	15,207 40
1,516 42	1,947 98	2,710 64	....	....	1,247 52	·269 92
82,099 59	77,858 17	91,531 67	174,733 58	179,294 93	162,553 86	170,982 98
30,460 41	37,292 12	45,528 08	43,664 83	53,412 42	54,667 89	54,798 85
540 50	1,254 90	43 22	3,652 53	3,268 30	7,173 12	5,783 85
733 05	1,468 03	1,255 04	2,140 94	4,323 79	....	585 15
3,897 65	1,592 39	1,888 83	9,013 80	8,003 88	6,357 20	2,987 89
161 05	240 75	148 83	1 75	454 62	284 10	695 92
711 63	756 35	912 62	112 13	670 91	827 62	1,228 18
....	....	....	322 64	945 31	239 00	....
1,380 19	1,343 16	1,236 44	1,543 03	2,146 96	1,764 92	1,297 59
			361 85	100 85	416 67	102 95
2,257 35	2,695 89	2,616 35	2,630 19	5,324 25	3,296 52	2,261 85
3,003 77	3,710 93	3,233 54	2,613 61	2,557 42	8,163 89	9,290 32
2,351 61	2,943 66	3,393 91	2,012 67	2,357 63	685 08	1,199 83
10,273 27	10,273 28	10,273 28	37,556 73	40,489 67	49,132 16	47,428 64
x 884 02	x 976 72	x 1,927 63	....	....	965 05	....
56,604 50	64,548 18	72,457 77	105,626 70	124,056 01	133,973 22	127,661 02
25,495 09	13,309 99	19,073 90	69,106 88	·55,238 92	28,560 64	43,321 96
....	....	....	....	....	....	....
10,200 00	10,500 00	10,700 00	13,647 55	16,469 79	11,723 21	....
15,295 09	2,809 99	8,373 90	55,459 33	38,769 13	16,837 43	43,321 96

"x"   Motor repairs.
xc, xg   See page 68.

STATEMENT

Comparative Detailed Operating Reports of Electric Departments of Hydro

Municipality Population	Chatham xa 12,863		Owen Sound xf 11,910	Galt xa 11,852		
—	1915	1916	1916	1913	1914	1915
EARNINGS	m					
	$ c.	$ c.	$ c.	$ c.	$ c.	$ c.
Domestic Light	5,581 54	10,155 37	16,003 61	10,535 38	15,797 16	17,024 42
Commercial Light	2,806 81	7,427 86	23,724 21	11,648 49	11,952 75	8,794 36
Power	449 70	3,766 87	13,772 61	16,575 61	23,826 87	30,547 84
Street Light	7,616 36	13,169 02	7,000 00	6,280 25	8,500 00	12,981 29
Miscellaneous	....	396 34	700 70	194 00	919 15	373 24
Total	16,454 41	34,914 46	61,201 13	45,233 73	60,995 93	69,721 15
EXPENSES						
Power Purchased	7,171 72	15,427 10	25,067 12	17,883 91	21,134 48	29,961 84
Sub-Stn. Operation	318 56	1,053 43	5,439 60	1,761 14	1,930 96	2,283 95
" " Maint'ce	23 48	50 20	....	180 76	99 42	280 66
Dist. System, Operation and Maintenance	102 09	839 35	2,742 65	446 24	1,729 80	1,499 76
Line Transformer M't'c'e	15 25	68 62	468 48	11 48	129 05	120 76
Meter Maintenance	45 94	92 43	318 35	2 00	91 88	57 81
Consumers' Premises—Exp.	....	535 22	....	....	208 64	....
Street Light Sys., Operation and Maintenance	396 40	1,817 32	2,806 42	296 88	2,234 06	3,066 10
Promotion of Business	326 00	353 85	....	....	....	....
Billing and Collecting	810 65	1,624 56	1,119 74	1,188 20	1,868 30	2,226 16
Gen. Office, Sal. and Exp.	1,630 14	2,079 44	3,120 54	1,792 40	1,618 71	2,713 64
Undistributed Expenses	871 85	1,515 83	806 41	....	187 55	475 21
Int. and Deb. Payments	5,463 85	8,855 45	11,281 56	9,721 64	10,337 35	13,269 15
Miscellaneous Expenses	....	....	....	....	....	....
Total Expenses	17,175 88	34,312 80	53,170 87	33,284 65	41,570 20	55,955 04
Surplus	....	601 66	8,030 26	11,949 08	19,425 73	13,766 11
Loss	721 47	....	....	....	....	....
Depreciation Charge	....	....	3,307 80	8,400 00	10,600 00	10,000 00
Surp. Less Depr. Chg.	721 47	601 66	4,722 46	3,549 08	8,825 73	3,766 11

"m" 10 months' operation.
Italics denote losses.
xa, xf See page 68.

"C"—Continued

Municipalities for the years ending December 31st, 1913, 1914, 1915 and 1916

Galt xa 11,852	Sarnia xa 11,676	Niagara xa Falls 11,147	Woodstock xb 10,084				Brockville xf 9,428
1916	1916	1916	1913	1914	1915	1916	1916
		h					
$ c.	$ c.	$ c.	$ c.	$ c.	$ c.	$ c.	$ c.
19,961 17	....	21,733 29	6,495 02	8,807 40	10,472 14	11,206 71	12,897 12
10,485 26	17,498 81	13,259 02	12,942 32	11,610 14	11,718 95	12,983 32	21,994 02
36,029 78	12,640 12	9,613 91	20,262 52	19,832 26	20,742 18	23,721 92	15,828 62
12,567 40	3,480 00	12,849 81	7,160 00	7,320 00	7,810 08	7,355 01	9,000 00
45 00	....	9 84	354 18	471 80	673 97	1,860 65	....
79,088 61	33,618 90	57,465 87	47,214 04	48,041 50	51,417 32	56,627 61	59,719 76
41,098 16	....	15,391 75	18,798 66	18,690 30	20,217 74	24,747 98	8,754 44
2,774 79	9,289 42	3,516 04	1,834 83	2,149 53	1,817 22	1,924 83	14,304 71
89 72	....	....	497 39	83 02	108 46	33 08	2,878 57
1,795 06	642 75	4,272 18	1,827 65	1,566 91	1,654 10	2,068 72	1,955 01
15 55	4 00	197 54	4 84	23 75	74 94	128 08	17 59
185 80	....	560 67	70 75	57 05	24 82	313 11	219 29
160 76			345 00				
2,620 53	137 26	3,959 08	1,142 30	1,665 72	584 03	502 77	494 27
							851 48
2,566 98	....	1,795 99	1,115 75	1,628 44	1,443 25	1,722 35	566 28
3,298 27	3,843 56	2,548 06	2,513 73	3,050 10	3,007 93	2,794 11	2,648 31
603 80	1,087 33	1,920 19	447 96	581 45	972 96	1,077 89	892 28
15,303 85	7,738 92	9,078 40	6,853 83	7,219 04	7,290 95	7,241 71	15,535 74
....	....	....	....	500 00	1,000 00	b 1,000 00	b 1,325 54
70,513 27	22,693 24	43,239 90	35,806 87	37,215 31	38,196 40	43,554 63	50,443 51
8,575 34	10,925 69	14,225 97	11,407 17	10,826 38	13,220 92	13,072 98	9,276 25
....			....				....
8,500 00	....	8,315 00	5,827 40	6,450 00	6,725 00	6,930 20	7,000 00
75 34	10,925 69	5,910 97	5,579 77	4,376 38	6,495 92	6,142 78	2,276 25

"b" Patriotic Fund contributions.
"h" 6 months' operation.
xa, xb, xf See page 68.

STATEMENT

Comparative Detailed Operating Reports of Electric Departments of Hydro

Municipality Population	xa	Welland 7,243			xb	Barrie 6,453	
—	1913	1914	1915	1916	1913	1914	1915
	f						
EARNINGS	$ c.	$ c.	$ c.	$ c.	$ c.	$ c.	$ c.
Domestic Light	1,369 67	4,411 20	4,643 16	4,800 06	10,071 55	11,149 49	11,087 68
Commercial Light	558 46	1,676 38	1,600 79	1,580 48	9,252 70	9,464 64	9,572 91
Power	4,307 21	8,305 71	33,541 88	78,184 81	3,393 45	3,712 24	4,567 76
Street Light	1,395 00	5,049 00	5,235 75	5,181 00	4,292 53	4,572 75	5,075 00
Miscellaneous	....	....	1,171 16	3,899 76	583 28	137 89	145 51
Total	7,630 34	19,442 29	51,192 74	93,646 11	27,593 51	29,037 01	30,448 86
EXPENSES							
Power Purchased	4,861 38	7,598 77	31,100 96	62,152 76	6,611 27	10,873 86	12,352 71
Sub-Stn. Operation	295 43	406 99	208 78	1,115 16	5,706 97	2,745 68	2,428 00
＂　　＂　Maint'ce.	....	32 30	96 66	387 59	....	....	....
Dist. System, Operation and Maintenance.......	191 18	138 94	590 33	841 42	679 16	448 87	1,008 10
Line Transformer M't'c'e.	32 82	107 53	318 22	1,010 32	....	....	58 50
Meter Maintenance.......	50	57 21	200 13	228 68	17 92	....	151 73
Consumers' Premises–Ex.	....	....	....	....	....	....	....
Street Light Sys., Operation and Maintenance...	123 82	446 23	192 52	156 28	402 06	108 02	675 44
Promotion of Business...	....	....	....	....	....	....	....
Billing and Collecting....	317 42	748 38	455 89	541 14	....	....	....
Gen. Office, Sal. and Exp.	798 53	2,790 59	3,720 01	5,431 25	3,578 67	2,294 92	2,567 43
Undistributed Expenses..	39 45	10 25	420 97	624 60	544 58	510 67	1,174 97
Int. and Deb. Payments..	2,638 54	5,080 20	8,474 79	8,199 77	5,590 40	6,052 29	6,052 29
Miscellaneous Expenses..	....	....	....	....	....	....	....
Total Expenses......	9,299 07	17,417 39	45,778 76	80,688 97	23,131 03	23,044 31	26,469 17
Surplus.·.............	....	2,024 90	5,413 98	12,957 14	4,462 48	5,992 70	3,979 69
Loss.................	1,668 73	....	....	....	....	....	....
Depreciation Charge.	....	....	4,425 00	4,000 00	3,350 00	3,500 00	3,500 00
Surp. Less Depr. Chg.	1,668 73	2,024 90	988 98	8,957 14	1,112 48	2,492 70	479 69

"f"　4 months' operation.
Italics denote losses.
xa, xb　See page 68.

"C"—Continued

Municipalities for the years ending December 31st, 1913, 1914, 1915 and 1916

Barrie xb 6,453	Collingwood xb 6,361				Midland xb 6,258			
1916	1913	1914	1915	1916	1913	1914	1915	1916
$ c.	$ c.	$ c.	$ c.	$ c.	$ c.	$ c.	$ c.	$ c.
11,907 10	8,775 83	7,857 86	7,094 27	8,320 44	6,095 11	6,941 07	6,580 45	7,145 74
10,635 67	7,600 00	7,555 54	5,688 26	6,213 86	6,104 16	5,048 06	4,462 54	4,624 85
6,918 33	896 72	5,165 39	9,527 70	23,152 41	5,700 22	6,484 43	10,229 52	12,262 89
5,323 67	3,802 88	4,647 00	4,715 00	3,940 00	3,463 07	3,728 76	3,100 00	3,330 46
237 09	106 21	....	....	91	....	13 71	33 26	113 10
35,021 86	21,181 64	25,225 79	27,025 23	41,627 62	21,362 56	22,216 03	24,405 77	27,477 04
14,417 95	7,480 48	10,450 24	13,733 50	24.922 78	6,059 33	6,539 10	8,367 74	11,787 55
1,254 53	1,952 60	2 25	....	....	....	....	....	....
....	....	10 51	3 97	....	....	....	....	....
182 06	1,374 21	749 16	530 27	493 42	989 11	1,284 29	1,104 58	981 34
....	9 19	36 83	....	....	57 20	420 06	122 60	35 34
1,039 54	13 37	15 25	....	98 44	....	....	-	605 31
....	....	....	....	....	....	....	....	....
506 46	133 20	664 19	477 36	382 60	526 53	1,020 22	1,020 86	961 47
....	252 08	302 39	526 63	816 33	221 04	157 89	282 69	494 20
2,560 26	2,066 94	1,916 97	1,988 80	1,988 08	1,435 86	1,692 75	2,088 81	1,771 67
726 93	209 90	173 18	128 76	....	....	107 63	....	175 46
6,052 29	4,277 77	4,369 96	3,556 84	3,393 33	4,134 55	4,267 05	3,827 60	3,955 47
....	....	....	250 00	....	....	....	....	....
26,740 02	17,769 94	18,690 93	21,196 13	32,094 98	13,423 62	15,488 49	16,814 39	20,767 81
8,281 84	3,411 70	5,534 86	5,829 10	9,532 64	7,938 94	6,727 54	7,591 39	6,709 23
....	....	....	....	....	....	....	....	....
2.575 00	2,390 00	2,400 00	2,600 00	2,150 00	2,950 00	3,200 00	3,400 00	3,100 00
5,706 84	1,021 70	4,134 86	3,229 10	7,382 64	4,988 94	3,527 54	4,191 39	3,609 23

xb See page 68.

STATEMENT

Comparative Detailed Operating Reports of Electric Departments of Hydro

Municipality Population	xb	Ingersoll 5,176			xa	Walkerville 5,096
—	1913	1914	1915	1916	1914	1915
EARNINGS	$ c.	$ c.	$ c.	$ c.	$ c.	$ c.
Domestic Light	3,595 03	5,085 82	5,480 52	6,857 94	337 96	12,640 03
Commercial Light	6,048 51	6,359 72	5,716 91	6,540 51	1,492 84	7,596 25
Power	15,293 44	12,818 27	16,251 18	20,380 90	6,042 11	38,580 74
Street Light	4,262 02	3,960 04	3,564 80	3,729 00	1,716 61	3,601 29
Miscellaneous	976 99	250 88	610 56	681 28	....	982 28
Total	30,176 00	28,474 73	31,623 97	38,189 63	12,289 52	63,400 59
EXPENSES						
Power Purchased	11,966 61	11,441 79	16,994 84	20,236 43	6,104 53	45,503 27
Sub-Stn. Operation	828 83	907 02	852 02	1,144 36	259 76	1,425 79
" " Maint'ce	....	....	....	....	1 75	39 86
Dist. System, Operation and Maintenance	422 13	535 79	446 05	1,219 74	502 81	1,132 37
Line Transformer M't'c'e.	187 39	113 54	277 77	47 31	3 00	163 19
Meter Maintenance	97 00	360 05	297 19	81 59	13 25	217 05
Consumers' Premises–Exp.	....	....	....	....	....	....
Street Light Sys., Operation and Maintenance	440 09	274 54	214 69	414 97	10 58	749 88
Promotion of Business	....	....	....	....	....	....
Billing and Collecting	560 15	543 73	668 26	834 79	562 05	2,039 70
Gen. Office, Sal. and Exp..	1,615 40	1,471 88	1,561 32	1,024 03	1,499 11	2,806 63
Undistributed Expenses	195 56	71 63	82 63	590 85	374 34	923 24
Int. and Deb. Payments..	5,337 25	5,198 90	5,046 35	4,905 00	1,908 19	8,758 92
Miscellaneous Expenses	....	....	....	....	....	....
Total Expenses	21,650 41	20,918 87	26,441 12	30,499 07	11,239 37	63,759 90
Surplus	8,525 59	7,555 86	5,182 85	7,690 56	1,050 15	....
Loss	....	....	....	....	....	359 31
Depreciation Charge .	2,862 00	3,168 00	3,200 00	2,650 00	....	....
Surp. Less Depr. Chg.	5,663 59	4,387 86	1,982 85	5,040 56	1,550 15	*359 31*

Italics denote losses.
xa xb   See page 68.

"C"—Continued

Municipalities for the years ending December 31st, 1913, 1914, 1915 and 1916

Walkerville xa 5,096	Waterloo xf 4,956				Goderich xb 4,655		
1916	1913	1914	1915	1916	1914	1915	1916
	p						
$ c.	$ c.	$ c.	$ c.	$ c.	$ c.	$ c.	$ c.
18,610 61	4,263 66	4,723 94	5,401 82	5,454 60	7,197 05	6,072 51	7,086 32
11.805 00	5,098 42	4,825 22	5,284 87	4,750 09	4,196 49	5,066 76	5,253 15
76,567 87	14,970 14	13,282 12	15,125 32	17,905 45	1,240 73	5,645 26	5,498 56
3,828 49	5,294 10	5,137 84	5,773 20	5,798 75	5,525 00	5,525 00	5,162 39
1,653 93	....	477 61	276 14	834 92	....	....	135 00
112,465 90	29,626 32	28,446 73	31,861 35	34,743 81	18,159 27	22,309 53	23,135 42
75,704 99	11,075 53	9,882 03	14,230 85	16,914 08	6,315 17	7,716 02	9,136 85
1,994 86	1,019 10	924 41	863 04	890 01	1,806 40	1,705 39	1,461 80
250 24	81 00	182 23	315 50	47 74	....	....	....
976 49	378 74	794 51	2,013 65	1,479 03	167 83	312 13	525 44
399 31	32 13	42 90	2 65	74 95	11 25	113 65	314 94
543 58	54 67	193 53	61 72	106 32	15 94	13 43	....
....	....	....	....	....	....	....	....
1,103 25	1,093 25	459 21	869 98	693 68	68 20	413 67	727 63
....	....	....	....	....	....	....	....
2,183 61	866 90	756 25	926 41	1,021 01	343 13	405 95	494 19
5,585 79	2,520 00	2,519 64	2,463 40	3,064 05	204 85	185 28	813 59
3,023 92	.709 44	323 72	431 95	473 57	154 40	113 35	119 44
11,092 60	3,676 92	3,473 33	4,284 71	3,475 25	4,182 09	4,447 27	5,302 27
....	....	....	....	....	....	....	....
102,858 64	21,507 68	19,551 76	26,463 86	29,139 69	13,269 26	15,426 14	18,896 15
9,607 26	8,118 64	8,894 97	5,397 47	5,604 12	4,890 01	6,883 39	4,239 27
....	....	....	....	....	....	....	....
3,773 06	3,100 00	3,500 00	4,000 00	3,700 00	2,920 00	3,750 00	2,600 00
5,834 20	5,018 64	5,394 97	1,397 49	1,904 12	1,970 01	3,133 39	1,639 27

"p" 13 months' operation.
xa xb, xf See page 68.

STATEMENT

Comparative Detailed Operating Reports of Electric Departments of Hydro

Municipality Population	xb	Dundas 4,652			xb	Preston 4,643
—	1913	1914	1915	1916	1913	1914
EARNINGS	$ c.	$ c.	$ c.	$ c.	$ c.	$ c.
Domestic Light	3,045 85	5,349 24	6,139 97	6,925 46	5,477 10	6,520 39
Commercial Light	4,193 27	4,198 64	4,310 96	4,714 78	5,366 77	5,011 15
Power	3,070 40	4,305 96	5,930 54	10,915 58	21,017 68	21,975 26
Street Light	60 10	3,050 85	3,460 35	3,547 73	2,594 55	2,778 48
Miscellaneous	930 81	....	....	....	232 47	98 53
Total .... :	11,300 43	16,904 69	19,841 82	26,103 55	34,688 57	36,383 81
EXPENSES						
Power Purchased	3,474 08	4,038 10	4,981 97	7,411 36	16,673 20	17,460 00
Sub-Stn. Operation	....	....	71 64	17 89	1,459 16	1,509 01
" " Maint'ce...	....	....	....	....	49 21	28 33
Dist. System, Operation and Maintenance	154 77	840 00	1,448 70	822 50	1,238 36	2,368 26
Line Transformer M't'c'e.	35 80	74 75	91 00	125 18	280 22	139 99
Meter Maintenance.......	4 40	31 18	61 42	36 86	79 67	86 01
Consumers' Premises–Exp.	....	84 68	28 54	....	....	....
Street Light Sys., Operation and Maintenance..	....	285 34	378 76	369 73	431 92	523 05
Promotion of Business ..	....	789 93	....	....	....	....
Billing and Collecting ...	689 51	937 59	1,026 26	1,120 00	656 75	739 90
Gen. Office, Sal. and Exp..	1,642 56	1,876 50	1,905 51	1,732 83	415 98	568 69
Undistributed Expenses ..	....	138 32	898 42	1,467 23	183 85	585 82
Int. and Deb. Payments..	1,970 14	4,504 12	5,706 69	5,565 89	4,120 54	7,300 84
Total Expenses	7,971 26	13,600 51	16,598 91	18,668 97	25,588 86	31,309 90
Surplus	3,329 17	3,304 18	3,242 91	7,434 58	9,099 71	5,073 91
Loss	....	....	....	....	....	....
Depreciation Charge .	1,508 00	1,675 00	2,900 00	2,830 00	2,924 00	3,400 00
Surp. Less Depr. Chg.	1,821 17	1,629 18	342 91	4,604 58	6,175 71	1,673 91

xb See page 68.

"C"—Continued

Municipalities for the years ending December 31st, 1913, 1914, 1915 and 1916

	Preston xb 4,643		Paris xb 4,370			Wallaceburg xb 4,107	
	1915	1916	1914	1915	1916	1915	1916
	$ c.	$ c.	$ c.	$ c.	$ c.	$ c. (n)	$ c.
	6,615 91	7,341 15	4,766 23	5,071 54	5,877 57	4,079 74	5.095 45
	4,488 76	4,779 76	2,778 00	4,063 03	3,805 95	4,239 30	4,589 30
	21,698 34	22,624 37	1,419 90	6,328 33	8,974 66	87 32	5,866 32
	2,830 50	3,044 92	4,103 00	4,576 00	4,576 00	2,680 61	3,094 56
	15 00	....	....	....	....	....	....
	35,648 51	**37,790 20**	**13,067 22**	**20,937 90**	**23,234 18**	**11,086 97**	**18,645 63**
	18,843 12	20,693 58	4,020 80	7,104 77	7,837 15	5,601 51	9,464 40
	1,667 38	1,727 51	1,082 57	1,647 07	1,387 25	....	59 43
	30 10	211 78	....	....	....	....	....
	1,656 67	1,093 91	1,299 26	·1,325 58	1,299 93	143 88	729 31
	149 14	197 11	13 45	20 00	....	....	....
	56 28	145 13	....	2 05	7 60	....	129 79
	....	....	....	....	....	....	....
	413 40	297 29	333 09	493 88	281 48	295 13	563 91
	822 42	1,046 83	....	....	83 50	....	1,955 13
	496 56	956 13	563 26	746 78	636 17	1,877 06	909 46
	1,340 06	531 01	115 30	100 00	348 64	....	....
	7,212 87	7,258 79	5,849 94	7,966 15	6,665 00	3,580 84	8,701 50
	32,688 00	**34,159 07**	**13,277 67**	**19,406 28**	**18,546 72**	**10,998 42**	**17,512 93**
	2,960 51	3,631 13	....	632 62	4,687 46	88 85	1,132 70
	....	....	210 45	....	....	....	....
	3,800 00	3,500 00	....	....	2,000 00	....	1,038 00
	839 49	131 13	*210 45*	632 62	2,687 46	88 85	94 70

"n"   11 months' operation.
Italics denote losses.
xb See page 68.

STATEMENT

Comparative Detailed Operating Reports of Electric Departments of Hydro

Municipality Population	Simcoe xa 4,061		Brampton xb 4,041			
—	1915	1916	1913	1914	1915	1916
EARNINGS	1					
	$ c.	$ c.	$ c.	$ c.	$ c.	$ c.
Domestic Light	351 67	857 61	5,617 61	6,798 89	6,860 48	6,660 66
Commercial Light	1,386 89	2,292 28	3,983 65	4,055 99	4,053 56	4,013 51
Power	766 42	1,386 33	10,557 72	10,658 33	11,624 83	12,922 72
Street Light	2,708 51	3,500 00	3,500 00	4,200 00	4,486 00	4,262 17
Miscellaneous	12 80	128 99	....	....	62 71	269 05
Total	5,226 29	8,165 21	23,661 98	25,713 21	27,087 58	28,128 11
EXPENSES						
Power Purchased	2,438 62	3,531 25	11,084 34	11,692 39	13,259 58	14,489 32
Sub-Stn. Operation	....	4 70	26 11	58 58	30 95	25 68
. " " Maint'ce..	....	....	....	....	....	....
Dist. System, Operation and Maintenance	3 70	40 48	231 54	522 54	1,032 33	954 36
Line Transformer M't'c'e.	....	26 37	16 00	197 15	150 45	....
Meter Maintenance.......	....	12 10	....	51 31	13 15	38 42
Consumers' Premises—Exp.	....	....	....	....	....	....
Street Light Sys., Operation and Maintenance..	19 81	59 45	168 79	429 60	282 72	191 62
Promotion of Business ..	....	....	....	....	....	....
Billing and Collecting ...	....	....	341 70	794 57	871 46	935 76
Gen. Office, Sal. and Exp..	441 53	1,020 71	1,694 67	1,904 94	1,854 65	1,744 33
Undistributed Expenses ..	232 50	124 65	371 28	66 47	28 12	147 14
Int. and Deb. Payments..	1,473 94	1,948 91	3,781 42	4,936 36	4,799 34	4,739 19
Total Expenses	4,610 10	6,768 62	17,716 05	20,653 91	22,322 75	23,265 82
Surplus	616 19	1,396 59	5,945 93	5,059 30	4,764 83	4,862 29
Loss	....	....	....	....	....	....
Depreciation Charge .	....	1,350 00	2,500 00	3,000 00	3,000 00	3,000 00
Surp. Less Depr. Chg.	616 19	46 59	3,445 93	2,059 30	1,764 83	1,862 29

"1" 9 months' operation.
xa, xb See page 68.

" C "—Continued

Municipalities for the years ending December 31st, 1913, 1914, 1915 and 1916

xb	St. Marys 3,958				xb	Penetanguishene 3,928				Petrolia 3,891 xa
	1913	1914	1915	1916		1913	1914	1915	1916	1916
										j
	$ c. 3,815 77	$ c. 4,614 95	$ c. 5,073 97	$ c. 5,020 33		$ c. 1,989 80	$ c. 1,936 73	$ c. 2,050 69	$ c. 2,314 37	$ c. 1,598 03
	4,553 73	4,733 33	4,222 53	3,161 26		4,511 16	3,064 83	2,676 60	2,706 74	1,840 35
	8,221 72	10,610 05	8,379 87	9,266 74		8,775 95	8,001 69	10,048 08	11,650 03	356 67
	3,582 00	3,441 00	3,850 00	5,390 33		2,042 00	2,016 00	2,095 00	2,095 00	2,074 32
	....	....	178 00	....		....	....	148 35	17 70	195 95
	20,173 22	23,399 33	21,704 37	22,838 66		17,318 91	15,019 25	17,018 72	18,783 84	6,065 32
	10,055 82	8,966 67	9,040 90	10,411 47		6,347 56	7,673 95	9,935 27	11,954 10	2,818 60
	728 39	803 25	729 98	784 83		967 84	725 24	734 23	742 17	....
	150 46	195 00	....	100 67		....	3 25	1 66	....	....
	556 05	400 29	582 11	475 54		301 41	166 21	92 25	78 45	....
	519 39	350 34	136 96	245 73		236 11	93 51	1 00	7 70	....
	202 56	175 22	102 77	196 43		....	178 86	27 60	182 69	....
	....	....	....	....		....	....	....	....	....
	554 36	423 60	502 85	640 39		144 56	335 99	373 93	220 76	143 29
	....	....	....	....		....	131 74	58 88	....	....
	263 21	257 03	296 57	238 61		44 45	133 00	227 56	196 25	....
	1,077 38	994 13	1,143 40	964 08		1,278 02	1,305 25	1,303 05	1,260 29	1,422 41
	75 63	138 54	72 80	528 22		....	3 00	....	216 66	....
	4,616 15	4,658 00	4,775 42	4,775 42		2,035 90	1,986 09	1,981 39	2,050 40	1,486 24
	18,799 40	17,362 07	16,507 87	19,361 39		11,355 85	12,736 09	14,736 82	16,909 47	5,994 49
	1,373 82	6,037 26	4,320 61	3,477 27		5,963 06	2,283 16	2,281 90	1,874 37	70 83
	....	....	....	....		....	....	....	....	....
	....	3,340 00	3,600 00	2,900 00		1,820 00	1,960 00	2,000 00	1,780 00	....
	1,373 82	2,697 26	720 61	577 27		4,143 06	323 16	281 90	94 37	70 83

"j"   7 months' operation.
xa, xb See page 68.

STATEMENT

Comparative Detailed Operating Reports of Electric Departments of Hydro

Municipality Population	Tillsonburg xb 3,084				Strathroy xb 2,998	
——	1913	1914	1915	1916	1915	1916
EARNINGS	$ c.	$ c.	$ c.	$ c.	$ c.	$ c.
Domestic Light	2,796 57	3,367 74	3,203 51	4,009 67	3,380 78	3,318 45
Commercial Light	4,677 38	4,579 37	4,236 42	4,493 51	4,701 76	3,817 38
Power	4,763 13	6,303 09	5,619 15	5,692 05	700 49	2,927 36
Street Light	2,601 00	2,463 96	2,507 81	2,595 96	4,221 76	4,654 59
Miscellaneous	1,163 11	863 28	667 61	436 69	....	368 88
Total	16,001 19	17,577 44	16,234 50	17,227 88	13,004 79	15,086 66
EXPENSES						
Power Purchased	6,249 35	6,999 79	7,248 93	7,761 57	5,541 40	7,507 66
Sub-Stn. Operation	950 05	753 91	713 91	750 71	....	....
" " Maint'ce..	....	....	....	....	....	....
Dist. System, Operation and Maintenance	332 50	570 90	471 99	333 93	78 62	75 14
Line Transformer M't'c'e.	4 89	11 55	....	....	....	....
Meter Maintenance.......	....	16 47	4 40	19 68	....	....
Consumers' Premises–Exp.	....	....	....	....	....	....
Street Light Sys., Opera- tion and Maintenance..	205 87	210 50	309 17	161 04	160 10	187 91
Promotion of Business ..	....	....	43 29	36 95	....	....
Billing and Collecting ...	907 04	923 46	1,003 63	993 63	....	....
Gen. Office, Sal. and Exp..	1,064 21	997 04	1,306 50	1,654 61	1,353 44	1,898 60
Undistributed Expenses ..	1,033 61	1,000 00	....	50 38	....	....
Int. and Deb. Payments..	2,137 07	2,727 41	2,674 75	2,594 83	2,719 74	2,188 26
Total Expenses	12,884 59	14,211 21	13,776 57	14,357 33	9,853 80	11,857 57
Surplus	3,116 60	3,366 23	2,457 93	2,870 55	3,151 49	3,229 09
Loss	....	....	....	....	....	....
Depreciation Charge .	1,782 75	1,830 00	1,875 00	1,600 00	1,500 00	1,050 00
Surp. Less Depr. Chg.	1,333 85	1,536 23	582 93	1,270 55	1,651 49	2,179 09

xb See page 68.

" C "—Continued

Municipalities for the years ending December 31st, 1913, 1914, 1915 and 1916

xb	Hespeler 2,740			xb	Prescott 2,740			Orange-ville 2,493 xa
1913	1914	1915	1916	1914	1915	1916	1916
							g
$ c.	$ c.	$ c.	$ c.	$ c.	$ c.	$ c.	$ c.
2,206 75	2,635 41	2,787 48	3,011 73	7,472 75	4,058 14	4,186 96	613 08
1,667 00	1,934 75	2,334 15	2,012 28	996 00	3,033 62	3,611 95	722 87
5,044 30	6,116 27	9,017 58	11,177 71	1,099 27	3,431 45	4,141 90	866 11
1,500 00	1,478 00	1,536 00	1,831 80	2,500 00	2,500 00	2,500 00	760 00
....	....	....	....	9 00	....	117 39	127 27
10,418 05	12,164 43	15,675 21	18,033 52	12,077 02	13,023 21	14,558 20	3,089 33
5,465 01	4,753 26	6,663 89	9,755 25	5,047 30	4,552 99	4,603 77	1,379 12
2,101 87	614 43	413 06	839 98	3,293 49	1,147 65	2,317 58	....
....	....	....	....	361 49	805 14	47 63	....
638 83	565 16	431 37	626 62	767 49	929 36	1,247 01	39 40
4 17	54 05	52 76	....	....	34 00	....	....
....	....	....	147 22	116 10	146 70	27 80	....
....	....	....	....	....	....	....	....
57 50	111 92	139 02	165 66	119 00	210 22	520 60	64 72
....	....	....	....	37 82	81 94	22 17	....
735 23	1,207 23	481 99	1,367 10	1,165 23	1,503 78	1,588 89	750 53
272 67	112 50	112 50	137 50	169 62	260 23	166 90	....
2,140 19	3,144 33	3,144 33	3,144 34	1,722 31	2,233 12	1,983 39	610 88
11,415 47	10,562 88	12,438 82	16,183 67	12,799 85	11,905 13	12,475 74	2,844 65
....	1,601 55	3,236 29	1,849 85	....	1,118 08	2,082 46	244 68
997 42	....	....	....	700 06	....	....	....
....	1,350 00	1,400 00	1,075 00	1,950 00	2,000 00	1,880 00	....
....	251 55	1,836 29	774 85	*2,650 06*	*881 92*	202 46	244 68

"g" 5 months' operation.
Italics denote losses.
xa, xb See page 68.

STATEMENT

Comparative Detailed Operating Reports of Electric Departments of Hydro

Municipality Population	Listowel 2,326 xb	Ridge- town 2,329 xa	xb	Elmira 2,270		Clinton 2,177 xb
—	1916	1916	1914	1915	1916	1914
	z		p			
EARNINGS	$ c.	$ c.	$ c.	$ c.	$ c.	$ c.
Domestic Light	*7,696 19	2,173. 64	1,968 41	2,059 11	2,211 16	2,023 70
Commercial Light	....	2,838 32	2,020 81	1,674 44	1,665 69	2,028 08
Power	605 03	740. 86	1,876 49	2,801 33	2,635 22	1,255 33
Street Light	2,163 16	2,853 00	1,680 00	1,680 00	1,740 00	1,105 66
Miscellaneous	....	390 90	....	3 75	18 24	....
Total	10,464 38	8,999 72	7,545 71	8,218 63	8,270 31	6,412 77
EXPENSES						
Power Purchased	2,010 78	3,950 44	3,077 56	3,361 63	3,494 69	2,291 20
Sub-Stn. Operation	2,121 60	....	....	....	....	911 74
" " Maint'ce...	....	....	....	....	....	....
Dist. System, Operation and Maintenance	351 71	215 56	....	....	....	80 99
Line Transformer M't'c'e.	....	....	....	....	....	....
Meter Maintenance.......	....	....	....	....	....	....
Consumers' Premises–Exp.	....	....	....	....	....	....
Street Light Sys., Opera' tion and Maintenance..	73 29	23 27	102 55	83 64	148 96	145 74
Promotion of Business ..	....	....	....	....	....	....
Billing and Collecting ...	....	....	....	....	....	....
Gen. Office, Sal. and Exp..	2,569 12	1,114 21	1,170 47	1,090 84	1,122 04	1,182 42
Undistributed Expenses ..	....	....	31 17	....	....	32 29
Int. and Deb. Payments..	2,928 48	1,840 86	1,425 22	1,356 67	1,877 58	1,838 56
Total Expenses	10,054 98	7,144 34	5,806 97	5,892 78	6,143 27	6,483 14
Surplus	409 40	1,855 38	1,738 74	2,325 85	2,127 04	....
Loss	....	....	....	....	....	70 37
Depreciation Charge .	....	425 00	650 00	750 00	620 00	....
Surp. Less Depr. Chg.	409 40	1,430 38	1,088 74	1,575 85	1,507 04	*70 37*

* Domestic and Commercial not separable.
" b " 13 months' operation.
" z " 6 months Hydro; 6 months steam.
Italics denote losses.
xa, xb See page 68.

" C "—Continued

Municipalities for the years ending December 31st, 1913, 1914, 1915 and 1916

	Clinton xb 2,177		Weston xb 2,156				Milton xa 2,072			
	1915	1916	1913	1914	1915	1916	1913	1914	1915	1916
	$ c.	$ c.	$ c.	$ c.	$ c.	$ c.	$ c.	$ c.	$ c.	$ c.
	2,930 57	3,161 29	4,117 20	3,741 84	4,407 36	5,477 65	1,149 28	1,961 22	1,981 80	2,219 28
	3,068 63	3,064 37	1,475 74	1,599 97	1,305 90	1,407 31	1,212 26	2,226 80	1,900 98	1,892 21
	2,108 24	2,498 64	6,170 36	4,958 59	4,798 33	5,202 84	6,462 38	11,325 61	5,364 29	10,428 79
	1,630 40	1,650 00	2,052 00	3,067 50	2,684 67	3,692 00	900 00	1,350 00	1,575 00	2,013 20
	118 31	273 61	24 88	....	31 79	17 55	143 18	455 62	....	262 42
	9,856 15	10,647 91	13,840 18	13,367 90	14,228 05	15,797 35	9,867 10	17,319 25	10,822 07	16,815 90
	3,835 94	4,190 07	5,159 49	5,783 87	5,536 71	6,121 26	4,902 34	7,696 45	6,511 50	9,332 39
	911 51	....	....	....	....	....	....	....	....	....
	....	....	....	....	....	....	....	....	....	....
	146 80	298 77	791 77	662 71	1,181 11	1,001 17	167 82	609 66	513 70	731 07
	....	....	....	....	....	....	....	....	....	417 42
	....	....	....	....	....	....	....	....	....	....
	298 61	106 26	574 25	451 99	419 20	189.66	....	86 16	169 82	50 65
	....	....	....	....	....	....	....	....	....	....
	1,569 57	1,323 31	927 35	1,668 62	1,264 78	1,428 12	42 27	572 05	819 70	889 31
	....	....	79 50	76 17	....	....	....	....	....	....
	2,643 15	3,089 21	1,588 48	1,588 42	2,310 20	2,096 09	1,582 93	2,277 04	2,270 34	2,178 67
	9,405 58	9,007 62	9,120 84	10,231 78	10,712 00	10,836 30	6,695 36	11,241 36	10,285 06	13,599 51
	450 57	1,640 29	4,719 34	3,136 12	3,516 05	4,961 05	3,171 74	6,077 89	537 01	3,216 39
	....	....	....	....	....	....	....	....	....	....
	380 20	1,200 00	1,390 00	1,450 00	1,520 00	1,600 00	900 00	1,250 00	1,090 00	900 00
	70 37	440 29	3,329 34	1,686 12	1,996 05	3,361 05	2,271 74	4,827 89	*552 99*	2,316 39

Italics denote losses.
xa, xb See page 68.

STATEMENT

Comparative Detailed Operating Reports of Electric Departments of Hydro

Municipality Population	xa	Mimico 1,976			Chesley 1,975 xa	xh	Seaforth 1,964
—	1913	1914	1915	1916	1916	1913	1914
			†	†	g		
EARNINGS	$ c.	$ c.	$ c.	$ c.	$ c.	$ c.	$ c.
Domestic Light	2,021 06	5,085 16	5,748 44	7,011 08	1,881 23	2,124 18	2,467 36
Commercial Light	*	*	346 49	506 44	*	2,876 47	2,581 30
Power	795 49	963 64	1,042 11	1,449 14	135 61	7,509 99	7,707 01
Street Light	987 00	1,049 34	2,015 66	2,496 75	521 65	1,815 81	1,869 96
Miscellaneous	....	....	....	52 23	49 89	61 63	110 14
Total	3,803 55	7,098 14	9,152 70	11,515 64	2,588 38	14,388 08	14,735 77
EXPENSES							
Power Purchased	1,740 66	2,801 90	3,342 50	4,217 02	1,332 68	7,931 55	8,646 18
Sub-Stn. Operation	....	....	....	....	....	....	....
" " Maint'ce...	....	....	....	....	....	....	....
Dist. System, Operation and Maintenance	144 79	53 29	167 16	698 69	25 98	1,573 93	1,078 00
Line Transformer M't'c'e.	....	....	....	....	....	....	....
Meter Maintenance.......	....	....	....	....	....	....	....
Consumers' Premises–Exp.	....	....	....	....	....	....	....
Street Light Sys., Opera- tion and Maintenance..	23 89	88 85	148 80	253 82	23 38	317 37	638 57
Promotion of Business ..	....	....	....	....	....	....	....
Billing and Collecting ...	....	....	....	....	....	....	....
Gen. Office, Sal. and Exp..	265 61	674 73	892 39	1,098 29	130 59	368 67	529 05
Undistributed Expenses ..	....	....	....	....	....	....	....
Int. and Deb. Payments..	845 02	1,561 45	2,300 32	2,580 10	482 05	1,653 65	1,704 25
Total Expenses	3,019 97	5,180 22	6,851 17	8,847 92	1,994 55	11 845 17	12,596 05
Surplus	783 58	1,917 92	2,301 53	2,667 72	593 70	2,542 9 1	2,139 72
Loss	....	....	....	....	....	....	....
Depreciation Charge .	740 00	920 00	1,200 00	1,000 00	....	1,300 00	1,400 00
Surp. Less Depr. Chg.	43 58	997 92	1,101 53	1,667 72	593 70	1,242 91	739 72

* Domestic and Commercial not separable.
† Domestic includes Rural Revenue.
"g" 5 months' operation.
xa, xh See page 68.

"C"—Continued

Municipalities for the years ending December 31st, 1913, 1914, 1915 and 1916

	Seaforth xh 1,964		Mount Forest 1,941 xb	xa Georgetown 1,905				Fergus xh 1,776	
	1915	1916	1916	1913	1914	1915	1916	1915	1916
			-	f				p	
	$ c.	$ c.	$ c.	$ c.	$ c.	$ c.	$ c.	$ c.	$ c.
	2,593 70	3,045 65	1,967 03	661 49	3,069 02	2,999 83	3,174 63	1,314 03	1,621 27
	2,724 84	2,941 03	2,420 75	842 87	2,362 33	2,276 41	2,101 00	2,367 91	2,111 16
	7,685 52	9,684 11	1,739 79	234 32	2,976 61	8,734 01	10,726 24	882 24	2,819 21
	1,869 96	1,869 96	1,963 00	541 67	1,843 67	1,834 03	1,724 17	1,744 75	1,575 00
	143 53	88 39	523 01	....	....	130 53	369 40	99 65	91 31
	15,017 55	17,629 14	8,613 58	2,280 35	10251 63	15,974 81	18,095 44	6,408 58	8,217 95
	9,305 22	11,625 46	3,544 42	759 00	4,183 72	8,893 20	9,790 20	2,598 37	3,382 69
	....	....	....	....	....	....	....	....	....
	891 49	1,170 86	969 92	12 85	192 11	137 03	290 19	23 77	123 40
	....	....	....	....	....	....	....	....	....
	314 55	228 17	74 92	201 06	128 09	192 12	259 17	97 28	132 70
	....	....	....	....	....	....	....	....	....
	548 30	559 54	315 09	....	895 46	955 08	1,102 70	1,208 84	681 81
	1,662 37	1,695 75	1,622 33	....	1,466 55	1,929 67	1,963 05	967 76	1,148 74
	12,721 93	15,279 78	6,526 68	972 91	6,865 93	12,107 10	13,405 31	4,896 01	5,469 34
	2,295 62	2,849 36	2,086 90	1,307 44	3,385 70	3,867 71	4,690 13	1,512 57	2,748 61
	....	....	....	....	....	....	....	....	....
	1,450 00	1,225 00	615 00	300 00	850 00	1,280 00	1,210 00	650 00	500 00
	845 62	1,124 86	1,471 90	1,007 44	2,535 70	2,587 71	3,480 13	862 57	2,248 61

"f" 4 months' operation.
"p" 13 months' operation.
xa, xb, xh See page 68.

STATEMENT

Comparative Detailed Operative Reports of Electric Developments of Hydro

Municipality	Palmerston	Tilbury		Acton			
Population	1,843 xb	xa 1,740		xa 1,735			
—	1916	1915	1916	1913	1914	1915	1916
EARNINGS	y	k					
	$ c.	$ c.	$ c.	$ c.	$ c.	$ c.	$ c.
Domestic Light	6,102 25	979 57	1,507 37	1,236 50	1,463 72	1,931 11	1,942 11
Commercial Light	*	1,476 53	2,071 77	1,567 48	1,496 18	1,725 73	1,592 62
Power	282 57	......	149 60	318 77	836 13	1,019 27	1,565 53
Street Light	1,542 33	715 00	938 73	1,000 00	1,563 00	1,555 00	1,497 50
Miscellaneous	......	19 39	12 85	286 72	83 60	188 76	136 31
Total	7,927 15	3,190 49	4,680 32	4,409 47	5,442 63	6,419 87	6,734 07
EXPENSES							
Power Purchased	1,480 74	1,601 33	2,267 40	1,801 50	2,344 50	2,495 70	2,500 20
Sub-Stn. Operation	1,133 63	......	......	......	......	......	......
" " Maint'ce	......	......	......	......	......	......	......
Dist. System, Operation and Maintenance	66 02	......	12 09	371 97	35 42	78 52	63 88
Line Transformer M't'c'e.	......	......	......	......	......	......	......
Meter Maintenance	......	......	......	......	......	......	......
Consumers' Premises—Exp.	......	......	......	......	......	......	......
Street Light Sys., Operation and Maintenance	44 00	10 60	23 10	7 20	147 12	144 16	112 23
Promotion of Business	......	......	......	......	......	......	......
Billing and Collecting	......	......	......	......	......	......	......
Gen. Office, Sal. and Exp.	1,044 29	643 64	1,054 03	841 70	943 77	667 70	999 19
Undistributed Expenses	......	......	......	......	......	......	......
Int. and Deb. Payments	1,840 00	668 57	864 00	442 00	1,124 06	1,124 06	1,101 41
Total Expenses	5,608 68	2,924 14	4,220 62	3,584 37	4,594 87	4,510 14	4,776 91
Surplus	2,318 47	266 35	459 70	825 10	847 76	1,909 73	1,957 16
Loss	......	......	......	......	......	......	......
Depreciation Charge	295 00	......	275 00	500 00	500 00	500 00	500 00
Surp. Less Depr. Chg.	2,023 47	266 35	184 70	325 10	347 76	1,409 73	1,457 16

* Domestic and Commercial not separable.
" k " 8 months' operation.
" y " 5 months Hydro; 7 months steam.
xa, xb See page 68.

" C "—Continued

Municipalities for the years ending December 31st, 1913, 1914, 1915 and 1916

Gravenhurst xh 1,702 xh	Mitchell xh 1,687				Durham 1,600 xb	Exeter 1,572 xh	Dresden xb 1,521	
1916	1913	1914	1915	1916	1916	1916	1915	1916
						h	k	
$ c.	$ c.	$ c.	$ c.	$ c.	$ c.	$ c.	$ c.	$ c.
3,553 06	2,424 59	2,470 29	2,379 58	2,311 80	1,518 72	727 88	1,093 68	1,995 51
4,575 10	2,813 92	2,712 55	2,684 01	2,677 35	1,057 33	677 73	1,223 25	1,986 21
2,469 19	6,160 53	3,944 91	2,333 08	3,231 56	....	361 73	....	....
1,172 49	1,675 00	1,950 00	2,100 00	2,100 00	1,068 00	1,473 88	1,100 00	1,650 00
....	385 50	443 90	63 20	9 74	....	50 78	153 51	286 29
11,769 84	13,459 54	11,521 65	9,559 87	10,830 45	3,644 05	3,292 00	3,570 44	5,918 01
2,470 59	6,858 86	4,882 39	4,424 38	4,966 61	2,005 89	1,477 19	1,917 34	2,685 88
....	12 35	....	....	....	....	....	....	....
....	....	....	....	....	....	....	....	....
1,252 54	81 25	66 52	486 96	201 04	254 48	23 04	25 82	40 62
....	....	....	....	....	....	....	....	....
....	....	....	....	....	....	....	....	....
50 72	44 64	34 12	26 10	38 40	43 50	21 65	11 24	124 30
....	....	....	....	....	....	....	....	....
2,156 21	1,223 80	1,315 10	1,258 61	2,004 69	166 31	567 86	729 57	1,259 82
....	100 00	....	....	....	....	....	....	....
3,483 41	2,224 07	2,224 06	2,124 46	1,808 33	1,277 28	665 47	754 98	1,492 65
9,413 47	10,544 97	8,522 19	8,320 51	9,019 07	3,747 46	2,755 21	3,438 95	5,603 27
2,356 37	2,914 57	2,999 46	1,239 36	1,311 38	....	536 79	131 49	314 74
....	....	....	....	....	103 41	....	....	....
1,650 00	1,150 00	1,200 00	1,000 00	1,000 00	....	....	....	314 74
706 37	1,764 57	1,799 46	239 36	311 38	*103 41*	536 79	131 49	000 00

"h" 6 months' operation.
"k" 8 months' operation.
Italics denote losses.
xb, xh See page 68.

STATEMENT

Comparative Detailed Operating Reports of Electric Departments of Hydro

Municipality Population	xh	New Hamburg 1,543			Victoria Harbor 1,477 xh		Blenheim 1,424 xh
—	1913	1914	1915	1916	1915	1916	1916
					e		
EARNINGS	$ c.	$ c.	$ c.	$ c.	$ c.	$ c.	$ c.
Domestic Light	1,589 21	1,779 90	1,888 04	1,816 44	105 79	642 29	2,231 76
Commercial Light	1,890 72	1,403 56	1,273 38	1,211 25	117 85	1,171 37	2,356 37
Power	5,792 20	5,209 51	2,825 57	1,646 90	....	....	
Street Light	1,827 00	1,827 00	1,827 00	1,827 00	141 00	720 00	2,536 00
Miscellaneous	325 44	....	351 77	400 90	....	....	31 78
Total	11,424 57	10,219 97	8,165 76	6,902 49	364 64	2,583 66	7,155 91
EXPENSES							
Power Purchased	5,206 00	4,770 26	3,144 80	2,934 14	172 82	954 00	3,326 29
Sub-Stn. Operation	....	....	....	....	....	....	....
" " Maint'ce...	....	....	....	....	....	....	....
Dist. System, Operation and Maintenance	323 40	380 19	469 01	480 61	17 89	51 45	76 54
Line. Transformer M't'c'e.	....	....	....	....	....	....	
Meter Maintenance.......	....	....	....	....	....	....	
Consumers' Premises—Exp.	....	....	....	....	....	....	
Street Light Sys., Opera- tion and Maintenance..	....	....	177 00	101 98	....	55 40	165 98
Promotion of Business ..	....	....	....	....	....	....	....
Billing and Collecting ...							
Gen. Office, Sal. and Exp..	1,194 68	995 47	1,055 70	1,056 52	30 00	157 26	684 53
Undistributed Expenses ..	....	107 21	....	....	....	....	18 48
Int. and Deb. Payments..	1,170 92	1,172 91	1,303 57	1,170 92	....	497 96	897 08
Total Expenses	7,895 00	7,426 04	6,150 08	5,744 17	220 71	1,716 07	5,168 90
Surplus	3,529 57	2,793 93	2,015 68	1,158 32	143 93	817 59	1,987 01
Loss	....	....	....	....			....
Depreciation Charge .	900 00	900 00	900 00	830 00	....	190 00	440 00
Surp. Less Depr. Chg.	2,629 57	1,893 93	1,115 68	328 32	143 93	627 59	1,547 01

"e" 3 months' operation.
xh See page 68.

" C "—Continued

Municipalities for the years ending 31st December, 1913, 1914, 1915 and 1916

Harriston 1,404 xb	Port Dalhousie xa 1,318				Caledonia xh 1,217			
1916	1913	1914	1915	1916	1913	1914	1915	1916
y								
$ c.	$ c.	$ c.	$ c.	$ c.	$ c.	$ c.	$ c.	$ c.
2,967 86	3,742 54	3,656 01	3,608 70	2,868 05	404 60	880 54	265 62	263 39
*	*	*	*	782 99	*	*	950 38	777 38
366 79	347 28	429 54	252 12	339 12	470 34	188 54	138 42	519 82
1,253 25	1,246 67	880 00	968 00	850 00	584 00	780 00	808 00	760 00
....	....	....	....	....	....	....	....	....
4,587 90	5,336 49	4,965 55	4,828 82	4,840 16	1,458 94	1,849 08	2,162 42	2,320 59
1,191 50	2,393 00	2,407 20	2,415 28	1,911 14	766 70	669 00	793 00	917 00
1,026 97	....	....	....	....	....	....	....	....
....								
254 98	253 81	421 83	225 52	600 76	23 05	92 95	53 58	91 65
....	....	....	....	....	....	....	....	....
....								
77 28	8 74	65 28	25 75	54 90	....	35 80	22 28	22 65
....	....	....	....	....				
205 45	302 30	712 50	1,014 54	1,092 59	48 28	66 82	92 76	82 85
522 46	112 98	218 83	....					
992 61	814 89	725 89	629 04	1,264 89	134 47	122 86	361 72	361 72
4,271 25	4,785 72	4,551 53	4,810 13	4,924 28	972 50	987 43	1,343 34	1,475 87
316 65	550 77	414 02	518 69	....	486 44	861 65	819 08	844 72
....	....	....	....	84 12	....	....	....	....
345 00	450 00	414 02	415 00	....	250 00	260 00	300 00	260 00
28 35	100 77	....	103 69	84 12	236 44	601 65	519 08	584 72

* Domestic and Commercial not separable.
" y " 5 months Hydro; 7 months steam.
Italics denote losses.
xa, xb, xh See page 68.

STATEMENT

Comparative Detailed Operating Reports of Electric Departments of Hydro

Municipality / Population-		Norwich 1,189 xh				New Toronto 1,186 xa	
→	1913	1914	1915	1916	1914	1915
EARNINGS	$ c.	$ c.	$ c. †	$ c. †	$ c.	$ c.
Domestic Light	1,926 78	2,168 13	2,529 91	2,319 58	653 56	1,416 10
Commercial Light	1,162 98	995 16	1,075 79	1,168 34	*	*
Power	1,978 55	1,893 72	2,169 31	2,642 97	....	2,140 36
Street Light	1,285 50	1,197 00	1,126 00	1,188 56	600 00	783 00
Miscellaneous	46 71	746 92	2,504 61	3,730 22	....	....
Total	6,400 52	7,000 93	9,405 62	11,044 67	1,253 56	4,339 46
EXPENSES						
Power Purchased	3,176 24	2,849 30	2,954 63	6,039 14	233 30	1,351 92
Sub-Stn. Operation	....	....	....	....	....	....
" " Maint'ce.	....	....	....	....	....	....
Dist. System, Operation and Maintenance	178 90	464 80	809 58	883 68	50 73	137 80
Line Transformer M't'c'e.	....	13 48	7 05	116 70	....	....
Meter Maintenance	....	37 11	1 32	1 35	....	....
Consumers' Premises—Exp.	....	....	....	....	....	....
Street Light Sys., Operation and Maintenance	79 51	95 40	75 95	88 14	137 85	55 00
Promotion of Business	....	....	....	....	....	....
Billing and Collecting	....	....	....	....	....	....
Gen. Office, Sal. and Exp.	838 27	534 15	595 76	574 16	318 01	629 49
Undistributed Expenses	....	....	....	....	....	....
Int. and Deb. Payments	886 40	960 58	1,985 15	2,452 31	178 44	654 10
Total Expenses	5,159 32	4,954 82	6,429 44	10,155 48	918 33	2,828 31
Surplus	1,241 20	2,046 11	2,976 18	889 19	335 23	1,511 15
Loss	....	....	....	....	....	....
Depreciation Charge	500 00	530 00	1,195 00	1,370 00	200 00	550 00
Surp. Less Depr. Chg.	741 20	1,516 11	1,781 18	*480 81*	135 23	961 15

* Domestic and Commercial not separable.
† Miscellaneous includes Rural Revenue.
xa, xh See page 68.

"C"—Continued

Municipalities for the years ending December 31st, 1913, 1914, 1915 and 1916

New Toronto xh 1,186 xa	Waterford xh 1,133		Shelburne 1,115 xa	Elora xh 1,115			Beaverton xh 1,015		Markdale 989 xa
1916	1915	1916	1916	1914	1915	1916	1915	1916	1916
			g	c			q		l
$ c.	$ c.	$ c.	$ c.	$ c.	$ c.	$ c.	$ c.	$ c.	$ c.
-1,571 03	685 22	1,112 28	538 29	101 98	1,044 49	1,253 03	1,484 62	1,417 39	934 65
143 32	546 08	796 50	494 38	167 25	1,820 07	1,828 25	1,149 67	1,065 23	972 28
9,744 31	....	1,007 74	....	....	197 78	972 12	456 74	383 45	35 76
838 00	892 50	1,174 82	446 23	110 33	1,000 00	1,000 00	1,057 72	923 04	540 46
....	....	....	....	....	214 97	7 86	109 08	62 20	252 79
12,296 66	2,123 80	4,091 34	1,478 90	379 56	4,277 31	5,061 26	4,257 83	3,851 31	2,735 94
6,547 34	931 11	2,063 38	650 50	133 05	1,711 73	2,004 97	3,188 00	3,423 94	1,039 68
....	....	....	....	....	....	....	....	....	....
228 19	26 30	212 03	....	....	274 00	85 28	83 17	107 54	80 13
....	....	....	....	....	....	....	....	....	....
83 02	23 16	90 00	....	24 78	61 52	53 80	....	32 22	43 09
....	....	....	....	....	....	....	....	....	....
678 32	78 41	184 20	238 33	66 19	785 52	817 85	152 02	432 41	288 23
922 31	978 56	1,366 37	34 33	125 35	846 15	875 17	884 64	855 20	657 86
8,459 18	2,037 54	3,915 98	923 16	349 37	3,678 92	3,837 07	4,257 83	3,851 31	2,108 99
3,837 48	86 26	175 36	555 74	30 19	598 39	1,224 19	....	....	626 95
....	....	....	....	....	....	....	....	....	....
450 00	....	....	....	....	460 00	375 00	....	....	....
3,387 48	86 26	175 36	555 74	30 19	138 39	849 19	....	....	626 95

"c"—1 month's operation.
"g" 5 months' operation.
"l" 9 months' operation.
"q" 14 months' operation.
xa, xh See page 68.

STATEMENT

Comparative Detailed Operative Reports of Electric Departments of Hydro

Municipality / Population	xa	Hagersville 1,105			xh	Winchester 1,065	
—	1913	1914	1915	1916	1914	1915	1916
EARNINGS	$ c. e	$ c.	$ c.	$ c.	$ c.	$ c.	$ c.
Domestic Light	81 42	1,222 33	1,172 85	1,606 80	2,972 09	1,608 40	1,812 29
Commercial Light	*	*	1,592 59	1,343 82	*	1,336 85	1,364 47
Power	746 85	2,679 08	2,434 62	2,527 92	......	......	227 52
Street Light	300 00	1,200 00	1,200 00	1,200 00	1,500 00	1,500 00	1,500 00
Miscellaneous	......	......	......	......	......	......	39 36
Total	1,128 27	5,101 41	6,400 06	6,678 54	4,472 09	4,535 25	4,943 64
EXPENSES							
Power Purchased	967 23	3,084 34	3,010 99	3,163 30	1,827 07	2,137 86	2,337 50
Sub-Stn. Operation	......	......	......	......	......	......	......
" " Maint'ce...	......	......	......	......	......	......	......
Dist. System, Operation and Maintenance	......	52 15	156 80	65 66	2 32	501 85	156 00
Line Transformer M't'c'e.	......	......	......	......	......	......	......
Meter Maintenance	......	......	......	......	......	......	......
Consumers' Premises–Exp.	......	......	......	......	......	......	......
Street Light Sys., Operation and Maintenance.	......	73 00	58 37	......	58 50	60 26	35 28
Promotion of Business	......	......	......	......	......	......	......
Billing and Collecting	......	......	......	......	......	......	......
Gen. Office, Sal. and Exp..	37 69	545 77	595 22	748 01	173 09	380 55	714 53
Undistributed Expenses	......	......	......	......	......	......	......
Int. and Deb. Payments..	97 60	383 93	577 57	550 80	541 80	795 91	773 70
Total Expenses	1,102 52	4,139 19	4,398 94	4,527 77	2,602 78	3,876 43	4,017 01
Surplus	25 75	962 22	2,001 12	2,150 77	1,869 31	658 82	926 63
Loss	......	......	......	......	......	......	......
Depreciation Charge	......	425 00	500 00	380 00	500 00	465 00	370 00
Surp. Less Depr. Chg.	25 75	537 22	1,501 12	1,770 77	1,869 31	193 82	556 63

* Domestic and Commercial not separable.
"e" 3 months' operation.
xa, xh See page 68.

" C "—Continued

Municipalities for the years ending December 31st, 1913, 1914, 1915 and 1916

xh	Port Credit 1,046			xh	Stayner 972			xa	Cannington 903
1913	1914	1915	1916	1913	1914	1915	1916	1915	1916
				d				q	
$ c.	$ c.	$ c.	$ c.	$ c.	$ c.	$ c.	$ c.	$ c.	$ c.
1,963 22	2,461 42	1,975 29	1,781 49	158 48	909 58	995 47	1,012 15	1,599 40	1,720 25
*	*	587 11	464 02	116 91	747 93	933 55	997 39	1,120 04	973 63
848 59	308 88	236 47	257 40	301 86	1,699 08	1,694 94	1,835 29	464 26	462 47
696 00	810 60	1,000 00	1,033 00	35 00	707 50	607 25	609 00	980 12	831 96
....	....	....	....	....	....	....	....	22 58	....
3,507,81	3,580 90	3,798 87	3,535 91	612 25	4,064 09	4,231 21	4,458 83	4,186 40	3,988 31
1,210 65	1,333 00	1,406 46	1,546 06	187 52	2,726 45	2,524 18	2,725 01	2,693 38	2,316 44
....	....	....	....	....	....	....	....	....	....
22 21	23 51	77 77	386 30	....	56 85	67 53	155 26	251 70	....
....	....	....	....	....	....	....	....	....	....
....	....	....	....	....	....	....	....	....	....
121 27	72 77	22 29	44 40	....	96 00	53 78	....	11 04	33 72
....	....	....	....	....	....	....	....	....	....
171 82	450 67	470 75	214 04	14 48	31 00	98 02	358 14	223 48	690 83
....	18 46	....	....	....	....	....	....	....	48 80
534 23	571 55	537 22	568 95	340 82	784 66	784 66	753 16	1,006 80	898 52
2,060 18	2,469 96	2,514 49	2,759 75	542 82	3,694 96	3,528 17	3,991 57	4,186 40	3,988 31
1,447 63	1,110 94	1,284 38	776 16	69 43	369 13	703 04	462 26	....	....
....	....	....	....	....	....	....	....	....	....
446 00	535 00	600 00	470 00	....	115 00	300 00	280 00	....	....
1,001 63	575 94	684 38	306 16	69 43	254 13	403 04	182 26	....	....

* Domestic and Commercial not separable.
" d "   2 months' operation.
" q "   14 months' operation.
xa, xh   See page 68.

STATEMENT

Comparative Detailed Operative Reports of Electric Departments of Hydro

Municipality / Population	Dutton xa 870		Pt. Stanley xa 849				Milverton 890 xh
—	1915	1916	1913	1914	1915	1916	1916
EARNINGS	e $ c.	$ c.	$ c.	$ c.	$ c.	$ c.	$ c.
Domestic Light	318 85	1,353 04	1,828 66	2,066 41	2,498 57	2,956 97	292 00
Commercial Light	206 59	960 27	1,771 70	1,753 60	1,736 42	1,551 37	406 95
Power	....	135 31	2,418 00	2,170 88	2,064 76	1,985 92	....
Street Light	364 23	1,469 88	2,199 50	1,961 35	1,900 50	1,714 00	665 98
Miscellaneous	....	111 39	....	157 77	226 18	214 00	....
Total	889 67	4,029 89	8,217 86	8,110 01	8,426 43	8,422 26	1,364 93
EXPENSES							
Power Purchased	442 18	1,813 70	3,506 43	3,682 26	4,735 96	4,753 04	593 81
Sub-Stn. Operation	....	....	....	....	....	....	....
" " Maint'ce	....	....	....	....	....	....	....
Dist. System, Operation and Maintenance	15 55	22 35	354 49	116 92	65 01	97 43	4 98
Line Transformer M't'c'e.	....	....	....	....	....	....	....
Meter Maintenance	....	....	....	....	....	....	....
Consumers' Premises—Exp.	....	....	....	....	....	....	....
Street Light Sys., Operation and Maintenance	12 04	69 91	....	....	63 13	191 12	33 48
Promotion of Business	....	....	....	....	....	....	....
Billing and Collecting	....	....	292 81	286 23	....	....	....
Gen. Office, Sal. and Exp.	79 30	204 36	368 47	581 96	919 21	940 24	8 08
Undistributed Expenses	....	....	....	....	....	....	....
Int. and Deb. Payments	144 70	476 04	1,188 91	1,232 82	1,232 82	1,232 82	690 86
Total Expenses	693 77	2,586 36	5,711 11	5,900 19	7,016 13	7,214 65	1,331 21
Surplus	195 90	1,443 53	2,506 75	2,209 82	1,410 30	1,207 61	33 72
Loss	....	....	....	....	....	....	....
Depreciation Charge	....	240 00	617 75	950 00	740 00	665 00	....
Surp. Less Depr. Chg.	195 90	1,203 53	1,889 00	1,259 82	670 30	542 61	33 72

"e" 3 months' operation.
xa, xh See page 68.

"C"—Continued

Municipalities for the years ending December 31st, 1913, 1914, 1915 and 1916

	Chesterville 854 xh			Ayr 800 xa		Waterdown 785 xh			
	1914	1915	1916	1915	1916	1913	1914	1915	1916
				n				†	†
	$ c.	$ c.	$ c.	$ c.	$ c.	$ c.	$ c.	$ c.	$ c.
	530 13	919 27	1,490 99	892 63	1,084 46	1,164 29	1,054 13	1,202 41	1,218 86
	791 67	1,187 54	1,240 56	773 08	804 00	*	535 83	567 65	575 10
	....	....	177 55	348 78	393 39	917 63	1,011 38	1,207 80	1,149 78
	465 00	689 00	798 00	1,091 83	1,092 00	435 00	510 00	580 80	590 00
	....	....	....	....	....	....	418 46	1,488 36	1,681 41
	1,786 80	2,795 81	3,707 10	3,105 82	3,373 85	2,516 94	3,529 80	5,046 22	5,215 15
	1,107 66	2,123 30	1,993 63	1,170 61	1,320 35	988 00	1,660 71	1,605 10	2,003 34
	....	....	....	....	....	....	....	....	....
	....	126 30	336 99	....	....	183 71	67 66	281 36	354 12
	....	....	....	....	....	....	....	....	....
	....	....	48 29	45 20	44 52	35 31	48 15	17 00	41 10
	....	....	....	....	....	....	....	....	....
	59 00	56 77	120 00	397 82	301 98	213 14	207 87	327 69	392 97
	....	....	....	....	115 74	....	....	....	....
	344 00	572 55	435 34	1,119 49	1,076 82	521 56	723 09	1,243 23	1,482 95
	1,510 66	2,878 92	2,934 25	2,733 12	2,859 41	1,941 72	2,707 48	3,474 38	4,274 48
	276 14	....	772 85	372 70	514 44	575 22	822 32	1,571 84	940 67
	....	83 11	....	....	....	....	....	....	....
	247 50	....	375 00	250 00	260 00	365 00	420 00	1,000 00	887 00
	28 64	*83 11*	397 85	122 70	254 44	210 22	402 32	571 84	53 67

* Domestic and Commercial not separable.
† Miscellaneous includes Rural Revenue.
"n" 11 months' operation.
Italics denote losses.
xa, xh See page 68.

STATEMENT

Comparative Detailed Operating Reports of Electric Departments of Hydro

Municipality Population	Thamesville xh 769		Bolton xh 727		Dundalk 721 –xh	Bothwell xh 703	
—	1915	1916	1915	1916	1916	1915	1916
	e		m			e	
EARNINGS	$ c.	$ c.	$ c.	$ c.	$ c.	$ c.	$ c.
Domestic Light	378 79	1,729 79	624 86	926 86	924 30	230 61	928 16
Commercial Light	283 86	1,021 17	553 80	882 26	960 58	191 21	768 59
Power			313 74	3,947 32	618 52	....	....
Street Light	255 00	1,030 00	811 25	893 75	744 00	219 25	1,186 06
Miscellaneous	....	25 42	....	186 00	....	....	....
Total	917 65	3,806 38	2,303 65	6,836 19	3,247 40	641 07	2,882 81
EXPENSES							
Power Purchased	537 22	1,872 38	1,126 94	4,120 46	1,362 22	440 00	1,604 92
Sub-Stn. Operation	....	....	....	....	....	....	....
" Maint'ce...	....	....	....	....	....	....	....
Dist. System, Operation and Maintenance	4 15	22 40	206 57	30 82	30 00	....	15 45
Line Transformer M't'c'e.	....	....	....	....	....	....	....
Meter Maintenance.......	....	....	....	....	....	....	....
Consumers' Premises–Exp.	....	....	....	....	....	....	....
Street Light Sys., Operation and Maintenance.	40 00	20	12 12	77·61	....	36 72	11 16
Promotion of Business ..	....	....	....	....	....	....	....
Billing and Collecting ...	....	....	....	....	....	....	....
Gen. Office, Sal. and Exp.	116 00	262 83	314 26	289 94	158 80	4 80	114 77
Undistributed Expenses ..	....	....	....	....	....	....	....
Int. and Deb. Payments..	....	740 65	552 82	866 16	818 56	....	565 99
Total Expenses	697 37	2,898 41	2,212 21	5,384 99	2,369 58	481 52	2,312 29
Surplus	220 28	907 97	91 44	1,441 20	877 82	159 55	570 52
Loss	....	....	....	....	....	....	....
Depreciation Charge ·	....	190 00	....	321 00	200 00	....	135 00
Surp. Less Depr. Chg.	220 28	717 97	91 44	1,120 20	677 82	159 55	435 52

"e" 3 months' operation.
"m" 10 months' operation.
xh See page 68.

"C"—Continued

Municipalities for the years ending December 31st, 1913, 1914, 1915 and 1916

Lucan xh 662		Woodbridge xh 639		Ailsa Craig 586 xa	Creemore xh 585			Embro xa 483	
1915	1916	1915	1916	1916	1914	1915	1916	1915	1916
n				n	d			n	
$ c.	$ c.	$ c.	$ c.	$ c.	$ c.	$ c.	$ c.	$ c.	$ c.
824 07	1,124 73	367 49	507 10	579 57	97 31	699 81	922 41	400 50	633 95
687 37	857 11	443 53	556 82	213 46	127 31	937 84	1,041 90	489 67	598 41
18 66	159 67	498 44	2,221 33	15 57	39 60	939 20	1,151 96	....	155 54
812 60	979 50	960 00	963 00	819 62	138 80	857 28	874 58	620 68	685 10
108 10	135 55	....				1 35	6 00		58 25
2,450 80	3,256 56	2,269 46	4,248 25	1,628 22	403 02	3,435 48	3,996 85	1,510 85	2,131 25
1,511 32	1,543 95	877 63	2,461 11	746 02	162 00	2,580 53	2,252 69	782 02	1,057 98
....	....	....	....	....	....	....	....	....	....
....	66 30	66 65	44 81	30 56	....	185 17	182 00	16 00	16 40
....	....	....	....	....	....	....	....	....	....
....	14 50	24 96	48 79	16 74	....	14 80	22 20	36 28	94 61
....	....	....	....	....	....	....	....	....	....
440 03	254 59	153 75	284 01	100 07	6 14	221 98	257 16	95 98	74 71
412 43	873 49	239 38	636 88	401 10	20 59	509 55	689 52	285 25	390 30
2,363 78	2,752 83	1,362 37	3,475 60	1,294 49	188 73	3,512 03	3,403 57	1,215 53	1,634 00
87 02	503 73	907 09	772 65	333 73	214 29	....	593 28	295 32	497 25
....	....	....	....	....	....	76 55	....	....	....
....	270 00	425 00	300 00	180 00	....	....	200 00	250 00	235 00
87 02	233 73	482 09	472 65	153 73	214 29	76 55	303 28	45 32	262 25

"d" 2 months' operation.
"n" 11 months' operation.
Italics denote losses.
xa, xh See page 68.

STATEMENT

Comparative Detailed Operating Reports of Electric Departments of Hydro

Municipality Population	xh	Coldwater 579			Wyoming 544 xh	Flesherton 428 xh
—	1913	1914	1915	•1916	1916	1916
					d	
EARNINGS	$ c.	$ c.	$ c.	$ c.	$ c.	$ c.
Domestic Light	735 68	853 56	874 94	977 62	96 84	568 76
Commercial Light	*	589 85	703 35	848 82	85 38	423 83
Power	247 19	617 26	363 88	247 91	....	....
Street Light'.............	532 00	528 00	528 00	528 00	128 00	504 00
Miscellaneous						
Total	1,514 87	2,588 67	2,470 17	2,602 35	310 22	1,496 59
EXPENSES						
Power Purchased	535 86	897 12	1,018 75	1,008 22	72 52	809 49
Sub-Stn. Operation	....	....	....	....	....	....
" " Maint'ce..	....	....	....	....	....	....
Dist. System, .Operation and Maintenance	74 58	139 37	138 72	147 60	....	....
Line Transformer M't'c'e.	....	....	....	....	....	....
Meter Maintenance.......	....	....	....	....	....	....
Consumers' Premises-Exp.	....	....	....	....	....	....
Street Light Sys., Operation and Maintenance..	32 92	32 00	20 00	22 32	22 32	· 22 32
Promotion .of Business ..	....	....	....	....	....	....
Billing and Collecting ...						
Gen. Office, Sal. and Exp..	1 50	68 00	80 00	100 00	21 48	185 46
Undistributed Expenses ..	....	....	300 00	226 90	....	....
Int. and Deb. Payments..	....	481 64	481 64	481 64	103 04	85 34
Total Expenses ..,...	644 86	1,618 13	2,039 11	1,986 68	219 36	1,102 61
Surplus	870 01	970 54	431 06	615 67	90 86	393 98
Loss	....	....	....	....	....	....
Depreciation Charge .	375 00	380 00	380 00	325 00	....	150 00
Surp. Less Depr. Chg.	495 01	590 54	51 06	290 67	90 86	243 98

`* Domestic and Commercial not separable.
" d " 2 months' operation.
xh See page 68.

"C"—Continued

Municipalities for the years ending December 31st, 1913, 1914, 1915 and 1916

xh	Woodville 388		Chats-worth 374 xh	Baden xh				Brechin xh	
	1915	1916	1916	1913	1914	1915	1916	1915	1916
	q		n						
	$ c.	$ c.	$ c.	$ c.	$ c.	$ c.	$ c.	$ c.	$ c.
	324 34	496 52	287 52	884 11	1,247 81	938 33	808 21	148 83	172 42
	563 68	512 07	193 15	*	*	*	*	407 78	404 70
	1,149 17	1,185 54	391 98	2,242 77	4,580 23	4,588 87	5,059 22	1,007 59	1,153 32
	507 60	423 44	325 00	830 95	705 68	580 06	683 58	117 00	117 00
	....	....	77 65	....	....	....	....	....	150 00
	2,544 89	2,617 57	1,275 30	3,957 83	6,533 72	6,107 26	6,551 01	1,681 20	1,997 44
	2,167 90	1,970 18	727 65	2,807 04	4,541 56	4,153 75	5,080 81	1,498 18	1,673 64
	....	....	....	....	....	....	....	....	....
	· 12 00	8 55	62 20	28 84	179 28	52 26	48 36	....	....
	....	....	....	....	....	....	....	....	....
	....	....	....	....	....	....	....	....	....
	26 64	11 04	2 50	....	14 52	43 53	11 04	....	....
	42 87	297 34	91 78	267 45	389 45	357 10	321 95	86 22	152 71
	295 48	330 46	310 81	325 26	325 26	373 71	325 28	96 80	171 09
	2,544 89	2,617 57	1,194 94	3,428 59	5,450 07	4,980 35	5,787 44	1,681 20	1,997 44
	....	....	80 36	529 24	1,083 65	1,126 91	763 57	....	....
	....	....	....	....	....	....	....	....	....
	....	....	....	277 00	280 00	300 00	275 00	....	....
	....	....	80 36	252 24	803 65	826 91	488 57	....	....

*   Domestic and Commercial not separable.
"n"   11 months' operation.
"q"   14 months' operation.
xh   See page 68.

STATEMENT

STATEMENT

Comparative Detailed Operating Reports of Electric Departments of Hydro

Municipality	Beachville				Burford	
Population	xh				xh	
—	1913	1914	1915	1916	1915	1916
	s				h	
EARNINGS	$ c.	$ c.	$ c.	$ c.	$ c.	$ c.
Domestic Light	562 37	587 33	363 33	400 81	176 14	577 69
Commercial Light	*	*	296 37	263 62	111 81	380 44
Power	5,993 81	5,368 04	5,593 15	5,393 02	235 76	519 72
Street Light	206 03	150 00	150 00	150 00	279 48	572 00
Miscellaneous						
Total	6,762 21	6,105 37	6,402 85	6,207 45	803 19	2,049 85
EXPENSES						
Power Purchased	4,221 68	3,283 89	4,522 88	5,352 36	571 55	1,129 67
Sub-Stn. Operation						
" " Maint'ce..						
Dist. System, Operation and Maintenance	54 34	34 85	27 76	56 33		25 84
Line Transformer M't'c'e.						
Meter Maintenance.......						
Consumers' Premises—Exp.						
Street Light Sys., Operation and Maintenance..	76 37	44 46	9 95	35 88		12 94
Promotion of Business ..						
Billing and Collecting ...						
Gen. Office, Sal. and Exp..	249 50	193 11	258 66	325 81	77 06	71 43
Undistributed Expenses ..	127 62	29 18		38 36		59 48
Int. and Deb. Payments..	288 88	501 45	357 79	369 82	201 21	413 25
Total Expenses	5,018 39	4,086 40	5,177 04	6,178 56	849 82	1,712 61
Surplus	1,743 82	2,018 97	1,225 81	28 89		337 24
Loss					46 63	
Depreciation Charge .	525 00	400 00	420 00	375 00		165 00
Surp. Less Depr. Chg.	1,218 82	1,618 97	805 81	*34 11*	*46 63*	172 24

* Domestic and Commercial not separable.
"h" 6 months' operation.
"s" 2 years' operation.
Italics denote losses.
xh See page 68.

" C "—Continued

Municipalities for the years ending December 31st, 1913, 1914, 1915 and 1916

Comber xh		Drumbo xh		Delaware xh		Dorchester xh		Granton xh	Grantham Twp. xh
1915	1916	1915	1916	1915	1916	1915	1916	1916	1916
j				m					†
$ c.	$ c.	$ c.	$ c.	$ c.	$ c.	$ c.	$ c.	$ c.	$ c.
214 87	538 57	304 39	340 75	146 16	354 60	579 23	613 03	180 84	3,030 72
274 49	678 58	288 99	277 43	114 18	141 64	309 88	275 82	70 90	....
....	....	159 85	116 57	....	....	287 95	667 93	....	....
448 37	779 51	455 00	420 00	188 18	241 50	85 72	326 74	240 01	....
....	....	....	....	....	....	....	....	....	....
937 73	1,996 66	1,208 23	1,154 75	448 52	737 74	1,262 78	1,883 52	491 75	3,030 72
620 24	1,159 98	795 36	602 85	217 11	352 26	583 47	785 60	248 72	668 09
....	....	....	....	....	....	....	....	....	....
....	38 38	....	3 35	....	7 87	....	33 19	8 32	471 33
....	....	....	....	....	....	....	....	....	....
....	40 94	....	11 04	....	34 20	....	22 77	2 40	....
....	....	....	....	....	....	....	....	17 80	474 86
135 76	137 15	51 29	54 64	71 89	45 63	58 54	102 37	....	....
....	50 40	....	....	....	....	....	....	....	....
172 92	378 26	281 33	271 11	.77 13	229 35	159 47	281 55	108 53	2,997 93
928 92	1,805 11	1,127 98	942 99	366 13	669 31	801 48	1,225 48	385 77	4,612 21
8 81	191 55	80 25	211 76	82 39	68 43	461 30	658 04	105 98	....
....	....	....	....	....	....	....	....	....	1,581 49
....	145 00	....	110 00	....	80 00	200 00	150 00	....	....
8 81	46 55	80 25	101 76	82 39	*11 57*	261 30	508 04	105 98	*1,581 49*

† Domestic includes Rural Revenue.
"j" 7 months' operation.
"m" 10 months' operation.
Italics denote losses.
xh See page 68.

STATEMENT

Comparative Detailed Operating Reports of Electric Departments of Hydro

Municipality	Elmvale				Holstein	Lambeth
Population	xh				xh	xh
—	1913	1914	1915	1916	1916	1915
	h				j	l
EARNINGS	$ c.	$ c.	$ c.	$ c.	$ c.	$ c.
Domestic Light	284 34	673 18	704 12	816 74	141 80	344 47
Commercial Light	358 60	896 11	778 98	736 74	169 63	119 00
Power	....	438 38	1,186 44	1,043 96	....	455 90
Street Light	302 00	624 00	624 00	624 00	124 00	295 16
Miscellaneous	....	....	....	....	....	....
Total	944 94	2,631 67	3,293 49	3,221 44	435 43	1,214 53
EXPENSES						
Power Purchased	506 33	898 78	1,335 80	1,352 32	213 51	800 72
Sub-stn. Operation	....	....	....	....	....	....
" " Maint'ce..	....	....	....	....	....	....
Dist. System, Operation and Maintenance	7 86	326 94	300 00	300 00	12 17	20 10
Line Transformer M't'c'e.	....	....	....	....	....	....
Meter Maintenance.......	....	....	....	....	....	....
Consumers' Premises–Exp.	....	....	....	....	....	....
Street Light Sys., Operation and Maintenance..	....	....	15 17	56 28	75	....
Promotion of Business ...	....	....	....	....	....	....
Billing and Collecting ...						
Gen. Office, Sal. and Exp..	75 12	434 67	213 27	147 24	37 56	44 71
Undistributed Expenses ..	....	....	....	....	....	....
Int. and Deb. Payments..	449 76	434 67	546 42	498 83	229 17	156 10
Total Expenses	1,039 07	2,108 42	2,410 66	2,354 67	493 16	1,021 63
Surplus	....	523 25	882 83	866 77	....	192 90
Loss	94 13	....	....	....	57 73	....
Depreciation Charge .	....	350 00	385 00	290 00	....	....
Surp. Less Depr. Chg.	94 13	173 25	497 83	576 77	57 73	192 90

"h" 6 months' operation.
"j" 7 months' operation.
"l" 9 months' operation.
Italics denote losses.
xh See page 68.

" C "—Continued

Municipalities for the years ending December- 31st, 1913, 1914, 1915 and 1916

Lambeth xh	Lynden xh		Mount Brydges xh		Otterville xh	Plattsville xh		Princeton xh	
1916	1915	1916	1915	1916	1916	1915	1916	1915	1916
	d		l		m			n	
$ c.	$ c.	$ c.	$ c.	$ c.	$ c.	$ c.	$ c.	$ c.	$ c.
575 65	60 00	254 76	427 45	644 75	476 40	551 39	666 30	440 42	657 80
208 96	28 94	227 57	*	170 46	111 14	477 71	580 62	71 57	127 81
249 36	....	650 38	517 50	760 58	22 50	1,128 27	1,436 62	....	192 92
420 00	67 50	360 00	449 66	532 00	269 15	498 00	534 00	340 00	340 00
....	....	....	....	....	....	....	....	....	6 61
1,453 97	156 44	1,492 71	1,394 61	2,107 79	879 19	2,655 37	3,217 54	851 99	1,325 14
819 20	55 95	920 13	1,025 71	1,308 69	429 36	2,031 19	2,079 85	507 23	919 15
....	....	....	....	....	....	....	....	....	....
3 09	....	23 89	22 05	12 57	3 15	....	- 49 30	....	9 90
....	....	....	....	....	....	....	....	....	....
....	....	....	....	....	....	....	....	....	....
70 99	....	24 54	....	28 00	11 04	14 02	19 49	....	15 93
....	....	....	....	....	....	....	....	....	....
58 32	....	70 10	117 38	79 10	74 29	85 42	86 58	11 84	132 49
				51 09					
382 49	....	315 32	358 60	296 20	346 74	386 29	346 17	263 35	239 57
1,334 09	55 95	1,353 98	1,523 74	1,775 65	864 58	2,516 92	2,581 39	782 42	1,317 04
119 88	100 49	138 73	~......	332 14	14 61	138 45	636 15	69 57	8 10
....	....	....	129 13	....	....	....	....	....	....
100 00	....	120 00	....	125 00	....	....	145 00	....	96 00
19 88	100 49	18 73	*129 13*	207 14	14 61	138 45	491 15	69 57	*87 90*

* Domestic and Commercial not separable
"d" 2 months' operation.
"l" 9 months' operation.
"m" 10 months' operation.
"n" 11 months' operation.
Italics denote losses.
xh See page 68.

STATEMENT

Comparative Detailed Operating Reports of Electric Departments of Hydro

Municipality Population	Port McNicoll xh		Rockwood xh				Sunder- land xh
—	1915	1916	1913	1914	1915	1916	1915
	n		f				q
EARNINGS	$ c.	$ c.	$ c.	$ c.	$ c.	$ c.	$ c.
Domestic Light	415 03	618 82	230 27	848 55	731 97	733 66	794 83
Commercial Light	311 20	301 92	*	*	251 27	388 05	939 85
Power	....	7 37	480 82	1,542 01	907 57	903 57	....
Street Light	351 00	336 00	196 00	549 50	507 50	506 00	323 82
Miscellaneous	....	....	....	....	....	....	20 08
Total	1,077 23	1,264 11	907 09	2,940 06	2,398 31	2,531 28	2,078 58
EXPENSES							
Power Purchased	616 27	670 51	237 50	1,113 49	1,154 85	870 81	1,621 28
Sub-stn. Operation	....	....	....	....	....	....	....
" " Maint'ce..	....	....	....	....	....	....	....
Dist. System, Operation and Maintenance	18 88	99 30	....	....	....	36 26	....
Line Transformer M't'c'e.	....	....	....	....	....	....	....
Meter Maintenance.......	....	....	....	....	....	....	....
Consumers' Premises–Exp.	....	....	....	....	....	....	....
Street Light Sys., Opera- tion and Maintenance..	24 24	33 48	....	36 14	13 92	46 97	24 96
Promotion of Business ...	....	....	....	....	....	....	....
Billing and Collecting ...							
Gen. Office, Sal. and Exp..	164 58	169 56	44 46	119 55	115 74	111 49	33 27
Undistributed Expenses ..							
Int. and Deb. Payments..	203 14	482 51	357 49	413 19	445 80	395 77	399 07
Total Expenses	1,027 11	1,455 36	639 45	1,682 37	1,730 31	1,461 30	2,078 58
Surplus	50 12	....	267 64	1,257 69	668 00	1,069 98	....
Loss	....	191 25	....	....	....	....	....
Depreciation Charge .	....	130 00	....	275 00	300 00	240 00	....
Surp. Less Depr. Chg.	50 12	*321 25*	267 64	982 69	368 00	829 98	....

* Domestic and Commercial not separable.
"f"   4 months' operation.
"n"   11 months' operation.
"q"   14 months' operation.
Italics denote losses.
xh See page 68. .

" C "—Continued

Municipalities for the years ending December 31st, 1913, 1914, 1915 and 1916

Sunderland xh	St. George xh		Stanford Twp. xh	Thorndale xh			Thamesford xh		
1916	1915	1916	1916	1914	1915	1916	1914	1915	1916
	f		f	m			⁻ m		
$ c.	$ c.	$ c.	$ c.	$ c.	$ c.	$ c.	$ c.	$ c.	$ c.
752 64	203 23	832 23	730 57	446 27	299 37	328 67	393 49	574 34	642 21
840 22	139 16	474 38	†	*	374 09	403 01	323 92	481 78	537 42
211 86	311 30	583 52	4,331 96	329 27	542 53	459 79	946 32	423 21	268 23
272 16	202 50	495 00	....	294 00	294 00	294 46	372 16	469 00	476 00
....	....	....	....	....	....	....	....	....	....
2,076 88	856 19	2,385 13	5,062 53	1,069 54	1,509 99	1,485 93	2,035 89	1,948 33	1,923 86
1,345 62	411 15	1,227 88	2,009 48	510 00	883 86	1,139 22	1,031 10	993 40	1,013 59
....	....	....	....	....	....	....	....	....	....
....	....	1 20	55 03	5 25	71 52	74 42	9 80	7 19	2 50
....	....	....	....	....	....	....	....	....	....
....	....	....	....	....	....	....	....	....	....
22 32	....	3 00	....	29 04	7 19	65 18	23 68	27 47	33 90
....	....	....	....	....	....	....	....	....	....
309 87	64 30	126 49	900 44	94 12	64 63	104 58	125 94	159 32	122 89
									48 84
399 07	172 00	412 83	737 19	109 92	11 74	205 60	249 94	209 41	477 08
2,076 88	647 45	1,771 40	3,702 14	748 33	1,138 94	1,589 00	1,440 46	1,396 79	1,698 80
....	208 74	613 73	1,360 39	321 21	371 05	....	595 43	551 54	225 06
....	....	....	....	....	....	103 07	....	....	....
....	....	150 00	....	130 00	135 00	85 00	250 00	250 00	235 00
....	208 74	463 73	1,360 39	191 21	236 05	*188 07*	345 43	301 54	*9 94*

* Domestic and Commercial not separable.
† Revenue all Rural.
"f"   4 months' operation.
"m"   10 months' operation.
Italics denote losses.
xh See page 68.

STATEMENT " C "—Concluded

Comparative Detailed Operative Reports of Electric Departments of Hydro Municipalities for the years ending December 31st, 1913, 1914, 1915 and 1916

Municipality Population	Toronto Township xh			Williamsburg xh		Waubaushene xh	
—	1914	1915	1916	1915	1916	1915	1916
EARNINGS	r					n	
	$ c.	$ c.	$ c.	$ c.	$ c.	$ c.	$ c.
Domestic Light	8,151 12	8,615 27	8,369 78	403 72	568 66	516 34	646 58
Commercial Light				139 26	224 29	220 50	496 47
Power					285 73	32 28	49 52
Street Light				156 00	220 67	377 00	348 00
Miscellaneous							
Total	8,151 12	8,615 27	8,369 78	698 98	1,299 35	1,146 12	1,540 57
EXPENSES							
Power Purchased	3,085 55	2,153 94	2,174 17	318 62	547 82	560 77	642 81
Sub-stn. Operation							
" " Maint'ce							
Dist. System, Operation and Maintenance	284 02	706 20	395 59	82 50	97 63	16 55	110 16
Line Transformer M't'c'e							
Meter Maintenance							
Consumers' Premises—Exp.							
Street Light Sys., Operation and Maintenance					16 04		17 38
Promotion of Business							
Billing and Collecting							
Gen. Office, Sal. and Exp.	374 61	376 04	462 21	30 02	41 60	175 55	112 77
Undistributed Expenses							
Int. and Deb. Payments	1,358 65	3,482 49	3,258 87	211 27	220 67	220 84	425 56
Total Expenses	5,102 83	6,718 67	6,285 84	642 41	923 76	973 21	1,308 68
Surplus	3,048 29	1,896 60	2,083 94	56 57	375 59	172 91	231 89
Loss							
Depreciation Charge		1,800 00	1,934 00		70 00		115 00
Surp. Less Depr. Chg.	3,048 29	96 60	149 94	56 57	305 59	172 91	116 89

"n" 11 months' operation.
"r" 17 months' operation.
xh See page 68.

COMPARATIVE STATEMENT

OF

REVENUE, NUMBER OF CONSUMERS, TOTAL CONSUMPTION,
AVERAGE MONTHLY CONSUMPTION PER CONSUMER,
AVERAGE MONTHLY BILL AND NET COST PER
KW-HR. FOR YEARS 1912, 1913, 1914,
1915 AND 1916

[113]

STATEMENT "D"

Showing Comparative Revenue, Number of Consumers, Average Monthly Bill, and Net Average Monthly Bill, and Total Kw-hr. Consumption, Average Monthly Consumption per Customer, Cost per Kw-hr. for the Years 1912, 19, 1914, 1915 and 1916

Municipality	Year	Domestic Light Revenue	Consumption Kw-hrs.	No. of Consumers	Av'g Monthly Consumption	Average Monthly Bill	Net Cost per Kw-hr.	Net Cost prior to Hydro	Commercial Light Revenue	Consumption Kw-hrs.	No. of Consumers	Av'g Monthly Consumption	Average Monthly Bill	Net Cost per Kw-hr.	Net Cost prior to Hydro	Power Revenue	No. of Consumers	Total Number Consumers
Toronto	1912	201,554 74		11,441					233,799 04	6,156,073	4,764		4 09			225,451 55	518	11,959
	1913	190,376 89	4,220,270	16,519	25	1 25	4.4	8 + 25	305,634 31	7,683,589	6,276	116	4 61	3.8	12 + 25	347,708 88	1,037	22,320
	1914	289,065 45	6,240,882	23,181	27	1 22	4.5		291,907 92	10,243,496	7,227	126	3 60	3.9		483,681 15	1,494	30,951
	1915	331,807 18	8,599,559	29,724	27	1 04	3.9		272,243 06	11,491,377	7,406	131	3 10	2.8		575,239 17	1,504	38,455
	1916	335,81 91	11,250,250	34,347	29	89	3.1							2.4		612,918 32	1,707	43,460
Hamilton	913	34,451 95	862,937	5,117	23	92	3.9	8 + 25	25,453 99	628,471	924	95	2 55	4.1	8	47,415 58	209	6,250
	1914	74,668 38	1,856,627	6,404	23	81	3.7		35,125 57	1,309,863	1,375	109	2 06	3.4		70,665 43	337	10,116
	1915	92,207 60	2,514,104	10,595	26	78	3		34,633 16	1,840,920	1,434	116	2 02	1.9		84,789 71	406	12,435
	1916	108,137 22	3,625,059	12,423					36,126 03	2,085,601	1,546			1.8		115,224 78	464	14,433
Ottawa	1912	62,598 18		5,390		1 02		7 + 8	51,365 91		440		7 08		7 + 8	25,299 94	90	5,920
	1913	68,082 27	1,376,353	5,766	19	95	5		53,438 04	1,061,263	818	106	5 16	4.9		26,978 76	152	6,736
	1914	68,767 48	1,767,519	6,342	22	82	3.8		51,769 72	1,501,978	852	131	4 07	3.1		31,748 23	156	7,350
	1915	67,441 19	2,131,307	7,338	23	80	3.4		46,636 99	1,786,603	1060	137	3 27	2.4		32,126 50	140	8,538
	1916	72,875 12		7,912					42,569 96		1,107					42,996 39	188	9,207
London	1912	28,196 62		3,851		77		9 + 25	28,527 44		792		3 63		9 + 25	52,633 00	158	4,801
	1913	41,932 42	920,000	5,201	17	83	4.5		39,256 07	1,350,000	1,007	125	3 81	3.0		79,758 96	198	5,406
	1914	57,473 08	1,192,000	6,299	18	70	4.8		47,593 44	1,580,000	1,075	127	3 44	3.5		130,396 35	249	7,649
	1915	57,184 75	1,732,435	7,326	21	76	3.3		43,751 37	1,452,896	1,046	137				148,567 23	271	8,643
	1916	71,146 90	2,378,144	8,282	24		2.9		48,747 74	1,930,269	1,129	147		2.5		180,204 33	295	9,706
Brantford	1914	7,103 77	148,427	1,184	19	82	4.8	8 + 13	5,392 87	166,469	300	94	2 89	3.6	8 + 13	647 69	111	1,495
	1915	13,629 36	319,480	1,615	21	79	4.3		10,746 67	347,349	321	107	2 68	3.1		12,901 29	18	1,954
	1916	17,504 44	468,324	2,056			3.7		10,530 19	419,933	334			2.5		24,213 00	26	2,316
Windsor	1914	3,143 41		1,802		89		12	1,107 38		257		3 16		8	9 77	10	2,069
	1915	23,161 57	468,386	2,519	18	104	4.9		12,009 99	309,757	377	82	3 44	3.9		3,734 81	43	2,939
	1916	35,565 79	726,442	3,180	21		4.9		16,831 60	465,683	439	95		3.6		7,370 82	60	3,685
Peterborough	1914	8,661 71		2,692		79		Flat	7,749 91		507		4 14		Flat	7,013 23	98	3,292
	1915	27,998 24	3,221	3,221	13	78	6.1		27,568 41		602	65	3 66	6.6		30,185 83	113	3,936
	1916	31,020 72	510,369	3,401					26,408 82	467,668	602					36,597 04	117	4,120

Kitchener	1912	14,585 02				1,022						19,080 32		422						28,654 23	105	1,549
	1913	15,291 37				1,291		99	11+25			19,548 91		470	91					85,665 90	127	1,888
	1914	17,757 08	859,307		1,694	20		4.9		19,549 45	562,630	519	95 3 65	3.5	49,173 17	130	2,343
	1915	19,108 60	494,725		2,032	22	85	3.9		16,807 15	579,303	646	91 2 63	2.9	54,732 50	138	2,716
	1916	20,876 63	582,754		2,407	22	79	3.6		17,323 67	801,789	643	123 2 65	2.2	62,436 31	147	3,097
St. Catharines	1914	2,013 49	53,572	833	19	65	3.7		412 75	22,843	92		1.9	12,742 98	20	945
	1915	9,540 70	273,389	1,612			3.5		3,810 11	196,056	192	115	1.9	25,193 30	34	1,838
	1916	16,419 57	591,765	2,410	24	68	2.8		5,925 49	318,877	247	121 2 23	1.5	40,688 67	48	2,705
St. Thomas	1912	7,596 01	187,000	620		1 18	5.9	11	18,741 74	272,000	300	72 4 26	5.9	14,761 30	60	980
	1913	11,125 50	277,539	961	19	90	4.8		16,097 41	346,994	329	81 3 15	3.9	36,550 26	70	1,350
	1915	13,221 00	460,103	1,499	19	81	4.6		13,480 75	504,679	384	102 3 73	2.7	44,247 13	92	1,975
	1916	16,517 37	629,102	1,903	23	81	3.2		13,422 48	607,131	434	2 81	2.5	44,780 45	104	2,438
		20,210 52		2,241	25				15,145 47		464	93		46,698 91	107	2,812
Stratford	1912	6,942 56		640		90		12+25	14,661 16		316			8,834 40	76	1,032
	1913	11,550 71	269,459	1,042	18	1 03	5.5		17,072 61	345,639	367	76 3 55	4.7	14,272 59	92	1,501
	1914	15,180 91	388,200	1,403	21	90	4.4		16,336 30	400,686	396	79 3 92	3.7	16,519 24	99	1,898
	1915	16,967 58	553,441	1,724	26	90	3.6		14,766 75	601,616	439	110 2 75	2.5	15,415 78	104	2,267
	1916	20,108 76		1,993					14,803 08		463			23,506 12	103	2,559
igh..	1912	10,251 87	224,373	960	17	87	5.2	8+25	16,400 57	287,561	345	67 3 38	5.2	30,139 01	73	1,378
	1913	11,528 07	286,032	1,260	17	1 00	5.9		15,075 61	325,080	400	65 3 16	4.9	42,091 34	85	1,745
	1915	16,920 54	366,928	1,573	18	76	4.2		15,923 51	437,567	441	83 2 32	2.8	38,148 46	80	2,094
	1916	17,221 76	469,528	1,824	20	74	3.7		12,692 86	522,526	474	91 2 36	2.6	38,404 28	81	2,379
				2,033					13,710 72		490			48,369 83	86	2,609
Pt. Arthur	1913	81,830 66		2,409				8+25	32,933 91		500		8+25	51,748 11	55	2,964
	1914	38,097 65		2,969					28,662 58		550			92,804 49	55	3,574
	1915	32,048 37		2,800							550			85,060 78	50	3,400
Chatham	1915	5,581 54	110,552	949	14	80	5.5	8+25	2,806 81	81,805	180	81 3 48	3.4	449 70	7	1,136
	1916	10,155 37	176,508	1,171			5.8		7,427 36	174,204	215		4.3	3,766 37	25	1,401
Owen Sound	1916	16,003 61	225,620	1,376			7.16.4+15		23,724 21	388,717	435		6.16.4+15	13,772 61	83	1,894
Galt	1912	8,183 69	300,121	830	1 22		11		9,732 86	289,857	250		11	10,042 59	47	1,127
	1913	10,535 38		1,122	1 10	5.3		11,648 49		353	68 3 25	10,575 61	65	1,540
	1914	15,797 16	512,443	1,745	1 08	3.3		11,952 75	350,788	339	92 2 80	4.1	23,826 87	70	2,154
	1915	17,024 42	716,396	2,038	23	75	2.8		8,794 36	532,860	375	2 10	2.3	30,547 84	75	2,488
	1916	19,961 17		2,236	28	78			10,485 26		386	115 2 30	2.0	36,029 78	79	2,701
Niagara Falls	1916	21,733 29		2,050		3.5		13,259 02		400		Flat	9,613 01	80	2,530
Woodstock	1912	4,914 92	100,000	464	1 08	6.5	8+20	13,316 02	298,000	265	77 3 95	5.2	21,087 61	43	772
	1913	6,495 02	169,054	636	17	1 08	5.2		12,942 32	289,982	282	78 3 12	4.0	20,262 52	55	973
	1915	8,807 40	230,297	949	21	88	4.5		11,610 14	371,787	337	90 2 80	3.1	19,832 26	57	1,343
	1916	10,472 14	288,201	1,099	20	80	3.9		11,718 95	503,977	360	114 2 95	2.6	20,742 18	62	1,521
		11,206 71		1,224	21				12,983 32		372			23,721 92	72	1,668
Brockville	1916	12,897 12	144,913	965		9.0		21,994 02	253,163	312		8.7	15,828 62	31	1,308

STATEMENT "D"—Continued

Showing Comparative Revenue, Number of [?], [?] Kw-hr. Consumption, Average Monthly [?] Kw-hr. [?]sumption per Customer, Average Monthly Bill, and Net Cost per Kw-hr. for the Years 1912, 1913, 1914, 1915 and 1916

Municipality	Year	Domestic Light Revenue	Consumption	No. of Consumers	Av'g Monthly Consumption	Average Monthly Bill	Net Cost per Kw-hr.	Net Cost prior to Hydro	Commercial Light Revenue	Consumption	No. of Consumers	Av'g Monthly Consumption	Average Monthly Bill	Net Cost per Kw-hr.	Net Cost prior to Hydro	Power Revenue	Power No. of Consumers	Total No. of Consumers
Welland	1913	1,369 67		408					558 46		53					4,307 21	18	479
	1914	4,411 20	117,328	492	27	82	3.7	8+25	1,676 38	64,449	53	100	2 64	2.6	8+25	8,305 71	23	568
	1915	4,643 16	154,534	467	27	81	3.6		1,600 79	69,340	57	105	2 42	2.3		38,541 88	23	547
	1916	4,800 06	154,706	536	26	79	3.1		1,580 48	94,582	75	141	2 40	1.7		78,184 81	24	635
Barrie	1913	10,071 55		563					9,252 70		200					3,390 29	13	776
	1914	11,149 49	152,095	651	20	1 54	7.3	9	9,464 64	138,948	200	58	3 85	6.8	9	3,712 24	13	864
	1915	11,087 68	147,307	843	18	1 24	7.1		9,572 91	177,000	252	65	3 93	5.4		4,567 76	14	1,109
	1916	11,907 10	204,420	896	21	1 14	5.8		10,635 67	189,409	257	63	3 50	5.6		6,918 33	18	1,171
[?]	1913	7,013 66	83,406	477	16	1 27	8.4		9,362 17	108,676	220	46	2 78	8.4		896 72	21	715
	1914	7,857 86	103,598	554	16	1 27		11+10	7,555 54	124,276	232	42	2 04	6.1	11+10	5,165 39	21	807
	1915	7,094 27	118,336	622	17	1 00	6.0		5,688 26	116,583	233	58	2 18	4.9		9,527 70	26	881
	1916	8,320 44	162,464	714	20	1 04	5.1		6,213 86	163,956	242			3.8		23,152 41	33	989
Midland	1912	5,878 05		420					5,878 05		165					3,188 03	18	663
	1913	6,095 11	88,228	491	16	1 11	6.9	9	6,104 16	118,267	172	58	3 01	5.1	9	6,484 43	25	688
	1914	6,580 45	127,397	621	19	1 06	3.3		5,084 06	117,741	176	56	2 44	4.6		10,229 52	39	829
	1915	6,941 07	199,257	689	25	84	4.0		4,462 54	97,300	188	45	2 05	2.5		12,262 89	31	916
	1916	7,145 74	180,735	732	21	83			4,624 85	186,953	184	84	2 07					947
Ingersoll	1912	3,073 73		220					6,648 28		142					14,430 66	38	400
	1913	3,595 03	43,406	278	14	1 20	8.3	8+25	6,048 51	81,724	170	44	3 23	7.4	8+25	15,293 44	44	492
	1914	5,085 32	68,342	416	12	1 22	7.5		6,359 72	106,689	194	46	2 32	5.1		12,818 27	48	658
	1915	5,480 52	102,537	497	19	1 00	5.3		5,716 91	139,428	197	60	2 46	4.1		16,251 18	52	746
	1916	6,857 94	127,449	590	20	1 05	4.0		6,540 51	176,757	206	51	2 70			20,380 90		847
Walkerville	1914	3,087 96		790				15-5	1,492 84		175				15-10-5	6,042 11	75	1,040
	1915	13,036 98	241,771	1,169	21	1 12			7,836 93	167,198	195	70	3 49	4.4		39,523 81	72	1,421
	1916	18,813 06	391,629	1,513	21	1 34	4.8		12,104 72	309,727	216	126	4 61	3.9		77,003 07	75	1,804
Waterloo	1912	4,057 46		239					4,524 93		112					11,545 93	35	386
	1913	4,263 66	69,576	321	21	1 27	6.1	12+25	5,098 42	87,718	125	62	3 58	5.8	12+25	14,970 14	44	490
	1914	4,723 94	85,199	430	19	1 05	5.5		4,825 22	98,924	153	59	2 90	4.9		13,282 14	51	634
	1915	5,401 82	106,570	524	19	94	5.1		5,284 87	107,821	162	57	2 80	3.6		15,125 32	53	739
	1916	5,454 60	145,196	592	22	81	3.8		4,750 09	130,418	150	69	2 54			17,905 45	50	792

Goderich	1914	7,197 05	83,805	400	....	....	8.6	9	4,196 49	79,874	155	....	....	5.3	9	1,240 73	10	565
	1915	6,072 51	92,406	441	.. 18	1 20	6.6	10+25	5,066 76	121,559	168	62 2 60	4.1		5,645 26	8	617
	1916	7,086 32	108,654	511	19	1 24	6.5		5,253 15	98,221	159	50 2 68	5.4		5,498 56	9	679
Hdas	1913	3,045 85	92,168	377	..	..	..	10+25	4,198 27	119,947	134	..	..	..	3,070 40	27	538
	1914	5,349 24	128,600	520	19	99	5.8		4,198 64	157,547	153	69 2 44	3.5		4,305 96	30	703
	1915	6,139 97	613	19	90	4.8		4,310 96	157,151	160	84 2 29	2.7		5,930 54	37	810
	1916	6,925 46	146,710	673	19	89	4.8		4,714 78	179,151	168	91 2 39	2.6		10,915 58	35	876
Preston	1912	4,234 68	83,852	341	..	..	..	9+20	5,237 99	103,000	131	..	..	9+20	15,478 14	21	492
	1913	5,477 10	108,257	526	16	1 05	6.5		5,366 77	106,675	151	61 3 18	5.2		21,017 68	28	705
	1914	6,520 39	129,896	629	14	90	6.		5,011 15	118,756	165	56 2 64	4.7		21,975 26	29	823
	1915	6,615 91	714	16	83	5.1		4,488 76	155,325	174	58 2 21	3.8		21,698 34	30	918
	1916	7,341 15	186,361	785	21	82	3.9		4,779 76	182	72 2 24	3.1		22,624 37	34	1,001
Paris	1914	4,766 23	65,037	354	..	..	5.8	7+10	2,778 09	65,108	142	..	..	4.3	8+20	1,419 90	1	497
	1915	5,071 54	87,239	477	17	1 01	4.6		4,063 03	100,259	150	57 2 32	4.1		6,328 33	4	631
	1916	5,877 57	127,382	552	21	96			3,805 95	96,750	150	53 2 11	3.9		8,974 66	4	706
Wallaceburg	1915	4,079 74	56,482	368	..	..	7.2	11	4,239 30	63,747	161	..	..	6.6	10	87 32	2	531
	1916	5,095 45	68,988	438	15	1 05	7.4		4,589 30	67,718	354	22 1 48	6.8		5,866 32	5	593
Simcoe	1915	351 67	5,227	35	..	..	6.7		1,386 89	26,852	61	..	..	5.1	8	766 42	8	104
	1916	1,857 61	13,238	57	..	..	6.5		2,292 28	46,254	84	53 2 63	5.0		1,386 33	12	153
Brampton	1912	3,004 66	409	..	..	..	9+15	2,893 74	101,751	104	..	..	9+15	3,531 34	12	525
	1913	5,617 61	142,178	643	..	..	4.9		3,986 65	116,717	138	55 2 17	4.0		10,557 72	16	797
	1914	6,798 89	159,435	627	18	89	4.3		4,055 99	153,542	174	56 1 94	3.5		10,658 33	21	822
	1915	6,860 48	691	20	86	4.0		4,053 56	174	73 1 92	2.6		11,624 83	21	886
	1916	6,660 66	165,435	722	20	79			4,013 51	175			12,922 72	24	921
St. Mary's	1912	4,967 16	44,801	240	..	..	8.5	9+15	4,069 20	62,486	143	..	..	7.3	9+15	6,001 30	20	403
	1913	3,815 77	67,375	396	12	1 00	6.7		4,553 73	75,257	160	34 2 50	6.3		8,221 72	29	588
	1914	4,614 95	72,819	454	13	90	6.9		4,733 33	75,644	161	39 2 46	5.5		10,610 05	30	645
	1915	5,073 97	528	12	86	3.9		4,222 53	151	40 2 25	4.0		8,379 87	33	712
	1916	5,020 33	127,274	563	19	77			3,161 26	79,768	161	42 1 69			9,266 74	28	752
Penetang	1912	1,676 26	27,199	101	..	..	7.3	9	3,836 30	58,111	87	..	..	7.7	9	2,207 51	13	201
	1913	1,989 80	35,163	128	19	1 44	5.5		4,511 16	66,489	91	55 4 23	4.6		8,775 95	15	234
	1914	1,936 73	42,843	153	21	1 15	4.8		3,064 83	78,657	100	58 2 68	3.4		8,001 69	15	268
	1915	2,050 69	49,242	174	22	1 04	4.7		2,676 60	83,448	102	65 2 21	3.2		10,048 08	15	291
	1916	2,317 37	189	23	1 06			2,706 74	95	71 2 30			11,650 03	16	290
Tillsonburg	1912	3,233 92	29,115	200	..	..	9.6	11+25	3,350 91	66,049	128	..	..	7.8	11+25	3,283 75	6	334
	1913	2,796 57	45,937	254	10	1 03	7.3		4,677 38	70,265	143	41 2 87	6.5		4,763 15	17	414
	1914	3,367 74	55,346	300	14	1 02	5.7		4,579 37	74,564	160	38 2 52	5.7		6,303 09	16	476
	1915	3,203 51	72,975	348	14	83	5.5		4,236 42	95,326	161	38 2 19	4.7		5,619 15	15	524
	1916	4,009 67	375	18	1 02			4,493 41	188	46 2 14			5,692 05	17	580
Strathroy	1915	3,380 78	36,200	233	..	..	9.3	12+25	4,701 76	50,469	147	..	..	9.3	12+25	704 49	5	385
	1916	3,318 45	51,191	314	16	1 01	6.5		3,817 38	66,325	152	37 2 12	5.8		2,927 36	8	574

STATEMENT "D"—Continued

Showing Comparative Revenue, Number of Consumers, Total Kw-hr. Consumption, Average Monthly Consumption per Customer, Average Monthly Bill, and Net Cost per Kw-hr. for the years 1912, 1913, 1914, 1915 and 1916

Municipality	Year	Domestic Light							Total Light							Power		Total Number of Consumers
		Revenue $ c.	Consumption Kw-hrs.	Number of Consumers	Av'g Monthly Consumption Kw-hr	Average Monthly Bill $ c.	Net Cost per Kw-hr Cents	Net Cost prior to Hydro Cents	Revenue $ c.	Consumption Kw-hrs.	Number of Consumers	Av'g Monthly Consumption Kw-hr	Average Monthly Bill $ c.	Net Cost per Kw-hr Cents	Net Cost prior to Hydro Cents	Revenue $ c.	Number of Consumers	
Hespeler	1913	2,189 00		174				10+15	1,684 75		76				10+15	5,044 30	11	261
	1914	2,635 41	34,848	229	14	1 00	7.6		1,934 75	35,979	85	37	2 00	5.4		6,116 27	13	327
	1915	2,787 48	39,580	272	11	90	7.0		2,334 15	39,657	90	38	2 22	5.9		9,017 58	14	376
	1916	3,011 73	54,239	277	17	92	5.5		2,012 28	44,900	84	43	1 93	4.5		11,177 71	12	273
Prescott	1914	4,868 75		342				9	3,609 00		122				9	1,099 27	10	474
	1915	4,058 14	67,130	369	16	95	6.0		3,033 62	62,647	145	39	1 89	4.8		3,431 45	11	525
	1916	4,186 96	63,304	380	15	93	6.6		3,611 95	71,794	133	43	2 16	5.0		4,141 90	22	525
Ridgetown	1916	2,173 64	24,975	174			8.7	10+25	2,838 32	32,594	101			8.7	10+25	740 86	3	278
Elmira	1914	1,908 41	20,875	158		1 00	9.5	11.4+10	2,020 81	28,490	65		1 85	7.1	11.4+1	1,876 49	8	231
	1915	2,059 11	27,576	185	13	88	7.5		1,674 44	28,368	85	32	1 56	5.9		2,801 33	10	280
	1916	2,211 16	30,817	233	12		7.2		1,665 69	35,414	92	33		4.7		3,635 22	12	338
Weston	1912	3,979 81		225				7.2*22.5	750 00		15				7.2*22.5	1,674 28	4	344
	1913	4,117 20		360					1,475 74		34					6,166 97	6	400
	1914	3,741 84	79,766	352	17	80	4.7		1,599 97	26,774	78	40	2 38	6.0		4,958 59	10	440
	1915	4,407 36	96,186	441	21	93	4.6		1,305 90	27,564	90	27	1 30	4.7		4,798 33	9	540
	1916	5,477 65	135,272	475	25	1 00			1,407 31	31,898	88	30	1 31			5,202 84	11	574
Clinton	1914	2,023 70	21,466	179	16	1 28	9.4	10+25	2,028 08	24,696	111	20	2 31	8.2	10+25	1,255 33	7	297
	1915	2,980 57	36,598	204	17	1 27	8.2		3,068 63	40,234	110	31	2 30	7.6		2,018 24	6	320
	1916	3,161 29	41,986	211	17		7.5		3,064 37	41,205	112			7.4		2,498 64	7	330
Milton	1913	1,149 28		110		1 51		10	1,212 26		74		2 43		10	6,462 38	5	189
	1914	1,961 22	25,649	150	19	1 03	7.6		2,226 80	41,015	79	44	2 00	5.4		11,325 61	6	235
	1915	1,981 80	28,900	170	15	1 01	6.8		1,900 98	41,520	80	44		4.6		5,364 29	7	257
	1916	2,219 28	36,573	197	16				1,892 21	44,445	84	45	1 93			10,428 79	6	287
Mimico	1913	2,021 06		250				8+25			10				8+25	795 49	5	255
	1914	5,085 16	91,184	462	17	90	5.4		346 49	3,462	7	40	2 14	5.4		963 64	5	477
	1915	5,748 44	105,884	609	18	95	5.4		506 44	6,551	31	38	1 76	5.3		1,042 11	3	619
	1916	7,011 08	137,318	621			5.1			10,982				4.6		1,449 14	8	660

Town	Year	(1)	(2)	(3)	(4)	(5)	head	(6)	(7)	(8)	(9)	(10)	head	(11)	(12)	(13)
Seaforth	1913	2,124 18	24,666	178			8.6	2,876 47	34,789	105	35	98	8.3	7,509 99	10	293
	1914	2,467 36	37,453	211	16	1 06	6.8	2,581 30	45,492	112	36	1 98	5.6	7,707 01	10	333
	1915	2,593 70	43,162	238	16	1 06	6.0	2,724 84	48,840	111	37	2 03	5.6	7,685 52	11	360
	1916	3,045 65	51,884	280	17	96	5.9	2,941 03	56,380	110	43	2 22	5.2	9,684 11	12	402
Fergus	1915	1,314 08	19,328	114			6.8	2,367 91	37,844	91			6.3 10+.25	882 24	7	212
	1916	1,621 27	24,275	149	16	1 03	6.7 10+.25	2,111 16	34,953	92	32	2 00	6.0	2,819 21	7	248
Mt. Forest	1916	1,967 03	27,337	106			7.2 10	2,420 75	39,059	164			6.2 10	1,739 79	7	277
Palmerston	1916	6,102 25		151			Flat	282 57		63			Flat		1	215
Durham	1916	1,518 72	17,091	155		95	8.9 Flat	1,057 33	13,949	67		2 25	8.8 Flat			222
Georgetown	1913	661 49		160			7.2 10+.10	842 87		50	59	3 15	8	234 32	5	285
	1914	3,069 02	42,328	242	17	27	6.9	2,362 33	29,544	75	34	3 20	8.9	2,976 61	17	334
	1915	2,999 83	43,392	294	14	93	5.6	2,276 41	35,318	97	45	1 79	3.3	8,734 01	16	407
	1916	3,174 63	56,191	306	16	88	10+.10	2,101 00	53,129	99			10+.10	10,726 24	21	426
Tilbury	1915	979 57		123			10	1,476 53		67		2 36	10	149 60		190
	1916	1,507 37	21,483	127	14	1 00	6.5	2,071 77	32,612	79	37		4.5		2	218
Acton	1913	1,236 50		82			10	1,567 48		62	28	2 08	10	318 77	3	147
	1914	1,463 72	21,192	146	15		6.9	1,496 18	19,878	58	36	2 59	7.5	836 13	5	209
	1915	1,931 11	29,079	183	15		6.6	1,725 73	24,336	58	52	2 35	7.1	1,019 27	5	241
	1916	1,942 11	29,685	185	15		6.5	1,592 62	35,227	60			4.5	1,565 53	7	252
Mitchell	1912	2,964 48		159			Flat	2,977 08		79			Flat	4,597 03	13	251
	1913	2,362 52		179				2,813 92		85				6,160 53	16	270
	1914	2,470 29		191				2,712 55		100		2 25		3,944 91	16	307
	1915	2,379 58		190	14		6.8	2,684 01		95	33		6.8	2,333 08	17	292
	1916	2,311 80	33,759	218				2,677 35	39,211	103				3,231 56	21	342
New Harg	1912	1,195 08		124			10	1,423 35		63			10	3,369 05	5	192
	1913	1,589 21		142			7.7	1,890 72		63	25	1 78	7.2	5,792 20	8	213
	1914	1,779 90	23,010	170	12	89	4.9	1,403 56	19,404	68	27	1 54	5.5	5,209 51	6	244
	1915	1,888 04	33,913	187	16	88	5.5	1,273 38	23,041	70	32	1 39	4.6	2,825 57	4	261
	1916	1,816 44	37,109	196	16	79		1,211 25	26,492	70				1,646 90	4	270
Dresden	1915	1,095 68		185			7.5 Flat	1,223 25		109			6.5 Flat			294
	1916	1,995 51	26,473	197	12	87		1,986 21	30,352	106	24	1 54				303
Victoria Harbor	1915	105 79		56				117 85		34						90
	1916	642 29		65				1,171 37		31						96
Pt. Dalhousie	1913	3,742 54		238			Flat			10			Flat	347 28	3	241
	1914	3,656 01		240						10				429 54	3	253
	1915	3,608 70		250				782 99		32				252 12	2	262
	1916	2,868 05		330										339 12	8	370
Caledonia	1913	404 60		17			None			16			None	470 34	1	34
	1914	880 54		21						32		2 44		188 54	1	54
	1915	265 62	4,618	24	16	98	5.4	950 38	18,325	33	47		5.4	138 42	3	58
	1916	263 39	4,800	27	16	86	5.5	777 38	20,000	37	47	1 85	4.	519 82		67

STATEMENT "D"—Continued

Showing Comparative Revenue, Number of ... Average Monthly ... Average Monthly ... Kw-hr., ... Kw-hr., consumption per Customer, Average Monthly Bill, and Net Cost per Kw-hr. for the Years 1912, 1913, 1914, 1915 and 1916

Municipality	Year	Domestic Light Revenue $ c.	Consumption Kwhrs.	No. of Consumers	Av'g Monthly Consumption kwhr	Average Monthly Bill $ c.	Net Cost per Kw-hr. Cents	Net Cost prior to Hydro Cents 10+25	Commercial Light Revenue $	Consumption Kw-hrs.	No. of Consumers	Av'g Monthly Consumption Kw-hr	Average Monthly Bill $ c.	Net Cost per Kw-hr. Cents	Net Cost prior to Hydro Cents 10+25	Power Revenue $ c.	Net Cost per Kw-hr. Cents	Net Cost prior to Hydro Cents 10+25	No. of Consumers	Total Number Consumers
Norwich	1912	862 17		128				8+25	674 48		64	20	1 38	6.5	10+25	263 93	6.5	10+25		194
	1913	1,926 78	28,172	166	15	1 09	6.8		1,162 98	17,917	76	22	1 04	6.4		1,978 55	6.4		2	245
	1914	2,168 13	35,578	198	16	99	5.5		995 16	20,690	84	26	1 09	4.2		1,893 72	4.2		3	286
	1915	2,529 91	37,082	228	16	99	6.2		1,075 79	25,880	80	25	1 16	4.7		2,169 31	4.7		5	313
	1916	2,319 58	49,858	234	18	84	4.7		1,168 34	24,909	87					2,642 97			6	327
New Toronto	1914	653 50	11,947	100		100	7.0	8+25			4			7.0	8+25		7.0	8+25	1	106
	1915	1,416 10	19,520	153			5.5		143 32	5,956	8			5.5		2,140 36	5.5		2	163
	1916	1,571 03	29,162	210							10					9,744 31			4	224
Waterford	1915	685 22		75	14	1 08	7.8.10		546 08		40	20	1 62	8.110		1,007 74	8.110			115
	1916	1,112 28	14,220	99					796 50	9,827	42								2	143
Elora	1915	1,044 49	14,009	89	18	1 08	7.4	10+25	1,820 07	25,431	60	38	2 48	7.1	10+25	197 78	7.1	10+25	1	150
	1916	1,253 03	20,500	105			6.1		1,828 25	27,945	63			6.5		972 12	6.5		3	170
Hagersville	1913	81 92		3				None	*		24				None	746 85	5.4	None		30
	1914	1,222 23	16,053	70	21	06	5.4			6,446	60	28	99	5.2		2,679 08	5.2		3	133
	1915	1,172 85	23,213	114	21	1 11	5.1		1,592 59	22,676	73	32	1 58	4.8		2,434 62	4.8		3	190
	1916	1,606 80	30,025	127	21	1 11	5.4		1,343 82	27,840	69					2,527 92			4	200
Winchester	1914	1,672 09		103	21	1 27	5.9	15	1,300 00		50	50	2 23	7.6	15	227 52	7.6	15	1	153
	1915	1,698 40	28,610	120	24	1 18	5.4		1,336 85	17,550	30	38	2 37	6.2			6.2			171
	1916	1,812 29	36,931	135					1,364 47	21,999	46									182
Pt. Credit	1913	1,963 42		93			6.0	None	*		21			6.0	None	848 59	6.0	None		116
	1914	2,461 42	41,862	125	23	1 24	5.4		587 11	17,934	35	44	1 18	3.3		308 88	3.3		2	162
	1915	1,975 29	36,484	141	26		4.0		464 02	13,800	33	35	1 17	3.3		236 47	3.3		2	177
	1916	1,781 49	44,251	145												257 40			3	181
Beaverton	1915	1,484 02		131	13	90	6.9	Flat	1,149 67		56	25	1 53	6.1	Flat	456 74	6.1	Flat	5	192
	1916	1,417 39	20,685	131					1,065 23	17,594	60					383 45			6	197
...ber	1913	158 48		120				Flat	116 91		30				Flat	301 86	6.7	Flat		152
	1914	909 58	9,200	108	7	66	9.9		747 93	11,000	56	20	45	6.7		1,699 08	6.8		2	156
	1915	995 47	11,845	106	9	78	8.4		933 55	13,725	56	20	39	6.8		1,694 94	7.7		2	164
	1916	1,012 15	11,995	115	9	76	9.2		997 39	12,955	65	18	1 37	7.7		1,835 29			3	183

Municipality	Year	1	2	3	4	5	6	7	8	9	10	11	12	13	14	15
Cannington	9 & 16	1,599 40		135				1,120 04		65				464 26	9	206
	1916	1,720 25		150				973 63		73				462 47	7	230
Dutton	1915	318 85	3,970	108	13 1 03	8.0	Flat	2,818	206 59	43	23 1 34	7.3	Flat	135 31	1	152
	1916	1,353 04	17,243	112		7.8		13,256	960 27	52		7.2			1	165
Pt. Stanley	1912	897 02		122				1,106 63		40				1,314 70	3	165
	1913	1,828 08		182			Flat	1,771 70		60			Flat	2,418 00	9	251
	1914	2,066 41		229				1,753 60		72				2,170 83	12	313
	1915	2,498 57		274				1,736 42		73				2,064 76	9	356
	1916	2,956 97		308				1,551 37		72				1,985 92	11	391
Chesterville	1914	530 13	7,672	68		6.9	None	10,176	791 67	35		7.7	None			103
	9 & 16	919 27	12,663	85	14 1 00	7.2		12,104	1,187 54	49	21 2 06	9.8		177 55		134
	1916	1,490 99	15,779	89	17 1 43	9.4		15,179	1,240 56	47	26 2 12	8.2			1	137
Ayr	1915	892 63	16,031	79		5.5		9,477	773 08	79		8.1		348 78		115
	1916	1,084 46	12,314	83	13 1 12	8.8	12.5+25	12,960	804 00	48	26 1 61	6.2	12.5+25	393 39	2	133
Waterdown	1913	774 40		41				340 00		20				614 42	2	63
	1914	1,003 09	13,360	70	16 1 25	7.9	None	361 20		34	20 1 31	6.5	None	917 65	2	106
	1915	1,054 13	18,017	71	19 1 30	6.7		535 83		34	23 1 48	6.7		1,011 38	5	110
	1916	1,202 41	18,622	84	18 1 15	6.5		567 65		30	24 1 55	6.4		207 80	7	121
		1,218 86		93				575 10		32				1,149 78	6	131
Thamesville	1915	378 79	19,061	107		9.1	9	13,087	283 36	53		7.8	11			160
	1916	1,729 79		137	13 1 18				1,021 17	59	20 1 52					196
Bolton	1915	624 86	6,563	59		9.5	10+25	7,298	553 80	42		7.6	10+25	313 74	3	104
	1916	926 86	9,322	70	12 1 20	9.9		13,081	882 26	36	28 1 88	6.7		3,947 32	4	110
Ailsa Craig	1916	579 57	6,270	61		9.2	None	1,910	213 46	11		11.2	None	15 67	1	63
Flesherton	1916	568 76		73			None		423 83	30			None			103
Dundalk	1916	924 30		88			Flat	960 58		63			Flat	618 52	2	153
Bothwell	1915	230 61		68			Flat		191 21	32			Flat			100
	1916	928 16	8,662	78	10 1 03	10.7		8,613	768 57	52	17 1 46	8.9				130
Lucan	1915	824 07		87					687 37	39				18 66	3	129
	1916	1,124 73	12,047	98	11 1 00	9.3		8,370	857 11	42	17 1 78	10.2		159 67	7	147
Woodbridge	1915	367 49	4,878	42		7.5	None	4,911	443 53	33		9.0	None	498 44	2	77
	1916	507 10	7,059	58	13 1 89	7.0		7,048	556 82	33	17 1 40	7.9		2,221 33	7	98
Creemore	1915	699 81	6,399	78		10.9	Flat	7,653	937 84	59		12.2	Flat	939 20	1	138
	1916	922 41	9,678	78	14 1 00	7.2		8,745	1,041 90	44	15 1 72	11.9		1,151 96	2	132
Coldwater	1913	405 43		48			None		330 25	32			None	247 19	1	81
	1914	853 56	12,466	62	19 1 30	6.8		10,382	589 85	39	24 1 40	5.7		617 26	2	103
	1915	874 94	16,706	66	21 1 15	6.3		13,686	703 35	37	31 1 54	5.1		363 88	2	105
	1916	977 62	16,599	70	20 1 20	5.9		16,644	848 82	39	36 1 85	5.1		247 91	2	111
Embro	1915	400 50		65			None		489 67	30			None			95
	1916	633 95	5,690	58	7 1 85	11.1		10,333	698 41	29	29 1 66	6.8		155 54	2	89

STATEMENT "D"—Continued

Showing Comparative Revenue, Number of ..., Total Kw-hr. Consumption; Average Monthly Consumption per ..., Average Monthly Bill, and Net Cost per Kw-hr. for the Years 1912, 19, 19, 1916.

Municipality	Year	Light							Commercial Light							Power		Total Number Consumers
		Revenue	Consumption Kw-hrs.	Number of Consumers	Av'g Monthly Consumption Kw-hr	Average Monthly Bill	Net Cost per Kw-hr. Cents	Net Cost prior to Hydro Cents 12.5	Revenue	Consumption Kw-hrs.	Number of Consumers	Av'g Monthly Consumption Kw-hr	Average Monthly Bill	Net Cost per Kw-hr. Cents	Net Cost prior to Hydro Cents 12.5	Revenue	Number of Consumers	
Witville	1915	324 34		35	9	92	9.8	None	563 68		28	28				1,149 17	3	66
	1916	496 52	5,049	41					512 07	6,618	21	21	1 62	7.7	12.5	1,185 54	3	68
Baden	1913	884 11		75	7	75	10.0	None	*		*	7	75	10.0	None	2,242 77	4	79
	1914	1,247 81	6,920	82	13	98	7.4		*	5,547	*	13	98	7.4		4,580 23	4	86
	1915	938 33	12,729	72	16	86	5.5		*		*					4,588 87	4	76
	1916	808 21	8,824	84					*	5,772	*	16	86	5.5		5,059 33	5	89
Brechin	1915	148 83		13	11	1 02	9.4	None	407 78		14	28	2 00	7.5	None	1,007 59	1	28
	1916	172 42	1,836	16					404 70	5,370	20	28				1,153 32	1	37
Beachville	1913	562 97		45	11	74	7.9	None	*		*			7.9	None	5,993 81	4	49
	1914	587 33	4,422	45	11	74	6.8		*	2,988	*	34	2 05	6.1		5,368 04	4	49
	1915	363 33	5,356	37	13	84	6.8		296 37	4,847	12	34	2 05	6.1		5,593 15	4	53
	1916	400 81	5,891	42					263 62	3,872	12	27	1 83	6.8		5,393 02	3	57
Burford	1916	577 69	9,005	64	14	1 32	6.4	Flat	380 44	7,569	30	30		5.0	Flat	519 72	1	95
Comber	1915	214 87		33	14	1 32	6.8	None	274 49	3,497	33	15	1 50	7.8	None			66
	1916	538 57	5,894	37			9.1		678 58	6,729	37	15		10.1				74
Drumbo	1915	304 49		40	10	77	7.5	None	288 99	3,718	30	15	1 12	7.6	None	159 85	1	71
	1916	340 75	4,481	35					277 43		22					116 57		57
Delaware	1915	146 16		22	11	1 35	12.5	None	114 18	1,823	10	14	1 07	7.8	None		1	33
	1916	354 60	2,835	23					141 64		12							35
Dorchester	1915	579 23		61	10	1 84	8.5	None	309 88	4,806	18	19	1 35	6.4	None	287 95	2	81
	1916	613 03	7,329	61			8.4		275 82	4,879	16	16		5.7		667 93	2	79
Lynden	1916	254 76	3,500	24			7.3	None	227 57	4,430	10			5.1	None	650 38		35
Elmvale	1913	284 34		52	10	1 03	9.9	None	358 60	15,402	52	25	1 49	5.8	None			105
	1914	673 18	6,866	57	10	87	9.1		896 11	16,193	48	25	1 16	3.9		438 38	2	107
	1915	704 12	7,728	78	11	85	7.7		778 93	18,644	64	25	97	5.0		1,186 44	2	144
	1916	816 74	10,562	81					736 74		62					1,043 96	3	146

Lambeth	1915	344 47	2,991	49				None	119 00	1,042	9		11.4	None	559 82	1	69
	1916	575 65	6,880	54	11	91	11.5	None	208 96		13	1 58	8.3	None	249 36	1	68
Mt. Brydges	1915	333 43		45	8			None	494 02		15				None	517 50		61
	1916	644 75	5,058	55		1 07	12.7	None	170 46	3,106	15	17	95	5.5	None	760 58	2	72
Plattsville	1915	551 39	6,001	56	11	96	9.1	None	477 71	5,091	20	14 1 35	9.4	None	1,128 27	4	80
	1916	666 30	7,422	60			9.0		580 62	5,900	22		9.8		1,436 62	3	85
Princeton	1915	440 42		30	17	1 48	8.5	None	81 57	1,278	15	8	83	10.6	None			45
	1916	657 80	7,739	44	17				127 81		11						55
Pt. McNicoll	1915	415 03	6,057	60	17	82	6.8	None	311 20	6,542	26	17 1 07	4.7	None	192 92		86
	1916	618 82	9,450	66	12		6.5		301 92	4,738	21		6.4		7 37	1	88
Rockwood	1913	230 27		48	13	1 38	8.8	None	*		9		8.8		480 82	1	58
	1914	848 55	7,824	54	13	1 03	7.7		251 27	3,300	7	32 2 46	7.7		1,542 01	3	64
	1915	731 97	9,500	65	13	89	6.5		388 05	5,930	10	47 3 08	6.4		907 57	3	78
	1916	733 66	11,263	72	14						11				903 57	5	87
Sunderland	1915	794 83		57	11	1 06	9.8	12.5	939 85	9,644	36	45 1 92	9.0	12.5	211 86		93
	1916	752 64	7,714	61					840 22		37					1	99
St. George	1915	208 23		39	20	1 46	7.8	None	139 16	7,031	14	31 2 08	6.7	None	311 30	1	54
	1916	832 23	11,483	56			7.2		474 38		24				583 52	2	82
Thorndale	1914	446 27	2,787	34	7	76	7.8	None	374 09	2,989	18	16 1 64	7.8	None	329 27	1	63
	1915	299 37	2,816	32	9	84	10.6		403 01	3,653	20	16 1 64	10.2		542 53		53
	1916	328 67	3,597	33			9.1			3,709	21		10.9		459 79		55
Thamesford	1914	383 49	3,686	44	9	78	10.9	None	323 92	3,445	26	12 1 20	9.4	None	946 32	2	72
	1915	574 34	6,676	59	10	87	8.6		481 78	5,886	26	20 1 63	8.2		423 21	2	87
	1916	642 21	7,540	64			8.5		537 42	6,768	29		7.9		268 23	2	95
Williamsburg	1915	403 72		44	14	1 11	7.7	None	139 26	3,934	9	36 2 08	5.7	None		1	54
	1916	568 66	7,392	41					224 29		9				285 73		51
Waubaushene	1915	516 34	7,296	49	13	1 01	7.0	None	220 50	2,979	15	36 2 37	7.7	None	32 28	1	65
	1916	646 58	8,233	58			7.9		496 47	7,534	20		6.6		49 52	1	79

STATEMENT "E"

Street Light Installation in Hydro Municipalities, December 31st, 1916, showing Cost per Year, Cost per Lamp, and Cost per Capita.

Municipality	Population	Number of Lamps	Size and Style of Lamps	Cost per Lamp	Total Cost	Cost per Capita
				$ c.	$ c.	$ c.
Toronto.........	463,705	24	500 w. Nitro m	45 00	361,920 32	78
		452	5 lt. Stds. m	40 00		
		41,789	100 watt m	8 00		
Hamilton........	100,461	401	500-Watt m	40 00	80,815 73	80
		501	250 " m	12 00		
		294	200 " m	12 00		
		7,270	100 " m	7 20		
		10	150 " m			
		6	60 " m	special		
		12	40 " m			
Ottawa...........	100,163	59	arcs s	45 00	60,632 48	61
		671	400-watt s	45 00		
		44	250 " s	35 00		
		429	75 " s	10 00		
		2,870	100 " m	60c. per ft.		
		313	100 " m	6 00		
London	58,055	2,461	75 " s		31,719 17	55
		193	200 " m			
		22	300 " s	Special		
		18	400 " s			
		96	500 " m			
		146	100 " m			
Brantford.......	25,420	147	mag. arcs s	40 00	27,500 83	1 08
		2,850	100-watt s	7 50		
		7	150 " s	9 00		
Windsor.........	24,162	280	500 " s	50 00	37,266 17	1 54
		1,948	75 " s	12 00		
Peterboro'.......	20,426	145	arcs	50 00	13,257 49	65
		56	magnetites s	50 00		
		350	60-watt s	9 00		
Kitchener	19,266	10	500 " m	33 00	18,621 19	97
		26	400 " m	29 00		
		1,973	100 " s	9 00		
St. Catharines....	17,880	1,970	100 " s	8 00	15,261 33	85
St. Thomas......	17,174	113	500 " s	37 50	14,690 24	85
		20	arcs s	55 00		
		987	75 " s	9 50		
Stratford........	17,081	11	500 " s	50 00	15,753 20	92
		164	500 " s	45 00		
		5	500 " s	40 00		
		767	75 " s	10 00		
Guelph	16,735	1,103	100 " m	8 50	9,518 72	57
Port Arthur	14,307	1,661	100 " m	7 49	15,207 40	1 06
		15	100 " m	5 62		
		724	60 " m	4 78		
Chatham	12,863	69	500-watt s	36 75	13,169 02	1 02
		83	400 " s	30 00		
		31	100 " s	11 00		
		646	100 " s	12 00		
Owen Sound.....	11,910	53	400 C. P. s	50 00	7,000 00	59
		114	75-watt s	11 00		
		249	60 " m	11 00		
Galt.............	11,852	78	500 " m	....	12,567 40	1 06
		97	300 " m	....		
		279	100 " m	....		
		853	75 " s	....		
Sarnia	11,676	....	....	....	3,480 00	*

STATEMENT "E"—Continued

Street Light Installation in Hydro Municipalities, December 31st, 1916, showing Cost per Year, Cost per Lamp, and Cost per Capita.

Municipality	Population	Number of Lamps	Size and Style of Lamps		Cost per Lamp	Total Cost	Cost per Capita
					$ c.	$ c.	$ c.
Niagara Falls....	11,147	30	arc C.	s	50 00		
		16	arc T.	s	50 00		
		101	ornam.	s	50 00	12,849 81	1 15
		57	32 C.P.	m	6 00		
		413	100-watt	s	12 00		
Woodstock.......	10,084	50	250 ''	s	24 00	7,355 01	73
		678	100 ''	s	9 00		
Brockville.......	9,428	52	5 lt. Stds.	m		9,000 00	95
		34	3 lt. Stds.	m	....		
		503	80 C.P.	m			
Welland.........	7,243	345	100-watt	m	9 00	5,181 00	72
		96	200 ''	m	18 00		
Barrie..........	6,453	433	100 ''	s	12 00	5,323 67	82
Collingwood	6,361	394	100 ''	m	10 00	3,940 00	62
Midland........	6,258	16	750 ''	s	40 00	3,330 46	53
		276	100 ''	s	10 00		
Ingersoll	5,176	26	650 ''	s	....		
		220	75 ''	s	11 50	3,729 00	72
		67	60 ''	s	11 00		
Walkerville......	5,096	691	60 ''	m	5 60	9,039 04	1 77
		94	100 ''	m	12 00		
		17	60 ''	m	12 00		
Waterloo........	4,956	44	5 lt. Stds.	m	40 00	5,798 75	1 17
		8	3 ''	m	25 00		
		38	60-watt	m	8 75		
		14	100 ''	m	10 50		
		382	100 ''	s	8 75		
Goderich	4,655	275	75-watt	s	14 00	5,162 39	1 11
		16	5 lt. Stds.	m	50 00		
		8	1 ''	m	40 00		
		8	1 . ''	m	25 00		
Dundas..........	4,652	301	100-watt	m	9 00	3,547 73	58
		30	W. Hamilton	m	14 00		
		24	Ancaster	m	12 00		
		5	Greensville	m	12 00		
Preston..........	4,643	222	75-watt	s	11 00	3,044 92	65
		47	100 ''	s	12 00		
Paris	4,370	400	100 ''		11 00	4,576 00	1 05
Wallaceburg	4,107	170	75 ''	s	13 50	3,094 56	75
		28	400 ''	s	30 00		
Simcoe	4,061	27	300 ''	s	38 00	3,500 00	86
		228	75 ''	s	14 00		
Brampton	4,041	570	100 ''	m	7 50	4,262 17	1 05
St. Mary's.......	3,958	113	250 ''		25 00	5,390 33	1 36
		198	100 ''		13 00		
Penetang........	3,928	170	100 ''		12 00	2,095 00	55
		2	....	s	27 50		
Petrolia.........	3,891	136	100-watt	s	15 50	....	*
		24	600 ''		55 00		
Tillsonburg......	3,084	216	75 ''	s	11 00	2,595 96	84
Strathroy........	2,998	32	200 ''	s	23 00	4,654 59	1 55
		283	75 ''	s	14 00		
Hespeler	2,740	18	200 ''	s	18 00	1,831 80	67
		128	100 ''	s	13 00		

STATEMENT "E"—Continued

Street Light Installation in Hydro Municipalities, December 31st, 1916, showing Cost per Year, Cost per Lamp, and Cost per Capita.

Municipality	Population	Number of Lamps	Size and Style of Lamps		Cost per Lamp	Total Cost	Cost per Capita
					$ c.	$ c.	$ c.
Prescott.........	2,740	400	100-watt	m	....	2,500 00	90
Orangeville......	2,493	32 / 116	250 C.P. / 150 "	s	15 00 } / 12 00 }	....	•
Listowel.........	2,326	12 / 230	350-watt / 60 "		.... }	....	•
Ridgetown	2,326	17 / 130	200 " / 100 "	s	37 00 } / 18 00 }	2,969 00	1 27
Elmira..........	2,270	145	100 "	m	12 00	1,740 00	77
Clinton	2,177	133 / 211	75 " / 75 "	s / s	12 50 / 12 00	1,650 00 / ---- . 4	76
Weston..........	2,156	8 / 26 / 26	5 lt. Stds. / York Tp. / Etobicoke Tp.	m / s / s	40 00 / 16 00 / 15 00	3,692 00	†1 30
Milton..........	2,072	203	100-watt	m	11 00	2,013 20	97
Mimico	1,976	152 / 61	100 " / 100 "	m / m	11 00 / 16 00	2,496 75	† 84
Chesley	1,975	81 / 16	100 " / 200 "	s / s	13 00 } /	....	•
Seaforth.........	1,964	10 / 70 / 60	80 " / 80 " / 100 "	s / s / s	13 00 / 12 00 } / 15 00	1,869 96	95
Mount Forest	1,941	171	100 "	s	12 00	1,963 00	1 01
Georgetown......	1,905	150 / 11	100 " / Glenwilliam	m / m	11 00 } / 12 00 }	1,724 17	† 83
Palmerston	1,843	103	100-watt	s	15 00	1,542 33	84
Fergus	1,776	126	100 . "	m	12 50	1,575 00	88
Tilbury.	1,740	61	100 "	m	15 00	938 73	54
Acton	1,735	72 / 60	75 " / 100	s / m	.... }	1,497 50	86
Gravenhurst	1,702	162 / 27	75 " / dock lights	s	.... }	1,172 49	* 69
Mitchell	1,687	156	100-watt	s	12 00	2,100 00	. 1 24
Durham ....;	1,600	90	100 "	s	12 00	1,068 00	67
Exeter ....;	1,572	23 / 150	250 " / 100 "	m / m	27 00 } / 14 00 }	....	.....
New Hamburg ...	1,543	215	100 "	m	8 50	1,827 00	1 18
Dresden	1,521	110	100 "	s	15 00	1,650 00	1 08
Victoria Harbor..	1,477	60	100 "	m	12 00	720 00	49
Blenheim	1,424	13 / 133	300 " / 100 "	s / s	36 50 } / 15 50 }	2,536 00	1 78
Harriston..	1,404	61	75 "	s	16 50	1,253 25	* 89
Pt. Dalhousie	1,318	85	100 "	m	10 00	850 00	64
Caledonia	1,217	69	100 "	m	12 00	760 00	62
Norwich.........	1,189	15 / 45 / 53	400 " / 100 " / 60 "	m / m / m	42 00 } / 10 50 } / 9 00 }	1,183 56	99

STATEMENT "E"—Continued

Street Light Installation in Hydro Municipalities, December 31st, 1916, showing Cost per Year, Cost per Lamp, and Cost per Capita.

Municipalities	Population	Number of Lamps	Size and Style of Lamps		Cost per Lamp	Total Cost	Cost per Capita
					$ c.	$ c.	$ c.
New Toronto.....	1,186	59 12	100-watt 100 ''		12 00 15 00	838 00	71
Waterford	1,133	96	100 ''	⊞	14 00	1,174 82	1 03
Shelburne.	1,115	86	100 ''	s	12 00	....	*
Elora	1,115	80	100 ''		12 50	1,000 00	90
Hagersville	1,105	100	100 ''		12 00	1,200 00	1 08
Winchester	1,065	113	100 ''		15 00	1,500 00	1 41
Pt. Credit	1,046	94	100 ''		11 00	1,033 00	99
Beaverton	1,015	71	100 ''	⊞	13 00	923 04	91
Markdale........	989	65	100 ''	s	10 50	....	*
Stayner.........	972	51 15	60 '' 100 ''	s s	9 00 12 00	609 00	63
Cannington	903	69	100 ''	m	12 00	831 96	92
Milverton........	893	88	100 ''	m	12 50	....	*
Dutton	870	95	100 ''	m	15 50	1,469 88	1 68
Port Stanley	849	111 46	100 '' 100 ''	m m	13 00 6 50	1,714 00	‖
Chesterville......	854	61	100 ''	m	13 00	798 00	93
Ayr.............	800	78	100 ''		14 00	1,092 00	1 35
Waterdown	785	59	100 ''		10 00	590 00	75
Thamesville.	769	70	100 ''		15 00	1,030 00	1 34
Bolton..........	727	60	100 ''		15 00	893 75	1 23
Dundalk.........	721	62	100 ''		12 00	744 00	1 03
Bothwell	703	74	100 ''		15 50	1,186 06	1 68
Lucan	662	65	100 ''		15 00	979 50	1 48
Woodbridge......	639	74	100 ''		13 00	963 00	1 51
Ailsa Craig......	586	51	100 ''		15 50	819 62	1 40
Creemore	585	54	100 ''		16 00	874 58	1 50
Coldwater	579	44	100 ''		12 00	523 00	91
Wyoming........	544	48	100 ''	⊞	16 50	....	*
Embro	483	49	100 ''	m	14 00	685 10	1 42
Flesherton.......	428	44	150 ''	m	11 50	....	*

STATEMENT "E"—Concluded

Street Light Installation in Hydro Municipalities, December 31st, 1916, showing Cost per Year, Cost per Lamp, and Cost per Capita.

Municipality	Population	Number of Lamps	Size and Style of Lamps		Cost per Lamp	Total Cost	Cost per Capita
					$ c.	$ c.	$ c.
Woodville........	388	33	100-watt		13 00	423 44	1 09
Chatsworth......	374	26	100 ''		12 00	325 00	87
Baden........................		62	100 ''		11 00	683 58	**
Brechin		9	100 ''		13 00	117 00	**
Beachville		42	100 ''		12 00	150 00	**
Burford		44	100 ''		13 00	572 00	**
Comber.................		42	100 ''		16 50	779 51	**
Drumbo		30	100 ''		14 00	420 00	**
Delaware		21	100 ''		14 00	241 50	**
Dorchester..............		27	100 ''		14 00	326 74	**
Elmvale		52	100 ''		12 00	624 00	**
Granton		32	100 ''		15 00	....	*-
Holstein		11	150 ''	m	15 50	....	**
Lambeth		30	100 ''	m	14 00	420 00	**
Lynden..................		35	100 ''	m	12 00	360 00	**
Mount Brydges		38	100 ''	m	14 00	532 00	**
Otterville..................		19	100 ''	m	17 00	....	*-
Plattsville......		32	100 ''	m	16 50	534 00	**
Princeton..............		20	100 ''	m	17 00	340 00	**
Port McNicoll....		28	100 ''	m	12 00	336 00	**
Rockwood..................		41 5	· 100 '' 60 ''	m	11 00	506 00	**
Sunderland		21	100 ''	m	13 00	272 16	**
St. George......		33	100 ''	m	15 00	495 00	**
Thorndale		21	100 ''	m	14 00	294 46	**
Thamesford..................		34	100 ''	m	14 00	476 00	**
Williamsburg		17	100 ''	m	13 00	220 67	**
Waubaushene		29	100 ''	m	12 00	348 00	**

NOTE:—

m Multiple system.
s Series system.
* Not a full year.
† Rural revenue not included.

‡ $5,210.54 Local Improvement debenture charges included.
‖ On account of large summer population figures not representative.
** Population not recorded in Government statistics, so no figures used.

STATEMENT "F"

Pump Rates in Municipalities

Street

M

Wood

Chat

Bad

Brec

Beac

Bur

Com

Dru

Del

Dor

Eln

Gra

Hol

Lai

Lyr

Mo

Ott

Ple

Pr

Po

R

St

St

T

T

W

Waubaushene ....

NOTE:—

m Multiple system.
s Series system.
* Not a full year.
† Rural revenue not included.

‡ $5,210.54 Local improvement charges included.
‖ On account of large summer figures not representative.
** Population not recorded in G statistics, so no figures used.

Ninth Annual Report

OF THE

HYDRO-ELECTRIC POWER COMMISSION

OF THE

PROVINCE OF ONTARIO

FOR THE YEAR ENDED OCTOBER 31st

1916

VOLUME III.

PRINTED BY ORDER OF

THE LEGISLATIVE ASSEMBLY OF ONTARIO

TORONTO:

Printed and Published by A. T. WILGRESS, Printer to the King's Most Excellent Majesty

1917

Printed by
WILLIAM BRIGGS
Corner Queen and John Streets
TORONTO

To His Honour, COLONEL SIR JOHN HENDRIE, K.C.M.G., C.V.O.,

Lieutenant-Governor of Ontario.

MAY IT PLEASE YOUR HONOUR:

The undersigned has the honour to present to Your Honour the third volume of the Ninth Annual Report of the Hydro-Electric Power Commission of Ontario for the fiscal year ending October 31st, 1916.

Respectfully submitted,

ADAM BECK,

Chairman.

TORONTO, ONT., February 17th, 1917.

COLONEL SIR ADAM BECK, K.B., LL.D.,

Chairman, Hydro-Electric Power Commission,

Toronto, Ont.

SIR,—I have the honour to transmit herewith the third volume of the Ninth Annual Report of the Hydro-Electric Power Commission of Ontario for the fiscal year ending October 31st, 1916.

I have the honour to be,

Sir,

Your obedient servant,

W. W. POPE,

Secretary.

HYDRO-ELECTRIC POWER COMMISSION
OF ONTARIO

COLONEL SIR ADAM BECK, K.B., LL.D., London, Chairman.

HON. I. B. LUCAS, M.P.P., Markdale, Commissioner.

COLONEL W. K. McNAUGHT, C.M.G., Toronto, Commissioner.

W. W. POPE, Secretary.

F. A. GABY, Chief Engineer.

HYDRAULIC INVESTIGATIONS AND CONSTRUCTION

MEASUREMENT OF STREAM FLOW

The systematic measurement of stream flow was begun in 1912, and has been carried on continuously up to the present time

This hydrometric study of the important rivers of the Province, though so far extending over a period of time too short to be really comprehensive, has nevertheless resulted in the accumulation of an appreciable amount of valuable data, and has provided an absolutely necessary basis of computation for the proper study of hydraulic development, river improvement, and flood prevention.

It is only by means of some governmental agency that information on stream flow can be adequately secured. The value of the data being directly proportional to the period of time over which it has been taken, the process is essentially continuous. No individual or private enterprise, therefore, possibly can carry on a work the utility of which is dependent solely upon the consistent accumulation and compilation of data over a continuous and long period of years.

The run-off from 47,000 square miles of watershed is now under continuous observation, but this is only about 12 per cent. of the total area of the basins within the boundaries of the Province, and the great number of enquiries received with reference to the flow of the rivers of Ontario, indicates not only that the Hydro-Electric Power Commission is becoming recognized as the source for dependable data of this kind, but also the necessity of increasing the scope of the work to cover a much greater territory within the Province than it does at present. In this connection it is especially necessary that the rivers flowing into James Bay and in the Lake Superior district be brought under observation, as the success of the large number of mining and pulp industries in this territory is absolutely dependent upon the power of the rivers, which cannot be gauged by any means other than the systematic study and recording of their flow.

During the year 1916, conditions did not permit of the addition of new stations, or even of the desired amount of work on those already established, and the rivers covered are practically the same as those of the previous year. The discharge curves, however, are better defined as a result of measurements secured at river stages not reached during previous years, and the accuracy of the daily flow estimates has been increased to a corresponding extent.

Many very valuable power sites are situated in uninhabited country often difficult of access, where river stages cannot be brought under continuous observation. In such cases the only information secured has consisted of intermittent flow measurements taken by the metering parties on the occasion of such visits as they were able to make.

As previously pointed out in the 1915 report, this report includes only the information that has been secured during the current water year, November 1st, 1915, to October 31st, 1916.

POWER AND STORAGE SURVEYS

Niagara Power Development.

During 1916 surveys were carried on continuously in connection with the gathering of the detailed information necessary for the design of the Chippawa-Queenston power plant. The initial surveys for this scheme are described in the report of the Commission for 1915.

These surveys have necessitated the use of a comparatively large field force of engineers, and have included the securing of the necessary topographical information, core drill explorations of the rock surface, and hydrometric data of the Welland and Niagara Rivers. The hydrometric information covered the continuous reading of water levels along the Niagara River at essential locations, the measurements of flow in the Welland River, and at its mouth, and the study of velocities and surface filaments in the Niagara River at Chippawa, and at the power house location at Smeaton's curve.

The office staff has been increased to transcribe the above information to the drawings, and to proceed with the design of the necessary structures. Good progress has been made on the studies of the best methods of construction for the work, and the preliminary designs are well advanced.

Nipissing Power Company.

The Nipissing Power Company, which was part of the assets of the Electric Power Company, taken over by the Provincial Government in May, 1916, is located on the South River near Powassan.

The natural flow of the stream must be augmented in the near future, by storage on its head waters. Studies were made during 1916, by the Commission on the possibilities of securing this storage at Cox's Chute, and designs of the necessary dams have been prepared.

The surge tank at present in use at the power plant is of wood construction, and has outlived its period of usefulness. During the summer surveys were made at, the power house, and information collected for the design of a new tank. The necessary drawings for a new steel structure have been prepared and the Commission are now calling for tenders for its construction and erection.

Lac Seul Gauge

Readings are taken twice daily on the gauge attached to the wharf at the main post of the Hudson's Bay Company, at Lac Seul. Considerable difficulty was experienced with this gauge during the high water of 1916, owing to movement taking place in the elevation of the wharf, and corrections have been applied for dates between which the gauge zero was checked. These water elevations are not used in connection with stream flow measurements, but only to obtain the stage of the lake.

CROWN LEASES

Under the terms of Water-Power Leases issued by the Department of Lands, Forests and Mines, the plans and specifications covering the development of any power site owned by the Province, must be approved by the Commission, as a condition governing the issue of the lease. Two important matters were dealt with under this head during the past year.

The first was the development of the Mattagami Pulp and Paper Company at Smooth Rock Falls on the Mattagami River. This scheme involved the building of a large power plant and pulp mill at Smooth Rock Falls. This plant is under construction at the present time, in accordance with approved plans and specifications. Inspection of the works has been made from time to time.

The Abitibi Pulp and Paper Company, who have already a development at Iroquois Falls, submitted plans in August for a further power installation at Twin Falls on the Abitibi River. The plans involve the elimination of the Company's dam at Couchiching Falls, which controls the storage of Lake Abitibi. These plans for this development have been submitted for approval, and preliminary construction work is now in progress.

POWER CONSTRUCTION

SOUTH FALLS

The South Falls plant is located on the south branch of the Muskoka river. A resumé of the negotiations leading up to the acquisition of this plant from the Town of Gravenhurst was given in the report of the Commission for 1915, and the contemplated changes and additions to the plant were noted therein.

The work of extending the plant was commenced during September, 1915. A permanent road to the power house, and the subgrade for the wood-stave pipe were completed during the next six weeks. Cofferdams were put in for unwatering the head-works and tail race, the discharge water from old unit was diverted, and good progress made in the enlarging of tail race cut.

The excavation for the tail race and power house foundations was completed on January 10th, 1916. The first concrete in the power house was poured on January 11th, 1916, and the substructure was completed on March 27th, 1916. All of the above work was done by day labour, under the supervision of the Commission's engineers.

The power house superstructure was built under contract by Witchall & Son, of Toronto. Work was started on March 13th, and completed on May 27th, 1916.

The steel penstock, supplied by the Wm. Hamilton Company, of Peterboro, was delivered to the site in December, 1915, and the erection was completed on January 31st, 1916. The material for the wood-stave pipe, with the exception of sills and chocks, was supplied by the Pacific Coast Pipe Company; the erection being done by the Commission's working staff. The work of erection was started on April 4th, 1916, but owing to delays in delivery of sills, etc., was not finally completed until the end of June.

Some alterations had also to be made on the head works to accommodate the second pipe, this work being completed by April 4th, 1916.

The turbine, flywheel, butterfly valve, etc., supplied by the Wm. Hamilton Company, were delivered at South Falls, on June 28th, and the governor and relief valve on July 15th. These were erected in place and grouted in by July 24th, and the new unit was put on commercial load on August 25th, 1916.

The old unit was then shut down and the steel penstock emptied. Concrete saddles were built under it, earth and debris removed, and the pipe painted.

The wood-stave pipe is 946 feet long and 60 inches inside diameter, and is connected to the head works by means of a steel thimble 5 feet in diameter. The penstock at the lower end of the pipe is 64 feet long and 5 feet in diameter. It is provided with a 48-inch diameter Tee connection for a future surge tank, and a 42-inch diameter cross-over connection to the old steel penstock in order that the capacity of the same may be increased when required.

The turbine is a 23-inch single runner horizontal Samson wheel in a cone-cylinder case, and is provided with a 3-ton, 60-inch diameter flywheel. The rated capacity is 1,060 mechanical horse-power at the generator coupling when operating at 102-foot head and 720 r.p.m. The unit is controlled by a Ludlow oil-pressure governor, and a governor-operated relief valve.

The turbine is direct connected to a 750 k.v.a., 60-cycle, three phase, 6,600-volt generator installed by the Canadian Westinghouse Company, of Hamilton, Ontario.

The capacity now installed in this plant, including the old unit, is about 1,500 electrical horse-power, and is now in continuous operation, supplying light and power to the municipalities of Gravenhurst and Huntsville.

COBDEN

A hydro-electric power plant of about 135 electric horse-power, was completed for the village of Cobden during 1916. The preliminary report and estimate covering this development was published in the report of the Commission for 1915. This plant is designed to carry the lighting load of the village, and a small 10-hour industrial load.

The designs for this plant were prepared, and the engineering work in general carried out by the Commission, on behalf of the municipality. The financing of the proposition was, however, a purely municipal undertaking, all costs being paid by the municipality.

The development scheme involved the construction of a storage dam at the outlet of Olmstead lake, from whence water is drawn through about 7 miles of natural channel to the pond at the original mill site, which is controlled by an old, but still serviceable stone and earth-fill dam. This old dam has been made part of the new development, and water is drawn from the pond through 200 feet of new head-race. After passing through a new concrete head-block, the water is carried to the wheels through a 30-inch wood-stave pipe.

The storage dam is a small earth-filled crib structure controlling about 96,000,000 cubic feet of water, this volume of storage being considered sufficient to meet the anticipated load requirements.

The power house is an entirely new structure throughout, and as the plant is situated about a mile from the village, it was provided with an upper residential storey, and a rear annex for the operator and his family, the whole being designed to combine practical utility with homelike architectural features. The foundations are of solid concrete, except for a portion where the stone foundations of the old mill were utilized. The lower storey of the main building is pressed brick, and the upper storey and annex is of wood with stained shingle trim and roof. The building contains eight residential rooms in addition to the machine room, which opens directly into the living-room.

The machine installation consists of one Boving globe casing single runner turbine, of 160 H.P. capacity, running at 720 r.p.m., and provided with a fly-wheel coupling. Direct connected to the turbine is a Canadian General Electric Company generator, 3 phase, 60 cycle, 2,300 volts, and 100 k.v.a. capacity, with a belt driven exciter. The unit is controlled by a type "C" Woodward mechanical governor.

Cobden Development—Storage Dam at Olmstead Lake

Cobden Development—Combined Residence and Power House

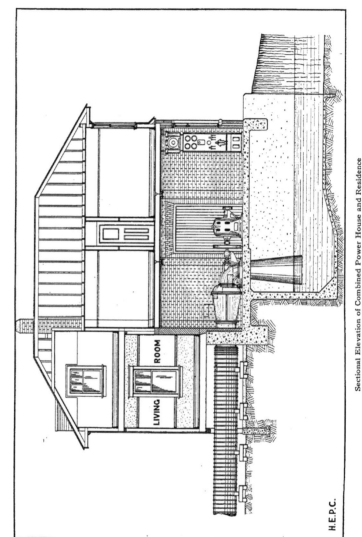

LIVING ROOM

Sectional Elevation of Combined Power House and Residence

H.E.P.C.

This plant was tested out and put in commercial operation on November 24th, 1916, and has been operating satisfactorily and continuously since that date.

The plant as originally designed did not include the operator's residence, but apart from the increase in cost, which this change involved, the work was completed within the original estimates, in spite of the high cost of labour and materials, which could not be reasonably anticipated when the estimates were prepared.

Almonte

In the spring of 1916, the Town of Almonte asked the Commission to investigate the possibilities of changing over their generating station and distribution system from direct to alternating current.

The station is located in the Town of Almonte on the Mississippi River, and operates under a 24-foot head.

A report on the hydraulic features involved, together with an estimate of the cost of changing over to alternating current was made in July. Following the recommendations made in this report, the town proceeded with the work of remodelling the plant under the direction of the engineers of the Commission.

The old equipment consisted of a pair of 42-inch diameter Barber turbines, horizontal setting, belt connected to a countershaft driving three-belted direct current generators of 130 k.w. total capacity.

The two wheels were originally coupled together with a flange coupling, but this coupling broke due to vibration in the setting, so that at the time of inspection the wheels were working independently, though belted to the same jack shaft.

It was decided to extend the turbine shaft through the power house wall and place a single new A.C. generator in a new building to be erected against the wall of the existing power house. This arrangement ensured a solid foundation for the generator, and placed the drive belt well away from any leakage or dampness from the turbine casing.

A pit for the drive pulley was excavated in rock and lined with concrete, and a concrete foundation constructed for the generator. A neat frame building 15 feet x 19 feet was erected, to house the generator and exciter, and a frame housing was built over the pulley pit and belt. The centre line of the generator was set eighteen feet five inches above, and nineteen feet over, from the centre line of the turbine shaft.

With this arrangement it was necessary to lengthen the turbine shaft six feet four inches, but as the drive was to be all from one end it was necessary to remove the old shaft from the near wheel, and replace it with a 5-inch shaft 19 feet 6 inches long. This new shaft was procured, the necessary key seats cut, and collars turned for thrust bearings. New thrust bearings were purchased, being standard bearings 4 15-16 inches x 15 inches with adjustable base plates, and babbitted to fit the thrust collars on the shaft.

When all was in readiness, the plant was shut down, the top of the wheel casing was dismantled and both shafts removed from the runners. One runner was taken to a local machine shop, where it was rebored to fit the new 5-inch shaft, and the end of the other shaft was turned and fitted to receive one-half of the jaw coupling.

The runner was then replaced and pressed onto the new shaft, and when the jaw coupling, new stuffing box and dome bushings had been placed, the shafts were lined up and the thrust bearings grouted.

New lignum vitae bearings were placed inside the casing, one on either side of the jaw coupling. These bearings were bolted to cast iron supports, resting on each side of the wooden wheel casing, and as the wet wood had proved to be far from rigid, new cast iron struts were placed so as to form knee braces from the bearings to the iron floor of the casing.

Owing to the bearings not being rigid, during the period of previous operation, the perimeter of the runners had become badly worn, causing considerable leakage. To remedy this a ¾-inch x 1½-inch bar bent to the radius of the runner, was riveted to the inside of the cowl close up to the runner to ensure a more efficient water seal.

The thrust bearings were located near the outer edge of the new shaft, one on either side of the 58-inch drive pulley. This pulley, as also the 46-inch pulley on the generator shaft, is an iron centre wood rim split pulley with a 20-inch face.

The belt is 3-ply leather 20-inch x 69 feet 3 inches, and drives the new 250 k.w. 60-cycle, 2,200-volt, three-phase Westinghouse generator.

The plant has been operating quite satisfactorily since the change has been made.

STREAM FLOW DATA

Regular Stations

EASTERN ONTARIO DISTRICT

River	Location	Drainage Area Sq.Miles	Township	County
Bonnechere	near Eganville	670	Wilberforce	Renfrew
"	near Golden Lake	575	South Algona	"
"	at Renfrew	910	Horton	"
Madawaska	at Flat Rapids	3,210	McNab	"
"	at Madawaska	800	Murchison	
Mississippi	at Ferguson's Falls	1,042	Drummond	
"	at Galetta	1,456	Fitzroy	Carleton
"	near Snow Road	446	Sherbrooke	Lanark
Moira	near Foxboro	1,038	Thurlow	Hastings
Napanee	near Napanee	300	Camden	Addington
Tay	near Glen Tay	204	Bathurst	Lanark
York	near Bancroft	374	Faraday	Hastings

Bonnechere River near Eganville

Location—400 feet downstream from McCrae's Power Plant, and one mile from the Village of Eganville, near lot 16, concession 6, Township of Wilberforce, County of Renfrew.

Records Available—Discharge measurements from September, 1916. Gauge readings from September 24, 1915.

Drainage Area—670 square miles.

Gauge—Points on the rock bottom of the river from which direct readings are made to the water surface.

Channel and Control—The channel is slightly curved from the power house above and straight for ½ mile below the section. The bed of the river is shale, solid rock, and stones in some places. The banks are high, rocky and wooded, and not liable to overflow.

Discharge Measurements—Made by wading in section with the gauge at most stages, but frequently a few hundred yards further upstream at suitable low stages for better results.

Winter Flow—The relation between gauge heights and discharge is seriously disturbed during winter months, and estimates for that period are not more than fair.

Regulation—McCrae's plant and dam is a short distance above the section, and there is another dam at Eganville, and one between.. The flow is further regulated by the operation of the Round Lake Dam and the lumber dams on tributary streams.

Accuracy—Good for open channel measurements.

Observer—H. Welk, Eganville.

Discharge Measurements of Bonnechere River near Eganville in 1915-6

Date	Hydrographer	Width in Feet	Area of Section in Sq. Feet	Mean Velocity in Feet per Sec.	Gauge Height in Feet	Discharge in Sec-Feet	Discharge in Second-feet per Square Mile
1915							
Nov. 20....	West, C. W.	55	71	2.47	100.50	177	....
Dec. 10....	" "	53	74	2.13	100.71 (a)	157	....
1916							
Jan. 27....	Campbell, L. L. .	53	96	2.43	101.83	233 (b)	....
Mar. 30....	Campbell, L. L. .	....	....	....	103.22	338 (c)	....
" 31....	" "	....	....	....	103.22	337 (c)	....
Apr. 14....	" "	....	....	....	101.67	542 (c)	....
May 22....	" "	....	....	....	103.09	1,408 (c)	....
June 16....	McLennan, C. C.	149	456	2.40	102.37	1,094 (d)	....
July 11....	" "	141	286	2.29	101.60	656	....

(a) Ice along edges of control causes considerable effect at section.
(b) Section almost entirely ice covered.
(c) Weir measurement.
(d) Measurement below regular section.

Bonnechere River near Golden Lake

Location—At the highway bridge between Golden Lake Station and Village, in the Township of South Algona, County of Renfrew.

Records Available—Discharge measurements from June, 1915. Daily gauge heights from June 26, 1915.

Drainage Area—575 square miles.

Gauge—Elevations of water surface made by indirect readings from a point on the bridge, whose elevation is checked monthly.

Channel and Control—Bays exist above and below the section, the current being very slow up to the bridge. The flow is confined between the abutments of the bridge at all stages. The bed of the river is well protected by large boulders, and is not subject to change.

Winter Flow—Slightly affected by ice.

Regulation—The flow is regulated to the capacity of the Round Lake Dam for storage purposes, and the lumber industry has flood dams on some of the tributary waters.

Accuracy—Mean of daily readings give good results for stage readings. Calculations have been applied to compensate for dam effect in the spring and autumn of 1916.

Observer—Mary Sunstrum, Golden Lake.

Discharge Measurements of Bonnechere River near Golden Lake in 1915-6

Date	Hydrographer	Width in Feet	Area of Section in Sq. Feet	Mean Velocity in Feet per Sec.	Gauge Height in Feet	Discharge in Sec-Feet	Discharge in Second-feet per Square Mile
1915							
Nov. 22....	West, C. W.	108	238	.80	555.24	193 (a)	....
Dec. 13....	"	108	239	.64	555.21	153 (a)	....
1916							
Jan. 29....	Campbell, L. L. .	110	273	.94	555.46	256 (a)	....
Feb. 26....	McLennan, C. C.	112	316	1.10	555.99	347 (b)	....
Mar. 24:...	"	112	304	1.01	555.82	306 (b)	....
May 8....	"	121	766	3.09	559.42	2,362 (c)	....
" 9....	"	121	722	3.74	559.31	2,700 (d)	....
" 9....	"	121	697	3.99	559.11	2,780 (e)	....
" 10....	"	121	686	3.89	559.01	2,670 (f)	....
" 18....	"	121	598	3.36	558.30	2,010 (f)	....
" 20....	"	121	586	3.24	558.24	1,900	....
June 10....	Campbell, L. L. .	121	447	2,41	557.19	1,078	....
July 13....	"	117	373	1.73	556.43	647	....
Sept. 9....	McLennan, C. C.	112	325	1.06	555.91	346	....
" 9....	"	126	209	1.65	555.90	344	....
Oct. 30....	Campbell L. L. .	109	303	.40	555.69	121 (g)	....

(a) Ice on lake, section free.
(b) Dam in course of construction just below control.
(c) Dam influence—high swell on lake.
(d) Dam influence—part spillway gone.
(e) Dam influence—all spillway gone.
(f) Dam influence.
(g) New dam under construction.

Daily Gauge Height and Discharge of Bonnechere River near Golden Lake for 1915-6

Drainage Area 575 Square Miles

Day	November Gauge Ht. (Feet)	November Dis-charge (Sec-ft.)	December Gauge Ht. (Feet)	December Dis-charge (Sec-ft.)	January Gauge Ht. (Feet)	January Dis-charge (Sec-ft.)	February Gauge Ht. (Feet)	February Dis-charge (Sec-ft.)	March Gauge Ht. (Feet)	March Dis-charge (Sec-ft.)	April Gauge Ht. (Feet)	April Dis-charge (Sec-ft.)	May Gauge Ht. (Feet)	May Dis-charge (Sec-ft.)	June Gauge Ht. (Feet)	June Dis-charge (Sec-ft.)	July Gauge Ht. (Feet)	July Dis-charge (Sec-ft.)	August Gauge Ht. (Feet)	August Dis-charge (Sec-ft.)	September Gauge Ht. (Feet)	September Dis-charge (Sec-ft.)	October Gauge Ht. (Feet)	October Dis-charge (Sec-ft.)
1	555.04	117	555.16	144	555.30	180	555.56	259	555.98	360	555.59	360	559.25	2460	557.66	1440	556.14	515	555.86	378	555.68	307	555.51	246
2	555.02	113	555.16	144	555.28	175	555.59	269	555.96	360	555.75	227	559.25	2460	557.53	1370	556.44	650	555.86	378	555.76	337	555.56	263
3	554.99	107	555.14	138	555.30	180	555.59	269	555.98	360	555.92	313	559.00	2200	557.53	1330	556.36	610	555.79	348	555.81	357	555.60	277
4	555.00	109	555.16	144	555.28	175	555.60	272	555.96	351	556.17	420	559.00	2200	557.49	1300	556.34	600	555.76	338	555.91	378	555.51	246
5	555.02	113	555.16	144	555.30	180	555.60	272	555.96	351	556.50	585	559.30	2510	557.45	1270	556.32	590	555.76	338	555.91	400	555.40	208
6	555.05	119	555.16	144	555.30	180	555.60	272	555.98	351	556.50	585	559.25	2510	557.37	1240	556.32	590	555.76	338	555.98	422	555.40	208
7	555.05	119	555.14	138	555.30	180	555.60	272	555.96	360	556.67	680	559.17	2420	557.37	1210	556.32	590	555.76	338	556.00	431	555.46	228
8	555.06	120	555.15	141	555.30	180	555.60	272	555.96	351	557.00	860	558.58	2360	557.32	1170	556.32	590	555.76	338	555.86	440	555.47	232
9	555.09	126	555.15	141	555.30	180	555.58	266	555.94	341	557.09	920	558.41	2780	557.22	1100	556.28	610	555.66	299	555.76	378	555.48	235
10	555.06	120	555.16	144	555.32	186	555.58	266	555.96	351	557.17	870	558.57	2670	557.22	1030	556.31	570	555.66	299	555.66	337	555.44	222
11	555.05	119	555.16	144	555.32	186	555.56	259	555.96	351	557.34	990	558.48	2240	557.11	1010	556.26	585	555.56	299	555.66	299	555.46	228
12	555.08	124	555.16	144	555.32	186	555.57	262	555.96	351	557.67	1250	558.55	2150	557.08	955	556.24	560	555.56	263	555.64	292	555.40	208
13	555.10	126	555.16	146	555.30	180	555.61	276	555.94	341	557.84	1390	558.38	2220	556.99	915	556.15	550	555.56	263	555.62	284	555.46	249
14	555.16	141	555.17	146	555.32	186	555.66	293	555.93	329	558.09	1490	558.28	2060	556.93	900	556.21	510	555.46	263	555.62	284	555.52	228
15	555.18	149	555.16	144	555.32	186	555.67	296	555.92	323	558.25	1640	558.36	1960	536.91	900	556.09	540	555.46	228	555.61	281	555.46	228
16	555.22	159	555.20	154	555.32	186	555.72	313	555.92	323	558.50	1870	558.51	2040	556.91	1030	556.06	480	555.46	228	555.56	263	555.46	228
17	555.22	159	555.20	154	555.32	186	555.78	329	555.92	317	558.75	2040	558.75	2180	557.11	900	556.06	468	555.46	228	555.51	245	555.46	228
18	555.20	154	555.18	149	555.31	183	555.80	329	555.88	317	559.00	2300	558.28	2040	557.07	870	556.03	454	555.46	228	555.51	245	555.48	236
19	555.20	159	555.20	154	555.31	183	555.81	337	555.88	317	559.00	2200	558.20	2010	556.91	810	556.06	454	555.46	211	555.59	245	555.46	228
20	555.20	154	555.20	154	555.30	180	555.86	337	555.86	309	559.09	2280	558.20	1890	556.86	755	556.03	468	555.36	195	555.53	274	555.46	228
21	555.22	159	555.20	154	555.30	180	555.86	337	555.87	313	559.17	2370	558.12	1900	556.76	715	556.03	468	555.36	195	555.53	242	555.56	263
22	555.22	159	555.20	157	555.30	180	555.86	337	555.90	325	559.25	2460	558.08	1820	556.66	675	556.06	454	555.36	195	555.52	242	555.61	281
23	555.22	159	555.21	157	555.32	186	555.88	337	555.89	321	559.42	2640	558.03	1780	556.59	645	555.98	454	555.41	211	555.51	245	555.63	288
24	555.26	170	555.24	164	555.32	186	555.88	337	555.90	306	559.42	2640	557.99	1740	556.46	645	555.98	431	555.46	228	555.48	236	555.61	281
25	555.26	170	555.26	170	555.36	197	555.88	384	555.90	305	559.42	2640	557.95	1720	556.32	645	555.94	431	555.46	228	555.46	228	555.61	281
26	555.23	162	555.26	170	555.40	208	555.99	379	555.90	305	559.25	2460	557.91	1680	556.46	595	555.86	468	555.46	299	555.42	215	555.61	281
27	555.22	159	555.30	180	555.46	227	555.98	371	555.90	305	559.34	2550	557.87	1640	556.46	620	555.86	431	555.66	299	555.48	236	555.61	281
28	555.18	149	555.29	177	555.50	240	555.96	371	555.90	305	559.42	2640	557.83	1610	556.36	500	555.86	378	555.68	307	555.46	228	555.66	299
29	555.18	149	555.28	174	555.56	259	555.96	371	555.91	310	559.25	2460	557.78	1570	556.41	570					555.66	299
30	555.16	144	555.28	174	555.56	259			556.01	422			557.74	1530	556.16	545						
31			555.30	177	555.56	259			556.01	422			557.70	1470								

Monthly Discharge of Bonnechere River near Golden Lake for 1915-6

Drainage Area, 575 Square Miles

Month	Discharge in Second-féet			Discharge in Second-feet per Square Mile			Run-off
	Maximum	Minimum	Mean	Maximum	Minimum	Mean	Depth in Inches on Drainage Area
November (1915)	170	107	139	.30	.19	.24	.27
December "	180	138	153	.31	.24	.27	.31
January .. (1916)	259	175	194	.45	.30	.34	.39
February	384	259	303	.67	.45	.52	.56
March	422	305	338	.73	.52	.59	.68
April	2,640	190	1,611	4.59	.33	2.80	3.12
May	2,780	1,470	2,050	4.83	2.56	3.57	4.12
June 26-30	1,440	545	934	2.50	.95	1.62	1.81
July	650	378	521	1.13	.66	.91	1.05
August	378	195	274	.66	.34	.48	.55
September	440	215	297	.77	.37	.52	.58
October	299	208	249	.52	.36	.43	.50
The year	2,780	107	588	4.83	.19	1.02	13.88

Bonnechere River at Renfrew

Location—One-half mile below Raglan St., Town of Renfrew, Township of Horton, County of Renfrew, on the Barnett Estate.

Records Available—Discharge measurements from September, 1916. Daily gauge readings from November 1, 1916.

Drainage Area—910 square miles.

Gauge—On the right bank of the river at the section, a box chain gauge with nine feet of standard gauge plates. Distance from end of weight to marker is 12.43 feet.

Channel and Control—The channel is straight for 100 feet above and 300 feet below the station, but both above and below the station long sharp curves occur. There is a high clay bank on the right, and a low clay bank on the left. At extreme high water there may be an escape from this channel of some water from higher above the section to points below the section. The bed of the stream is composed of clean small stones.

Winter Flow—Little ice effect expected, though on occasions frazil ice from the rapids above may make meter measurements difficult.

Regulation—The Round Lake Dam, the Golden Lake Dam for power purposes, and the dams on the upper river for lumbering purposes have large regulating effects on this river. The power plants in Renfrew, running twenty-four hours to their full capacity, and having little pondage, will not seriously affect the estimate of mean gauge heights.

Observer—William Collie, 88 Bank St., Renfrew.

Discharge Measurements of Bonnechere River at Renfrew for 1916

Date	Hydrographer	Width in Feet	Area of Section in Sq. Feet	Mean Velocity in Feet per Sec.	Gauge Height in Feet	Discharge in Sec–Feet	Discharge in Second-feet per Square Mile
1916							
Sept. 11....	McLennan, C. C.	83	170	2.09	103.13	356	....
" 11....	" "	83	171	2.11	103.13	361	....
Oct. 26....	" "	81	134	1.90	102.81	254	....

Madawaska River at Flat Rapids

Location—Near lot 7, concession 9, Township of McNab, County of Renfrew, half mile below Flat Rapids.

Records Available—High-water measurements during 1915 and 1916 to be used in con-junction with low-water measurements at this section for application to gauge readings taken at Claybank by the Ottawa River Storage Survey, from April 15, 1909. Discharge measurements commenced in October, 1916, at this section, and September, 1915, at high-water section.

Drainage Area—3,210 square miles.

Gauge—Nine feet of standard gauge plates on the boom crib 1,000 feet below the Clay-bank bridge, about 1,500 feet below the high water section, and 3 miles below the low water section.

Channel and Control—Channel is straight for 3,000 feet above and 500 feet below the station and favorably fast current exists for metering purposes. Clay and gravel banks, high on the right bank, medium, to low on the left bank, but the river is not liable to overflow. The flow is through one channel at high and low stages and through two channels at medium stages. Possibly frazil ice may be expected on some days.

Discharge Measurements—From boat and ice.

Winter Flow—Gauge height discharge relation will be considerably affected by ice, but likely to be capable of close estimation from discharge measurements.

Regulation—There are no powers developed on the river as yet, though construction has started on one at the foot of Calabogie Lake, which will have considerable regulating effect on the river below, but possibly not acting rapidly enough to disturb the gauge height discharge daily estimate. The storage works for lumbering purposes on the upper river and its tributaries are still in use.

Observer—Narcisse Jandreau, R. R. Arnprior.

Discharge Measurements of Madawaska River at Claybank in 1915-6

Date	Hydrographer	Width in Feet	Area of Section in Sq. Feet	Mean Velocity in Feet per Sec.	Gauge Height in Feet	Discharge in Sec–Feet	Discharge in Second-feet per Square Mile
1915							
Nov. 25....	West, C. W	322	4,696	.32	260.54	1,485	....
Dec. 17....	"	316	4,543	.27	260.59	1,235 (a)	....
1916							
Jan. 24....	Campbell, L. L...	318	4,283	.39	260.88	1,669 (a)	....
Feb. 12....	McLennan, C. C..	324	4,484	.66	260.79	2,954 (a)	....
Apr. 19....	Campbell, L. L...	348	6,584	2.08	265.96	13,694	....
May 23....	" ..	344	5,962	1.70	264.29	10,125	....
June 14....	McLennan, C. C..	337	5,520	1.31	262.92	7,255	....
July 10....	" ..	331	5,083	.73	261.83	3,701	....
Oct. 12....	Campbell, L. L...	230	2,085	.56	260.29	1,176	....

(a) Ice measurement.

Madawaska River at Madawaska

Location—50 feet above the G.T. Ry. bridge, Canada Atlantic branch, 500 yards east of the Madawaska Station, Township of Murchison, District of Nipissing.

Records Available—Discharge measurements from September, 1915, and monthly thereafter, and gauge readings from September 27, 1915.

Drainage Area—800 square miles.

Gauge—Three feet of standard gauge plates secured vertically, to pile, three feet west of face of east abutment.

Channel and Control—Channel is straight for about 400 feet above the section, curving slightly to the right under the bridge. The banks are sandy, and not liable to overflow. The bed of the river is soft, and there are some weeds above the section. The point of control is not clearly defined.

Discharge Measurements—Made about fifty feet above gauge from a boat.

Winter Flow—Affected by ice conditions.

Regulation—Lumber interests on the river above the section operate dams for driving purposes.

Accuracy—Open water rating curve for ordinary stages likely to be very good.

Observer—G. Wormke, Madawaska.

Discharge Measurements of Madawaska River at Madawaska in 1915-6

Date	Hydrographer	Width in Feet	Area of Section in Sq. Feet	Mean Velocity in Feet per Sec.	Gauge Height in Feet	Discharge in Sec-Feet	Discharge in Second-feet per Square Mile
1915							
Nov. 22....	West, C. W.	75	461	.55	101.75	253 (a)	....
Dec. 13....	" "	75	421	.57	101.69	238 (b)	....
1916							
Jan. 31....	Campbell, L. L..	70	520	1.21	104.92	633 (b)	....
Feb. 28....	McLennan, C. C.	78	487	.92	104.33	446 (b)	....
Mar. 25....	" "	75	409	.68	103.50	279 (b)	....
Apr. 17....	Campbell, L. L..	104	1,180	2.15	109.30	2,531	....
May 20....	McLennan, C.C..	102	1,129	1.89	108.89	2,132	....
June 16....	Campbell, L. L..	86	644	.96	104.00	620	....
July 13....	" "	81	563	.80	103.07	449	....
Sept. 9....	McLennan, C.C..	76	474	.46	101.60	216 (c)	....
Oct. 27....	Campbell, L. L..	79	498	.54	102.25	267	....

(a) Weeds may effect, ice on both edges of section.
(b) Ice measurement.
(c) Weeds near left bank caused very irregular flow.

Daily Gage Height and Discharge of Madawaska River at Madawaska, for 1915-6

Drainage Area 800 Square Miles.

Day	Nov. Gauge Ht. (Feet)	Nov. Dis-charge (Sec-ft.)	Dec. Gauge Ht. (Feet)	Dec. Dis-charge (Sec-ft.)	Jan. Gauge Ht. (Feet)	Jan. Dis-charge (Sec-ft.)	Feb. Gauge Ht. (Feet)	Feb. Dis-charge (Sec-ft.)	Mar. Gauge Ht. (Feet)	Mar. Dis-charge (Sec-ft.)	Apr. Gauge Ht. (Feet)	Apr. Dis-charge (Sec-ft.)	May Gauge Ht. (Feet)	May Dis-charge (Sec-ft.)	June Gauge Ht. (Feet)	June Dis-charge (Sec-ft.)	July Gauge Ht. (Feet)	July Dis-charge (Sec-ft.)	Aug. Gauge Ht. (Feet)	Aug. Dis-charge (Sec-ft.)	Sep. Gauge Ht. (Feet)	Sep. Dis-charge (Sec-ft.)	Oct. Gauge Ht. (Feet)	Oct. Dis-charge (Sec-ft.)
1	101.83	261	103.50	525	102.00	284	105.17	675	104.25	432	107.00	1270	110.04	3280	106.88	1220	103.79	575	101.60	227	101.50	213	101.46	207
2	101.79	255	102.92	429	102.12	297	105.17	670	104.21	424	107.00	1270	110.00	3240	106.50	1140	103.92	600	101.62	230	101.48	211	101.42	202
3	101.75	249	102.79	408	102.25	312	105.17	670	104.08	402	108.67	1930	109.88	3120	106.48	1130	104.08	625	101.62	230	101.42	202	101.35	192
4	101.75	249	102.67	389	102.17	297	105.08	650	104.00	388	108.00	1590	109.83	3070	106.29	1090	104.10	630	101.62	230	101.42	202	101.27	181
5	101.75	249	102.25	324	102.38	326	105.08	645	104.02	389	107.00	1270	109.62	2860	106.25	1070	103.94	600	101.62	230	101.71	244	101.25	178
6	101.75	249	102.00	287	102.38	321	105.08	645	103.82	356	106.33	1090	109.33	2570	106.17	1060	103.73	565	101.62	230	101.88	269	101.23	175
7	101.75	249	101.62	230	102.27	302	105.08	640	103.83	356	106.25	1080	109.12	2360	106.17	1060	103.62	545	101.62	230	101.77	253	101.17	167
8	101.75	249	101.50	213	102.21	288	105.00	625	103.92	468	105.92	995	108.71	1970	105.75	950	103.52	530	101.71	244	101.73	246	101.17	167
9	101.75	249	101.52	216	102.33	303	105.75	755	104.00	380	105.85	980	108.42	1780	105.38	875	103.25	498	101.77	253	101.60	227	101.17	167
10	101.75	249	101.75	249	102.46	318	105.83	770	103.83	351	105.92	995	108.12	1640	105.46	890	103.25	482	101.75	249	101.52	216	101.17	167
11	101.75	249	101.67	237	102.50	320	105.50	705	103.83	350	105.83	975	108.46	1800	105.58	915	103.17	469	101.75	253	101.48	211	101.17	167
12	101.75	249	101.67	237	102.23	276	105.33	670	103.88	356	106.35	1100	108.50	1820	105.48	895	103.15	466	101.69	240	101.42	202	101.15	164
13	101.75	249	101.67	237	102.54	320	105.00	605	103.92	360	106.33	1090	108.33	1730	105.38	875	103.04	448	101.65	234	101.40	199	101.19	170
14	101.75	249	101.71	244	102.50	309	104.83	570	103.79	359	106.67	1180	107.92	1560	105.27	850	102.92	429	101.62	230	101.34	191	101.25	178
15	101.67	237	101.75	249	102.50	305	104.71	550	103.75	338	107.54	1430	107.67	1500	105.15	825	102.92	429	101.62	230	101.33	189	101.25	178
16	101.67	237	101.79	255	102.50	302	104.71	545	103.75	331	108.60	1890	107.90	1550	104.83	765	102.92	426	101.62	230	101.33	189	101.25	178
17	101.67	237	101.58	224	102.42	287	104.58	535	103.75	329	109.04	2720	109.04	2280	104.17	635	102.83	415	101.58	224	101.33	189	101.25	224
18	101.67	237	101.92	275	102.50	294	104.58	515	103.71	321	110.15	3390	109.48	2720	103.98	610	102.83	415	101.58	224	101.29	184	101.58	240
19	101.71	244	101.83	261	102.50	294	104.58	515	103.67	314	109.88	3120	109.25	2490	104.04	620	102.77	405	101.58	224	101.31	186	101.69	238
20	101.75	249	101.81	259	102.79	324	104.54	505	103.58	299	109.73	2970	109.17	2410	104.12	635	102.75	402	101.58	224	101.33	189	101.67	313
21	101.83	261	101.75	249	102.79	327	104.54	500	103.62	304	109.73	2970	108.94	2180	104.15	640	103.08	455	101.58	224	101.31	186	102.54	368
22	101.83	261	101.83	261	103.21	388	104.46	485	103.67	309	109.90	3140	108.67	1940	104.10	630	102.90	426	101.52	216	101.33	189	102.69	392
23	101.83	261	101.83	261	103.58	442	104.27	453	103.50	299	110.50	3470	108.29	1710	104.02	615	102.75	402	101.50	213	101.33	189	102.35	339
24	101.83	261	101.83	261	103.77	453	104.27	442	103.50	283	110.17	4430	108.19	1670	103.88	590	102.62	399	101.42	202	101.31	186	102.27	328
25	101.83	261	102.00	287	103.77	466	104.25	444	103.50	287	110.92	4160	107.96	1580	103.73	580	102.25	381	101.52	216	101.33	189	102.17	313
26	101.83	261	102.00	287	103.83	471	104.56	490	103.52	287	110.81	4240	107.79	1510	103.83	580	101.79	324	101.50	213	101.33	189	102.23	321
27	101.83	261	102.08	287	103.96	487	104.25	453	103.75	386	110.67	4050	107.44	1370	103.71	560	101.69	255	101.48	211	101.40	199	101.24	323
28	103.50	525	102.08	299	104.46	570	104.44	464	105.31	690	110.67	3910	107.25	1340	103.92	600	101.67	240	101.44	205	101.33	189	102.25	324
29	103.50	525	102.08	299	104.62	595	104.44	464	105.92	850	110.42	3660	107.25	1340	103.75	565	101.67	238	101.40	199	101.52	216	102.25	324
30	103.50	525	102.00	287	104.67	600			106.50	1030	110.12	3360	107.08	1290	103.69	555	101.67	238			101.54	219	102.17	313
31			102.00	287	104.92	635			106.83	1160			107.12	1300			101.67	238					102.17	313

Monthly Discharge of Madawaska River at Madawaska for 1915-6

Drainage area 800 square miles

Month.	Discharge in Second-feet.			Discharge in Second-feet. per square mile			Run-off
	Maximum	Minimum	Mean	Maximum	Minimum	Mean	Depth in Inches on Drainage Area
November (1915)	525	237	287	.66	.30	.36	.40
December........	525	213	285	.66	.27	.36	.42
January .. (1916)	635	276	371	.79	.34	.46	.53
February	770	434	581	.96	.54	.73	.79
March..........	1,160	279	425	1.45	.35	.53	.61
April..........	4,430	915	2,333	5.54	1.14	2.92	3.26
May............	3,280	1,290	1,985	4.10	1.61	2.48	2.86
June	1,220	555	784	1.52	.69	.98	1.09
July...........	630	238	437	.78	.30	.55	.63
August.........	253	199	228	.32	.25	.29	.33
September......	269	184	205	.34	.23	.26	.29
October	392	164	242	.49	.20	.30	.35
The year	4,430	164	679	5.54	.20	.85	11.57

Mississippi River at Ferguson's Falls

Location—At the highway on the road through the Village of Ferguson's Falls, near lots 16 and 17, concession 12, Township of Drummond, County of Lanark.

Records Available—Discharge measurements from July, 1915, and gauge readings from July 13, 1915.

Drainage Area—1.042 square miles.

Gauge—0 to 6 feet of standard gauge plates secured to the inner face of the first pier from the south end of the bridge and near the downstream corner of the pier.

Channel and Control—Channel is straight for 300 feet above and ½ mile below the gauging station. The banks are not liable to overflow. There are 7 channels, formed by the piers of the bridge. The present control is a short distance below the section, and ice action there will affect the discharge relation at low winter stages, but this will not be the point of control for high-water stages. At certain stages measurements are made 1,500 feet below bridge.

Winter Flow—Discharge relation will be affected by ice.

Regulation—The river is regulated throughout its length by power and storage dams, as well as dams in connection with the timber industry.

Accuracy—Open flow relation will be good.

Observer—A. M. Sheppard, Ferguson's Falls.

Discharge Measurements of Mississippi River at Ferguson's Falls in 1915-6

Date	Hydrographer	Width in Feet	Area of Section in Sq. Feet	Mean Velocity in Feet per Sec.	Gauge Height in Feet	Discharge in Sec-Feet	Discharge in Second-feet per Square Mile
1915							
Nov. 9....	West, C. W	187	233	1.74	101.25	406	....
Dec. 1....	"	189	255	1.97	101.40	502	....
1916							
Jan. 11....	"	168	248	2.00	101.50	496 (a)	....
Feb. 8....	McLennan, C. C..	198	442	3.58	102.29	1,581 (b)	....
Apr. 12....	"	211	772	5.93	103.88	4,579	....
May 25....	" ..	211	693	5.56	103.46	3,857	....
June 20....	" ..	211	733	5.77	103.71	4,225	....
Sept. 28....	" ..	210	195	1.59	101.12	310 (c)	....
" 28....	" ..	172	201	1.68	101.14	339	....

(a) Ice above section and at piers.
(b) Ice covered above and below section.
(c) Metering taken 600 ft. below regular section.

Daily Gauge Height and Discharge of Mississippi River at Ferguson's Falls for 1915-6

Drainage Area, 1,042 Square Miles

Day	Nov Gauge Ht. (Feet)	Nov Dis-charge (Sec-ft)	Dec Gauge Ht.	Dec Dis-charge	Jan Gauge Ht.	Jan Dis-charge	Feb Gauge Ht.	Feb Dis-charge	Mar Gauge Ht.	Mar Dis-charge	Apr Gauge Ht.	Apr Dis-charge	May Gauge Ht.	May Dis-charge	Jun Gauge Ht.	Jun Dis-charge	Jul Gauge Ht.	Jul Dis-charge	Aug Gauge Ht.	Aug Dis-charge	Sep Gauge Ht.	Sep Dis-charge	Oct Gauge Ht.	Oct Dis-charge
1	101.27	419	101.39	510	101.35	478	102.25	1380	101.81	555	103.12	3150	104.10	4980	103.10	3110	103.19	3270	101.83	945	101.25	405	101.13	328
2	101.28	426	101.39	510	101.38	500	102.45	1740	101.78	630	103.50	3860	104.03	4850	103.08	3070	103.13	3160	101.81	920	101.25	405	101.10	310
3	101.28	419	101.38	500	101.38	500	102.49	1830	101.80	565	103.83	4480	104.00	4790	103.05	3020	103.11	3130	101.78	890	101.25	405	101.08	298
4	101.26	412	101.35	478	101.42	530	102.50	1850	101.78	485	104.10	4980	103.97	4740	103.02	2960	103.08	3070	101.75	855	101.25	405	101.08	298
5	101.24	398	101.35	478	101.43	540	102.46	1750	101.76	470	104.25	5270	103.88	4480	102.97	2860	103.08	3070	101.72	820	101.25	405	101.08	298
6	101.25	405	101.34	470	101.42	530	102.41	1660	101.77	492	104.29	5340	103.83	4380	102.93	2790	103.06	3030	101.68	780	101.26	410	101.08	298
7	101.25	405	101.33	462	101.42	492	102.35	1560	101.77	470	104.23	5230	103.78	4280	102.85	2630	102.99	2900	101.67	770	101.32	455	101.08	298
8	101.23	391	101.33	462	101.42	450	102.33	1520	101.75	455	104.17	5110	103.67	4170	102.83	2600	102.93	2790	101.67	770	101.36	485	101.08	298
9	101.23	391	101.35	478	101.42	470	102.31	1470	101.75	470	104.23	5230	103.52	3900	102.95	2820	102.83	2600	101.67	770	101.38	500	101.07	292
10	101.23	391	101.38	500	101.45	462	102.31	1410	101.75	448	104.06	4900	103.52	3900	102.83	2600	102.73	2420	101.62	720	101.33	472	101.06	286
11	101.23	391	101.48	585	101.49	462	102.21	1300	101.78	419	103.98	4750	103.48	3820	102.83	2600	102.65	2270	101.66	760	101.30	440	101.11	316
12	101.23	391	101.45	555	101.49	510	102.18	1230	101.75	426	103.88	4570	103.38	3630	102.86	2650	102.59	2060	101.59	690	101.26	412	101.13	328
13	101.21	377	101.29	433	101.54	530	102.18	1230	101.75	419	103.94	4680	103.29	3420	102.94	2810	102.54	2060	101.57	670	101.24	398	101.18	358
14	101.21	377	101.31	448	101.57	550	102.19	1290	101.78	426	104.04	4870	103.15	3200	102.98	2890	102.44	1870	101.54	640	101.25	405	101.20	370
15	101.20	370	101.38	500	101.58	550	102.11	1140	101.78	455	104.15	5080	103.08	3070	102.98	2890	102.39	1770	101.51	610	101.22	384	101.21	377
16	101.21	377	101.31	462	101.61	585	102.06	1070	101.76	500	104.27	5300	102.96	2920	102.98	2890	102.34	1680	101.47	575	101.17	358	101.21	377
17	101.21	377	101.31	448	101.63	620	101.96	935	101.78	515	104.35	5450	103.12	3150	103.00	2920	102.32	1650	101.43	540	101.17	352	101.23	391
18	101.19	364	101.33	462	101.67	340	101.92	890	101.80	585	104.45	5630	103.29	3460	103.26	3400	102.28	1570	101.40	515	101.17	352	101.33	462
19	101.21	377	101.32	455	101.66	650	101.92	910	101.81	600	104.52	5770	103.52	3900	103.46	3780	102.26	1540	101.32	455	101.15	340	101.28	426
20	101.29	433	101.29	433	101.67	650	101.97	935	101.81	620	104.54	5810	103.65	4130	103.66	4150	102.21	1460	101.28	425	101.15	340	101.30	440
21	101.34	470	101.31	462	101.78	770	101.90	945	101.79	660	104.52	5770	103.71	4250	103.80	4420	102.16	1380	101.25	405	101.15	340	101.31	448
22	101.33	462	101.30	440	101.85	845	101.90	820	101.84	660	104.48	5690	103.71	4250	103.91	4630	102.12	1320	101.25	405	101.14	334	101.31	448
23	101.33	462	101.33	462	101.88	865	101.84	750	101.84	720	104.46	5650	103.65	4130	103.92	4650	102.09	1280	101.25	405	101.12	322	101.31	448
24	101.33	462	101.29	433	101.90	910	101.83	740	101.79	780	104.46	5650	103.56	3970	103.90	4610	102.06	1230	101.25	405	101.17	352	101.30	440
25	101.33	462	101.32	455	101.96	995	101.80	700	101.83	810	104.46	5650	103.46	3780	103.79	4400	102.03	1190	101.25	405	101.16	346	101.26	412
26	101.35	478	101.33	462	102.02	1070	101.83	585	101.83	875	104.42	5580	103.46	3780	103.64	4120	102.00	1150	101.25	405			101.26	412
27	101.38	500	101.33	462	102.10	1160	101.80	590	101.89	890	104.40	5540	103.29	3460	103.54	3940	101.98	1110	101.25	405			101.25	405
28	101.36	485	101.33	470	102.17	1250	101.94	630	101.94	995	104.35	5450	103.16	3220	103.49	3820	101.97	1110	101.25	405			101.22	384
29	101.36	485	101.33	462	102.17	1260	101.83	610	102.09	1080	104.27	5300	103.11	3130	103.34	3560	101.93	1070	101.25	405			101.20	370
30	101.41	525	101.34	470	102.17	1260			102.40	1280	104.19	5160	103.09	2990	103.27	3420	101.89	1020	101.25	405			101.17	352
31			101.35	478	102.19	1300			102.75	1790			103.12	3150			101.84	960	101.25	405				

Monthly Discharge of Mississippi River at Ferguson's Falls for 1915-6

Drainage Area 1,042 Square Miles

Month	Discharge in Second-feet			Discharge in Second-feet per Square Mile			Run-off
	Maximum	Minimum	Mean	Maximum	Minimum	Mean	Depth in Inches on Drainage Area
November.(1915)	525	364	422	.50	.35	.40	.45
December "	585	433	470	.56	.42	.45	.52
January...(1916)	1,300	455	697	1.25	.44	.67	.77
February.......	1,850	585	1,154	1.78	.56	1.11	1.20
March..........	2,450	398	726	2.35	.38	.70	.81
April..........	5,810	3,150	5,145	5.58	3.62	4.94	5.51
May............	4,980	2,840	3,807	4.78	2.73	3.65	4.21
June	4,650	2,600	3,377	4.46	2.50	3.24	3.61
July	3,270	960	1,967	3.14	.92	1.89	2.18
August	945	405	599	.91	.39	.57	.66
September......	500	322	387	.48	.31	.37	.41
October........	462	286	371	.44	.27	.36	.42
The year	5,810	286	1,588	5.58	.27	1.52	20.69

Mississippi River at Galetta

Location—In the Village of Galetta, Township of Fitzroy, County of Carleton, about one hundred feet above, and parallel to the highway bridge over the river. It is only a few hundred yards below the dam and power house of the Galetta Power & Milling Company.

Records Available—Discharge measurements from June, 1915, and gauge readings twice daily from June 24, 1915.

Drainage Area—1,456 square miles.

Gauge—0 to 9 feet of standard gauge plates secured to the left abutment of the highway bridge. High stages measured by rule from gauge.

Channel and Control—Channel is straight for 200 feet above and below the section to a little rapid. The river bed is composed of gravel and stones, with solid rock on the right bank and gravel on the left bank. The point of control is through a solid rock formation a hundred and fifty yards below the section.

Discharge Measurements—Made by wading and from a boat held up to tag line by cable. Extreme high-water measurements have to be made from the highway bridge.

Winter Flow—The winter conditions here will not seriously affect the gauge height and discharge relations.

Regulation—The river is subject to regulation throughout its entire length. In the headwaters are storage dams for power purposes, as well as timber dams for driving purposes.

Accuracy—Owing to the wet season the wasted water has been considerably more than would usually be the case. This season's relations between gauge height and discharge are likely better than those of the ordinary year.

Co-operation—Discharge measurements made at the bridge by the Department of Public Works of Canada.

Observer—J. P. Coyne, Galetta.

Discharge Measurements of Mississippi River at Galetta in 1915-6

Date	Hydrographer	Width in Feet	Area of Section in Sq. Feet	Mean Velocity in Feet per Sec.	Gauge Height in Feet	Discharge in Sec-Feet	Discharge in Second-feet per Square Mile
1915							
Nov. 24....	West, C. W.	88	140	3.44	244.47	481	....
Dec. 9....	" "	90	148	3.42	244.47	508 (a)	....
1916							
Jan. 24....	Campbell, L. L. .	60	196	4.60	245.49	902 (b)	....
Feb. 21....	McLennan, C. C.	96	300	3.45	246.05	1,034 (c)	....
Mar. 20....	" "	100	222	3.00	245.24	667 (d)	....
April 19....	Campbell, L. L. .	....	....	....	252.07	5,656	....
May 22....	" "	....	....	....	250.82	3,961	....
June 14....	McLennan, C. C.	102	902	2.62	248.82	2,363	....
July 10....	" "	101	894	3.26	248.86	2,333	....
Sept. 7....	" "	68	131	3.34	244.28	437	....
Oct. 24....	Campbell, L. L. .	75	150	3.47	244.55	519	....

(a) Ice at gauge.
(b) Ice at left edge of section.
(c) Ice at edges of section.
(d) Ice at edges of section and control.
3 H (iii)

Daily Gauge Height and Discharge of Mississippi River at Galetta for 1915-6

Drainage Area, 1,456 Square Miles

Day	November Gauge Ht. Feet	Nov. Dis-charge Sec-ft.	December Gauge Ht. Feet	Dec. Dis-charge Sec-ft.	January Gauge Ht. Feet	Jan. Dis-charge Sec-ft.	February Gauge Ht. Feet	Feb. Dis-charge Sec-ft.	March Gauge Ht. Feet	Mar. Dis-charge Sec-ft.	April Gauge Ht. Feet	Apr. Dis-charge Sec-ft.	May Gauge Ht. Feet	May Dis-charge Sec-ft.	June Gauge Ht. Feet	June Dis-charge Sec-ft.	July Gauge Ht. Feet	July Dis-charge Sec-ft.	August Gauge Ht. Feet	Aug. Dis-charge Sec-ft.	September Gauge Ht. Feet	Sept. Dis-charge Sec-ft.	October Gauge Ht. Feet	Oct. Dis-charge Sec-ft.
1	244.15	391	244.61	565	244.49	486	247.90	1840	245.99	915	251.11	4380	251.32	4670	249.61	2850	249.53	2790	245.49	900	244.11	276	243.99	330
2	244.26	433	244.53	535	244.49	521	248.15	1960	245.76	830	252.15	5780	251.24	4560	249.53	2790	249.57	2820	245.59	935	244.15	391	243.92	304
3	244.24	425	244.49	520	244.36	471	248.01	1870	245.78	840	251.86	5390	251.15	4440	249.49	7602	249.86	3040	245.53	915	244.07	361	244.03	345
4	244.20	410	244.45	520	244.45	506	247.90	1800	245.82	850	251.65	5110	251.03	12670	249.36	2670	249.74	2940	245.57	930	244.07	361	243.90	296
5	244.15	391	244.42	495	244.61	565	247.90	1780	245.70	805	251.53	4950	250.90	4090	249.36	5002	249.44	2730	245.53	915	244.20	410	243.50	296
6	244.15	391	244.30	391	244.82	650	247.70	1730	245.65	740	251.91	5570	250.82	3980	249.07	2480	249.32	2640	245.28	825	244.20	410	243.95	315
7	244.15	391	244.44	448	244.80	640	247.63	1670	245.53	790	251.57	5000	250.61	3720	249.07	2480	249.24	2590	244.86	660	244.24	425	243.90	296
8	244.05	353	244.53	500	244.90	675	247.61	1680	245.74	840	251.90	5450	250.49	3600	248.99	2430	249.11	2510	245.07	740	244.36	471	243.74	295
9	244.11	376	244.44	535	244.82	640	247.40	1510	245.78	860	252.10	5450	250.36	3470	248.94	2400	248.94	2400	245.24	805	244.28	440	243.78	250
10	244.11	376	244.30	376	244.82	650	247.15	1440	245.70	820	252.53	5730	250.24	3360	249.07	2480	248.82	2330	245.28	825	244.20	410	243.82	265
11	244.11	376	244.54	448	244.54	540	247.15	1430	245.70	805	252.86	6290	250.15	3450	248.94	2400	248.61	2280	245.22	840	244.36	471	243.94	311
12	244.13	383	244.36	495	244.57	495	246.94	1370	245.59	745	252.57	6730	249.89	3060	248.82	2330	248.44	2210	245.03	725	244.36	471	243.94	311
13	244.11	376	244.24	425	244.65	550	247.11	1140	245.59	745	252.32	6350	249.70	2910	248.82	2320	248.11	1940	244.90	575	244.42	494	244.03	345
14	244.09	368	244.44	500	244.82	580	246.55	1280	245.57	780	252.32	6010	249.49	2760	248.61	2310	247.99	1880	244.90	675	244.36	471	244.03	345
15	244.03	345	244.49	500	244.86	740	246.74	1140	245.61	775	252.11	5720	249.44	2730	248.44	2460	247.90	1840	244.90	675	244.40	486	243.99	330
16	244.07	361	244.74	500	244.74	660	246.74	1220	245.65	790	252.20	5850	250.76	2900	248.11	2940	247.94	1860	244.82	650	244.36	471	244.13	383
17	244.15	391	244.42	495	244.78	620	246.49	1220	245.59	745	252.49	6240	250.49	4960	247.90	2850	247.70	1790	244.82	650	244.36	440	244.19	406
18	244.15	383	244.44	500	244.94	630	246.36	1160	245.40	706	252.40	6120	251.49	6120	247.94	2760	247.53	1680	244.74	615	244.28	410	244.28	440
19	244.20	410	244.40	486	244.84	690	246.07	1050	245.44	735	252.07	5680	251.11	4380	247.70	2820	247.53	1680	244.65	580	244.20	391	244.53	486
20	244.40	486	244.40	486	244.90	655	246.32	940	245.40	735	251.90	5450	250.53	3870	247.53	2760	246.40	1250	244.57	550	244.09	368	244.70	535
21	244.59	555	244.40	555	244.90	675	246.36	990	245.42	760	252.07	5450	250.53	3640	247.50	2910	246.40	1250	244.53	535	244.15	391	244.49	600
22	244.42	495	244.40	486	245.02	740	246.32	930	245.44	835	252.15	5680	250.57	3600	246.61	3100	246.44	1250	244.11	410	244.03	345	244.49	615
23	244.42	495	244.42	495	245.53	915	246.00	935	245.38	800	252.03	5620	250.57	3600	246.40	3170	246.40	1260	244.20	391	243.99	330	244.53	520
24	244.40	471	244.40	486	245.42	875	245.99	865	245.38	820	251.86	5390	250.49	3680	246.44	3280	246.24	1250	244.34	462	243.90	296	244.70	535
25	244.40	471	244.40	486	246.15	1030	246.03	835	245.32	865	251.86	5390	250.11	3020	246.40	3210	246.24	1190	244.07	433	243.90	296	244.61	565
26	244.38	478	244.50	525	246.29	1150	246.05	905	245.32	865	251.86	5180	249.99	3240	246.24	3140	246.09	1130	244.11	361	243.97	323	244.65	580
27	244.38	478	244.49	520	246.74	1200	246.06	935	246.07	1120	251.70	5180	249.80	3140	246.09	3020	246.07	1120	244.09	376	243.95	355	244.42	494
28	244.38	478	244.57	520	246.82	1380	245.99	905	246.76	1380	251.53	4950	249.78	3020	245.99	2910	245.99	1090	244.07	376	244.07	361	244.18	402
29	244.38	478	244.59	550	246.82	1410	246.05	935	249.25	2590	251.40	4770	249.80	2970	245.99	2910	245.61	940	244.07	361			244.03	345
30	244.57	550	244.57	550	246.82	1410			250.57	3680			249.78	2970					244.01	358			243.99	330
31			244.57	550	247.05	1490																		

Monthly Discharge of Mississippi River at Galetta for 1915-6

Drainage Area. 1,456 Square Miles

Month	Discharge in Second-feet			Discharge in Second-feet per Square Mile			Run-off
	Maximum	Minimum	Mean	Maximum	Minimum	Mean	Depth in Inches on Drainage Area
November .(1915)	555	345	428	.38	.24	.29	.32
December. ''	565	425	504	.39	.29	.35	.40
January ..(1916)	1,490	471	786	1.02	.32	.54	.62
February	1,960	865	1,291	1.35	.59	.89	.96
March..........	3,680	670	973	2.53	.46	.67	.76
April..........	6,730	4,380	5,563	4.62	3.01	3.82	4.26
May...........	4,900	2,730	3,604	3.37	1.88	2.48	2.86
June...........	3,280	2,310	2,743	2.25	1.59	1.88	2.10
July...........	3,040	940	1,891	2.09	.65	1.30	1.50
August........	935	338	641	.64	.23	.44	.51
September	494	296	402	.34	.20	.28	.31
October........	615	235	398	.42	.16	.27	.31
The year	6,730	235	1,596	4.62	.16	1.10	14.97

Mississippi River near Snow Road

Location—At the highway bridge about two miles below the Village of Snow Road, Township of Sherbrooke, County of Lanark.

Records Available—Discharge measurements from July, 1915, and gauge readings on week days since July 30, 1915.

Drainage Area—496 square miles.

Gauge—0 to 6 ft. of standard gauge plates secured vertically to the downstream side of the left abutment of the highway bridge. The elevation of the zero on gauge is assumed as 100.00.

Channel and Control—The channel approaches and leaves the section at a slight angle. The banks are high, and are not liable to overflow. The bridge pier forms two channels at the gauging section. Earth, rocks and gravel in the river bed, not shifting. Control for ordinary stages not well defined. At very high water stages the point of control is probably the head of the rapids just above High Falls.

Discharge Measurements—Measurements made from bridge at all stages.

Winter Flow—Discharge relation affected by ice.

Regulation—The power and lumber companies operating on this river have storage dams above this point.

Accuracy—No Sunday readings have been secured by gauge-readers, but the fluctuation in stage is slow. The open-water relation should be good.

Observer—Fred. Jackson, Snow Road.

Discharge Measurements of Mississippi River near Snow Road in 1915-6

Date	Hydrographer	Width in Feet	Area of Section in Sq. Feet	Mean Velocity in Feet per Sec.	Gauge Height in Feet	Discharge in Sec-Feet	Discharge in Second-feet per Square Mile
1915							
Nov. 23....	West, C. W......	58	322	.90	102.10	291	....
Dec. 16....	"	58	320	.99	102.02	317 (a)	....
---1916							
Feb. 1....	Campcell, L. L..	58	380	1.59	103.00	605 (b)	....
" 23....	McLennan, C. C..	58	309	1.21	102.58	374 (c)	....
Mar. 21....	"	58	307	1.17	102.92	361 (c)	....
Apr. 8....	"	58	443	2.80	104.17	1,239	....
June 28....	"	58	496	3.80	105.00	1,885	....
July 14....	Campbell, L. L..	58	426	2.35	103.75	1,000	....
Sept. 12....	"	58	318	1.00	102.17	316	....
Oct. 1....	"	58	300	.69	101.92	208	....

(a) Ice on ponds above and below section.
(b) Ice on ponds above and below section. Section partly ice-covered.
(c) Ice measurement.

Daily Gauge Height and Discharge of Mississippi River near Snow Road for 1915-6

Drainage Area, 446 Square Miles

Day	November Gauge Ht. Feet	November Dis-charge Sec-ft.	December Gauge Ht. Feet	December Dis-charge Sec-ft.	January Gauge Ht. Feet	January Dis-charge Sec-ft.	February Gauge Ht. Feet	February Dis-charge Sec-ft.	March Gauge Ht. Feet	March Dis-charge Sec-ft.	April Gauge Ht. Feet	April Dis-charge Sec-ft.	May Gauge Ht. Feet	May Dis-charge Sec-ft.	June Gauge Ht. Feet	June Dis-charge Sec-ft.	July Gauge Ht. Feet	July Dis-charge Sec-ft.	August Gauge Ht. Feet	August Dis-charge Sec-ft.	September Gauge Ht. Feet	September Dis-charge Sec-ft.	October Gauge Ht. Feet	October Dis-charge Sec-ft.
1	102.08	265	102.17	288	102.23	302	103.00	605	102.58	359	104.38	2720	106.33	2720	104.08	1220	104.50	1520	103.00	605	102.25	307		243
2	102.08	265	102.19	292	102.24	305	103.02	600	102.58	356	104.38	2670	106.25	2670	104.00	1160		1540	103.00	605	102.33	329	101.96	237
3	102.04	255	102.19	292	102.25	308	103.02	600	102.58	356	104.75	2630	106.17	2630	104.08	1160	104.58	1570	103.04	625		329	101.96	237
4	102.02	250	102.17	288	102.25	308	103.00	580	102.62	356	104.38	1430	106.08	2560		1390	104.67	1640	103.00	605	102.33	329	101.96	237
5	102.02	250			102.25	308	103.83	495		353	104.17	1280	105.88	2430	104.00	1160	104.58	1570	102.92	560	102.33	329	101.92	229
6	102.04	255	102.17	288	102.25	308	103.83	486	102.58	353	104.17	1280	105.75	2350	104.00	1160	104.42	1460		560	102.33	329	101.92	229
7	102.00	250	102.17	288	102.25	308	103.79	459	192.58	350	104.08	1280		2240	104.00	1160	104.17	1280	102.92	560	102.25	307	101.92	229
8		247	102.17	288	102.25	308	103.71	438	102.58	350		1380	105.42	2130	104.00	1160	104.52	1110	102.92	560	102.25	307		329
9	102.00	245	102.17	288	102.25	308	103.71	433	102.60	350	104.33	1380	105.17	1970	103.92	1220		1530	102.83	510	102.25	307	102.33	329
10	102.00	245	102.17	288	102.25	308	103.69	422	102.62	350	104.33	1390	105.17	1860	104.08	1220		1530	102.83	510		304	102.38	344
11	102.00	245	102.17	288	102.33	308	103.69	418	102.65	365	104.50	1520	104.83	1860	104.17	1280		1060	102.75	472	102.21	298	102.42	356
12	102.00	245	102.17	288	102.33	308	103.67	410	102.65	365	104.75	1700	104.75	1700		1350	103.83	1030	102.75	472	122.21	298	102.38	344
13	101.92	229	102.17	288	102.33	308			162.65	365	105.25	2020	104.50	1520	104.38	1390	103.79	1020		426	102.17	288	102.33	329
14		227	102.17	288	102.33	308	103.62	401	102.65	365	105.50	2180	104.50	1430	104.33	1390	103.77	1020	102.50	380	102.17	288	102.33	318
15	101.90	225	102.17	288	102.33	308	103.62	395	102.62	365	105.75	2350	104.50	1340	104.33	1360	103.77	1920	102.50	380	101.17	288	102.29	308
16	101.85	214	102.15	282		308	103.60	389	102.62	365			104.25	1360	104.33	1390	103.75	1010	102.35	335	102.17	288		308
17	101.85	214	102.17	288	102.33	308	103.60	386	102.62	365	106.25	2510	104.29	1360	104.33	1390	103.75	1010	102.35	335	102.17	288	102.21	298
18	101.92	229	102.19	292	102.38	308	103.60	383	102.75	365	106.42	2780	104.67	1390		2240	103.67	960	102.25	307	102.18	289	102.21	298
19		229			102.38	308	103.60	380	102.92	365	106.58	2890	104.83	2510	103.58	2510	103.58	910	102.08	265	102.08	290	102.21	298
20	102.02	250	102.17	288	102.38	335	130.60	377	102.92	365	106.33	2720	104.79	2510	106.00	2510	103.54	890		277	102.08	265	102.23	302
21		250	102.17	288	102.38	344	103.58	374	102.94	365	106.25	2670		1750	106.08	720	103.50	865	102.17	288	102.08	265	102.25	308
22	102.10	270	102.19	292	102.50	380	103.58	374	102.92	374		2670	104.50	620	106.00	2560	103.50	865	102.17	288	102.08	265		298
23	102.10	270	102.21	298		389	103.58	371	102.92	371	106.25	2890	104.42	1520	105.83	2400		835	102.25	307	102.08	265	102.12	288
24	102.10	270	102.21	298	102.56	398	103.58	371	102.88	374	106.58	2890	104.42	1460	105.58	2240		805	102.33	329	102.08	265	102.12	275
25	102.10	270	192.25	305	102.62	418	103.58	365		380	106.58	2940	104.38	1460	105.33	2070	103.38	780	102.42	356	102.08	265	102.08	265
26	102.10	270	102.67	305	102.67	438	103.67	362	102.83	418	106.67	2940	104.21	1340	105.17	1970	102.33	740	102.42	356	102.02	245	102.08	245
27	102.13	278	102.23		102.75	472		359	102.83	464	106.67	2940		1310	105.08	1910	103.25	740		350	102.00	245	102.00	245
28		282	102.21	298		510	103.58		102.85	510	106.50	2840	104.08	1220	105.00	1860	103.25		102.38	344	102.00	250	102.00	245
29	102.15	282	102.19	298	102.83	510	103.58		102.96	580		2780	104.17	1280	104.92	1810	103.17	625	102.38	329	102.02	250	101.92	237
30	102.17	288	102.21	298	102.83	535			103.79	1030			104.08	1280	104.67	1640		650	102.33	329	102.02	250	101.92	229
31			102.23	302	102.92	560							104.17	1280			103.08							

Monthly Discharge of Mississippi River near Snow Road for 1915-6

Drainage Area, 446 Square Miles

Month	Discharge in Second-feet			Discharge in Second-feet per Square Mile			Run-off
	Maximum	Minimum	Mean	Maximum	Minimum	Mean	Depth in Inches on Drainage Area
November (1915)	288	214	253	.65	.48	.57	.64
December "	307	282	292	.69	.63	.65	.75
January ..(1916)	560	302	360	1.26	.68	.81	.93
February	605	359	427	1.36	.80	.96	1.04
March	1,030	350	405	2.31	.78	.91	1.02
April	2,940	1,220	2,183	6.59	2.74	4.89	. 5.46
May	2,720	1,220	1,712	6.10	2.74	3.84	4.43
June............	2,560	1,110	1,663	5.74	2.49	3.73	4.16
July	1,640	600	1,051	3.68	1.35	2.36	2.72
August	625	265	419	1.40	.59	.94	1.08
September	329	245	286	.74	.55	.64	.71
October	356	229	278	.80	.51	.62	.71
The year	2,940	214	776	6.59	.48	1.74	23.68

Moira River near Foxboro

Location—Three hundred feet above G.T.R. Crossing, and six hundred feet east of Foxboro Station, on the G.T.R.-Belleville, Peterboro Branch. Near Lot 5, Concession VI, Township of Thurlow, County of Hastings.

Records Available—Monthly discharge measurements from September, 1915, and gauge readings from October 12, 1915.

Drainage Area—1,038 square miles.

Gauge—Four points on the bed of the river, about 50 feet above the section have been selected from which the elevation of the water surface is measured twice daily. One of these points is used at a time, according to the stage of the river.

Channel and Control—At one side of the river at the section are boulders and rocks, but the rest of the section is smooth, solid rock, liable to no movement at all. The control is only a few feet below the section and is not likely to freeze over in winter except for short periods of time.

Discharge Measurements—At ordinary stages the measurements are made by wading, at tag line.

Winter Flow—The relation of gauge height to discharge will be but slightly affected by ice, but likely in a fairly uniform manner throughout the winter.

Regulation—The river above the section has dams in many places besides the regulation for the lumber interest, on different tributary lakes and streams.

Accuracy—Open water relation will be good.

Observer—C. Stewart, Foxboro P.O.

Discharge Measurements of Moira River near Foxboro in 1915-6

Date	Hydrographer	Width in Feet	Area of Section in Sq. Feet	Mean Velocity in Feet per Sec.	Gauge Height in Feet	Discharge in Sec–Feet	Discharge in Second-feet per Square Mile
1915							
Nov. 13....	West, C. W......	163	192	1.13	321.95	217	....
Dec. 4....	"	166	323	2.52	322.75	816 (a)	....
1916							
Jan. 5....	"	164	273	1.75	322.46	478 (a)	....
Feb. 12....	McLennan, C. C..	178	507	2.96	323.93	1,500 (a)	....
Mar. 10....	" ..	162	297	2.25	322.68	669	....
May 8....	" ..	181	505	4.10	324.05	2,073	....
June 27....	Campbell, L. L ..	190	673	5.87	325.17	3,952	....
July 26....	" ..	164	268	1.80	322.47	482	....
Sept. 19....	" ..	120	126	.95	321.66	121	....
Oct. 12....	" ..	115	107	.67	321.50	72	....

(a) Ice covered above section.

Daily Gauge Height and Discharge of Moira River near Foxboro for 1915-6

Drainage Area, 1,038 Square Miles

Day	November Gauge Ht. (Feet)	November Dis-charge (Sec-ft.)	December Gauge Ht. (Feet)	December Dis-charge (Sec-ft.)	January Gauge Ht. (Feet)	January Dis-charge (Sec-ft.)	February Gauge Ht. (Feet)	February Dis-charge (Sec-ft.)	March Gauge Ht. (Feet)	March Dis-charge (Sec-ft.)	April Gauge Ht. (Feet)	April Dis-charge (Sec-ft.)	May Gauge Ht. (Feet)	May Dis-charge (Sec-ft.)	June Gauge Ht. (Feet)	June Dis-charge (Sec-ft.)	July Gauge Ht. (Feet)	July Dis-charge (Sec-ft.)	August Gauge Ht. (Feet)	August Dis-charge (Sec-ft.)	September Gauge Ht. (Feet)	September Dis-charge (Sec-ft.)	October Gauge Ht. (Feet)	October Dis-charge (Sec-ft.)
1	322.01	264	322.89	730	322.44	464	325.32	4200	322.84	695	326.69	6510	325.02	3700	324.37	2610	324.50	2830	322.27	382	321.79	174	321.60	105
2	321.97	246	322.87	720	322.44	464	325.55	4560	322.84	695	327.09	7180	324.90	3500	324.39	2640	324.35	2570	322.20	349	321.79	174	321.60	105
3	321.99	254	322.84	700	322.46	475	325.54	4580	322.83	690	327.34	7610	324.82	3360	324.52	2860	324.26	2430	322.18	340	321.77	167	321.58	98
4	321.99	254	322.77	655	322.42	454	325.37	4290	322.77	655	327.59	8020	324.77	3290	324.60	3000	324.21	2350	322.16	331	321.76	164	321.56	92
5	322.01	254	322.73	630	322.48	485	325.20	4010	322.74	635	327.79	8360	324.74	3240	324.60	3000	324.13	2210	322.10	304	321.76	164	321.54	85
6	322.00	259	322.69	605	322.54	519	324.98	3630	322.67	590	327.79	8360	324.66	3100	324.58	2970	324.04	2060	322.10	304	321.74	163	321.52	79
7	321.98	251	322.65	580	322.56	530	324.75	3250	322.68	600	327.49	7850	324.66	3100	324.51	2850	323.89	1820	322.08	295	321.73	161	321.54	85
8	321.98	251	322.61	555	322.56	530	324.43	2710	322.70	610	327.04	7100	324.47	2780	324.45	2 40	323.80	1690	322.16	331	321.79	174	321.54	85
9	321.97	246	322.59	545	322.54	519	324.36	2590	322.66	585	326.29	5830	324.36	2590	324.39	2840	323.62	1450	322.16	331	321.78	170	321.55	88
10	321.98	251	322.48	485	322.59	545	324.18	2290	322.66	585	326.10	5540	324.25	2410	324.39	2640	323.48	1299	322.14	322	321.74	163	321.54	85
11	321.98	251	322.48	485	322.62	560	324.00	1990	322.65	580	325.90	5180	324.14	2230	324.41	2680	323.58	1400	322.12	313	321	151	321.54	85
12	321.96	242	322.44	464	322.61	555	323.89	1830	322.62	565	325.79	4990	324.07	2110	324.48	2800	323.48	1290	322.10	304	321	144	321.54	85
13	321.98	251	322.43	459	322.73	630	323.79	1680	322.63	570	325.73	4900	323.98	1960	324.63	3050	323.38	1180	322.08	295	321.68	133	321.58	98
14	321.97	246	322.39	439	322.75	640	323.73	1590	322.62	565	325.78	4980	323.83	1730	324.71	3190	323.29	1080	322.05	281	321.68	133	321.56	92
15	321.97	246	322.39	439	322.79	665	323.65	1490	322.63	570	326.06	5450	323.75	1620	324.70	3170	323.24	1040	322.03	272	321.70	140	321.54	85
16	321.97	246	322.66	585	322.83	690	323.45	1330	322.60	550	326.18	5660	323.64	1480	324.90	3500	322.91	750	321.98	250	321.68	133	321.54	98
17	322.33	410	322.31	410	322.85	690	323.39	1190	322.60	550	326.24	5760	323.78	1640	325.52	4540	322.93	765	321.97	246	321.68	133	321.54	85
18	321.99	254	322.31	401	322.85	705	323.27	1000	322.57	535	326.27	5810	323.94	1800	325.51	4520	322.85	705	321.96	242	321.68	133	321.54	85
19	321.99	254	322.39	439	322.89	730	323.39	1190	322.59	545	326.16	5620	324.15	2240	325.01	3660	322.80	670	321.96	242	321.66	125	321.62	112
20	322.08	295	322.35	420	322.96	800	323.20	1000	322.59	545	326.16	5620	324.26	2430	326.31	5870	322.60	635	321.94	233	321.74	165	321.74	165
21	322.08	401	322.37	430	322.89	755	323.14	960	322.58	540	325.79	4990	324.34	2570	326.48	6160	322.60	635	321.92	225	321.62	116	321.74	165
22	322.49	490	322.37	439	322.97	795	323.14	935	322.57	535	325.65	4760	324.34	2570	326.50	6190	322.68	595	321.92	216	321.64	119	321.74	155
23	322.49	490	322.36	425	323.38	1080	322.56	925	322.56	525	325.69	4830	324.36	2590	326.39	6000	322.68	545	321.90	216	321.63	116	321.72	148
24	322.84	690	322.39	435	323.47	1280	323.11	910	322.54	525	325.69	4870	324.33	2540	325.79	4990	322.59	520	321.90	205	321.61	109	321.69	137
25	322.96	785	322.39	439	323.55	1370	323.02	835	322.54	520	325.71	4870	324.33	2470	325.58	4650	322.51	500	321.87	193	321.62	112	321.67	130
26	322.94	770	322.38	434	323.95	1920	322.94	810	322.59	545	325.60	4680	324.20	2530	325.45	4420	322.47	480	321.84	193	321.64	119	321.68	133
27	322.94	750	322.38	444	324.30	2490	322.94	725	322.59	545	325.71	4680	324.11	2180	325.14	4680	322.47	485	321.85	197	321.64	119	321.67	130
28	322.91	730	322.42	454	324.73	3220	322.85	725	322.88	2490	325.60	4680	324.20	2180	324.93	3550	322.38	434	321.85	197	321.60	112	321.68	133
29	322.89	750	322.42	454	324.58	2960	322.85	660	324.30	3150	325.60	4360	323.87	1800	324.75	3250	322.34	415	321.80	178	321.63	116	321.64	119
30	322.90	730	322.39	439	324.58	3350		705	324.30	4290	325.16	3940	324.07	2110	324.65	3080	322.33	410	321.80	178	321.60	85	321.64	119
31	322.90	740	322.37	430	325.14	3910			326.40	6020			324.30	2490			322.30	396	321.81	182		105	321.59	102

Monthly Discharge of Moira River near Foxboro for 1915-6.

Drainage Area 1,038 Square Miles　–

Month.	Discharge in Second-feet.			Discharge in Second-feet per Square Mile.			Run-off.
	Maximum.	Minimum.	Mean.	Maximum.	Minimum.	Mean.	Depth in inches on Drainage Area.
November (1915)	785	242	411	.76	.23	.40	.45
December　''	730	401	501	.70	.39	.48	.55
January　(1916)	3,910	454	1,151	3.77	.44	1.11	1.28
February	4,580	660	1,989	4.41	.64	1.92	2.07
March..........	6,020	520	1.025	5.80	.50	.99	1.14
April..........	8,360	3,940	5,761	8.05	3.80	5.55	6.19
May............	3,700	1,480	2,434	3.56	1.43	2.33	2.69
June............	6,190	2,610	3,790	5.96	2.51	3.65	4.07
July............	3,830	396	1,148	2.73	.38	1.11	1.28
August	382	178	264	.37	.17	.25	.29
September	174	82	136	.17	.08	.13	.15
October,........	155	79	108	.15	.08	.10	.12
The year	8,360	79	1,540	8.05	.08	1.48	20.10

Napanee River near Napanee

Location—At Mink's Bridge, three miles from Napanee, near lot 1, concession 1, Township of Camden, County of Addington.

Records Available—Discharge measurements from August, 1915, and gauge readings from September 8, 1915.

Drainage Area—300 square miles.

Gauge—Standard gauge plates 0 to 6 ft. firmly secured to a 4 x 4 in. pine driven in river bottom and spiked and wired to one of three elms in one cluster on the right bank 400 ft. above the bridge and section.

Channel and Control—The channel is curved above the section to within 20 feet of the bridge, and is straight for 300 feet below. The right bank is high, while the left is comparatively low and liable to overflow. The bed of the stream is composed of rocks and gravel, not likely to shift.

Discharge Measurements—Made by wading at low stages and from bridge at high stages.

Winter Flow—Relation of gauge height to discharge is affected by ice.

Regulation—There are several power developments on the upper part of the river, and also lumber dams on tributary waters.

Accuracy—Two daily readings give only fair mean daily gauge heights.

Observer—Mrs. Dan. O'Shaughnessy, Napanee.

Discharge Measurements of Napanee River near Napanee in 1915-6

Date	Hydrographer	Width in Feet	Area of Section in Sq. Feet	Mean Velocity in Feet per Sec.	Gauge Height in Feet	Discharge in Sec-Feet	Discharge in Second-feet per Square Mile
1915							
Nov. 12	West. C. W.....	64	74	1.02	101.77	76 (a)	....
Dec. 4 "	"	64	100	1.43	102.20	143 (b)	....
1916							
Jan. 6, ...	"	64	196	2.07	103.58	407 (c)	....
Feb. 12 "	Campbell, L. L.	64	299	2.23	105.62	668 (d)	....
Mar. 11 "	"	64	123	2 04	103.50	251	....
Apr. 4 "	"	64	490	4 66	108.23	2286	....
May 30 "	"	64	298	3.36	105.25	1003	....
June 27 "	"	64	350	3.98	106.08	1392	....
July 27 "	McLennan, C. C.	64	87	1.49	101.99	130	....
Sep. 19 "	Campbell, L. L.	48	31	1.17	101.07	36 (e)	....

(a) Weeds may affect.
(b) Ice at edges of river, above and below section.
(c) Ice above and below section.
(d) Ice measurement.
(e) Dam under construction at Colbrook. Water being held at Petworth dam.

Daily Gauge Height and Discharge of Napanee River near Napanee for 1915-16

Drainage Area 300 Square miles

Day	Nov. Gauge Ht. (Feet)	Nov. Dis-charge (Sec-ft.)	Dec. Gauge Ht. (Feet)	Dec. Dis-charge (Sec-ft.)	Jan. Gauge Ht. (Feet)	Jan. Dis-charge (Sec-ft.)	Feb. Gauge Ht. (Feet)	Feb. Dis-charge (Sec-ft.)	Mar. Gauge Ht. (Feet)	Mar. Dis-charge (Sec-ft.)	Apr. Gauge Ht. (Feet)	Apr. Dis-charge (Sec-ft.)	May Gauge Ht. (Feet)	May Dis-charge (Sec-ft.)	June Gauge Ht. (Feet)	June Dis-charge (Sec-ft.)	July Gauge Ht. (Feet)	July Dis-charge (Sec-ft.)	Aug. Gauge Ht. (Feet)	Aug. Dis-charge (Sec-ft.)	Sept. Gauge Ht. (Feet)	Sept. Dis-charge (Sec-ft.)	Oct. Gauge Ht. (Feet)	Oct. Dis-charge (Sec-ft.)
1	101.83	100	102.12	137	102.33	167	106.17	1040	103.50	215	108.29	2310	105.25	1030	105.08	960	105.96	1330	102.05	127	101.38	54	101.30	48
2	101.79	95	102.12	137	102.29	161	106.08	1010	103.54	226	108.38	2390	105.29	1050	105.08	960	106.00	1340	102.09	133	101.38	54	101.38	54
3	101.79	95	102.12	137	102.21	150	106.75	1280	103.56	233	108.25	2290	105.42	840	105.17	995	106.29	1470	101.88	106	101.30	48	101.30	48
4	101.75	91	102.12	137	102.46	188	107.17	1440	103.50	226	108.29	2310	104.79	805	105.17	995	106.67	1630	101.97	117	101.30	48	101.22	43
5	101.75	91	102.12	137	102.75	238	108.00	1770	103.5b	243	108.35	2330	104.71	720	105.08	960	106.62	1610	101.97	117	101.26	46	101.22	43
6	101.67	91	102.12	137	102.71	231	102.75	1430	103.50	233	108.88	2550	104.50	655	104.92	890	105.58	1170	101.51	66	101.22	43	101.22	43
7	101.71	86	102.08	131	102.71	231	107.25	1290	103.54	243	108.62	2450	104.33	640	104.58	755	104.50	720	101.80	96	101.22	43	101.26	43
8	101.71	95	102.12	137	102.29	155	106.96	1400	103.50	240	108.67	2470	104.29	580	104.71	805	104.33	675	101.80	96	101.22	43	101.18	38
9	101.79	95	102.12	137	102.67	212	107.25	1290	103.50	243	108.12	2230	104.12	580	104.75	805	104.04	555	101.88	87	101.22	43	101.13	38
10	101.75	91	102.08	131	102.71	212	106.17	1400	103.42	243	108.08	2220	104.04	580	105.33	1060	103.88	505	101.72	106	101.26	46	101.22	43
11	101.79	86	102.12	137	102.62	192	105.71	935	103.42	236	108.04	2200	104.12	580	105.42	1130	103.71	452	101.88	106	101.30	48	101.22	43
12	101.79	95	102.21	150	102.67	193	105.66	730	103.42	256	107.25	1870	104.12	475	105.42	1100	103.67	441	101.88	70	101.22	43	101.22	43
13	101.75	91	102.33	167	103.39	368	105.33	705	103.42	261	107.50	1980	103.79	464	105.17	995	103.58	418	101.55	54	101.22	43	101.22	43
14	101.79	95	102.29	161	102.71	185	105.17	575	103.44	267	107.00	1770	103.75	464	105.50	1130	103.50	394	101.34	51	101.26	43	101.22	43
15	101.75	91	102.33	167	102.71	197	105.08	530	103.33	275	108.50	2390	103.75	464	108.04	2200	103.50	394	101.34	43	101.13	38	101.30	48
16	101.71	91	102.29	161	102.79	183	105.04	510	103.33	256	108.52	2400	103.33	1340	107.29	1890	103.12	308	101.30	48	101.09	36	101.30	48
17	101.71	86	102.29	161	102.79	190	104.92	505	103.33	265	108.10	2230	106.00	1220	106.67	1630	103.22	308	101.47	62	101.05	35	101.30	48
18	101.71	95	102.29	161	102.79	183	104.62	394	103.33	271	108.02	2190	105.71	1150	106.67	1630	102.71	231	101.47	62	101.05	35	101.30	48
19	101.96	116	102.29	161	102.75	172	104.42	352	103.29	276	108.00	2180	105.54	1170	106.67	1630	102.58	208	101.30	48	101.05	35	101.30	48
20	102.12	137	102.29	161	102.75	173	104.12	292	103.29	275	108.00	2180	105.58	1130	106.67	1630	102.50	195	101.30	48	101.05	35	101.30	48
21	102.71	231	102.29	161	102.67	161	104.04	292	103.42	306	107.35	1910	105.50	1170	106.58	1560	102.50	195	101.30	48	101.22	43	101.34	51
22	102.71	245	102.25	156	102.75	150	104.04	280	103.38	304	106.67	1640	105.58	1120	106.50	1690	102.33	167	101.34	54	101.30	48	101.47	62
23	102.29	161	102.29	161	102.67	157	103.88	258	103.29	292	106.71	1770	105.46	1100	106.83	1630	102.42	181	101.30	48			101.42	62
24	101.92	111	102.33	167	104.00	380	103.88	254	103.26	290	107.25	1870	105.42	995	106.67	1430	102.33	167	101.38	54			101.30	58
25	101.71	86	102.42	181	103.83	332	103.71	231	103.25	296	107.60	1760	105.42	975	106.50	1420	102.29	161	101.38	54			101.30	58
26	102.29	161	102.67	224	104.25	427	103.71	234	103.54	365	107.25	1770	105.12	975	106.83	1420	102.12	137	101.38	54			101.22	48
27	102.29	161	102.58	209	105.38	810	103.69	226	104.29	595	107.02	1770	105.12	995	106.21	1430	102.00	121	101.38	54			101.38	43
28	102.12	137	102.46	188	106.00	1050	103.62	229	106.21	1390	107.00	1350	105.12		106.17	1420	102.00	121	101.38	54			101.42	48
29	102.21	150	102.42	181	104.83	575	103.54	219	108.75	2470	106.02	1340	105.17		106.17	1420	102.08	131					101.38	54
30	102.21	150	102.38	175	105.42	700			109.50	2800	106.00				106.08	1380							101.42	58
31					105.67	870			109.00	2600			105.17	995									101.38	54

Monthly Discharge of Napanee River near Napanee for 1915-6

Drainage Area, 300 Square Miles

Month	Discharge in Second-feet			Discharge in Second-feet per Square Mile			Run-off
	Maximum	Minimum	Mean	Maximum	Minimum	Mean	Depth in Inches on Drainage Area
November (1915)	245	82	117	.82	.27	.39	.44
December.......	224	126	158	.75	.42	.53	.61
January ..(1916)	1,050	141	307	3.50	.47	1.02	1.18
February	1,770	219	700	5.90	.73	2.33	2.51
March.........	2,800	215	538	9.33	.72	1.79	2.06
April..........	2,550	1,340	2,052	8.50	4.47	6.84	7.63
May...........	1,340	464	899	4.47	1.55	3.00	3.46
June	2,200	805	1,277	7.33	2.68	4.26	4.75
July...........	1,630	121	519	5.43	.40	1.73	1.99
August	133	43	73	.44	.14	.24	.28
September.....	54	35	43	.18	.12	.14	.16
October........	62	38	48	.21	.13	.16	.18
The year	2,800	35	557	9.33	.12	1.86	25.32

Petawawa River near Petawawa

Location—About 1½ miles southwest of Petawawa station above C.P.R. bridge, near lot 15, concession 7, Township of Petawawa, County of Renfrew.

Records Available—Discharge measurements from October, 1915, and daily gauge heights from November 5, 1915.

Drainage Area—1,572 square miles.

Gauge—Temporary mark used from December 15, 1915, to February 29, 1916, to obtain water elevations afterwards reduced to same datum as permanent gauge, screwed to plank, bolted to large rock in river, back of Rantzs' house, 1,000 feet above the station, and 200 feet above the head of the rapids. This gauge has been used for gauge readings since March 1, 1916.

Discharge Measurements—The discharge measurements for normal and low flows, summer and winter, are made by wading in fast water near the end of the straight stretch in the river downstream from the gauge. At high water measurements are made opposite the hotel in the lower village from a boat.

Channel and Control—The controlling section is a few hundred yards above the metering section. The river is straight for a few hundred feet each side of the section, but is crooked and fast for two miles below the section. The soundings for depth are taken for each metering as the water is fast and the river bed of stones may change slightly between meterings, and the depths do not change the same as the gauge readings.

Winter Flow—The control here is at fast water and only slightly affected by ice.

Accuracy—Gauge readings twice daily give good mean daily gauge height as the fluctuation at the gauge is slow.

Observer—Elsa Rantz, Petawawa.

Discharge Measurements of Petawawa River near Petawawa in 1915-6

Date	Hydrographer	Width in Feet	Area of Section in Sq. Feet	Mean Velocity in Feet per Sec.	Gauge Height in Feet	Discharge in Sec-Feet	Discharge in Second-feet per Square Mile
1915							
Nov. 5....	West, C. W.....	163	231	2.91	101.58	673	....
Dec. 15....	"	162	231	2.91	101.57	605 (a)	....
1916							
Jan. 28....	Campbell, L. L..	160	215	2.90	101.74	623 (a)	....
Feb. 25....	McLennan, C. C.	158	234	3.18	101.78	745 (a)	....
Mar. 23....	"	145	203	3.10	101.71	629 (b)	....
June 15....	"	319	1,805	1.61	103.50	2,921	....
July 12....	"	312	1,466	1.28	102.79	1,879	....
Sept. 8....	"	169	260	3.40	101.92	882	....
Oct. 28....	Campbell, L. L. .	197	327	3.62	102.33	1,186	....

(a) Section open. Lake above frozen.
(b) Ice at edges of section.

Daily Gauge Height and Discharge of Petawawa River near Petawawa for 1915-6

Drainage Area 1.572 Square Miles

Day	Nov Gauge Ht. (Feet)	Nov Dis-charge (Sec-ft.)	Dec Gauge Ht. (Feet)	Dec Dis-charge (Sec-ft.)	Jan Gauge Ht. (Feet)	Jan Dis-charge (Sec-ft.)	Feb Gauge Ht. (Feet)	Feb Dis-charge (Sec-ft.)	Mar Gauge Ht. (Feet)	Mar Dis-charge (Sec-ft.)	Apr Gauge Ht. (Feet)	Apr Dis-charge (Sec-ft.)	May Gauge Ht. (Feet)	May Dis-charge (Sec-ft.)	Jun Gauge Ht. (Feet)	Jun Dis-charge (Sec-ft.)	Jul Gauge Ht. (Feet)	Jul Dis-charge (Sec-ft.)	Aug Gauge Ht. (Feet)	Aug Dis-charge (Sec-ft.)	Sep Gauge Ht. (Feet)	Sep Dis-charge (Sec-ft.)	Oct Gauge Ht. (Feet)	Oct Dis-charge (Sec-ft.)
1					101.55	595	101.76	740	101.83	790	102.29	1180	104.42	4630	104.00	3830	103.92	3680	102.50	1410	101.67	675	101.54	585
2					101.57	610	101.78	755	101.83	790	102.46	1370	104.42	4630	103.96	3750	103.88	3620	102.46	1370	101.71	705	101.71	560
3					101.59	620	101.78	755	101.83	790	102.62	1550	104.54	4860	103.92	3680	103.75	3350	102.50	1410	101.75	735	101.50	560
4					101.57	610	101.78	770	101.80	790	102.83	1820	104.67	5000	103.62	3620	103.62	3020	102.42	1320	101.75	735	101.50	560
5					101.57	610	101.78	755	101.79	765	102.92	1950	104.67	5000	103.88	3510	103.29	2560	102.38	1280	101.75	735	101.50	560
6					101.57	610	101.80	770	101.75	735	102.92	1950	104.67	5000	103.83	3280	103.12	2270	102.33	1230	101.75	735	101.50	560
7					101.57	610	101.80	770	101.79	735	102.92	1950	104.50	4780	103.71	3210	103.00	2070	102.21	1110	101.75	735	101.50	560
8					101.59	620	101.82	785	101.82	790	102.92	1950	104.54	4630	103.67	3060	102.96	2010	102.29	1180	101.75	735	101.50	560
9					101.59	610	101.80	770	101.79	765	102.92	1950	104.29	4380	103.58	3060	103.00	2070	102.33	1230	101.75	735	101.50	560
10				610	101.57	610	101.80	770	101.83	790	102.93	1970	104.21	4230	103.50	2920	102.88	1890	102.25	1150	101.75	735	101.50	560
11				595	101.53	580	101.80	770	101.83	790	103.00	2070	104.17	4150	103.58	2920	102.79	1770	102.17	1070	101.75	735	101.50	560
12				620	101.55	595	101.82	785	101.75	735	103.08	2210	104.21	4230	103.50	2920	102.75	1720	102.17	1070	101.75	735	101.50	560
13				595	101.55	595	101.78	755	101.75	735	103.21	2430	104.08	3980	103.42	2780	102.79	1770	102.17	1070	101.75	735	101.50	560
14			101.57	595	101.57	610	101.78	755	101.75	735	103.33	2630	104.04	3910	103.50	2920	102.83	1820	102.08	990	101.75	735	101.50	560
15			101.55	595	101.57	610	101.78	755	101.75	735	103.42	2780	104.00	3830	103.42	2780	102.83	1820	102.04	960	102.00	675	101.50	560
16			101.59	610	101.55	595	101.80	770	101.75	735	103.50	2920	104.00	3830	103.92	3680	102.92	1950	102.00	925	102.00	675	101.50	560
17			101.59	620	101.55	595	101.80	770	101.75	735	103.62	3120	104.21	4380	103.83	3510	102.92	1950	102.00	925	102.00	675	101.62	640
18			101.57	595	101.55	595	101.80	770	101.75	735	103.75	3350	104.29	4380	103.83	3510	102.92	1950	102.00	925	101.92	640	101.67	675
19			101.59	610	101.55	595	101.80	770	101.75	735	103.79	3430	104.33	4460	103.79	3430	102.92	1950	101.92	860	101.92	675	101.67	675
20			101.57	620	101.55	595	101.80	770	101.75	735	103.75	3350	104.33	4460	104.08	3980	103.00	2070	101.92	860	101.83	675	101.83	790
21			101.59	640	101.55	595	101.80	770	101.71	705	103.67	3210	104.33	4460	104.29	4380	103.00	2070	101.83	790	101.67	675	101.83	860
22			101.55	595	101.65	660	101.76	740	101.75	735	103.54	2990	104.29	4380	104.29	4380	103.33	2630	101.79	765	101.67	640	101.92	860
23			101.59	620	101.65	660	101.78	755	101.75	735	103.67	3210	104.33	4310	104.33	4460	103.33	2630	101.79	735	101.62	615	102.25	1050
24			101.61	635	101.65	660	101.80	740	101.75	735	103.75	3350	104.33	4310	104.29	4380	103.21	2430	101.75	735	101.58	615	102.25	1050
25			101.61	650	101.65	660	101.80	770	101.75	735	103.83	3510	104.29	4310	104.33	4460	103.04	2140	101.75	735	101.58	615	102.25	1050
26			101.63	650	101.68	685	101.80	770	101.71	705	103.96	3750	104.38	4550	104.25	4310	103.00	2070	101.71	705	101.58	615	102.25	1230
27			101.59	620	101.70	695	101.78	755	101.79	765	104.12	4060	104.38	4310	104.17	4150	102.88	1890	101.71	705	101.58	615	102.33	1230
28			101.57	620	101.74	725	101.76	740	101.83	790	104.25	4300	104.17	4150	104.17	4150	102.79	1770	101.71	705	101.58	615	102.33	1230
29			101.59	610	101.74	725	101.78	755	101.92	860	104.42	4630	104.17	4150	104.04	3910	102.75	1720	101.67	675			102.33	1230
30			101.57	610	101.74	725			102.08	990	104.50	4780	104.12	4060	103.92	3680	102.75	1720	101.67	675			102.33	1230
31			101.55	595	101.74	725							104.00	3830			102.71	1660	101.67	675			102.33	1230

Monthly Discharge of Petawawa River near Petawawa for 1915-6

Drainage Area, 1,572 Square Miles

.Month	Discharge in Second-feet			Discharge in Second-feet per Square Mile			Run-off
	Maximum	Minimum	Mean	Maximum	Minimum	Mean	Depth in Inches on Drainage Area
1915							
November	....	....	....	....	....	....	....
December 15-31..	650	595	615	.41	.38	.39	.25
January (1916).	725	580	631	.46	.37	.40	.46
February	785	740	761	.50	.47	.48	.51
March.........	990	705	762	.63	.45	.48	.55
April..........	4,780	1,180	2,791	3.04	.75	1.78	1.99
May	5,000	3,830	4,358	3.18	2.44	2.77	3.19
June...........	4,460	2,780	3.579	2.84	1.77	2.28	2.54
July...........	3,680	1,660	2,201	2.34	1.06	1.40	1.61
August	1,410	675	992	.90	.43	.63	.73
September	735	615	692	.46	.39	.44	.49
October.........	1,230	560	738	.78	.36	.46	.53
The period......	5,000	560	1,691	3.18	.36	1.08	12.93

Tay River near Glen Tay

Location—Near lots 20 and 21, concession 11, Township of Bathurst, County of Lanark. At the highway bridge north of the Village of Glen Tay, and east of the auxiliary plant of the Canadian Electric & Water Company, Limited, of Perth and Ottawa.

Records Available—Discharge measurements July, 1915, and gauge readings from July 10, 1915.

Drainage Area—204 square miles.

Gauge—Vertical steel staff 0 to 3 feet fastened to the pier of bridge one foot above section.

Channel and Control—The channel is straight from the dam 150 feet above and straight for 250 feet below the section. The banks are high, and not liable to overflow. The bed of the river is composed of shale and stones, not shifting. The flow is confined between the bridge abutments at all stages. The control is a short distance below the section, and the flood flow is likely to disturb it to some extent.

Discharge Measurements—Made by wading at ordinary stages, and from the bridge at very high stages.

Winter Flow—Channel at section likely free from ice during winter, but will be affected by ice formation below the section.

Regulation—The river is dammed immediately above the section and one mile further up, for power purposes, and the Department of Railways and Canals operate a dam at the foot of Bob's Lake for regulating canal purposes.

Accuracy—The open-water rating will be very good.

Observer—Paul Griffin, Manion P.O.

Discharge Measurements of Tay River near Glen Tay in 1915-6

Date	Hydrographer	Width in Feet	Area of Section in Sq. Feet	Mean Velocity in Feet per Sec.	Gauge Height in Feet	Discharge in Sec-Feet	Discharge in Second-feet per Square Mile
1915							
Nov. 8......	West, C. W	48	60	2.78	94.38	166	....
" 30......	"	48	58	2.69	94.34	157	....
1916							
Jan. 10	"	40	37	2.02	94.05	74	....
Feb. 9	"	42	56	2.90	94.38	161(a)	....
Mar. 7......	McLennan, C. C.	29	56	3.15	94.80	175(b)	....
Apr. 3......	Campbell, L. L. .	43	172	5.72	96.71	981	....
May 26.....	McLennan, C. C..	48	104	5.49	95.38	573	....
June 21.....	Campbell, L. L. .	47	158	5.89	96.38	927	....
Sept. 20	"	46	45	1.70	94.05	76	....
Oct. 12	"	35	32	2.27	94.05	72	....

(a) Ice at north edge of section.
(b) Ice below section.

Daily Gauge Height and Discharge of Tay River near Glen Tay for 1915-6

Drainage Area, 204 Square Miles

Day	November Gauge Ht. (Feet)	November Dis-charge (Sec-ft.)	December Gauge Ht. (Feet)	December Dis-charge (Sec-ft.)	January Gauge Ht. (Feet)	January Dis-charge (Sec-ft.)	February Gauge Ht. (Feet)	February Dis-charge (Sec-ft.)	March Gauge Ht. (Feet)	March Dis-charge (Sec-ft.)	April Gauge Ht. (Feet)	April Dis-charge (Sec-ft.)	May Gauge Ht. (Feet)	May Dis-charge (Sec-ft.)	June Gauge Ht. (Feet)	June Dis-charge (Sec-ft.)	July Gauge Ht. (Feet)	July Dis-charge (Sec-ft.)	August Gauge Ht. (Feet)	August Dis-charge (Sec-ft.)	September Gauge Ht. (Feet)	September Dis-charge (Sec-ft.)	October Gauge Ht. (Feet)	October Dis-charge (Sec-ft.)
1	93.63	28	94.34	146	94.05	71	95.55	590	94.42	86	97.75	1400	94.88	342	95.55	590	95.67	635	94.55	220	94.46	188	94.46	188
2	93.96	56	94.36	152	94.46	188	95.01	390	94.55	113	97.46	1300	95.01	390	95.46	555	95.63	620	94.55	220	94.46	188	94.05	71
3	93.94	53	94.01	63	94.01	63	94.92	357	94.59	121	96.67	1010	95.01	390	95.63	620	95.63	620	94.55	220	94.46	188	94.09	79
4	93.94	53	94.01	63	94.09	79	94.82	320	94.67	79	96.21	835	95.13	442	95.55	590	95.55	590	94.46	188	94.46	188	94.09	79
5	93.96	56	93.96	56	94.09	79	94.61	243	94.67	142	95.63	620	95.09	420	95.63	620	95.42	540	94.46	188	94.46	188	94.05	71
6	93.96	56	93.98	58	94.25	119	94.55	220	94.63	124	95.57	595	94.96	372	95.63	620	95.30	498	94.46	188	94.42	173	94.25	119
7	94.01	63	93.98	58	94.01	63	94.48	195	94.80	173	95.25	479	94.92	372	95.55	590	95.38	530	94.46	188	94.55	220	94.05	71
8	94.26	152	94.01	63	94.13	88	94.63	250	94.69	132	95.30	498	94.92	357	95.55	590	95.21	464	94.46	188	94.55	220	94.05	71
9	94.34	146	93.96	56	93.96	56	94.40	166	94.80	173	95.21	464	94.88	342	95.84	700	95.09	420	94.42	173	94.46	188	94.05	71
10	93.96	56	93.96	56	93.96	56	94.36	152	94.98	250	95.13	435	94.88	342	95.84	700	94.96	372	94.46	188	94.21	108	94.05	71
11	93.96	56	94.01	63	93.92	51	94.32	132	95.11	246	95.05	405	94.80	313	96.17	820	94.88	342	94.38	169	94.30	132	94.05	71
12	93.96	56	94.40	166	94.19	102	94.30	124	95.13	298	95.09	405	94.80	280	96.21	835	94.88	342	94.34	159	94.30	132	94.05	71
13	93.94	53	94.05	71	93.98	58	94.35	142	95.13	306	95.01	390	94.71	280	96.09	790	94.80	313	94.42	173	94.46	188	94.05	63
14	93.96	56	94.05	71	94.21	108	94.25	102	95.15	316	94.96	372	94.71	280	95.92	725	94.75	294	94.51	146	94.51	206	94.05	63
15	93.96	56	94.05	71	93.88	46	94.17	79	95.15	346	95.05	405	95.96	740	95.80	685	94.80	313	94.46	188	94.34	146	94.01	56
16	93.96	56	94.05	71	93.96	56	94.25	95	95.10	335	95.25	479	96.38	900	95.92	725	94.80	313	94.51	206	94.51	206	94.01	63
17	93.96	56	94.05	71	93.96	56	94.21	81	95.05	213	95.05	420	96.51	945	95.92	960	94.80	294	94.51	206	94.25	119	94.01	56
18	93.96	56	93.98	58	94.19	102	94.23	83	95.03	261	94.94	365	96.01	760	96.55	960	94.75	294	94.55	220	94.25	119	93.96	63
19	93.96	56	94.05	79	94.19	102	94.23	83	95.23	324	94.80	313	96.67	635	96.55	960	94.84	327	94.55	220	94.25	119	94.01	63
20	94.03	67	94.09	79	94.19	102	94.03	46	95.15	313	94.71	280	95.46	555	96.59	990	94.80	313	94.55	220	94.30	132	94.01	71
21	94.13	88	94.09	88	94.42	280	94.19	65	95.19	394	94.63	250	95.59	605	96.46	975	94.71	280	94.55	220	94.25	119	94.01	63
22	94.11	83	94.51	152	94.71	280	94.19	67	95.19	368	94.73	287	95.55	590	96.13	925	94.71	280	94.55	220	94.25	119	94.01	56
23	94.36	152	94.15	206	94.59	235	94.23	86	94.96	390	95.25	479	95.46	555	96.05	860	94.71	280	94.55	220	94.42	173	93.96	56
24	94.28	159	94.21	93	94.96	372	94.33	88	94.92	394	95.28	490	95.38	530	95.96	805	94.71	280	94.55	220	94.05	63	93.96	56
25	93.98	58	94.09	108	94.71	450	94.36	88	96.17	313	95.09	420	95.34	515	95.84	805	94.71	280	84.55	220	94.01	71	93.92	51
26	94.34	146	93.98	79	95.11	427	94.21	45	95.13	320	95.05	405	95.38	530	96.25	805	94.63	250	94.63	188	94.09	79	93.92	88
27	94.34	146	94.13	88	95.13	435	94.21	54	95.11	405	94.96	372	95.55	590	96.13	805	94.59	235	94.46	188	94.17	98	93.92	98
28	93.96	56	94.34	132	95.05	250	94.38	83	95.05	394	94.96	372	95.63	620	96.05	775	94.55	220	94.46	188	94.13	88	94.13	98
29	94.01	63	94.30	146	94.63	235	94.38	79	95.42	376	94.92	357	95.55	590	95.96	740	94.55	220	94.46	188	94.05	79		
30	93.98	58	94.63	250	94.59	235			97.38	520	94.92	357	95.80	685	95.80	725	94.55	220	94.46	188	94.17	98	94.13	98
31			94.17	98	94.71	280			97.80	1420			95.63	620	95.75	665	94.46	188	94.46	188			94.13	88

Monthly Discharge of Tay River near Glen Tay for 1915-6

Drainage Area 204 Square Miles

Month	Discharge in Second-feet			Discharge in Second-feet per Square Mile			Run-off
	Maximum	Minimum	Mean	Maximum	Minimum	Mean	Depth in Inches on Drainage Area
November (1915)	159	28	76	.78	.14	.37	.41
December . ''	250	56	98	1.23	.27	.48	.55
January .. (1916)	450	46	158	2.21	.23	.77	.89
February	590	45	153	2.89	.22	.75	.81
March..........	1,420	86	354	6.96	.42	1.74	2.01
April...........	1,400	250	509	6.86	1.23	2.50	2.79
May............	945	280	497	4.63	1.37	2.44	2.81
June........ ...'	990	555	752	4.85	2.72	3.69	4.12
July...........	635	220	363	3.11	1.08	1.78	2.05
August	220	146	197	1.08	.72	.97	1.12
September	220	63	149	1.08	.31	.73	.81
October.........	188	51	74	.92	·25	.36	.42
The year	1,400	28	281	6.96	.14	1.38	18.78

York River near Bancroft

Location—At the highway bridge one and a half miles below Bancroft, near lots 53 and 54, west of the Hastings Road, Township of Faraday, County of Hastings.

Records Available—Discharge measurements from July, 1915. Daily gauge heights from July 16, 1915.

Drainage Area—374 square miles.

Gauge—Vertical standard gauge plates 0 to 6 ft. secured on the upstream face of the right bridge pier near the west corner.

Channel and Control—The channel is straight for 400 feet above and 250 feet below the section. The banks are high and sandy, not liable to overflow. The bed is composed of gravel. Flow takes place in two channels under the bridge at high stages, and in one channel at lower stages.

Discharge Measurements—Made from the bridge at all stages.

Winter Flow—Ice will materially affect the open-water relation of gauge heights to discharge, and frazil ice at times makes meterings difficult.

Regulation—The dam at Bancroft gives very small storage, and the plants there do not use the entire flow. On account of the electrical plant working at night, and the other mills during the day, daily gauge readings give fairly accurate figures for the mean daily stage. Some of the tributary streams are controlled by dams for storage and driving purposes for the lumber industry.

Accuracy—As the river bed is composed of gravel, slight movement no doubt takes place without changing the general profile and section.

Observer—J. L. Churcher, Bancroft.

Discharge Measurements of York River near Bancroft in 1915-6

Date	Hydrographer	Width in Feet	Area of Section in Sq. Feet	Mean Velocity in Feet per Sec.	Gauge Height in Feet	Discharge in Sec–Feet	Discharge in Second-feet per Square Mile
1915							
Nov. 11....	West, C. W.	55	207	1.06	101.21	220	....
Dec. 3....	"	55	212	1.17	101.31	248 (a)	....
1916							
Jan. 7....	"	55	205	1.05	101.71	216 (b)	....
Feb. 10....	McLennan, C. C.	55	262	1.14	102.24	298 (c)	....
Mar. 8....	"	55	308	1.82	103.38	561 (d)	....
April 5....	Campbell, L. L. .	69	485	2.54	105.29	1,232	....
May 31....	"	68	376	2.04	103.70	769	....
June 28....	"	68	269	1.41	102.06	380	....
July 24....	McLennan, C. C..	56	·223	1.28	101.54	286	....
Oct. 11....	Campbell, L. L..	56	184	.73	100.83	135●	....

(a). Ice along edges of river, above and below section.
(b) Ice on both sides of river.
(c) Frazile ice at section. Sides of section frozen.
(d) Section almost entirely ice covered.

Daily Gauge Height and Discharge of York Ri or near Bancroft for 1915-6

Drainage Area, 374 Square Mes

Day	Nov. Gauge Ht. (Feet)	Nov. Dis-charge (Sec-ft.)	Dec. Gauge Ht. (Feet)	Dec. Dis-charge (Sec-ft.)	Jan. Gauge Ht. (Feet)	Jan. Dis-charge (Sec-ft.)	Feb. Gauge Ht. (Feet)	Feb. Dis-charge (Sec-ft.)	Mar. Gauge Ht. (Feet)	Mar. Dis-charge (Sec-ft.)	Apr. Gauge Ht. (Feet)	Apr. Dis-charge (Sec-ft.)	May Gauge Ht. (Feet)	May Dis-charge (Sec-ft.)	June Gauge Ht. (Feet)	June Dis-charge (Sec-ft.)	July Gauge Ht. (Feet)	July Dis-charge (Sec-ft.)	Aug. Gauge Ht. (Feet)	Aug. Dis-charge (Sec-ft.)	Sep. Gauge Ht. (Feet)	Sep. Dis-charge (Sec-ft.)	Oct. Gauge Ht. (Feet)	Oct. Dis-charge (Sec-ft.)
1	101.33	234	101.40	248	101.49	186	102.12	266	102.67	368	105.25	1220	107.00	1730	103.59	735	101.65	298	101.51	270	101.31	230	100.67	113
2	101.31	230	101.40	248	101.60	200	102.11	262	102.53	344	105.48	1290	107.00	1730	103.58	735	101.65	298	101.50	268	101.31	230	100.79	133
3	101.25	219	101.35	238	101.52	186	102.18	274	102.56	352	105.43	1280	107.00	1730	103.35	670	101.62	292	101.44	256	101.31	230	100.88	149
4	101.29	226	101.35	238	101.73	224	102.20	278	102.61	362	105.41	1270	106.83	1680	103.25	650	101.63	294	101.38	246	101.32	232	100.88	149
5	101.29	226	101.33	234	101.52	196	102.10	258	102.46	338	105.33	1250	106.67	1640	103.31	660	101.61	290	101.35	238	101.35	238	100.92	157
6	101.28	224	101.33	234	101.56	200	102.06	248	103.48	560	105.33	1250	106.25	1520	103.54	720	101.58	284	101.38	246	101.32	232	100.88	157
7	101.28	224	101.30	228	101.65	217	102.10	258	103.50	560	105.05	1170	106.08	1460	102.84	550	101.59	286	101.35	238	101.29	226	100.88	149
8	101.28	224	101.30	228	101.96	250	102.27	268	103.32	560	105.00	1150	103.42	690	102.83	550	101.59	281	101.33	234	101.16	201	100.88	149
9	101.27	222	101.31	230	102.02	262	102.28	282	103.34	575	105.00	1150	102.59	491	102.84	550	101.54	276	101.33	238	101.20	209	100.96	164
10	101.27	221	101.44	256	102.04	256	102.33	298	103.48	590	105.04	1160	102.60	493	102.85	550	101.58	284	101.40	248	101.15	200	100.94	160
11	101.29	226	101.68	304	101.96	266	102.50	328	102.49	590	104.95	1130	102.75	525	102.56	515	101.40	248	101.40	248	101.17	203	100.92	157
12	101.29	226	101.66	300	102.00	256	102.49	328	103.89	540	105.02	1160	102.56	485	102.70	525	101.38	244	101.41	250	101.22	213	100.92	157
13	101.26	221	101.39	246	102.04	260	102.49	328	102.71	493	105.33	1250	103.08	605	102.60	493	101.44	256	101.40	248	101.28	224	100.92	157
14	101.25	219	101.60	288	102.04	264	103.12	466	102.95	605	105.67	1340	103.87	815	102.17	438	101.42	252	101.33	234	101.27	222	100.91	155
15	101.25	219	101.80	328	102.17	268	103.24	493	103.07	605	105.92	1420	103.92	830	102.65	565	101.50	268	101.33	234	101.26	220	100.92	157
16	101.25	219	101.88	344	102.17	290	103.00	443	104.74	1020	106.02	1450	103.94	835	102.73	520	101.48	264	101.33	234	101.24	217	100.92	157
17	101.27	222	101.82	332	102.25	306	102.88	417	104.57	970	106.06	1460	104.29	940	102.81	540	101.47	262	101.33	234	101.24	217	100.92	157
18	101.19	207	101.83	334	102.27	308	102.77	392	104.41	970	106.35	1540	104.87	1110	102.82	545	101.51	270	101.33	234	101.24	217	100.92	157
19	101.25	219	101.36	240	102.31	318	102.80	396	104.33	1130	106.42	1570	105.08	1170	102.79	540	101.57	282	101.33	234	101.25	220	101.09	188
20	101.32	232	101.35	234	102.31	316	102.94	430	104.94	1300	106.33	1540	105.33	1250	102.83	550	101.55	278	101.33	234	101.25	220	101.12	190
21	101.34	236	101.39	234	102.31	316	103.06	449	104.44	980	106.21	1510	105.21	1210	103.15	620	101.56	280	101.33	234	101.25	220	101.08	186
22	101.35	238	101.39	232	102.33	316	102.94	434	104.34	955	106.17	1490	105.17	1200	103.01	590	101.53	278	101.33	234	101.24	217	101.06	182
23	101.33	234	101.36	234	102.35	318	102.68	374	104.31	960	106.21	1490	105.17	1170	102.71	520	101.56	280	101.33	234	101.25	220	101.04	179
24	101.31	230	101.33	220	102.39	318	102.43	320	104.31	960	106.17	1500	105.08	1170	102.46	463	101.52	274	101.35	238	101.22	213	101.04	179
25	101.31	230	101.38	205	102.40	324	102.48	334	104.13	895	106.21	1660	105.04	1160	102.40	436	101.55	274	101.33	234	101.08	186	101.04	179
26	101.29	226	101.38	203	102.43	332	102.47	330	104.12	890	106.75	1660	102.62	497	102.29	428	101.54	276	101.33	234	101.06	182	101.04	179
27	101.32	232	101.40	203	102.44	334	102.46	326	104.23	925	107.00	1730	102.64	500	102.21	411	101.52	272	101.33	234	101.04	179	101.04	179
28	101.32	232	101.40	200	102.29	308	102.46	368	104.12	940	107.00	1730	102.81	540	102.12	390	101.52	272	101.33	234		213	101.04	179
29	101.46	260	101.49	205	102.21	290	102.65	364	104.23		107.00	1730	102.75	390	102.12	390			101.33	234		186	101.04	179
30	101.48	264	101.63	228	102.12	273		273	104.44		107.00	1730	102.75	525	101.79	326			101.30	228		182	101.04	179
31			101.67	234	102.25	294		294	104.73	1070			103.67	760					101.32	232		179		

Monthly Discharge of York River near Bancroft for 1915-6

Drainage Area 374 square miles

Month.	Discharge in Second-feet.			Discharge in Second-feet, per square mile			Run-off
	Maximum	Minimum	Mean	Maximum	Minimum	Mean	Depth in Inches on Drainage Area
November (1915)	264	194	227	.71	.52	.60	.67
December "	344	200	248	.92	.53	.66	.76
January ..(1916)	338	186	274	.90	.50	.73	.84
February	493	248	345	1.32	.66	.92	.99
March..........	1,300	338	752	3.48	.90	2.01	2.32
April	1,730	1,130 *	1,420	4.63	3.02	3.80	4.24
May....:.......	1,730	485	1,000	4.63	1.30	2.67	3.08
June	735	326	544	1.97	.87	1.45	1.62
July...........	298	244	275	.80	.65	.74	.85
August	270	228	240	.72	.61	.64	.74
September......	238	179	216	.64	.48	.58	.65
October........	207	113	165	.55	.30	.44	.51
The year	1,730	113	475	4.63	.30	1.27	17.29

Regular Stations

NORTHERN ONTARIO DISTRICT

River	Location	Drainage Area Sq. Miles	Township	District
aux Sables	at Massey	524	Salter..............	Sudbury
Blanche	near Englehart........	230	Evanturel	Timiskaming
Frederickhouse......	at Frederickhouse	1,252	Clute...............	"
Kagawong	at Kagawong..........	94	Allan...............	Manitoulin Island
Maganetawan, North.	near Burk's Falls	107	Armour.............	Parry Sound
" South.	" " "	257	"	"
Mississagi	at Iron Bridge	3,565	Gladstone	Algoma
Muskoka, N. Branch.	near Port Sydney	560	Stephenson	Muskoka
Muskoka, S. Branch.	at Tretheway's Falls..	668	Draper..............	"
Seguin	near Parry Sound	380	McDougall..........	Parry Sound
South	near Powassan........	294	Himsworth	Parry Sound
Spanish	at Espanola...........	4,490	Merritt.......... ...	Sudbury
Sturgeon	at Smoky Falls	2,250	Field	Nipissing
Vermilion...........	near Whitefish	1,580	Graham	Sudbury
Wanapitei	at McVitties		Secord	"

aux Sables River at Massey

Location—About 800 feet upstream from C.P. Ry bridge, and ¼ mile north-east of railway station, in the Village of Massey, Township of Salter, Sudbury District.

Records Available—Discharge measurements from August, 1914, to October, 1916. Daily gauge heights from June 10, 1915, to October 31, 1916.

Drainage Area—524 square miles.

Gauge—Vertical steel staff with enamelled face, graduated in feet and inches, fastened to rock on left shore 400 feet above railway bridge. Zero of the gauge (elev. 15.00 feet) is referred to bench mark (elev. 29.76 feet) painted on top of rock near gauge.

Channel and Control—Straight for 1,000 feet above and 500 feet below the gauging station to a rapid. Both banks are high, rocky, wooded, and are not liable to overflow. The bed of the stream is composed of clay and gravel, practically permanent. The velocity is moderate, and one channel exists at all stages.

Discharge Measurements—Made by wading during low water periods. At high stages measurements are made from boat with a Price current meter.

Regulation—The operation of logging dams above cause fluctuations in gauge heights during the log-driving season.

Observer—Jas. Blight, Massey.

Discharge Measurements of aux Sables River at Massey in 1915-6

Date	Hydrographer	Width in Feet	Area of Section in Sq. Feet	Mean Velocity in Feet per Sec.	Gauge Height in Feet	Discharge in Sec-Feet	Discharge in Second-feet per Square Mile
1915							
Nov. 20, ...	Murray, W. S.	96	392	1.91	20.33	752	....
Dec. 6	"	95	578	1.95	21.70	1.129 (a)	....
1916							
Feb. 4, ...	"	75	154	2.55	18.04	393 (b)	....
Mar. 9	"	77	127	2.27	17.25	287 (b)	....
Apr. 14	"	96	963	2.32	26.40	2,241 (c)	....
May 11	"	97	822	2.15	24.20	1,772	....

(a) Ice on control.
(b) Ice measurement.
(c) River rising rapidly.

Daily Gauge Height and Discharge of aux Sables River at Massey for 1915-6

Drainage Area 524 Square Miles

Day	Nov Gauge Ht.	Nov Discharge	Dec Gauge Ht.	Dec Discharge	Jan Gauge Ht.	Jan Discharge	Feb Gauge Ht.	Feb Discharge	Mar Gauge Ht.	Mar Discharge	Apr Gauge Ht.	Apr Discharge	May Gauge Ht.	May Discharge	Jun Gauge Ht.	Jun Discharge	Jul Gauge Ht.	Jul Discharge	Aug Gauge Ht.	Aug Discharge	Sep Gauge Ht.	Sep Discharge	Oct Gauge Ht.	Oct Discharge
1	18.29	434	22.62	1330	16.58	228	18.66	390	17.66	349	21.41	1040	27.82	2580	22.33	1260	26.54	2270	16.04	179	15.04	112	17.37	314
2	18.50	465	22.50	1300	16.58	228	18.83	390	17.58	340	24.00	1660	27.32	2460	23.46	1530	26.54	2270	16.04	179	15.04	112	17.37	314
3	18.50	465	22.62	1330	16.58	228	18.00	390	17.50	330	26.00	2140	27.20	2430	26.04	2150	26.04	2270	16.04	179	15.04	112	17.37	314
4	18.37	445	22.39	1270	16.58	228	18.04	390	17.50	330	26.00	2140	26.37	2230	26.04	2150	26.54	2270	16.04	179	15.04	112	17.37	314
5	18.29	434	21.66	1100	16.58	228	18.00	390	17.33	310	26.00	2140	26.42	2240	26.04	2150	26.54	2270	16.04	179	15.04	112	17.37	314
6	18.16	414	21.54	1070	21.70	390	18.00	390	17.33	310	25.50	2020	26.00	2140	26.04	2150	26.54	2270	16.04	179	15.04	112	17.37	314
7	18.16	414	21.45	1050	20.62	390	18.00	390	17.33	310	25.40	2000	25.33	1980	24.79	1850	26.54	2270	16.04	179	15.04	112	17.37	314
8	18.08	402	21.29	1010	19.91	390	18.00	390	17.33	310	25.00	1900	24.79	1850	24.33	1740	22.62	1330	16.04	179	15.04	112	17.37	314
9	18.16	414	21.16	798	19.16	390	18.00	390	17.33	310	24.70	1830	24.91	1880	24.12	1690	21.95	1170	16.04	179	15.04	112	17.37	314
10	18.25	428	20.87	911	19.08	390	18.00	390	17.33	310	25.04	1910	25.16	1940	24.04	1670	21.33	1170	16.04	179	15.04	112	17.45	324
11	18.33	440	18.16	414	19.08	390	18.00	390	17.33	310	25.37	1990	24.70	1830	24.04	1670	21.95	1170	16.04	179	15.04	112	17.57	338
12	18.45	458	18.00	390	19.08	390	18.66	405	17.33	310	25.70	2070	25.00	1900	24.42	1760	21.54	1070	16.04	179	15.62	148	17.57	338
13	19.66	662	18.00	390	19.08	390	18.66	420	17.33	310	26.12	2170	24.70	1830	24.79	1850	21.12	970	16.04	179	16.12	186	17.57	335
14	20.16	762	17.83	370	19.08	390	18.66	435	17.66	349	26.62	2290	25.04	1910	24.98	1900	20.75	885	16.04	179	16.50	220	17.54	335
15	20.33	796	17.62	344	19.08	390	18.58	450	17.66	349	27.20	2430	25.25	1960	25.25	1960	20.62	855	16.04	179	16.12	257	17.54	335
16	20.62	856	17.37	314	19.08	390	18.50	465	17.58	340	27.20	2430	25.12	1930	25.37	1990	20.79	895	16.04	179	16.87	275	18.04	396
17	20.62	856	17.16	289	19.08	390	18.29	433	17.58	340	27.58	2520	24.95	1890	25.37	1990	20.04	740	16.04	179	17.04	294	18.33	440
18	20.50	830	16.83	263	19.08	390	18.29	433	17.50	330	28.11	2650	24.87	1870	28.61	2770	18.91	525	16.04	179	17.20	289	19.29	590
19	20.37	804	19.16	568	19.08	390	18.04	396	17.50	330	28.36	2710	24.66	1820	28.61	2770	18.37	445	16.04	179	17.16	284	19.62	655
20	20.29	788	18.95	533	19.08	390	18.00	390	17.41	314	28.57	2760	24.96	1890	28.40	2720	17.95	384	16.04	179	17.12	261	20.12	755
21	20.37	804	18.75	503	19.08	390	18.00	390	17.37	314	29.07	2880	23.79	1610	28.28	2690	17.70	354	16.04	179	16.91	257	20.12	755
22	20.25	780	18.58	477	19.00	390	18.00	390	17.37	314	30.03	3110	23.70	1590	28.15	2660	17.20	294	15.50	140	16.87	257	21.04	950
23	20.16	762	18.66	489	19.00	390	18.00	390	17.37	314	30.36	3190	23.79	1610	27.65	2540	17.20	294	15.75	158	16.87	257	22.04	1190
24	20.08	746	18.55	473	19.00	390	18.00	390	17.33	310	30.36	3190	24.04	1670	27.99	2620	17.12	284	15.70	154	16.87	257	22.54	1310
25	19.95	720	18.33	440	19.00	390	18.00	390	17.62	344	30.36	3190	24.04	1670	27.45	2490	16.95	265	15.66	151	16.87	257	23.16	1460
26	19.79	688	16.58	228	19.00	390	17.87	374	18.49	463	30.36	3190	24.04	1670	27.40	2550	16.83	253	15.54	143	16.87	257	23.70	1590
27	19.75	680	16.58	228	19.00	390	17.75	360	18.99	538	30.36	3190	23.54	1550	26.95	2370	16.70	240	15.54	143	16.87	257	24.37	1750
28	23.16	1460	16.58	228	19.00	390	17.66	349	19.08	554	30.03	3110	22.50	1300	26.83	2340	16.66	236	15.45	137	16.91	261	24.95	1890
29	23.00	1420	16.58	228	19.00	390			20.54	837	29.44	2970	21.70	1110	26.59	2280	16.54	224	15.33	130	16.99	269	25.20	1950
30			16.55	228	19.08	390					29.03	2870	21.79	1180			16.37	208	15.20	122	17.08	280	25.20	1950
31			16.58	228	18.91	390							22.03	1190			16.08	182	15.08	115	17.12	284		

Monthly Discharge of aux Sables River at Massey for 1915-6

Drainage Area 524 Square Miles

Month	Discharge in Second-feet			Discharge in Second-feet per Square Mile			Run-off
	Maximum	Minimum	Mean	Maximum	Minimum	Mean	Depth in Inches on Drainage Area
November (1915)	1,460	402	703	2.78	.77	1.34	1.50
December "	1,330	228	606	2.54	.44	1.16	1.34
January .. (1916)	390	228	364	.74	.44	.69	.80
February.......	465	349	398	.89	.67	.76	.82
March..........	835	310	359	1.59	.59	.69	.80
April	3,190	1,040	2,454	6.08	1.98	4.68	5.22
May...........	2,580	1,110	1,828	4.92	2.12	3.49	4.02
June...........	2,770	1,260	2,170	5.29	2.40	4.14	4.62
July...........	2,270	182	978	4.33	.35	1.87	2.16
August	179	115	166	.34	.22	.32	.37
September	294	112	203	.56	.21	.39	.44
October	1,950	314	735	3.72	.60	1.40	1.61
The year	3,190	112	911	6.08	.21	1.74	23.70

Blanche River near Englehart

Location—At the highway bridge near the High Falls, 3½ miles north-west of the Town of Englehart, north half of lot 12, concession 3, Township of Evanturel, Temiskaming District.

Records Available—Discharge measurements, August, 1914, to October, 1916. Daily gauge heights, October 8, 1914, to October 31, 1916.

Drainage Area—430 square miles.

Gauge—Vertical steel staff with enamelled face, graduated in feet and inches, and located on the southwest corner of the wing wall of the bridge. The zero on the gauge (elev. 10.00) is referred to a bench mark (elev. 23.39), painted on a prominent rock on the right bank, 75 feet below the bridge.

Channel—At a point 200 feet above the station, the river curves from the right and then flows straight, up to a point 700 feet below the station. Both banks are high, rocky, wooded, and will not overflow. The bed of the stream is composed of clay, practically permanent. The current is very slow, flowing through 2 channels at low stages and 3 channels during high water periods.

Discharge Measurements—Made from the highway bridge with a Price current meter.

Regulation—A temporary dam is built above the station during the summer months. This dam is used for storing water during the period when the river is used for log driving. The gauge heights at the section are therefore affected during the log driving periods.

Winter Flow—During the winter months measurements are made through the ice to determine the winter discharge. The relation of gauge height to discharge is seriously affected by ice.

Accuracy—Rating curve fairly well defined between gauge heights 10.50 feet and 12.00 feet.

Observer—Roy Robinson, Englehart.

Discharge Measurements of Blanche River near Englehart in 1915-6

Date	Hydrographer	Width in Feet	Area of Section in Sq. Feet	Mean Velocity in Feet per Sec.	Gauge Height in Feet	Discharge in Sec-Feet	Discharge in Second-feet per Square Mile
1915 Nov. 25.	Murray, W. S..	97	640	.52	10.75	334	....
1916 Jan. 22, ...	" " ..	72	560	.50	10.66	280(a)	....
April 18	" " ..	116	1,122	2.51	15.42	2,811	....
May 2	" " ..	....	1,284	3.06	16.50	3,936	....
June 13	" " ..	90	627	.47	10.58	295	....
July 8	" " ..	88	613	.45	10.39	276	....
Sept. 4	" " ..	91	603	.43	10.37	259	....
Oct. 4	" " ..	91	614	.43	10.25	263	....

(a) Ice measurement.

Daily Gauge Height and Discharge of Blanche River near Englehart for 1915-6

Drainage Area, 430 Square Miles

Day	Nov Gauge Ht. (Feet)	Nov Dis-charge (Sec-ft.)	Dec Gauge Ht. (Feet)	Dec Dis-charge (Sec-ft.)	Jan Gauge Ht. (Feet)	Jan Dis-charge (Sec-ft.)	Feb Gauge Ht. (Feet)	Feb Dis-charge (Sec-ft.)	Mar Gauge Ht. (Feet)	Mar Dis-charge (Sec-ft.)	Apr Gauge Ht. (Feet)	Apr Dis-charge (Sec-ft.)	May Gauge Ht. (Feet)	May Dis-charge (Sec-ft.)	June Gauge Ht. (Feet)	June Dis-charge (Sec-ft.)	July Gauge Ht. (Feet)	July Dis-charge (Sec-ft.)	Aug Gauge Ht. (Feet)	Aug Dis-charge (Sec-ft.)	Sep Gauge Ht. (Feet)	Sep Dis-charge (Sec-ft.)	Oct Gauge Ht. (Feet)	Oct Dis-charge (Sec-ft.)
1	11.26	460	10.91	372	10.50	270	10.20	200	10.12	184	12.00	680	15.75	3120	....	312	10.58	290	10.46	260	10.33	228	10.25	210
2	11.25	458	11.00	395	10.50	270	10.08	176	10.08	176	12.04	690	15.50	2900	....	315	10.62	300	10.41	248	10.39	242	10.25	210
3	11.33	479	12.83	1020	10.50	270	10.12	184	10.08	176	12.00	680	15.50	2900	....	318	10.66	310	10.41	248	10.25	210	10.25	210
4	11.16	435	12.83	1020	10.33	228	10.08	176	10.08	176	12.33	800	15.33	2750	....	322	10.71	332	10.37	238	10.29	218	10.25	210
5	11.25	458	12.75	975	10.33	210	10.08	192	10.08	176	12.75	975	15.08	2520	....	327	10.75	322	10.33	228	10.33	228	10.25	210
6	11.00	395	12.83	1020	10.33	228	10.16	192	10.16	192	12.91	1060	14.66	2180	....	332	10.66	332	10.39	242	10.33	228	10.25	210
7	11.00	395	12.83	1020	10.25	210	10.13	186	10.20	200	13.00	1100	14.66	2180	10.75	335	10.75	332	10.50	270	10.33	228	10.25	210
8	11.00	372	12.75	975	10.25	210	10.08	176	10.25	210	13.33	1300	14.33	1920	10.76	352	10.58	290	10.37	238	10.25	210	10.27	214
9	10.91	352	12.66	935	10.33	228	10.12	184	10.25	210	13.33	1300	13.91	1650	10.83	372	10.41	248	10.41	248	10.25	210	10.27	214
10	10.83	352	12.58	900	10.25	210	10.08	176	10.20	200	13.50	1920	13.79	1570	10.91	372	10.37	238	10.37	248	10.23	206	10.27	214
11	11.00	395	12.66	935	10.25	210	10.16	192	10.29	218	13.33	1400	13.62	1470	10.66	310	10.46	260	10.62	300	10.16	192	10.27	214
12	10.83	352	12.66	935	10.16	192	10.16	192	10.25	210	11.83	1300	13.33	1300	10.66	332	10.39	242	10.58	290	10.25	210	10.25	210
13	10.91	372	12.50	870	10.16	192	10.16	192	10.29	218	11.66	680	13.16	1 02	10.58	290	10.37	238	10.54	280	10.21	192	10.25	210
14	11.00	395	12.41	835	10.12	184	10.12	184	10.75	332	11.75	630	12.91	1060	10.58	290	10.33	228	10.54	280	10.25	202	10.29	218
15	11.16	435	12.33	800	10.16	192	10.20	200	10.66	310	11.66	605	12.50	870	10.50	270	10.25	210	10.50	270	10.25	210	10.29	218
16	11.08	415	12.08	705	10.16	192	10.16	192	10.71	322	12.58	580	12.83	1020	10.58	300	10.29	218	10.46	260	10.25	210	10.29	218
17	11.00	395	12.00	680	10.16	192	10.12	184	10.66	310	13.70	900	13.00	1109	10.62	290	10.33	228	10.43	252	10.21	202	10.29	218
18	10.91	372	11.91	655	10.08	176	10.08	176	10.62	300	15.42	1520	12.91	1060	10.66	310	10.37	238	10.41	248	10.16	192	11.16	435
19	11.00	395	11.83	630	10.38	240	10.12	184	10.58	290	15.00	2830	12.83	1020	10.58	300	10.41	248	10.41	248	10.21	202	11.16	435
20	11.08	415	11.75	605	10.56	285	10.08	176	10.62	300	12.83	2450	12.79	995	10.66	310	10.41	248	10.37	238	10.41	210	11.16	435
21	11.00	395	11.66	580	10.66	310	10.16	192	10.62	300	15.33	2750	12.75	975	10.62	300	10.46	260	10.37	238	10.41	248	11.16	435
22	10.91	372	11.66	580	10.25	210	10.12	184	10.62	300	15.50	2900	12.66	935	10.66	300	10.41	248	10.33	228	10.41	248	11.16	435
23	10.83	352	11.50	530	10.25	210	10.08	176	10.58	290	16.00	3250	12.50	870	10.62	300	10.37	238	10.41	248	10.39	242	11.16	435
24	10.91	372	11.41	505	10.16	192	10.08	184	10.62	300	17.50	4850	12.25	770	10.58	290	10.37	238	10.37	238	10.35	232	11.16	435
25	10.91	395	11.33	480	10.16	192	10.12	184	10.70	320	17.00	6950	12.66	935	10.62	300	10.33	228	10.33	228	10.30	220	11.16	435
26	10.83	352	11.25	480	10.12	184	10.25	210	10.75	332	19.60	7350	11.00	395	10.66	310	10.33	228	10.20	200	10.30	220		
27	10.83	352	11.16	435	10.16	192	10.33	228	10.75	332	20.00	7350	11.50	530	10.71	322	10.41	248	10.16	228	10.29	218		
28	10.91	372	10.91	372	10.20	200			11.00	395	20.00	6750	10.91	372	10.71	322	10.46	260	10.33	228	10.25	210		
29	11.00	395	10.75	332	10.12	184			10.95	382	19.40	6750	10.75	332	10.66	310	10.37	248	10.25	210				
30	11.00	395	10.71	322	10.16	192			11.04	405	17.00	4350	10.75	332	....	....	10.41	248	10.33	228				
31			10.50	270					11.58	555	16.50	3850	10.66	310			10.51	272	10.37	238				

Monthly Discharge of Blanche River near Englehart for 1915-6

Drainage Area, 430 Square Miles

Month	Discharge in Second–feet			Discharge in Second–feet per Square Mile			Run-off
	Maximum	Minimum	Mean	Maximum	Minimum	Mean	Depth in Inches on Drainage Area
November.(1915)	479	352	396	1.11	.82	.90	1.00
December "	1,020	270	682	2.37	.63	1.59	1.83
January .. (1916)	285	176	214	.66	.41	.50	.58
February	228	176	188	.53	.41	.44	.48
March..........	555	176	277	1.29	.41	.64	.74
April	7,350	580	2,519	17.09	1.35	5.86	6.54
May............	3,120	310	1,340	7.26	.72	3.12	3.60
June............	372	270	313	.87	.63	.73	.81
July	332	210	260	.77	.49	.60	.69
August	300	192	247	.70	.45	.57	.66
September	248	192	217	.58	.45	.50	.56
October	435	210	285	1.01	.49	.66	.76
The year	7,350	176	577	17.09	.41	1.34	18.24

Frederickhouse River at Frederickhouse

Location—On the T.C. Ry, bridge at the Frederickhouse station, Township of Clute, Sudbury District, 6 miles west of the Town of Cochrane.

Records Available—Discharge measurements from July, 1915, to October, 1916. Daily gauge heights from July 7, 1915, to October 31, 1916.

Drainage Area—1,260 square miles.

Gauge—Vertical steel staff with enamelled face, graduated in feet and inches, and fastened to downstream side of right abutment. Zero of gauge (elev. 9.00 feet) is referred to a bench mark (elev. 10.00 feet) on top of base of same abutment, to which gauge is attached.

Channel and Control—The channel is straight and consists of a number of rapids for about 1 mile above and below the station. The banks are high and wooded, and not liable to overflow. The bed of the stream is composed of clay and boulders, and is shifting. The velocity is high.

Discharge Measurements—Made from bridge with a Price current meter.

Regulation—Temporary dams on river above used for log driving cause fluctuations at gauge.

Observer—Frank Prior, Frederickhouse.

Discharge Measurements of Frederickhouse River at Frederickhouse in 1915-6

Date	Hydrographer	Width in Feet	Area of Section in Sq. Feet	Mean Velocity in Feet per Sec.	Gauge Height in Feet	Discharge in Sec-Feet	Discharge in Second-feet per Square Mile
1915							
Nov. 26....	Murray, W. S..	185	657	4.28	11.93	2,814	....
Dec. 10....	"	190	463	3.69	10.91	1,711(a)	....
1916							
May 3....	"	190	1,246	10.87	15.00	12,202(b)	....
June 14....	"	190	478	4.47	10.96	2,145	....
July 9....	"	190	430	3.67	10.69	1,577	....
" 9....	"	....	....	....	10.69	1,235(c)	....

(a) Section partly ice-covered.
(b) Coefficient applied to calculated discharge.
(c) Measurement two miles above regular section.

Daily Gauge Height and Discharge of Frederickhouse River at Frederickhouse for 1915-6

Drainage Area 1,260 Square Miles

Day	November Gauge Ht. (Feet)	November Dis-charge (Sec-ft.)	December Gauge Ht.	December Dis-charge	January Gauge Ht.	January Dis-charge	February Gauge Ht.	February Dis-charge	March Gauge Ht.	March Dis-charge	April Gauge Ht.	April Dis-charge	May Gauge Ht.	May Dis-charge	June Gauge Ht.	June Dis-charge	July Gauge Ht.	July Dis-charge	August Gauge Ht.	August Dis-charge	September Gauge Ht.	September Dis-charge	October Gauge Ht.	October Dis-charge
1	11.56	2410	11.14	1910	12.91	1860	13.33	2200	11.75	1860	11.33	2140	13.66	10110	11.75	2640	11.16	1930		880	9.58	280	9.62	320
2	11.56	2410	11.12	1880	12.91	1860	13.33	2200	11.66	1860	11.33	2140	14.83	10800	11.66	2530	11.25	2040		860	9.58	280	9.58	280
3	11.56	2410	11.10	1860	12.95	1860	13.33	2160	11.58	1800	11.33	2140	15.00	11500	11.62	2480	11.25	2040		840	9.58	280	9.58	280
4	11.52	2360	11.08	1840	13.00	1950	13.33	2160	11.50	1750	11.33	2140	15.00	11500	11.62	2480	11.25	2040		820	9.58	280	9.58	280
5	11.50	2340	11.02	1770	13.02	1980	13.33	2160	11.41	1750	11.33	2140	15.00	11500	11.58	2440	11.16	1930		800	9.58	270	9.58	280
6	11.48	2320	11.00	1750	13.04	1980	13.33	2160	11.41	1750	11.33	2140	14.91	11130	11.54	2390	11.16	1930		780	9.62	320	9.58	280
7	11.45	2280	10.97	1720	13.06	1920	13.33	2160	11.41	1750	11.33	2140	14.91	11130	11.50	2340	11.16	1930		760	9.62	320	9.58	280
8	11.47	2300	10.95	1700	12.91	1950	13.31	2160	11.37	1750	11.33	2140	14.91	11130	11.45	2280	11.16	1930		740	9.60	300	9.58	280
9	11.54	2390	10.93	1670	13.08	1980	13.29	2160	11.37	1750	11.33	2140	14.87	10970	11.37	2180	11.16	1930		720	9.58	280	9.58	280
10	11.52	2360	10.91	1650	13.12	2020	13.29	2200	11.35	1750	11.37	2180	14.87	10970	11.33	2140	11.12	1880		700	9.58	280	9.58	280
11	11.50	2340	10.95	1700	13.12	1980	13.25	2180	11.33	1750	11.37	2180	14.87	10970	11.29	2090	11.08	1840		680	9.58	280	9.58	280
12	11.45	2280	11.06	1720	13.12	1980	13.16	2120	11.33	1750	11.41	2230	14.87	10970	11.25	2040	11.08	1840		660	9.62	320	9.58	280
13	11.37	2180	11.12	1710	13.12	1980	13.08	2100	11.33	1750	11.46	2290	14.91	11130	11.21	1990	11.04	1790		640	9.83	550	9.58	280
14	11.37	2180	11.12	1710	13.14	1920	13.00	2100	11.33	1750	11.33	2140	14.83	10800	11.12	1880	10.83	1560		620	9.83	550	9.58	280
15	11.37	2180	11.21	1710	13.18	1990	12.91	2100	11.33	1750	11.58	2440	14.75	10470	11.08	1840	10.91	1560		600	9.83	530	9.60	300
16	11.37	2180	11.39	1690	13.20	2060	12.83	2100	11.33	1750	11.75	2640	14.66	10110	11.08	1840	10.91	1650		580	9.78	480	9.58	280
17	11.37	2180	11.52	1690	13.25	2100	12.83	2100	11.33	1750	11.91	2830	14.58	9780	11.12	1880	10.75	1470		560	9.70	400	9.58	280
18	11.33	2140	11.58	1690	13.29	2160	12.75	2100	11.33	1750	12.00	2940	14.58	9780	11.12	1880	10.66	1380		540	9.66	260	9.58	280
19	11.33	2140	11.75	1710	13.29	2160	12.58	2100	11.29	1750	12.16	3150	14.58	9780	11.16	1930	10.58	1290		520	9.62	320	9.62	280
20	11.33	2140	11.91	1720	13.31	2100	12.50	2100	11.25	1750	12.41	3520	14.83	10800	11.16	1930	10.50	1200		500	9.58	280	9.77	470
21	11.29	2090	12.12	1730	13.33	2100	12.41	2080	11.20	1750	12.66	3920	14.00	7400	11.16	1930	10.41	1110		480	9.58	280	9.83	530
22	11.25	2040	12.27	1720	13.33	2160	12.33	2070	11.16	1750	12.58	3790	13.66	6280	11.16	1930		1080		460	9.58	280	9.91	610
23	11.20	1980	12.39	1710	13.33	2160	12.25	2040	11.16	1750	12.91	4370	13.50	5760	11.16	1930		1050		440	9.58	280	9.91	610
24	11.16	1930	12.50	1710	13.33	2160	12.16	2020	11.12	1750	13.16	4930	13.16	4950	11.16	1930		1020		420	9.58	280	10.08	860
25	11.12	1880	12.69	1690	13.33	2180	12.66	2100	11.12	1750	13.50	5750	12.83	4220	11.25	2040		1000		400	9.58	280	10.16	780
26	11.08	1840	12.83	1730	13.37	2180	12.08	1980	11.12	1750	13.83	6840	12.50	3660	11.25	1930		980		380	9.62	320	10.21	860
27	11.16	1930	12.91	1690	13.37	2180	12.27	2130	11.16	1800	13.83	6840	12.50	3660	11.16	1930		960		360	9.66	360	10.21	910
28	11.16	1930	12.91	1750	13.37	2180	11.91	1920	11.16	1930	13.91	7100	12.25	3280	11.16	1930		960		340			10.25	950
29	11.16	1930	12.91	1800	13.33	2180	11.83	1920	11.25	2040	13.83	6840	12.16	3150	11.16	1930		940		320			10.25	950
30	11.16	1930	12.91	1840	13.33	2180			11.33	2140	14.50	9450	12.08	3040	11.16	1930		920		300				
31			12.91	1910	13.33	2220							11.91	2830				900		280				

Monthly Discharge of Frederickhouse River at Frederickhouse for 1915-6

Drainage Area, 1,260 Square Miles

Month	Discharge in Second-feet			Discharge in Second-feet per Square Mile			Run-off
	Maximum	Minimum	Mean	Maximum	Minimum	Mean	Depth in Inches on Drainage Area
November. (1915)	2,410	1,840	2,167	1.91	1.46	1.72	1.92
December　"	1,910	1,650	1,744	1.52	1.31	1.38	1.59
January .. (1916)	2,220	1,860	2,060	1.76	1.48	1.63	1.88
February	2,220	1,920	2,112	1·76	1.52	1,68	1.81
March	2,140	1,750	1,788	1.70	1.38	1.42	1.64
April	9,450	2,140	3,588	7.50	1.70	2.85	8.18
May	11,500	2,830	8,501	9.13	2.25	6.75	7.28
June...........	2,640	1,840	2,092	2.09	1.46	1.66	1.85
July...........	2,040	900	1,498	1.62	.71	1.19	1.37
August	880	280	580	.70	.22	.46	.53
September	530	280	328	.42	.22	.26	.29
October.........	950	280	437	.75	.22	.35	.40
The year	11,500	280	2,244	9.13	.22	1.78	24.24

Kagawong River at Kagawong

Location—150 feet below Kagawong Falls in the Village of Kagawong, Township of Billings, Manitoulin Island.

Records Available—Discharge measurements from July, 1915, to October, 1916. Daily gauge heights from July 11, 1915, to October 31, 1916.

Drainage Area—94 square miles.

Gauge—Vertical steel staff with enamelled face, graduated in feet and inches, connected to a 2 x 4 scantling and attached to a large rock in stream 20 feet below the gauging station. Zero of the gauge (elev. 10.00 feet) is referred to a bench mark (elev. 15.86 feet) painted on a rock on right bank at the gauging station. The initial point for soundings is located on an iron post on the left bank opposite the bench mark.

Channel—Straight for about 100 feet above and below the gauging station. Both banks are high and wooded, and are not liable to overflow. The bed of the stream is composed of rock and clay, slightly shifting, one channel existing at all stages.

Discharge Measurements—Made by wading with a small Price current meter.

Regulation—The flow is controlled by the dam 200 feet above the falls.

Accuracy—The daily gauge readings have heretofore been taken before the mill opens and after it ·closes, so that the estimates of daily discharge made from the mean daily gauge reading are very much too low.

Observer—Stuart Hunt, Kagawong.

Discharge Measurements of Kagawong River at Kagawong in 1915-6

Date	Hydrographer	Width in Feet	Area of Section in Sq. Feet	Mean Velocity in Feet per Sec.	Gauge Height in Feet	Discharge in Sec-Feet	Discharge in Second-feet per Square Mile
1915 Nov. 18 ..	Murray, W. S..	21	14	3.80	11.20	53	....
1916 June 6	''	22	27	3.82	11.58	103	....
'' 6	''	22	23	3.19	11.41	73	....
Oct. 17	''	22	31	1.61	11.25	49(a)	....

(a) Section has been somewhat improved since previous measurement.

Daily Gauge Height and Discharge of Kagawong River at Kagawong for 1915-6

Drainage Area, 94 Square Miles

Day	Nov Gauge Ht. (Feet)	Nov Dis-charge (Sec-ft.)	Dec Gauge Ht. (Feet)	Dec Dis-charge (Sec-ft.)	Jan Gauge Ht. (Feet)	Jan Dis-charge (Sec-ft.)	Feb Gauge Ht. (Feet)	Feb Dis-charge (Sec-ft.)	Mar Gauge Ht. (Feet)	Mar Dis-charge (Sec-ft.)	Apr Gauge Ht. (Feet)	Apr Dis-charge (Sec-ft.)	May Gauge Ht. (Feet)	May Dis-charge (Sec-ft.)	Jun Gauge Ht. (Feet)	Jun Dis-charge (Sec-ft.)	Jul Gauge Ht. (Feet)	Jul Dis-charge (Sec-ft.)	Aug Gauge Ht. (Feet)	Aug Dis-charge (Sec-ft.)	Sep Gauge Ht. (Feet)	Sep Dis-charge (Sec-ft.)	Oct Gauge Ht. (Feet)	Oct Dis-charge (Sec-ft.)
1	11.00	32	10.75	18	11.00	32	11.33	62	12.20	110	11.92	175	12.25	245	11.75	140	11.58	104	11.08	38	11.08	38	10.91	27
2	11.00	32	10.75	18	11.00	32	11.54	96	11.83	116	12.00	192	12.15	245	11.66	121	11.41	74	11.08	38	11.08	38	11.00	32
3	11.00	32	11.25	63	10.83	22	11.24	52	11.75	118	12.00	192	12.25	245	11.66	121	11.58	104	11.08	38	11.00	32	10.95	29
4	11.00	32	10.77	18	10.83	22	11.20	48	12.37	121	12.16	226	12.25	245	11.50	88	11.49	86	11.08	38	11.00	32	10.83	22
5	11.00	32	10.77	18	10.83	22	11.33	48	11.91	125	12.16	226	12.25	245	11.41	74	11.41	74	11.00	38	11.00	32	10.83	22
6	11.00	32	10.79	20	11.29	53	11.29	47	11.83	72	12.20	234	12.08	209	11.58	104	11.49	74	11.00	32	11.04	32	10.91	27
7	10.70	15	10.79	20	12.08	72	11.20	47	11.66	48	12.20	234	12.16	226	11.58	104	11.41	86	11.00	32	11.00	32	10.91	27
8	10.87	24	10.79	20	12.16	53	11.33	44	11.45	48	12.16	226	12.12	217	11.58	104	11.41	86	11.00	32	11.00	32	10.91	27
9	10.76	18	10.79	20	11.16	45	11.33	44	11.49	46	12.16	226	12.16	226	11.38	74	11.41	74	11.00	32	11.00	32	10.91	27
10	10.66	13	10.79	20	10.83	22	11.54	44	11.45	40	12.16	226	12.16	226	11.41	104	11.41	74	11.00	32	11.00	32	10.91	27
11	10.87	24	10.87	24	11.00	32	11.37	42	11.33	40	12.33	261	12.00	192	11.58	104	11.41	74	11.00	32	11.08	32	10.91	27
12	10.83	22	10.91	27	11.01	35	12.04	42	11.41	40	12.20	245	12.08	209	11.58	104	11.41	74	11.00	32	11.00	32	10.87	24
13	10.62	11	10.96	30	11.00	32	12.91	41	11.54	53	12.25	245	12.16	226	11.58	104	11.41	74	11.00	32	10.91	38	10.87	27
14	10.62	11	11.08	38	11.50	88	11.41	40	11.37	40	12.33	245	12.16	226	11.58	104	11.16	45	11.00	32	11.00	38	10.91	27
15	10.62	11	11.25	53	11.20	48	11.31	40	11.33	40	12.25	245	11.91	173	11.41	74	11.08	38	11.00	35	10.91	27	10.91	27
16	10.62	11	11.00	18	11.08	38	11.10	40	11.37	40	12.33	261	11.83	156	11.58	104	11.00	32	11.00	32	11.00	27	10.91	27
17	11.16	45	10.75	18	11.00	32	11.16	40	11.33	40	12.33	261	12.00	192	11.58	104	11.08	38	11.00	38	11.00	32	10.91	27
18	11.16	45	10.75	20	11.00	36	11.29	40	11.33	40	12.16	261	12.00	192	11.58	104	11.16	38	11.00	32	11.00	32	10.91	27
19	11.16	45	10.79	20	11.08	38	11.45	40	11.33	40	12.33	245	12.00	192	11.41	74	11.08	45	11.04	35	11.00	32	10.91	27
20	10.66	13	10.77	18	11.08	38	11.58	42	11.33	40	12.25	261	12.00	192	11.50	88	11.08	38	11.00	32	11.00	32	10.91	27
21	10.66	13	10.79	20	11.08	38	11.37	42	11.33	40	12.33	226	11.83	156	11.58	104	11.00	38	11.08	38	11.00	32	10.91	27
22	10.66	13	10.79	20	11.12	38	11.12	68	11.33	40	12.16	261	11.83	156	11.58	104	11.08	38	11.04	35	11.00	32	10.91	27
23	10.67	14	10.79	20	11.12	38	11.37	68	11.37	40	12.33	261	11.83	156			11.08	38	11.04	38	11.00	32	10.91	27
24	10.69	15	10.83	22	11.16	45	11.37	104	11.41	44	12.16	226	11.75	140			11.08	38	11.00	32	11.00	32	10.91	27
25	10.71	16	10.83	22	11.16	45	11.58	104	11.37	44	12.25	245			11.50										
26	10.75	18	10.83	22	11.75	140	12.50	108	11.50	88	12.16	226												
27	10.73	18	10.83	22	11.41	74	12.04	110	11.74	137														
28	10.75	18	11.08	38	11.25	53			11.91	173														
29	11.25	53			11.25	53			11.91	173														
30					11.25	53			11.91	173														
31			10.41	3	11.25	53			11.91	173														

5 H (iii)

Monthly Discharge of Kagawong River at Kagawong for 1915-6

Drainage Area 94 Square Miles

Month	Discharge in Second-feet			Discharge in Second-feet per-Square Mile			Run-off
	Maximum	Minimum	Mean	Maximum	Minimum	Mean	Depth in inches on Drainage Area
November (1915).	53	11	23	.56	.12	.24	.27
December ··	53	3	24	.56	.03	.26	.30
January ..(1916).	140	22	45	1.49	.23	.48	.55
February	110	40	54	1.17	.43	.57	.61
March..........	73	40	74	1.84	.43	.79	.91
April	261	175	237	2.78	1.86	2.51	2.80
May............	245	140.	207	2.61	1.49	2.20·	2.54
June	140	74	101	1.49	.79	1.07	1.19
July............	104	32	62	1.11	.34	.66	.76
August	38	32	34	.40	.34	.36	.42
September......	38	27	32	.40	.29	.34	.38
October	32	22	26	.34	.23	.28	.32
The year	261	3	76	2.78	.03	.81	11.02

Maganetawan River (North Branch) Near Burk's Falls

Location—One mile north of Burk's Falls station, 200 feet upstream from the Grand Trunk Railway bridge, on lot 7, concession 10, Township of Armour, District of Parry Sound.

Records Available—Monthly discharge measurements from June, 1915, to October, 1916. Daily gauge readings from August 1, 1915, to October 31, 1916.

Drainage Area—107 square miles.

Gauge—Vertical steel staff with enamelled face fastened to a 2 x 4 scantling and connected to a wooden platform on the right shore 20 feet above gauging station. Zero of the gauge (elev. 27.09 feet) is referred to a bench mark (elev. 35.00 feet) painted on top of 5-ft. iron pipe 20 feet above gauging station.

Channel and Control—Straight for about 200 feet above and 100 feet below the gauging station to the falls. The banks are high and wooded, and are not liable to overflow. The bed of the stream is composed of clay and a few rocks, practically permanent. The velocity is moderate.

Discharge Measurements—Made by wading with a small Price current meter.

Accuracy—The rating curve is fairly well defined between limits, for which gauge height records are available.

Observer—Henry Stroud, Burk's Falls.

Discharge Measurements of Maganetawan River (North Branch) near Burk's Falls in 1915-6

Date	Hydrographer	Width in Feet	Area of Section in Sq. Feet	Mean Velocity in Feet per Sec.	Gauge Height in Feet	Discharge in Sec-Feet	Discharge in Second-feet per Square Mile
1915							
Nov. 10, ...	Murray, W. S. ...	47	99	1.41	29.64	140	....
1916							
Jan. 17, ...	"	40	68	1.60	29.77	109 (a)	....
Feb. 15 ..	"	49	91	2.19	30.34	199 (a)	....
Mar. 13	"	46	80	1.41	29.88	114 (a)	....
Apl. 12 ..	"	60	197	3.25	31.54	642 (b)	....
May 15 ..	"	60	182	2.44	31.00	444	....
June 20	"	55	139	2.01	30.42	280	....
Aug. 30 ....¹	"	36	50	.50	25.70	26	....
Oct. 11	"	38	72	1.09	29.42	78	....

(a) Ice measurement.
(b) Logs on control.

Daily Gauge Height and Discharge of Maganetawan River (North Branch) near Burk's Falls for 1915-6

Drainage Area, 707 Square Miles

Day	November Gauge Ht. (Feet)	November Dis-charge (Sec-ft)	December Gauge Ht. (Feet)	December Dis-charge (Sec-ft)	January Gauge Ht. (Feet)	January Dis-charge (Sec-ft)	February Gauge Ht. (Feet)	February Dis-charge (Sec-ft)	March Gauge Ht. (Feet)	March Dis-charge (Sec-ft)	April Gauge Ht. (Feet)	April Dis-charge (Sec-ft)	May Gauge Ht. (Feet)	May Dis-charge (Sec-ft)	June Gauge Ht. (Feet)	June Dis-charge (Sec-ft)	July Gauge Ht. (Feet)	July Dis-charge (Sec-ft)	August Gauge Ht. (Feet)	August Dis-charge (Sec-ft)	September Gauge Ht. (Feet)	September Dis-charge (Sec-ft)	October Gauge Ht. (Feet)	October Dis-charge (Sec-ft)
1	29.84	168	30.25	262	29.50	100	31.17	520	29.96	134	31.50	620	31.67	670	30.63	358	30.09	199	29.09	44	28.75	26	29.46	82
2	29.75	150	30.34	285	29.50	100	31.17	520	29.84	114	31.91	760	31.59	640	30.67	370	30.09	199	29.00	38	28.79	27	29.42	77
3	29.71	142	30.34	285	29.50	100	31.17	520	29.75	88	32.09	820	31.59	640	30.75	392	30.04	186	28.96	36	28.80	27	29.42	77
4	29.71	142	30.34	285	29.50	100	31.17	520	29.67	82	32.67	1020	31.59	640	30.84	466	30.00	176	28.88	33	28.92	33	29.42	72
5	29.75	150	30.34	272	29.63	126	31.09	497	29.75	88	32.67	1020	31.50	615	30.92	443	29.92	158	28.88	31	29.34	67	29.38	72
6	29.67	134	30.25	262	29.55	110	31.09	470	29.75	88	32.59	995	31.42	590	30.84	419	29.84	141	28.88	29	29.38	67	29.42	72
7	29.71	142	30.25	262	29.55	100	31.00	410	29.79	100	32.34	910	31.42	590	30.75	393	29.75	124	28.92	31	29.38	72	29.25	57
8	29.71	142	30.17	242	29.50	100	30.84	380	29.84	100	32.00	790	31.38	580	30.71	381	29.75	124	28.92	33	29.42	77	29.17	51
9	29.71	142	30.25	262	29.59	100	30.75	350	29.84	100	31.75	700	31.34	565	30.59	346	29.67	112	28.84	33	29.42	67	29.21	54
10	29.63	126	30.25	262	29.59	100	30.75	350	29.88	100	31.84	735	31.42	590	30.50	319	29.63	105	28.84	33	29.38	62	29.34	67
11	29.67	134	30.25	262	29.59	100	30.67	325	29.88	110	31.88	750	31.25	540	30.50	319	29.59	100	28.84	31	29.25	58	29.44	79
12	29.75	150	30.25	262	29.59	100	30.67	312	29.88	110	31.67	675	31.17	515	30.50	319	29.55	94	28.84	29	28.84	58	29.44	79
13	29.75	150	30.25	262	29.59	100	30.50	250	29.88	110	31.50	620	31.09	490	30.50	319	29.50	87	28.84	29	28.67	23	29.44	79
14	29.67	134	30.00	222	29.67	100	30.38	200	29.88	110	31.92	760	31.00	490	30.67	370	29.46	82	28.84	29	28.75	29	29.46	82
15	29.63	126	29.92	200	29.67	100	30.34	200	29.88	110	32.17	850	30.96	455	30.71	381	29.42	77	28.84	29	28.84	26	29.50	87
16	29.42	88	29.80	184	29.67	100	30.29	190	29.88	110	32.42	885	30.96	455	30.75	393	29.42	77	28.84	29	29.00	38	29.59	100
17	29.09	44	29.75	168	29.67	100	30.30	180	29.88	110	32.75	980	31.00	466	30.75	393	29.34	67	28.84	29	29.09	44	29.59	124
18	29.42	88	29.75	160	29.75	104	30.25	180	29.88	110	32.92	1030	31.04	478	30.75	393	29.25	58	28.84	29	30.09	199	29.92	370
19	29.67	134	29.75	160	29.75	110	30.25	184	29.79	100	33.17	1100	31.09	490	30.42	295	29.30	51	28.84	28	29.92	158	29.92	392
20	29.67	134	29.84	150	29.84	134	30.25	184	29.88	100	33.00	1060	31.09	490	30.59	346	29.38	63	28.82	44	29.75	124	30.75	407
21	29.67	134	29.67	134	29.92	130	30.25	184	29.71	100	32.67	955	31.09	490	30.59	346	29.34	72	28.80	67	29.34	67	31.09	492
22	29.67	134	29.59	118	30.38	250	30.25	184	29.71	100	32.75	980	31.09	490	30.50	319	29.34	67	28.80	67	29.34	72	31.09	492
23	29.75	150	29.59	118	30.38	250	30.17	170	29.71	100	32.54	920	31.04	478	30.42	295	29.30	63	28.80	63	29.42	77	31.17	515
24	29.84	168	29.59	118	30.38	250	30.09	160	29.75	104	33.09	1080	31.04	466	30.42	283	29.25	58	28.79	58	29.42	67	31.21	530
25	29.84	168	29.59	118	30.50	275	30.09	160	29.75	150	32.54	920	31.00	466	30.38	283	29.25	58	28.75	58	29.34	72	31.25	540
26	30.09	222	29.59	118	30.50	275	30.00	140	30.00	200	32.42	885	30.92	443	30.38	259	29.21	54	28.75	54	29.38	72	31.25	540
27	30.09	222	29.55	110	30.75	395	30.00	140	30.25	262	32.34	860	30.84	419	30.30	245	29.17	51	28.75	51	29.42	77	31.25	540
28	30.46	315	29.55	110	30.92	446	29.96	134	30.67	371	32.09	785	30.75	393	30.17	221	29.13	47	28.75	51	29.42	77	31.25	540
29	30.59	348	29.55	110	31.09	497			31.00	470	31.75	685	30.59	346										
30	30.42	305	29.55	110	31.17	520			31.17	520	31.59	640												
31			31.17	520																				

Monthly Discharge of Maganetawan River (North Branch) near Burk's
Falls for 1915-6

Drainage Area, 107 Square Miles

Month	Discharge in Second-feet			Discharge in Second-feet per Square Mile			Run-off
	Maximum	Minimum	Mean	Maximum	Minimum	Mean	Depth in Inches on Drainage Area
November (1915).	348	44	166	3.25	.44	1.55	1.73
December ''	285	110	189	2.66	1.03	1.77	2.04
January ..(1916).	520	100	190	4.86	.93	1.78	2.05
February	520	134	282	4.86	1.25	2.64	2.84
March	520	82	148	4.86	.77	1.38	1.59
April..........	1,100	620	859	10.28	5.79	8.03	8.96
May............	670	346	515	6.26	3.23	4.81	5.55
June	466	221	346	4.36	2.07	3.23	3.60
July...........	199	47	96	1.86	.44	.90	1.04
August	44	26	30	.41	.24	.28	.82
September	199	23	70	1.86	.21	.65	.73
October........	540	51	225	5.05	.48	2.10	2.42
The year	1,100	23	259	10.28	·21·	2.42	32.94

Maganetawan River (South Branch) near Burk's Falls

Location—One-half mile south of Burk's Falls station, and 200 feet east of G.T. Ry. tracks on lot 8, concession 8, Township of Armour, Parry Sound District.

Records Available—Discharge measurements from June, 1915, to October, 1916. Daily gauge heights from August 1, 1915, to October 31, 1916.

Drainage Area—257 square miles.

Gauge—Vertical steel staff with enamelled face, graduated in feet and inches, fastened to 2 x 8 scantling wedged between two hardwood trees on the left shore 20 feet above gauging station. Zero of the gauge (elev. 22.00 feet) is referred to a bench mark (elev. 35.00 feet) painted on top of a 5-ft. iron pipe located near the gauge on the north branch of the river.

Channel and Control—Straight for about 250 feet above and 500 feet below the rapids. The banks are high and wooded, and are not liable to overflow. The current is moderate.

Discharge Measurements—Made by wading with a small price meter.

Regulation—Temporary dams above, which are used during log driving season, cause fluctuations at the gauge.

Accuracy—Rating curve fairly well defined between gauge heights 23.50 and 24.00 feet. There are not sufficient data available to define a good curve above and below these limits.

Observer—Henry Stroud, Burk's Falls.

Discharge Measurements of Maganetawan River (South Branch) near Burk's Falls in 1915-6

Date	Hydrographer	Width in Feet	Area of Section in Sq. Feet	Mean Velocity in Feet per Sec.	Gauge Height in Feet	Discharge in Sec-Feet	Discharge in Second-feet per Square Mile
1915 Nov. 10....	Murray, W.S ...	65	132	2.13	24.00	283	....
1916 Feb. 15....	"	70	178	3.06	24.70	546 (a)	....
Mar. 13....	"	67	126	2.34	23.92	294 (b)	....
April 5....	"	77	242	4.51	25.52	1,090	....
May 15....	"	77	249	3.48	25.66	866	....
June 20....	"	78	210	3.18	25.14	670	....
Aug. 30....	"	62	81	1.74	23.37	142	....
Oct. 11....	"	64	88	1.71	23.49	151	....

(a) River ice-covered above section.
(b) Floating ice at section.

Daily Gauge Height and Discharge of Maganetawan River (South Branch) near Burk's Falls for 1915-6

Drainage Area 257 Square Miles

Day	Nov. Gauge Ht. (Feet)	Nov. Dis-charge (Sec-ft.)	Dec. Gauge Ht. (Feet)	Dec. Dis-charge (Sec-ft.)	Jan. Gauge Ht. (Feet)	Jan. Dis-charge (Sec-ft.)	Feb. Gauge Ht. (Feet)	Feb. Dis-charge (Sec-ft.)	Mar. Gauge Ht. (Feet)	Mar. Dis-charge (Sec-ft.)	Apr. Gauge Ht. (Feet)	Apr. Dis-charge (Sec-ft.)	May Gauge Ht. (Feet)	May Dis-charge (Sec-ft.)	June Gauge Ht. (Feet)	June Dis-charge (Sec-ft.)	July Gauge Ht. (Feet)	July Dis-charge (Sec-ft.)	Aug. Gauge Ht. (Feet)	Aug. Dis-charge (Sec-ft.)	Sept. Gauge Ht. (Feet)	Sept. Dis-charge (Sec-ft.)	Oct. Gauge Ht. (Feet)	Oct. Dis-charge (Sec-ft.)
1	24.16	346	24.16	346	24.16	346	24.75	605	24.29	396	25.0.	780	26.33	1610	25.37	815	25.00	685	23.25	114	23.41	151	23.66	229
2	24.12	332	24.20	360	24.12	332	24.83	645	24.16	346	25.16	825	26.25	1555	25.33	790	25.00	685	23.25	114	23.45	162	23.62	216
3	24.08	318	24.25	380	24.08	318	24.91	685	24.16	346	25.58	1085	26.25	1555	25.33	790	24.91	650	23.25	114	23.41	132	23.60	209
4	24.16	346	24.25	380	24.37	428	24.83	645	24.16	346	25.41	975	26.21	1525	25.37	815	24.83	625	23.25	114	23.33	151	23.58	202
5	24.08	318	24.25	380	24.37	428	24.83	645	24.16	346	25.62	1115	26.21	1525	25.33	790	24.75	600	23.25	114	23.33	132	23.58	202
6	24.00	290	24.25	380	24.58	520	24.91	685	24.16	346	25.66	1140	26.00	1380	25.25	770	24.66	570	23.25	114	23.33	132	23.58	202
7	24.08	318	24.25	380	24.42	448	24.83	645	24.16	346	25.71	1175	26.00	1380	25.25	770	24.58	540	23.29	123	23.33	132	23.54	189
8	24.08	318	24.25	380	24.37	428	24.83	645	24.16	346	25.75	1205	25.91	1315	25.21	755	24.58	540	23.33	132	23.33	132	23.54	189
9	24.00	290	24.25	380	24.00	290	24.75	605	24.00	290	25.66	1140	25.91	1315	25.25	770	24.54	530	23.33	132	23.33	132	23.50	176
10	24.00	290	24.33	412	24.00	290	24.66	580	24.04	304	25.71	1175	25.91	1315	25.25	770	24.50	515	23.33	132	23.33	132	23.50	171
11	24.00	290	24.33	412	24.08	318	24.70	605	23.95	278	25.79	1235	25.83	1260	25.21	755	24.46	500	23.37	141	23.33	132	23.50	176
12	24.08	318	24.16	346	24.00	290	24.75	605	23.91	268	25.83	1260	25.83	1260	25.21	755	24.41	483	23.45	162	23.33	132	23.50	176
13	24.02	297	24.16	346	24.00	290	24.75	605	23.91	268	25.83	1260	25.75	1205	25.29	780	24.37	470	23.45	162	23.33	132	23.50	176
14	24.00	290	24.16	346	24.08	318	24.66	560	23.91	268	26.00	1380	25.66	1140	25.37	815	24.33	457	23.52	183	23.41	151	23.54	189
15	24.00	290	24.16	346	24.08	318	24.67	565	23.91	268	26.08	1435	25.66	1140	25.37	815	24.33	457	23.54	189	23.41	176	23.58	202
16	24.00	290	24.16	346	24.16	346	24.62	540	23.91	268	26.08	1435	26.75	1270	25.29	780	24.37	470	23.54	202	23.50	216	23.62	216
17	23.95	278	24.12	332	24.16	346	24.58	520	23.87	258	26.08	1435	26.50	1190	25.29	780	24.37	470	23.54	189	23.62	216	23.75	260
18	24.00	290	24.08	318	24.08	318	24.62	540	23.83	249	26.25	1555	25.83	1190	25.25	770	23.46	165	23.50	176	23.58	202	23.83	287
19	24.00	290	24.08	318	24.08	318	24.50	480	23.83	249	26.33	1610	25.83	960	25.16	735	23.46	165	23.50	176	23.58	202	24.00	345
20	24.00	290	24.08	318	24.00	290	24.50	480	23.83	249	26.41	1665	25.83	960	25.16	735	23.46	165	23.50	176	23.58	202	24.08	371
21	24.00	290	24.08	318	24.08	318	24.41	444	23.58	254	26.33	1610	25.87	980	25.08	710	23.50	176	23.50	176	23.58	202	24.00	399
22	24.00	290	24.08	318	24.16	346	24.41	444	24.50	260	26.41	1665	26.16	1070	25.04	695	23.46	165	23.16	96	23.58	202	24.16	457
23	24.00	290	24.08	318	24.25	380	24.41	444	24.25	295	26.41	1665	26.50	1190	25.00	685	23.41	151	23.33	132	23.58	202	24.33	483
24	24.00	290	24.04	304	24.29	396	24.33	412	24.29	380	26.41	1665	26.33	1130	25.00	685	23.41	151	23.41	151	23.58	202	24.41	555
25	24.00	290	24.04	304	24.33	412	24.29	396	24.41	396	26.37	1640	25.91	990	25.00	685	23.39	146	23.41	162	23.58	202	24.66	625
26	24.00	290	24.04	304	24.33	412	24.29	396	24.29	412	26.33	1610	25.41	820	25.04	695	23.27	132	23.16	176	23.62	216	24.83	650
27	24.04	304	24.08	318	24.33	412	24.29	396	24.33	520	26.33	1610	25.33	790	25.00	685	23.29	123	23.50	132	23.66	229	24.91	710
28	24.08	318	24.12	332	24.50	480	24.29	396	24.58	605	26.33	1585	25.37	815	25.00	685	23.25	118	23.33	132			25.08	725
29	24.16	346	24.12	332	24.62	540			24.75	605	26.29	1585	25.41	820	25.00	685	23.25	114	23.41	151			25.12	
30	24.08	318	24.12	332	24.66	560			24.91	685	26.25	1555	25.45	835	25.00	685	23.25	114						
31			24.16	346	24.66	560																		

Monthly Discharge of Maganetawan River (South Branch) near Burk's
Falls for 1915-6

Drainage Area, 257 Square Miles

Month	Discharge in Second-feet			Discharge in Second-feet per Square Mile			Run-off
	Maximum	Minimum	Mean	Maximum	Minimum	Mean	Depth in Inches on Drainage Area
November (1915).	346	278	304	1.35	1.08	1.18	1.32
December. ··	412	304	348	1.60	1.18	1.35	1.56
January ..(1916).	560	290	381	2.18	1.13	1.48	1.71
February	685	396	555	2.67	.54	2.16	2.33
March..........	685	249	339	2.67	.97	1.32	1.52
April...........	1,665	780	1,379	6.48	3.04	5.37	5.99
May............	1,610	790	1,173	6.26	3.07	4.56	5.26
June	815	685	750	3.17	2.67	2.92	·3.26
July...........	685	114	364	2.67	.44	1.42	1.64
August	202	96	149	.78	.37	.58	.67
September......	229	132	171	.89	.51	.67	.75
October........	725	171	312	2.82	.67	1.21	1.39
The year	1,665	132	517	6.48	.51	2.01	27.36

Mississagi River at Iron Bridge

Location—At highway bridge in the village of Iron Bridge, south half of lot 3, concession 2, Township of Gladstone, District of Algoma.

Records Available—Discharge measurements from September, 1915, to October, 1916. Daily gauge heights from November 16, 1915, to October 31, 1916.

Drainage Area—3,565 square miles.

Gauge—Vertical steel staff with enamelled face graduated in feet and inches, 0 to 6 foot section placed on pile on left shore 350 feet down stream from bridge, 6 to 12 foot section placed on down stream side of right abutment of bridge. Zero on the gauge (elev. 32.00 feet) referred to bench mark (elev. 55.50 feet) on top of right abutment on down stream side, painted thus " B.M. 55.50."

Channel—Straight for about 300 feet above and about 1 mile below the gauging station. The bed of the stream consists of clay and sand, slightly shifting.

Discharge Measurements—Made from highway bridge with small Price current meter.

Control—About eleven miles below the gauging station there is a small falls and rapids known as the Mississagi rapids. Log jams sometimes occur on these rapids during low water period, which may cause back water at the gauging station.

Winter Flow—During the winter months measurements are made through the ice to determine the winter flow. The relation of gauge height to discharge is seriously affected by ice.

Observer—Lorne Arnill, Iron Bridge.

Discharge Measurements of Mississagi River at Iron Bridge in 1915-6

Date	Hydrographer	Width in Feet	Area of Section in Sq. Feet	Mean Velocity in Feet per Sec.	Gauge Height in Feet	Discharge in Sec-Feet	Discharge in Second-feet per Square Mile
1915							
Nov. 16....	Murray, W. S...	177	3,117	2.09	36.09	6,515	....
Dec. 3....	"	183	3,513	2.42	38.25	8,550	....
1916							
Feb. 8....	"	170	2,705	.94	33.50	2,520(a)	....
Mar. 8....	"	150	2,174	.63	33.00	1,366(a)	....
Aug. 23....	"	160	2,288	.62	31.25	1,430	....
Oct. 19....	"	165	2,464	1.02	32.39	2,516	....

(a) Ice measurement.

Daily Gage Height and Discharge of Mississagi River at Iron Bridge for 1915-6

Drainage area: 3,565 Square Miles

Day	Nov. Gauge Ht.	Nov. Dis-charge	Dec. Gauge Ht.	Dec. Dis-charge	Jan. Gauge Ht.	Jan. Dis-charge	Feb. Gauge Ht.	Feb. Dis-charge	Mar. Gauge Ht.	Mar. Dis-charge	Apr. Gauge Ht.	Apr. Dis-charge	May Gauge Ht.	May Dis-charge	June Gauge Ht.	June Dis-charge	July Gauge Ht.	July Dis-charge	Aug. Gauge Ht.	Aug. Dis-charge	Sept. Gauge Ht.	Sept. Dis-charge	Oct. Gauge Ht.	Oct. Dis-charge
1			38.67	8950	34.84	4350	33.50	2910	33.25	1350	33.83	4090	41.00	12300	36.66	6930	36.58	6850	31.84	2090	30.88	1130	32.33	2580
2			38.25	8530	34.84	4330	33.67	3000	33.17	1350	34.12	4380	40.80	11090	36.50	6770	36.08	6350	31.84	2090	30.84	1090	32.29	2540
3			37.84	8120	34.75	4150	33.75	3000	33.17	1350	34.37	4630	40.60	10890	36.50	6770	36.08	6350	31.75	2000	30.84	1090	32.16	2410
4			37.50	7780	34.42	4040	33.84	3050	33.17	1350	34.41	4670	40.58	10870	36.41	6680	35.91	6180	31.67	2000	31.42	1670	32.00	2250
5			36.84	7110	34.67	4260	33.84	2750	33.17	1350	34.41	4670	40.50	10790	36.25	6520	35.50	5770	31.67	1920	32.58	2830	32.00	2250
6			36.67	6940	34.34	4010	33.75	2650	33.17	1350	34.58	4840	45.50	10790	36.83	7100	35.41	5680	31.59	1840	32.08	2330	31.92	2170
7			36.50	6770	34.00	3950	33.67	2580	33.17	1350	34.58	4840	40.50	10450	36.33	6600	35.33	5600	31.59	1840	31.75	2000	32.00	2090
8			36.50	6770	34.59	3790	33.59	2520	33.17	1350	34.66	4920	40.50	10790	36.25	6520	35.33	5600	31.50	1750	31.59	1840	31.84	2000
9			36.25	6520	34.59	3790	33.50	2420	33.00	1330	34.75	5010	40.00	10290	35.83	6100	35.08	5350	31.42	1670	31.59	1710	31.75	1920
10			36.25	6520	34.00	3560	33.50	2350	33.00	1330	35.25	5520	39.91	10200	35.50	5770	34.83	5090	31.67	1920	31.46	1630	31.67	1840
11			36.42	6570	34.09	3770	33.50	2210	33.00	1330	35.25	5270	39.58	9870	35.08	5350	35.08	5350	31.67	1920	31.38	1570	31.59	1840
12			37.00	6970	33.67	3260	33.50	2150	33.00	1330	35.41	5680	39.08	9370	35.33	5600	34.91	5170	31.67	1920	31.32	1570	31.59	1920
13			37.42	7170	33.50	3130	33.50	2150	33.00	1330	35.91	6180	38.58	8860	35.33	5600	34.66	4920	31.67	1920	31.42	1670	31.67	2090
14			37.75	7280	33.50	3030	33.50	2150	33.08	1330	36.16	6430	38.58	8780	36.50	6100	34.50	4760	31.67	1920	31.75	2000	31.84	1840
15			37.92	7360	33.50	2930	33.50	2550	33.00	1330	36.70	6970	38.25	8530	36.50	6770	34.33	4670	31.67	1920	32.08	2330	31.92	2090
16			37.75	7360	33.50	2930	33.50	2550	33.00	1430	37.16	7440	38.50	8780	37.16	7440	34.33	4590	31.67	1920	32.00	2250	31.96	2170
17			37.42	7170	33.50	2890	33.59	2550	33.00	1470	37.70	7980	38.25	8530	37.50	7780	34.08	4340	31.67	1920	31.92	2170	32.16	2410
18	36.09	6360	37.59	7170	33.50	2850	33.50	2550	33.00	1530	38.40	8680	38.08	8360	38.00	8280	34.08	4090	31.50	1750	31.84	2090	32.58	2830
19	35.84	6110	37.67	6870	33.50	2850	33.50	2550	33.00	1590	38.90	9180	37.91	8190	38.33	8610	33.83	4090	31.50	1670	31.67	1920	32.58	2830
20	35.59	5860	36.84	6670	33.42	2780	33.50	1850	33.00	1700	40.00	10290	37.58	7860	38.58	8860	33.83	3840	31.42	1670	31.59	1840	32.66	2910
21	35.59	5860	36.59	6370	33.42	2750	33.42	2750	33.00	2000	40.50	10790	37.58	7610	38.58	8860	33.33	3590	31.34	1590	31.46	1710	32.83	3030
22	35.59	5860	36.42	5970	33.67	3130	33.34	1750	33.00	2550	41.00	12300	37.25	7530	38.58	8860	33.16	3220	31.34	1590	31.54	1790	34.00	4260
23	35.50	5770	36.25	5770	33.92	3130	33.34	1750	33.00	2550	40.95	12240	37.16	7440	38.00	8280	32.83	3080	31.25	1500	31.40	1650	34.33	4590
24	35.34	5610	35.67	5470	33.92	3260	33.34	1750	33.00	2550	41.40	12700	37.00	7280	37.41	7440	32.58	2830	31.25	1500	31.50	1750	34.58	4840
25	35.17	5440	35.34	5220	34.00	3260	33.34	1680	33.00	2550	41.80	13100	37.00	7100	37.16	7100	38.58	2830	31.17	1420	31.59	1840	36.33	6600
26	34.84	5160	35.34	5160	34.00	3260	33.34	1550	33.08	2550	42.00	13300	37.00	7280	37.00	7280	32.50	2750	31.17	1420	31.59	1840	37.08	7360
27	35.84	6110	37.50	7780	34.00	3200	33.34	1450	33.08	2550	41.80	13100	37.50	7780	36.50	6770	32.41	2660	31.09	1340	31.55	1800	37.08	7360
28	37.50	7780	38.84	9120	33.92	3200	33.25	1350	33.16	2550	41.50	12800	37.83	8110	36.50	6770	32.25	2500	31.09	1340	31.84	2090	37.08	7360
29	38.84	9120	35.00	4960	33.75	3030	33.25	1350	33.33	3150	41.35	12650	37.83	8110	36.66	6930	32.16	2410	31.00	1250	32.12	2370	37.25	7530
30	39.00	9290	34.67	4660	33.59	2850			33.50	3760	41.20	12500	37.83	8110	36.83	7100	32.08	2330	30.92	1170	32.33	2580	37.08	7360
31	39.09	9380	34.50	4060	33.42	2850							37.66	7940			31.92	2170	30.92	1170			37.08	7360

Monthly Discharge of Mississagi River at Iron Bridge for 1915-6

Drainage Area 3565 Square Miles.

Month	Discharge in Second-feet			Discharge in Second-feet per Square Mile			Run-off
	Maximum	Minimum	Mean	Maximum	Minimum	Mean	Depth in Inches on Drainage Area
Nov. 15-30, (1915)	9,380	5,100	6,595	2.63	1.43	1.85	1.03
December	8,950	4,060	6,522	2.51	1.14	1.83	2.11
January ..(1916)	4,350	2,750	3,378	1.22	.77	.95	1.10
February.......	3,050	1,350	2,237	.86	.38	.63	.68
March..........	3,760	1,330	1,805	1.05	.37	.51	.59
April..........	13,300	4,090	8,238	3.73	1.15	2.31	2.58
May	12,300	7,100	9,028	3.45	1.99	2.53	2.92
June	8,860	5,350	7,160	2.49	1.50	2.01	2.24
July...........	6,850	2.170	4,302	1.92	.61	1.21	1.39
August.........	2,090	1,170	1,697	.59	.33	.48	.55
September......	2,830	1,090	1,878	.79	.31	.53	.59
October	7,530	1,840	3,817	2.11	.52	1.07	1.23
The period......	13,300	1,090	4,641	3.45	.31	1.30	17.70

Muskoka River (North Branch) near Port Sydney

Location—At the highway bridge near the Village of Port Sydney and ¼ mile below
Mary Lake, on lot 25, concession 5, Township of Stephenson, Muskoka District.

Records Available—Discharge measurements from April, 1915, to October, 1916. Daily
gauge heights from April 16, 1915, to Oct. 31, 1916.

Drainage Area—560 square miles.

Gauge—Vertical steel staff with enamelled face graduated in feet and inches and
fastened to abutment on left upstream side of bridge. Zero of gauge (elev. 7.00
feet) is referred to a bench mark (elev. 24.78 feet) painted on top of right abutment, downstream side.

Channel—Straight for about 1,500 feet above and 500 feet below gauging station. Both
banks are high, wooded, and not liable to overflow. The bed of the channel is composed of clay and gravel.

Discharge Measurements—Made from highway bridge with a small Price current meter.

Regulation—The operation of dam at Mary Lake during certain periods of the year will
cause fluctuation at the gauge.

Accuracy—The rating curve is fairly well defined, and estimates of discharge are fair.

Observer—A. E. McInnes, Port Sydney.

Discharge Measurements of Muskoka River (North Branch) near Port Sydney in 1915-6

Date	Hydrographer	Width in Feet	Area of Section in Sq. Feet	Mean Velocity in Feet per Sec.	Gauge Height in Feet	Discharge in Sec-Feet	Discharge in Second-feet per Square Mile
1915							
Nov. 11....	Murray, W. S..	53	302	1.86	8.58	563	....
Dec. 23....	"	52	308	1.72	8.66	533	....
1916							
Jan. 19....	Murray, W. S...	50	292	1.55	8.41	452(a)	....
Feb. 17....	" ..	53	313	2.24	8.80	704	....
Mar. 16....	" ..	48	293	1.67	8.52	495	....
Apr. 11....	" ..	58	444	5.90	11.16	2,622	....
" 29....	" ..	58	499	7.12	12.00	3,552	....
May 23....	" ..	55	366	3.77	9.75	1,482	....
June 22....	" ..	55	331	3.09	9.34	1,023	....
July 11....	" ..	47	260	.62	7.85	163	....

(a) River ice-covered below section.

Daily Gauge Height and Discharge of Muskoka River (North Branch) near Port Sydney for 1915-6

Drainage area, 560 Square Miles

Day	Nov Gauge Ht.	Nov Dis-charge	Dec Gauge Ht.	Dec Dis-charge	Jan Gauge Ht.	Jan Dis-charge	Feb Gauge Ht.	Feb Dis-charge	Mar Gauge Ht.	Mar Dis-charge	Apr Gauge Ht.	Apr Dis-charge	May Gauge Ht.	May Dis-charge	Jun Gauge Ht.	Jun Dis-charge	Jul Gauge Ht.	Jul Dis-charge	Aug Gauge Ht.	Aug Dis-charge	Sep Gauge Ht.	Sep Dis-charge	Oct Gauge Ht.	Oct Dis-charge
	Feet	Sec-ft.	Feet	Sec-ft.	Feet	Sec-ft.	Feet	Sec-ft.	Feet	Sec-ft.	Feet	Sec-ft.	Feet	Sec-ft.	Feet	Sec-ft.	Feet	Sec-ft.	Feet	Sec-ft.	Feet	Sec-ft.	Feet	Sec-ft.
1	8.41	446	9.41	1130	8.66	605	10.62	2060	8.41	446	11.08	2440	10.91	2290	9.25	1010	9.00	840	7.83	125	7.71	88	7.83	125
2	8.41	446	9.41	1130	8.66	605	10.58	2020	8.41	446	10.95	2320	11.41	2740	9.25	1010	9.00	840	7.83	125	7.71	88	7.83	125
3	8.41	446	9.41	1130	8.66	605	10.58	2020	8.41	446	10.83	2220	11.41	2740	9.58	1260	9.00	840	7.83	125	7.71	88	7.83	125
4	8.41	446	9.41	1130	8.33	400	10.41	1890	8.50	500	10.83	2220	11.33	2670	9.50	1200	8.91	775	7.83	125	8.33	398	7.71	125
5	8.83	720	9.41	1130	8.33	400	10.33	1820	8.50	500	10.83	2220	11.16	2510	9.29	1040	8.91	775	7.83	125	8.25	350	7.71	88
6	8.83	720	9.41	1130	8.33	400	10.25	1760	8.66	605	11.33	2900	11.16	2510	9.08	895	8.50	500	8.83	720	8.16	296	7.71	88
7	8.83	720	9.41	1130	8.33	400	10.16	1700	8.37	422	11.33	2900	11.20	2550	9.25	1010	8.70	620	8.83	720	7.83	155	7.83	125
8	8.58	550	9.16	950	8.33	400	10.16	1700	8.41	446	12.66	4140	11.00	2370	9.25	1010	8.50	500	8.83	720	7.54	125	7.83	155
9	8.58	550	9.16	950	8.33	400	10.08	1630	8.50	500	11.00	2670	10.58	2020	9.33	1070	7.83	125	8.25	350	7.70	63	7.91	155
10	8.58	550	9.00	840	8.66	605	10.08	1630	8.50	500	11.33	2510	10.33	1820	9.29	1040	7.83	125	8.08	249	7.66	77	7.85	132
11	8.58	550	8.16	296	8.66	605	9.91	1510	8.50	500	11.16	2510	10.08	1630	9.33	1070	7.83	125	7.91	155	7.75	85	7.87	140
12	8.58	550	8.16	296	8.66	605	9.50	1200	8.50	500	11.16	2510	10.00	1575	8.70	775	7.83	125	7.75	100	7.75	100	7.87	140
13	8.58	550	8.16	296	8.66	605	9.42	1140	8.50	500	11.75	3070	8.83	720	8.50	630	7.87	140	7.75	100	7.75	100	7.87	140
14	8.58	550	8.16	296	8.66	605	9.41	1130	8.50	500	11.75	3070	9.33	1070	8.58	500	7.87	155	7.75	100	7.83	100	7.87	140
15	8.58	550	8.16	296	8.66	605	9.04	870	8.50	500	12.25	3620	9.83	1450	8.75	665	7.91	155	7.83	125	7.83	125	8.08	249
16	8.58	550	8.16	296	8.66	605	8.75	665	8.50	500	12.25	3620	10.62	2060	9.33	1070	7.91	205	7.83	125	7.83	125	8.16	296
17	7.83	129	8.41	446	8.41	446	8.83	720	8.50	500	12.20	3560	10.50	1960	9.50	1200	8.00	205	7.83	125	7.83	125	8.45	470
18	8.58	550	8.41	446	8.41	446	8.75	665	8.41	446	12.20	3560	10.37	1880	9.75	1290	8.62	580	7.83	125	7.83	125	8.46	476
19	8.58	550	8.41	446	8.41	446	8.41	446	8.33	398	12.50	3930	10.33	1820	9.91	1510	8.58	249	7.83	125	7.83	125	8.41	446
20	8.58	550	8.41	296	8.41	446	8.41	446	8.25	350	12.50	3930	9.33	1070	9.70	1350	8.58	550	7.83	112	7.83	125	9.41	1130
21	8.58	550	8.41	446	8.45	470	8.50	500	8.25	350	12.33	3720	9.91	1510	9.33	1070	8.25	350	7.79	77	7.83	125	9.50	1200
22	8.58	550	8.66	605	9.08	895	8.50	500	8.25	350	12.00	2370	9.91	1510	9.33	1070	7.91	155	7.66	77	7.83	125	9.54	1230
23	9.16	950	8.66	605	9.33	1070	8.50	500	8.25	350	12.83	4360	9.75	1390	9.33	1070	7.83	125	7.66	77	7.83	125	9.78	1410
24	9.16	950	8.66	605	9.37	1100	8.75	665	8.25	350	12.66	4140	9.75	1390	9.41	1130	7.83	125	7.66	205	7.83	125	10.08	1630
25	9.16	950	8.66	605	9.70	1350	8.58	550	8.25	350	12.58	4030	9.75	1390	9.37	1070	7.83	125	8.00	88	7.83	125	10.00	1570
26	9.16	950	8.66	605	10.41	1890	8.58	550	8.70	630	12.50	3930	9.83	1450	9.00	840	7.83	77	7.71	88	7.83	125	9.91	1510
27	9.16	950	8.66	605	10.58	2020	8.58	550	8.75	665	12.37	3760	9.08	895	9.00	840	7.83	77	7.71	88	7.83	125	9.91	1510
28	9.41	1130	8.66	605	10.66	2020	8.58	550	10.63	1980	12.33	3720	9.41	1130	9.00	840	7.58	205			7.83	125	9.62	1290
29	9.41	1130	8.66	605	10.58	2090			8.75	630	12.04	3380	9.41	1130	9.00	840	7.58	88	8.00	205	7.83	125		
30	9.41	1130	8.66	605	10.66	2090			10.53	665	11.00	2370	9.41	1130	9.00	840	7.62	69	7.71	88	7.83	125		
31			8.66	605	10.66	2090			11.00	2370			9.41	1130			7.62	69	7.71					

Monthly Discharge of Muskoka River (North Branch) near Port
Sydney for 1915-6

Drainage Area 560 Square Miles

Month	Discharge in Second-feet			Discharge in Second-feet per Square Mile.			Run-off
	Maximum	Minimum	Mean	Maximum	Minimum	Mean	Depth in Inches on Drainage Area
November (1915)	1,130	129	636	2.02	.23	1.14	1.27
December. ''	1,130	296	681	2.02	.53	1.22	1.41
January .. (1916)	2,090	400	798	3.73	.71	1.42	1.64
February	2,060	446	1,104	3.68	.80	1.97	2.12
March..........	2,370	350	573	4.23	.62	1.02	1.18
April	4,360	2,220	3,206	7.79	3.96	5.72	6.38
May	2,740	720	1,746	4.89	1.29	3.12	3.60
June	1,510	500	998	2.70	.89	1.78	1.99
July............	840	61	326	1.50	.11	.58	.67
August	720	77	194	1.29	.14	.35	.40
September.....	398	53	136	.71	.09	.24	.27
October	1,570	88	552	2.80	.16	.99	1.14
The year	4,360	53	908	7.79	.09	1.62	21.95

Muskoka River (South Branch) at Tretheway's Falls

Location—At small steel highway bridge known as Tretheway's Falls Bridge, about 1 mile south of the Muskoka Falls Post Office, and about 7 miles south of the Town of Bracebridge, Township of Draper, Muskoka District.

Records Available—Discharge measurements, August, 1912, to October, 1916. Daily gauge heights, June 4, 1914, to October 31, 1916.

Drainage Area—668 square miles.

Gauge—As there is no available place for establishing a permanent staff gauge, a bench mark (elevation 25.00), painted on a stringer, on the up-stream side of the bridge, is used in ascertaining the water elevation, by measuring down to the surface of the stream with a graduated staff. It is referred to a bench mark (elevation 33.08) painted on a large rock on the right bank, 90 feet to the right of the downstream side of the bridge.

Channel and Control—Straight for about 300 feet above and 300 feet below the station. The banks are fairly high, rocky and wooded and will not overflow. The current is very swift and the bed of stream is rough and rocky, with a heavy slope about 250 feet below the section.

Discharge Measurements—Made from the upstream side of the bridge with a Price current meter and a stay line.

Winter Flow—The gauge is located where the current is swift and ice seldom forms across the river for the entire width. The relation of gauge height to discharge is but slightly affected by ice.

Accuracy—Measurements made at Black's Bridge 1 mile above, were used in conjunction with those made at Tretheway's Falls, and a fairly well-defined rating curve has been established. Open water curve used throughout the year.

Observer—Wesley Morrow, Muskoka Falls.

Discharge Measurements of Muskoka River at Tretheway's Falls in 1915-6

Date	Hydrographer	Width in Feet	Area of Section in Sq. Feet	Mean Velocity in Feet per Sec.	Gauge Height in Feet	Discharge in Sec-Feet	Discharge in Second-feet per Square Mile
1915							
Nov. 9....	Murray, W. S...	50	174	3.45	13.92	602	....
Dec. 15....	"	50	193	3.33	14.00	644 (d)	....
1916							
Jan. 19....	"	49	198	3.53	14.48	700 (a)	....
Feb. 17....	"	50	211	4.89	14.75	1,032	....
Mar. 15....	"	50	230	5.44	15.17	1,251	....
April 11....	"	89	1,595	1.23	16.25	1,940 (b)	....
" 28....	"	125	1,960	2.21	19.34	4,338 (c)	....
May 17....	"	89	1,657	1.50	17.00	2,569 (c)	....
June 22....	"	91	1,665	1.17	16.25	1,958 (c)	....
July 13....	"	89	1,390	.56	14.50	781 (c)	....
" 13....	"	49	198	4.57	14.50	908	....
Oct. 12....	"	42	129	2.55	12.92	330	....

(a) River ice-covered above section.
(b) Reading taken at Black's Bridge. Logs in stream.
(c) Reading taken at Black's Bridge.

Daily Gauge Height and Discharge of Muskoka River (South Branch) at Tretheway's Falls for 1915-6

Drainage Area, 668 Square Miles

Day	Nov. Gauge Ht. (Feet)	Nov. Dis-charge (Sec-ft.)	Dec. Gauge Ht.	Dec. Dis-charge	Jan. Gauge Ht.	Jan. Dis-charge	Feb. Gauge Ht.	Feb. Dis-charge	Mar. Gauge Ht.	Mar. Dis-charge	Apr. Gauge Ht.	Apr. Dis-charge	May Gauge Ht.	May Dis-charge	June Gauge Ht.	June Dis-charge	July Gauge Ht.	July Dis-charge	Aug. Gauge Ht.	Aug. Dis-charge	Sept. Gauge Ht.	Sept. Dis-charge	Oct. Gauge Ht.	Oct. Dis-charge
1	14.00	580	14.34	700	14.09	610	16.00	1560	14.59	935	15.50	1460	19.00	4050	16.17	1910	15.50	1460	13.84	565	13.17	385	13.17	385
2	14.00	580	14.34	700	14.09	610	16.25	1710	14.50	890	16.00	1790	19.00	4050	16.09	1850	14.67	975	13.84	565	13.17	385	13.17	385
3	14.00	580	14.34	700	14.09	610	16.00	1560	14.50	890	16.00	1790	19.00	4050	15.84	1710	14.50	890	13.84	565	13.17	385	13.17	385
4	13.92	550	14.34	700	14.09	610	16.00	1560	14.50	890	16.00	1790	19.17	4190	15.50	1460	14.59	935	13.84	565	13.17	385	13.17	385
5	13.92	550	14.34	700	14.09	610	16.25	1710	14.50	890	16.25	2140	18.84	3920	16.00	1790	14.59	935	13.84	565	13.17	385	13.09	374
6	13.92	550	14.25	665	14.17	640	16.50	2140	15.00	1160	16.50	2260	18.67	3790	16.50	2140	14.50	890	13.67	501	13.17	385	13.09	374
7	13.92	550	14.17	640	14.17	640	16.00	1790	14.59	935	16.67	2490	18.50	3650	17.00	2490	14.50	890	13.50	450	13.17	385	13.09	374
8	13.92	550	14.17	640	14.17	640	16.00	1790	14.59	935	17.00	2680	18.50	3650	17.50	2860	14.50	890	13.34	413	13.17	385	13.09	374
9	13.92	550	14.17	640	14.09	610	16.00	1790	14.75	1020	17.25	2865	18.34	3520	17.50	2860	14.50	890	13.25	398	13.17	385	13.09	374
10	13.92	550	14.17	640	14.09	610	15.92	1730	15.00	1160	17.50	2865	18.00	3390	17.34	2740	14.50	890	13.25	398	13.17	385	13.09	374
11	13.92	550	14.17	640	14.17	640	15.92	1730	16.00	1790	17.50	3050	17.84	3250	17.17	2740	14.42	850	13.17	385	13.17	385	13.00	365
12	13.92	550	14.09	610	14.17	640	15.84	1680	16.00	1790	17.75	3050	17.50	3120	17.17	2740	14.42	850	13.25	398	13.17	385	13.00	365
13	13.92	550	14.09	610	14.25	665	15.67	1560	15.75	1620	17.75	3050	17.50	2865	16.67	2260	14.34	810	13.25	398	13.17	385	13.00	365
14	13.92	550	14.17	640	14.17	640	15.50	1460	16.00	1790	18.00	3250	17.25	2865	16.67	2260	14.34	810	13.25	398	13.17	385	13.00	365
15	13.92	550	14.09	610	14.09	610	15.67	1560	15.75	1620	18.25	3450	17.34	2620	16.50	2140	14.34	810	13.25	398	13.17	385	13.09	365
16	13.92	550	14.09	610	14.09	610	15.50	1460	15.50	1460	18.50	3650	17.50	2680	16.34	2030	14.34	810	13.25	398	13.17	385	13.17	374
17	13.84	525	14.09	610	14.09	610	15.50	1460	15.50	1460	18.67	3790	17.50	2680	16.67	2260	14.34	810	13.25	398	13.17	385	13.25	385
18	13.84	525	14.00	580	14.09	610	15.17	1260	15.25	1310	18.67	3790	17.25	2740	16.67	2260	14.25	765	13.25	398	13.17	385	13.34	398
19	13.84	525	14.00	580	14.09	610	14.84	1060	15.25	1310	18.84	3790	17.00	2865	16.42	2080	14.34	810	13.17	385	13.13	380	13.34	413
20	14.17	640	14.09	610	14.00	580	14.67	975	15.00	1160	18.50	3920	17.00	2680	16.25	1960	14.25	765	13.17	385	13.13	380	13.34	413
21	14.00	580	14.09	610	14.00	580	14.67	975	15.00	1160	19.00	4050	17.00	2490	16.25	1960	14.34	810	13.17	385	13.13	380	13.34	413
22	14.00	580	14.09	610	14.75	865	14.58	930	14.50	890	19.00	4050	17.00	2490	16.17	1910	14.25	765	13.17	385	13.13	380	13.42	430
23	13.92	550	14.09	610	15.09	1040	14.50	890	14.00	660	19.34	4340	17.00	2490	16.00	1790	14.25	765	13.17	385	13.13	380	13.42	430
24	13.92	550	14.09	610	15.09	1040	14.50	890	14.00	660	19.50	4470	17.00	2490	16.00	1790	14.25	765	13.17	385	13.13	380	13.42	430
25	14.00	580	14.09	610	15.00	995	14.50	890	14.00	660	19.50	4470	17.00	2490	16.25	1960	14.25	765	13.17	385	13.09	374	13.50	450
26	14.00	580	14.09	610	15.00	995	14.50	890	14.00	660	19.34	4340	17.00	2490	16.50	2140	14.25	685	13.17	385	13.09	374	13.50	450
27	14.00	580	14.09	610	15.50	1260	14.50	890	14.25	765	19.34	4470	17.00	2490	16.50	2140	14.09	640	13.17	385	13.09	374	13.59	477
28	14.34	700	14.09	610	15.25	1130	14.50	890	14.34	765	19.00	4060	17.00	2490	16.17	1910	14.00	640	13.17	385	13.09	374	13.59	477
29	14.00	580	14.09	610	15.25	1130	14.50	890	14.45	865	19.00	4050	17.00	2490	15.75	1610	14.00	600	13.17	385	13.09	374	13.59	477
30	14.34	700	14.00	580	15.75	1410			14.84	1060	19.00	4050	16.50	2140			13.92	600	13.17	385			13.59	477
31			14.09	610	16.00	1560							16.34	2030			13.84	565	13.17	385				

Monthly Discharge of Muskoka River (South Branch) at Tretheway's Falls in 1915-6

Drainage Area, 668 Square Miles

Month	Discharge in Second-feet			Discharge in Second-feet per Square Mile			Run-off
	Maximum	Minimum	Mean	Maximum	Minimum	Mean	Depth in Inches on Drainage Area
November (1915)	700	525	574	1.05	.79	.86	.96
December "	700	580	628	1.05	.87	.94	1.08
January .. (1916)	1,560	580	787	2.34	.87	1.18	1.36
February	2,140	890	1,405	3.20	1.33	2.10	2.27
March	1,790	660	1,099	2.68	.99	1.65	1.90
April	4,470	1,460	3,110	6.69	2.19	4.66	5.20
May	4,190	2,030	3,000	6.27	3.04	4.49	5.18
June	2,860	1,610	2,142	4.28	2.41	3.21	3.58
July	1,460	565	824	2.19	.84	1.23	1.42
August	565	385	426	.84	.58	.64	.74
September	385	374	382	.58	.56	.57	.64
October	477	365	401	.71	.55	.60	.69
The year	4,470	365	1,227	6.69	.55	1.84	25.02

6 II (iii)

Seguin River near Parry Sound

Location—700 feet below Mountain Dam, two miles above the highway bridge, and about seven miles above the Town of Parry Sound, Township of McDougall, Parry Sound District.

Records Available—Discharge measurements from June, 1914, to October, 1916. Daily gauge heights from August 1, 1915, to October 31, 1916.

Drainage Area—380 square miles.

Gauge—Vertical steel staff with enamelled face, graduated in feet and inches, firmly wedged in rock on left shore 200 feet below dam. Zero of gauge (elev. 8.00 feet) is referred to a bench mark (elev. 15.00 feet) painted on a large rock directly across stream from gauge.

Channel—Both banks are high, wooded and not liable to overflow. The bed of the stream is composed of rocks and boulders, slightly shifting. The current is swift, and flows through one channel at all stages.

Discharge Measurements—Made by wading with a Price current meter. During high water, measurements are made at the highway bridge at the head of Mill Lake, 2 miles below wading section.

Regulation—The dam 700 feet above gauging station causes fluctuation of river at gauge.

Winter Flow—Ice forms along the banks of river at the station during the winter months. The river is entirely covered with ice for a considerable distance above and below station.

Accuracy—Discharges for gauge heights below 10.6 feet are considered fair. Rating curve above this point not very well defined.

Observer—Percy Burnside, Parry Sound.

Discharge Measurements of Seguin River near Parry Sound in 1915-6

Date	Hydrographer	Width in Feet	Area of Section in Sq. Feet	Mean Velocity in Feet per Sec.	Gauge Height in Feet	Discharge in Sec-Feet	Discharge in Second-feet per Square Mile
1915 Dec. 14, ...	Murray, W. S....	63	538	1.23	11.61	665(a)	....
1916 Feb. 16, ...	" "	63	553	1.65	12.62	916(a)	....
Mar. 14	" "	63	364	.72	11.12	262(b)	....
April10	" "	63	551	5.00	13.00	2,857(a)	....
May 16	" "	63	516	2.65	12.39	1,369(a)	....
June 21	" "	63	494	.92	11.33	456(a)	....
July 12	" "	63	423	.64	10.87	270(a)	....
Sept. 18	" "	63	152	1.78	10.97	270(a)	....
Oct. 11	" "	91	125	1.52	10.66	190	....

(a) Measurement made at highway bridge.
(b) Ice measurement.

Daily Gage Height and Discharge of Seguin River near Parry Sound (Min Dam) for 1915-6

Drainage Area. 380 Square Miles

Day	Nov Gauge Ht. (Feet)	Nov Dis-charge (Sec-ft)	Dec Gauge Ht. (Feet)	Dec Dis-charge (Sec-ft)	Jan Gauge Ht. (Feet)	Jan Dis-charge (Sec-ft)	Feb Gauge Ht. (Feet)	Feb Dis-charge (Sec-ft)	Mar Gauge Ht. (Feet)	Mar Dis-charge (Sec-ft)	Apr Gauge Ht. (Feet)	Apr Dis-charge (Sec-ft)	May Gauge Ht. (Feet)	May Dis-charge (Sec-ft)	Jun Gauge Ht. (Feet)	Jun Dis-charge (Sec-ft)	Jul Gauge Ht. (Feet)	Jul Dis-charge (Sec-ft)	Aug Gauge Ht. (Feet)	Aug Dis-charge (Sec-ft)	Sep Gauge Ht. (Feet)	Sep Dis-charge (Sec-ft)	Oct Gauge Ht. (Feet)	Oct Dis-charge (Sec-ft)
1	11.81	840	11.76	795	11.25	448	12.91	2470	11.16	334	12.00	1010	13.50	4000	12.16	1180	11.08	361	10.58	186	10.58	186	10.50	170
2	11.91	930	11.83	855	11.16	400	12.83	2200	11.16	334	12.00	1010	13.50	4000	11.91	930	11.08	361	10.58	186	10.66	208	10.50	170
3	12.00	1010	11.93	945	11.08	361	12.83	2200	11.16	334	12.00	1010	13.75	4650	11.91	930	11.08	361	10.58	186	10.66	208	10.41	156
4	12.12	1130	12.08	1090	11.00	325	12.83	2200	11.16	334	12.08	1090	13.75	4650	12.00	1010	11.00	325	10.50	170	10.66	208	10.41	156
5	12.28	1330	12.12	1130	11.16	400	12.83	2200	11.16	334	12.16	1180	13.75	4650	11.91	930	11.00	325	10.50	170	10.66	208	10.33	145
6	12.43	1510	11.79	820	11.12	380	12.83	1970	11.16	334	12.00	1010	13.16	4650	11.85	855	11.08	361	10.50	170	10.66	208	10.33	145
7	12.43	1510	11.54	630	11.16	400	12.91	1840	11.20	343	12.00	1010	13.50	4000	11.75	785	11.08	361	10.50	170	10.75	235	10.33	145
8	12.56	1710	11.41	540	11.29	470	12.83	1470	11.25	370	12.00	1010	13.16	3120	11.66	715	11.00	325	10.50	170	10.83	260	10.33	145
9	12.58	1750	11.39	530	11.00	325	12.75	170	11.25	370	12.50	1610	13.08	2910	11.58	655	10.83	260	10.50	157	10.83	260	10.33	145
10	12.82	2240	11.50	600	10.83	260	12.91	1290	11.25	325	12.50	2080	13.00	2700	11.58	655	10.91	289	10.41	170	10.83	260	10.41	156
11	11.94	955	11.62	685	10.66	208	12.66	1110	11.08	285	12.75	2700	13.00	2700	11.62	685	10.91	289	10.50	170	10.91	289	10.50	156
12	11.71	755	11.77	805	10.41	157	12.83	1230	11.08	305	13.00	2700	12.50	1610	11.58	655	11.00	325	10.50	170	10.91	289	10.50	170
13	11.45	565	11.61	715	10.33	144	12.91	1350	11.00	305	13.00	2700	12.25	1290	11.62	685	11.00	325	10.58	196	11.00	325	10.54	170
14	11.28	464	11.61	680	10.25	135	12.83	144	11.00	268	13.16	3120	12.25	1290	11.66	715	11.00	325	10.66	208	11.00	325	10.58	178
15	11.47	580	11.58	655	10.50	180	12.75	1010	11.00	250	13.25	3350	12.25	1290	11.58	655	10.91	289	10.66	208	11.00	325	10.58	186
16	11.75	785	11.50	600	10.66	208	11.91	170	11.00	250	13.00	2700	12.33	1390	11.58	655	10.83	260	10.58	186	11.00	325	10.66	186
17	11.62	685	11.50	600	10.83	260	12.62	920	11.00	250	13.00	2700	12.33	1390	11.53	493	10.75	235	10.58	186	11.00	325	10.75	208
18	11.22	431	11.50	600	10.03	26	12.16	535	11.00	250	13.00	2700	12.15	1290	11.33	540	10.66	208	10.50	170	11.00	325	10.83	235
19	11.12	380	11.50	600	10.91	289	12.04	535	11.00	250	13.00	2700	12.25	1290	11.41	540	10.58	186	10.41	157	11.00	325	11.00	260
20	11.00	325	11.41	540	10.96	309	12.04	420	11.08	274	13.00	2700	12.25	1180	11.41	540	10.58	186	10.33	144	11.00	260	11.16	325
21	11.08	261	11.41	540	10.92	293	11.83	420	11.08	285	13.00	2700	12.16	1180	11.41	493					11.00	170	11.41	400
22	11.24	442	11.37	515	11.33	325	11.58	370	11.12	325	13.00	2700	12.08	1090	11.33	448					10.50		11.58	540
23	11.58	730	11.25	448	11.33	493	11.50	285	11.16	325	13.00	2910	12.08	1090	11.25	400							11.75	655
24	11.54	630	11.16	400	11.58	655	11.54	285	11.41	400	13.08	2910	12.12	1120	11.16	400							11.91	785
25	11.41	540	11.29	470	11.83	855	11.50	325	11.50	540	13.08	2910	12.12	1180									12.08	930
26	11.77	805	11.42	550	11.91	930	11.58	325	11.50	600	13.08	2910	12.16	1180									12.08	1090
27	11.16	400	11.50	600	12.00	1010	11.58	325	11.58	475	13.16	3120	12.16	1180					10.41	157	11.00	260	12.08	1090
28	11.46	575	11.54	630	12.16	1180	11.41	475	11.58	655	13.16	3120	12.16	1180			10.58	186	10.33	144	10.83	260	12.08	1090
29	11.56	640	11.50	600	12.25	1290	11.46	325	11.58	655	13.25	3350	12.00	1010			10.58	186	10.41	157	10.58	186	12.08	1090
30	11.66	715	11.41	540	12.41	1480	11.37	464	11.66	715	13.50	4000	12.16	1180	11.16	400	10.58	170	10.50	170	10.50	170	12.08	1090
31			11.32	487	12.50	1610			11.91	930			12.16	1180			10.58	178	10.54	178			12.08	1090

Monthly Discharge of Seguin River near Parry Sound for 1915-6

Drainage Area, 380 Square Miles

Month.	Discharge in Second-feet			Discharge in Second-feet per Square Mile			Run-off
	Maximum	Minimum	Mean	Maximum	Minimum	Mean	Depth in Inches on Drainage Area.
November (1915)	2,240	325	857	5.89	.86	2.26	2.52
December "	1,130	400	651	2.97	1.05	1.71	1.97
January (1916)	1,610	185	517	4.24	.86	1.36	1.57
February	2,470	285	1,005	6.50	.75	2.64	2.85
March..........	930	250	380	2.45	.66	1.00	1.15
April	4,000	1,010	2,370	10.53	2.66	6.24	6.96
May	4,650	1,010	2,198	12.24	2.66	5.78	6.66
June	1,180	400	677	3.11	1.05	1.78	1.99
July............"	361	186	272	.95	.49	.72	.83
August.........	208	144	177	.55	.38	.47	.54
September......;	325	170	272	.86	.45	.72	.80
October	1,090	156	375	2.87	.41	.99	1.14
The year........	4,650	135	809	12.24	.36	2.13	28.99

South River near Powassan

Location—At highway bridge known as Healey's Bridge, about 2½ miles north-west of the Town of Powassan, on lot 21, concession 13, Township of Himsworth, District of Parry Sound.

Records Available—Discharge measurements from March, 1912, to October, 1916. Daily gauge heights from March 11, 1914, to October 31. 1916.

Drainage Area—294 square miles.

Gauge—Vertical steel staff with enamelled face, graduated in feet and inches, which was removed from old bridge and located on the north-west corner of the left abutment of the new Gough's highway bridge, about one mile below gauging station. Zero of gauge (elev. 23.00) is referred to bench mark (elev. 56.15) painted on a rock on the top corner of barn foundation known as Gough's barn, about 350 feet from gauge.

Channel—Straight for about 200 feet above and 1,500 feet below the gauging station. Both banks are high and not liable to overflow. The bed of the stream consists of clay and boulders, slightly shifting. The current is moderate.

Discharge Measurements—Made from Healey's highway bridge during high water, and, during low water periods, by wading 100 feet above bridge.

Control—About 5 miles below gauging station there is a dam used by the Nipissing Power Company plant. There is a two-foot fall 3 miles below section.

Winter Flow—During the winter months measurements are made through ice to determine the winter flow. The relation of gauge height to discharge is seriously affected by ice.

Accuracy—The rating curve is fairly well defined. Discharges for open water period are considered good. Measurements are made of flow of Genesee Creek entering between section. and gauge.

Observer—Owen Gough, Powassan.

Remarks—The old Gough's Bridge was replaced in April, 1915, by a new bridge 150 feet upstream.

Discharge Measurements of South River near Powassan in 1915-6

Date	Hydrographer	Width in Feet	Area of Section in Sq. Feet	Mean Velocity in Feet per Sec.	Gauge Height in Feet	Discharge in Sec-Feet	Discharge in Second-feet per Square Mile
1915							
Nov. 29....	Murray,W. S....	111	421	1.17	25.80	493	....
1916							
Jan. 15....	''	70	132	1.27	24.83	168 (a)	....
Feb. 11....	''	74	201	1.65	26.02	333 (b)	....
April 7....	''	120	1,052	1.48	31.08	1,567 (c)	....
'' 12....	''	125	809	1.60	28.91	1,295 (c)	....
May 8....	'	115	702	1.42	28.33	998 (d)	....
June 26....	''	110	385	.84	25.66	322	....
Aug. 18....	''	56	89	.90	23.83	81	....

(a) Measurement made on ice at wading section. Water on ice.
(b) Measurement made on ice at wading section.
(c) Ice broken up but not out of river. -
(d) Logs in stream.

Daily Gauge Height and Discharge of South River near Powassan for 1915-6

Drainage Area, 294 Square Miles

Day	November Gauge Ht. (Feet)	November Dis-charge (Sec-ft)	December Gauge Ht. (Feet)	December Dis-charge (Sec-ft)	January Gauge Ht. (Feet)	January Dis-charge (Sec-ft)	February Gauge Ht. (Feet)	February Dis-charge (Sec-ft)	March Gauge Ht. (Feet)	March Dis-charge (Sec-ft)	April Gauge Ht. (Feet)	April Dis-charge (Sec-ft)	May Gauge Ht. (Feet)	May Dis-charge (Sec-ft)	June Gauge Ht. (Feet)	June Dis-charge (Sec-ft)	July Gauge Ht. (Feet)	July Dis-charge (Sec-ft)	August Gauge Ht. (Feet)	August Dis-charge (Sec-ft)	September Gauge Ht. (Feet)	September Dis-charge (Sec-ft)	October Gauge Ht. (Feet)	October Dis-charge (Sec-ft)
1	24.95	256	25.83	421	24.20	105	27.79	750	25.00	170	33.58	4050	28.87	1300	26.80	645	25.16	291	23.70	81	23.70	81	25.54	363
2	24.70	216	25.70	395	24.29	117	27.54	695	25.08	178	33.95	4270	30.20	2020	26.58	590	24.95	256	23.66	76	24.41	172	25.21	300
3	24.70	216	25.54	362	24.33	113	27.29	570	25.00	178	32.45	3370	29.74	1740	26.41	550	24.91	250	23.66	76	24.83	237	24.91	250
4	24.66	210	25.41	337	24.16	105	26.79	525	25.00	178	31.87	3030	29.28	1490	26.29	520	24.91	250	23.70	81	24.70	216	24.79	230
5	24.79	230	25.41	337	24.12	105	26.75	500	24.91	163	31.37	2720	28.91	1310	26.16	490	24.83	237	23.75	87	25.33	322	24.52	203
6	24.95	256	25.37	329	24.37	123	26.58	479	24.91	163	31.00	2500	28.66	1210	26.04	466	24.70	216	23.66	76	26.08	475	24.50	185
7	25.00	264	25.37	329	24.45	149	26.50	446	24.91	163	30.03	2170	28.50	1150	25.95	446	24.70	216	23.70	81	25.87	430	24.46	179
8	24.87	243	25.29	314	24.54	156	26.33	415	24.83	163	29.74	1740	28.29	1080	25.83	421	24.66	210	23.87	101	25.41	337	24.41	172
9	24.83	237	25.29	314	24.41	143	26.25	375	24.83	163	29.29	1600	27.95	965	25.91	438	24.66	210	23.91	106	25.16	291	24.33	161
10	24.25	150	25.25	306	24.41	143	26.16	345	24.91	163	29.04	1370	27.66	880	25.95	446	24.58	197	24.00	117	24.83	237	24.33	161
11	24.70	216	25.16	291	24.45	130	26.08	335	24.91	163	28.95	1330	27.83	930	26.00	457	24.54	191	24.20	143	24.66	210	24.29	155
12	25.04	271	25.00	264	24.45	136	25.91	320	24.91	163	28.99	1350	27.83	930	25.78	411	24.50	185	24.04	122	24.37	191	24.25	150
13	25.41	336	25.00	264	24.54	143	25.83	307	25.08	163	29.54	1630	27.62	805	25.45	345	24.66	210	23.91	106	24.29	166	24.33	161
14	25.37	330	25.00	240	24.66	149	25.83	295	24.75	163	29.95	1870	27.29	775	25.16	291	24.45	178	23.83	97	24.29	155	24.33	269
15	25.25	307	24.91	216	24.79	166	25.70	281	25.08	163	31.08	2550	27.20	750	25.12	284	24.04	122	23.91	122	24.16	145	25.03	307
16	25.25	307	24.91	216	24.79	170	25.58	264	24.87	170	31.00	2500	27.16	740	25.24	306	23.91	106	23.83	106	24.04	138	25.25	322
17	25.25	307	24.83	208	24.83	178	25.58	264	24.83	170	31.00	2500	27.49	830	25.87	430	23.87	101	23.79	97	24.04	122	25.58	371
18	25.12	284	24.83	208	24.75	185	25.50	256	24.87	178	30.85	2470	27.74	900	26.00	457	24.08	127	23.79	91	24.00	117	26.00	457
19	25.08	278	24.83	208	24.75	195	25.41	248	24.91	188	31.00	2170	27.95	965	26.16	466	24.08	127	23.66	76	24.04	122	25.91	438
20	25.33	322	24.83	208	24.75	200	25.41	240	24.75	200	30.00	1900	28.33	1090	26.16	492	24.08	127	23.66	76	24.58	197	26.95	685
21	25.33	322	24.75	193	24.83	865	25.33	232	24.75	216	30.00	1720	27.70	899	26.00	466	24.04	122	23.66	76	24.83	203	27.75	905
22	25.45	345	24.75	193	27.62	1010	25.33	224	24.83	216	30.12	1970	27.54	840	26.00	457	24.00	117	23.66	76	24.62	203	28.41	1120
23	25.37	329	24.75	193	28.08	855	25.25	216	24.83	237	31.21	2190	27.37	795	25.70	430	24.00	117	23.66	76	24.54	191	28.08	1010
24	25.33	322	24.75	193	27.58	805	25.25	200	24.95	237	31.03	2520	27.12	725	25.75	405	24.00	117	23.66	76	24.66	210	27.79	915
25	25.37	329	24.75	193	27.41	855	25.25	185	25.33	256	30.49	2190	26.95	685	25.75	405	24.00	117	23.66	76	24.79	230	27.62	865
26	25.29	314	24.75	193	27.58	785	25.08	185	27.33	322	30.08	1950	26.70	620	25.66	387	23.95	106	23.66	76	24.87	243	27.87	940
27	25.37	329	24.75	193	27.33	845	25.08	185	28.43	785	29.58	1660	27.12	785	25.66	387	23.91	101	23.63	73	24.75	224	28.00	980
28	25.62	379	24.66	193	28.00	845	25.08	185	30.58	2250	29.29	1500	27.33	785	25.62	405	23.87	97	23.62	71	24.79	230	27.96	970
29	25.79	413	24.54	136	28.25	920	26.08	185	30.58		29.04	1370	27.16	740	25.62	379	23.83	97	23.66	76	25.41	337	27.71	895
30	25.91	438	24.20	105	28.08	905			32.99	3690	28.74	1250	27.33	740	25.45	345	23.83	97	23.62	97	25.79	413	27.33	785
31					27.95	845							27.12	725			23.80	93	23.66	76			27.29	775

Monthly Discharge of South River near Powassan for 1915-6

Drainage Area, 294 Square Miles

Month	Discharge in Second-feet			Discharge in Second-feet per Square Mile			Run-off
	Maximum	Minimum	Mean	Maximum	Minimum	Mean	Depth in Inches on Drainage Area
November .(1915)	438	150	293	1.49	.51	1.00	1.12
December "	421	105	246	1.43	.36	.84	.97
January ..(1916)	1,010	105	382	3.43	.36	1.30	1.50
February	750	185	335	2.55	.63	1.14	1.23
March	3,690	163	415	12.55	.55	1.41	1.63
April	4,270	1,250	2,183	14.52	4.25	7.43	8.29
May	2,020	620	983	6.87	2.11	3.34	3.85
June	645	284	434	2.19	.97	1.48	1.65
July	291	93	161	.99	.32	.55	.63
August	155	71	89	.53	.24	.30	.35
September	475	81	229	1.62	.28	.78	.87
October	1,120	150	506	3.81	.51	1.72	1.98
The year	4,270	71	519	14.52	.24	1.77	24.09

Spanish River at Espanola

Location—At highway bridge, about 200 yards below Espanola Falls and about the same distance below the Spanish River Pulp and Paper Mills, in the Town of Espanola, Township of Merritt, Sudbury District.

Records Available—Discharge measurements from March, 1914, to October, 1916. Daily gauge heights from May 6, 1915, to October 31, 1916.

Drainage Area—4,490 square miles.

Gauge—Vertical steel staff with enamelled face, graduated in feet and inches, fastened to pile near left abutment on upstream side of bridge. Zero of gauge (elev. 19.00 feet) is referred to bench mark (elev. 25.38 feet) located on top of nose of left abutment.

Channel—Above the station the water from the Falls and Power House flows into a pool about 700 feet wide and then narrows down to 225 feet at the bridge, thence flowing straight for about 1,000 feet. Both banks are high, rocky, wooded, and will not overflow. The bed of the stream is composed of clay and boulders, practically permanent. The current is fast, one channel existing at low stages. At high stages the stream flows through two channels, separated by the centre pier of the bridge.

Discharge Measurements—Made from highway bridge with a Price current meter. Occasional check measurements are made at Webbwood bridge.

Regulation—The paper plant uses all the water coming down the river at low stages during the summer, discharging through the tail race and past the section. The river is used throughout the spring and summer for log driving.

Winter Flow—Ice forms about one mile below the station, but remains open at the gauging section during the entire year.

Accuracy—Conditions at station are not very favorable for making accurate discharge measurements. The discharge relation is affected by logs during the log driving period. As there are not sufficient records available to compute discharges for that period, the open water rating curve was assumed applicable.

Observer—Thos. Lynch, Espanola.

Discharge Measurements of Spanish River at Espanola in 1915-6

Date	Hydrographer	Width in Feet	Area of Section in Sq. Feet	Mean Velocity in Feet per Sec.	Gauge Height in Feet	Discharge in Sec-Feet	Discharge in Second-feet per Square Mile
1915							
Nov. 17....	Murray, W. S..	228	3,116	1.69	23.56	5,279	....
Dec. 7....	"	228	3,493	2.21	25.25	2,710	....
1916							
Jan. 12...	"	220	2,960	1.18	22.91	3,484 (a)	....
Feb. 9....	"	217	2,619	.93	21.58	2,424 (b)	....
Mar. 9...	"	214	2,831	1.09	22.41	3,087 (c)	....
Apr. 25...	"	228	7,233	4.08	37.84	29,503	....
May 30....	"	228	3,840	2.66	26.75	10,231 (d)	....
June 7...	"	234	3,543	1.77	24.16	6,270 (e)	....
Aug. 24....	"	198	2,681	1.07	22.00	2,851	....
" 24....	"	212	3,205	.80	22.00	2,575 (e)	....
Oct. 18....	"	246	2,599	1.06	21.37	2,750	....
" 18....	"	193	3,026	.85	21.35	2,504 (e)	....

(a) Ice on river 300 ft. below section.
(b) Side and back current at centre pier. Ice on part of section.
(c) Ice on part of section.
(d) Logs on control.
(e) Reading taken at Webbwood.

Daily Gauge Height and Discharge of Spanish River at Espanola for 1915-6

Drainage Area 4,490 Square Miles

Day	November Gauge Ht. (Feet)	November Dis-charge (Sec-ft)	December Gauge Ht.	December Dis-charge	January Gauge Ht.	January Dis-charge	February Gauge Ht.	February Dis-charge	March Gauge Ht.	March Dis-charge	April Gauge Ht.	April Dis-charge	May Gauge Ht.	May Dis-charge	June Gauge Ht.	June Dis-charge	July Gauge Ht.	July Dis-charge	August Gauge Ht.	August Dis-charge	September Gauge Ht.	September Dis-charge	October Gauge Ht.	October Dis-charge
1	23.29	4580	25.16	7560	23.16	4390	22.33	3280	22.50	3500	27.95	12220	34.83	24090	26.28	9380	25.98	8870	21.75	2550	21.85	2670	21.08	1750
2	22.66	3710	25.12	7490	23.08	4270	22.31	3250	22.41	3380	29.75	15280	34.00	22600	25.90	8740	26.08	9040	21.71	2500	21.83	2650	21.50	2250
3	22.50	3500	25.16	7560	23.25	4520	22.25	3180	22.35	3300	30.83	17110	33.83	22290	25.83	8630	25.66	8360	22.00	2850	21.79	2600	21.46	2200
4	22.27	3200	25.33	7830	22.83	3930	22.20	3110	21.95	3180	30.62	16750	33.33	21390	25.17	7760	25.38	7910	22.08	2950	21.83	2600	21.41	2140
5	22.46	3450	25.08	7430	23.00	4150	22.18	3080	21.12	1790	31.08	17540	33.00	20800	24.41	6360	24.87	7090	22.08	2950	21.83	2650	21.45	2190
6	22.39	3360	25.47	8050	23.25	4060	21.75	2550	22.58	3600	31.25	17820	32.75	20370	23.83	5430	24.58	6630	22.15	3040	21.91	2650	21.50	2250
7	22.25	3180	25.41	7960	23.08	3960	21.66	2440	22.83	3930	31.35	17960	32.50	19950	24.50	6500	24.08	5830	21.91	2740	21.95	2740	21.37	2090
8	22.80	3890	25.39	7920	22.91	3760	21.62	2390	22.54	3550	31.33	17960	32.50	19950	24.39	6320	23.91	5560	22.04	2900	22.12	2790	21.03	1690
9	23.31	4620	24.73	6870	22.91	3700	21.60	2370	22.29	3230	31.16	17670	32.00	19100	24.50	6500	23.58	5030	22.04	2900	22.08	3010	20.87	1510
10	23.27	4560	24.54	6560	22.91	3560	21.56	2320	22.12	3010	33.33	21390	31.50	18250	24.54	6560	23.58	5030	22.06	2930	21.91	2950	21.08	1750
11	23.35	4680	24.42	6370	22.83	3500	21.45	2190	21.98	2830	29.83	15410	31.50	18250	24.35	6260	23.75	5300	22.00	2850	22.15	2740	21.41	2140
12	23.35	4680	24.68	6790	22.91	3570	21.33	2050	20.10	755	29.74	15260	30.95	17740	25.62	8290	23.70	5220	22.08	2930	22.25	2650	21.41	2140
13	24.00	5700	24.54	6560	22.83	3340	20.66	1290	21.54	2300	29.45	14760	30.75	16980	25.29	7760	23.52	4930	22.06	2900	20.25	3040	21.16	1840
14	23.47	4860	24.43	6390	22.75	3300	21.35	2070	21.87	2690	29.70	15190	29.00	14000	25.20	7620	23.33	4640	22.06	2900	21.62	3180	21.25	1950
15	23.54	4960	24.54	6560	22.66	3270	21.33	2050	22.00	2850	29.70	15190	30.00	15700	25.16	7560	23.22	4480	22.04	2790	21.58	3180	21.66	2440
16	23.56	5000	24.45	6420	22.64	3240	21.27	1970	22.16	2900	31.16	17670	30.00	15700	24.97	7250	23.08	4270	21.95	2740	21.66	885	21.95	2790
17	23.54	4960	24.31	6200	22.62	3210	21.25	1950	22.04	2690	31.16	17670	29.60	15020	24.97	7250	22.83	3930	21.91	2740	21.66	2390	21.74	2540
18	23.43	4800	24.12	5890	22.54	3180	21.25	1950	21.87	2600	33.50	21700	29.00	14000	25.45	8020	22.54	3550	21.91	2740	21.50	2350	21.16	1840
19	23.33	4530	24.12	5890	22.58	3180	21.18	1870	20.25	885	33.75	22150	29.00	14000	25.45	8020	22.37	3330	21.87	2690	21.41	2440	21.00	1650
20	23.83	5430	24.00	5700	22.56	3180	20.54	1170	21.79	2600	34.00	22600	29.00	14000	26.40	9580	22.18	3080	21.95	2790	21.41	2440	21.91	2740
21	23.41	4760	23.91	5560	22.33	3280	21.75	2550	21.95	2790	34.00	22600	28.75	13580	27.12	10800	22.04	2900	22.00	2850	21.50	2250	21.96	2800
22	24.00	5700	23.83	5430	22.33	3930	21.81	2620	22.00	2850	34.16	22980	28.00	12300	27.12	10800	21.91	2740	21.91	2740	21.46	2250	21.91	2050
23	23.66	5160	23.81	5430	22.89	4010	22.22	3140	21.91	2900	34.33	23190	27.75	11880	28.41	13000	21.91	2740	21.87	2740	22.00	2200	23.50	4900
24	23.21	4460	23.54	5400	23.41	4760	22.29	3230	20.33	960	34.58	23640	27.50	11450	28.00	12300	22.00	2850	21.83	2690	21.41	2140	21.83	2650
25	23.35	4680	22.75	4960	23.29	4590	22.22	3140	22.33	3280	34.75	23950	26.83	10310	27.79	11940	22.00	2850	21.83	2650	21.41	2140	22.33	3280
26	23.45	4820	23.08	3820	23.16	4390	22.22	3140	23.72	5250	35.50	25300	25.75	8500	27.74	11860	22.08	2950	21.89	2720	23.50		23.91	5560
27	23.75	5300	23.16	4270	23.16	4390	22.08	2950	22.95	4080	35.66	25590	25.25	7700	27.54	11520	22.29	3230	21.83	2650	23.33		24.00	5700
28	23.91	5560	23.12	4390	23.12	4330	22.50	3500	23.62	5090	35.16	24690	25.00	7300	27.20	10940	22.29	3230			23.91		23.91	5560
29	25.50	8100	23.12	4330	22.95	4080	22.58	3600	25.37	7890	35.00	24400	26.50	9750	26.60	9920	22.45	3440			24.00		24.83	7160
30	25.16	7560	23.21	4460	22.90	4020					35.50	25300	26.66	10020	26.74	10160	22.16	3060			23.91		24.33	7030
31				4020	22.90	4020							26.64	9990										6230

Monthly Discharge of Spanish River at Espanola for 1915-6

Drainage Area. 4,490 Square Miles

Month	Discharge in Second-feet			Discharge in Second-feet per Square Mile			Run-off
	Maximum	Minimum	Mean	Maximum	Minimum	Mean	Depth in Inches on Drainage Area
November (1915)	8,100	3,180	4,793	1.80	.71	1.07	1.19
December " "	8,050	3,820	6,091	1.79	.85	1.36	1.57
January...(1916)	4,760	3,180	3,860	1.06	.71	.86	.99
February	3,600	1,170	2,566	.80	.26	.57	.61
March..........	7,890	755	3,116	1.76	.17	.69	.80
April...........	25,590	12,220	19,854	5.70	2.72	4.42	4.93
May	24,090	7,300	15,227	5.37	1.63	3.39	3.91
June	13,000	5,430	8,846	2.90	1.21	1.97	2.20
July...........	9,040	2,740	4,675	2.01	.61	1.04	1.20
August.........	3,040	2,500	2,803	.68	.56	.62	.71
September......	3,180	885	2,498	.71	.20	.56	.62
October.........	7,160	1,510	3,058	1.59	.33	.68	.78
The year	25,590	885	6,442	5.70	.20	1.43	19.46

Sturgeon River at Smoky Falls

Location—At the highway bridge at Smoky Falls Post Office, and two miles above the Smoky Falls, Township of Springer, Nipissing District.

Records Available—Discharge measurements, August, 1912, to October, 1916. Daily gauge heights, January 12 to 31, 1914, and March 15, 1914, to October 31, 1916.

Drainage Area—2,250 square miles.

Gauge—Vertical steel staff with enamelled face, graduated in feet and inches, and attached to a wooden pile on the right, upstream side of the bridge. The zero on the gauge (elevation 32.00) is referred to a bench mark (elevation 53.47) painted on a rock on the right bank of the river, about 175 feet above the bridge.

Channel—Straight for about 700 feet above and about 1 mile below the station. The banks are fairly high, clean, sandy and not liable to overflow. The bed of the stream is composed of clay and sand, slightly shifting. The current is fast and smooth, flowing through six channels, formed by bridge piers and abutments.

Discharge Measurements—Made from highway bridge with a Price current meter.

Regulation—Dams above are used for power and log driving purposes.

Winter Flow—During the winter months the river is covered with ice, and measurements are made through the ice to determine the winter discharge. The relation of gauge height to discharge is seriously affected by ice.

Accuracy—The open water rating curve is fairly well defined. The relation of gauge height to discharge is affected during the log-driving season.

Observer—A. Pineault, Smoky Falls.

Discharge Measurements of Sturgeon River at Smoky Falls in 1915-6

Date	Hydrographer	Width in Feet	Area of Section in Sq. Feet	Mean Velocity in Feet per Sec.	Gauge Height in Feet	Discharge in Sec-Feet	Discharge in Second-feet per Square Mile
1915							
Dec. 1....	Murray, W. S ..	210	2,293	1.84	35.58	4,208	....
1916							
Jan. 27....	" "	210	1,663	1.10	33.74	1,843 (a)	....
Feb. 25....	" "	205	1,622	1.18	33.91	1,913 (a)	....
Mar. 24...	" "	205	1,538	1.29	34.08	1,979 (a)	....
May 5....	" "	210	3,410	4.70	40.91	16,027	....

(a) Ice measurement.

Daily Gauge Height and Discharge of Sturgeon River at Smoky Falls for 1915-6

Drainage Area 2,250 Square Miles

Day	November Gauge Ht. (Feet)	November Discharge (Sec-ft.)	December Gauge Ht.	December Discharge	January Gauge Ht.	January Discharge	February Gauge Ht.	February Discharge	March Gauge Ht.	March Discharge	April Gauge Ht.	April Discharge	May Gauge Ht.	May Discharge	June Gauge Ht.	June Discharge	July Gauge Ht.	July Discharge	August Gauge Ht.	August Discharge	September Gauge Ht.	September Discharge	October Gauge Ht.	October Discharge
1	34.00	2090	35.58	4380	33.89	1970	33.83	1905	34.08	2185	36.12	5255	41.12	15620	36.66	6170	34.83	3220	33.74	1800	33.20	1310	32.71	975
2	34.00	2090	35.58	4480	33.79	1860	33.75	1815	34.08	2185	36.62	6105	41.25	15930	36.45	5820	34.83	3220	33.45	1510	33.08	1210	32.87	1060
3	34.00	2090	35.45	4170	33.75	1815	33.75	1815	34.08	2185	36.54	5970	41.25	15930	36.37	5680	34.99	3460	33.20	1310	32.79	1010	32.79	1090
4	33.91	1990	35.33	3980	33.66	1720	33.75	1815	34.08	2185	36.41	5745	41.12	15620	36.25	5480	34.95	3400	33.29	1380	32.70	970	32.91	1090
5	33.83	1905	35.54	4315	33.79	1860	33.75	1815	34.08	2185	36.41	5745	40.91	15110	36.25	5480	34.70	3020	33.50	1560	33.10	1280	32.91	1090
6	33.70	1760	35.41	4105	33.75	1815	33.83	1905	34.08	2185	36.33	5610	40.50	14130	36.04	5120	34.58	2850	33.29	1380	33.16	1230	33.00	1150
7	33.58	1640	35.41	4105	33.66	1720	33.83	1905	34.08	2185	36.42	5765	40.33	13720	35.95	4970	34.58	2850	33.41	1480	33.08	1210	32.91	1120
8	33.50	1560	35.21	3785	33.58	1640	33.83	1905	34.08	2185	36.33	5610	40.16	13310	35.91	4910	34.70	3020	33.62	1680	33.03	1170	32.95	1090
9	33.50	1560	35.00	3470	33.58	1640	33.75	1815	34.16	2280	36.33	5610	40.16	13310	35.87	4840	34.54	2800	33.95	2030	33.00	1150	32.91	1090
10	33.41	1480	34.83	3215	33.58	1640	33.75	1815	34.16	2280	36.33	5610	39.91	12710	35.83	4780	34.45	2670	33.99	2080	32.70	970	32.91	1090
11	33.41	1480	34.66	2965	33.58	1640	33.83	1905	34.08	2185	36.41	5745	39.58	11940	35.83	4780	34.41	2610	33.58	1640	32.58	910	32.79	1020
12	33.54	1600	33.54	2795	33.58	1640	33.75	1815	34.00	2090	36.62	6105	39.33	11380	35.83	4780	34.50	2740	33.54	1600	32.50	870	32.81	1030
13	33.70	1760	34.45	2680	33.58	1640	33.95	2035	34.00	2090	37.29	7300	39.08	10840	35.91	4910	34.41	2610	33.54	1600	32.50	870	32.83	1040
14	33.95	2035	34.41	2615	33.58	1640	34.00	2090	34.00	2090	37.45	7605	38.95	10560	36.20	5390	34.29	2450	33.58	1640	32.54	890	32.87	1060
15	33.95	2035	34.41	2615	33.50	1560	34.00	2090	33.91	1990	37.75	8175	38.41	9450	35.91	4910	34.25	2400	33.50	1560	32.62	930	32.91	1090
16	33.83	1905	34.41	2615	33.50	1560	33.91	1990	33.91	1990	37.70	8080	38.87	10400	35.83	4780	34.12	2230	33.62	1680	32.87	1060	32.91	1090
17	33.79	1860	34.37	2560	33.41	1480	33.91	1990	33.91	1990	37.91	8480	38.54	9710	35.75	4650	34.08	2190	33.50	1560	33.04	1180	33.12	1250
18	33.66	1720	34.33	2500	33.41	1480	33.91	1990	33.91	1990	38.37	9370	38.37	9470	35.87	4840	33.91	1990	33.41	1410	33.08	1210	33.16	1280
19	33.66	1720	34.33	2500	33.41	1480	33.91	1990	33.91	1990	37.95	8660	38.12	8880	35.70	4570	33.75	1990	33.33	1450	32.91	1090	33.25	1350
20	33.87	1945	34.29	2445	33.42	1490	33.91	1990	33.91	1990	38.75	10145	37.95	8660	35.58	4610	33.66	1820	33.41	1410	32.71	1090	33.66	1720
21	34.33	2500	34.25	2395	33.54	1600	33.91	1990	33.91	1990	38.91	10480	37.87	8400	35.56	4610	33.87	1720	33.33	1460	32.66	975	34.37	2420
22	34.33	2500	34.08	2280	33.54	1600	33.83	1905	33.91	1990	39.29	11290	37.48	7660	35.66	4040	33.99	1950	33.50	1560	32.66	950	34.66	2960
23	33.79	1860	34.08	2185	33.58	1640	33.83	1905	33.83	1905	39.79	12425	37.41	7530	35.37	3910	34.03	2080	33.83	1900	32.66	950	34.66	2960
24	34.00	2090	33.83	2185	33.66	1720	33.91	1990	34.08	2185	39.91	12715	37.29	7300	35.25	3850	33.74	2130	33.54	1600	32.66	950	34.66	2960
25	34.00	2090	34.00	2090	33.66	1720	33.91	1990	34.08	2185	40.12	13220	37.16	7060	35.20	3770	33.50	1800	33.50	1560	32.66	950	34.66	2960
26	34.28	2435	34.00	2090	33.75	1815	34.04	2140	34.00	2090	40.37	13820	37.00	6670	35.16	3710	33.50	1600	33.45	1510	32.66	975	34.75	3090
27	34.95	3395	34.00	2090	33.75	1815	34.04	2140	34.04	2140	40.91	15115	36.87	6540	35.12	3650	33.41	1560	33.33	1410	32.71	995	34.83	3160
28	34.95	3395	33.91	1990	33.91	1990	34.08	2185	34.16	2280	41.08	15520	36.75	6320	35.08	3590	33.50	1560	33.16	1280	32.75	995	34.79	3220
29	35.16	3710	33.91	1990	33.75	1615			34.37	2560	41.12	15620	36.66	6170	35.04	3530	33.50	1480	33.20	1310	32.75	995	34.83	3220
30	35.45	4170	34.00	2090	33.75	1815			34.95	3395	41.08	15520	36.66	6320	35.00	3470	33.50	1680	33.04	2140	32.66	950	34.88	3220
31			33.79	1860	33.83	1905			35.41	4105			36.75	6320	34.45	2670	33.62	1680					34.83	3220

Monthly Discharge of Sturgeon River at Smoky Falls for 1915-6

Drainage Area 2,219 Square Miles

Month	Discharge in Second-feet.			Discharge in Second-feet per Square Mile			Run-off
	Maximum	Minimum	Mean	Maximum	Minimum	Mean	Depth in Inches on Drainage Area.
November (1915)	4,170	1,480	2,096	1.85	.66	.93	1.04
December "	4,380	1,860	2,815	1.95	.83	1.25	1.44
January .. (1916)	1,970	1,480	1,687	.88	.66	.75	.86
February	2,185	1,815	1,953	.97	.81	.87	.94
March..........	4,105	1,990	2,243	1.82	.88	1.00	1.15
April...........	15,620	5,255	9,153	6.94	2.34	4.07	4.54
May...........	15,930	6,170	10,224	7.08	2.74	4.54	5.23
June	6,170	2,670	4,528	2.74	1.19	2.01	2.24 .
July...........	3,460	1,480	2,355	1.54	.66	1.05	1.21
August.........	2,140	1,180	1,577	.95	.48	.70	.81
September.....	1,310	870	1,042	.58	.39	.46	.51
October.........	3,220	975	1,812	1.43	.43	.81	.93
The year	15,930	870	3,450	7.08	.39	1.53	20.83

Vermilion River near Whitefish

Location—At the old highway bridge 50 feet above the rapids, 300 feet north of C.P.R. bridge, and two miles east of the Town of Whitefish, Township of Graham, Sudbury District.

Records Available—Discharge measurements from August, 1913, to October, 1916. Daily gauge heights from June 11, 1915, to October 31, 1916.

Drainage Area—1,580 square miles.

Gauge—Vertical steel staff with enamelled face, graduated in feet and inches, attached to pile at the left abutment of old highway bridge. Zero of gauge (elev. 25.00 feet) is referred to bench mark (elev. 38.39) painted on rock on right bank 15 feet above gauging station.

Channel and Control—Straight for about 300 feet above and 700 feet below the station. Both banks are high, rocky and wooded, and not liable to overflow. Bed of stream is rocky and permanent, current is swift, two channels existing at all stages on account of the centre pier of the bridge. Log jams sometimes occur on the rapids during low flows, causing back water at the station.

Discharge Measurements—Made from old highway bridge with a Price current meter.

Winter Flow—On account of the fast current the channel at gauging station remains open during the winter months, ice forming at banks, allowance for this being made in estimates.

Accuracy—Rating curve fairly well defined between gauge heights 27.00 feet and 32.00 feet. As there are not sufficient data available for computing the discharge during the log driving period the open water curve was assumed applicable.

Observer—A. Boucher, Whitefish.

Discharge Measurements of Vermilion River near Whitefish in 1915-6

Date	Hydrographer	Width in Feet	Area of Section in Sq. Feet	Mean Velocity in Feet per Sec.	Gauge Height in Feet	Discharge in Sec–Feet	Discharge in Second-feet per Square Mile
1915							
Nov. 22	Murray, W. S..	169	853	1.97	28.35	1.685	....
Dec. 4 "	"	184	1.069	2.73	29.58	2,626(a)	....
1916							
Jan. 28 .ⱼ..	"	144	735	1.52	27.74	1,116(b)	....
Feb. 5	"	104	730	1.38	27.76	1,008(c)	....
Mar. 7	"	135	594	1.32	27.33	784(d)	....
April 13	"	196	1,397	4.40	31.26	6,139	....
May 9	"	206	1,465	5.13	31.57	7,511	....
June 8	"	188	928	2.37	28.82	2,207	....

(a) Floating ice at section.
(b) Section partly ice-covered.
(c) Section partly ice-covered and at gauge.
(d) Ice measurement.

Daily Gauge Height and Discharge of Vermilion River near Whitefish for 1915-6

Drainage Area 1,590 Square Miles

Day	Nov Gauge Ht.	Nov Dis-charge	Dec Gauge Ht.	Dec Dis-charge	Jan Gauge Ht.	Jan Dis-charge	Feb Gauge Ht.	Feb Dis-charge	Mar Gauge Ht.	Mar Dis-charge	Apr Gauge Ht.	Apr Dis-charge	May Gauge Ht.	May Dis-charge	Jun Gauge Ht.	Jun Dis-charge	Jul Gauge Ht.	Jul Dis-charge	Aug Gauge Ht.	Aug Dis-charge	Sep Gauge Ht.	Sep Dis-charge	Oct Gauge Ht.	Oct Dis-charge
1	28.16	1420	28.99	2380	27.99	1250	27.74	1025	27.49	805	27.83	1105	33.95	13120	28.78	2130	29.08	2500	27.25	635	26.16	152	26.16	152
2	28.08	1340	29.83	3580	27.91	1180	27.74	1025	27.41	745	29.66	3320	33.61	12240	28.70	2030	29.00	2390	27.08	515	26.16	152	26.16	152
3	28.16	1420	29.74	3440	27.91	1180	27.74	1025	27.41	745	30.33	4465	33.45	11820	28.43	1710	28.91	2280	26.33	186	26.16	152	26.16	152
4	28.24	1500	29.58	3200	27.91	1180	27.74	1025	27.41	745	31.16	6100	33.32	11480	28.45	1740	28.91	2280	26.75	335	26.33	186	26.16	152
5	28.25	1510	28.99	2380	27.83	1105	27.74	1025	27.41	745	31.33	6480	33.15	11040	28.45	1740	28.91	2280	26.50	220	26.50	220	26.16	152
6	28.25	1510	28.83	2185	27.83	1105	27.74	1025	27.41	745	31.49	6845	32.95	10620	28.28	1550	28.91	2280	26.50	220	26.50	220	26.16	152
7	28.29	1550	28.83	2185	27.83	1105	27.74	1025	27.41	745	31.49	6845	31.53	6940	28.20	1460	28.91	2280	26.50	220	26.50	220	26.25	170
8	28.24	1500	28.74	2080	27.74	1025	27.74	1025	27.41	745	31.49	6845	31.28	6370	29.08	2500	29.08	2500	26.50	220	26.58	252	26.25	170
9	28.24	1500	28.66	1980	27.74	1025	27.74	1025	27.41	745	31.41	6665	31.03	5820	29.08	2500	29.08	2500	26.50	220	26.58	252	26.25	170
10	28.24	1500	28.66	1980	27.74	1025	27.74	1025	27.41	745	31.33	6480	30.95	5650	29.08	2500	29.00	2390	26.41	202	26.58	252	26.25	170
11	28.24	1500	28.49	1780	27.74	1025	27.66	955	27.41	745	31.24	6280	30.78	5320	29.83	3580	28.91	2280	26.50	220	26.50	220	26.25	170
12	28.24	1500	28.41	1690	27.74	1025	27.66	955	27.41	745	31.33	6480	30.70	5170	29.75	3460	28.83	2190	26.75	335	26.58	252	26.25	170
13	28.33	1605	28.41	1690	27.74	1025	27.66	955	27.41	745	31.33	6480	30.61	5000	29.66	3320	28.83	2190	26.75	335	26.50	220	26.25	170
14	28.33	1605	28.41	1690	27.74	1025	27.66	955	27.41	745	31.49	6845	30.45	4700	29.66	3320	28.66	1980	26.66	296	26.50	220	26.33	186
15	28.33	1605	28.33	1605	27.74	1025	27.66	955	27.41	745	31.74	7425	30.28	4370	29.66	3320	28.58	1890	26.66	296	26.50	220	26.33	186
16	28.33	1605	28.33	1605	27.74	1025	27.66	955	27.41	745	31.83	7640	30.20	4220	29.66	3320	28.58	1790	26.58	252	26.33	186	26.33	186
17	28.33	1605	28.33	1605	27.74	1025	27.66	955	27.33	690	31.91	7835	29.95	3780	29.66	3320	28.50	1790	26.58	252	26.16	152	26.41	222
18	28.35	1605	28.24	1500	27.74	1025	27.66	955	27.33	690	31.91	7835	29.86	3630	29.75	3450	28.50	1790	26.50	220	26.16	136	26.58	252
19	28.35	1605	28.24	1420	27.74	1025	27.66	955	27.16	570	31.91	7835	29.78	3500	29.83	3580	28.50	1790	26.50	220	26.08	136	26.75	335
20	28.33	1605	28.16	1420	27.74	1025	27.66	955	27.16	570	31.91	7835	29.70	3380	29.91	3710	28.41	1690	26.33	186	25.91	102	26.08	136
21	28.33	1605	28.16	1420	27.74	1025	27.66	955	27.16	570	31.99	8025	29.53	3130	29.91	3710	28.41	1690	26.33	186	26.00	120	27.08	516
22	28.33	1605	28.16	1420	27.83	1105	27.58	880	27.08	515	32.66	9765	30.36	4520	29.91	3710	28.16	1420	26.33	186	26.00	120	27.25	635
23	28.33	1605	28.16	1420	27.83	1105	27.58	880	27.08	515	32.66	9765	29.28	2780	29.83	3580	28.08	1240	26.25	170	26.00	120	27.25	635
24	28.24	1500	28.16	1420	27.83	1105	27.49	805	27.08	515	34.49	14525	29.28	2780	29.83	3580	28.00	1260	26.25	170	26.00	120	27.33	690
25	28.33	1605	28.16	1500	27.83	1105	27.49	805	27.08	570	34.73	15175	29.28	2780	29.75	3450	28.00	1260	26.25	170	26.00	120	27.66	955
26	28.08	1340	28.08	1340	27.83	1105	27.49	805	27.08	570	34.36	14185	29.20	2670	29.66	3320	27.91	1180	26.25	170	26.00	120	27.66	955
27	28.33	1605	28.08	1340	27.83	1105	27.49	805	27.24	630	34.16	13665	29.03	2430	29.66	3320	27.83	1110	26.25	170	26.08	136	27.75	1030
28	28.49	1780	28.08	1340	27.83	1105	27.49	805	27.41	745	34.16	14185	28.95	2330	29.50	3090	27.75	1030	26.25	170	26.16	152	27.75	1030
29	28.74	2080	28.08	1340	27.74	1025			27.41	745	33.49	11925	28.86	2220	29.33	2850	27.91	1180	26.25	170	26.16	152	27.75	1030
30	28.83	2185	28.08	1340	27.74	1025			27.41	745	33.09	10885	28.86	2220	29.16	2610	27.75	1180	26.25	170			27.75	1030
31			27.99	1250	27.74	1025			27.74	1025			28.86	2220			27.41	745	26.25	170			27.75	1030

Monthly Discharge of Vermilion River near Whitefish for 1915-6

Drainage Area, 1,580 Square Miles

Month	Discharge in Second-feet			Discharge in Second-feet per Square Mile			Run-off
	Maximum	Minimum	Mean	Maximum	Minimum.	Mean.	Depth in Inches on Drainage Area
November (1915)	2,185	1,340	1,585	1.38	.85	1.00	1.12
December "	3,580	1,250	1,821	2.27	.79	1.15	1.33
January (1916)	1,250	1,025	1,073	-.79	.65	.68	.78
February	1,025	805	943	.65	.51	.60	.65
March	-1,025	515	696	.65	.33	.44	.51
April..........	15,175	1,105	9,024	9.60	.70	5.71	6.37
May............	13,120	2,220	5,442	8.30	1.41	3.44	3.97
June	3,710	1,460	2,915	2.35	.92	1.84	2.05
July	2,500	745	1,836	1.58	.47	1.16	1.34
August	635	170	241	.40	.11	.15	.17
September......	252	102	177	.16	.06	.11	.12
October.........	1,030	136	341	.65	.09	.22	.25
The year........	15,175	102	2,168	9.60	.06	1.37	18.65

Wanapatei River at McVittie's

Location—Along the C. N. Ry, line, twenty miles south of the Town of Sudbury, and about two miles up stream from McVittie's power house, and 300 feet above Water Falls, southeast corner of the Township of Secord, District of Sudbury (Mining Division).

Records Available—Discharge measurements from September, 1916, to October, 1916. Daily gauge heights from October 1, 1916, to October 31, 1916.

Drainage Area—1,175 square miles.

Gauge—Vertical steel staff with enamelled face, graduated in feet and inches, fastened on a 2 x 4 scantling and secured to a large tree on right shore on the cross section line. The zero of the gauge (elev: 5.00 ft.) is referred to a bench mark (elev. 11.15 feet) on top of spike riven in stump, 6½ feet downstream from initial point, right shore.

Channel—Straight for about 400 feet above and 300 feet below the station. Banks are high, rocky, and wooded, and not liable to overflow. The bed of the stream is composed of clay, practically permanent; the current is slow.

Discharge Measurements—Made from boat with a small Price current meter.

Control—During log driving periods logs may jam at the head of the falls, which is 300 feet below station. The jam may cause a back water affect at the gauging station.

Observer—J. S. McVittie, McVittie's Siding.

Discharge Measurements of Wanapitei River at McVittie's

Date	Hydrographer	Width in Feet	Area of Section in Sq. Feet	Mean Velocity in Feet per Sec.	Gauge Height in Feet	Discharge in Sec-Feet	Discharge in Second-feet per Square Mile
1916							
Sept. 8....	Murray, W. S....	142	2,195	.85	102.08	770	....
" 28....	" ..	142	2,190	.32	101.83	704	....

Wanapitei River near Wanapitei

Location—100 feet above the falls known as Timmins Chute, six miles above the Village of Wanapitei, Township of Dryden, Sudbury District.

Records Available—Monthly discharge measurements from June, 1914 to August, 1916. Daily gauge heights from August 15, 1915, to October 31, 1916.

Drainage Area—940 square miles.

Gauge—Vertical steel staff with enamelled face, graduated in feet and inches, and fastened on a 2 x 8 scantling to a large elm tree on left bank 150 feet above falls. Zero of gauge (elev. 24.00 feet) is referred to bench mark (elev. 30.00 feet) painted on top of prominent rock at brink of falls on right shore.

Channel—Straight for about 500 feet above and 100 feet below gauging station. Banks are high, rocky and wooded, and do not overflow. The bed of the stream is composed of clay and gravel, slightly shifting. The current is moderate.

Discharge Measurements—Made by boat with Price current meter. Affected by construction work August-September.

Winter Flow—River is covered with ice during the winter months, and measurements are made through ice to determine the winter discharge.

Observer—Wilfred Rioux, Wanapitei.

Discharge Measurements of Wanapitei River near Wanapitei in 1915-6

Date	Hydrographer	Width in Feet	Area of Section in Sq. Feet	Mean Velocity in Feet per Sec.	Gauge Height in Feet	Discharge in Sec–Feet	Discharge in Second-feet per Square Mile
1915 Nov. 23	Murray, W. S..	108	642	1.03	25.81	667	....
1916 Jan. 13	" "	111	562	1.25	25.75	702(a)	....
Feb. 3	" "	104	532	1.39	25.66	738(a)	....
Apr. 26	" "	143	2,207	1.68	28.75	3,704(b)	....
May 31	" "	145	1,262	3.15	30.64	3,978	....
Aug. 25	" "	112	641	1.39	25.50	894(c)	....

(a) Ice measurement.
(b) Measurement taken at C. P. R. bridge at Wanapitei.
(c) Control changed by construction of power plant three-quarter mile above section.

Daily Gauge Height and Discharge of Wanapitei River near Wanapitei for 1915-6

Drainage Area, 940 Square Miles

Day	Nov Gauge Ht. (Feet)	Nov Dis-charge (Sec-ft.)	Dec Gauge Ht. (Feet)	Dec Dis-charge (Sec-ft.)	Jan Gauge Ht. (Feet)	Jan Dis-charge (Sec-ft.)	Feb Gauge Ht. (Feet)	Feb Dis-charge (Sec-ft.)	Mar Gauge Ht. (Feet)	Mar Dis-charge (Sec-ft.)	Apr Gauge Ht. (Feet)	Apr Dis-charge (Sec-ft.)	May Gauge Ht. (Feet)	May Dis-charge (Sec-ft.)	June Gauge Ht. (Feet)	June Dis-charge (Sec-ft.)	July Gauge Ht. (Feet)	July Dis-charge (Sec-ft.)	Aug Gauge Ht. (Feet)	Aug Dis-charge (Sec-ft.)	Sep Gauge Ht. (Feet)	Sep Dis-charge (Sec-ft.)	Oct Gauge Ht. (Feet)	Oct Dis-charge (Sec-ft.)
1	25.79	700	26.12	835	25.79	700	25.75	665	25.62	625	25.42	555	31.08	4360	28.66	2280	28.60	2240	27.41	1470	25.31	520	...	...
2	25.79	700	26.08	815	25.79	700	25.75	650	25.66	650	25.50	585	31.41	4590	28.16	1930	28.71	2320	27.33	1420	25.31	520	...	...
3	25.75	685	26.00	785	25.83	715	25.66	653	25.66	650	25.02	635	31.50	4780	27.91	1770	28.91	2460	27.29	1390	25.25	498	...	...
4	25.79	700	26.00	785	25.83	715	25.81	665	25.81	710	25.79	700	31.58	4860	28.25	1990	28.93	2470	27.25	1370	25.33	525	...	...
5	25.79	700	25.95	765	26.00	785	25.75	685	25.79	700	25.79	700	31.66	4940	28.50	2170	28.93	2470	27.16	1320	25.35	535	...	...
6	25.79	700	25.95	765	25.91	750	25.75	685	25.79	700	25.79	700	31.66	4940	28.50	2170	28.93	2470	27.16	1320	25.33	525	...	...
7	25.79	700	25.95	765	25.83	715	25.75	685	25.75	685	25.83	715	31.65	4940	27.95	1790	28.25	1790	27.18	1330	25.31	520	...	...
8	25.79	700	25.95	765	25.83	715	25.75	685	25.75	685	25.83	715	31.62	4900	27.96	1800	28.25	1790	27.29	1390	25.27	505	...	...
9	26.83	715	25.95	685	25.83	715	25.75	685	25.79	700	25.83	715	31.54	4820	27.95	1790	27.83	1720	27.21	1350	25.27	505	...	...
10	26.83	715	25.58	615	25.79	700	25.75	685	25.79	700	25.91	750	31.54	4820	27.91	1770	27.81	1710	27.21	1350	25.16	466	...	...
11	25.79	700	25.58	615	25.83	715	25.75	685	25.75	685	25.91	800	31.41	4690	27.91	1770	27.75	1670	27.00	1270	25.16	466	...	...
12	25.79	700	25.54	565	25.83	715	25.66	650	25.71	670	26.04	835	31.41	4690	27.54	1540	27.66	1620	26.68	1080	25.16	466	...	...
13	25.87	715	25.70	600	25.83	685	25.66	650	25.71	670	26.12	870	31.29	4570	27.12	1290	27.64	1600	26.58	1030	25.16	466	...	...
14	25.83	635	25.70	645	25.75	685	25.66	650	25.71	670	26.25	885	31.12	4400	27.79	1690	27.58	1570	26.54	1010	25.12	452	...	...
15	25.83	715	25.83	715	25.75	685	25.64	640	25.66	650	26.25	955	31.62	4900	27.52	1530	27.58	1570	26.54	1010	25.12	452	...	...
16	25.79	700	25.79	700	25.83	715	25.66	650	25.71	670	26.41	955	31.00	4280	27.54	1540	27.58	1570	26.54	1010	25.08	438	...	...
17	25.79	700	25.75	685	25.83	715	25.66	650	25.71	670	26.41	965	31.00	4280	27.91	1770	27.58	1570	26.50	995	25.08	438	...	...
18	25.79	700	25.75	685	25.87	735	25.66	660	25.71	670	26.41	965	30.96	4240	27.54	1540	27.58	1570	26.45	970	25.08	438	...	...
19	25.83	715	25.75	685	25.91	750	25.73	675	25.66	650	26.25	885	30.83	4110	28.08	1880	27.58	1570	26.41	955	25.08	438	...	...
20	25.83	715	25.75	685	25.91	750	25.70	665	25.66	650	26.25	865	30.83	4110	28.08	1880	27.58	1570	26.39	945	25.04	424	...	...
21	25.83	715	25.75	685	25.91	750	25.66	650	25.66	650	26.41	955	31.54	4940	28.08	1880	27.75	1670	26.37	935	25.08	438	...	...
22	25.81	710	25.75	685	25.96	770	25.58	615	25.66	650	26.41	955	31.39	4820	27.98	1810	27.58	1670	26.35	925	25.08	438	...	...
23	25.81	710	25.79	700	25.79	700	25.58	615	25.60	625	26.83	1060	31.27	4670	27.85	1720	28.16	1720	25.00	410	25.08	438	...	...
24	25.83	715	25.83	715	25.75	685	25.50	585	25.58	615	27.00	1140	31.23	4550	28.81	2390	27.83	1690	24.91	383	25.18	473	...	...
25	25.83	715	25.83	700	25.75	650	25.33	615	25.58	625	28.50	1220	31.16	4510	28.77	2360	27.79	1660	25.50	585	25.33	525	...	...
26	25.83	715	25.79	700	25.66	650	25.50	585	25.58	615	28.75	2170	31.12	4440	29.16	2660	27.73	1660	25.46	570	25.23	490	...	...
27	26.16	850	25.79	700	25.66	615	25.58	525	25.54	600	28.75	2340	31.12	4400	28.93	2510	27.66	1620	25.41	555	25.25	498	...	...
28	26.16	885	25.79	700	25.62	635	25.50	585	25.54	585	29.66	3050	31.66	4860	28.83	2400	27.58	1570	25.41	555	25.21	484	...	...
29	26.25	885	25.83	715	25.75	675	25.58	615	25.54	585	30.29	3620	31.47	4750	28.66	2240	27.54	1540	25.37	540	25.21	484	...	...
30	26.25	885	25.83	715	25.75	685			25.42	555	30.70	3990	31.33	4610	28.60	2240	27.50	1520	25.33	525	25.21	484	...	...
31	26.22	875	25.79	700	25.75	685			25.41	555			30.58	3880			27.50	1520	25.31	520			...	...

Monthly Discharge of Wanapitei River near Wanapitei for 1915‑6

Drainage Area, 940 Square Miles

Month	Discharge in Second-feet			Discharge in Second-feet per Square Mile			Run-off
	Maximum	Minimum	Mean	Maximum	Minimum	Mean	Depth in Inches on Drainage Area
November (1415)	885	685	729	.94	.73	.78	.87
December "	835	565	710	.89	.60	.76	.88
January ..(1916)	785	615	706	.84	.65	.75	.86
February	685	525	643	.73	.56	.68	.73
March..........	710	555	649	.76	.59	.69	.80
April..........	4,110	555	1,311	4.37	.59	1.39	1.55
May............	4,940	3,880	4,609	5.26	4.13	4.90	5.64
June	2,650	1,290	1,985	2.82	1.37	2.08	2.32
July............	2,470	1,520	1,787	2.63	1.62	1.90	2.19
August	1,470	383	979	1.56	.41	1.04	1.20
September......	535	424	478	.57	.45	.51	..57
October.........	....	....	....	....	....	....	....
The year........	4,940	383	1,330	5.26	.41	1.41	17.58

Regular Stations

NORTH-WESTERN ONTARIO DISTRICT

River	Location	Drain-age Area Sq. Miles	Township	District
Eagle	at Eagle River........	970	....	Kenora ....
English.............	at Caribou Falls......	21,600	....	" ....
"	at Ear Falls...........	11,700	....	" ....
"	at Manitou Falls......	14,600	....	" ....
"..	near Oak Falls.......	15,570	....	" ....
"	at Sturgeon Falls.....	....	....	" ....
Footprint	at Rainy Lake Falls ..	590	....	Rainy River .....
Manitou	at Devil's Cascades....	435	....	" ....
Seine	at Skunk Rapids......	2,300	....	. " ....
Turtle	at Mountain Rapids...	1,760	....	" ....
Wabigoon...........	near Quibell	2,400	....	" ....
"	at Wabigoon Falls	3,120	....	Kenora...........

Eagle River at Eagle River

Location—At the highway bridge 1,000 feet south of the C.P. Ry. crossing of the river, and above the "Cascades," in the Township of Aubrey, District of Kenora. This river is a branch of the Wabigoon River.

Records Available—Discharge measurements from January, 1914, to October, 1916. Daily gauge heights February 12, 1914, to October 31, 1916.

Drainage Area—970 square miles.

Gauge—Vertical staff with enamelled face screwed to a 2 x 4 inch scantling, which is nailed to the south side of the bridge crib near the south-east corner, and next to the left bank of the river. The zero on the gauge (elev. 1,172.99) is referred to a bench mark (elev. 1,176.56, C.P.R. datum) painted on a point of rock on the left bank a few feet south-west of gauge.

Channel and Control—Straight for about 100 feet above the station, with the water flowing slowly. Below the section the channel is straight for about 20 feet, with the water running swiftly to the Cascades. The banks are clean, high, rocky and not liable to overflow. The bed consists of rock, and is permanent. At extreme highwater the flow is cut up by the bridge piers, but under normal conditions the flow is all through one channel.

Discharge Measurements—Made from the highway bridge with a small Price current meter.

Winter Flow—Not affected by ice. The water at the section never freezes.

Accuracy—The station rating curve is well defined. Fluctuation in gauge heights is occasionally augmented by wind on Eagle Lake. This is in every way an exceptionally good station.

Observer—J. Nelson, Eagle River.

Discharge Measurements of Eagle River at Eagle River in 1916

Date	Hydrographer	Width in Feet	Area of Section in Sq. Feet	Mean Velocity in Feet per Sec.	Gauge Height in Feet	Discharge in Sec-Feet	Discharge in Second-feet per Square Mile
1916							
June 13....	Taylor, J, R. ...	95	391	5.84	1177.66	2,283	........,....
" 17....	"	95	351	5.13	1177.24	1,801	....
" 17....	"	95	351	4.95	1177.24	1,737	....
July 5....	"	95	320	4.88	1176.91	1,564	....
" 5....	"	95	320	4.90	1176.91	1,570	....

Daily Gage Height and Discharge of Eagle River at Eagle River for 1915-6

Drainage Area 970 Square Miles

Day	Nov Gauge Ht. (Feet)	Nov Dis-charge (Sec-ft.)	Dec Gauge Ht. (Feet)	Dec Dis-charge (Sec-ft.)	Jan Gauge Ht. (Feet)	Jan Dis-charge (Sec-ft.)	Feb Gauge Ht. (Feet)	Feb Dis-charge (Sec-ft.)	Mar Gauge Ht. (Feet)	Mar Dis-charge (Sec-ft.)	Apr Gauge Ht. (Feet)	Apr Dis-charge (Sec-ft.)	May Gauge Ht. (Feet)	May Dis-charge (Sec-ft.)	Jun Gauge Ht. (Feet)	Jun Dis-charge (Sec-ft.)	Jul Gauge Ht. (Feet)	Jul Dis-charge (Sec-ft.)	Aug Gauge Ht. (Feet)	Aug Dis-charge (Sec-ft.)	Sep Gauge Ht. (Feet)	Sep Dis-charge (Sec-ft.)	Oct Gauge Ht. (Feet)	Oct Dis-charge (Sec-ft.)
1	1173.93	270	1174.09	310	1174.16	329	1174.32	376	1174.24	358	1174.16	329	1175.74	970	1177.74	2110	1176.74	1510	1176.16	1155	1175.32	780	1175.37	800
2	1173.91	265	1174.09	310	1174.14	324	1174.37	392	1174.24	352	1174.16	329	1175.82	1010	1177.78	2140	1176.74	1510	1176.11	1155	1175.28	760	1175.39	810
3	1173.89	261	1174.11	316	1174.16	329	1174.39	399	1174.24	352	1174.16	329	1175.95	1070	1177.82	2160	1176.74	1510	1176.16	1180	1175.32	780	1175.39	810
4	1173.86	254	1174.11	316	1174.16	329	1174.39	399	1174.22	346	1174.16	329	1176.03	1115	1177.87	2190	1176.70	1490	1176.16	1180	1175.37	800	1175.37	800
5	1173.82	245	1174.14	324	1174.18	335	1174.39	399	1174.22	346	1174.14	324	1176.11	1155	1177.91	2220	1176.66	1470	1176.07	1135	1175.37	800	1175.37	800
6	1173.82	245	1174.14	324	1174.20	340	1174.39	399	1174.22	346	1174.14	324	1176.24	1220	1177.91	2220	1176.61	1440	1176.11	1155	1175.45	835	1175.32	835
7	1173.82	245	1174.11	316	1174.22	346	1174.37	392	1174.22	346	1174.14	324	1176.32	1265	1177.95	2240	1176.57	1410	1176.11	1155	1175.49	855	1175.32	780
8	1173.89	261	1174.11	316	1174.22	346	1174.37	392	1174.22	346	1174.14	324	1176.41	1320	1177.99	2240	1176.53	1390	1176.07	1135	1175.53	875	1175.32	780
9	1173.93	270	1174.09	310	1174.24	352	1174.34	383	1174.22	346	1174.11	316	1176.49	1360	1177.95	2240	1176.45	1340	1176.11	1155	1175.53	875	1175.32	780
10	1174.05	285	1174.07	305	1174.24	352	1174.34	383	1174.24	352	1174.11	316	1176.49	1360	1177.91	2220	1176.45	1340	1176.11	1155	1175.49	855	1175.32	780
11	1174.05	300	1174.07	305	1174.28	364	1174.34	383	1174.24	352	1174.11	316	1176.49	1360	1177.87	2190	1176.41	1320	1176.11	1155	1175.53	875	1175.28	760
12	1174.03	295	1174.07	305	1174.30	370	1174.37	392	1174.24	352	1174.11	316	1176.57	1410	1177.82	2160	1176.32	1265	1175.99	1095	1175.49	855	1175.26	750
13	1174.03	295	1174.14	324	1174.30	370	1174.34	383	1174.24	352	1174.14	324	1176.66	1470	1177.74	2110	1176.24	1220	1175.99	1095	1175.45	835	1175.26	750
14	1174.03	295	1174.14	324	1174.30	370	1174.34	383	1174.24	352	1174.14	324	1176.74	1510	1177.66	2070	1176.20	1200	1175.91	1055	1175.41	820	1175.16	705
15	1174.03	295	1174.16	329	1174.32	376	1174.37	392	1174.22	346	1174.14	324	1176.78	540	1177.57	2010	1176.16	1180	1175.91	1055	1175.41	820	1175.16	705
16	1174.07	305	1174.16	329	1174.32	376	1174.37	392	1174.22	346	1174.20	340	1176.91	1660	1177.57		1176.07	1135	1175.87	1035	1175.41	820	1175.16	705
17	1174.07	305	1174.14	324	1174.32	376	1174.37	392	1174.22	346	1174.28	364	1176.99	1920	1177.41	1920	1175.99	1095	1175.82	1010	1175.41	820	1175.16	705
18	1174.02	292	1174.14	324	1174.30	370	1174.37	392	1174.22	346	1174.47	326	1177.07	1710	1177.32	1860	1176.07	1135	1175.78	990	1175.37	800	1175.16	705
19	1174.03	294	1174.16	329	1174.30	370	1174.37	392	1174.22	346	1174.57	363	1177.24	1810	1177.24	1810	1176.16	1180	1175.66	930	1175.32	780	1175.14	700
20	1174.03	294	1174.14	324	1174.30	370	1174.34	383	1174.20	340	1174.66	499	1177.24	1810	1177.16	1770	1176.24	1220	1175.61	910	1175.37	800	1175.14	700
21	1174.11	316	1174.16	329	1174.30	370	1174.32	376	1174.20	340	1174.74	530	1177.32	1890	1177.07	1710	1176.24	1220	1175.57	890	1175.37	800	1175.14	700
22	1174.14	324	1174.11	316	1174.30	370	1174.30	370	1174.20	340	1174.87	585	1177.37	1890	1176.99	1660	1176.28	1245	1175.49	855	1175.37	800	1175.11	685
23	1174.14	324	1174.09	310	1174.28	364	1174.30	370	1174.20	340	1174.91	600	1177.41	1920	1176.91	1620	1176.28	1245	1175.45	835	1175.32	780	1175.11	685
24	1174.14	324	1174.11	316	1174.26	358	1174.30	370	1174.18	335	1175.07	665	1177.49	1960	1176.82	1560	1176.24	1220	1175.41	820	1175.32	780	1175.11	685
25	1174.11	316	1174.11	316	1174.26	358	1174.30	370	1174.18	335	1175.16	705	1177.53	1990	1176.87	1590	1176.16	1180	1175.32	780	1175.37	800	1175.09	675
26	1174.09	310	1174.14	324	1174.28	364	1174.28	364	1174.18	335	1175.28	760	1177.57	2010	1176.87	1590	1176.11	1155	1175.39	780	1175.37	800	1175.11	685
27	1174.11	316	1174.14	324	1174.24	352	1174.28	364	1174.18	335	1175.37	800	1177.57	2010	1176.91	1620	1176.11	1155	1175.32	780	1175.39	810	1175.09	675
28	1174.11	316	1174.16	329	1174.24	352	1174.26	358	1174.16	329	1175.49	855	1177.61	2040	1176.87	1590	1175.99	1095	1175.32	760	1175.39	810	1175.09	675
29	1174.11	316	1174.16	329	1174.24	352	1174.26	358	1174.16	329	1175.57	890	1177.66	2070	1176.87	1590	1175.99	1135	1175.32	780	1175.39	810	1175.09	675
30	1174.11	316	1174.16	329	1174.24	364			1174.14	324	1175.66	930	1177.68	2080	1176.82	1560	1176.32	1135	1175.32	780	1175.57	800	1175.07	665
31			1174.16	329	1174.30	370			1174.14	324			1177.68	2080			1176.07		1175.32	780			1175.09	675

Monthly Discharge of Eagle River at Eagle River for 1915-6

Drainage Area, 970 Square Miles

Month	Discharge in Second-feet			Discharge in Second-feet per Square Mile			Run-off
	Maximum	Minimum	Mean	Maximum	Minimum	Mean	Depth in Inches on Drainage Area
November (1915)	324	245	293	.33	.25	.30	.33
December ''	329	305	320	.34	.31	.33	.38
January .. (1916)	376	324	357	.39	.33	.37	.43
February	399	358	382	.41	.37	.39	.42
March	358	324	343	.37	.33	.35	.40
April	930	316	469	.96	.33	.48	.54
May	2,080	970	1,597	2.14	1.00	1.65	1.90
June...........	2,260	1,560	1,932	2.33	1.61	1.99	2.22
July	1,510	1,095	1,267	1.56	1.13	1.31	1.51
August	1,180	760	992	1.22	.78	1.02	1.18
September	875	760	815	.90	.78	.84	.94
October.........	810	665	729	.84	.69	.75	.86
The year	2,260	245	798	2.33	.25	.82	11.16

English River at Caribou Falls

Location—About 1,200 feet above Caribou Falls, the last falls on the river, and about five miles from the Winnipeg River, District of Kenora.

Records Available—Discharge measurements from May, 1914, to October, 1916.

Drainage Area—21,600 square miles.

Gauge—Vertical staff located on the left bank of the river 25.6 feet north of a blazed jack pine, which is used as the initial point for soundings. The zero on the gauge (elevation 100.00) is referred to a bench mark (elevation 109.45) painted on a point of rock 16 feet south of the blazed jack pine.

Channel and Control—Above the station the channel takes a 90 degree curve to the right, thence following comparatively straight to the head of the falls. Both banks are high, rocky and wooded, and not liable to overflow. The bed of the stream is rocky, with large boulders or protruding shelves of rock and practically permanent. The water at the left bank is still, backflow existing at higher stages. The natural control is wide and unobstructed.

Discharge Measurements—Made from a canoe, and occasionally through ice, with a small Price current meter or from raft in winter.

Winter Flow—Ice conditions make little or no difference, the channel being rarely frozen over.

Accuracy—A well defined curve has been secured here.

Discharge Measurements of English River at Caribou Falls in 1916

Date	Hydrographer	Width in Feet	Area of Section in Sq. Feet	Mean Velocity in Feet per Sec.	Gauge Height in Feet	Discharge in Sec-Feet	Discharge in Second-feet per Square Mile
1916 June 26....	Carmichael, R.M	245	10,819	2.39	105.04	25,845	....

English River at Ear Falls

Location—At the foot of Lac Seul, about three miles below Pine Ridge Hudson's Bay Co's. Post, and about ¼ mile above upper Ear Falls, District of Kenora.

Records Available—Discharge measurements from July, 1914, to October, 1916. Bi-weekly gauge heights, February 1st, 1915, to October 31st, 1916.

Drainage Area—11,700 square miles.

Gauge—Vertical staff with enamelled face screwed to a 6-inch hewn spruce post which is firmly wedged in the rock of the left bank 200 feet below a 2-inch poplar, which is painted white and used as the initial point for soundings. The zero on the gauge (elev. 115.12) is referred to a bench mark (elev. 122.75) painted on a point of rock 5 feet above the gauge.

Channel and Control—Straight for about 300 feet above and below the station, then turning to the left widens out to the top of the falls. Both banks are high, rocky and wooded, and will not overflow. The bed of the stream at the section is apparently permanent; the current sluggish, and flowing through one channel at all stages. The natural control is wide, shallow and unobstructed.

Discharge Measurements—Made from a canoe with a small Price current meter.

Winter Flow—Ice conditions make little difference, the channel rarely freezing over.

Accuracy—Backwater at the left bank causes a little difficulty in making accurate discharge measurements.

Observer—Chas. McIvor, care of Hudson Bay Co's. Lac Seul Post, Sioux Lookout P.O.

Remarks—The very steady regimen of the English River, together with the lack of gauge readers, makes it possible and necessary to apply the gauge heights at Ear Falls to gauges at Manitou and Oak Falls. Gauge readings taken on nearly the same day were used in making up curves for the three stations, and the results obtained justify the assumptions made. No allowance is made for lag. With additional data it may be possible to extend the system to points farther down the river.

Discharge Measurements of English River at Ear Falls in 1916

Date	Hydrographer	Width in Feet	Area of Section in Sq. Feet	Mean Velocity in Feet per Sec.	Gauge Height in Feet	Discharge in Sec-Feet	Discharge in Second-feet per Square Mile
1916 July 28....	Taylor, J. R.....	359	9,753	2.04	122.70	19,862	....
" 28....	"	359	9,753	2.04	122.70	19,872	....

Daily Gauge Height and Discharge of English River at Ear Falls for 1915-6

Drainage Area, 11,700 Square Miles

Day	November Gauge Ht. (Feet)	November Dis-charge (Sec-ft.)	December Gauge Ht. (Feet)	December Dis-charge (Sec-ft.)	January Gauge Ht. (Feet)	January Dis-charge (Sec-ft.)	February Gauge Ht. (Feet)	February Dis-charge (Sec-ft.)	March Gauge Ht. (Feet)	March Dis-charge (Sec-ft.)	April Gauge Ht. (Feet)	April Dis-charge (Sec-ft.)	May Gauge Ht. (Feet)	May Dis-charge (Sec-ft.)	June Gauge Ht. (Feet)	June Dis-charge (Sec-ft.)	July Gauge Ht. (Feet)	July Dis-charge (Sec-ft.)	August Gauge Ht. (Feet)	August Dis-charge (Sec-ft.)	September Gauge Ht. (Feet)	September Dis-charge (Sec-ft.)	October Gauge Ht. (Feet)	October Dis-charge (Sec-ft.)
1	119.41	6920					119.37	6800							121.41	14740			122.62	19480	121.22	12980		
2			119.87	8630									119.29	6570										
3		7050							119.04	5910														
4					119.62	7680	119.37	6800			118.70	5160							122.50	19000				
5	119.45	7050											119.45	7040	121.62	15580	122.62	19480			121.20	13900		
6									119.00	5810	118.70	5160												
7			119.95		119.62	7680																		
8				00																				
9	119.37	6810	119.87	8630	119.62		119.33	6690					119.62	7680	121.87	16580	122.62	19480	122.35	18500	120.97	12980		
10									118.95	5700														
11					119.62	7630	119.33	6690			118.74	5240												
12													119.79	8360							121.02	13180		
13			119.79	8360					118.87	5510					122.08	17420	122.70	19800	122.22	17980			120.16	9840
14					119.60	7600	119.29	6570																
15											118.79	5340					122.74	19960						
16	119.29	6570											119.95	9000	122.20	17900			121.97	16980	120.95	12900		
17			119.74	8160	119.58	7520			118.83	5430					122.24	18060							120.12	9680
18							119.24	6430			118.79	5340												
19	119.33	6690											120.24	10160			122.93	20720	121.95	16900	120.83	12420		
20			119.70	8000	119.56	7440									122.37	18580							120.04	9360
21							119.22	6380	118.79	5340	118.83	5430					122.72	19880						
22															122.45	18850			121.87	16580	120.77	12210		
23	119.20	6320											120.62	11680	122.54	19160								
24			119.66	7840																				
25					119.45	7040	119.20	6320	118.79	5340	118.91	5600			122.62	19480	122.72	19880	121.72	15980	120.62	11680	119.95	9000
26	119.95	9000											120.87	12580										8880
27															122.66	19640								
28			119.62	7680	119.41	6320	119.12	6110	118.79	5340	118.95	5700					122.70	19800	121.50	15100	120.56	11440	119.87	8680
29															122.70	19800							119.83	8520
30	119.87	8680	119.62	7680									121.04	13260	122.74	19960								
31									118.74	5240														

Monthly Discharge of English River at Ear Falls for 1915-6

Drainage Area, 11,700 Square Miles

Month	Discharge in Second-feet			Discharge in Second-feet per Square Mile			Run-off
	Maximum	Minimum	Mean	Maximum	Minimum	Mean	Depth in Inches on Drainage Area
November..(1915)	9,000	6,320	7,255	.77	.54	.62	.69
December ''	9,000	7,680	8,231	.77	.66	.70	.81
January ...1916)	7,680	6,920	7,445	.66	.59	.64	.74
February	6,800	6,110	6,532	.58	.52	.56	.60
March	5,910	5,240	5,513	.51	.45	.47	.54
April	5,700	5,160	5,371	.49	.44	.46	.51
May............	13,260	6,570	9,592	1.13	.56	.82	.95
June............	19,960	14,740	18,135	1.71	1.26	1.55	1.73
July	20,720	19,480	19,875	1.77	1.66	1.70	1.96
August	19,480	15,100	17,389	1.66	1.29	1.49	1.72
September	13,980	11,440	12,743	1.19	.98	1.09	1.22
October	9,840	8,520	9,109	.84	.73	.78	.90
The year	20,720	5,240	10,935	1.77	.45	.93	12.66

Daily Gauge Height of English River at Lac Seul for 1915-6

Day.	Nov.	Dec.	Jan.	Feb.	Mar.	April	May	June	July	Aug.	Sept.	Oct.
1	105.27	105.73	105.77	105.44	105.10	104.83	105.33	108.17	109.63	109.41	107.81	106.66
2	105.27	105.77	105.77	105.44	105.10	104.83	105.39	108.25	109.63	109.36	107.73	106.77
3	105.27	105.77	105.77	105.44	105.02	104.77	105.45	108.31	109.63	109.26	107.69	106.56
4	105.23	105.77	105.77	105.44	105.02	104.77	105.48	108.46	109.63	109.21	107.65	106.58
5	105.27	105.77	105.73	105.44	105.02	104.75	105.56	108.50	109.65	109.19	107.61	106.61
6	105.31	105.77	105.73	105.35	105.02	104.75	105.62	108.58	109.61	109.11	107.56	106.49
7	105.35	105.81	105.73	105.35	105.02	104.78	105.64	108.71	109.63	109.13	107.51	106.43
8	105.44	105.81	105.73	105.35	105.02	104.69	105.81	108.75	109.61	109.06	107.46	106.33
9	105.44	105.81	105.69	105.35	105.02	104.69	105.83	108.83	109.61	109.01	107.41	106.33
10	105.44	105.81	105.69	105.35	105.02	104.69	106.23	108.96	109.73	108.96	107.36	106.31
11	105.44	105.85	105.69	105.35	105.02	104.64	106.43	108.98	109.88	109.06	107.31	106.29
12	105.44	105.85	105.65	105.35	105.02	104.69	106.43	109.06	109.90	108.96	107.26	106.24
13	105.52	105.85	105.65	105.35	105.02	104.71	106.48	109.13	109.88	108.91	107.21	106.21
14	105.52	105.85	105.65	105.35	105.02	104.78	106.48	109.21	109.88	108.86	107.21	106.21
15	105.52	105.85	105.62	105.35	104.94	104.69	106.56	109.25	109.90	108.73	107.16	106.16
16	105.52	105.85	105.62	105.35	104.94	104.71	106.78	109.33	109.88	108.66	107.11	106.16
17	105.56	105.85	105.60	105.27	104.92	104.77	106.85	109.42	109.88	108.58	107.01	106.13
18	105.56	105.85	105.52	105.27	104.94	104.81	106.83	109.54	109.94	108.56	106.96	106.01
19	105.60	105.85	105.52	105.27	104.96	104.83	106.89	109.56	110.03	108.49	106.91	106.01
20	105.60	105.85	105.52	105.19	104.85	104.85	106.98	109.56	110.07	108.47	106.86	106.01
21	105.60	105.77	105.52	105.19	104.85	104.94	107.00	109.58	109.92	108.41	107.11	106.01
22	105.64	105.77	105.52	105.19	104.85	105.00	107.04	109.58	109.94	108.36	107.01	105.95
23	105.64	105.77	105.52	105.19	104.79	105.00	107.14	109.58	109.92	108.26	106.94	105.91
24	105.64	105.77	105.52	105.27	104.77	105.02	107.39	109.71	109.94	108.26	106.91	105.87
25	105.67	105.77	105.52	105.19	104.77	105.10	107.52	109.67	109.84	108.18	106.88	105.93
26	105.67	105.77	105.52	105.10	104.85	105.17	107.60	109.67	109.86	108.16	106.83	105.83
27	105.69	105.77	105.52	105.10	104.85	105.23	107.73	109.71	109.51	108.06	106.79	105.76
28	105.69	105.77	105.52	105.10	104.83	105.23	107.85	109.71	109.51	108.03	106.76	105.71
29	105.69	105.77	105.52	105.10	104.85	105.38	107.91	109.71	109.51	107.99	106.71	105.78
30	105.69	......	105.52	......	104.85	105.85	107.98	109.67	109.46	107.91	106.69	105.71
31	......	......	105.52	......	104.83	......	108.06	......	109.41	107.86	......	105.71

English River at Manitou Falls

Location—About 800 feet above the first chute of the Manitou Falls, and five miles below the mouth of the Mattawa River and the old Mattawa H. B. Co's. Post. Cedar River enters the English River ½ mile below the metering section.

Records Available—Discharge measurements from July, 1914, to October, 1916. Bi-weekly gauge heights interpolated from Ear Falls gauge heights, February 1st, 1915, to October 31st, 1916.

Drainage Area—14,600 square miles.

Gauge—Vertical staff with enamelled face screwed to a 6-inch pine post and firmly wedged and wired to the right bank 15 feet south of a 2-inch jack pine, which is used as the initial point for soundings. The zero on the gauge (elev. 89.42) is referred to a bench mark (elev. 100.43) painted on a point of rock 2.5 feet south-east of the initial point.

Channel and Control—About 1,200 feet above the station the channel begins to narrow down and turns to the right out of the lake above. It is comparatively straight thence to the station and falls. Both banks are high, rocky and wooded, and will not overflow. The bed of the stream is rocky and permanent. The current is slow above and moderately swift at the section.

Discharge Measurements—Made from a canoe with a small Price current meter.

Remarks—The very steady regimen of the English River, together with the lack of gauge readers, makes it possible and necessary to apply the gauge heights at Ear Falls to the gauge at Manitou Falls. Gauge readings taken on nearly the same day were used in making up curves for the two stations, and the results obtained justify the assumptions made. No allowance is made for " lag."

Discharge Measurements of English River at Manitou Falls in 1916

Date	Hydrographer	Width in Feet	Area of Section in Sq. Feet	Mean Velocity in Feet per Sec.	Gauge Height in Feet	Discharge in Sec–Feet	Discharge in Second-feet per Square Mile
1916 July 30....	Taylor, J. R.....	247 ₰	5,801	3.73	101.86	21,666	....
" 30....	"	247	5,801	3.75	101.86	21,742	....

Daily Gauge Height and Discharge of English River at Manitou Falls for 1915-6

Drainage Area, 14,500 Square Miles

Day	November Gauge Ht. Feet	November Dis-charge Sec-ft.	December Gauge Ht. Feet	December Dis-charge Sec-ft.	January Gauge Ht. Feet	January Dis-charge Sec-ft.	February Gauge Ht. Feet	February Dis-charge Sec-ft.	March Gauge Ht. Feet	March Dis-charge Sec-ft.	April Gauge Ht. Feet	April Dis-charge Sec-ft.	May Gauge Ht. Feet	May Dis-charge Sec-ft.	June Gauge Ht. Feet	June Dis-charge Sec-ft.	July Gauge Ht. Feet	July Dis-charge Sec-ft.	August Gauge Ht. Feet	August Dis-charge Sec-ft.	September Gauge Ht. Feet	September Dis-charge Sec-ft.	October Gauge Ht. Feet	October Dis-charge Sec-ft.
1	92.31	8250					92.20	8110					92.00	7850	98.07	16250			101.75	21400	97.50	15450		
2																								
3	93.55	9860	93.55	9860	92.86	8970	92.20	8110	91.35	7030									101.40	20910				
4																								
5	92.45	8440									90.45	5980	92.45	8430	98.73	17170	101.75	21400			97.47	15410		
6																								
7	93.75	10120	93.75	10120	92.86	8970	92.10	7980	91.25	6910	90.45	5980												
8	93.55	9860	93.55	9860																				
9	92.20	8110			92.86	8930	92.10	7980	91.10	6730	90.35	6100	92.90	9020	99.55	18320	101.75	21400	100.92	20240	96.75	14400		
10																								
11																								
12																								
13			93.30	9540	92.83	8930			90.92	6510	90.67	6250	93.30	9640	100.15	19160	102.00	21750	100.35	19440	96.95	14680	94.40	11110
14																								
15																								
16	92.00	7850	93.20	9410	92.78	8860	92.00	7850	90.80	6370	90.67	6250	93.75	10120	100.47	19800	102.10	21890	99.80	18670	96.47	14010	94.16	10770
17																								
18	92.10	7980					91.89	7710	90.80	6370			94.49	11090	100.65	19860	102.66	22660	99.75	18600	96.60	14190		
19																								
20			93.08	9250	92.71	8770			90.69	6250	90.80	6370			101.05	20420	102.05	21820			96.15	13560	93.95	10480
21																								
22	91.80	7590					91.85	7660					95.75	13000	101.27	20730	102.05	21820	99.55	18320				
23			92.98	9120											101.55	21120								
24	93.75	10120			92.45	8420	91.80	7500	90.69	6250	91.02	6630							99.05	17620	95.75	13000	93.72	10160
25													95.50	14050									93.50	9850
26																								
27															101.75	21400								
28			92.86	8970	92.32	8270	91.55	7270	90.69	6250	91.10	6730			101.85	21540	102.00	21750	98.37	16670	95.55	12720		
29															102.00	21750								
30	93.55	9860	92.86	8970									97.00	14750	102.10	21890							93.50	9850
31																							93.40	9710

NOTE.—Gauge heights interpolated from at Falls and discharges applied from Manitou Falls rating curve.

Monthly Discharge of English River at Manitou Falls for 1915-6

Drainage Area, 14,600 Square Miles

Month	Discharge in Second-feet			Discharge in Second-feet per Square Mile			Run-off
	Maximum	Minimum	Mean	Maximum	Minimum	Mean	Depth in Inches on Drainage Area
November. (1915)	19,120	7,850	8,525	.69	.54	.58	.65
December. "	10,120	8,970	9,455	.69	.61	.65	.75
January ..(1916)	8,970	8,270	8,770	.61	.57	.60	.69
February	8,110	7,270	7,807	.56	.50	.53	.57
March	7,080	6,090	6,488	.48	.42	.44	.51
April ....:......	6,730	5,980	6,281	.46	.41	.43	.48
May	14,750	7,850	10,872	1.01	.54	.74	.85
June...........	21,890	16,250	19,940	1.50	1.11	1.37	1.53
July	22,660	21,400	20,811	1.55	1.47	1.43	1.65
August	21,400	16,670	19,097	1.47	1.14	1.31	1.51
September	15,450	12,720	14,158	1.06	.87	.97	1.08
October........	11,110	9,710	10,276	.76	.67	.70	.81
The year	22,660	5,980	12,313	1.55	.41	.84	11.43

English River near Oak Falls

Location—About one mile above the upper fall of Oak Falls, and about one-half mile below Wilcox Lake, District of Kenora.

Records Available—Discharge measurements from August, 1914, to October, 1916. Bi-weekly gauge heights interpolated from observations at Ear Falls, February 1st, 1915, to October 31st, 1916.

Drainage Area—15,570 square miles.

Gauge—Vertical staff with enamelled face screwed to a cedar post and firmly wedged in rock on the right bank 200 feet above the metering section. The zero on the gauge (elev. 194.09) is referred to a bench mark (elev. 200.00 painted on a rock in the river near the right bank and 20 feet above the final point for soundings. The initial point for soundings is located on the left bank, and consists of the head of a nail driven in the side of a 12-inch poplar blazed and marked I.P., N. 70° W.

Channel and Control—Straight for about 300 feet above and ½ mile below the station. Both banks are high, rocky and wooded, and not liable to overflow. The bed of the stream is rocky and practically permanent. The current is sluggish above and moderately swift below the station, a small rapid existing about 800 feet below.

Discharge Measurements—Made from a canoe with a small Price current meter.

Remarks—The very steady regimen of the English River, together with the lack of gauge readers, makes it possible and necessary to apply the gauge heights at Ear Falls to the gauge at Oak Falls. Gauge readings taken on nearly the same day were used in making up curves for the two stations, and the results obtained justify the assumptions made. No allowance is made for lag.

Discharge Measurements of English River near Oak Falls in 1916

Date	Hydrographer	Width in Feet	Area of Section in Sq. Feet	Mean Velocity in Feet per Sec.	Gauge Height in Feet	Discharge in Sec-Feet	Discharge in Second-feet per Square Mile
1916 Aug. 2....	Taylor, J. R....	443	8,348	2.83	200.30	235.95	....

Daily Gage Height and Discharge of English River near Oak Falls for 1915-6

Drainage Area, 15,570 Square Miles

Day	November Gauge Ht. (Feet)	November Dis-charge (Sec-ft)	December Gauge Ht. (Feet)	December Dis-charge (Sec-ft)	January Gauge Ht. (Feet)	January Dis-charge (Sec-ft)	February Gauge Ht. (Feet)	February Dis-charge (Sec-ft)	March Gauge Ht. (Feet)	March Dis-charge (Sec-ft)	April Gauge Ht. (Feet)	April Dis-charge (Sec-ft)	May Gauge Ht. (Feet)	May Dis-charge (Sec-ft)	June Gauge Ht. (Feet)	June Dis-charge (Sec-ft)	July Gauge Ht. (Feet)	July Dis-charge (Sec-ft)	August Gauge Ht. (Feet)	August Dis-charge (Sec-ft)	September Gauge Ht. (Feet)	September Dis-charge (Sec-ft)	October Gauge Ht. (Feet)	October Dis-charge (Sec-ft)
1	196.29	8820					196.23	8640					196.14	8500	198.75			40	200.33	23720	198.52	460		
2			196.92	10710					195.80	7620														
3	196.36	9030					196.23	8640			196.35	6620	196.35	9000			200.20	23200	200.06	22640				
4			196.56	9630	196.56	9630									199.00									
5											195.35	6620												
6	196.36	9030			196.56	9630	196.18	8500	195.75	7520								60			198.50	16400		
7			197.01	10980																				
8			196.92	10710																				
9	196.23	8640			196.56	9630	196.18	8500	195.67	7260	195.40	6720	196.58	9690	199.34	19760	200.20	23200	199.87	21880	198.23	15320		
10																								
11			196.56	9630			196.18	8500																
12							196.12	8350	195.57	7060	195.47	6860	196.78	10290	199.57	20680	200.29	23560	199.75	21400	198.30	15600	197.29	11860
13																								
14			196.80	10350	196.55	9600									199.70	21200	200.33	23720	199.44	20160	198.22	15280	197.29	11860
15																								
16	196.12	8350	196.74	10170	196.53	9540	196.06	8200	195.52	6960	195.47	6860	197.02	11010	199.77	21480			199.42	20080	198.07	14660	197.24	11690
17																								
18	196.18	8500																						
19	196.18		196.53	9540			196.06		195.52		195.47		197.37	12140	199.92	22080	200.55	24600	199.34	19760	198.07	14660	197.13	11340
20																								
21			196.67	9960					195.46	6840	195.53	6980			200.00	22400	200.52	23630	199.34	19760	197.73	13600	197.13	11340
22															200.12	22880								
23	196.02	8100	196.49	9420			196.05	8170					197.82	13760					199.34	19760			197.02	11010
24			196.11	8330			196.02	8100	195.46	6840	195.63	7180					200.32	23680	199.13	18920	197.73	13600	196.91	10680
25																								
26	197.01	10980	196.36	9030	196.36	9030					195.63	7280	198.12		200.20	23200			199.13	18920	187.82	13760	196.91	10680
27							196.02								200.24	23280	200.29	23560	198.87	17880				
28			196.29	8820	196.29	8820			195.46	6840	195.63	7280			200.29	23560	200.29	23560	198.87	17880	197.82	13760	196.85	10500
29							195.90						198.32	15680	200.29	23560					197.73	13410		
30	196.92	10710	196.56	9630			195.90	7820					198.32	15680	200.33	23720								
31			196.56	9630					195.40	6710														

NOTE.—Gauge heights interpolated from Ear Falls and discharges applied from Oak Falls rating curve.

Monthly Discharge of English River near Oak Falls for 1916

Drainage Area, 15,570 Square Miles

Month	Discharge in Second-feet			Discharge in Second-feet per Square Mile			Run-off
	Maximum	Minimum	Mean	Maximum	Minimum	Mean	Depth in Inches on Drainage Area
November (1915)	10,980	8,100	9,140	.70	.52	.59	.66
December. ''	10,980	8,330	10,050	.70	.53	.64	.74
January ...(1916)	9,620	8,820	9,410	.62	.57	.60	.69
February	8,640	7,820	8,320	.55	.50	.53	.57
March	7,620	6,710	7,070	.49	.43	.45	.52
April.	7,280	6,620	6,590	.47	.43	.49	.55
May.	15,680	8,500	11,641	1.01	.55	.75	.86
June............	23,720	17,400	21,542	1.52	1.12	1.38	1.54
July	24,600	23,200	23,650	1.58	1.49	1.52	1.75
August	23,720	17,880	20,716	1.52	1.15	1.33	1.53
September	16,480	13,410	14,945	1.06	.86	.96	1.07
October.........	11,860	10,500	11,109	.76	.67	.71	.82
The year........	24,600	6,620	13,260	1.58	.43	.85	11.57

English River at Sturgeon Falls

Location—About 300 feet above the lowest of the three falls known as Sturgeon Falls, District of Kenora, and about 30 miles above the Winnipeg River.

Records Available—Discharge measurements from June, 1914.

Drainage Area—Not measured.

Gauge—Vertical staff with enamelled face, screwed to a 5" hewn spruce post firmly wedged and braced to the left bank about 150 feet below the metering section. The zero on the gauge (elevation 91.52) is referred to a bench mark (elevation 100.00) painted on the left bank 10 feet from the initial point and two feet below the line of section. The initial point for soundings is a nail driven in the side of a 6-inch blazed poplar on the left bank, and marked I.P., N. 10° E.

Channel and Control—There are deep bays on both sides of the river above the station, from which the channel takes a gentle curve to the left, thence flowing comparatively straight and narrowing to the station and falls. The bed is composed of rock with a little gravel in the centre, and practically permanent. Both banks are high, rocky and wooded, and will not overflow. The velocity is low at the right bank, and very slight backflow exists at the left.

Discharge Measurements—Made from a canoe with a small Price current meter.

Footprint River at Rainy Lake Falls

Location—100 feet above the crest of the lowest fall, at the mouth of the Footprint River where it flows into the north-west bay of Rainy Lake, on Indian Reserve 17A, District of Rainy River.

Records Available—Monthly discharge measurements from July, 1914. Daily gauge heights, Sept. 18, 1914, to Oct. 31, 1916.

Drainage Area—425 square miles.

Gauge—Vertical steel staff gauge, graduated in feet and inches. The zero on the gauge (elevation 101.30) is referred to a bench mark (elevation 110.51) painted on the ledge of a rock on right bank.

Channel—About 40 feet above the station the channel curves to the left and then runs straigth for about 140 feet, dropping into Rainy Lake. The banks are high, rocky, wooded, and not liable to overflow. The right bank has been burnt over. The bed of the river contains large boulders, and one channel exists at all stages.

Discharge Measurements—Made from a canoe with a small Price current meter.

Winter Flow—Relation of gauge height to discharge not affected by ice.

Regulation—Occasional operations of the dam at Footprint Lake cause fluctuations in the river at the gauge.

Accuracy—The rating curve is well defined. Open water curve used throughout the year.

Observer—John Lyons, Fort Frances P.O.

Discharge Measurements of Footprint River at Rainy Lake Falls in 1916

Date	Hydrographer	Width in Feet	Area of Section in Sq. Feet	Mean Velocity in Feet per Sec.	Gauge Height in Feet	Discharge in Sec-Feet	Discharge in Second-feet per Square Mile
1916							
June 4....	Taylor, J. R.....	137	455	2.74	104.72	1246	....
July 12....	" "	66	177	3.56	103.53	628(a)	....

(a) Reading taken 70 ft. above regular section.

Daily Gauge Height and Discharge of Footprint River at Rainy Lake Falls for 1915-6

Drainage Area. 590 Square Miles

Day	Nov Gauge Ht (Feet)	Nov Dis-charge (Sec-ft)	Dec Gauge Ht (Feet)	Dec Dis-charge (Sec-ft)	Jan Gauge Ht (Feet)	Jan Dis-charge (Sec-ft)	Feb Gauge Ht (Feet)	Feb Dis-charge (Sec-ft)	Mar Gauge Ht (Feet)	Mar Dis-charge (Sec-ft)	Apr Gauge Ht (Feet)	Apr Dis-charge (Sec-ft)	May Gauge Ht (Feet)	May Dis-charge (Sec-ft)	Jun Gauge Ht (Feet)	Jun Dis-charge (Sec-ft)	Jul Gauge Ht (Feet)	Jul Dis-charge (Sec-ft)	Aug Gauge Ht (Feet)	Aug Dis-charge (Sec-ft)	Sep Gauge Ht (Feet)	Sep Dis-charge (Sec-ft)	Oct Gauge Ht (Feet)	Oct Dis-charge (Sec-ft)
1	101.34	79	101.38	83	101.38	83	101.38	83	101.38	83	101.63	108	103.63	680	104.83	1300	103.72	725	102.97	390	102.47	252	102.01	159
2	101.34	79	101.38	83	101.38	83	101.38	83	101.38	83	101.63	108	103.76	745	104.73	1250	103.72	725	102.97	390	102.42	240	102.01	159
3	101.34	79	101.38	83	101.38	83	101.38	83	101.38	83	101.63	108	103.80	765	104.73	1250	103.72	725	102.97	390	102.42	240	102.01	159
4	101.34	79	101.38	83	101.38	83	101.38	83	101.38	83	101.63	108	103.80	765	104.63	1190	103.74	735	102.97	390	102.42	240	101.97	153
5	101.34	79	101.38	83	101.38	83	101.38	83	101.38	83	101.63	108	103.82	775	104.72	1240	103.74	735	102.97	390	102.42	240	101.92	146
6	101.34	79	101.38	83	101.38	83	101.38	83	101.38	83	101.59	104	103.84	785	104.76	1260	103.74	735	102.97	390	102.42	240	101.92	146
7	101.34	79	101.38	83	101.38	83	101.38	83	101.38	83	101.59	104	103.88	805	104.63	1190	103.74	735	102.92	372	102.38	230	101.92	146
8	101.34	79	101.38	83	101.38	83	101.38	83	101.38	83	101.59	104	103.97	850	104.63	1190	103.74	735	102.92	372	102.38	230	101.92	146
9	101.34	79	101.38	83	101.38	83	101.38	83	101.38	83	101.59	104	104.01	870	104.55	1150	103.63	680	102.88	360	102.38	230	101.88	140
10	101.34	79	101.38	83	101.38	83	101.38	83	101.38	83	101.59	104	104.05	890	104.51	1130	103.57	650	102.84	360	102.38	230	101.88	140
11	101.34	79	101.38	83	101.38	83	101.38	83	101.38	83	101.59	104	104.13	930	104.47	1100	103.55	640	102.84	347	102.38	230	101.84	135
12	101.34	79	101.38	83	101.38	83	101.38	83	101.38	83	101.59	104	104.22	975	104.47	1100	103.55	640	102.88	360	102.34	222	101.84	135
13	101.34	79	101.38	83	101.38	83	101.38	83	101.38	83	101.59	104	104.30	1030	104.38	1060	103.51	620	102.88	360	102.34	222	101.84	135
14	101.34	79	101.38	83	101.38	83	101.38	83	101.38	83	101.59	104		1030	104.38	1060	103.51	620	102.84	347	102.30	213	101.80	129
15	101.34	79	101.38	83	101.38	83	101.38	83	101.38	83	101.59	104		1065	104.38	1060	103.47	600	102.72	315	102.30	213	101.80	129
16	101.34	79	101.38	83	101.38	83	101.38	83	101.42	87	101.63	108		1065	104.33	1060	103.47	600	102.68	305	102.30	213	101.80	129
17	101.34	79	101.38	83	101.38	83	101.38	83	101.42	87	101.80	129		1120	104.34	1035	103.37	600	102.68	305	102.30	213	101.76	124
18	101.34	79	101.38	83	101.38	83	101.38	83	101.47	92	101.97	153		1120	104.47	1100	103.42	575	102.63	292	102.30	213	101.76	124
19	101.34	79	101.38	83	101.38	83	101.38	83	101.55	100	102.22	196		1175	104.47	1100	103.42	575	102.63	292	102.22	196	101.76	124
20	101.34	79	101.38	83	101.38	83	101.38	83	101.55	100	102.42	240		1175	104.47	1100	103.38	555	102.63	292	102.22	196	101.72	119
21	101.34	79	101.38	83	101.38	83	101.38	83	101.55	100	102.55	272	104.70	1250	104.47	1100	103.47	600	102.59	282	102.22	179	101.72	119
22	101.34	79	101.38	83	101.38	83	101.38	83	101.57	102	102.68	305	104.74	1250	104.42	1080	103.22	480	102.51	262	102.13	179	101.72	119
23	101.34	79	101.38	83	101.38	83	101.38	83	101.57	102	102.80	335	104.78	1270	104.22	980	103.18	470	102.51	262	102.15	172	101.72	119
24	101.38	83	101.38	83	101.38	83	101.38	83	101.57	102	102.92	372	104.78	1270	104.05	890	103.13	445	102.51	262	102.09	172	101.72	119
25	101.38	83	101.38	83	101.38	83	101.38	83	101.59	104	103.05	417	104.86	1320	103.90	815	103.13	445	102.51	262	102.09	172	101.72	119
26	101.38	83	101.38	83	101.38	83	101.38	83	101.59	104	103.22	483	104.95	1370	103.80	765	103.13	445	102.51	262	102.05	165	101.76	124
27	101.38	83	101.38	83	101.38	83	101.38	83	101.59	104	103.26	499	105.03	1410	103.72	725	103.13	445	102.51	262	102.05	165	101.76	124
28	101.38	83	101.38	83	101.38	83	101.38	83	101.59	104	103.38	555		1410	103.72	725	103.13	445	102.47	252			101.76	124
29	101.38	83	101.38	83	101.38	83			101.59	104	103.47	600		1360	103.72	725	103.06	418	102.47	252			101.76	124
30	101.38	83	101.38	83	101.38	83			101.59	104	103.55	640		1360			103.01	403	102.47	252			101.76	124
31			101.38	83	101.38	83			101.63	108				1300										

Monthly Discharge of Footprint River at Rainy Lake Falls for 1915-6

Drainage Area, 590 Square Miles

Month	Discharge in Second-feet			Discharge in Second-feet per Square Mile			Run-off
	Maximum	Minimum	Mean	Maximum	Minimum	Mean	Depth in Inches on Drainage Area
November (1915)	83	79	80	.14	.13	.14	.16
December "	83	83	83	.14	.14	.14	.16
January.. (1916)	83	83	83	.14	.14	.14	.16
February	83	83	83	.14	.14	.14	.15
March	108	83	92	.18	.14	.16	.18
April	640	104	229	1.08	.18	.39	.45
May	1,410	680	1,070	2.39	1.15	1.81	2.09
June	1,300	725	1,061	2.20	1.23	1.80	2.01
July	735	403	594	1.25	.68	1.01	1.16
August	390	252	325	.66	.43	.55	.63
September	252	165	212	.43	.28	.36	.40
October	159	119	137	.27	.20	.23	.27
The year	1,410	79	338	2.39	.14	.57	7.76

Manitou River at Devil's Cascades

Location—About 150 feet above the old dam, at the head of the Devil's Cascades, Rainy River District.

Records Available—Monthly discharge measurements from July, 1914. Daily gauge heights, July 15, 1914, to June 30th, 1916.

Drainage Area—435 square miles.

Gauge—An inclined steel staff, graduated in feet and inches, and located on the face of the old dam. The zero of the gauge is at an elevation of 139.38 feet referred to a bench mark (elevation 147.37) painted on a rock 1 foot east of the initial point for soundings.

Channel—Straight for about 150 feet above and 400 feet below the station. The right bank is high, rocky, wooded, and not liable to overflow, but the left bank is low and wooded, with a gradually rising bank, which is not liable to overflow unless the dam is operated. The bed of the stream is composed of rock, and the current is slow, one channel existing at all stages.

Discharge Measurements—Made from canoe or ice with a small Price current meter.

Winter Flow—The relation of gauge height to discharge is affected by ice during the cold period, and measurements are made to determine the winter flow.

Regulation—Several dams exist on the river between the section and Manitou Lake, which are not in operation at present. The operation of the dam just above the station causes fluctuations at the gauge.

Accuracy—A fairly well-defined rating curve has been developed, and records are considered fair.

Discharge Measurements of Manitou River at Devil's Cascades in 1916

Date	Hydrographer	Width in Feet	Area of Section in Sq. Feet	Mean Velocity in Feet per Sec.	Gauge Height in Feet	Discharge in Sec-Feet	Discharge in Second-feet per Square Mile
1916							
June 4....	Taylor, J. R.	117	797	2.02	146.89	1613	....
July 12....	"	116	699	1.25	145.99	874	....

Seine River at Skunk Rapids

Location—About 200 feet above Skunk Rapids, and 1 mile upstream from the Canadian Northern Ry. bridge. One-half mile north of the C. N. Ry. tracks, and 1 mile west of La Seine Station, in the District of Rainy River.

Records Available—Discharge measurements from August, 1914. Daily gauge heights, Sept. 22, 1914, to April 30, 1915, and Oct. 1st, 1915, to Oct. 31st, 1916. ..

Drainage Area—2,300 square miles.

Gauge—Vertical steel staff gauge with enamelled face, graduated in feet and inches, and located near La Seine station, on the C. N. Ry. The zero on the gauge is at an elevation of 1,138.21 feet, which is referred to a bench mark (elevation 1,152.73) painted on a large boulder, on the right bank of the river, 6 feet from a 6-inch poplar tree used as a final point for soundings. The initial point is on the left bank and consists of a 2-inch spruce tree, blazed and marked I.P. with white paint. "H. E. P. Comm." is painted on the rock directly below the spruce tree.

Channel and Control—Straight for about 500 feet above and 200 feet below the station to the rapids. The right bank of the river curves into a point at the rapids forming a narrow channel. The velocity of the river is slow and the banks are high, rocky and wooded. This land has been burnt over, but most of the trees are still standing. The bed of the stream is sandy and clean, with a few boulders near the right bank. One channel exists at all stages.

Discharge Measurements—Made from a canoe with a small Price current meter.

Winter Flow—The relation of gauge height to discharge is affected by ice during the winter months and measurements are made to determine the winter flow.

Accuracy—Open water rating curve is fairly well defined and estimates are considered good.

Observer—Wm. Clark, Flanders.

Discharge Measurements of Seine River at Skunk Rapids in 1916

Date	Hydrographer	Width in Feet	Area of Section in Sq. Feet	Mean Velocity in Feet per Sec.	Gauge Height in Feet	Discharge in Sec-Feet	Discharge in Second-feet per Square Mile
1916							
June 6....	Taylor, J. R....	290	3,045	2.39	101.45	7261	....
" 6....	"	209	3,045	2.40	101.45	7305	....
July 13....	"	206	2,449	1.33	98.93	3258	....

Daily Gauge Height of Seine River at Skunk Rapids for 1915-6

Drainage Area, 2,300 Square Miles

(Gauge Ht. in Feet; Discharge columns, in Sec-ft., are blank throughout.)

Day	Nov.	Dec.	Jan.	Feb.	March	April	May	June	July	Aug.	Sept.	Oct.
1	97.39	96.93	95.97	95.34	94.97	95.05	99.64	102.22	99.49	97.81	96.78	97.43
2	97.39	96.89	95.97	95.30	94.97	95.14	99.70	102.14	99.43	97.74	96.76	97.43
3	97.40	96.89	95.93	95.30	94.97	95.18	99.78	101.93	99.43	97.70	96.81	97.43
4	97.41	96.80	95.93	95.26	94.97	95.22	99.89	101.80	99.35	97.64	96.85	97.41
5	97.41	96.80	95.95	95.22	94.93	95.22	100.10	101.72	99.26	97.55	96.85	97.33
6	97.41	96.80	95.89	95.22	94.89	95.22	100.18	101.45	99.24	97.60	96.85	97.27
7	97.44	96.72	95.89	95.18	94.84	95.26	100.39	101.31	99.14	97.55	96.85	97.26
8	97.47	96.72	95.87	95.14	94.84	95.30	100.68	101.14	99.08	97.47	96.85	97.26
9	97.47	96.51	95.84	95.14	94.84	95.30	100.93	101.14	99.03	97.41	96.81	97.26
10	97.52	96.47	95.87	95.10	94.80	95.39	101.14	101.03	98.99	97.39	96.83	97.26
11	97.60	96.47	95.80	95.05	94.80	95.43	101.14	100.93	98.93	97.31	96.81	97.24
12	97.70	96.41	95.76	95.01	94.80	95.45	101.14	100.91	98.89	97.24	96.78	97.22
13	97.72	96.34	95.72	95.01	94.80	95.89	101.34	100.91	98.85	97.20	96.76	97.20
14	97.39	96.26	95.68	94.97	94.80	96.14	101.43	100.76	98.78	97.18	96.70	97.18
15	97.30	96.22	95.64	94.97	94.80	96.55	101.43	100.68	98.72	97.12	96.74	97.18
16	97.22	96.22	95.64	94.97	94.80	96.72	101.64	100.64	98.66	97.12	96.76	97.16
17	97.14	96.16	95.64	94.97	94.80	97.05	101.60	100.51	98.60	97.18	96.76	97.18
18	97.05	96.16	95.64	94.97	94.80	97.84	101.72	100.39	98.51	97.12	97.76	97.18
19	97.14	96.10	95.57	94.97	94.80	98.39	101.78	100.31	98.43	97.14	96.76	97.18
20	97.05	96.05	95.55	94.97	94.80	98.64	101.82	100.16	98.35	97.08	96.76	97.18
21	97.05	96.05	95.55	94.97	94.80	98.72	101.89	99.93	98.31	97.08	97.01	97.12
22	97.05	96.01	95.51	94.97	94.80	99.05	101.89	99.89	98.24	97.16	97.18	97.03
23	97.01	96.01	95.51	94.97	94.80	99.14	101.91	99.89	98.18	97.16	97.26	97.01
24	96.97	96.01	95.51	94.97	94.80	99.18	101.97	99.85	98.16	97.12	97.51	97.01
25	96.97	95.99	95.47	94.97	94.80	99.22	101.84	99.76	98.10	97.08	97.60	97.01
26	96.97	95.97	95.47	94.97	94.89	99.34	101.80	99.68	98.08	97.03	97.60	96.99
27	96.97	95.97	95.47	94.97	94.89	99.43	101.80	99.74	98.01	96.99	97.60	97.01
28	96.97	95.97	95.43	94.97	94.93	99.51	101.80	99.60	97.92	96.91	97.51	
29	96.97	95.97	95.43		94.97	99.55	101.80	99.55	97.88	96.87	97.45	96.99
30	96.93	95.97	95.39		95.01		101.89		97.84	96.85		97.01
31		95.97										

Turtle River at Mountain Rapids

Location—About 300 feet above Mountain Rapids, and about 8 miles from the Olive Mine, 12 miles from Mine Centre, which is on the C. N. Ry., in the Rainy River District.

Records Available—Monthly discharge measurements from August, 1914. Daily gauge heights, Aug. 9, 1914, to Oct. 31, 1916.

Drainage Area—1,760 square miles.

Gauge—Vertical steel staff gauge with enamelled face, graduated in feet and inches, and fastened on a crib pier at the C. N. Ry. saw mill, 12 miles from the station. The gauge is located 1,000 feet south of the mouth of Little Turtle River, on the east shore of Little Turtle Lake. Zero on gauge (elevation 83.45) is referred to a bench mark established on a rock with white paint, on the left bank of the river, four feet south of a blazed pine tree, marked I.P. with white paint, which is used as the initial point for soundings. The elevation of this bench mark is 96.00, which is referred to another bench mark (assumed elevation 100.00) established on a rock with white paint, 35 feet north-east of the gauge, at the C. N. Ry. Mill at Mine Centre.

Channel and Control—Straight for about 1,000 feet above and below the station, the water running slowly. The banks are high, wooded and rocky. The bed of the stream is sandy and clean, one channel existing at all stages. The river is used extensively for log driving, and the log jams in Otter Falls affect the section somewhat.

Discharge Measurements—Made from a canoe with a small Price current meter.

Winter Flow—The relation of gauge height to discharge is seriously affected by ice and measurements are made during the winter to determine the flow.

Accuracy—Open water rating curve fairly well defined between gauge heights 91.50 and 94.50. The relation of gauge height to discharge during the log-driving period is affected by back water from log jams.

Observer—Hiram Smith, Mine Centre.

Discharge Measurements of Turtle River at Mountain Rapids in 1916

Date	Hydrographer	Width in Feet	Area of Section in Sq. Feet	Mean Velocity in Feet per Sec.	Gauge Height in Feet	Discharge in Sec-Feet	Discharge in Second-feet per Square Mile
1916							
May 24....	Taylor, J. R....	183	3,668	1.40	96.60	5,143	....
" 24....	"	183	3,668	1.41	96.60	5,187	....
July 13....	"	177	3,510	.88	95.33	3,089 (a)	....

(a) River almost filled with logs below rapids.

Daily Gauge Height of Turtle River at Mountain Rapids for 1915-6

Drainage Area 1,760 Square Miles.

Day	November Gauge Ht. (Feet)	Nov. Discharge (Sec-ft)	December Gauge Ht. (Feet)	Dec. Discharge (Sec-ft)	January Gauge Ht. (Feet)	Jan. Discharge (Sec-ft)	February Gauge Ht. (Feet)	Feb. Discharge (Sec-ft)	March Gauge Ht. (Feet)	Mar. Discharge (Sec-ft)	April Gauge Ht. (Feet)	Apr. Discharge (Sec-ft)	May Gauge Ht. (Feet)	May Discharge (Sec-ft)	June Gauge Ht. (Feet)	June Discharge (Sec-ft)	July Gauge Ht. (Feet)	July Discharge (Sec-ft)	August Gauge Ht. (Feet)	Aug. Discharge (Sec-ft)	September Gauge Ht. (Feet)	Sept. Discharge (Sec-ft)	October Gauge Ht. (Feet)	Oct. Discharge (Sec-ft)
1	91.33		91.58		91.31		91.31		91.16		91.14				96.64		95.62		93.66		92.92		94.00	
2	91.31		91.56		91.31		91.31		91.14		91.14				96.81		95.81		93.62		92.89		93.95	
3	91.22		91.56		91.31		91.31		91.14		91.16				96.80		95.81		93.60		92.87		93.90	
4	91.22		91.52		91.31		91.29		91.14		91.16				96.89		95.82		93.59		92.81		93.83	
5	91.20		91.51		91.31		91.29		91.14		91.16				96.97		95.89		93.54		92.97		93.74	
6	91.22		91.51		91.31		91.27		91.14		91.14				96.97		95.89		93.58		92.87		93.67	
7	91.18		91.47		91.31		91.27		91.16		91.14				96.97		95.89		93.56		93.08		93.62	
8	91.18		91.47		91.31		91.27		91.16		91.14				96.72		95.81		93.54		93.14		92.57	
9	91.45		91.47		91.31		91.27		91.16		91.14				96.72		95.74		93.48		92.93		92.50	
10	91.51		91.47		91.31		91.24		91.16		91.14				96.69		95.72		93.52		92.89		93.41	
11	91.70		91.47		81.31		91.24		91.16		91.16				96.64		95.67		93.47		92.99		93.34	
12	91.99		91.45		91.31		91.24		91.14		91.16				96.70		95.37		93.41		93.14		93.29	
13	92.06		91.43		91.31		91.24		91.14		91.22				96.65		95.29		93.37		93.17		93.23	
14	92.12		91.43		91.31		91.22		91.14		91.47				96.65		95.22		93.30		93.17		93.15	
15	92.10		91.43		91.31		91.22		91.12		91.56				96.58		95.16		93.24		93.14		94.10	
16	92.10		91.39		91.29		91.22		91.12		91.64				96.56		94.99		93.21		93.15		93.05	
17	92.06		91.39		91.29		91.22		91.12						96.49		94.91		93.16		93.20		92.95	
18	91.97		91.39		91.29		91.22		91.12						96.43		94.83		93.20		93.22		92.90	
19	91.97		91.39		91.29		91.20		91.10						96.27		94.74		93.14		93.43		92.89	
20	91.94		91.35		91.29		91.20		91.10						96.01		94.66		93.12		93.72		92.89	
21	91.87		91.35		91.29		91.18		91.10						95.81		94.52		93.06		94.18		92.88	
22	91.81		91.37		91.29		91.18		91.10						95.66		94.41		93.12		94.22		92.84	
23	91.74		91.37		91.29		91.18		91.10						95.58		94.29		93.14		94.26		92.81	
24	91.72		91.37		91.31		91.18		91.10						95.49		94.16		93.16		94.26		92.62	
25	91.68		91.37		91.31		91.18		91.10				96.64		95.47		94.06		93.14		94.24		92.56	
26	91.64		91.37		91.31		91.16		91.10				96.64		95.47		93.99		93.13		94.22		92.55	
27	91.63		91.35		91.31				91.10				96.56		95.49		93.91		93.08		94.08		92.54	
28	91.64		91.35		91.31				91.10				96.56		95.53		93.83		93.02				92.55	
29	91.62		91.31		91.31				91.10				96.47				93.81		92.96				92.53	
30					91.33				91.10				96.47				93.76						92.60	
31					91.33				91.14															

Wabigoon River near Quibéll

Location—About 200 feet above the second fall from the G.T.P. Railway bridge, and ½ mile below the bridge which spans the first fall. One mile east from Quibell Station, Township of Wabigoon, District of Kenora.

Records Available—Discharge measurements from June, 1914, to October, 1915. Daily gauge heights from August 1, 1914, to October 31, 1916.

Drainage Area—2,400 square miles.

Gauge—Vertical staff with enamelled face screwed to a 5-inch hewn spruce post firmly wedged and braced to the rock on the right bank of the river 1,200 feet above the metering station. The zero on the gauge (elev. 1,061.64) is referred to a bench mark (elev. 1,069.46, G.T.P. datum) painted on a point of rock just below the gauge. The initial point for soundings is a spike driven in the rock on the left bank.

Channel and Control—1,200 feet above the station the channel takes a sharp bend to the right, thence running comparatively straight to the station and falls. The water is sluggish above and moderately swift at the station. The banks are high, rocky and wooded. The bed of the stream is full of boulders and crevices. One channel exists at all stages.

Discharge Measurements—Made from canoe and ice with a small Price current meter.

Regulation—The Dryden Timber and Power Company operate a plant on the Wabigoon River at Dryden, which runs 24 hours per day with the exception of Sundays and holidays.

Winter Flow—Ice formation is very heavy here, and the winter flow is somewhat disturbed by it.

Accuracy—Rating curve fairly well defined, and estimates for open water flow are good.

Observer—D. C. Warner, Quibell.

Discharge Measurements of Wabigoon River near Quibell, in 1916

Date	Hydrographer	Width in Feet	Area of Section in Sq. Feet	Mean Velocity in Feet per Sec.	Gauge Height in Feet	Discharge in Sec-Feet	Discharge in Second-feet per Square Mile
1916							
June 14....	Carmichael, R.M.	248	3,890	1.43	1070.64	5,548 (a)	....
" 14....	"	248	3,890	1.57	1070.59	6,121 (b)	....
July 7....	"	92	959	2.95	1066.59	2,832	....
" 7....	"	92	959	2.91	1066.59	2,788	....
" 7....	"	92	959	2.88	1066.59	2,764	....

(a) Backwater 30 ft. from left bank due to two large boulders. Trees growing in water 15 ft. from left bank. Not taken at regular section.

(b) Discharge increased by strong wind down stream. Not taken at regular section.

Daily Gauge Height of Wabigoon River near Quibell for 1915-6

Drainage Area 2,400 Square Miles

Day	November Gauge Ht. Feet	November Discharge Sec-ft.	December Gauge Ht. Feet	December Discharge Sec-ft.	January Gauge Ht. Feet	January Discharge Sec-ft.	February Gauge Ht. Feet	February Discharge Sec-ft.	March Gauge Ht. Feet	March Discharge Sec-ft.	April Gauge Ht. Feet	April Discharge Sec-ft.	May Gauge Ht. Feet	May Discharge Sec-ft.	June Gauge Ht. Feet	June Discharge Sec-ft.	July Gauge Ht. Feet	July Discharge Sec-ft.	August Gauge Ht. Feet	August Discharge Sec-ft.	September Gauge Ht. Feet	September Discharge Sec-ft.	October Gauge Ht. Feet	October Discharge Sec-ft.
1	1063.20		1063.60		1063.22		1063.85		1063.37		1063.20		1068.97		1071.31		1069.24		1065.74		1064.24		1065.29	
2	1063.12		1063.52		1062.22		1063.87		1063.41		1063.18		1069.06		1071.24		1069.18		1065.72		1064.22		1065.33	
3	1063.06		1063.47		1063.22		1063.89		1063.68		1063.14		1069.06		1071.22		1068.72		1065.64		1064.20		1065.79	
4	1063.04		1063.43		1063.20		1063.91		1063.76		1063.10		1069.06		1071.18		1067.85		1065.56		1064.72		1066.10	
5	1062.97		1063.39		1063.20		1063.72		1063.79		1063.12		1069.18		1071.14		1067.22		1065.41		1065.39		1066.20	
6	1062.97		1063.39		1063.18		1063.81		1063.81		1063.81		1069.29		1071.12		1066.64		1065.39		1065.33		1066.24	
7	1063.12		1063.39		1063.16		1063.81		1063.83		1062.10		1069.35		1071.06		1066.31		1065.33		1065.26		1066.43	
8	1063.43		1063.37		1063.14		1063.81		1063.87		1063.14		1069.31		1071.04		1066.16		1065.31		1065.16		1066.41	
9	1063.35		1063.39		1063.14		1063.89		1063.81		1063.81		1069.47		1071.02		1066.06		1065.24		1065.06		1066.39	
10	1064.43		1063.39		1063.14		1063.85		1063.72		1063.20		1069.64		1070.99		1065.97		1065.16		1064.81		1066.06	
11	1064.81		1063.39		1063.14		1063.95		1063.64		1063.22		1069.66		1070.93		1065.91		1065.12		1064.72		1065.33	
12	1064.93		1063.39		1063.16		1063.97		1063.60		1063.41		1069.87		1070.83		1065.81		1065.06		1064.62		1065.68	
13	1065.14		1063.35		1063.24		1063.87		1063.52		1063.81		1069.89		1070.68		1065.72		1064.91		1064.49		1064.97	
14	1064.99		1063.31		1063.33		1063.89		1063.54		1064.39		1069.85		1070.60		1065.64		1064.83		1064.41		1064.83	
15	1064.89		1063.33		1063.35		1063.85		1063.89		1065.47		1063.91		1070.47		1065.56		1064.72		1064.35		1064.56	
16	1064.60		1063.33		1063.33		1063.81		1063.47		1067.06		1070.12		1070.39		1065.47		1064.70		1064.31		1064.47	
17	1064.43		1063.33		1063.31		1063.72		1063.47		1067.72		1070.31		1070.31		1065.56		1064.72		1064.26		1064.43	
18	1064.26		1063.33		1063.33		1063.64		1063.47		1063.31		1070.39		1070.06		1066.33		1064.68		1064.22		1064.41	
19	1061.26		1063.33		1063.33		1063.60		1063.47		1063.39		1070.43		1069.97		1067.14		1064.66		1064.60		1064.37	
20	1061.08		1063.33		1063.31		1063.54		1063.47		1068.64		1070.45		1069.91		1067.41		1064.62		1065.31		1064.35	
21	1063.97		1063.26		1063.47		1063.45		1063.42		1068.79		1070.47		1069.85		1067.33		1064.60		1065.54		1064.33	
22	1063.91		1063.24		1063.54		1063.43		1063.37		1068.39		1070.39		1069.66		1067.24		1064.56		1065.83		1064.33	
23	1063.85		1063.24		1063.56		1063.43		1063.35		1068.06		1070.52		1069.56		1067.02		1064.54		1065.89		1064.31	
24	1063.76		1063.22		1063.60		1063.39		1063.31		1067.97		1070.68		1069.47		1066.85		1064.49		1065.93		1064.29	
25	1063.68		1063.22		1063.64		1063.39		1063.22		1068.20		1071.02		1069.37		1066.60		1064.47		1065.72		1064.29	
26	1063.64		1063.18		1063.70		1063.35		1063.18		1068.31		1071.06		1069.35		1066.41		1064.45		1065.58		1064.26	
27	1063.64		1063.18		1063.72		1063.33		1063.16		1068.54		1071.10		1069.31		1066.26		1064.39		1065.43		1064.24	
28	1063.64		1063.18		1063.76		1063.31		1063.14		1068.60		1071.20		1069.33		1066.20		1064.35		1065.31		1064.31	
29	1063.62		1063.20		1063.79				1063.16		1058.47		1071.22		1069.33		1065.97		1064.31				1064.31	
30	1063.62		1063.22		1063.81				1063.22		1068.72		1071.31		1069.33		1065.85		1064.26				1064.33	
31			1063.24		1063.81				1063.22				1071.31										1064.35	

Wabigoon River at Wabigoon Falls

Location—About 100 feet above Wabigoon Falls, the last fall on the river, and three miles from its junction with the English River, District of Kenora.

Records Available—Discharge measurements from June, 1914, to October, 1915.

Drainage Area—3,120 square miles.

Gauge—Vertical staff with enamelled face screwed to a 5-inch hewn spruce post firmly wedged and braced to the left bank about 200 feet above the metering section. The zero on the gauge (elev. 111.37) is referred to a bench mark (elev. 120.07), consisting of a nail driven in the head of a 4-inch tamarac stump two feet up-stream from the gauge. Another bench mark (elev. 118.51) is painted on a point of rock on the left bank 75 feet below the metering section. The initial point for soundings is on the right bank, the edge of a 5-inch blazed poplar tree, and marked I. P., S. 12° E.

Channel and Control—Straight for about ½ mile above and 100 feet below the station to the falls. Both banks are high, rocky and wooded, and will not overflow. The bed of the stream is composed of rock, with a few boulders and weeds at the right bank. The current is sluggish at and above the station, but swift just below the section.

Discharge Measurements—Made from canoe and ice with a small Price current meter.

Regulation—The Dryden Timber & Power Company operate a plant at Dryden, Ontario. The power is used for the mill and for lighting the town. This plant runs 24 hours per day with the exception of Sundays and holidays, when it runs 12 hours. Part of the flow is utilized for operating a saw mill on the opposite side of the river.

Accuracy—The station rating curve is fairly well defined.

Regular Stations

SOUTH-WESTERN ONTARIO DISTRICT

River	Location	Drain-age Area Sq. Miles	Township	County
Ausable	near Arkona	408	West Williams......	Middlesex
Beaver	near Kimberley........	100	Euphrasia..........	Grey
Bighead	at Meaford	132	St. Vincent.........	"
Black	near Washago	585	Rama	Ontario
Credit.............	at Cataract Jct	85	Caledon	Peel
Maitland	at Ben Miller........	950	Colborne	Huron
Nottawasaga........	near Nicolston.......	416	Essa	Simcoe
Rocky Saugeen......	near Markdale.......	96	Glenelg.............	Grey
Saugeen............	near Port Elgin	1,565	Saugeen............	Bruce
"	near Walkerton......	895	Brant..............	"
Sydenham	near Owen Sound.....	71	Derby........	Grey
Thames, main stream	near Byron...........	1,270	Delaware	Middlesex
" north branch	near Fanshaw.........	650	London.............	"
" south branch	near Ealing...........	515	London and West-minster.........	"

Ausable River near Arkona

Location—At the highway bridge at Marsh's Mills, about two miles east of the village of Arkona, near lot 22, concession 7, Township of West Williams, County of Middlesex.

Records Available—Discharge measurements from May 14th, 1915, to October 31st, 1916. Gauge readings from June 24th, 1915, to October 31st, 1916.

Drainage Area—408 square miles.

Gauge—Vertical staff gauge 0 to 12 feet on the downstream side of the first pier. The elevation of the zero of the gauge is 0.00 and a B.M. is established on top of the right girder, elevation 23.31.

Channel and Control—The discharge measurements are made in the medium fast water between the two rapids. The flow is confined between the abutments at all stages. The stream bed is composed of shale, and will not shift. The channel is straight for 400 yards above and below the section.

Discharge Measurements—Made from the bridge, except in low water, when they are made at a wading section 300 feet above the bridge.

Accuracy—Discharge measurements have not yet been made covering the range of stage.

Observer—Milton Marsh, Arkona P.O.

Discharge Measurements of Ausable River near Arkona in 1915-6

Date	Hydrographer	Width in Feet	Area of Section in Sq. Feet	Mean Velocity in Feet per Sec.	Gauge Height in Feet	Discharge in Sec-Feet	Discharge in Second-feet per Square Mile
1915 Nov. 9....	Yeates, W.	29	45	1.34	1.54	60	....
1916 Jan. 14....	''	89	416	2.23	3.42	927(a)	....
Feb. 24....	''	54	151	.83	1.87	95(b)	....
Mar. 30....	'' —	104	752	7.52	6.75	5650(c)	....
Aug. 24....	''	39	57	1.68	1.78	96(d)	....

(a) Slush at low-water section; control clear.
(b) Ice and slush on control; section clear.
(c) Control clear; co-efficient used to reduce observed velocities.
(d) Not at regular section.

Daily Gauge Height and Discharge of Ausable River near Arkona for 1915-6

Drainage Area, 408 Square Miles

Day	November Gauge Ht. (Feet)	November Dis-charge (Sec-ft.)	December Gauge Ht. (Feet)	December Dis-charge (Sec-ft.)	January Gauge Ht. (Feet)	January Dis-charge (Sec-ft.)	February Gauge Ht. (Feet)	February Dis-charge (Sec-ft.)	March Gauge Ht. (Feet)	March Dis-charge (Sec-ft.)	April Gauge Ht. (Feet)	April Dis-charge (Sec-ft.)	May Gauge Ht. (Feet)	May Dis-charge (Sec-ft.)	June Gauge Ht. (Feet)	June Dis-charge (Sec-ft.)	July Gauge Ht. (Feet)	July Dis-charge (Sec-ft.)	August Gauge Ht. (Feet)	August Dis-charge (Sec-ft.)	September Gauge Ht. (Feet)	September Dis-charge (Sec-ft.)	October Gauge Ht. (Feet)	October Dis-charge (Sec-ft.)
1	1.44	48	3.17	820	2.60	475	5.71	3705	1.71	62	5.42	3230	2.54	442	3.79	1310	1.63	88	1.25	24	1.17	19	1.33	32
2	1.38	38	3.00	710	4.96	2550	4.93	2505	1.71	62	5.00	2600	2.50	420	3.04	735	1.58	76	1.25	24	1.21	21	1.29	27
3	1.44	48	3.00	710	5.71	3705	2.96	685	1.71	62	4.25	1750	2.56	453	2.75	560	1.52	64	1.25	24	1.21	21	1.29	27
4	1.44	48	2.87	630	4.79	2350	2.46	298	1.67	54	3.77	1295	2.79	585	2.52	432	1.50	60	1.33	22	1.21	21	1.29	27
5	1.54	68	2.37	352	5.79	3845	2.31	244	1.67	54	3.43	1000	2.83	610	2.58	464	1.50	60	1.23	23	1.17	19	1.27	26
6	1.54	68	2.35	342	7.38	7000	2.27	244	1.67	54	3.21	845	2.71	535	2.44	387	1.50	60	1.24	23	1.26	25	1.25	24
7	1.54	68	2.29	316	5.04	2660	2.23	212	1.75	70	2.96	685	2.50	420	2.44	387	1.48	56	1.21	21	1.33	32	1.25	24
8	1.54	68	2.29	316	4.34	1840	2.29	228	1.92	110	2.77	570	2.52	431	3.96	1460	1.46	52	1.21	21	1.36	35	1.25	24
9	1.54	68	2.27	308	3.89	975	2.29	236	1.92	110	2.62	486	2.64	497	3.19	830	1.42	44	1.25	24	1.31	29	1.23	22
10	1.53	66	2.27	300	3.56	453	2.31	244	1.92	110	2.45	431	3.33	930	2.83	610	1.46	48	1.21	22	1.21	24	1.19	20
11	1.51	62	2.25	300	2.39	368	2.31	244	1.92	110	2.54	442	5.25	2980	2.96	685	1.39	38	1.22	22	1.21	21	1.17	19
12	1.51	62	2.25	300	2.64	520	1.98	125	1.87	98	3.02	720	4.29	1790	2.44	387	1.37	36	1.25	24	1.21	21	1.17	19
13	1.51	62	2.23	308	4.88	2455	1.98	125	1.85	92	4.42	1920	3.37	960	2.28	312	1.37	36	1.25	24	1.21	21	1.29	27
14	1.51	62	2.29	316	3.13	790	1.93	112	1.88	100	3.85	1365	2.85	620	2.17	268	1.37	36	1.21	21	1.21	21	1.33	32
15	1.51	62	2.31	324	2.56	535	1.89	102	1.90	105	3.46	1020	4.83	2400	2.08	232	1.37	36	1.21	21	1.21	21	1.33	33
16	1.52	64	2.25	300	3.00	453	1.94	115	1.92	110	3.29	905	4.50	2010	2.00	200	1.37	36	1.27	26	1.21	21	1.25	29
17	1.52	64	2.19	276	3.23	360	1.92	115	1.92	110	3.29	905	3.92	1430	2.29	316	1.37	36	1.30	28	1.21	21	1.33	32
18	1.52	64	2.27	308	3.23	292	1.94	115	1.92	110	3.21	845	3.60	1140	2.50	420	1.33	32	1.25	24	1.21	21	1.33	32
19	1.73	112	2.98	700	2.29	376	1.91	108	1.92	98	3.21	845	3.31	915	2.50	420	1.33	32	1.33	32	1.21	21	1.62	85
20	3.00	710	3.06	745	2.29	316	1.92	110	1.87	92	3.04	735	3.46	1020	2.46	398	1.33	32	2.00	200	1.21	21	1.89	157
21	3.00	710	2.81	595	2.38	356	1.90	106	1.85	88	3.44	1010	3.19	835	2.29	316	1.31	29	1.71	108	1.21	21	1.62	85
22	2.83	610	2.98	700	4.71	2250	1.88	100	1.83	78	3.44	1010	3.00	710	2.12	248	1.31	29	1.46	52	1.21	21	1.50	60
23	2.62	486	2.89	645	5.96	4130	1.85	92	1.75	80	3.21	845	4.17	1670	1.96	184	1.29	27	1.32	32	1.21	21	1.44	48
24	2.31	324	3.06	745	5.21	2915	1.85	92	1.80	375	2.96	685	3.46	1020	1.87	151	1.27	26	1.31	29	1.21	21	1.33	32
25	2.25	300	3.23	860	4.38	1880	1.83	88	5.17	2855	2.85	620	2.83	610	2.04	216	1.44	48	1.30	28	1.21	21	1.33	32
26	2.37	352	3.10	770	3.46	1020	1.79	78	7.58	7420	2.92	660	2.54	442	2.06	224	1.50	60	1.25	24	1.33	32	1.33	32
27	3.17	820	3.06	745	3.34	940	1.71	62	7.83	7940	2.92	875	2.37	352	1.89	157	1.38	38	1.21	21	1.33	32	1.33	32
28	3.37	960	2.98	700	5.71	3705	1.71	62	6.71	5590	3.25	875	2.50	420	1.81	133	1.31	29			1.33	32	1.33	32
29	3.71	1240	2.85	620	5.21	2915			5.75	3775	3.23	860	2.73	550	1.69	102	1.27	26					1.33	32
30			2.89	645	3.96	1465					2.83	610	4.92	2500	1.67	98							1.33	42
31			2.81	595	6.38	4920							4.73	2280										

Monthly Discharge of Ausable River near Arkona for 1915-6

Drainage Area 408 Square Miles

Month	Discharge in Second-feet			Discharge in Second-feet per Square Mile			Run-off
	Maximum	Minimum	Mean	Maximum	Minimum	Mean	Depth in Inches. on Drainage Area
November (1915)	1,240	38	272	3.06	.09	.67	.75
December	860	276	525	2.11	.68	1.29	1.49
January ..(1916)	7,000	292	1,900	17.16	.72	4.65	5.36
February	3,705	62	872	9.08	.15	.91	.98
March	7,940	54	975	19.46	.13	2.38	2.74
April	3,230	·393	1,000	7.92	.96	2.45	2.78
May	2,980	352	1,030	7.30	.86	2.53	2.92
June	1,460	98	422	3.58	.24	1.03	1.15
July..........	88	26	42	.22	.06	.10	.12
August........	200	21	33	.49	.05	.08	.09
September.....	35	19	23	.09	.05	.05	·.06
October	157	19	37	.38	.05	.09	.10
The year	7,940	19	555	19.46	.05	1.36	18.51

Beaver River near Kimberley

Location—At Hill's Bridge, about 2 miles above Kimberley, on the south half of lot 2, concession 5, Township of Euphrasia, County of Grey.

Records Available—Discharge measurements at Weber's Bridge September, 1914, to January, 1915. Discharge measurements and daily gauge heights April 25, 1915, to October 31, 1916, at Hill's Bridge.

Drainage Area—100 square miles.

Gauge—Vertical staff 0 to 6 feet on tree on left bank 20 feet downstream from bridge. Zero on gauge is 0.00.

Channel and Control—Channel straight above and below for a distance of 200 feet. The banks and control are permanent under ordinary conditions. The bed is composed of stones and gravel, one channel existing at all stages.

Discharge Measurements—Made from the bridge during the high-water period, and from a permanent wading section located 20 feet above the bridge for the low-water stages.

Regulation—The Hydro-Electric Power Commission's power plant located three-quarters of a mile upstream, though a twenty-four hour power, has a marked effect on the river stage at this section.

Accuracy—The rating curve is fairly well defined, but open-water estimates are subject to errors, due to fluctuations in stage caused by operation of power plant.

Observer—A. Hill, Kimberley, P.O.

Discharge Measurements of Beaver River near Kimberley in 1915-6

Date	Hydrographer	Width in Feet	Area of Section in Sq. Feet	Mean Velocity in Feet per Sec.	Gauge Height in Feet	Discharge in Sec-Feet	Discharge in Second-feet per Square Mile
·--1915							
Dec. 8	Cunnington, G...	56	40	2.05	.96	83	....
‡1916							
Jan. 14....	'' ''	58	66	1.94	1.37	128	....
Feb. 8....	Roberts, E.	·57	90	2.19	1.92	197 (a)	....
‚ʳ ·· 9....	''	57	93	2.40	2.00	223 (a)	....
‚ʳ ·· 24....	Cunnington, G...	56	73	2.50	1.75	184 (a)	....
June 13..	Roberts, E.	57	62	2.18	1.39	135	... .
Oct. 4....	Yeates, W.	57	22	1.74	.62	38	....

(a) Ice at island above section diverting current to left bank.

Daily Gauge Height and Discharge of Beaver Ri or near Kimberley for 1915-6

Drainage Area, 100 Square Miles

Day	Nov Gauge Ht. (Feet)	Nov Dis-charge (Sec-ft)	Dec Gauge Ht. (Feet)	Dec Dis-charge (Sec-ft)	Jan Gauge Ht. (Feet)	Jan Dis-charge (Sec-ft)	Feb Gauge Ht. (Feet)	Feb Dis-charge (Sec-ft)	Mar Gauge Ht. (Feet)	Mar Dis-charge (Sec-ft)	Apr Gauge Ht. (Feet)	Apr Dis-charge (Sec-ft)	May Gauge Ht. (Feet)	May Dis-charge (Sec-ft)	Jun Gauge Ht. (Feet)	Jun Dis-charge (Sec-ft)	Jul Gauge Ht. (Feet)	Jul Dis-charge (Sec-ft)	Aug Gauge Ht. (Feet)	Aug Dis-charge (Sec-ft)	Sep Gauge Ht. (Feet)	Sep Dis-charge (Sec-ft)	Oct Gauge Ht. (Feet)	Oct Dis-charge (Sec-ft)
1	0.83	57	1.08	87	1.81	206	1.96	237	2.29	311	3.21	520	1.87	218	1.46	144	0.92	67	0.71	45	0.71	45	0.58	33
2	0.85	59	1.04	82	1.64	174	2.04	254	1.96	237	2.87	444	1.96	237	1.46	144	0.92	67	0.71	45	0.67	41	0.62	37
3	0.96	71	1.08	87	1.42	137	2.08	263	2.08	341	2.83	435	1.92	228	1.46	144	0.92	67	0.71	45	0.67	41	0.62	37
4	1.08	87	1.08	84	1.54	157	2.04	254	2.21	292	2.62	387	2.00	245	1.42	137	1.00	77	0.71	45	0.67	41	0.60	35
5	1.08	87	1.06	82	2.08	263	2.19	288	2.00	245	2.46	350	2.04	254	1.50	150	1.00	77	0.67	41	0.62	37	0.67	41
6	0.83	57	1.04	82	1.92	228	1.71	187	2.17	283	2.37	329	2.00	245	1.46	144	0.96	72	0.71	49	0.67	41	0.62	37
7	0.81	55	1.08	87	1.92	228	1.48	147	2.08	263	2.25	302	1.92	228	.42	137	0.92	67	0.75	49	0.64	39		37
8	0.79	53	1.12	93	2.33	320	1.92	196	1.75	195	2.17	283	1.96	237	1.42	137	0.96	72	0.75	45	0.58	33		37
9	0.79	53	1.08	87	2.75	416	2.00	224	1.83	210	2.08	263	1.92	228	1.46	144	0.83	57	0.71	45	0.56	31	0.71	45
10	0.81	55	1.25	112	2.08	262	2.31	224	1.75	195	2.04	254	1.83	210	1.50	150	0.92	67	0.71	45	0.60	35	0.81	55
11	0.77	51	1.25	112	1.33	124	2.37	290	1.92	228	2.12	272	1.75	195	1.46	144	0.92	67	0.71	45	0.62	37		55
12	0.75	49	0.83	57	1.56	160	2.17	283	1.75	195	2.17	283	1.75	195	1.42	137	0.87	61	0.71	45	0.62	37	0.87	61
13	0.81	55	0.79	53	1.46	144	2.71	382	1.67	180	2.33	320	1.67	180	1.42	137	0.87	61	0.71	45	0.64	39	0.83	57
14	0.77	51	0.85	59	1.54	157	3.33	508	1.42	137	2.87	444	1.58	164	1.46	144	0.87	61	0.71	45	0.67	41	0.75	49
15	0.75	49	0.87	62	1.85	214	2.17	474	1.77	198	2.54	368	1.67	180	1.54	157	0.79	53	0.71	45	0.62	37	0.79	53
16	0.75	49	0.83	57	1.92	228	2.21	292	1.67	180	2.33	320	1.67	180	1.64	174	0.75	49	0.71	45	0.58	33	0.96	72
17	0.79	53	0.83	57	2.08	263	2.21	210	1.67	180	2.42	341	1.75	195	1.54	157	0.88	57	0.71	45	0.58	33	0.79	53
18	0.79	53	0.83	59	2.17	283	1.83	228	1.71	187	2.37	329	1.83	210	1.50	150	0.83	57	0.71	45	0.69	43	0.96	72
19	1.00	77	0.89	64	2.58	377	1.92	220	1.71	187	2.25	302	1.75	195	1.42	137	0.83	57	0.71	45	0.69	43	0.87	61
20	1.08	87	0.87	67	2.54	368	2.17	224	1.50	150	2.42	341	1.62	171	1.33	124	0.83	57	0.71	45	0.67	43	0.79	41
21	1.00	77	0.94	70	2.19	288	2.54	302	1.42	137	2.29	311	1.58	164	1.21	105	0.75	49	0.71	45	0.60	41	0.67	53
22	1.00	77	0.89	64	3.00	474	2.92	375	1.21	106	2.87	444	1.54	157	1.17	100	0.75	49	0.71	45	0.60	35	0.79	57
23	1.00	77	0.87	57	1.75	195	2.12	185	1.12	93	2.50	359	1.56	160	1.04	82	0.75	49	0.71	45	9.62	37	0.83	72
24	1.00	82	0.83	57	1.92	228	1.71	187	1.29	118	2.37	329	1.50	150	1.00	77	0.75	49	0.71	45	0.67	41	0.96	67
25	1.04	103	0.83	53	1.83	210	1.71	87	1.37	130	2.21	292	1.50	150	1.12	93	0.71	45	0.71	45	0.67	35	0.92	57
26	1.19	124	0.79	59	2.04	254	1.75	195	1.04	82	2.17	283	1.42	137	1.04	82	0.71	45	0.71	45	0.75	37	0.83	57
27	1.33	106	1.39	132	2.46	350	1.73	91	1.21	106	2.08	263	1.75	195	0.96	72	0.71	45	0.71	45	0.67	41	0.79	53
28	1.21	106	0.85	59	2.71	407	2.12	272	1.50	150	2.08	263	1.62	171	1.00	77			0.71	45		49	0.92	67
29	1.27	115	0.92	67	2.21	292	2.17	283	1.62	171	2.04	254	1.50	150		77			0.71	45		49	0.81	55
30	1.21	106	0.87	62	2.00	245			2.29	311	1.83	210	1.50	150					0.71	45				
31					2.50	359			2.83	435			1.50	150					0.71	45				

Monthly Discharge of Beaver River near Kimberley for 1915-6

Drainage Area, 100 Square Miles   .

Month	Discharge in Second-feet			Discharge in Second-feet per Square Mile.			Run-off
	Maximum	Minimum	Mean	Maximum	Minimum	Mean	Depth in Inches on Drainage Area
November (1915)	124	49	70	1.24	.49	.70	.78
December ``	132	53	73	1.32	.53	.73	.84
January .. (1916)	474	124	258	4.74	1.24	2.58	2.97
February	508	147	263	5.08	1.47	2.63	2.84
March	435	82	206	4.35	.82	2.06	2.37
April..........	520	210	330	5.20	2.10	3.30	3.68
May...........	254	137	191	2.54	1.37	1.91	2.20
June...........	174	72	129	1.74	.72	1.29	1.44
July...........	77	45	58	.77	.45	.58	.67
August	49	41	45	.49	.41	.45	.52
September	49	31	39	.49	.31	.39	.44
October........	72	33	51	.72	.33	.51	.59
The year........	520	31	142	5.20	.31	1.42	19.33

Bighead River at Meaford

Location—At the Georgian Bay Milling & Power Co. grist mill bridge outside of the Town of Meaford, near lot 15, concession 5, Township of St. Vincent, County of Grey.

Records Available—Discharge measurements and daily gauge heights from June 10, 1915, to Oct. 31, 1916.

Drainage Area—132 square miles.

Gauge—Vertical staff 0 to 12 feet on right abutment. Elevation of zero on gauge is 0.00.

Channel and Control—The channel is straight for 100 feet above and 500 feet below the gauging station. The bed of the stream is composed of stones and gravel, and is shifting. During the freshet stage, banks and control are not stationary. During a freshet in January, 1916, the stream scoured badly, completely changing the rating curve.

Discharge Measurements—Made at the bridge, also at a wading station 100 feet downstream.

Regulation—Low-water flow is controlled by the Georgian Bay Milling & Power Co.'s dam located four miles upstream. As the plant is usually run for 24 hours each day, except Sunday, the fluctuations will not be great.

Accuracy—The rating curve has not yet been well defined for new conditions.

Observer—Wilbert Baker, Meaford.

Discharge Measurements of Bighead River at Meaford in 1915-6

Date	Hydrographer	Width in Feet	Area of Section in Sq. Feet	Mean Velocity in Feet per Sec.	Gauge Height in Feet	Discharge in Sec-Feet	Discharge in Second-feet per Square Mile
1915 Dec. 10....	Cunnington, G...	29	33	2.00	2.04	66	....
1916 Jan. 21....	" "	45	110	1.23	3.29	135 (a)	....
Feb. 11....	Roberts, E......	65	76	2.68	2.56	205 (b)	....
June. 11....	" "	95	77	1.98	1.83	152 (c)	....
Oct. 4....	Yeates, W......	13	7	.87	.96	6	....
" 4....	" "	43	29	.20	.96	6	....

(a) Reading not taken at regular section; river jammed; ice on control.
(b) Section badly scoured.
(c) Section completely scoured; control washed out.

Daily Gauge Height and Discharge of Bighead River at Meaford for 1915-6

Discharge Area 132 Square Miles

Day	November Gauge Ht. (Feet)	November Dis-charge (Sec-ft.)	December Gauge Ht. (Feet)	December Dis-charge (Sec-ft.)	January Gauge Ht. (Feet)	January Dis-charge (Sec-ft.)	February Gauge Ht. (Feet)	February Dis-charge (Sec-ft.)	March Gauge Ht. (Feet)	March Dis-charge (Sec-ft.)	April Gauge Ht. (Feet)	April Dis-charge (Sec-ft.)	May Gauge Ht. (Feet)	May Dis-charge (Sec-ft.)	June Gauge Ht. (Feet)	June Dis-charge (Sec-ft.)	July Gauge Ht. (Feet)	July Dis-charge (Sec-ft.)	August Gauge Ht. (Feet)	August Dis-charge (Sec-ft.)	September Gauge Ht. (Feet)	September Dis-charge (Sec-ft.)	October Gauge Ht. (Feet)	October Dis-charge (Sec-ft.)
1	2.08	99	2.54	191	2.46	76	2.69	194	2.33	184	5.77	630	2.44	198	2.00	141	1.67	98	1.35	56	1.23	41	0.62	0
2	1.75	47	2.64	211	3.17	190	2.17	163	2.33	184	5.19	555	2.60	219	2.00	141	1.62	92	1.33	54	1.27	46	1.27	46
3	2.02	88	2.60	203	3.29	190	2.17	163	2.33	184	3.42	326	2.58	216	1.94	133	1.62	92	1.33	54	1.25	43	1.25	43
4	1.94	74	2.58	199	2.92	154	2.10	154	2.33	184	3.25	303	2.50	206	1.92	131	1.67	98	1.27	46	1.25	43	0.67	0
5	2.00	84	2.50	183	3.79	241	2.48	203	2.29	179	3.14	289	2.33	192	1.89	127	1.60	89	1.25	41	1.23	43	0.69	0
6	2.00	99	2.52	187	3.87	285	2.75	239	2.27	172	2.83	249	2.39	184	1.83	119	1.58	86	1.23	41	1.19	41	1.31	51
7	2.00	84	2.46	175	3.23	241	2.58	216	2.27	176	2.83	249	2.33	184	1.79	114	1.52	79	1.27	46	0.92	1	0.67	0
8	2.00	84	2.46	175	3.04	167	2.58	216	2.17	163	2.58	216	2.33	184	1.75	108	1.50	76	1.35	56	1.17	36	1.25	43
9	2.00	84	2.37	157	3.25	194	2.42	196	2.17	163	2.56	214	2.17	163	1.73	106	1.50	76	1.33	54	0.83	1	1.23	41
10	2.00	84	2.37	157	3.25	212	2.42	196	2.25	176	2.96	201	2.19	166	1.75	108	1.50	76	1.33	54	1.19	36	0.67	0
11	2.06	85	2.27	121	3.67	249	2.52	209	2.35	186	2.52	209	2.17	163	1.83	119	1.42	66	1.31	51	1.17	33	1.27	46
12	2.10	103	2.33	103	3.33	149	2.50	206	2.42	196	2.94	263	2.17	163	1.74	107	1.44	68	1.27	46	1.12	33	1.29	49
13	2.06	84	2.42	121	3.08	212	2.50	206	2.37	189	3.00	271	2.10	154	1.75	108	1.35	55	1.27	46	1.14	27	1.50	76
14	2.08	99	2.54	140	3.75	258	2.64	224	2.33	184	3.54	341	2.08	151	1.73	106	1.33	54	1.25	43	1.12	29	1.56	84
15	2.08	99	2.54	158	3.25	212	2.75	239	2.25	172	3.25	303	2.08	151	2.14	159	1.33	54	1.25	43	0.67	0	1.58	86
16	2.14	111	2.58	140	3.00	140	2.75	239	2.35	186	3.00	271	2.00	141	2.87	254	1.33	54	1.25	43	1.19	36	1.75	108
17	2.27	137	2.54	140	3.00	140	2.64	224	2.33	184	2.98	268	2.00	141	3.04	276	1.33	54	1.29	49	1.17	33	1.85	121
18	2.21	125	2.54	140	3.08	140	2.50	206	2.33	184	2.81	246	2.00	141	2.89	257	1.33	54	1.25	43	1.25	43	1.77	111
19	2.56	195	2.54	140	3.06	140	2.33	184	2.33	184	2.35	241	1.96	136	2.65	231	1.42	66	1.25	43	1.27	46	1.73	106
20	2.46	175	2.50	121	3.04	140	2.33	184	2.29	179	2.77	241	1.92	131	2.56	221	1.37	59	1.25	43	1.25	43	1.67	98
21	2.48	179	2.50	121	3.29	121	2.46	201	2.25	172	3.17	293	1.92	131	2.48	203	1.33	54	1.27	46	0.69	0	1.64	94
22	2.44	171	2.37	103	5.87	613	2.60	228	2.33	184	4.25	432	1.87	124	2.33	184	1.33	54	1.25	43	1.27	46	1.58	86
23	2.46	175	2.52	94	3.17	121	2.67	219	2.35	186	4.50	466	1.83	119	2.08	151	1.31	51	1.19	41	1.25	43	1.50	76
24	2.46	175	2.54	121	2.92	94	2.50	206	2.37	189	4.00	401	1.83	119	2.00	141	1.31	46	1.17	33	1.25	43	1.50	76
25	2.46	175	2.56	130	2.87	121	2.35	186	2.37	189	3.77	371	1.83	119	1.94	133	1.25	43	1.27	46	1.29	49	1.46	71
26	2.25	133	2.54	132	2.96	103	2.33	184	3.31	311	2.87	254	1.83	119	1.79	114	1.25	43	1.25	43	1.25	43	1.42	66
27	2.42	167	2.56	136	3.08	131	2.37	189	6.25	693	2.50	206	2.58	216	1.73	106	1.25	43	1.25	43			1.42	66
28	2.30	167	2.56	136	3.37	158	2.33	184	4.92	520	2.25	172	2.29	179	1.67	98	1.25	43	1.25	43			1.42	66
29	2.54	191	2.64	140	3.19	167			4.75	498	2.25	172	2.06	149	1.67	98	1.25	43	1.25	43			1.52	79
30			2.87	149	3.00	185			4.75	498	2.25	172	2.00	141			1.39	62	1.25	43			1.50	76
31			3.00	158	3.29	190			4.79	505									1.23	41				

Monthly Discharge of Bighead River at Meaford for 1915-6

Drainage Area, 132 Square Miles

Month	Discharge in Second-feet			Discharge in Second-feet per Square Mile			Run-off
	Maximum	Minimum	Mean	Maximum	Minimum	Mean	Depth in Inches on Drainage Area
November (1915)	195	47	124	1.48	.36	.94	1.05
December. ''	211	94	146	1.60	.71	1.11	1.28
January.. (1916)	285	67	182	2.16	.51	1.38	1.59
February	239	154	201	1.81	1.17	1.52	1.64
March	693	163	234	5.25	1.23	1.77.	2.04
April...........	630	172	292	4.77	1.30	2.21	2.47
May............	219	119	158	1.66	.90	1.20	1.38
June	276	98	146	2.09	.74	1.11	1.24
July............	98	43	64	.74	.33	.48	.55
August	56.	33	46	.42	.25	.35	.40
September	49	0	34	.37	.00	.26	.29
October.........	121	0	64	.92	.00	.48	.55
The year... ...	693	0	140	5.25	.00	1.06	14.43

Black River near Washago

Location—At the highway bridge known as Kennedy's Bridge, about 5 miles southeast of the Town of Washago, on lot 1, concession G, Township of Rama, County of Ontario.

Records Available—Discharge measurements at first bridge from August, 1913, to January, 1914. Discharge measurements at Kennedy's Bridge from February, 1914, and daily gauge heights from May 5, 1915, to October 31, 1916.

Drainage Area—585 square miles.

Gauge—Vertical staff 0 to 12 feet on tree on left bank. Elevation of zero is 19.00, which is referred to a B.M. (elevation 30.00) on tie rod on downstream side of bridge, latter used for water elevations since gauge went out in spring of 1916.

Channel and Control—The channel is straight for 150 feet above and 700 feet below the gauging section. The banks and control can be considered permanent, as the velocity here is never very high. The bed of the stream is composed of rock.

Discharge Measurements—Made from the bridge and wading section 50 feet below.

Winter Flow—Owing to the somewhat sluggish flow at this section, ice from December to March forms to a great thickness, and relation of gauge height to discharge is seriously affected during that period. Measurements are made to determine the winter flow.

Regulation—The flow at this section during May, June and July is controlled to a large extent by logging dams above. The operation of gates at these dams causes fluctuations in gauge heights, amounting to several feet at the gauge. At times logs lodge below section, causing considerable backwater.

Accuracy—For three months in the early summer the river stage is subject to large fluctuations, and the accuracy of the discharge depends upon accuracy of mean daily gauge heights. Rating curve not well defined at all stages.

Observer—John Carrick, Washago.

Discharge Measurements of Black River near Washago in 1915-6

Date	Hydrographer	Width in Feet	Area of Section in Sq. Feet	Mean Velocity in Feet per Sec.	Gauge Height in Feet	Discharge in Sec–Feet	Discharge in Second-feet per Square Mile
1915 Nov. 1....	Roberts, E.	119	492	.65	21.67	322	....
1916 Jan. 20....	Cunnington, G...	119	459	1.09	22.78	486 (a)	........,....
Feb. 22...	`` ..	119	632	1.39	24.00	883 (b)	....
Oct. 3....	Yeates, W.	31	43	1.09	19.80	47 (c)	....

(a) Ice measurement.
(b) Ice-covered above and below section; small ice jam below.
(c) Measurement made at wading section.

Daily Gauge Height and Discharge of Black River near Washago, for 1915-6

Drainage Area 585 Square Miles

Day	Nov. Gauge Ht. (Feet)	Nov. Dis-charge (Sec-ft.)	Dec. Gauge Ht. (Feet)	Dec. Dis-charge (Sec-ft.)	Jan. Gauge Ht. (Feet)	Jan. Dis-charge (Sec-ft.)	Feb. Gauge Ht. (Feet)	Feb. Dis-charge (Sec-ft.)	Mar. Gauge Ht. (Feet)	Mar. Dis-charge (Sec-ft.)	Apr. Gauge Ht. (Feet)	Apr. Dis-charge (Sec-ft.)	May Gauge Ht. (Feet)	May Dis-charge (Sec-ft.)	June Gauge Ht. (Feet)	June Dis-charge (Sec-ft.)	July Gauge Ht. (Feet)	July Dis-charge (Sec-ft.)	Aug. Gauge Ht. (Feet)	Aug. Dis-charge (Sec-ft.)	Sept. Gauge Ht. (Feet)	Sept. Dis-charge (Sec-ft.)	Oct. Gauge Ht. (Feet)	Oct. Dis-charge (Sec-ft.)
1	21.69	327	23.10	850	22.46	375	26.77	2770	23.64	720	28.63	4740	25.71	2550	24.50	1660	21.79	357	20.67	107	19.79	46	19.92	51
2	21.64	312	23.10	850	22.46	360	26.85	2640	23.58	700	28.88	4930	25.56	2440	23.90	1260	21.73	339	20.54	94	19.81	46	19.90	50
3	21.62	306	22.98	790	22.42	369	26.73	2760	23.56	690	28.77	4850	25.62	2480	23.50	1050	21.75	345	20.63	103	19.86	48	19.88	49
4	21.60	300	22.81	675	22.42	375	26.73	2760	23.48	690	28.65	4760	25.79	2440	23.40	1000	21.79	357	20.54	94	19.81	48	19.86	47
5	21.69	327	23.08	675	22.42	390	26.48	2540	23.42	690	28.50	4640	25.58	2450	23.29	945	21.94	402	20.56	96	19.81	46	19.79	46
6	21.69	327	23.00	620	22.46	390	26.08	2240	23.39	690	27.73	4070	26.14	2870	23.40	1000	21.98	414	20.54	94	19.83	47	19.79	45
7	21.79	357	22.83	590	22.52	405	25.71	1970	23.33	670	27.48	3880	25.54	2420	23.36	980	21.81	363	20.56	96	20.00	56	19.71	42
8	21.83	369	22.71	550	22.58	411	25.56	1800	23.37	700	27.31	3750	25.75	2580	23.23	910	21.75	345	20.58	98	19.98	53	19.71	42
9	21.87	381	22.62	550	22.58	417	25.37	1650	23.37	700	27.13	3620	25.75	2580	23.08	835	21.58	295	20.63	103	19.87	49	19.79	46
10	21.77	351	22.75	510	22.60	450	25.21	1590	23.33	690	26.90	3440	25.67	2520	23.17	885	21.56	290	20.54	94	19.83	47	19.79	46
11	21.71	333	22.83	510	22.60	453	24.98	1400	22.33	690	26.71	3300	25.64	2500	23.11	850	21.37	243	20.52	92	19.77	45	19.73	43
12	21.69	327	22.94	520	22.69	459	24.87	1380	23.44	710	26.63	3240	24.60	1730	23.00	800	21.44	260	20.63	103	19.75	44	19.71	43
13	21.69	327	22.83	510	22.71	480	24.77	1280	23.46	720	26.63	3240	24.04	1340	22.94	770	21.50	270	20.63	103	19.73	43	19.73	42
14	21.71	333	22.92	497	22.71	480	24.67	1200	23.46	730	26.63	3240	23.92	1270	22.83	720	21.44	260	20.63	103	19.73	43	19.90	43
15	21.67	321	22.79	480	22.73	480	24.52	1150	23.39	730	27.73	3840	24.06	1360	22.75	690	21.40	250	20.50	90	19.73	43	19.73	50
16	21.62	306	22.77	480	22.73	480	24.37	1110	23.35	700	27.71	4070	23.98	1310	22.71	675	21.33	232	20.50	90	19.77	45	20.13	62
17	21.58	294	22.75	450	22.71	480	24.25	1050	23.33	690	27.75	4080	24.17	1430	22.65	650	21.31	228	20.48	88	19.69	45	20.19	65
18	21.50	270	22.67	450	22.75	486	24.17	1000	23.33	690	27.71	4050	24.12	1390	22.65	650	21.29	222	20.44	85	19.69	42	20.60	100
19	21.44	255	22.60	429	22.81	510	24.17	1000	23.25	670	27.54	3920	24.14	1400	22.67	660	21.25	212	20.35	76	19.71	42	20.94	141
20	21.67	321	22.56	420	22.77	485	24.14	980	23.17	590	27.29	3740	24.14	1390	22.50	595	21.08	170	20.67	107	19.67	41	21.08	170
21	21.96	408	22.56	399	22.81	510	24.08	950	23.17	580	27.27	3900	24.12	1390	22.42	565	21.08	170	20.98	147	19.75	44	21.87	381
22	22.10	450	22.48	390	22.81	510	23.98	875	23.25	580	27.87	4170	24.17	1430	22.31	530	21.08	170	20.87	130	19.75	43	22.90	755
23	22.21	483	22.50	390	23.10	550	23.87	840	23.23	630	27.87	4170	23.90	1260	22.25	505	21.06	165	20.77	117	19.73	43	23.08	835
24	22.19	477	22.50	390	23.79	900	23.71	775	23.21	670	27.63	3990	24.29	1510	22.15	470	21.00	150	20.64	104	19.79	44	22.96	780
25	22.14	462	22.44	390	24.21	800	23.67	775	23.29	710	27.42	3840	24.12	1390	22.12	463	21.02	155	20.48	88	19.75	46	22.50	665
26	22.29	505	22.44	390	24.35	1230	23.67	780	23.48	925	27.15	3630	24.19	1440	22.04	432	21.02	155	20.42	83	19.75	44	22.46	590
27	22.44	565	22.42	381	24.50	320	23.69	790	24.12	1390	26.83	3390	24.25	1480	21.98	414	21.08	170	20.36	77	19.87	49	22.42	585
28	22.73	680	22.44	369	24.89	1520	23.71	800	24.87	1920	26.60	3390	24.25	1480	22.00	420	21.06	165	20.00	69	19.90	50	22.52	560
29	22.92	760	22.46	366	26.08	2170	23.67	720	26.32	3000	26.10	2840	24.40	1590	21.98	414	21.06	144	20.25	54			22.52	600
30	23.02	810	22.46	360	26.50	2540			27.75	4080			24.67	1780	21.92	396	20.96	144	19.87	49			22.56	605
31			22.46	369	26.56	2640							24.73	1820			20.73	113	19.79	46			22.52	600

Monthly Discharge of Black River near Washago for 1915-6

Drainage Area. 585 Square Miles

Month	Discharge in Second-feet			Discharge in Second-feet per Square Mile			Run-off
	Maximum	Minimum	Mean	Maximum	Minimum	Mean	Depth·in Inches on Drainage᾿ Area
November. (1915)	810	255	401	1.38	.44	.69	.77
December "	850	360	501	1.45	.62	.86	.99
January .. (1916)	2,720	360	837	4.65	.62	1.43	1.65
February	2,840	720	1,440	4.85	1.23	2.46	2.65
March	4,080	580	934	6.97	.99	1.60	1.84
April	4,930	2,840	3,882	8.43	4.85	6.64	7.41
May	2,870	`1,260	1,840	4.91	2.15	3.15	3.63
June...........	1,660	396	740	2.84	.68	1.26	1.41 ·
July	414	113	248	.71	.19	.42	.48
August	147	46	92	.25	.08	.16	.18
September	54	41	46	.09	.07	.08	.09
October........	835	42	282	1.43	.07	.48	.55
The year........	4,930	41	931	8.43	.07	1.59	21.64

Credit River at Cataract Junction

Location—About 500 feet from C.P.R. station at Cataract Junction, lot 14, concession 3, Township of Caledon, County of Peel.

Records Available—Discharge measurements from June, 1912, to October 31st, 1916. Daily gauge heights from May 7, 1915, to October 31, 1916.

Drainage Area—85 square miles.

Gauge—Vertical staff 0 to 6 feet on tree on right bank. Zero on gauge (elevation 8.00) is referred to a B.M. (elevation 10.00) painted on rock 100 feet downstream from metering section.

Channel and Control—The channel is straight for about 350 feet above and 300 feet below the section. The right bank is low, and overflows during high stages. The bed is composed of gravel, which is shifting during flood stages.

Discharge Measurements—Made at permanent wading section at all stages.

Winter Flow—The ice, unless jammed, has but little effect at this section. The open channel curve can be used with a fair degree of accuracy.

Regulation—The dam at Erin, about four miles upstream, causes serious fluctuations in the river stage at this section. Semi-daily gauge readings will not give a representative mean.

Accuracy—A fairly well-defined rating curve has been established for this station. The accuracy of the estimates of discharge depends upon the accuracy of the mean daily gauge heights.

Observer—Alfred Riches, Cataract Junction.

Discharge Measurements of Credit River at Cataract Junction in 1916

Date	Hydrographer	Width in Feet	Area of Section in Sq. Feet	Mean Velocity in Feet per Sec.	Gauge Height in Feet	Discharge in Sec–Feet	Discharge in Second-feet per Square Mile
1916							
Jan. 7....	Roberts, E.	41	53	1.80	9.82	96 (a)	....
" 27....	"	41	51	3.30	9.46	.169 (b)	....
Feb. 19....	"	45	55	1.06	9.25	58 (c)	....

(a) Slush ice on control.
(b) Thin ice on river below section.
(c) Heavy ice; slush ice on control.

Daily Gauge Height and Discharge of Credit River at Cataract Junction for 1915-6

Drainage Area 85 Square Miles

Day	November Gauge Ht. (Feet)	November Dis-charge (Sec-ft.)	December Gauge Ht. (Feet)	December Dis-charge (Sec-ft.)	January Gauge Ht. (Feet)	January Dis-charge (Sec-ft.)	February Gauge Ht. (Feet)	February Dis-charge (Sec-ft.)	March Gauge Ht. (Feet)	March Dis-charge (Sec-ft.)	April Gauge Ht. (Feet)	April Dis-charge (Sec-ft.)	May Gauge Ht. (Feet)	May Dis-charge (Sec-ft.)	June Gauge Ht. (Feet)	June Dis-charge (Sec-ft.)	July Gauge Ht. (Feet)	July Dis-charge (Sec-ft.)	August Gauge Ht. (Feet)	August Dis-charge (Sec-ft.)	September Gauge Ht. (Feet)	September Dis-charge (Sec-ft.)	October Gauge Ht. (Feet)	October Dis-charge (Sec-ft.)
1	8.70	41	8.73	46	9.23	59	9.52	117	9.67	151	11.12	940	8.88	74	8.84	65	8.71	43	8.57	24	8.55	22	8.60	27
2	8.66	35	8.71	43	8.81	59	9.94	270	9.35	67	10.54	705	9.04	114	8.79	55	8.67	37	8.59	26	8.47	16	8.57	24
3	8.67	37	8.73	46	8.87	72	10.12	330	9.73	170	9.94	466	9.00	102	8.79	55	8.69	40	8.60	23	8.50	18	8.50	23
4	8.66	37	8.72	38	8.89	76	10.00	290	9.14	27	9.59	326	9.03	111	8.81	59	8.63	40	8.50	27	8.54	22	8.50	18
5	8.67	35	8.68	38	8.81	59	10.04	306	9.12	26	9.27	198	8.96	92	8.83	63	8.64	31	8.56	25	8.49	17	8.61	28
6	8.67	35	8.71	43	9.02	83	9.67	151	9.39	72	9.25	190	8.87	72	8.78	54	8.60	33	8.57	18	8.47	16	8.57	24
7	8.72	44	8.69	40	9.42	95	9.34	59	9.39	72	9.12	140	8.89	76	8.76	51	8.60	30	8.54	19	8.50	18	8.55	24
8	8.64	33	8.69	40	10.02	330	9.49	*102	9.44	78	8.96	92	8.83	63	8.81	59	8.60	30	8.56	23	8.50	18	8.50	22
9	8.72	44	8.69	40	10.19	390	9.51	*114	9.44	78	8.92	83	8.84	65	8.80	57	8.64	34	8.55	24	8.47	16	8.57	18
10	8.64	33	8.73	46	9.03	27	9.39	78	9.54	102	8.95	88	8.80	57	8.84	65	8.58	33	8.55	23	8.50	18	8.59	24
11	8.62	30	8.76	51	8.81	12	9.57	117	9.31	57	8.96	92	8.93	85	8.96	117	8.62	35	8.55	22	8.51	19	8.58	22
12	8.63	31	8.67	37	8.14	21	9.69	151	9.27	49	9.02	108	8.89	85	9.05	102	8.60	30	8.48	18	8.52	20	8.53	26
13	8.71	43	8.69	40	8.94	27	9.87	230	9.10	10	9.22	178	8.78	54	9.00	72	8.53	27	8.67	23	8.54	20	8.59	25
14	8.64	33	8.79	55	9.34	67	10.07	306	9.75	75	9.85	430	8.86	66	8.87	114	8.59	26	8.55	22	8.52	20	8.52	21
15	8.64	33	8.67	37	9.60	123	9.87	230	9.04	10	9.35	430	8.93	80	9.04	123	8.60	25	8.59	22	8.50	18	8.62	26
16	8.64	33	8.67	37	9.64	132	9.46	90	9.17	46	9.29	206	8.95	83	9.07	100	8.60	27	8.56	16	8.47	16	8.60	23
17	8.54	25	8.60	33	9.74	170	9.72	170	9.14	37	9.44	266	8.88	90	8.92	88	8.84	65	8.47	16	8.56	13	8.58	20
18	8.54	22	8.67	37	9.75	182	8.87	14	9.83	49	9.36	234	8.80	57	8.99	63	8.79	51	8.55	22	8.55	23	8.62	30
19	8.81	59	8.67	55	9.69	159	9.39	57	9.29	30	9.10	132	8.78	54	8.83	63	8.63	33	8.59	22	8.51	23	8.87	27
20	8.79	450	8.79	140	9.56	126	9.37	210	9.12	30	9.25	190	8.77	54	8.77	52	8.64	30	8.54	23	8.47	19	8.96	71
21	8.90	72	8.88	83	10.19	390	9.83	108	8.67	37	9.28	202	8.83	63	8.75	49	8.62	28	8.55	22	8.53	16	8.83	92
22	8.87	59	8.81	33	10.19	143	9.55	90	8.93	37	10.06	515	8.98	97	8.94	68	8.61	24	8.59	22	8.47	16	8.72	63
23	8.81	52	8.71	33	9.50	170	9.44	12	8.94	85	9.89	446	8.92	83	8.85	88	8.67	27	8.56	23	8.50	16	8.71	44
24	8.77	44	8.77	52	9.70	80	8.85	11	8.71	89	9.37	230	8.80	57	8.82	49	8.61	21	8.47	16	8.55	18	8.61	43
25	8.71	40	8.98	166	9.31	78	8.85	14	8.96	43	9.35	230	8.75	49	8.71	40	8.53	21	8.67	22	8.59	23	8.59	28
26	8.69	54	8.67	44	9.29	78	8.87	22	8.89	61	9.50	198	8.82	61	8.75	43	8.59	24	8.55	25	8.47	18	8.62	26
27	8.78	54	9.19	49	9.62	170	9.04	51	9.58	92	9.27	166	8.93	83	8.69		8.67		8.59		8.50		8.60	30
28	8.78	90	8.67	54	10.08	310	9.29	47	10.52	76	9.19	102	8.88	74	8.71		8.61		8.56		8.55		8.62	27
29	8.95	78	9.27	90	9.64	159	9.27	47	11.58	322	9.00	92	9.06	120			8.53		8.59		8.59		8.73	46
30	8.90	65	9.67	54	9.56	140			11.29	1120	8.96		9.02	108			8.59		8.54		8.58		8.64	33
31	8.84		9.74		10.58	470				1010														

Monthly Discharge of Credit River at Cataract Junction for 1915-6

Drainage Area, 85 Square Miles

Month	Discharge in Second-feet			Discharge in Second-feet per Square Mile			Run-off
	Maximum	Minimum	Mean	Maximum	Minimum	Mean	Depth in Inches on Drainage Area
November (1915)	450	22	59	5.29	.26	.69	.77
December . "	166	27	52	1.95	.32	.61	.70
January .. (1916)	470	12	147	5.53	.14	1.73	1.99
February	330	12	131	3.88	.14	1.54	1.66
March	1,120	10	155	13.18	.12	1.82	2.10
April	940	83	266	11.06	.98	3.13	3.49
May	120	49	77	1.41	.58	.91	1.05
June...........	123	40	69	1.45	.47	.81	.90
July	43	20	31	.51	.24	.36	.42
August	37	16	22	.44	.19	.26	.30
September	26	13	19	.31	.15	.22	.25
October	92	18	32	1.08	.21	.38	.44
The year	1,120	10	88	13.18	.12	1.04	14.16

Maitland River at Ben Miller

Location—At the highway bridge in the Village of Ben Miller, five miles south-west of the Town of Goderich, Township of Colborne, County of Huron.

Records Available—Discharge measurements from May, 1911, to Feb., 1915. Daily gauge heights from June 1st, 1911, to Oct. 31st, 1916.

Drainage Area—950 square miles.

Gauge—Vertical steel staff gauge with enamelled face graduated in feet and inches and located on the downstream side of the first pier from the left abutment. The zero on the gauge (elev. 12.00) is referred to a bench mark (elev. 29.07) painted on the downstream side of the right wing wall.

Channel and Control—The channel is straight for 300 feet above and ¼ mile below the section. Both banks are low, clean and liable to overflow at high stages. The control is permanent during all stages, being composed of limestone.

Discharge Measurements—Made from the bridge at ordinary and high stages, and at a permanent wading section during the low water period.

Winter Flow—Ice greatly affects relation of gauge height to discharge. The section being wide and shallow, ice frequently freezes to the bottom, rendering meter measurements impossible.

Accuracy—For the low water a well-defined rating curve has been established.

Observer—E. Pfrimmer, Ben Miller P.O.

Daily Gauge Height and Discharge of Maitland River at Ben Miller for 1915-6

Drainage Area, 950 Square Miles

Day	Nov Gauge Ht. (Feet)	Nov Discharge (Sec-ft)	Dec Gauge Ht. (Feet)	Dec Discharge (Sec-ft)	Jan Gauge Ht. (Feet)	Jan Discharge (Sec-ft)	Feb Gauge Ht. (Feet)	Feb Discharge (Sec-ft)	Mar Gauge Ht. (Feet)	Mar Discharge (Sec-ft)	Apr Gauge Ht. (Feet)	Apr Discharge (Sec-ft)	May Gauge Ht. (Feet)	May Discharge (Sec-ft)	Jun Gauge Ht. (Feet)	Jun Discharge (Sec-ft)	Jul Gauge Ht. (Feet)	Jul Discharge (Sec-ft)	Aug Gauge Ht. (Feet)	Aug Discharge (Sec-ft)	Sep Gauge Ht. (Feet)	Sep Discharge (Sec-ft)	Oct Gauge Ht. (Feet)	Oct Discharge (Sec-ft)
1	13.62	348	15.08	3060	14.83	30	16.50	7850	14.00	780	17.25	11800	14.67	2060	14.33	1290	13.58	313	13.25	125	13.12	94	13.21	113
2	13.62	348	15.17	3300	15.00	2220	15.58	4510	14.25	1150	17.00	10300	14.67	2060	14.21	1090	13.58	313	13.25	125	13.08	87	13.17	104
3	13.62	348	15.33	3750	15.33	2550	15.25	3520	14.21	1090	16.33	7180	14.75	2220	14.33	890	13.54	279	13.25	113	13.08	87	13.12	94
4	13.62	348	15.17	3300	15.29	2800	14.83	2420	14.08	890	15.83	5340	14.92	2650	14.00	780	13.50	245	13.25	125	13.12	87	13.12	94
5	13.62	348	15.00	2850	15.25	2680	14.50	1640	14.00	780	15.54	4380	14.58	1830	14.33	1290	13.46	121	13.17	113	13.12	94	13.12	94
6	13.62	348	14.92	2650	16.67	6950	14.33	1290	14.00	780	15.25	3520	14.58	1830	14.33	1290	13.46	221	13.17	104	13.17	94	13.12	94
7	13.62	348	14.75	2220	16.17	4570	14.00	780	13.92	670	15.04	2960	14.58	1830	14.25	1150	13.37	197	13.21	104	13.17	104	13.12	94
8	13.58	313	14.50	1640	15.83	3950	14.00	780	13.83	555	14.83	2420	14.67	2060	14.33	1290	13.37	172	13.19	113	13.12	94	13.12	94
9	13.58	313	14.33	1290	15.25	2850	14.25	1090	13.79	555	14.75	2260	14.75	2220	14.25	1150	13.33	172	13.27	108	13.08	94	13.12	94
10	13.58	313	14.21	1090	15.08	2680	14.50	890	13.75	510	14.67	2060	14.92	2650	14.23	1120	13.33	154	13.21	131	13.04	87	13.12	94
11	13.58	313	14.12	950	15.00	2650	14.33	1000	13.83	470	14.62	1930	14.75	2220	14.25	1150	13.29	137	13.17	113	13.04	87	13.12	94
12	13.58	313	14.04	785	14.75	2220	14.50	1070	13.92	555	14.58	1830	14.48	1600	14.25	1150	13.33	154	13.17	104	13.08	83	13.33	154
13	13.58	313	14.00	780	14.67	2050	14.75	1070	13.92	670	15.21	3410	14.25	1150	14.17	1020	13.33	154	13.17	104	13.08	83	13.08	154
14	13.56	296	13.96	725	14.58	1830	15.00	1070	13.79	670	15.50	4250	14.25	1150	14.08	890	13.33	154	13.17	104	13.12	83	13.29	137
15	13.56	296	13.96	725	14.50	1640	15.17	1070	13.96	510	16.00	5950	14.42	1460	14.08	890	13.25	154	13.12	104	13.12	87	13.25	125
16	13.56	296	13.96	725	14.58	1830	16.33	1070	16.33	725	15.92	5660	14.50	1640	14.08	890	13.33	126	13.10	90	13.12	87	13.29	137
17	13.54	279	14.21	1090	14.42	1460	14.50	1070	14.00	725	15.58	4510	14.50	1640	14.92	2650	13.33	154	13.08	87	13.14	94	13.46	221
18	13.54	313	14.42	1460	14.42	1460	14.17	1070	13.96	725	15.25	3520	14.50	1640	14.58	1830	13.33	154	13.23	119	13.14	94	13.50	245
19	14.00	780	14.37	1360	14.42	1460	14.04	1070	13.92	1070	15.25	3520	14.42	1460	14.50	1640	13.42	197	13.19	108	13.14	94	13.46	245
20	14.83	26	14.37	1360	14.33	1290	14.29	1210	13.83	1070	15.25	3520	14.23	1290	14.33	1290	13.50	245	13.12	94	13.25	98	13.46	245
21	14.92	2650	14.33	1290	16.37	7330	14.17	1020	13.83	670	15.42	4010	14.23	1120	14.29	1210	13.50	197	12.08	87	13.25	98	13.42	221
22	14.79	2320	14.33	1290	16.83	5660	14.12	950	13.79	725	15.67	4900	14.23	1020	14.17	1020	13.42	162	13.08	87	13.25	98	13.42	221
23	14.75	2220	14.46	1550	15.92	5340	14.21	1090	13.75	565	15.33	3750	14.17	1020	13.92	670	13.35	162	13.04	81	13.25	98	13.42	221
24	14.50	1640	14.54	1740	15.57	9340	14.08	950	13.75	565	14.92	2650	14.12	950	13.83	555	13.35	162	13.08	87	13.14	113	13.39	197
25	14.42	1460	14.52	1690	15.83	5070	14.04	835	13.83	510	15.08	3060	14.17	1020	13.79	510	13.33	154	13.12	94	13.14	125	13.42	197
26	14.58	1830	14.71	2120	15.83	5340	14.00	780	14.50	555	15.25	3520	14.12	950	13.67	393	13.29	154	13.12	94	13.25	113	13.39	180
27	14.83	2420	14.83	1880	15.92	5340	13.79	510	17.75	1640	15.08	3060	14.08	835	13.67	393	13.35	154	13.12	94	13.25	125	13.33	180
28	15.29	3630	14.92	1880	16.33	12280	13.71	430	19.33	4250	15.75	5070	14.04	725	13.62	348	13.33	154	13.12	94			13.39	180
29	15.42	4010	14.87	1880	17.33	7180	13.83	555	18.25	29690	15.08	3060	14.08	890	13.58	313	13.29	137	13.12	94			13.33	154
30	15.17	3300	14.83	1880	15.58	4510			14800	18620	14.67		14.25	1150									13.33	154
31			14.83	1880	16.00	5950							14.42	1460				137						

10 H (iii)

Monthly Discharge of Maitland River at Ben Miller for 1915-6

Drainage Area 950 Square Miles

Month	Discharge in Second-feet.			Discharge in Second-feet per Square Mile.			Run-off
	Maximum	Minimum	Mean	Maximum	Minimum	Mean	Depth in Inches on Drainage Area
November (1915)	4,010	279	1,148	4.22	.29	1.21	1.35
December. ''	8,750	725	1,745	3.95	.76	1.84	2.12
January ..(1916)	12,280	1,290	4,145	12.93	1.36	4.36	5.03
February	7,850	430	1,450	8.26	.45	1.53	1.65
March	29,690	470	2,779	31.25	.49	2.93	3.38
April	11,800	1,830	4,314	12.42	1.93	4.54	5.06
May	2,650	725	1,581	2.79	.76	1.66	1.91
June............	2,650	313	1,017	2.79	.33·	1.07	1.19
July	313	125	185	.33	.13	.19	.22
August	131	81	103	.14	.09	.11	.13
September	125	83	95	.13	.09	.10	.11
October	245	87	152	.26	.09	.16	.18
The year........	29,690	81	1,559	31.25	.09	1.64	22.32

Nottawasaga River near Nicolston

Location—At McLean's Bridge, 4 miles north of the Town of Nicolston, near lot 5, concession 6, Township of Essa, County of Simcoe.

Records Available—Discharge measurements from June, 1912, to Feb., 1916. Daily gauge heights, from August 18, 1914, to October 31, 1916.

Drainage Area—416 square miles.

Gauge—Vertical staff 0 to 12 feet on right abutment, upstream side. Zero on the gauge (elevation 4.00) is referred to B.M. (elevation 20.00) on tension rod of bridge 60 feet from initial point for soundings.

Channel and Control—The channel below the section is straight for about 600 feet. Above the section it is straight for about 100 feet, when it takes a sharp turn to the right, causing an angle at the bridge. Both banks and control are subject to change under high-water conditions.

Discharge Measurements—Made from the bridge at all stages.

Winter Flow—The relation of gauge height to discharge is affected by ice during the winter months and measurements are made to compute the winter flow.

Regulation—The dams above have little effect this section.

Accuracy—These records, with the reduction made for the angle at section, can be considered good up to discharges of 800 second feet. There are not sufficient records available to compute discharges very accurately above gauge height 8.00 feet. The estimate made is probably close to the actual discharge.

Observer—John Scott, Egbert P.O.

Discharge Measurements of Nottawasaga River near Nicolston in 1916

Date	Hydrographer	Width in Feet	Area of Section in Sq. Feet	Mean Velocity in Feet per Sec.	Gauge Height in Feet	Discharge in Sec-Feet	Discharge in Second-feet per Square Mile
1916							
Jan. 15....	Cunnington, G...	90	378	1.24	7.67	468 (a)	....
Feb. 12....	Roberts, E.....	90	264	.89	6.46	236 (a)	....
" 23....	Cunnington, G...	90	264	.84	6.42	224 (a)	....

(a) Ice measurement.

Daily Gauge Height and Discharge of Nottawasaga River at Nicolston for 1915-6

Drainage Area 416 Square Miles

Day	Nov Gauge Ht. (Feet)	Nov Dis-charge (Sec-ft.)	Dec Gauge Ht. (Feet)	Dec Dis-charge (Sec-ft.)	Jan Gauge Ht. (Feet)	Jan Dis-charge (Sec-ft.)	Feb Gauge Ht. (Feet)	Feb Dis-charge (Sec-ft.)	Mar Gauge Ht. (Feet)	Mar Dis-charge (Sec-ft.)	Apr Gauge Ht. (Feet)	Apr Dis-charge (Sec-ft.)	May Gauge Ht. (Feet)	May Dis-charge (Sec-ft.)	Jun Gauge Ht. (Feet)	Jun Dis-charge (Sec-ft.)	Jul Gauge Ht. (Feet)	Jul Dis-charge (Sec-ft.)	Aug Gauge Ht. (Feet)	Aug Dis-charge (Sec-ft.)	Sep Gauge Ht. (Feet)	Sep Dis-charge (Sec-ft.)	Oct Gauge Ht. (Feet)	Oct Dis-charge (Sec-ft.)
1	5.94	178	6.58	306	6.27	244	13.75	2720	6.58	246	17.92	4390	7.33	468	7.64	545	5.87	164	5.33	75	5.33	75	5.54	106
2	5.90	170	6.44	278	6.67	324	11.31	1740	6.54	230	15.37	3370	7.62	540	7.08	406	5.75	140	5.35	78	5.19	59	5.44	91
3	5.94	178	6.27	244	7.00	390	9.42	1060	6.54	230	13.27	2530	7.77	580	7.02	394	5.73	136	5.25	65	5.10	50	5.44	91
4	5.94	178	6.04	198	7.98	388	8.12	665	6.50	226	11.98	2010	8.39	745	6.71	382	5.75	140	5.23	63	5.21	61	5.42	88
5	6.14	218	5.98	186	7.08	406	7.56	525	6.42	220	10.70	1610	8.02	640	6.52	294	5.58	112	5.21	61	5.19	59	5.54	106
6	6.23	236	6.08	206	8.29	585	7.17	428	6.64	250	9.27	1010	7.52	515	6.46	282	5.54	106	5.19	59	5.31	72	5.50	100
7	6.08	206	5.92	174	7.04	510	6.89	382	7.04	290	8.60	810	7.12	453	6.27	244	5.58	94	5.75	140	5.31	72	5.48	97
8	6.10	210	6.14	218	7.62	455	6.67	368	6.85	290	8.27	710	7.06	402	6.17	224	5.58	112	5.50	100	5.27	67	5.25	65
9	6.02	194	6.10	210	8.04	370	6.62	340	6.69	270	7.89	610	6.87	364	6.17	224	5.54	88	5.31	72	5.25	65	5.31	72
10	6.08	206	5.92	174	7.62	390	6.73	242	6.73	270	7.73	570	7.12	415	6.23	236	5.58	106	5.35	78	5.23	63	5.50	100
11	5.87	164	6.02	194	7.37	378	6.62	260	6.71	270	7.69	570	6.96	382	7.71	565	5.48	112	5.42	88	5.37	80	5.44	109
12	6.04	198	5.87	164	7.21	382	6.50	240	6.79	290	8.23	700	6.48	286	7.96	625	5.54	97	5.46	94	5.25	65	5.56	103
13	6.02	194	6.21	232	7.21	493	6.60	230	6.85	290	8.75	855	6.44	244	7.37	478	5.37	106	5.14	54	5.31	72	5.62	118
14	5.96	182	6.00	198	7.83	560	6.62	228	6.83	228	10.67	1500	6.27	278	7.21	357	5.29	80	5.08	48	5.33	80	5.54	106
15	6.00	190	6.06	202	8.14	472	6.58	226	6.73	226	12.64	2280	6.79	348	6.83	278	5.39	69	5.12	52	5.39	84	5.67	91
16	6.02	194	6.25	190	7.64	410	6.58	226	6.67	254	10.89	1590	7.02	394	8.37	348	5.56	80	5.12	52	5.17	57	5.81	96
17	6.02	194	6.37	240	7.48	398	6.64	230	6.75	270	9.96	1250	7.00	390	7.54	740	5.37	109	5.17	52	5.29	69	5.87	152
18	5.90	170	6.34	261	7.04	318	6.44	214	6.56	254	9.89	1250	6.77	344	7.25	520	5.58	80	5.19	57	5.35	78	6.83	164
19	6.02	194	6.39	232	6.64	282	6.54	220	6.73	196	9.67	900	6.54	298	6.98	448	6.62	112	5.14	54	5.37	65	7.06	356
20	7.17	428	6.19	228	6.46	306	6.56	230	6.79	230	10.37	1150	6.29	248	6.67	386	6.04	314	5.27	67	5.39	80	6.58	402
21	7.25	447	6.27	228	6.58	282	6.50	230	6.79	212	12.50	1390	6.19	228	6.44	324	5.69	198	5.14	54	5.25	84	6.08	306
22	6.72	334	6.31	244	6.46	282	6.62	250	6.83	298	13.92	2220	7.06	398	6.21	278	5.67	125	5.25	65	5.39	65	6.04	206
23	6.35	260	6.21	252	9.19	1040	6.42	210	6.75	212	11.98	2790	6.31	402	6.06	248	5.52	103	5.21	61	5.42	88	5.85	198
24	6.33	256	6.19	232	9.37	1120	6.54	234	6.85	230	10.60	2010	6.64	318	5.94	232	5.37	80	5.29	69	5.35	78	5.75	160
25	6.33	236	6.37	228	9.60	1200	6.62	250	6.92	250	9.73	1480	6.31	252	6.79	232	5.33	75	5.29	69	5.37	80	5.88	140
26	6.58	306	6.31	264	9.83	1240			8.45	374	9.21	1170	7.04	495	6.44	402	5.35	78	5.27	67	5.64	121	5.79	156
27	6.31	236	6.31	252	9.92	1240			10.79	765	8.42	995	6.31	252	6.21	178	5.21	61	5.23	63	5.58	112	5.71	148
28	7.08	306	6.31	232	10.10	1300			13.87	1540	7.87	755	9.79	1190	6.17	278	5.35	78	5.29	69			5.79	132
29	7.00	390	6.29	252	11.06	1650			19.77	2770	7.60	600	8.23	700	5.94	224			5.27	67			5.71	148
30	6.92	374	6.31	248	10.58	1470			19.25	5130	7.60	535	8.10	660	5.89	178	5.21	61	5.23	63			5.71	132
31			6.29	248	9.06	950				4920			8.37	740		168	5.35	78	5.29	69				

Monthly Discharge of Nottawasaga River near Nicolston for 1915-6

Drainage Area 416 Square Miles

Month	Discharge in Second-feet			Discharge in Second–feet per Square Mile			Run-off
	Maximum	Minimum	Mean	Maximum	Minimum	Mean	Depth in Inches on Drainage Area
November (1915)	447	164	245	1.07	.39	.59	.66
December "	306	164	228	.74	.39	.55	.63
January. (1916)	1,680	244	677	4.04	.59	1.63	1.88
February	2,720	196	438	6.54	.47	1.05	1.13
March	5,130	220	722	12.33	.53	1.74	2.01
April	4,390	535	1,450	10.55	1.29	3.49	3.89
May	1,190	228	456	2.86	.55	1.10	1.27
June...........	740	168	384	1.78	.40	.92	1.03
July	164	61	111	.39	.15	.27	.31
August	140	48	68	.34	.12	.16	.18
September	121	50	75	.29	.12	.18	.20
October	402	65	143	1.97	.16	.34	.39
The year........	5,130	48	415	12.33	.12	1.00	13.61

Rocky Saugeen River near Markdale

Location—At the Glen Cross highway bridge, three-quarters of a mile above Hayward's Falls, near lot 5, concession 8, Township of Glenelg, County of Grey.

Records Available—Discharge measurements and daily gauge heights June 8, 1915, to October 31, 1916.

Drainage Area—96 square miles.

Gauge—Vertical staff 0 to 6 feet on the downstream side of the centre pier of bridge. The zero of gauge (elevation 0.00) is referred to a B.M. (elevation 29.65) painted on a rock projecting from bank 40 feet north from first telephone pole on left bank.

Channel and Control—The channel is straight for 200 feet above and 500 feet below the station. The bed and banks are permanent, as flood conditions do not exist on this stream.

Discharge Measurements—Made at a permanent wading section. When the river is extremely high measurements will be made from the bridge.

Winter Flow—Ice does have a serious effect at this section.

Regulation—The dam above has little effect on the river stage at this section.

Accuracy—The rating curve is well defined except for maximum flows.

Observer—Arthur McNally, Markdale.

Discharge Measurements of Rocky Saugeen River near Markdale in 1915-6

Date	Hydrographer	Width in Feet	Area of Section in Sq. Feet	Mean Velocity in Feet per Sec.	Gauge Height in Feet	Discharge in Sec-Feet	Discharge in Second-feet per Square Mile
1915 Dec. 9....	Cunnington, G..	75	75	1.04	1.87	78 (a)	....
1916 Jan. 13....	''	85	150	1.48	2.25	223 (b)	....
Feb. 10....	Roberts, E.	85	158	1.38	2.25	218	....
'' 24....	Cunnington, G..	82	125	1.08	1.83	138	....
June 12....	Roberts, E.	85	128	1.18	1.92	150	....
Oct. 4....	''	68	61	.83	1.14	50	....

(a) Logs in stream.
(b) Ice measurement.

Daily Gauge Height and Discharge of Rocky Saugeen River near Markdale for 1915-6

Drainage Area, 96 Square Miles

Day	Nov Gauge Ht. (Feet)	Nov Dis-charge (Sec-ft.)	Dec Gauge Ht. (Feet)	Dec Dis-charge (Sec-ft.)	Jan Gauge Ht. (Feet)	Jan Dis-charge (Sec-ft.)	Feb Gauge Ht. (Feet)	Feb Dis-charge (Sec-ft.)	Mar Gauge Ht. (Feet)	Mar Dis-charge (Sec-ft.)	Apr Gauge Ht. (Feet)	Apr Dis-charge (Sec-ft.)	May Gauge Ht. (Feet)	May Dis-charge (Sec-ft.)	Jun Gauge Ht. (Feet)	Jun Dis-charge (Sec-ft.)	Jul Gauge Ht. (Feet)	Jul Dis-charge (Sec-ft.)	Aug Gauge Ht. (Feet)	Aug Dis-charge (Sec-ft.)	Sep Gauge Ht. (Feet)	Sep Dis-charge (Sec-ft.)	Oct Gauge Ht. (Feet)	Oct Dis-charge (Sec-ft.)
1	1.25	58	1.75	123	1.67	111	2.58	291	1.92	115	3.50	520	2.33	234	2.08	181	1.75	122	1.33	67	1.25	59	1.17	53
2	1.33	67	1.75	123	1.75	123	2.67	313	1.83	101	3.42	500	2.50	273	1.92	151	1.75	122	1.33	67	1.25	59	1.17	53
3	1.33	67	1.75	123	1.75	123	2.75	332	1.83	101	3.25	457	2.50	273	1.92	151	1.67	111	1.33	67	1.25	59	1.17	53
4	1.33	67	1.67	111	1.67	111	2.67	313	1.83	101	3.25	457	2.50	273	1.92	151	1.67	111	1.33	67	1.25	59	1.17	53
5	1.33	58	1.58	98	1.67	111	2.58	291	1.75	91	3.00	395	2.42	255	1.92	151	1.67	111	1.33	67	1.25	59	1.17	53
6	1.33	58	1.58	98	1.75	123	2.50	273	1.75	91	2.83	353	2.42	255	1.92	151	1.58	98	1.33	67	1.25	59	1.17	53
7	1.25	58	1.50	88	1.75	123	2.50	273	1.75	91	2.67	313	2.33	234	1.92	151	1.58	98	1.33	67	1.25	59	1.17	53
8	1.25	58	1.50	88	1.75	123	2.50	273	1.67	81	2.58	291	2.25	216	1.92	151	1.58	98	1.33	67	1.33	67	1.17	53
9	1.25	58	1.42	78	1.67	111	2.50	273	1.67	81	2.58	291	2.25	200	2.00	151	1.50	88	1.33	67	1.33	67	1.17	53
10	1.25	58	1.42	78	1.75	123	2.33	234	1.67	81	2.58	291	2.17	200	1.92	151	1.50	88	1.42	78	1.25	59	1.17	53
11	1.25	58	1.42	78	1.75	123	2.33	234	1.67	81	2.67	313	2.17	200	1.92	151	1.50	88	1.33	67	1.25	59	1.17	53
12	1.25	58	1.42	78	1.83	135	2.67	313	1.67	81	2.75	332	2.17	200	1.92	151	1.50	88	1.25	59	1.25	59	1.33	67
13	1.25	58	1.50	88	1.92	151	2.67	259	1.58	70	2.83	353	2.00	165	2.0	165	1.50	88	1.25	59	1.17	53	1.25	59
14	1.25	58	1.50	88	2.00	165	2.58	239	1.67	81	2.83	353	2.17	200	2.25	216	1.50	88	1.25	59	1.08	47	1.25	59
15	1.25	58	1.50	88	1.83	135	2.58	239	1.67	81	2.75	332	2.17	200	2.50	273	1.50	88	1.25	59	1.08	47	1.25	59
16	1.25	58	1.58	98	1.92	151	2.50	239	1.67	81	2.67	313	2.08	181	2.33	234	1.50	88	1.25	59	1.08	47	1.33	59
17	1.25	58	1.50	88	1.92	151	2.42	216	1.58	69	2.75	332	2.08	181	2.25	216	1.42	78	1.25	59	1.17	53	1.42	78
18	1.33	67	1.58	98	2.00	165	2.33	200	1.58	69	3.08	415	2.08	181	2.17	200	1.42	78	1.25	59	1.25	59	1.33	67
19	1.50	98	1.67	111	2.08	181	2.33	185	1.67	69	2.92	375	2.08	165	2.0	165	1.42	78	1.25	59	1.25	59	1.33	67
20	1.58	88	1.58	98	2.33	234	2.25	171	1.75	111	2.83	353	2.00	165	1.92	151	1.50	88	1.25	53	1.25	59	1.25	59
21	1.58	88	1.58	98	2.83	353	2.25	171	1.75	123	2.83	353	2.00	165	1.83	135	1.50	88	1.17	53	1.25	59	1.25	59
22	1.50	88	1.58	88	2.83	353	2.08	138	1.75	123	2.67	313	2.00	165	1.83	135	1.42	78	1.17	53	1.33	67	1.25	59
23	1.42	78	1.58	98	2.83	353	2.08	138	1.75	123	2.50	273	2.00	151	1.83	135	1.42	78	1.17	59	1.25	59	1.25	59
24	1.42	78	1.58	88	2.75	332	2.08	138	1.83	135	2.50	273	1.92	151	1.83	135	1.33	67	1.25	59	1.25	59	1.25	59
25	1.50	78	1.50	88	2.67	313	2.00	125	2.00	165	2.42	255	1.92	151	1.83	135	1.33	67	1.25	59	1.25	59	1.25	59
26	1.67	111	1.58	98	2.92	375	1.92	115	2.42	255	2.33	234	1.92	165	1.83	135	1.33	67	1.25	59	1.25	59	1.25	59
27	1.75	123	1.67	111	2.92	375			2.67	313			2.00	181	1.83	135	1.33	67	1.25	59	1.33	67	1.25	59
28	1.75	123	1.58	98	2.92	375			3.17	438			2.08	181			1.33	67	1.25	59	1.25	59	1.25	59
29	1.75	123	1.92	98	2.92	375							2.08	181					1.25	59	1.25	67	1.25	59
30	1.75	123	1.58	98	2.75	332							2.08	181					1.25	59	1.25	59	1.25	59
31			1.58	98	2.58	291							2.08	181					1.25	59			1.25	59

Monthly Discharge of Rocky Saugeen River near Markdale for 1915-6

Drainage Area, 96 Square Miles

Month.	Discharge in Second-feet.			Discharge in Second-feet per Square Mile			Run-off
	Maximum	Minimum	Mean	Maximum	Minimum	Mean	Depth in Inches on Drainage Area
November (1915).	123	58	77	1.28	.60	.80	.89
December	123	78	96	1.28	.81	1.00	1.15
January (1916).	375	111	208	3.91	1.16	2.17	2.50
February	332	115	226	3.46	1.20	2.35	2.53
March	438	69	119	4.56	.72	1.24	1.43
April	520	234	344	5.42	2.44	3.58	3.99
May	273	151	198	2.84	1.57	2.06	2.37
June	273	135	162	2.84	1.41	1.69	1.89
July	122	67	88	1.27	.70	.92	1.06
August	78	53	62	.81	.55	.65	.75
September	67	47	58	.70	.49	.60	.67
October	78	53	59	.81	.55	.61	.70
The year	520	47	141	5.42	.49	1.47	20.01

Saugeen River near Port Elgin

Location—At the highway bridge known at McCalder's Bridge, 4 miles north-east of the Town of Port Elgin, near lot 5, concession 12, Township of Saugeen, County of Bruce.

Records Available—Discharge measurements from July, 1911, to October, 1916. Daily gauge heights from April 19, 1914, to October 31, 1916.

Drainage Area—1,565 square miles.

Gauge—Vertical staff 0 to 12 feet on right abutment downstream side. Zero on gauge (elevation 4.00) is referred to a B.M. (elevation 25.00) painted on wooden handrail of bridge.

Channel and Control—The channel is straight for about 350 feet above and below the section. The bed of the stream, with two submerged piers at the section, is composed of fairly large boulders, which will only shift during high flood stages. The current is moderate and flows through two channels, which are separated by the centre pier of the bridge.

Discharge Measurements—Made from the bridge at all stages.

Winter Flow—Ice greatly affects relation of gauge height to discharge. Measurements are made during the winter to determine the flow.

Regulation—Fluctuations occur in the river stage at this section. This is no doubt caused by the plants at Walkerton, Chesley and Paisley.

Accuracy—Semi-daily reading should give a fair representative mean. The fluctuations that have been noted are not large, consequently the gauge height records can be classified as good. A well-defined curve is shown for flows up to 20,000 sec. feet. A slight angle in cross-section No. 1 may affect accuracy of meter measurements.

Observer—John Shanks, Southampton.

Discharge measurements of Saugeen River near Port Elgin in 1915-6

Date	Hydrographer	Width in Feet	Area of Section in Sq. Feet	Mean Velocity in Feet per Sec.	Gauge Height in Feet	Discharge in Sec-Feet	Discharge in Second-feet per Square Mile
1915							
Nov. 23....	Yeates, W.	197	1,060	1.81	6.80	1,922	....
1916							
Jan. 12....	Cunnington, G...	210	1,439	2.41	8.67	3,462 (a)	....
" 28....	Yeates, W.	210	2,431	4.59	13.33	11,166 (b)	....
" 28....	" "	210	2,410	4.59	13.26	11,070 (b)	....
" 28....	" "	210	2,389	4.50	13.17	10,762 (b)	....
Feb. 2....	" "	210	1,696	3.68	9.88	6,234 (c)	....
" 2....	" "	210	1,675	3.64	9.79	6,095 (c)	....
Mar. 30....	Roberts, E.	210	2,578	6.45	14.03	16,637 (c)	....
" 30....	" "	210	2,557	6.45	13.96	16,488 (c)	....
" 31....	" "	210	2,431	5.96	13.81	14,477 (c)	....
" 31....	" "	210	2,431	6.01	13.81	14,600 (c)	....
" 31....	" "	210	2,578	6.44	14.00	16,576 (c)	....
Apr. 2....	Yeates, W.	220	2,765	6.73	14.75	18,605 (c)	....
" 2....	" "	220	2,699	6.62	14.48	17,880 (c)	....
" 3....	" "	210	2,452	6.02	13.45	14,768 (c)	....
" 4....	Roberts, E.	210	2,305	5.45	12.75	12,556 (c)	....
" 4....	" "	210	2,284	5.42	12.69	12,374 (c)	....
" 4....	" "	210	2,242	5.22	12.49	11,694 (c)	....
" 4....	" "	210	2,242	5.11	12.44	11,458 (c)	....
" 4....	" "	210	2,221	5.14	12.39	11,423 (c)	....
" 5....	" "	210	2,116	4.90	11.88	10,369 (c)	....
" 5....	" "	210	2,074	4.66	11.66	9,652 (c)	....
" 5....	" "	210	2,074	4.61	11.61	9,562 (c)	....
" 6....	" "	210	1,927	4.25	10.96	8,185 (c)	....
" 7....	" "	210	1,759	3.77	10.18	6,625 (c)	....
" 7....	" "	210	1,811	3.82	10.40	6,922 (c)	....
" 8....	" "	210	1,654	3.49	9.68	5,770 (c)	....
" 11....	Yeates, W.	210	1,381	2.79	8.33	3,852 (c)	....
" 11....	" "	210	1,381	2.76	8.33	3,803 (c)	....
" 12....	" "	210	1,444	2.84	8.67	4,103 (c)	....
" 12....	" "	210	1,444	2.92	8.67	4,216 (c)	....
" 12....	" "	210	1,444	2.95	8.69	4,266 (c)	....
" 12....	" "	210	1,444	2.89	8.69	4,176 (c)	....
" 13....	" "	210	1,538	3.19	9.19	4,905 (c)	....
" 13....	" "	210	1,538	3.21	9.19	4,940 (c)	....
Oct. 5....	" "	191	673	.65	4.79	436	....

(a) Too many estimated velocities for accurate results.
(b) Ice and slush in stream; co-efficient applied to observed surface velocities.
(c) Co-efficient applied to observed surface velocities.

Daily Gauge Height and Discharge of Saugeen River near Port Elgin for 1915-6

Drainage Area 1.565 Square Mes

Day	Nov Gauge Ht (Feet)	Nov Dis-charge (Sec-ft)	Dec Gauge Ht (Feet)	Dec Dis-charge (Sec-ft)	Jan Gauge Ht (Feet)	Jan Dis-charge (Sec-ft)	Feb Gauge Ht (Feet)	Feb Dis-charge (Sec-ft)	Mar Gauge Ht (Feet)	Mar Dis-charge (Sec-ft)	Apr Gauge Ht (Feet)	Apr Dis-charge (Sec-ft)	May Gauge Ht (Feet)	May Dis-charge (Sec-ft)	Jun Gauge Ht (Feet)	Jun Dis-charge (Sec-ft)	Jul Gauge Ht (Feet)	Jul Dis-charge (Sec-ft)	Aug Gauge Ht (Feet)	Aug Dis-charge (Sec-ft)	Sep Gauge Ht (Feet)	Sep Dis-charge (Sec-ft)	Oct Gauge Ht (Feet)	Oct Dis-charge (Sec-ft)
1	5.29	694	7.83	3195	6.94	2215	10.58	7420	8.14	2995	14.87	19185	7.71	3060	6.54	1770	6.00	1220	4.85	460	4.69	402	5.02	540
2	5.27	682	7.50	2830	8.56	4085	9.85	6045	8.04	2885	14.92	19345	8.42	3900	6.48	1710	5.81	1070	4.83	452	4.67	396	4.98	520
3	5.23	658	7.27	2575	8.98	4670	9.42	5530	7.96	2775	13.58	15140	8.42	3900	6.42	1640	5.75	1040	4.81	444	4.69	402	4.89	476
4	5.21	646	7.06	2345	8.23	3675	7.77	3125	7.92	2720	12.57	12195	8.60	4140	6.35	1570	5.69	970	4.81	444	4.67	396	4.83	452
5	5.23	658	6.94	2215	9.25	5075	7.67	3015	7.83	2610	11.75	10025	8.46	3950	6.27	1490	5.62	915	4.77	430	4.67	396	4.79	436
6	5.29	694	6.79	2050	10.25	6775	7.48	2810	7.83	2610	11.10	8530	8.29	3750	6.33	1490	5.50	820	4.75	422	4.67	396	4.75	422
7	5.29	694	6.69	1940	8.71	4380	11.08	8485	7.75	2555	10.33	6925	7.83	3200	6.23	1450	5.37	740	4.79	437	4.67	396	4.75	422
8	5.25	670	6.60	1840	8.71	3880	10.12	6430	7.67	2500	9.54	5520	7.50	2830	6.14	1360	5.29	695	5.00	530	4.67	396	4.75	415
9	5.25	670	6.62	1860	8.60	3520	10.29	6395	7.58	2390	9.04	4760	7.37	2690	6.17	1390	5.27	680	5.04	550	4.67	396	4.69	402
10	5.23	658	6.37	1590	8.60	3520	10.46	6300	7.60	2390	8.52	4030	7.33	2640	6.12	1340	5.23	660	4.87	468	4.67	396	4.73	415
11	5.21	646	6.27	1490	8.69	3520	10.79	6215	7.69	2500	8.10	3520	7.39	2710	6.10	1340	5.25	695	4.83	452	4.67	396	4.56	365
12	5.29	694	6.46	1685	8.67	3495	10.46	6130	7.81	2610	8.67	4240	7.39	2710	6.19	1410	5.21	670	4.79	437	4.67	396	4.52	355
13	5.33	718	6.17	1390	9.14	4140	10.29	5960	7.77	2610	9.19	4985	7.31	2620	6.28	500	5.14	645	4.77	422	4.64	387	4.52	355
14	5.31	706	5.77	1035	8.75	3520	10.08	5620	7.69	2500	10.33	6925	7.08	2370	6.29	510	5.08	605	4.75	430	4.64	387	4.85	460
15	5.27	682	5.67	955	8.35	3105	10.00	5450	7.63	2555	11.25	8875	7.02	2300	6.27	490	4.96	570	4.73	422	4.67	396	4.87	468
16	5.25	670	6.08	1300	8.14	2610	9.96	5375	7.60	2610	10.85	7985	7.06	2350	6.37	1590	4.96	510	4.75	422	4.56	375	4.96	510
17	5.29	694	6.50	1730	7.71	2335	10.19	5790	7.58	2390	10.14	6565	7.42	2740	6.42	5330	4.92	510	4.85	415	4.52	365	5.10	580
18	5.31	706	6.46	1685	7.50	2060	10.08	5300	7.48	2335	9.73	5840	7.35	2660	9.31	5760	5.02	490	4.94	460	4.60	355	5.19	635
19	5.75	1020	6.50	1730	7.17	1840	9.54	4700	7.39	2280	9.59	5605	7.27	2580	8.73	4320	5.12	540	4.89	500	4.67	375	5.29	695
20	6.87	2135	6.52	1750	7.10	1785	9.29	4420	7.29	2280	10.12	6530	7.23	2530	8.08	3500	5.19	540	4.85	476	4.67	396	5.44	785
21	7.35	2665	6.48	1710	7.12	1730	9.02	4000	7.37	2335	10.52	7290	7.04	2320	7.50	2830	5.33	590	4.79	460	4.69	402	5.46	795
22	7.14	2435	6.51	1740	13.37	13400	8.96	3940	7.35	2390	11.04	8390	6.89	2160	7.00	2250	5.29	635	4.81	437	4.75	422	5.50	820
23	6.90	2170	6.62	1860	11.02	8300	8.89	3880	7.25	2390	11.48	9405	6.87	2140	6.69	1940	5.25	720	4.81	444	4.77	430	5.54	850
24	6.60	1840	6.77	2025	10.33	6300	8.89	3700	7.27	2390	11.31	9015	6.83	2090	6.33	1550	5.19	695	4.81	444	4.75	430	5.48	810
25	6.64	1885	6.85	2115	10.39	6300	8.77	3280	7.17	2445	11.31	7545	6.77	2030	6.23	1450	5.14	670	4.75	422	4.85	422	5.42	770
26	6.56	1795	6.72	1970	10.92	7250	8.42	2940	7.29	2600	9.83	6010	6.75	2000	6.12	1340	5.08	635	4.75	422	4.92	460	5.39	755
27	7.14	2435	6.81	2070	11.08	7460	8.12	2885	8.92	4590	9.35	3225	6.92	2190	6.21	1430	4.98	605	4.73	416	4.96	490	5.33	720
28	8.12	3545	6.86	2125	13.25	10880	8.08	1995	12.33	11525	8.89	4545	7.21	2510	6.21	1430	4.94	570				510	5.29	695
29	8.46	3950	6.75	2005	12.27	8875	8.14		14.33	17455	8.23	3675	7.33	2640	6.21	1430	4.89	520					5.39	755
30	8.42	3905	6.79	2050	11.44	8760			13.87	16010	7.85	3230	7.08	2370	6.21	1430		500					5.35	730
31			6.81	2070	11.20	8300			13.71	15530			6.85	2110				475					5.31	705
																							5.25	670

Monthly Discharge of Saugeen River near Port Elgin for 1915-6

Drainage Area, 1,565 Square Miles

Month	Discharge in Second-feet			Discharge in Second-feet per Square Mile			Run-off
	Maximum	Minimum	Mean	Maximum	Minimum	Mean	Depth in Inches on Drainage Area
November (1915).	3,950	645	1,400	2.53	.41	.90	1.00
December '' .	3,195	955	1,900	2.05	.61	1.22	1.40
January ((1916).	13,400	1,730	5,089	8.59	1.11	3.26	3.76
February	8,485	2,810	4,890	5.44	1.80	3.13	3.37
March..........	17,455	2,280	4,213	11.19	1.46	2.70	3.11
April..........	19,345	3,220	7,702	12.40	2.06	4.94	5.51
May	4,140	2,000	2,716	2.65	1.28	1.74	2.01
June	5,330	1,320	1,984	3.42	.85	1.27	1.42
July............	1,220	475	683	.78	.30	.44	.51
August	550	415	446	.35	.27	.29	.33
September......	510	355	405	.33	.23	.26	.29
October.........	850	355	593	.54	.23	.38	.44
The year	19,345	355	2,654	12.40	.23	1.70	23.14

Saugeen River near Walkerton

Location—At the south line bridge, 3½ miles above the Town of Walkerton, near lot 39, concession 2, Township of Brant, County of Bruce.

Records Available—Discharge measurements from June, 1912, to October, 1916. Daily gauge heights from March 26, 1914, to October 31, 1916.

Drainage Area—895 square miles.

Gauge—Vertical staff 0 to 12 feet on post driven in bed of stream and protected by overhanging tree on right bank 100 feet downstream from bridge. Zero on the gauge is 12.00 feet, which is referred to a B.M. (elevation 35.00) on tension rod of bridge.

Channel and Control—Channel is straight for about 500 feet above and below the section. Both banks are high, and do not overflow. The river bed is composed of clay, one channel existing at all stages.

Discharge Measurements—Made from the bridge at all stages.

Winter Flow—Ice greatly affects relation of gauge height to discharge. Measurements are made to determine the winter flow.

Regulation—The dam at Walkerton, about 3½ miles downstream, has no effect on the river stage at this section.

Accuracy—Weeds below the section have a decided effect on the accuracy of the measurements. During the period when weeds are present, a different rating curve has been established. There are not sufficient records available to define the two curves at all stages, and therefore discharges cannot be classed as very good.

Observer—James Preston, Walkerton.

Discharge Measurements of Saugeen River near Walkerton in 1915-6

Date	Hydrographer	Width in Feet	Area of Section in Sq. Feet	Mean Velocity in Feet per Sec.	Gauge Height in Feet	Discharge in Sec-Feet	Discharge in Second-feet per Square Mile
1915							
Nov. 24....	Yeates, W.	126	598	1.47	16.52	884	....
1916							
Jan. 29....	''	135	1,485	3.66	23.04	5,439 (a)	....
April' 3....	''	135	1,566	4.86	23.60	7,605	....
June 13....	Roberts, E.....	125	621	1.61	16.68	1,001	....
Oct. 4....	Yeates, W.	119	436	.54	15.08	234	....

(a) Heavy slush in river.

Daily Gauge Height and Discharge of Saugeen River near Walkerton for 1915-6

Drainage Area 850 Square Miles

Day	Nov Gauge Ht. (Feet)	Nov Dis-charge (Sec-ft)	Dec Gauge Ht. (Feet)	Dec Dis-charge (Sec-ft)	Jan Gauge Ht. (Feet)	Jan Dis-charge (Sec-ft)	Feb Gauge Ht. (Feet)	Feb Dis-charge (Sec-ft)	Mar Gauge Ht. (Feet)	Mar Dis-charge (Sec-ft)	Apr Gauge Ht. (Feet)	Apr Dis-charge (Sec-ft)	May Gauge Ht. (Feet)	May Dis-charge (Sec-ft)	Jun Gauge Ht. (Feet)	Jun Dis-charge (Sec-ft)	Jul Gauge Ht. (Feet)	Jul Dis-charge (Sec-ft)	Aug Gauge Ht. (Feet)	Aug Dis-charge (Sec-ft)	Sep Gauge Ht. (Feet)	Sep Dis-charge (Sec-ft)	Oct Gauge Ht. (Feet)	Oct Dis-charge (Sec-ft)
1	15.50	385	17.79	1,810	16.17	685	21.04	3,700	16.37	600		6,480	17.79	1,810	16.98	1,190	16.33	770	15.37	288	15.17	261	15.12	246
2	15.54	400	17.42	1,495	16.92	1,145	19.58	3,250	16.35	600			18.25	2,250	16.71	995	16.04	620	15.33	312	15.25	285	15.29	297
3	15.62	435	17.12	1,285	17.25	1,375	18.42	2,420		600	23.60	7,	18.58	2,580	16.62	940	15.96	940	15.25	285	15.12	246	15.21	273
4	15.67	455	16.83	1,080	17.25	1,375	17.37	1,460	16.29	600	22.00	6,	18.96	0	16.50	870	15.83	525	15.29	297	15.17	261	15.12	246
5	15.75	490	16.62	940	17.87	1,560	17.42	1,495	16.29	600	21.50	5,500	18.71	2,710	16.67	970	15.87	540	15.21	273	15.14	252	15.25	255
6	15.71	470	16.50	870	18.29	1,640	17.67	1,705	16.29	600	21.50	5,500	18.29	2,290	16.54	895	15.77	497	15.00	210	15.25	285	15.21	273
7	15.58	415	16.42	820	18.33	1,730	17.46	1,530	16.25	575	20.75	4,750	17.87	1,880	16.48	860	15.67	451	15.25	285	14.96	198	15.21	273
8	15.67	455	16.42	820	18.37	1,865	17.37		16.33	575	19.75	3,750	17.71	1,740	16.37	790	15.67	451	15.51	396	15.25	246	15.12	246
9	15.58	415	16.29	745	18.67	2,	17.75	1,560	16.37	575	19.12	3,120	17.71	1,740	16.50	870	15.58	412	15.46	380	15.12	246	15.04	222
10	15.46	370	16.00	620	18.58	1,910	18.42	1,640	16.33	625	18.58	2,580	17.69	1,720	16.29	745	15.58	412	15.50	328	14.92	186	15.25	222
11	15.46	370	16.04		18.21	1,775	18.17	1,730	16.29	700	18.29	2,290	17.54	1,590	17.0	1,230	15.54	396	15.37	312	15.04	222	15.25	255
12	15.50	385	16.00	620	18.04	1,560	18.02	1,640	16.42	700	18.29	2,290	17.79	1,810	16.92	1,140	15.54	429	15.33	312	15.00	210	15.04	222
13	15.58	415	16.08	640	18.25	1,640	17.69	1,270	16.46	700	18.83	2,830	17.71	1,740	16.71	995	15.62	429	15.12	297	15.00	210	15.29	297
14	15.33	325	16.02	610	18.12		17.69	1,200	16.50	700	19.71	3,710	17.46	1,530	16.46	845	15.54	396	15.29	396	15.12	246	15.37	328
15	15.54	400	15.96	580	18.00	1,520	17.79	1,200	16.33	650	19.21	3,210	17.41	1,230	16.46	845	15.54	396	15.31	304	15.00	210	15.29	297
16	15.46	370	16.14	670	18.00	1,410	17.79	1,130	16.37	650	22.58	6,580	17.35	1,440	17.37	1,460	15.46	364	15.25	285	15.04	222	15.37	228
17	15.46	370	16.12	660	17.52		17.42	1,095	16.37	650	21.46	5,460	17.04	1,230	17.42	1,500	15.46	364	15.12	261	14.83	159	15.37	280
18	15.46	370	16.21	725	17.42	990	17.08	1,060	16.29	675	20.58	4,580	17.42	1,500	18.96	2,980	15.46	364	15.12	246	15.04	222	15.50	364
19	15.83	525	16.25	755	17.42	990	16.75	930	16.35	675	20.60	4,	17.42	1,500	19.62	3,620	15.46	364	15.12	261	15.04	222	15.58	380
20	16.71	1,000	16.21	725	17.29	990	16.62	725	16.29	675	20.33	4,330	17.64	1,680	19.08	2,080	16.00	0	15.21	273	15.08	234	15.71	412
21	17.12	1,285	16.21		17.50	1,200		650	16.33	675	20.42	4,420	17.54	1,590	18.08	2,080	16.00	705	15.12	246	15.08	234	15.79	470
22	17.00	1,200	16.31		17.08	990	16.83	650	16.21	685	20.75	4,750	17.37	1,280	16.71	1,160	15.75	488	15.12	246	15.04	222	15.75	505
23	16.58	920	16.42	820	20.53	4,400		810	16.17	920	21.21	5,210	17.12	1,200	16.79	1,050	15.54	396	15.08	234	15.12	246	15.67	487
24	16.52	880	16.29	745	20.71	4,200	16.77	750	16.33	920	22.62	6,620	17.00	1,200	16.50	870	15.48	372	15.12	246	15.12	234	15.54	433
25	16.58	920	16.21	705	20.56	4,100	16.67	700	16.58		21.67	5,670	17.08	1,260	16.42	820	15.37	348	15.12	246	15.08	234	15.50	396
26	16.62		16.33		20.60	4,100	16.46	700	17.83	1,850	20.27	4,270	17.04	1,230	16.37	790	15.42	328	15.08	234	15.04	285	15.50	380
27	17.50	1,560	16.33		21.23	4,650	16.46	700	20.25	4,250	19.42	3,420	16.87	1,110	16.42	820	15.31	304	15.04	222	15.12	246	15.37	396
28	18.35	2,350	16.25	725	23.75	6,200	16.46	650		4,800	19.21	3,210	16.67	970	16.33	770	15.25	285	15.12	246	15.12	285	15.37	328
29	18.58	2,580	16.29	745	22.79	5,450	16.37	600		4,800	18.75	2,750	16.71	995	16.25	725	15.29	297	15.12	285	15.25	285	15.54	348
30	18.46	2,460	16.42	820	21.17	4,500				5,360	18.33	2,330	17.58	1,620					15.21	273	15.42	348	15.37	328
31			16.45	840	20.83	4,200				5,920	17.92	1,930	17.17	1,320					15.08	234	15.46	366	15.46	364

Monthly Discharge of Saugeen River near Walkerton for 1915-6

Drainage Area 850 Square Miles

Month	Discharge in Second-feet			Discharge in Second-feet per Square Mile			Run-off
	Maximum	Minimum	Mean	Maximum	Minimum	Mean	Depth in Inches on Drainage Area
November (1915)	2,580	325	796	3.04	.38	.94	1.05
December "	1,810	580	819	2.13	.68	.96	1.11
January .. (1916)	6,200	685	2,448	7.29	.81	2.88	3.32
February	3,700	600	1,313	4.35	.71	1.54	1.66
March	5,920	577	1,267	6.96	.68	1.49	1.72
April	7,600	1,930	4,443	8.94	2.27	5.23	5.84
May	2,960	970	1,631	3.48	1.14	1.92	2.21
June	3,620	725	1,235	4.26	.85	1.45	1.62
July	770	297	437	.91	.35	.51	.59
August	396	210	278	.47	.25	.33	.38
September	366	159	244	.43	.19	.29	.32
October	505	222	328	.59	.26	.39	.45
The year	7,600	159	1,268	8.94	.19	1.49	20.28

Sydenham near Owen Sound

Location—At the highway bridge above the Town of Owen Sound's filtration plant, near lot 9, concession 1, Township of Derby, County of Grey.

Records Available—Discharge measurements and daily gauge heights from June 9, 1915, to October 31, 1916.

Drainage Area—71 square miles.

Gauge—Vertical staff 0 to 6 feet on upstream side of first pier from right abutment. Zero on the gauge is 0.00.

Channel and Control—The channel is straight for 200 feet above and below the section, both banks are low, but do not overflow, the stream never assuming flood proportions. The bed is composed of solid rock, with two channels during the low-water period. During the high-water stages all the water is confined between the two abutments of the bridge.

Discharge Measurements—Made from the bridge during the high-water period, and from a permanent wading section located 30 feet upstream during the low stages.

Winter Flow—Ice has little effect.

Regulation—The Town of Owen Sound has a dam 300 feet above this section that is used to supply water for the filtration beds.

Diversions—An additional 750,000 gallons of water per day should be added to the daily flow at this section, which is the approximate amount diverted.

Accuracy—There are not sufficient readings to define a curve at all stages. Discharges between gauge heights .90 and 1.40 are fair.

Observer—Myrtle Cook, Ashley P.O.

Discharge Measurements of Sydenham River near Owen Sound in 1915-6

Date	Hydrographer	Width in Feet	Area of Section in Sq. Feet	Mean Velocity in Feet per Sec.	Gauge Height in Feet	Discharge in Sec-Feet	Discharge in Second-feet per Square Mile
1915 Dec. 9....	Cunnington, G..	52	39	1.76	1.33	67	....
1916 June 12....	Roberts, E....	60	47	1.73	1.42	81	....
Oct. 4....	Yeates, W....	46	19	.91	.92	18	....

Daily Gauge Height and Discharge of Sydenham River near Owen Sound for 1915-6

Drainage Area, 71 Square Miles

Day	November Gauge Ht. (Feet)	November Dis-charge (Sec-ft.)	December Gauge Ht. (Feet)	December Dis-charge (Sec-ft.)	January Gauge Ht. (Feet)	January Dis-charge (Sec-ft.)	February Gauge Ht. (Feet)	February Dis-charge (Sec-ft.)	March Gauge Ht. (Feet)	March Dis-charge (Sec-ft.)	April Gauge Ht. (Feet)	April Dis-charge (Sec-ft.)	May Gauge Ht. (Feet)	May Dis-charge (Sec-ft.)	June Gauge Ht. (Feet)	June Dis-charge (Sec-ft.)	July Gauge Ht. (Feet)	July Dis-charge (Sec-ft.)	August Gauge Ht. (Feet)	August Dis-charge (Sec-ft.)	September Gauge Ht. (Feet)	September Dis-charge (Sec-ft.)	October Gauge Ht. (Feet)	October Dis-charge (Sec-ft.)
1	1.06	33	1.64	130	1.37	43	2.25	278	1.69	61	3.02	576	1.75	152	1.69	140	1.37	77	1.00	26	0.92	19	1.00	26
2	1.06	33	1.62	126	1.54	71	2.10	234	1.69	61	3.00	568	1.79	160	1.60	122	1.33	71	0.96	22	0.92	19	0.92	19
3	1.08	35	1.50	102	1.71	112	2.04	217	1.83	74	2.71	448	1.87	177	1.54	110	1.29	64	0.96	22	0.92	19	0.92	19
4	1.10	37	1.46	94	2.10	122	1.94	193	1.79	69	2.54	380	1.92	188	1.50	102	1.25	58	0.92	19	0.96	22	0.96	15
5	1.17	46	1.42	86	2.10	184	1.83	169	1.83	74	2.37	318	1.85	173	1.50	102	1.25	58	0.92	19	0.92	19	0.87	15
6	1.17	46	1.42	86	2.19	220	1.81	112	1.71	58	2.19	259	1.79	160	1.46	94	1.21	52	0.92	19	0.92	19	0.87	15
7	1.17	46	1.37	77	2.23	234	2.06	132	1.73	63	2.06	223	1.75	152	1.39	80	1.17	46	0.92	19	0.92	19	0.87	15
8	1.12	40	1.37	77	2.08	206	2.00	128	1.85	66	2.00	206	1.71	144	1.33	71	1.17	46	0.96	22	0.87	15	0.92	19
9	1.08	35	1.33	71	1.96	173	1.83	116	1.87	68	1.89	182	1.71	144	1.33	71	1.12	40	1.00	26	0.87	15	0.92	19
10	1.08	35	1.29	64	1.87	152	1.75	102	2.08	71	1.83	169	1.67	136	1.44	90	1.12	40	1.00	26	0.92	19	0.92	19
11	1.06	33	1.37	77	1.89	156	1.71	88	1.98	86	1.87	177	1.67	136	1.42	84	1.08	35	1.00	26	0.92	19	0.92	22
12	1.08	35	1.33	71	1.85	142	1.69	77	1.87	74	1.98	202	1.67	136	1.42	84	1.08	35	1.00	26	0.92	19	0.96	26
13	1.08	35	1.37	77	2.02	173	1.81	96	1.85	61	2.08	228	1.58	118	1.33	71	1.08	35	1.00	26	0.92	19	1.00	26
14	1.08	35	1.27	47	2.01	184	1.85	82	1.87	61	2.12	240	1.56	114	1.29	64	1.08	35	1.00	26	9.92	19	1.00	26
15	1.08	35	1.29	45	1.94	162	1.64	66	1.87	61	2.27	284	1.54	110	1.37	77	1.04	30	1.00	26	0.92	19	1.04	30
16	1.08	35	1.31	42	1.83	146	1.62	63	2.00	74	2.12	240	1.58	118	1.87	177	1.00	26	0.96	22	0.87	15	1.08	35
17	1.08	35	1.25	37	1.96	162	1.62	61	1.92	66	2.00	206	1.58	118	1.87	335	1.04	30	0.96	22	0.92	19	1.12	40
18	1.06	33	1.27	43	1.89	152	1.64	61	2.08	74	2.00	206	1.58	118	2.42	394	1.08	26	0.92	19	0.92	19	1.17	46
19	1.21	52	1.33	43	1.81	144	1.79	58	2.17	74	2.00	206	1.58	118	2.58	304	1.04	26	0.96	22	0.92	19	1.17	46
20	1.40	82	1.33	37	1.73	132	1.67	69	2.17	90	1.98	202	1.54	110	2.33	228	1.00	30	1.04	30	0.92	19	1.12	46
21	1.54	110	1.29	41	1.69	140	1.79	58	2.00	86	2.06	223	1.50	102	2.08	188	1.08	35	0.92	19	0.92	19	1.08	40
22	1.58	118	1.33	41	2.35	311	1.62	58	1.89	79	2.10	234	1.50	102	1.92	169	1.04	35	0.96	22	0.92	19	1.08	35
23	1.58	118	1.33	41	2.79	434	1.58	49	2.12	74	2.35	311	1.46	94	1.83	B6	1.00	30	0.92	19	0.92	19	1.04	35
24	1.44	90	1.33	43	2.62	412	1.58	49	2.12	112	2.23	272	1.42	86	1.67	126	1.08	26	0.92	19	0.96	22	1.04	30
25	1.42	86	1.37	43	2.39	325	1.62	49	1.87	106	2.04	217	1.42	86	1.54	170	1.04	26	1.04	30	1.00	26	1.08	35
26	1.44	90	1.35	43	2.39	325	1.71	56	1.89	142	1.94	193	1.71	144	1.50	102	1.00	26	0.92	19	1.00	26	1.04	30
27	1.52	106	1.39	43	2.46	350	1.62	56	2.12	182	1.85	173	1.92	188	1.50	102	1.00	22	0.96	22			1.04	30
28	1.58	118	1.42	43	2.73	456			2.46	240	1.81	164	1.83	169	1.50	102	0.96	26	0.92	19			1.00	30
29	1.62	126	1.42	43	2.48	357			2.83	350	1.75	152	1.77	156	1.42	86	1.00	26	0.92	19			1.00	30
30			1.42	43	2.25	278			2.92	500	1.75	152					1.00	26	0.92	19				
31			1.37	43	2.23	272				536														

Monthly Discharge of Sydenham River near Owen Sound for 1915-6

Drainage Area 71 Square Miles

Month	Discharge in Second-feet			Discharge in Second-feet per Square Mile			Run-off
	Maximum	Minimum	Mean	Maximum	Minimum	Mean	Depth in Inches on Drainage Area
November.(1915)	126	33	62	1.77	.46	.87	.97
December "	130	37	58	1.83	.52	.82	.95
January .. (1916)	484	43	219	6.82	.61	3.08	3.55
February	278	49	100	3.92	.69	1.41	1.52
March..........	536	58	124	7.55	.82	1.75	2.02
April...........	576	152	254	8.11	2.14	3.58	3.99
May	188	86	134	2.65	1.21	1.89	2.18
June............	394	64	134	5.55	.90	1.89	2.11
July............	77	22	39	1.08	.31	.55	.63
August	26	19	23	.37	.27	.32	.37
September	26	15	19	.37	.21	.27	.30
October........	46	15	27	.65	.21	.38	.44
The year	576	15	99	8.11	.21	1.39	18.92

Thames River (Main Stream) near Byron

Location—At the highway bridge known as Kilworth Bridge, 2 miles north-west of the Town of Byron, near the Village of Komoka, Township of Delaware, County of Middlesex.

Records Available—Monthly discharge measurements from March, 1912, to August, 1916. Daily gauge heights from March 13, 1914, to October 31, 1916.

Drainage Area—1,270 square miles.

Gauge—Vertical staff 0 to 12 feet on centre pier. The zero on gauge (elevation 6.00), which has remained unchanged since established, is referred to a B.M. (elevation. 31.21) on downstream side of right abutment.

Channel and Control—The channel is straight above and below section for about 600 feet. The banks are high, and do not overflow or shift to a great extent. The control, however, is not stationary under high-water conditions. The velocity is high.

Discharge Measurements—Made from the bridge at all stages.

Winter Flow—Ice is present during the winter period, and measurements are made to determine the winter flow.

Accuracy—During flood stages the high velocity necessitates the taking of surface readings. The station rating curve is fairly well defined for ordinary flows.

Observer—James Bourne, Komoka.

Discharge Measurements of Thames River (main stream) near Byron in 1915-6

Date	Hydrographer	Width in Feet	Area of Section in Sq. Feet	Mean Velocity in Feet per Sec.	Gauge Height in Feet	Discharge in Sec-Feet	Discharge in Second-feet per Square Mile
1915 Nov. 12....	Yeates, W.	197	229	1.34	6.63	319	....
1916 Jan. 25....	``	239	964	4.73	9.90	4,563 (a)	....
Feb. 23....	``	201	267	2.25	6.87	600 (b)	....
Mar. 29....	``	256	2,154	7.49	14.67	16,139	....
`` 31....	``	262	1,828	7.24	13·48	13,593	....
Aug. 22....	``	181	175	.76	6.38	133	....

(a) Surface velocities.
(b) Ice on control.

Daily Gauge Height and Discharge of Thames River (main stream) near Byron for 1915-6

Drainage Area, 1270 Square Miles

Day	Nov Gauge Ht.	Nov Dis-charge	Dec Gauge Ht.	Dec Dis-charge	Jan Gauge Ht.	Jan Dis-charge	Feb Gauge Ht.	Feb Dis-charge	Mar Gauge Ht.	Mar Dis-charge	Apr Gauge Ht.	Apr Dis-charge	May Gauge Ht.	May Dis-charge	Jun Gauge Ht.	Jun Dis-charge	Jul Gauge Ht.	Jul Dis-charge	Aug Gauge Ht.	Aug Dis-charge	Sep Gauge Ht.	Sep Dis-charge	Oct Gauge Ht.	Oct Dis-charge
1	6.67	402	8.87	3000	7.50	1180	12.58	10650	6.83	525	12.04	9300	7.42	1100	9.96	4830	6.75	440	6.33	118	6.33	118	6.46	208
2	6.71	428	8.29	2200	9.46	3940	9.83	4590	6.83	525	11.92	9010	7.29	970	8.71	2760	6.75	440	6.50	240	6.33	118	6.42	176
3	6.67	402	7.96	1770	11.29	7540	8.62	2640	6.87	555	10.37	5640	7.54	1230	8.92	3080	6.75	440	6.42	176	6.33	118	6.42	176
4	6.58	352	7.75	1500	10.71	6320	7.29	970	6.83	525	9.58	4140	8.54	2530	8.62	2640	6.67	376	6.33	118	6.33	118	6.37	142
5	6.62	372	7.62	1330	11.54	8100	7.29	970	6.75	460	9.17	2470	8.12	1980	8.46	2420	6.67	376	6.33	118	6.33	118	6.33	118
6	6.67	402	7.50	1380	15.50	18450	7.21	1100	6.83	525	8.96	3140	7.67	1380	8.29	2200	6.67	376	6.33	118	6.29	95	6.33	118
7	6.67	402	7.46	1140	11.96	9100	7.21	890	6.87	555	8.50	2470	7.42	1100	7.96	1770	6.67	376	6.27	85	6.33	118	6.33	118
8	6.54	336	7.33	1010	10.71	6320	6.87	402	6.92	600	8.17	2040	7.58	1280	7.58	1380	6.50	240	6.29	95	6.33	118	6.33	118
9	6.58	352	7.33	1010	9.46	3940	6.67	555	7.00	680	8.00	1820	8.04	1870	11.12	7160	6.58	240	6.37	142	6.33	95	6.25	75
10	6.58	352	7.25	930	9.08	3330	7.08	680	7.04	720	7.83	1600	8.08	1920	10.29	5480	6.58	240	6.33	118	6.29	118	6.33	75
11	6.58	352	7.17	850	9.29	3660	7.12	760	6.92	600	7.67	1390	10.96	6820	9.08	3330	6.62	336	6.46	208	6.33	118	6.25	75
12	6.58	352	7.00	680	8.87	3000	7.12	800	6.96	640	8.08	1920	9.42	3870	8.54	2530	6.71	408	6.37	142	6.25	75	6.33	118
13	6.67	402	6.92	600	12.79	11170	7.37	1050	6.96	680	8.83	2940	8.21	2090	8.62	2640	6.58	304	6.37	142	6.33	118	6.37	142
14	6.67	402	6.79	460	10.96	6820	7.67	1390	7.00	680	10.79	6480	7.79	1550	8.17	2040	6.54	272	6.42	176	6.25	75	6.46	208
15	6.62	372	7.04	720	9.71	4380	7.33	1010	7.08	680	11.29	7540	9.01	3250	7.71	1440	6.71	408	6.33	118	6.25	95	6.50	240
16	6.67	402	7.08	760	8.58	2580	7.12	800	7.25	640	9.71	4380	10.96	6820	7.46	1140	6.50	240	6.33	118	6.29	95	6.46	240
17	6.67	402	7.17	850	9.10	3010	7.04	720	7.00	640	9.46	3940	10.79	6480	7.04	720	6.50	240	6.29	95	6.29	118	6.42	208
18	6.67	402	7.50	1180	11.92	7630	7.00	680	7.00	680	9.87	5670	9.46	3940	7.58	1280	6.46	208	6.29	95	6.29	118	6.42	176
19	9.42	3870	7.62	760	11.33	8100	6.92	600	6.87	555	9.04	3290	9.83	4590	7.71	1440	6.42	208	6.33	118	6.33	95	6.62	336
20	9.29	3860	7.58	1180	11.62	8290	6.83	525	6.83	525	8.42	2370	9.08	3330	7.71	1440	6.42	176	6.37	142	6.29	75	6.75	440
21	8.62	2640	7.54	1330	11.83	8790	6.92	600	6.96	600	8.46	2420	8.75	2820	7.54	1230	6.46	208	6.33	118	6.25	75	6.71	408
22	8.08	1920	7.46	1280	14.12	14720	6.83	525	6.87	555	8.46	2420	8.58	2580	7.37	1050	6.46	208	6.33	118	6.25	95	6.58	304
23	8.17	2040	7.58	1230	13.54	13160	6.87	555	7.58	1280	8.37	2300	8.58	2580	7.21	890	6.42	176	6.33	118	6.33	118	6.50	240
24	7.71	1440	7.67	1140	12.46	10350	6.83	525	7.58	680	8.21	2090	10.58	6060	7.04	720	6.42	176	6.33	118	6.33	118	6.42	176
25	7.83	1600	7.58	1280	10.04	4980	6.83	525	11.33	7630	7.87	1650	9.87	4670	7.33	1010	6.54	272	6.33	118	6.33	118	6.50	240
26	8.25	2140	7.79	1390	10.04	4000	6.87	525	14.71	16320	8.08	1920	8.79	2380	7.33	1010	6.42	176	6.33	118	6.33	142	6.42	176
27	7.83	2710	7.75	1280	10.04	4980	6.83	525	14.33	15290	8.79	2880	8.00	1820	7.42	1100	6.42	176	6.33	118	6.37	142	6.42	176
28	9.75	4450	7.62	1550	13.50	13050	6.92	600	14.25	15080	8.67	2710	7.67	1390	7.12	800	6.25	75	6.33	118	6.46	208	6.46	208
29	9.50	4000	7.42	1500	10.67	6240			12.96	11600	8.00	1820	8.29	2200	6.92	600			6.33	118	6.50	240	6.46	208
30	9.96	4830	7.50	1330	9.67	4310					7.67	1390	8.54	2530	6.83	510			6.33	240			6.50	240
31			7.42	1100	12.42	10250							13.00	11700			6.33	118	6.33	118				
				1180									11.79	8700										

Monthly Discharge of Thames River near Byron for 1915-6

Drainage Area, 1,270 Square Miles

Month	Discharge [in Second-feet			Discharge in Second-feet per Square Mile.			Run-off
	Maximum	Minimum	Mean	Maximum	Minimum	Mean	Depth in Inches on Drainage Area
November. (1915)	4,830	336	1,336	3.80	.26	1.05	1.17
December . ``	3,000	460	1,202	2.36	.36	.95	1.10
January...(1916)	18,450	1,180	7,345	14.53	.93	5.78	6.66
February	10,650	402	1,277	8.39	.32	1.01	1.09
March	16,320	460	2,665	12.85	.36	2.10	2.42
April	9,300	1,390	3,437	7.32	1.09	2.71	3.02
May............	11,700	970 .	3,334	9.21	.76	2.63	3.03
June............	7,160	510	2,001	5.64	.40	1.58	1.76
July............	440	75	276	.35	.06	.22	.25
August	240	85	129	.19	.07	.10	.12
September	240	75	116	.19	.06	.09	.10
October........	440	75	197	.35	.06	.16	.18
The year	18,450	75	1,949	14.53	.06	1.53	20.82

Thames River (North Branch) near Fanshawe

Location—At the highway bridge near Fanshawe Post Office, between lots 8 and 9, concessions 4 and 5, Township of London, County of Middlesex.

Records Available—Daily gauge heights and discharge measurements from May 13, 1915, to October 31, 1916.

Drainage Area—650 square miles.

Gauge—Vertical staff 0 to 12 feet on right abutment, downstream side. Elevation of zero on gauge 4.00 is referred to a B.M. (elevation 30.00) on tension rod, downstream side, 170 feet from the initial point of soundings.

Channel and Control—The channel is straight above and below section for 500 feet. The bed of the stream is composed of clay and gravel, the banks are high and will not overflow. The channel and control is shifting during high-water periods.

Discharge Measurements—Made from the bridge and at a permanent wading section about 500 feet above during low water.

Accuracy—There are not sufficient records available to define rating curve at all stages.

Observer—Allen Donley, London.

Discharge Measurements of Thames River (North Branch) near Fanshawe in 1915-6

Date	Hydrographer	Width in Feet	Area of Section in Sq. Feet	Mean Velocity in Feet per Sec.	Gauge Height in Feet	Discharge in Sec-Feet	Discharge in Second-feet per Square Mile
1915 Nov. 12....	Yeates, W	90	155	.82	6.87	127	....
1916 Jan. 25....	''	-171	904	2.25	9.15	2,038 (a)	....
Mar. 29....	''	171	1,264	4.71	11.29	5,953 (b)	....
'' 31....	''	171	1,230	4.14	11.00	5,091	....
Aug. 22....	''	28	17	1.08	6.10	18	....

(a) Heavy swell at gauge.
(b) Reading taken 500 feet above gauge.

Daily Gauge Height and Discharge of Thames River (North Branch) near Fanshawe for 1915-6

Drainage Area, 650 Square Miles

Day	Nov Gauge Ht. (Feet)	Nov Dis-charge (Sec-ft.)	Dec Gauge Ht. (Feet)	Dec Dis-charge (Sec-ft.)	Jan Gauge Ht. (Feet)	Jan Dis-charge (Sec-ft.)	Feb Gauge Ht. (Feet)	Feb Dis-charge (Sec-ft.)	Mar Gauge Ht. (Feet)	Mar Dis-charge (Sec-ft.)	Apr Gauge Ht. (Feet)	Apr Dis-charge (Sec-ft.)	May Gauge Ht. (Feet)	May Dis-charge (Sec-ft.)	Jun Gauge Ht. (Feet)	Jun Dis-charge (Sec-ft.)	Jul Gauge Ht. (Feet)	Jul Dis-charge (Sec-ft.)	Aug Gauge Ht. (Feet)	Aug Dis-charge (Sec-ft.)	Sep Gauge Ht. (Feet)	Sep Dis-charge (Sec-ft.)	Oct Gauge Ht. (Feet)	Oct Dis-charge (Sec-ft.)
1	7.02	156	8.67	1360	8.75	1460	8.83	940	9.25	350	10.35	4000	7.58	390	9.83	3080	7.62	412	6.25	28	6.10	18	6.54	58
2	6.98	145	8.50	1160	9.75	2950	8.79	795	8.98	380	9.98	3330	7.79	520	9.96	3300	7.48	340	6.33	35	6.14	23	6.48	51
3	6.96	140	8.12	770	13.33	10840	8.92	705	8.69	375	9.83	3080	8.04	695	9.58	2680	7.39	296	6.25	28	6.14	20	6.52	56
4	6.94	135	8.08	730	13.00	9980	12.46	660	8.50	365	9.69	2850	8.21	850	9.25	2170	7.31	264	6.35	37	6.10	18	6.39	41
5	6.81	102	7.89	645	12.62	9000	11.81	625	8.46	355	9.58	2680	8.08	730	8.87	1630	7.23	232	6.27	30	6.06	16	6.29	31
6	6.77	95	7.85	555	12.29	8170	11.81	625	8.42	350	9.04	1870	7.81	530	8.50	1160	7.21	232	6.21	25	6.10	14	6.27	30
7	6.71	85	7.75	490	11.75	6850	11.76	590	8.23	350	9.04	1360	7.69	454	8.27	910	7.13	197	6.23	26	6.10	18	6.19	23
8	6.67	80	7.71	465	11.58	6450	12.03	590	8.17	350	8.67	1280	7.67	442	8.06	715	7.10	187	6.23	26	6.14	14	6.19	23
9	6.71	85	7.67	440	11.25	5720	11.94	590	8.10	350	8.60	1070	7.60	400	7.85	555	7.04	169	6.27	30	6.19	20	6.14	20
10	6.79	98	7.58	390	10.71	4670	11.79	590	7.87	340	8.42	730	7.85	555	8.48	1140	6.94	145	6.19	23	6.10	20	6.08	17
11	6.87	118	7.58	390	9.75	2950	11.60	555	7.75	330	8.08	660	8.87	1630	8.27	910	6.96	139	6.10	18	6.14	20	6.04	18
12	6.98	145	7.56	380	8.96	1750	11.14	555	7.79	325	8.37	1020	8.62	1300	8.12	770	6.98	151	6.10	18	6.19	18	6.06	14
13	6.85	112	7.75	490	9.33	2290	9.87	545	7.83	315	8.71	1410	8.04	695	8.14	785	7.02	163	6.23	26	6.10	23	6.14	16
14	6.85	112	7.75	490	8.67	1360	9.75	525	7.73	305	8.54	1210	7.71	466	7.96	630	6.94	139	6.14	20	6.14	23	6.19	20
15	6.75	92	7.75	490	8.54	1210	9.75	525	7.64	300	9.75	2950	9.08	1920	7.77	505	6.81	104	6.10	18	6.10	23	6.14	23
16	6.87	118	8.08	730	8.50	1160	9.75	525	7.63	296	9.83	3080	9.37	2350	6.81	442	6.73	88	6.10	20	6.04	14	6.08	20
17	6.81	102	8.08	730	8.50	1160	9.75	525	7.44	288	9.81	3050	8.75	1460	7.67	412	6.69	80	6.19	18	6.08	17	6.14	17
18	6.79	98	8.25	890	8.50	1160	9.75	505	7.42	288	9.69	2850	9.17	2050	7.62	412	6.64	72	6.19	23	6.10	18	6.23	20
19	6.96	140	8.54	1210	8.50	1160	9.50	480	7.37	284	9.56	2650	8.37	1020	7.62	360	6.64	72	6.23	18	6.10	23	6.31	26
20	9.46	2490	8.54	1180	10.29	2250	9.50	460	7.37	280	9.40	2400	8.17	850	7.52	400	6.62	69	6.10	23	6.14	23	6.46	33
21	8.04	1750	8.52	1210	9.42	2250	9.50	460	7.33	288	9.04	1870	8.21	645	7.0	412	6.54	57	6.14	26	6.14	26	6.42	49
22	8.96	695	8.50	1160	9.37	2250	9.50	460	7.29	288	8.67	1360	7.98	815	7.62	370	6.39	41	6.06	20	6.14	20	6.39	44
23	7.96	620	8.50	1160	9.33	2250	9.50	448	7.27	272	8.12	770	9.25	2170	7.54	545	6.42	44	6.12	16	6.10	26	6.37	44
24	7.94	870	8.50	1160	9.50	2550	9.50	442	7.26	256	8.29	930	8.73	1440	7.67	555	6.25	28	6.17	16	6.27	30	6.42	39
25	8.23	2300	8.50	1160	11.17	5560	9.48	430	10.25	244	8.08	730	8.42	1070	7.83	530	6.29	31	6.14	22	6.12	19	6.42	44
26	9.33	2550	8.50	1160	10.62	6270	9.44	412	11.50	770	8.25	890	7.67	605	7.85	492	6.25	28	6.12	19			6.39	41
27	9.50	2300	8.50	1160	8.54	4500	9.47	400	11.27	3820	7.92	605	7.54	442	7.81	480	6.25	28	6.14	20			6.23	39
28	9.33	2230	8.50	1160	8.50	1210		400	10.77	6270	7.92	605	7.46	370	7.75	454	6.25	28	6.17	22			6.19	26
29	9.29	1920	8.50	1160	8.71	1160			10.42	5760			7.46	330	7.69	454	6.25	28	6.12	19				23
30	9.08		8.50	1160	8.71	1100				4780			8.42	1070	7.69		6.25	28	6.14	20				
31			8.50	1160						4130							6.25	28	6.17	22				

Monthly Discharge of Thames River (North Branch) near Fanshawe for 1915-6

Drainage Area 650 Square Miles

Month	Discharge in Second-feet			Discharge in Second-feet per Square Mile			Run-off
	Maximum	Minimum	Mean	Maximum	Minimum	Mean	Depth in Inches on Drainage Area
November (1915).	2,550	80	684	3.92	.12	1.05	1.17
December ··	1,360	380	864	2.09	.58	1.33	1.53
January (1916).	10,840	1,100	3,544	16.68	1.69	5.45	6.28
February	940	400	541	1.45	.62	.83	.90
March..........	6,270	244	1,077	9.65	.38	1.66	1.91
April...........	4,000	605	1,786	6.25	.93	2.75	3.07
May	2,350	330	922	3.62	.51	1.42	1.64
June	3,300	360	923	5.08	.66	1.42	1.58
July	412	28	126	.64	.04	.19	.22
August.........	37	16	23	.06	.02	.04	.05
September	30	14	20	.05	.02	.03	.03
October.........	58	14	32	.09	.02	.05	.06
The year	10,840	14	881	16.68	.02	1.36	18.51

Thames River (South Branch) near Ealing

Location—At the highway bridge known as Vauxhall Bridge between lots 10 and 11, concession B, between Townships of London and Westminster, County of Middlesex.

Records Available—Daily gauge heights and discharge measurements from May 11, 1915, to October 31, 1916.

Drainage Area—515 square miles.

Gauge—Vertical staff 0 to 12 feet on downstream side of first right pier. Elevation of zero on gauge is 4.00, referred to B.M., elevation 30.00.

Channel and Control—The channel is straight above and below for 800 feet. The banks and control are shifting under high-water conditions.

Discharge Measurements—Made from the bridge. During the extreme low water a wading section is used.

Winter Flow—The relation of gauge height to discharge is affected by ice during the winter months.

Accuracy—The rating curve is fairly well defined up to gauge height 11.00 feet.

Observer—Geo. Leathorn, London.

Discharge Measurements of Thames River (South Branch) near Ealing in 1915-6

Date	Hydrographer	Width in Feet	Area of Section in Sq. Feet	Mean Velocity in Feet per Sec.	Gauge Height in Feet	Discharge in Sec-Feet	Discharge in Second-feet per Square Mile
1915							
Nov. 12....	Yeates, W....	151	235	.85	6.46	201	....
1916							
Jan. 24....	" "	193	1,185	2.40	11.83	2,849 (a)	....
Mar. 29....	" "	193	1,358	3.81	12.71	5,178	....
" 31....	" "	193	1,107	3.15	11.35	3,485	....
Aug. 23....	" "	86	87	1.06	6.09	92 (b)	....

(a) Ice on both sides and bed of stream.
(b) Reading taken 500 feet above gauge.

Daily Gauge Height and Discharge of Thames River (South Branch) near Ealing for 1915-6

Drainage Area, 515 Square Miles

Day	Nov. Gauge Ht. (Feet)	Nov. Dis-charge (Sec-ft.)	Dec. Gauge Ht. (Feet)	Dec. Dis-charge (Sec-ft.)	Jan. Gauge Ht. (Feet)	Jan. Dis-charge (Sec-ft.)	Feb. Gauge Ht. (Feet)	Feb. Dis-charge (Sec-ft.)	Mar. Gauge Ht. (Feet)	Mar. Dis-charge (Sec-ft.)	Apr. Gauge Ht. (Feet)	Apr. Dis-charge (Sec-ft.)	May Gauge Ht. (Feet)	May Dis-charge (Sec-ft.)	June Gauge Ht. (Feet)	June Dis-charge (Sec-ft.)	July Gauge Ht. (Feet)	July Dis-charge (Sec-ft.)	Aug. Gauge Ht. (Feet)	Aug. Dis-charge (Sec-ft.)	Sep. Gauge Ht. (Feet)	Sep. Dis-charge (Sec-ft.)	Oct. Gauge Ht. (Feet)	Oct. Dis-charge (Sec-ft.)
1	6.50	210	8.33	955	7.83	705	12.25	4540	7.33	500	10.79	2890	7.21	455	9.64	1840	6.62	246	6.10	100	5.92	64	6.12	105
2	6.52	210	7.83	705	9.50	890	9.96	2100	7.29	485	10.42	2520	7.42	540	8.80	1230	6.50	210	6.12	105	5.92	64	6.00	80
3	6.42	186	7.54	585	13.46	2600	8.75	1200	7.25	470	9.69	1880	7.60	610	9.14	1470	6.60	240	6.12	105	5.92	64	6.00	80
4	6.44	192	7.25	470	13.83	6540	7.37	520	7.33	500	9.04	1400	8.14	860	8.71	1180	6.52	216	6.08	96	5.92	64	5.96	72
5	6.44	192	7.27	478	13.08	6540	7.83	705	7.25	470	8.79	1220	7.89	735	8.75	1200	6.54	222	6.12	105	5.92	64	5.96	72
6	6.54	222	7.21	454	12.87	5290	7.31	495	7.25	470	8.69	1130	7.50	570	8.58	1100	6.37	173	6.02	84	5.92	64	5.96	72
7	6.37	173	7.21	454	11.75	3940	7.42	490	7.33	500	8.33	955	7.29	485	8.42	1000	6.39	177	6.08	96	5.92	64	5.96	72
8	6.33	163	7.10	410	10.25	2360	8.08	490	7.46	553	8.12	850	7.33	500	11.06	3170	6.25	137	6.12	105	5.92	118	5.83	80
9	6.33	163	7.08	403	9.37	1630	9.12	490	7.58	600	7.85	715	7.67	640	10.67	2770	6.31	158	6.12	105	6.17	96	6.00	50
10	6.42	186	7.08	403	9.00	1370	8.62	490	7.58	570	7.79	685	7.89	735	9.25	1540	6.33	162	6.00	80	6.08	92	6.04	88
11	6.42	186	7.00	375	9.00	1370	8.08	490	7.50	570	8.00	790	9.67	1870	8.83	1250	6.31	158	6.12	105	6.06	80	5.92	64
12	6.48	204	7.12	418	9.00	1370	8.08	490	7.54	585	8.98	1360	8.75	1200	8.56	1090	6.29	147	6.14	110	5.83	72	5.92	64
13	6.39	177	7.21	454	11.58	3740	8.08	490	7.62	620	10.12	2250	8.02	800	7.71	850	6.29	147	6.17	117	5.96	64	6.25	80
14	6.46	198	7.37	520	10.79	2890	8.08	490	7.50	570	10.25	2360	7.52	580	7.37	655	6.23	132	5.96	72	5.92	64	6.25	137
15	6.40	180	7.31	494	9.75	1930	8.08	490	7.50	570	9.29	1570	9.25	1540	7.35	520	6.25	137	6.10	100	5.92	72	6.19	137
16	6.42	186	7.25	470	8.71	1180	8.08	490	7.50	570	9.29	1570	10.37	2470	7.62	510	6.23	132	6.04	88	5.96	50	6.23	122
17	6.37	173	7.17	438	7.54	585	8.08	490	7.42	540	9.75	1930	10.77	2870	7.71	620	6.29	147	6.10	100	5.83	64	6.08	132
18	6.37	173	7.21	454	7.50	570	8.08	490	7.42	540	8.87	1280	9.61	1870	7.71	655	6.17	117	5.94	68	5.92	64	6.23	96
19	7.71	655	7.50	570	7.37	520	7.79	490	7.42	500	8.29	935	8.87	1280	7.54	595	6.25	137	6.06	92	5.92	64	6.50	132
20	8.62	1120	7.83	705	7.42	540	7.75	490	7.42	540	8.27	925	8.44	1010	7.33	585	6.23	132	5.89	58	5.92	64	6.54	210
21	8.75	1200	7.81	695	7.67	640	7.75	490	7.35	520	8.17	875	8.12	850	7.23	500	6.25	132	6.00	80	5.92	64	6.69	267
22	8.42	875	7.67	640	7.50	570	7.62	490	7.33	500	8.08	830	7.89	735	7.06	462	6.12	105	5.98	76	5.92	47	6.54	222
23	8.17	670	7.58	600	10.29	1440	7.58	490	7.44	545	7.94	760	10.94	3040	7.06	375	6.12	105	6.04	88	5.81	64	6.35	167
24	7.75	670	7.71	655	9.75	1440	7.46	490	8.87	1280	7.77	680	9.52	1750	7.23	396	6.27	142	6.08	96	5.92	64	6.39	177
25	7.56	595	7.64	625	9.33	1440	7.31	495	10.54	2640	7.89	735	8.85	1260	7.23	462	6.17	117	5.92	80	5.92	64	6.31	157
26	7.50	570	7.54	585	9.12	1670	7.25	540	13.67	6330	8.04	810	8.02	800	7.44	426	6.08	96	6.17	80	6.25	138	6.21	127
27	7.83	705	7.94	760	9.42	1670	7.42	540	12.25	5510	8.89	1290	7.46	655	6.89	545	6.04	88	6.00	80	6.29	148	6.12	105
28	8.42	1000	7.79	685	11.58	3740	7.42	540	13.04	4540	7.69	645	8.19	885	6.75	337	6.04	88	5.87	55	....	....	6.10	100
29	8.54	1070	7.67	640	10.08	2210	....	....	11.29	3420	7.37	520	8.08	830	6.71	288	6.08	96	5.96	80	....	....	6.12	100
30	8.69	1160	7.50	570	9.33	1600	....	....	....	....	....	....	9.98	2120	6.71	280	5.96	72	6.00	72	....	....	6.00	80
31	....	....	7.83	705	11.67	3840	....	....	....	....	....	....	11.02	3120	....	....	....	....	6.00	80	....	....	6.10	100

Monthly Discharge of Thames River (South Branch) near Ealing for 1915-6

Drainage Area 515 Square Miles

Month	Discharge in Second-feet			Discharge in Second-feet per Square Mile			Run-off
	Maximum	Minimum	Mean	Maximum	Minimum	Mean	Depth in Inches on Drainage Area
November (1915).	1,200	163	468	2.33	.32	.91	1.02
December ··	955	375	565	1.85	.73	1.10	1.27
January (1916).	6,540	520	2,140	12.70	1.01	4.16	4.80
February	4,540	470	719	8.82	.91	1.40	1.51
March..........	6,330	470	1,198	12.29	.91	2.33	2.69
April..........	2,890	520	1,233	5.61	1.01	2.39	2.67
May	3,120	455	1,212	6.06	.88	2.35	2.71
June	3,170	280	933	6.16	.54	1.81	2.02
July...........	246	72	145	.48	.14	.28	.32
August.........	105	55	124	.20	.11	.24	.28
September......	148	50	72	.29	.10	.14	.16
October.........	267	64	115	.52	.12	.22	.25
The year.......	6,540	50 ·	745	12.70	.10	1.45	19.74

Regular Stations

SOUTH-WESTERN ONTARIO DISTRICT

Grand River and Tributaries

River	Location	Drainage Area Sq. Miles	Township	County or District
Grand	at Belwood	280	Garafraxa	Wellington Co. .....
"	at Brantford..........	2,000	Brantford...........	Brant Co..........
"	near Conestogo.......	550	Woolwich...........	Waterloo Co.......
"	at Galt	1,360	North Dumfries	" ......
"	at Glen Morris........	1,390	South Dumfries	Brant Co ....
"	at York	2,280	Oneida..............	Haldimand Co.....
Boston Creek	near York	125	"	" .....
Conestogo	at St. Jacob's	305	Woolwich	Waterloo Co.......
Fairchild's Creek ...	near Onondaga	115	Onondaga	Brant Co. ....
Galt Creek	at Galt	45	North Dumfries	Waterloo Co ....
Irvine	near Salem	67	Nichol..............	Wellington Co.....
Nith	near Canning..........	365	Blenheim	Oxford Co ....
Speed	near Guelph..........	77	Guelph	Wellington Co .....
"	at Hespeler,..........	250	Waterloo............	Waterloo Co.......
Whiteman's Creek ..	near Burford..........	154	Brantford...........	Brant Co..........

Grand River at Belwood

Location—At the bridge in the Village of Belwood, on the 7th concession, Township of Garafraxa, County of Wellington.

Records Available—August 31, 1913, to October 31, 1916.

Drainage Area—280 square miles.

Gauge—Vertical steel staff 0 to 12 feet on right abutment. Elevation of zero on gauge is 1366.00, which has remained unchanged since established.

Channel and Control—The channel is straight for about 400 feet above and 600 feet below gauging section. The channel bed at the bridge is solid rock, and permanent at all stages. At the permanent low water section, however, the channel is shifting under high water conditions.

Winter Flow—During the winter months the relation of gauge height to discharge is greatly affected by ice, and readings are taken to determine the winter discharge.

Accuracy—The river stage at this section is not affected by any power plants above or below. The rating curve is well defined, and estimates are considered good.

Observer—Lloyd Mosure, Belwood P.O.

Discharge Measurements of Grand River at Belwood in 1915-6

Date	Hydrographer	Width in Feet	Area of Section in Sq. Feet	Mean Velocity in Feet per Sec.	Gauge Height in Feet	Discharge in Sec-Feet	Discharge in Second-feet per Square Mile
1915							
Nov. 9....	Cunnington G...	65	43	1.69	1,367.29	73	....
1916							
Feb. 3....	Roberts E.	110	552	1.90	1,369.00	1,050 (a)	....
" 18....	"	95	59	1.16	1,367.82	69 (b)	....
Mar. 30....	Cunnington G...	110	718	3.73	1,370.50	2,680	....
" 30....	" ...	110	718	3.70	1,370.44	2,646	....
Apr. 1....	" ...	110	806	5.57	1,371.33	4,487	....
" 1....	" ...	110	806	5.84	1,371.33	4,708	....
May 9....	Roberts E	110	410	.60	1,367.76	246	....
Oct. 6....	"	63	14	.38	1,366.83	5	....

(a) Slush and ice in stream; section has been scoured by freshets.
(b) Ice on control.

Daily Gauge Height and Discharge of Grand River at Belwood for 1915-6

Drainage Area, 280 Square Miles

Day	Nov Gauge Ht. (Feet)	Nov Dis-charge (Sec-ft)	Dec Gauge Ht. (Feet)	Dec Dis-charge (Sec-ft)	Jan Gauge Ht. (Feet)	Jan Dis-charge (Sec-ft)	Feb Gauge Ht. (Feet)	Feb Dis-charge (Sec-ft)	Mar Gauge Ht. (Feet)	Mar Dis-charge (Sec-ft)	Apr Gauge Ht. (Feet)	Apr Dis-charge (Sec-ft)	May Gauge Ht. (Feet)	May Dis-charge (Sec-ft)	June Gauge Ht. (Feet)	June Dis-charge (Sec-ft)	July Gauge Ht. (Feet)	July Dis-charge (Sec-ft)	Aug Gauge Ht. (Feet)	Aug Dis-charge (Sec-ft)	Sept Gauge Ht. (Feet)	Sept Dis-charge (Sec-ft)	Oct Gauge Ht. (Feet)	Oct Dis-charge (Sec-ft)
1	1367.33	72	1368.16	444	1367.98	145	1369.87	1960	1367.46	55	1371.42	4910	1367.67	205	1367.83	293	1367.17	25	1366.83	5	1366.75	2	1366.85	6
2	1367.29	62	1368.08	393	1368.17	155	1368.96	1070	1367.50	55	1370.46	2650	1367.87	317	1367.62	180	1367.10	15	1366.83	5	1366.81	4	1366.83	5
3	1367.29	62	1367.87	275	1368.21	175	1368.42	680	1367.50	55	1370.17	2300	1368.12	474	1367.67	205	1367.12	18	1366.83	5	1366.79	4	1366.83	5
4	1367.29	62	1367.83	255	1368.14	218	1368.42	530	1367.50	55	1369.58	1640	1368.50	740	1367.58	160	1367.08	14	1366.83	5	1366.79	5	1366.83	5
5	1367.33	72	1367.83	255	1368.42	255	1368.42	395	1367.50	55	1369.37	1430	1368.00	395	1367.58	160	1367.08	14	1366.83	5	1366.75	4	1366.83	5
6	1367.33	72	1367.58	72	1368.42	290	1368.37	365	1367.50	55	1369.14	1230	1367.75	248	1367.50	120	1367.04	13	1366.83	5	1366.75	2	1366.83	5
7	1367.31	68	1367.58	147	1369.33	860	1368.12	305	1367.54	70	1369.00	1100	1367.50	120	1367.39	82	1367.02	11	1366.83	5	1366.75	2	1366.83	5
8	1367.29	68	1367.58	147	1369.96	1250	1368.08	275	1367.58	85	1368.83	970	1367.54	140	1367.42	92	1367.00	11	1366.83	5	1366.75	2	1366.89	7
9	1367.29	68	1367.58	147	1369.62	1185	1368.08	248	1367.58	85	1368.54	770	1367.71	225	1367.42	92	1367.00	11	1366.83	5	1366.79	2	1366.92	8
10	1367.31	68	1367.46	108	1369.31	1120	1368.08	248	1367.54	65	1368.50	740	1367.71	225	1367.35	70	1366.96	9	1366.83	5	1366.77	2	1366.87	8
11	1367.29	72	1367.46	108	1369.25	990	1368.00	220	1367.54	248	1369.00	1100	1368.04	421	1367.42	170	1366.96	9	1366.83	5	1366.75	2	1366.92	8
12	1367.33	72	1367.58	72	1369.17	665	1367.92	220	1367.50	220	1368.83	970	1367.60	293	1367.60	170	1365.92	8	1366.83	5	1366.75	2	1366.96	9
13	1367.31	68	1367.58	68	1369.79	890	1367.87	170	1367.50	220	1369.00	1100	1367.54	106	1367.54	140	1365.92	8	1366.79	4	1366.75	2	1367.00	11
14	1367.33	72	1367.58	72	1369.75	990	1367.87	70	1367.50	70	1370.75	3110	1367.46	150	1367.42	92	1366.92	6	1366.79	4	1366.75	2	1366.96	9
15	1367.37	62	1367.62	62	1369.37	960	1367.87	85	1367.58	85	1370.08	2200	1367.56	205	1367.42	92	1365.87	6	1366.75	4	1366.75	2	1366.96	9
16	1367.37	62	1367.62	62	1369.31	795	1367.87	600	1367.58	85	1369.42	1480	1367.67	360	1368.00	395	1366.96	9	1366.75	2	1366.75	2	1366.94	9
17	1367.29	72	1367.67	72	1369.08	600	1367.79	85	1367.58	85	1369.75	1820	1367.77	210	1368.25	565	1366.96	8	1366.75	2	1366.77	2	1366.92	8
18	1367.33	72	1367.69	72	1369.08	535	1367.83	438	1367.83	438	1369.50	1550	1367.69	215	1368.21	535	1366.92	9	1366.75	2	1366.77	2	1367.02	12
19	1367.96	323	1367.69	323	1368.83	438	1367.77	85	1367.50	85	1369.17	1250	1367.58	160	1368.04	421	1366.92	9	1366.75	2	1366.75	2	1367.02	18
20	1367.67	690	1367.67	690	1368.75	345	1367.75	85	1367.50	85	1370.08	2200	1367.54	140	1367.81	281	1366.94	9	1366.75	3	1366.79	2	1367.12	18
21	1368.08	393	1367.75	393	1368.71	318	1367.75	85	1367.50	85	1369.54	1590	1367.44	99	1367.58	160	1367.17	25	1366.75	13	1366.79	2	1367.12	18
22	1367.87	275	1367.75	275	1368.62	195	1367.62	85	1367.50	55	1371.37	4740	1367.39	82	1367.60	82	1367.06	13	1366.77	13	1366.83	5	1367.08	14
23	1367.67	183	1367.75	183	1371.67	1770	1367.75	86	1367.50	55	1370.46	2650	1367.42	236	1367.42	92	1367.00	11	1366.79	4	1366.83	5	1367.08	9
24	1367.71	200	1367.75	200	1370.33	1280	1367.62	70	1367.54	55	1370.46	2650	1367.62	180	1367.50	76	1367.00	11	1366.79	4	1366.83	5	1366.94	9
25	1367.75	217	1367.75	217	1369.71	1020	1367.67	70	1367.79	102	1369.37	1270	1367.54	140	1367.42	120	1366.96	9	1366.83	5	1366.83	5	1366.92	8
26	1368.83	880	1367.75	880	1369.12	1020	1367.50	605	1368.31	270	1369.19	1290	1367.35	70	1367.42	70	1366.92	8	1366.83	5	1366.83	5	1366.92	8
27	1369.08	1040	1367.79	605	1369.33	1400	1367.58	55	1369.04	605	1369.21	1100	1367.50	120	1367.33	64	1366.89	7	1366.82	5	1366.85	6	1366.92	8
28	1369.06	1030	1367.81	1040	1370.42	2600	1367.58	55	1369.04	1140	1368.83	970	1368.87	1000	1367.25	42	1366.83	8	1366.80	4	1366.85	6	1366.92	8
29	1368.46	640	1367.81	640	1371.50	5200			1370.46	2650	1368.65	845	1368.17	510	1367.25	42	1366.83	5	1366.75	2	1366.96	9	1366.92	8
30	1367.62	163	1367.83	163	1369.25	1320			1371.37	4740	1368.58	795	1368.50	740	1367.25	42	1366.83	5	1366.75	2	1366.92	8	1366.92	8
31			1367.83		1370.83	3270			1371.46	5060			1368.21	535			1366.83	5	1366.75	2			1366.94	9

Monthly Discharge of Grand River at Belwood for 1915-6

Drainage Area, 280 Square Miles

Month	Discharge in Second-feet			Discharge in Second-feet per Square Mile			Run-off
	Maximum	Minimum	Mean	Maximum	Minimum	Mean	Depth in Inches on Drainage Area
November. (1915)	1,040	62	241	3.71	.22	.86	.96
December. ``	444	90	159	1.59	.32	.57	.66
January .. (1916)	5,200	145	1,137	18.57	.52	4.06	4.68
February	1,960	55	273	7.00	.20	.95	1.05
March	5,060	55	520	18.07	.20	1.86	2.14
April	4,910	470	1,735	17.54	1.68	6.20	6.91
May	1,000	70	288	3.57	.25	1.03	1.19
June	565	42	174	2.02	.15	.62	.69
July	25	5	11	.09	.02	.04	.05
August	5	2	4	.02	.01	.01	.01
September	9	2	3	.03	.01	.01	.01
October	18	5	9	.06	.02	·03	.03
The year	5,200 ·	2	378	18.57	.01	1.35	18.38

Grand River at Brantford

Location—At the Toronto-Hamilton-Brantford Railway bridge in the City of Brantford, County of Brant.

Records Available—Discharge measurements from August, 1912, to October 31, 1916. Daily gauge heights from July 8, 1913, to October 31, 1916.

Drainage Area—2,000 square miles.

Gauge—Vertical steel staff, 0 to 12 feet on left abutment. Elevation of zero on gauge is 643.00, which has remained unchanged since established.

Channel and Control—The bed is not shifting under ordinary conditions. The channel above has been narrowed considerably by the building of the Lake Erie & Northern Railway right-of-way. Directly below section a bridge for this same railway is now built that has four piers, the back water from which is quite apparent. During the freshet, ice is liable to jam at this point. During the spring floods of 1916, the bed of stream scoured, so that former curve at low gauge heights is applicable.

Discharge Measurements—Made from the bridge at all stages.

Winter Flow—The relation of gauge height to discharge is seriously affected by ice, and measurements are made to determine the winter flow.

Regulation—The Western Counties Electric Company have a dam 1,000 feet above this section that causes fluctuations that are noticeable in the river stage. Their plant is running at its full capacity. The observed mean gauge height does not give the correct mean daily stage.

Diversions—The Western Counties Electric Company use about 50 second feet for power purposes at times.

Accuracy—With the exception of a slight angle at section these records can be classified as good. The back water caused through the construction work of the Lake Erie & Northern Railway bridge, 150 feet below this section, necessitated the use of more than one curve.

Observer—John Anguish, Brantford.

Discharge Measurement of Grand River at Brantford in 1915-6

Date	Hydrographer	Width in Feet	Area of Section in Sq. Feet	Mean Velocity in Feet per Sec.	Gauge Height in Feet	Discharge in Sec-Feet	Discharge in Second-feet per Square Mile
1915							
Nov. 3....	Yeates, W	341	960	.81	645.18	779 (a)	....
Dec. 29....	"	341	1,040	.86	645.59	897 (b)	....
1916							
Jan. 3....	Roberts, E	364	1,264	1.35	646.21	1,707 (c)	....
" 29....	"	373	3,383	3.19	651.64	10,788 (d)	....
Feb. 1....	Yeates, W, ...	373	3,756	4.82	652.77	18,100 (e)	....
" 16....	Roberts, E, ...	359	1,203	.89	646.08	1,071 (f)	....
" 21....	"	278	834	.77	645.08	638 (g)	....
Mar. 2....	"	278	842	.79	645.35	670 (h)	....
" 8....	Yeates, W, ...	278	816	.95	645.40	778 (f)	....
" 13....	"	278	771	.99	645.21	765 (f)	....
" 22....	"	278	761	.94	645.21	721 (h)	....
" 23....	"	278	761	.93	645.19	719 (h)	....
" 24....	"	278	782	.97	645.31	768 (h)	....
" 25....	"	278	782	.96	645.26	651 (i)	....
June 19....	"	371	1,721	2.16	646.88	3,711 (j)	....
" 20....	"	366	1,646	1.96	646.65	3,226 (j)	....
" 21....	"	364	1,501	1.81	646.33	2,712 (j)	....
" 22....	"	364	1,391	1.49	646.00	2,076	....
" 23....	"	363	1,355	1.32	645.87	1,782	....
" 26....	"	365	1,574	1.84	646.50	2,889	....
" 27....	"	364	1,428	1.57	646.08	2,244	....
" 28....	"	363	1,283	1.23	645.70	1,576	....
" 29....	"	361	1,173	1.14	645.43	1,346	....
" 30....	"	361	1,210	1.21	645.49	1,466	....
Aug. 5....	"	306	908	.48	644.58	433	....
" 7....	"	306	908	.61	644.64	453	....
Sept. 7....	"	288	877	.52	644.50	556	....
" 8....	"	290	869	.47	644.48	405	....
" 11....	"	307	906	.54	644.60	494	....
" 12....	"	273	780	.31	644.17	244	....
" 13....	"	246	756	.24	644.04	178	....
" 15....	"	288	877	.47	644.48	415	....
" 19....	"	288	877	.50	644.50	438	....
" 28....	"	219	703	.16	643.87	110	....
" 29....	"	278	840	.38	644.31	319	....

From 7 p.m. to 7 a.m. the only water passing this section is leakage from the dams above during low-water periods.

(a) Construction work below section.
(b) Ice above, control clear.
(c) Ice on section and control.
(d) Ice jams forming and breaking.
(e) New piers completed below section.
(f) Ice on section and control.
(g) Thin ice on control.
(h) Ice on control.
(i) Thawing—ice effect diminishing.
(j) Section scouring.

Daily Gauge Height and Discharge of Grand River at Brantford for 1915-6

Drainage Area, 2,000 Square Miles

Day	November Gauge Ht. (Feet)	November Dis-charge (Sec-ft.)	December Gauge Ht. (Feet)	December Dis-charge (Sec-ft.)	January Gauge Ht. (Feet)	January Dis-charge (Sec-ft.)	February Gauge Ht. (Feet)	February Dis-charge (Sec-ft.)	March Gauge Ht. (Feet)	March Dis-charge (Sec-ft.)	April Gauge Ht. (Feet)	April Dis-charge (Sec-ft.)	May Gauge Ht. (Feet)	May Dis-charge (Sec-ft.)	June Gauge Ht. (Feet)	June Dis-charge (Sec-ft.)	July Gauge Ht. (Feet)	July Dis-charge (Sec-ft.)	August Gauge Ht. (Feet)	August Dis-charge (Sec-ft.)	September Gauge Ht. (Feet)	September Dis-charge (Sec-ft.)	October Gauge Ht. (Feet)	October Dis-charge (Sec-ft.)
1	645.04	725	647.17	3520	645.48	1150	652.54	17330	645.25	600	651.96	15480	646.31	2560	648.04	5790	645.21	1080	644.44	408	644.35	345	644.52	465
2	645.00	790	646.50	2480	645.64	1350	649.21	7820	645.14	520	651.54	14170	646.17	2330	646.96	3680	645.14	1000	644.50	450	644.39	373	644.56	495
3	645.04	725	646.21	2040	646.04	1790	647.37	3880	645.17	560	649.79	9280	646.54	2940	647.79	2580	645.08	945	644.48	436	644.37	359	644.37	359
4	645.08	760	645.96	1690	646.60	2630	645.96	1690	645.27	600	649.04	7420	647.06	3860	648.33	6440	645.00	865	644.46	422	644.31	317	644.39	373
5	644.96	655	645.77	1460	647.17	3520	645.79	1490	645.21	600	648.08	5260	647.10	3920	647.33	4360	644.81	685	644.39	373	644.62	540	644.44	408
6	645.08	760	645.69	1370	648.48	6130	645.46	1130	645.33	690	647.75	4600	646.62	3090	647.33	4130	644.79	670	644.42	394	644.42	394	644.44	408
7	645.17	845	645.62	1290	649.37	8225	645.46	1130	645.29	690	647.31	3770	646.25	2460	646.73	3280	644.75	635	644.46	422	644.39	373	644.37	359
8	645.12	800	645.52	1190	648.37	5880	645.37	1040	645.33	735	646.25	2860	646.08	2200	646.71	3240	644.75	635	644.50	450	644.29	304	644.29	304
9	645.12	800	645.44	1110	647.46	4040	645.42	1020	645.33	690	646.75	2540	646.14	2290	646.71	3240	644.79	670	644.42	450	644.02	163	644.25	278
10	645.17	845	645.17	840	647.17	3520	645.17	1020	645.17	620	646.29	2160	646.23	2430	645.08	5880	644.77	650	644.50	450	644.06	179	644.31	317
11	644.87	575	645.10	780	647.00	3230	645.71	1120	645.12	560	646.25	2100	646.50	2880	647.92	5540	644.71	610	644.35	345	644.29	304	644.33	331
12	644.94	635	645.06	745	647.04	6170	645.75	1170	645.29	760	646.56	2570	646.75	2570	647.44	4580	644.71	610	644.46	422	644.23	264	644.33	331
13	644.92	620	645.12	735	647.54	6170	645.71	1120	645.29	760	647.87	4840	646.21	2400	647.08	3890	644.56	495	644.48	436	644.17	230	644.42	394
14	644.92	620	645.35	780	654.08	7320	645.67	1020	645.25	735	650.37	10820	645.87	1900	646.50	2890	644.58	670	644.50	450	644.25	278	644.44	408
15	664.96	655	645.21	710	651.12	6170	645.75	1020	645.17	665	651.92	15350	646.17	2330	646.12	2260	644.83	720	644.54	480	644.19	240	644.44	450
16	645.06	745	645.25	780	654.06	4700	645.58	1020	645.25	760	649.33	8120	647.17	4050	646.62	3080	644.58	510	644.64	480	644.02	163	644.39	373
17	644.98	670	645.17	710	653.00	2030	645.71	1020	645.27	760	648.58	6350	647.25	4200	646.83	3450	644.62	540	644.58	510	644.25	278	644.44	408
18	644.88	845	645.17	960	652.42	1500	645.71	1020	645.23	710	649.21	7820	647.25	5450	647.21	4130	644.62	540	644.58	510	644.12	205	644.56	495
19	645.17	845	645.25	920	649.37	960	645.79	1020	645.21	760	648.17	5450	646.75	3310	647.04	3820	644.62	540	644.52	465	644.37	359	644.79	670
20	646.29	2160	645.25	920	652.42	1170	645.27	1020	645.23	760	647.33	3800	646.33	2590	646.67	3170	644.58	510	644.58	510	644.23	373	645.04	885
21	647.50	4120	645.25	920	652.37	3230	645.71	1020	645.12	1020	647.87	4840	646.08	2200	646.02	2100	644.56	495	644.58	510	644.02	163	644.96	825
22	646.79	2920	645.25	920	652.83	6170	645.58	6170	645.29	890	648.54	6260	646.81	3420	646.25	1740	644.64	670	644.42	392	644.29	304	644.85	720
23	646.29	2160	645.29	920	652.37	13450	645.54	3230	645.21	870	649.51	7460	647.25	4200	645.75	1740	644.39	670	644.44	408	644.31	317	644.75	640
24	645.98	1720	645.14	815	654.42	9820	645.37	890	649.67	1150	649.06	4720	647.25	3240	645.75	1890	644.79	670	644.44	408	644.17	230	644.75	640
25	645.98	1720	645.33	760	654.33	9820	645.29	780	645.48	2280	647.81	4390	646.17	2340	646.42	2740	644.56	495	644.56	436	644.46	422	644.75	640
26	645.92	1640	645.12	800	652.87	12550	645.33	690	646.37	8980	647.64	5800	646.08	2200	646.33	2130	644.64	555	644.56	495	644.50	450	644.72	615
27	647.08	3370	645.17	845	651.29	13420	645.12	600	649.67	23060	648.33	4940	646.33	2590	645.62	1570	644.62	540			644.17	317	644.56	495
28	648.34	6260	645.29	960	653.33	19860	649.67	645	654.33	21870	647.92	3370	646.73	3310	645.33	1280	644.60	525			644.17	230	644.62	495
29	647.83	4750	645.44	1110	652.54	12550	645.38	790	653.96	20780	647.08	2600	646.33	5360	645.25	1120	644.46	422			644.46	450	644.56	495
30	647.96	5020	645.37	1040	649.17	7730			653.62		646.58		645.25										644.67	580
31			645.67	1350	650.00	9820							649.96	106510										

Monthly Discharge of Grand River at Brantford for 1915-6

Drainage Area, 2,000 Square Miles

Month	Discharge in Second-feet			Discharge in Second-feet per Square Mile.			Run-off
	Maximum	Minimum	Mean	Maximum	Minimum	Mean	Depth in Inches on Drainage Area
November (1915).	6,260	620	1,645	3.13	.31	.82	.91
December ''	3,520	710	1,138	1.76	.35	.57	.66
January (1916).	19,860	1,150	6,337	9.93	.58	3.17	3.65
February	17,330	600	1,918	8.66	.30	.96	1.04
March	23,060	520	3,069	11.53	.26	1.53	1.76
April...........	15,480	2,100	6,419	7.74	1.05	3.21	3.58
May...........	10,510	1,900	3,284	5.26	.95	1.64	1.89
June	6,440	1,120	3,387	3.22	.56	1.69	1.89
July	1,080	422	633	.54	.21	.32	.37
August	510	373	441	.26	.19	.22	.25
September	540	163	295	.27	.08	.15	.17
October	905	278	498	.46	.14	.25	.29
The year.......	23,060	163	2,419	11.53	.08	1.21	16.46

Grand River near Conestogo

Location—At the highway bridge ¼ mile below the Village of Conestogo, Township of Woolwich, County of Waterloo.

Records Available—July 16, 1913, to October 31, 1916.

Drainage Area—550 square miles.

Gauge—Vertical steel staff 0 to 12 feet on the centre pier of bridge. Elevation of zero is 1017.00 feet.

Channel and Control—The channel is straight for about 300 feet above and below the gauging section. The banks are low and liable to overflow. The bed is composed of gravel, and all the water is confined between the abutments of the bridge, except at a very serious flood. In flood stages the banks and bed are liable to shift.

Discharge Measurements—Made from the bridge during high water, and at a permanent low water section located 600 feet upstream during the low water period.

Winter Flow—The relation of gauge height to discharge is seriously affected by ice during the winter season, and measurements are made to determine the winter flow.

Accuracy—The slight shifting of the channel has little affect. The rating curve is well defined, and records are good.

Observer—E. Schinbein, Conestogo.

Discharge Measurements of Grand River near Conestogo in 1915-6

Date	Hydrographer	Width in Feet	Area of Section in Sq. Feet	Mean Velocity in Feet per Sec.	Gauge Height in Feet	Discharge in Sec-Feet	Discharge in Second-feet per Square Mile
1915							
Nov. 10....	Roberts, E.	130	107	1.37	1,018.42	147	....
1916							
Jan. 7....	" "	238	662	2.33	1,020.60	1,539(a)	....
" 26....	Cunnington, G..	247	712	2.44	1,020.83	1,735(b)	....
Feb. 2....	Roberts, E.....	235	612	2.25	1,020.43	1,378(c)	....
" 19....	" "	135	156	1.10	1,019.00	173(d)	....
Mar. 21....	Cunnington, G..	266	1,349	4.03	1,023.83	5,489	....
Apr. 4....	" " ..	248	809	3.00	1,021.17	2,430	....
" 4....	" " ..	248	809	2.97	1,021.17	2,401	....
" 4....	" " ..	248	809	2.96	1,021.17	2.397	....
May 9....	Roberts, E.....	182	356	1.79	1,019.25	634	....
Oct. 6....	" "	118	45	.60	1,017.77	27	....

(a) Anchor ice at section.
(b) Ice at both sides of section.
(c) Slush at section and ice at left side.
(d) Measurement not taken at regular section; ice at gauge.

Daily Gauge Height and Discharge of Grand River near Conestogo for 1915-6

Drainage Area, 550 Square Miles

Day	November Gauge Ht. (Feet)	Nov. Dis-charge (Sec-ft.)	December Gauge Ht.	Dec. Dis-charge	January Gauge Ht.	Jan. Dis-charge	February Gauge Ht.	Feb. Dis-charge	March Gauge Ht.	Mar. Dis-charge	April Gauge Ht.	Apr. Dis-charge	May Gauge Ht.	May Dis-charge	June Gauge Ht.	June Dis-charge	July Gauge Ht.	July Dis-charge	August Gauge Ht.	Aug. Dis-charge	September Gauge Ht.	Sept. Dis-charge	October Gauge Ht.	Oct. Dis-charge
1	1018.39	147	1019.85	1060	1018.96	335	1022.04	3290	1018.87	150	1024.29	6990	1019.25	575	1019.58	835	1018.46	168	1017.94	49	1017.67	18	1017.89	42
2	1018.37	142	1019.48	755	1019.31	470	1020.54	1500	1018.87	150	1022.33	4910	1019.75	975	1019.64	880	1018.50	180	1017.77	32	1017.71	22	1017.85	37
3	1018.35	125	1019.31	620	1019.52	610	1019.96	975	1018.77	110	1022.08	3660	1020.04	1240	1020.92	2180	1018.42	156	1017.77	28	1017.75	26	1017.89	42
4	1018.31	130	1019.12	485	1019.60	690	1019.46	505	1018.79	110	1021.46	2850	1020.37	1570	1020.04	905	1018.33	130	1017.75	28	1017.75	26	1017.79	30
5	1018.33	125	1018.98	400	1021.17	2160	1018.96	260	1018.71	97	1020.89	2150	1019.87	1080	1020.18	1280	1018.29	130	1017.75	26	1017.64	16	1017.81	32
6	1018.39	147	1019.00	410	1021.46	2520	1018.92	240	1018.77	122	1020.64	1850	1019.58	835	1019.67	905	1018.25	119	1017.69	26	1017.67	18	1017.79	32
7	1018.35	136	1018.96	390	1020.79	1790	1019.12	260	1018.87	150	1020.08	1280	1019.35	650	1019.12	484	1018.08	119	1017.71	20	1017.64	16	1017.71	32
8	1018.35	136	1018.94	380	1020.62	1550	1019.62	260	1018.96	180	1019.94	1150	1019.27	590	1019.54	800	1018.08	109	1017.75	22	1017.67	18	1017.81	32
9	1018.46	168	1018.79	305	1020.23	1110	1019.17	260	1018.98	180	1019.54	800	1019.48	755	1019.75	975	1017.94	71	1017.73	24	1017.75	18	1017.67	18
10	1018.44	162	1018.58	212	1019.83	850	1019.58	310	1019.08	180	1019.62	865	1019.58	755	1020.50	1700	1017.96	71	1017.73	24	1017.64	16	1017.71	22
11	1018.40	150	1018.50	180	1019.92	875	1019.58	360	1018.98	180	1019.83	1050	1019.37	665	1019.62	865	1017.96	49	1017.71	22	1017.62	14	1017.71	22
12	1018.42	156	1018.60	220	1020.02	975	1019.62	360	1018.79	220	1020.52	1720	1019.17	520	1019.48	755	1017.94	51	1017.71	22	1017.67	18	1017.87	33
13	1018.42	156	1018.62	228	1020.69	1600	1019.52	360	1019.08	220	1021.96	3500	1019.04	434	1019.29	605	1017.94	51	1017.77	24	1017.71	22	1017.94	49
14	1018.31	125	1018.56	204	1020.50	1450	1019.46	335	1019.00	220	1023.83	6230	1018.87	345	1019.08	458	1017.94	49	1017.64	28	1017.71	22	1017.94	49
15	1018.37	142	1018.60	220	1020.39	1350	1019.29	310	1018.98	165	1022.37	4070	1019.21	545	1019.08	458	1017.96	49	1017.75	16	1017.67	18	1017.96	51
16	1018.44	162	1018.62	228	1020.04	975	1019.23	285	1019.02	200	1021.08	2380	1019.42	705	1021.00	2280	1017.96	49	1017.69	26	1017.71	22	1017.75	30
17	1018.40	150	1018.62	228	1019.54	540	1019.17	240	1018.94	165	1021.71	3170	1019.56	820	1020.21	1410	1017.96	51	1017.79	24	1017.73	18	1017.79	26
18	1018.37	142	1018.58	212	1019.08	285	1019.17	240	1018.87	150	1021.33	2680	1019.48	755	1020.21	1410	1017.96	51	1017.69	30	1017.73	24	1018.29	119
19	1018.75	285	1018.73	248	1018.83	285	1019.00	180	1018.77	170	1021.25	2580	1019.17	520	1019.83	975	1018.17	90	1017.73	30	1017.67	18	1018.33	130
20	1020.31	1510	1018.58	212	1018.75	200	1018.92	136	1018.87	220	1021.08	2380	1019.17	520	1019.50	770	1018.00	57	1017.69	24	1017.67	18	1018.21	100
21	1019.75	975	1018.73	275	1018.79	200	1018.87	136	1918.98	220	1021.27	2600	1019.04	434	1019.25	575	1017.98	54	1017.73	24	1017.73	24	1918.14	83
22	1019.56	820	1018.67	248	1022.87	4390	1018.87	136	1018.87	260	1022.67	4490	1018.87	345	1018.96	390	1018.10	74	1017.85	37	1017.75	26	1018.21	100
23	1019.21	545	1018.62	228	1021.25	2210	1018.87	136	1018.96	260	1021.08	2380	1019.62	865	1018.62	228	1018.00	57	1017.75	26	1017.71	22	1018.04	64
24	1019.21	545	1018.69	180	1020.62	1500	1018.87	117	1018.85	285	1020.81	2050	1019.35	650	1018.75	285	1018.00	57	1017.67	18	1017.89	42	1017.94	49
25	1019.29	605	1018.60	136	1020.83	1760	1018.83	110	1018.89	370	1020.79	2030	1019.00	410	1019.33	635	1017.96	51	1017.79	18	1017.67	18	1017.87	39
26	1019.75	975	1018.33	97	1020.96	1860	1018.73	136	1018.92	1740	1020.12	1320	1018.75	285	1019.00	410	1017.92	46	1017.79	30	1017.79	30	1017.87	39
27	1020.60	1810	1018.69	165	1022.08	3290	1018.85	110	1020.54	3660	1020.79	2030	1018.75	285	1018.75	285	1017.81	32	1017.81	32	1017.81	32	1017.85	37
28	1020.94	2210	1018.69	220	1025.46	8470	1018.75	110	1022.08	5380	1020.12	1320	1018.75	285	1018.62	228	1017.89	42	1017.98	54	1017.98	54	1017.89	39
29	1020.52	1720	1018.81	252	1021.08	2040			1023.29	6920	1019.73	955	1018.69	256	1018.58	212	1017.92	32			1017.96	51	1017.85	37
30	1020.33	1539	1019.06	360	1020.54	1590			1024.25	7550	1019.46	740	1021.06	2350	1018.54	196	1017.81	32					1017.89	39
31			1019.08	385	1023.92	6020			1024.62				1020.35	1550			1017.89	42					1017.94	49

Monthly Discharge of Grand River near Conestogo for 1915-6

Drainage Area 550 Square Miles.

Month	Discharge in Second-feet			Discharge in Second-feet per Square Mile			Run-off
	Maximum	Minimum	Mean	Maximum	Minimum	Mean	Depth in inches on Drainage Area
November (1915)	2,210	125	.538	4.02	.23	.98	1.09
December.. ''	1,060	97	312	1.93	.18	.57	.66
January. . (1916)	8.470	200	1,735	15.40	.36	3.15	3.63
February	3,290	110	411	5.98	.20	.75	.81
March..........	7,550	97	970	13.73	.18	1.76	2.03
April...........	6,990	740	2,694	12.71	1.35	4.90	5.47
May............	2,350	256	730	4.27	.47	1.33	1.53
June.	2,280	196	811	4.15	.36	1.47	1.64
July...........	180	32	76	.33	.06	.14	.16
August	49	18	25	.09	.03	.05	.06
September	54	14	24	.10	.03	.04	.04
October........	130	18	47	.24	.03	.08	.09
The year	8,470	14	696	15.40	.03	1.26	17.29

Grand River at Galt

Location—At the Concession Street bridge, in the City of Galt, Township of North Dumfries, County of Waterloo.

Records Available—July 21, 1913, to October 31, 1916.

Drainage Area—1,360 square miles.

Gauge—Vertical steel staff 0 to 12 feet on first left pier of the bridge. Elevation of zero on gauge is 851.00, which has remained unchanged since established.

Channel and 'Control—The channel is straight for 1,000 feet above and below the section. The bed is solid rock formation. Residents each year encroach on the natural channel by building up the banks to protect their lots from washing away.

Discharge Measurements—Made from bridge for high stages, and at a permanent wading section 150 feet upstream during low stages.

Winter Flow—Ice slightly affects the relation of gauge height to discharge during the winter, and measurements are made to determine the winter flow. The open-water rating curve is applicable.

Regulation—This section is subject to serious fluctuations in the river stage caused by the operation of the Galt dam situated ¼ mile above.

Accuracy—The rating curve is fairly well defined, and records are good.

Observer—Charles Parker, Galt.

Discharge Measurements of Grand River at Galt in 1915-6

Date	Hydrographer	Width in Feet	Area of Section in Sq. Feet	Mean Velocity in Feet per Sec.	Gauge Height in Feet	Discharge in Sec-Feet	Discharge in Second-feet per Square Mile
1915							
Nov. 16....	Cunnington, G...	142	234	1.60	852.48	375	....
Dec. 22....	Yeates, W.....	185	662	.66	852.79	437 (a)	....
1916							....
Jan. 5....	Cunnington, G...	194	984	1.82	854.46	1,794 (b)	....
" 21....	Yeates. W.....	187	746	1.00	853.33	751 (c)	....
Feb. 17....	" "	186	680	.99	852.93	600 (d)	....
" 23....	Roberts, E.	180	609	.94	852.72	573 (e)	....
Mar. 1....	Yeates, W.....	180	606	.79	852.64	478 (f)	. ...
" 30....	Cunnington, G...	214	2,393	5.96	861.25	14.256 (g)	....
Apr. 1....	Yeates, W.....	114	2,350	6.87	860.98	16,145	....
" 6....	Cunnington. G...	204	1,247	2.50	855.84	3,122	....
" 6....	" "	204	1,247	2.51	855.83	3,131	....
Oct. 12....	Roberts, E.	138 .	192	.99	852.96	189	....

(a) Ice at both sides of section; slush ice in stream.
(b) Section partly ice-covered.
(c) Thin ice on control and at gauge; slush ice in stream.
(d) Ice above and below section.
(e) Probably affected by heavy wind down stream.
(f) Ice measurement.
(g) Grass probably interferes with meter.

Daily Gauge Height and Discharge of Grand River at Galt for 1915-6

Drainage Area 1,360 Square Miles

Day	November Gauge Ht. (Feet)	November Dis-charge (Sec-ft.)	December Gauge Ht. (Feet)	December Dis-charge (Sec-ft.)	January Gauge Ht. (Feet)	January Dis-charge (Sec-ft.)	February Gauge Ht. (Feet)	February Dis-charge (Sec-ft.)	March Gauge Ht. (Feet)	March Dis-charge (Sec-ft.)	April Gauge Ht. (Feet)	April Dis-charge (Sec-ft.)	May Gauge Ht. (Feet)	May Dis-charge (Sec-ft.)	June Gauge Ht. (Feet)	June Dis-charge (Sec-ft.)	July Gauge Ht. (Feet)	July Dis-charge (Sec-ft.)	August Gauge Ht. (Feet)	August Dis-charge (Sec-ft.)	September Gauge Ht. (Feet)	September Dis-charge (Sec-ft.)	October Gauge Ht. (Feet)	October Dis-charge (Sec-ft.)
1	852.55	345	854.64	1890	852.94	515	859.00	9250	853.00	4605	860.67	15080	854.17	15080	855.35	2650	852.87	530	851.86	142	851.83	136	852.02	174
2	852.53	335	854.27	1550	853.29	725	856.37	4010	852.64	4010	859.04	9380	854.25	9380	854.54	1800	852.73	448	851.86	142	851.81	132	852.14	202
3	852.62	382	854.06	1360	853.87	1110	854.92	2170	852.67	4120	853.08	6940	854.67	6940	857.25	5340	852.68	418	851.85	140	851.77	124	852.07	184
4	852.52	330	853.69	1040	854.19	1390	853.87	1190	852.52	1190	857.08	5070	855.69	5070	856.08	3600	852.62	382	851.87	144	851.67	104	852.02	174
5	852.60	370	853.46	885	855.02	2870	853.62	995	852.50	995	856.21	3780	855.42	3780	855.50	2840	852.52	330	851.85	140	851.68	106	852.08	186
6	852.62	382	853.37	830	856.08	3460	853.15	700	852.44	700	855.81	3240	855.42	3240	855.04	2300	852.51	304	851.76	122	851.71	112	852.02	174
7	852.51	325	853.37	830	853.37	885	853.00	610	852.58	610	855.17	2450	854.58	2450	854.27	1550	852.46	265	851.73	116	851.79	128	851.98	166
8	852.60	370	853.23	750	853.23	750	853.44	875	852.58	875	854.56	1810	854.12	1810	854.67	1910	852.35	296	851.77	124	851.78	126	851.92	154
9	852.75	460	853.28	780	853.50	3390	853.00	271	852.44	271	854.60	1480	853.96	1480	854.75	1990	852.44	271	851.81	132	851.78	126	851.88	146
10	852.60	370	853.19	725	854.77	1910	852.57	284	852.58	284	854.19	1550	854.02	1550	855.29	2580	852.37	271	851.81	132	851.68	106	851.97	164
11	852.56	350	852.96	585	854.52	1910	852.61	335	852.87	335	854.27	1550	854.10	1400	855.62	4370	852.44	296	851.92	154	851.71	112	852.14	202
12	852.64	394	852.39	277	854.54	1710	852.73	382	852.61	382	854.87	2120	854.27	2120	854.44	1930	852.37	271	851.85	140	851.83	136	851.97	164
13	852.61	376	852.21	223	854.98	2150	852.82	382	852.37	382	857.20	5260	853.83	1160	854.50	1760	852.33	259	851.84	140	851.77	124	852.08	186
14	852.54	394	852.29	247	856.00	2150	852.78	360	852.37	360	858.90	8970	854.00	965	854.29	1570	852.29	247	851.78	126	851.71	116	851.97	182
15	852.68	418	852.29	247	855.08	2240	852.81	382	853.25	360	859.08	9510	854.00	1310	854.29	1570	852.21	211	851.81	132	851.71	112	852.08	186
16	852.70	430	852.48	312	853.46	1450	852.82	382	852.69	382	856.87	4740	854.67	1910	855.92	3390	852.12	196	851.67	104	851.66	102	852.09	190
17	852.67	412	852.29	247	854.00	1050	853.00	490	852.69	490	857.18	4820	854.75	4820	854.67	3390	852.00	186	851.80	130	851.69	108	852.10	188
18	852.62	394	852.48	312	853.58	780	853.00	490	852.69	490	857.10	5230	854.69	1930	855.92	2670	852.10	170	851.87	144	851.73	116	852.06	182
19	852.67	394	852.89	545	853.62	780	853.14	605	852.54	575	855.23	3490	854.25	1530	854.96	186	852.08	186	851.73	146	851.95	160	852.09	223
20	855.42	2740	852.81	585	853.50	830	853.00	800	852.54	540	855.71	2510	854.04	1350	854.50	1760	852.06	190	851.85	140	851.81	132	852.21	330
21	854.96	2220	852.96	585	853.62	839	853.14	575	852.46	388	857.58	4500	854.04	4500	854.75	2220	851.96	182	851.82	134	851.83	136	852.52	460
22	854.33	1610	852.98	600	853.50	2840	852.56	388	852.56	345	852.52	5920	853.64	5920	853.75	1420	852.48	312	851.90	134	851.82	134	852.75	460
23	853.85	1180	852.75	460	858.50	8220	852.88	345	852.50	350	859.25	10060	859.25	10060	853.27	1010	852.37	271	851.83	136	851.69	108	852.59	365
24	853.85	1070	852.64	394	856.17	3730	852.75	400	852.50	400	856.96	4880	854.79	2030	853.27	1460	852.37	271	851.86	142	851.64	98	852.52	330
25	853.71	1070	852.64	394	856.79	3780	852.71	325	853.67	325	855.96	3440	854.17	3440	854.17	1500	852.23	229	851.86	142	851.64	98	852.64	325
26	853.71	1060	852.71	460	853.92	3220	852.67	308	853.79	308	856.12	3660	853.62	995	854.21	1060	852.12	196	851.85	140	851.61	92	852.42	288
27	855.50	2840	852.75	460	856.92	4820	852.60	296	856.83	296	857.00	4940	853.56	950	853.71	1060	851.94	190	851.75	120	851.82	134	852.34	262
28	856.33	3950	852.77	472	864.33	13710	852.79	365	860.44	280	855.67	3060	854.33	1610	853.46	885	851.92	196	851.77	116	851.84	138	852.29	247
29	855.60	2970	853.00	610	857.58	5920			861.92	4690	854.96	2220	853.33	1950	853.71	750	851.94	158	851.73	124	852.08	186	852.17	211
30	855.83	3270	853.17	610	856.42	4080			861.92	14300	854.54	1800	853.75	1950	853.00	610	851.92	154	851.83	136	852.10	190	852.23	229
31			853.12	680	858.67	8350			861.42	17850			856.87	4710			851.89	148	851.82	134			852.25	235

Monthly Discharge of Grand River at Galt for 1915-6

Drainage Area, 1,360 Square Miles

Month	Discharge in Second-feet			Discharge in Second-feet per Square Mile			Run-off
	Maximum	Minimum	Mean	Maximum	Minimum	Mean	Depth in Inches on Drainage Area
November. (1915)	3,950	325	1,045	2.90	.24	.77	.86
December. ''	1,890	223	643	1.39	.16	.47	.54
January .. (1916)	13,710	515	3,029	10.08	.88	2.23	2.57
February.......	9,250	186	954	6.80	.14	.70	.76
March.........	19,700	247	2,167	14.49	.18	1.59	1.83
April.........	15,080	1,480	4,792	11.09	1.09	3.52	3.93
May..........	4,740	950	1,705	3.49	.70	1.25	1.44
June..........	5,340	610	2,052	3.93	.45	1.51	1.68
July..........	530	148	256	.39	.11	.19	.22
August........	154	104	134	.11	.08	.10	.12
September	190	92	126	.14	.07	.09	.10
October........	460	146	231	.34	.11	.17	.20
The year.......	19,700	92	1,424	14.49	.07	1.05	14.29

Grand River at Glen Morris

Location—At the Glen Morris bridge, in the Village of Glen Morris, Township of South Dumfries, County of Brant.

Records Available—Discharge measurements from August, 1912, to October 31, 1916. Daily gauge heights, July 21, 1913, to October 31, 1916.

Drainage Area—1,390 square miles.

Gauge—Vertical steel staff 0 to 6 feet on a post and 6 to 12 feet on a tree on left bank. Elevation of the zero on gauge is 801.00, which has remained unchanged since established.

Channel and Control—The channel is straight for 1,000 feet above and below the section. The bed of the river is composed of gravel and boulders, and banks are permanent. The bed and control is shifting under high water conditions.

Discharge Measurements—Made from bridge during the high water stages, and at permanent wading section located 150 feet upstream during the lower water periods.

Winter Flow—This section is seriously affected by ice which usually floods, forming as many as three or four layers of ice with water between them. Measurements are made during the winter months to determine the winter flow.

Regulation—This section is subject to fluctuations in the river stage, due to the storing of water, during the night and at week ends, by the Galt dam, located eight miles above.

Accuracy—Owing to poor natural conditions, the liability of the control to shift and back water caused by ice, the records cannot be considered better than fair.

Observer—Alfred Forbes, Glen Morris P.O.

Discharge Measurements of Grand River at Glen Morris in 1915-6

Date	Hydrographer	Width in Feet	Area of Section in Sq. Feet	Mean Velocity in Feet per Sec.	Gauge Height in Feet	Discharge in Sec-Feet	Discharge in Second-feet per Square Mile
1915							
Nov. 6....	Yeates, W.	265	404	1.02	802.52	415	....
Dec. 21....	"	222	315	1.81	802.83	571 (a)	....
1916							
Jan. 4....	Cunnington, G...	281	770	2.78	804.06	2,137 (b)	....
Feb. 17....	"	266	537	1.57	803.27	843 (c)	....
" 24....	Roberts, E.	266	438	1.30	802.83	589 (d)	....
" 25....	Yeates, W.	266	495	1.22	802.87	606 (e)	....
Mar. 1....	"	266	544	.98	803.23	537	....
" 16....	"	266	471	1.33	803.12	626	....
Apr. 1....	"	410	2,669	7.47	809.19	19,942	....
" 8....	Cunnington, G...	281	829	2.74	804.08	2,274	....
" 8....	"	281	801	2.73	804.04	2,185	....
July 5....	Yeates, W.	271	468	1.18	802.79	553	....
Oct. 12....	Roberts, E.	171	167	1.15	802.87	192	....

(a) Ice at both sides of section.
(b) Ice at piers.
(c) Ice on section half-way across.
(d) Section partly ice-covered.
(e) Ice measurement.

Daily Gauge Height and Discharge of Grand River at Glen Morris for 1915-6

Drainage Area. 1.399 Square Miles

Day	Nov Gauge Ht (Feet)	Nov Dis-charge (Sec-ft)	Dec Gauge Ht	Dec Dis-charge	Jan Gauge Ht	Jan Dis-charge	Feb Gauge Ht	Feb Dis-charge	Mar Gauge Ht	Mar Dis-charge	Apr Gauge Ht	Apr Dis-charge	May Gauge Ht	May Dis-charge	Jun Gauge Ht	Jun Dis-charge	Jul Gauge Ht	Jul Dis-charge	Aug Gauge Ht	Aug Dis-charge	Sep Gauge Ht	Sep Dis-charge	Oct Gauge Ht	Oct Dis-charge
1	802.52	464	804.00	950	802.77	2270	806.92	9140	803.08	560	809.25	16420	803.79	1940	804.58	3380	802.96	855	802.25	320	802.33	355	802.37	375
2	802.54	478	803.69	1800	803.77	1800	806.75	6870	802.83	840	808.33	13460	803.79	1940	804.00	1940	802.75	645	802.29	336	802.33	355	802.37	375
3	802.35	365	803.60	1670	803.97	1670	806.71	14510	803.17	520	806.17	7050	804.12	2490	805.83	6180	802.67	575	802.33	355	802.33	355	802.33	355
4	802.44	414	803.54	1480	804.08	1480	805.75	2810	802.87	450	805.00	6180	804.62	3450	804.96	4200	802.67	575	802.29	336	802.33	336	802.37	375
5	802.52	464	803.04	1590	804.04	1590	805.83	1670	803.00	450	805.00	4290	804.46	3130	804.54	3290	802.71	610	802.29	336	802.29	336	802.33	355
6	802.44	414	802.94			2260	803.12	960	803.00	520	804.92	4110	804.00	2270	804.42	3050	802.67	575	802.25	320	802.25	320	802.33	355
7	802.46	426	802.81			2130	803.17	960	803.00	520	804.67	3570	803.79	1940	803.92	2140	802.62	535	802.25	320	802.33	355	802.33	355
8	802.50	450	802.73			2050	803.21	1020	803.00	520	804.08	2410	803.58	1640	804.58	3570	802.58	505	802.29	336	802.33	355	802.33	355
9	802.46	426	802.64			2020	803.08	790	803.00	520	803.92	2140	803.71	1820	804.12	2480	802.58	505	802.29	336	802.33	355	802.21	304
10	802.54	478	802.54			1960	803.00	690	803.00	520	803.75	1880	803.71	1820	804.71	4470	802.58	505	802.33	336	802.25	320	802.29	336
11	802.52	464	802.60			1890	802.96	690	803.00	520	803.67	1770	803.71	1820	804.04	2570	802.50	480	802.33	336	802.17	288	802.29	336
12	802.52	464	802.67			1810	804.21	1140	802.79	450	803.71	1820	803.83	2000	803.75	1880	802.50	450	802.33	336	802.12	268	802.17	336
13	802.48	438	802.56			1750	803.25	900	802.92	390	805.83	6180	804.00	1640	803.92	2340	802.50	450	802.42	402	802.25	304	802.29	336
14	802.23	312	802.64			1700	803.21	945	802.92	485	805.83	4750	803.33	1590	804.21	2640	802.42	402	802.42	402	802.46	426	802.37	375
15	802.26	324	802.60			1640	803.29	900	803.08	450	805.07	4800	803.54	1590	804.29	2800	802.42	402	802.35	355	802.46	426	802.46	375
16	802.35	365	802.56			1590	803.29	840	803.12	520	805.21	5480	804.04	2340	804.67	3570	802.42	402	802.33	355	802.46	426	802.46	426
17	802.14	276	802.52			1530	803.17	790	803.17	645	805.23	4380	804.12	2480	804.33	2870	802.42	402	802.33	355	802.21	304	802.42	402
18	802.31	345	802.54			1470	803.12	760	802.96	690	805.04	3210	803.83	2480	804.04	2340	802.42	402	802.42	402	802.21	288	802.37	375
19	804.64	3500	802.56	803.42	1430	803.12	760	803.00	520	805.04	4370	803.54	2000	803.75	1880	802.42	402	802.35	355	802.25	320	802.46	375
20	804.69	3610	802.52	803.17	1140	803.08	740	803.00	600	805.04	6180	803.96	1770	803.54	1590	802.42	426	802.33	355	802.29	336	802.79	426
21	804.19	2600	802.44	803.83	2000	803.08	600	803.12	645	805.54	5390	803.79	1470	803.37	1350	802.58	505	802.33	355	802.33	355	802.96	855
22	803.19	1130	802.64	808.67	10880	802.87	590	803.17	670	805.00	11630	803.46	1300	803.21	1150	802.58	575	802.29	320	802.29	355	802.87	760
23	804.04	2340	802.69	805.08	4470	802.83	620	803.00	520	805.83	6180	803.33	1300	803.67	1770	802.58	610	802.33	336	802.21	304	802.83	720
24	804.15	2530	802.64	804.92	4110	802.87	450	802.92	520	805.83	6180	803.75	1880	803.83	2000	802.71	575	802.33	355	802.21	288	802.75	645
25	804.31	2830	802.73	805.08	4470	802.87	450	802.92	670	805.04	4370	804.08	2410	803.50	1530	802.67	450	802.33	355	802.29	336	802.67	665
26	804.44	3090	802.77	806.08	6820	802.92	420	803.00	810	805.04	4290	805.12	4550	803.46	1250	802.50	550	802.33	355	802.33	355	802.58	505
27	805.50	5390	802.85	808.83	15110	803.00	450	803.75	1880	805.00	5210	805.71	5880	803.29	1040	802.50	450	802.33	355	802.21	304	802.54	478
28	805.62	5670	803.06	805.75	5980	803.00	450	805.83	6180	804.83	3920			803.50	900	802.50	402	802.25	320	802.29	336	802.46	426
29	805.60	5620		804.79	3830			808.33	13460	804.29	2790					802.42	320	802.29	336	802.25	320	802.46	426
30	804.10	2440		807.00	9380			809.92	18840	803.96	2210					802.25	288	802.33	355	802.29	336	802.50	450
31									809.42	17100					802.17		802.33				802.46	426

Monthly Discharge of Grand River at Glen Morris for 1915-6

Drainage Area, 1,390 Square Miles

Month	Discharge in Second-feet			Drainage in Second-feet per Square Mile			Run-off
	Maximum	Minimum	Mean	Maximum	Minimum	Mean	Depth in Inches on Drainage Area
November (1915)	5,670	276	1,602	4.08	.20	1.15	1.28
December.. ''	2.270	360	726	1.63	.26	.52	.60
January .. (1916)	15,110	665	3,305	10.87	.48	2.38	2.74
February	9,140	420	1,504	6.58	.30	1.08	1.16
March.........	18,840	390	2,315	13.55	.28	1.67	1.93
April..........	16,420	1,700	5,312	11.81	1.22	3.82	4.26
May..,.........	5,880	1,300	2,245	4.23	.94	1.61	1.86
June	6,180	900	2,463	4.45	.65	1.77	1.97
July...........	855	288	483	.62	.21	.35	.40
August.........	402	320	347	.29	.23	.25	.29
September	426	268	336	.31	.19	.24	.27
October........	855	304	453	.62	.22	.33	.38
The year........	18,840	268	1,752	13.55	.19	1.26	17.15

Grand River at York

Location—At the highway bridge in the Village of York, Township of Oneida, County of Haldimand.

Records Available—June 25, 1913, to October 31, 1916.

Drainage Area—2,280 square miles.

Gauge—Vertical steel staff 0 to 6 feet on the first pier from left abutment and 6 to 12 feet on the left abutment. The elevation of zero is 593.00, and has remained unchanged since established.

Channel and Control—The flow is confined between the abutments of the bridge at all stages. The bed of the river is well protected, but shifting during flood stages. A partly demolished dam about 200 feet downstream affects flow, especially at low stages. Part of this old dam is washed out at each flood period.

Discharge Measurements—Taken from the highway bridge, and at a permanent low water section located 800 feet above during the low water period.

Floods—No floods of a serious nature have occurred here since the spring of 1912, when the dam below the bridge was wrecked, the water cutting around the right abutment, greatly increasing the width of the channel. Village residents state the water rose to a gauge height of 606 feet, which would mean approximately 100,000 second feet.

Winter Flow—The relation of gauge height to discharge is seriously affected by ice, and measurements are made to determine the winter flow.

Regulation—The nearest dam is at Caledonia, five miles above. The intermittent operation of the mills causes daily fluctuations in the gauge heights.

Accuracy—The conditions of flow are good, except for the fluctuations caused through the Caledonia Mills. Well-defined rating curves have been established, and the records can be considered good. Semi-daily gauge heights will not give a good representative mean.

Observer—Fred. Brown, York P.O.

Discharge Measurements of Grand River at York in 1915-6

Date	Hydrographer	Width in Feet	Area of Section in Sq. Feet	Mean Velocity in Feet per Sec.	Gauge Height in Feet	Discharge in Sec-Feet	Discharge in Second-feet per Square Mile
1915							
Nov. 18....	Cunnington, G..	293	492	1.51	593.87	746	....
1916							
Jan. 10....	"	387	2,229	2.11	596.79	4,706 (a)	....
" 22....	Yeates, W.....	382	2,653	1.34	598.02	3,543 (a)	....
Apr. 1....	Roberts, E.....	400	3,444	6.37	600.00	21,937 (b)	....
" 1....	" ...	400	3,364	6.32	599.75	21,256	....
" 3....	" ...	382	2,610	4.59	597.92	11,970	....
" 3....	" ...	378	2,418	4.20	597.33	10,168	....
" 4....	" ...	378	2,229	3.68	596.92	8,213	....
" 4....	" ...	378	2,229	3.44	596.83	7,660	....
July 6....	" ...	341	1,177	.67	593.94	789	....

(a) Heavy ice piled on crest of dam causing backwater.
(b) Control changing.

Daily Gauge Height and Discharge of Grand River at ⅍ for 1915-6

Drainage Area, 2,286 Square Miles

Day	Nov. Gauge Ht. (Feet)	Nov. Discharge (Sec-ft)	Dec. Gauge Ht. (Feet)	Dec. Discharge (Sec-ft)	Jan. Gauge Ht. (Feet)	Jan. Discharge (Sec-ft)	Feb. Gauge Ht. (Feet)	Feb. Discharge (Sec-ft)	Mar. Gauge Ht. (Feet)	Mar. Discharge (Sec-ft)	Apr. Gauge Ht. (Feet)	Apr. Discharge (Sec-ft)	May Gauge Ht. (Feet)	May Discharge (Sec-ft)	June Gauge Ht. (Feet)	June Discharge (Sec-ft)	July Gauge Ht. (Feet)	July Discharge (Sec-ft)	Aug. Gauge Ht. (Feet)	Aug. Discharge (Sec-ft)	Sept. Gauge Ht. (Feet)	Sept. Discharge (Sec-ft)	Oct. Gauge Ht. (Feet)	Oct. Discharge (Sec-ft)
1	593.94	765	596.42	5060	594.50	1340	599.87	21180	596.00	1500	00.0	21800	595.42	3210	596.87	7810	594.39	1370	593.44	424	593.31	355	593.14	276
2	594.02	840	595.48	2910	593.48	1520	597.871	870	596.00	440	599.00	17000	595.29	2900	596.17	5340	594.25	1200	593.42	412	593.31	355	593.39	305
3	593.83	660	595.33	2520	595.83	2140	596.46	6270	595.85	1440	597.54	10610	595.33	2990	596.21	5470	594.17	1100	593.46	436	593.27	335	593.50	460
4	593.87	700	595.79	2050	596.71	2830	596.04	3040	595.69	1380	596.62	6860	596.04	4130	596.75	7350	594.00	950	593.52	474	593.31	355	593.48	448
5	593.94	765	594.96	1930	596.17	3420	597.42	3040	595.69	1380	596.33	5860	596.04	4530	596.75	6140	594.00	900	593.42	412	593.19	296	593.42	412
6	593.79	625	594.71	1600	597.46	5300	598.29	2810	595.83	1380	596.40	6080	595.83	3290	596.08	4930	594.00	900	593.31	355	592.96	208	593.42	412
7	593.83	660	594.60	1460	597.48	9500	598.00	2600	595.83	1320	596.62	6860	595.44	2940	596.19	5060	593.96	855	593.42	412	593.21	305	593.46	436
8	593.98	800	594.54	100	598.21	10000	597.60	2400	595.77	1320	596.62	6860	595.17	2640	596.06	5310	593.81	700	593.31	424	593.48	448	593.23	315
9	594.00	820	594.50	1340	598.50	7160	597.33	2210	595.48	1260	595.62	3740	595.25	2810	596.17	4990	593.67	585	593.44	305	593.44	424	593.33	365
10	593.90	725	594.50	1340	597.29	4460	597.31	2210	595.27	1260	595.50	3400	595.44	3260	596.71	5340	593.71	620	593.21	315	593.06	244	593.42	412
11	593.88	700	594.42	1250	597.48	3680	597.33	2120	595.64	1200	595.44	3260	595.44	3260	596.37	7200	593.81	700	593.23	305	593.21	305	593.42	412
12	593.94	765	594.50	1250	596.83	3540	597.33	2120	595.58	1140	595.64	3790	595.69	3930	596.12	5980	593.83	720	593.21	306	593.25	325	593.33	365
13	593.96	590	594.42	1250	596.42	3680	597.25	2030	595.69	1140	595.87	3790	595.71	3990	595.42	5180	593.75	650	593.42	412	593.29	345	593.33	365
14	593.75	590	594.08	1270	596.46	6780	597.25	1940	595.75	1140	597.96	535.87	595.12	2540	595.42	3680	593.75	650	593.37	385	593.12	268	593.46	436
15	593.96	780	594.44	1270	597.37	7160	597.08	1940	595.44	1140	599.33	18580	595.33	2990	595.96	3210	593.58	650	593.21	268	593.17	288	593.27	335
16	593.12	780	595.37	2600	597.08	7160	597.08	1940	595.48	1140	597.87	370	596.04	4930	595.75	2900	593.75	515	593.46	436	593.21	305	593.42	412
17	593.96	715	595.27	2420	597.08	5700	597.00	1780	595.44	1080	596.96	8150	596.21	5470	595.75	4690	593.71	650	593.25	325	592.96	208	593.71	620
18	593.89	880	595.17	2250	597.37	6400	597.00	1780	595.42	900	597.29	490	596.21	5470	595.94	4100	593.71	620	593.27	335	593.33	325	593.48	448
19	594.06	4970	595.06	2080	598.29	940	596.89	1780	595.44	1140	597.29	900	595.83	4320	595.67	4630	593.52	515	593.35	375	593.37	335	593.50	460
20	594.33	3800	595.39	1930	597.48	7160	596.62	1710	595.33	1080	596.69	5730	595.58	3620	595.37	3880	593.58	474	593.33	365	593.31	375	593.79	680
21	596.39	2700	594.85	1780	597.42	6970	596.71	1710	595.31	1040	596.29	5860	585.34	3020	595.04	3090	593.52	515	593.25	325	593.31	385	594.12	1040
22	595.98	880	594.83	1760	597.87	6780	596.71	1640	595.19	1500	596.33	8000	585.14	2580	595.04	2380	593.58	474	593.37	385	593.31	355	594.21	1100
23	595.43	3800	594.75	1660	597.87	8300	596.48	1640	595.04	1500	599.33	11050	595.83	4320	594.87	2070	593.52	474	593.44	424	593.29	325	594.21	1150
24	545.43	2700	594.80	1660	598.67	12400	596.42	1640	595.04	2380	596.87	7810	595.43	4140	594.62	1740	393.52	810	593.42	412	593.25	345	594.04	950
25	594.06	880	594.73	1630	598.79	12490	596.31	1640	595.04	1500	596.67	7050	596.00	4800	594.42	1670	593.85	740	593.04	365	593.04	236	593.87	760
26	594.89	1840	594.44	1270	598.02	7810	596.17	1570	595.71	3990	596.54	6550	595.42	3210	594.71	1500	593.67	585	593.27	355	593.25	335	593.81	700
27	594.81	1730	594.46	1300	596.87	7500	596.08	1600	597.42	10020	596.23	5540	595.33	2850	594.50	1800	593.58	515	593.23	355	593.31	355	593.79	680
28	594.83	1760	594.71	1600	596.79	14700	595.98	1600	598.96	16820	596.23	4380	595.62	3740	594.46	1450	593.58	515	593.17	288	593.23	315	593.69	600
29	596.54	5440	594.50	1410	598.50	11420			600.08	22220	595.85	4380	596.54	6550	594.42	1400	597.25	448	593.25	325	593.58	515	
30	596.79	6360	594.56	1410	599.92	980			600.67	25280	595.71	3990	596.54	6550			593.48	474	593.25	315	593.62	545	
31	596.42	5060	594.37	1200	597.17	9000			601.02	27100			597.12	8790			593.52		593.23		593.64	560	

Monthly Discharge of Grand River at York for 1915-6

Drainage Area, 2,280 Square Miles

Month	Discharge in Second-feet			Discharge in Second-feet per Square Mile			Run-off
	Maximum	Minimum	Mean	Maximum	Minimum	Mean	Depth in Inches on Drainage Area
November (1915)	6,360	590	1,669	2.80	.26	.73	.81
December "	5,060	900	1,815	2.22	.39	.80	.92
January (1916)	21,420	1,340	7,565	9.39	.59	3.32	3.83
February	21,180	1,500	3,167	9.29	.66	1.39	1.50
March..........	27,100	900	4,430	11.89	.39	1.94	2.24
April...........	21,800	3,260	8,369	9.56	1.43	3.67	4.09
May ., ...	8,790	2,640	3,972	3.86	1.16	1.74	2.01
June............	7,810	1,400	4,056	3.43	.61	1.78	1.99
July............	1,370	448	689	.60	.20	.30	.35
August	474	288	373	.21	.13	.16	.18
September	448	208	324	.20	.09	.14	.16
October.........	1,150	276	550	.50	.12	.24	.28
The year	27,100	208	3,076	11.89	.09	1.35	18.38

Boston Creek near York

Location—At the second highway bridge known as Anderson's Bridge, above the junction with the Grand River, between Concessions 5 and 6, Township of Oneida, County of Haldimand.

Records Available—June 23, 1913, to May 31, 1915, at first highway bridge. At Anderson's Bridge, June 1, 1915, to August 31, 1916.

Drainage Area—125 square miles.

Gauge—Vertical steel staff 0 to 9 feet, attached to downstream side of left abutment. Elevation of zero on gauge is 600.00.

Channel and Control—The channel is straight for 400 feet above and below the gauging section. The river bed is composed of slab rock and is not shifting under normal conditions. The flow passes between the two abutments of the bridge at all stages.

Discharge Measurements—Made from the bridge during freshet stages and from a permanent wading section 100 feet above, during the low water period.

Winter Flow—Relation of gauge height to discharge is affected by ice and measurements are made to determine the winter flow.

Accuracy—Records previous to June 1st, 1915, are not very reliable on account of being affected by backwater from the Grand River. Insufficient records to define rating curve at high stages. Gauge reading discontinued after August 31, 1916.

Observer—H. J. Anderson, Caledonia.

Discharge Measurements of Boston Creek near York in 1915-6

Date	Hydrographer	Width in Feet	Area of Section in Sq. Feet	Mean Velocity in Feet per Sec.	Gauge Height in Feet	Discharge in Sec-Feet	Discharge in Second-feet per Square Mile
1915							
Nov. 18....	Cunnington, G...	42	21	.92	600.75	19	....
1916							
Apr. 3....	Roberts, E	79	206	2.13	602.29	438	....
" 3....	"	79	206	2.14	602.29	440	....
" 4....	"	79	190	1.65	602.00	314	....
" 4....	"	79	190	1.74	602.00	330	....

Daily Gauge Height and Discharge of Boston Creek near York for 1915-6

Drainage Area, 125 Square Miles

Day	Nov Gauge Ht. (Feet)	Nov Dis-charge (Sec-ft.)	Dec Gauge Ht. (Feet)	Dec Dis-charge (Sec-ft.)	Jan Gauge Ht. (Feet)	Jan Dis-charge (Sec-ft.)	Feb Gauge Ht. (Feet)	Feb Dis-charge (Sec-ft.)	Mar Gauge Ht. (Feet)	Mar Dis-charge (Sec-ft.)	Apr Gauge Ht. (Feet)	Apr Dis-charge (Sec-ft.)	May Gauge Ht. (Feet)	May Dis-charge (Sec-ft.)	Jun Gauge Ht. (Feet)	Jun Dis-charge (Sec-ft.)	Jul Gauge Ht. (Feet)	Jul Dis-charge (Sec-ft.)	Aug Gauge Ht. (Feet)	Aug Dis-charge (Sec-ft.)	Sep Gauge Ht. (Feet)	Sep Dis-charge (Sec-ft.)	Oct Gauge Ht. (Feet)	Oct Dis-charge (Sec-ft.)
1	600.75	22	600.98	49	601.62	66	603.33	850	601.35	27	602.79	635	601.21	84	602.37	468	600.81	28	600.58	6	....	....	....	....
2	600.77	24	601.04	58	602.58	320	602.54	535	601.25	22	602.58	550	601.10	72	602.50	520	600.77	24	600.58	6	....	....	....	....
3	600.75	22	601.04	58	603.04	400	602.21	404	601.17	16	602.50	520	601.21	66	602.54	535	600.75	22	600.60	7	....	....	....	....
4	600.75	22	601.00	52	602.83	360	602.12	368	601.17	17	602.04	336	601.33	84	602.37	468	600.75	22	600.62	9	....	....	....	....
5	600.75	22	600.87	35	602.79	320	602.21	404	601.31	27	601.81	244	601.33	106	602.29	436	600.75	22	600.62	9	....	....	....	....
6	600.69	15	600.92	42	603.62	620	602.17	388	601.42	39	601.67	191	601.29	106	602.00	320	600.75	22	600.67	13	....	....	....	....
7	600.73	19	600.87	35	603.42	540	601.96	304	601.54	59	601.54	154	601.21	98	602.17	388	600.75	22	600.67	13	....	....	....	....
8	600.75	22	600.85	33	603.37	380	602.50	240	601.60	59	601.50	144	601.17	84	602.67	590	600.73	19	600.67	13	....	....	....	....
9	600.75	22	600.87	35	603.21	200	602.58	170	601.54	66	601.42	126	601.10	77	602.62	570	600.69	22	600.60	7	....	....	....	....
10	600.73	19	601.04	58	602.37	185	602.33	200	601.52	66	601.42	126	601.39	66	602.29	400	600.67	15	600.64	11	....	....	....	....
11	600.67	13	601.00	52	601.96	185	602.08	144	601.50	66	601.44	119	601.58	135	602.00	320	600.69	13	600.58	6	....	....	....	....
12	600.73	19	600.96	47	601.96	280	601.96	100	601.50	66	603.00	131	601.56	160	601.71	204	600.75	22	600.60	9	....	....	....	....
13	600.73	19	600.85	33	602.17	280	601.98	82	601.67	82	603.04	720	601.39	165	601.62	176	600.69	15	600.62	7	....	....	....	....
14	600.75	22	600.87	39	602.25	480	601.85	66	601.75	91	602.17	735	601.52	119	601.62	176	600.67	13	600.60	6	....	....	....	....
15	600.81	28	600.92	22	602.75	600	601.71	58	601.83	110	602.17	388	601.79	149	601.81	252	600.60	13	600.58	6	....	....	....	....
16	600.73	19	600.87	16	602.87	680	601.62	33	601.77	110	602.08	388	601.92	236	601.79	191	600.67	13	600.58	6	....	....	....	....
17	600.71	17	600.85	12	603.29	780	601.46	22	601.75	110	601.85	260	601.87	288	601.67	115	600.67	13	600.58	6	....	....	....	....
18	600.75	22	600.85	12	603.50	760	601.62	22	601.75	110	601.62	149	601.69	268	601.37	98	600.67	13	600.53	13	....	....	....	....
19	600.94	44	600.92	16	603.12	620	601.25	22	601.67	110	601.52	570	601.48	197	601.29	80	600.67	13	600.60	6	....	....	....	....
20	601.04	58	601.10	33	602.92	560	601.25	33	601.62	110	602.75	352	601.33	176	601.19	77	600.71	17	600.67	9	....	....	....	....
21	601.58	165	601.14	52	602.75	480	601.44	46	601.58	110	602.62	236	601.25	139	601.17	77	600.69	15	600.62	6	....	....	....	....
22	601.54	154	601.29	59	602.42	520	601.33	33	601.58	110	602.08	191	601.71	106	601.17	58	600.67	13	600.58	6	....	....	....	....
23	601.42	136	601.08	39	601.83	360	601.33	27	601.58	165	602.79	165	601.92	91	601.04	52	600.62	9	600.58	9	....	....	....	....
24	601.31	102	601.08	39	601.67	252	601.21	22	602.46	505	601.67	165	601.83	204	601.00	49	600.71	17	600.58	7	....	....	....	....
25	601.19	80	601.17	52	601.75	220	601.08	16	603.67	990	601.58	134	601.62	288	600.98	42	600.69	15	600.58	6	....	....	....	....
26	601.12	69	601.42	82	602.00	320	601.06	7	604.12	1170	601.58	106	601.46	252	600.92	31	600.64	13	600.62	6	....	....	....	....
27	601.00	52	601.42	82	602.29	436	601.19	12	603.96	1100	601.46	134	601.33	176	600.87	35	600.67	11	600.60	7	....	....	....	....
28	601.00	52	601.54	91	601.37	268	601.37	22	604.12	935	601.33	106	603.17	135	600.83	31	600.62	9	600.58		....	....	....	....
29	601.00	52	601.79	110	601.87	256		33	603.54	820			602.83	106	600.83	31	600.62	9	600.60		....	....	....	....
30	601.00	52	602.00	121	602.79				603.25				603.17	790	600.83		600.62	9			....	....	....	....
31			602.08	91									602.83	650			600.62				....	....	....	....

13 H (iii)

Monthly Discharge of Boston Creek near York for 1915-6

Drainage Area, 125 Square Miles

Month	Discharge in Second-feet			Discharge in Second-feet per Square Mile			Run-off
	Maximum	Minimum	Mean	Maximum	Minimum	Mean	Depth in Inches on Drainage Area
November (1915)	165	13	46	1.32	.10	.37	.41
December "	121	12	50	.97	.10	.40	.46
January (1916)	780	66	403	6.24	.53	3.22	3.71
February	850	7	161	6.80	.06	1.29	1.39
March	1,170	16	240	9.36	.13	1.92	2.21
April...........	735	106	308	5.88	.85	2.46	2.74
May...........	790	66	181	6.32	.53	1.45	1.67
June	590	31˙	234	4.72	.25	1.87	2.09
July...........	28	9	16	·.22	.07	.13	.15
August.........	13	6	۲8	.10	.05	.06	.07
September	....	....	....	....	....	....	....
October.........	....	....	....	....	....	....	....
The period	1,170	7	164	9.36	.05	1.31	14.90

NOTE.—Gauge reading discontinued from September 1st, 1916.

Conestogo River at St. Jacob's

Location—At the highway bridge in the Village of St. Jacob's, Township of Woolwich, County of Waterloo.

Records Available—July 16, 1913, to August 31, 1916.

Drainage Area—305 square miles.

Gauge—Vertical steel staff 0 to 3 feet on pile near left bank and 3 to 12 on the right abutment. Elevation of zero on the gauge is 1057.00, which has remained unchanged since established.

Channel and Control—The channel is straight for about 500 feet above and 1,000 feet below the gauging section. The banks are low, shifting, and liable to overflow. Fine gravel forms the bed of the stream and is not very permanent. The disposal of garbage from the bridge affects the area of the section to some extent.

Discharge Measurements—Made from the bridge during high stages, and at a permanent wading section located 800 feet down stream during the low water period.

Winter Flow—The relation of gauge height to discharge is affected by ice during the winter season.

Regulation—The Snyder mill is located just above this bridge, and its intermittent operation causes variations in the river stage. During the dry season it is possible, when the dam is closed and flash boards on, to hold back practically all the water for a period of 24 hours.

Accuracy—The constantly changing channel and control has necessitated the use of a number of rating curves, and therefore the records cannot be considered very reliable.

Observer—A. Niebergall, St. Jacob's.

Gauge reading discontinued after August 31, 1916.

Discharge Measurements of Conestogo River at St. Jacob's in 1915-6

Date	Hydrographer	Width in Feet	Area of Section in Sq. Feet	Mean Velocity in Feet per Sec.	Gauge Height in Feet	Discharge in Sec-Feet	Discharge in Second-feet per Square Mile
1915							
Nov. 10....	Roberts, E.	65	42	1.35	1,058.14	57	....
1916							
Mar. 31....	Cunnington. G...	166	949	2.88	1,061.46	2,738	....
Apr. 4....	"	165	768	1.63	1,060.33	1,256	....
" 4....	"	165	768	1.54	1,060.21	1,181	....
" 4....	"	165	751	1.62	1,060.21	1,216	....
May 9....	Roberts. E.	160	558	.64	1,059.00	359	....

14 H (iii)

Daily Gauge Height and Discharge of Conestogo River at St. Jacobs for 1915-6

Drainage Area 305 Square Miles

Day	Nov Gauge Ht. Feet	Nov Dis-charge Sec-ft.	Dec Gauge Ht. Feet	Dec Dis-charge Sec-ft.	Jan Gauge Ht. Feet	Jan Dis-charge Sec-ft.	Feb Gauge Ht. Feet	Feb Dis-charge Sec-ft.	Mar Gauge Ht. Feet	Mar Dis-charge Sec-ft.	Apr Gauge Ht. Feet	Apr Dis-charge Sec-ft.	May Gauge Ht. Feet	May Dis-charge Sec-ft.	June Gauge Ht. Feet	June Dis-charge Sec-ft.	July Gauge Ht. Feet	July Dis-charge Sec-ft.	Aug Gauge Ht. Feet	Aug Dis-charge Sec-ft.	Sept Gauge Ht. Feet	Sept Dis-charge Sec-ft.	Oct Gauge Ht. Feet	Oct Dis-charge Sec-ft.
1	1058.12	59	1059.46	570	1058.96	220	1061.67	2950	1058.25	55	1061.71	3000	1058.56	173	1058.79	252	1058.19	73	1057.77	20				
2	1058.04	46	1059.29	475	1059.31	340	1060.27	1280	1058.37	75	1061.52	2770	1058.29	98	1060.33	1350	1058.14	63	1057.56	9				
3	1058.04	46	1059.00	340	1060.52	1310	1059.08	275	1066.33	65	1060.44	1480	1059.54	620	1059.87	875	1058.08	52	1057.48	6				
4	1058.29	98	1058.71	224	1060.60	1430	1058.64	125	1058.39	75	1059.98	970	1058.92	304	1959.12	1394	1058.00	40	1057.46	6				
5	1058.35	112	1058.71	112	1062.17	2750	1058.50	100	1058.21	55	1059.54	620	1058.67	259	1059.02	349	1058.04	46	1057.46	6				
6	1058.08	52	1058.60	185	1060.46	1490	1058.33	65	1058.37	75	1059.59	530	1058.67	210	1058.71	224	1057.96	36	1057.42	5				
7	1057.92	32	1058.46	32	1060.79	1310	1058.33	65	1058.37	75	1058.46	435	1058.46	143	1058.56	173	1057.98	38	1057.46	0				
8	1058.08	52	1058.48	52	1060.02	1090	1058.31	65	1058.31	65	1059.14	403	1059.02	349	1058.89	291	1057.85	26	1057.42	5				
9	1058.17	69	1058.42	69	1060.23	835	1058.31	65	1058.37	75	1059.04	358	1059.10	385	1059.39	530	1057.89	28	1057.46	6				
10	1058.08	49	1058.40	125	1060.83	1430	1058.52	100	1058.37	100	1058.96	322	1058.56	173	1060.37	1390	1057.96	36	1057.48	6				
11	1058.08	52	1058.29	98	1060.92	1490	1058.29	55	1058.35	55	1058.58	179	1058.73	230	1059.37	520	1057.83	24	1057.39	4				
12	1058.10	55	1058.21	55	1059.02	835	1058.12	55	1058.46	55	1059.28	470	1058.37	118	1059.23	445	1057.73	18	1057.54	9				
13	1057.96	55	1058.17	78	1061.69	295	1058.29	55	1058.48	40	1061.52	2770	1058.44	137	1059.25	455	1057.73	18	1057.73	6				
14	1058.12	59	1058.21	78	1060.50	340	1058.46	88	1058.37	55	1063.17	4750	1058.52	358	1059.04	358	1057.64	13	1057.44	5				
15	1058.12	63	1058.29	98	1060.39	295	1058.46	88	1058.44	88	1062.04	3400	1058.54	167	1059.21	435	1057.69	16	1057.39	4				
16	1058.14	63	1058.04	63	1059.04	255	1058.44	255	1058.46	88	1059.87	870	1058.35	496	1059.33	496	1057.67	15	1057.37	3				
17	1058.12	59	1058.17	69	1059.42	318	1058.42	318	1058.44	88	1059.67	710	1058.14	63	1059.87	875	1057.62	12	1057.29	4				
18	1058.08	52	1058.31	102	1059.08	255	1058.39	75	1058.42	75	1060.09	1030	1058.48	149	1059.67	710	1057.60	11	1057.35	3				
19	1059.33	275	1058.27	92	1058.83	255	1058.37	75	1058.44	65	1060.09	1450	1058.29	98	1060.50	1550	1057.35	24	1057.60	11				
20	1059.71	480	1058.37	118	1059.75	238	1058.35	65	1058.44	65	1060.08	1070	1058.23	82	1059.54	620	1057.83	167	1057.37	3				
21	1059.69	362	1058.37	362	1062.79	1790	1058.35	65	1058.50	100	1060.08	080	1058.27	92	1059.33	496	1058.54	313	1057.35	3				
22	1059.60	220	1058.33	220	1061.87	1790	1058.44	88	1058.56	112	1062.83	4350	1058.46	143	1059.12	394	1058.46	143	1057.37	3				
23	1059.71	255	1058.42	255	1060.25	480	1058.35	75	1058.54	112	1060.77	1870	1058.29	98	1059.23	445	1058.31	102	1057.33	4				
24	1058.87	185	1058.39	340	1060.02	660	1058.44	88	1058.73	202	1060.89	2020	1058.14	63	1058.81	259	1058.08	52	1057.39	2				
25	1058.96	340	1058.29	65	1060.96	1670	1058.37	88	1059.14	403	1060.79	585	1058.17	69	1058.46	63	1058.04	46	1057.31	3				
26	1060.42	1090	1058.46	88	1060.96	65	1058.37	75	1060.42	1450	1059.48	100	1058.39	122	1058.96	322	1057.89	29	1057.35	3				
27	1061.06	2220	1058.71	122	1061.08	88	1060.42	88	1062.48	3930	1060.60	1670	1058.33	108	1058.71	93	1057.83	24	1057.33	3				
28	1060.85	1970	1058.62	125	1063.46	5120	1058.46	100	1063.94	4680	1060.96	2100	1058.46	143	1058.27	77	1057.77	20	1057.35	5				
29	1060.21	1210	1058.60	112	1063.08	4650	1058.35	75	1063.08	4650	1059.81	820	1060.67	545	1058.21	77	1057.77	21	1057.42	4				
30	1059.37	520	1058.62	125	1061.54	2800			1062.87	4390	1059.37	520			1058.23		1057.79	21	1057.39	4				
31			1058.60	125	1061.92	3250											1057.81	23	1057.46	6				

Monthly Discharge of Conestogo River at St. Jacobs for 1915-6

Drainage Area 305 Square Miles

Month	Discharge in Second-feet			Discharge in Second-feet per Square Mile			Run-off
	Maximum	Minimum	Mean	Maximum	Minimum	Mean	Depth in Inches on Drainage Area
November (1915)	2,220	32	339	7.28	.10	1.11	1.24
December. ''	510	55	147	1.87	.18	.48	.55
January .. (1916)	5,120	220	1,379	16.79	.72	4.52	5.21
February	2,950	40	224	9.67	.13	.73	.79
March	5,680	55	732	18.62	.18	2.40	2.77
April	4,350	179	1,497	14.26	.59	4.91	5.48
May	1,750	63	234	5.74	.21	.77	.89
June...........	1,550	77	474	5.08	.25	1.55	1.73
July	313	11	50	1.03	.04	.16	.18
August	20	2	5	.07	.01	.02	.02
September.....	....	....	....	....	....	....	....
October	....	....	....	....	....	....	....
The period......	5,680	2	507	18.62	.01	1.66	18.82

Gauge reading discontinued from September 1st, 1916.

Fairchild's Creek near Onondaga

Location—At the highway bridge called Howell's Bridge, lot 16, concession 3, Township of Onondaga, County of Brant.

Records Available—June 28, 1913, to August 31, 1916.

Drainage Area—115 square miles.

Gauge—Vertical steel staff 0 to 12 feet on left abutment of bridge. Elevation of zero is 621.00.

Channel and Control—Clay and silt decidedly shifting. This section is affected by Grand River backwater during the freshet period.

Discharge Measurements—Made from the bridge at all stages.

Winter Flow—The relation of gauge height to discharge is affected by ice, and measurements are made to determine the winter discharge.

Accuracy—The records for low flows are good. There are not sufficient records available to define rating curve at intermediate and high stages.

Observer—Gertrude Ludlow, Cainsville P.O.

Gauge readings discontinued after August 31, 1916.

Discharge Measurements of Fairchild's Creek near Onondaga in 1915-6

Date	Hydrographer	Width in Feet	Area of Section in Sq. Feet	Mean Velocity in Feet per Sec.	Gauge Height in Feet	Discharge in Sec-Feet	Discharge in Second-feet per Square Mile
1915 Nov. 2....	Yeates, W.	46	26	.83	622.06	21 (a)	....
1916 Mar. 27....	Roberts, E.	78	426	1.89	629.13	866 (b)	....
July 3....	Yeates, W.	47	28	.96	622.14	27	....

(a) Control has changed since last high water.
(b) Backwater from ice jam.

Daily Gauge Height and Discharge of Fairchild's Creek near Onondaga for 1915-6

Drainage Area 115 Square Miles

Day	November Gauge Ht. Feet	November Dis-charge Sec-ft.	December Gauge Ht. Feet	December Dis-charge Sec-ft.	January Gauge Ht. Feet	January Dis-charge Sec-ft.	February Gauge Ht. Feet	February Dis-charge Sec-ft.	March Gauge Ht. Feet	March Dis-charge Sec-ft.	April Gauge Ht. Feet	April Dis-charge Sec-ft.	May Gauge Ht. Feet	May Dis-charge Sec-ft.	June Gauge Ht. Feet	June Dis-charge Sec-ft.	July Gauge Ht. Feet	July Dis-charge Sec-ft.	August Gauge Ht. Feet	August Dis-charge Sec-ft.	September Gauge Ht. Feet	September Dis-charge Sec-ft.	October Gauge Ht. Feet	October Dis-charge Sec-ft.
1	622.06	27	622.48	88	622.10	31	630.87	1770	622.21	22	629.62	1520	622.77	146	623.52	296	622.09	30	621.84	12				
2	622.08	29	622.37	68	622.94	180	627.08	1010	622.25	26	628.08	1210	622.71	146	622.85	162	622.08	29	621.84	12				
3	622.04	26	622.35	64	624.44	480	624.92	575	622.21	22	625.69	780	622.89	170	622.98	188	622.08	29	621.86	13				
4	622.04	26	622.31	57	623.67	326	624.50	492	622.17	22	624.08	408	623.50	292	622.83	158	622.09	30	621.86	13				
5	622.04	26	622.42	77	625.23	640	624.00	640	622.17	22	623.67	326	623.00	242	622.69	130	622.04	28	621.85	13				
6	622.04	26	622.25	48	629.92	1580	623.73	392	622.27	26	623.67	326	623.25	192	622.58	108	622.04	26	621.87	13				
7	622.02	26	622.27	48	629.79	1550	623.42	338	622.48	31	623.50	292	622.87	176	622.58	108	622.01	23	621.85	12				
8	622.02	24	622.23	46	629.04	1400	623.21	262	622.64	64	623.67	292	622.89	170	624.02	396	622.00	22	651.85	12				
9	622.04	26	622.23	51	627.42	1080	622.89	192	622.98	142	623.83	368	622.85	166	623.08	208	622.00	22	621.85	12				
10	622.04	26	622.46	54	626.31	855	622.64	132	622.89	132	623.67	326	622.85	170	623.08	154	622.00	22	621.85	12				
11	622.04	24	622.25	48	625.94	780	622.71	92	622.81	112	623.87	388	623.19	230	622.81	196	622.00	22	621.92	16				
12	622.04	24	622.10	31	625.25	640	622.64	102	622.73	102	623.87	326	622.98	188	623.02	154	621.96	19	621.92	16				
13	622.06	27	622.12	33	627.87	1170	622.54	73	622.81	112	628.12	366	622.73	188	622.67	126	621.96	18	621.87	13				
14	622.01	23	622.00	22	628.00	1190	622.42	55	622.96	152	627.75	1220	622.69	130	622.54	100	621.95	18	621.87	13				
15	621.96	23	622.00	22	626.50	890	622.42	48	622.96	152	625.02	595	624.31	454	622.60	112	621.93	20	621.84	13				
16	622.06	27	622.00	19	626.50	890	622.37	42	622.75	112	624.52	496	625.00	592	622.60	96	621.97	16	621.85	12				
17	622.06	27	621.98	21	624.23	438	622.43	48	622.54	55	624.81	555	623.69	330	622.52	96	621.92	18	621.84	12				
18	622.12	33	621.98	27	623.62	316	622.42	48	622.39	42	623.75	342	623.33	258	623.33	92	621.94	18	621.87	13				
19	622.17	150	622.14	35	623.25	242	622.46	48	622.31	36	623.90	372	622.89	170	622.58	108	621.94	18	621.87	18				
20	622.79	154	622.17	39	623.23	238	622.39	42	622.25	31	624.00	392	622.81	154	622.56	104	621.94	20	621.94	16				
21	622.81	116	622.12	33	623.08	208	622.31	36	622.25	31	625.52	695	622.71	134	622.46	84	621.92	16	621.92	16				
22	622.62	84	622.04	29	626.00	792	622.31	31	622.29	42	627.04	1000	622.67	126	622.39	71	621.92	16	621.87	13				
23	622.46	68	622.06	26	628.04	1200	622.31	31	622.42	64	624.58	510	625.58	708	622.31	57	621.89	14	621.87	14				
24	622.37	68	622.06	27	628.92	1380	622.25	31	624.29	450	623.69	330	624.10	412	622.48	54	621.89	14	621.86	13				
25	622.37	64	622.14	35	626.75	940	622.27	26	629.12	1420	623.44	280	622.98	188	622.35	88	621.89	14	621.89	13				
26	622.35	66	622.10	31	625.64	720	622.27	26	630.75	1740	623.75	342	622.64	120	622.50	64	621.87	14	621.89	14				
27	622.36	92	622.12	33	625.73	740	622.29	26	633.00	2190	623.10	212	623.37	142	622.23	46	621.87	14	621.87	13				
28	622.50	108	622.14	39	628.08	1210	622.21	22	634.00	2390	622.98	188	623.23	266	622.15	36	621.87	14	621.87	13				
29	622.58	108	622.17	39	628.58	1310			631.54	1900	622.87	166	626.06	238	622.12	33	621.87	14	621.86	13				
30	622.58		622.08	29	624.87	565							623.23	804			621.87	14						
31			622.08	29	628.12	1220							625.33	660										

Monthly Discharge of Fairchild's Creek near Onondaga for 1915-6

Drainage Area, 115 Square Miles

Month	Discharge in Second-feet			Discharge in Second-feet per Square Mile			Run-off
	Maximum	Minimum	Mean	Maximum	Minimum	Mean	Depth in Inches on Drainage Area
November (1915)	154	22	52	1.34	.19	.45	.50
December ``	88	19	41	.77	.17	.36	.42
January.. (1916)	1,580	31	813	13.47	.27	7.07	8.15
February	1,770	22	208	15.39	.19	1.81	1.96
March..........	2,390	22	380	20.78	.19	3.30	3.80
April..........	1,520	166	521	13.21	1.44	4.53	5.05
May............	804	120	268	6.99	1.04	2.33	2.69
June	396	33	125	3.44	.29	1.09	1.22
July...........	30	14	20	.26	.12	.17	.20
August.........	18	12	13	.16	.10	.11	.13
September.....	......	.....	....	....	....	....	....
October	....	.....	....	....	....	....	....
The period.....;	2,390	12	245	20.78	.10	2.12	24.05

Gauge reading discontinued from September 1st, 1916.

Galt Creek at Galt

Location—At the Kerr Street Bridge in the City of Galt, Township of North Dumfries, County of Waterloo.

Records Available—July 9, 1913, to August 31, 1916.

Drainage Area—45 square miles.

Gauge—Vertical steel staff 0 to 9 feet on the right abutment of bridge. Elevation of zero on gauge is 893.00, which has remained unchanged since established.

Channel and Control—The channel is straight for 500 feet above and below section. The river bed and banks are both practically permanent. It is bounded on both sides by the G.T.R. and C.P.R.

Discharge Measurements—Made from the upstream side of the bridge at all stages.

Winter Flow—The relation of gauge height to discharge is affected by ice during the winter months, and measurements are made to determine the winter flow.

Accuracy—The rating curve is fairly well defined, and the records can be classed as good.

Observer—Charles Parker, Galt.

Gauge readings discontinued after August 31, 1916.

Discharge measurements of Galt Creek at Galt in 1915-6

Date	Hydrographer	Width in Feet	Area of Section in Sq. Feet	Mean Velocity in Feet per Sec.	Gauge Height in Feet	Discharge in Sec-Feet	Discharge in Second-feet per Square Mile
1915							
Dec. 21....	Yeates, W....	18	9	2.13	893.79	19 (a)	....
1916							
Apr. 6....	Cunnington, G...	24	35	2.78	894.17	98	....
" 6....	" "	24	36	2.69	894.17	96	....
" 6....	" "	24	36	2.88	894.17	104	....

(a) Ice on section; ice jam below section.

Daily Gauge Height and Discharge of Galt Creek at Galt for 1915-6

Drainage Area 45 Square Miles

Day	November Gauge Ht. (Feet)	November Dis-charge (Sec-ft)	December Gauge Ht. (Feet)	December Dis-charge (Sec-ft)	January Gauge Ht. (Feet)	January Dis-charge (Sec-ft)	February Gauge Ht. (Feet)	February Dis-charge (Sec-ft)	March Gauge Ht. (Feet)	March Dis-charge (Sec-ft)	April Gauge Ht. (Feet)	April Dis-charge (Sec-ft)	May Gauge Ht. (Feet)	May Dis-charge (Sec-ft)	June Gauge Ht. (Feet)	June Dis-charge (Sec-ft)	July Gauge Ht. (Feet)	July Dis-charge (Sec-ft)	August Gauge Ht. (Feet)	August Dis-charge (Sec-ft)	September Gauge Ht. (Feet)	September Dis-charge (Sec-ft)	October Gauge Ht. (Feet)	October Dis-charge (Sec-ft)
1	893.43	18	893.75	45	894.06	40	894.58	171	893.54	12	894.92	239	893.67	37	894.29	117	893.46	20	893.30	12	....	....	....	....
2	893.44	18	893.56	27	894.19	45	894.56	167	893.56	14	894.79	213	893.89	61	894.12	91	893.42	17	893.25	11	....	....	....	....
3	893.45	19	893.58	29	894.31	50	894.44	145	893.48	10	894.46	148	894.00	74	893.96	69	893.46	20	893.27	11	....	....	....	....
4	893.44	18	893.54	26	894.33	56	894.58	137	893.54	12	894.12	91	894.08	85	993.75	45	893.44	18	893.31	11	....	....	....	....
5	893.44	18	893.46	20	894.39	68	894.77	119	893.46	10	894.12	91	894.04	80	893.69	39	893.43	12	893.31	12	....	....	....	....
6	893.44	18	893.46	20	894.44	74	894.96	96	893.48	12	894.12	91	893.96	69	893.71	41	893.53	25	893.29	13	....	....	....	....
7	893.43	18	893.52	24	894.46	68	895.37	111	893.42	10	893.87	80	893.85	56	893.87	58	893.39	18	893.31	13	....	....	....	....
8	893.43	18	893.54	26	894.35	56	895.69	96	893.58	10	893.75	58	893.81	51	894.04	80	893.39	16	893.33	13	....	....	....	....
9	893.35	14	893.51	23	894.21	40	896.12	96	893.46	9	893.75	45	893.69	45	894.10	88	893.51	23	893.33	15	....	....	....	....
10	893.36	14	893.52	24	894.14	45	895.83	96	893.44	8	893.71	45	893.77	43	894.02	77	893.44	18	893.33	16	....	....	....	....
11	893.40	16	893.94	40	894.14	45	895.96	96	893.44	22	893.81	51	893.73	43	893.81	64	893.52	24	893.33	16	....	....	....	....
12	893.48	21	893.96	16	894.31	56	895.71	96	893.54	22	893.81	105	893.69	39	893.67	51	893.58	29	893.27	17	....	....	....	....
13	893.45	19	893.85	21	894.48	62	895.54	96	893.73	22	894.21	105	893.67	37	893.77	47	893.52	24	893.27	11	....	....	....	....
14	893.46	19	893.77	16	894.67	62	895.04	96	893.73	14	894.58	179	893.81	41	894.04	80	893.43	18	893.25	11	....	....	....	....
15	893.50	22	893.73	12	894.64	62	895.04	96	893.60	14	894.62	132	893.71	51	894.37	64	893.35	11	893.28	11	....	....	....	....
16	893.48	21	893.64	17	894.50	45	895.00	96	893.44	12	894.37	132	893.92	88	894.08	85	893.31	14	893.28	11	....	....	....	....
17	893.42	17	893.71	18	894.37	31	894.92	96	893.44	12	894.33	124	894.21	105	894.12	80	893.35	14	893.25	11	....	....	....	....
18	893.42	18	893.64	12	894.12	26	894.64	92	893.39	10	894.25	111	894.33	91	894.62	64	893.37	14	893.25	11	....	....	....	....
19	893.53	18	893.64	18	893.77	22	894.37	64	893.50	10	894.04	85	893.98	72	893.92	58	893.31	15	893.25	13	....	....	....	....
20	893.77	47	893.96	26	893.69	39	894.04	40	893.54	14	893.89	61	893.77	47	893.79	49	893.37	15	893.33	13	....	....	....	....
21	893.96	69	893.81	14	894.48	152	894.17	50	893.60	26	894.04	80	893.87	58	893.73	39	893.31	11	893.33	20	....	....	....	....
22	893.85	56	893.75	14	894.75	205	894.17	31	893.71	31	894.08	121	893.67	85	893.48	21	893.27	12	893.46	12	....	....	....	....
23	893.83	54	893.71	12	894.71	197	893.69	16	893.87	43	894.31	98	894.17	98	893.48	33	893.25	12	893.28	12	....	....	....	....
24	893.69	39	893.81	14	894.71	148	893.73	19	894.00	58	894.12	105	894.00	54	893.60	35	893.31	12	893.31	12	....	....	....	....
25	893.67	37	893.85	22	894.21	105	893.67	16	894.08	74	894.08	98	893.83	69	893.64	29	893.29	11	893.23	10	....	....	....	....
26	893.58	31	894.04	19	894.25	111	893.71	16	894.71	85	894.71	98	893.96	88	893.96	33	893.33	11	893.27	11	....	....	....	....
27	893.60	30	894.02	19	894.12	205	896.71	197	894.71	197	894.71	111	894.10	111	893.62	33	893.33	11	893.27	11	....	....	....	....
28	893.59	30	893.96	16	894.75	209	893.92	22	895.04	263	894.08	80	894.25	132	893.96	33	893.33	11	893.23	11	....	....	....	....
29	893.68	38	894.06	22	894.77	148	893.62	14	895.42	339	894.08	56	894.25	111	893.56	24	893.27	11	893.25	11	....	....	....	....
30	893.73	43	894.23	38	894.46	156	....	....	895.37	329	893.85	..	894.37	132	893.52	..	893.27	11	893.25	11	....	....	....	....
31	....	....	894.04	19	894.50	..	....	....	895.17	289	....	....	894.52	160	....	....	893.31	..	893.27	..	....	....	....	....

Monthly Discharge of Galt Creek at Galt for 1915-6

Drainage Area. 45 Square Miles

Month	Discharge in Second-feet			Discharge in Second-feet per Square Mile			Run-off
	Maximum	Minimum	Mean	Maximum	Minimum	Mean	Depth in Inche on Drainage Area
November (1915)	69	14	27	1.53	.31	.60	.67
December. "	61	12	23	1.36	.27	.51	.59
January .. (1916)	209	22	86	4.64	.49	1.91	2.20
February	171	14	81	3.80	.31	1.80	1.94
March..........	339	8	64	7.53	.18	1.42	1.64
April..........	239	41	103	5.31	.91	2.29	2.55
May............	160	37	71	3.56	.82	1.58	1.82
June	117	21	55	2.60	.47	1.22	1.36
July...........	29	10	16	.64	.22	.36	.42
August.........	20	10	12	.44	.22	.27	.31
September......	....	....	....	....	....	....	....
October.........	....	....	....	....	....	....	....
The period	339	8	54	7.53	.18	1.20	13.61

Gauge reading discontinued from September 1st, 1916.

Irvine River near Salem

Location—At the highway bridge known as Watt's Bridge about 1½ miles above Salem on the blind line between the 11th and 12th concessions, lot 14, Township of Nichol, County of Wellington.

Records Available—Old section, July to October, 1913; present section, November 1, 1913, to August 31, 1916.

Drainage Area—67 square miles.

Gauge—Vertical steel staff 0 to 9 feet attached to the centre pier of bridge. Elevation of zero on gauge is 1297.00, which has remained unchanged since established.

Channel and Control—The river bed and banks are composed of solid rock, and consequently permanent.

Discharge Measurements—During the flood of 1914 an attempt was made to obtain a meter reading from the bridge, but owing to a velocity of about 14 feet per second it was found impossible to keep the meter in the water. During the low stages a permanent wading section is located 100 feet upstream.

Winter Flow—The relation of gauge height to discharge is somewhat affected when ice is present at the station. Meter measurements are made during that period to determine the winter discharge.

Accuracy—The open channel rating curve is well defined up to gauge height 1289.50 feet, and records of discharge up to 400 sec. feet are good.

Observer—Annie Barber, Salem.

Gauge reading discontinued after August 31, 1916.

Discharge Measurements of Irvine River near Salem in 1915-6

Date	Hydrographer	Width in Feet	Area of Section in Sq. Feet	Mean Velocity in Feet per Sec.	Gauge Height in Feet	Discharge in Sec–Feet	Discharge in Second-feet per Square Mile
1915 Nov. 10....	Roberts, E	44	15	1.00	1,297.42	15 (a)	....
1916 Apr. 1....	Cunnington, G..	77	134	7.60	1,299.08	1,019	....
May 9....	Roberts, E.	47	28	2.43	1,297.77	68	....

(a) Rocks affect accuracy of reading.

Daily Gauge Height and Discharge of Irvine River near Salem for 1915-6

Drainage Area, 67 Square Miles

Day	November Gauge Ht. Feet	November Dis-charge Sec-ft.	December Gauge Ht. Feet	December Dis-charge Sec-ft.	January Gauge Ht. Feet	January Dis-charge Sec-ft.	February Gauge Ht. Feet	February Dis-charge Sec-ft.	March Gauge Ht. Feet	March Dis-charge Sec-ft.	April Gauge Ht. Feet	April Dis-charge Sec-ft.	May Gauge Ht. Feet	May Dis-charge Sec-ft.	June Gauge Ht. Feet	June Dis-charge Sec-ft.	July Gauge Ht. Feet	July Dis-charge Sec-ft.	August Gauge Ht. Feet	August Dis-charge Sec-ft.	September Gauge Ht. Feet	September Dis-charge Sec-ft.	October Gauge Ht. Feet	October Dis-charge Sec-ft.
1	297.54	32	298.06	27	297.93	8	299.17	470	297.45	8	299.04	950	297.83	79	297.84	81	297.39	16	297.08	2				
2	297.51	28	298.00	27	298.17	5	298.75	120	297.43	8	298.71	480	298.00	120	297.87	87	297.37	15	297.08	2				
3	297.48	25	297.98	25	298.50	72	298.75	107	297.42	8	298.33	234	298.17	175	298.04	132	297.37	15	297.08	2				
4	297.49	26	297.96	27	298.25	54	298.75	94	297.42	8	298.33	234	297.99	87	297.87	87	297.34	13	297.06	2				
5	297.50	27	297.96	27	298.25	39	298.75	94	297.42	8	298.33	234	297.99	117	298.04	132	297.35	14	297.06	2				
6	297.50	27	297.96	27	298.44	39	299.12	94	297.42	8	298.21	188	297.64	45	297.87	87	297.27	9	297.06	2				
7	297.50	27	297.93	27	298.54	39	299.25	83	297.50	10	297.81	87	297.62	42	297.96	110	297.27	9	297.04	1				
8	297.50	27	297.85	27	298.52	39	299.08	72	297.50	10	297.42	19	297.67	50	297.87	87	297.25	8	297.06	2				
9	297.49	26	297.74	27	298.67	39	299.00	54	297.50	10	297.29	10	297.67	50	297.89	92	297.25	8	297.04	2				
10	297.44	21	297.69	22	299.17	39	298.96	39	297.50	10	298.08	120	298.00	120	297.87	87	297.25	8	297.06	2				
11	297.40	17	297.65	10	299.17	27	298.85	39	297.50	10	298.17	144	298.17	120	298.12	157	297.22	6	297.06	2				
12	297.39	16	298.37	10	298.92	27	298.77	27	297.50	10	298.17	176	297.82	76	298.17	175	297.17	4	297.06	2				
13	297.37	15	298.42	16	298.96	27	298.62	17	297.50	10	299.25	1300	297.85	83	298.10	150	297.17	4	297.06	2				
14	297.35	13	297.75	15	299.75	27	298.31	17	297.50	10	300.46	3362	297.71	56	297.94	120	297.17	4	297.06	2				
15	297.48	21	297.75	13	299.25	17	298.17	10	297.50	10	298.83	615	297.69	52	297.85	83	297.17	4	297.06	2				
16	297.48	25	297.75	21	298.67	10	298.04	10	297.50	10	298.37	252	297.83	79	297.94	104	297.17	4	297.06	2				
17	297.52	29	297.62	25	298.75	10	297.87	10	297.50	10	298.75	520	297.85	83	300.08	2720	297.17	4	297.06	2				
18	297.54	32	297.64	29	298.75	10	297.64	10	297.50	10	298.52	333	298.00	120	299.04	950	297.17	4	297.04	1				
19	298.12	46	297.71	32	299.17	10	297.58	10	297.52	14	298.31	224	297.87	87	298.33	234	297.17	4	297.04	1				
20	298.48	54	297.67	46	298.92	22	297.54	10	297.58	14	297.80	880	297.87	72	298.27	210	297.17	7	297.02	1				
21	298.48	54	297.65	54	298.96	575	297.54	10	297.54	14	299.00	298	298.04	63	298.31	132	297.24	5	297.00	1				
22	298.00	39	297.63	54	299.75	385	297.50	10	297.54	10	298.46	810	297.9	63	297.80	100	297.19	4	297.00	1				
23	297.98	27	297.58	39	299.25	242	297.50	10	297.50	10	300.17	2870	297.79	42	297.79	70	297.17	4	297.00	1				
24	297.94	17	297.58	27	298.67	265	297.50	10	297.50	10	298.96	810	297.85	61	297.49	42	297.17	4	297.00	1				
25	298.00	22	297.58	17	298.75	265	297.50	10	297.50	10	298.42	276	297.81	83	297.69	26	297.17	4	297.06	2				
26	298.46	27	297.62	22	298.75	880	297.50	10	297.56	27	298.27	210	297.81	74	297.87	52	297.11	4	297.06	2				
27	298.83	320	297.67	27	299.58	3430	297.50	10	298.83	615	298.27	210	297.71	56	297.71	87	297.12	3	297.08	2				
28	298.77	265	297.69	10	300.50	1930	297.47	8	299.54	1800	299.04	950	297.60	39	297.61	56	297.09	2	297.08	2				
29	298.69	150	297.75	10	299.62	1930			300.19	2900	298.89	695	297.67	50	297.53	40	297.08	2	297.08	2				
30	298.42	94	297.83	10	299.62	1930			299.96	2510	298.83	234	297.75	63	297.47	31	297.08	2	297.08	2				
31			297.92	10	299.79	1220			299.14	1120			297.75	63			297.08	2	297.06	2				
			297.87	10							297.81	74	298.33	234	297.53	24								
											297.62	42	297.98	114	297.42	19								

Monthly Discharge of Irvine River near Salem for 1915-6

Drainage Area 67 Square Miles

Month	Discharge in Second-feet			Discharge in Second-feet per Square Mile			Run-off
	Maximum	Minimum	Mean	Maximum	Minimum	Mean	Depth in Inches on Drainage Area
November (1915)	320	13	54	4.78	.19	.81	.90
December ''	27	10	15	.40	.15	.22	.25
January (1916)	3,430	5	461	51.19	.07	5.67	6.54
February	470	8	50	7.01	.12	.75	.81
March	2,900	8	297	43.28	.12	4.43.	5.11
April...........	3,362	10	560	50.18	.15	8.36	9.33
May............	234	39	86	3.49	.58	1.28	1.48
June..........: ..	2,720	19	213	40.60	.28	3.18	3.55
July...........	16	2	6	.24	.03	.09	.10
August.........	2	1	2	.03	.02	.03	.03
September	....	....	....	....	....	....	....
October.........	....	....	....	....	....	....	....
The period	3,430	1	166	51.19	.02	2.49	28.10

Gauge reading discontinued from September 1st, 1916.

Nith River near Canning

Location—At the highway bridge 200 feet upstream from the Grand Trunk Railway bridge, lot 2, concession 2, Township of Blenheim, County of Oxford, 1 mile from the Village of Canning.

Records Available—July 5, 1913, to October 31, 1916.

Drainage Area—365 square miles.

Gauge—Vertical steel staff 0 to 3 feet on pile in centre of stream and 3 to 12 feet on left abutment. Elevation of zero on gauge is 799.00, which has remained unchanged since established.

Channel and Control—Slightly shifting bed; both banks permanent under ordinary conditions. Control only affected by ice jams during the early freshet.

Discharge Measurements—Made from the bridge during high-water stages, and from a permanent wading section 100 feet above during the low-water period.

Winter Flow—The relation of gauge height to discharge is seriously affected by ice during the winter, and measurements are made to determine the winter flow.

Regulation—Fluctuations of a serious nature occur in the river stage at this section, caused through the intermittent operation of the milling plant at Canning, 1½ miles above.

Accuracy—On account of stage variations, these records are not very reliable.

Observer—Lewis Baker, Canning P.O.

Discharge Measurements of Nith River near Canning in 1915-6

Date	Hydrographer	Width in Feet	Area of Section in Sq. Feet	Mean Velocity in Feet per Sec.	Gauge Height in Feet	Discharge in Sec-Feet	Discharge in Second-feet per Square Mile
1915							
Nov. 5....	Yeates, W......	93	76	1.72	801.21	131	....
" 23....	Cunnington, G...	95	139	3.30	802.21	459	....
Dec. 20....	Yeates, W......	95	142	1.39	802.54	197 (a)	....
1916							
Jan. 26....	"	119	388	3.30	803.76	1,277 (b)	....
" 31....	Roberts, E.	125	517	4.03	804.75	2,083 (c)	....
Mar. 28....	Yeates, W......	126	568	4.03	805.12	2,287 (d)	....
Apr. 2....	Roberts, E......	125	567	4.22	805.10	2,396	....
" 7....	Cunnington, G...	114	263	2.24	802.62	588	....
" 7....	"	114	263	2.45	802.62	645	....
" 7....	" ..	114	263	2.23	802.67	587	....
July 4....	Yeates W......	92	75	1.63	801.07	122	....

(a) Ice on control.
(b) Ice below section.
(c) Ice on both sides of section.
(d) Ice on sides below section.

Daily Gauge Height and Discharge of Nith River near Canning for 1915-6

Drainage Area, 365 Square Miles

Day	Nov Gauge Ht. (Feet)	Nov Dis-charge (Sec-ft.)	Dec Gauge Ht.	Dec Dis-charge	Jan Gauge Ht.	Jan Dis-charge	Feb Gauge Ht.	Feb Dis-charge	Mar Gauge Ht.	Mar Dis-charge	Apr Gauge Ht.	Apr Dis-charge	May Gauge Ht.	May Dis-charge	Jun Gauge Ht.	Jun Dis-charge	Jul Gauge Ht.	Jul Dis-charge	Aug Gauge Ht.	Aug Dis-charge	Sep Gauge Ht.	Sep Dis-charge	Oct Gauge Ht.	Oct Dis-charge
1	801.25	158	802.96	910	803.23	230	806.00	2480	....	610	805.12	2340	802.02	434	803.35	1120	801.71	299	801.04	116	800.67	72	800.98	107
2	801.23	152	802.37	605	803.42	315	804.58	1380	....	610	804.85	2120	802.37	605	802.60	720	801.73	307	800.96	104	800.73	78	800.77	82
3	801.10	125	802.04	443	804.42	425	803.02	670	....	610	803.96	1480	802.25	545	803.17	1020	801.71	299	800.92	98	800.71	76	800.92	98
4	801.18	141	801.89	376	805.19	545	802.35	470	....	610	803.42	1160	802.58	710	804.31	1700	801.21	148	800.89	94	800.60	65	800.98	107
5	801.17	139	801.77	323	805.62	670	802.56	470	....	610	803.10	985	802.69	765	802.94	900	801.19	143	800.98	107	800.89	94	801.04	116
6	801.17	133	801.81	340	806.73	720	802.44	470	....	610	802.92	885	802.29	565	802.75	710	801.14	133	800.83	88	800.89	94	800.94	101
7	800.96	104	801.64	274	806.64	770	802.39	520	....	610	802.58	710	802.31	575	802.58	885	801.19	143	800.67	72	800.77	82	800.98	107
8	801.12	129	801.56	248	804.33	820	802.52	570	....	610	802.46	650	802.27	555	802.92	950	800.87	92	800.94	101	800.73	78	800.85	90
9	801.23	152	801.56	248	803.50	875	802.67	570	....	610	802.14	490	801.89	376	803.04	730	801.10	125	800.94	107	800.92	98	800.87	92
10	801.23	152	801.56	248	803.50	930	802.73	570	....	610	802.06	452	802.37	605	803.62	995	801.04	116	800.81	86	800.83	88	800.81	88
11	801.14	133	801.60	260	803.35	930	802.81	570	....	610	802.12	480	802.56	700	803.12	1170	801.08	122	800.94	101	800.48	59	800.89	94
12	801.23	152	801.52	236	803.79	1010	802.85	570	....	610	802.37	480	802.62	730	803.44	1080	801.04	116	800.92	116	800.92	98	800.94	101
13	801.23	143	801.67	285	803.29	930	802.79	570	....	610	803.87	1420	802.12	480	803.27	565	801.04	122	800.98	107	800.87	92	801.04	116
14	801.12	143	801.56	248	804.29	1095	802.81	570	....	610	806.14	3160	802.02	434	803.02	434	801.08	139	800.94	119	800.94	101	801.04	133
15	801.19	143	801.64	274	805.34	1320	802.92	570	....	610	805.50	2640	802.71	775	802.12	480	801.02	113	801.06	119	800.89	94	801.04	116
16	801.29	168	801.60	260	804.87	1150	802.71	448	....	610	803.58	1250	803.25	1070	802.12	730	801.06	119	801.00	107	800.54	62	801.00	63
17	801.27	162	801.56	248	804.79	1040	802.48	335	....	610	803.58	1250	803.37	1130	802.62	480	801.00	119	801.02	113	800.62	67	801.00	110
18	801.25	158	801.52	236	803.21	1050	802.14	425	....	610	803.60	1260	803.29	1090	802.54	690	800.98	107	800.96	104	800.44	57	801.27	162
19	801.23	236	801.52	236	803.21	1050	802.50	425	....	610	803.44	1170	803.10	985	802.27	555	801.02	113	801.02	107	800.73	78	801.37	191
20	802.89	870	802.52	185	803.31	1100	802.37	402	....	610	803.60	1250	803.27	1080	802.27	425	801.08	122	800.98	113	800.96	104	801.44	212
21	803.31	1060	802.33	185	803.31	1340	802.48	380	....	610	802.48	650	803.37	1080	801.77	323	801.14	133	801.02	107	801.35	185	801.44	212
22	802.52	680	802.44	170	804.71	2010	802.58	425	....	610	802.75	795	802.37	605	801.71	299	801.10	125	800.92	98	800.85	90	801.31	173
23	802.73	545	802.48	170	805.19	2390	802.73	470	....	610	803.87	1420	802.87	860	801.83	348	801.06	119	800.94	101	800.89	94	801.29	167
24	801.83	376	802.48	170	806.25	3240	802.54	425	....	610	803.25	1070	803.25	1070	801.81	505	801.08	122	800.96	104	800.96	104	801.23	152
25	801.83	348	802.48	170	804.71	2010	802.06	380	....	610	803.04	950	802.29	565	802.23	535	800.79	84	801.00	110	800.96	104	801.23	139
26	801.85	857	802.58	170	803.71	1330	802.08	358	805.12	2340	802.67	755	802.02	434	802.00	425	800.94	101	800.94	101	800.77	82	801.14	133
27	802.81	825	802.73	170	803.58	1250	802.17	380	805.12	2340	803.37	1130	802.04	443	801.81	340	800.52	61	800.85	90	800.89	94	801.17	133
28	804.06	1540	802.85	170	804.83	2100	802.25	402	807.08	3900	803.33	1110	802.04	630	801.69	292	800.87	92	801.06	119	800.94	101	801.12	129
29	803.37	1130	802.96	170	806.46	2450			808.33	4900	802.67	755	802.42	1500	801.69	292	800.92	98	801.00	110	801.04	116	800.81	86
30	803.94	1460	803.19	170	803.92	1450			807.21	4010	801.44	398	804.00	2940			800.81	98	800.83	88	801.25	158	801.08	122
31	....				804.54	1870							805.87				800.96	104	800.62	67	....		801.04	116

Monthly Discharge of Nith River near Canning for 1915-6

Drainage Area 365 Square Miles

Month	Discharge in Second-feet			Discharge in Second-feet per Square-mile			Run-off
	Maximum	Minimum	Mean	Maximum	Minimum	Mean	Depth in Inches on Drainage Area
November (1915)	1,540	104	417	4.22	.28	1.14	1.27
December.　"	910	170	270	2.49	.47	.74	.85
January.. (1916)	3,240	230	1,239	8.88	.63	3.39	3.91
February	2,480	335	571	6.79	.92	1.56	1.68
March..........	4,900	610	1.076	13.42	1.67	2.95	3.40
April	3,160	398	1,148	8.66	'1.09	3.15	3.51
May............	2,940	376	798	8.05	1.03	2.19	2.52
June	1.700	292	683	4.66	.80	1.87	2.09
July............	307	61	131	.84	.17	.36	.42
August	116	67	103	.32	.18	.28	.32
September	158	57	92	.43	.16	.25	.28
October	212	63	124	.58	.17	.34	.39
The year........	4,900	57	554	13.42	.16	1.52	20.69

Speed River near Guelph

Location—At Caraher's highway bridge above the junction of the Speed and Eramosa Rivers and 3¾ miles from the City of Guelph, Township of Guelph, County of Wellington.

Records Available—October 27, 1913, to October 31, 1916.

Drainage Area—77 square miles.

Gauge—Vertical steel staff 0 to 12 feet, one on each abutment of bridge. Elevation of zero on each gauge is 1126.00, which has remained unchanged since established.

Channel and Control—The channel is straight for 250 feet above and 500 feet below the gauging section. During flood stages the control and banks are liable to shift, as the bed is composed of loose gravel. One channel exists at all stages.

Discharge Measurements—Made from the bridge and from a permanent low water section 300 feet down stream.

Winter Flow—The relation of gauge height to discharge is seriously affected by ice during the winter season, and measurements are taken during that period to determine the winter flow.

Regulation—A small mill is operated one mile and a half upstream. Slight fluctuations are caused only in the dry season, and are hardly noticeable at the gauge.

Accuracy—The open channel rating curve is fairly well defined for flows up to 500 second feet, the discharge for low flows being considered good.

Observer—Hugh Caraher, Guelph.

Discharge Measurements of Speed River near Guelph in 1915-6

Date	Hydrographer	Width in Feet	Area of Section in Sq. Feet	Mean Velocity in Feet per Sec.	Gauge Height in Feet	Discharge in Sec-Feet	Discharge in Second-feet per Square Mile
1915							
Nov. 9....	Roberts, E......	45	25	.84	1,128.14	21	
1916							
April 5....	Cunnington, G...	70	162	1.70	1,129.14	276	
" 5....	"	70	162	1.63	1,129.14	264	
" 5....	" "	70	162	1.63	1,129.17	265	
May 10....	Roberts, E......	56	57	1.44	1,128.58	82	
Oct. 6....	Yeates, W.......	49	13	.26	1,127.98	3	

Daily Gauge Height and Discharge of Speed River near Guelph for 1915-6

Drainage Area, 77 Square Miles.

Day	Nov Gauge Ht. (Feet)	Nov Dis-charge (Sec-ft.)	Dec Gauge Ht. (Feet)	Dec Dis-charge (Sec-ft.)	Jan Gauge Ht. (Feet)	Jan Dis-charge (Sec-ft.)	Feb Gauge Ht. (Feet)	Feb Dis-charge (Sec-ft.)	Mar Gauge Ht. (Feet)	Mar Dis-charge (Sec-ft.)	Apr Gauge Ht. (Feet)	Apr Dis-charge (Sec-ft.)	May Gauge Ht. (Feet)	May Dis-charge (Sec-ft.)	Jun Gauge Ht. (Feet)	Jun Dis-charge (Sec-ft.)	Jul Gauge Ht. (Feet)	Jul Dis-charge (Sec-ft.)	Aug Gauge Ht. (Feet)	Aug Dis-charge (Sec-ft.)	Sep Gauge Ht. (Feet)	Sep Dis-charge (Sec-ft.)	Oct Gauge Ht. (Feet)	Oct Dis-charge (Sec-ft.)
1	128.33	47	128.50	74	128.75	43	131.37	635	128.83	50	130.29	710	128.64	103	128.87	163	128.25	37	127.83	4	127.83	4	127.92	8
2	128.17	28	128.50	43	129.04	74	131.12	515	128.89	66	129.67	463	128.75	130	128.96	191	128.17	28	127.83	4	127.92	8	127.92	8
3	128.08	19	128.46	31	129.12	84	130.56	395	128.94	74	128.87	163	129.00	204	130.08	623	128.17	28	127.75	2	127.92	8	127.92	8
4	128.08	28	128.42	26	129.17	94	130.21	257	129.00	84	128.83	152	129.12	246	129.14	254	128.17	28	127.67	2	127.92	8	127.92	8
5	128.17	28	128.42	28	129.29	117	129.62	204	128.87	74	128.96	191	128.85	158	129.04	218	128.08	19	127.67	2	127.92	8	127.92	8
6	128.17	28	128.42	26	129.75	239	129.58	143	128.83	66	128.96	191	128.71	120	128.87	163	128.08	19	127.67	2	127.92	8	127.92	8
7	128.17	28	128.42	26	129.75	239	129.21	84	128.98	84	128.69	115	128.58	90	128.69	115	128.08	19	127.58	1	127.92	4	127.92	8
8	128.21	32	128.39	21	129.75	239	129.29	117	129.21	84	128.71	120	128.62	99	128.67	110	128.08	19	127.71	1	127.83	4	127.92	8
9	128.21	28	128.39	21	129.54	188	129.17	106	129.00	84	128.75	130	128.60	94	128.67	110	128.17	28	127.83	2	127.83	4	127.92	8
10	128.14	25	128.54	31	129.42	157	128.96	74	129.00	84	128.67	110	128.60	94	128.54	82	128.12	23	127.92	4	127.83	4	127.92	8
11	128.17	29	122.54	31	129.37	117	129.08	74	129.08	84	128.67	110	128.96	191	128.62	99	128.08	19	127.92	8	127.83	4	127.92	11
12	128.21	32	128.56	31	129.46	172	128.92	66	129.08	94	128.98	198	128.67	110	128.58	90	128.08	19	127.92	8	127.83	4	127.92	11
13	128.21	32	128.56	31	129.46	276	128.75	43	129.08	94	129.58	427	128.60	94	128.50	74	128.00	13	127.92	8	127.83	4	127.96	19
14	128.25	37	128.58	37	130.06	204	128.83	57	129.04	94	130.33	725	128.54	82	128.46	67	128.08	19	127.92	8	127.83	4	128.08	19
15	128.21	32	128.58	31	129.83	204	129.04	204	129.08	94	129.71	479	128.83	152	128.46	67	128.00	13	127.92	8	127.83	4	128.08	19
16	128.17	32	128.54	26	129.79	172	128.83	57	129.08	94	129.00	204	128.83	152	128.83	152	128.12	23	127.92	8	127.83	4	128.08	19
17	128.25	37	128.54	26	129.64	143	128.83	57	129.00	74	129.77	505	128.85	158	128.52	78	128.04	16	127.92	8	127.83	4	128.08	13
18	128.42	60	128.62	31	129.54	117	128.79	50	129.14	94	129.30	315	128.77	135	128.54	82	128.00	13	127.92	8	127.83	4	128.00	13
19	129.00	204	128.67	37	129.46	94	128.79	50	128.92	74	128.96	191	128.58	90	128.54	82	128.00	13	127.92	8	127.83	4	128.12	23
20	128.75	130	128.67	37	129.42	84	128.79	50	129.08	94	128.79	140	128.58	90	128.50	74	128.04	16	127.92	8	127.83	4	128.46	67
21	128.50	74	128.62	31	129.35	74	128.79	50	129.08	94	129.54	411	128.52	78	128.44	64	128.04	16	128.06	8	127.83	4	128.42	60
22	128.52	78	128.67	43	129.44	117	128.73	50	129.00	84	130.29	710	128.62	99	128.42	60	128.00	13	127.83	8	127.83	4	128.35	50
23	128.48	71	128.79	57	132.12	315	128.75	50	128.96	74	129.75	495	129.08	232	128.12	23	128.00	13	127.96	8	127.83	4	128.42	47
24	128.48	71	128.54	31	132.33	375	128.87	66	128.96	74	129.17	265	128.85	158	128.33	47	128.00	13	127.92	8	127.83	4	128.37	52
25	128.46	67	128.42	31	131.67	204	128.87	66	128.96	84	129.00	204	128.60	94	128.83	152	128.00	13	127.92	8	127.83	4	128.37	52
26	128.71	120	128.54	31	131.19	143	128.92	66	129.21	204	128.96	191	128.46	67	128.58	90	127.87	6	127.92	8	127.83	4	128.08	19
27	128.79	140	128.92	74	131.00	130	128.87	57	129.62	443	129.62	443	128.58	90	128.44	64	127.87	6	127.83	8	127.83	4	128.37	19
28	129.00	204	128.96	84	131.33	204	128.87	57	131.33	1130	129.02	211	128.67	110	128.33	47	127.83	4	127.92	8	127.83	4	128.08	19
29	128.83	152	128.92	74	132.17	475			133.08	1830	128.83	152	128.50	74	128.29	42			127.92	8	127.92	8	128.08	16
30	128.73	125	128.87	66	131.39	204			133.81	1920	128.69	115	129.87	545	128.29	42			127.92	8	127.92	8	128.04	13
31			128.87	50	130.37	74			131.52	1200			129.35	335					127.92	8			128.00	13
					132.32	915																		

Monthly Discharge of Speed River near Guelph for 1915-6

Drainage Area, 77 Square Miles

Month	Discharge in Second-feet			Discharge in Second-feet per Square Mile			Run-off
	Maximum	Minimum	Mean	Maximum	Minimum	Mean	Depth in Inches on Drainage Area
November (1915)	204	19	66	2.65	.25	.86	.96
December "	84	21	39	1.09	.27	.51	.59
January (1916)	915	43	196	11.86	.56	2.55	2.94
February	635	37	124	8.25	.48	1.61	1.74
March..........	1,920	50	283	24.94	.65	3.68	4.24
April...........	725	110	295	9.42	1.43	3.83	4.27
May...........	545	74	145	7.08	.96	1.88	2.17
June...........	625	23	116	8.12	.30	1.51	1.68
July...........	37	4	17	.48	.05	.22	.25
August	18	1	7	.23	.01	.09	.10
September	8	4	5	.10	.05	.06	.07
October.........	67	8	21	.87	.10	.27	.31
The year	1,920	1	109	2,494	.01	1.42	19.33

Speed River at Hespeler

Location—At a point 100 feet below the jail, which adjoins the power house, in the Town of Hespeler, Township of Waterloo, County of Waterloo.

Records Available—Discharge measuréments from July 10, 1913, to October 31, 1916. Daily gauge heights from October 23, 1913, to October 31, 1916.

Drainage Area—250 square miles.

Gauge—Vertical steel staff 0 to 12 feet on jail wall adjoining power house. The elevation of zero on the gauge is 935.00.

Channel and Control—Straight for about 300 feet above and below the gauging section. Loose gravel forms the bed of this stream, which is decidedly shifting. The banks are low, and overflow when the water raises 2 feet above normal. Weeds at the control and in channel have a decided effect at the gauging section.

Discharge Measurements—Made from a permanent wading section 100 feet below the gauge during the low stages, and the dam 400 feet above will be used as a weir during the flood season.

Winter Flow—The relation of gauge height to discharge is somewhat affected by the presence of ice for a short period during the winter season.

Regulation—A dam 400 ft. above this section causes serious fluctuations in the river stage during the low water period.

Accuracy—Owing to the shifting bed and the presence of weeds at and below section, greatly interfering with the metering of stream, these records can only be classed as fair.

Observer—W. D. Scott, Hespeler.

Discharge Measurements of Speed River at Hespeler in 1915-6

Date	Hydrographer	Width in Feet	Area of Section in Sq. Feet	Mean Velocity in Feet per Sec.	Gauge Height in Feet	Discharge in Sec-Feet	Discharge in Second-feet per Square Mile
1915							
Nov. 16....	Cunnington, G.	90	99	1.92	936.43	152	....
Dec. 23....	Yeates, W	86	80	1.04	936.21	83 (a)	....
1916							
Jan. 8....	Roberts, E....	102	182	2.40	937.31	436	....
" 21....	Yeates, W	97	150	1.58	936.92	238 (b)	....
Feb. 17....	"	93	131	1.38	936.68	181 (b)	....
Mar. 1....	Cunnington, G.	94	105	1.27	936.42	132 (c)	....
May 10....	Roberts, E....	100	166	2.27	937.08	378	....

(a) Section has been badly scoured; large quantities of gravel have been taken from bed of stream.

(b) Ice-covered below section.

(c) Section partly ice-covered.

Daily Gauge Height and Discharge of Speed River at Hespeler for 1915-6

Drainage Area, 250 Square Miles

Day	Nov Gauge Ht. (Feet)	Nov Dis-charge (Sec-ft.)	Dec Gauge Ht. (Feet)	Dec Dis-charge (Sec-ft.)	Jan Gauge Ht. (Feet)	Jan Dis-charge (Sec-ft.)	Feb Gauge Ht. (Feet)	Feb Dis-charge (Sec-ft.)	Mar Gauge Ht. (Feet)	Mar Dis-charge (Sec-ft.)	Apr Gauge Ht. (Feet)	Apr Dis-charge (Sec-ft.)	May Gauge Ht. (Feet)	May Dis-charge (Sec-ft.)	Jun Gauge Ht. (Feet)	Jun Dis-charge (Sec-ft.)	Jul Gauge Ht. (Feet)	Jul Dis-charge (Sec-ft.)	Aug Gauge Ht. (Feet)	Aug Dis-charge (Sec-ft.)	Sep Gauge Ht. (Feet)	Sep Dis-charge (Sec-ft.)	Oct Gauge Ht. (Feet)	Oct Dis-charge (Sec-ft.)
1	936.48	150	937.05	330	936.48	150	939.98	2190	936.62	186	939.83	2080	937.23	405	938.42	1090	936.64	191	936.31	109	936.23	94	936.00	57
2	936.39	128	937.12	358	936.69	205	938.39	1070	936.50	155	939.23	1660	937.25	415	937.73	670	936.60	180	936.31	109	936.19	86	936.23	94
3	936.42	135	936.98	305	936.81	244	937.64	615	936.52	160	938.69	1280	937.21	395	938.96	1470	936.60	180	936.35	118	936.04	63	936.27	101
4	936.42	135	936.77	230	936.83	250	937.19	386	936.52	160	938.37	1060	937.12	358	938.73	1310	936.52	160	936.33	114	935.98	55	936.25	98
5	936.48	150	936.58	175	937.06	334	937.04	326	936.56	165	938.04	855	937.10	350	938.27	990	936.52	160	935.96	90	936.23	94	936.23	98
6	936.44	140	936.50	155	937.33	455	937.00	275	936.54	170	937.62	600	937.10	405	938.27	705	936.48	145	935.89	52	936.27	101	936.23	94
7	936.35	118	936.48	150	937.52	550	936.79	202	936.64	191	937.23	485	937.10	350	937.79	560	936.46	145	936.34	44	936.21	101	936.08	69
8	935.42	135	936.50	155	937.42	500	936.71	186	936.60	180	937.23	405	937.12	358	937.62	510	936.42	135	936.35	116	936.21	90	936.25	98
9	935.42	145	936.39	128	937.19	386	936.73	186	936.50	155	937.23	378	937.12	358	937.54	455	936.50	155	936.29	118	936.04	63	936.27	101
10	936.46	128	936.37	123	937.23	405	936.79	208	936.48	150	937.06	334	937.14	364	937.44	510	936.62	160	936.31	105	936.27	101	936.25	101
11	936.39	106	936.37	123	937.10	350	936.73	194	936.48	150	937.37	475	937.14	358	937.33	378	936.42	135	936.31	109	936.30	107	936.27	98
12	936.29	106	936.37	123	936.96	296	936.73	240	936.50	160	938.42	1090	937.12	358	937.44	378	936.39	128	936.02	60	936.27	101	936.10	72
13	936.33	114	936.37	123	937.56	570	936.87	310	936.48	155	938.58	1210	937.14	358	937.17	378	936.37	123	936.33	114	936.25	98	936.23	94
14	936.35	118	936.35	118	937.21	395	937.08	310	936.46	155	938.96	1470	937.14	364	937.17	364	936.35	118	936.23	94	936.25	98	936.23	94
15	935.39	128	936.35	118	937.08	342	937.06	275	936.39	145	938.35	1060	937.29	435	937.17	364	936.31	109	936.27	101	935.96	52	936.25	98
16	936.46	145	936.35	118	937.08	310	937.00	258	936.62	128	938.39	1070	937.44	510	937.14	364	936.30	118	936.21	101	936.25	98	936.29	98
17	936.42	135	936.46	145	937.19	292	936.96	296	936.64	186	938.37	1060	937.33	455	937.14	350	936.33	128	936.00	90	936.29	98	936.04	63
18	936.52	160	936.52	160	937.60	257	936.75	257	936.64	191	938.37	1060	937.23	405	937.10	318	936.33	123	936.31	57	936.21	105	936.27	101
19	936.64	191	936.48	150	937.52	258	936.71	194	936.44	191	937.54	560	937.17	378	937.02	282	936.31	114	936.27	105	936.21	101	936.23	101
20	937.21	395	936.48	150	937.44	240	936.71	194	936.50	140	938.35	1040	937.08	358	936.92	386	936.21	109	936.23	109	935.83	90	936.23	101
21	937.19	386	936.31	145	937.02	240	936.96	296	936.44	155	938.35	930	937.08	342	937.04	425	936.21	94	936.31	101	936.21	39	936.27	94
22	937.10	350	936.31	109	936.92	334	936.79	237	936.37	140	938.67	1270	937.06	334	937.19	296	936.31	105	936.20	94	936.23	86	936.29	101
23	936.87	265	936.39	128	937.06	109	936.58	175	936.30	123	937.87	750	937.04	326	937.27	244	936.19	105	936.19	88	936.25	90	936.27	101
24	936.75	224	936.31	128	938.14	128	936.50	155	936.71	107	937.83	730	937.17	378	936.81	218	936.00	98	936.27	88	936.25	94	936.23	78
25	936.75	224	936.27	118	937.85	128	936.50	155	937.08	211	937.71	665	938.69	1060	936.73	218	935.89	101	936.27	101	936.25	98	936.14	104
26	936.81	310	936.27	101	937.71	101	936.64	191	937.37	342	937.58	580	938.37	1280	936.69	205	936.31	99	936.20	101	936.23	94	936.28	104
27	937.00	310	936.35	101	937.71	118	936.62	186	937.08	1060	937.37	475					936.00	98	936.27	99			936.29	105
28	937.33	455	936.37	123	937.98	123	936.67	200	938.37	2020							935.89	57	936.27	98				
29	937.25	415	936.31	109	938.71	1340			939.75	2550							936.00	44	926.25					
30	937.17	278	936.42	118	938.19	945			940.50	2620							935.89	60						
31			936.42	135	938.67	1270			940.60								936.31	109						

Monthly Discharge of Speed River at Hespeler for 1915-6

Drainage Area, 250 Square Miles

Month	Discharge in Second-feet			Discharge in Second-feet per Square Mile			Run-off
	Maximum	Minimum	Mean	Maximum	Minimum	·Mean	Depth in Inches on Drainage Area
November (1915)	455	105	203	1.82	.42	.81	.90
December ''	358	101	154	1.43	.40	.62	.71
January (1916)	1,300	150	500	5.20	.60	2.00	2.31
February	2,190	155	336	8.76	.62	1.34	1.45
March..........	2,620	107	410	10.48	.43	1.64	1.89
April	2,080	334	906	8.32	1.34	3.62	4.04
May............	1,280	326	428	5.12	1.30	1.71	1.97
June	1,470	205	517	5.88	.82	2.07	2.31
July............	191	44	121	.76	.18	.48	.55
August.........	118	44	96	.47	18	.38	.44
September	107	39	89	.43	.16	.36	.40
October	105	57	94	.42	.23	.38	.44
The year	2,620	39	320	10.48	.16	1.28	17.42

Whiteman's Creek near Burford

Location—At the first concrete bridge above the confluence of the creek with the Grand River, lot 14, concession 3, Township of Brantford, County of Brant.

Records Available—June 30, 1913, to August 31, 1916.

Drainage Area—154 square miles.

Gauge—Vertical steel staff 0 to 12 feet on the left abutment of bridge. Elevation of zero on the gauge is 690.00, which has remained unchanged since established.

Channel and Control—All the water passes between the two abutments. The river bed directly under the bridge is solid concrete. During flood conditions on the Grand River this section may be affected by backwater.

Discharge Measurements—Made from the bridge at all stages.

Winter Flow—Seriously affected by ice.

Regulation—A mill located 2 miles upstream known as App's Mill causes serious daily fluctuations in the river stage at this section.

Accuracy—The fluctuations caused by chopping mill make it difficult to obtain the representative mean daily gauge height. The rating curve is fairly well defined up to 700 second feet.

Observer——J. R. Davis, Brantford.

Gauge readings discontinued after August 31, 1916.

Discharge Measurements of Whiteman's Creek near Burford in 1915-6

Date	Hydrographer	Width in Feet	Area of Section in Sq. Feet	Mean Velocity in Feet per Sec.	Gauge Height in Feet	Discharge in Sec-Feet	Discharge in Second-feet per Square Mile
1915 Nov. 4....	Cunnington, G ..	61	35	1.70	690.83	52	....
1916 May 2....	Yeates, W......	60	69	2.49	691.33	171	....

Daily Gauge Height and Discharge of Whiteman's Creek near Burford for 1915-6

Drainage Area, 154 Square Miles

Day	Nov. Gauge Ht. (Feet)	Nov. Dis-charge (Sec-ft.)	Dec. Gauge Ht. (Feet)	Dec. Dis-charge (Sec-ft.)	Jan. Gauge Ht. (Feet)	Jan. Dis-charge (Sec-ft.)	Feb. Gauge Ht. (Feet)	Feb. Dis-charge (Sec-ft.)	Mar. Gauge Ht. (Feet)	Mar. Dis-charge (Sec-ft.)	Apr. Gauge Ht. (Feet)	Apr. Dis-charge (Sec-ft.)	May Gauge Ht. (Feet)	May Dis-charge (Sec-ft.)	June Gauge Ht. (Feet)	June Dis-charge (Sec-ft.)	July Gauge Ht. (Feet)	July Dis-charge (Sec-ft.)	Aug. Gauge Ht. (Feet)	Aug. Dis-charge (Sec-ft.)	Sept. Gauge Ht. (Feet)	Sept. Dis-charge (Sec-ft.)	Oct. Gauge Ht. (Feet)	Oct. Dis-charge (Sec-ft.)
1	690.75	50	691.67	251	691.52	88	693.19	860	692.08	190	693.12	825	691.21	130	692.73	640	690.89	70	690.46	16	690.39	9		
2	690.71	44	691.50	203	691.48	107	692.69	620	691.83	151	692.92	725	691.17	151	692.19	417	690.85	64	690.58	29	690.58	29		
3	690.69	42	691.42	182	691.69	164	692.35	478	691.71	140	692.50	540	691.35	164	691.94	334	690.87	66	690.62	33	690.54	24		
4	690.73	47	691.33	158	691.92	203	692.23	433	692.23	190	692.02	360	691.96	190	691.87	312	690.75	50	690.54	24	690.46	16		
5	690.67	39	691.23	135	692.50	355	691.71	263	692.00	195	691.87	312	691.25	140	691.85	306	690.73	47	690.54	24	690.42	12		
6	690.87	66	691.10	107	693.44	538	691.37	169	691.87	176	691.79	287	691.23	135	691.67	251	690.62	33	690.60	20	690.29	4		
7	690.67	39	691.27	144	692.85	458	691.69	203	692.08	203	691.54	214	691.29	149	691.60	231	690.60	33	690.58	22	690.50	20		
8	690.60	31	691.19	126	692.64	421	693.14	246	691.98	151	691.52	209	691.29	135	691.60	231	690.67	39	690.52	20	690.50	29		
9	690.67	39	691.12	111	692.37	386	693.50	290	691.85	151	691.50	203	691.29	149	692.02	360	690.77	52	690.58	27	690.58	29		
10	690.67	39	691.33	98	692.25	353	693.31	266	691.81	157	691.48	198	691.42	149	692.25	439	690.73	47	690.56	29	690.58	27		
11	690.75	50	691.19	98	692.23	321	693.11	246	691.92	176	691.58	225	691.50	203	692.17	411	690.75	50	690.58	27	690.50	20		
12	690.75	50	691.39	118	692.23	353	693.21	260	691.96	176	691.83	299	691.94	334	692.83	685	690.69	42	690.56	20	690.42	12		
13	690.75	50	691.37	107	692.50	353	693.04	231	691.83	151	692.33	470	691.89	319	692.79	665	690.67	39	690.50	20	690.37	8		
14	690.81	58	691.14	80	692.29	353	692.92	203	691.25	140	692.79	665	691.62	237	692.54	555	690.60	31	690.54	24	690.39	9		
15	690.77	52	691.06	71	692.29	306	693.00	203	691.08	103	692.87	705	691.46	192	692.08	380	690.62	33	690.39	9	690.42	12		
16	690.81	58	691.02	64	692.29	321	692.69	203	691.83	156	692.54	556	691.85	306	691.71	263	690.67	39	690.39	9	690.52	22		
17	690.77	52	691.10	71	694.75	518	692.69	203	691.46	128	692.08	379	692.49	620	691.58	225	690.58	29	690.62	33	690.50	20		
18	690.87	66	691.12	80	696.12	1025	692.27	176	691.62	133	692.00	353	692.48	530	691.54	214	690.58	29	690.37	8				
19	691.17	122	691.31	88	696.08	970	692.27	203	691.46	118	692.04	340	691.94	334	691.46	192	690.58	29	690.54	24				
20	691.94	334	691.27	80	696.23	915	692.60	203	691.04	96	691.67	251	691.54	214	691.50	203	690.37	37	690.54	20				
21	691.83	299	691.21	71	696.33	840	692.58	203	691.04	96	691.44	187	691.58	220	691.42	181	690.62	29	690.58	29				
22	691.56	220	691.17	71	694.27	740	692.12	176	691.21	130	691.50	203	691.56	225	691.33	158	690.50	36	690.67	29				
23	691.44	187	691.12	64	693.04	497	692.31	217	691.46	192	691.52	209	692.25	140	691.31	153	690.67	39	690.67	33				
24	691.35	164	691.10	71	692.31	462	692.27	190	691.00	88	691.35	164	692.25	140	691.10	107	690.54	24	690.62	33				
25	691.31	154	691.14	64	692.33	470	692.14	176	691.25	140	691.48	203	692.04	366	691.29	149	690.58	24	690.58	24				
26	691.33	158	691.12	64	692.44	515	692.23	164	692.25	439	691.64	209	691.69	257	691.37	168	690.54	16	690.54	27				
27	691.52	209	691.10	64	693.12	825	692.23	217	693.79	1200	691.50	209	691.64	243	691.25	140	690.46	16	690.56	24				
28	691.58	225	691.14	71	692.62	590	692.19	217	693.79	1200	691.52	198	691.60	231	691.14	115	690.50	20	690.46	16				
29	691.75	275	691.56	56	692.50	540			694.58	1660	691.35	164	691.54	214	691.04	96	690.54	31	690.50	20				
30	691.75		691.56	71	693.12	825			693.96	1300			692.56	565	691.00	88	690.58	29	690.60	31				
31													692.73	640			690.50	33	690.62	33				

Monthly Discharge of Whiteman's Creek near Burford for 1915-6

Drainage Area 154 Square Miles

Month	Discharge in Second-feet			Discharge in Second-feet per Square Mile			Run-off
	Maximum	Minimum	Mean	Maximum	Minimum	Mean	Depth in Inches on Drainage Area
November (1915)	334	31	117	2.17	.20	.76	.85
December "	251	56	101	1.63	.86	.66	.76
January (1916)	1,025	88	489	6.66	.57	3.18	3.67
February	860	164	267	5.58	1.06	1.73	1.86
March..........	1,660	88	312	10.78	.57	2.03	2.34
April...........	825	164	376	5.36	1.06	2.44	2.72
May............	640	122	271	4.16	.79	1.76	2.03
June.	685	88	284	4.45	.57	1.84	2.05
July............	70	16	36	.45	.10	.23	.27
August.........	39	8	25	.25	.05	.16	.18
September......	29	4	17	.19	.03	.11	.07
October.........	....	....	....	....	....	....	....
The period	1,660	4	217	10.78	.03	.41	16.83

Gauge reading discontinued from November 1st, 1916.

Miscellaneous Measurements

River	Location	Date	Discharge in Sec-ft.
Beaver.....................	Feversham	..Dec. 8, 1915....	22
"	"	..Jan. 14, 1916....	39
"	"	..Feb. 9, 1916....	76
"	"	..Feb.10, 1916....	78
"	"	..Feb.24, 1916....	54
Kabuskong	Bonfield	..Nov. 4, 1915....	33
"	"	..Dec. 21, 1915....	28
"	"	..June 2, 1916....	139
"	"	..July 7, 1916....	79
Rainy	Emo	..May 30, 1916....	41,584
Snake Creek..............	Port Elgin	..Nov. 23, 1915....	85
Sydenham.................	Florence	..Nov. 11, 1915....	69
Winnipeg.................	Dalles Rapids...........	..Aug. 30, 1916....	27,141
"	" "	..Sept. 4, 1916....	24,731
"	" "	..Sept. 9, 1916....	24,205
"	Throat Rapids	..Sept. 8, 1916....	5,807
.. ..	White Dog Falls	..June 28, 1916....	40,746
.. ..	White Dog Falls, S. Chan..	..June 19, 1916....	35,674
.. ..	White Dog Falls, N.Chan..	..Sept.30, 1916....	27,404

EASTERN ONTARIO DISTRICT

Summary of Discharge

Summary of discharge in second-feet per square mile for regular and near stations in Eastern Ontario District for which such data are available in this report

Station	Drainage Area Sq. miles	1915		1916										
		Nov.	Dec.	Jan.	Feb.	Mar.	April	May	June	July	Aug.	Sept.	Oct.	Year.
Bonnechere River at Glen Lake	575	.24	.27	.34	.52	.59	2.80	3.57	1.62	.91	.48	.52	.43	1.02
Madawaska River at Madawaska	800	.36	.36	.46	.73	.53	2.92	2.48	.98	.55	.29	.26	.30	.85
Mississippi River at Ferguson's Falls	1,042	.40	.45	.67	1.11	.70	4.94	3.55	3.24	1.89	.57	.37	.36	1.52
Mississippi River at	1,456	.29	.35	.54	.89	.67	3.82	2.48	1.88	1.30	.44	.28	.27	1.10
Mississippi River near Snow Road	446	.57	.65	.81	.96	.91	4.89	3.84	3.73	2.36	.94	.64	.62	1.74
Moira River near Foxboro	1,038	.40	.48	1.11	1.92	.99	5.55	2.36	3.65	1.11	.25	.13	.10	1.48
Napanee River near	300	.39	.53	1.02	2.33	1.79	6.84	3.00	4.26	1.73	.24	.14	.16	1.86
Petawawa River near Petawawa	1,572	*	.39	.40	.48	.48	1.78	2.77	2.28	1.40	.63	.44	.46	1.08
Tay River near Glen Tay	204	.37	.48	.77	.75	1.74	2.50	2.44	3.69	1.78	.97	.73	.36	1.38
York River near Bancroft	374	.60	.66	.73	.92	2.01	3.80	2.67	1.45	.74	.64	.58	.44	1.27

*December 15-31.

NORTHERN ONTARIO DISTRICT

Summary of Discharge

Summary of discharge in second-feet per square mile for regular river stations in the Northern Ontario District for hih u**h** data are **late** in this report.

Station	Drainage rea Sq. miles	1915		1916										Year
		Nov.	Dec.	Jan.	Feb.	Mar.	Apr.	May	June	July	Aug.	Sept.	Oct.	
Aux Sables River near Massey	524	1.34	1.16	.69	.76	.69	4.68	3.49	4.14	1.87	.32	.39	1.40	1.74
Blanche River near Englehart	430	.90	1.59	.50	.44	.64	5.86	3.12	.73	.60	.57	.50	.66	1.34
Frederickhouse River at Frederickhouse	1,260	1.72	1.38	1.63	1.68	1.42	2.85	6.75	1.66	1.19	.46	.26	.35	1.78
Kagawong River at Kagawong	94	.24	.26	.48	.57	.79	2.51	2.20	1.07	.66	.36	.34	.28	.81
Maganetawan River (So. Branch) nar Burk's Falls	107	1.55	1.77	1.78	2.64	1.38	8.03	4.81	3.23	.90	.28	.65	2.10	2.42
Maganetawan River (So. Branch) near Hk's Falls	257	1.18	1.35	1.48	2.16	1.32	5.37	4.56	2.92	1.42	.58	.67	1.21	2.01
Mississagi River at Iron Bridge	3,565	*1.85	1.83	.95	.63	.51	2.31	2.53	2.01	1.21	.48	.53	1.07	1.30
Muskoka River (North Branch) near Port Sydney	560	1.14	1.22	1.42	1.97	1.02	5.72	3.12	1.78	.58	.35	.24	.99	1.62
...a River (So. h) at Trethewey's Falls	668	.86	.94	1.18	2.10	1.65	4.66	4.49	3.21	1.23	.64	.57	.60	1.84
Seguin River near Parry Sound	380	2.26	1.71	1.36	2.64	1.00	6.24	5.78	1.78	.72	.47	.72	.99	2.13
South River nar Powassan	294	1.00	.84	1.30	1.14	1.41	7.43	3.34	1.48	.55	.30	.78	1.72	1.77
Spanish River at Espanola	4,490	1.07	1.36	.86	.57	.69	4.42	3.39	1.97	1.04	.62	.56	.68	1.43
Sturgeon River nar i Ry Falls	2,250	.93	1.25	.75	.87	1.00	4.07	4.54	2.01	1.05	.70	.46	.81	1.53
Vermilion River near Whitefish	1,580	1.00	1.15	.68	.60	.44	5.71	3.44	1.84	1.16	.15	.11	.22	1.37
Wanapitei River nar Wanapitei	940	.78	.76	.75	.68	.69	1.39	4.90	2.08	1.90	1.04	.51	.....	1.41

*November 15-30.

NORTH-WESTERN ONTARIO DISTRICT

Summary of Discharge

Summary of discharge in second-feet per square mile for regular river stations in the North-Western Ontario District for which such data are available in this report

Station	Drainage Area Sq. miles	1915		1916											Year
		Nov.	Dec.	Jan.	Feb.	Mar.	Apr.	May	June	July	Aug.	Sept.	Oct.	
Eagle River at Eagle River...........	970	.30	.33	.37	.39	.35	.48	1.65	1.99	1.31	1.02	.84	.75	.82
English River at Ear Falls..........	11,700	.62	.70	.64	.56	.47	.46	.82	1.55	1.70	1.49	1.09	.78	.93
English River at Manitou Falls......	14,600	.58	.65	.60	.53	.44	.43	.74	1.37	1.43	1.31	.97	.70	.84
English River at Oak Falls.........	15,570	.59	.64	.60	.53	.45	.49	.75	1.38	1.52	1.33	.96	.71	.85
Footprint River at Rainy Lake Falls......	590	.14	.14	.14	.14	.16	.39	1.81	1.80	1.01	.55	.36	.23	.57

SOUTH-WESTERN ONTARIO DISTRICT

Summary of Discharge

Summary of discharge in second-feet per square mile for regular river stations in South-Western Ontario District for which uch ata are available in this report.

Station	Drainage area Sq. miles	1915		1916										
		Nov.	Dec.	Jan.	Feb.	Mar.	Apr.	May	June	July	Aug.	Sept.	Oct.	Year.
Ausable River nr Arkona	408	.67	1.29	4.65	.91	2.38	2.45	2.53	1.03	.10	.08	.05	.09	1.36
Beaver River nr Kimberley	100	.70	.73	2.58	2.63	2.06	3.30	1.91	1.29	.58	.45	.39	.51	1.42
Bighead River at rd	132	.94	1.11	1.38	1.52	1.77	2.21	1.20	1.11	.48	.35	.26	.48	1.06
Black River nr Washago	585	.69	.86	1.43	2.46	1.60	6.64	3.15	1.26	.42	.16	.08	.48	1.59
Credit River at Cataract Junction	85	.69	.61	1.73	1.54	1.82	3.13	.91	.81	.36	.26	.22	.38	1.04
Maitland River at Ben Miller	950	1.21	1.84	4.36	1.53	2.93	4.54	1.66	1.07	.19	.11	.10	.16	1.64
Nottawasaga River nr son	416	.59	.55	1.63	1.05	1.74	3.49	1.10	.92	.27	.16	.18	.34	1.00
oRky Saugeen River near Markdale	96	.80	1.00	2.17	2.35	1.24	3.58	2.06	1.69	.92	.65	.60	.61	1.47
Saugeen River nr Port Elgin	1,565	.90	1.22	3.26	3.13	2.70	4.94	1.74	1.27	.44	.29	.26	.38	1.70
Saugeen River nr n	850	.94	.96	2.88	1.54	1.49	5.23	1.92	1.45	.51	.33	.29	.39	1.49
Sydenham River near wen Sound	71	.87	.82	3.08	1.41	1.75	3.8	1.89	1.89	.55	.32	.27	.38	1.39
hes River (Main Stream) near yrds	1,270	1.05	.95	5.78	1.01	2.10	2.71	2.63	1.58	.22	.10	.09	.16	1.53
hes River (South Branch) near Ealing	515	.91	1.10	4.16	1.40	2.33	2.39	2.35	1.81	.28	.24	.14	.22	1.45
hes River (North nch) nr Fanshawe	650	1.05	1.33	5.45	.83	1.66	2.75	1.42	1.42	.19	.04	.03	.05	1.36

SOUTH-WESTERN ONTARIO DISTRICT

GRAND RIVER BASIN

Summary of Discharge

Summary of discharge in second-feet per square mile for regular ... stations on Grand ... river and ... times for ... such data are available in this report

Station	Drainage Area Sq. miles	1915		1916											
		Nov.	Dec.	Jan.	Feb.	M.	April	May	June	July	Aug.	Sept.	d.	Year
Grand River at Belwood	280	.86	.57	4.06	.95	1.86	6.20	1.03	.62	.04	.01	.01	.03	1.35
Grand River near Conestogo	550	.98	.57	3.15	.75	1.76	4.90	1.33	1.47	.14	.05	.04	.08	1.26
Grand River at Galt	1,360	.77	.47	2.23	.70	1.59	3.52	1.25	1.51	.19	.10	.09	.17	1.05
Grand River at Glen Morris	1,390	1.15	.52	2.38	1.08	1.67	3.82	1.61	1.77	.35	.25	.24	.33	1.26
Grand River at Brantford	2,000	.82	.57	3.17	.96	1.53	3.21	1.64	1.69	.32	.22	.15	.25	1.21
Grand River at York	2,280	.73	.80	6.32	1.39	1.94	6.67	1.74	1.78	.30	.16	.14	.24	1.35
Irvine River at Salem	67	.81	.22	5.67	.75	4.43	8.36	1.28	3.18	.09	.03	......	......	2.48
Conestogo River at St. ...	305	1.11	.48	4.52	.73	2.40	4.91	.77	1.55	.16	.02	.06	.27	1.66
Speed River near ...	77	.86	.51	2.55	1.61	3.68	6.83	1.8	1.51	.22	.09	.36	.38	1.42
Speed River at Hespeler	250	.81	.62	2.00	1.34	1.64	3.62	1.71	2.07	.48	.38	......	......	1.28
Galt Crk at Galt	45	.60	.51	1.91	1.80	1.42	2.29	1.58	1.22	.36	.27	.25	.34	1.20
Nith River nr Canning	365	1.14	.74	3.39	1.56	2.95	3.15	2.19	1.87	.36	.28	.11	......	1.52
Whiteman's Creek near Rurford	154	.76	.66	3.18	1.73	2.03	2.44	1.76	1.84	.23	.16	......	......	1.41
Fairchild's Creek at Onondaga	115	.45	.36	7.07	1.81	3.30	4.53	2.33	1.09	.17	.11	......	......	2.12
Boston Creek nr York	125	.37	.40	3.22	1.29	1.92	2.46	1.45	1.87	.13	.06	......	......	1.31

INDEX

PAGE

Almonte Construction 5
Ausable River 117-119
Aux Sables River 43-45

Beaver River 120-122
Bighead River 123-125
Black River 126-128
Blanche River 46-48
Bonnechere River 9-13
Boston Creek 180-182

Cobden Construction 4
Conestogo River 183-185
Credit River 129-131
Crown Leases 2

Discharge Summary 208-212

Eagle River 90-92
Eastern Ontario Metering Sections ... 8
English River—
    Caribou Falls 93
    Ear Falls 94-96
    Manitou Falls 98-100
    Oak Falls 101-103
    Sturgeon Falls 104

Fairchild's Creek 186-188
Footprint River 105-107
Frederickhouse River 49-51

Galt Creek 189-191
Grand River—
    Belwood 161-163
    Brantford 164-167
    Conestogo 168-170
    Galt 171-173
    Glen Morris 174-176
    York 177-179

Irvine River 192-194

Kagawong River 52-54

Lac Seul 2

Madawaska River 14-17
Magnetawan River 55-60
Maitland River 132-134
Manitou River 108
Measurement of Stream Flow 1

PAGE

Miscellaneous Measurements 207
Mississagi River 61-63
Mississippi River 18-26
Moira River 27-29
Muskoka River 64-69

Napanee River 30-32
Niagara Power Development 2
Nipissing Power Company 2
Nith River 195-197
Northern Ontario Metering Sections.. 42
Northwestern Ontario Metering Sec-
    tions 89
Nottawasaga River 135-137

Petawawa River 33-35
Power Construction 3

Rocky Saugeen River 138-140

Saugeen River 141-147
Seguin River 70-72
Seine River 109-110
South Falls Construction 3
South River 73-75
Southwestern Ontario Metering Sec-
    tions 116
Grand River Metering Sections 160
Spanish River 76-78
Speed River 198-203
Sturgeon River 79-81
Summary of Discharge—
    Eastern Ontario 208
    Northern Ontario 209
    Northwestern Ontario 210
    Southwestern Ontario 211
    Southwestern Ontario, Grand River
    Basin 212
Sydenham River 148-150

Tay River 36-38
Thames River 151-159
Turtle River 111-112

Vermilion River 82-84

Wabigoon River 113-115
Wanapitei River 85-88
Whiteman's Creek 204-206

York River 39-41

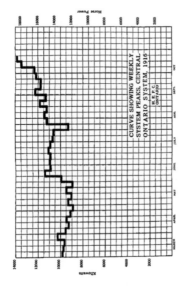

CURVE SHOWING WEEKLY
SYSTEM PEAKS, CENTRAL
ONTARIO SYSTEM, 1916

H. E. P. C.
ONTARIO

Map to accompan[y]
Sen. Jt. No. 48, 1917

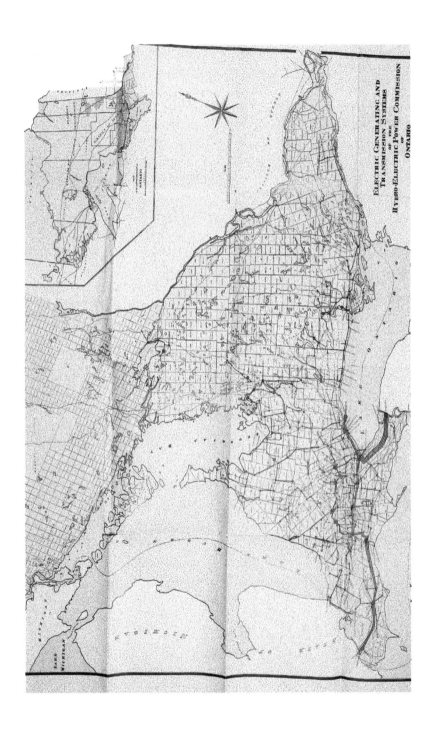

ELECTRIC GENERATING AND
TRANSMISSION SYSTEMS
OF THE
HYDRO-ELECTRIC POWER COMMISSION
OF
ONTARIO

Lightning Source UK Ltd.
Milton Keynes UK
UKHW012121180219
337529UK00012B/1484/P